Great Events from History

The 20th Century

1901-1940

Great Events from History

The 20th Century

1901-1940

Volume 4
1923-1930

Editor
Robert F. Gorman
Southwest Texas State University

SALEM PRESS
Pasadena, California   Hackensack, New Jersey

Editor in Chief: Dawn P. Dawson

Editorial Director: Christina J. Moose	*Production Editor:* Andrea E. Miller
Acquisitions Editor: Mark Rehn	*Design, Layout, and Graphics:* James Hutson
Research Supervisor: Jeffry Jensen	*Additional Layout and Graphics:* William Zimmerman
Manuscript Editors: Judy Selhorst,	*Photo Editor:* Cynthia Breslin Beres
Andy Perry, Anna A. Moore	*Editorial Assistant:* Dana Garey
Research Assistant Editor: Tim Tiernan	

Cover photos (pictured clockwise, from top left): Marlene Dietrich in *The Blue Angel*, 1930. (The Granger Collection, New York); Orville Wright in flight, 1909. (The Granger Collection, New York); Hammer and Sickle. (The Granger Collection, New York); Gold coffin of King Tut, photographed in 1922. (The Granger Collection, New York); Picasso's *Guernica*. (The Granger Collection, New York); American troops landing in France, 1918. (The Granger Collection, New York)

Some of the essays in this work originally appeared in the following Salem Press sets: *Chronology of European History: 15,000 b.c. to 1997* (1997, edited by John Powell; associate editors, E. G. Weltin, José M. Sánchez, Thomas P. Neill, and Edward P. Keleher); *Great Events from History: North American Series, Revised Edition* (1997, edited by Frank N. Magill); *Great Events from History II: Science and Technology* (1991, edited by Frank N. Magill); *Great Events from History II: Human Rights* (1992, edited by Frank N. Magill); *Great Events from History II: Arts and Culture* (1993, edited by Frank N. Magill); *Great Events from History II: Business and Commerce* (1994, edited by Frank N. Magill), and *Great Events from History II: Ecology and the Environment* (1995, edited by Frank N. Magill). New material has been added.

Library of Congress Cataloging-in-Publication Data

Great events from history. The 20th century, 1901-1940 / editor, Robert F. Gorman.
    p. cm.
Some of the essays in this work originally appeared in various Salem Press publications.
Includes bibliographical references and index.
ISBN 978-1-58765-324-7 (set : alk. paper) -- ISBN 978-1-58765-325-4 (v. 1 : alk. paper) -- ISBN 978-1-58765-326-1 (v. 2 : alk. paper) -- ISBN 978-1-58765-327-8 (v. 3 : alk. paper) -- ISBN 978-1-58765-328-5 (v. 4 : alk. paper) -- ISBN 978-1-58765-329-2 (v. 5 : alk. paper) -- ISBN 978-1-58765-330-8 (v. 6 : alk. paper) 1. Twentieth century. I. Gorman, Robert F. II. Title: 20th century, 1901-1940. III. Title: Twentieth century, 1901-1940.

D421.G629 2007
909.82'1—dc22

2007001930

First Printing

PRINTED IN THE UNITED STATES OF AMERICA

CONTENTS

1923 *(continued)*

1924

1925

Contents

1928

1929

CONTENTS

1930

KEYWORD LIST OF CONTENTS

LIST OF MAPS, TABLES, AND SIDEBARS

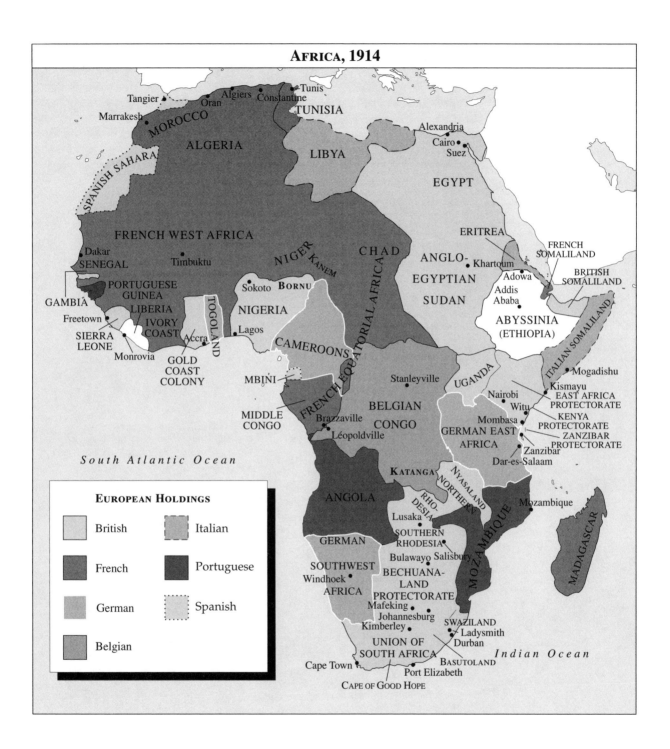

AFRICA, 1914

Tangier
Marrakesh
MOROCCO
Oran
Algiers
Constantine
Tunis
TUNISIA
ALGERIA
LIBYA
SPANISH SAHARA
Alexandria
Cairo
Suez
EGYPT
FRENCH WEST AFRICA
Dakar
SENEGAL
Timbuktu
NIGER
KANEM
CHAD
ANGLO-
EGYPTIAN
SUDAN
ERITREA
FRENCH
SOMALILAND
Khartoum
BRITISH
SOMALILAND
Adowa
Addis
Ababa
ABYSSINIA
(ETHIOPIA)
GAMBIA
PORTUGUESE
GUINEA
LIBERIA
Freetown
SIERRA
LEONE
Monrovia
IVORY
COAST
Accra
TOGOLAND
GOLD
COAST
COLONY
Sokoto
BORNU
NIGERIA
Lagos
CAMEROONS
MBINI
MIDDLE
CONGO
FRENCH EQUATORIAL AFRICA
Brazzaville
Léopoldville
Stanleyville
BELGIAN
CONGO
UGANDA
Nairobi
Witu
Mombasa
GERMAN EAST
AFRICA
Zanzibar
Dar-es-Salaam
ITALIAN SOMALILAND
Mogadishu
Kismayu
EAST AFRICA
PROTECTORATE
KENYA
PROTECTORATE
ZANZIBAR
PROTECTORATE
South Atlantic Ocean
ANGOLA
KATANGA
NYASALAND
NORTHERN
RHO-
DESIA
Lusaka
SOUTHERN
RHODESIA
Bulawayo
Salisbury
MOZAMBIQUE
Mozambique
MADAGASCAR
GERMAN
SOUTHWEST
AFRICA
Windhoek
BECHUANA-
LAND
PROTECTORATE
Mafeking
Johannesburg
Kimberley
UNION OF
SOUTH AFRICA
Cape Town
CAPE OF GOOD HOPE
Port Elizabeth
SWAZILAND
Ladysmith
Durban
BASUTOLAND
Indian Ocean

EUROPEAN HOLDINGS

- British
- French
- German
- Belgian
- Italian
- Portuguese
- Spanish

EUROPE, 1914

Arctic Ocean

Iceland

Atlantic Ocean

Northern Ireland

North Sea

IRELAND

GREAT BRITAIN

DENMARK

NETHERLANDS

NORWAY

SWEDEN

Baltic Sea

RUSSIA

BELGIUM

GERMAN EMPIRE

FRANCE

SWITZERLAND

AUSTRO-HUNGARIAN EMPIRE

ROMANIA

Black Sea

PORTUGAL

SPAIN

Corsica

ITALY

Adriatic Sea

MONTE-NEGRO

SERBIA

ALBANIA

BULGARIA

Thrace

GREECE

OTTOMAN EMPIRE

Sardinia

Sicily

ALGERIA

TUNISIA

Mediterranean Sea

Crete

Cyprus

MOROCCO

AFRICA

LIBYA

EGYPT

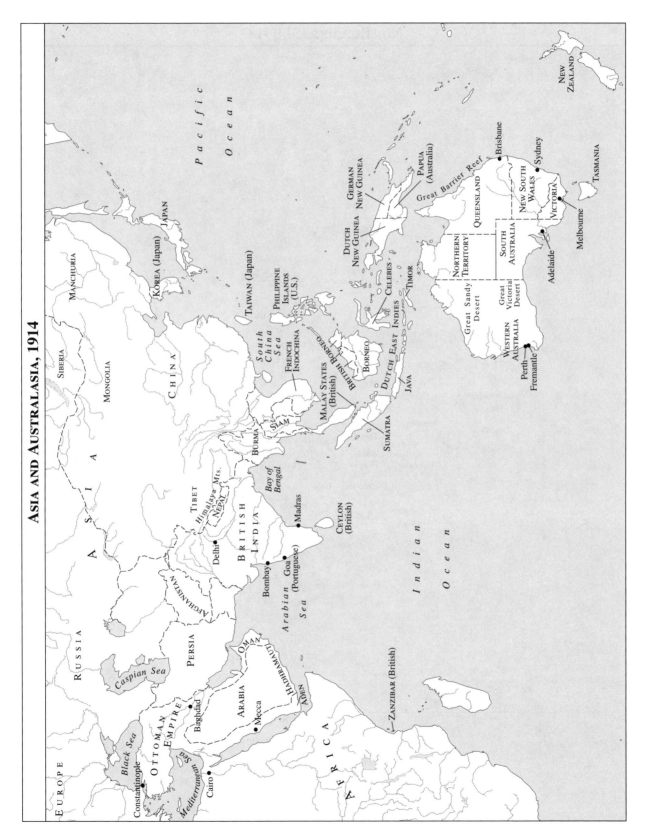

ASIA AND AUSTRALASIA, 1914

EUROPE

Constantinople

Black Sea

OTTOMAN EMPIRE

Baghdad

ARABIA

Mecca

Cairo

AFRICA

Mediterranean Sea

Caspian Sea

RUSSIA

PERSIA

AFGHANISTAN

OMAN

HADHRAMAUT

ADEN

ZANZIBAR (British)

Arabian Sea

Goa (Portuguese)

Bombay

Delhi

BRITISH INDIA

TIBET

Himalaya Mts.

NEPAL

Bay of Bengal

Madras

CEYLON (British)

Indian Ocean

ASIA

SIBERIA

MONGOLIA

MANCHURIA

CHINA

BURMA

SIAM

FRENCH INDOCHINA

South China Sea

KOREA (Japan)

JAPAN

TAIWAN (Japan)

PHILIPPINE ISLANDS (U.S.)

MALAY STATES (British)

BRITISH BORNEO

BORNEO

SUMATRA

JAVA

DUTCH EAST INDIES

CELEBES

TIMOR

Pacific Ocean

DUTCH NEW GUINEA

GERMAN NEW GUINEA

PAPUA (Australia)

Great Barrier Reef

QUEENSLAND

NORTHERN TERRITORY

SOUTH AUSTRALIA

WESTERN AUSTRALIA

Great Sandy Desert

Great Victoria Desert

Perth

Fremantle

Adelaide

NEW SOUTH WALES

VICTORIA

Brisbane

Sydney

Melbourne

TASMANIA

NEW ZEALAND

North America, 1914

Bering Sea

Bering Strait

Arctic Ocean

GREENLAND (Denmark)

TERRITORY OF ALASKA

KLONDIKE

Baffin Bay

Northwest Territories

Hudson Bay

DOMINION OF CANADA

NEWFOUNDLAND

British Columbia

Alberta

Saskatchewan

Manitoba

Ontario

Quebec

St. Lawrence River

Washington

Oregon

Idaho

Montana

North Dakota

South Dakota

Minnesota

Wisconsin

Michigan

Great Lakes

New York

Maine

Vermont

New Hampshire

Massachusetts

Rhode Island

Connecticut

Nevada

Wyoming

Nebraska

Iowa

Illinois

Indiana

Ohio

Pennsylvania

New Jersey

Delaware

California

Utah

Colorado River

Colorado

Kansas

Missouri

Missouri River

Ohio

Ohio River

Kentucky

Maryland

Virginia

West Virginia

Arizona

New Mexico

Rio Grande

Oklahoma

Arkansas River

Mississippi River

Tennessee

North Carolina

South Carolina

Texas

Louisiana

Mississippi

Alabama

Georgia

Florida

MEXICO

Gulf of Mexico

Pacific Ocean

Atlantic Ocean

CUBA

HAITI

PUERTO RICO

JAMAICA

DOMINICAN REPUBLIC

Caribbean Sea

BELIZE

CENTRAL AMERICA

HONDURAS

GUATEMALA

EL SALVADOR

COSTA RICA

NICARAGUA

PANAMA

SOUTH AMERICA

SOUTH AMERICA, 1914

Caracas

BRITISH
GUIANA

VENEZUELA

DUTCH
GUIANA

FRENCH
GUIANA

North

Atlantic

Ocean

Bogotá

COLOMBIA

**Galápagos
Islands**

ECUADOR

Quito

Amazon River

A m a z o n   B a s i n

BRAZIL

São Francisco River

PERU

Lima

A n d e s

La Paz

BOLIVIA

Sucre

M o u n t a i n s

PARAGUAY

Paraná River

Rio de Janeiro

South

Pacific

Ocean

CHILE

Santiago

ARGENTINA

URUGUAY

Buenos Aires

Montevideo

South

Atlantic

Ocean

Negro River

**Falkland
Islands**
(British)

Stanley

**South
Georgia**

**Cape
Horn**

Great Events from History

The 20th Century

1901-1940

1923

DISCOVERY OF THE COMPTON EFFECT

Arthur Holly Compton's explanation for the change in wavelength of X rays scattered from matter provided an important confirmation of the quantum theory of radiation.

LOCALE: St. Louis, Missouri
CATEGORIES: Science and technology; physics; chemistry

KEY FIGURES
Arthur Holly Compton (1892-1962), American physicist, educator, and philosopher
Joseph John Thomson (1856-1940), English physicist
Charles Thomson Rees Wilson (1869-1959), English physicist
Charles Glover Barkla (1877-1944), English physicist
Ernest Rutherford (1871-1937), English physicist

SUMMARY OF EVENT

The importance of the phenomenon known as the Compton effect to the fields of chemistry and physics can be appreciated only within the context of early twentieth century science. By the end of the nineteenth century, physical scientists were experiencing a general feeling of complacency. All material substances were known to be composed of molecules, which were understood to be specific combinations of atoms of the ninety or so elemental substances found in nature. The research of Joseph John Thomson indicated clearly that the negatively charged electron is a constituent of all atoms, which, because they are all neutral, had to have some type of positive particle also. Ernest Rutherford's famous experiment in which he scattered alpha particles from a thin film of gold provided evidence for his theory of atomic structure. Rutherford's atom was composed of a tiny, but massive, positive nucleus surrounded by space occupied by tiny electrons. Chemists and atomic physicists believed that they had a fairly clear picture of the structure of the material world.

Physicists were enamored of the laws of motion of Sir Isaac Newton, which had explained successfully the motion of objects varying in size from the near microscopic to the planets in the solar system. Equally well accepted were the laws of James Clerk Maxwell, which described the behavior of electromagnetic radiation. Set in this theory, light was seen as a type of electromagnetic wave phenomenon. The attitude of physicists was that the basic laws of nature had been discovered and that it was necessary only to continue their application in explaining natural phenomena.

One of the clear distinctions made by scientists by the end of the nineteenth century was the classification of natural phenomena as either particle or wave phenomena. Particles were thought of as bundles of matter possessing mass, which determines the way in which the particles respond to applied force. In addition to mass, two fundamental properties were associated with particles because of their motion. These are momentum and kinetic energy, both of which are conserved in the absence of interaction with some outside force. A particle of mass m and velocity v has kinetic energy equal to $mv2/2$ and momentum equal to mv. During a collision (any interaction in which the particles exert forces on one another) between two particles, momentum is always conserved. In some collisions, known as elastic collisions, kinetic energy is conserved also. Conservation of kinetic energy and momentum requires only that the total of each quantity is the same after the collision as before. The particles involved may exchange all or some of their momentum and kinetic energy with one another. Moving particles, then, may be seen as a means of transporting energy from one place to another.

Another means of transporting energy is the wave; familiar examples are water waves, sound waves, and electromagnetic waves such as light. All waves are characterized by wavelength lambda (distance between two identical points on adjacent waves) and frequency v (number of waves per unit time). Waves can be unambiguously identified by their ability to interfere with each other. Whenever two harmonic waves of equal amplitude intersect at some point in a medium, the net effect is the sum of the two waves. If the waves are always in phase at the intersection point, the net wave is twice that of either wave; but, if they are out of phase, they cancel. Two wave systems interfering in a medium give a pattern of amplitudes that is constant in time. Whenever a wave moves around some object or passes through a small opening, an interference pattern between waves coming from different points near the edge of the barrier is set up. This is known as a diffraction pattern. Observation of interference and diffraction patterns is regarded as a confirming test of the wave nature of a phenomenon. There was no doubt in the minds of early twentieth century physicists that light was a wave phenomenon. Diffraction and interference patterns had been observed and

Arthur Holly Compton. (The Nobel Foundation)

used in wavelength measurements.

X rays were discovered by Wilhelm Conrad Röntgen in the mid-1890's, and Max von Laue demonstrated the diffraction of X rays by crystals in 1912. It was determined quickly that X rays (electromagnetic waves of wavelength much shorter than that of light) provided a powerful new tool for the investigation of matter. Thomson studied the scattering of X rays by matter using the theory that the X rays interacted with bound electrons, causing them to oscillate at the same frequency as the incident radiation. The oscillating electrons, in turn, reradiated the energy at the same frequency as the incident radiation. Charles Glover Barkla investigated this phenomenon and found that the scattered X rays were of two kinds: One type had the same wavelength as the incident radiation and the second type had a longer wavelength.

It was at this point that Arthur Holly Compton investigated this secondary type of scattered radiation. His explanation helped to change the direction of physics. Compton's career as a research physicist began in 1919 when, as a Fellow of the National Research Council, he

studied at Rutherford's laboratory in Cambridge. He studied the scattering and absorption of gamma rays and observed that the scattered radiation was more absorbable than the primary. This observation led eventually to his discovery of the Compton effect. He thought that the increased absorption indicated a change in the wavelength of the scattered rays and, if light could be described as having particle-like behavior, a decrease in its momentum. Compton did not think that the accuracy of the gamma-ray data was enough to allow him to defend a photonic interpretation with confidence.

After his year at Cambridge, Compton moved to Washington University, where he intended to extend his gamma-scattering experiments into the X-ray region. Using a Bragg crystal spectrometer, he was able to analyze the scattered and primary radiation with great precision. Compton used monochromatic X rays from a molybdenum source, scattered from a target of graphite (a form of carbon), and found that the scattered rays contained radiation that had the same wavelength as the incident radiation as well as radiation of a longer wavelength. The wavelength of this second type of scattered radiation varied in a systematic way with the scattering angle.

This change in wavelength could not be explained in terms of the classical theories of electrodynamics. In 1922, after all attempts to use classical explanations had failed, Compton arrived at his revolutionary quantum theory for the interaction. He treated the process as a collision between a free electron and an X-ray quantum having kinetic energy and momentum. Applying the laws of conservation to the collision, Compton was able to derive the equations for the Compton effect in the form in which they are used today and found exact agreement with his data. The kinetic energy and the momentum of the scattered photon were decreased by an amount equal exactly to that acquired by the electron, which then recoiled. When Compton first proposed his explanation, there was no experimental evidence for the recoil electron, but this evidence was provided shortly afterward by Charles Thomson Rees Wilson, who observed tracks in the cloud chamber, which could be explained in terms of Compton's theory.

SIGNIFICANCE

The Compton effect holds a position of primary importance in the development of modern physics. From the time of its first discovery and explanation, it has stimulated the development of quantum mechanics by providing experimental evidence that classical mechanics and electrodynamics were powerless to explain. During the entire early period of quantum theory (from 1920 to 1930), the Compton effect was a central phenomenon against which the theory could be tested. It provided conclusive proof that Albert Einstein's concept of the photon (introduced early in the 1900's to explain the photoelectric emission of electrons) as having both energy and momentum was correct. It also indicated that material particles have a wave nature and show interference effects. This wave-particle duality found in both radiation and matter lies at the heart of modern quantum theory.

This remarkable discovery had consequences that went far beyond the photon concept; it became the basis for Werner Heisenberg's uncertainty principle, one of the most important developments in quantum theory. For an electron to be located, it must be irradiated with photons of high energy, because errors in position are minimized by radiation of short wavelength. To be seen, the photon must enter the objective of the observing microscope, which gives a range of directions because of the finite width of the opening. As only the approximate direction of the photon is known after the collision, the recoil of the electron may be known only approximately. Attempts to increase accuracy of the position measurement increase uncertainty in the recoil momentum, because even shorter wavelengths must be used. The net result of this is that the more information is gained about one of these variables, the less is known about the other variable. This forms the essence of the uncertainty principle.

The Compton effect has played an important role in many diverse areas of science. For example, it has affected radiation shielding in nuclear physics. A beam of radiation is attenuated as it passes through matter as the photons are absorbed or scattered by the material. One of the experimental facts that Compton found was that the relative intensities of the primary and secondary radiation depend on the wavelength of the exciting radiation. The importance of the processes involved in attenuating the beam depends on the photon energies. Information of this type is useful for the design of radiation shielding.

The Compton effect has been used directly in the early diagnosis of osteoporosis, a disease indicated by changes in bone density. The Compton scattering of gamma rays from bone has an intensity that depends on the number of scattering centers. This, in turn, is related to the density of the bone material. Similar techniques have been developed for the diagnosis of lung diseases that affect tissue density.

Scientists have also obtained information about the electronic structure of molecules and crystals from the Compton effect. A Doppler shift resulting from the motion of the electrons toward or away from the photon either adds to or subtracts from the Compton shift. Extensive study of the line broadening because of this Doppler shift has provided physicists and chemists information about the momenta of electrons in matter.

—Grace A. Banks

FURTHER READING

Boorse, Henry A., and Lloyd Motz. "The Compton Effect." In *The World of the Atom*. New York: Basic Books, 1966. Brief description of the Compton effect and its importance to the development of physics. Also features reprints of a 1962 essay on Compton by S. K. Allison originally published in *Science* and two of Compton's early papers.

Crease, Robert P., and Charles C. Mann. *The Second Creation: Makers of the Revolution in Twentieth-Century Physics*. Rev. ed. New Brunswick, N.J.: Rutgers University Press, 1996. Follows the development of physics from its nineteenth century roots to the enigmatic mysteries of the late twentieth century. Examines characters and personalities as well as the issues of physics. Includes brief discussion of the Compton effect.

Ford, Kenneth W. *The Quantum World: Quantum Physics for Everyone*. Cambridge, Mass.: Harvard University Press, 2004. Explains the concepts of quantum physics in nontechnical language for lay readers. Illustrated.

Heathcote, Niels H. de V. *Nobel Prize Winners in Physics, 1901-1950*. New York: Henry Schuman, 1953. The chapter on Compton contains a clear, nonmathematical description of the Compton effect. Quotes extensively from Compton's Nobel lecture. Suitable for readers with little background in physics.

Hendry, John. *The Creation of Quantum Mechanics and the Bohr-Pauli Dialogue*. Boston: D. Reidel, 1984. History of quantum mechanics intended for readers who have had at least an introduction to quantum mechanics at the beginning college level. Includes discussion of the Compton effect and its importance to American physicists.

Massey, Sir Harrie. *The New Age in Physics*. 2d ed. New York: Harper, 1967. Provides a clear and interesting account of the development of twentieth century physics. Discusses the wave-particle question in the first two chapters, as well as other topics important to an understanding of the Compton effect.

Stuewer, Roger H. *The Compton Effect: Turning Point in Physics*. New York: Science History Publications, 1975. Detailed analysis of the theoretical and experi-

1923

mental work in the field of radiation physics related to the background, discovery, and impact of the Compton effect. Accessible to readers with a general background in college-level physics.

SEE ALSO: 1906: Barkla Discovers the Characteristic X Rays of the Elements; Dec. 10, 1906: Thomson Wins the Nobel Prize for Discovering the Electron; 1920-1930: Millikan Investigates Cosmic Rays.

1923
FEDERAL POWER COMMISSION DISALLOWS KINGS RIVER DAMS

The Federal Power Commission rejected the San Joaquin Light and Power Company's application for a permit to build hydroelectric plants in Kings Canyon in the Sierra Nevada. The decision demonstrated that the fledgling commission had the will and the power to stand up to the energy industry, and it helped safeguard Kings Canyon from development until 1940, when it became a national park.

LOCALE: Kings Canyon, California
CATEGORIES: Environmental issues; natural resources; government and politics; energy

KEY FIGURES
Oscar C. Merrill (fl. early twentieth century), chief engineer of the U.S. Forest Service and later executive secretary of the Federal Power Commission
William Kelly (fl. early twentieth century), chief engineer for the Federal Power Commission
John Muir (1838-1914), American naturalist and wilderness advocate
Gifford Pinchot (1865-1946), American conservationist

SUMMARY OF EVENT
Kings Canyon National Park is located in California's Sierra Nevada. Established in 1940, the park is noted for its spectacular mountain scenery, as well as for its groves of sequoias, or giant redwoods. The park's pristine beauty was almost lost to future generations in the 1920's, however, when speculators made plans to develop a series of dams and powerhouses on the forks of the Kings River. Only the timely intervention of the Federal Power Commission (FPC) in 1923 prevented an industrial development from occurring in what has since been recognized as one of North America's most scenic wilderness areas.

When the FPC rejected the San Joaquin Light and Power Company's application for a permit for hydropower development on the Kings River, the agency

was barely three years old. Congress had created the Federal Power Commission in 1920 following nearly forty years of lobbying and debate. The first hydropower development in the United States occurred in 1882, but despite the advantages noted by conservationists such as Gifford Pinchot—that hydroelectric power was a clean and a continually self-renewing resource—hydropower construction in general lagged well behind construction of steam-powered generating plants. For many years, the typical hydropower facility was a small run-of-the-river plant employing a simple diversion dam. Industrialists were reluctant to rely on hydropower, as its availability was often subject to seasonal fluctuations.

As the scale of power plants increased, moreover, steam plants also presented fewer legal complications. Many of the early hydropower plants were constructed on privately owned lands, and the electricity was generated within a single state. The legal questions that arose initially regarding permits and licenses did not seem too different from the concerns revolving around steam plants, such as ownership of the land on which the plant was to be built and rights-of-way for transmission lines. Federal jurisdiction came into play in only a few situations, for example if the waters involved were subject to international treaties or if the waters were located on federal reserves. The Federal Dam Act of 1906 added a third area of federal jurisdiction—navigable waters—and these three separate areas became the basis of federal authority over waterpower.

Riparian rights for the early developers of hydropower were also relatively simple. Because a hydroelectric plant does not permanently remove water from a river, downstream users and landowners in most states had little say in upstream development. A developer had only to purchase the land for the proposed dam and powerhouse, along with any area to be flooded by the reservoir the dam would create. As advances in both civil and electrical engineering led to increases in the scale of projects—from small diversion dams impounding a few acre-feet of water to large gravity and arch dams impounding reservoirs several miles in length and from transmission lines reaching five or ten miles to transmission lines stretching for hundreds of miles—the legal situation became more complicated.

By 1900, both conservationists and industrialists were citing the lack of a coherent federal water policy as a reason for the lack of development of hydropower. Despite the general agreement that definite policies were necessary, however, Congress accomplished nothing concrete until the outbreak of hostilities in Europe. Following the entry of the United States into World War I, with both conservationists and industrialists urging Congress to pass a comprehensive waterpower bill to help cope with a potential power shortage brought on by a scarcity of fuel oil, the legislative deadlock was finally broken. Still, it was not until late in 1918 that a compromise bill was introduced. Written by Oscar C. Merrill, chief engineer for the U.S. Forest Service, the bill proposed creating a commission that would consist of the

three departments already involved in waterpower regulation—the Departments of War, Interior, and Agriculture—and that would oversee waterpower on navigable streams, public lands, and national forests. Legislative inertia following the end of the war slowed the bill's passage, so it was not until June 10, 1920, that the Federal Water Power Act was signed into law.

Developers almost immediately swamped the newly created Federal Power Commission with applications for power development projects, including development on the Kings River. The application by the San Joaquin Light and Power Company called for three storage reservoirs, eight diversion dams, thirty-five miles of power tunnels and ditches, and seven powerhouses. The development, designed with a capacity of 266,000 horsepower, would have covered fourteen thousand acres in the Kings Canyon region. Two of the plants would have operated with effective heads of more than two thousand feet. ("Head" refers to the difference in elevation between the point at a dam where water enters the power tunnel leading to the hydroelectric turbines and the point where the water exits the turbine.)

The pristine natural beauty of Kings Canyon had already been recognized for decades by the time San Joaquin Light and Power applied to the FPC to build there. John Muir, one of the founders of the Sierra Club, was an early advocate of the creation of Kings Canyon National Park. Many preservationists, including Muir, had been urging that a national park be created south of Yosemite, a park that would include Kings Canyon, even before Yosemite was officially designated a national park in 1890. As early as 1891, in an article published in *The Century* magazine, Muir had described the region as even grander than the already famous Yosemite Valley. Muir made numerous trips into the Kings River area, often accompanied by other preservationists, but he died in 1914, before his goal of preserving all of the High Sierra could be accomplished.

The chronically understaffed FPC was able to act on only a handful of

KINGS CANYON, CALIFORNIA

the applications it received (more than two hundred by 1924). While Secretary Merrill pleaded for additional staff to handle the backlog, other engineers began to question the merits of many of the applications. William Kelly, chief engineer for the Federal Power Commission, toured the western states in 1922. Kelly reportedly noted that many of the conditions following World War I that had led to the passage of the Federal Water Power Act in 1920—scarcity of fuel oil, for example—were no longer valid. Kelly observed that the rapid development of hydroelectric sites seemed in some cases to be outpacing justification for their development.

The combination of an overwhelming backlog of applications and the perception that additional development was unnecessary may have led to Merrill's decision to reject multiple pending applications. Trade publications such as *Power* reported that the FPC had decided to clear its record of applications for preliminary permits for a number of sites around the country. The proposed Kings River project was one such project, and the San Joaquin Light and Power Company was informed that they would not receive a permit. Before the company could reapply, the demand for hydropower development abated. As Kelly had noted, fuel oil was no longer in short supply. The pressure to develop hydroelectric sites as an alternative to fossil fuels eased, and the project no longer seemed as lucrative an investment.

SIGNIFICANCE

The Federal Power Commission's action proved significant for two very different reasons. First, Merrill's decision to reject so many applications at once had the seemingly contradictory effect of both helping to establish the authority of the FPC in regulating hydroelectric development and highlighting the young agency's many structural weaknesses. As authorized under the Federal Water Power Act of 1920, the FPC had only one employee, its executive secretary, Oscar Merrill. Congress had failed to allocate funding for even one clerk-typist for the FPC; all support staff had to be borrowed from the component departments, as the FPC could not hire anyone independently.

For example, William Kelly, who in 1922 had recommended against approving many of the applications on file, had been borrowed from the War Department and the Army Corps of Engineers. Prior to being assigned to the FPC, Colonel Kelly had worked on fortification construction for most of his engineering career. He was not an electrical engineer by training, but few military engineers at that time were. Merrill's reli-

ance on Kelly's advice showed how limited the personnel resources of the Federal Power Commission actually were.

In addition, conservationists who had lobbied for the creation of the FPC noticed the often cursory reviews given to permit applications. Rather than weighing the merits of each application in terms of the best use of natural resources, as Gifford Pinchot and others had hoped the FPC would do, the young commission was quickly accused of too often considering only engineering design criteria. Merrill's action in rejecting so many applications out of hand emphasized that the FPC was so understaffed that it was unable to fulfill its mission properly.

At the same time, until the FPC acted in 1923 to reject dubious applications, such as that for the Kings Canyon project, many observers in both the hydroelectric industry and the conservation movement may have doubted the commission's willingness to stand up to industry. Chronically shorthanded and hounded by would-be developers, the FPC might easily have become little more than a licensing bureau that passively collected permit fees and gave rubber-stamped approvals to all applications. Rejecting applications such as the one proposed by San Joaquin Light and Power for development on the Kings River demonstrated to the hydroelectric industry that the FPC was willing to turn down a developer. Despite the doubts of conservationists, the days of wildcat speculation in hydroelectric development on federal lands had ended.

Second, rejection of the application for development on the Kings River preserved the essential wilderness character of the region. A few years earlier, wilderness preservationists had lost the battle to prevent construction of the O'Shaughnessy Dam in Yosemite National Park's Hetch Hetchy Valley. The timely intervention of the FPC, although motivated by nonaesthetic concerns, meant that Kings Canyon would not be similarly modified. Even though the canyon did suffer depredations from logging, its river was not dammed, nor were any of its canyons inundated by reservoirs. If not a totally virgin wilderness, Kings Canyon is still far more unspoiled than many national parks. Visitors to Kings Canyon can still enjoy a mountain wilderness little different from that visited by John Muir in the late nineteenth century.

Muir believed that, like Yosemite, Kings Canyon's depth, width, and flat valley floor were the result of glacial action. The notebooks Muir filled with his impressions of the High Sierra contain numerous sketches of Kings Canyon rock formations and the evidence they displayed of extensive glaciation. Because the FPC seemingly saved Kings Canyon almost by accident rather than by acting deliberately to preserve the region, it is hard to say if Muir's many years of drawing attention to the beauty of the High Sierra played any role in Merrill's decision to reject the San Joaquin Light and Power application. While lobbying for passage of the Federal Water Power Act, Merrill had voiced strong preservationist sentiments regarding unique natural areas such as the Grand Canyon, so it is possible that he based his decision on more than simple economic analyses of the projected need for electricity in California. In any case, whether initially saved deliberately or by accident, Kings Canyon was designated as a national park in 1940. It remains natural and unspoiled, a uniquely beautiful national treasure.

—*Nancy Farm Mannikko*

Further Reading

Baum, Robert David. *The Federal Power Commission and State Utility Regulation*. Washington, D.C.: American Council on Public Affairs, 1942. Hard to find, but one of the few books to examine the history of the Federal Power Commission.

Blehm, Eric. *The Last Season*. New York: Harper-Collins, 2006. Story of the disappearance of a ranger who spent twenty-eight years working in the Kings Canyon and Sequoia National Parks. Although focused on the tragic life of one man, it contains a wealth of information about the parks, their history, and the day-to-day routine of the people who work to preserve them. Includes maps and illustrations.

Despain, Joel. *Hidden Beneath the Mountains: The Caves of Sequoia and Kings Canyon National Parks*. Dayton, Ohio: Cave Books, 2003. Useful guide to one of the least-known but most breathtaking resources of Kings Canyon National Park.

Grunsky, Frederic R., ed. *South of Yosemite: Selected Writings by John Muir*. Garden City, N.Y.: Natural History Press, 1968. Vivid descriptions of the Sierra Nevada range and Kings Canyon. Illustrated with Muir's sketches and black-and-white photographs.

Gulliver, John S., and Roger E. A. Arndt. *Hydropower Engineering Handbook*. New York: McGraw-Hill, 1991. While much of the mathematics may be comprehensible only to civil engineers, the lucid explanations of the different factors involved in hydroelectric development and the numerous accompanying illustrations make this book an invaluable resource for anyone interested in the topic.

Hughes, Thomas P. *Networks of Power*. Baltimore: The Johns Hopkins University Press, 1983. Fascinating history of electrification in the United States and Europe. Lavishly illustrated. A classic in the history of technology.

Jones, Holway R. *John Muir and the Sierra Club: The Battle for Yosemite*. San Francisco: Sierra Club Books, 1965. Excellent history of the early years of the Sierra Club and one of its first preservation battles, the attempt to prevent the construction of the dam in the Hetch Hetchy Valley. Lavishly illustrated with excellent photographs.

See also: Dec. 19, 1913: U.S. Congress Approves a Dam in Hetch Hetchy Valley; Aug. 25, 1916: National Park Service Is Created; July 18, 1932: St. Lawrence Seaway Treaty; Jan., 1937-Feb., 1940: Adams Lobbies Congress to Preserve Kings Canyon; June 21, 1938: Natural Gas Act.

1923

1923
GERMANS BARTER FOR GOODS IN RESPONSE TO HYPERINFLATION

When inflation made the German mark virtually worthless, Germans resorted to barter as a replacement for currency transactions.

LOCALE: Germany
CATEGORIES: Trade and commerce; government and politics; economics

KEY FIGURES
Charles G. Dawes (1865-1951), American attorney, politician, and financier
Hans Luther (1879-1962), German minister of finance, 1923-1925
Gustav Stresemann (1878-1929), chancellor of the Weimar Republic
Benjamin Strong (1872-1928), governor of the Federal Reserve Bank of New York, 1914-1928

SUMMARY OF EVENT
In 1923, inflation of the German mark, begun during World War I, reached such proportions that Germans resorted to barter for many of their economic transactions. Stores closed every day at noon so that clerks could change prices on products. Prices often rose during the morning hours to double what they were at opening time. Germans who were paid wages or salaries rushed to buy things with the money, because within hours it would lose half its value. Farmers refused to sell their produce, for the money received had no value except to pay taxes and to pay off any mortgages they had. Businesspeople rushed to take out loans at banks and then hastened to spend the money, buying virtually anything, because by the next day it could be sold for far more than the amount of the loan. People with mortgages on their property paid them off in money that was scarcely worth the paper on which it was printed. Debtors reaped a bonanza, and creditors were impoverished.

The roots of the German hyperinflation go back to World War I. Like all major nations in 1914, Germany was on the gold standard. Any citizen could turn in bank notes and receive gold coins of equivalent value. The first measure to pass the German Reichstag in August of 1914 relieved the Reichsbank, the German central bank, of this requirement. It was the passage of this act that represented Germany's commitment to go to war to aid its Austrian ally. Relieved of the need to redeem bank notes in gold, the Reichsbank financed the war on credit. Semiannual war-bond drives were held (the bonds were per-

petual, meaning that the principal would never be repaid, and carried a low rate of interest), and special loan banks were created to handle the sale of war bonds.

Many of the war bonds were discounted (used as collateral for loans) at the banks, which in turn rediscounted them at the Central bank. These bonds provided the "reserves" behind the increasing amount of bank notes issued by the central bank. By the end of World War I, the amount of money in circulation was about five times what it had been in 1914. In neutral markets, where gold redemption still prevailed, the mark was worth no more than half what it had been before the war. The domestic price index rose 100 percent in four years.

Once stable government was restored following the German Revolution of 1918-1919, the new republic that emerged found itself faced with a formidable financial problem. It had lost 10 percent of its territory and more than 10 percent of its tax base, as many of the lands it was forced to cede to its neighbors were among the most productive economically. It owed 98 billion marks, in the form of war bonds, to its citizens. In the first years of the republic, paying the interest on this obligation absorbed most of the central government's revenue. In addition, it owed immense sums in gold to the victorious Allies in the form of reparations. Where reparations were demanded in the form of goods and equipment, it had to compensate the private owners of those goods. Between 1919 and 1923, governmental revenues never exceeded 35 percent of outlays, and a formidable debt accumulated.

One major source of financial problems were the reparations demanded by the Allies, on the grounds that Germany had caused the war. The German government had to make the payments, but it could get the money to do so only by taxing its citizens or by borrowing. Because a large portion of the economic base of Germany was decimated, either through territorial losses or reparations in kind, the nation's resources to generate taxes were reduced. The German government was required to make cash reparations payments in gold. Because Germany had negligible gold deposits of its own, this gold could be acquired only through a massive excess of exports over imports. Even then, the government somehow had to acquire the gold earned by private firms and individuals through their exporting activities.

The German government resorted to printing money to pay obligations that could be met with marks. The result was inflation of prices and a tremendous increase in borrowing. Private individuals borrowed money to buy things they wanted or needed, knowing that when they had to pay the money back it would be worth far less. Governments at the federal, state, and local levels borrowed money both to finance ongoing operations and to pay off old debt. Any old debt that could be paid off made money for the debtor. Debts expressed in marks required only to be paid off in the same number of paper marks, even though they were worth, in terms of purchasing power, only a fraction of the original indebtedness. Lenders had failed to provide for inflation in setting the terms of their loans. As all these new debt instruments were presented at banks for discount, the banks needed currency to pay them off. They turned to the Reichsbank, which began printing more and more bank notes. In the early fall of 1923, the need for new bank notes became so great that although 30 paper mills and 150 printing plants were devoted exclusively to printing money, they could not keep up with the demand. As the German mark steadily became less meaningful as a way of expressing value, everyone began valuing everything in dollars, based on the exchange rate of the moment.

In January, 1923, the French and Belgians, alleging minor defaults in reparations payments, marched into the Ruhr Valley, Germany's industrial heartland. The object was to seize the industrial plants of the Ruhr and force these to produce directly for the Allies. The German response was "passive resistance," as both labor and management refused to operate the plants. Eventually, the French and Belgians brought in operators of their own, but in the meantime the German government assumed responsibility for paying support to all those engaged in passive resistance. Money was being paid out by the government, even though no salable goods were being produced. Passive resistance and the cost shouldered by the government in connection with it caused inflation to spin out of control.

By September, it was clear that something would have to be done. The existing government resigned and was replaced by one headed by Gustav Stresemann. Passive resistance was ended. At the suggestion of Hans Luther, the German finance minister, the government decided to issue a new currency, to be called the Rentenmark, which would be backed by the agricultural and industrial real estate of Germany. The decree authorizing the Rentenmark was issued on October 15, 1923. One month later, paper marks were declared worthless and exchanged at the rate of one trillion Reichsmarks for one Rentenmark, declared to be the equivalent of one gold mark.

A new bank called the Rentenbank was created and authorized to issue up to 3.2 billion Rentenmark notes. Of this sum, 1.2 billion were to be made available to the government for the payment of salaries and other obligations. The remainder was available for loans to business, in an effort to get the economy started again. Over the succeeding six months, Rentenmarks gradually replaced the old paper currency in circulation. As the government reformed taxes, it began to receive revenue in the new, stable currency to carry on its affairs. The entire system was made possible by a moratorium on reparations payments while the issue was studied by an international committee headed by Charles G. Dawes, an attorney and financier who later became vice president of the United States. Eventually, in what is known as the Dawes Plan, a scaled-down version of reparations was put in place, and the economic situation in Germany returned to relative normalcy.

SIGNIFICANCE

Assessing the impact of the German hyperinflation involves determining who were the winners and who were the losers. Generally, debtors were the winners. These included both public debtors and private debtors. Public debtors included both the central government, the Reich, and state and local governments. Old obligations could be paid off with paper marks worth a fraction of the old marks that were convertible to gold. As a result, the central government, which owed its citizens 98 billion marks in war debt in 1918, reduced its debt to almost nothing. Many states and municipalities also paid off old debts.

Many private debts were also paid off at a fraction of their former worth. Many mortgages contracted in an earlier era were paid off. When debts were bills for purchased goods, late in the inflation the courts began to hold that the constitutional requirement of equity meant that a sum more nearly equal to the current value of the goods in question had to be paid. Large businesses in particular profited from the inflation. Banks had been accustomed to financing much business activity, and the time spread between the date of a loan to buy raw materials or machinery and the time when those raw materials were converted into salable items enormously magnified their value in paper marks. In effect, the interest rate on revalued debts was adjusted to compensate lenders for inflation.

Even the banks made money, thanks to the inveterate Reichsbank policy of keeping interest rates low. Commercial banks could make loans to businesses at relatively high interest rates, then discount the bills at the

Reichsbank at a much lower rate. The spread represented a substantial profit.

Losers from the inflation included savers and creditors. Those who had invested their money in mortgages found the mortgages paid off in worthless paper marks. Somewhere between one-fourth and one-half of the German electorate had savings that disappeared in the inflation, and the Germans have never forgotten this. Almost 10 percent of the German population had lived off income from savings and investments prior to World War I. These people were reduced to abject poverty.

After the stabilization plan was put in place, a bitter battle ensued concerning the revaluation of old debts. Initially, many government officials favored a ban on revaluation, but as the outcry of the dispossessed increased, politicians changed their position. Moreover, Stresemann, who became chancellor in August of 1923, opposed a ban. Furthermore, courts were increasingly responding to pleas from creditors that the repayment of debts in worthless paper marks did not accord with equity. Several court decisions in late 1922 and early 1923 required the renegotiation of contracts as a result of the inflation. By November, 1923, the courts were stating unequivocally that creditors were entitled to relief.

The difficulty with revaluation was that the stabilization of the currency would be vitiated if revaluation amounted to any significant percentage of debts. New money would have to be printed to pay the higher debts, and inflation would return. The original proposal called for 10 percent revaluation, but this meager amount resulted in protests forcing upward revision of the percentage. In February of 1924, the government issued the Tax Decree, in which guidelines for revaluation were laid down. The level of revaluation was raised from 10 percent to 15 percent and would include municipal bonds that had been issued for income-producing activities such as gas works. Under pressure from the Social Democratic Party, the government agreed that savings deposits in banks and life insurance policies would also be revalued. This proposal won the support of the banking, industrial, and commercial interests of Germany.

Nevertheless, there was sufficient opposition to these terms in the Reichstag that the government decided to call for a new election, to take place in May of 1924. New claims for revaluation began to be heard from savings banks, the portfolios of which were full of government bonds. They began to demand revaluation of government bonds, given that they were going to have to revalue the savings accounts of their depositors. Churches, especially the Catholic Church, called for substantial revalua-

tion. Many of their charitable activities were financed by endowments, especially mortgages. Moreover, some courts were responding to individual pleas for revaluation and setting their own rates. It was clear that a new mandate from the populace, to be followed by legislation by the new Reichstag, was the only answer.

Unfortunately, the election of May, 1924, yielded no solid majority for any political party or grouping of parties. A weak minority government was formed. It decided to appoint a Committee on Revaluation to draft legislation on the subject. It was now recognized that government bonds would have to be revalued; however, as Finance Minister Luther pointed out, any significant revaluation would reduce the interest rate to a negligible amount. It was now also agreed that mortgages would have to be revalued, with a revaluation rate of 25 percent finding general favor. At the same time that creditors were pressing for upward revision of the revaluation percentages, the U.S. government was working in the opposite direction. Benjamin Strong, governor of the Federal Reserve Bank of New York, stated explicitly that any major upward revision of revaluation would cause American loans to German firms to dry up, as Americans would believe that the added debt burden would prevent German firms from earning enough to repay their foreign loans.

The final compromise on revaluation was reached in a law passed on July 15, 1925. The legislation specified different percentages of revaluation for various kinds of financial assets. Mortgages were to be revalued at 25 percent and industrial obligation bonds at 15 percent (with an additional 10 percent in special cases). Government bonds were revalued at 12.5 percent provided that the holder had purchased the bond before July 1, 1920; bonds purchased after that date were revalued at 2.5 percent. All government bonds were required to be surrendered for new redemption bonds. Repayment of these would not take place until at least 1932. One-thirtieth of the bonds would be repaid each year, with a lottery determining which bonds those would be.

Commercial bank accounts were not revalued. Savings bank accounts were subjected to revaluation according to a complex formula that pooled claims and then divided the repayments according to the size of the claim. The interest rate for private debt was set at 1.2 percent in 1925, with incremental additions until it reached 5 percent in 1928. Employee savings accounts with employers were revalued at varying amounts resulting from individual negotiation.

Although most creditors received something from the revaluation, many remained deeply embittered. Moreover, the burden of repayment falling on the government, the restrictions imposed by the Allies on the operations of the Reichsbank, and the fear of a repetition of the inflationary debacle forced all levels of government to balance their budgets. When the Great Depression hit Germany in 1930, with greater impact in 1931 and 1932, the central government found it impossible to respond with fiscal stimulus. Throughout the twentieth century, German governments remained hampered in their fiscal and monetary policies because of deep-rooted fears of a repetition of the hyperinflation of the 1920's.

—*Nancy M. Gordon*

FURTHER READING

Feldman, Gerald D. *The Great Disorder: Politics, Economics, and Society in the German Inflation, 1914-1924*. New York: Oxford University Press, 1997. In-depth examination of the economic crisis in Germany includes discussion of the Dawes Plan. Features illustrations, tables, bibliography, and index.

Guttmann, William, and Patricia Meehan. *The Great Inflation: Germany, 1919-1923*. Farnborough, England: Saxon House, 1975. Account of Germany's financial crisis written in nontechnical language.

Holtfrerich, Carl-Ludwig. *The German Inflation, 1914-1923*. Translated by Theo Balderston. Berlin: De Gruyter, 1986. Economist's account of the German crisis. Highly technical; includes many statistics.

Hughes, Michael L. *Paying for the German Inflation*. Chapel Hill: University of North Carolina Press, 1988. Focuses on the struggle over revaluation and presents many details that illuminate who won and who lost as a result of the inflation.

Ringer, Fritz, ed. *The German Inflation of 1923*. New York: Oxford University Press, 1969. Collection of materials from other sources provides a handy resource for readers interested in a variety of interpretations of the inflation. Concludes with a section on the contribution of the inflation to Adolf Hitler's rise.

Stolper, Gustav. *German Economy, 1870-1940*. New York: Reynal & Hitchcock, 1940. Provides a wealth of details and a broad perspective on Germany's financial history.

Wueschner, Silvano A. *Charting Twentieth-Century Monetary Policy: Herbert Hoover and Benjamin Strong, 1917-1927*. Westport, Conn.: Greenwood Press, 1999. Examination of the influence of Hoover, as secretary of commerce, and Strong, as governor of the Federal Reserve Bank of New York, on U.S. monetary policy, both domestic and international, in the period when the Dawes Plan was formulated. Chapters 2 and 3 include discussion of the Dawes Plan.

SEE ALSO: Jan. 11, 1923-Aug. 16, 1924: France Occupies the Ruhr; Sept. 1, 1924: Dawes Plan.

1923

KAHN DEVELOPS A MODIFIED SYPHILIS TEST

Reuben Leon Kahn's development of a simplified test for detection of the venereal disease syphilis made better control of syphilis possible and also led eventually to Kahn's development of the universal serologic test, an advance in immunology.

LOCALE: University of Michigan, Ann Arbor
CATEGORY: Health and medicine

KEY FIGURES
Reuben Leon Kahn (1887-1974), Soviet-born American serologist and immunologist
August von Wassermann (1866-1925), German physician and bacteriologist

SUMMARY OF EVENT

Syphilis is one of the chief venereal diseases, a group of diseases whose name derives from that of Venus, the Roman goddess of love. The term "venereal" arose from the idea that the diseases were transmitted solely through sexual contact with infected individuals. Although syphilis is almost always contracted in this way, it occasionally arises after contact with objects used by syphilis-infected people in highly unhygienic surroundings, particularly in the underdeveloped countries of the world.

Many believe that syphilis was first introduced in Europe by the members of Christopher Columbus's crew, supposedly after they were infected by sexual contact with West Indian women during their voyages of exploration. Columbus is reported to have died of heart and brain problems very similar to symptoms produced by advanced syphilis. According to many historians, syphilis spread rapidly throughout sixteenth century Europe.

New diseases are always devastating, partly because

1923

1817

of lack of immunity, and early syphilis was no exception. Regrettably, the limited medicine of the time was of little help, and the early death rate from the disease was high. Every country blamed the high incidence of syphilis on some other nation (for example, the French called syphilis the Spanish disease, and vice versa). It was not until 1530 that the Italian physician and poet Fracastor coined the name "syphilis" in an epic poem.

The origin of syphilis in the Western Hemisphere is supported by the reported paleontological evidence of its existence in pre-Columbian skeletons throughout North, South, and Central America. In contrast, no such evidence has been obtained—according to proponents of this theory—in the pre-Columbian remains found in Europe or Asia. Another group of researchers has argued that this theory of the origin of syphilis is not correct, and controversy over the issue continues in the twenty-first century.

Modern syphilis is much milder than the original disease, and relatively uncommon, but if it is not identified and treated appropriately, it can be devastating and even fatal. When syphilis is passed from a pregnant woman to her unborn child, the results are often serious health problems for the child that can include paralysis, insanity, and heart disease. Given the potential negative effects of the disease, the detection and cure of syphilis are important worldwide.

Syphilis is caused by a spiral-shaped germ, called a spirochete, *Treponema pallidum.* Spirochetes enter the body through breaks in the skin or through the mucous membranes, regardless of how they are transmitted. Once spirochetes enter the body, they spread rapidly. During the first four to six weeks after infection—that is, in its primary phase—syphilis is very contagious. During this time, it is identified by the appearance of a sore, or chancre, at the entry site of the infecting spirochetes. The chancre disappears quickly, and within six to twenty-four weeks, the disease shows itself as a skin rash, feelings of malaise, and other flulike symptoms (secondary syphilis). These problems also disappear quickly in most cases, and latent syphilis begins. In latent syphilis, the individual has no symptoms, but spirochetes are spreading through the body. If they localize in the brain or the heart, they produce paralysis, mental derangement, and/or death. A person in this stage of syphilis can still infect sexual partners.

Today, the cure for syphilis is simple, consisting of treatment with penicillin or other types of antibiotics. Very frequently, such treatment is carried out in a venereal disease clinic or in the office of a family physician.

Because one of the most serious results of syphilis is infection of unborn children, Americans who apply for marriage licenses are required to prove that they are free of the disease, and obstetricians routinely test their pregnant patients for the disease. The early detection of syphilis remains very important because no vaccine is yet available against the disease.

The first viable test for syphilis was originated by August von Wassermann in 1906. In this test, blood samples are taken and treated in a medical laboratory. The treatment of the samples is based on the fact that the blood of afflicted persons has formed antibodies to fight *Treponema pallidum*, and these antibodies can react with other substances (an extract of lipid—fatlike—body chemicals) that cause changes in the blood component called complement. When this reaction occurs, complement is said to be "fixed" and the test is positive. After syphilis is cured, the antibodies disappear and complement is no longer fixed, so the Wassermann test becomes negative.

The Wassermann test is a useful indicator of syphilis in 95 percent of all infected persons, but it is also very time-consuming (requiring a two-day incubation period), complex, and somewhat lacking in sensitivity. In 1923, serologist and immunologist Reuben Leon Kahn developed a modified syphilis test, the "standard Kahn test," that was simpler, faster, and more sensitive. This test, which is based on the reaction of serum from the tested individual with an extract of certain lipid components of beef heart, is complete after a few minutes. By 1925, Kahn's test had become the standard syphilis test used by the U.S. Navy and later was employed worldwide for the detection of the disease.

SIGNIFICANCE

Kahn soon realized that his test for syphilis was not perfect, however. For example, in some cases, related to other diseases, false positive reactions and false negative reactions occurred. This led him to a broader study of the immune reactions that produced the Kahn test. He investigated the role of various tissues in immunity, as differentiated from the role of blood antibodies and white blood cells. Kahn showed, for example, that different tissues of immunized and nonimmunized animals possessed differing immunologic capabilities. Furthermore, the immunologic capabilities of test animals varied with their ages, being very limited in newborns and increasing as they matured.

By 1951, this effort led to Kahn's development of the "universal serological reaction," a precipitation reaction in which blood serum is tested against reagent composed of tissue lipids. Kahn viewed the reaction as a "potential serologic indicator of various situations in health and in different diseases." This effort constitutes an important landmark in the development of the science of immunology.

As W. Montague Cobb has noted, Kahn's scientific contributions represent three investigative careers: The first was the development of his practical, rapid precipitation test for syphilis and special procedures that helped to clarify reactions with lipid antigens (1920 to 1928), the second was a study of tissue immunity that identified differences of tissue localization of bacteria and foreign proteins in test animals of different ages and immune states (1930 to 1957), and the third was a study of radiation effects on this tissue localization (1957 to 1973). Kahn is most widely known, however, for his efforts in the serological testing for syphilis. His endeavors also served to stimulate other developments in the field of immunology, including the VDRL test (originated by the Venereal Disease Research Laboratory), which replaced the Kahn test as one of the most often used screening tests for syphilis.

—Sanford S. Singer

FURTHER READING

Allen, Peter Lewis. *The Wages of Sin: Sex and Disease, Past and Present*. Chicago: University of Chicago Press, 2002. Discusses societal attitudes toward the victims of disease, especially sexually transmitted diseases, from the Middle Ages to the beginning of the twenty-first century. Chapter 3 looks specifically at responses to syphilis sufferers in early modern Europe. Includes bibliography and index.

Cobb, W. Montague. "Reuben Leon Kahn, D.Sc, LL.D., M.D., Ph.D.—1887." *Journal of the National Medical Association* 63 (September, 1971): 388-394. One of the few available sources of biographical material on Kahn. Describes Kahn as both scientist and person, providing insight into his youth, education, and highlights of his life. Includes a complete list of Kahn's publications.

Kahn, Reuben L. *The Kahn Test: A Practical Guide*. Baltimore: Williams & Wilkins, 1928. Presents a summary of the precipitation phenomenon in syphilis and a detailed discussion of the technical use of the Kahn test. Meant as a guide for laboratory workers, includes information on apparatus, reagents, standardization of the antigen, use of the test, procedure, and special aspects.

_____. "Rapid Precipitation Phase of the Kahn Test for Syphilis, with New Method for Indicating Results." *Journal of the American Medical Association* 81 (July 14, 1923): 88-92. The original report of the Kahn test. Details the methodology and equipment utilized and indicates the advantages of the test over older methods and over Kahn's own earlier efforts.

_____. *Universal Serologic Reaction in Health and Disease*. New York: Commonwealth Fund, 1951. Presents data to support Kahn's contention that serologic reactions with lipid antigen are widely applicable as indicators of health and disease.

Parran, Thomas. *Shadow on the Land: Syphilis*. New York: Reynal & Hitchcock, 1937. Describes the impact of syphilis on U.S. public health and society in the early twentieth century. Includes a history of syphilis and discussion of its occurrence in North America and elsewhere.

Stansfield, William D. *Serology and Immunology: A Clinical Approach*. New York: Macmillan, 1981. Contains a comprehensive chapter on the etiology and serology of syphilis. Highly technical, rewarding information source for readers seeking details about methodology.

U.S. Public Health Service. *Syphilis: A Synopsis*. Washington, D.C.: Author, 2001. Brief text designed as a primer for physicians explains the tools of diagnosis and management of syphilis, the course of the disease, problems associated with congenital syphilis, and other topics.

SEE ALSO: Dec. 2-5, 1902: Founding of the International Sanitary Bureau; Apr., 1910: Ehrlich Introduces Salvarsan as a Cure for Syphilis; 1913: Schick Introduces a Test for Diphtheria; Jan., 1928: Papanicolaou Develops a Test for Diagnosing Uterine Cancer; Sept., 1928: Fleming Discovers Penicillin in Molds; 1932-1935: Domagk Discovers That Sulfonamides Can Save Lives; May, 1940: Florey and Chain Develop Penicillin as an Antibiotic.

1923

1923
THE TEN COMMANDMENTS ADVANCES AMERICAN FILM SPECTACLE

Cecil B. DeMille became Hollywood's preeminent producer-director of motion-picture spectacle with the critical and box-office success of The Ten Commandments *in 1923.*

LOCALE: United States
CATEGORY: Motion pictures

KEY FIGURES

Cecil B. DeMille (1881-1959), American film director-producer
Samuel Goldwyn (1882-1974), American film producer
Jesse L. Lasky (1880-1958), American show business entrepreneur
Jeanie Macpherson (1884-1946), American screenwriter
Adolph Zukor (1873-1976), American film producer

SUMMARY OF EVENT

When Cecil B. DeMille's epic *The Ten Commandments* opened in Los Angeles and New York in December, 1923, its enthusiastic reception immediately solidified DeMille's reputation as Hollywood's preeminent showman. Fans, critics, and Hollywood itself, with only a few exceptions, were dazzled. Completed at a cost of slightly less than $1.5 million, DeMille's silent-era spectacle rang up a box-office take of more than $4 million. James R. Quirk, the influential editor of *Photoplay* magazine, called it "the best photoplay ever made" and "the greatest theatrical spectacle in history." Hollywood's moguls rejoiced as well, because the film's epochal retelling of the story of Moses leading the Children of Israel out of bondage from Egypt to the Promised Land helped to defuse the efforts of conservative activists seeking to control the content of films through various forms of censorship.

Produced by the Famous Players-Lasky Corporation and released through its Paramount Pictures distribution arm, *The Ten Commandments* consolidated DeMille's reputation as the foremost American director of movie spectacles. Although esteemed for having codirected one of Hollywood's first feature-length films, *The Squaw Man* (1914), and for such popular and critically acclaimed productions as *The Cheat* (1915) and *Male and Female* (1919), in 1923 DeMille needed a hit to counter a recent downward spiral of such lackluster releases as *Adam's Rib* (1923), which had received only tepid box-office and critical support. DeMille knew as well as any-

one that in Hollywood he was considered only as good as his last picture. With the rousing success of *The Ten Commandments*, DeMille was again atop the short list of bankable and therefore elite Hollywood directors. Also, the epic was the first in a long line of lavish and successful extravaganzas—including his last directorial assignment, a second rendition of *The Ten Commandments* (1956)—that forever would be linked to the name of Cecil B. DeMille.

The Ten Commandments consists of two parts. The first, the spectacle, depicts biblical stories taken from the book of Exodus, including the persecution of the Jews by the Egyptians, the flight of the Israelites through the parted waters of the Red Sea, the giving to Moses of the Ten Commandments, and Moses' defiant breaking of the tablets upon his discovery of the Israelites' worship of the golden calf. The film's second part, a contemporary family melodrama set in San Francisco, centers on the moral conflicts between two brothers, one who is good and keeps the commandments, the other who is bad and breaks them. In essence, the second story is an allegory designed by DeMille and his dependable scenarist Jeanie Macpherson as a warning to modern society to heed God's injunctions. Therefore, when critics and historians refer to *The Ten Commandments* as a spectacle, they generally have in mind the film's sumptuously mounted prologue.

The larger-than-life dimensions of *The Ten Commandments* can be gauged in several ways. In 1923, a film budget of $1.5 million was staggering, especially given that the expense of a typical feature production of the period was about $100,000. Indeed, the film's epic budget, while making for headline-grabbing publicity, exacerbated already strained relations between DeMille and his partners, Adolph Zukor and Jesse L. Lasky, Famous Players-Lasky's president and vice president in charge of production, respectively. At one point in the midst of shooting, DeMille, fatigued by the constant carping from New York on such matters as an invoice for $2,500 for a pair of magnificent coal-black horses to draw a chariot, offered to buy the film outright for $1 million. DeMille's bold demonstration of faith in his project shocked Zukor and Lasky, who wisely decided to relent. Although each of the New York-based executives sent warm congratulatory telegrams to DeMille on the film's successful debut, the animosity created by the incessant budgetary wrangling during production eventually re-

Actor Theodore Roberts as Moses in a scene from The Ten Commandments. *(Hulton Archive/Getty Images)*

sulted in DeMille's painful resignation from Famous Players-Lasky in 1925.

Budgets aside, what most impressed moviegoers of 1923 and 1924 was the film's on-screen display of spectacle. Although thwarted by the cost-conscious Zukor from shooting on location in Egypt, DeMille bolted the confines of Hollywood for Guadalupe, an arid desert area near Santa Maria in central California, where a construction gang of more than one thousand carpenters, electricians, painters, and landscape gardeners erected a still-amazing facsimile of the ancient Egyptian city of Per-Ramses. As construction progressed, DeMille commuted to Los Angeles in order to shoot some of the film's interior scenes. Eventually, twenty-five hundred actors and forty-five hundred animals, including two hundred camels, were settled in Camp DeMille, itself a virtual replica of an army camp. For added authenticity, DeMille, in part reflecting the influence of David Belasco, the great theatrical realist with whom he had worked as a young man, hired a contingent of Orthodox Jews to play the Children of Israel.

DeMille's special-effects expert, Roy Pomeroy, played a pivotal role in the film's success by achieving such still-convincing miracles as the parting of the Red Sea, the drowning of the Egyptians, and Moses' reception of the Ten Commandments from the incendiary heavens. Indeed, most film historians have judged Pomeroy's effects of 1923 more convincing than those he created for DeMille's 1956 version of *The Ten Commandments*. The element of spectacle in the 1923 production was heightened even further by DeMille's decision to shoot parts of the prologue in an early and then experimental version of the Technicolor process (in contrast to the conventional black-and-white treatment given the modern story). Audiences and critics alike were impressed by the enhanced sense of realism.

SIGNIFICANCE

The Ten Commandments emphatically confirmed DeMille's reputation as one of Hollywood's most astute judges of public taste. Sensing that the vogue for Jazz Age depictions of fast living had begun to alienate a

1923

DeMille's Filmography

Cecil B. DeMille directed an exceptionally large number of motion pictures and became one of the most recognized names in American film.

Release Date	Title	Release Date	Title
1913	The Squaw Man	1921	Forbidden Fruit
1914	The Virginian		The Affairs of Anatol
	The Call of the North	1922	Fool's Paradise
	What's-His-Name		Saturday Night
	The Man from Home		Manslaughter
1915	The Rose of the Rancho	1923	Adam's Rib
	The Girl of the Golden West		The Ten Commandments
	The Warrens of Virginia	1924	Triumph
	The Unafraid		Feet of Clay
	The Captive	1925	The Golden Bed
	The Wild Goose Chase		The Road to Yesterday
	The Arab	1926	The Volga Boatman
	Chimmie Fadden	1927	The King of Kings
	Kindling		
	Maria Rosa	1928	The Godless Girl
	Carmen	1929	Dynamite
	Temptation	1930	Madam Satan
	Chimmie Fadden out West		
	The Cheat	1931	The Squaw Man
1916	The Golden Chance	1932	The Sign of the Cross
	The Trail of the Lonesome Pine	1933	This Day and Age
	The Heart of Nora Flynn	1934	Four Frightened People
	The Dream Girl		Cleopatra
1917	Joan the Woman	1935	The Crusades
	A Romance of the Redwoods	1937	The Plainsman
	The Little American	1938	The Buccaneer
	The Woman God Forgot	1939	Union Pacific
	The Devil Stone	1940	North West Mounted Police
1918	The Whispering Chorus		
	Old Wives for New	1942	Reap the Wild Wind
	We Can't Have Everything	1944	The Story of Dr. Wassell
	Till I Come Back to You	1947	Unconquered
	The Squaw Man		
1919	Don't Change Your Husband	1949	Samson and Delilah
	For Better, for Worse	1952	The Greatest Show on Earth
	Male and Female		
1920	Why Change Your Wife?	1956	The Ten Commandments
	Something to Think About		

growing number of Americans—a shift in public attitude hastened by the day's lurid headlines screaming the latest off-screen Hollywood scandals—DeMille devised a narrative dramatic formula that offered both gaudy titillation and moral rectitude. Given the approval *The Ten Commandments* received from all segments of the public, including the clergy, a high moral tone became a basic thematic component of DeMille's subsequent films. In his condemnations of wrongdoing, however, DeMille felt it dramatically and commercially necessary to portray sin and sexuality with lingering, graphic detail. It was a solution that helped to ensure not only DeMille's own future but that of the industry as well. Indeed, when Hollywood was again threatened by censorious pressures in the early days of synchronized sound, DeMille's "have your cake and eat it too" strategy was institutionalized in the canons set forth by the Motion Picture Production Code of 1930 (the Hays Code).

An extensive press campaign during the production of *The Ten Commandments* kept the director's image before the public. With his drooping pipe, puttees, pistols, riding boots, and silver whistle, DeMille became the public's flesh-and-blood embodiment of the archetypal Hollywood director. DeMille loved the attention and the perks his meticulously choreographed image helped secure. He even appeared in cameo roles, most notably in *Hollywood* (1923) and *Sunset Boulevard* (1950), playing himself. Perhaps most significant, "DeMille" was a name the public knew and responded to with the kind of devotion otherwise given only to stars such as Charles Chaplin, Mary Pickford, and Douglas Fairbanks.

Another consequence of the success achieved by *The Ten Commandments* was the type-casting of its director as a maestro of the film spectacle. Indeed, DeMille's name remains inextricably linked to the genre of the spectacular epic, conjuring up images not only of the director's two versions of *The Ten Commandments* but also of a succession of mammoth epics that included *The King of Kings* (1927), *The Sign of the Cross* (1932), *Cleopatra* (1934), *The Crusades* (1935), *The Plainsman* (1937), *The Buccaneer* (1938), *Union Pacific* (1939), *Samson and Delilah* (1949), and *The Greatest Show on Earth* (1952).

In assessing DeMille's overall impact, the director's crucial role as a founding partner of the Jesse L. Lasky Feature Play Company in 1913 should not be forgotten. As the fledgling firm's director-general, it was DeMille who was responsible for deciding to make its first production, *The Squaw Man*, a six-reel "feature" film. Subsequent features directed and produced by DeMille and employing such well-known personalities as Metropolitan Opera diva Geraldine Farrar and silent-film star Mary Pickford solidified the Lasky Company's leadership in the growing feature-film market. Consequently, DeMille is justly regarded as one of the individuals who established Hollywood as the film capital of the world.

DeMille's unique role as a master showman with tremendous ability to anticipate and play to the shifting tastes of the public should also not be discounted. Indeed, his sexual melodramas such as *Old Wives for New* (1918) and *Male and Female* accurately gauged the public's appetite for vicariously sampling the lifestyles of the era's rich and famous, a natural enough manifestation of human curiosity that had been made urgent by the deprivations and sacrifices required by the U.S. involvement in World War I. In the process, DeMille's parade of high fashion, his elevation of bathing to an art form, and his detailed depictions of the rules of etiquette required by high society for getting on in life educated and titillated Americans and influenced their behavior.

—Charles Merrell Berg

FURTHER READING

Birchard, Robert S. *Cecil B. DeMille's Hollywood*. Lexington: University Press of Kentucky, 2004. Study of DeMille's life and work and of the effects of his work on the history of American filmmaking. Bibliographic references and index.

Brownlow, Kevin. "Cecil B. DeMille." In *The Parade's Gone By*. New York: Alfred A. Knopf, 1968. Brownlow's incisive assessment of DeMille's silent film career includes telling and balanced quotations from actors Gloria Swanson, Leatrice Joy, Bessie Love, Adela Rogers St. Johns, and Gary Cooper, director William Wellman, producer David O. Selznick, and historian William Everson.

DeMille, Cecil B. *The Autobiography of Cecil B. DeMille*. Edited by Donald Hayne. Englewood Cliffs, N.J.: Prentice-Hall, 1959. A thorough and personal accounting of DeMille's life, times, and career with important insights on the rise of Hollywood, DeMille's switch from theater to motion pictures, and the controversies swirling about his larger-than-life epic films.

Essoe, Gabe, and Raymond Lee. *DeMille: The Man and His Pictures*. New York: Castle Books, 1970. A valuable if flawed source. Includes useful appreciations by Charlton Heston, Henry Wilcoxon, and Elmer Bernstein, an impressive collection of production stills and photos, a filmography, and a listing of DeMille's various honors.

Higham, Charles. *Cecil B. DeMille: A Biography of the Most Successful Film Maker of Them All*. New York: Charles Scribner's Sons, 1973. A lively and indispensable account of DeMille as an initially great director contented, finally, to be a great showman. Higham's penetrating insights are grounded in DeMille's voluminous correspondence and notebooks and extensive interviews with more than two hundred of DeMille's colleagues. Includes a filmography.

Jacobs, Lewis. *The Rise of the American Film: A Critical History*. 1939. Reprint. New York: Teachers College Press, 1968. Jacobs's masterful history includes a candid essay on DeMille's social-cultural impact and, in Jacobs's view, DeMille's severe limitations as a director.

Koszarski, Richard. "Cecil B. DeMille." In *An Evening's Entertainment: The Age of the Silent Feature Picture, 1915-1928*. New York: Charles Scribner's Sons, 1990. Koszarski provides an overview of DeMille's artistic and cultural importance set against the evolution of the American silent feature film.

Orrison, Katherine. *Written in Stone: Making Cecil B. DeMille's Epic, "The Ten Commandments."* Lanham, Md.: Vestal Press, 1999. In-depth study of the making of the film, including photographs taken on location during production.

Pratt, George C. "Cecil B. DeMille." In *Spellbound in Darkness: A History of the Silent Film*. Rev. ed. Greenwich, Conn.: New York Graphic Society, 1973. Includes Pratt's brief yet trenchant assessment of DeMille's silent-era career as well as reprints of contemporary reviews of several of DeMille's films.

1923

Rotha, Paul. *The Film Till Now: A Survey of World Cinema*. Rev. ed. London: Spring Books, 1967. Classic work, first published in 1930, is one of the first attempts to survey the international film. Conveys the British author's candid assessments of the most prominent American directors, including DeMille.

Zukor, Adolph. *The Public Is Never Wrong: The Autobiography of Adolph Zukor*. Edited by Dale Kramer. London: Cassell, 1954. Zukor's recollections are gentlemanly yet candid and are especially useful in cor-roborating and expanding on DeMille's pivotal role in the formation and evolving fortunes of Paramount Pictures.

SEE ALSO: Dec. 4, 1924: Von Stroheim's Silent Masterpiece *Greed* Premieres; 1925: Eisenstein's *Potemkin* Introduces New Film Editing Techniques; 1925-1927: Gance's *Napoléon* Revolutionizes Filmmaking Techniques; 1927: Lang Expands the Limits of Filmmaking with *Metropolis*; 1930's-1940's: Studio System Dominates Hollywood Filmmaking.

1923-1939
CAMBRIDGE ANCIENT HISTORY APPEARS

Cambridge University Press published the Cambridge Ancient History *with the goal of creating a comprehensive English-language, multiauthored compilation of scholarship in the field of ancient history. Edited by the British historian J. B. Bury, the premiere edition of the* Cambridge Ancient History *set the standard for historical studies. Revised and expanded since its original edition, it remains the world's most comprehensive collection of scholarship regarding the ancient world.*

ALSO KNOWN AS: *CAH*
LOCALE: Cambridge, England
CATEGORIES: Publishing and journalism; historiography; archaeology

KEY FIGURES
J. B. Bury (1861-1927), British historian
Lord Acton (1834-1902), British historian
Eugénie Sellers Strong (1860-1943), British archaeologist and art historian

SUMMARY OF EVENT
The *Cambridge Ancient History* (1923-1939; also known as *CAH*) was published in the context of a profound change in historical thinking and archaeological practices. The study of the ancient world, which had previously been the realm of wealthy aristocrats and amteur archaeologists, had developed into a group of specialized academic disciplines. Early archaeological efforts, consisting mainly of hunts for valuable artworks for private collections, matured into a more scientific endeavor with added attention paid to the accurate recording of stratigraphy and an increased interest in the cultural context of recovered artifacts.

These developments arose out of the heady archaeological climate of the nineteenth and early twentieth centuries, which had witnessed the discovery of spectacular archaeological remains, among them the fabled Homeric site of Troy in Asia Minor (now Turkey), the legendary citadel of Agamemnon at Mycenae on mainland Greece, and the palace of the mythological King Minos at Knossos on Crete. News of these exciting finds captured the interest not only of classicists and antiquarians but also of the general public. The study of the ancient world, which had previously been the domain of solely the rich and privileged, became available to virtually any young man. Departments of classics, history, and archaeology expanded as a result of the increased interest in classical education, and new departments were founded.

The increased interest in the study of history and archaeology, along with the growth of academic departments specializing in those fields, created a need for more scholarly and dependable publications than the somewhat sporadic and often inaccurate site reports that had been published previously. At the forefront of this new development in academic historical publication was Cambridge University Press, the oldest publisher in the world, which had received its charter from Henry VIII in 1534. Aware that German, Italian, and Greek publishers were producing scholarly encyclopedias and historical journals in their native languages, the Cambridge University Press began planning a series of historical publications in the English language.

In 1896, the syndics of Cambridge University Press decided to produce a *Cambridge Modern History* (1902-1912; also known as *CMH*). They invited Lord Acton to plan and edit the new series. Acton held the position of Regius Professor of Modern History at Cambridge University, and he was widely regarded as one of the foremost political historians of his time. Acton's planning for the *CMH* established the guidelines for later Cambridge publications, including the *Cambridge Ancient History*.

For the new *CMH*, Acton envisioned a multiauthored compendium of modern history, entirely in the English language but without any national bias. In addition, Acton wanted the *CMH* to be accessible to scholars and interested laypersons alike, which meant that notes of any kind and all foreign-language quotations would be omitted. Acton hoped that a multiauthored publication, with separate specialists writing separate chapters, would avoid the myopic pitfalls that were found in the single-author historical studies available at the time. Acton died before the *CMH* was published, but his guidelines for the publication remained intact and the resulting volumes, appearing between 1902 and 1912, met with scholarly and public approval.

Following Acton's vision and guidelines for an English-language, multiauthored compendium with broad reader appeal, Cambridge University Press published the *Cambridge Medieval History* (1911-1936) under the guidance of J. B. Bury. A noted British historian and Regius Professor of History at Cambridge University, Bury had written on subjects as widely diverse as ancient Greece and the Byzantine Empire. Bury's wide range of interests made his writings accessible to a broad audience, from academics to the general public, which made Bury well suited to follow his predecessor Acton's vision. Published between 1911 and 1936, the *Cambridge Medieval History* garnered praise from scholars and laypersons alike.

When, in 1923, it was decided to create a similar historical compendium on the ancient world, Bury was invited to oversee its production. At first conception, the *Cambridge Ancient History* was intended to be eight volumes, however by the time of its final publication, the series had expanded to twelve volumes of text and five volumes of plates. Between 1923 and 1939, volumes were published with the following titles:

Prolegomena and Prehistory
Early History of the Middle East
History of the Middle East and the Aegean Region, c. 1800-1380 B.C.
History of the Middle East and the Aegean Region, 1380-1000 B.C.
The Prehistory of the Balkans: The Middle East and the Aegean World, Tenth to Eighth Centuries B.C.
The Assyrian and Babylonian Empires and other States of the Near East from the Eighth to the Sixth Centuries B.C.

The Expansion of the Greek World, Eighth to Sixth Centuries B.C.
Persia, Greece, and the Western Mediterranean c. 525-479 B.C.
The Fifth Century B.C.
The Fourth Century B.C.
The Hellenistic World
The Rise of Rome to 220 B.C.
Rome and the Mediterranean to 133 B.C.
The Last Age of the Roman Republic, 146-43 B.C.
The Augustan Empire, 43 B.C.-A.D. 69
The High Empire, A.D. 70-192
The Imperial Crisis and Recovery, A.D. 193-324

Even though the new series was to be published in English, the goal of the *CAH* was to present an overview of ancient history that was not wholly English in focus. As the series developed, the authorship expanded to include non-English authors such as Robert Armstrong Stewart Macalister of Dublin and William Scott Ferguson of Harvard. As publication progressed further, authors from numerous countries were invited to contribute. The first edition had only one female contributor, Eugénie Sellers Strong, who contributed a section on Roman art. Although it was unusual at the time for a woman to contribute to a premier scholarly publication such as the *CAH*, Strong was well qualified for the task. Strong was a graduate of Cambridge University, one of the very first women in England to acquire a university education. Strong was a professional archaeologist; she served as the assistant director of the British School at Rome, and she was a noted author in the field of art and archaeology. Other women were permitted to contribute to the first edition of the *CAH* by making English translations of articles contributed by men writing in other languages.

As a testimony to the popularity of the new *CAH* series, many of the first editions went into second editions by the year following that of their initial publication. Still, not all scholars were pleased with the new *CAH*. Some complained that it was too academic for the general public, while others complained that it was not academic enough for professional scholars. Because the *CAH* was a compendium of chapters written by different authors, some subjects were repeated in different chapters, while other subjects were omitted altogether. Disconcerting to many readers was the fact that in various sections some authors actually disagreed with one another. Probably the most sharp criticism of the original *CAH* was that the coverage had too heavy an emphasis on political and military history. Through careful editorial oversight, these weaknesses were rectified in later editions.

1923

SIGNIFICANCE

The concept of a multiauthored compendium of historical scholarship revolutionized academic publishing. Within the covers of a single volume, readers could compare the theories of multiple specialists and witness how those specialists grappled with historical evidence, argued their points, and even disagreed with one another. By examining the various editions, students of history experienced the process by which historians construct history. The *CAH* reflects the evolution of historical thinking, and it contains the combined scholarship of the finest historians of the ancient world.

One of the greatest strengths of the *CAH* is its adaptability to change. For the later editions of the *CAH*, authors were permitted to add scholarly notes to their texts, which provided academics with the depth they demanded, and the weighty emphasis on political and military history of the earlier volumes gave way to a more complete and balanced coverage of the various areas of ancient studies. In response to other perceived weaknesses in the early editions, later editors exercised more oversight on the continuity of the narrative throughout the volumes, thereby eliminating many lacunae in the information provided and avoiding much of the repetition contained in the original texts. The original edition dealt with the ancient world up to the year 324 C.E., whereas later editions were expanded to cover history through 600 C.E. In keeping with accepted historical practice, the editors continued to allow contributing authors to express opposing opinions. Careful and substantive changes have kept the *CAH* abreast of current historical thinking without jeopardizing its high academic standards. In its broad scope, sound scholarship, and wide appeal, the *CAH* remains the definitive publication on the history of the ancient world.

—*Sonia Sorrell*

FURTHER READING

Cambridge Ancient History. 1st-3d ed. New York: Cambridge University Press, 1923-2001. The individual volume introductions, the selection and scope of coverage of the text, and the organization of the chapters provide a good overview of the development of the discipline of ancient history through the decades.

Chadwick, Owen. *Acton and History*. New York: Cambridge University Press, 1998. Compilation of the writings on Lord Acton's contributions to the fields of history and historiography by the foremost expert on the subject. Bibliographic references and index.

Rhodes, P. J. "The *Cambridge Ancient History*." http://www.dur.ac.uk/Classics/histos/1999/rhodes.html. In this lecture summary, Rhodes presents an overview of the origins and development of the *Cambridge Ancient History*, and he discusses the shift in scholarly emphases from the time of the original publication through the intervening editions.

SEE ALSO: 1907: Meinecke Advances the Analytic Method in History; Summer, 1918: Rise of Cultural Relativism Revises Historiography; 1934: Toynbee's Metahistorical Approach Sparks Debate.

January 11, 1923-August 16, 1924
FRANCE OCCUPIES THE RUHR

French and Belgian troops occupied Germany's industrial center in response to the German government's failure to make prompt reparations for the consequences of World War I. The occupation devastated Germany's economy and stimulated the growth of extreme nationalism.

LOCALE: Ruhr Valley, Germany
CATEGORIES: Diplomacy and international relations; economics; military history

KEY FIGURES

Raymond Poincaré (1860-1934), premier of France and foreign minister, 1922-1924

Wilhelm Cuno (1876-1933), chancellor of Germany, 1922-1933

Gustav Stresemann (1878-1929), chancellor of Germany, 1923, foreign minister, 1923-1929

Édouard Herriot (1872-1957), premier of France, 1924-1925

Charles G. Dawes (1865-1951), American attorney and financier, later vice president of the United States, 1925-1929

Adolf Hitler (1889-1945), Nazi leader who attempted to seize power in November, 1923

SUMMARY OF EVENT

The Ruhr industrial district, which spans some two thousand square miles, lies between the Ruhr and the Lippe

THE RUHR VALLEY

Rivers, extending from the Dutch frontier on the west to Hamm in the east. After the middle of the nineteenth century, it became one of the world's most important industrial concentrations, primarily because of its huge coal deposits. In the 1920's, the area produced more than 80 percent of Germany's coal as well as 80 percent of its iron and steel. Most of the iron ore processed in the region came from Sweden and the French province of Lorraine.

The French occupation of the Ruhr district was a consequence of the French government's unrealistically high demands for German reparations. At the Paris Peace Conference of 1919, the delegates had been unable to agree on an amount of reparations, and so they established a Reparations Commission to determine the total bill. In the meantime, the Allies demanded that Germany begin making preliminary payments, which included deliveries of coal to France as compensation for the French mines flooded by retreating German troops. Germans

were horrified by these and other conditions included in the Treaty of Versailles.

From the election of 1919 until the elections of 1924, the French parliament was dominated by conservatives and nationalists who supported a hard-line position toward reparations. In March of 1921, even before the final amount of reparations had been decided, the French government asserted that the Germans were behind in their coal deliveries and sent troops to occupy Dusseldorf and two other Ruhr cities. The following year, Raymond Poincaré, who had served as president during the war, became prime minister. Poincaré was firmly committed to a legalistic interpretation of the Versailles treaty, and he made it clear that he would not hesitate to use military force if Germany fell behind in its payments.

In April of 1922, the Reparations Commission decided that Germany had to pay a total figure of thirty-three billion dollars, a huge amount that dwarfed the reparations charged after previous European conflicts. Even though many economists argued that the amount exceeded Germany's capacity, French public opinion vehemently opposed making any concessions. The people of Germany, in contrast, viewed the reparations as exorbitant and entirely unjust. German chancellor Wilhelm Cuno, who headed a nonpartisan, conservative ministry, failed in his attempts to secure a moratorium on the payments.

During the latter part of 1922, all European nations were faced with serious economic problems. The German government informed the Allies that it could not meet its schedule of cash payments but that it would continue to make deliveries of coal and natural resources. With the United States pressuring France and other countries to repay their war debts, Poincaré became increasingly insistent that Germany make full and prompt payments. When Germany's coal shipments fell 10 percent short of the promised amount, Poincaré decided—against the advice of the British government—to use military force.

On January 11, 1923, Poincaré dispatched a technical mission and two army divisions to Essen, the headquar-

1923

Raymond Poincaré. (Library of Congress)

become serious. In order to pursue its policy of passive resistence, Germany had printed large amounts of money to pay companies and workers for nonactivity. As a result, German money lost almost all of its value: In 1919, fourteen German marks were worth one U.S. dollar, but by January of 1923 it took eighteen thousand marks to purchase a dollar, and by November of 1923 it took more than four trillion marks. A significant number of Germans became too poor to buy basic items, and many lost their life savings.

The Ruhr occupation also did serious damage to the French economy. It greatly increased the size of France's budget deficit and further debilitated the already weak French franc. Since the occupation was an economic failure, informed observers realized that France would not be able to rely on regular reparations payments. Then, in August of 1923, just as Germany appeared to be threatened with chaos, all the moderate political parties in the country united to form a Great Coalition to deal with the emergency. Gustav Stresemann, the leader of the conservative Peoples' Party, served as chancellor during the next hundred days, a period usually considered one of the more successful periods of German history. Stresemann ordered an end to passive resistance, took steps to reach an understanding with France, dealt with inflation by issuing a new German currency, and helped suppress communist and Nazi uprisings.

Poincaré finally acknowledged that the size and schedule of German payments would have to be modified. In November of 1923, he agreed to the appointment of an international commission to examine the practical question of Germany's ability to pay. By June of 1924, the new French premier, Édouard Herriot, was firmly committed to reaching a settlement and withdrawing troops from the Ruhr district as soon as possible.

On August 16, 1924, the commission, which was headed by American financier Charles G. Dawes, reached agreements on a more realistic schedule of German payments and a reduction of the French debt to the United States. As part of the Dawes Plan, the French government agreed to evacuate the Ruhr. The signing of the agreements on September 1, 1924, alleviated Franco-German tensions and helped prepare the way for the Locarno Agreements of 1925, which included France's renunciation of another military intervention in Germany.

SIGNIFICANCE

The occupation of the Ruhr produced a great deal of political instability and economic dislocation, which in turn

ters of the German Coal Syndicate. The Belgian government assisted the operation with a token number of troops. The stated purpose of the mission was to ensure that coal and timber deliveries were made according to schedule. Internationally, the occupation, which was inconsistent with the principles of the League of Nations, was unpopular and provoked much sympathy for Germany.

In response to the occupation, Chancellor Cuno decided to pursue a policy of passive resistance, and he ordered Ruhr residents not to work in the coal mines or to cooperate with occupying forces. The French received their coal, but Cuno's policy made the coal extremely expensive. Angry Ruhr residents committed numerous acts of sabotage, and their demonstrations sometimes developed into violent confrontations. In one of these clashes, thirteen people were killed. In order to keep the shipments flowing, Poincaré was forced to send five army divisions (amounting to seventy-five thousand troops), as well as thousands of administrators, engineers, and railway workers.

The occupation of the Ruhr greatly exacerbated Germany's problem of postwar inflation, which had already led to a great deal of anger and bitterness, especially in Germany. One of the manifestations of this anger was a growth in political extremism. On the left, the German Communist Party attracted large numbers of new followers. On the extreme right, Adolf Hitler attempted a November, 1923, takeover of the Bavarian government in his unsuccessful Beer Hall Putsch in Munich.

The withdrawal of French troops from the Ruhr, combined with the accommodating policies of Chancellor Stresemann, helped to bring about the conciliatory climate in European diplomatic relations that prevailed from 1924 until the beginning of the Great Depression in 1929. However, in many sectors of German society, bitter resentments about the Ruhr occupation continued to exist, and these unpleasant memories were skillfully exploited by Hitler and the Nazis.

—*Thomas Tandy Lewis*

FURTHER READING

Balderston, Theo. *Economics and Politics in the Weimar Republic*. Cambridge, England: Cambridge University Press, 2002. Informative survey emphasizes the German economy during the period.

Bassel, Richard. *Germany After the First World War*. New York: Oxford University Press, 1995. A good discussion of the legacies of the war and the ways in which the Weimar government dealt with overwhelming financial and political challenges.

Fischer, Conan. *Ruhr Crisis, 1923-1924*. New York: Oxford University Press, 2003. The most complete work devoted to the occupation; particularly valuable for its depiction of daily life in the Ruhr region.

Keiger, John F. *Raymond Poincaré*. Cambridge, England: Cambridge University Press, 2002. The most scholarly and readable political biography available on Poincaré.

McDougall, Walter. *France's Rhineland Diplomacy, 1914-1924*. Princeton, N.J.: Princeton University Press, 1978. A scholarly and readable account of French policies toward postwar Germany.

Paxton, Robert. *Europe in the Twentieth Century*. Belmont, Calif.: Wadsworth, 2004. Highly recommended as an excellent introduction to the crisis within the broader context of European history and international conflict.

Schmidt, Royal J. *Versailles and the Ruhr: Seedbed of World War II*. The Hague, the Netherlands: Martinus Nijhoff, 1968. Useful account of the economy of the Ruhr Valley, the diplomacy of German reparations, and the impact of France's military occupation.

Wright, Jonathan. *Gustav Stresemann: Weimar's Greatest Statesman*. New York: Oxford University Press, 2004. The most scholarly of several political biographies devoted to Stresemann.

SEE ALSO: Mar. 3, 1918: Treaty of Brest-Litovsk; 1919-1933: Racist Theories Aid Nazi Rise to Political Power; July 31, 1919: Weimar Constitution; 1923: Germans Barter for Goods in Response to Hyperinflation; Nov. 8, 1923: Beer Hall Putsch; Sept. 1, 1924: Dawes Plan; Oct., 1925: Germany Attempts to Restructure the Versailles Treaty; 1929-1940: Maginot Line Is Built; Jan. 30, 1933: Hitler Comes to Power in Germany; May 10-June 22, 1940: Collapse of France.

1923

February 15, 1923
BESSIE SMITH RECORDS "DOWNHEARTED BLUES"

The results of a modest recording session in 1923 helped make Bessie Smith the most celebrated blues singer in history.

LOCALE: New York, New York
CATEGORY: Music

KEY FIGURES
Bessie Smith (1894-1937), American blues singer
Mamie Smith (1883-1946), American blues singer
Ma Rainey (1886-1939), American blues singer
Clarence Williams (1898-1965), American jazz pianist

SUMMARY OF EVENT
Long before her first recording session in 1923, Bessie Smith had sung for audiences in cities throughout the American Southeast and Midwest. She began to sing publicly in 1903, when, at age nine, she stood on street corners in her hometown of Chattanooga, Tennessee, and shouted out Baptist hymns she learned from her father, a part-time preacher. In 1912, she joined a traveling vaudeville show, where she met Ma Rainey, a singer whose powerful, lusty voice influenced the style of singing Smith eventually followed. Moving from city to city appealed to Smith, because Chattanooga had become for her a virtual prison of poverty. She suffered indignities as part of the traveling show, however: She was considered too fat, too tall, and too black for featured roles. Smith greatly resented the preferential treatment that light-skinned black female performers received, but she channeled her hostility toward a positive goal—she was determined to succeed.

By 1921, Smith had her own show, and black audiences considered her a star. She had an arresting presence on stage that some likened to that of an evangelist, and the way she delivered her songs reflected her innermost hurts. She sang the blues as no one had heard them sung before. Smith's rise to prominence coincided with growing recognition by recording companies that there was a market for black music. The OKeh Record Company first recorded a black singer, Mamie Smith, in 1920. Her recording of "Crazy Blues" sold enough copies to convince executives that there was a future for the blues on records. Ma Rainey recorded more than ninety songs in the early 1920's.

Bessie Smith had two auditions with OKeh, but she was turned down each time because her voice was judged too rough to have general appeal. Black Swan Records, founded by blues composer W. C. Handy, also turned her down, choosing instead to promote the less strident singing of Ethel Waters, Smith's principal competitor in the 1920's. Smith's chance finally came when Frank Walker, a producer of "race records" for Columbia Records, decided to give her an opportunity. Walker dispatched pianist Clarence Williams to Philadelphia to bring Smith to New York City for a recording session that began on February 15, 1923.

It took two days, under the patient guidance of Williams, for the nervous Smith to record "Downhearted Blues" and "Gulf Coast Blues." Whatever doubts there were about Smith's rough manner, her voice and phrasing proved to be explosive on record. "Downhearted Blues" sold more than 750,000 copies. After that modest recording session in 1923, Bessie Smith quickly became known as the "Empress of the Blues." By 1924, her record sales passed the two million mark, and she made featured appearances on Milton Stan's black vaudeville circuit.

In January, 1925, Smith made what some critics believe to be her best recordings when she teamed for one memorable session with Louis Armstrong, who was then a member of Fletcher "Smack" Henderson's orchestra.

Bessie Smith. (Library of Congress)

Smith was reluctant to record with Armstrong, but her favorite accompanist, cornetist Joe Smith, was not in New York at the time. As it happened, Smith and Armstrong had an instant rapport, and from this session came the version of "St. Louis Blues" that became the standard. In that song and others that she recorded with Armstrong, Smith diverged markedly from a literal reading of the lyrics and, in so doing, created something new and exciting.

As her singing career continued to gain momentum in the second half of the 1920's, however, Smith's personal life collapsed. Wrangling over the distribution of her royalties as well as her excessive drinking, boorish behavior at parties and social gatherings, and unhappy marriage to a Philadelphia policeman brought her considerable public disfavor and misery. While she was blossoming as a professional, such problems remained of secondary importance, but when her career started to slide after 1929, they became open wounds.

The beginning of the end for Smith came from a combination of factors, some of which were out of her control. A failed Broadway show left her depressed, and her appearance in the 1929 film *St. Louis Blues*, in which she sang the title song, made it clear that she had little acting talent. In 1929, the sale of blues records declined, and promoters demanded that Smith and other black stars fill their music with double entendres. With the United States in the midst of the Great Depression, such efforts did not help sales very much. Also working against Smith in the early 1930's were the expansion of radio and the development of new recording technology. She had difficulty adapting to the new technology, which demanded a softer, more intimate sound to appeal to nationwide audiences listening in their living rooms. The new technology tended to favor the styles of singing displayed by performers such as Ethel Waters, Ella Fitzgerald, and Louis Armstrong.

Smith's last great recording session was in 1929, when she recorded "Nobody Knows You When You're Down and Out," "Alexander's Ragtime Band," and "There'll Be a Hot Time in the Old Town Tonight." To each of these songs, Smith imparted an air of hovering tragedy, a reflection of the circumstances in her life at the time. These recordings reveal her to be as much a jazz singer as a blues singer. "Nobody Knows You When You're Down and Out" became the song with which Smith would be most associated over the years, even more than "St. Louis Blues."

Smith's career went steadily downhill in the 1930's. She no longer received top dollar for appearances, and

her recordings did not sell particularly well. Although her voice remained powerful, numerous comeback efforts between 1933 and 1937 failed. She died in an automobile accident near Clarksdale, Mississippi, while traveling to a singing engagement on September 26, 1937. Stories at the time said she might have lived if she had been admitted to a white hospital that turned her away, but such stories were not accurate.

SIGNIFICANCE

More than any other black artist, Bessie Smith opened the door for black musicians to the commercial market. She sang "country blues," as opposed to the "urban blues" of Ma Rainey and Mamie Smith. She sang with a passion, pain, and verve that rang true to black listeners throughout the United States. Her audience appreciated her complete defiance of the white world; she refused to yield to white conventions in her music or in her personal life. In her singing, she refused to surrender blandly to lyrics or melody; therefore, her songs usually bore her personal stamp. This was an attribute that not only endeared her to her faithful followers but also left its mark on other entertainers.

British jazz musician and critic Humphrey Lyttelton has argued that Smith was one of only three 1920's musicians (Louis Armstrong and Sidney Bechet were the other two) who had the talent and confidence to change the "rhythmic conventions of the day." Smith was able to move away from the legacy of ragtime rhythm by adjusting lyrics (dropping or adding words and syllables) to suit her personal interpretation of a song. Many artists of the 1930's, including some of the highly popular "crooners" of the time, were much influenced by Smith's molding of lyrics to give proper emphasis to a phrase. Armstrong's recording session with Smith in 1925 no doubt also encouraged his departure from standard phrasing.

It is difficult to gauge Smith's influence on other artists in the 1940's and early 1950's. She was not forgotten, but the recorded music of the war and postwar eras was scarcely of the same brilliance as that of the 1920's. In the late 1950's, however, the mix of blues and gospel music began to inspire a new era for black artists. Gospel singer Mahalia Jackson, while rejecting Bessie Smith's rather seamy way of life, essentially emulated her stage presence and style of singing to gain considerable popularity.

In addition to Jackson, Dinah Washington and Linda Hopkins were the 1950's singers most obviously in the Bessie Smith mold. Washington studied Smith closely. In many ways, Washington's life, with its evangelical

1923

roots, poverty, and sorrowful personal problems, paralleled Smith's. Washington, like Smith, had begun by singing hymns; also like Smith, she developed a powerful, expressive, pain-ridden style marked by immaculate phrasing and diction. To hear Washington's version of "This Bitter Earth" is to experience the same emotional reaction evoked by Smith's "Nobody Knows You When You're Down and Out." It was appropriate that Washington recorded an album titled *Dinah Washington Sings Bessie Smith* shortly before her death in 1963.

Linda Hopkins proved to be the most thorough student of Bessie Smith's life and the most exacting emulator of her style. In 1936, when Hopkins was only eleven years old, she heard Smith sing in New Orleans; the experience left an indelible impression. One year later, Mahalia Jackson "discovered" Hopkins, and her career as a blues singer ascended. In 1959, Hopkins began to portray Bessie Smith in her performances, and in 1974 she developed a one-woman show in which she played Smith. That show became the musical *Bessie and Me* in 1976. More than fifty years after Smith's first recording session in 1923, Hopkins had revived a great interest in Smith's life.

In the 1970's, rhythm-and-blues star Aretha Franklin built substantially on the foundation laid by Bessie Smith. To a great extent, Franklin learned of Smith through Hopkins. By helping to introduce the world to modern soul music, Franklin became the most influential female singer since Smith's era of the 1920's.

Bessie Smith's black successors enjoyed something that she never experienced—enthusiastic approval and acceptance from white audiences. Ironically, Smith's own recordings, rereleased in 1958 and then reissued in their entirety by Columbia Records in 1970, gained wide popularity and sold more than half a million copies. It is no exaggeration to say that the music of Smith and her later counterparts communicated to white listeners the fact that the black experience in the United States was not adequately expressed by the lighthearted sounds of much popular black music.

—*Ronald K. Huch*

FURTHER READING

Albertson, Chris. *Bessie*. Rev. ed. New Haven, Conn.: Yale University Press, 2003. A solid biography with, perhaps, a little too much emphasis on the rough side of Smith's life. A good portion of the book is based on interviews with Smith's niece, Ruby Walker. Includes many photographs, discography, and index.

Feinstein, Elaine. *Bessie Smith*. New York: Viking Press, 1985. Brief and highly impressionistic look at Smith's life includes little about her music but does carefully analyze the controversial events surrounding her death. Suitable for readers seeking an introduction to Smith's life. Features photographs, select discography, brief bibliography, and index.

Jones, LeRoi. *Blues People: The Negro Experience in White America*. 1963. Reprint. New York: William Morrow, 1999. Interesting volume discusses how blues and jazz evolved in white America. Filled with insights about how blacks survived and how their music flourished in difficult circumstances. Places Bessie Smith's work in historical context. Includes index.

Lyttelton, Humphrey. *The Best of Jazz: Basin Street to Harlem*. New York: Taplinger, 1978. Outstanding collection of essays on the great names in jazz from the 1920's and 1930's by a well-known British jazz musician and critic. Includes an essential essay on Smith. Features select bibliography, discography, and index.

Priestley, Brian. *Jazz on Record: A History*. London: Elm Tree Books, 1988. Impressive history of jazz recordings from the 1920's to the 1980's contains much of interest regarding Bessie Smith. Features a record guide, photographs, brief bibliography, and index.

Southern, Eileen. *The Music of Black Americans: A History*. 3d ed. New York: W. W. Norton, 1997. Excellent scholarly account of the subject provides both background and important detail. Includes a splendid critical bibliography and discography as well as numerous selections from scores and an extensive index.

Wardlow, Gayle Dean. *Chasin' That Devil Music: Searching for the Blues*. San Francisco: Backbeat Books, 1998. Describes the author's search for early recordings and documentation of the stories and songs of blues artists (many of which appear on an accompanying CD). Focuses on Delta blues singers of the early twentieth century.

SEE ALSO: 1910's: Handy Ushers in the Commercial Blues Era; 1920's: Harlem Renaissance; Nov., 1925: Armstrong Records with the Hot Five; 1930's: Guthrie's Populist Songs Reflect the Depression-Era United States; 1933: Billie Holiday Begins Her Recording Career.

March 3, 1923
LUCE FOUNDS *TIME* MAGAZINE

Henry R. Luce revolutionized American journalism by introducing, with his partner Briton Hadden, the first newsmagazine. He then went on to build one of the most influential publishing empires in the United States.

LOCALE: New York, New York
CATEGORIES: Publishing and journalism; organizations and institutions

KEY FIGURES

Henry R. Luce (1898-1967), cofounder of *Time* magazine
Briton Hadden (1898-1929), cofounder of *Time* magazine
John Stuart Martin (1900-1977), managing editor of *Time* magazine, 1929-1937
Clare Boothe Luce (1903-1987), American playwright and wife of Henry R. Luce
Roy E. Larsen (1899-1979), first circulation manager of *Time* magazine, later president of Time Inc., 1939-1960

SUMMARY OF EVENT

Henry R. Luce was born on April 3, 1898, in Tengchow, China, where his father was a Presbyterian missionary. He attended the British-run Chefoo School from 1908 to 1913 before attending the Hotchkiss School in Lakeville, Connecticut. There he became interested in journalism and began his friendship with fellow student and aspiring journalist Briton Hadden. Hadden edited the Hotchkiss school newspaper, the *Weekly Record*, while Luce was the editor of the *Literary Monthly*. The two went on to Yale University in 1916, where they joined the staff of the *Yale Daily News*, Hadden becoming its chairman and Luce its managing editor. Despite service in the army in 1918-1919, both received their bachelor of arts degrees in 1920. After spending a year studying history at the University of Oxford, Luce became a reporter for the *Chicago Daily News* before rejoining Hadden at the *Baltimore News*.

By the fall of 1922, Luce and Hadden had succeeded in raising almost eighty-six thousand dollars in capital to start *Time: The Weekly News-Magazine*. The first issue appeared in late February, 1923, with a cover date of March 3, 1923. Hadden appears to have been the source of many of the ideas behind the magazine, but Luce supplied the organizational talents required to implement

Hadden's ideas. The magazine's purpose, Hadden and Luce's prospectus explained, was to fill the informational gap that existed "because no publication has adapted itself to the time which busy men are able to spend on simply keeping informed." Major emphasis was placed on conciseness; initially, no entry was to be more than four hundred words. Perhaps most important, the young publishers did not even pay lip service to reportorial objectivity. "*Time* gives both sides," they declared, "but clearly indicates which side it believes to have the stronger position."

Through a preferred-stock arrangement, Luce and Hadden retained full control of Time Incorporated. Hadden was president from 1923 to 1925, when Luce assumed that title. Hadden largely handled the editorial side for four years while Luce was business manager; they then traded roles.

The basic subscription rate was five dollars per year, with a cover price of fifteen cents an issue. *Time* started with nine thousand subscribers recruited on a three-week trial basis through a mail campaign. The first years were financially difficult, but by the end of 1927, *Time* was on its way to success. Circulation had risen to 175,000, annual advertising revenue was almost half a million dollars, and the magazine showed a profit. After Hadden's death in late February, 1929, from a streptococcus infection, Luce acquired majority control of the undertaking. Roy E. Larsen, a Harvard graduate who joined *Time* during the planning stage and was its first circulation manager, became Luce's second in command as president of Time Inc. from 1939 to 1960.

The cover of the first issue featured a picture of former Speaker of the House of Representatives Joseph G. Cannon, on the occasion of his retirement from Congress. Thereafter, the cover almost invariably featured a portrait of an individual. *Time*'s news coverage similarly focused on personalities. Along with conciseness, *Time* boasted of its comprehensive coverage of "all available information on all subjects of importance and general interest." Entries were arranged by subject matter into departments. Departments in the first issue that became permanent features were "National Affairs" (later shortened to "The Nation"), "Foreign News" (later retitled "The World"), "Books," "Art," "The Theatre" (expanded in 1958 to include television and renamed "Show Business"), "Cinema," "Music," "Education," "Religion," "Medicine," "Finance" (later divided into "U.S.

Business" and "World Business"), "Sport," "The Press" (newspapers and magazines), and "Milestones" (a column of brief paragraphs recording births, marriages, divorces, and deaths of well-known personalities). A "Letters" department was added in *Time*'s second year and became one of the magazine's most popular features.

After Hadden's death, his cousin John Stuart Martin became managing editor, acting in that position until 1937. By that date, circulation had passed the 750,000 mark. Martin was largely responsible for *Time*'s distinctive style: an aura of omniscience coupled with what one historian of American magazines has termed "use of word coinages, blends, puns, inverted syntax, esoteric words, tropes and epithets of various kinds." *Time*'s contributions to the American language include the popularization of the words "tycoon," "pundit," and "kudos." Another feature of *Time* was its proclivity for the "upended sentence," the most famous example of which is its often-repeated introduction to death notices, "As it must to all men, death came last week to . . ."

Occasional full-color covers began as early as 1929, but use of color in the body of the magazine did not come until 1945. At first, *Time* relied for copy largely on rewriting newspaper clippings, particularly from *The New York Times*. Contemporary newspapers adhered to a rigid structure developed by the national wire services, such as the Associated Press, whereby all the important facts were jammed into the first paragraph, or "lead." *Time* rewrote the stories in dramatic narrative form, with a beginning, middle, and end. Another favorite *Time* technique to make old news appear fresh was to lace accounts with colorful but mostly insignificant details such as the appearance, ages, or middle names of persons in the news. Only in the late 1930's did *Time* begin to build up its own staff of reporters and stringers. Even then, the final product followed a standardized formula. Reporters' stories were heavily edited, writers had little autonomy, and no authors' names, or bylines, were attached to entries.

Even while *Time* was still in shaky financial condition, Luce was looking to expand. In 1924, he and Hadden became publishers of the new *Saturday Review of Literature*, but they withdrew from involvement two years later. In 1928, Time Inc. launched an advertising trade journal titled *Tide*, which the company sold in 1930. Luce's willingness to take risks was shown by his decision to launch a new monthly business magazine, *Fortune*, in February, 1930, when the economy was reeling from the shock of the stock market crash. Covering far more than business and finance, *Fortune* included

first-rate, in-depth analysis of national politics, foreign affairs, and developments in art and culture. Luce also acquired *Architectural Forum* in the early 1930's. Roy E. Larsen was responsible for introducing, in 1931, a weekly radio program called *The March of Time* broadcast over the Columbia Broadcasting System. The program, modeled on *Time* magazine, reenacted the more important news stories of the week. A monthly newsreel version produced by Twentieth Century-Fox was begun in 1935. *The March of Time* continued on the radio until 1945, and the newsreel lasted for another six years before transfer to television. The television show was terminated in 1954.

Next to *Time*, Luce's most important innovation was the introduction of the weekly picture magazine *Life* in November, 1936. *Life* was made possible by technological advances in photography and photoengraving that had been made independent of Luce. Luce's contribution lay in recognizing the mass-audience appeal of photographs. That potential had first been exploited in Germany, and the German photographers Luce brought over to advise him were responsible for what became *Life*'s most distinctive feature—the grouping together of photographs into "photoessays" in which pictures largely substituted for words. *Life* was an immediate sales success. Circulation reached 500,000 within four weeks and 1.7 million by late in 1937. Financially, however, *Life* was a money loser during its first years, and it almost bankrupted Time Inc. *Life* did not begin to make money until early in 1939, when circulation passed the 2 million mark.

SIGNIFICANCE

Time's most direct antecedent was the *Literary Digest*, the pages of which were largely filled with quotations from newspapers. The *Literary Digest* focused on the conflict of editorial opinion, not on presenting a comprehensive summary of the news. *Time*'s success stimulated a host of imitators. Only two, however, survived to remain long-term competitors. *News-week* (the hyphen was later dropped) was started in February, 1933, by former *Time* staffer Thomas S. Martyn. Its continuing financial losses led to Martyn's ouster and *Newsweek*'s merger in February, 1937, with *Today*, another would-be *Time* rival edited by former New Deal Brain Truster Raymond Moley. Generous financial infusions from its chief backer, Vincent Astor, kept *Newsweek* afloat until its purchase in the 1960's by *The Washington Post* placed the magazine on a more solid competitive footing vis-à-vis *Time*. *Time*'s second major competitor was *United*

States News (later *U.S. News & World Report*), begun in early 1933 by conservative syndicated columnist David Lawrence.

Like *Time*, *Life* had its rivals. The most successful was *Look*, launched in early 1937. Luce's innovations had an impact reaching beyond the magazine realm. *Time*'s demonstration of the existence of a large middle-class audience for synthesis led many newspapers to introduce news analysis in their own pages, in the form of weekly reviews and daily commentaries. *Life* gave a major boost to the new way of reporting events known as photojournalism, whereby visual images became the primary carriers of stories.

At first, *Time* was largely apolitical, lacking even an editorial page. Its attitude toward politics and politicians was basically irreverent and skeptical. By the late 1930's, however, Luce was moving to a more highly politicized stance. The potential influence represented by the circulation of his magazines inflated his sense of self-importance, and he had grown increasingly disillusioned with President Franklin D. Roosevelt's New Deal, blaming its hostility toward business for prolonging the Depression. Also pulling him into politics was his second marriage. Luce had married Lila Hotz in 1923; they had two children. He was divorced from her and in 1935 married Clare Boothe Brokaw, a playwright and former editor of *Vanity Fair*. She went on to become active in Republican Party affairs and was a member of the House of Representatives from Connecticut from 1943 to 1947.

Thinking that the Republican Old Guard was hopelessly out of touch with the electorate, Luce aspired to formulate a moderate Republicanism that could offer a viable alternative to the New Deal. Foreign policy became the major focus of Luce's political activism. By 1939, he had become convinced that Germany's Adolf Hitler represented a threat not only to the United States but also to Western civilization as a whole. He personally favored U.S. intervention after the outbreak of the war in Europe. He worked through his magazines to alert the country to the dangers that would result from a Hitler triumph, and he played a leading role in the capture of the 1940 Republican presidential nomination by the pro-Allied Wendell Willkie. In an influential article, "The American Century," published in the February 17, 1941, issue of *Life* under his own name, he set forth his vision of the future role of the United States in spreading throughout the world the benefits of democratic capitalism.

Sometime between late 1943 and 1944, Luce became alarmed over the potential threat of the Soviet Union. Much to the unhappiness of many members of his staff, Luce had his magazines take an increasingly anti-Soviet line. By the late 1940's, he was attacking the containment policy of President Harry S. Truman as too defensive. The transformation of Luce into a hard-line Cold Warrior was reinforced by his longtime support for China's Chiang Kai-shek. Like most other members of what might be termed the missionary lobby, Luce had embraced Chiang as the instrument for the Americanization of China and blamed the Truman administration's lack of support

Briton Hadden (left) and Henry R. Luce (center) in 1925 with Cleveland, Ohio, city manager William R. Hopkins, who is reading an article in Time *magazine. (Hulton Archive/Getty Images)*

1923

for Chiang's defeat by the Chinese Communists. In 1952, *Life* openly and *Time* more subtly supported Republican presidential nominee Dwight D. Eisenhower and the Republican platform's call for an aggressive policy to roll back Communism.

Eisenhower named Clare Boothe Luce to the post of U.S. ambassador to Italy, but Henry Luce did not have much influence in the new administration. Although his magazines refrained from open criticism, he was privately disappointed at the administration's failure to carry through on its promise of a more aggressive foreign policy. As an alternative way of combating Communism, Luce took up championship of the glories of the Western European cultural tradition. Starting in the late 1940's, he required that each issue of *Life* carry at least one "serious offering" on the great art, religions, and ideas of Western civilization. Luce strongly backed U.S. involvement in Vietnam; *Time* even edited its own Vietnam correspondent's dispatches to accord with Luce's interventionist position.

Luce retired as editor in chief of Time Inc. in 1964. He died of a heart attack on February 28, 1967. Even before Luce stepped down, cracks had begun to appear in his empire. The consistently money-losing *Architectural Forum* was given as a gift to the American Planning and Civic Association in 1964. Faced with the competition of more narrowly focused business news periodicals, Luce in the 1940's directed *Fortune* to limit its coverage exclusively to business matters. Its shift from monthly to biweekly publication in 1982 undercut what had been its forte of in-depth analysis. The rise of television hit all magazines hard. *Life* continued to prosper because of its color pictures and advertising displays as long as television remained black-and-white. By the 1960's, however, *Life* began to slide in both circulation and advertising. Its end came with the issue of December 29, 1972. *Life* was resurrected in October, 1978, as a monthly publication focusing on feature articles rather than news, but the new *Life* never came near the circulation of its namesake.

During Luce's last years, *Time* came under increasing attack for its politically motivated slanting of the news. Under his successors, the magazine drifted toward a bland middle-of-the-roadism politically. Deeper problems remained: oversimplification of complex issues, masses of trivial and insignificant details, and exaggeration of the role of the individual "newsmaker." Much of *Time*'s remaining reputation was shredded by a libel suit brought by Israeli general Ariel Sharon in 1985. Although *Time* was saved from paying damages by a constitutional technicality, the trial exposed the shoddiness

of *Time*'s reportorial and editorial practices. Worse, circulation remained stagnant, at approximately 4.5 million, from the mid-1960's through the 1980's, despite the vast expansion of the magazine's target audience of college graduates. In a bid to boost sales, *Time* underwent an extensive format revamping in 1988 (including the addition of bylines) that was accompanied by a shift from "hard" to more "soft" news.

By the 1980's, Time Inc. had become a gigantic conglomerate with a primary business of entertainment rather than journalism. Its magazines division had become one of four separately incorporated subsidiaries. The other three were Home Box Office (HBO), a leading cable television programmer; the American Television and Communication Corporation, the second-largest cable television system; and Time Books. Within the magazine division, the stars were *Sports Illustrated* and *People*. *Sports Illustrated* had been launched in 1954 to appeal to the growing market of young and affluent sports fans. First appearing in 1974, *People* jumped within two years to a circulation of 2.5 million thanks to its photograph-laden focus on celebrities. The shift was personified by J. Richard Munro, the chief executive officer of Time Inc. from 1980 to 1990. Munro had come to the top spot after first serving as publisher of *Sports Illustrated* and group vice president for video. He was a moving force behind the controversial merger in 1990 with rival entertainment conglomerate Warner Communications to form Time Warner, which became one of the leading global information technology, media, and entertainment companies.

—John Braeman

FURTHER READING

Baughman, James L. *Henry R. Luce and the Rise of the American News Media.* 1987. Reprint. Baltimore: The Johns Hopkins University Press, 2001. Essentially favorable biography sets its subject in the broader context of twentieth century news media. Explains how Luce's innovative summary and synthesis of the news using a short-story format and visual images changed American journalism. Portrays Luce as a proponent of Republican Party politics and middle-class American values. Includes bibliography and index.

Busch, Noel F. *Briton Hadden: A Biography of the Co-founder of "Time."* 1949. Reprint. Westport, Conn.: Greenwood Press, 1975. Thorough account of Hadden's role in creating *Time* and developing its style. Written by Hadden's cousin, who wrote for the magazine in its early years. Very valuable for understanding the origins of *Time*, but does little to illuminate Hadden's character.

Clurman, Richard M. *To the End of Time: The Seduction and Conquest of a Media Empire.* New York: Simon & Schuster, 1992. A detailed account of the wheeling and dealing involved in Time Inc.'s merger with Warner Communications. Sharply indicts Time's top management.

Donovan, Hedley. *Right Places, Right Times: Forty Years in Journalism, Not Counting My Paper Route.* New York: Henry Holt, 1989. An insider's look at the workings of the Luce empire during the post-World War II years by a man who rose to be editorial director of Time Inc. from 1960 to 1964 and succeeded Luce as editor in chief from 1964 to 1979.

Elson, Robert T. *Time Inc.: The Intimate History of a Publishing Enterprise.* 3 vols. New York: Atheneum, 1968-1986. Official company history uses oral histories and records in the Time Inc. archives not available to outside researchers. First volume covers 1923 to 1940: the founding of *Time* and *Life*, *Time*'s approach to journalism and the development of its style, and the personalities of the individuals involved. Remarkably candid for an official history, but nevertheless portrays Time Inc. very favorably. Includes photographs and index.

Griffith, Thomas. *Harry and Teddy: The Turbulent Friendship of Press Lord Henry R. Luce and His Favorite Reporter, Theodore H. White.* New York: Random House, 1995. Describes the friendship and working relationship between Luce and White, with particular focus on White's reporting on China. Includes photographs.

Herzstein, Robert E. *Henry R. Luce, "Time," and the American Crusade in Asia.* New York: Cambridge University Press, 2005. Focuses on Luce's publishing activities aimed at shaping U.S. policy toward Asian nations. Includes illustrations, endnotes, and index.

Kobler, John. *Luce: His Time, Life, and Fortune.* Garden City, N.Y.: Doubleday, 1968. Lively and balanced account of Luce's founding of and control over Time Inc., its internal feuds, its influence in foreign affairs, and Luce's skill as a businessman. Written by a senior editor of the *Saturday Evening Post* and first published as a series of articles in that magazine. Includes photographs of key individuals, reproductions of covers of publications, cartoons, and bibliography.

Luce, Henry. *The Ideas of Henry Luce.* Edited by John K. Jessup. New York: Atheneum, 1969. Collection of Luce's speeches, article excerpts, and other statements on journalism, politics, law and order, business, art and architecture, Christianity, the New Deal, communism, China, American presidents, and many other subjects. Useful for understanding Luce's biases, which influenced his publications and provoked much controversy. Includes a brief insightful biographical introduction by a former aide to Luce.

Mott, Frank Luther. *A History of American Magazines.* 5 vols. Cambridge, Mass.: Harvard University Press, 1938-1968. Massive work by a leading historian of American magazines. The account of *Time* up to the early 1960's in volume 5 provides especially interesting information on matters of physical format and style.

Swanberg, W. A. *Luce and His Empire: A Biography.* New York: Charles Scribner's Sons, 1972. Polemical biography, based on substantial research, castigates Luce's motives, commitments, and achievements. Argues primarily that Luce was a megalomaniac who used *Time* and its sister publications to try to shape U.S. policies. Engaging and entertaining, but lacks subtlety and balance, often ignores historical contexts, and presents some trivial information. Includes a splendid collection of photographs, endnotes, and index.

Tebbel, John, and Mary Ellen Zuckerman. *The Magazine in America, 1741-1990.* New York: Oxford University Press, 1991. History draws on scholarly and popular examinations of the periodical press, primarily in the post-1918 years.

SEE ALSO: Nov. 7, 1914: Lippmann Helps to Establish *The New Republic*; Sept. 15, 1917: *Forbes* Magazine Is Founded; Feb., 1922: *Reader's Digest* Is Founded; Feb. 21, 1925: Ross Founds *The New Yorker*; Feb., 1930: Luce Founds *Fortune* Magazine; Nov. 23, 1936: Luce Launches *Life* Magazine.

March 5, 1923
NEVADA AND MONTANA INTRODUCE OLD-AGE PENSIONS

Before Nevada and Montana approved old-age pensions in 1923, the United States trailed far behind the rest of the industrialized world in providing relief for older citizens.

LOCALE: Nevada; Montana
CATEGORIES: Laws, acts, and legal history; business and labor

KEY FIGURES
Joseph M. Dixon (1867-1934), governor of Montana, 1921-1925
James G. Scrugham (1880-1945), governor of Nevada, 1923-1927
Abraham Epstein (1892-1942), American crusader for old-age pensions and founder of the American Association for Old Age Security

SUMMARY OF EVENT

At the same hour and on the same day, March 5, 1923, Montana governor Joseph M. Dixon and Nevada governor James G. Scrugham signed the first old-age pension legislation in the United States. The issue of providing pensions for older Americans had become prominent in the years after World War I. Proponents of old-age pensions, propelled to a great extent by the politics of Progressivism, pointed to the fact that the United States stood alone among industrialized nations in failing to provide assistance to those considered too old to hold regular jobs. The United States continued to apply the nineteenth century doctrine of laissez-faire at a time when circumstances cried out for assistance to retired wage earners. It was no longer realistic to expect that life-long wage earners could set aside enough money to live comfortably in their retirement years.

Supporters of old-age pensions had statistics on their side, and they used them effectively. In 1880, 3 percent of the U.S. population was age sixty-five or older, but by 1920 the proportion in this age group had risen to 5 percent. In addition, more people than ever before worked for wages, the average life span was increasing rapidly, businesses were tending to retire workers forcibly, and industrialization had brought about greater dispersal of family members. Given these facts, there could be little doubt that the need for old-age pensions was going to increase in the future. This led Abraham Epstein, a prominent advocate of old-age relief, to ask in the 1920's, "If the sunset of life is to continue unproductive, wretched and humiliating, is it worth prolonging?"

Much of the information that pension advocates used to expose the problems of retired American workers came from a study conducted by a legislative commission created in Pennsylvania in 1917. It was not in Pennsylvania, however, or in any other highly industrialized northeastern state, that an old-age pension bill was first enacted. Instead, the underpopulated and far less industrialized states of Montana and Nevada led the way. The circumstances under which these two states first provided old-age assistance included staggering local economies, progressive politics, and inadequate care facilities for the destitute elderly.

Like many other states, Montana and Nevada had a certain number of county homes that housed the old and poor. These were modeled roughly on the poorhouses prescribed by the 1834 New Poor Law in England. Although some of the more onerous aspects of the poorhouses had been eliminated, the county homes were scarcely desirable residences. Moreover, with physician fees and food costs, they were expensive to maintain, and the numbers of persons seeking refuge continued to increase. It was evident that these homes would soon be incapable of handling the demands placed on them. Those who supported the creation of old-age allowances made compelling economic and humanitarian arguments against housing the destitute elderly in county homes. They pointed out that the homes were becoming too expensive to maintain and that, because of the notorious conditions in many of the homes, people feared living in them more than they feared starving.

Early in 1923, the state legislatures in Montana and Nevada began to consider another kind of relief for the retired and poor. In each state, the presence of a governor who favored social reform contributed to the momentum for new measures. In Montana, Governor Dixon, a long-time Republican progressive who had served in the U.S. House of Representatives (1903-1907) and the U.S. Senate (1907-1913) and managed Theodore Roosevelt's 1912 presidential campaign, gave his support to a pension plan that would allow individual counties to provide relief for persons seventy years of age and older who had incomes of less than three hundred dollars per year. Each person given a pension had to have been a citizen of the United States and a resident of Montana for at least fifteen years. The maximum that any person could receive was twenty-five dollars each month. The Montana law placed the burden of administering and financing the pension in the hands of county officials. County commissioners were to decide who qualified for the old-age pension and how much each pensioner would receive. There was no state authority to oversee the pension plan, and the state would not reimburse counties for the pensions they paid.

In Nevada, the old-age pension bill gained the support of Democrats and progressive Republicans. The Democratic governor, James Scrugham, gave his approval to the measure as it proceeded through the state legislature. The Nevada law provided for a form of administration much different from that approved in Montana. In Nevada, the governor, lieutenant governor, and attorney general were established as the State Old Age Pension Commission. The governor then appointed three residents from each county to serve on county pension boards. These boards received applications for relief from eligible persons and then made recommendations to the state commission. Pensions could be granted to individuals sixty years of age or older who had been U.S. citizens for at least fifteen years and residents of Nevada for at least ten years. No one could be given an old-age allowance in excess of one dollar per day. Applicants who owned property valued at three thousand dollars or more were automatically disqualified. The money to support the Nevada system came from a special tax on property within each county.

SIGNIFICANCE

Although it remained to be seen whether the centralized Nevada system or the decentralized Montana system would work more efficiently, supporters of old-age pensions from around the nation were buoyed by the legislation. Beginning with Pennsylvania in May, 1923, many other states took similar action.

In the specific cases of Montana and Nevada, however, the impacts of the 1923 old-age pension measures appear to have been slight. A survey of Montana counties undertaken by Abraham Epstein in 1926 is quite revealing in this regard. Epstein received information from fifty-one of the state's fifty-six counties. Fourteen counties did not participate in the system because they had either no applications or no money to provide pensions. The largest county, which included the city of Butte, fell into the latter category. Epstein further found that, in the counties responding, only 2.6 out of every 1,000 eligible inhabitants applied for old-age pensions. At the end of 1926, there were only 448 pensioners in the thirty-two counties reporting that they had granted any pensions.

Statistics gathered from the Associated Industries of Montana and the U.S. Department of Labor showed that each citizen of the participating counties paid about twenty-eight cents per year to support the pension plan and that money spent on old-age relief was less than a quarter of that spent to maintain the county homes.

The Nevada old-age pension law was so ineffective that the state legislature repealed it early in 1925. In March of that year, a new bill was passed that adopted the Montana system of putting all decisions in the hands of county officials; the state no longer supervised the granting of old-age allowances. The 1925 Nevada legislation also raised the eligible age for assistance to sixty-five. A survey undertaken in 1926 found only one person in the entire state who had been granted an old-age pension. In both Montana and Nevada, as well as in other states, private insurance interests tried to discourage implementation of the pension laws.

The Montana and Nevada laws did not have much impact within the respective populations of those states, but on a national level the legislation gave momentum to the old-age pension cause. Legislators in highly populated industrial states were embarrassed that sparsely populated Montana and Nevada had taken the first steps to provide relief for the aged poor. Ultimately, it took the Great Depression, when many well-to-do elderly lost their savings, to force the U.S. government to devise a federally funded program to ensure income for the elderly. The result was the national Social Security Act, passed during the Franklin D. Roosevelt administration. This legislation did not abandon the notion that individuals should provide as much as possible for their own retirement through personal savings, but it added a safety net to ensure that the elderly would have a degree of financial security in retirement.

—*Ronald K. Huch*

FURTHER READING

Axinn, June, and Mark J. Stern. *Social Welfare: A History of the American Response to Need*. 6th ed. Newton, Mass.: Allyn & Bacon, 2004. History of welfare programs and legislation in America from the colonial period to the present includes discussion of the introduction of old-age pensions in the 1920's.

Douglas, Paul H. *Social Security in the United States*. 1936. Reprint. New York: Beard Books, 2000. A comprehensive, if somewhat thin, look at efforts to provide relief for the nonworking aged. Explains why employers in every state opposed pension legislation on the basis of cost. Includes index.

1923

Elliott, Russell R. *History of Nevada.* 2d ed. Lincoln: University of Nebraska Press, 1987. Splendid general history of Nevada includes thorough annotated bibliography and index.

Epstein, Abraham. *The Challenge of the Aged.* 1928. Reprint. New York: Ayer, 1976. One of the most useful and significant works on the plight of the aged in the United States through 1927 by a leader in the campaign for old-age relief. Provides substantial, well-organized information and statistics that illuminate the subject. Includes notes, appendix, and index.

Karlin, Jules A. *Joseph M. Dixon of Montana.* 2 vols. Missoula: University of Montana Press, 1974. Well-researched and inclusive biography of one of Montana's most important politicians. Does not discuss old-age pension laws, but describes convincingly the circumstances in Montana from which such laws

emerged. Includes excellent bibliography and index.

Katz, Michael B. *In the Shadow of the Poorhouse: A Social History of Welfare in America.* Rev. ed. New York: Basic Books, 1996. History of the development of social programs aimed at relieving the plight of the poor in the United States. Chapter 8 discusses the period in which the Nevada and Montana legislation was passed. Includes notes and indexes.

Spense, Clark C. *Montana: A History.* New York: W. W. Norton, 1978. Limited state history provides a very good introduction to Montana's politics and society. Includes suggestions for further reading and index.

SEE ALSO: Nov. 7, 1916: First Woman Is Elected to the U.S. Congress; Nov. 23, 1921-June 30, 1929: Sheppard-Towner Act; Oct. 29, 1929-1939: Great Depression; Aug. 14, 1935: Roosevelt Signs the Social Security Act.

March 14, 1923
AMERICAN MANAGEMENT ASSOCIATION IS ESTABLISHED

The founding of the American Management Association was a milestone in efforts to professionalize management and in the ascendancy of a conservative position on personnel relations.

LOCALE: New York, New York

CATEGORIES: Business and labor; organizations and institutions

KEY FIGURES

Meyer Bloomfield (1878-1938), American social worker

Clarence J. Hicks (1863-1944), American welfare worker

Sam A. Lewisohn (1884-1951), American industrialist and publicist

Alfred P. Sloan (1875-1966), American automobile executive

SUMMARY OF EVENT

On March 14, 1923, the members of the National Personnel Association convened in New York City to discuss broadening that organization's membership. The board of directors recognized that managers outside personnel departments were coping with personnel issues on a daily basis and clearly were qualified to join personnel managers in an expanded national association. At the same time, the establishment of such an organization would mark an

important step in the development of a professional reputation for managers. The American Management Association (AMA) grew out of this decision.

The roots of the AMA stretch back to a series of organizational efforts by groups concerned with personnel issues and dedicated to achieving a recognized standing in the business community. The National Association of Corporate Training (NACT), the Industrial Relations Association of America (IRAA), and the Special Conference Committee (SCC) played central roles in the events leading to the formation of the AMA.

The NACT and the IRAA each traced its origins to some aspect of personnel matters. The NACT arose out of the dissatisfaction of many in the corporate world over the lack of appropriate training in public schools, which no longer provided industry with workers who were able to meet the demands of a competitive society. In response, corporations initiated their own educational programs and called for more market-oriented training in the public schools.

The vocational movement grew directly from this dissatisfaction with inadequately trained workers. It concentrated on testing and counseling workers in an effort to identify their abilities and then match these with appropriate jobs in industry. By 1915, proponents of manual training had established the National Vocational Conference (NVC), which was headed by Meyer Bloomfield, a social worker with a law degree who had long participated in the personnel movement.

In his capacity as president of the NVC, Bloomfield sponsored a major conference on personnel management in 1917, during which participants established a committee charged with setting up a national organization of employment managers. In 1918, a subsequent national conference launched the National Association of Employment Managers. It brought together local organizations such as the Boston Employment Association, founded by Bloomfield, and gave the field of personnel management an increasingly professional cast. In 1919, this group renamed itself the Industrial Relations Association of America.

Members of the SCC engineered the merger of the IRAA and the NACT. The SCC also had grown out of personnel issues. Its founder, Clarence J. Hicks, had created the employee representation plan for John D. Rockefeller's Colorado Fuel. That plan established a mechanism through which employees could express their grievances and simultaneously gave personnel managers some sense of the workers' daily concerns. Hicks also developed one of the most expansive benefits programs of the time and a personnel department with substantial powers for Rockefeller's Standard Oil of New Jersey. He designed the department specifically to improve and sustain productive employer-employee relationships. He brought these notions to the SCC, the members of which considered company unions and welfare work to be fundamental in their promotion of personnel management.

SCC members served on the boards of the IRAA and the NACT, and thus assumed critical roles in the founding of the National Personnel Association. The members of this organization hoped to gain the authority in employee relations that engineers and line managers had achieved over production workers, both skilled and unskilled.

The SCC's influence persisted in the AMA. For the most part, those who joined the AMA came from large companies (such as Standard Oil, Westinghouse, and Du Pont) that had the resources to sustain personnel departments. Adopting the SCC philosophy, the AMA pinpointed human relations as its main area of concern. Sam A. Lewisohn, the AMA's president, noted that labor relations among company officials had generated little attention from the business community, a neglect the AMA intended to remedy. The AMA united the various strands of the personnel movement, from company union and welfare work to vocational training.

The AMA's journal, the *American Management Review*, energetically promoted human relations as an essential ingredient in industrial success. First published in April, 1923, the journal gained increasing notoriety by featuring individual and industry opinions on the issues affecting employee relations. It raised important topics ranging from declining productivity to the fragility of the work ethic. The *American Management Review* also continued the debate on educational training of workers to improve their productivity and ensure their loyalty to their companies.

The AMA reinforced its professional orientation by cosponsoring, with the educational director of the American Telephone and Telegraph Company, a series of conferences on engineering education. The AMA hoped to promote management instruction in the country's leading engineering schools. Scores of universities introduced courses and full-scale programs in business administration during the 1920's, a definite sign of the maturing of management as a professional career. The AMA also maintained relations with the American Council on Higher Education, which was founded during World War I to handle wartime activities in four-year institutions and continued as a permanent body determined to make institutions of higher education more amenable to cooperation with industry.

Business leaders in the 1920's also contributed to this increasingly professional image of personnel management. Many had performed years of public service before joining the ranks of business, an experience that gave them a self-perception as professionals. Other figures in the business community, including Alfred P. Sloan of General Motors, actually had participated in educational training in management skills as they prepared for careers in business. They argued that managers must broaden their concerns from satisfying investors to cooperating with workers, the public, and customers. Few considered themselves to be solely managers of private enterprises; most believed that their positions made them trustees of the public welfare. By the 1930's, the AMA, its journal, and the efforts of managers had imbued management with the professional character it had so desperately sought.

SIGNIFICANCE

The formation of the AMA marked the ascendancy of the conservative philosophy of personnel management. The founders of the AMA and their allies among those in personnel management refused to endorse the independent position that personnel departments had achieved during

1923

World War I. They urged the restriction of the capacity of personnel departments to interfere with line organizations. The AMA stated that production workers remained well outside the authority of the personnel department, which had only the capacity to serve in a consulting, rather than an active, role in matters relating to the line.

World War I had created labor market conditions that encouraged the promotion of personnel departments. Labor shortages and government demands for nonstop production forced company officials to seek the aid of personnel managers in confronting an increasingly aggressive workforce. Absences, tardiness, and other signs of worker unrest had become far more common. The threat of strikes and demands for collective bargaining punctuated negotiations between capital and labor. The federal government in fact endorsed collective bargaining to prevent work stoppages that could endanger the production of materials needed for the war effort.

Personnel departments flourished in this new environment, because their skills accommodated the needs of both employers and employees. This newfound opportunity enabled personnel managers and their departments to carve out an independent niche in corporate enterprise and achieve a standing on a par with the line organization. Proponents of personnel management established highly centralized personnel departments that seized the powers of line supervisors in the area of employee relations. The federal government contributed to this development by ordering all companies with which it carried on extensive business operations to adopt many of the personnel measures that had proven effective in stabilizing workforces. In an unexpected move, supporters of the late Frederick Winslow Taylor, the best-known advocate of scientific management, acknowledged the importance of worker morale, a point stressed by personnel managers. Taylor saw workers as cogs in the production process and rarely discussed the wants and needs of the individual employee.

The war nurtured the personnel movement, but the end of hostilities presaged a series of setbacks to personnel department enthusiasts. The inevitable labor surplus and an economic depression in 1921-1922 reduced the overflow of jobs typical of the wartime years. In the face of this reversal, enhanced by the intense mechanization of the 1920's, companies sought a return to prewar labor conditions. Control over wages and decisions to hire and fire, among other powers, returned to the shop floor. Individual supervisors in these decentralized systems were freed from interference in their daily management of workers by those in the personnel department. A declaration presented at the first meeting of the AMA expressed the view that personnel managers could only advise those in line departments. Supervisors had regained their lost autonomy. Members of the AMA declared that in the past, personnel departments had vastly overstepped their limits by interfering in line organizations on matters such as disciplining workers.

The antipathy of the SCC toward trade unions and their negotiators also carried over into the AMA. Giants in the SCC such as Standard Oil of New Jersey had long harbored strident opposition to trade unions and collective bargaining, opposition that the war had forced them to suspend. The traditional negative view of such activities reemerged with a vengeance as corporations backed off from their cooperative position. This view clashed with the position of liberals among personnel managers who advocated strict neutrality on the issue of union organizing and urged this perspective on the national association. The position of the conservative, practical manager dovetailed with the widespread probusiness attitude of American society during the 1920's.

Despite this position, the legacy of SCC attitudes toward company unions and welfare work, in addition to notions inherited from vocational guidance groups that joined the AMA, blunted the worst characteristics of line autonomy. Training programs designed to make line supervisors more sensitive to employees' interests appeared throughout the decade. Company unions also placed restraints on authority by providing grievance outlets for workers.

The pro-union laws of the New Deal and the resurgence of independent worker organizations forced a sudden shift in these positions. Strikes, labor unrest, and government intrusion revived many of the labor market conditions that had been pervasive during World War I. Companies turned to dynamic personnel managers for solutions in dealing with a defiant workforce, and personnel departments began to recover their independence and to exercise authority equal to that held by the line and other departments in the corporation. Personnel managers also engineered the return of standardized employment procedures, which replaced the idiosyncratic and unpredictable methods of line supervisors. This shift in authority significantly enhanced the power of the personnel department over employees in production while correspondingly diminishing that of the line supervisors. Line forepersons reluctantly surrendered their voice in employee evaluation, wage determination, recruiting procedures, and even employee dismissal as personnel departments eagerly assumed control over these matters.

These trends intensified during World War II, when worker shortages and government intrusion reminiscent of the 1917-1919 period reappeared in the labor markets. In the midst of this turbulence, the AMA continued to serve as an outlet for managers' discussion of the renewed threat of unions and the constant battle for control of the workplace. By the 1940's, the more pragmatic and conservative element in the AMA, after years of interaction with the liberal wing, had adopted many of the liberals' sophisticated methods of personnel management to deal with a more independent and hostile workforce. The association, through its journal and other publications, provided effective indicators of the diversity of thought and attitudes among corporate managers during these decades.

—*Edward J. Davies II*

FURTHER READING

Bernstein, Irving. *The Lean Years: A History of the American Worker, 1920-1933*. 1960. Reprint. New York: Da Capo Press, 1983. Chapter 3 contains an effective discussion of key issues such as company unions and welfare capitalism. Includes an insightful discussion of the personnel management movement during the 1920's and the relative lack of experience company officials had in dealing with personnel issues. Examines the motivation of managers to reduce the power of the foreperson in the workplace.

Commons, John R., ed. *History of Labor in the United States, 1896-1932*. Vol. 3 in *History of Labor in the United States*. New York: Macmillan, 1935. Chapter 16 briefly describes scientific management and rationalization. Chapter 17 focuses on personnel management, including the AMA and the attitudes of those involved in the association.

Eilbert, Henry. "The Development of Personnel Management in the United States." *Business History Review* 33 (Autumn, 1959): 345-364. Reviews the beginnings of personnel management in the early twentieth century. Explains the roles of welfare work, vocational guidance, and scientific management in the evolution of personnel management. Discusses the importance of World War I in shaping personnel management and the relationship between personnel managers and line supervisors.

Harris, Howell John. *The Right to Manage: Industrial Relations Policies of American Business in the 1940s*. Madison: University of Wisconsin Press, 1982. Opening chapter provides a concise description of the personnel movement from its inception through 1940.

Relies on AMA publications and the *American Management Review* for source material and reveals much about management attitudes.

Heald, Morrell. *The Social Responsibilities of Business: Company and Community, 1900-1960*. 1970. Reprint. New Brunswick, N.J.: Transaction, 2005. Chapter 3 focuses on managerial leadership and includes descriptions of the American Management Association and the debates in the *American Management Review*. Also contains a discussion of professionalism and business education.

Jacoby, Sanford. *Employing Bureaucracy: Managers, Unions, and the Transformation of Work in the Twentieth Century*. Rev. ed. Mahwah, N.J.: Lawrence Erlbaum, 2004. Comprehensive and insightful discussion of the personnel movement and the place of the AMA in its development. Covers a number of key themes, including welfare work, vocational guidance, and attitudes toward personnel management. Provides illuminating analysis of the tensions among personnel managers concerning their place in the corporation.

Nelson, Daniel. "The Company Union Movement, 1900-1937: A Reexamination." *Business History Review* 56 (Autumn, 1982): 335-357. Offers effective analysis of the growth and expansion of company unions and explanation of why these organizations prosper or fail. Provides particularly useful information on the role of Clarence J. Hicks in this movement.

Noble, David F. *America by Design: Science, Technology, and the Rise of Corporate Capitalism*. New York: Alfred A. Knopf, 1977. Critical and provocative account of the impact of corporations uses science as a centerpiece in production. Includes a discussion of corporate educational efforts, the impact of World War I, and ties between management and higher education.

Pusateri, C. Joseph. *A History of American Business*. 2d ed. Arlington Heights, Ill.: Harlan Davidson, 1988. Chapter 13 contains a broad and important discussion of the rise of corporate administration in the twentieth century. Places the AMA and the efforts to professionalize management in this broader context.

Stone, Florence. "AMA: Building Management Excellence for Eighty Years." *MWorld* (Fall, 2003): 74-81. History of the AMA from the organization's own viewpoint and in one of its own publications. Includes illustrations and time line.

Wood, Norman J. "Industrial Relations Policies of American Management, 1900-1933." *Business His-*

tory Review 34 (Winter, 1960): 403-420. Discusses the characteristics of three periods: 1900-1916, 1917-1919, and 1920-1933. Themes include scientific management, industrial safety, and welfare work in the first time frame, the professionalization of personnel management in the second, and the expansion of the personnel department's responsibilities into areas such as employee health programs in the third.

SEE ALSO: Apr. 8, 1908: Harvard University Founds a Business School; Mar., 1914: Gilbreth Publishes *The Psychology of Management*; July, 1916: Fayol Publishes *General and Industrial Management*; 1920's: Donham Promotes the Case Study Teaching Method at Harvard; 1925: McKinsey Founds a Management Consulting Firm; 1938: Barnard Publishes *The Functions of the Executive*.

April 9, 1923
U.S. SUPREME COURT RULES AGAINST MINIMUM WAGE LAWS

By ruling that minimum wage legislation was unconstitutional, the U.S. Supreme Court declared its support of laissez-faire policy and upheld the doctrine of freedom of contract.

ALSO KNOWN AS: *Adkins v. Children's Hospital*
LOCALE: Washington, D.C.
CATEGORIES: Laws, acts, and legal history; business and labor

KEY FIGURES

George Sutherland (1862-1942), associate justice of the United States, 1922-1938
William Howard Taft (1857-1930), chief justice of the United States, 1921-1930
Oliver Wendell Holmes, Jr. (1841-1935), associate justice of the United States, 1902-1932
Felix Frankfurter (1882-1965), American attorney

SUMMARY OF EVENT

On April 9, 1923, the U.S. Supreme Court ruled five to three in the case of *Adkins v. Children's Hospital* that minimum wage laws violated the freedom of contract between employers and workers as well as the due process clause of the Fifth Amendment to the U.S. Constitution. The Court's decision, surprising to many, was consistent with established laissez-faire economic policies of the time as well as the Court's own doctrine of freedom of contract, which it had been developing since the late 1890's but would eventually repudiate in its 1937 decision in *West Coast Hotel Company v. Parrish*. This doctrine held that private parties to a contract were to be free from state intervention except in those limited cases in which public health, welfare, or the morals of the community were involved.

Massachusetts had adopted a minimum wage law in 1912, which was quickly followed by similar laws in

several other states. The *Adkins* case stemmed from a 1918 federal law that created the Minimum Wage Board within the District of Columbia. The board's function was to inspect working conditions and then establish a legal minimum wage after negotiating with representatives of employers and employees. Moreover, the board was given the power to enforce its standards of minimum wages in order to protect female and teenage workers within the District of Columbia from economic conditions detrimental to their "health and morals." Failure of an employer to abide by the act was classified as a misdemeanor and carried a possible fine and imprisonment.

In 1920, the Minimum Wage Board determined that the cost of the "necessaries of life" had risen to a minimum of $16.50 a week and that many of the women working in the district's hotels, restaurants, and hospitals were being paid less, often much less, than the estimated living wage. The Children's Hospital, which employed a large proportion of women, refused to pay the wage set by the board. The hospital, along with others, brought suit to challenge the authority of the board to set wages.

The case was argued before the Court by Harvard Law School professor Felix Frankfurter in collaboration with the National Consumers League (Frankfurter would later take a seat on the Court as an associate justice in 1939). In his argument, Frankfurter stressed that the law had not harmed local industry or reduced the level of employment and in fact had improved the welfare of the district's women and children. He and his supporters submitted a large volume of documentary evidence in support of their arguments, but they ultimately failed to convince the Court that minimum wage legislation was valid. The opponents of the legislation held to a basic conservative argument of the need to protect private property and stressed the importance of freedom of contract.

Writing for the majority, Associate Justice George

Sutherland held that the 1918 law not only disrupted the right of a private contract but also violated the right of property protected by the due process clause of the Fifth Amendment. He asserted that the right of private contracts could be restrained only in exceptional cases and that in the view of the Court, at least for the time being, labor relations were largely beyond the police powers and regulatory powers of the states, Congress, and the courts.

Because in earlier rulings the Court had given mixed signals about when and where it was appropriate to set maximum work hours, the opinion in *Adkins* drew a sharp distinction between minimum wage laws and maximum hour laws. In *Adkins*, the Court held that contractual wages are appropriately set by the value of labor in the free market and that any attempt to fix wages places a burden on private employers concerning what in fact is a social issue. In the 1908 case of *Muller v. Oregon*, the Court had ruled that because of the state's interest in women's health it could, because of gender, legitimately set maximum hours. Because the decision in *Adkins* was handed down after the adoption of the Nineteenth Amendment in August of 1920, the Court's opinion also held that gender differences did not constitute a valid reason to ignore freedom of contract.

Chief Justice William Howard Taft, normally fairly conservative, issued a rare written dissent to the Court's decision in *Adkins*. Taft contended that laws could, in certain situations, be enacted to limit freedom of contract. It was, for example, within the police powers of the states, or Congress, to set maximum hours as well as to establish minimum wages. His dissent questioned the majority's distinction between wages and hours as a test of the liberty of contract, noting that one was as important as the other. Taft went on to note that although the adoption of the Nineteenth Amendment provided women with some political power, it did nothing to alter the physical distinctions between women and men. Constitutional issues therefore did not need to be recast simply because of its adoption.

Also dissenting in the *Adkins* decision was Associate Justice Oliver Wendell Holmes, Jr., who accepted the notion that Congress had the power to establish minimum wage rates for women in the District of Columbia but then questioned the constitutionality of liberty of contract. As Holmes noted, laws exist to forbid people from doing things they want to do. He questioned why labor contracts should be singled out for exemption, and he listed several cases in which liberty of contract had been limited by statute with validation by the Court. Holmes's attempt to get the Court to abandon its doctrine of liberty

of contract would not be accepted by a majority of the Court for some years, but in his dissent he expressed the differences in approach among the justices concerning economic issues and labor relations. In Holmes's view, an appointed board could be held to reasonably determine a standard for a living minimum wage. Such a standard need not come from the operations of a free market.

SIGNIFICANCE

The Court's decision in *Adkins* demonstrates the impact that laissez-faire policies had on judicial temperaments, the economy, and the citizens of the United States in the 1920's and 1930's. The decision reflected popular, although not universal, attitudes toward labor relations in the late nineteenth and early twentieth centuries. A direct impact of the *Adkins* decision was its use throughout the 1920's and early 1930's to overturn several states' minimum wage laws and other early New Deal legislation. The times and opinions were changing, however, and the Court's earnest endorsement of freedom of contract in *Adkins* would be overturned in 1937.

Initial reactions to the Court's ruling in *Adkins* were mixed. Those who favored a free and open market hailed it as an important and necessary endorsement of private property and the protection of freedom of contract under the due process clause. Those who favored direct regulation of economic and social conditions attacked it as a shameful example of inhumanity. *The New Republic*, for example, ran an editorial stating that the Court had in effect endorsed the legal right to starve.

Regardless of whether one agrees with the Court's ruling in *Adkins*, the case makes it clear that wages and prices are central to the operation of an economy. For that reason, various groups followed the case very closely. Groups opposed to minimum wage legislation had long stressed that such laws were potentially harmful not only to industry but also to labor itself, as unemployment would rise in response to higher legislated wages. Rising labor costs would be imposed on business and passed along to consumers, and labor groups themselves would have diminished ability to bargain. Those in favor of minimum wage legislation attempted to refute these claims. They argued that such laws protect the weak, raise standards of living, improve the general health and welfare, improve workers' bargaining power, and provide benefits to employers by increasing morale and worker efficiency.

Others debated the significance of an absolute power to fix wages. Did, for example, the right to set a minimum wage then also imply the ability to set a maximum wage?

Was it feasible to determine and then fix a workable wage or a living wage? How would work performed at home be legislated? How would the enforcement of a minimum wage be handled?

Because of the importance it placed on freedom of contract, the Court's decision in *Adkins* was a major setback to the progressive labor movement. During the early decades of the twentieth century, progressive groups sought legislative remedies for many of the inequities and other problems they believed existed in labor relations. The gains made by these groups were, at least for the time being, stalled by this ruling. The Court had ruled in essence that the free marketplace and not mandated regulation would guide the decisions of society. Because minimum wage legislation was seen as a means to regulate as well as to prohibit certain labor practices, progressive groups had hoped that the Court would rule to uphold the minimum wage as a means of protecting the health and welfare of women and children. Conservatives saw minimum wage legislation simply as an unconstitutional intrusion into private affairs between employers and employees.

The Court's ruling in this case, among others, provides a good deal of insight into the role of women and children in the American economy during the early years of the twentieth century. Minimum wage legislation often specified that the health and welfare of women and children were to be protected by a minimum living wage. This emphasis can be explained by the fact that gender- and age-specific legislation was more likely to be accepted, or, alternatively, that women and children were employed in less productive industries, had lower wages, and had less bargaining power in the market, thus legislation on their behalf was necessary.

By ruling minimum wage legislation unconstitutional, the Court demonstrated a belief in the merits of a marketplace free from government intervention. The decision in *Adkins* affirmed the Court's belief that the freedom of contract doctrine remained, at least for the time, paramount to the operation of the free market. Moreover, if the freedom of contract doctrine were broadly applied, the nation, the economy, and labor relations would remain dominated by laissez-faire policies. The significance of this was made obvious in the *West Coast Hotel v. Parrish* decision, which upheld a Washington State minimum wage law and overturned *Adkins*. In that decision, Chief Justice Charles Evans Hughes dismissed the primacy of freedom of contract and instead argued that due process was of paramount importance to the interests of the community.

With the repudiation of the *Adkins* decision and abandonment of a laissez-faire approach to social and economic problems, the roles of federal, state, and local governments clearly changed. The relative impact of the legislation that followed in the wake of the Court's later ruling remains a matter of considerable debate in the early twenty-first century.

—*Timothy E. Sullivan*

FURTHER READING

Brandeis, Louis D., and Josephine Goldmark. *Women in Industry*. Reprint. New York: Arno Press, 1969. A summary of the Supreme Court's decision upholding the constitutionality of the ten-hour workday. Helps to place labor issues and the debate on gender and the workplace in the context of the early twentieth century.

Hall, Kermit L., ed. *The Oxford Companion to the Supreme Court of the United States*. New York: Oxford University Press, 1992. A useful guide to the history of the Court, its major decisions, every justice who has served on the Court, and doctrines that have guided and influenced the Court since its founding in 1789. Concise yet detailed entries help to make landmark cases and legal terms accessible to a variety of users.

_____. *The Oxford Guide to United States Supreme Court Decisions*. New York: Oxford University Press, 1999. Collection of essays on more than four hundred significant Court decisions, with supporting glossary and other aids.

Levin-Waldman, Oren M. *The Case of the Minimum Wage: Competing Policy Models*. Albany: State University of New York Press, 2001. Discusses the evolution of minimum wage policy and law in the United States, focusing on how the nature of arguments concerning a minimum wage has changed over time as the strength of organized labor has declined. Includes tables and figures, bibliography, and index.

Nichols, Egbert Ray, and Joseph H. Baccus, eds. *Selected Articles on Minimum Wages and Maximum Hours*. New York: H. W. Wilson, 1936. Outlines and defines the debate on whether Congress has the power to fix minimum wages and maximum hours for workers. Reprints of editorials and other commentary offer a variety of legal, political, and economic interpretations.

Nordlund, Willis J. *The Quest for a Living Wage: The History of the Federal Minimum Wage Program*. Westport, Conn.: Greenwood Press, 1997. Traces the process through which the U.S. government has attempted to develop a fair method of ensuring that workers receive a living wage. Discusses the theories behind minimum wage programs and gives an overview of the first fifty years of the operation of the Fair Labor Standards Act. Includes tables and figures, bibliography, and index.

Stigler, George J. "The Economics of Minimum Wage Legislation." *American Economic Review* 36 (June, 1946): 358-365. Concise and nontechnical discussion of the relative efficiencies of minimum wage legislation. Provides and uses evidence on employment and wages in Minnesota in the late 1930's.

Welch, Finis. *Minimum Wages: Issues and Evidence.* Washington, D.C.: American Enterprise Institute for Public Policy Research, 1978. A reexamination of the issues forty years after the enactment of the federal minimum wage law.

SEE ALSO: Apr. 17, 1905: U.S. Supreme Court Strikes Down Maximum Hours Law; June 4, 1912: Massachusetts Adopts the First Minimum Wage Law in the United States; Feb. 5-July 22, 1937: Supreme Court-Packing Fight; June 25, 1938: Fair Labor Standards Act.

Summer, 1923
ZDANSKY DISCOVERS PEKING MAN

Otto Zdansky discovered a tooth that provided the first evidence that Homo erectus *had existed outside Java.*

ALSO KNOWN AS: Beijing man
LOCALE: Zhoukoudian, China
CATEGORIES: Anthropology; prehistory and ancient cultures

KEY FIGURES
Otto Zdansky (fl. 1920's), Austrian paleontologist
Johan Gunnar Andersson (1874-1960), Swedish mining expert
Davidson Black (1884-1934), Canadian professor of anatomy
Franz Weidenreich (1873-1948), German anotomist and anthropologist
Pei Wenzhong (W. C. Pei; 1904-1982), Chinese paleontologist

SUMMARY OF EVENT
The story of the discovery (and subsequent loss) of Peking man is one of the most engrossing in the history of anthropology. It began in 1899 when K. A. Haberer, physician to the German legation at China's capital city of Beijing (then known in the West as Peking), found his movements seriously restricted by the violent Boxer Rebellion and wisely limited his avocation of fossil hunting to urban drugstores. (It had long been traditional in China to grind up vertebrate mammalian fossils and use them for medicine.) Haberer then sent his voluminous collection of fossils in several shipments to Munich, where his friend Max Schlosser described them in a monograph ti-

tled *Die fossilen Säugethiere Chinas* (1903; *Fossil Primates of China*, 1924).

All the fossils in the collection were mammalian—it included no fossils of reptiles or birds—and one particularly distinctive tooth seemed to be either apelike or human. Eventually, it proved to be that of a prehistoric ape, but as a significant body of evidence from a previously little known locality the collection as a whole, and the enigmatic tooth especially, aroused interest throughout the West, in large part because Schlosser boldly predicted that some new form of prehistoric fossil would soon be found in China. Nothing further took place, however, until 1918, when Johan Gunnar Andersson turned to professional fossil collecting in China on behalf of Swedish institutions. When his discoveries proved to be not only abundant but also interesting, the Swedish Paleontological Institute of Uppsala sent Otto Zdansky, a professionally trained paleontologist, to China to improve the scientific quality of Andersson's work.

Zdansky arrived in the summer of 1921 and began operations of his own at an abandoned limestone quarry approximately thirty miles (roughly forty-eight kilometers) southwest of Beijing near the village of Zhoukoudian. Andersson had already described the site two years before and recommended it to Zdansky. The site was known locally as Chicken Bone Hill. After excavations began, however, Zdansky's workmen told him of a richer site, called Dragon Bone Hill, adjacent to another abandoned quarry on the other side of the village. On his first visit to the site, Zdansky was accompanied by Andersson, who immediately noticed a number of incongruous quartz fragments and identified them as chipped tools.

1923

Zdansky, however, did not agree that the fragments were tools.

Later, while excavating by himself in 1923, Zdansky found a single molar tooth at Dragon Bone Hill, the first fossil evidence of Peking man. Curiously, however, he did not inform Andersson of his find (relations between the two men were somewhat strained), and he made no mention of it in his publications until 1926, when he had returned to Sweden. By that time, Zdansky's longtime patron (as chairman of the Swedish China Research Committee), Crown Prince Gustav Adolf, was scheduled to visit China. Asked to contribute finds, Zdansky informed Andersson of the two teeth he had earlier discovered (a second example having turned up before he left China). At a reception in Beijing on October 22, 1926, Andersson, in turn, informed the prince and the world. The news caused a sensation everywhere in the educated world, as the fossil remains now called Peking man were thought to represent the oldest form of humanity known.

Among those present at the Beijing meeting was Davidson Black, a professor of anatomy who had long been interested in the biological history of humankind. Without having seen Zdansky's actual specimens (which were still in Sweden), Black wrote two short papers proclaiming that "the actual presence of early man in Eastern Asia is no longer a matter of conjecture" and concluding that the hypothesis that humans had originated in Asia was now considerably substantiated. In a more cautious paper of his own, Zdansky pointedly failed to endorse either assertion, regarding the teeth as only probably human and the evidence too scant to support any far-reaching conclusions.

With support from Crown Prince Gustav Adolf, the Geological Survey of China, and the Rockefeller Foundation, Black now undertook a further round of excavations at Zhoukoudian. Having accepted an appointment at Cairo University, Zdansky declined to head the project and was replaced by Birger Bohlin, another Swedish paleontologist. Only three days before the end of the first season's work, on October 16, 1927, Bohlin found a beautifully preserved left lower molar tooth. On the basis of only three teeth, two of which he had never seen, Black confidently proposed a new hominid genus called *Sinanthropus pekinensis*.

Despite extensive efforts, further excavations yielded nothing of fundamental importance until December, 1929, when Black's Chinese assistant Pei Wenzhong found an almost complete skull of Peking man partially embedded in a cave. Black (and several coauthors) described this skull, jawbone fragments found earlier, vari-

ous teeth, and a large collection of nonhuman fossils from the site in 1933 in the well-known publication *Fossil Man in China*. After Black's premature death in 1934, however, a comparison of the skull that Pei had found with fragments discovered by Eugène Dubois in Java (known as Java man) revealed them to be so nearly identical that separate designations for the two finds seemed inappropriate. The name *Sinanthropus* was therefore discarded in favor of *Homo erectus*, which applied to both examples.

From 1934 to 1937, when military conditions forced a halt, continuing excavations at Zhoukoudian revealed a wonderful collection of skulls, jaws, teeth, and even some limb bones. Anthropologist Franz Weidenreich then studied, described, and made casts of these specimens, publishing his findings in a series of admirably competent monographs. In April, 1941, he brought the casts, photographs, and his notes with him to the United States. In December, 1941, an attempt was made to evacuate the specimens from Beijing to a waiting American ship. Unfortunately, war between Japan and the United States broke out, forcing the interruption of the shipment, and the precious fossils disappeared.

SIGNIFICANCE

The most immediate consequence of the discovery of Peking man was that it appeared to confirm—with fossil evidence for the first time—a long-prevalent belief that humankind originated in Asia. Earlier work in archaeology (the discovery of the Sumerians by Sir Leonard Woolley in particular) had already established Asia as the home of human civilization. It seemed logical, then, to assume that Asia had also been the original habitat for uncivilized humankind. It is believed today that humankind originated in Africa, as Charles Darwin suggested. The first significant fossil evidence in support of this hypothesis was the discovery of *Australopithecus* (the Taung child) by Raymond Arthur Dart in 1924. *Australopithecus* was still not fully human, and some assert that it was never part of human ancestry at all. The more obviously human *Sinanthropus* distracted attention from *Australopithecus* and the African-origin hypothesis, thereby delaying its acceptance. As a result, early African discoverers such as Robert Bloom and L. S. B. Leakey found it somewhat more difficult to obtain a hearing for their beliefs.

Prior to its identification as *Homo erectus*, moreover, Peking man further complicated human genealogy by appearing to be a separate genus. Leakey cleverly utilized this perception in his book *Adam's Ancestors*

(1934), in which he argued that the known diversity of prehistoric human types (Java man, Peking man, the since-discredited Piltdown man, and the since-redated Kanam man) was evidence of an extremely long period of prior evolution and therefore pushed human origins back into the Miocene epoch. Eventually, further discoveries by the Leakeys and others would indeed place *Homo erectus* closer to the end of human evolution than to the beginning. The fact that *Homo erectus* had been found both in Java and China attested to the migratory diversity of early humans and tended to affirm their unity.

Finally, discoveries in the cave and quarry deposits of Zhoukoudian were revolutionary in that they offered more information regarding the daily living of human ancestors than was available from any previous fossil evidence. Peking man, for example, had used fire, but perhaps without knowing how to make it. He was, moreover, a cannibal and a primitive toolmaker. Many speculations followed as to what life in the caves must have been like. Whatever his merits, Peking man represented the first opportunity that reputable scientists had to study not only early humans but also the society they created.

—Dennis R. Dean

FURTHER READING

Black, Davidson, et al. *Fossil Man in China: The Choukoutien Cave Deposits, with a Synopsis of Our Present Knowledge of the Late Cenozoic in China*. Peiping: Geological Survey of China, 1933. Although intended for specialists, this classic account is necessary to any serious consideration of Black's work. Includes a useful bibliography of Black's early papers.

Day, Michael H. *Guide to Fossil Man*. 4th ed. Chicago: University of Chicago Press, 1986. Excellent source of information regarding any type of fossil, although readers should bear in mind that all books in this fast-moving field quickly become out of date.

Lewin, Roger. *Bones of Contention: Controversies in the Search for Human Origins*. 2d ed. Chicago: University of Chicago Press, 1997. A onetime close associate of the Leakeys, Lewin is primarily concerned with the history of discovery in Africa and how researchers' finds struggled for acceptance in the learned world. He has little to say about the discovery of Peking man, as such, beyond emphasizing its originally negative impact on researchers studying possible African origins of humankind.

Oosterzee, Penny van. *Dragon Bones: The Story of Peking Man*. New York: Perseus Books, 2000. Historical account for lay readers describes the activities that led to the discovery of Peking man and the events that followed. The author is an Australian ecologist and science writer.

Reader, John. *Missing Links: The Hunt for Earliest Man*. 1981. Reprint. New York: Penguin Books, 1994. Focuses primarily on Africa, but surveys the entire topic of early man in chronological order, with the first five chapters (of twelve) dealing with Neanderthal man, Java man, Piltdown man, *Australopithecus*, and Peking man. Provides excellent discussion of the context in which Peking man emerged. Includes excellent photographs and a very helpful bibliography.

Wendt, Herbert. *In Search of Adam: The Story of Man's Quest for the Truth About His Earliest Ancestors*. Translated by James Cleugh. 1955. Reprint. Westport, Conn.: Greenwood Press, 1973. Although dated, this popular account is comprehensive and well illustrated. Provides an adequate section on Peking man, given the book's brevity.

SEE ALSO: Dec., 1908: Boule Reconstructs the First Neanderthal Skeleton; Summer, 1924: Dart Discovers the First Australopithecine Fossil; Fall, 1937-Winter, 1938: Weidenreich Reconstructs the Face of Peking Man; Sept. 12, 1940: Lascaux Cave Paintings Are Discovered.

1923

June 26, 1923
OKLAHOMA IMPOSES MARTIAL LAW IN RESPONSE TO KKK VIOLENCE

Oklahoma governor Jack Walton's declaration of martial law in response to Ku Klux Klan terrorism led to a controversy that resulted in his impeachment and removal from office.

LOCALE: Oklahoma

CATEGORIES: Civil rights and liberties; terrorism; government and politics

KEY FIGURES

Jack Walton (1881-1949), governor of Oklahoma, January-November, 1923

Edwin DeBarr (1859-1950), vice president of Oklahoma University and Grand Dragon of the Oklahoma Ku Klux Klan

N. Clay Jewett (fl. early twentieth century), Oklahoma City businessman and Grand Dragon of the Oklahoma Ku Klux Klan

Martin E. Trapp (1877-1951), lieutenant governor of Oklahoma

SUMMARY OF EVENT

The original Ku Klux Klan began in Tennessee in late 1865, shortly after the Civil War. A secret organization whose members wore masks, hoods, and robes, it spread throughout the South, using threats, beatings, and murder to prevent recently freed slaves from exercising their newly won political and civil rights. In the early 1870's the federal government forcibly suppressed the first Klan movement, yet racial violence continued. By the turn of the century, southern blacks had lost virtually all of the rights supposedly guaranteed under the 1868 Fourteenth Amendment (equal citizenship) and the 1870 Fifteenth Amendment (suffrage) to the U.S. Constitution.

In 1915, William Joseph Simmons organized a second Ku Klux Klan in Atlanta, Georgia. By 1920, this organization had spread beyond the old Confederacy and found varying degrees of support throughout the United States. The Klan's targets included not only African Americans but also Catholics, Jews, and aliens as well as native-born Americans who violated the moral code of rural, Protestant America. By the mid-1920's, the Klan had attained a membership of several million and exercised political influence in a number of states and communities.

The Klan became a visible presence in Oklahoma in 1921. This former Indian territory, admitted to statehood in 1907, had a tradition of frontier vigilantism, lynch-ings, labor tensions, and mistreatment of its large Native American population, which was systematically cheated of its land. Blacks in 1920 formed about 7 percent of Oklahoma's two million residents and had been subjected to disfranchisement and racial segregation well before the Klan's arrival. In the spring of 1921, lynching rumors triggered a Tulsa race riot in which nearly eighty people, mostly blacks, perished. Catholics, Jews, and aliens were few in number and were regarded with some suspicion by the white Protestant majority.

Under the leadership of its first Grand Dragon, Edwin DeBarr, a chemistry professor and vice president of the University of Oklahoma, the Oklahoma Klan by the spring of 1922 reached a membership of seventy thousand. Unlike many of its sister organizations in other states, it focused little attention on Catholics, Jews, and aliens and generally refrained from initiating economic boycotts against these groups. Although the Klan played no clear role in the Tulsa riot, it occasionally targeted blacks. In El Reno, a black hotel porter was whipped for being insufficiently deferential toward white guests, and in Enid the Klan drove out more than twenty blacks whom its members viewed as posing a criminal threat. In 1922, a prominent Tulsa black was whipped and mutilated for attempting to register blacks to vote.

The primary targets of Klan violence, however, were native-born whites. The oil boom of the early twentieth century had generated rowdy boomtowns accompanied by an upsurge of crime, vice, and labor strife. State "dry laws" and national Prohibition were flagrantly violated. Oklahoma was thus fertile ground for Klan recruiters who pledged to restore order and reaffirm traditional values. Local whipping squads formed, and alleged adulterers, loose women, wife beaters, bootleggers, and criminals were abducted and beaten. The first evidence of the Klan in Oklahoma was the July, 1921, abduction and whipping of a Muskogee dishwasher accused of criminal behavior. Later that year, a shoot-out in Wilson between Klan members and suspected bootleggers left three of the latter dead. Although hundreds of floggings occurred, victims feared reporting the incidents because many officials and police had Klan affiliations. Indeed, by 1922 the Klan had become a significant political force in Oklahoma, locally and on the state level. Klansmen dominated the state legislature.

At first, there was little open opposition to the Klan, but this would change under the administration of Governor Jack Walton. As mayor of Oklahoma City, Walton had earlier expressed opposition to the Klan. He had warned police that he would not tolerate their membership in the order, and he had launched an investigation of Klan use of the local fairgrounds. Following his successful 1922 gubernatorial election campaign, backed by the Democratic party and the new Farmer-Labor Reconstruction League, Walton made an effort to conciliate the diverse elements of his constituency, which included not only the reformist Reconstruction Leaguers who were anti-Klan but also a significant proportion of Klansmen. Walton opportunistically appointed Klansmen to state positions and even secretly joined the order. He used patronage ineptly and caused an outrage when he appointed a poorly qualified Reconstruction League leader as president of the Agricultural and Mining College.

Walton's efforts to please all sides backfired. Rumors circulated that Walton had taken money from the oil interests and had misappropriated state funds. By the spring of 1923, there was considerable talk of impeachment. At the same time, there was a new outbreak of masked attacks. Walton announced that if local law officers failed to correct the problem, he would employ the National Guard. On June 26, he briefly imposed martial law in Okmulgee County. In August, six unmasked men kidnapped and severely whipped Nate Hantaman, a Jewish boardinghouse operator in Tulsa suspected of dealing in narcotics and liquor. There was evidence of possible police collusion with the kidnapping. After officials failed to apprehend Hantaman's assailants, Walton on August 13 placed Tulsa under martial law, sending in National Guard troops and then establishing a court of inquiry that indicted several floggers. Such actions won praise from both the Oklahoma press and the national press, but then Walton seemed to abandon all restraint. On August 30, in violation of the state constitution, he announced a suspension of habeas corpus for the entire county and sent in two hundred more troops. When the *Tulsa Tribune* protested, Walton briefly placed the paper's editorial page under military censorship. He advised citizens to shoot any masked men who attempted to assault them, promising to grant them pardons.

Open warfare ensued between Walton and the Klan. The Oklahoma City businessman who had recently replaced DeBarr as Grand Dragon, N. Clay Jewett, declared that Walton would never break the Klan's power in Oklahoma. Walton then ordered a statewide ban on Klan parades and demonstrations, threatening to place the entire state under martial law if his order were disobeyed. Jewett shrewdly complied and exhorted his followers to refrain from vigilante action. On September 15, just as a grand jury was to convene to investigate the governor's misuse of power, Walton placed all of Oklahoma under martial law. Labeling Klansmen enemies of the state, he called up six thousand additional National Guard troops and forcibly prevented the grand jury from proceeding with its investigation. Testimony given before an Oklahoma City military court revealed that high local officials had joined the Klan. The general sentiment, however, was that the governor had gone too far.

By now, a determined effort to impeach Walton was under way. The governor used threats, military force, and legal action in a desperate attempt to prevent such action, but on October 2 Oklahoma voters overwhelmingly approved an initiative proposal permitting a special legislative session in which the issue of impeachment and removal could be considered. On October 8, the governor terminated military rule in Oklahoma. Three days later, he convened the legislature to consider anti-Klan proposals, but when the lower house met, it made impeachment proceedings its first priority and adopted twenty-two charges against Walton. In November, the state senate upheld eleven of the charges by the two-thirds majority needed for conviction and removal from office. The charges included the suspension of habeas corpus, use of the National Guard to prevent a grand jury from convening, misuse of state funds, excessive use of pardons, and incompetence.

SIGNIFICANCE

Governor Walton's decision to invoke martial law provoked considerable controversy. Oklahomans had been sharply divided on the Klan issue, with the organization receiving its greatest support in the central, northern, and eastern sections of the state. Among followers of the Reconstruction League, with its strongest base in southern Oklahoma, there was deep opposition to the hooded order. The league condemned the Klan as antilabor and denounced its violence and bigotry, and at least initially supported Walton's war on the Klan. Most Oklahomans, however, recoiled at the governor's decision to invoke martial law. Tulsans, for example, found it insulting to have troops patrolling their streets and to be subjected to sundown curfews. On the eve of the October 2 initiative election that ultimately paved the way for Walton's ouster, the governor proclaimed a postponement of the balloting and threatened that National Guard troops and police were prepared to shoot those who went to the

1923

polls. Nevertheless, more than half of the eligible voters defied the threat and voted 209,452 to 70,638 in favor of the proposal.

Many Oklahomans, including members of the Reconstruction League, concluded that Walton posed a greater menace than did the Klan, and they rallied around the cry that they wanted "neither Klan nor king." Historians generally agree that Walton used his war on the Klan to divert attention from his own corruption and incompetence. Tactics nominally directed against the Klan in actuality posed threats to the constitutional rights of all Oklahoma citizens. Moreover, at the time of Walton's ouster, politically and numerically the Oklahoma Klan was stronger than ever: In 1924 its membership hit a peak of more than 100,000, placing the state near the nation's top in terms of its percentage of Klansmen. The unpopularity of Walton's actions may well have bolstered the Oklahoma Klan, which had seemed to be waning prior to his declaration of martial law.

At the same time, however, Klan abuses clearly warranted corrective action. Oklahoma's Klan reputedly was the most violent in the nation, and local authorities were ineffective in controlling it, sometimes even collaborating with the hooded order. Oklahoma military court hearings admittedly yielded few convictions, but the several floggers who were indicted and convicted were probably the first Klansmen whose guilt was clearly demonstrated by a court of law.

Under Walton's successor, Martin E. Trapp, the legislature in late 1923 adopted a moderate bill that regulated the wearing of masks and slightly increased the penalties for masked offenses. Furthermore, as most Oklahomans came to reject the excesses of vigilantism, Klan leaders like Jewett attempted to discourage such activities, and the Klan wave of terror ceased. The Klan's political success also proved fleeting. The majority of Oklahoma Klansmen were Democrats who took offense when Jewett, a Republican, engaged in machinations designed to benefit his own party. Klansmen also tired of the order's internal bickering, its authoritarian structure, and the continual financial burdens of dues and "taxes." As in other states, the Klan failed to deliver politically despite its nominal control over the legislature. As the decade ended, the Oklahoma Klan was a virtually powerless force claiming only two thousand members.

Oklahoma's black population continued to hold a subordinate social and political position until the Civil Rights revolution of the late 1950's and the 1960's. A third Klan movement, with a penchant toward violence, developed in reaction to these human rights advances,

but it never came close to approaching the Klan of the 1920's either in scale or in political influence.

—*Allen Safianow*

FURTHER READING

Alexander, Charles C. *The Ku Klux Klan in the Southwest.* 1965. Reprint. Norman: University of Oklahoma Press, 1995. Contends that the Klan's appeal in southwestern states rested primarily on its attempts to enforce crumbling Victorian moral values, and asserts that Walton's war on the Klan was in reality an attempt to cloak the ineptness and corruption of his own administration. Includes glossary of Klan terminology and annotated bibliography.

Chalmers, David M. *Hooded Americanism: The History of the Ku Klux Klan.* 3d ed. New York: F. Watts, 1981. Comprehensive history of the Klan. Chapter titled "Mayhem and Martial Law in Oklahoma" offers a brief introduction to the events but not much in the way of analysis. Includes bibliography and index.

Morgan, H. Wayne, and Anne Hodges Morgan. *Oklahoma: A History.* New York: W. W. Norton, 1984. Presents a clear, concise consideration of the Klan's rise in Oklahoma and Walton's crusade against the organization. Argues that Walton lacked the experience and intelligence necessary to govern the state and that the alliance formed to remove him from office served to fortify the Klan politically, at least temporarily. Includes references and index.

Neuringer, Sheldon. "Governor Walton's War on the Ku Klux Klan: An Episode in Oklahoma History, 1923 to 1924." *Chronicles of Oklahoma* 45 (Summer, 1967): 153-179. Provides a detailed and balanced assessment of Walton's political struggle against the Klan. Suggests that initially there was some justification for establishing military courts, but Walton resorted to measures that were clearly unconstitutional, unwarranted, and counterproductive. Includes references.

Scales, James R., and Danney Goble. *Oklahoma Politics: A History.* Norman: University of Oklahoma Press, 1982. Presents an informative analysis of Oklahoma politics of the 1920's and portrays Walton's war on the Klan as a largely ineffective political maneuver. Argues that "the Klan richly deserved punishment, but not subversion of civil liberties with unparalleled ruthlessness." Includes illustrations, references, and index.

Schrems, Suzanne H. *Who's Rocking the Cradle? Women Pioneers of Oklahoma Politics from Socialism to the KKK, 1900-1930.* Norman, Okla.: Horse

Creek, 2004. Surveys the political activities of women in Oklahoma during the period covered. Chapter 6 is devoted to women's involvement in the Oklahoma Ku Klux Klan. Includes index.

Tucker, Howard A. *History of Governor Walton's War on Ku Klux Klan, the Invisible Empire*. Oklahoma City: Southwest, 1923. Brief work written by an Oklahoma journalist shortly before Walton's impeachment provides a vivid if disjointed depiction of

Klan violence, often through the testimony of its victims. Presents Walton's behavior in a more sympathetic light than most later sources. Marred by some inaccuracies and dubious claims.

SEE ALSO: Sept., 1913: Anti-Defamation League Is Founded; Mar. 3, 1915: Griffith Releases *The Birth of a Nation*; June, 1917: First Pulitzer Prizes Are Awarded; 1921-1924: Ku Klux Klan Spreads Terror in the American South.

August 27-September 29, 1923
CORFU CRISIS

Italian leader Benito Mussolini bombarded and occupied the Greek island of Corfu after the murder of an Italian envoy and his party. Reluctant to come to Greece's aid, the League of Nations deferred to the Conference of Ambassadors, which forced Greece to issue an apology and pay compensation.

LOCALE: Corfu, Greece; Italy; Geneva, Switzerland; Paris, France

CATEGORIES: Diplomacy and international relations; colonialism and occupation

KEY FIGURES

Benito Mussolini (1883-1945), prime minister and dictator of Italy, 1922-1943

Enrico Tellini (d. 1923), Italian general

Emilio Solari (1864-1954), Italian admiral

Petros Euripéos (fl. early twentieth century), prefect of Corfu

Jules Cambon (1845-1935), president of the Conference of Ambassadors

Nikolaos Sokrates Politis (1872-1942), Greek delegate to the League of Nations

SUMMARY OF EVENT

On August 27, 1923, five Italians—members of an international-boundary commission charged with defining the border between Greece and Albania—were murdered on Greek territory. Italian leader Benito Mussolini, who had been waiting for such a provocation, held Greece responsible for the murders and issued an ultimatum consisting of a series of largely unreasonable demands. When the Greek government rejected some of these demands, Mussolini ordered the Italian fleet to occupy the Greek island of Corfu, a step widely interpreted as a prelude to the permanent Italian annexation of Corfu

and the rest of the Ionian Islands. A bombardment preceding the occupation led to casualties among a group of Armenian refugees, and Greece turned to the newly formed League of Nations for help.

Corfu (sometimes referred to as Kerkyra), the northernmost of the Ionian Islands, lies in a strategic position between the Adriatic and Ionian seas: It is opposite the large Italian Gulf of Taranto and within sight of the present-day border between Greece and Albania. Ceded to Greece in 1864 by Great Britain, the Ionian Islands were coveted by Italy, which hoped to establish control over not only the eastern Adriatic but also the entire Mediterranean region.

Albania had secured its independence from the Ottoman Empire in 1912, and in the years following World War I, Great Britain, Albania, Yugoslavia, and Greece asked the League of Nations to delimit Albania's boundaries. The League referred the matter to the Conference of Ambassadors, which had been created to oversee the provisions of the Treaty of Versailles (which had concluded World War I), and the conference set up a Commission of Delimitation to study the borders. The group working on the issue of the Greco-Albanian border included five Italian members, including General Enrico Tellini.

On the morning of August 27, 1923, Tellini, his Italian colleagues, and an Albanian interpreter were ambushed and murdered on the Greek side of the border near Janina. Within two days, Mussolini, who had come to power late in the preceding year, issued an ultimatum to the Greek government. Among other demands, Mussolini insisted that Greece pay Italy an indemnity of fifty million lire, and that it fully agree to all of Italy's demands within twenty-four hours.

There was no evidence that Greeks had been responsible, and in fact there was good reason to believe that Al-

1923

banians were to blame, as Albanian bandits had been active in the area as early as 1921. Since the crime had taken place on its soil, however, Greece was willing to accede to some of Italy's demands. It rejected other demands as unreasonable, however, and Mussolini probably expected this. The Italian leader then dispatched a fleet under the command of Admiral Emilio Solari to occupy Corfu and hold it until the Italian demands were met.

When Corfu's prefect, Petros Euripéos, was hesitant to surrender to Solari, the admiral quickly ordered that the island be bombarded—apparently against Mussolini's instructions—to avoid the use of unnecessary force. The bombardment began shortly after 5:00 P.M. on August 31, and was concentrated on the forts overlooking the capital of the island (a town also known as Corfu) and its harbor. At this time, the forts held no artillery, and in fact one contained a hospital and had been converted into a temporary shelter for refugees from Armenia. Sixteen people (mostly Armenians) were killed, and more than fifty were wounded in the bombardment. The prefect surrendered after about twenty minutes, and Italian troops then occupied the town.

The following day, September 1, Greek delegate Nikolaos Sokrates Politis (who was born in Corfu) presented an official appeal to the League of Nations in Geneva, Switzerland. Although Italy had been one of the first countries to endorse the League, it now rejected the organization's jurisdiction and threatened to withdraw. In the ensuing flurry of diplomatic activity, it became clear that the members of the League Council (which at this time included the four permanent members of France, Great Britain, Italy, and Japan, as well as four nonpermanent members) were for the most part intent on advancing their own strategic interests. In particular, French Prime Minister Raymond Poincaré was anxious to retain Italy's support on other issues. While Great Britain initially favored League action, the country was eventually persuaded to side with France. As a result, the Council deferred once again to the Conference of Ambassadors, which had after all overseen the initial border delimitation. Even Greece fell into line with this decision, and Politis lost whatever chance he and his country had of forcing the issue in the League.

The Conference of Ambassadors sat in Paris, and its president at the time was French diplomat Jules Cambon. After intense and complicated negotiations, Italy agreed in mid-September to withdraw its forces from Corfu, although the evacuation was not completed until September 27. When a commission of inquiry charged with investigating the murders of the Italians failed to identify the culprits within the allotted time, the conference insisted that Greece apologize to Italy and pay the indemnity of fifty million lire. Delays in arranging the payment led Mussolini to order his warships back to Corfu, and it was only on September 29 that the ships left Greek waters for good.

SIGNIFICANCE

Although Italy evacuated Corfu under the agreement arbitrated by the Conference of Ambassadors, the affair was Mussolini's first foreign policy success, and it made him a hero in his own country. He quickly went on to increase Italy's power at the expense of its neighbors, wresting the Fiume region at the northern end of the Adriatic from Yugoslavia, redoubling Italian pacification efforts in its North African colonies of Tripoli and Cyrenaica, and consolidating Italian influence over Albania.

Even though further military confrontation had been avoided, the actions of the League of Nations and the Conference of Ambassadors during the crisis amounted to a capitulation to Italy and its belligerent new leader, and helped pave the way for another world war. The affair highlighted the League's reluctance to enforce its own covenant and undermined its authority in dealing with future disputes. An inquiry subsequently commissioned by the League's secretary-general, British diplomat Sir James Eric Drummond, concluded that the League did indeed have the authority to act in such situations, but in Corfu's case it no longer mattered.

—*Grove Koger*

FURTHER READING

Barros, James. *The Corfu Incident of 1923: Mussolini and the League of Nations*. Princeton, N.J.: Princeton University Press, 1966. Argues that the League was not designed to deal with situations such as the Corfu crisis. The single best work on the subject in English. Supplemented by an excellent chronology.

Boatswain, Timothy, and Colin Nicolson. *A Traveller's History of Greece*. 2d ed. London: Phoenix, 2003. Sees the incident as one of a series of debilitating events in modern Greek history.

Kallis, Aristotle A. *Fascist Ideology: Expansionism in Italy and Germany, 1922-1945*. New York: Routledge, 2000. Considers the crisis and the occupation of Corfu as emblematic of fascist leadership and expansionist philosophy.

Neville, Peter. *Mussolini*. New York: Routledge, 2004. Popular biography that considers the Corfu crisis as a step in Mussolini's rise to international power.

Ostrower, Gary B. *The League of Nations: From 1919 to 1929*. Garden City Park, N.Y.: Avery, 1996. Includes a thorough account of the affair and its implications for the new organization.

Woodhouse, C. M. *Modern Greece: A Short History*. 5th ed. London: Faber & Faber, 1998. Treats the incident as an element in the modern nation's first national crisis and an early prelude to World War II.

SEE ALSO: Oct. 24-30, 1922: Mussolini's "March on Rome"; 1925-1926: Mussolini Seizes Dictatorial Powers in Italy; Oct. 23, 1925: Greece Invades Bulgaria; Oct. 11, 1935-July 15, 1936: League of Nations Applies Economic Sanctions Against Italy; Apr. 7, 1939: Italy Invades and Annexes Albania.

September 1, 1923
EARTHQUAKE ROCKS JAPAN

After Japan experienced one of the most destructive earthquakes in history, building codes were improved and modern architectural standards were established.

ALSO KNOWN AS: Great Kanto earthquake
LOCALE: Yokohama and Tokyo, Japan
CATEGORIES: Disasters; earth science; urban planning

KEY FIGURE
Gotō Shimpei (1857-1929), mayor of Tokyo

SUMMARY OF EVENT
On September 1, 1923, an earthquake that would have registered a magnitude 8.3 on the modern Richter scale shook the heavily populated Japanese cities of Yokohama and Tokyo on the island of Honshū. Often called the great Kanto earthquake because it affected cities on the Kanto Plain, the quake is remembered as among the most costly natural disasters in history. Scientists have estimated that it created a shock wave three hundred times more powerful than that produced by the atomic bomb that devastated Hiroshima in 1945.

The Japanese archipelago is located within the "Pacific Ring of Fire," a narrow zone of tectonic activity and volcanoes surrounding the Pacific Ocean. About 80 percent of the world's earthquakes take place within this area. Japan experiences about three thousand tremors each day and averages one large earthquake every seventy years. Before 1923, the most serious Japanese quakes were the Hizen earthquake on February 10, 1792, which resulted in the deaths of fifteen thousand people, and the Sinano earthquake on May 8, 1844, which killed twelve thousand.

The morning of September 1, 1923, was warm, with wind gusts followed by rain. When the quake struck at 11:58 A.M., many residents of Yokohama and Tokyo were busy preparing their midday meals. The quake's epicenter was located about fifty miles southwest of Tokyo Bay in an area called the Sagami Trough. Within this region, the northeastern edge of the Philippine Sea plate converges with the southeastern edge of the Eurasian plate. The ground shaking associated with the initial shock lasted five minutes. The quake was registered in Hawaii, Washington, D.C., and northern Great Britain.

It has been estimated that more than fifteen thousand people were killed in the first two minutes of the quake, as buildings toppled and loose debris fell. In Yokohama's harbor, the shaking caused liquefaction of soil material, damaging buildings and other structures. Elsewhere, shock waves produced hundreds of landslides and mudflows, especially along the Boso and Miura Peninsulas. One mudflow buried the entire village of Nebukawa. The entire Boso Peninsula was tilted toward the northeast and uplifted, in some places as much as six feet. In addition to collapsing homes and office buildings, the force of the quake displaced roads and railroad tracks. In Kamakura the quake tore the Great Buddha statue from its foundation. In addition to damage caused by shaking, shock waves produced a tsunami wave thirty-nine feet high that struck the north shore of Oshima and was felt as far away as Ecuador in the eastern Pacific Ocean. Hundreds of smaller tremors were felt in the hours after the initial quake.

After the quake, numerous fires, many ignited by overturned cooking ranges, burned uncontrollably in Tokyo and Yokohama. In Yokohama more than eighty separate fires swept through areas with tightly packed wood and paper houses. The wind, which was blowing at speeds up to eighteen miles per hour, became a major obstacle to containing the flames. More than thirty thousand people fleeing the firestorm in Tokyo's Fukagawa and Honjo neighborhoods were forced into open areas that offered little refuge from the flames and heat. Many perished in wind-spawned cyclones. Emergency responders seeking to extinguish fires could do little because the quake had broken water mains. In Yokohama Harbor, leaking oil caught fire the morning after the

1923

quake. Many fires continued to burn until September 3, and afterward it was difficult to distinguish regions devastated by the quake from those destroyed by fire.

Thousands died while trapped inside collapsed structures. More than forty thousand persons who fled to the Military Clothing Depot died when a firestorm devastated the building. Survivors described the flames as sounding like heavy surf with occasional thunderous crashes. The total number of dead has been estimated at more than one hundred thousand, with forty thousand others missing. Even in rural areas, where fewer buildings were destroyed than in the cities, more than twelve thousand people died.

Panic in the aftermath of the quake led to rumors that Koreans living in the region had set fires, poisoned water sources, and looted homes. As a result, civilian militias killed thousands of Koreans. On September 8, Tokyo was placed under martial law and the army was given responsibility for distributing food, seizing property, and taking other actions needed to maintain order. Engineering corps worked night and day to repair roads, bridges, and communications facilities.

Seven prefectures were affected by the quake: Tokyo, Kanagawa, Saitama, Ibaraki, Shizuoka, Chiba, and Yamanashi. Most people in these areas were without information about the magnitude of destruction or the status of friends and relatives. Damaged telephone and telegraph lines isolated survivors from the outside world. The first news reports about the quake were transmitted by radio from ships anchored in Yokohama and Tokyo Bays. In the absence of functioning newspapers, signs were posted to coordinate relief efforts and share information about missing persons.

Nearly seven hundred thousand homes were completely or partially destroyed in the affected areas, leaving almost two million persons homeless. In addition to severe damage to buildings, many other structures—such as tunnels, storage tanks, canals, sewers, and dams—were destroyed or damaged by the quake and subsequent fires. Twisted train tracks and rubble left in the streets made road travel nearly impossible. A few buildings did escape damage, however. The Royal Palace was spared because of its thick walls and water-filled moat. Concrete and steel-reinforced structures, such as the headquarters of the Mitsubishi Corporation and the Nippon Kogyo Building, experienced only minor damage.

In the weeks after the quake, severe damage to businesses—including facilities in Yokohama's port—caused the unemployment rate to soar. Damage to farms and warehouses brought requests for immediate international assistance. Gotō Shimpei, Tokyo's mayor, organized the rebuilding of the city. An emergency requisition ordinance was implemented to allow government officials to obtain any goods needed in the relief effort. The Japanese government set aside ten million yen to assist with the relief effort, and monetary support for rebuilding damaged areas came from countries around the world.

SIGNIFICANCE

The devastation of the Kanto earthquake served as a catalyst for the development of improved engineering to minimize future earthquake-related damage. In 1929, the World Engineering Congress held a conference in Tokyo with earthquake construction as a central topic. Attendees introduced designs for buildings that would be resistant to wind forces but remain flexible during seismic events.

Basic building codes were substantially changed in Japan following the quake. Many one- and two-story buildings made out of wood or brick were replaced with modern five- and six-story structures of concrete and steel. New parks and open areas were planned throughout Tokyo as places where citizens could take refuge in the event of an earthquake.

The process of rebuilding began slowly, but it built momentum significantly after 1926. An underground rail system was introduced in 1927 and a new airport in 1931. By 1932, Yokohama and Tokyo were again bustling urban areas, and by 1935 the population of Tokyo was larger than it had been before the quake. The new emphasis on designing structures to withstand severe earthquakes did not carry over into a concern for preventing fire damage, however, and many of the structures built in Tokyo and Yokohama after the quake were made with flammable materials. As a result, a large number of structures in these areas were burned in Allied bombing raids during World War II.

Although the Kanto earthquake was not the largest ever to strike Japan, its proximity to cities with combined populations of more than two million made it among the most costly natural disasters in history. The earthquake was responsible for one of the two largest peacetime fires in modern history, the other being the fire caused by the 1906 San Francisco earthquake. Few buildings that stood in Yokohama and Tokyo before the 1923 quake remain today. Among its long-term impacts, the earthquake raised awareness throughout Japan and the world about the importance of disaster management. Since 1960,

September 1 has been designated Disaster Prevention Day in Japan, and each year on that date private and public organizations sponsor disaster preparation drills.

—*Thomas A. Wikle*

FURTHER READING

Busch, Noel F. *Two Minutes to Noon*. New York: Simon & Schuster, 1962. Presents a historical account of the 1923 quake based on extensive research conducted in Japan.

Clancey, Gregory. *Earthquake Nation: The Cultural Politics of Japanese Seismicity, 1868-1930*. Berkeley: University of California Press, 2006. Focuses on social issues tied to earthquakes in Japanese life.

Ryang, S. "The Great Kanto Earthquake and the Massacre of Koreans in 1923: Notes on Japan's Modern National Sovereignty." *Anthropological Quarterly* 76, no. 4 (2003): 731-748. Examines issues associated with the deaths of nearly six thousand Koreans as a result of the earthquake, fires, and subsequent killings.

Utsu, T. "Japanese Earthquakes 1885-1925." *Bulletin of the Earthquake Research Institute* 57 (1982): 111-117. A technical look at the large earthquakes that affected Japan in the late nineteenth and early twentieth centuries.

SEE ALSO: 1906-1910: Oldham and Mohorovičić Determine the Earth's Interior Structure; Apr. 18, 1906: San Francisco Earthquake; Dec. 28, 1908: Earthquake and Tsunami Devastate Sicily; Jan., 1935: Richter Develops a Scale for Measuring Earthquake Strength.

October, 1923
TEAPOT DOME SCANDAL

The Teapot Dome scandal resulted in the establishment of the Federal Oil Conservation Board and increased federal regulation of the U.S. petroleum industry.

ALSO KNOWN AS: Oil Reserves scandal; Elk Hills scandal

LOCALE: Washington, D.C.

CATEGORIES: Crime and scandal; trade and commerce; government and politics

KEY FIGURES

Albert B. Fall (1861-1944), U.S. secretary of the interior, 1921-1923

Josephus Daniels (1862-1948), U.S. secretary of the Navy, 1913-1921

Robert M. La Follette (1855-1925), U.S. senator from Wisconsin

Thomas J. Walsh (1859-1933), U.S. senator from Montana

Warren G. Harding (1865-1923), president of the United States, 1921-1923

Calvin Coolidge (1872-1933), president of the United States, 1923-1929

Gifford Pinchot (1865-1946), former chief of the Division of Forestry in the U.S. Department of Agriculture

Harry F. Sinclair (1876-1956), president of the Mammoth Oil Company

Edward L. Doheny (1856-1935), president of the Pan-American Petroleum and Transport Company

SUMMARY OF EVENT

In 1921 and 1922, Secretary of the Interior Albert B. Fall, after transferring U.S. federal lands designated for naval oil reserves from the secretary of the Navy's jurisdiction to his own department, awarded leases on the Teapot Dome area in Wyoming and Elk Hills, California, to the Mammoth Oil Company and the Pan-American Petroleum and Transport Company. Senate investigations of Fall's actions, conducted in October, 1923, revealed that Fall had accepted $400,000 in loans from executives of those companies. The resulting political scandal forced Fall to resign and heightened public concerns over federal regulation of petroleum resources. On December 18, 1924, President Calvin Coolidge, under pressure from the American public, conservationists, and a number of leaders of the petroleum industry, created the Federal Oil Conservation Board (FOCB), which was composed of the secretaries of war, navy, interior, and commerce. The FOCB was to bring greater federal involvement in petroleum conservation regulation, but it also provided a forum for the industry to voice its concerns to the federal government.

The idea of reserving petroleum-bearing lands for exclusive federal use, especially for the military, went back to the early twentieth century. The U.S. Navy had changed its coal-burning engines to petroleum-based internal combustion engines in 1904, and the army would increasingly use trucks and automobiles. Thus the U.S. military was becoming dependent on petroleum prod-

1923

ucts. On September 27, 1909, President William Howard Taft issued an executive order that withdrew from private use 3,041,000 acres of land in California and Wyoming for exclusive federal use. From late 1909 through 1910, the federal government withdrew lands in western states for the maintenance of petroleum reserves.

The issue of federal petroleum reserves came to the forefront during World War I. American oil played a crucial part in the war effort, and thus petroleum was established as a commodity of strategic importance. Secretary of the Navy Josephus Daniels, seeking to ensure that the Navy had an adequate supply of oil during and after the war, in 1917 planned to have lands set aside for exclusive federal petroleum reserves. In 1920, as the Navy faced a shortage of oil and as pressure from private interests to open up federal lands for oil production intensified, Daniels drafted an amendment to the general Mineral Leasing Act of 1920 allowing the secretary of the interior to grant leases to private companies to produce crude oil on federal lands, thus making petroleum supplies available to the Navy.

High production levels during the war, fed by rising prices and endless federal demand, heightened concerns over waste, exhaustion of oil reserves, price, and industrial stability. Production across the nation rose from 265 million barrels of oil in 1914 to 355 million in 1918. Oil production continued to increase, at an even greater rate, after the war, rising from 472 million barrels in 1921 to 732 million in 1923. Oil prices fell from $3.08 per barrel in 1920 to $1.78 in 1921, then to $1.34 in 1923. The price remained around $1.30 for the rest of the decade before declining precipitously with the economic depression of the 1930's. Leaders of the oil industry feared an immediate and severe price deflation and consequent economic collapse in the industry. In addition, with production levels reaching new highs each year, conservationists, government officials, and a number of oil executives began to fear exhaustion of domestic petroleum reserves in the near future. During the early 1920's, fears of an oil shortage were overshadowed by concerns of oversupply, price deflation, and economic chaos for the petroleum industry. Conservation of petroleum increasingly came to be seen as an answer to each of these problems. It was in this context that pressure from the Teapot Dome scandal led to creation of the FOCB.

When Albert B. Fall became secretary of the interior under President Warren G. Harding, he faced immediate suspicion from conservationists. Fall, a former U.S. senator from New Mexico, represented southwestern interests that advocated unrestrained development of natural resources by the private sector. In May, 1921, using the amendment that Daniels wrote to the Mineral Leasing Act of 1920, Fall had authority over federal reserves transferred from the secretary of the Navy to the Department of the Interior. In July, 1921, Fall leased federal lands in Elk Hills, California, to Edward L. Doheny of the Pan-American Petroleum and Transport Company. In April, 1922, Fall leased the Teapot Dome tract in Wyoming to Harry F. Sinclair, president of the Mammoth Oil Company.

The transfer of naval reserves to private interests not only further enraged Fall's critics but also gave them something to focus on. Fall already had been branded as anticonservationist by critics such as Senator Robert M. La Follette (a Republican from Wisconsin) and Gifford Pinchot, former chief forester under Theodore Roosevelt. Daniels, who had drafted the amendment allowing the secretary of the interior to oversee the naval supply, distrusted Fall's intentions. With Daniels's support, in 1923 Pinchot and La Follette investigated Fall's actions. Ultimately, La Follette persuaded Senator Thomas J. Walsh, a Democrat from Montana and a member of the Senate Public Lands Committee, to open Senate hearings on the matter.

A rising tide of protest against Fall forced him to resign even before the hearings began in October, 1923. The Senate investigation revealed that Fall had accepted $400,000 in loans from Sinclair and Doheny in return for the public land leases. Historians have noted that had Fall truly desired to profit by exploiting his office, he could have obtained much larger loans from oil interests. Both Doheny and Sinclair were acquitted of bribery, but Sinclair spent several months in jail in 1929 for contempt of the Senate and of court. Fall was later found guilty of accepting a bribe while secretary of the interior and was sentenced to a year in jail.

The Teapot Dome scandal, coming to attention during the presidential election campaign of 1924, occurred in the context of a public arena of heightened political rhetoric. The scandal resulted in much more focus being placed on federal regulation of the petroleum industry. Calvin Coolidge, who became president after Harding's death in 1923, created a Naval Petroleum Reserve office in the Department of the Navy in March, 1924. He attempted to shift federal policy from private exploitation back to federal conservation. Coolidge also came under pressure from public opinion, conservationists, and a number of leaders from the petroleum industry to increase federal regulation of the oil industry.

On December 18, 1924, Coolidge created the Federal

Key figures in the Teapot Dome and Elk Hills oil scandals stand outside a Washington, D.C., courthouse in 1929 (from left): Albert B. Fall and Edward L. Doheny, and defense lawyers Frank J. Hogan and Mark Thompson. (Hulton Archive/Getty Images)

Oil Conservation Board (FOCB). The purpose of the FOCB was to study the government's responsibilities, with cooperation from representatives of the oil industry. The FOCB was to focus on the three main industry concerns: the size of crude oil reserves, the technical conditions of production, and the economic disruption caused by overproduction. Coolidge commented on the direct relationship between oil conservation and economic stability, stating that overproduction encourages low prices, which in turn led to wastefulness. The FOCB would also advise the president on the best policy to ensure the future supply of fuel oil for the U.S. Navy and to safeguard national security through conservation of oil. From its inception the FOCB was cooperative with and even deferential to the petroleum industry, especially to the American Petroleum Institute (API), the major trade association for the industry.

SIGNIFICANCE

In 1926, the FOCB held hearings and attempted to build consensus among the representatives of various concerns within the petroleum industry on the conservation issue. The FOCB encountered an industry divided on the issue of production controls but united against federal intervention. Larger integrated companies traditionally supported production controls, and smaller companies opposed restrictions. Representatives from the API stated to the FOCB during these hearings that there was no danger of exhausting petroleum reserves, that waste was negligible, and that the government should let the oil industry determine its own prices.

The hearings and subsequent actions of the FOCB focused on technical problems of petroleum production. The API's assertions of the industry's ability to regulate itself were undermined by continued heavy production in the mid-1920's. Nevertheless, there were no significant federal production controls imposed in the 1920's.

As production levels increased across the nation in the 1920's, oil prices continued to fluctuate but primarily fell. The industry and the API abandoned the policy of relying solely on the market to determine prices, realizing that more stringent cooperative private efforts at production control were needed. In early January, 1929, the API announced a policy of voluntary production controls to limit production for the next three or four years, based on 1928 levels. The FOCB approved a version of this code on May 28, 1930. In December, 1928, industry leaders and members of the API set out to institute an industrywide code of ethics designed to eliminate price and nonprice competition in an attempt to bring stability. In July, 1929, the Federal Trade Commission approved this code, with deletions of restrictions on price cutting and extension of credit. The FOCB still refused to implement federal production controls, stating that voluntary efforts would have to be the largest part of any production control program. In March, 1930, the FOCB initiated a program of demand forecasts to help the petroleum industry project market need and produce accordingly. In 1932, the FOCB worked out a system of voluntary informal restrictions with the leading oil importers in the United States. In all these actions, the FOCB helped the petroleum industry to regulate itself.

These efforts at industrial self-regulation and production control were swamped by new and even more productive fields in Oklahoma City in late 1929 and East Texas in late 1930. President Herbert Hoover, formerly a member of the FOCB as secretary of commerce under Coolidge, took an even stronger laissez-faire approach, stating that the FOCB had no legal power to control production. Hoover believed that responsibility for such actions lay with the Congress, not the executive branch. The FOCB ultimately urged various forms of self-regulation and left the industry to solve its own problems. The problem of oil conservation regulation was left to the industry itself and to state governments until Franklin D. Roosevelt assumed the presidency in 1933. The Teapot Dome scandal returned federal policy on naval reserves back toward conservation and preservation. Ironically, despite the political scandal Fall created, his policy may have been the more correct one. Within a decade after the scandal, planners for the Navy realized that some of their reserves had been depleted as a result of drainage. This occurred when production crews drilled on private property adjacent to the federal lands and drained the neighboring petroleum reservoirs.

With the New Deal programs of President Franklin D. Roosevelt, the federal government generally increased its regulatory role. The Petroleum Administration Board (PAB) continued in the manner that the FOCB had established. The PAB replaced the FOCB, assuming its duties and taking over its files. The PAB came to an end in May, 1935, when the Supreme Court ruled the National Industrial Recovery Act unconstitutional. The PAB had been created under that act. The Bureau of Mines then began forecasting demand for the oil industry. In response to continuing problems of overproduction, Congress passed the "Hot" Oil Act of 1935, restricting interstate shipment of oil. It also set up, under the Department of the Interior, the Federal Petroleum Board (FPB), which enforced the prohibition against "hot" oil. This federal regulatory agency, like the ones before it, worked closely with the industry and with the state regulatory commissions.

The concept of maintaining strategic petroleum reserves was renewed during World War II and the Korean War, when concerns again arose over exhaustion. President Roosevelt created the Petroleum Reserves Corporation (PRC), a government corporation that would exploit Saudi Arabian oil reserves, to conserve petroleum in the United States and counteract British influence in that region. The PRC was short-lived, however, because of opposition from U.S. oil companies, which did not want federal interference in their private efforts to produce oil in the Middle East. During the Korean War, Congress passed the Defense Production Act of 1950, which enabled President Harry Truman to establish the Petroleum Administration for Defense (PAD), which, like the FOCB, made demand forecasts for the industry. The PAD facilitated collective voluntary efforts from nineteen of the largest oil companies to coordinate petroleum supplies. The PAD was dissolved after the war, but in 1954 President Dwight D. Eisenhower began to implement a policy of maintaining reserves equal to 20 percent of domestic annual production. Also in 1954, Eisenhower created the Committee on Energy Supplies. Composed of the secretaries of state, treasury, interior, and commerce, this committee studied the extent of available domestic petroleum resources as well as the growing problem of U.S. dependence on oil imports from the Middle East.

As the United States grew increasingly dependent on oil imports from the Middle East in the 1960's and 1970's, the idea of national strategic petroleum reserves was again revived. The Strategic Petroleum Reserve was begun in 1973; as of 2005, it continued to operate, with a capacity of 727 million barrels and an actual inventory of about 700 million barrels.

—*Bruce Andre Beaubouef*

FURTHER READING

Bates, J. Leonard. *The Origins of Teapot Dome: Progressives, Parties, and Petroleum, 1909-1921.* Urbana: University of Illinois Press, 1963. Focuses primarily on the political events that led up to the Teapot Dome scandal rather than on the actions and policies of the Federal Oil Conservation Board. Useful for its thorough account of the development of the Mineral Leasing Act of 1920, the political debates over federal lands policy, the naval reserves issue, and pressures for legislation during this period.

Davis, Margaret Leslie. *Dark Side of Fortune: Triumph and Scandal in the Life of Oil Tycoon Edward L. Doheny.* Berkeley: University of California Press, 1998. Biography of one of the leading figures in the Teapot Dome scandal. Includes photographs, bibliography, and index.

Melosi, Martin V. *Coping with Abundance: Energy and Environment in Industrial America.* New York: Alfred A. Knopf, 1985. Excellent overview of the growth of the major energy industries in the United States includes a concise yet detailed account of the Teapot Dome scandal and the formation and actions of the Federal Oil Conservation Board.

Nash, Gerald D. "After Teapot Dome: Calvin Coolidge and the Management of Petroleum Resources, 1924-1929." In *United States Oil Policy, 1890-1964.* Pittsburgh: University of Pittsburgh Press, 1968. Excellent source for an introduction to the development of the U.S. petroleum industry and the growth of federal and state regulations. Deals especially well with the relationship between the industry and the federal government. Includes thorough discussion of the Teapot Dome scandal and the Federal Oil Conservation Board.

Noggle, Burl. *Teapot Dome: Oil and Politics in the 1920's.* 1965. Reprint. Westport, Conn.: Greenwood Press, 1980. Deals with the politics of petroleum and the U.S. government. Focuses mostly on the Teapot Dome scandal, but includes brief discussion of the Federal Oil Conservation Board and the concerns of the petroleum industry in oil conservation regulation.

Stratton, David H. *Tempest over Teapot Dome: The Story of Albert B. Fall.* Norman: University of Oklahoma Press, 1998. Biography places the Teapot Dome scandal within the context of Fall's life and times. Includes illustrations and index.

Yergin, Daniel. *The Prize: The Epic Quest for Oil, Money, and Power.* New York: Simon & Schuster, 1991. Deals only briefly with Teapot Dome and the Federal Oil Conservation Board but provides a useful, informative, and readable account of the growth of the oil industry in the United States and in the international arena.

Zimmerman, Erich W. *Conservation in the Production of Petroleum.* New Haven, Conn.: Yale University Press, 1957. Excellent monograph on the development of petroleum conservation policies in the United States. Deals at some length with the Federal Oil Conservation Board. Intended for readers who have some familiarity with conservation issues.

SEE ALSO: June, 1917: First Pulitzer Prizes Are Awarded; Nov. 5, 1918-Nov. 2, 1920: Republican Resurgence Ends America's Progressive Era; 1921-1923: Scandals of the Harding Administration; Nov. 4, 1924: Coolidge Is Elected U.S. President; Dec. 10, 1924: Hoover Becomes the Director of the U.S. Bureau of Investigation.

1923

October 1, 1923
GREAT BRITAIN GRANTS SELF-GOVERNMENT TO SOUTHERN RHODESIA

Southern Rhodesia had been administered by the British South Africa Company, founded by Cecil Rhodes, but by the early 1920's this arrangement was no longer satisfactory to the company or the white settlers. An elected assembly chose internal self-government as the way forward, and the British parliament accepted this decision.

LOCALE: Southern Rhodesia (now Zimbabwe), Africa
CATEGORIES: Colonialism and occupation; government and politics; indigenous peoples' rights

KEY FIGURES

Sir Charles Patrick John Coghlan (1863-1927), first premier of Southern Rhodesia, 1923-1927, and cofounder of the Responsible Government Association

Ethel Tawse Jollie (1876-1950), cofounder of the Responsible Government Association and the first woman parliamentarian in the British Empire

Jan Christian Smuts (1870-1950), prime minister of South Africa, 1919-1924, who drafted the South African constitution to allow Southern Rhodesia to enter as a fifth province

Alfred Milner (Viscount Milner; 1854-1925), high commissioner of South Africa, 1897-1901, and colonial secretary, 1919-1921, the British minister who agreed to self-government for Southern Rhodesia

Winston Churchill (1874-1965), colonial secretary, 1921-1922, the British minister who oversaw the latter stages the implementation of self-government in Southern Rhodesia

First Earl Buxton (Sydney Charles Buxton; 1853-1934), colonial undersecretary, 1892-1895, and later governor-general of South Africa

Cecil Rhodes (1853-1902), diamond magnate and prime minister of the Cape Colony, 1890-1896

SUMMARY OF EVENT

The interior of southern Africa was not settled or developed until the late nineteenth century, when Cecil Rhodes pioneered the exploitation of the area's resources by setting up the British South Africa Company. In 1889 the company received a charter that enabled it to administer large areas of land north of the Transvaal on behalf of the British crown and gave it rights over the use of land and exploitation of minerals. The company built railways and settled towns. Particularly notable were Bulawayo, the commercial center, and Salisbury, which later became the territory's capital. In this process, however, the British expropriated large areas of land and significant numbers of cattle belonging the indigenous African population. Not surprisingly, this led to revolts, especially by the Ndebele (1896) and Shona (1897). In response to these insurrections and other factors, the British government established a direct presence in the area in the form of a resident commissioner who reported to the high commissioner in South Africa.

The British-controlled area was at first called Rhodesia, but in 1898 a government order-in-council divided it into three sections: Southern Rhodesia, Northern Rhodesia, and Nyasaland. Today these regions are independent states: Zimbabwe, Zambia, and Malawi. At the time the order was issued, however, the Boer War (1899-1902) was beginning in South Africa. When the war ended, South Africa was unified under British rule, and the independent Boer (Dutch settler) states were made provinces under the South Africa Act (1909).

The company encouraged colonization by white farmers and miners. The climate in the highlands was pleasant, and some of the land could sustain cattle, tobacco, and corn. By 1901, the white population had reached approximately eleven thousand. In contrast, the indigenous African population numbered approximately eight hundred thousand. Local government established a ten-member legislative council, and though the majority of this group's seats were initially appointed by the British South Africa Company, the addition of seats gave the elected members a small majority by 1907. The electoral role was officially color-blind, but so few Africans met the requirements for registration that it was effectively a white electorate. A separate Department of Native Affairs was set up to look after the tribal reserves and other native matters, but this department was always mindful of the British South Africa Company's need for a steady source of African labor in its mines, which were primarily devoted to gold extraction.

Although both the gold and tobacco markets were unpredictable, the two sectors generally brought prosperity to the province. By 1899, 15.8 million acres of land were controlled by whites, although much of it was still unused. White farmers began to move north from South Africa, and by 1904 there were some 545 farmers. Seven years later, this number had increased to 1,324. In that year, 1911, these farmers began to exercise their political influence by refusing to pay a labor tax imposed by the company. In 1908, Charles Patrick John Coghlan, a Bulawayo lawyer of Irish extraction, was elected to the legislative council. His political and rhetorical skills soon made him a leader in the growing movement concerned with maintaining white settler privileges and opposed to the British South Africa Company's hold on power.

In 1908 and 1909, Southern Rhodesia sent delegates to a national convention was held in South Africa. At the convention, part of the discussion concerned the future of the province, since the leaders of the British South Africa Company had realized that serving as the area's administrator was beyond both their ability and their desire. Several possibilities were considered: Southern Rhodesia could become South Africa's fifth province some time after 1910, it could become a Crown Colony and be administered from London, it could remain part of the company under a modified charter, or it could become its own self-governing area. The option of becoming a

Crown Colony was sometimes tied in with the concept of a Central African Federation, which would reunite the three provinces.

In 1917, a new political party, the Responsible Government Association (RGA), was formed out of the Rhodesia Agricultural Union. Its cofounder was Ethel Tawse Jollie, the wife of a white farmer, and its first president was John McChlery. In 1919, Coghlan joined the party, which wanted Southern Rhodesia to retain its connection to Great Britain and opposed both the Afrikaaners (as the Dutch-speaking South Africans were called) and the British South Africa Company.

In the meantime, the company had lost a significant legal battle in the British Privy Council, the highest court in the British Empire. The court ruled that the company did not have rights to any "unalienated" land—land not already assigned to blacks or whites—and that all such land belonged to the British crown. The company's possession of the area's railways and mines was affirmed, however. After the Privy Council's decision, the British government established a commission to look into the cost of purchasing the company's administrative role in Southern Rhodesia, but the commission's report was not released until February of 1921, after elections in Southern Rhodesia had already taken place.

The 1920 election in Southern Rhodesia proved crucial. Coghlan led the RGA's efforts, and the party won a resounding majority over the Rhodesia Unionist Association, which had just been founded on a platform promoting unity with South Africa. The unionists were supported by many businesses, while the RGA was primarily supported by the farmers and clerks. By this time, the white population had grown to 33,000, approximately 20 percent of whom were ethnic Afrikaners (South Africans of European, usually Dutch, descent). In the 1920 election, there were 11,000 electors, 6,765 of whom actually voted. The legislative council felt it had a mandate to request of Alfred Milner, head of the Colonial Office in London and a former high commissioner to South Africa, that the country become self-governing. Milner agreed to follow the British

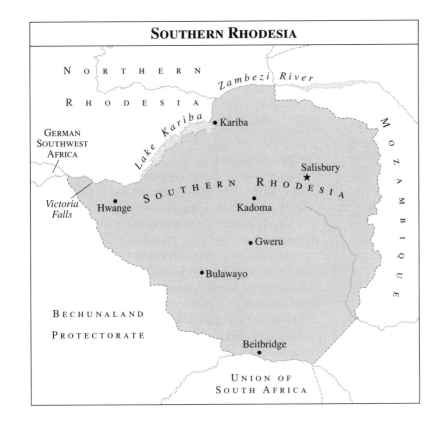

SOUTHERN RHODESIA

NORTHERN RHODESIA

Zambezi River

GERMAN SOUTHWEST AFRICA

Lake Kariba

Kariba

SOUTHERN RHODESIA

MOZAMBIQUE

Salisbury

Victoria Falls

Hwange

Kadoma

Gweru

Bulawayo

BECHUNALAND PROTECTORATE

Beitbridge

UNION OF SOUTH AFRICA

1923

practice of allowing self-government in parts of southern Africa in which whites were capable of defending themselves, and he promised self-government by October, 1924.

Although Milner resigned in February of 1921, his successor, Winston Churchill, felt obliged to continue the process. He appointed a committee to advise him on the establishment of self-government in Northern Rhodesia and Southern Rhodesia, although the committee was not given the option of unifying the two areas. The First Earl Buxton, another former high commissioner of South Africa (1916-1920), was appointed its chairman. The Buxton Committee, set up March 7, 1922, had reported on Southern Rhodesia by April 12, and on Northern Rhodesia by April 29. It advised that a referendum be held on a constitution, which would be drafted by the Colonial Office on the model created by the constitution of South Africa. This constitution, the committee said, should be shown first to the Southern Rhodesian delegates in London.

However, Jan Christian Smuts, prime minister of South Africa, and the British South Africa Company both wanted Rhodesia to be unified with South Africa. Smuts and the company pressured the British government to include this option in the referendum, which the British refused to hold until Smuts issued his terms for joining the regions. A petition signed by more than eight thousand Rhodesian voters who supported the union helped promote Smuts's goal, and his terms, issued on July 30, 1922, were generous to both the Rhodesians and the company. Among other rules, Smuts required that the South African policy of bilingualism be imposed and that white labor have freedom of movement.

Coghlan campaigned against Smuts and his supporters under the slogan "Rhodesia for the Rhodesians, Rhodesia for the Empire." Although the region's most powerful groups were against the RGA, the party was still able to secure a majority. The white population had increased slightly, to 35,000, some 20,000 of whom were entitled to vote. By contrast, the native African population now numbered near 900,000, but only 60 were entitled to vote.

The election's results were announced November 6, 1922, at the Bulawayo courthouse: The RGA received 8,774 votes, while the unionists received 5,989. The union vote was higher than might have been expected, especially in the light of political upheavals caused by the trades unions in South Africa. The British South Africa Company accepted the terms offered by the Colonial Office, and they ceased rule on October 1, 1923. In the 1923 elections, the RGA, which had since been renamed the Rhodesia Party, was opposed by only four independent candidates in a thirty-seat legislature. The party's new hold on power made Coghlan the first premier of Southern Rhodesia, and he held this post (with the help of five cabinet ministers) until his death in 1927.

SIGNIFICANCE

Southern Rhodesia's successful bid for self-government brought Cecil Rhodes's and Jan Smuts's dream for a greater South Africa to an end. Although the new legislature in Southern Rhodesia could only legislate for white affairs and the British government was allowed a veto over many areas, in practice the new council, its cabinet, and the new governor were allowed as much independence as any of the dominions. The adoption of self-government entrenched white minority rule in the country and kept both land and capital firmly in white hands. The British South Africa Company continued to operate, although it gradually sold its railways and mineral rights.

For nearly a half century, self-government appeared to have been a successful solution. The country's tobacco, cattle, and corn industries prospered, white settlers continued to emigrate to Southern Rhodesia, and the region was able to avoid the harsh apartheid system that was to disfigure South African politics. The desire for white supremacy, however, pushed politicians toward total independence from Britain, and then the weight of the inequality between the races led to a bitter civil war and a shaky transition to power by a black-led government unused to democracy. Later, an insatiable desire for the reapportionment of land from the white farmers led to economic collapse.

—*David Barratt*

FURTHER READING

Banana, Canaan S., ed. *Turmoil and Tenacity: Zimbabwe, 1890-1990*. Harare, Zimbabwe: College Press, 1989. A collection of essays by modern African scholars, edited by a noted academic.

Birmingham, D., and P. M. Martin, eds. *History of Central Africa*. 1983. Rev. ed. 2 vols. London: Longman, 1998. One of the most recent British contributions to Rhodesian history. A series of separate essays.

Blake, Robert. *A History of Rhodesia*. London: Eyre Methuen, 1977. Part 2 deals with Rhodesia as a self-governing colony. A sound if somewhat dated history.

Kennedy, Dane. *Islands of White: Settler Society and Culture in Kenya and Southern Rhodesia*. Durham, N.C.: Duke University Press, 1987. A detailed study from the Duke University Center for International

Studies. Compares two white minority cultures and governments in Africa.

Mazrui, Ali, ed. *Africa Since 1935.* Vol. 8 in *The UNESCO General History of Africa.* Berkeley: University of California Press, 1993. This volume deals with the 1920's and sets the Rhodesian question in a wider context.

Mutambirwa, James A. Chamunorwa. *The Rise of Settler Power in Southern Rhodesia, 1898-1923.* Madison, N.J.: Fairleigh Dickinson University Press, 1981. An account from the perspective of an African historian.

Summers, Carol. *From Civilisation to Segregation and Social Control in Southern Rhodesia, 1890-1934.* Athens: Ohio University Press, 1994. A critical study of the growth of white minority rule, focusing on the interaction of the settlers, company officials, missionaries, societies in the United Kingdom, and the most vocal of the African groups.

Wallis, J. P. R. *One Man's Hand: The Story of Sir Charles Coghlan and the Liberation of Southern Rho-desia.* New York: Longmans, Green, 1950. The only biography of the main figure in the self-government of the country.

Willis, A. J. *An Introduction to the History of Central Africa: Zambia, Malawi, and Zimbabwe.* 4th ed. Oxford, England: Oxford University Press, 1985. Sets the history of Southern Rhodesia in the context of British Central Africa and the British South Africa Company.

SEE ALSO: Dec. 19, 1901: Completion of the Mombasa-Lake Victoria Railway; Jan., 1904-1905: Herero and Nama Revolts; Nov. 1, 1908: Belgium Annexes the Congo; May 31, 1910: Formation of the Union of South Africa; Mar. 28, 1911: Baro-Kano Railroad Begins Operation in Nigeria; Apr. 14, 1911: Lever Acquires Land Concession in the Belgian Congo; Jan. 8, 1912: South African Native National Congress Meets; Early 1920: Britain Represses Somali Rebellion.

October 18, 1923
STRAVINSKY COMPLETES HIS WIND OCTET

Igor Stravinsky's Octet was one of the most critical compositions that defined a post-World War I musical aesthetic based on objective rather than emotive elements. It exemplified not only Stravinsky's personal neoclassical period but also the neoclassical movement in music generally.

ALSO KNOWN AS: Octet for Wind Instruments
LOCALE: Paris, France
CATEGORY: Music

KEY FIGURES
Igor Stravinsky (1882-1971), Russian-born composer
Sergei Diaghilev (1872-1929), Russian impresario
Serge Koussevitzky (1874-1951), Russian-born conductor
Nadia Boulanger (1887-1979), French music instructor
Vera de Bosset (1888-1982), private dedicatee of the Octet and later Stravinsky's second wife
Jean Cocteau (1889-1963), French poet, dramatist, and filmmaker

SUMMARY OF EVENT

Following the success of his score for the 1910 ballet *L'Oiseau de feu* (*The Firebird*), Igor Stravinsky lived in Paris for several years. The outbreak of World War I in 1914 cut him off from his native Russia, and he took refuge in Switzerland. Compelled to write for reduced instrumental resources rather than the large orchestras he had used for the ballet *Le Sacre du printemps* (1913; *The Rite of Spring*) and the opera *Le Rossignol* (1914; *The Nightingale*), he experimented with limited scorings, often for unusual instrumental combinations: *L'Histoire du soldat* (1918; *The Soldier's Tale*) was scored for violin, string bass, clarinet, bassoon, cornet, trombone, and percussion, and the final scoring for *Les Noces* (1923; *The Wedding*) called for four pianos and six percussion players to accompany the vocal soloists and chorus.

The Russian Revolution of October, 1917, further cut Stravinsky off from his native land, to which he would not return until 1962. His Russian works composed in Switzerland, such as the burlesque *Renard* (1916), featured limited orchestration and use of Russian folktales. Other popular materials in Stravinsky's works of this period include the Spanish *paso doble* (a souvenir of a visit to Spain with Sergei Diaghilev) and American ragtime; both appear in *The Soldier's Tale*.

Stravinsky's aesthetic began to evolve from an expressive to an objective and austere one. Denied the ex-

1923

pressive resources of the large orchestra for economic reasons, he came to eschew this sound in his reaction against the overblown sonorities of older composers such as Gustav Mahler in Austria and Aleksandr Scriabin in Russia. Reducing the number of strings, and finally eliminating them altogether, was one way of getting away from the soaring, lush emotionalism that he particularly detested in Scriabin's music; Stravinsky sought to achieve a more objective sound.

The relatively cool and objective strains of the eighteenth century were a final attraction. During World War I, many composers sought an antidote to the heavily Germanic post-Romantic sound, resulting in such works as Maurice Ravel's *Le Tombeau de Couperin* (1919; Couperin's tomb) and Sergei Prokofiev's *Classical Symphony* (1917), works with piquant modern harmonies but classical orchestration, balance, and restraint. After the war, Diaghilev reorganized his Ballets Russes and commissioned Stravinsky to write a ballet using music purporting to be by the eighteenth century Italian composer Giovanni Battista Pergolesi; Stravinsky did not change the melodies or basses but made subtle modifications to the harmony and scored *Pulcinella* (1920) for classical orchestra.

The strands of Stravinsky's new developments came together for the first time in the *Symphonies of Wind Instruments* (1920), written as a memorial to Claude Debussy, who had died in 1918. The musical materials were Russian, and the harmonies and counterpoint were reminiscent of *The Rite of Spring*, but the form was very advanced (the German composer Karlheinz Stockhausen took it as a model for his works), and the sonorities, written for the wind section of a large symphony orchestra but without the strings or percussion, are astringent and biting.

With the Octet of 1923, Stravinsky abandoned Russian musical materials, and the classical ethos of balance and restraint became paramount. The scoring is for flute, clarinet, two bassoons, two trumpets, and two trombones, and each instrument is directed to play solo. This scoring differs from the standard wind octet of the classical period, which consisted of two each of oboes, clarinets, bassoons, and horns.

The work is in three movements. The first movement, "Sinfonia," consists of a slow introduction followed by a fast movement in a modified sonata form; the key center of E-flat major is clearly recognizable. A theme and variations form the second movement; the theme undergoes various transformations, first in a recurring trombone-centered variation, then as a march. After the trombone

variation comes a waltz in which the theme is embedded, then a gallop (the music used for bareback riders in the circus) as a counterpoint to the theme. The trombone variation returns, followed by a fugato wherein the counterpoint grows increasingly denser and more dissonant; after it thins out, the solo flute plays material similar to that which linked the slow introduction to the allegro moderato of the first movement. This linkage, however, is to a finale that pays homage to Johann Sebastian Bach, in the manner of one of Bach's two-part inventions. This movement is in sonata form, with a very free reprise and a coda that incorporates ragtime elements.

At the work's first performance at the Paris Opera on October 18, 1923, Stravinsky made his debut as a conductor in the place of Serge Koussevitzky, who had commissioned the work for one of his concerts. Koussevitzky conducted the other two works on the program. Although the published score of the Octet bears no dedication, Stravinsky privately dedicated it to Vera de Bosset, who became his wife seventeen years later.

In an article written the following year for *The Arts* (January, 1924), Stravinsky stated that his Octet was "a

Igor Stravinsky. (Library of Congress)

musical object" with a form "influenced by the musical matter with which it is composed." He added that the work was "not an 'emotive' work but a musical composition based on objective elements which are sufficient in themselves." The form of his music, he maintained, was derived from counterpoint, and he remarked that his music "has no other aim than to be sufficient in itself . . . the play of the musical elements is the thing." The Octet sums up the contrapuntal devices of Bach, the structural ideas of Wolfgang Amadeus Mozart, and elements of musical culture associated with popular entertainments such as the circus.

SIGNIFICANCE

The Octet determined the future shape of musical neoclassicism. Its atmosphere was one of musical detachment rather than of the intense involvement of such expressionists as Arnold Schoenberg and his pupils. Although the name of the movement suggests an imitation of the works of Mozart, in reality neoclassicism embraced nearly all the musically remembered past, principally the works of the composers of the eighteenth century and some early Romantics. Elements from popular musical cultures were employed in neoclassicism, much as they had been in the eighteenth century. Excluded, however, were the highly emotive musical devices of the late Romantic and post-Romantic composers such as Richard Wagner, Johannes Brahms, Gustav Mahler, and Aleksandr Scriabin. Thus the neoclassicists differed from such composers as Jean Sibelius, Ralph Vaughan Williams, and Carl Nielsen, whose music represented an evolution of the late Romantic musical tradition.

By 1923, Stravinsky had become fully converted to the neoclassical idiom; his last Russian work of the post-war period, the chamber opera *Mavra* (1922), paid homage to Alexander Pushkin, Mikhail Glinka, and Peter Ilich Tchaikovsky rather than to the "uncultured" folk music of *The Wedding*. The internationalism of Stravinsky's neoclassicism is best seen in his largest-scale 1920's work, the 1927 opera-oratorio *Oedipus Rex* for narrator, soloists, male chorus, and large orchestra. The text, based on Sophocles' drama, was written by Jean Cocteau and then (except for the narrator's summaries) translated into Ciceronian Latin to provide an atmosphere of timelessness. The music was in the Anglo-Italian style of George Frideric Handel's oratorios of the early eighteenth century. Despite the detachment of both librettist and composer from the often-violent plot, the work was highly moving.

An equally monumental (but shorter) counterpart was the *Symphony of Psalms* of 1930, commissioned for the fiftieth anniversary of the Boston Symphony Orchestra by Koussevitzky, its new conductor. The work's texts were portions of psalms from the Latin (Vulgate) Bible. Its form was not that of the conventional symphony, and some of its techniques had been used in Bach's church cantatas. The scoring was for mixed chorus and large orchestra, without violins or violas. Stravinsky had returned to the Orthodox Church in 1926, and the work reflected better than any his newly restored faith.

After the Octet, Stravinsky decided to become more active as a conductor and pianist, allowing him less time for composition but facilitating the more frequent performance and wider dissemination of his music. For this purpose, he wrote the spiky Concerto for Piano and Wind Instruments (1924), the Serenade in A Major (1925), a 1924 sonata for solo piano, and *Capriccio* (1929), a three-movement piano concerto in all but name, one of his most popular works of the period. Stravinsky did not have any pupils, but he found the French music pedagogue Nadia Boulanger a person who communicated his ideas on music effectively. Boulanger's advocacy in addition to Stravinsky's own performances helped to spread the composer's influence. Boulanger's pupils included Aaron Copland, Walter Piston, Virgil Thomson, Sir Lennox Berkeley, Elliott Carter, and Karel Husa.

Although Stravinsky became a French citizen in 1934, thus protecting some of his copyrights, he was not thoroughly accepted as a French composer (he was denied election to the French Academy to succeed Paul Dukas), and he felt the pressure of events leading to World War II. He did not tour foreign countries as frequently, his music was condemned in the Soviet Union as bourgeois formalism and in Nazi Germany as degenerate, and his oldest daughter, mother, and wife died in the late 1930's while Stravinsky himself was suffering from tuberculosis. His music at the time became more practical: The Concerto for Two Solo Pianos (1935) was written for him and his son Soulima to play in smaller cities that lacked a professional orchestra, and his 1938 chamber concerto in E-flat known as *Dumbarton Oaks* (from the estate near Washington where Stravinsky's patron commissioned the work) contains very specific markings for the conductor. These two works are among Stravinsky's most accessible neoclassic works, and both show the strong influence of Bach.

Stravinsky began his Symphony in C Major in 1938 as a commission for the fiftieth anniversary of the Chicago Symphony Orchestra. Two movements were written in France but interrupted by the composer's trip to the

United States, where he was to occupy a chair at Harvard University and deliver the lectures later published as *The Poetics of Music in the Form of Six Lessons* (1947). Stravinsky had been very favorably impressed by the vigor of American musical life, and he welcomed the idea of moving to the United States. The third movement was finished in Cambridge, Massachusetts, the city where he married Vera de Bosset (the marriage endured until the composer's death in 1971); the fourth in Beverly Hills, California. He admitted that he had studied symphonies by Franz Joseph Haydn, Beethoven, and even Tchaikovsky as models. The work is in quite standard symphonic form, but with the instruments often treated in concerto fashion. With this work, one of Stravinsky's masterpieces and a capstone of his neoclassic style, his French period concluded and his American period began.

—*R. M. Longyear*

FURTHER READING

Adorno, Theodor W. *Philosophy of New Music*. Translated and edited by Robert Hullot-Kentor. Minneapolis: University of Minnesota Press, 2006. A comparison of Stravinsky and Schoenberg by one of the leaders of the Frankfurt School of social theory and aesthetic philosophy. Bibliographic references and index.

Asafyev, Boris. *A Book About Stravinsky*. Translated by Richard F. French. Ann Arbor: UMI Research Press, 1982. Completed in 1929, Asafyev's volume is the main study by a Soviet-era musicologist. It contains a perceptive analysis of the Octet, but the author deprecates many of Stravinsky's neoclassic works.

Austin, William W. *Music in the Twentieth Century*. New York: W. W. Norton, 1966. A thorough treatment of Stravinsky's neoclassic period within the context of twentieth century music, in a volume that is still the best study of the period.

Dushkin, Samuel. "Working with Stravinsky." In *Igor Stravinsky*, edited by Edwin Corle. Freeport, N.Y.: Books for Libraries Press, 1969. A vivid account of Stravinsky as a musical collaborator. Also contains a firsthand account of Stravinsky's personal and family life during the 1930's.

Lubaroff, Scott. *An Examination of the Neo-classical Wind Works of Igor Stravinsky: The Octet for Winds and Concerto for Piano and Winds*. Lewiston, N.Y.: E. Mellen Press, 2004. Close reading of two of Stravinsky's most important neoclassical pieces. Bibliographic references and index.

Stravinsky, Igor. *Stravinsky: An Autobiography*. New York: W. W. Norton, 1962. Originally published in 1936, this volume contains the composer's firsthand account of his work on the Octet and other neoclassical compositions during his French years. Unfortunately, the translation is poor.

Stravinsky, Igor, and Robert Craft. *Dialogues and a Diary*. London: Faber & Faber, 1968. When Stravinsky was in his eighties, Robert Craft had him reminisce about his early days and give his current opinions about music. This volume covers the Paris years and the genesis of the Octet.

Stravinsky, Vera. *Dearest Bubushkin*. Edited by Robert Craft. New York: Thames and Hudson, 1985. The correspondence of Vera and Igor Stravinsky, with excerpts from Vera's diary from 1922 on. The text is illustrated with numerous photographs.

White, Eric Walter. *Stravinsky: The Composer and His Works*. 2d ed. Berkeley: University of California Press, 1979. The standard English biography of the composer. Includes detailed analyses of his compositions as well as a chronicle of his life.

SEE ALSO: June 25, 1910: *The Firebird* Premieres in Paris; Mar. 15, 1911: Scriabin's *Prometheus* Premieres in Moscow; May 29, 1913: *The Rite of Spring* Stuns Audiences; 1921-1923: Schoenberg Develops His Twelve-Tone System; 1930's: Hindemith Advances Music as a Social Activity.

November 8, 1923
BEER HALL PUTSCH

Adolf Hitler, a disaffected German nationalist and disgruntled ideologue, attempted a local uprising but ended up under arrest. Although his effort to seize power failed and he was convicted of treason, he emerged as a national hero, and the event became a celebrated moment in the history of the Nazi Party.

LOCALE: Munich, Germany
CATEGORIES: Wars, uprisings, and civil unrest; government and politics

KEY FIGURES
Adolf Hitler (1889-1945), leader of the Nazi party and chancellor of Germany, 1933-1945
Rudolf Hess (1894-1987), one of Hitler's earliest followers
Ernst Röhm (1887-1934), leader of Hitler's paramilitary organization, the Sturm Abteilung (SA)
Hermann Göring (1893-1946), famous World War I fighter pilot who took over the leadership of the SA from Ernst Röhm in early 1923
Erich Ludendorff (1865-1937), World War I German general and one of Hitler's earliest supporters
Gustav Ritter von Kahr (1862-1934), prime minister of Bavaria, 1920-1921, Staats Komissav (state commissioner), 1923-1924
Julius Streicher (1885-1946), one of Hitler's chief ideologues who founded the anti-Semitic newspaper *Der Stürmer*

SUMMARY OF EVENT
Inspired by Benito Mussolini's fascist March on Rome of October 28, 1922, which resulted in Mussolini's appointment as Italy's prime minister, Adolf Hitler and his followers believed that they too could stage a putsch (the sudden overthrow of a government) and establish rule by a führer, the German equivalent of *duce*, the Italian term for the leader of the Fascist Party. Mussolini had been able to take charge of Italian cities using paramilitary groups: The threat of force intimidated the Italian king and the country's governing class, which capitulated to the fascists and acceded to Mussolini's assumption of one-man rule. Collaborating with Ernst Röhm, Hitler began organizing a group of approximately eight hundred men. Hitler saw this group as the core of a larger force that would be loyal to him alone and would provide the momentum he needed to overthrow the weakening

Weimar government that had been established in the wake of Germany's defeat in World War I.

Like other right-wing German groups, Hitler's Nazis attacked the Weimar government's inability to deal with the aftermath of World War I, especially with France's demand that Germany pay reparations for the destruction caused by invading German armies. Hitler's speeches denounced the Weimar government's failure to repudiate the very idea of reparations, and like other extremist groups on the left and the right, the Nazis believed that the Weimar government would soon be pushed from power. The only question was who would have the will and the support to engineer a successful putsch.

Röhm, acting independently of Hitler, organized his paramilitary groups in Bavaria in preparation for a sudden seizure of power. Meanwhile, Hermann Göring used discipline to shape the Sturm Abteilung (SA) into a militant cadre. Hitler, suspecting that he would lose control of his own movement if he did not act quickly, set November 9 as the putsch's date; he chose the anniversary of William II's 1918 deposition as the German emperor in the belief that his cohort would rally around the anniversary.

On the evening of November 8, Hitler, escorted by his faithful aide Rudolf Hess and Nazi storm troopers, disrupted a meeting of about three thousand people held by Gustav Ritter von Kahr, head of the Bavarian government. Firing a shot into the ceiling, Hitler took charge of the meeting room, a large beer hall just outside Munich's center. Announcing that his men had surrounded the building, Hitler declared that Kahr's Bavarian government had been deposed.

Leaving Göring in charge of the crowded room, Hitler informed the shaken but recalcitrant Kahr that he was about to march on Berlin and form a new national government. Not until General Erich Ludendorff arrived at his side, however, was Hitler able to force Kahr to announce to the meeting that he recognized the new government. "The national revolution has begun!" Hitler shouted. Ludendorff seconded the claim by calling the putsch a watershed event, and Rudolf Hess took Kahr and his entourage into custody.

At the same time, Röhm captured the German army's headquarters in Munich, and other fascist paramilitaries took over the police headquarters. Nevertheless, Hitler had not secured all elements of the army and police, and he had no plans to extend his power. Julius Streicher

CASUALTIES OF THE BEER HALL PUTSCH

The sixteen Nazi supporters listed below died in the Beer Hall Putsch. Adolf Hitler considered them martyrs and praised them in the foreword to his book Mein Kampf *(1925-1926; English translation, 1939).*

- Felix Alfarth
- Andreas Bauriedl
- Theodor Casella
- William Ehrlich
- Martin Faust
- Anton Hechenberger
- Oskar Körner
- Karl Kuhn
- Karl Laforce
- Kurt Neubauer
- Klaus von Pape
- Theodor von der Pfordten
- Johann Rickmers
- Max Erwin von Scheubner-Richter
- Lorenz Ritter von Stransky
- Wilhelm Wolf

urged Hitler to capitalize on his initiative by organizing a mass rally, but Hitler began to sense that he was not in control of events, and, according to Hitler biographer Joachim C. Fest, the Nazi leader suffered a nervous collapse.

With other reports suggesting that the public favored the putsch, Hitler momentarily revived and began planning several large rallies. He was stymied, however, by the fact that he had prepared for use of force but not for an actual violent revolution. Since his followers had not secured the support of the police and army, Hitler was not in a position to mount an attack against significant resistance. General Ludendorff made matters worse by releasing Kahr from custody, and Kahr and his associates immediately regrouped. By the time Hitler and his cohort marched toward the Ministry of War in Munich, armed police were there to meet them. Shots were fired: Göring was hit in the leg, and Hitler was shoved to the ground and dislocated his shoulder. Ludendorff, Streicher, Hitler, and others were arrested. Göring managed to escape, but the Nazi bid for power had become a debacle.

SIGNIFICANCE

Even though the Beer Hall Putsch was a failure, the event itself made Hitler a national figure. His trial became political theater: Hitler attacked the Weimar government and portrayed himself as a patriot who hoped to revive Germany's spirits and its sense of greatness. His efforts were bolstered by the knowledge that elements of the Bavarian government had colluded with his attempted takeover, and so it would be difficult to treat him harshly. The sentence for treason was life imprisonment, but Hitler received only a five-year prison term in rather comfort-

able surroundings in Landsberg am Lech, an ancient fortress west of Munich, where he served only part of his sentence and began writing *Mein Kampf* (1925-1926; English translation, 1939).

Ultranationalists considered Hitler a hero because he took complete responsibility for the putsch. His self-confidence buoyed his followers, and by shielding figures such as Ludendorff, Hitler actually enhanced his role as the leader of a movement dedicated to Germany's rebirth. Concealing the facts of his own vacillation during the putsch, Hitler played the decisive leader, and he treated his failure to overthrow a despised government as just the first step in his rightful path to power. Although German law dictated that, as an Austrian, Hitler should have been deported, the court ruled that Hitler could serve his sentence in Germany, a decision that delighted the trial's audience.

The failed putsch convinced Hitler that he would have to acquire power by legal means: He needed to use the very institutions of the state to subvert the state. The putsch also became part of Nazi ideology, and it was remembered as the moment in history when Nazis were martyred for a cause (sixteen Nazis were killed in confrontations with the police on November 9). The event was commemorated each year in a celebration that Hitler called the "real birthday" of his party.

—*Carl Rollyson*

FURTHER READING

Burleigh, Michael. *The Third Reich: A New History.* New York: Hill & Wang, 2000. Informative, but not as accessible to the general reader as the other three works cited here. Addresses the Beer Hall Putsch only briefly, but thoroughly examines this event's role in the rise of Nazism.

Evans, Richard J. *The Coming of the Third Reich.* New York: Penguin Books, 2004. A work of impressive and engaging scholarship. Includes a perceptive chapter on the Beer Hall Putsch.

Fest, Joachim C. *Hitler.* New York: Harcourt Brace Jovanovich, 1973. One of the best single-volume biographies of Hitler available. Includes a detailed chapter on the Beer Hall Putsch.

Shirer, William L. *The Rise and Fall of the Third Reich: A History of Nazi Germany.* 30th anniversary ed. New York: Ballantine, 1991. Classic work is still one of the most readable and informative histories of the Third

Reich. Although Shirer's research has been superseded in some respects, this remains one of the best introductions to the Nazi era. Chapter on the Beer Hall Putsch presents lively details that amount to one of the most thorough explanations of the role this event played in Hitler's biography and in the rise of Nazism.

SEE ALSO: July 31, 1919: Weimar Constitution; July 18, 1925-Dec. 11, 1926: *Mein Kampf* Outlines Nazi Thought; Jan. 30, 1933: Hitler Comes to Power in Germany; Feb. 27, 1933: Reichstag Fire; Mar. 23, 1933: Enabling Act of 1933; June 30-July 2, 1934: Great Blood Purge; Nov. 9-10, 1938: Kristallnacht.

December 10, 1923
PROPOSAL OF THE EQUAL RIGHTS AMENDMENT

The Equal Rights Amendment was intended to ensure women's right to equal treatment under the law in the United States. Passage of the amendment succeeded suffrage as a major goal of the American women's movement.

LOCALE: Washington, D.C.
CATEGORIES: Civil rights and liberties; social issues and reform; women's issues

KEY FIGURE
Alice Paul (1885-1977), American social reformer

SUMMARY OF EVENT
After the passage in 1920 of the Nineteenth Amendment to the U.S. Constitution, which gave women the right to vote, many women who had worked for the amendment's ratification disengaged from political activity. However, some realized that although women could vote, they still faced many obstacles to real freedom. Among other things, women did not have the same educational opportunities as men, economic independence, or access to information about family planning.

As people began to address these concerns, issues that had been put aside during the push for suffrage started to come to the surface. Some women, mainly members of the National Woman's Party (NWP), believed in complete equality between women and men; others, primarily those associated with the National American Woman Suffrage Association (NAWSA), believed that there were some areas in which women needed special protective legislation. In the 1908 case of *Muller v. Oregon*, the U.S. Supreme Court had stated:

The two sexes differ in structure of body, in the functions to be performed by each, in the amount of physical strength, in the capacity for long-continued labor, particularly when done standing. . . .

This difference justifies a difference in legislation, and upholds that which is designed to compensate for some of the burdens which rest upon her.

Although this decision protected some women, it proved discriminatory in many cases. Because of the assumption that women were weaker and more vulnerable than men, women were prohibited from practicing certain professions, such as law, even when they were fully qualified to do so. They were forbidden to lift weights, even those no heavier than an eighteen-month-old child. Women were forbidden to serve in bars at night, although they were able to work as cleaners or entertainers at the same hour.

These issues, which had been submerged while the women's movement focused on suffrage, now became increasingly important. The women's movement, which had been so united before 1920, began to show factions among its members, dividing into groups such as pacifists, social feminists, and professional women.

It was into this dilemma that Alice Paul stepped. Born in 1885 of Quaker parents in Moorestown, New Jersey, she had graduated from Swarthmore College in 1905. She went as a student to England, where she had been an active participant in the British woman suffrage movement. A woman of strong will and ambition, Paul

1923

TEXT OF THE EQUAL RIGHTS AMENDMENT

The Equal Rights Amendment as proposed in 1923 and as finally defeated in 1982 was simple, brief, and comprehensive:

SECTION 1. Equality of rights under the law shall not be denied or abridged by the United States or by any state on account of sex.
SECTION 2. The Congress shall have the power to enforce, by appropriate legislation, the provisions of this article.
SECTION 3. This amendment shall take effect two years after the date of ratification.

adopted the militant techniques of the British suffragists. In 1913, she broke with the NAWSA, which had always lobbied state legislatures, and founded the Congressional Union for Woman Suffrage to work with the U.S. Congress in Washington, D.C. This group eventually became known as the National Woman's Party. In 1917, Paul and the NWP organized around-the-clock picketing of the White House, and, as a result, Paul was arrested and jailed. Such actions received international press coverage and were ultimately good for the cause of woman suffrage, but they also left Paul thousands of dollars in debt and without the physical stamina to continue.

However, many women realized that the time was ripe for further action, and they also realized they needed Paul's leadership. A ceremony was planned at the U.S. Capitol Building on February 15, 1921, Susan B. Anthony's birthday, both to celebrate women's right to vote and to launch a campaign for the removal of legal disabilities of women. Representatives of more than one hundred women's organizations attended the ceremony; the only group noticeably absent was the NAWSA, which complained that the NWP was unconcerned about the problems of working women (the NAWSA believed that factory women, for example, still required special legislation). The idea of the Equal Rights Amendment was conceived during this convention.

Paul took a leave of absence from the NWP to earn a law degree. She received an LL.B. from Washington College of Law in 1922, an LL.M. in 1927, and a DC.L. in 1928 from American University in Washington. In 1923, the NWP again held a convention, this time in Seneca Falls, New York, where the first Women's Rights Convention had been held in 1848. In memory of Elizabeth Cady Stanton and Lucretia Mott, Paul presented a proposal, originally called the Lucretia Mott Amendment: "Men and women shall have equal rights throughout the United States and in every place subject to its jurisdiction." The proposal was not unanimously accepted. As before, there was a concern that it would invalidate all protective legislation for women, especially laws regarding labor. Paul, however, believed that most protective legislation only furthered discrimination against women. If the women had been able to compromise on these issues, perhaps they could have strengthened their ranks and consolidated their new power, but such was not to be.

Although the majority of women supported the protectionists, the proposed text of the Equal Rights Amendment (ERA) was introduced in Congress on December 10, 1923. It read simply:

Equality of rights under the law shall not be denied or abridged by the United States or by any state on account of sex.

Paul decided that the next step for the National Woman's Party would be to elicit the support of other women's groups. The NWP conducted studies to determine the legal positions of women in individual states in relation to divorce, marriage, child custody, work, education, family planning, and career opportunities. The party also planned to reveal the fundamental inadequacy of protectionist legislation. The members lobbied to get representation on an investigative panel of the U.S. Department of Labor's Woman's Bureau, which met in January, 1926. However, the gap between the goals of the NWP and the attitudes of the rest of the country widened, and antagonisms prevented any progress. In November, 1928, the Woman's Bureau panel found that legislative protection was good for women.

SIGNIFICANCE

Despite the passage of the Nineteenth Amendment, the decade of the 1920's was in many ways antifeminist. Women were not considered capable of combining marriage and career. Feminists were attacked as unfeminine and asexual. Freudian theories, which saw women as either temptresses or slaves, were popular. Feminism did not appeal to many women of the younger generation, who rebelled against the repressive, Victorian culture identified with the older generation, which had given birth to the ERA. Despite this milieu, in 1928 the National Federation of Business and Professional Women's Clubs expressed its support of the ERA. Gradually, more groups promoted it. The ERA was publicly championed by the Republican Party in 1940, the General Federation of Women's Clubs in 1943, and the Democratic Party in 1944.

Not until 1959, however, did the NAWSA, which by then had become the League of Women Voters, support the amendment. During the 1960's and 1970's, feminist activity was rekindled, and in 1972, the ERA passed the U.S. House of Representatives and the Senate. According to law, it then had seven years to be ratified by three-fourths of the states. In her later years, Alice Paul dedicated all her time to passage of the ERA. She died in 1977, still hoping for its passage. Although Congress extended the deadline to 1982, and many states did ratify the amendment, time ran out, and the ERA did not become law.

—Winifred O. Whelan

FURTHER READING

Baker, Jean H. *Sisters: The Lives of America's Suffragists*. New York: Hill & Wang, 2005. Discusses the lives and work of the five most prominent activists in the U.S. suffrage movement: Lucy Stone, Susan B. Anthony, Elizabeth Cady Stanton, Frances Willard, and Alice Paul. Blends personal information on the subjects with political and historical analysis. Includes index.

Flexner, Eleanor, and Ellen Fitzpatrick. *Century of Struggle: The Woman's Rights Movement in the United States*. Enlarged ed. Cambridge, Mass.: Belknap Press, 1996. Sound standard account of the American women's rights movement. Includes illustrations and index.

Hammer, Roger A. *American Woman: Hidden in History, Forging the Future*. 2d ed. Golden Valley, Minn.: Place in the Woods, 1993. A concise collection of stories about women, both contemporary and historical, including Alice Paul. Illustrations.

Lunardini, Christine A. *From Equal Suffrage to Equal Rights: Alice Paul and the National Woman's Party, 1910-1928*. 1986. Reprint. Lincoln, Nebr.: iUniverse, 2000. Focuses on Paul's role in the suffrage movement and examines the importance of the NWP in continuing the fight for gender equality after American women had won the right to vote.

Pole, J. R. *The Pursuit of Equality in American History*. 2d ed. Berkeley: University of California Press, 1993. Includes discussion of the divisions that arose among American women after the passage of the Nineteenth Amendment in 1920.

Woodward, Carolyn. "The Growth of the Modern Women's Movement." In *Changing Our Power: An Introduction to Women's Studies*, edited by Jo Whitehorse Cochran, Donna Lengston, and Carolyn Woodward. 2d ed. Dubuque, Iowa: Kendall/Hunt, 1991. Describes what happened to the ERA and how it was defeated.

SEE ALSO: Oct. 10, 1903: Pankhursts Found the Women's Social and Political Union; Nov. 7, 1916: First Woman Is Elected to the U.S. Congress; 1917: National Woman's Party Is Founded; Sept. 20, 1917: Canadian Women Gain the Vote; Feb. 6, 1918: British Women Gain the Vote; Feb. 14, 1920: League of Women Voters Is Founded; Aug. 26, 1920: U.S. Women Gain the Right to Vote.

December 29, 1923
ZWORYKIN APPLIES FOR PATENT ON AN EARLY TYPE OF TELEVISION

Zworykin's concept of an all-electronic television receiver foreshadowed the development of modern television systems. His initial prototype was lackluster at best, but his later invention of the kinescope, or picture tube, provided the basis for mass-produced consumer-operated television sets.

LOCALE: Pittsburgh, Pennsylvania
CATEGORIES: Inventions; science and technology; radio and television; communications and media

KEY FIGURES

Vladimir Zworykin (1889-1982), Soviet electronic engineer and director of the medical electronics center of the Rockefeller Institute for Medical Research
Paul Gottlieb Nipkow (1860-1940), German engineer and inventor
Alan A. Campbell Swinton (1863-1930), Scottish engineer
Guglielmo Marconi (1874-1937), Italian physicist and inventor
Charles Francis Jenkins (1867-1934), American physicist, engineer, and inventor
Heinrich Hertz (1857-1894), German physicist

SUMMARY OF EVENT

Although Vladimir Zworykin is popularly known as the father of television, his work in the 1920's actually built on the contributions of numerous scientists and electrical engineers who began theorizing about possible applications of electricity as early as the 1830's. Antecedents of all-electronic television can be found in several different but related areas in electrical engineering. The invention of the telegraph in the 1830's demonstrated the possibility of modulating an electrical current to transmit coded signals; the invention of the telephone in 1876 showed that sound waves could be converted into electrical impulses and back again. Heinrich Hertz's measurements of electromagnetic waves in the late 1880's provided empirical evidence of earlier theoretical speculations about the nature of electricity. According to Orrin E. Dunlap, Jr., Guglielmo Marconi's work with radio was a direct response to Marconi's reading of Hertz's paper. In any event, engineers and scientists who had been working on the electrical transmission of images by wire responded to the challenge of achieving the wireless projection of visual images almost simultaneously with the development of radio.

In 1894, an American inventor, Charles Francis Jenkins, described a scheme for electrically transmitting moving pictures. Jenkins's idea, however, was only one of an already long tradition in electrical engineering of theoretical television systems. Even before invention of the telephone or detection of electromagnetic waves, scientists had begun to consider how images might be transmitted with electricity. American and European scientists began attempting to transmit still images over telegraph wires in the 1840's. In 1842, for example, the English physicist Alexander Bain invented an automatic copying telegraph for sending still pictures. Although Bain's system scanned images line by line, many early attempts assumed the simultaneous transmission of every portion of an image was necessary and so involved multiple wires—that is, a separate electrical current for each point on the image. By the 1870's, wide recognition of persistence of vision—retention of a visual image by the eye for a short period of time after the removal of the stimulus that produced it—led to experiments with systems in which the image to be projected was scanned line by line but required one wire only. Rapid scanning of images became the underlying principle of all television

systems, both electromechanical and all-electronic.

Although almost sixty years were to pass between the emergence of the concept of scanning and the development of working all-electronic systems, electromechanical systems began to appear in the 1880's. In 1884, a German inventor, Paul Gottlieb Nipkow, patented a complete television system that utilized a mechanical sequential scanning system and a photoelectric cell sensitized with selenium for transmission. The selenium photoelectric cell converted the light values of the image being scanned into electrical impulses to be transmitted to a receiver where the process would be reversed: The electrical impulses led to light of varying brightnesses being produced and projected onto a rotating disk that was scanned to reproduce the original image. If the system—that is, the transmitter and the receiver—were in perfect synchronization and if the disk rotated quickly enough, persistence of vision enabled the viewer to see a complete image rather than a series of moving points of light.

As attempts to refine mechanical systems progressed, it became clear that all possessed a major handicap: Because the image to be projected was mechanically scanned, a barrier existed regarding potential improvements in sensitivity. Edward W. Constant II, a historian of technology, has referred to such barriers or perceived theoretical limitations as "presumptive anomalies" that could lead to revolutionary changes within a technology.

For a television image to be projected onto a screen of reasonable size and retain good quality and high resolution, any system employing only thirty to one hundred lines, as early mechanical systems did, would clearly be inadequate. A few systems were developed that utilized two hundred or more lines, but the difficulties these presented made the possibility of an all-electronic system increasingly attractive. These difficulties were not generally recognized until the early 1930's, when television began to move out of the laboratory and into commercial production. John Swift has noted that although inventors such as John Logie Baird in England, who had developed a mechanical system based on the Nipkow principle, and Jenkins in the United States were aware of Zworykin's all-electronic

Schematic of a television picture tube.

work for Westinghouse Electric Corporation and RCA (Radio Corporation of America), they continued to refine mechanical systems until the government intervened.

Many Americans witnessed television for the first time in the form of electromechanical television during the 1930's demonstrations of Jenkins's motor-driven mechanical scanners. The receiver had a large glass bull's-eye-like screen, and Baird's system had been adopted for initial television broadcasts by the British Broadcasting Corporation. It was not until the English government set broadcast standards mandating high-definition television that Baird's development work on those mechanical systems ceased.

Interest in all-electronic television paralleled interest in mechanical systems, but solutions to technical problems proved harder to achieve. In 1908, a Scottish engineer, Alan A. Campbell Swinton, proposed what was essentially an all-electronic television system. Swinton theorized that the use of magnetically deflected cathode-ray tubes for both the transmitter and receiver in a system was possible. In 1911, Swinton formally presented his idea to the Röntgen Society in London, but the technology available did not allow for practical experiments.

On December 29, 1923, Zworykin filed a patent application for the iconoscope, or television transmission tube. His interest in all-electronic television dated back to his days in the Soviet Union as a student of Boris L. Rosing, in prerevolutionary St. Petersburg. Zworykin credited Rosing's work with cathode-ray tubes as a major influence on his own ideas. Zworykin's patent application for a camera tube differed from Swinton's 1911 plan, in that rather than disclosing a mosaic of rubidium cubes, Zworykin disclosed a layer of photoelectric material. On March 17, 1924, Zworykin applied for a patent for a two-way system. The first cathode-ray tube receiver had a cathode, a modulating grid, an anode, and a fluorescent screen. Condenser plates produced electrostatic horizontal deflection, and coils produced magnetic vertical deflection.

According to Albert Abramson, Zworykin later admitted the results were very poor and the system, as shown, was still far removed from a practical television system. Zworykin's employers were so unimpressed that they admonished him to forget television and work on something more useful. Zworykin's interest in television was thereafter confined to his nonworking hours, as he spent the next year working on phonographic sound recording. It was not until the late 1920's that he was able to devote his full attention to television. Ironically, West-

inghouse had by then resumed research in television, but Zworykin was not part of the team. After he returned from a trip to France in 1928, during which he had witnessed an exciting demonstration of an electrostatic tube, Westinghouse indicated it was not interested. This lack of corporate support in Pittsburgh led Zworykin to approach RCA. Zworykin reportedly demonstrated his system to the Institute of Radio Engineers at Rochester, New York, on November 18, 1929, claiming to have developed a working picture tube, a tube that would revolutionize television development; RCA recognized the potential.

Significance

The picture tube, or kinescope, developed by Zworykin changed the history of television. Abramson noted that the kinescope made it possible to have a practical receiver in the home of the viewer, a device that the average person could operate, that required no technical knowledge to use, and that could be viewed under normal lighting conditions. Within a few years, mechanical systems disappeared and television technology began to utilize systems similar to Zworykin's by use of cathode-ray tubes at both ends of the system.

At the transmitter, in Zworykin's system, the image is focused on a mosaic screen composed of light-sensitive cells. A stream of electrons sweeps the image and each cell sends off an electric current impulse as it is hit by the electrons, the light and shade of the focused image regulating the amount of current. This string of electrical impulses, after amplification and modification into ultrahigh-frequency wavelengths, is broadcast by antenna to be picked up by any attuned receiver, where it is retransformed into a moving picture in the cathode-ray tube receiver. The cathode-ray tubes contain no moving parts, as the electron stream is guided entirely by electric attraction. Although both the iconoscope and the kinescope were far from perfect when Zworykin initially demonstrated them, they set the stage for all future television development.

This television development had impacts far beyond mere popular entertainment systems. As influential as television broadcasting may be on everyday lives, cathode-ray tubes also have had many other important applications. Although Zworykin developed the cathode-ray tube to serve as part of a broadcasting system and saw television as analogous to radio, it definitely has not been limited to this one use. Military radar systems, for example, display information on cathode-ray tubes, as do numerous other information display systems. Cathode-ray

1923

tubes have proved to be especially valuable in electronics applications, as the use of computers has become more widespread. Computer terminals were routinely paired with monitors—that is, CRTs or cathode-ray tubes—so that the operators would have immediate access to a visual display for both input and output data. Cathode-ray technology was adapted to produce a whole new range of high-definition television screens, gel screen monitors, flat-screen televisions, and laptop and desktop computer monitors.

Cathode-ray tubes have been used also in experimental communications systems similar to telephones, by including visual images along with sound, and in security systems in a variety of settings. What Zworykin may have envisioned as a simple entertainment device available for home use has spread far beyond its limited, originally intended, application. The cathode-ray tube has uses that range from supermarket cash registers to closed-circuit television security systems to large-screen color television sets, now equipped with the capability of providing sound in stereo. Zworykin's developments served as the beginning of modern television.

—*Nancy Farm Mannikko*

FURTHER READING

Abramson, Albert. *The History of Television, 1880-1941*. Jefferson, N.C.: McFarland, 1987. Comprehensive history of television in the United States, Europe, and the Soviet Union. Includes endnotes, glossary, and bibliography.

_____. *Zworykin: Pioneer of Television*. Urbana: University of Illinois Press, 1995. Detailed biography focusing on Zworykin's work on televisual apparatuses. Bibliographic references and index.

Constant, Edward W., II. *Origins of the Turbojet Revolution*. Baltimore: The Johns Hopkins University Press, 1980. Constant utilizes a case study of the development of the turbojet to speculate about the origins of technological change. Although the work does not deal directly with television, it provides interesting insights into the processes of invention and innovation, which are applicable in any field.

De Forest, Lee. *Television: Today and Tomorrow*. New York: Dial Press, 1942. This book provides a thorough explanation of the technical principles of television. Written for the layperson by an electrical engineer who was responsible for many of the innovations that made television possible.

Dunlap, Orrin E., Jr. *Radio's One Hundred Men of Science*. New York: Harper & Brothers, 1944. This book provides brief biographies of one hundred scientists and engineers associated with the history of electricity, radio, and television, including Luigi Galvani, Oliver Heaviside, Nipkow, Zworykin, and Philo T. Farnsworth. Excellent reference work.

Hubbell, Richard W. *Four Thousand Years of Television: The Story of Seeing at a Distance*. New York: G. P. Putnam's Sons, 1942. Hubbell traces the history of television back to the invention of papyrus paper in ancient Egypt. Provides lucid explanations of the technical aspects of television and its ancestors.

McMahon, Morgan E. *A Flick of the Switch, 1930-1950*. Palos Verdes Peninsula, Calif.: Vintage Radio, 1975. Although this book primarily contains a pictorial history of radio and television, it also provides clear illustrations of the underlying concepts of both electromechanical and all-electronic television systems.

Shiers, George, ed. *Technical Development of Television*. New York: Arno Press, 1977. This book includes both histories of television and reprints of original articles by Zworykin, Jenkins, and others. The evaluations by observers of competing television systems in the 1920's and 1930's are particularly enlightening.

Swift, John. *Adventure in Vision: The First Twenty-five Years of Television*. London: John Lehmann, 1950. Details the history of television in England, the work of John L. Baird, and the demise of low-definition mechanical systems. Lavishly illustrated, with both line drawings and photographs.

Webb, Richard C. *Tele-Visionaries: The People Behind the Invention of Television*. Hoboken, N.J.: John Wiley & Sons, 2005. Details the contributions of each of television's major inventors. Bibliographic references and index.

SEE ALSO: Nov. 2, 1936: BBC Airs the First High-Definition Television Program; Apr. 30, 1939: American Television Debuts at the World's Fair; Sept. 1, 1940: First Color Television Broadcast.

1924

HUBBLE DETERMINES THE DISTANCE TO THE ANDROMEDA NEBULA

Edwin Powell Hubble used the Cepheid variables to determine the distance to the Andromeda galaxy, a finding that eventually led to the development of the big bang theory.

LOCALE: Mount Wilson Observatory, California
CATEGORIES: Science and technology; astronomy

KEY FIGURES

Edwin Powell Hubble (1889-1953), American astronomer
Harlow Shapley (1885-1972), American astronomer and director of Harvard College Observatory
Henrietta Swan Leavitt (1868-1921), American astronomer
Willem de Sitter (1872-1934), Dutch astronomer

SUMMARY OF EVENT

The question of how the cosmos began has always fascinated humanity. The Babylonians measured the positions of stars and the planets and concluded that those bodies affected human lives. Their answer was based on myths and therefore was not scientific. The ancient Greeks were the first to explain the cosmos in a scientific manner: They saw the cosmos as a series of spheres, with the stars attached to the outer sphere. They considered the entire universe to be a few million kilometers in diameter. This work culminated with Ptolemy and his theory of the geocentric cosmos, in which everything—the Moon, the planets, the Sun—moves around Earth. His theory, which accounted for all the known motions of the objects in the sky, was so successful that scientists, astronomers, philosophers, and religious leaders alike accepted it as valid for almost fifteen hundred years.

This consensus changed gradually starting in the early sixteenth century with the work of Nicolaus Copernicus, who quietly asserted the case for heliocentricity—that is, that Earth is not the center of the universe but merely a planet that moves around the Sun. The edge of the universe was as far away as the planet Saturn. In the seventeenth century, Galileo championed this cause, leading to the famous controversy over cosmological understanding and its theological implications. In time, although Galileo's specific arguments were found to be inaccurate, the principle of heliocentricity was proved as a fact.

As technology improved, the importance of the universe continued to diminish. In 1838, Friedrich Wilhelm Bessel measured the angular movement (stellar parallax) of star 61 Cygnus against its background stars and determined that it was six light-years away from Earth. The inability to measure this stellar parallax was one of the reasons the ancients concluded from their observations that Earth was not moving, and, therefore, the geocentric theory was correct. The stars were simply too far away for them to measure the parallax.

From 1915 to 1920, Harlow Shapley used the 100-inch (254-centimeter) telescope at the Mount Wilson Observatory to study globular clusters. These densely packed assemblies of gravitationally bound stars are, in turn, bound to Earth's galaxy, the Milky Way. Shapley noted that the clusters are not evenly distributed in the sky. He knew also that certain stars, the Cepheid variables, have an interesting property: Their average luminosity correlates with the period of their variability. Luminosity is the amount of energy a star gives off per second and determines the star's absolute brightness. If two stars have the same luminosity, the one closer to Earth will appear brighter. The brightness of a star as viewed from Earth is termed its apparent brightness. A star's apparent brightness is dependent on its absolute brightness and its distance from Earth, and astronomers developed an equation to show that relationship.

For the Cepheids, the luminosity varies in a predictable manner and is in concert with the period of oscillation. Henrietta Swan Leavitt established this relationship in 1904, when she cataloged a large number of variable stars. She saw that for the Cepheids, the longer the period of light variation, the greater the average brightness of the star. If a variable's distance could be determined to calibrate the relationship, this would establish the star's absolute brightness. Astronomers could then reverse the process and use the period-luminosity relationship to measure the distances of other Cepheid variables and objects associated with them.

The method to determine the distance works in the following manner. An astronomer measures a Cepheid's apparent brightness and period. The period-luminosity curve yields the star's absolute brightness, and the two brightnesses are entered into the distance-brightness equation. The calculation yields the Cepheid's distance from Earth. Because globular clusters contain Cepheids, Shapley was able to measure the distance to the clusters. Knowing the distances and the direction of the clusters, Shapley plotted their location relative to the location of Earth in the Milky Way. Because the number of clusters

1924

increased toward the portion of the Milky Way in the constellation Sagittarius, Shapley concluded that Earth's location is about two-thirds the distance from the center of the galaxy in Sagittarius and that the Milky Way is shaped like a disk about 100,000 light-years in diameter.

With the realization that the Milky Way is a grouping of billions of stars came the question of whether there are more of these groupings. Up to this point, astronomers did not have telescopes powerful enough to find out, but in 1919, Edwin Powell Hubble gained access to what was then the world's most powerful telescope: the Mount Wilson 100-inch telescope. By 1924, he was able to resolve the fuzzy patches of light that Charles Messier had cataloged into individual stars a century and a half before. These "nebulas" were not clouds of glowing gas like those found within our galaxy; rather, they were galaxies similar to the Milky Way.

Hubble was able to detect Cepheid variables in the Andromeda nebula, and, after determining the apparent brightness and period of oscillation for several Cepheids, he was able to calculate the distance to the nebula at roughly 800,000 light-years. This is more than eight times the distance to the most distant stars in our galaxy. Hubble's work proved that the light patches are separate, gravitationally bound groups of stars and independent of our own galaxy. Hubble went on to measure the distances to other nearby galaxies.

Two decades later, Walter Baade determined that the Andromeda nebula is actually 2 million light-years from Earth. He discovered that there are two types of Cepheid variables: the classic variety and another set with a different brightness-period relationship. These other Cepheids are brighter for a given period of oscillation than the classic Cepheids. Hubble assumed that his Cepheids were fainter than they were, and therefore closer than they were.

Once Hubble determined that the nebulas were other galaxies, he gathered information about them. This led to their classification and the plotting of their possible evolution. With improvement in photography and other techniques, astronomers were able to analyze the light spectra of galaxies. The spectrum of a galaxy looks like a rainbow with dark lines through it and is the total of all frequencies of light coming from the galaxy. The lines are caused by the absorption of certain light frequencies by cooler gases in the galaxy. If there is relative motion between the light's source and the detector, the spectrum is shifted; this is known as the Doppler effect. If a galaxy is moving toward Earth, the entire spectrum shifts toward the blue end of the spectrum. If the galaxy is mov-

Edwin Powell Hubble at the Mount Wilson Observatory near Pasadena, California. (NASA/GSFC)

ing away, the shift is toward the red end of the spectrum. The amount of shift is proportional to the velocity of the galaxy. With this method, Hubble determined that the farther the galaxy is from Earth, the faster it is receding. This suggests that the galaxies are moving away from one another and leads to the conclusion that the universe is expanding, as maintained by Dutch astronomer Willem de Sitter.

SIGNIFICANCE

In order to answer the question of the origin of the cosmos, one must determine its characteristics. The universe could be small or large. It may have a boundary or it may continue forever. It may be static or dynamic. Therefore, astronomers devote much of their time to determining the distances of various objects—such as planets, stars, nebulas, and galaxies—from Earth and how those distances change over time. Such distances obviously cannot be measured directly, so astronomers have developed ingenious methods of indirect measurement, such as the use of trigonometry. As larger telescopes have been built, astronomers have devised new methods that utilize the data these instruments allow them to gather, as Hubble did in using the Mount Wilson telescope to locate the Cepheid variables in the Andromeda nebula.

Astronomers continued the work that Hubble began, establishing the distances and the velocities of nearby galaxies. This permitted them to measure the more distant galaxies through such methods as the comparison of image sizes. Linking this information with the galaxies' velocities—found using the Doppler effect—scientists have determined that the universe is from 13 to 18 billion years old and is expanding.

Two theories have been put forward to explain the age and expansion of the universe: the big bang theory of Georges Lemaître and George Gamow and the steady state theory of Thomas Gold and Fred Hoyle. The steady state theory proposes that the universe is expanding but remains the same because new matter is created to take the place of the galaxies that are moving away from Earth. Astronomers are uncomfortable with the assertion that the matter appears from nowhere—something that is very difficult to verify.

Most astronomers now accept the big bang theory as the best explanation of how the universe began. According to this theory, at some time between 13 and 18 billion years ago, a very hot, very dense "object" exploded. As the temperature dropped, matter as it is now known came into existence: electrons, protons, neutrons, and other particles. As the universe cooled, hydrogen formed, along with a small amount of helium. The matter formed into the first stars and galaxies. There were no planets, because the elements—such as silicon, oxygen, and iron—necessary for planets' formation did not exist. Before planets could form, stars had to undergo supernova explosions that would cause the formation of these elements and others.

Although astronomers continue to gather information and form theories, the eventual likely fate of the universe remains unknown. It may continue to expand forever. It could "die" as its stars use up their hydrogen fuel and become white dwarfs, neutron stars, or black holes. Or, if the universe has enough mass, its expansion will stop because of the gravitational attraction of that mass, and it will then collapse into its original condition. It may then start to expand again to produce another universe, one that may be completely different from our present universe, with physical laws we cannot even imagine.

—*Stephen J. Shulik*

FURTHER READING

Baade, Walter. *Evolution of Stars and Galaxies*. Cambridge, Mass.: Harvard University Press, 1963. Baade's work on stellar populations led to the discovery that there are two varieties of Cepheid variables and resulted in the doubling of the estimated distance to the Andromeda nebula to 2 million light-years. Compiled from a series of lectures Baade gave in the fall of 1958.

Clark, David H., and Matthew D. H. Clark. *Measuring the Cosmos: How Scientists Discovered the Dimensions of the Universe*. New Brunswick, N.J.: Rutgers University Press, 2004. Relates the stories of the scientists who have contributed to current knowledge about the size, mass, and age of the universe. Chapters 4 and 5 include discussion of the work of Hubble and Leavitt. Features glossary, bibliography, and index.

Ferris, Timothy. *The Red Limit: The Search for the Edge of the Universe*. Rev. ed. New York: Harper Perennial, 2002. Well-presented volume discusses the history of the major discoveries in astronomy, paying particular attention to the individuals who made these discoveries. A comprehensible, accurate discussion of astronomy written in an engaging style for readers who have no familiarity with modern cosmological ideas. Includes extensive glossary, selected bibliography, and index.

Kaufmann, William J., III. *Galaxies and Quasars*. San Francisco: W. H. Freeman, 1979. Explains in nontechnical language the implications of Hubble's discoveries. Discusses the Cepheid variable luminosity-period relationship, the Doppler effect, and the geometry of the universe. Includes many figures and photographs.

Silk, Joseph. *The Big Bang*. 3d ed. New York: W. H. Freeman, 2000. Presents a sweeping account of the formation and evolution of the universe. Recounts the history of astronomical speculation about the universe and examines evidence for the big bang theory. Includes glossary and index.

_____. *On the Shores of the Unknown: A Short History of the Universe*. New York: Cambridge University Press, 2005. A history of the universe and the development of humankind's knowledge about it that is accessible to lay readers. Includes illustrations and index.

SEE ALSO: 1912: Slipher Obtains the Spectrum of a Distant Galaxy; Mar. 3, 1912: Leavitt Discovers How to Measure Galactic Distances; Early 1920's: Slipher Presents Evidence of Redshifts in Galactic Spectra; Dec. 13, 1920: Michelson Measures the Diameter of a Star; Dec., 1924: Hubble Shows That Other Galaxies Are Independent Systems; 1929: Hubble Confirms the Expanding Universe.

1924

1924

MANN'S *THE MAGIC MOUNTAIN* REFLECTS EUROPEAN CRISIS

The debate concerning the condition of the European soul in Thomas Mann's The Magic Mountain *reflected the sense of crisis that prevailed in Europe between World Wars I and II.*

LOCALE: Germany
CATEGORY: Literature

KEY FIGURE
Thomas Mann (1875-1955), German novelist

SUMMARY OF EVENT
As with any literary text, the significance of Thomas Mann's most powerful novel, *Der Zauberberg* (1924; *The Magic Mountain*, 1927), should first be understood in the context of the author's life and creative output. Mann was born June 6, 1875, in the city of Lübeck, Germany, to a wealthy merchant family. After the death of his father, the family business was closed, and Mann's mother moved to Munich. Mann worked for a brief time with an insurance company but embarked on a full-time writing career after publishing a short story in a prestigious literary magazine. During this period, he became immersed in the writings of the philosophers Arthur Schopenhauer and Friedrich Nietzsche as well as in the music of composer Richard Wagner. In 1905, Mann married Katja Pringsheim, the daughter of a wealthy Munich family, and they had a total of six children over the ensuing years.

Mann's first literary success was the huge novel *Buddenbrooks: Verfall einer Familie* (1901; English translation, 1924), the story of four generations of a Lübeck merchant family. The novel begins in 1835 with the founding of the family firm by the hardy Johann Buddenbrooks and ends with the premature death of Johann's great-grandson, the young and frail Hanno. In this first novel, Mann established one of his most prominent themes: that spirit, or self-consciousness, is essentially a disease and is inimical to the vitality of existence. In this view, strongly influenced by the ideas of Schopenhauer, the artistic or reflective temperament appears as a perennial outsider, a kind of parasite that sucks the very blood of life. Each succeeding generation of the family becomes more introspective and consequently physically weaker. Mann developed similar themes in his well-known novella *Tonio Kröger* (1903; English translation, 1914).

In *Buddenbrooks*, Mann also employed the technique of the leitmotif, which he adapted from the music of Wagner. In this technique, a certain phrase or image is associated with a theme or character and is later repeated, with slight variations, to evoke that particular figure or idea.

Der Tod in Venedig (1912; *Death in Venice*, 1925) is Mann's most famous novella. It is the story of the writer Gustav von Aschenbach, a rigid and highly disciplined man who travels to the decaying city of Venice. On the beach there, he sees a handsome young Polish boy, Tadzio, and gradually becomes erotically obsessed with him. Thus begins Aschenbach's slow decline, both physical and moral, and he finally dies of the plague when his obsession prohibits him from leaving the city. Mann sounds here again his theme of the artist and intellectual as an outsider, a decadent and diseased individual.

The outbreak of World War I saw Mann as a conservative champion of traditional German values. This led him into a bitter conflict with his brother Heinrich, a prominent liberal and democratic author. During the postwar Weimar period, however, Mann became a staunch defender of democracy. His well-known 1929 short story "Mario und der Zauberer" ("Mario and the Magician"), which was written as a result of his experiences in Benito Mussolini's Italy, is a veiled condemnation of fascism; ironically, the story predicted what would later happen in Adolf Hitler's Germany.

In 1926, Mann began work on an enormous tetralogy of novels devoted to the Joseph story of the Old Testament. He finally completed it in 1943 while in exile. He had left Germany in 1933 for a lecture tour, but his reputation with the Nazi Party was so bad that his children warned him not to return. He stayed for a while in France and Switzerland and then moved to the United States in 1938. He worked on his writing and taught for a time at Princeton University and finally moved to Southern California, home to many prominent German exiles, in 1940. He became an American citizen in 1944.

During this time, Mann wrote one of his most ambitious novels, *Doktor Faustus: Das Leben des deutschen Tonsetzers Adrian Leverkühn, erzählt von einem Freunde* (1947; *Doctor Faustus: The Life of the German Composer Adrian Leverkühn as Told by a Friend*, 1948), the story of the tragic fate of a composer as narrated by the bourgeois intellectual Serenus Zeitblom. The novel is a parable of the succumbing of middle-class Germany, with its long tradition of humanism and spiritual values, to the demoniac forces of Hitler's racist ideology. As the title suggests, Leverkühn is a Faustian individual who sells his soul to the devil in order to produce a new kind of music. Here, Mann was influenced by the work of Arnold Schoenberg, the modernist composer who also was residing in exile in California. Mann suggested that the romantic German spirit, in its quest for ever-new experiences and its exploration of self-consciousness, had flirted with an abyss of subjectivity and irrationalism that had dangerous consequences. Elements of Nietzsche's biography also figure in the Leverkühn character.

In 1952, Mann moved to Switzerland, where he remained until his death on August 12, 1955. His last novel, *Bekenntnisse des Hochstaplers Felix Krull: Der Memoiren erster Teil* (1954; *Confessions of Felix Krull, Confidence Man: The Early Years*, 1955), again dealt with the theme of the artist, here a con artist who fools himself and the public through a series of poses. Throughout his writings, Mann maintained a sense of ambivalence toward his art, a feeling that he often mediated through a subtle sense of irony.

Thomas Mann. (The Nobel Foundation)

The plot of *The Magic Mountain* begins in 1907, when the young Hans Castorp from northern Germany goes to the elegant and international tuberculosis sanatorium Berghof in Davos, Switzerland, to visit his ailing cousin. Although he participates in the daily routine of the patients, which involves long periods of rest in the thin Alpine air as well as opulent meals, Castorp is not really ill, and at first he remains merely an observer. He stays, however, for a period of seven years, even after the death of his cousin. His own condition worsens and then improves.

His stay becomes a period of education for Castorp, as he is exposed to a variety of experiences, both sensual and intellectual. Indeed, Mann imitates and parodies the nineteenth century genre of the *Bildungsroman*, or novel of education. Castorp falls in love with an elegant and beautiful Russian woman, Clawdia Chauchat, and has a passionate, and at times rather morbid, affair. He reads numerous books on topics ranging from the medical and natural sciences to Freudian psychology and the occult. He goes skiing and almost dies in a snowstorm, during which he has a frightening vision. Most important, he meets two older intellectuals who become his mentors. The first is Settembrini, an Italian humanist who upholds the values of European liberalism and rationalism. The other is Naphta, a dogmatic, formerly Jewish, and charismatic Jesuit priest who speaks for a blind and irrational faith. These two ideologues engage in a battle of minds for the prize of Castorp's intellectual spirit. The contest climaxes in a pistol duel in which the enraged Naphta commits suicide when Settembrini refuses to fire at him.

When Clawdia Chauchat leaves Berghof after their brief affair, Castorp pines for her. He is both disappointed and impressed when she returns accompanied by her lover, the robust and completely unintellectual businessman Mynheer Peeperkorn, whose unbridled vitality serves as a counterpoint to the sterile intellectuality of Settembrini and Naphta. Here Mann's view of the artist and intellectual as fundamentally alienated from the vital forces of life is again apparent. Castorp leaves the sanatorium after his seven-year stay, presumably to join the army at the outbreak of the war.

SIGNIFICANCE

Mann himself regarded *The Magic Mountain* as a statement about the constitution of the European soul and the intellectual and spiritual impasse it confronted during the first part of the twentieth century. Hans Castorp is to be understood as a kind of Everyman, the average bourgeois European. The Berghof sanatorium, with its interna-

1924

THE JESUIT AND THE HUMANIST

In The Magic Mountain, *Thomas Mann uses the characters of Naphta and Settembrini to represent opposite poles in European thought. In this excerpt from one of the characters' arguments, Naphta asserts the importance of faith:*

"Permit me to remark that any system of pains and penalties which is not based upon belief in a hereafter is simply a bestial stupidity. And as for the degradation of humanity, the history of its course is precisely synchronous with the growth of the bourgeois spirit. Renaissance, age of enlightenment, the natural sciences and economics of the nineteenth century, have left nothing undone or untaught which could forward this degradation. Modern astronomy, for example, has converted the earth, the centre of the All, the lofty theatre of the struggle between God and the Devil for the possession of a creature burningly coveted by each, into an indifferent little planet, and thus—at least for the present—put an end to the majestic cosmic position of man—upon which, moreover, all astrology bases itself."

"For the present?" Herr Settembrini asked, threateningly. His own manner of speaking had something in it of the inquisitor waiting to pounce upon the witness so soon as he shall have involved himself in an admission of guilt.

"Certainly. For a few hundred years, that is," assented Naphta, coldly. "A vindication, in this respect, of scholasticism is on the way, is even well under way, unless all signs fail. Copernicus will go down before Ptolemy. The heliocentric thesis is meeting by degrees with an intellectual opposition which will end by achieving its purpose. Science will see itself philosophically enforced to put back the earth in the position of supremacy in which she was installed by the dogma of the Church."

"What? What? Intellectual opposition? Science philosophically enforced? What sort of voluntarism is this you are giving vent to? And what about pure knowledge, what about science? What about the unfettered quest for truth? Truth, my dear sir, so indissolubly bound up with freedom, the martyrs in whose cause you would like us to regard as criminals upon this planet but who are rather the brightest jewels in her crown?"

Herr Settembrini's question, and its delivery, were prodigious. He sat very erect, his righteous words rolled down upon little Naphta, and he let his voice swell out at the end, so that one could tell how sure he was his opponent could only reply with shamefaced silence. . . .

Naphta responded, with disagreeable composure: "My good sir, there is no such thing as pure knowledge. The validity of the Church's teaching on the subject of science, which can be summed up in the phrase of Saint Augustine: *Credo, ut intellegam:* I believe, in order that I may understand, is absolutely incontrovertible. Faith is the vehicle of knowledge, intellect secondary. Your pure science is a myth."

Source: Thomas Mann, *The Magic Mountain*, translated by H. T. Lowe-Porter (New York: Alfred A. Knopf, 1927).

tional clientele, becomes a microcosm of European society, and with its high altitude, thin air, and febrile atmosphere, it produces a hermetic intensification of all aspects of the individual's sensual and intellectual life.

The dilemma of European intellectuals as posited in Mann's novel can be approached first through an examination of the horrible vision that Castorp sees during the snowstorm. Initially, he perceives an idyllic landscape, sunny and populated by a seemingly healthy and happy people. In the dark interior of a temple, however, he comes upon a group of ugly and frightening old women who are dismembering a child. Here Mann echoes some of the ideas of Nietzsche concerning the origins of Greek tragic art and culture. Given that the Greco-Roman tradition is central to Western culture, he is suggesting that at the heart of the European spirit there is a conflict of light and dark, of an enlightened, civilized, Apollonian world and a Dionysian one of utter barbarism and cruelty.

Prior to World War I, Europeans had regarded themselves as a highly cultured and refined people who had produced the likes of William Shakespeare, Voltaire, Leo Tolstoy, and Johann Wolfgang von Goethe. The years 1914 to 1918, however, saw the advent of modern warfare and terrible and unprecedented human destruction. Among European intellectuals, there was a profound sense of shock at the depths to which European culture had sunk. Culture had revealed itself to be nothing more than a thin veneer that masked a mindless, raging beast. A feeling of crisis gradually emerged in which the powers of the critical intellect and reason were devalued.

Mann gives more in-depth explanation of the dialectical forces that seemed to tear at the European spirit in the long conversations between Castorp and his two ideological mentors that take up much of the latter half of the novel. Indeed, much of the novel is taken up by conversation; it includes little overt action. Settembrini, the ailing but elegant man from the land in which the Renaissance began, is presented as the champion of the eighteenth century Enlightenment spirit, the dualistic belief that the use of reason can bring about progress and lead humanity out of its spiritual darkness into a more humane world. He stands in the European tradition of rationalistic philosophers such as Gottfried Wilhelm Leibniz, Immanuel Kant, René Descartes, Denis Diderot, and Voltaire. During the course of the Weimar era in the 1920's, Germany became more and more polarized between conflicting political and social ideologies. Settembrini is the spokesman for a liberal democracy in which the educated masses can be trusted to exercise their critical judgment and elect the most suitable representatives. His character echoes the political stance of Mann's brother, the liberal democrat Heinrich.

If Settembrini represents one cultural and ideological pole of the European scene, then the volatile and cynical Jesuit priest Naphta (whose character Mann modeled, in part, on the Marxist literary critic György Lukács) speaks for its opposite. Whereas Settembrini lauds the rationality of the eighteenth century, Naphta praises the Middle Ages, the era of blind (or irrational) faith in forces that are far more powerful than the mere intellect of humankind. Where the former speaks of the free exercise of the critical intellect, the latter advocates nonrational belief and a fanatical discipline of the body. Naphta eschews the critical debate of the liberal democrats and urges the extremist rhetoric of the demagogues. His political views touch on those of the radical socialist who sees only violent political change in the terrorist mass movements of ideological zealots.

The Magic Mountain captured the spirit of Mann's age: the dialectical forces of rationalism and irrationalism, intellect and emotion, that seemed to tear at the fabric of the European soul in the years following World War I. In the figures of Settembrini and Naphta, this conflict is presented in the form of ideological debate. It is the great irony of the novel that although Naphta dies, his ideological position lived on in the fanatical yet mesmerizing ravings of Adolf Hitler and in the racist and fascist programs of the Nazis.

—*Thomas F. Barry*

FURTHER READING

Feuerlicht, Ignace. *Thomas Mann*. 1968. Reprint. New York: Macmillan, 1983. A thorough critical introduction to the author's life and writings. Recommended for beginning students. Includes notes and bibliography.

Hatfield, Henry, ed. *Thomas Mann: A Collection of Critical Essays*. Englewood Cliffs, N.J.: Prentice-Hall, 1964. A fine collection of academic essays on Mann's work by leading American and European scholars, some of which have been translated from the German. Includes notes and chronology.

Heller, Erich. *The Ironic German: A Study of Thomas Mann*. Boston: Little, Brown, 1958. An early but still important study of Mann's major texts and themes by a leading American scholar. Includes notes and bibliography.

Kurzke, Hermann. *Thomas Mann: Life as a Work of Art*. Translated by Leslie Willson. Princeton, N.J.: Princeton University Press, 2002. In-depth biography of Mann translated from the German examines Mann's works to show how his art and his life influenced each other. Includes forty photographs.

Prater, Donald. *Thomas Mann: A Life*. New York: Oxford University Press, 2006. One of few full-scale biographies of Mann available in English. Focuses on the events of his life rather than on his writings, drawing on diaries, correspondence, and other documents to place Mann in the context of his times. Includes photographs.

Stern, J. P. *Thomas Mann*. New York: Columbia University Press, 1967. A brief but first-rate introduction to Mann's life and major writings. Includes a selected bibliography of Mann's works as well as of important critical texts.

Winston, Richard. *Thomas Mann: The Making of an Artist, 1875-1911*. New York: Alfred A. Knopf, 1981. An excellent biography that focuses on Mann's formative years. Includes notes and bibliography.

Ziolkowski, Theodore. "Thomas Mann: *The Magic Mountain*." In *Dimensions of the Modern Novel: German Texts and European Contexts*. Princeton, N.J.: Princeton University Press, 1969. Stimulating essay situates Mann's novel within the thematic contexts of European fiction. Includes notes.

SEE ALSO: 1915: *The Metamorphosis* Anticipates Modern Feelings of Alienation; 1918-1919: Germans Revolt and Form a Socialist Government; 1925: Gide's *The Counterfeiters* Questions Moral Absolutes.

1924

1924
SOVIETS ESTABLISH A SOCIETY FOR THE PROTECTION OF NATURE

Volunteer organizations were established in the Soviet republics to serve as public information agencies to assist in the protection of nature.

ALSO KNOWN AS: All-Russian Society for the Protection of Nature

LOCALE: Soviet Union

CATEGORIES: Environmental issues; organizations and institutions; natural resources

KEY FIGURES

Vladimir Ilich Lenin (Vladimir Ilich Ulyanov; 1870-1924), leader of the Russian Communist Party and chairman of the Council of People's Commissars of Soviet Russia, 1917-1924

Anatoly Lunacharsky (1875-1933), Soviet minister of education and culture, 1917-1929

Joseph Stalin (Joseph Vissarionovich Dzhugashvili; 1878-1953), first secretary of the Soviet Communist Party and leader of the Soviet Union, 1929-1953

SUMMARY OF EVENT

After the Russian Revolution of November, 1917, which brought the Communist Party to power, the Russians paid little attention to environmental concerns. The leaders of Soviet Russia had expected their revolution to be a stimulus to turn World War I into a class war, bringing into existence an international socialist state in Europe. When this did not occur, the Communists were faced with the prospect of building socialism not in an industrialist state, as Marxist theory envisioned, but in a backward, rural state. The emphasis of the new regime would thus have to be on economic development—the antithesis of environmental protection.

Ecological themes were not entirely neglected in Marxist-Leninist theory and practice. Although it is difficult to find references to the natural environment in the writings of Karl Marx, a few writings do express concern that the land, which would be the legacy of the working class, or proletariat, not be despoiled or destroyed. Marx's collaborator, Friedrich Engels, was more direct in stating that the human community is not the possessor of the earth but its custodian for future generations.

Indeed, under Vladimir Ilich Lenin's leadership between 1917 and 1922, the Soviets passed a number of environmental laws, although whether Lenin ordered these or they originated from lower levels of the Soviet bureaucracy is difficult to say. One of the most important such laws was the nationalization law of November 8, 1917, enacted the day after the revolt, which made all land in the Soviet Union the property of the state. In 1918, the new Soviet government enacted laws concerning irrigation, forests, hunting, and fishing.

In 1919, the government established the Astrakhan National Forest Preserve and passed legislation regarding hunting and natural resources, particularly the protection of water resources. Laws affected irrigation and drainage, established water conservancy districts, registered water services, and established sanitary districts. These laws, however—with a few exceptions, such as the forest preserve—were little more than sanitation regulations, concerned with daily living. Environmental issues remained subordinate to the major political and economic problems confronting Soviet society in its first years.

From 1917 to 1922, Lenin's government concluded the war with Germany, fought a civil war against the Soviet government's Russian opponents, and battled an Allied invasion after World War I ended. Moscow, which became the seat of the government in 1918, established a policy called War Communism, a euphemism for centralized economic and social control. All resources were put into the war effort. Because most environmental concerns were of a local or regional nature, these issues received little attention during this period.

In 1922, Lenin introduced the New Economic Policy (NEP), which represented a partial return to a market economy. Again, Soviet emphasis was on production rather than on ecological preservation, especially after the destruction wreaked by World War I and the Russian Civil War. The NEP reintroduced a measure of decentralization that allowed local concerns, where they existed, to be heard. Yet part of the NEP was to invite foreign entrepreneurs into the country to exploit its resources in exchange for technology and necessary foreign currency. Soviet environmentalists reported that Lenin personally stopped a work crew from cutting down trees in a Moscow park. Under the NEP, however, Lenin approved the destruction of whole forests in order to achieve his economic goals.

The NEP was accompanied by a loosening of restrictions on Soviet society, with considerable freedom granted to ordinary Soviet citizens, including the ability to organize in various associations. In those first years of Soviet rule, many idealists organized clubs and associations for various purposes. The Soviet minister of education and culture, Anatoly Lunacharsky, especially encouraged the preservation of traditional Russian education, historical monuments, and national heritage. It was in this context that public opinion brought about the formation in 1924 of the All-Russian Society for the Protection of Nature.

In 1922, after the victory in the civil war, the Soviet government restructured itself into the Soviet Union, which encompassed several Soviet republics, eventually growing to a union of fifteen. Volunteer organizations similar to the 1924 Russian society were formed in all the republics. By the 1970's, the All-Russian Society alone comprised more than twenty-two million members. The purposes of the society were to teach love and respect for nature and to involve the Soviet people in the conservation, proper use, and replenishment of natural resources. One of the society's tangible goals was the planting of parks and gardens in cities, towns, villages, and rural areas. The society used its resources to promote natural conservation and educational activities for children and adults. Councils of the society were established in autonomous republics, in regions and districts, and in cities and neighborhoods. The local and central organizations worked with factories, collective farms, schools, and various other organizations to encourage the protection of the natural environment.

SIGNIFICANCE

In 1929, Joseph Stalin emerged as the supreme dictator of the Soviet Union. Defeating his rivals and eventually having them executed, he not only succeeded to Lenin's mantle but in fact outdid the former Soviet leader in the scope of his supreme power as well. Stalin brought the NEP to an end and introduced a program of rapid industrialization. This was accompanied in Soviet society by the creation of a modern totalitarian system through which the Soviet government attempted to regulate almost all aspects of the lives of individual citizens.

From 1941 to 1945, the Soviet Union engaged in World War II, which on the Eastern European front was fought mainly on Soviet territory; vast areas of the country were devastated. Then began a process of rebuilding and reindustrialization. Under the circumstances, the Soviets paid little more than lip service to environmental concerns. With a few exceptions, the Soviet Union engaged in very little serious environmental activity until the 1960's. Given the rudimentary industrial development of the Soviet Union and its low standard of living, however, the nation's environmental problems were not

as serious as those in the high-technology regions of Western Europe and North America.

Stalin believed in the manipulation of nature and had some concerns for its preservation, so long as such preservation was compatible with his modernization program. The local and regional societies for the protection of nature thus remained active during the Stalinist period and beyond and were organized by the vast Communist Party apparatus. The societies spread information on conservation through the press and published and disseminated posters and pamphlets. They also used motion pictures, radio, and, later, television to disseminate their messages.

The societies helped organize exhibits and displays in schools and factories, and they planted trees, shrubs, and flowers throughout the Soviet Union. They stressed the conservation of natural resources and helped organize programs to protect air and water quality, especially in heavily populated areas. The societies also worked to protect recreation areas from industrial and domestic pollution, and they were responsible for organizing national environmental celebrations such as Bird Day, Forest Week, and Nature Month. In cooperation with local soviets (cities, towns, and village councils), they organized conservation inspections as well as environment-related competitions and contests.

The first All-Union Congress on Conservation convened in 1933. Its resolutions emphasized the protection of natural resources and their regeneration. In 1956, the Soviet Union joined the International Union for the Conservation of Nature and Natural Resources.

In addition to the supposedly volunteer public organizations, the State Committee for Conservation in the Russian Republic and similar groups in the other republics were also active. These groups came under the jurisdiction of the Commissariat for Education, Lunacharsky's ministry, which was charged with coordinating all conservation activities. In 1930, the Committee for Conservation was changed to the Interdepartmental State Committee for Promoting the Development and Protection of Natural Resources, still under the authority of the Commissariat for Education. In 1933 and 1938, the committee underwent further reorganization, eventually becoming the Central Board for Preserves, which was charged with overseeing the rational use of natural resources. This board was directly responsible to the Russian cabinet. Similar evolution took place in conservation agencies in the other republics.

In the post-World War II Soviet Union, many different agencies and ministries had responsibilities concerning the environment, including the State Committee for

Science and Technology, the Ministry of Agriculture, the Ministry of Land Reclamation and Water-Use Management, and the State Committee of Forest Economy. In general, however, those agencies in charge of protecting the environment were also in charge of its use and exploitation. The Soviet authorities ignored this conflict of interest.

In the late 1960's and the 1970's, environmental degradation in the Soviet Union became too serious to ignore. The Soviet government passed many laws, but these did not stem the increasing tide of pollution. The attitude that nature was to be mastered permeated the thinking of Soviet authorities, as it did that of the Communist leaders of Eastern Europe, where environmental problems were equally bad. For example, Soviet leader Nikita S. Khrushchev's virgin lands campaign, which introduced monoculture agriculture into marginal soils despite warnings against the practice, was an environmental disaster. Furthermore, pervasive government censorship prevented any widespread Soviet conservation campaign.

Growing danger to the Soviet Union's water resources brought ecological concerns to the forefront as fresh water became dangerously scarce. Poor harvests in the 1960's compelled the Soviets to import grain and stimulated massive irrigation plans, leading to grandiose schemes to divert Siberian waters. Despite damage to the environment in many different areas, plans for the use of Siberian water for Soviet industry increased. Bodies of water such as the Caspian Sea and the unique Lake Baikal in Siberia were destroyed by loss of water and contamination by sewage and industrial pollutants. The valuable Caspian sturgeon catch was devastated. Rivers turned into sewers as untreated water was pumped into them, and agricultural chemicals produced water pollution by way of drainage and air-blown particles that filtered into the water supply.

Criticism concerning environmental problems proved to be one of the most powerful means of dissent within the Soviet Union. The first significant issue of public debate in this regard was the pollution of Lake Baikal, the deepest and hence the largest (by volume) lake in the world. The damage to the water and the fish it contained, including unique species, as well as to the lake's formerly pristine surroundings, aroused the ire of private citizens and public officials alike. The protesters forced the government to recommit itself to the protection of nature, particularly in Siberia.

Even with such government concessions, environmental protests continued in the Soviet Union and eventually contributed to the formulation of the policy of glasnost, or openness, in the late 1980's. Soviet citizens called for a government committee for the protection of nature that would have more power than the volunteer committee and would be free of the conflicts of interest that undermined the effectiveness of the existing groups. When further liberalization occurred under Mikhail Gorbachev, environmental issues became an important factor in the unraveling of the Soviet Union in 1991.

—Frederick B. Chary

FURTHER READING

Goldman, Marshal I. *The Spoils of Progress: Environmental Pollution in the Soviet Union.* Cambridge, Mass.: MIT Press, 1972. A classic American work on Soviet environmental problems. Discusses the history of the conservation movement, particularly in the years since World War II. An appendix lists major Soviet conservation laws.

Komarov, Boris. *The Destruction of Nature in the Soviet Union.* White Plains, N.Y.: M. E. Sharpe, 1980. This dissident essay protesting the despoliation of nature in the Soviet Union was influential in the organization of the Green movement in the last years of the Soviet Union.

Pavlínek, Petr, and John Pickles. *Environmental Transitions: Transformation and Ecological Defence in Central and Eastern Europe.* London: Routledge, 2000. Discusses the environmental changes that have taken place in Central and Eastern Europe with the transition away from state socialism after the fall of the Soviet Union. Includes maps, tables, figures, bibliography, and index.

Pelloso, Andrew J. *Saving the Blue Heart of Siberia: The Environmental Movement in Russia and Lake Baikal.* Bloomington: Indiana University School of Public and Environmental Affairs, 1993. Presents two aspects of conservation activity in Siberia after World War II. Analyzes the efforts of both official and dissident environmental groups.

Shaposhnikov, L. K. "Societies for the Conservation of Nature." In *Great Soviet Encyclopedia*, edited by A. M. Prokhorov. New York: Macmillan, 1983. One of the best English-language accounts available of the All-Russian Society for the Protection of Nature.

Treadgold, Donald W., and Herbert J. Ellison. *Twentieth Century Russia.* 9th ed. Boulder, Colo.: Westview Press, 2000. Comprehensive history of Russia in the twentieth century provides excellent coverage of the political background of the Soviet period. Includes maps and index.

Völgyes, Iván, ed. *Environmental Deterioration in the Soviet Union and Eastern Europe*. New York: Praeger, 1974. Collection of scholarly essays about pollution problems provides an excellent survey of the state of the environment in the Soviet Union in the 1960's and 1970's.

SEE ALSO: Aug. 25, 1916: National Park Service Is Created; Feb. 1, 1919: Lenin Approves the First Soviet Nature Preserve; May 20, 1919: National Parks and Conservation Association Is Founded; 1926: Vernadsky Publishes *The Biosphere*; Nov. 19, 1929: Serengeti Game Reserve Is Created.

1924
STEENBOCK DISCOVERS SUNLIGHT INCREASES VITAMIN D IN FOOD

With his discovery that the ultraviolet component of sunlight increases vitamin D in food, Harry Steenbock stimulated extensive research on vitamins.

LOCALE: Madison, Wisconsin
CATEGORIES: Science and technology; biology

KEY FIGURES
Harry Steenbock (1886-1967), American biochemist
Adolf Windaus (1876-1959), German chemist
Christiaan Eijkman (1858-1930), Dutch physician
Frederick Hopkins (1861-1947), British biochemist
Elmer Verner McCollum (1879-1967), American biochemist

SUMMARY OF EVENT
The discovery that exposure to sunlight increases the amount of vitamin D in food arose from two separate areas of research involving biochemistry and medicine. The first part of the investigation involved sterol, specifically cholesterol. In 1901, the importance of this substance was not yet known, and a number of able chemists had attempted to unravel the components of the substance without success. Cholesterol is one of a large group of related compounds called sterols that are found in animal and vegetable cells. In Germany, Adolf Windaus began by comparing this group of substances and found that they have a common feature in a tetracyclic carbon skeleton. He was convinced that other natural products would share in this basic skeleton. By 1919, he had demonstrated that cholesterol could be transformed into cholanic acid. By 1932, the work of Heinrich Wieland and Windaus had paid off, and the correct structure of the sterol ring was discovered.

The story of vitamins began in 1906, when Christiaan Eijkman was seeking a cure for the tropical disease beriberi. He observed that chickens fed on polished rice exhibited symptoms similar to the disease in humans. When the chickens were fed rice with the hulls intact, however, the disease disappeared. Consequently, Eijkman demonstrated that the disease is caused by a dietary deficiency, which was later found to be a substance called thiamine, or vitamin B. In the same year, Sir Frederick Hopkins proposed that several substances are essential for the maintenance of health and, with his colleague, Casimir Funk, named these substances "vitamins."

In 1907, Elmer Verner McCollum was on the faculty of the University of Wisconsin, where Harry Steenbock was an undergraduate student. McCollum, who was involved in dietary and nutritional research, learned of Eijkman's work and became convinced that a small quantity of a substance called vitamin is as essential to life as all the nutritional value of food. In 1913, he discovered a substance similar to vitamin B, except that it was found in fats; this turned out to be vitamin A. Nine years later, he contributed to the identification of vitamin D.

By the 1920's, vitamin research was being pursued in a number of laboratories in England, Germany, and the United States. One area of research involved the disease rickets, which scientists knew could be prevented through the ingestion of fish liver oil. By the early 1920's, it was discovered that the active agent in the fish liver oil was vitamin D. Although vitamin D could effect a cure for rickets, exposure to sunlight also proved to be effective. Scientists thus began to examine whether there were several paths toward a cure or these paths were all part of a single therapeutic process.

Steenbock brought together the two strands of medical and biochemical research in his work, in which he concentrated on the chemical analysis of livestock nutrition. He had participated in an experiment in which components of a plant were mixed in such a way that they were chemically identical but produced different nutritional results. The influence of McCollum's experimental methods, which included the use of white mice, and Steenbock's livestock experiment led to the beginning of

1924

the inclusion of live animal subjects in nutritional studies. Steenbock continued his research activities in nutrition through the field of vitamin studies. In 1920, he isolated a compound called carotene, which is associated with yellow foods and contains vitamin A. By 1924, Alfred F. Hess and Steenbock had independently exposed certain foods to sunlight and found that these foods were also effective in the cure of rickets. Somehow, light converted chemicals in the food into vitamin D. The precise mechanism for this conversion was not resolved for some time.

In 1925, Hess invited Windaus to take part in the work on vitamin D. Windaus began a collaborative effort on the study of vitamin D and continued his work on the photochemical nature of sterol. Over the years, he identified a number of other compounds with similar characteristics. Windaus believed that cholesterol was the source of vitamin D, as cholesterol exhibits similar properties when exposed to ultraviolet light. Working in Germany, Robert Pohl had identified an impurity in cholesterol, called ergosterol, that Hess and Windaus later proved could convert to vitamin D. Thus, by 1927, the major features of both the chemistry and the structure of sterol and vitamin D had become clear.

Through further research, Windaus found several variations of vitamin D and eventually isolated one form that was identical to the one purified from tuna fish liver oil; this was confirmed by Hans Brockman in Windaus's laboratory. After Windaus received the 1928 Nobel Prize in Chemistry for this work, the April, 1929, issue of the *Scientific Monthly* published an article that analyzed why the work on rickets conducted by several noteworthy American and English scientists had been overlooked. The article expressed the opinion that Hess and Steenbock should have been given greater credit for discovering the effects of exposure to ultraviolet light on vitamin D in food and living animals.

SIGNIFICANCE

Long before the discovery of vitamins, scientists had observed the effects of restricted diets on both human and animal populations. Diseases that had resulted from dietary deficiencies had been described in detail. For example, the lack of fresh fruits and vegetables during long sea voyages produced scurvy, a disease caused by the absence of vitamin C. Although it was well known that scurvy could be remedied through the ingestion of fruits and vegetables, little was known about why this was so.

Steenbock's discovery of the effects of ultraviolet light on the production of vitamin D coincided with an extensive period of research on vitamins. The culmination of Eijkman's initial identification of vitamin B came in 1926 with the further refinement of the vitamin. The work of B. C. P. Jansen and W. F. Donath resulted in the isolation of a component called vitamin B_1 (thiamine). These researchers began with more than 300 kilograms (about 661 pounds) of rice polishings (husks removed from rice grains) and produced less than 100 milligrams (about 0.004 ounce) of thiamine crystal. Another resolution of an existing vitamin problem involved Steenbock's initial observation of a relationship between vitamin D and carotene, which was later solved by Thomas Moore and Hans von Euler-Chelpin. In 1928, the final piece in the vitamin alphabet was provided by Albert Szent-Györgyi, who isolated vitamin C from oranges and cabbage.

The next stage in vitamin research was the discovery of the functions of these substances. It had been demonstrated already that vitamins could cure diseases and function as growth factors. Research suggested that vitamins act on enzyme systems to regulate the respiration of cells and metabolism. In a series of experiments involving pigeons and thiamine, it was demonstrated that pigeons lacking this vitamin suffered from spasms. Thiamine is essential in the process of glucose metabolism, and without this vitamin, the mechanism for the breakdown of glucose is impaired. It became clear that thiamine directly influences five metabolic reactions that, in turn, regulate the energy flow necessary for the maintenance of the cells. These experiments thus showed the relationship between vitamin B and beriberi.

Subsequent explorations on more than twenty vitamins provided a complex picture of the roles of these substances as regulators of various mechanisms at the cellular level. Vitamins, in very small amounts, are indispensable components of food and organic life.

—*Victor W. Chen*

FURTHER READING

Bailey, Herbert. *The Vitamin Pioneers*. Emmaus, Pa.: Rodale Books, 1968. Discusses the history of the development of medical and biochemical knowledge about vitamins. The sections on vitamins B and D are comprehensive and suitable for the general reader.

Carpenter, Kenneth J. "A Short History of Nutritional Science: Part 3 (1912-1944)." *Journal of Nutrition* 133 (October, 2003): 3023-3032. Third part of a four-part series includes discussion of the research on vitamin D, placing this work in the context of the history of nutritional science in general.

Feldman, David, J. Wesley Pike, and Francis H. Glorieux, eds. *Vitamin D*. 2d ed. 2 vols. New York: Academic Press, 2004. Comprehensive reference set geared toward professionals working in endocrinology, osteology, cancer research, and related fields. First chapter provides a historical overview. Includes illustrations and index.

Ihde, Aaron J. *The Development of Modern Chemistry*. 1964. Reprint. Mineola, N.Y.: Dover, 1984. Comprehensive history of the different areas of chemistry. Chapter 24 covers the developments in biochemistry that led directly to Steenbock's research. Topics discussed include nutrition, the search for vitamins, and metabolism.

Leicester, Henry M. *Development of Biochemical Concepts from Ancient to Modern Times*. Cambridge, Mass.: Harvard University Press, 1974. Provides a valuable overview of biochemical concepts. Chapters 15, 16, and 17 cover enzymes and cell constituents, energy production and biological oxidation, and intermediary metabolism.

SEE ALSO: 1901: Grijns Suggests the Cause of Beriberi; 1901: Hopkins Announces the Discovery of Tryptophan; 1906: Hopkins Postulates the Presence of Vitamins; 1922: McCollum Names Vitamin D and Pioneers Its Use Against Rickets; 1928-1932: Szent-Györgyi Discovers Vitamin C.

1924
SVEDBERG DEVELOPS THE ULTRACENTRIFUGE

Theodor Svedberg's development of the ultracentrifuge enabled scientists to separate colloidal particles, including proteins, carbohydrates, cell organelles, and viruses.

LOCALE: Uppsala, Sweden
CATEGORIES: Science and technology; chemistry; biology

KEY FIGURES
Theodor Svedberg (1884-1971), Swedish physical chemist
John B. Nichols (fl. early twentieth century), American chemist
Herman Rinde (fl. early twentieth century), Swedish chemist

SUMMARY OF EVENT

Many essential aspects of modern knowledge in the fields of chemistry, biochemistry, and biology are indebted to Theodor Svedberg's development of the machine he called the ultracentrifuge. By definition, an ultracentrifuge is a fast centrifuge that produces a convection-free centrifugal field. Such a device is useful for the study of the properties of dissolved solutes, including the measurement of their molecular weights through sedimentation velocity and sedimentation equilibrium techniques, the identification of both their molecular sizes and their shapes, and the characterization of synthetic and natural macromolecules on the basis of the property called buoyant density. A centrifuge is a machine in which a compartment (rotor) is spun around a central axis to develop centrifugal force, which is measured in gravities and can be used to separate colloid particles and materials of different densities.

Svedberg was a Swedish physical chemist with a great interest in biology. Svedberg's decision to become a physical chemist is said to have been based in part on his belief that numerous unsolved biological problems could be explained as chemical phenomena that could be studied best with the techniques of physical chemistry. He received B.S. and Ph.D. degrees in 1905 and 1907, respectively, from the University of Uppsala. In 1912, the university appointed him to the first Swedish chair of physical chemistry. One of Svedberg's main lifelong interests was an understanding of the chemistry of colloids. It was this interest that led him to develop the ultracentrifuge.

A colloid is a mixture in which tiny particles of one or several substances are dispersed in another substance (very often water). Colloid particles are much larger than crystalloidal molecules (for example, sugar) or crystalloidal ions (for example, sodium and chloride ions). They are usually too small to settle out under the force of gravity or to be seen with light microscopes. The size of colloid particles ranges from 5 to 200 nanometers. Examples of very important biological colloid particles are proteins, deoxyribonucleic acid (DNA), and the viruses.

In his thesis, Svedberg described an electrical method for producing very pure colloidal suspensions of metals. Through continued efforts, he identified many other im-

1924

Theodor Svedberg. (The Nobel Foundation)

portant aspects of the physical chemistry of colloids. A particularly frustrating aspect of carrying out these studies was that it was very important to identify the exact sizes of the colloid particles. This was difficult to do because the available methodology involved examining the rate of their settling out (sedimentation), and only the very largest colloid particles sedimented at rates that were useful.

Svedberg believed that sedimentation of colloid particles could be hastened to a point where their study would be practical if they could be subjected to the increased gravitational fields produced in a high-speed centrifuge. He proposed to design such a centrifuge in a fashion that would allow the sedimentation of the particles to be followed photographically. Svedberg began his work on this "optical" centrifuge while he was a visiting professor at the University of Wisconsin, Madison, in 1923. The centrifuge he developed there, in collaboration with John B. Nichols, was not entirely successful because, although the user could follow the sedimentation of colloid particles, convection problems prevented the unequivocal identification of their sizes.

After returning to Sweden, Svedberg continued his efforts and aimed to develop convection-free centrifugal sedimentation. In 1924, he and his colleague Herman Rinde succeeded in doing so. At first, Svedberg and Rinde studied inorganic colloids. They soon discovered, however, that the very important, poorly understood biological macromolecules called proteins would also sediment in their centrifugal fields. The researchers then quickly made important discoveries in fundamental protein chemistry. First, they demonstrated that all the molecules of any particular protein are of one size (monodisperse particles). These data contrasted greatly with those obtained with metal colloids, which are composed of particles of many sizes (polydisperse), and flew in the face of the established belief that proteins were also polydisperse. The Svedberg centrifuge, which he named the ultracentrifuge, allowed scientists to measure the sizes and the shapes of proteins, making it an invaluable research tool for biology, biochemistry, and medicine.

Svedberg received the 1926 Nobel Prize in Chemistry for his work on disperse systems. The Nobel Committee stated that these endeavors "proved the real existence of molecules and atoms." In his Nobel acceptance lecture, Svedberg described the great potential he foresaw for the use of the ultracentrifuge in chemistry, medicine, physics, and biology. Over the next sixteen years, he improved the device's design and function, and by 1936 he had produced an ultracentrifuge capable of spinning a centrifuge rotor at 120,000 revolutions per minute and of producing a centrifugal force of 525,000 times the force of gravity.

Using the improved ultracentrifuge, Svedberg and his coworkers examined hundreds of proteins from many different kinds of plants and animals. They found that the molecular weights of different proteins vary greatly, and they learned that proteins are round, monodisperse molecules possessed of high molecular weights. They also discovered that the same proteins from different species have similar or identical molecular weights. Svedberg and his colleagues also studied the properties of carbohydrates (for example, cellulose and starch) in the ultracentrifuge and learned that these biomolecules are very long, thin, polydisperse molecules. This work, much of which is described in Svedberg's coauthored book *The Ultracentrifuge* (1940), was essential to the development of modern life science.

In addition to his work with the ultracentrifuge, Svedberg made many other important scientific contributions, including a seminal study of radioactivity and important participation in the development of the Swedish synthetic rubber industry. Svedberg's scientific endeavors were reported in more than two hundred publications. He received many honors and awards for his efforts, including the Nobel Prize, the Berzelius Medal of the Royal Swedish Academy of Sciences, the Franklin Medal of the Franklin Institute, and honorary doctorates from Harvard University, Oxford University, the Sorbonne, and the University of Delaware.

SIGNIFICANCE

Svedberg's development of the ultracentrifuge had significant impacts on many aspects of chemistry and physics, but nowhere has this device been more generally valuable than in life science research. In fact, most life scientists view the advent of the general availability of ultracentrifuges as one of the outstanding technological events in the field. The great credit given to Svedberg is emphasized by the fact that the sizes of many biological particles, determined by ultracentrifugation, are denoted in "svedberg" units (s units). The impact of ultracentrifugation in the field of biology is made evident by scientists' use of such "s values" to describe many important components of living cells that mediate or participate in life processes. For example, bacterial ribosomes (which mediate the synthesis of proteins) are described as being composed of 30 and 50 s subunits. Other examples of such usage abound throughout the literature of life science.

Furthermore, the ultracentrifuge enabled biologists, biochemists, physicians, and other life scientists to shift the focus of their endeavors from taxonomic and morphologic study of whole organisms to examination of smaller and smaller parts of such organisms. Examples of such research include the isolation of viruses and identification of the basis for their method of attacking cells, the separation of the subcellular organelles (for example, cell nuclei) and the elucidation of their biological functions, the development of understanding of the molecular basis for storage and utilization of hereditary information, the visualization and description of individual protein and nucleic acid molecules, and the discovery of the methodology for carrying out genetic engineering. Truly, the ultracentrifuge hastened the development of life science into molecular biology.

As Howard K. Schachman points out in *Ultracentrifugation in Biochemistry* (1959), the utilization of the ultracentrifuge as a research tool has evolved continually, leading to changes "almost as dramatic as the era beginning in 1923 when Svedberg and his collaborators first began to exploit centrifugal fields for the study of macromolecules and colloid particles." In 1947, fewer than twenty ultracentrifuges were in operation worldwide. By 1959, three hundred sophisticated ultracentrifuges were available to the world scientific community. By the early 2000's, thousands of these instruments were in service, and they had become routine tools—viewed as necessities—for most life science endeavors.

At the beginning of the twenty-first century, scientists can make measurements that were not even conceptualized by the most advanced early researchers in the field of ultracentrifugation. Many new techniques have been added to supplement the classical methodology, and many new aspects of ultracentrifugation have been developed. One outstanding example is the design of zonal rotors that allow large-scale use of ultracentrifugal technique suitable for industrial application.

—*Sanford S. Singer*

FURTHER READING

Bloomfield, Victor A. "Ultracentrifuge." *McGraw-Hill Encyclopedia of Science and Technology*. 6th ed. New York: McGraw-Hill, 1987. Brief summary presents a diagram of an ultracentrifuge, an explanation of the instrument's design, diagrams of common rotors, and an explanation of usage in molecular weight determination by sedimentation equilibrium or sedimentation velocity. Includes suggestions for further reading.

Chervenka, C. H., and L. H. Elrod. *A Manual of Methods for Large Scale Zonal Centrifugation*. Palo Alto, Calif.: Spinco Division of Beckman Instruments, 1972. Practical text describes operating principles, equipment needed, and procedures used in large-scale zonal centrifugation. Also discusses methods used for industrial-scale isolation of viruses, subcellular organelles, proteins, and nucleic acids. Includes useful diagrams.

Claesson, Stig, and Kai O. Pederson. "The (Theodor) Svedberg." In *Dictionary of Scientific Biography*, edited by Charles Coulston Gillispie. New York: Charles Scribner's Sons, 1970. Brief biographical article provides an excellent picture of Svedberg and his contributions to science. Discusses his early study of colloid chemistry and his development of the ultracentrifuge as well as other contributions. Includes references.

Koehler, Christopher S. W. "Developing the Ultracentrifuge." *Today's Chemist at Work*, February, 2003, 63-66. Brief article describes Svedberg's work as well as that of other scientists who contributed to the development of modern ultracentrifuges.

1924

Schachman, Howard K. *Ultracentrifugation in Biochemistry*. New York: Academic Press, 1959. Classical, highly technical treatise on ultracentrifugation describes many aspects of the construction and biochemical use of ultracentrifuges. Thoroughly covers sedimentation velocity, sedimentation equilibrium, and data interpretation. Recommended for readers seeking in-depth coverage of the topic.

Svedberg, Theodor, and Kai O. Pederson. *The Ultracentrifuge*. Oxford, England: Clarendon Press, 1940. Describes the development of the ultracentrifuge by Svedberg and his colleagues' group. Covers most of the theory and methodology of ultracentrifuges of the time and describes the ultracentrifugation of natural

and synthetic colloids. Provides a vivid picture of Svedberg and his work.

Tiselius, Arne, and Stig Claesson. "The Svedberg and Fifty Years of Physical Chemistry in Sweden." *Annual Review of Physical Chemistry* 18 (1967): 1-8. Discusses Svedberg's impact on physical chemistry in Sweden. Concisely covers many aspects of his contributions to the chemistry of colloids, from the development of the ultracentrifuge to his overall role in academic science and technology.

SEE ALSO: 1902: Zsigmondy Invents the Ultramicroscope; Sept., 1915-Feb., 1916: McLean Discovers the Natural Anticoagulant Heparin.

1924
U.S. GOVERNMENT LOSES ITS SUIT AGAINST ALCOA

A circuit court dismissed charges against Aluminum Company of America for acquisition of the Cleveland Products Company's stock, showing that not all monopolies would be prosecuted.

ALSO KNOWN AS: *Alcoa v. Federal Trade Commission*
LOCALE: Philadelphia, Pennsylvania
CATEGORIES: Trade and commerce; laws, acts, and legal history

KEY FIGURES
Alfred Hunt (1855-1899), American metallurgist and president of the Pittsburgh Reduction Company and later Aluminum Company of America
Andrew Mellon (1855-1937), founder of Mellon National Bank and U.S. secretary of the treasury
Pierce Butler (1866-1939), justice of the Third Circuit Court
Charles Martin Hall (1863-1914), American chemist

SUMMARY OF EVENT
Founded in 1902, Aluminum Company of America (commonly known as Alcoa) immediately attained monopoly power in the aluminum industry. After signing a consent decree with the government in 1912, the company was charged by the Federal Trade Commission in 1918, under section 7 of the Clayton Antitrust Act of 1914, for acquiring stocks of the Cleveland Products Company. *Alcoa v. Federal Trade Commission* was dismissed in 1924, leaving Alcoa with monopoly status until it was prosecuted again in 1945.

The formation of Alcoa was a result of a patent for processing aluminum alloys by electrolysis, a process discovered by Charles Martin Hall in 1886. Despite the abundance of bauxite ore, until the discovery of the Hall process, aluminum had been difficult to extract and was used only in expensive costume jewelry. In 1888, a group of Pittsburgh investors including Alfred Hunt, Arthur Vining Davis, and Andrew and Richard B. Mellon formed the Pittsburgh Reduction Company and acquired the right to the Hall patent.

Meanwhile, Alfred and Eugene Cowles of Cowles Electric Smelting Company of Lockport also began using the Hall process to make aluminum alloys. After winning a patent infringement suit against the Cowles brothers in 1893, Pittsburgh Reduction became the sole producer of virgin aluminum by the Hall process until 1906. The Cowles brothers acquired rights to a process similar to Hall's that was patented in 1892 by Charles Schenck Bradley.

By 1891, Pittsburgh Reduction had been recapitalized as a million-dollar company. In 1907, after Hall's patent expired, the company changed its name to Aluminum Company of America to reflect the nature and national scope of its business. Between 1907 and 1910, Alcoa became the sole aluminum producer by purchasing the exclusive right to the Bradley patent from the Cowles brothers.

The Hall and Bradley processes dramatically reduced the cost of aluminum production. A few years after its formation, Pittsburgh Reduction was able to undercut most other smelting companies in aluminum price. By the beginning of the twentieth century, aluminum's price had fallen enough to make commercial aluminum production and use practical for the first time.

Immediately after its formation, Pittsburgh Reduction began the process of vertical integration to ensure the company's position against potential competition once Hall's patent expired. First, it integrated backward by acquiring bauxite mines to secure its own ore supply, aluminum refineries in Illinois, fabricating facilities in New Kensington, and a number of waterpower electricity-generating sites in New York State and Canada. By the late 1890's, Pittsburgh Reduction had purchased about 90 percent of bauxite reserves in the United States. Even after Hunt died during the Spanish-American War, the integration process continued under Richard B. Mellon and later under Arthur Davis, who became the presidents of Alcoa in 1899 and 1910, respectively.

With the increased production of and the creation of a potential market for aluminum, the Pittsburgh company began to make efforts to expand its demand. First, it began to integrate forward, acquiring consumers of its product. In 1901, it formed its own cookware subsidiary, Aluminum Cooking Utensil Company, to promote the use of aluminum cooking utensils. Through its efforts, aluminum came to be used in many household products ranging from cooking utensils and heat conductors to electric wire and cables, gradually replacing other metals, particularly steel.

In the 1910's, mass production of automobiles by the Ford Motor Company, the beginning of the aircraft industry, and the outbreak of World War I increased the demand for aluminum. By 1915, more than half of all aluminum production was devoted to automobile parts. Three years later, Alcoa's annual production reached 150 million pounds, much of the increase a result of military applications of aluminum during World War I.

As a result of increased demand for aluminum and economies of scale achieved through increased production, Alcoa expanded its production at an annual rate of 10 percent throughout the first two decades after its formation. Declining aluminum prices accompanied expanded production. During the 1910's, Alcoa had operations across most of the United States east of the Mississippi, including mining, reduction, fabricating, and electric power sites. It produced about 90 percent of primary aluminum alloy and mill-fabricated products used in the United States, with the other 10 percent accounted for by imports, mostly from Switzerland, France, and Great Britain.

Through its Canadian subsidiary, the Northern Aluminum Company, Alcoa joined European cartels between 1901 and 1912 in order to control its domestic markets. The United States contains only a small amount of the world's bauxite reserves. By the end of the 1920's, through the purchase of bauxite reserves in South America, waterpower plants on waterfalls in eastern Canada, and various aluminum smelting and fabricating companies, Alcoa controlled thirty-two operations in eleven countries.

Even after Hall's patent expired, Alcoa proved successful in maintaining its monopoly position in the aluminum industry. Attempts to enter the industry of primary aluminum failed to challenge Alcoa's dominant position. In 1912, for example, a group of French financiers representing the central sales agency of the French aluminum industry, L'Aluminum Français, organized the Southern Aluminum Company and began constructing aluminum reduction facilities in North Carolina. The company planned to use French imported bauxite ore, which was cheaper than the American counterpart. The outbreak of World War I in August, 1914, however, terminated the French financing and ended construction of the plant. A year later, Alcoa bought the Southern Aluminum Company. The Uihlein family, known for its Schlitz breweries, acquired some bauxite ore in Guyana but soon decided to quit aluminum production. The Guyana ore eventually was sold to Alcoa.

Passage of the Sherman Antitrust Act in 1890 had begun intense public scrutiny of "trusts," or holding companies, and monopolies in the U.S. market. Even though the prosperity of Alcoa was the result of a patent, the legality of the company's monopoly status was no longer warranted after 1907, when Hall's patent expired. Throughout the 1910's and 1920's, Alcoa was able to continue expanding its operation by acquiring aluminum reduction plants, mines, and power-generating facilities not only in the United States but also in Canada, Western Europe, and Scandinavia.

Meanwhile, major victories over big trusts in the early 1910's encouraged the U.S. Department of Justice to prosecute other big corporations for violation of antitrust law. Alcoa was an obvious candidate for such action. In May, 1912, the Justice Department charged Alcoa with violating section 2 of the Sherman Act by monopolizing and restraining trade in the aluminum industry. The next month, the District Court of Western Pennsylvania ruled Alcoa guilty and ordered a consent decree in which Alcoa agreed to drop its participation in the international cartels through its Canadian subsidiary and to end its pol-

1924

icy of restricting bauxite companies from supplying competing aluminum manufacturers. Alcoa denied the charges that it had controlled the price of aluminum and discriminated in price or service of primary aluminum against competing fabricators and in favor of its own subsidiary.

Largely because of abolition of the international agreement, aluminum imports to the United States increased sharply following the decree in 1912. Even though the decree signified a victory for the government and temporarily reduced public hostility against monopoly, it had little effect on Alcoa's industry position. Alcoa remained the dominant firm in the aluminum industry.

In 1914, new major antitrust legislation was passed in the form of the Clayton Antitrust Act and the Federal Trade Commission Act. The new laws resulted in a new government agency, the Federal Trade Commission, which was responsible for enforcing the modified antitrust law. Because the 1912 consent decree had not resulted in dissolution of Alcoa, the government continued to press charges. Between 1912 and 1940, Alcoa was subject to five major antitrust charges and three Federal Trade Commission complaints.

In 1915, the Cleveland Products Company's aluminum rolling mill in Ohio went bankrupt, largely because of the federal government's price control over aluminum sheet during World War I. Alcoa agreed to invest in the plant in return for a controlling stock interest. In 1922, the Federal Trade Commission challenged this transaction for violating section 7 of the Clayton Act, which prohibits both acquisitions of competing firms and interlocking directorates that may potentially lessen competition.

In February, 1923, in the Third Circuit Court of Appeals, the prosecution was sustained by a vote of two to one. Alcoa sold Cleveland Products' stock interest to avoid further charges. Later, Cleveland Products found itself in debt again. Alcoa purchased the company's ingot supply in a government auction, and the Federal Trade Commission filed against the transaction. In 1924, the same judges in the Third Circuit Court, headed by Pierce Butler, unanimously ruled in favor of Alcoa. The court decision demonstrated the judiciary's tendency to be tolerant of monopolies if they were "well behaved." The government temporarily halted its actions against Alcoa.

SIGNIFICANCE

Alcoa's history provides many interesting legal as well as economic lessons. The decision in the 1924 case, together with that in the U.S. Steel case in 1920, reflected

the government's attitude toward existing monopolies. It reaffirmed the courts' principle of "rule of reason," established in the Standard Oil antitrust suit in 1911. It also reflected pressure from the administration favoring Alcoa, in which Secretary of the Treasury Andrew Mellon was a major stockholder. The court's interpretation that not all monopolies are offenses against the antitrust laws extended the era of the rule of reason as the basis of enforcing the antitrust laws. The rule of reason stated that large firms were legal as long as their size was not accompanied by "unreasonable" conduct.

After its victory over the government, Alcoa continued to expand. From 1925 to 1928, it acquired waterpower sites and expanded its reduction capacity in Canada. Alcoa's victory also initiated a new merger movement in many American industries over the next two decades. The president of Alcoa, Arthur Davis, began to refocus the company's attention on domestic operations. In 1928, he divested Alcoa of all overseas operations except for bauxite mines in South America. The assets were sold to Davis's brother, Edward, who operated Aluminum Limited in Montreal, Canada. The Canadian company, which was renamed Alcan Aluminum Limited in 1966, grew to become the dominant aluminum company in Canada.

After its early defeat, the Department of Justice did not give up on Alcoa. Before the second major antitrust suit, which began in 1937, the government made nearly 140 individual charges against Alcoa, including conspiracy with foreign aluminum manufacturers and monopolization of bauxite reserves, waterpower sites, alumina and ingot aluminum, and aluminum castings. In addition, the Federal Trade Commission continued to file charges against Alcoa for violating the 1912 consent decree by delaying shipment of ore supply to competitors and by discriminating in prices. In 1930, all these complaints were dismissed. Alcoa also successfully defended itself against charges by the Baush Company in 1935 and the Sheet Aluminum Corporation in 1934 that it had monopolized the industry through price discrimination.

The second major antitrust suit against Alcoa lasted for eight years, ending with a U.S. Supreme Court decision in 1945 that held Alcoa had monopolized virgin ingot aluminum. That court decision reversed the interpretation in the 1924 case and stressed that the sheer existence of a monopoly can be an offense against antitrust law.

Alcoa provides a classic example of monopoly in the United States. The company was able to maintain its monopoly power in the aluminum industry beyond that warranted by the government patent through the skilled management of full (forward and backward) integration in the aluminum business as well as by maintaining continued expansion of the demand for aluminum. Amid the government hostility against monopoly in the early 1900's, the court ruling in favor of Alcoa reversed more than two decades of rulings against big corporations, notably Standard Oil and American Tobacco. The new judicial attitude toward big corporations led to the rise of many large companies and to mergers in the next few decades. As for the aluminum industry, Alcoa maintained its monopoly status until the second major antitrust suit ended in 1945. The period following that defeat saw the rise of two competitors, Reynolds Metals and Kaiser Aluminum & Chemical Corporation.

—Jim Lee

FURTHER READING

Armentano, Dominick T. *Antitrust and Monopoly: Anatomy of a Policy Failure.* 2d ed. Oakland, Calif.: Independent Institute, 1990. Covers major antitrust lawsuits since the Sherman Act. Discusses their relationship to economic theory and the development of antitrust legislation. Chapter 4 addresses the Alcoa case. Includes an appendix of relevant sections of antitrust laws. Written for an undergraduate audience.

Carr, Charles C. *Alcoa: An American Enterprise.* New York: Rinehart, 1952. Covers the birth of the modern aluminum industry and the history of Alcoa until the end of World War II. Also discusses Alcoa's labor relations and antitrust cases.

Hovenkamp, Herbert. *Federal Antitrust Policy: The Law of Competition and Its Practice.* 2d ed. Eagan, Minn.: West, 1999. Covers nearly all aspects of U.S. antitrust policy in a manner understandable to people with no background in economics. Chapter 2 discusses "history and ideology in antitrust policy."

Parry, Charles W. *Alcoa: A Retrospection.* New York: Newcomen Society of the United States, 1985. A pamphlet containing Parry's speech on the history of Alcoa, beginning with the life of Charles Martin Hall.

Peck, Merton J. *Competition in the Aluminum Industry, 1945-1958.* Cambridge, Mass.: Harvard University Press, 1961. An industry study of supply and demand conditions and of pricing behavior in the industry. Includes a chapter on economic theory and public policy.

Peritz, Rudolph J. R. *Competition Policy in America: History, Rhetoric, Law.* Rev. ed. New York: Oxford University Press, 2001. Explores the influences on U.S. public policy of the concept of free competition. Discusses congressional debates, court opinions, and the work of economic, legal, and political scholars in this area.

Smith, George David. *From Monopoly to Competition: The Transformation of Alcoa, 1888-1986.* Cambridge, England: Cambridge University Press, 1988. Provides interesting discussion of the changing dynamic structure of the aluminum industry over the course of the twentieth century.

Wallace, Donald H. *Market Control in the Aluminum Industry.* Cambridge, Mass.: Harvard University Press, 1937. A thorough study of the early development of the aluminum industry in the United States as well as in Europe before World War II. Includes an appendix that presents a record of the 1924 legal case.

Weiss, Leonard. *Economics and American Industry.* New York: John Wiley & Sons, 1961. Chapter 5 provides good coverage of the evolution of the structure of the aluminum industry. Offers a useful illustration of the industry's pricing behavior with economic models. Valuable for undergraduate economics students.

Whitney, Simon N. *Antitrust Policies: American Experience in Twenty Industries.* 2 vols. New York: Twentieth Century Fund, 1958. Chapter 2 of volume 2 contains succinct discussions of the antitrust cases in the aluminum industry in the first half of the twentieth century and a good end-of-chapter survey of events. Other chapters provide case studies of other major industries. Appendix contains critiques of the studies by economists and government officials.

SEE ALSO: Mar. 14, 1904: U.S. Supreme Court Rules Against Northern Securities; May 15, 1911: U.S. Supreme Court Establishes the "Rule of Reason"; May 29, 1911: U.S. Supreme Court Breaks Up the American Tobacco Company; Sept. 26, 1914: Federal Trade Commission Is Organized; Oct. 15, 1914: Clayton Antitrust Act; Mar. 1, 1920: *United States v. United States Steel Corporation*; Feb. 21, 1927: Eastman Kodak Is Found to Be in Violation of the Sherman Act; Nov., 1932: Antitrust Prosecution Forces RCA to Restructure.

1924

1924-1932
HAWTHORNE STUDIES EXAMINE HUMAN PRODUCTIVITY

The Hawthorne studies, which constituted one of the first major scientific efforts to examine human productivity and motivation, led to the development of the field of industrial sociology.

ALSO KNOWN AS: Hawthorne effect
LOCALE: Cicero, Illinois
CATEGORIES: Business and labor; sociology

KEY FIGURES

George Elton Mayo (1880-1949), American
   psychologist and professor of industrial research
George A. Pennock (fl. twentieth century),
   superintendent of inspection at the Hawthorne plant
T. North Whitehead (1891-1969), American statistician
Fritz Jules Roethlisberger (1898-1974), American
   professor of industrial research
William Lloyd Warner (1898-1970), American
   professor of social anthropology

SUMMARY OF EVENT

The Hawthorne studies were a series of experiments conducted between 1924 and 1932 by Harvard University professors and employees of the Hawthorne Works of the Western Electric Manufacturing Company in Cicero, Illinois. The initial purpose of the experiments was to investigate determinants of worker output. Among the results of the studies, however, were the emergence of the field of industrial sociology and recognition of the importance of social factors in worker behavior.

Three sets of experiments were conducted at the Hawthorne plant: the illumination studies, the relay assembly experiments, and the bank wiring experiments. The illumination studies were conducted between November, 1924, and April, 1927. The primary investigator in these experiments was George A. Pennock, superintendent of inspection at the Hawthorne plant. In cooperation with the National Research Council, Western Electric studied the relationship between worker efficiency and the quality and quantity of illumination in the workplace.

The experimental design included a control group and an experimental group. The first test examined whether efficiency in the experimental group would be increased with increased illumination. The efficiency of the experimental group did increase when the lighting in the group's work area was improved, but the efficiency of

the control group simultaneously improved in similar magnitude. When the reverse hypothesis was tested, with lighting reduced in the experimental group's workplace, the efficiency of both groups again improved. This was contrary to all expectations. Despite continued reductions in illumination, efficiency continued to improve until workers in the experimental group were scarcely able to see what they were doing. Pennock concluded that light was only one of many variables that might affect the rate of production. He further concluded that researchers must control other variables effectively in testing the impact of a given factor postulated to influence productivity. Pennock's report on the illumination studies, published in *Personnel Journal* in 1930, was the first description of the studies at the Hawthorne plant to appear in the management literature.

In 1927, Pennock met George Elton Mayo at a meeting of the National Industrial Conference Board in New York. Pennock noted the parallels between his work at the Hawthorne plant and the experimental work that Mayo presented at the meeting. Ultimately, he convinced Mayo to travel to Illinois and look into the possible reasons for the results documented in the illumination experiments. Mayo did not take on the Hawthorne project alone. He was accompanied by a well-recognized group of his colleagues from Harvard University that included Fritz Jules Roethlisberger, another professor of industrial research; William Lloyd Warner, a social anthropologist; and T. North Whitehead, a statistician. Along with this group of academicians, other leaders from Western Electric became involved in the studies, including the directors of employee relations and personnel research.

The second set of experiments accepted Pennock's earlier conclusions. These new experiments were designed to determine the environmental factors influencing efficiency, using an experimental design that, in the estimation of the research team, adequately controlled all the variables believed to be critical. The researchers hoped that the greater rigidity of control in this set of experiments would overcome the problems of the earlier attempt. They did everything that was within their power to minimize the number of variables involved in determination of the efficiency in question and to control those variables as strictly as possible. They chose to work with a small group and endeavored to observe and record all the changes that took place on an individual basis. Further, there would be no changes in type of work, the work waiting for each operator would be kept constant, no inexperienced operators would be used, no personnel would be shifted, all operators would be involved in the same task, the job would be of short duration, the work would be enduring enough to keep the operators employed throughout the experimental period, the work pace would not be influenced by mechanical equipment, and the subjects would participate voluntarily.

Because of these and other considerations, the experimenters chose the relay assembly operation to test their hypotheses. A separate test room was established in which a workbench for the operators faced the observers' stations. The subjects were selected with the aid of the guidance of two experienced operators who were friendly toward each other and would themselves be subjects. When the experiments were completed, Whitehead had an enormous volume of data for analysis. Despite several years of analysis by Whitehead and his staff, the researchers found no statistically significant correlations between variations in physical circumstances and variations in the output of workers in the relay assembly test room.

It is fair to say that the second experiment at the Hawthorne plant failed to achieve its stated objectives, but it would be unfair to suggest that the researchers failed to learn. They discovered that the six individuals in the experiment became a team, developed a team spirit, and, as a team, cooperated with the experimenters. Further, the close supervision they received seemed to have positive effects, and, as a result, Western Electric began an interviewing program to improve the supervision of its workers. This interviewing program yielded many fruitful insights into employee morale, particularly the benefits of eliminating employee fears of authority. Further, the program documented the impacts of outside concerns on employee morale and led to the belief that satisfaction or dissatisfaction with work is in part a function of an individual's position or status within both the organization and society. The influences of the worker's social environments within the plant and outside the plant were thus recognized as key determinants of worker behavior.

The third set of experiments at the Hawthorne plant sought to use nonintrusive observation and interview processes to explore informal social influences on worker behavior. This set of studies used a bank wiring observation room, selected by the researchers specifically to allow effective study of group influences. The researchers collected baseline data on worker behavior

prior to placing the study group under observation. Six months of observation then ensued. Individual potential for productivity was measured through dexterity and intelligence tests, among others. The conclusions of the bank wiring experiment underscored the importance of informal group controls on productivity. The researchers noted that the group controls had greater influences on behavior than did piece-rate incentives or management expectations, that the group itself actually set the rate of production informally, along with many other norms, and that group controls had greater influences on behavior than did individual capacities.

SIGNIFICANCE

The field of industrial sociology was created during the Hawthorne experiments. The recognition of the importance of social systems to worker behavior is clearly the one greatest impact of the years of effort put forth at the Hawthorne plant by the researchers from Harvard University and Western Electric. Industrial sociology later became one of the key scientific foundations supporting an understanding of labor productivity. Without the contributions of this field, the development of management thought would have been vastly different in the remainder of the twentieth century.

The "Hawthorne effect" is the common name given to the result that Pennock observed in the first set of experiments at the Hawthorne plant. The Hawthorne effect is the change that takes place in individuals' behavior when they perceive that they are being treated differently from others. This explains why efficiency improved no matter how the illumination was varied: The workers perceived that they were receiving special treatment. Contrary to popular belief, however, the discovery of the Hawthorne effect was not the most important finding of the Hawthorne studies. The Hawthorne effect is only one manifestation of the experiments' greater contribution, which was the discovery of the general influence of social systems on worker behavior.

The practice of management was significantly altered as a result of the experiments' demonstration of the impact of social systems on workers. It is generally recognized that the era of scientific management came to an end following the Hawthorne studies. Traditional managerial beliefs and assumptions of the day, such as the Machiavellian and laissez-faire assumption that individuals act primarily out of enlightened self-interest, were rejected as a result of the studies. Scientifically designing work for the individual and scientifically selecting the ideal individual to perform the work, as advocated by

1924

Frederick Winslow Taylor, were no longer viewed as adequate to ensure efficient production.

As old ideas were rejected, new ideas were endorsed. The Hawthorne studies ushered in a "human relations" or "social man" era in the workplace. Industrial sociology provided a new and different way of looking at motivation and productivity, changing the nature of management-labor relations. The focus of theoretical attention was shifted from the individual to the group and from determinants of worker productivity to determinants of worker motivation. The Hawthorne studies made clear the importance of human and social skills to effective management. Workers no longer were believed to be motivated solely by wages, and managers came to recognize that antagonistic labor relations practices could have detrimental long-term effects on productivity.

Managerial practices and patterns of workplace supervision certainly changed as a result of the Hawthorne studies. It also can be argued that the studies changed industrial engineering and its applications of time-and-motion studies, industrial psychology and physiology, with their emphasis on the individual, and even economic theory. Mayo, in fact, endeavored to draw conclusions from the Hawthorne studies that extended well beyond managerial issues to societal processes. In his view, rapid industrial growth and rapid technological innovation in manufacturing, use of large-scale mass-production systems, and impersonal relations within the workplace had disturbed the "communal integrity" of the United States. Cultural and societal social development had not kept pace with technological progress, and these factors required attention. These broad conclusions regarding society were not validated by the Hawthorne studies, but as principal investigator in the studies, Mayo gained prominence and a platform to advance his theories.

Some have described the relay assembly experiment performed at the Hawthorne plant as the first great scientific experiment in industry. The Hawthorne studies verified the value of applying the scientific process and experimentation in the development of management theory. As a consequence, the development of management theory since that time has required a basis in valid scientific experimental projects. Dogmatic prescriptions such as Lillian Gilbreth's *The Psychology of Management* (1914) no longer suffice. The Hawthorne studies were not minor investigations of esoteric topics: Their impact on all managerial disciplines is widely recognized to be immense.

—*Mark D. Hanna*

FURTHER READING

Faunce, William A., ed. *Readings in Industrial Sociology*. New York: Appleton-Century-Crofts, 1967. Collection contains the landmark works in the field of industrial sociology, including early and modern writings.

George, Claude S., Jr. *The History of Management Thought*. Englewood Cliffs, N.J.: Prentice-Hall, 1968. Comprehensive treatment of the history of management thought from prehistoric times through the 1960's. Provides an outstanding description of the ancient history of managerial thought and developments in the twentieth century. Includes a time line of critical events.

Korman, Abraham K. *Industrial and Organizational Psychology*. Englewood Cliffs, N.J.: Prentice-Hall, 1971. A thorough review, geared toward college students of the subject, of the psychological theory and research relating to industrial and organizational psychology. Introductory chapter presents a succinct yet complete description of the development of industrial and organizational psychology.

Miller, Delbert C., and William H. Form. *Industrial Sociology*. 3d ed. New York: Harper & Row, 1980. An outstanding and thorough treatment of industrial sociology and its development. Includes many figures and foldouts.

Miner, John B. *Organizational Behavior: Foundations, Theories, and Analyses*. New York: Oxford University Press, 2002. Comprehensive discussion of organizational behavior includes background on early research in the field. Chapter 2 addresses Mayo's work and the Hawthorne studies. Includes bibliographic references and index.

Rose, Michael. *Industrial Behaviour: Theoretical Development Since Taylor*. London: Allen Lane, 1975. Divided chronologically into five parts: "Taylorism," "Human Factor Industrial Psychology," "Human Relations," "Some Methodological and Theoretical Consequences of the Tavistock Institute of Human Relations," and "Action Approaches." Focuses on the development of theories regarding management of the human element of organizations.

Trahair, Richard C. S. *The Humanist Temper*. 1984. Reprint. New Brunswick, N.J.: Transaction, 2005. Exhaustive personal biography of George Elton Mayo. Reprint edition features a foreword by leadership expert Abraham Zaleznik.

Wren, Daniel A. *The Evolution of Management Thought*. 5th ed. New York: John Wiley & Sons, 2004. Provides definitive treatment of the development of early management thought, the scientific management era, the "social man" era, and the modern era. Includes an extensive bibliography.

SEE ALSO: Mar., 1914: Gilbreth Publishes *The Psychology of Management*; July, 1916: Fayol Publishes

General and Industrial Management; Mar. 14, 1923: American Management Association Is Established; 1925: McKinsey Founds a Management Consulting Firm; Jan. 1, 1925: Bell Labs Is Formed; 1938: Barnard Publishes *The Functions of the Executive*.

1924-1976
HOWARD HUGHES BUILDS A BUSINESS EMPIRE

A young aviation hero and one of the wealthiest men in the United States, Howard Hughes drew on his fortune to create a business and political empire.

LOCALE: United States

CATEGORIES: Business and labor; trade and commerce; government and politics

KEY FIGURES

Howard Hughes (1905-1976), billionaire who created a controversial business empire

Howard Hughes, Sr. (1869-1924), founder of the Hughes Tool Company

Robert Aime Maheu (b. 1917), Central Intelligence Agency operative and a longtime Hughes influence peddler

Hubert H. Humphrey (1911-1978), vice president of the United States and presidential candidate who received secret campaign funds from Maheu and Hughes

Richard Nixon (1913-1994), president of the United States, 1969-1974

Frank William Gay (b. 1920), executive who worked for Hughes

SUMMARY OF EVENT

The Hughes cone bit, an ingeniously engineered rock drill patented in 1909 by Howard Hughes, Sr., established the Hughes Tool Company of Houston, Texas, as the sole supplier of a tool essential to the world's petroleum industry. Described as one of the greatest inventions affecting that industry, the cone bit was the basis for the Hughes fortune. Howard Hughes, Jr., inherited the Hughes Tool Company in 1924 and subsequently controlled it until its sale in 1972. The company provided the profits, credit, financial leverage, and basis of influence that made possible the assemblage and maintenance of his business empire.

Young Hughes worshiped his father and enjoyed a sheltered upbringing. From his early years, he was shy and awkward, obsessed with the state of his health, and indifferent to his educational opportunities. He dropped out of college, showing few signs of independence or indications of purpose. Howard Hughes, Jr., was an apparently unpromising, although good-looking, eighteen-year-old millionaire at the time of his inheritance. Within a few years, however, Hughes's growing (if carefully disguised) egomania, his ruthless instrumentalism, and his iron will brought him national attention because of his attempts to conquer Hollywood. Beginning in the 1920's and continuing into the 1940's, he produced a series of controversial films, including *Hell's Angels* (1930), *Scarface* (1932), and more than a dozen other films with which his name and those of stars he ostensibly created were identified. In 1947, he bought a controlling interest in Radio-Keith-Orpheum (RKO), then later sold it and founded his own studio. His playboy activities as well as his reserved manner, which eventually devolved into phobias and reclusiveness, further ensured public fascination with his exploits and the mystique that soon surrounded him.

It was as a flyer that Hughes joined the ranks of the nation's heroes. Although his father had wanted Hughes to become an engineer, young Hughes's maiden flight in a Curtiss seaplane in 1921 revealed what became his sole undying passions: flying and aviation. By 1932, having acquired an Army Boeing pursuit plane from the Department of Commerce and work space in Burbank, California, leased from Lockheed Aircraft Corporation, Hughes established the Hughes Aircraft Company. He modified the plane into his H-1, eventually the most advanced aircraft of its time. Decades later, Hughes Aircraft was one of the country's leading defense contractors.

The 1920's and 1930's were marked by the public's infatuation with Hollywood and captivation by the accomplishments of fliers and aircraft designers, Hughes included. Hughes, and indirectly his aircraft company, earned his earliest aviation encomiums by setting speed and distance records. In 1934 and 1935, for example, fly-

1924

ing his H-1, he garnered first place in various air meets and established new short-distance "flight over land" speed records. In 1935 and 1936, he broke records for transcontinental flights and won the coveted Harmon Trophy.

These accomplishments paled in 1938 when, piloting a twin-engine Lockheed, Hughes circled the world in less than four days, eclipsing the record set for that feat by veteran flyer Wiley Post. All these flights and the tests that preceded them were dangerous, and Hughes experienced three serious crashes. Like his wartime construction of the world's largest airplane, the *Spruce Goose*, all were immensely expensive. All these efforts and achievements, as Hughes then acknowledged, were made possible by the expert teams of designers and mechanics that his tool company fortune allowed him to enlist.

Hughes also displayed a more important, if less apparent, ability to sell. His capacity to wheel and deal, to marshal and manipulate the hopes, ambitions, and loyalties of a wide range of people, and to invoke his public image to influence the curiosity of the media gave him tremendous power in his business affairs. The Hughes Tool Company, the operations of which he largely ignored, reliably supplied his capital; his personal talents helped bring together a remarkable array of enterprises.

By the early 1950's, in addition to his control over the economically invaluable tool company, Hughes owned Hollywood's Hughes Production Company and Hughes Aircraft. By 1944, he had acquired 45 percent of the stock in Trans World Airlines (TWA), a major international carrier with exclusive foreign and domestic routes. TWA became his favorite possession, one to which he made significant initial contributions. He helped conceive the Lockheed-built Constellation, the fastest long-range piston-driven passenger aircraft in the United States when it entered service in 1946. He selected other

Howard Hughes (center, in hat and facing camera) is greeted by a crowd at Floyd Bennett Airport in New York in July, 1938, after setting a new speed record for an around-the-world flight. (AP/Wide World Photos)

outstanding aircraft for the TWA fleet, and his salesmanship, publicity, and governmental influence were exploited on TWA's behalf.

During the 1960's, Hughes increased his holdings. Through stock ownership in the Atlas Corporation, for example, he gained control in 1961 of Northeast Airlines, a regional carrier. After moving to Las Vegas in 1966, he spent $65 million in one year acquiring four of the Nevada city's larger hotel-casinos and hundreds of acres of valuable real estate that were available for more casinos and housing subdivisions as well as an air charter service (Alamo Airlines), North Las Vegas Airport and its ancillary motel and dining facilities, the KLAS television station, several luxury ranches, and two hundred Nevada mining claims. Such acquisitions made Hughes Nevada's biggest private landowner. He reputedly was the nation's wealthiest individual.

SIGNIFICANCE

The Hughes empire, from its inception until its founder's death in 1976, bore the imprint and suffered the consequences of Hughes's increasingly distorted perceptions and priorities. Hughes paid scant attention to the chief personnel or to the fundamental operations of most of his enterprises. Few of his top executives or his chief aides ever met or spoke to him directly; other key figures may have done so only once or twice in a quarter of a century. This was true even for the Hughes Tool Company in Houston, the principal source of his wealth and operating capital. He never visited the company after 1938. Fortunately, the firm for years was under the capable direction of Noah Dietrich.

Hughes owned or controlled what at best was a mixed collection of enterprises. The Hughes Tool Company pumped out capital almost in complete isolation from Hughes's other ventures. The general affairs and accountings of the other business interests were recorded for Hughes by Frank William Gay, a Mormon whom Hughes dissuaded from an academic career when he recruited him in 1947. Gay's job was to reorganize and manage Hughes's inconspicuous Romaine Street operational base in Los Angeles. Gay and his Romaine Street staff specialized in catering to Hughes's personal eccentricities, including his phobia about germs, his passion for starlets, and his drug addiction. The staff also handled the paperwork generated by Hughes's complex business adventures, legal battles, secret political dealings, and ongoing business and governmental negotiations. Like the tool company, Gay's Romaine Street operations were rarely visited by Hughes.

HUGHES AND HOLLYWOOD

In addition to his other business interests, Howard Hughes produced these Hollywood films:

Release Date	Title
1926	*Everybody's Acting*
	Swell Hogan
1927	*Two Arabian Knights*
1928	*The Mating Call*
	The Racket
1930	*Hell's Angels*
1931	*The Age for Love*
	The Front Page
1932	*Cock of the Air*
	Scarface
	Sky Devils
1943	*Behind the Rising Sun*
	The Outlaw
1947	*The Sin of Harold Diddlebock*
1950	*The Tattooed Stranger*
	Vendetta
1951	*His Kind of Woman*
	Two Tickets to Broadway
	The Whip Hand
1952	*The Las Vegas Story*
	Macao
1953	*Louisiana Territory*
	Second Chance
1954	*The French Line*
1955	*Son of Sinbad*
	Underwater!
1956	*The Conqueror*
1957	*Jet Pilot*

Hughes operated under the assumption that anyone could be bought. Friendless and egocentric, he authorized—or, out of negligence, permitted—lavish salaries and perquisites for his immediate aides and even for a number of associates with whom he never deigned to meet. In exchange, such persons were expected to behave as if their lives and loyalties were fully under his control. They might be called on to minister to his whims, to suborn politicians, or to conduct clandestine negotiations on his behalf. Through the years, he fortuitously attracted people of genuine talent to his organizations, few of whom stayed for long. He was less interested in utilizing engineering skills, scientific training, or executive abilities than he was in manipulating subjects.

Accordingly, by the end of the 1960's, Hughes's im-

1924

mediate aides and those with whom he did business were largely an unsavory lot. They included Las Vegas's Mafia casino owners, corrupt judges, cash-hungry politicians, sycophantic newspaper publishers, purveyors of worthless mining claims, quack doctors who plied Hughes with codeine and other narcotics (and were presumably culpable for his death), and pliable public officials, including a Nicaraguan dictator, a Bahamian president, U.S. attorney general John Mitchell, Vice President Hubert H. Humphrey, and President Richard Nixon.

Robert Aime Maheu symbolized much that was characteristic of all these men, namely, an addiction to influence, power, and wealth. Maheu was an intelligence agent for the United States during World War II, a former agent of the Federal Bureau of Investigation, and an employee of the Central Intelligence Agency, for which he had been detailed to mastermind the assassination of Cuban dictator Fidel Castro. He was familiar with organized crime figures and enjoyed a large number of legal, business, and governmental contacts that were deployed on behalf of Hughes's firms.

Although he never met Hughes and eventually would sue him, Maheu was nevertheless an important front man and dealer for Hughes during the 1960's. He was one of Hughes's chosen instruments in the Northeast Airlines buyout. For a time, Maheu directed Hughes's fight against the multimillion-dollar lawsuit TWA had filed against Hughes, and he negotiated with crime-syndicate acquaintances for Hughes in his Las Vegas ventures. It was Maheu who arranged for influence money to be supplied to Hubert Humphrey and, through Bebe Robozo, to Nixon's presidential campaign. With such dubious figures on salary, Hughes the hustler was himself hustled. He increasingly took to self-imposed, almost hermetic seclusion. His lust for unquestioning loyalty and control actually cost him tens of millions of dollars that unaccountable associates bled from him.

Nearly all of Hughes's acquisitions lost money while he was in nominal control. All of Hughes's wartime ventures, for example, were expensive failures. Even the fabulous *Spruce Goose* proved too large to qualify as a museum piece. Similarly, while its electronic missile teams performed well, Hughes Aircraft consistently incurred heavy losses until Hughes sold it, after which it recovered sensationally. RKO and TWA also lost money, as did other constituents of Hughes's empire. In addition, in his quest for influence Hughes badly tainted the nation's political process. The aviation hero ended life as a rich but largely unloved man whom few admired other than for his wealth.

—*Clifton K. Yearley*

FURTHER READING

Ambrose, Stephen. *Nixon: The Education of a Politician 1913-1962*. New York: Simon & Schuster, 1987. The best portrait of Nixon and those around him. Good for context on the political world with which Hughes interacted. Chapters 26 and 27 deal with Hughes's money and influence. An excellent historical account.

Barlett, Donald L., and James B. Steele. *Empire: The Life, Legend, and Madness of Howard Hughes*. New York: W. W. Norton, 1979. Detailed, authoritative, and objective. Contains photos, a chronology, appendixes, chapter notes, and an unusually fine index.

Brown, Peter Harry, and Pat H. Broeske. *Howard Hughes: The Untold Story*. Cambridge, Mass.: Da Capo Press, 2004. The authors focus on Hughes's personal life, particularly on his romantic entanglements and his more hedonistic exploits.

Dean, John W. *Blind Ambition: The White House Years*. New York: Simon & Schuster, 1976. An insider's sketch of the character of those in government. Chapter 3 treats specifics of Hughes's involvement in the Nixon administration. No notes or bibliography. Useful index.

Drosnin, Michael. *Citizen Hughes: The Power, the Money, and the Madness*. New York: Broadway Books, 2004. Covers less ground than Barlett and Steele's book but was the first to use thousands of documents stolen from Hughes's headquarters as well as a thief's testimonial. More information on personal relations between Hughes and Maheu. Good essays, photos of documents, and a useful index.

Lukas, J. Anthony. *Nightmare: The Underside of the Nixon Years*. New York: Viking Press, 1976. Lukas was the first journalist to explore Hughes's involvement in the Watergate scandal and the extent of Hughes's influence with the CIA, administrative agencies, and politicians. Very valuable and an easy read.

SEE ALSO: Jan. 10, 1901: Discovery of Oil at Spindletop; 1908: Hughes Revolutionizes Oil Well Drilling; 1930's-1940's: Studio System Dominates Hollywood Filmmaking; 1931-1932: Gangster Films Become Popular.

January 25-February 5, 1924
FIRST WINTER OLYMPIC GAMES

The International Winter Sports Week, sponsored by the International Olympic Committee, brought together athletes from sixteen nations to compete in sixteen events. It was so successful that two years later it was declared to have been the First Winter Olympic Games.

ALSO KNOWN AS: International Winter Sports Week
LOCALE: Chamonix, France
CATEGORIES: Sports; diplomacy and international relations

KEY FIGURES
Sonja Henie (1912-1969), Norwegian figure skater and later a Hollywood movie star
Thorleif Haug (1894-1934), Norwegian cross-country skier
Gillis Grafström (1893-1938), Swedish figure skater
Jacob Tullin Thams (1898-1954), Norwegian ski jumper
Clas Thunberg (1893-1973), Finnish speed skater
Julius Skutnabb (1889-1965), Finnish speed skater
Anders Haugen (1888-1984), American ski jumper
Pierre de Coubertin (1863-1937), French politician who was the driving force behind the revival of the Olympic Games

SUMMARY OF EVENT
Although Pierre de Coubertin's vision for the Olympics was rooted in the sports of the ancient Greek Olympic Games, organizers of the first modern Olympic Games wanted to hold Winter Games as well as Summer Games. Most of the nations that would have participated in the Winter Games, however, already held similar events. The success of the Nordic Games, held in Stockholm, meant that the Norwegians, Swedes, and Finns resisted the organization of a competing event. France sponsored a Winter Sports Week at Chamonix in 1908 that drew two thousand spectators, and another in 1912 brought twelve thousand people to Chamonix.

As a result of the appeal generated by France's Winter Sports Week, in 1922 the International Olympic Committee voted in favor of an International Winter Sports Week, which would be held in Chamonix in 1924 to correspond with the Summer Games being held that year in Paris. The Scandinavians continued to resist, but when the Games finally began on January 25, 1924, the Norwegians, Finns, and Swedes were there. Although the

Scandinavians were expected to dominate the Games, the very first event was won by an American, speed skater Charles Jewtraw, who upset the powerful Finnish speed skater Clas Thunberg and Norwegian Oskar Olsen in the 500-meter race. Overall, however, the Scandinavians did dominate the Games. Norway and Finland won twenty-eight of the forty-three medals available, and Norway alone won eleven of the twelve total medals in the four Nordic events. Finland won the other, a bronze, and together the two nations won fifteen of the sixteen speed skating races (one of which ended in a tie).

Among the medal winners were some of the most impressive individual performances of the Chamonix Olympic Games. Finnish speed skater Thunberg won three gold medals, one silver medal, and two bronze medals, and one of his gold medals was for the combination of all four events. His teammate, Julius Skutnabb, won a gold, a silver, and a bronze (in the combined event), in spite of the fact that he was thirty-four years old and that his career had been interrupted by World War I. Norwegian Jacob Tullin Thams became the first Olympic ski-jump champion, and the Norwegian team dominated this event. Thams's teammate, Thorleif Haug, was Norway's biggest winner: He earned gold medals in the 50-kilometer cross-country, the 18-kilometer cross-country, and the combined cross-country and ski jump. He also won a bronze medal in the ski jump.

Although the Norwegians and Finns won many of the medals, the single most impressive display of athletic ability was offered by the Canadian ice-hockey team. In their first game, the Canadians beat Switzerland 33-0, and followed that win with a 30-0 triumph over Czechoslovakia, a 22-0 victory over Sweden, and a 19-2 victory over Great Britain. In the finals, they defeated the team from the United States 6-1 and won the tournament with a 110-3 scoring advantage over their opponents.

The most celebrated participant to emerge from the Chamonix Games did not win any medals. Sonja Henie, an eleven-year-old Norwegian figure skater, was such a novice that she frequently paused in her freestyle routine to skate to the sidelines and ask her coach a question. By 1927, however, she had begun a series of ten consecutive World Championships that was punctuated by gold medals at the Winter Olympic Games of 1928, 1932, and 1936. Her fame soared: By the early 1930's, she needed a police escort during appearances in Europe and the United States. After her skating career ended, she be-

1924

came a Hollywood movie star and toured with ice shows, inspiring generations of figure skaters from the United States and establishing figure skating as one of the most popular sports of the Winter Olympic Games.

At the Chamonix Games, the standard in figure skating was set by an innovative Swede named Gillis Grafström. Grafström changed the nature of figure skating from a series of gliding dance routines to an athletic sport by inventing jumps and spins—the spiral, the change-sit spin, the flying-sit spin—that altered the routines in dramatic ways. After winning gold at Antwerp, when figure skating was an event in the Summer Games, Grafström won again at Chamonix. He would subsequently take gold medals at St. Moritz, Switzerland, and Lake Placid, New York, making him the most successful figure skater in Olympic history.

The medal ceremony for all events was held at the closing of the Games. Since many of the medal winners had already left Chamonix, at the ceremony their medals were presented to other members from their delegations. At the same event, Pierre de Coubertin, the father of the modern Olympic movement and winner of an Olympic literary prize at the 1912 Summer Games, presented a prize for alpinism to Charles Bruce, who had led a 1922 expedition that tried to climb Mount Everest.

It was 1974 before the final medal was awarded for the Chamonix Games. During the ski-jumping competition, an American named Anders Haugen had finished fourth, behind three Norwegians, after losing style points on an extraordinary jump. When the Norwegian team met in 1974 on the fiftieth anniversary of their victory, they discovered a calculation error that showed Haugen had actually finished in third place. In a remarkable demonstration of the Olympic sprit, the widow of the bronze medal winner, Nordic champion Thorleif Haug, insisted that Haugen be brought to Norway at age eighty-six and awarded the bronze medal (still in her possession) for his jump fifty years earlier.

Competitors Sonja Henie and Gillis Grafström at the Olympic Games in Chamonix, France. (AP/Wide World Photos)

SIGNIFICANCE

The International Winter Sports Week was so successful that in 1926 the event was designated the First Winter Olympic Games. The success ultimately proved to be significantly broader, however, as the first Winter Olympics (and its predecessors) showcased skills that had long been developed by Scandinavian armies and residents of cold-weather climates. Because the competitions were held exclusively on ice or snow, for many years participation in the quadrennial Games was largely confined to countries with long, cold winters. As the Winter Games grew more popular, however, nations began to adapt local conditions or build facilities in which athletes could train for Winter Olympic events. As a result, the 1928

Games in St. Moritz saw an 84 percent increase in participants, and the numbers of athletes competing continued to grow in the years to follow.

—*Devon Boan*

FURTHER READING

Greenspan, Bud. *Frozen in Time: The Greatest Moments at the Winter Olympics*. Toronto: Stoddart, 1997. More than fifty-five brief but dramatic accounts of memorable events during the Winter Olympics by the Olympic movement's most famous film historian and documentarian. Includes the story of Anders Haugen.

Strait, Raymond. *Queen of Ice, Queen of Shadows: The Unsuspected Life of Sonja Henie*. Bath, England: Scarborough House, 1990. A candid and inspiring, although sometimes dark and disturbing, biography of Henie. Focuses on the effect of early fame and her father's expectations on her personal development.

Wallechinsky, David. *The Complete Book of the Winter Olympics, 2006 Edition: Turin*. Toronto: Sport- Classic Books, 2005. An exhaustive reference work with complete descriptions and histories of the events of the Winter Olympics, including lists of winners for each event throughout Olympic history.

Wukovits, John. *The Encyclopedia of the Winter Olympics*. Princeton, N.J.: Franklin Watts, 2002. A concise introduction to the history of the Winter Games, its events, and its most celebrated participants, including Sonja Henie.

SEE ALSO: July 1, 1903: First Tour de France; Oct. 1-13, 1903: Baseball Holds Its First World Series; Dec. 26, 1908: First Black Heavyweight Boxing Champion; May 5-July 27, 1912: Stockholm Hosts the Summer Olympics; June, 1922: New Wimbledon Tennis Stadium Is Dedicated; Aug. 6, 1926: Ederle Swims the English Channel; July 6, 1933: First Major League Baseball All-Star Game; Aug. 1-16, 1936: Germany Hosts the Summer Olympics; Sept. 17, 1938: First Grand Slam of Tennis.

February, 1924
IBM CHANGES ITS NAME AND PRODUCT LINE

The conglomerate Computing-Tabulating-Recording signaled a new corporate direction when it discarded its old name and became International Business Machines.

LOCALE: New York, New York
CATEGORIES: Computers and computer science; science and technology; organizations and institutions

KEY FIGURES

Thomas J. Watson, Sr. (1874-1956), general manager of the company that became IBM
Thomas J. Watson, Jr. (1914-1993), general manager who took over from his father and led IBM into the computer age
Charles Ranlett Flint (1850-1934), promoter who organized CTR and selected Watson to be its leader
Herman Hollerith (1860-1929), inventor of census tabulating machines, which became CTR's most important product
George Fairchild (1854-1924), first chairman of CTR, who left most of the real work to Watson

SUMMARY OF EVENT

In 1910, Charles Ranlett Flint created Computing-Tabulating-Recording (CTR). Flint was a colorful promoter who had earlier created American Woolen, United States Rubber, and American Chicle; he was also a founder of the Automobile Club of America. Today CTR would be called a conglomerate, given that its divisions were largely unrelated to one another. International Time Recording manufactured workplace time clocks and time cards onto which workers punched their hours of arrival and departure. The Computing Scale Company of America's primary product was a scale that came equipped with a chart enabling a clerk to calculate the price of an item from its weight and price per pound. Tabulating Machine Company produced machines used to tabulate results from the 1890 census and the cards on which information was punched.

The last of these companies was to prove the key element of CTR's success. Its founder, inventor Herman Hollerith, worked at the U.S. Census Bureau, where difficulties had developed in the tabulation of the 1880 census. It seemed clear that unless some mechanical way could be invented to speed calculations, the 1890 counting would take more than ten years to complete and would thus continue into the 1900 census year. Hollerith developed a machine that punched census information such as race, sex, age, and address onto cards. The cards could be fed into a sorter that would group them according to any desired set of data that had been punched. An operator could then count them, thus completing the task. The machines were a huge success, but the government insisted on leasing them rather than buying them outright. Hollerith agreed to this arrangement, noting later that although the machines eventually turned a profit, the real returns came from the sale of the punch cards on which data were recorded.

Flint considered International Time to be the most promising of the CTR divisions, so that division's executives dominated the first CTR board of directors. Hollerith was given the job of chief engineer and was not consulted when the company's officers were chosen. Flint arranged for a $7 million loan to get the company started. The loan had a term of thirty years at an interest rate of 6 percent, high by the standards of the time. Lenders apparently considered the company a relatively high-risk venture. As the former president of International Time, George Fairchild was a logical choice for CTR's first chairman. Fairchild had been elected to the House of Representatives in 1906 and had just been named by President William Howard Taft to a ministerial post in Mexico. Fairchild thus became the firm's nominal leader, but Frank Kondolf, the former chief operating officer at International Time, performed the day-to-day management. Kondolf did not impress Flint, who embarked on a search for another leader.

Flint discovered Thomas J. Watson, today considered to be one of America's premier businessmen. Watson came from the small town of Painted Post, near Corning, in Upper New York. After holding several jobs in sales, in 1895 Watson accepted a trainee position at National Cash Register (NCR), where the chief executive officer, John Patterson, was a pioneering figure in the fledgling business-machine industry. Patterson extolled the role of salesperson, which he considered to be the key role in the firm. At a time when salespeople were considered to be somewhat disreputable, NCR trained its sales force to be straightforward, prompt, and solicitous of customers' interests. Watson learned well and quickly rose through the ranks to become NCR's star salesman in upper New York.

In 1903, Watson was summoned to NCR's Dayton, Ohio, headquarters and told of a plan to smash the company's competition. He would establish a company, to be known as Watson's Cash Register & Second-Hand Exchange, that would undersell competitors and force them out of the business. He began operating in New York City and then went on to Philadelphia and Chicago. The company was quite successful, but its secret ties with NCR constituted a violation of antitrust laws.

In 1910, American Cash Register filed antitrust complaints against NCR. Two years later, the federal government joined in the case, charging Patterson, Watson, and others with criminal violations. They were found guilty in 1913 and sentenced to fines and prison terms. Appeals followed, and in 1915 the courts found deficiencies and unfairness in the original trial, ordering a new one. The matter was eventually dropped, but in the process Patterson and Watson had quarreled. Patterson had fired Watson, who now was available to Flint and CTR.

Flint offered Watson the post of general manager at a salary of $25,000 per year until the criminal charges were settled. He accepted and began work in May, 1914. After an examination of the CTR businesses, Watson decided that Tabulating Machine Company had the most promising line of products. In addition to the general managership of CTR, he assumed the presidency of that company. After the antitrust suit against him was dropped, he became president of CTR as well.

Watson placed his own men in positions of leadership and devised new markets for tabulating machines. The Hollerith model was employed by corporations to keep inventories and by railroads to maintain schedules. The machines were leased, and the cards used to operate them were sold outright. As with the census machines, the leases provided a steady cash flow and sales of the cards supplied large profits. By 1918, CTR was producing thirty million cards monthly for the Midwest alone. All the while, sales of time clocks and scales stagnated.

Fairchild died in December, 1924, and Watson assumed the title of chairman along with the position of chief executive officer. Earlier in the year, he had decided to change the company's name to reflect its new business concentration. In 1917, he had christened the company's Canadian subsidiary International Business Machines. In February, 1924, he replaced CTR's corporate designation with the same name.

SIGNIFICANCE

The alteration of a company's name is hardly a major event in itself, but CTR's change signaled a change in corporate direction. In time, scales and clocks would be discarded from the company's product lines, and Watson would concentrate on business machines.

Under Watson's leadership, IBM's engineers designed accounting and other machines, breaking through into new areas. IBM purchased a small company that manufactured electric typewriters and made it the leader in a growing field. Columbia University professors conceived a plan to develop multiple-choice tests that could be taken on standard forms and graded by machine. Watson provided the researchers with materials and machines, and out of this came standardized tests graded by machines—IBM machines. The company also produced millions of forms to be used with various machines.

IBM produced large calculators capable of performing computations in minutes that previously had taken hours. It developed machines to process payrolls, with the payroll checks created on IBM cards. During World War II, IBM created machines for the military. By the war's end, IBM had annual revenues of $142 million and earnings of $10.9 million. Remington Rand, a competitor in some fields, had sales of $133 million but earnings of only $5.3 million.

Remington Rand then purchased UNIVAC, a small entity attempting to develop the first computer, from American Totalizator. Remington Rand and its large electromechanical computers won the contract for the 1950 census from a stunned IBM. Thomas J. Watson, Jr., who had come into contact with military computers during the war, urged his father to develop an interest in them. The elder Watson demurred. Research indicated that at best only a dozen or so computers might be sold. Besides, IBM was the master in large calculators, which really were computers without programs or memories. He wondered about the wisdom of giving up a leadership position to devote more energy to an untested technology. The younger Watson persisted, and IBM entered the computer arena. With superior research and salesmanship, IBM drew close to UNIVAC and then surpassed it. In 1953, UNIVAC had most of the computer market; by 1955, IBM had the greatest share of placements.

Other firms soon entered the field, including Burroughs, NCR, Honeywell, General Electric, and RCA. There were also some new companies to contend with, led by Control Data, Digital Equipment, and Scientific Data Systems (soon to be acquired by Xerox).

In the mid-1960's, IBM created a new line of data-processing equipment known as the 360 series. Based on integrated circuits, these machines would make obsolete many highly successful machines then in production. Tom Watson, Jr., was taking the same kind of gamble as general manager of IBM that he had when entering the computer market. The line was a success, and it increased IBM's lead over its rivals. Several left the field or sold off their computer operations, but this prompted the appearance of new companies that attempted to emulate IBM machines and sell them at lower prices. In response, IBM accelerated the introduction of new mainframe computers, and the upstarts faltered. They could not copy the IBM products quickly enough to earn a profit before IBM introduced a new product that made the old copies unsalable.

Watson retired in 1971 and was succeeded in turn by Vincent Learson, Frank Cary, John Opel, and John Akers. IBM remained the industry leader into the 1970's. Although rivals complained that their machines delivered more power for the buyer's dollar, IBM's support system was such that users of equipment still preferred IBM, which was affectionately called "Big Blue." Change was coming, however, and this time IBM faltered. In the mid-1970's, few people had heard of the small desktop computers fashioned from parts by enthusiasts. Soon, however, desktop computers were on sale to office managers. Sales to individuals followed shortly thereafter. The first buyers used their word-processing capacities as replacements for typewriters. As more programs were written and marketed, the small machines were used for other functions, many of which had previously required much larger computers. Each company had its own software, and these programs rarely worked on competitors' machines.

IBM entered the personal computer market in 1981 and announced that its architecture—the basic structure of its machines—would be available to competitors. Programs could be written to be compatible with machines produced by more than one company. This move was hailed by the industry but may have been an error. Using basic operating software from Microsoft and computer chips from Intel, IBM made it possible for many rivals to enter the field by purchasing components rather than seeking permission to use IBM patents.

Small computers became increasingly powerful, cutting into IBM's sales and leases of larger units. They became "commodity" products, ones for which brand name was relatively unimportant to buyers. They knew what a personal computer was supposed to do, and almost all the machines on the market performed those tasks with approximately the same proficiency and speed. IBM had a difficult time marketing its products as superior. The company responded by purchasing ROLM, a manufacturer of sophisticated telephonic equipment, and by taking an interest in MCI Communications, a rival to American Telephone and Telegraph (AT&T) in long-line telephonics. Clearly, IBM intended to branch out into areas related to data transmission. Both forays failed, and IBM abandoned the fields.

Although IBM made a promising start in the personal computer (PC) field, the company soon stumbled. Its small PC Jr. was a flop, and the company did not have a

1924

plausible entry in the laptop and notebook markets until the early 1990's, far behind competitors. By then, Akers had embarked on a series of restructurings, and it was clear that the company was foundering. In late 1992, Akers announced further cutbacks and a $6 billion charge against restructuring, hinting that more was to come, including a dividend cut. In 1993, IBM hired its first chairman and CEO from the outside, Louis V. Gerstner, who quickly stabilized the company, resisted calls to split it, and aggressively exploited strategies and markets in the newly emerging Internet and network computing arenas. Acquisitions of profitable businesses, such as Lotus Development Corporation and Tivoli Systems, added to its growth. A major public relations event in 1997 was IBM's unveiling of its Deep Blue supercomputer that defeated World Chess Champion Garry Kasparov. IBM was a major innovator in the development of e-business, but with the collapse of the dot-com industry in the late 1990's, its fortunes waned. The economic downturn of 2002 saw a slight drop in revenue and net earnings, but IBM quickly recovered, and by 2006 the company employed about 329,000 people and earned $96 billion in revenue and $8.4 billion in net earnings.

—*Robert Sobel*

FURTHER READING

Belden, Thomas. *The Lengthening Shadow: The Life of Thomas J. Watson*. Boston: Little, Brown, 1962. The first biography of Watson, written with IBM's support. Unduly flattering but useful in showing the kind of image the company hoped establish.

Maisonrouge, Jacques. *Inside IBM: A Personal Story*. New York: McGraw-Hill, 1989. Maisonrouge was a senior officer at IBM who worked closely with both the Watsons.

Maney, Kevin. *The Maverick and His Machine: Thomas Watson, Sr. and the Making of IBM*. New York: John Wiley & Sons, 2003. Maney takes a penetrating look at Watson's life: his ruthless business strategies, his self-absorption, and his inability to differentiate himself from his company. Highly recommended.

Pugh, Emerson W. *Building IBM: Shaping an Industry and Its Technology*. Cambridge, Mass.: MIT Press, 1995. Useful history, both as a case study of IBM and as an overview of the computer industry generally. Contains an extensive bibliography and an index.

Rodgers, William. *Think: A Biography of the Watsons and IBM*. New York: Stein & Day, 1969. An early history and biography. Valuable for its point of view on the company during the early years of the computer.

Sobel, Robert. *I.B.M.: Colossus in Transition*. New York: Times Books, 1981. A standard history of the company during its period of growth and power.

Watson, Thomas J., Jr. *A Business and Its Beliefs: The Ideas That Helped Build IBM*. Rev. ed. New York: McGraw-Hill, 2003. First published in 1963 and delivered as part of the McKinsey Foundation Lecture Series, sponsored by Columbia University. This is the clearest statement of the IBM philosophy available.

Watson, Thomas J., Jr., and Peter Petre. *Father, Son, and Company: My Life at IBM and Beyond*. New York: Bantam, 2000. Describes Watson's relations with his father, with some material on the early history of IBM.

Watson, Thomas J., Sr. *Men-Minutes-Money*. New York: IBM, 1934. Watson's interpretation of IBM's philosophy and policies. Indicates how money was spent on research and production.

SEE ALSO: 1903: Delaware Revises Corporation Laws; 1932: Berle and Means Discuss Corporate Control; Fall, 1934-May 6, 1953: Gibbon Develops the Heart-Lung Machine.

February 12, 1924
GERSHWIN'S *RHAPSODY IN BLUE* PREMIERES IN NEW YORK

George Gershwin's composition and performance of Rhapsody in Blue *combined elements of American popular music with the European classical tradition.*

LOCALE: New York, New York
CATEGORY: Music

KEY FIGURES
George Gershwin (1898-1937), American composer
Paul Whiteman (1890-1967), American bandleader
Ferde Grofé (1892-1972), American pianist and music orchestrator

SUMMARY OF EVENT
While visiting Great Britain with his dance orchestra in 1923, New York bandleader Paul Whiteman began thinking of performing a concert of American popular music in a major concert hall. When a rival bandleader announced similar plans, Whiteman—goaded into action—developed a program to show that popular music had moved from simple dance music to a true art form. He booked New York City's Aeolian Hall for a performance to take place on February 12, 1924.

Whiteman had worked with composer George Gershwin in the Broadway show *George White's Scandals of 1922* and had suggested a future collaboration. Gershwin, however, did not learn about his role in Whiteman's upcoming concert until the *New York Herald Tribune* announced on January 4, 1924, that Gershwin was writing a jazz concerto for the program. By that time, the twenty-five-year-old Gershwin had acquired a considerable reputation as a writer of Broadway songs, but his composition of a movement for string quartet in 1919 and a one-act "jazz opera" in 1922 indicated greater ambitions. Drawing on his notebooks, where he found the opening clarinet passage, Gershwin began composing a work he called *American Rhapsody* on January 7. He later stated that he had no real plan for the piece, but rather only the object of showing that jazz did not need to be written or performed in strict time. While traveling by train to Boston, he developed a structure for the composition, calling it "a sort of musical kaleidoscope of America." After he returned to New York, he conceived the middle theme of the piece while improvising on a piano at a party.

Gershwin wrote the orchestra accompaniment as a second piano part to be scored by Ferde Grofé, Whiteman's arranger. Apparently completing his composition

by January 29, Gershwin left a blank section for improvisation on which he noted "wait for nod." Grofé's orchestration is dated February 4, 1924. Gershwin's brother Ira, meanwhile, suggested a new title, *Rhapsody in Blue*.

Whiteman added nine musicians to his fourteen-member orchestra and held rehearsals for five days at the Palais Royal nightclub, to which he invited critics and writers. During one of these rehearsals, clarinetist Ross Gorman, for a joke, played the opening passage of *Rhapsody in Blue* as a wailing glissando. Taken with the sound, Gershwin asked Gorman to play it that way at the concert.

Despite Whiteman's fears, the Aeolian Hall was filled on February 12. Titled "An Experiment in Modern Music," the concert began with an address by Whiteman's manager, Hugh Ernst, who stated that the program was educational and was meant to show the development of jazz (an ill-defined term at the time) from discordance to sophistication. An expensive printed program, with notes by Ernst and writer Gilbert Seldes, provided additional information, organizing the concert around such themes as "True Form of Jazz" and "Contrast—Legitimate Scoring vs. Jazzing." The music ranged from "Livery Stable Blues" to "Pomp and Circumstance" and serenades by Victor Herbert.

The audience included luminaries from the New York social and artistic scenes as well as people from vaudeville and Tin Pan Alley. They were receptive, but after twenty-three selections, they had become noticeably restless by the time Gershwin walked to the piano to perform *Rhapsody in Blue*. The opening glissando brought everyone to attention, however, and soon they recognized that this loosely constructed Lisztian rhapsody, with its blues-tinged harmonies and jazzlike rhythms, was a truly new sound. At the work's close they broke into tumultuous applause and called Gershwin back for several bows.

The critical reaction to *Rhapsody in Blue* was mixed, with most writers noting both the technical immaturity of the composer and the freshness of his approach. Deems Taylor wrote for the *New York World*, "It was crude, but it hinted at something new, something that has not hitherto been said in music."

Whiteman repeated the concert at Aeolian Hall on March 7 and then performed the program at New York's Carnegie Hall in April and November. He then took it to Rochester, Pittsburgh, Cleveland, Indianapolis, and St.

Louis, after which Gershwin left the program. In June, 1924, Gershwin and Whiteman recorded *Rhapsody in Blue* for the Victor Blue label; the recording sold more than a million copies. Later that same year, T. B. Harms and Company published the sheet music for *Rhapsody in Blue*. Grofé reorchestrated the piece for symphony orchestra in 1926 and 1942, the latter being the version most familiar today.

In 1925, the Symphony Society of New York commissioned Gershwin to write a concerto to be performed with the New York Symphony Orchestra in December. Like *Rhapsody in Blue*, *Concerto in F* did not adhere to textbook formalities and drew on jazz and popular music, but it had greater structural integrity than the earlier work and was orchestrated by the composer.

Continuing to write hit musicals for the theater, Gershwin also pursued his "serious" composing. His first performance of *Preludes for Piano* took place in 1926, and in 1928 the New York Philharmonic presented his orchestral tone poem *An American in Paris*. After the relatively unsuccessful *Second Rhapsody* of 1931, Gershwin concentrated on his opera *Porgy and Bess*, a story about poor southern blacks first performed in 1935. Although criticized for being merely a succession of hit songs and scorned by many African Americans as a white interpretation of black music and life, the opera survived because of its songs. After a revival in New York in 1942, *Porgy and Bess* grew in both popularity and critical reputation. Gershwin, however, did not live to see this success; he died from a brain tumor on July 11, 1937.

SIGNIFICANCE

Before *Rhapsody in Blue*, various composers had attempted to draw on elements of American popular music. Antonín Dvořák's Ninth Symphony (1893) reflected the spirituals of the African American, but the more specific influence of commercial popular music appeared in Igor Stravinsky's *Ragtime* (1918) and *Piano Rag-Music* (1919) and Darius Milhaud's *Le Boeuf sur le toit* (1919) and *La Création du monde* (1923). Other works revealing this influence included Erik Satie's *Parade* (1917) and John Alden Carpenter's *Piano Concertino* (1915) and *Krazy Kat* (1921). In the mid-nineteenth century, the American composer and pianist Louis Moreau Gottschalk wrote a number of piano pieces reflecting the musical idioms of the American South. Later, Scott Joplin, the "Ragtime King," used ragtime idioms for some of the songs in his opera *Treemonisha* (1911), and Charles Ives incorporated ragtime elements into his compositions.

None of these works, however, gained the attention for combining "jazz" and the European tradition the way Gershwin's did. The division between classical music and American popular music remained, for the most part, wide.

Paul Whiteman's attempt to lift American popular music to an art form also had its predecessors. In 1914, James Reese Europe's black Clef Club Symphony Orchestra had appeared at Carnegie Hall, and on February 10, 1924, only a few days before the Aeolian Hall concert, bandleader Vincent Lopez held a lecture-concert at the Anderson Art Galleries in New York. The announcement of Lopez's planned performance was the factor that had provoked Whiteman into action. At the program, Harvard University professor and composer Edward Burlington Hill discussed the history of jazz and Lopez's band provided musical illustrations. Although these efforts had relatively little impact, they suggested that the attempt to combine the elite European tradition with American popular culture was more than Whiteman's individual concern. Furthermore, writers such as Gilbert Seldes, the author of *The Seven Lively Arts* (1924), were arguing for the aesthetic validity and importance of American popular culture.

Gershwin's *Rhapsody in Blue* opened the door to further experimentation, particularly because of Whiteman's carefully developed publicity campaign for his concert. Furthermore, Henry O. Osgood, one of the music critics who attended the Aeolian Hall program, was inspired to write *So This Is Jazz* (1926), perhaps the first serious examination of the subject.

There now appeared to be a market for compositions drawing on jazz elements, and "serious" American composers responded. Aaron Copland used jazz idioms in his *Music for the Theater* (1925) and *Concerto for Piano and Orchestra* (1926), as did John Alden Carpenter in his ballet *Skyscrapers* (1926). Other composers incorporated the term "jazz" into the very titles of their works: Louis Gruenberg's *Daniel Jazz* (1923, antedating Gershwin's *Rhapsody*) and *Jazz Suite* (1925), George Antheil's *Jazz Symphony* (1925), Werner Janssen's *Chorale and Fugue in Jazz* (1929), and—changing the terminology slightly—Morton Gould's *Swing Sinfonietta* (1936).

More popularly oriented composers pursued similar goals. Whiteman's arranger Ferde Grofé wrote *The Mississippi Suite* in 1924, drawing on jazz colors and idioms, and in 1931 made subtler use of these elements in his now-famous *Grand Canyon Suite*. Another orchestrator, Robert Russell Bennett, drew as Gershwin had on his experience in musical stage works to write *Charleston Rhapsody* (1926) and *Concerto Grosso* (1932) for jazz band and orchestra. James P. Johnson, the black ragtime and stride piano composer, wrote *Yamekraw: A Rhapsody in Black and White* (1925), which was scored by William Grant Still, who in turn composed *Africa* (1930) and *Afro-American Symphony* (1930).

European composers, some specifically influenced by Gershwin, were also drawn to this American music. Among the more significant efforts were Ernst Krenek's *Jonny spielt auf* (1927), Paul Hindemith's *Neues vom Tage* (1928-1929), Maurice Ravel's Piano Concerto in D Major for Left Hand (1931) and Piano Concerto in G Major (1931)—both of which have been described as "Gershwinesque"—and Kurt Weill's *Mahagonny Songspiel* (1927) and *Die Dreigroschenoper* (1928). Alban Berg, whom Gershwin met in 1928, included a clarinet glissando in the second song of *Der Wein* (1929) that is clearly reminiscent of *Rhapsody in Blue*'s opening.

Drawn to such elements as syncopation and polyrhythm, the relationship of soloists to accompanying instruments, and special instrumental techniques and sonorities, these composers did not write "jazz"; rather, they produced music in the classical tradition with a distinctively modern sound, one that sometimes reached a wide audience. As Ravel stated in 1928, "These popular forms are but the materials of construction, and the work of art appears only on mature conception where no detail has been left to chance."

The cross-fertilization of musical worlds popularized by George Gershwin brought recognition to American music and American composers, contributing greatly to the eclecticism of twentieth century "serious" music. When composers draw on rock music for inspiration, as Leonard Bernstein did in his *Mass* (1971), or when jazz musicians such as Duke Ellington or Dave Brubeck seek to work with classical forms, they are further exploring the path blazed by Gershwin in 1924. Indeed, interest in emphasizing the influence of popular idioms led to the effort to move beyond the familiar 1942 orchestral arrangement of *Rhapsody in Blue* and restore the jazzier sound of Gershwin's original performance, most notably in 1984 with Maurice Peress's re-creation of the entire Aeolian Hall concert.

—*Gary Land*

FURTHER READING

Alpert, Hollis. *The Life and Times of "Porgy and Bess": The Story of an American Classic*. New York: Alfred A. Knopf, 1990. Examines the development of the opera from its beginnings in DuBose Heyward's novel to performances in 1987. Relates the opera to Gershwin's earlier work and also presents the opera's history as a mirror of American social change. Includes synopsis, photographs, bibliography, and index.

Ewen, David. *George Gershwin: His Journey to Greatness*. Reprint. Westport, Conn.: Greenwood Press, 1977. A rewritten version of the author's earlier work *George Gershwin: A Journey to Greatness* (1956). Although sometimes inaccurate, important as the first major biography of Gershwin. Particularly useful for its discussion of the development of Gershwin's reputation. Appendixes list Gershwin's works and various stage and motion-picture adaptations and productions. Includes photographs and index.

Goldberg, Isaac. *George Gershwin: A Study in American Music*. New York: Frederick Ungar, 1931. The first serious examination of Gershwin's music. Interesting for quotations from contemporaries, particularly reviewers of the Aeolian Hall concert, and for analysis of specific musical examples. Includes photographs, selected discography with critical discussion, and index.

Hyland, William G. *George Gershwin: A New Biography*. New York: Praeger, 2003. Comprehensive, in-depth biography examines both Gershwin's life and his music, placing the composer's work in the context of the times. Chapter 4 is devoted to *Rhapsody in Blue*. Includes photo essay, select bibliography, and index.

Jablonski, Edward. *Gershwin*. 1988. Reprint. New York: Da Capo Press, 1998. Careful biography, generally regarded as definitive, concentrates largely on Gershwin's career and social relationships rather than on probing his mind or his music. Includes numerous quotations from those who knew Gershwin. Reprint edition features a revised critical discography. Also includes photographs, bibliography, list of compositions by George and Ira Gershwin, and index.

Kimball, Robert, and Alfred Simon. *The Gershwins*. New York: Atheneum, 1973. Published on the occasion of the seventy-fifth anniversary of Gershwin's birth. Contains tributes from family, friends, and admirers. Most significant for memoirs from Gershwin show participants. Includes photographs, chronology, discography, and bibliography.

Rosenberg, Deena. *Fascinating Rhythm: The Collaboration of George and Ira Gershwin*. New York: E. P. Dutton, 1991. Concentrates on Gershwin's songs and

1924

includes excerpts from both music and lyrics. Features reference notes, chronology of works, alphabetical list of Gershwin and Gershwin songs, photographs, bibliography, discography, and index.

Schwartz, Charles. *Gershwin: His Life and Music*. Indianapolis: Bobbs-Merrill, 1973. A thorough but sometimes inaccurate discussion of both Gershwin's life and his music. Notable for attention to Gershwin's vanity and self-absorption. Includes photographs, catalog of Gershwin compositions and films based on Gershwin's works, discography, bibliography, and index.

Whiteman, Paul, and Mary Margaret McBride. *Jazz*. 1926. Reprint. New York: Arno Press, 1974. Chapter 4 presents Whiteman's own account of the Aeolian Hall concert. Includes photographs.

Wyatt, Robert, and John Andrew Johnson, eds. *The George Gershwin Reader*. New York: Oxford University Press, 2004. Collection of more than eighty writings by and about Gershwin sheds light on the composer's work. Pieces by musicians such as Irving Berlin and Leonard Bernstein and by critics such as Robert Benchley and Alexander Woollcott are accompanied by excerpts from Gershwin's personal correspondence. Includes chronology of Gershwin's life.

SEE ALSO: 1920's: Radio Develops as a Mass Broadcast Medium; Jan. 16, 1920: Formation of Les Six; July 17, 1927: Brecht and Weill Collaborate on the *Mahagonny Songspiel*; Dec. 4, 1927: Ellington Begins Performing at the Cotton Club; Oct. 10, 1935: Gershwin's *Porgy and Bess* Opens in New York.

March, 1924
EDDINGTON FORMULATES THE MASS-LUMINOSITY LAW FOR STARS

Arthur Stanley Eddington's demonstration of the relationship between a star's mass and its luminosity led to an understanding of how stars evolve.

LOCALE: Cambridge, England
CATEGORIES: Science and technology; astronomy

KEY FIGURES
Arthur Stanley Eddington (1882-1944), English astronomer, mathematician, and physicist
Jacob Karl Ernst Halm (1866-1944), German astronomer
William Wallace Campbell (1862-1938), American astronomer and educator
Ejnar Hertzsprung (1873-1967), Danish astronomer
Henry Norris Russell (1877-1957), American astronomer and astrophysicist

SUMMARY OF EVENT
In the early twentieth century, astronomy was changing. Until that time, astronomers had concerned themselves chiefly with the motions of heavenly objects and the laws and forces that describe those motions. With the advent of the analysis of starlight (spectrography) and the use of photography, the science of astrophysics began to take shape. Scientists could now learn more about the properties of stars other than their motions and could begin the task of understanding what stars are like internally, how they form, and what fuels their existence. New data were

becoming available that scientists could use to discover patterns or relationships among different properties of stars, as revealed by their light. The interpretation of these patterns and relationships was to be one of the first tasks of the science of astrophysics.

One type of new data concerned the luminosities (brightnesses) and spectral types of stars. A star's spectral type is a classification assigned to it after a study of its light, as spread out by a prism or a grating (its spectrum). A program at Harvard College Observatory and other research provided astronomers with catalogs of spectral type and luminosity for many stars. In 1905, Ejnar Hertzsprung, a Danish astronomer, revealed a relationship between a star's brightness and its type. This relationship was demonstrated in the Hertzsprung-Russell (H-R) diagram, developed by Hertzsprung and Henry Norris Russell in the United States. Its discovery raised issues regarding the meaning of this relationship and its implications for why stars are of differing colors and brightnesses.

Another type of new data concerned the masses of stars. When studying double-star systems, astronomers can use one of the laws formulated by Johannes Kepler in the seventeenth century to determine the sum of the masses of the two stars in the system. In some cases, a ratio of the masses of the two stars can also be obtained, and this information can be used to determine the mass of each individual star. This can be done either with stars that are visibly pairs of stars (visual doubles) or with stars that look like a single star to the eye but have spectra that reveal that two stars are actually present.

Jacob Karl Ernst Halm, at the Cape Observatory in South Africa, reviewed research conducted by William Wallace Campbell and by Russell with these double-star masses and postulated a relationship between a star's mass and its spectral class. Halm then combined these two relationships in 1911 (spectral type-brightness and mass-spectral type) and suggested that there is a relationship between a star's mass and its brightness. This possible relationship was also discussed by Russell in 1913 and by Hertzsprung in 1918.

In 1924, Arthur Stanley Eddington was a professor of astronomy at the University of Cambridge in England and director of the Royal Observatory in Greenwich. He analyzed mass and luminosity data for many stars and plotted a diagram of mass versus luminosity. The diagram showed a relationship between the two that generally indicated that the brighter a star is, the more massive it is. Stars range from dim low-mass stars to bright high-mass stars along a diagonal line stretching across the plot. Eddington not only demonstrated this relationship but also began the discussion of its cause and implications.

Eddington's theoretical explanation for the mass-luminosity relationship was based on the law of perfect gases. This law describes the relationship between the pressure, volume, and temperature of a gas. The temperature of a star is related to its luminosity, which is actually a measure of the amount of energy radiated away from the star in a given amount of time ("brightness" is commonly used as an equivalent term for luminosity, given that energy is seen in the form of visible light). At the time, H-R diagrams of spectral type versus luminosity for groups of stars showed that there are two types of stars: those recognized by Hertzsprung as being larger (the giants) and the main-sequence stars, or dwarf stars. The giant stars occupy one place on the diagram, with fairly constant luminosity and varying spectral types. The dwarf stars demonstrate Hertzsprung's color-luminosity relationship: Blue stars are brighter than yellow stars, which, in turn, are brighter than red stars. At the time when Eddington formulated this explanation, it was thought that only giant stars were composed of gases that would follow the perfect gas laws (which applied only under certain conditions), thus the mass-luminosity relationship should apply only to giant stars. Eddington tested the idea that only giants should exhibit the relationship between their masses and their luminosities and

was surprised to discover that the relationship held for stars on the main sequence too. This was in conflict with the prevailing assumption that main-sequence stars were too dense for the perfect gas laws to apply to them and their relatively low luminosities (relative to the giants) were accounted for by their high densities. Eddington's discovery indicated that their low luminosities could be accounted for simply by their low masses. He explained that the perfect gas laws applied at higher densities than expected for stars, because the material of which the stars were composed was highly ionized; that is, the individual atoms were missing some of their electrons because of the presence of high temperatures. This ionization reduced the bulk of the atoms, and the net result was that the perfect gas laws "worked" for much higher densities than could otherwise have been expected.

An interesting feature of the mass-luminosity diagram is the relatively broad range of luminosities and much smaller range of masses. The most massive star then known was estimated to be about one hundred times the mass of the Sun; the least massive was about one-

Arthur Stanley Eddington. (Library of Congress)

sixth the mass of the Sun. Eddington had also considered the problem of radiation pressure in a star, and he used radiation pressure to explain the relatively small range of stellar masses. He showed that there is a condition of equilibrium in a star, with gravitational pressure inward balanced by gas pressure and radiation pressure outward. Beyond a certain mass, the radiation pressure becomes so great that a star would be blown apart by it; therefore, mass is the upper limit to stellar masses. (Today, the most massive star known has been estimated to be only about sixty-five times the mass of the Sun.) Eddington developed an equation to describe equilibrium in a star that is still used today. This equation involved the assumption of perfect gas conditions and therefore at first he thought it should apply only to giant stars. The discovery that perfect gas conditions are also maintained in dwarf or main-sequence stars extended the applicability of this equation and the model of a star's interior that resulted.

The demonstration of the mass-luminosity relationship for stars gave astronomers new areas to investigate and revealed something about the conditions in main-sequence stars that had not been known before. It was an important step in the development of the current understanding of what makes stars shine and how they change over time.

SIGNIFICANCE

After documenting the mass-luminosity relationship, Eddington began sorting out problems of the structure of stars and their energy sources. The fact that the perfect gas law can be applied to both main-sequence and giant stars was a great help to scientists studying stellar structure. The basic problem of stellar structure is that of producing a model star, that is, a description of the physical properties of a star at various depths below the star's surface, such as the temperature and density. In order to know these properties, one must know the degree to which the gas prevents the free outward flow of radiation. The perfect gas law gives astronomers a tool for calculating this quantity, calculating the temperature and density at various depths in the star, and producing stellar models that are compared with actual stars. Eddington's calculations assumed an average particle mass (for the particles of gas in stars) that today is known to be too high. This resulted from the fact that at the time the proportions of the various gases composing the stars were not known. It was not until Russell's discovery that the Sun is almost entirely hydrogen that astronomers could use a particle weight more closely corresponding to reality.

The discovery of the mass-luminosity relation was important to theories of how stars change with time. In 1913, Russell had presented a scheme of stellar evolution in which all the stars on the main sequence were of different ages. The main sequence represented the path a star took throughout its lifetime, beginning as a bright blue star and cooling down to a dim red star as its energy source (heat from contraction under gravitational force) ran out. With Eddington's discovery, however, astronomers realized that stars on the main sequence had differing masses (because mass and luminosity are related and they have different luminosities): The stars on the dim red end of the main sequence were less massive than stars at the bright blue end. If the main sequence is an evolutionary path that stars follow, then mass loss must occur as stars age. This was difficult to explain; it was not until later discoveries on stellar evolution that astronomers realized that the main sequence is not an evolutionary path.

The questions of how stars evolve and what their energy source is were solved in the 1930's with the discovery of atomic fusion and the realization that fusion is occurring in stars. When two atoms fuse in the interior of a star, energy is released, and it is this energy that is seen as starlight and other types of radiation. Scientists now know that the mass of a star determines how quickly the fusion reactions take place inside it (how long it lives) and its place on the main sequence. A more massive star is brighter, hotter, and bluer, and when it comes to the end of its fuel supply, it has a more spectacular ending to its life than do less massive, cooler stars.

—*Mary Hrovat*

FURTHER READING

Abell, George O. *Realm of the Universe*. 5th ed. Philadelphia: Saunders College Publishing, 1994. Introductory college textbook explains various stellar properties and introduces the mass-luminosity relation and the diagram of this relation. Explains how data are gathered on masses of binary stars and discusses the Hertzsprung-Russell diagram and its relevance to stellar masses and evolutions. Includes illustrations, diagrams, glossary, and annotated bibliography.

Degani, Meir H. *Astronomy Made Simple*. Rev. ed. Garden City, N.Y.: Doubleday, 1976. Explains the mass-luminosity law in the context of the sequences of stars on the Hertzsprung-Russell diagram. Discussion of stellar evolution emphasizes the importance of a star's mass in determining how it will change with time. Includes line diagrams and glossary.

Eddington, A. S. *Stars and Atoms*. New Haven, Conn.:

Yale University Press, 1927. Collection of a series of lectures given in 1926. Describes the then-current knowledge of stellar structure in a manner intended for the amateur willing to apply new ideas. First section concerns stellar interiors and the mass-luminosity relation. Dated, but valuable for Eddington's own view of the work he performed and for his clear, engaging style.

Motz, Lloyd, and Jefferson Hane Weaver. *The Story of Astronomy*. New York: Plenum, 1995. Presents the history of astronomy from ancient times to the end of the twentieth century. Chapter 15 is devoted to the origin and development of the field of astrophysics. Features bibliography and index.

Pannekoek, A. *A History of Astronomy*. 1961. Reprint. Mineola, N.Y.: Dover, 1989. Scholarly classic work includes a chapter titled "Common Stars" that discusses the mass-luminosity relation in the context of the development of astrophysics in the early twentieth century, the development of the H-R diagram, and theories of stellar evolution. Includes some line drawings and black-and-white photographs.

Struve, Otto, and Velta Zebergs. *Astronomy of the Twentieth Century*. New York: Macmillan, 1962. Discusses the work on stellar properties that culminated in Eddington's discovery of the mass-luminosity law, including mass determination for binary stars. Also gives background on stellar evolution and H-R diagrams. Cowritten by an astronomer who participated in some of the astronomical history he describes. Includes drawings, diagrams, black-and-white photographs, glossary, and bibliography.

Zeilik, Michael, and Stephen A. Gregory. *Introductory Astronomy and Astrophysics*. 4th ed. Monterey, Calif.: Brooks/Cole, 1997. Provides a useful overview of general astronomy, including basic spectral issues and the use of H-R diagrams.

SEE ALSO: Nov. 6, 1919: Einstein's Theory of Gravitation Is Confirmed over Newton's Theory; Dec. 13, 1920: Michelson Measures the Diameter of a Star; July, 1926: Eddington Publishes *The Internal Constitution of the Stars*; 1931-1935: Chandrasekhar Calculates the Upper Limit of a White Dwarf Star's Mass.

March 31, 1924
FORMATION OF THE BLUE FOUR ADVANCES ABSTRACT PAINTING

When four leading abstract painters in Germany formed a partnership to promote their work, they made a significant contribution to the worldwide revolution in modern art.

ALSO KNOWN AS: Die Blaue Vier
LOCALE: Europe; United States; Mexico
CATEGORY: Arts

KEY FIGURES
Wassily Kandinsky (1866-1944), Russian painter
Paul Klee (1879-1940), Swiss painter
Lyonel Feininger (1871-1956), American cartoonist
    and painter
Alexey von Jawlensky (1864-1941), Russian painter
Emmy Scheyer (1889-1945), German art student
J. B. Neumann (1887-1961), American art dealer

SUMMARY OF EVENT

Emmy Scheyer was born in Braunschweig, Germany. As a young student, she discovered the paintings of Russian immigrant Alexey von Jawlensky and was so impressed by the new art form they represented that she decided to devote her life to publicizing Jawlensky's work. Through Jawlensky, she met many other avant-garde painters, including Wassily Kandinsky, Paul Klee, and Lyonel Feininger, who were teaching at the Bauhaus school of design. Because their art was revolutionary and as yet unpopular, all four men were chronically in need of money.

This was especially true after Germany's defeat in World War I and during the period of devastating inflation that followed. In 1924, Scheyer (who was given the nickname "Galka"—Russian for "black bird"—by Jawlensky) volunteered to promote their paintings in the affluent United States, which was famous for its receptivity to new ideas. On March 31, 1924, an agreement was signed designating Scheyer as the artists' American representative. For publicity purposes they christened their group Die Blaue Vier (the Blue Four), a reference to Der Blaue Reiter (the blue rider), a group of painters who had been inspired and led by the mystical Kandinsky.

In May of 1924, the aggressive, charismatic Scheyer went to New York and began sending out thousands of pamphlets to universities, museums, and art associa-

1924

tions, offering them exhibits and her services as a lecturer. In New York, she met and collaborated with J. B. Neumann, another ardent admirer of the new German avant-garde art who eventually became a wealthy Manhattan art dealer.

The first Blue Four exhibition was arranged by Scheyer at the Daniel Gallery, New York, in 1925. Sales were disappointing. Hoping for a better reception in the West, Scheyer traveled to California, lecturing about her artists along the way. Over the next three years, she gave lectures and arranged Blue Four exhibitions in San Francisco, Los Angeles, Portland, Oregon, and Spokane, Washington.

Scheyer returned to Europe several times before World War II in order to collect new paintings. In 1929, the Oakland Art Gallery across the bay from San Francisco opened a traveling Blue Four exhibition under the sponsorship of the Western Association of Art Museums. A big show was held in Hollywood at the Braxton Gallery in 1930. In 1931, the prestigious Palace of the Legion of Honor in San Francisco held a Blue Four exhibition under Scheyer's direction. That same year, Scheyer was invited by the famous Mexican artist Diego Rivera to arrange an exhibition at the national library in Mexico City.

By that time, Scheyer was a resident of Hollywood. She became a social celebrity and sold modern German paintings to members of the affluent film colony. The deepening worldwide depression of the 1930's created havoc in the international art market, and Scheyer was forced to earn her living mainly by giving art lessons to children. She never stopped devoting the bulk of her boundless energies to promoting the works of her Blue Four friends, however.

The American public was slow to accept avant-garde German art, both because the new art was revolutionary in nature and because Germany had only recently been an enemy in World War I. Although Americans had become attuned to French Impressionism, they were not ready to accept the radical notions embodied in the new German works. In fact, many critics and connoisseurs regarded the new art as little more than a hoax, calling the works crude, primitive, childish, incompetent, vulgar, or deliberately ugly and offensive.

A few, however, like Scheyer, immediately understood and responded to what the Blue Four were trying to do. These perceptive individuals, mostly artists themselves, were delighted with the possibility of being liberated from the tradition that held that the artist should copy nature.

An important factor in the appeal of the Blue Four was the rapid development of photography. Just as live performers were being threatened by cinematic photography, painters were being threatened by still photography. Why pay a high price for a painting or drawing when a camera could produce an even better likeness for a much cheaper price? The artists' defense of painting held that it was the element of human emotion that made the difference between painting and photography, which led to various experiments to capture the essential human emotion while either distorting the subject or doing without a subject altogether.

The Blue Four lasted for only one decade. The group broke up in the face of the growing repression of the Nazi government under Adolf Hitler, who hated what he called "degenerate art" and who favored art that served to promote patriotism, militarism, and totalitarianism. Klee returned to Switzerland in 1933; Kandinsky emigrated to France in 1933 and never returned to Germany. Feininger returned to the United States in 1936. Jawlensky remained in Nazi Germany until his death in 1941, but from 1933 on he was forbidden to exhibit his works.

During its brief life span, the Blue Four spread the message—particularly to the United States—that pictorial art had a potential that exceeded the mere copying of people, places, and things or the creation of attractive pictures to adorn the walls of wealthy patrons. Instead, they demonstrated, art could be used to explore the depths of human consciousness and communicate a vast range of ideas and feelings in a universal language.

SIGNIFICANCE

It is hard to overestimate the impact of German expressionist art. It had not only an unmistakable direct influence on oil painting and watercolors but also a far more important influence on the public at large through such things as package design, newspaper and magazine advertising, textile design, and the design of record covers, book jackets, greeting cards, wallpaper, stage scenery, billboards, posters, comic strips, animated cartoons, and television commercials. The masses have come to accept the concepts of German expressionist art without for the most part realizing where such concepts originated.

In the Walt Disney film *Fantasia*, which was a bold experiment in filmmaking at the time of its release in 1940, there are many examples of the influence of German expressionism to be seen. One of the most striking is the sequence in which abstract shapes of assorted colors are generated and modified to correspond to the music of Johann Sebastian Bach's Toccata and Fugue in D Minor.

In this instance, the main influence is probably that of Kandinsky.

In the 1930's, when Fred Astaire and Ginger Rogers danced against stylized backdrops representing the skyscrapers of Manhattan and other modernistic settings, most of the members of the motion-picture audience were appreciating artistic concepts first introduced by Feininger, although they would not have recognized his name. For many years, the covers of *The New Yorker* magazine also reflected the influence of all four members of the Blue Four and other German expressionist artists. The most notable example is the work of William Steig. The influence of both Klee and Jawlensky, moreover, is evident in the phenomenally popular comic strip *Peanuts*.

The impact of German expressionists on other painters has also been tremendous. Visitors to any major art museum are likely to wander through many rooms full of pictures of fat cherubs and portraits of men and women in lace and suddenly to feel as if they have entered a different universe when they find their way into exhibits marked "modern art." Even if such viewers do not fully understand abstract painting, they are likely to feel refreshed by the vivid colors and the whole sense of creative liberation represented by such canvases. The influence of such artists as Kandinsky and Klee is unmistakable. So dramatic has been the influence of such artists that many members of the art world have come to regard artists working in the traditional vein with contempt, calling them "illusionists," "illustrators," or, perhaps worst of all, "bourgeois painters." Such attitudes are clearly unfair to sincere and gifted traditional artists.

The impact of German expressionism and related movements has not been an unmitigated good; expressionism has spawned myriad untalented imitators whose main attraction to nonrepresentational art is in being freed from the need to develop technical expertise, the need to work long, hard hours to perfect a piece of art, and the need to have anything in particular to communicate. Many poseurs have capitalized on the sacrifices of true artists such as Kandinsky, Klee, Feininger, and Jawlensky, and some have made substantial money and seen their works displayed in the best museums.

The Blue Four artists and their colleagues had a definite political impact, too. Both the German dictator Adolf Hitler and the Soviet dictator Joseph Stalin hated the new expressionist art. Both recognized it for what it was: the proclamation of the freedom of the individual.

—*Bill Delaney*

FURTHER READING

Beale, Penny. "J. B. Neumann and the Introduction of Modern German Art to New York, 1923-1933." *Archives of American Art Journal* 29, nos. 1 and 2 (1989): 3-15. Interesting profile of a colorful character who was influential in introducing modern German art to the United States.

Droste, Magdalena. *Bauhaus, 1919-1933.* Cologne, Germany: Benedikt Taschen Verlag, 1998. Focuses on the collection of the Bauhaus Archiv Museum of Design in Berlin in examining the progression of the Bauhaus movement. Extensively illustrated. Includes artist and architect biographies, bibliography, and index.

Joachimides, Christos M., Norman Rosenthal, and Wieland Schmied, eds. *German Art in the Twentieth Century: Painting and Sculpture, 1905-1985.* Munich: Prestel-Verlag, 1985. Comprehensive collection of essays on all aspects of twentieth century German art, including its historical background and its international influence, by many different authorities in the field. Features hundreds of full-color and black-and-white illustrations. Kandinsky, Klee, Feininger, and Jawlensky are all discussed and represented with many color reproductions. Includes biographies of all important twentieth century German artists, with bibliographic references for each individual.

Kentgens-Craig, Margret. *The Bauhaus and America: First Contacts, 1919-1936.* Cambridge, Mass.: MIT Press, 1999. Scholarly examination of the reception of the Bauhaus in the United States and the reasons for American reactions to the movement's concepts. Includes bibliography and index.

Roters, Eberhard. *Painters of the Bauhaus.* Translated by Anna Rose Cooper. New York: Praeger, 1969. A history of Bauhaus painters and art instruction, with considerable attention given to the methods and personalities of Klee, Kandinsky, and Feininger. Illustrated.

Sandback, Amy Baker. "Blue Heights Drive." *Artforum* 28 (March, 1990): 123-127. A rare profile of Emmy Scheyer, the colorful woman who devoted much of her life to publicizing the Blue Four. Contains photographs of her in her modernistic home in the Hollywood Hills, where she entertained such film figures as Charles Laughton, Edward G. Robinson, and Greta Garbo.

Tolstoy, Leo. *What Is Art?* Translated by Almyer Maude. New York: Bobbs-Merrill, 1960. Neglected masterpiece by one of the world's greatest writers of-

1924

fers a simple definition of art, summarizes the history of aesthetics, and voices a conservative reaction to the modernistic art theories that were emerging at the beginning of the twentieth century.

Whitford, Frank. *Bauhaus*. London: Thames and Hudson, 1984. Complete history of the most celebrated and influential art school of modern times. Useful for understanding the relationship between Bauhaus ideas about architecture and fine art. Includes many illustrations, mostly photographs of historical interest.

Wolfe, Tom. *The Painted Word*. 1975. Reprint. New York: Bantam Books, 1999. Funny, irreverent history of abstract art in the United States illustrates the ways in which the principles behind abstract art have been exploited, abused, and misunderstood.

SEE ALSO: Sept., 1911: Der Blaue Reiter Abandons Representation in Art; 1912: Kandinsky Publishes His Theory of Abstract Art; 1919: German Artists Found the Bauhaus; 1934: Soviet Union Bans Abstract Art.

May 21, 1924
FARMERS DYNAMITE THE LOS ANGELES AQUEDUCT

Farmers in California's Owens Valley, angered by the drainage of their lands by the Los Angeles Aqueduct, resorted to the use of explosives when legal negotiations failed to achieve their goals in one of California's early battles over water.

LOCALE: Owens Valley, California

CATEGORIES: Agriculture; business and labor; trade and commerce

KEY FIGURES

William Mulholland (1855-1935), superintendent of the Los Angeles Department of Water and Power, 1902-1928

Joseph Barlow Lippincott (1864-1942), California supervisor for the Federal Reclamation Service who concurrently contracted with the city of Los Angeles

Fred Eaton (1855-1934), city engineer who first envisioned an aqueduct from Owens Valley to Los Angeles

Mark Watterson (1876?-1948), Owens Valley banker who led opposition to the Los Angeles Aqueduct

Wilfred Watterson (1869?-1943), Owens Valley banker and Mark Watterson's brother and partner

SUMMARY OF EVENT

Owens Valley, located in central California, is one hundred miles long and ten miles wide, bordered on the west by the Sierra Nevada and on the east by the White Mountains and Inyo Range. This region was long well supplied with water from the Owens River, which ran the length of the valley from its headwaters in the High Sierras to alkaline Owens Lake. In 1913, however, the Los Angeles Aqueduct tapped this river and transported the valley's

water 240 miles south to meet the growing needs of the city of Los Angeles. This was accomplished at the expense of Owens Valley farmers, ranchers, and townspeople, who found their livelihoods threatened.

Embittered by repeated attempts to come to terms with the Los Angeles Department of Water and Power (DWP) and its chief engineer, William Mulholland, and frustrated by court decisions against them, these citizens finally resorted to violent destruction to call the public's attention to their plight. On the morning of May 21, 1924, a group of forty men dynamited the aqueduct near Lone Pine. The damage was minimal and the action was largely symbolic, but this was only one battle in the twenty-year war waged over Owens Valley water. The Los Angeles Aqueduct's impact on valley commerce demonstrated the connection between business and natural resource utilization.

By the late 1800's, the Owens Valley was populated by miners, pioneers, Chinese laborers, and dislocated Paiute Indians. Homesteaders used the irrigation method previously practiced by the Paiutes. Canals and ditches diverted water from the Owens River, creating rich farmland from barren stretches of sagebrush. By the turn of the century, the Owens Valley was a prosperous agricultural region supporting farmers, ranchers, and the towns of Bishop, Independence, Lone Pine, and Big Pine. In 1903, the U.S. Reclamation Service studied the feasibility of a water system project in Owens Valley. Under the supervision of Joseph Barlow Lippincott, the project was designed to irrigate an additional 100,000 acres. Local citizens supported this plan and made potential reservoir sites readily available. Lippincott, however, also worked for Los Angeles during his employment with the Reclamation Service. According to William Chalfant, editor of the *Inyo Register*, Lippincott received five thousand dollars for providing the city with government maps and data. In 1905, he was accompanied on a valley survey by Fred Eaton, a Los Angeles city engineer.

Eaton first realized the potential for a gravity-powered aqueduct during a trip through the Owens Valley in 1892. His alliance with Lippincott enabled him to buy up about one million dollars' worth of land along the Owens River; he took advantage of the popular misconception that this property would be used for the reclamation project. The Reclamation Service decided not to pursue the project in view of the conflicting interests shown by Los Angeles city officials and businesspeople. Mulholland had known for years about Eaton's plan to bring Owens River water south, and by 1905 he was ready to initiate the aqueduct's construction. Southern California was suffering through the tenth year of a drought. Los Angeles's population had grown to 200,000 and was increasing rapidly. In July, the *Los Angeles Times* publicized the project for the first time. Angelenos were delighted. Owens Valley residents felt uneasy because the city failed to state a definite water development policy for the valley. Negotiations with the city met with resistance or bogged down in legal technicalities. The aqueduct was built with neither adequate storage facilities for excess floodwaters nor any guaranteed water supply for Owens Valley.

The Los Angeles Aqueduct's gates opened on November 15, 1913. As the water rushed into the northern San Fernando Valley, Mulholland said to the crowd, "There it is—take it." To the delight of real estate speculators who had purchased land at two dollars per acre, this transported water turned the arid San Fernando Valley into an agricultural gold mine. The "unlimited" water also accelerated the pace of industrial and individual relocation to sunny Southern California.

For the next decade, Owens Valley residents attempted to coexist with the aqueduct, but another drought in 1921 caused the DWP to increase groundwater pumping in the valley. The water table fell, drying out farmlands adjacent to city-owned properties. Farmers tried to consolidate their position by forming irrigation districts. Their efforts were encouraged by Mark and Wilfred Watterson, owners of the Inyo County Bank. While other banks and institutions refused to deal with residents because of the valley's uncertain future, the Wattersons' bank took land mortgages and offered financial assistance.

Owens Valley residents' attempts to unify were broken up by city agents, who often resorted to misrepresentations. Angered by their coercive tactics, the farmers responded with violence. The blast of May 21, 1924, began an alternating pattern of destruction and negotiation. Over the next three years, and despite the presence of armed guards, the aqueduct was blown up eleven times. City wells were also dynamited. On November 16, 1924, a group of men led by Mark Watterson took over the Alabama Gates. They opened the spillway, causing aqueduct water to pour into the dry riverbed. During the next four days, an estimated five hundred to eight hundred valley residents picnicked and camped at the gates. To the protesters' disappointment, the state militia was not called out, but the occupation received national sympathy.

Despite favorable attention from the press, the controversy continued for several years. The Owens Valley Property Owners Protective Association, led by the Wattersons, advertised grievances in state newspapers. It fought for financial restitution in the state's courts, where it won, and in the Senate Committee on Conservation, where a resolution died without a hearing. The final blow to the resistance movement occurred on August 4, 1927, when the state superintendent of banks discovered a shortage of funds at the Inyo County Bank. All five branches closed at noon, virtually wiping out the savings of Owens Valley residents. The Wattersons were tried and sentenced to ten years in San Quentin State Penitentiary.

SIGNIFICANCE

By the early 1930's, Los Angeles owned 85 percent of the Owens Valley. Although ranchers leased some city lands, their water rights were not guaranteed and could be revoked at any time. The towns of Laws and Big Pine were abandoned. Bishop lost 35 percent of its 1920 population. Agricultural production dropped 84 percent between 1920 and 1930. Orchards were bulldozed, and fields of alfalfa gave way to sagebrush. The Owens Valley, once irrigated into agricultural fertility, reverted to its naturally barren state.

Initially, the aqueduct provided Los Angeles with a surplus of water. Adjacent communities were permitted to use the extra water in exchange for their annexation by the city. Businesspeople supported this plan because it increased real estate values and encouraged development. From 1915 through 1917, the city expanded from 108 to 350 square miles. The population increased from 200,000 in 1905 to 1,192,000 in 1925. To Mulholland's surprise, Los Angeles soon needed to look for another source of water.

1924

The 1920's water war collapsed the economy of the Owens Valley, but the following fifty years saw the development of new business in tourism, recreation, and government employment. In 1941, the Long Valley dam granted Owens Valley a new lease on life. Crowley Lake, the reservoir created by the dam, became a recreational center for fishing and boating. Hikers, hunters, and skiers flocked to the Sierra Nevada and the White Mountains. Tourist dollars revitalized the valley towns' economies. City land no longer suitable for farming was consolidated into five-thousand-acre cattle ranches. Economic recovery, aided by jobs brought in by state and federal agencies, aided in tripling the valley's population between 1930 and 1990.

When the Los Angeles Aqueduct was constructed, no laws prevented the transportation of water from one region to another. The Owens Valley controversy made the public aware that legislation applicable to water-rich states spelled disaster in California. In 1931, the state passed the "county of origin" law, which set guidelines for jurisdiction of water development, guaranteeing that local needs would be considered. No longer could those with money and power appropriate this vital resource.

The law was not retroactive, and so it affected neither the situation in the Owens Valley nor the Mono extension. As early as 1920, Mulholland considered adding sixty miles to the aqueduct to tap several streams feeding Mono Lake. This lake, although saline and with no outlet, was a unique biosphere supporting a network of insects and birds. Following in the footsteps of their neighbors to the south, residents formed the Mono Basin Land Owners' Protective Association in 1931. Their protests fell on deaf ears, and in 1941 the city completed the extension. The lake level dropped slowly from 1941 to 1970, when a second aqueduct was constructed alongside the original one. The amount of water exported doubled within a few years. By 1981, the lake had fallen forty-six feet, and its surface area had receded from ninety to sixty square miles. In 1974, the environmental crisis at Mono Lake received public attention through the efforts of David Gaines, a biologist from the University of California, Davis. He formed the Mono Lake Committee in 1978 to inform the public and legally challenge the DWP. Although primarily an environmental group, the Mono Lake Committee empathized with the Owens Valley struggle and based its philosophy on the same principle of citizens protecting their natural resources.

Simultaneously, the environmental movement as a whole developed into a powerful force influencing business and political decisions. U.S. government policies began to reflect the public's concern with natural resources. Beginning in 1969, with creation of the Environmental Protection Agency (EPA) and passage of the National Environmental Policy Act, federal agencies took a larger role in setting guidelines and influencing state and local decisions regarding the development and allocation of resources. National policy had come a long way since 1906, when Theodore Roosevelt, pressured by Los Angeles businesspeople, put through a bill granting the city free access to federal lands along the aqueduct route.

The 1920's water war culminated in the economic upheaval of Owens Valley. Los Angeles drained water from the land without considering citizens' needs. Farms and ranches were sold or dried up. The towns depended on farmers for their economic livelihood and so lost much of their business. The valley managed to survive by making the transition from agricultural production to a service-oriented economy dependent on tourist dollars. The Owens Valley conflict became a California legend, and the story has been retold with varying accuracy in books and films. It showed how the exploitation of natural resources can devastate a region's commerce. The DWP's lack of forethought demonstrated the necessity of careful evaluation of present and future demands as well as environmental impact. Finally, almost one hundred years after the construction of the Los Angeles Aqueduct, an agreement was reached to return water to the Owens River, and water began to flow in December of 2006. A new era of revitalized ecology and recreational tourism was predicted, although the option to divert water back through the aqueduct to Los Angeles remained in place.

—*Susan Frischer*

FURTHER READING

Arrandale, Tom. *The Battle for Natural Resources*. Washington, D.C.: Congressional Quarterly Press, 1983. Easy-to-read discussion of government management of natural resources. Concentrates on post-1950's legislature and Bureau of Land Management decisions. One chapter is devoted to water resources, but it does not mention the Los Angeles Aqueduct. Includes tables, maps, photos, and selected bibliography.

California Division of Engineering and Irrigation. *Letter of Transmittal and Report of W. F. McClure, State Engineer: Concerning the Owens Valley-Los Angeles Controversy*. Bishop, Calif.: Chalfant Press, 1974. The California state engineer's official report to Governor Friend William Richardson after the Alabama

Gates takeover in 1924. Informal and sympathetic to valley residents. This report facilitated the Reparations Act of May, 1925. Includes reprints of letters and many newspaper articles.

Cooper, Erwin. *Aqueduct Empire*. Glendale, Calif.: Arthur H. Clark, 1968. Overview of California water resources, legislation, and projects written during the emergence of environmental awareness. Informal and conjectural in style. Devotes one chapter to the Owens Valley water war. Presents extensive information, although the author's pronuclear, protechnological attitude is dated. Includes photographs, bibliography, and time line.

Hoffman, Abraham. *Vision or Villainy: Origins of the Owens Valley-Los Angeles Water Controversy*. 1981. Reprint. College Station: Texas A&M University Press, 1992. Lengthy history of the Los Angeles Aqueduct focuses primarily on the personalities involved, especially Joseph Lippincott and William Mulholland. Photos. Extensive bibliography includes archival material and dissertations.

Hundley, Norris. *The Great Thirst: Californians and Water; A History*. Rev. ed. Berkeley: University of California Press, 2001. Excellent historical treatment of California's water issues that also provides discussion of how these issues continue to shape the state's development. Interesting analysis of the Owens Valley conflict and its consequences.

Kahrl, William L. *Water and Power*. Berkeley: University of California Press, 1982. Lengthy historical account of the Owens Valley buyout, similar in style and scope to the Hoffman volume cited above. Includes maps of the aqueduct in Owens Valley and water-supply systems for Los Angeles and other parts of California. Extensive bibliography.

Mulholland, Catherine. *William Mulholland and the Rise of Los Angeles*. 2d ed. Berkeley: University of California Press, 2002. Written by Mulholland's granddaughter, this biography sympathizes (unsurprisingly) with its subject, but it is also a good, scholarly treatment of Mulholland's vision for Los Angeles. Persuasively argues that Mulholland was not at fault—although he was blamed—for the 1928 catastrophe at the St. Francis Dam.

Walton, John. *Western Times and Water Wars*. Berkeley: University of California Press, 1993. Complete history of the Owens Valley, from the days of the Paiute Indians to publication. Emphasis on collective action in a broad historical and sociological context. Well researched, informative, and objective, although esoteric and theoretically dense. Includes interesting photos, statistical tables, graphics showing the layouts of early towns, and comprehensive bibliography.

Wood, R. Coke. *The Owens Valley and the Los Angeles Water Controversy: Owens Valley as I Knew It*. Stockton, Calif.: University of the Pacific, 1973. Written in 1934 as a master's thesis. Wood's viewpoint is surprisingly objective for someone reared in the Owens Valley during the water war. His personal experiences and remarks, although limited to the first chapter and footnotes, are possibly of greatest interest to the general reader. Includes photos and bibliography as well as several poems.

SEE ALSO: Nov. 5, 1913: Completion of the Los Angeles Aqueduct; Dec. 19, 1913: U.S. Congress Approves a Dam in Hetch Hetchy Valley; 1930's: Wolman Begins Investigating Water and Sewage Systems; Mar., 1937: Delaware River Project Begins; Dec. 30, 1940: Arroyo Seco Freeway Opens in Los Angeles.

1924

May 26, 1924

IMMIGRATION ACT OF 1924

The Immigration Act of 1924, which reflected widespread restrictionist sentiment in the United States after World War I, severely limited the numbers of immigrants from southern and eastern Europe permitted to enter the country each year.

ALSO KNOWN AS: Johnson-Reid Act; National Origins Act

LOCALE: Washington, D.C.

CATEGORIES: Laws, acts, and legal history; business and labor; immigration, emigration, and relocation

KEY FIGURES

Albert Johnson (1869-1957), U.S. congressman from Washington

David A. Reed (1880-1953), U.S. senator from Pennsylvania

William Paul Dillingham (1843-1923), U.S. senator from Vermont

Charles Evans Hughes (1862-1948), U.S. secretary of state, 1921-1925

A. Mitchell Palmer (1872-1936), attorney general of the United States, 1919-1921

Samuel Gompers (1850-1924), leader of the American Federation of Labor

SUMMARY OF EVENT

The Immigration Act of 1924 provided for a system of quotas for immigration into the United States, drastically limiting the numbers of people from southern and eastern Europe who could enter the country, especially in comparison with more "favored" national groups from northern and western Europe. As a result of strong pressure from American employers dependent on Latin American laborers, the measure included few restrictions on immigrants from nations in the Western Hemisphere. Otherwise, it severely curtailed the immigration of groups deemed by restrictionists to be not "American" enough.

The U.S. Congress had passed immigration legislation, after contentious debate, on several occasions prior to 1924. A quota system instituted in 1921 provided that people of each European nationality could enter the United States based on the percentage of their group's population in the United States in 1910. The Immigration Act of 1921 allowed only about 350,000 immigrants from Europe per year, most of them from the "preferred" national groups in northern and western Europe. It had several loopholes, however. By 1924, few voices were

raised against the further restriction of immigration, and some individuals called for a complete shutdown.

The Immigration Act of 1924, also known as the Johnson-Reed Act for its congressional sponsors, Congressman Albert Johnson of Washington and Senator David A. Reed of Pennsylvania, set national quotas based on estimates of the national origins of residents in the United States at the 1890 census. That the Senate Immigration Committee, headed by Senator William Paul Dillingham, chose 1890 as the date from which to calculate national origins was significant. That year was prior to the most extensive immigration from southern and eastern Europe, particularly Italy and the Balkan countries.

Immigration to the United States from all areas rose tremendously in the late nineteenth century, but after 1896 most European immigrants came from areas different from those of previous immigrants. A large proportion of immigrants in the mid-1800's had been from western Europe, particularly the British Isles and Germany. Pressures such as the Irish potato famine of the 1840's and the Franco-German conflicts in the third quarter of the century created these immigrant flows. The "new" immigrants, as they were called to distinguish them from immigrant groups already established in the United States by the 1890's, stood out in part simply because they came from other parts of Europe and the world, not only southern and eastern Europe but also, in significant numbers, Japan and the Far East.

The new immigrants could be differentiated from native-born residents of the United States and earlier immigrant groups on grounds other than their national origins. They were often physically distinguishable, with darker skin or non-"white" color (such as olive-skinned Italians or the Asian peoples), or smaller stature. They were different religiously from earlier groups, with many southern Europeans being Catholic and Asian immigrants being non-Christians, in contrast to the Protestantism (excepting the Irish) of earlier immigrant groups. The new immigrants settled in unprecedented patterns as well. Generally, they were not as drawn to farms in the Midwest as to urban and industrial communities and mining areas in the Northeast.

Restriction of immigration through legislation had broad support in 1924. A few efforts to moderate the provisions of the Johnson-Reed Act, such as the attempt by Secretary of State Charles Evans Hughes to make the act comport with earlier diplomatic agreements allowing residency for certain Japanese aliens, were rebuffed by Congress. The reasons advanced for limiting or stopping new immigrant groups from coming to the United States included humanitarian concerns about urban overcrowding, arguments about preserving the purity of a supposed "Nordic" race, scientific and pseudo-scientific concerns about racial characteristics, pleas to limit the labor supply, and arguments about the alleged links between the new immigrants and radical political movements. A few groups, including organizations representing business such as the National Organization of Manufacturers, consistently argued against limitations on immigration, hoping that immigration would provide continued flows of inexpensive (and often nonunion) factory and unskilled labor. Their desires were drowned out in the calls for restriction.

U.S. Health Service officers inspect Japanese immigrants as they arrive on the West Coast of the United States several months before Congress passed the restrictive Immigration Act of 1924. (NARA)

Labor leaders such as Samuel Gompers, who in the 1910's had been uncomfortable with the tone of restrictionist proposals, became convinced of the need to ensure the "Americanism" of the labor force after World War I. The hiring of immigrant laborers as strikebreakers in several incidents increased organized labor's fear that the new immigrants were too tractable in the hands of employers and would undercut existing pay rates. The inflation and massive unemployment of the early 1920's made the labor movement even more desperate to eliminate "foreign" (that is, new immigrant) competition for jobs.

The supporters of immigration restrictions in the years prior to passage of the 1924 act found justifications for their ideas among authors who wrote about the physical classification of human beings. Such writers on race ranged from trained biologists, geologists, and geneticists such as Francis Galton of England to amateur scientists and historians such as the widely read Madison Grant of New York City. Many of the restrictionists believed that they were practicing the science of "eugenics," or "good breeding," when they recommended that "inferior" national groups such as southern Europeans should not be allowed to "water down" the primarily whiter, Protestant, and "Nordic" groups that had arrived in the United States earlier. Such arguments found acceptance among some supporters of social Darwinism,

who believed that the "Nordic" northern Europeans were engaged in a battle for species survival. Among highly educated people in the United States, an acceptance of tenets of eugenicism and social Darwinism was widespread. Many offered it as an explanation for the success of their own well-established families. To even more extreme groups such as the Ku Klux Klan, which was at its height in influence in the postwar years, eugenics provided a "scientific" explanation for the most vicious forms of xenophobia and racism.

Nativism had been given powerful impetus by several high-profile governmental officials in the wake of World War I and the Bolshevik Revolution. Attorney General A. Mitchell Palmer launched a series of actions against radical groups and rounded up foreign agitators for deportation from the United States in 1920. Although these "Palmer raids" netted only a small number of people who finally were forced to leave the country and Palmer's "Red Scare" helped discredit its instigator, a number of political leaders, including the young J. Edgar Hoover, who had been appointed head of the new General Intelligence Division in the Department of Justice, remained convinced that radicalism, disloyalty to the United States, and new immigrants were intimately linked. The assumption that Italians, for example, were prone to anarchism and violence pervaded the internationally famous trial of Nicola Sacco and Bartolomeo Vanzetti in the mid-1920's.

1924

SIGNIFICANCE

The strong provisions of the Immigration Act of 1924 cut immigration to levels much lower than prior to the beginning of the new immigration, especially as supplemented by stepped-up enforcement in the late 1920's and 1930's, when fears about unemployment were even more pressing. Because some countries (such as Great Britain, a "preferred" nation to the restrictionists) never filled their yearly quotas, actual annual immigration under the act was much lower than the total of 150,000 persons allowed. In contrast, 1,285,000 immigrants entered the United States in 1907, the year in which immigration was highest. Nonetheless, despite the restrictive features of the 1921 and 1924 congressional immigration actions, more than 4 million people immigrated to the United States during the 1920's, compared with about 5.7 million in the previous decade. The years of the Great Depression saw a precipitous decline in immigration, with only about 528,000 immigrants. Although migration from Mexico had not been formally regulated by the 1924 act, enough small farmers began complaining about immigrants serving as cheap labor for large-scale cotton producers to pressure diplomats into restricting Mexican immigration through much stricter enforcement of visa regulations.

The fervor of restrictionist arguments moderated somewhat by the 1930's, especially as eugenics fell into disfavor because of its increasing association with fascism in Europe and as scandals smeared the reputation of the Ku Klux Klan. Ironically, however, despite Americans' mounting dismay at arguments about racial purity being advanced by Adolf Hitler, immigration restrictions (motivated in some instances by anti-Semitism) served as a powerful method for limiting immigration by Europeans seeking refuge from Nazi persecution. President Franklin D. Roosevelt refused to press for changes in immigration regulations and in the law of political asylum that would have granted admission to the United States to thousands of individuals, including children.

Immigration restriction as a national policy was severely tested by refugees from several areas of the world in the late 1940's, including people fleeing from new communist governments. The Cold War saw renewed fears within the United States that foreigners, especially from certain areas, might be spies or anti-American. Despite some administrative sympathy for refugees, notably in the administration of Harry S. Truman, legislation such as the Internal Security Act of 1950 and the McCarran-Walter Act of 1952 (both passed over presidential veto) contained strict regulation of potential subversives, strengthened the authority of government agencies to enforce immigration legislation, and kept the quota system in place.

The quota system remained as a guiding principle in U.S. immigration policy until 1965, when new grounds for establishing a person's suitability for entry into the country as a resident were established. Incremental changes in immigration law in the 1950's and early 1960's had provided for the reuniting of some immigrant families, but sweeping reforms of the quota system were blocked for a time by key members of Congress who still advocated restriction. Wholesale reform of immigration law was urged by organized labor, which long since had absorbed "new" immigrants as members, and by religious and intellectual groups that viewed the quota system as needlessly discriminatory. The authors of the Immigration Act of 1965 allowed for a "brain drain" of skilled and professional immigrants from the rest of the world into the United States, in part as a compromise with congressional restrictionists, to assure them that immigrants would be productive additions to American society.

With the passage of the 1965 act, national origin was no longer the primary determinant of an individual's ability to enter the United States. Quotas by regions of the world were retained, and a 20,000-person cap per country was applied to immigrants from the Eastern Hemisphere and later applied to those from Western Hemisphere nations. The usefulness of an individual's occupation, which first was provided as a consideration in the McCarran-Walter Act, and the necessity for political asylum could count in favor of a potential immigrant. Despite the worry that U.S. immigration policy is overly restrictive, actual levels of immigration increased steadily after World War II. The war years of the 1940's saw immigration rise to more than a million, to 2.5 million in the 1950's, 3.3 million in the 1960's, and nearly 4.5 million in the 1970's. In the 1980's and 1990's, immigration increased even more dramatically, to 71.3 million in the 1980's and more than 9 million in the 1990's, as Congress raised legal limits.

—Elisabeth A. Cawthon

FURTHER READING

American Council of Learned Societies. "Report of the Committee on Linguistic and National Stocks in the Population of the United States." In *Annual Report of the American Historical Association by the American Historical Society*. Washington, D.C.: Government Printing Office, 1932. Presents the findings of the committee assigned to determine the national origins of the population of the United States. Useful for information on the methods used by social scientists to circumvent problems resulting from gaps in early census data.

Bolino, August C. *The Ellis Island Source Book*. Washington, D.C.: Kensington Historical Press, 1985. Volume intended as a resource for families researching immigrant history includes a history of Ellis Island and U.S. immigration restriction.

Calavita, Kitty. *U.S. Immigration Law and the Control of Labor, 1820-1924*. London: Academic Press, 1984. Theoretical discussion of U.S. immigration policy is heavily informed by neo-Marxist analysis of the role of the state in promoting capitalism. Argues that pressure for the 1924 act was widespread and not attributable to any single group or set of interests.

Curran, Thomas J. *Xenophobia and Immigration, 1820-1930*. Boston: Twayne, 1975. Basic overview of the reasons for immigration restriction throughout U.S. history, focusing on nativism and groups such as the Ku Klux Klan.

Daniels, Roger. *Guarding the Golden Door: American Immigration Policy and Immigrants Since 1882*. New York: Hill & Wang, 2004. Examines trends in and influences on U.S. immigration policy from late in the nineteenth century to the beginning of the twenty-first century. Chapter 2 addresses the period of the 1920's. Includes tables and charts, bibliography, and index.

Divine, Robert A. *American Immigration Policy, 1924-1952*. New Haven, Conn.: Yale University Press, 1957. Reprint. New York: Da Capo Press, 1972. One of the most comprehensive treatments available of the history of immigration restriction from the 1924 act through the mid-1950's. Provides a detailed summary of the attitudes of both restrictionists and their opponents and describes the reasons behind the move to a national-origins system. Includes bibliography and index.

Garis, Roy. *Immigration Restriction*. New York: Macmillan, 1927. Work by a Vanderbilt University economist who supported restriction and the national-origins system demonstrates the prorestrictionist perspective of the time. Senate and House committees used some of the charts and graphs in this book to support a change from the 1921 method of using the census. Includes an index and a bibliography prepared by the Library of Congress for Congress.

Higham, John. *Strangers in the Land: Patterns of American Nativism, 1860-1925*. 2d ed. New Brunswick, N.J.: Rutgers University Press, 1988. Classic account of anti-immigrant hostility in the United States from the Civil War to the imposition of the national-origins system. Gives a complete account of the congressional struggle for immigration restriction and presents a detailed analysis of the 1924 legislative victory. Includes bibliography and index.

Hutchinson, E. P. *Legislative History of American Immigration Policy, 1798-1965*. Philadelphia: University of Pennsylvania Press, 1981. Encyclopedic discussion of all major pieces of immigration legislation considered and passed by Congress. Chronicles changes in the forms of various bills as they passed through committees and floor discussions.

Kessner, Thomas. *The Golden Door: Italian and Jewish Immigrant Mobility in New York City, 1880-1915*. New York: Oxford University Press, 1977. Uses a variety of local records, including census materials, to argue that "new" Italian and Jewish immigrants in New York City were upwardly mobile, despite the fears of nativists.

LeMay, Michael, and Elliott Robert Barkan, eds. *U.S. Immigration and Naturalization Laws and Issues: A Documentary History*. Westport, Conn.: Greenwood Press, 1999. Collection of primary documents on immigration history. Includes bibliographical references and index.

Taylor, Philip. *The Distant Magnet: European Emigration to the U.S.A*. New York: Harper & Row, 1971. Vivid and readable account of the motivations for and experience of immigration to the United States, drawn from diverse source materials. Captures the pathos and richness of a variety of cultures and the venom of restrictionist arguments. Includes photographs.

Tichenor, Daniel J. *Dividing Lines: The Politics of Immigration Control in America*. Princeton, N.J.: Princeton University Press, 2002. Examines the history of immigration policy in the United States since the nation's founding, focusing on the factors that have influenced attitudes toward immigration and immigrants. Includes tables, figures, and index.

SEE ALSO: Feb. 5, 1917: Immigration Act of 1917; May 19, 1921: Emergency Quota Act; Nov. 13, 1922: *Ozawa v. United States*; May 28, 1924: U.S. Congress Establishes the Border Patrol; Early 1930's: Mass Deportations of Mexicans.

1924

May 28, 1924
U.S. CONGRESS ESTABLISHES THE BORDER PATROL

The U.S. Congress established the U.S. Border Patrol to prevent undocumented immigrants from Latin America and Canada from entering the United States.

LOCALE: Washington, D.C.

CATEGORIES: Government and politics; civil rights and liberties; business and labor; immigration, emigration, and relocation

KEY FIGURES

John Box (1871-1941), U.S. congressman from Texas

James J. Davis (1873-1947), U.S. secretary of labor, 1921-1929

William Green (1873-1952), president of the American Federation of Labor

Claude Hudspeth (1877-1941), U.S. congressman from Texas

Charles Evans Hughes (1862-1948), U.S. secretary of state, 1921-1925

SUMMARY OF EVENT

The United States Border Patrol was created in 1924 to curtail illegal immigration from Latin America and Canada. Previously, a force of fewer than forty mounted inspectors rode the borders looking for Chinese migrants attempting to enter the country in violation of the 1882 Chinese Exclusion Act. Mexican workers were so valuable to the economy of the American Southwest that little effort was made to prevent them from crossing the Rio Grande to work as agricultural laborers for cotton and sugar beet growers. The addition of a literacy test to immigration requirements in 1917, during World War I, made it more difficult for farmhands to enter, but they could easily avoid the test by sneaking into the country at night. Enforcement was lax because farm owners depended on a cheap labor supply for their economic livelihood.

In the early 1920's, illegal immigration from Mexico far exceeded the average of fifty thousand legitimate immigrants per year. In 1921, the U.S. Congress adopted a restrictive immigration policy based on a national quota system. Some legislators asserted that the peoples of the Western Hemisphere should be included in the limitations, but their argument did not succeed because of opposition from the State Department and from agricultural interests in Texas, Arizona, and California. Secretary of State Charles Evans Hughes told Congress that limiting immigration from Latin America would harm U.S. at-

tempts to improve diplomatic relations with that part of the world, and farmers and growers claimed that they needed a steady supply of migrant labor from south of the border to stay in business. For these reasons, both the Senate and the House agreed to put no immigration restrictions on New World peoples.

When Congress passed a law in 1924 establishing a system of immigration quotas based on national origins, it again excluded people from the Western Hemisphere. A proposal to include Latin Americans and Canadians under this more restrictive policy failed by large margins in both the House and the Senate. Hughes once again testified in opposition to the amendment and repeated his statement that the foreign policy of the United States demanded favorable treatment for migrants from Western nations. A new element entered this debate in Congress, however, as several legislators, led by Representative John Box of Texas, emphasized what they perceived as the racial and cultural inferiority of the Mexican population. The discussion in Congress focused on Mexicans because they made up the largest portion of immigrants from nations in the Western Hemisphere. Almost one hundred thousand had crossed the border legally in 1924, and thousands more had entered illegally to avoid paying the eighteen-dollar visa fee required of all immigrants under the new law. Fewer than five thousand Central and South Americans came into the United States that year, and they were not perceived as a threat.

Advocates of ending both legal and illegal immigration argued that Mexicans were taking away American jobs and working for starvation wages. The American Federation of Labor, under its new president, William Green, and the American Legion were major proponents of this viewpoint. "Scientific racists," who believed that white America was disappearing, argued about the dangers of "colored blood" polluting the population and contaminating the American way of life. Most Mexicans had some Indian blood in their ancestry, and, according to racial theorists of the time, Indians were inferior to Nordic types in intelligence and physical ability. The 1924 law was aimed at keeping the "inferior" races of southern and eastern Europe out of the country. It made no sense, therefore, to allow free access to inferiors from other parts of the world. These arguments had been successful in winning approval of the 1921 quota system, whereby each nationality group in the United States was limited in immigration each year to 3 percent of its total number in the United States according to the 1910 census. The 1924 law reduced the total to 2 percent of the population according to the census base of 1890. Congress decided to remove Latin America and Canada from these restrictions principally because of the belief that cheap Mexican labor was necessary to keep American farmers prosperous.

Labor unions had frequently challenged that view. During the 1921-1922 depression in the United States, unions began a campaign to include Latin Americans under the immigration quota system. They had a strong ally in Secretary of Labor James J. Davis, a former union president. In 1922, Davis ordered all unemployed Mexicans to leave the United States. Resentment and violence mounted because of the economic hard times, and in some Texas towns starving Mexicans were physically expelled. When the short depression ended and job opportunities opened up, agricultural interests petitioned Congress to reopen the borders. Mexican labor was too valuable to the economy to exclude completely, because Mexicans did the jobs Americans simply would not do, and for wages that Americans would not accept. The Spanish-speaking aliens would not become permanent residents, Congress was reassured, and they offered no political threat because the poll tax still in effect in Texas and other southern states prevented them from voting. Sugar beet growers and cotton farmers tried to appease the labor unions by arguing that the aliens were unskilled laborers and therefore not a threat to American workers.

The same reasoning kept Canadians from inclusion in the new immigration system. These immigrants were mostly from French-speaking Quebec and worked in New England textile mills for very low wages. Most of the congressional debate centered on Mexicans, with little discussion of immigration from the north. The major fear in Congress seemed to be that large numbers of "peons" from south of the border were entering the United States illegally and that they posed a threat to American values and customs because they were Catholics and spoke a foreign language. Something had to be done to stop the flood, but the economic interests of southwestern farmers would also have to be protected. If, for foreign policy and economic reasons, Latin Americans could not be in the quota system, the reasoning went, perhaps the borders of the United States could be secured from illegal immigration by tighter controls. The smuggling of impoverished workers from south of the border was a major problem, and no agency of the American government existed to control it.

Concern over the flow of laborers from the south led to the establishment of the U.S. Border Patrol on May 28, 1924. Congressman Claude Hudspeth, who owned a large farm in East Texas but was not dependent on Mexican labor, proposed the agency's creation and got Congress to provide one million dollars for this new branch of the Bureau of Immigration and Naturalization in the Department of Labor. The Border Patrol initially had 450 officers whose main job was to ride the Mexican border on horseback to seek out smugglers and the hiding places of illegal aliens. Patrol officers were told to expel any alien who could not prove that he or she had paid the visa fee.

Opposition to the Border Patrol proved to be considerable. Ranchers and farmers protested and interfered with the arrests of their laborers. The growers bitterly assailed the increasingly difficult requirements for legal immigration. The 1924 law mandated not only a ten-dollar visa fee, which had to be paid to an American consul in the nation of origin, but also a six-dollar head tax for each applicant. Few Mexicans could afford these fees, given that their average wage was twelve cents for a ten-hour day in their homeland, thus illegal entry and the smuggling of laborers increased. By paying a small sum to a smuggler, a Mexican peasant could avoid the fees and the literacy test and easily find jobs paying more than a dollar per day in Texas, Arizona, and California.

In its first year of operation, the small Border Patrol staff reported turning back fifteen thousand aliens seeking illegal entry, but an estimated one hundred thousand farmworkers successfully evaded the border guards. In an attempt to improve the Border Patrol's success rate, in 1926 Congress doubled the number of officers and made the agency a permanent part of the Bureau of Immigration and Naturalization.

SIGNIFICANCE

During its first three years of operation, the Border Patrol turned back an annual average of fifteen thousand Mexicans seeking illegal entry. It did not have enough personnel to end all illegal entry, and Mexican workers were too valuable to the economy of the Southwest to eliminate completely. Ranchers and farmers who benefited greatly by using Mexican labor continued to oppose the patrol's efforts to pick up and deport field hands who preferred to deal with smugglers rather than pay the visa fee and head tax.

In 1926, the Immigration Service backed away from strict enforcement of the law and entered into a "gentlemen's agreement" with agricultural interests in California and Texas that called for registration of all Mexican

1924

workers in the states. Each worker would receive an identification card that allowed him or her to work in exchange for an eighteen-dollar fee payable at three dollars per week. When Congressman John Box of Texas heard about this "immigration on the installment plan," he was outraged and called for an end to the "outlaw's agreement." He denounced Mexicans as racially inferior to white Europeans and warned that their illegal influx had been so large that it threatened to reverse the results of the Mexican War of 1846-1848. After that conflict, the United States had acquired California, Arizona, and much of the rest of the Southwest, but now, according to Box, "blood-thirsty, ignorant" bandits from Mexico were becoming the largest population in those areas and retaking them.

In part because of such fears, in 1929 Congress voted to double the size of the Border Patrol and demanded a crackdown on illegal entry. Congress was also responding to union demands for increased border security. Steel corporations had recently begun to recruit Mexicans from the Southwest to work in places such as Chicago and Gary, Indiana, where they were paid less than Anglo-Americans. As the pool of European immigrant labor became more restricted because of requirements concerning national origins, northern industrialists began to see Mexico and Latin America as new sources of cheap labor, much to the annoyance of labor unions. For many impoverished Mexican agricultural workers, the economic rewards seemed worth the risk, and many moved north to Illinois, Michigan, and Ohio. In response, the Texas state legislature passed a law that required labor recruiters to pay a fee of one thousand dollars before they could begin operating in the state. The growers and farmers did not want all their cheap labor to move north.

Congress also passed a new law, suggested by the State Department, according to which anyone caught entering the United States after having been deported previously could be charged with a felony and be liable for up to two years' imprisonment. This legislation greatly decreased illegal entry into North America. The Border Patrol was also authorized to cover the borders of Florida and Canada. The gentlemen's agreement was ended, and full immediate payment of fees was again required of all immigrants. These measures, plus the economic insecurity brought about by the worldwide depression that began in 1929, temporarily ended the conflict over illegal immigration from Mexico and other nations of the Western Hemisphere. The issue did not reemerge as an important problem until after World War II.

The most significant impact of the creation of the U.S.

Border Patrol was that it made illegal entry into the United States much more difficult than it ever had been before. A government agency now had the authority to arrest and deport illegal aliens.

—Leslie V. Tischauser

FURTHER READING

Daniels, Roger. *Guarding the Golden Door: American Immigration Policy and Immigrants Since 1882*. New York: Hill & Wang, 2004. Examines trends in and influences on U.S. immigration policy from late in the nineteenth century to the beginning of the twenty-first century. Includes tables and charts, bibliography, and index.

Divine, Robert. *American Immigration Policy, 1924-1952*. New Haven, Conn.: Yale University Press, 1957. Detailed history of immigration policy, the debate about the national-origins system, and attempts to include the Western Hemisphere under immigration law provisions. Good background material on the most significant immigration laws and their enforcement. Includes bibliography and index.

Fogel, Walter. *Mexican Illegal Alien Workers in the United States*. Los Angeles: University of California, Institute of Industrial Relations, 1979. Provides brief description of the history, activities, and purposes of the Border Patrol. Contains useful information on the attitudes of Mexican workers and their reasons for illegally entering the United States as well as statistics concerning apprehensions and deportations. Focuses mainly on California.

Higham, John. *Strangers in the Land: Patterns of American Nativism, 1860-1925*. 2d ed. New Brunswick, N.J.: Rutgers University Press, 1988. Classic account of anti-immigrant hostility in the United States describes the attitudes of Texans and Californians toward their neighbors south of the border. Offers extensive discussion of anti-Catholic motivations for immigration restriction. Includes bibliography and index.

Perkins, Clifford A. *Border Patrol: With the U.S. Immigration Service on the Mexican Boundary, 1910-1954*. El Paso: Texas Western Press, 1978. Presents the recollections and adventures of a former Border Patrol district officer. Discusses the founding, staffing, and organization of the Border Patrol and the contributions of some of its early members. Provides useful information on the education, attitudes, and responsibilities of officers and relates many anecdotes concerning the methods they use.

Reisler, Mark. *By the Sweat of Their Brow: Mexican Immigrant Labor in the United States, 1900-1940*. Reprint. Westport, Conn.: Greenwood Press, 1976. Detailed, well-written history of Mexican immigration and the problem of illegal aliens. Discusses the organization and purpose of the Border Patrol and summarizes its accomplishments and problems. Presents an excellent discussion of the motivations of agricultural interests and restrictionists and provides complete statistics on the impact of enforcement on the movement of people across the border. Includes extensive bibliography and index.

Tichenor, Daniel J. *Dividing Lines: The Politics of Immigration Control in America*. Princeton, N.J.: Princeton University Press, 2002. Examines the history of immigration policy in the United States since the nation's founding, focusing on the factors that have influenced attitudes toward immigration and immigrants. Includes tables, figures, and index.

SEE ALSO: Feb. 5, 1917: Immigration Act of 1917; May 19, 1921: Emergency Quota Act; May 26, 1924: Immigration Act of 1924; Early 1930's: Mass Deportations of Mexicans.

June 2, 1924
INDIAN CITIZENSHIP ACT

The Indian Citizenship Act conferred U.S. citizenship on all Native Americans born within territorial limits of the United States, thus encouraging the dissolution of tribal nations.

LOCALE: Washington, D.C.
CATEGORIES: Laws, acts, and legal history; indigenous peoples' rights

KEY FIGURES
Henry Laurens Dawes (1816-1903), U.S. senator from Massachusetts
James Rood Doolittle (1815-1897), U.S. senator from Wisconsin
John Elk (fl. early twentieth century), American Indian who voluntarily separated from his tribe but was denied the right to vote in Nebraska
Homer P. Snyder (1863-1937), U.S. congressman from New York

SUMMARY OF EVENT

American Indians hold a unique position in U.S. society and law, so the question of their citizenship has been complicated. By the time of the Revolutionary War, it was established practice for European colonial powers to negotiate treaties with American Indian tribes, as they were considered to be independent nations, and this policy was continued by the United States. The U.S. Constitution regards tribes as distinct political units, separate and apart from the United States, although not foreign nations, so as long as American Indians were members of tribes or nations that negotiated treaties with the U.S. government as semi-independent political units, they could not be considered U.S. citizens. Two significant court rulings made it clear that an act of Congress would be required to grant citizenship to American Indians.

The issue of whether American Indians were citizens came into question when the Fourteenth Amendment to the Constitution was adopted in 1868. The amendment states that "all persons born or naturalized within the United States and subject to the jurisdiction thereof, are citizens of the State wherein they reside." This amendment was intended to grant citizenship to newly emancipated slaves; however, there was a question as to whether it covered American Indians as well. In 1868, Senator James Rood Doolittle of Wisconsin led the opposition to the extension of citizenship to American Indians under the Fourteenth Amendment. Many tribes were not yet settled on reservations and tribal wars were taking place in the Great Plains, and Doolittle felt strongly that Indians were not yet prepared for citizenship. There was considerable confusion in the Senate as to whether Indians living with tribal connections were subject to the jurisdiction of the United States. It was decided that Fourteenth Amendment rights did not extend to American Indians when the Senate Committee on the Judiciary ruled, in 1870, that tribal Indians were not granted citizenship under the Fourteenth Amendment because they were not subject to the jurisdiction of the United States in the sense meant by the amendment.

Once this matter was settled, issues arose over the status of American Indians who voluntarily severed relationships with their tribes. John Elk, an American Indian who had terminated relations with his tribe and lived and worked in Omaha, Nebraska, sought to register to vote in

1924

a local election. Elk met all the requirements to vote in the state of Nebraska, but he was refused the right to vote because election officials, and later the courts, ruled that as an American Indian, he was not a U.S. citizen. In 1884, the U.S. Supreme Court upheld the lower court decisions, ruling in *Elk v. Wilkins* that an Indian born as a member of a tribe, although he disassociated himself from that tribe and lived among whites, was not a citizen and therefore was ineligible to vote. This ruling indicated it would take a specific act of Congress to naturalize American Indians.

By the 1880's, many persons in the United States sought to end tribal sovereignty, individualize Indians (end their status as tribal members), and grant citizenship to them so they eventually would be amalgamated into the general population. As a means toward this end, Senator Henry Laurens Dawes of Massachusetts, a leader in reform legislation for American Indian issues, sponsored the General Allotment Act, which became law in 1887. This act carried provisions for citizenship as a reward for Indians who would leave their tribes and adopt "the habits of civilized life." In part, this meant that American Indians had to accept small plots of land, successfully farm their land, and learn the English language. Provisions in the General Allotment Act meant that eventually every American Indian could become a citizen, except for members of tribes specifically excluded in legislation. Indians in Oklahoma were originally excluded from these provisions, but in 1901, a congressional act granted Indians in Oklahoma Territory citizenship. By 1917, through a variety of federal statutes, as many as two-thirds of all Native Americans were U.S. citizens. However, U.S. involvement in World War I reopened the debate about citizenship for American Indians as a whole.

American Indians actively supported the war effort by working to increase food production, by purchasing war bonds, by contributing to the Red Cross, and, most dramatically, by enlisting in the armed forces. Between 6,000 and 10,000 Indians, many of whom were not citizens, enlisted for military service. In return for their service to the country, Representative Homer P. Snyder of New York authored the Veterans Citizenship Bill, which became law on November 6, 1919. This law granted any American Indian who had received an honorable discharge from U.S. military service during World War I the right to apply for citizenship with no restrictions on the right to tribal property. Still, by 1920, some 125,000 American Indians were not citizens. Many people in the United States believed that all Indians should be rewarded for their patriotism during World War I, and

Snyder introduced a bill in Congress that would make U.S. citizens of all remaining noncitizen Indians born in the United States. Political maneuvering began at once.

Many people favored citizenship for Indians as a way to sever the legal relationship between the tribes and the federal government, and many American Indians were aware that citizenship could alter their tribal governments and possibly dissolve the reservation land base. In particular, full-blooded members of many tribes were fearful that citizenship would end tribal sovereignty, bring them under state jurisdiction, and ultimately destroy tribal life and values. Compromise was required to resolve these conflicting views. In January, 1924, Congressman Snyder introduced House Resolution 6355, authorizing the secretary of the interior to grant citizenship to all American Indians but ensuring that "the granting of such citizenship shall not in any manner impair or otherwise affect the right of any Indian to tribal or other property." The bill was approved by Congress, and the Indian Citizenship Act, signed into law on June 2, 1924, by President Calvin Coolidge, made Native Americans both citizens of the United States and persons with tribal relations.

SIGNIFICANCE

Ultimately, citizenship had little impact on the lives of most American Indians. The Bureau of Indian Affairs continued its policy of treating tribal members as wards of the government and administering affairs for American Indian citizens. The right to vote was denied to many American Indians until the 1960's, because the states had the power to determine voter eligibility and many did not consider tribal members living on reservations to reside in the states. Since that time, federal protections such as those embodied in the Voting Rights Act of 1965 have ensured that American Indians have the right to vote in federal, state, and local elections, and, as members of tribes, they also can vote in tribal elections.

—*Carole A. Barrett*

FURTHER READING

Debo, Angie. *A History of the Indians in the United States*. 1970. Reprint. Norman: University of Oklahoma Press, 1989. Comprehensive, in-depth historical survey of the Indians of the United States emphasizes tribal relations with the U.S. government. Includes index.

Hauptman, Laurence M. *Tribes and Tribulations: Misconceptions About American Indians and Their Histories*. Albuquerque: University of New Mexico Press, 1995. Collection of essays seeks to set straight a number of common misunderstandings about American Indians. Includes discussion of the topic of Indians' U.S. citizenship.

Newton, Nell Jessup, ed. *Cohen's Handbook of Federal Indian Law*. Rev. ed. New York: Matthew Bender, 2005. The most complete sourcebook on American Indian legal issues available.

Olson, James S., and Raymond Wilson. *Native Americans in the Twentieth Century*. Chicago: University of Illinois Press, 1984. Interprets major trends, events, and attitudes affecting American Indian peoples, including the myriad issues involved in the citizenship debate.

Prucha, Francis Paul. *The Great Father: The United States Government and the American Indians*. 2 vols. Lincoln: University of Nebraska Press, 1995. Semi-

nal work addresses federal-tribal relationships and the development of American Indian policy. Traces the controversies surrounding citizenship for Indians.

Smith, Michael T. "The History of Indian Citizenship." In *The American Indian Past and Present*. 2d ed. New York: John Wiley & Sons, 1981. Traces the major factors that made it difficult for American Indians to obtain citizenship.

Washburn, Wilcomb E. *Red Man's Land/White Man's Law*. 2d ed. Norman: University of Oklahoma Press, 1995. Discusses the American Indian in the complex federal-tribal context, including information on citizenship. Features footnotes and index.

SEE ALSO: Jan. 5, 1903: *Lone Wolf v. Hitchcock*; Oct. 12, 1912: First Conference of the Society of American Indians; June 18, 1934: Indian Reorganization Act.

June 3, 1924
GILA WILDERNESS AREA IS DESIGNATED

Aldo Leopold's success in having approximately 755,000 acres of the Gila National Forest preserved as wilderness marked the beginning of formal wilderness preservation in the United States.

LOCALE: Gila National Forest, New Mexico
CATEGORIES: Environmental issues; government and politics; natural resources

KEY FIGURES
Aldo Leopold (1887-1948), American wildlife biologist, ecologist, and author
Arthur H. Carhart (1892-1978), American landscape architect and conservation writer
Frank C. W. Pooler (b. 1882), head of the U.S. Forest Service in Arizona and New Mexico
William B. Greeley (1879-1955), chief of the U.S. Forest Service, 1920-1928
Stephen T. Mather (1867-1930), first director of the National Park Service
Henry C. Wallace (1866-1924), U.S. secretary of agriculture, 1921-1924

SUMMARY OF EVENT
On June 3, 1924, District Forester Frank C. W. Pooler approved a recreation plan for the Gila National Forest in New Mexico. The plan incorporated Aldo Leopold's proposal for a Gila Wilderness Area of approximately 755,000 acres. This decision is widely regarded as the

first formal designation of an area to be managed as wilderness in the national forests of the United States.

In the first decades after its establishment in 1905, the U.S. Forest Service was militantly utilitarian, committed to using the resources of the national forests to foster the economic development of the nation. Timber harvesting, mining, grazing, and the development of roads, resorts, and communities were encouraged. Recreation was tolerated as a secondary use, but wilderness preservation was resisted. Despite calls for wilderness preservation from organizations such as the Ecological Society of America and the American Association for the Advancement of Science, the idea of prohibiting economic development in any part of the national forests was alien to most in the Forest Service.

Not every forester shared this view. Two who did not were Arthur H. Carhart and Aldo Leopold. Carhart was a landscape architect working for the Forest Service in Colorado as a recreation engineer. Carhart accepted appointment to the Forest Service in April, 1919, and before the year was out, he had made three major contributions to national forest wilderness preservation.

First, he was asked to survey the Trappers Lake area of Colorado's White River National Forest for home sites and a road. He completed the survey but argued that neither the road nor the homes should be built. He contended that the area was best left undeveloped. Carhart's superiors agreed, and his proposal to preserve the Trap-

1924

pers Lake area was incorporated in a district recreation plan. The 118,000-acre Flat Tops Primitive Area, protecting a part of the Trappers Lake region, was eventually set aside by the Forest Service. In 1975, the U.S. Congress designated the 235,000-acre Flat Tops Wilderness.

Second, Carhart traveled the Superior National Forest of Minnesota by canoe and prepared a preliminary report recommending protection of natural features and exclusion of roads. A revised report and proposal for a Superior Roadless Area was approved by Secretary of Agriculture Henry C. Wallace in April, 1923, a year before the Gila reservation. For forty years, the Superior Roadless Area enjoyed varying levels of protection from Congress and the Forest Service. Congress gave the area statutory protection in the Wilderness Act of 1964 and enlarged the area in 1978. As of 2006, nearly 800,000 acres were being managed as the Boundary Waters Canoe Area Wilderness.

Third, Carhart attracted the attention of Leopold, who traveled to Denver to meet Carhart in December, 1919. After a day of conversation, Leopold asked Carhart to put his thoughts in writing. The resulting memorandum to Leopold described the kinds of areas Carhart believed should be protected from development and predicted that, in time, the protected areas would be among the most cherished in the national forests.

Environmental historian Donald N. Baldwin argues persuasively that Carhart is the true father of the wilderness concept, but the Forest Service and most conservationists have bestowed that title on Aldo Leopold, who, above all others, gave voice to the growing movement for wilderness preservation. Leopold was a gifted and frequently published writer. Where others spoke of limiting development of or providing opportunities for primitive recreation, Leopold used the term "wilderness" and argued that its preservation was consistent with the utilitarian mission of the Forest Service.

Indeed, Leopold's initial interest in wilderness preservation was itself utilitarian. His advocacy predated by decades the ecological consciousness for which he would eventually be well known. Whereas Carhart was a landscape architect concerned with aesthetics, Leopold was an avid hunter and was preoccupied with wildlife of every description. To Leopold, wilderness meant game and public recreational space. Wilderness preservation meant preservation of the hunt. Writing in the *Journal of Forestry* in 1921, Leopold defined wilderness as "a continuous stretch of country preserved in its natural state, open to lawful hunting and fishing, big enough to absorb a two weeks' pack trip, and kept devoid of roads, artificial trails,

cottages, or other works of man." He asked whether the Forest Service's "principle of highest use does not itself demand that representative portions of some forests be preserved as wilderness," and he proposed protection of nearly half a million acres encompassing the headwaters of the Gila River in the Gila National Forest.

Leopold toured the Gila area during the summer of 1920. His inspection report, completed in July, contained a wilderness area recommendation. Leopold's supervisor, Pooler, approved the report in August and invited Leopold to prepare a more formal wilderness area proposal for discussion at the winter meeting of district foresters. The proposal was completed in October, discussed in nearby communities, mislaid for some time in the district office, and eventually approved by Pooler on June 3, 1924, five days after Leopold had left the Southwest for a new assignment as assistant director of a forest-products laboratory in Madison, Wisconsin. Historians are not unanimous on this point, but the U.S. Forest Service recognizes June 3, 1924, as the birth date of the national forest wilderness system.

LEOPOLD ON DEVELOPMENT

In an article published a little more than a year after official designation of the Gila Wilderness Area, Aldo Leopold continued to argue for the need to protect wilderness lands against development:

If in a city we had six vacant lots available to the youngsters of a certain neighborhood for playing ball, it might be "development" to build houses on the first, and the second, and the third, and the fourth, and even the fifth, but when we build houses on the last one, we forget what houses are for. The sixth house would not be development at all, but rather it would be mere short-sighted stupidity. "Development" is like Shakespeare's virtue, "which grown into a pleurisy, dies of its own too-much."

In objection to the dedication of the Gila as a permanent wilderness hunting ground, it has been truly said that a part of the area which would be "locked up" bears valuable stands of timber. I admit that this is true. Likewise, might our sixth lot be a corner lot, and hence very valuable for a grocery store or a filling station. I still insist *it is the last lot* for a needed playground, and this being the case, I am not interested in grocery stores or filling stations, of which we have a fair to middling supply elsewhere.

Source: Aldo Leopold, "A Plea for Wilderness Hunting Grounds," *Outdoor Life*, November, 1925.

SIGNIFICANCE

The Gila Wilderness was the first large tract officially designated as a wilderness area by a federal land-management agency. Its initial size was approximately 755,000 acres. Under changing Forest Service regulations, the Gila reservation was designated a Primitive Area in 1933, and about 438,000 acres of it were designated a Wilderness Area in 1953. The Gila Wilderness Area received statutory protection with the passage of the 1964 Wilderness Act, and in 1980, Congress created the Aldo Leopold Wilderness to the east of the Gila Wilderness. The Gila Wilderness is composed of 558,000 acres, and the Aldo Leopold is made up of an additional 202,000 acres. The total acreage protected as wilderness is approximately the size that Leopold proposed, but the acreage is in two units divided by a road, the construction of which Leopold had tried to prevent.

Despite Leopold's initial success with the Gila reservation, the nation was far from having a wilderness system in the 1920's. During the next several years, Leopold wrote extensively. He targeted different audiences in different journals, but always he sought to build a political constituency for wilderness preservation. Nevertheless, most of the Forest Service leadership remained committed to a narrower view of utility.

A catalyst was required to awaken the Forest Service to the value of wilderness preservation that catalyst was provided by the National Park Service. The National Park Service had been established in 1916, and it was aggressively led by Stephen T. Mather. Mather saw his own agency as the only legitimate keeper of the nation's scenic and recreational space and the only legitimate recipient of federal recreational dollars. He envisioned a multitude of new national parks protecting scenic areas in the American West. Most of the areas Mather envisioned as future national parks were already national forests. Growth of the national park system would come at the expense of the national forests. This was an unhappy prospect for policy makers in the national headquarters of the Forest Service.

Both agencies recognized a growing public interest in outdoor recreation, and both agencies attempted to exploit it. Under Mather's leadership, the National Park Service emphasized development, spectacle, and public enjoyment over nature preservation. The service built miles of roads, developed numerous campgrounds, and encouraged the construction of railroads and hotels. It organized ranger walks, held public bear feedings, tunneled a road through a standing sequoia tree, and perpetuated the "firefall," a bonfire built each evening on Glacier Point in Yosemite National Park to be pushed over the cliff into the valley below. These activities were popular with the traveling public but left the Park Service vulnerable to the charge that it was insufficiently sensitive to its preservation mission.

For Chief Forester William B. Greeley and his Washington staff, the wilderness proposals of Carhart and Leopold provided a possible means of defense against bureaucratic aggression from the National Park Service. If the national parks were to be turned into playgrounds, perhaps the Forest Service could champion real wilderness preservation. This was not an easy choice for an agency that contemplated trees primarily in terms of board feet of lumber. Greeley moved slowly, but gradually he embraced wilderness preservation. He canceled highly publicized plans for scenic highways in California and a cable car to the summit of Mount Hood, and he ordered foresters in the West to safeguard areas appropriate for preservation as wilderness. At the same time, Greeley publicly criticized the National Park Service for its policy of encouraging the construction of roads and hotels and the use of buses. The national forests, he wrote, would "provide some sizeable areas of real wilderness."

Greeley's use of wilderness preservation as a shield against national park expansion was remarkably successful. Between 1920 and 1928, the National Park Service proposed removing 2.3 million acres from the national forests for new or expanded national parks. It received fewer than 600,000 acres. In the course of saving the remaining 1.7 million acres, the Forest Service created 5 million acres of designated primitive areas. These areas were not as well protected as modern wilderness areas, and the designations might have been withdrawn at any time by the Forest Service. Still, the primitive areas set aside by the Forest Service in the 1920's constituted the nation's first wilderness preservation system.

The Forest Service primitive areas, inspired by Carhart and Leopold and motivated by fear of national park expansion, have been critical to the subsequent development of the wilderness system in the United States. The Forest Service institutionalized its primitive area system through the promulgation of Regulation L-20 in 1929. The regulation stipulated maintenance of primitive conditions for public education and recreation, but it nevertheless allowed limited development of timber, forage, and water resources. By 1937, the primitive area system had grown to seventy-two units and more than 13 million acres. In 1939, a new set of regulations went into effect.

1924

The primitive areas were to be reclassified as "wilderness," "wild," or "roadless/canoe," and boundary revisions were to be made. The reclassified areas were subject to more restrictive wilderness management, and their preserved status was understood to be permanent.

Even the Wilderness Act of 1964 and its administrative aftermath have been significantly shaped by the decisions to create primitive areas in the 1920's. When Congress established a statutory wilderness system in 1964, areas classified wilderness, wild, or roadless/canoe became charter members. Primitive areas that had not yet been reclassified by the Forest Service were protected by the law but not formally classified as wilderness. Instead, the secretary of agriculture was ordered to study the areas' wilderness potential and make recommendations to Congress.

The 1964 Wilderness Act designated 9 million acres as wilderness exempt from most forms of development, all of it in the national forests. By the early 2000's, the statutory wilderness system in the United States had grown to more than 106 million acres of public lands, in 663 wilderness areas, with units managed by the Forest Service, the National Park Service, the Fish and Wildlife Service, and the Bureau of Land Management. Most Americans accept Aldo Leopold's Gila recommendation as the first significant step on the path to wilderness preservation in the United States.

—Craig W. Allin

FURTHER READING

Allin, Craig W. *The Politics of Wilderness Preservation.* Westport, Conn.: Greenwood Press, 1982. Political history of the movement to preserve wilderness areas in the United States includes discussion of the establishment of national parks and national forests in the nineteenth century, the creation of the Forest Service and the National Park Service, and the rivalry between them regarding wilderness preservation.

Baldwin, Donald N. *The Quiet Revolution: Grass Roots of Today's Wilderness Preservation Movement.* Boulder, Colo.: Pruett, 1972. Examines the history of wilderness preservation and argues that Carhart deserves recognition at least equal to that of Leopold as an early and successful champion of wilderness preservation in the U.S. national forests.

Flader, Susan L. *Thinking Like a Mountain: Aldo Leopold and the Evolution of an Ecological Attitude Toward Deer, Wolves, and Forests.* 1974. Reprint. Madison: University of Wisconsin Press, 1994. Excellent biography emphasizes the development of Leopold's conservation philosophy. Chapter 3 examines "the Gila experience."

Knight, Richard L., and Susanne Riedel, eds. *Aldo Leopold and the Ecological Conscience.* New York: Oxford University Press, 2002. Collection of essays on Leopold's contributions to the environmental movement by ecologists, wildlife biologists, and conservationists who knew Leopold personally. Includes index.

Leopold, Aldo. *Aldo Leopold's Wilderness.* Harrisburg, Pa.: Stackpole Books, 1990. Collection of many of Leopold's early wilderness advocacy articles is a much-needed addition to the Leopold literature.

Meine, Curt. *Aldo Leopold: His Life and Work.* Madison: University of Wisconsin Press, 1988. Definitive traditional biography places Leopold's wilderness preservation work in the context of his overall life and times. Includes bibliography and index.

Meine, Curt, and Richard L. Knight, eds. *The Essential Aldo Leopold: Quotations and Commentaries.* Madison: University of Wisconsin Press, 1999. Unique collection joins quotations from Leopold's writings with commentaries on his work and ideas from historians, conservationists, philosophers, and biologists.

Murray, John A. *The Gila Wilderness Area: A Hiking Guide.* Albuquerque: University of New Mexico Press, 1988. Volume aimed at hikers includes informative chapters on the natural and human history of the Gila area. Features an excellent bibliography.

Nash, Roderick Frazier. *Wilderness and the American Mind.* 4th ed. New Haven, Conn.: Yale University Press, 2001. One of the best single sources on the role of wilderness in American intellectual history. Chapter 11, titled "Aldo Leopold: Prophet," presents an excellent synopsis of Leopold's role in the wilderness movement.

Tanner, Thomas, ed. *Aldo Leopold: The Man and His Legacy.* Ankeny, Iowa: Soil Conservation Society of America, 1987. Collection resulting from an Aldo Leopold centennial celebration at Iowa State University. Brings together work by most of the nation's leading Leopold scholars and reminiscences by members of the Leopold family.

SEE ALSO: May 20, 1919: National Parks and Conservation Association Is Founded; Sept., 1933: Marshall Writes *The People's Forests*; Mar. 16, 1934: Migratory Bird Hunting and Conservation Stamp Act; Oct. 19, 1934: Marshall and Leopold Form the Wilderness Society; Feb. 4, 1936: Darling Founds the National Wildlife Federation.

June 7, 1924
OIL POLLUTION ACT SETS PENALTIES FOR POLLUTERS

The Oil Pollution Act of 1924 was the first U.S. law to establish civil and criminal penalties for the grossly negligent or intentional discharge of oil from a vessel into U.S. waters.

LOCALE: Washington, D.C.
CATEGORIES: Environmental issues; laws, acts, and legal history; natural resources

KEY FIGURES
Calvin Coolidge (1872-1933), president of the United States, 1923-1929
Frank B. Willis (1871-1928), U.S. senator from Delaware
Walter F. Lineberger (1883-1943), U.S. congressman from California

SUMMARY OF EVENT
On June 7, 1924, President Calvin Coolidge signed into law the Oil Pollution Act, the first U.S. law to deal specifically with oil pollution of the navigable waters of the United States and its shorelines. The law imposed civil and criminal penalties for grossly negligent or willful discharge of oil into the sea from U.S. and foreign ships. It made exceptions for unavoidable accidents and for cases in which oil was discharged to avoid danger to life or property. In the context of the law, "oil" is defined as petroleum hydrocarbons that are obtained from underground deposits and that may exist in the form of crude oil, fuel oil, heavy diesel oil, and lubricating oil. The scope of the law was limited to offshore pollution within fifty nautical miles of land.

In 1924, preventing the deliberate discharge of oil by transport tankers was impeded by the technical inability of ships to separate residue oil, called "clingage," from water in their ballast tanks (ballast is the water used in a ship to balance it on heavy and stormy seas, especially when the ship is empty of cargo, as on a return voyage to its home port). A ship's oily ballast water had to be discharged before the ship reached port in order to avoid polluting the harbor. The process of cleaning the tank required pumping the entire contents overboard; the tank was then refilled with seawater. If the journey was long enough and the seas were not too heavy, the oil in the ballast tanks would float to the top. This small amount of oil from each ship—0.3 percent of a tank—could have been saved, but a practical method to do so was not generally available. (Some British ports had barges in their harbors

for pumping clingage oil off the top layer of ballast.)

Upon nearing their home ports, most ships simply dumped their oily ballast water over the side and refilled their tanks with water. The oil pumped out this way, however, eventually washed to shore along all the tanker routes of the world. In addition, harbors became intolerably polluted, because some oil was dumped from engines and pipelines in harbors and at docks. One of the worst examples of such pollution was in New York Harbor, where in 1921 it was reported that the wharves and pilings on the harbor front were saturated with oil and the water was coated with a layer of oil. This oil saturation devastated marine life and posed a fire hazard.

Various organizations such as the Audubon Society and the National Coast Anti-Pollution League, as well as newspaper editors speaking for local groups, began to urge congressional action to address the problem of oil pollution. The Audubon Society reported that thousands of waterfowl were dying annually as a result of their plumage being covered with oil. The fishing industry was also being affected to a serious extent. In 1880, the coastal waters of the United States produced 600,000 barrels of salt mackerel in one year; by 1921, the catch had dropped to 43,000 barrels, in large part because of the destruction of spawning fish from the effects of oil pollution. It was also estimated that between 1918 and 1923 oil pollution caused an 80 percent decrease in oyster production off the coast of Connecticut. In 1923, Los Angeles had become the world's largest oil market. There, the editor of the newspaper the *Express* reported that oil-pollution damage to ships, port, fishermen's income, and residents had become a paramount issue.

The problem of oil dumping was reaching dramatic levels: The number of oil-burning and oil-carrying ships rose from 364 in 1911 to 2,536 in 1921. In 1924, the United States exported more than 4 billion gallons of petroleum products. If 0.3 percent of this amount was clingage, then nearly 13 million gallons of oil products were dumped from that source alone.

Prior to passage of the Oil Pollution Act of 1924, the only law that could be applied to tanker dumping was the Refuse Act of 1899, under which it was illegal to discard any detrimental substance into the sea in territorial waters to a three-mile limit. That law also applied to dumping from land locations. Those found guilty of violating the law were required to pay fines and removal costs, and the law also provided for rewards for informants. In

1924

1868, the Canadian government prohibited the discharge of ballast, coal, chemicals, and other polluting substances into waters where fishing was practiced, although the law did not mention oil specifically. In 1918, the United States and Canada signed the Migratory Bird Treaty Act to protect migratory birds, but that act did not recognize damage to birds by oil pollution until 1948, when an addendum was written. Although it is one of the few treaties in North America that acknowledges that valuable resources cross political boundaries, it has not been consistently applied.

The debate in Congress that produced two bills leading to the Oil Pollution Act elicited strong opinions from the oil industry. The Willis Bill, written by Senator Frank B. Willis of Delaware on January 8, 1924, proposed to make it unlawful to dump any kind of oil product, crude or refined, from either ships or land-based refineries. The law would have been administered by the War Department, because the issue it sought to address concerned navigable waters. The Willis Bill also imposed fines and imprisonment at the option of the courts. The oil industry objected to the provisions of this bill and wanted to exempt land operations from controls. The Lineberger Bill, proposed by Walter F. Lineberger, a House representative from Long Beach, California, was different from the Willis Bill in several respects: It included regulation of oil from ships only, it imposed no prison penalties, and the law would be administered by the Department of Commerce. The Lineberger Bill also provided for investigations of land industry. The oil industry, the secretary of the interior, and the deputy commissioner of fisheries supported this bill.

The two houses of Congress reached a compromise on the two bills in order to protect the interests of the public and industry as quickly as possible. The law limited liability to vessels in coastal navigable waters. Violation of the act could result in fines and prison terms, and the Coast Guard was given authority to revoke the licenses of ship captains who broke the law. Administration of the law was the responsibility of the War Department until 1966, when it was transferred to the Department of the Interior.

SIGNIFICANCE

Public concern over conservation problems associated with oil pollution began to surface after World War I, when the shipping industry began using oil rather than coal to power ships. This shift added to the oil-pollution problem, which was further exacerbated by vessel accidents, nonmarine accidents, and operations that dumped automobile waste oil into water systems. About 70 percent of the world's oil traveled by sea.

The Oil Pollution Act of 1924 was a starting point for the regulation of an industry that was growing so quickly technology could not keep up with safety and pollution standards. Shipbuilders constructed tankers of such enormous size that, at first, the ships' engines were not powerful enough to stop the giant ships in time to avert accidents. At the request of Congress, President Coolidge called an International Conference on Oil Pollution, which was held June 8-17, 1926. The conference was attended by representatives of thirteen maritime nations that recognized coastal oil pollution as a problem. The recommendations that came out of the conference included extending the prohibition on dumping from 50 to 150 nautical miles in order to protect marine life and encouraging ships to install oil separators to conserve oil and protect natural resources.

Traditionally, international laws concerning liability for accidents on the open sea have focused on damage to the beneficial uses of the sea, and prosecution has been vested in the governments of origin of the ships involved. When enforcement has conflicted with economic concerns, it has often been lax. To the extent that oil pollution resulted in public protest and damage of domestic resources, the laws that were passed in each country called attention to the need for international action. This was the case with the Oil Pollution Act of 1924. In practice, the law proved difficult to enforce, because the high seas of international territory constitute a vast region. Adherence to a law that depended on international commitment to an honor code was difficult to verify. The 1924 law relied primarily on the Coast Guard to discipline domestic vessels polluting territorial waters and to control foreign ships that acted with negligence. Unless a ship was caught in the act of committing a violation, however, there was no way to prove responsibility for an infraction.

The deficiencies in the 1924 law eventually set in motion legislation that culminated in the 1970 Water Quality Improvement Act, which amended the 1924 act. The 1970 law prohibited discharges of oil from offshore and onshore facilities and empowered the president to order measures to prevent damage to the environment and to remove spilled oil. The 1970 law removed the need for criminal prosecution when a violation is reported by the ship owner. Any other domestic or foreign ship owned by a person operating a violating ship can be denied permission to gain access to a domestic port. Responsibility was thus placed on ship owners to keep all their ships in good operating condition. In this way, Congress attempted to focus attention on prevention of oil spills rather than on after-the-fact punishment.

The establishment of oil-pollution laws motivated the oil industry to develop the technology to prevent excess discharge of oil in the cleaning of tanks and in the handling of dirty ballast water. The new methods included load-on-top systems, by which oil and water are separated and the water is drawn out. The new load of oil is added on top of the remaining oil, and all of it is discharged at the port of destination. Another method, called crude-oil washing, uses the oil itself to disperse and clean the tank residues. Ballast water is taken onboard after the cleaning. These methods are cleaner than the methods of tank washing used in the 1920's. The load-on-top method discharges only 25 percent of the oil of older methods, and the crude-oil washing method discharges only 10 percent of the oil of the load-on-top method.

The Oil Pollution Act of 1924 set a precedent for action on a federal level to control oil pollution from domestic and foreign vessels. The deficiencies of the law encouraged stronger laws and public action, which eventually required industry to develop technology to prevent spills.

—*Laura R. Broyles*

FURTHER READING

Abbott, Lawrence F. "Oil on Troubled Waters." *Outlook* 136 (April 16, 1924): 638. Editorial expresses the public's sense of urgency in calling for congressional action on oil pollution. Describes the House and Senate bills in detail and emphasizes the need for a bill to save the environment, not to serve the special interests of government organizations or industry.

_____. "To Clean the Ocean of Oil." *Outlook* 143 (May 5, 1926): 16. Editorial discusses the progress made in controlling oil pollution since the passage of the Oil Pollution Act of 1924. Advocates more cooperation among nations to curb pollution.

Edwards, Max N. "Oil Pollution and the Law." In *Oil Pollution: Problems and Policies*, edited by Stanley E. Degler. Washington, D.C.: Bureau of National Affairs, 1969. Provides a good background review on laws related to oil pollution. Includes a full copy of the Oil Pollution Act of 1924.

Mitchell, Ronald B. *Intentional Oil Pollution at Sea: Environmental Policy and Treaty Compliance*. Cambridge, Mass.: MIT Press, 1994. Focuses on the issue of how to ensure that nations comply with the terms of international treaties aimed at reducing oil pollution. Combines theoretical analysis with an evaluation of changes in compliance over time.

Ross, William M. *Oil Pollution as an International Problem*. Seattle: University of Washington Press, 1973. Excellent legal resource contains a review of state and national jurisdictions, forms of liability used in courts that cover oil-pollution claims, and information on the historical development of oil-pollution laws. Explains the weaknesses in international laws regarding oil pollution.

Tan, Alan Khee-Jin. *Vessel-Source Marine Pollution: The Law and Politics of International Regulation*. New York: Cambridge University Press, 2005. Examines the history of international oil-pollution regulation and discusses how political, economic, and social forces affect antipollution treaties.

Wagnalls, Adam W. "The Oil Trouble on the Waters." *Literary Digest* 79 (November 10, 1923): 14. Editorial details environmental damage caused by oil pollution in every coastal region of the United States. Explains the seriousness of the problem and asserts that legislation that includes international action can solve the problem.

Wardley-Smith, J., ed. *The Control of Oil Pollution*. London: Graham & Trotman, 1983. Provides detailed discussion of shipping methods for transportation, loading, and unloading of oil as well as chapters on the environmental effects of oil pollution on birds, fisheries, and plankton. Good resource for the general reader.

SEE ALSO: June 27-29, 1906: International Association for the Prevention of Smoke Is Founded; 1910: Steinmetz Warns of Pollution in "The Future of Electricity"; Jan., 1922: Izaak Walton League Is Formed; Apr. 15, 1935: Arbitration Affirms National Responsibility for Pollution; Feb. 4, 1936: Darling Founds the National Wildlife Federation.

1924

Summer, 1924

DART DISCOVERS THE FIRST AUSTRALOPITHECINE FOSSIL

Raymond Arthur Dart discovered the first australopithecine, or link between ape and man, cast in limestone recovered from a quarry in Taung, South Africa.

LOCALE: University of Witwatersrand, Johannesburg, South Africa

CATEGORIES: Anthropology; prehistory and ancient cultures

KEY FIGURES

Raymond Arthur Dart (1893-1988), Australian anatomist

Robert Broom (1866-1951), Scottish physician

SUMMARY OF EVENT

In 1871, Charles Darwin suggested in *The Descent of Man and Selection in Relation to Sex* that it was quite likely that Africa would prove to be the continent where humankind first appeared. Darwin's suggestion was to become the center of a debate that greatly influenced the field of paleoanthropology. He made his suggestion despite the fact that the only human fossils known at the time had been found in Europe; for example, the first paleontological human remains were those of Neander-

thal man, found in Germany in 1856. Indeed, the first hominid remains discovered outside Europe were those from Java found in 1891 by Eugène Dubois, which prompted Western scientists to believe that humans first appeared in Asia, not Africa. Dubois's find, better known as Java man, has since been reclassified into the genus and species *Homo erectus*.

In 1907, a fossil known as the Heidelberg man was discovered in Germany. The next hominid remains believed to be of major significance were those found by Charles Dawson in 1911 in Sussex in southern England. This fossil was placed into a new genus and species known as *Eoanthropus dawsoni*, meaning "Dawson's dawn man." The fossil is perhaps best known as Piltdown man. Although fossil discoveries that are given a new name create controversy, this was not true of Dawson's find, because it looked the way most anthropologists of the time thought it should. In other words, the cranium was large and modern-looking, and the face was primitive and apelike. At the time, it was widely believed that intellect was an important step in the evolution between humans and apes, an idea supported by the large cranium. Additionally, as a human ancestor would need to possess some primitive traits, these might be found in the face and lower jaw.

In 1924, Raymond Arthur Dart was a young professor of anatomy in his second year of teaching in the Medical School at the University of Witwatersrand in Johannesburg, South Africa. Early during that summer, a fossil was brought to him from the Taung quarry by a student, Josephine Salmons. Dart determined that the fossil was that of a previously found extinct form of baboon, but it prompted his interest in the limestone quarry at Taung. He made arrangements to receive any other fossils the workers might find in the quarry, and he later received some boxes from Taung that contained more fossils. In one box was an unusual endocast, or fossilized cast, representing the interior of a cranium, notable for its size and unique structure. Dart recognized the anatomy as that of a higher primate, but unlike that of any living ape by virtue of its increased size. Also included was a single large fragment of a fossilized facial skeleton. The endocast and face were portions of the same animal. To Dart, the remains revealed a never-before-seen combination of traits, suggesting an anthropoid halfway between man and ape.

In February, 1925, Dart introduced his find to the scientific community with a brief article in the British journal

Raymond Arthur Dart.

DART AND THE FOSSILIZED BRAIN

On a Saturday afternoon in 1924, Raymond Dart was dressing for a wedding reception when he received a shipment of fossils from Taung and decided to take a peek before leaving:

A thrill of excitement shot through me. On the very top of the rock heap was what was undoubtedly an endocranial cast or mold of the interior of the skull. Had it been only the fossilised brain cast of any species of ape it would have ranked as a great discovery, for such a thing had never before been reported. But I knew at a glance that what lay in my hands was no ordinary anthropoidal brain. Here in lime-consolidated sand was the replica of a brain three times as large as that of a baboon and considerably bigger than that of an adult chimpanzee. The startling image of the convolutions and furrows of the brain and the blood vessels of the skull were plainly visible.

It was not big enough for primitive man, but even for an ape it was a big bulging brain and, most important, the forebrain was so big and had grown so far backward that it completely covered the hindbrain.

But was there anywhere among this pile of rocks, a face to fit the brain? I ransacked feverishly through the boxes. My search was rewarded, for I found a large stone with a depression into which the cast fitted perfectly.

I stood in the shade holding the brain as greedily as any miser hugs his gold, my mind racing ahead. Here I was certain was one of the most significant finds ever made in the history of anthropology.

Source: Raymond A. Dart, *Adventures with the Missing Link* (New York: Harper and Brothers, 1959).

Nature. He described the fossil as a juvenile member of a new genus, *Australopithecus*, and new species, *africanus*. *Australo* means "of the Southern Hemisphere," *pithecus* means "simian" or "apelike," and *africanus* means "of Africa." Thus *Australopithecus africanus* literally means "the South African ape."

Except for Robert Broom, a Scottish physician who had become a well-known paleontologist as a result of his South African discoveries bridging the gap between reptiles and mammals, the scientific community immediately opposed the acceptance of Dart's discovery. A major criticism was related to Dart's introduction of the new name based on a juvenile specimen. There was no question that the fossil was that of a juvenile, because the specimen retained some of its deciduous, or baby, teeth. As a result, Dart's discovery has frequently been called Taung child, Taung baby, or Taung boy.

Some critics seized this issue and argued that new names should not be based on juvenile specimens because dramatic differences between juveniles and adults of the same species might exist. Some argued that Dart may have simply found a juvenile member of an already documented fossil primate. Criticisms also were based on the fact that the discovery was made in South Africa and not Asia, where the world's attention had become focused since Dubois's discovery in 1891. Additionally, Dart's discovery possessed a small brain and a relatively modern-looking face and dentition, unlike Dawson's Piltdown man.

By the mid-1950's, however, the discoveries of adult forms of *Australopithecus* and other intermediate forms in the same area compelled many of Dart's critics to accept his 1924 discovery. Many critics were converted to Dart's ideas as a result of the 1947 Pan-African Congress of Prehistory held in Nairobi, Kenya. The congress, organized by L. S. B. Leakey, allowed several widely respected physical anthropologists to examine some of the early African hominids firsthand.

The last barrier to acceptance was torn down in the early 1950's. In 1953, Kenneth Page Oakley and others began a reexamination of *Eoanthropus dawsoni*. Fluorine dating, a new technique, revealed that the cranium was from the late Pleistocene epoch and the mandible belonged to a modern orangutan. Both portions had been modified and stained in order to appear as though they had come from the same animal. Piltdown man was thus exposed as a fraud, and its existence could no longer hinder the acceptance of the South African australopithecines as the link between modern *Homo sapiens* and living apes.

SIGNIFICANCE

Although the limestone and sedimentary contexts from which the South African fossils were recovered did not lend themselves to accurate geological dating, one could suggest that the fossils were from the lower Pleistocene epoch, approximately one million years ago. Moreover, the South African discoveries led paleoanthropologists to conclude that early hominids first appeared in a grassland or savanna environment, as opposed to the tropical forests others were suggesting. In addition, *Australopithecus africanus* and the remaining australopithecines provided clear evidence that human ancestors possessed more or less modern jaws and were walking upright before the expansion of the brain. This idea con-

1924

tradicted the previous notions about the significance of increased cranial capacity during human evolution.

Some have called Dart's discovery of the first *Australopithecus* one of the most significant scientific events of the twentieth century. Although such claims are debatable, there can be little question that the discovery must rank near the top of any list of important events in the fields of anthropology, paleontology, and prehistory.

—*Turhon A. Murad*

FURTHER READING

Campbell, Bernard G. *Human Evolution.* 4th ed. Chicago: Aldine, 1998. Presents the major findings concerning the evolution of human beings, including discussion of the work of Dart and others in the early twentieth century as well as more recent developments in the field. Includes illustrations, glossary, bibliography, and index.

Campbell, Bernard G., and James D. Loy. *Humankind Emerging.* 8th ed. Newton, Mass.: Allyn & Bacon, 1999. Comprehensive introduction to the field of physical anthropology. Chapter 6 discusses Dart's and Broom's work. Includes glossary, selected bibliography, and index. Individual chapters feature lists of suggested further reading.

Dart, Raymond A. *Adventures with the Missing Link.* New York: Harper & Brothers, 1959. A firsthand retrospective view of the discovery of *Australopithecus africanus* and the controversies that followed.

_____. "*Australopithecus Africanus:* The Man-Ape of South Africa." *Nature* 115 (February, 1925): 195-199. The publication that announced the discovery of the first australopithecine ever recovered. Presents details about the limestone quarry site at Taung, South Africa, and the circumstances of the fossil's discovery and describes the fossil cranium and accompanying endocast. Concludes that the remains are those of a juvenile member of a new genus and species, *Australopithecus africanus.*

Johanson, Donald C., and Maitland A. Edey. *Lucy: The Beginnings of Humankind.* 1981. Reprint. New York: Simon & Schuster, 1990. Coauthored by a prominent figure in the field of paleoanthropology, this volume offers a popular account of hominid discoveries from the Pleistocene of East Africa. Addresses the financial problems encountered in such research and describes the various strong personalities and controversies that have influenced attempts to document the human fossil record.

Leakey, Richard E., and Roger Lewin. *Origins.* New York: E. P. Dutton, 1977. Draws, in part, on the work of Leakey's parents, but also discusses paleontological discoveries at Lake Turkana in northern Kenya. Suggests that three or more species of hominids may have existed as contemporaries in East Africa approximately two million years ago. Emphasizes the question of why the lineage of *Homo* survived and the others did not.

Pfeiffer, John E. *The Emergence of Humankind.* 4th ed. New York: HarperCollins, 1985. Although not written in the style of most textbooks, this volume is used frequently as a textbook in introductory physical anthropology courses. Addresses the various lines of research often employed by paleoanthropologists in their attempts to learn about the hominid fossil record.

SEE ALSO: Dec., 1908: Boule Reconstructs the First Neanderthal Skeleton; Summer, 1923: Zdansky Discovers Peking Man; Fall, 1937-Winter, 1938: Weidenreich Reconstructs the Face of Peking Man; Sept. 12, 1940: Lascaux Cave Paintings Are Discovered.

September 1, 1924
DAWES PLAN

The United States developed a plan to assist Germany in recovering from World War I.

LOCALE: Washington, D.C.; London, England; Paris, France; Berlin, Germany

CATEGORIES: Diplomacy and international relations; economics

KEY FIGURES

Charles G. Dawes (1865-1951), American lawyer, politician, and financier

Charles Evans Hughes (1862-1948), U.S. secretary of state, 1921-1925

David Lloyd George (1863-1945), former prime minister of Great Britain

Henry M. Robinson (1868-1937), American financial expert

Owen D. Young (1874-1962), American financial expert

Gustav Stresemann (1878-1929), German foreign minister

SUMMARY OF EVENT

In the aftermath of World War I, it appeared that the Treaty of Versailles had raised more problems than it solved. Among the more pressing and complicated issues were the interrelated problems of German reparations and Allied war debts. The terms of the peace treaty had forced Germany to accept blame for the war and to promise to pay damages suffered by the Allies. A special Reparations Commission fixed the sum owed by Germany at 132 million gold marks, about $33 million in gold. Even some members of the commission recognized that Germany would be unable to pay this staggering sum. The Allied governments, especially those of Great Britain and France, expressed a willingness to scale down German reparations if the United States would forgo war debts owed to it by the Allies.

The U.S. government had lent more than $10 billion to twenty nations before and after the armistice, and it refused to forget these debts or to link them with the problem of German reparations. Moreover, while European countries could repay their debts only by selling goods and services in the United States, the latter embarked in the immediate postwar period on a tariff program that represented aggressive economic nationalism and crushed any hope that European goods would be able to compete in the U.S. market. Consequently, the Allies had

to press Germany for reparations in order to repay their own debts. The German government made a few token payments, but when faced with catastrophic inflation, it defaulted. In 1923, France occupied the Ruhr, Germany's principal industrial region, and took other steps to coerce the Weimar Republic into resuming payments. The Germans replied with a policy of passive resistance. The crisis was so serious that Europe appeared to be on the verge of financial and political disintegration.

It was to avoid economic disaster in Europe that the United States intervened. Although most people in the United States supported the government's insistence on repayment of the Allied war debts and refused to accept the Anglo-French argument that reparations and war debts were interdependent, some also saw that European trade was essential to U.S. prosperity. Something had to be done to ensure that trade and financial intercourse returned to normal channels. Secretary of State Charles Evans Hughes was one of those deeply concerned about the problem, even though he was a tariff protectionist. He could not propose direct U.S. involvement in European financial affairs because of congressional and public opposition; however, he might be able to help Europe through unofficial action while avoiding serious objections at home.

In a speech before the American Historical Association in December, 1922, Secretary Hughes proposed the creation of a commission of financial experts to investigate Germany's financial situation and to make recommendations concerning how and to what extent reparations should be paid. He did not say that the United States would participate directly in these negotiations, although he did admit, "I have no doubt that distinguished Americans would be willing to serve in such a commission."

Hughes apparently hoped this public proposal would cause the French to postpone occupation of the Ruhr, but the French went ahead with this act in January, 1923, and it appeared that Secretary Hughes's scheme was dead. In the fall of 1923, however, after it had become clear that the Ruhr operation was a failure, David Lloyd George, former prime minister of Great Britain, urged the French government to reconsider the U.S. secretary of state's idea. After further discussion, France agreed to a restricted version of the Hughes proposal. The Reparations Commission in late November created two special commissions: one to attempt to balance the budget and stabilize the currency of Germany and the other to deal with

German holdings abroad. The next step was to appoint a battery of experts. Not surprisingly, the Reparations Commission wanted several U.S. representatives to participate in this work. Apparently, the U.S. State Department was asked unofficially to recommend candidates. The names of Charles G. Dawes, Owen D. Young, and Henry M. Robinson, all noted financial experts, were put forward.

Dawes was appointed chairman of the first committee, and subsequent agreements were called the Dawes Plan. Credit must have gone equally to Hughes. After several months of deliberation, Dawes announced the committee's recommendations on April 9, 1924. The report recognized two distinct problems: the need for Germany to return to economic solvency and the need for an acceptable method of transferring surplus revenue to the Allies. The Dawes Committee proposed the reorganization of the Reichsbank under Allied supervision, a loan of $200 million in gold, and the creation of a new monetary unit, the Reichsmark. No precise figure was set for total reparations, but the Dawes Plan posited a sliding scale of payments based on expected German financial prospects. For 1924-1925, the payment was set at $250 million, and it was to rise over a period of five years to $625 million. The German government was committed to making these payments, but provisions were made to ensure that the payments would not threaten the stability of the German currency. One such provision was the appointment of an agent general for reparations payments to supervise and coordinate financial relations.

The Dawes Plan went into effect on September 1, 1924. Gustav Stresemann, the German foreign minister, persuaded his government that the Dawes Plan presented Germany with an opportunity to rebuild its economy. Despite criticism from extreme nationalists, he convinced the German people that the plan offered Germany many advantages, freeing the nation from French occupation of the Ruhr and attracting needed foreign investments.

SIGNIFICANCE

In terms of its limited goals, the Dawes Plan worked amazingly well. The international loan was oversubscribed, mostly by U.S. investors. An officer of the banking House of Morgan was appointed agent general. From 1925 to 1927, all went well, and the revival of the German economy seemed assured; only later was the Dawes Plan seen to be a stopgap measure. Germany able to meet its obligatory reparations only by borrowing from outside. U.S. loans to Germany under the Dawes Plan and

Charles G. Dawes. (Library of Congress)

the subsequent Young Plan exceeded $3 billion, while a total of only $2.6 billion was paid by the Allies to the United States during the same period. Despite the obvious connection between German reparations and Allied war debts, the United States continued to repudiate such a relationship.

—*Theodore A. Wilson and Leslie V. Tischauser*

FURTHER READING

Adler, Selig. *The Uncertain Giant, 1921-1941: American Foreign Policy Between the Wars.* New York: Harper & Row, 1965. A popular survey of the role of the United States in Europe between World Wars I and II.

Craig, Gordon. *Germany: 1866-1945.* New York: Oxford University Press, 1978. Presents a useful discussion of Germany's economic and social problems in the 1920's and an assessment of the impact of the Dawes Plan.

Dawes, Charles Gates. *A Journal of Reparations*. London: Macmillan, 1939. Dawes reviews his role in the investigation of Germany's financial fight.

Feldman, Gerald D. *The Great Disorder: Politics, Economics, and Society in the German Inflation, 1914-1924*. New York: Oxford University Press, 1997. In-depth examination of the economic crisis in Germany during and after World War I. Includes discussion of the Dawes Plan. Features illustrations, tables, bibliography, and index.

Hoff, Joan. *American Business and Foreign Policy, 1920-1933*. Lexington: University Press of Kentucky, 1971. Describes the role of the Dawes Plan in the economic rebuilding of Germany.

Schuker, Stephen A. *The End of French Predominance in Europe: The Financial Crisis of 1924 and the*

Adoption of the Dawes Plan. 1976. Reprint. Chapel Hill: University of North Carolina Press, 1988. An interpretation of the writing of the plan, with a useful discussion of the role of the United States in the negotiations.

Wueschner, Silvano A. *Charting Twentieth-Century Monetary Policy: Herbert Hoover and Benjamin Strong, 1917-1927*. Westport, Conn.: Greenwood Press, 1999. Examination of the influence of Hoover, as secretary of commerce, and Strong, as governor of the Federal Reserve Bank of New York, on U.S. monetary policy, both domestic and international, in the period when the Dawes Plan was formulated. Chapters 2 and 3 include discussion of the Dawes Plan.

SEE ALSO: 1923: Germans Barter for Goods in Response to Hyperinflation; Jan. 11, 1923-Aug. 16, 1924: France Occupies the Ruhr; Oct., 1925: Germany Attempts to Restructure the Versailles Treaty.

October, 1924
SURREALISM IS BORN

After the publication of André Breton's Manifesto of Surrealism, *avant-garde artists used the new term "Surrealism" to define their artistic movement.*

ALSO KNOWN AS: *Manifeste du surréalisme*; *Manifesto of Surrealism*
LOCALE: Paris, France
CATEGORIES: Arts; literature

KEY FIGURES
André Breton (1896-1966), French writer and critic
Max Ernst (1891-1976), German painter
Joan Miró (1893-1983), Spanish painter
Salvador Dalí (1904-1989), Spanish painter
René Magritte (1898-1967), Belgian painter
Yves Tanguy (1900-1955), American painter

SUMMARY OF EVENT
When the young French writer and critic André Breton published his first *Manifeste du surréalisme* (*Manifesto of Surrealism*, 1969) in October, 1924, he did not merely provide a friendly group of writers and artists with a new theory for their new art, he also gave this art its name and thus fostered the birth of Surrealism. The painters Max Ernst, André Masson, and Joan Miró readily accepted the theories outlined in Breton's manifesto, and so did many

of Breton's writer friends, among whom Louis Aragon, Paul Éluard, and Philippe Soupault were very influential.

As Breton's manifesto defined it, Surrealism sought to break down the boundary between dream and reality and to unite, in one picture or one text, the unconscious and the conscious. "Surrealism is based on the belief in the superior reality of certain forms of associations hitherto neglected, in the omnipotence of dream, in the disinterested play of thought," Breton explained. To capture this new "surreality," Breton and his friends strongly recommended "automatic," instead of premeditated, painting and writing. Surrealist theory thus emphasized a revolution in both the form and content of art.

In the fall of 1924, a distinctive body of new art already existed for which Breton created his theory. The early works of Max Ernst, for example, exhibit many of the Surrealists' ideas. By inviting the viewer to see an elephant in the form of a huge steel cauldron to which the artist has given legs and tusks, Ernst's painting *The Elephant of the Celebes* (1921) traces how dreams create irrational analogies between different objects. Ernst's depiction of a sky filled with fish shows in action the Surrealist principle of "conscious incongruous combination": By placing objects in an impossible context, the picture encourages the viewer to transcend the limits re-

1924

1943

ality imposes on relationships between objects.

Similar in theory, but quite different in its style, Joan Miró's *Catalan Landscape (The Hunter)* (1923-1924) invites a viewer to follow dream logic and see the hills of Catalonia in the painter's mere outline of pencil-thin, wavy lines; the hunter's head can be discovered in a mustachioed, one-eyed triangle at the top left of the picture.

In literature, the field of Breton's own experiments, 1924 saw the publication of two major Surrealist texts. Breton's *Les Pas perdus* (the lost steps) reflects in its antinovelistic form and apparently random content the antirational convictions of its author. In Louis Aragon's *Une Vague de rêves* (a wave of dreams), form and content focus on dreams and "automatic" unmediated writing.

Although the Surrealists initially defined it, their art had deep roots in earlier experiments with "antiart." Like the Dadaists, they rebelled against artistic tradition and conventional values. Both Dadaists and Surrealists were committed to experimenting with art. Surrealists, however, wanted art to have meaning and were ready for a theory to give coherence to their divergent goals. Breton's manifesto filled this void. It was only with its publication, then, that Surrealism was truly born as a forceful movement with a clear sense of artistic identity.

Breton admitted freely that the term "Surrealism" was the invention of his deceased friend Guillaume Apolli-

naire. Breton, however, insisted on his exclusive rights to the new word. Indeed, rival claims to the term literally died out: The three French magazines that used the word independently ceased publication by the spring of 1925. This left only the new review *La Révolution Surréaliste*, of which Breton quickly became the editor. Until 1929, when it was retitled, the journal served as an influential vehicle for disseminating Surrealist literature and theory. Beginning with its first issue—the cover of which was graced by an anonymous drawing of a fish bearing the word "SURRÉALISME" on its side—the magazine also carried illustrations by important Surrealists such as Max Ernst and André Masson.

Because of Breton's forceful promotion of their work, more painters felt drawn to the movement, which had originally favored writers and poets. After a one-man show of Masson's work in the Galérie Simon in Paris in 1924, the Surrealists staged their first major collective exhibition in the Galérie Pierre in Paris in 1925. At the exhibition, a wide audience reviewed works by the founding members of the Surrealist group, including Ernst, Masson, Miró, and Man Ray, and by such relative newcomers as Pierre Roy and Hans Arp. Also included were works by Pablo Picasso and Paul Klee, who were not strictly Surrealists. Giorgio De Chirico's early work was shown because of its initial influence on Surrealist painters, even though the Surrealists despised his current art.

A steady stream of exhibitions followed. The acquisition of the Surrealist Gallery, which opened on March 26, 1926, gave Surrealist painting a permanent exhibition space. Increasingly, international artists such as the Spaniard Salvador Dalí and the Belgian René Magritte joined the Surrealists, whose influence spread throughout Europe, the United States, and Japan. With Dalí and his fellow Spaniard Luis Buñuel, Surrealists turned to film; Dalí and Buñuel's *Un Chien andalou* (1928; *An Andalusian Dog*) became the first of several internationally acclaimed Surrealist films. The painters' frequent exhibitions, together with the flourishing review *La Révolution Surréaliste* and the energetic mentorship of Breton, contributed to the strong and quick growth of Surrealism after its well-tended birth in 1924.

SIGNIFICANCE

The energy and creativity of its founders helped to make Surrealism the most influential artistic movement between 1924 and World War II. In the field of the visual arts, the Surrealists' fascination with the unconscious yielded a rather unexpected result, for even though they

---

BRETON'S DEFINITION OF SURREALISM

In his Manifesto of Surrealism, *André Breton provides this definition:*

SURREALISM, *n.* Psychic automatism in its pure state, by which one proposes to express—verbally, by means of the written word, or in any other manner—the actual functioning of thought. Dictation of thought, in the absence of any control exercised by reason, exempt from any aesthetic or moral concern.

ENCYCL. *Philos.* Surrealism is based on the belief in the superior reality of certain forms of previously neglected associations, in the omnipotence of dreams, in the disinterested play of thought. It tends to ruin once and for all all other psychic mechanisms and to substitute itself for them in solving all the principal problems of life.

Source: André Breton, *Manifesto of Surrealism* (1924), in *Manifestoes of Surrealism*, translated by Richard Seaver and Helen R. Lane (Ann Arbor: University of Michigan Press, 1969).

strove to discard realist modes of representation, they desired to convey the new meaning that their dream logic gave familiar objects. Consequently, despite techniques that pointed in a different direction, Surrealist painting reemphasized the object, and the idea of meaning, in art.

These divergent artistic aspirations, which would ultimately separate and lead to both abstract expressionism and neorealism, were powerfully unified in such Surrealist paintings as Yves Tanguy's *Genesis* (1926). In Tanguy's painting, the background openly defies any notion of realist presentation: Painted in virtually the same pastel tones, sky and ground are separated only by a hovering, blue-black fog. In the midst of this dreamscape, however, grows a distinctly fernlike tree of knowledge, beyond which is a tightrope on which walks Eve, a naturalistically drawn woman.

To uncover the meaning that Tanguy invests in his objects, one must look at Freudian psychology, which Surrealism greatly helped to popularize. With Sigmund Freud, the Surrealists shared a keen interest in the unconscious and the erotic. Tanguy and other Surrealists readily accepted the sexual connotations Freud saw in everyday objects and incorporated such ideas into their own art. Eve's passage on the tightrope—a walk into adolescent sexuality—thus will lead her to a phallic tower of fog, out of which rises an outstretched palm holding a long nail (vagina and phallus); her route continues beneath the vaginal leaves of the tree to its terminus, the top of the phallic obelisk. A green snake and a black triangle complete the Freudian imagery on the fog-infested ground.

Whereas Freud used psychoanalysis to heal patients, however, the Surrealists were interested in the method alone. At the extreme, Dalí became fascinated with psychopathology and the sickness of the soul and developed his own branch of Surrealism. The famous melting watches of Dalí's *The Persistence of Memory* (1931) seek to capture the frame of mind of the individual paranoiac. His frightening *Soft Construction with Boiled Beans: Premonition of Civil War* (1936) reveals the collective horror of a nation, Spain, which was killing itself in civil war. Here, a violently deformed female torso is split in two, and while one hand squeezes an inflamed breast, a calcified leg presses bulging buttocks against spinal bones.

In the quest for the unconscious, Breton exhorted the Surrealists to experiment continuously with new techniques. Ironically, the idea of "automatic" writing and painting, which the *Manifesto of Surrealism* had called the key to Surrealism, soon proved a dead end. It was

André Breton.

abandoned despite such isolated successes as Miró's *The Gentleman* (1924), the major features of which appeared in the artist's mind at the moment of painting.

Overall, the Surrealists created many techniques that entered the repertoire of contemporary art. Among these lasting inventions are Ernst's collages, which, as in his *The Hundred-Headed Woman* (1929), create strange bird-people out of mixed-up illustrations cut from the pages of nineteenth century novels. Other innovations included Ernst's *frottage* (the rubbing of canvas over natural objects) and *grattage* (the scraping of the canvas). Oscar Dominguez's discovery of "decalcomania" (the spreading of black ink between two sheets of paper), first exhibited in the new Surrealist magazine *Minotaure* in 1936, quickly inspired other Surrealist painters.

Together, the goal of these techniques was to create accidental structures that the artist invests with a subjective meaning. For Masson's *Battle of Fishes* (1927), the artist spread glue randomly on his canvas. After pouring sand on the glue, he was left with a sandscape created by accident, which he turned into an ocean floor, the battle zone of his fish. The invitation of the unplanned became an important Surrealist legacy. It directly influenced the action painting of the American Jackson Pollock, who personally observed Max Ernst in the 1940's.

Just as influential were the methods of Surrealist painters, such as Magritte, who painted their objects with

1924

often photographic precision but placed them in impossible contexts. Magritte's *The Human Condition, I* (1943) offers a view of a window that is partially blocked by a painting that shows exactly the part of the landscape outside the window that the painting obscures. Magritte's style, Verism, became widely popular among the pop artists of the 1960's; its appeal even reached the point that Magritte's motifs were used for advertising posters.

Despite its powerful impact, Surrealism was persistently plagued by internal strife. Because Breton looked at the movement as an all-encompassing lifestyle, he took a personal interest in guarding its purity and expelled many offenders. His continuous development of Surrealist theory is linked to this control over the movement. Breton's discussion of the visual arts, *Le Surréalisme et la peinture* (1928; Surrealism and painting), which appeared in the same year as his novel *Nadja* (English translation, 1960), was written to refute a rival's idea that there was no Surrealist painting. Similarly, Breton's *Second Manifeste du surréalisme* (1930; *Second Manifesto of Surrealism*, 1969) came on the heels of mass expulsions, including Masson's.

The Surrealists' relationship with the French communists was characterized by the former's tenacious fight for artistic freedom. In *Légitime Défense* (1926; legitimate defense), Breton defended the Surrealists' interest in dreams. Even though he would briefly join the communists—at one point, he renamed his magazine *Le Surréalisme au service de la Révolution* (Surrealism in the service of the revolution)—from 1930 on, he knew that Surrealist art remained incompatible with the dogma of Socialist Realism.

Pierre Roy's painting *Rural Electrification* (1930) illustrates this difference. The work's electric poles are relegated to the background, where they are literally dwarfed by four bamboo sticks and small scraps of paper, the artist's childhood toys. By placing the subjective and personal over the communal and objective, Roy provided artists with an alternative to communist art.

After World War II, which caused most European Surrealists to flee to the United States after the Nazis occupied France in 1940, Surrealism, although still productive, lost its initial influence. The last great international Surrealist exhibitions were held in Chicago and Paris in 1947. After the deaths of many Surrealist artists in the 1960's and 1970's, however, major retrospectives of their works opened in Europe and the United States. Since then, interest in their art has remained strong, and in 1992, a Magritte retrospective received a warm welcome upon opening in London. Arrival of the exhibition

was also greeted eagerly in the United States, where European Surrealists had flourished late but had left strong traces.

—R. C. Lutz

FURTHER READING

Hopkins, David. *Dada and Surrealism: A Very Short Introduction.* New York: Oxford University Press, 2004. Concise introduction to these art movements discusses their international nature and the range of media employed. Also addresses the debates surrounding them, including issues of quality and attitudes toward women.

Jean, Marcel, ed. *The Autobiography of Surrealism.* New York: Viking Press, 1980. Anthology of writings by Surrealist painters and writers presents primary texts that shaped Surrealist art theory, which the artists took very seriously. Most selections are fine translations of crucial French texts. Richly illustrated with photos of the artists and their works. Includes bibliography.

_____. *The History of Surrealist Painting.* Translated by Simon Watson Taylor. New York: Grove Press, 1960. Definitive history of Surrealism up to the date of its publication. Includes reproductions of the most important Surrealist artworks (most in black and white, however) and photos of the artists themselves. Readable and extremely informative.

McShane, Megan. *Genesis of a Revolution from Dada to Surrealism.* New York: Parkstone Press, 2006. Describes the emergence of Surrealism and its relation to Dadaism, focusing on the common goals of the two movements. Includes more than one hundred illustrations.

Picon, Gaetan. *Surrealists and Surrealism, 1919-1939.* Translated by James Emmons. 1983. Reprint. New York: Hacker Art Books, 1996. Richly illustrated, detailed look at the development and growth of Surrealist art. Discusses many major Surrealist works and celebrates Surrealism's impact on art and artists all over the world. Includes chronological survey, bibliography, and "dictionary-index" with a brief entry for each major surrealist artist.

Polizzotti, Mark. *Revolution of the Mind: The Life of André Breton.* New York: Farrar, Straus and Giroux, 1995. First full-length biography of Breton in English places the man and his work in the context of his times. Includes photographs, notes, and index.

Read, Herbert Edward. *Surrealism.* 1936. Reprint. New York: Praeger, 1971. The first serious academic discussion of Surrealism in English, written at the height of Surrealism's artistic influence on modern art. Aimed at readers with some familiarity with art history. Intelligent, informative, and valuable for anyone interested in the origins and reception of the Surrealist movement.

Russell, John. *Max Ernst.* New York: Harry N. Abrams, 1967. One of the most comprehensive surveys of Ernst's work available for the general reader. Draws on interviews with Ernst to recount Ernst's impact on the birth of Surrealism and his later conflict with Breton. Includes reproductions of most of Ernst's major works, chronological survey of Ernst's works, biographical notes, and useful bibliography.

Schneede, Uwe M. *Surrealism.* Translated by Maria Pelikan. New York: Harry N. Abrams, 1974. Intro-

ductory survey aimed at a general audience. Presents forty-one discussions of individual Surrealist paintings (reproduced in color) and a concise but brief introductory text with black-and-white reproductions. Includes short chronology (1924-1971) and limited bibliography.

SEE ALSO: 1907: Bergson's *Creative Evolution* Inspires Artists and Thinkers; 1910: Gaudí Completes the Casa Milá Apartment House; 1913: Duchamp's "Readymades" Redefine Art; 1928: Buñuel and Dalí Champion Surrealism in *An Andalusian Dog*; Jan., 1935: Schiaparelli's Boutique Mingles Art and Fashion; 1940: García Lorca's *Poet in New York* Is Published; 1940-1941: Moore's Subway Sketches Record War Images.

October 21, 1924
HALIBUT TREATY

After five years of negotiation, the United States and Canada reached an agreement to save the fisheries of the North Pacific.

LOCALE: Ottawa, Ontario, Canada; Washington, D.C.
CATEGORIES: Environmental issues; diplomacy and international relations

KEY FIGURES

Julian Byng (1862-1935), British governor-general of Canada
Charles Evans Hughes (1862-1948), U.S. secretary of state
William Lyon Mackenzie King (1874-1950), prime minister of Canada, 1921-1926, 1926-1930, and 1935-1948

SUMMARY OF EVENT

On March 21, 1919, a Canadian-American Fisheries Conference called for a closed season on halibut fishing in the North Pacific every year for the next ten years. The commission, made up of scientists and fisheries experts, reported that halibut would totally disappear from the seas unless fishing could be prohibited for at least this period. In October of the same year, the Canadian government sent a draft treaty to the U.S. secretary of state calling for an end to halibut fishing from November 15, 1920, to February 15, 1921, and similar dates each year until 1930. According to the terms of the treaty, boats vi-

olating this season would be seized by either country's navy and their owners suitably punished. The treaty also contained provisions concerning regulations on lobster fishing, tariffs on fish traded between the two nations, rules for port privileges for fishing boats, and a call for a scientific investigation into the life history of the Pacific halibut.

The United States took no immediate action on the proposal. In February, 1921, however, another commission of fisheries experts issued another report predicting disaster unless halibut received protection. This conference report likened the troubles of the halibut industry to the terrible conditions faced by salmon fishermen on the Pacific coast. The value of salmon shipped from U.S. and Canadian canneries had dropped by more than 90 percent since 1913 (from $30 million to $3 million) and was heading quickly toward zero. The halibut industry faced similarly depressed conditions unless something could be done quickly to save the fish.

In the United States, Secretary of State Charles Evans Hughes and Secretary of Commerce Herbert Hoover recognized the need for action on the treaty. President Warren G. Harding sent the document to the Senate for advice and consent to ratification, a procedure requiring a two-thirds vote of approval. Senators began debating the various sections of the proposal but refused to give consent after objections from the governor and fisheries authorities in Washington State as well as members of Con-

1924

gress. These objections were based on the claim that the halibut question properly belonged in the hands of state officials, not the federal authorities; thus the province of British Columbia should be discussing limits with the state of Washington. Canadian authorities argued in turn that the provinces had no jurisdiction over such international questions as fisheries, so direct negotiations with the state of Washington were not permitted.

Another problem had to do with punishing violators of the closed season. Canada suggested that ships caught with halibut during the closed season could be tried in both countries if authorities desired. Several senators argued that this would constitute double jeopardy, a violation of the U.S. Constitution. Anyone suspected of breaking the law should be tried only once and in only one court for the same crime. Because of these objections, the treaty was withdrawn from Senate consideration in late August. It seemed to have no chance of ratification.

Canadian fisheries experts expressed outrage at the U.S. Senate's failure to ratify the treaty and asked Secretary Hughes whether any modifications would change the results. He replied that he knew of no modifications that would change the minds of those senators who were opposed, but he did suggest a meeting between Washington State officials and Canadian experts in the Pacific Northwest, and both sides agreed to that proposal. In February, 1922, representatives from the Canadian Marine and Fisheries Department met with the Fisheries Board of the state of Washington. They reached no agreement on protecting halibut, but they did decide to stop sockeye salmon fishing totally for five years, so desperately low was the population of that species. Washington State officials refused to give any assurances that they would help control halibut fishing.

In August, 1922, the Canadian government, tired of waiting for action by the United States, sent a new draft of a treaty proposal to Washington, D.C., asking for immediate action. On December 14, the United States agreed in principle to the new treaty, although it still needed Senate approval. The new treaty provided for a closed season on halibut. Violators would be turned over either to the U.S. Department of Commerce or to the Canadian Ministry of Marine and Fisheries of the Dominion of Canada, but not to both agencies. Representatives of the United States suggested that halibut taken accidentally during the closed season be used only to feed the crew of the detained vessel but not be sold. This provision was added to the final draft of the treaty.

A new complication arose when the revised treaty was sent back to Canada. In February, 1923, the British Colonial Office in London demanded that the treaty's title be changed before it could be given final approval by the English government. Canada, at this time, was still officially part of the British Empire, and the British authorities insisted that the title be changed from "A Convention for the Regulation of Halibut Fisheries on the Pacific Coast of Canada and the United States" to "A Convention for the Regulation of Halibut Fisheries on the Pacific Coast of His Majesty the King of the United Kingdom, of Great Britain and Ireland and the British Dominions Beyond the Seas, Emperor of India and the United States." The first version of the titled would have signified that Canada had the right to negotiate its own treaties, something that had never happened before and that the British wished to ensure never would.

Governor-General Julian Byng of Canada suggested that, because the treaty concerned only the United States and Canada, the signature of a Canadian minister should be enough to make it official. The British government extended plenipotentiary powers to Canada's representative, Ernest Lapointe, minister of marine and fisheries, to sign the treaty on behalf of His Majesty the king.

The proposed treaty established the closed season for each year as November 16 to February 15; halibut taken during this season could be used only for food for the crew of the boat that took the fish. Violators would have their boats seized and would be tried in the courts in the nation from which they came. The treaty also established the four-member International Fisheries Commission to study the life and environment of halibut and present recommendations for future regulations needed to save the fish. The treaty and ban would be in effect for five years and then be renewed if both parties agreed.

The Senate began debate on the treaty in March and gave consent to ratification with only one change: It added a provision stating that none of the nationals and inhabitants of any other part of Great Britain should engage in halibut fishing. This prohibition included people from all parts of the British Empire. Canadian officials raised an objection to this change, because it put the Canadians in an embarrassing position. It seemed to champion the British cause at the expense of Canada, by insisting that Canada had to secure the consent of the entire British Empire before agreeing to the treaty. Canada could not accept this demand; the document would not be presented to the Parliament in Ottawa because it would face certain defeat. The government of Prime Minister William Lyon Mackenzie King wanted to make the point that it could sign treaties without British consent, and it would block passage of the Halibut Treaty if necessary.

In October, the Harding administration agreed to resubmit the treaty without the offensive reservation. The Senate, however, was not scheduled to meet again until December, too late to approve a closed season for 1923-1924. Canada asked if the president could impose a ban on halibut fishing but was told that such action was beyond the powers of the chief executive of the United States. Halibut fishing had suffered greatly reduced supplies of fish since the first draft treaty had been proposed, more than four years earlier. Still, both sides reluctantly had to announce there would be no closed season that winter either.

By January, 1924, Canadian authorities declared that as the waters off Washington State and southern British Columbia had almost been depleted of halibut, fishing vessels would have to move north to the coast of Alaska, where supplies were more abundant. Still, the halibut industry faced serious trouble and possible bankruptcy if the catching of fish could not be halted quickly. Both sides eventually backed down from their positions. President Calvin Coolidge ratified the treaty on June 4, 1924. The British king, George V, ratified the Halibut Treaty on July 21, and the formal exchange of ratifications took place in Washington, D.C., on October 21, 1924. A closed season began in November, 1924, and persisted into the twenty-first century.

SIGNIFICANCE

The Halibut Treaty was important in part because it was the first treaty ever promulgated to address the conservation of a badly depleted deep-sea fishery. In addition, in negotiating the treaty with the United States, Canada took a significant step toward its eventual independence from Great Britain. Historians have also noted that this occasion of cooperation between Canada and the United States marks the point at which British influence in Canada began to decline and American influence began to increase.

—*Leslie V. Tischauser*

FURTHER READING

Clark, Lovell C., ed. *1919-1925*. Vol. 3 in *Documents on Canadian External Relations*. Ottawa: Department of External Affairs, 1970. Official information on the Halibut Treaty from the Canadian government.

McInnis, Edgar. *Canada: A Political and Social History*. 4th ed. Toronto: Holt, Rinehart and Winston of Canada, 1982. Includes a brief discussion of the treaty.

SEE ALSO: 1921-1948: King Era in Canada; Dec. 11, 1931: Formation of the British Commonwealth of Nations; July 18, 1932: St. Lawrence Seaway Treaty; Apr. 15, 1935: Arbitration Affirms National Responsibility for Pollution; Nov. 11, 1936: Reciprocal Trade Act; Aug. 16, 1940: Ogdensburg Agreement.

November 4, 1924
COOLIDGE IS ELECTED U.S. PRESIDENT

Calvin Coolidge's business-friendly presidential administration helped to trigger the Roaring Twenties.

LOCALE: United States
CATEGORIES: Government and politics; economics; business and labor

KEY FIGURES

Calvin Coolidge (1872-1933), president of the United States, 1923-1929
Warren G. Harding (1865-1923), president of the United States, 1921-1923
Herbert Hoover (1874-1964), U.S. secretary of commerce and later president of the United States, 1929-1933
Andrew Mellon (1855-1937), U.S. secretary of the treasury

SUMMARY OF EVENT

Calvin Coolidge's famous statement "The chief business of the American people is business" and Warren G. Harding's "Less government in business, more business in government" captured the spirit of the United States after World War I. A nation weary of Woodrow Wilson's idealistic crusade to "make the world safe for democracy" and of Progressive attempts to regulate business and individual life elected three consecutive Republican administrations in the 1920's and continued Republican dominance of the Oval Office for all but sixteen years of the period 1860 to 1932. During the decade of the 1920's, the United States reached unparalleled levels of prosperity and sustained a decade without a war.

Technological changes, including the automobile, radio, and widespread use of electrical energy, gave U.S. industry the capability to produce goods and provide em-

1924

Calvin Coolidge (left), with his wife and Senator Charles Curtis, rides to the Capitol to be sworn in as president of the United States.
(Library of Congress)

ployment at unprecedented levels. More than technology accounted for the Roaring Twenties, however: Secretary of the Treasury Andrew Mellon created dramatic tax cuts that unleashed productivity, paid off one-third of the national debt, and resulted in federal budget surpluses for most years in the decade. During the 1920's, unemployment levels dropped to the unequaled level of 1 percent, and confidence in business drove stock prices to new heights.

Harding had won the presidency with the promise to Americans of a "return to normalcy," by which he meant an end to wartime constraints and high levels of taxation. Railroads, telephone, and telegraph systems were returned to private ownership, and government-built and -owned merchant vessels to the private maritime industry. Harding's administration suffered, however,

from scandals such as Teapot Dome and accusations that the president had a mistress. When Harding died in office in June, 1923, his vice president, New Englander Calvin Coolidge, assumed the presidency. In November, 1924, Coolidge was elected to the office, defeating Democratic candidate John W. Davis and Progressive candidate Robert La Follette.

Coolidge aptly characterized wealth as the product of industry, ambition, character, and untiring effort. He put people before industry, as when he observed that the country needed a business government, by which he meant not "a government *by* business, not government *for* business, but . . . a government that will *understand* business." Critics, however, maintained that Coolidge merely granted easier access to government for business, and that he ignored antitrust laws and other regulatory efforts that business disliked. Although Coolidge had no control over the Federal Reserve Board, critics contended that his administration encouraged loose credit policies by the board that resulted in a "speculative bubble" in the stock market.

SIGNIFICANCE

Coolidge may have represented the era, but it began with the election of Warren G. Harding in 1920 and was characterized by Harding's appointment of Andrew Mellon as treasury secretary. Mellon observed that the rich had avoided paying taxes under the high rates, mainly by finding tax shelters. To boost government revenue, Mellon reduced tax rates, especially on the rich, making it less profitable for them to engage in accounting or investment manipulations to avoid taxation. As a result, the rich paid more in taxes than at any previous time in history, both in total dollar amounts and as a share of all taxes paid. Revenues rose as well, with the amount collected from those earning more than $100,000 per year rising from $194 million to $361 million. Mellon's tax cuts benefited the poorest groups the most, as their share of total taxes paid declined from $155 million to $32 million in 1926. Mellon's cuts increased government revenues to such an extent that the government reduced the national debt—not annual deficits—by one-third.

"Coolidge prosperity" bathed the nation. Families bought radios, electrical appliances, and other conveniences. Henry Ford's automobile company, manufacturing Model T's with mass-production methods, cut prices to the extent that an average U.S. family could acquire a car for a year's wages. Increases in automobile sales and the expansion of electrical energy made transportation and commerce cheaper and more widely available, reducing prices on virtually all manufactured goods.

Some did not participate in the Coolidge prosperity, however. Wealth inequality increased during the 1920's, largely because the number of millionaires grew rapidly. Stock manipulations during the "great bull

COOLIDGE'S INAUGURAL ADDRESS

Best remembered for his conservative and business-friendly administration, interwar president Calvin Coolidge occupied a period in American history when the nation was evolving from a young, isolationist country still forming its identity to a burgeoning superpower. On Wednesday, March 4, 1925—six years after the end of World War I and four years before the start of the Great Depression—Coolidge delivered his inaugural address. In it, he articulated the need to balance the nation's new world role and a reluctant stance toward war—an ideal that stood for the remainder of the twentieth century:

No one can contemplate current conditions without finding much that is satisfying and still more that is encouraging. Our own country is leading the world in the general readjustment to the results of the great conflict. . . . Realizing that we cannot live unto ourselves alone, we have contributed of our resources and our counsel to the relief of the suffering and the settlement of the disputes among the European nations. Because of what America is and what America has done, a firmer courage, a higher hope, inspires the heart of all humanity. . . .

. . . In the defense of our own ideals and in the general cause of liberty we entered the Great War. When victory had been fully secured, we withdrew to our own shores unrecompensed save in the consciousness of duty done. . . .

This Nation believes thoroughly in an honorable peace under which the rights of its citizens are to be everywhere protected. It has never found that the necessary enjoyment of such a peace could be maintained only by a great and threatening array of arms. In common with other nations, it is now more determined than ever to promote peace through friendliness and good will, through mutual understandings and mutual forbearance. We have never practiced the policy of competitive armaments. We have recently committed ourselves by covenants with the other great nations to a limitation of our sea power. As one result of this, our Navy ranks larger, in comparison, than it ever did before. Removing the burden of expense and jealousy, which must always accrue from a keen rivalry, is one of the most effective methods of diminishing that unreasonable hysteria and misunderstanding which are the most potent means of fomenting war. This policy represents a new departure in the world. It is a thought, an ideal, which has led to an entirely new line of action. It will not be easy to maintain. Some never moved from their old positions, some are constantly slipping back to the old ways of thought and the old action of seizing a musket and relying on force. America has taken the lead in this new direction, and that lead America must continue to hold. If we expect others to rely on our fairness and justice we must show that we rely on their fairness and justice. . . .

Some of the best thought of mankind has long been seeking for a formula for permanent peace. . . . But all these plans and preparations, these treaties and covenants, will not of themselves be adequate. . . . Peace will come when there is realization that only under a reign of law, based on righteousness and supported by the religious conviction of the brotherhood of man, can there be any hope of a complete and satisfying life. Parchment will fail, the sword will fail, it is only the spiritual nature of man that can be triumphant.

1924

market" involved more than a few shady characters: Samuel Insull, for example, created a pyramid of utilities that collapsed. Margin buying—seen as contributing to the speculation in the stock market—rose from $1 billion in 1920 to $8 billion in 1929. Many analysts, including the famous economist John Kenneth Galbraith, have argued that the inequities in wealth, stock speculation, and unsustainable consumer demand of the 1920's led directly to the Great Depression.

The fantastic rise in stock prices, however, may have only reflected the real growth of new industries, and, not surprisingly, utility, radio, automobile, and steel stocks witnessed some of the most rapid gains. The manufacturing boom also stimulated the stock market, even without assistance from the Federal Reserve or margin buying. Securities pioneers such as Charles E. Merrill developed sales plans to place securities in the hands of ordinary families, who found that they could own pieces of major corporations at low cost. The incentive to purchase such stocks was not necessarily brokers' loans, but the fact that share prices did not fall for more than five years. The stock market was, many people thought, a sure thing.

Coolidge was eligible to run for reelection in 1928, but he stepped down. In his place came Secretary of Commerce Herbert Hoover, who had a reputation as a planner who would merge the best parts of government and business. Rather than continuing the Coolidge policies, however, Hoover was a throwback to Wilson—a Progressive who sought to encourage the formation of voluntary trade associations in various industries that would establish quality standards, develop joint advertising campaigns, and force businesses into a net of cooperative efforts at a time when competition had led to the highest standard of living in the world. Nevertheless, business had few reservations about such a policy and welcomed an administration that would return to the World War I era of restricted competition. For example, the large population of small, unit banks supported passage of the McFadden Act of 1927, which essentially stymied the expansion of nationwide branch banking, out of concern that large banks would compete with them in local markets.

Hoover had experience in agriculture and hoped to help the struggling farm economy recover. His administration established the Federal Farm Board to make low-interest loans to farm cooperatives and to absorb surpluses, thus raising prices. Farm income recovered in some areas, but the low-interest loans increased production, lowering prices and contributing to the general business decline by keeping the farm sector in distress.

In other ways, Hoover—who has been criticized as "probusiness"—represented a break from Coolidge and Harding by championing planning as the solution to save the economy, especially after the 1929 stock market crash. The Federal Reserve Board had made a number of critical errors in the management of the nation's banking and monetary system. In 1928, misled into thinking that the stock market boom fueled inflation, the board tightened the money supply, curtailing production and sending international markets further into a tailspin. Congress passed the Hawley-Smoot Tariff Act in 1930, but key deliberations occurred just days before "Black Thursday," leading many persons to conclude that concern over the ruinous tariff rates (increases up to 34 percent on most goods) prompted the Great Crash. Foreign markets, already in depression, could no longer export to the United States or import U.S. goods; U.S. companies, sensing that their foreign markets were about to clamp shut, laid off workers and liquidated stock to gain capital.

Hoover instituted other policies that represented sharp breaks with the Harding-Coolidge approach to the economy, especially his creation of the Reconstruction Finance Corporation (RFC), which gave loans to troubled banks and businesses. However, the RFC published the names of loan recipients, and the public response was to withdraw money from banks or cease to conduct business with firms on the list. Bank runs accelerated. The policies of the Federal Reserve Board, Hoover, and Congress, combined with adherence to the gold standard long after other nations had abandoned gold, effectively ended the Coolidge prosperity. One of Hoover's first attempts to remedy the situation was to raise taxes, marking the final separation from Coolidge and Harding as the Roaring Twenties crashed to an end.

—Larry Schweikart

FURTHER READING

Atack, Jeremy, and Peter Passell. *A New Economic View of American History.* 2d ed. Boston: W. W. Norton, 1994. Historiographic look at economists' findings regarding the key economic events of U.S. history. In regard to the Great Depression, suggests that the monetarist views of Milton Friedman and the case against the gold standard have risen to high levels of acceptability among scholars.

Ferrell, Robert H. *The Presidency of Calvin Coolidge.* Lawrence: University Press of Kansas, 1998. Comprehensive account of Coolidge's years in office draws on materials unavailable previously. Includes bibliographic essay and index.

Folsom, Burton, Jr. *The Myth of the Robber Barons*. Herndon, Va.: Young America's Foundation, 1991. Contains an insightful chapter on Mellon and the effects of his tax policies in the 1920's. Includes a criticism of contentions that significant wealth disparities existed during the decade.

Schlesinger, Arthur M., Jr. *The Crisis of the Old Order*. 1957. Reprint. Boston: Houghton Mifflin, 2003. Influential book details the 1920's from a liberal perspective. Relies heavily on descriptions of Coolidge supplied by William White, whose accounts have not stood the test of time. White, for example, ignored substantial evidence that Coolidge viewed the economy as an integrated force of employees, capitalists, and consumers.

Silver, Thomas B. *Coolidge and the Historians*. Durham, N.C.: Carolina Academic Press, 1982. Well-balanced book addresses historical misinformation about Coolidge's policies and words. Provides full texts of Coolidge's speeches, unlike many other volumes.

Sobel, Robert. *Coolidge: An American Enigma*. Washington, D.C.: Regnery, 1998. Biography attempts to balance previous views of Coolidge as uninteresting and cold. Addresses Coolidge's views on big business and emphasizes his personal and political integrity. Includes selected bibliography and index.

White, William Allen. *Calvin Coolidge: The Man Who Is President*. New York: Macmillan, 1925. The earliest, and most flawed, interpretation of Coolidge, followed by White's 1938 book, *A Puritan in Babylon: The Story of Calvin Coolidge* (New York: Macmillan).

Wilson, Joan Hoff. *Herbert Hoover: Forgotten Progressive*. 1975. Reprint. Prospect Heights, Ill.: Waveland Press, 1992. A liberal revisionist portrays Hoover as consistent with the Progressive movement earlier in the century and argues that Hoover had sharp differences with Coolidge and Harding.

SEE ALSO: Nov. 5, 1918-Nov. 2, 1920: Republican Resurgence Ends America's Progressive Era; 1921-1923: Scandals of the Harding Administration; Oct., 1923: Teapot Dome Scandal; June 7, 1924: Oil Pollution Act Sets Penalties for Polluters; Dec. 10, 1924: Hoover Becomes the Director of the U.S. Bureau of Investigation.

December, 1924
HUBBLE SHOWS THAT OTHER GALAXIES ARE INDEPENDENT SYSTEMS

Hubble demonstrated that the Milky Way galaxy is only one of many in the universe and founded the astronomical study of galaxies external to the Milky Way.

LOCALE: Mount Wilson Observatory, California
CATEGORIES: Science and technology; astronomy

KEY FIGURES
Edwin Powell Hubble (1889-1953), American astronomer
Heber Doust Curtis (1872-1942), American astronomer
Harlow Shapley (1885-1972), American astronomer
Adriaan van Maanen (1884-1946), Dutch astronomer

SUMMARY OF EVENT
At the beginning of the twentieth century, there were two theories about spiral nebulas—groups of stars that appear as spiraling streams flowing outward from a central core. One theory held that such nebulas were part of the Milky Way galaxy. The other held that they were "island universes," large, distant, independent systems. To resolve this question, it was important to measure the distances of the nebulas. The island universe theory held that the nebulas were remote from the Milky Way; the other theory held that they were closer.

In 1914, the American astronomer Vesto Melvin Slipher announced that the spiral nebulas were moving away from the Milky Way at high speeds. He had drawn his conclusions from his spectral analysis of Doppler shifts in these star groups. His announcement was taken as evidence that these nebulas could not possibly be part of the Milky Way. Slipher had not conclusively solved the problem, however, because he had not determined the distances of these nebulas.

Distance has always been a difficult question for astronomers. By the early twentieth century, astronomers had measured distances to some nearby stars using the parallax method, which compares the different angles of nearby stars in relation to Earth and the Sun as Earth moves around the Sun. Unfortunately, spiral nebulas are too far away for parallax to be useful.

1924

Working at the Mount Wilson Observatory, the Dutch astronomer Adriaan van Maanen compared the positions of bright spots within spiral nebulas in photographs taken at different times in order to observe the motions of the spots. In 1916, he published his results, which suggested that the spirals were rotating and that the rotation was rapid. If large distances and sizes were assumed for the nebulas, the nebulas would have to be rotating at immensely fast speeds, in some cases exceeding the speed of light. As this was known to be impossible, van Maanen's results were taken as evidence that the spiral nebulas must be nearby parts of the Milky Way.

In April, 1920, Harlow Shapley and Heber Doust Curtis debated their differing views before the National Academy of Sciences. Using a new distance determination method involving a type of star, a Cepheid variable, Shapley had arrived at a much larger size for our galaxy than had been previously deduced. Because of van Maanen's studies, Shapley argued that the spiral nebulas were part of this large Milky Way.

Curtis agreed with previous studies that indicated a smaller Milky Way. He also believed in the "island universe" theory—that the spiral nebulas were other galaxies similar to and outside the Milky Way. As evidence, Curtis used Slipher's measurements of the speed at which the nebulas were moving away from the Milky Way. Today it is recognized that Shapley's results for the size and shape of the galaxy were substantially correct. Yet the island universe hypothesis was strongly supported by evidence presented by Edwin Powell Hubble to the American Association for the Advancement of Science in December, 1924.

In 1923, Hubble was working at Mount Wilson Observatory, studying photographs taken with the 100-inch (254-centimeter) Hooker telescope. He was the first to isolate Cepheid variables in the Andromeda nebula. Cepheid variables are stars whose brightnesses varies periodically and whose period of variation is related to their actual brightness. Once a star's actual brightness is known and its apparent brightness as seen from Earth is measured, its distance can be determined. This was the same method used by Shapley to determine the size of the Milky Way galaxy.

Hubble used the Cepheids to calculate that the nebulas are, in fact, at great distances and must be huge, independent systems. The distance Hubble found for the Andromeda nebula is about 900,000 light-years and the diameter almost 33,000 light-years (a light-year is the distance light travels in a vacuum in one year, approximately 5.88 trillion miles, or 9.46 trillion kilometers). These results later required correction, as it was found that there are two types of Cepheid variables, and the ones that Hubble studied had a different period-luminosity relationship; the distance is closer to 2 million light-

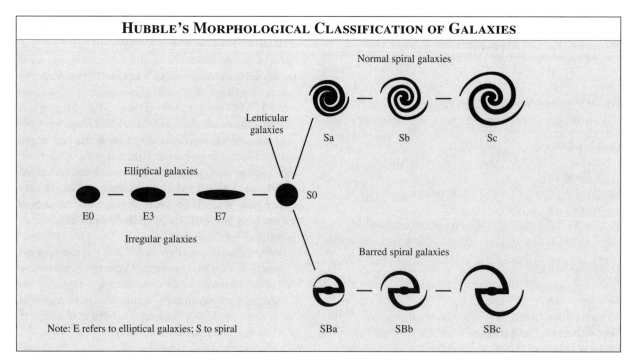

HUBBLE'S MORPHOLOGICAL CLASSIFICATION OF GALAXIES

Normal spiral galaxies

Lenticular galaxies

Sa   Sb   Sc

Elliptical galaxies

E0   E3   E7   S0

Irregular galaxies

Barred spiral galaxies

SBa   SBb   SBc

Note: E refers to elliptical galaxies; S to spiral

years. Yet Hubble's results changed scientists' idea of the scale of the universe and of Earth's place in it.

Hubble was at first reluctant to publish his results, because he could not explain why van Maanen's results would be incorrect. Although many influential astronomers were immediately convinced by Hubble's results, controversy lingered for some years after these results were presented. Van Maanen's results could not be duplicated by others, and all other evidence indicated that the galaxies were distant and separate from the Milky Way; therefore, his work was gradually forgotten.

SIGNIFICANCE

The philosophical consequences of Hubble's conclusions were immense. The great sizes and distances of the spirals meant not only that the Sun was only one of many in a huge galaxy but also that the Milky Way was merely one of many independent systems. This realization shifted humankind's place in the cosmos, a shift that could be said to be equal to that which the Polish astronomer Nicolaus Copernicus inaugurated when he suggested that the Sun, not the Earth, was the center of the solar system.

Hubble's work led to the beginning of the classification and study of galaxies. Once galaxies were identified as separate units of the cosmos, their shapes and sizes, their distances, and their distribution in space were studied. During the 1920's, Hubble presented a classification scheme for galaxies that is still in use.

There were important follow-ups to Hubble's work. Once Cepheids were found in other spirals and distances were known, Hubble was able to work out a plot of distance versus velocity; he found that the farther away a galaxy is, the faster it is moving away from Earth. This means that the universe is expanding. By using this plot to extrapolate backward in time to the so-called big bang, astronomers could estimate the age of the universe. Studies are still being conducted to determine the exact age, but data from the Wilkinson Microwave Anisotropy Probe have pinpointed it with incredible accuracy at 13.7 billion years. Hence the discoveries surrounding Cepheid variables created a drastically different picture of the universe: a universe in motion, rushing way from an energetic beginning, rather than the static and stable universe that scientists had previously assumed.

—Mary Hrovat

FURTHER READING

Berendzen, Richard, Richard Hart, and Daniel Seeley. *Man Discovers the Galaxies*. New York: Columbia University Press, 1984. Excellent history of early twentieth century work in studying the Milky Way and external galaxies, including much information on the process by which these galaxies were determined to be independent systems. Accessible to the nonscientist. Presents archival materials, including correspondence, and includes many photographs, charts, and graphs.

Gribbin, John. *In Search of the Big Bang: The Life and Death of the Universe*. Rev. ed. New York: Penguin Books, 1998. History of modern cosmology presents the story of the discovery of the nature of external galaxies. Puts Hubble's work into the fuller context of the development of cosmological thought. Intended for the general reader. Includes illustrations, bibliography, and index.

Hetherington, Norriss S. "The Purported Rotation of Spiral Nebulas." In *Science and Objectivity: Episodes in the History of Astronomy*. Ames: Iowa State University Press, 1988. Investigates the possible sources of van Maanen's error when he measured rapid rotation in the spiral nebulas, with emphasis on how preconceptions and subjective ideas may have influenced the gathering of data. Discusses the influence of van Maanen's work on Hubble.

Hubble, Edwin. *The Realm of the Nebulae*. 1936. Reprint. Mineola, N.Y.: Dover, 1991. Text of lectures given by Hubble at Yale in 1935 on spiral nebulas. Chapters 1 and 4 deal with the discovery of the nebulas' distances; the remainder of the book describes then-current knowledge on types of galaxies, their distribution, and the overall view of the universe. Dated, but valuable for Hubble's view of his studies.

Rowan-Robinson, Michael. *Cosmology*. 4th ed. New York: Oxford University Press, 2004. Comprehensive volume discusses advances in technology that have allowed scientists to gain increasing understanding of the origin and evolution of the universe. Topics include the formation and aging of various types of stars and galaxies, the big bang theory, quasars, and black holes. Also examines a number of controversies in the field. Includes illustrations and index.

Shapley, Harlow. *Through Rugged Ways to the Stars*. New York: Charles Scribner's Sons, 1969. Autobiography contains a chapter on the Shapley-Curtis debate (chapter 6) and one that contains descriptions of Hubble and van Maanen (chapter 4). Written in a conversational style. Includes photographs.

Struve, Otto, and Velta Zebergs. "Galaxies." In *Astron-*

1924

omy of the Twentieth Century. New York: Macmillan, 1962. Cowritten by an astronomer who lived through some of the advances in astronomy described. Tells the story of the discovery of galaxies as independent systems and of the resulting work in classifying and understanding galaxies. Includes photographs, drawings, and a time line of twentieth century astronomy.

Whitney, Charles A. *The Discovery of Our Galaxy.* 1971. Reprint. Ames: Iowa State University Press, 1988. Presents the history of cosmological thought. Part 3 discusses the discovery and study of external galaxies as well as the study of our own galaxy. De-

scribes actual observations and telescopes used to make discoveries. Includes photographs, drawings, glossary, and bibliography.

SEE ALSO: 1912: Slipher Obtains the Spectrum of a Distant Galaxy; Mar. 3, 1912: Leavitt Discovers How to Measure Galactic Distances; 1913: Hertzsprung Uses Cepheid Variables to Calculate Distances to the Stars; Early 1920's: Slipher Presents Evidence of Redshifts in Galactic Spectra; Dec. 13, 1920: Michelson Measures the Diameter of a Star; 1924: Hubble Determines the Distance to the Andromeda Nebula; 1929: Hubble Confirms the Expanding Universe.

December 4, 1924
VON STROHEIM'S SILENT MASTERPIECE *GREED* PREMIERES

Erich von Stroheim probed beneath the surface of life and human behavior to create a triumph of cinematic naturalism in his motion picture Greed.

LOCALE: United States
CATEGORY: Motion pictures

KEY FIGURES
Erich von Stroheim (1885-1957), American film director
Gibson Gowland (1872-1951), British-born film actor
ZaSu Pitts (1898-1963), American film actor
Jean Hersholt (1886-1956), Danish-born film actor

SUMMARY OF EVENT
Motion picture director Erich von Stroheim began production of *Greed*, his film adaptation of Frank Norris's naturalistic 1899 novel *McTeague*, in the spring of 1923. Von Stroheim intended to present Norris's story of avarice and human degradation in authentic detail. His film begins by showing McTeague (played by Gibson Gowland) as a burly young miner at the Big Dipper gold mine in Placer County, California. McTeague, the son of an alcoholic father who dies of delirium tremens in a saloon at the mine, is a giant man with supreme strength and slow wits. He appears to be gentle and good-natured, but the brute within him lies just beneath the surface. McTeague is shown as a victim of circumstance, environment, and heredity, unable to control his own destiny. His mother, an overworked drudge in the camp's kitchen, desperately wants her son to leave the mine to seek a profession. When a traveling dentist stops at the camp, Mother

McTeague persuades the dentist to take her son with him as an apprentice.

Several years later, after having learned the basic skills of dentistry, McTeague has opened a dental parlor on Polk Street in San Francisco. His practice is going well and his life seems comfortable when he meets Marcus Schouler (played by Jean Hersholt). Marcus is an arrogant, vulgar blowhard who works as an attendant at a nearby dog hospital, but McTeague finds him a likable, colorful character, and they soon become good friends. Marcus introduces McTeague to his fiancé, Trina (played by ZaSu Pitts), the shy daughter of German immigrant parents. Trina has a broken tooth, and Marcus has brought her to McTeague to have it fixed. McTeague develops a passion for Trina and finally confesses his love for her to Marcus, who, with a false sense of generosity, gives up Trina to his friend. After a few months, McTeague and Trina marry. On the eve of their wedding, Trina learns that she has won five thousand dollars in a lottery drawing.

The lottery win marks the film's descent into tragedy. Marcus feels cheated in having given up the newly rich Trina and, in a moment of anger and self-pity, throws a knife at McTeague. The former friend is now an enemy, and Marcus begins to plot his revenge on the newlyweds. Marcus informs the state medical board that McTeague is practicing without a license, and McTeague is forced to curtail his practice. Trina then becomes a miser, unwilling to spend a cent of her lottery winnings. With the loss of income, the McTeagues slowly sink into poverty. McTeague, once again a victim of circumstance, takes to drinking, and Trina is forced to work as a carver of wooden toys. McTeague begins to act more and more like a brute, and he torments his wife in an unsuccessful attempt to get her money. Eventually, he abandons her. Trina's only comfort (more accurately, her passion) is her money, which she continues to hoard in the form of gold coins. Finally, the beast in McTeague rises to full force. He breaks into his wife's room, murders her, and flees with the coins.

McTeague, now on the run, briefly returns to his mountain home. Before long, however, he senses pursuit and sets off across the Mojave Desert. At this juncture, Marcus reappears in the film to join the posse in pursuit of McTeague. The posse turns back when the chase reaches Death Valley, but Marcus continues to pursue McTeague on his own. Driven onward by greed, Marcus overtakes McTeague on the salt flats of Death Valley. There, miles from water and in 130-degree heat, they fight to the death. McTeague manages to kill Marcus but finds himself handcuffed to a corpse. McTeague dies in the desert with the gold coins scattered around him.

Von Stroheim completed production of *Greed* in October, 1923. The shooting had lasted 198 days at a cost of roughly half a million dollars. Von Stroheim immediately began editing, and on January 12, 1924, he presented a forty-two-reel, nine-and-a-half-hour preview to a small group of associates. The studio demanded that further cuts be made, and von Stroheim complied, producing a twenty-four-reel version.

While von Stroheim struggled to cut his film to a marketable length, his parent company (Goldwyn) merged with the Metro Pictures Corporation. Louis B. Mayer took over as head of production, and Irving Thalberg became von Stroheim's new production manager. Both executives foresaw a financial disaster in *Greed*, with its excessive length and pessimistic message, and demanded further cuts. Von Stroheim then sent the film to one of his closest friends, director Rex Ingram, who edited the film to eighteen reels. Von Stroheim took this version to Mayer, who insisted that it be cut to ten reels. Von Stroheim protested that the artistic qualities of the film would be destroyed in the process, but he was powerless to prevent further cutting.

Von Stroheim had broken the rules in his pursuit of artistic integrity, and he paid the price. *Greed* was given to an outside "cutter" for final editing. The studio first showed this truncated version of the film on December 4, 1924, at William Randolph Hearst's Cosmopolitan Theatre in New York City. The film was shown twice daily and ran for six weeks to mixed reviews. Von Stro-

heim, who felt his most creative work had been ruined, refused even to look at the final product.

SIGNIFICANCE

Erich von Stroheim's *Greed* is now considered a silent film classic. Von Stroheim was a disciple of the legendary D. W. Griffith and had worked for several years under his tutelage. Von Stroheim's uses of close-ups, camera angles, lighting, composition, and symbolism show the influences of Griffith's work, but von Stroheim's films in general, and *Greed* in particular, go beyond Griffith's in their stark, realistic analysis and in their attention to authentic detail.

Von Stroheim was one of the first directors to struggle with the problem of how to adapt a work of written fiction to the screen realistically. Just as Frank Norris had rebelled against the popular fiction of the 1890's, von Stroheim rebelled against the sentimental Hollywood products of the 1920's. Critics attacked both artists for the vulgarity and sordidness of their "realism," and both defended themselves as having merely presented life in a truthful manner. They noted that individuals can be good, kind, noble, and idealistic, but they can also be selfish, mean, jealous, and greedy. Norris's and von Stroheim's uncompromising portrayals of life and human behavior are more accurately described as "naturalism." Both men believed that heredity and environment control human actions and that individuals are at the mercy of irresistible natural forces. Both were concerned about psychological and sociological nuances outside the accepted cultural definition of what should be openly displayed as art.

Von Stroheim relied entirely on actual locations to add force and meaning to the more grotesque aspects of his story. For the scenes that took place in the Placer County mining area, von Stroheim had the Goldwyn Company lease and restore to operation the actual mine described in Norris's novel. When the story shifted to San Francisco, von Stroheim moved shooting there as well. Because the San Francisco earthquake and fire of 1906 had destroyed the seedy Polk Street area described in Norris's novel, von Stroheim had to improvise. He rented a house at the corner of Hayes and Laguna Streets, furnished the rooms exactly as Norris's novel describes them, and then had the actors actually live in the rooms to get the feel of their surroundings.

Von Stroheim filled each scene with interesting and important details. He believed that objects could be used to create atmosphere and that an emphasis on detail would both enrich the scene and accentuate the dramatic importance of the film. He kept the backgrounds of his

1924

scenes in deep focus, so that details were not lost on the viewer and so that contrasting themes and symbols, plots and subplots, could be ironically juxtaposed.

Von Stroheim's obsession with realistic detail was also evident in the scenes shot in Death Valley. The director rejected the studio's advice that he film the desert scenes on the sand dunes near Los Angeles; instead, he took a film crew consisting of forty-one men and one woman to Death Valley. There, again for the sake of realism and to stay true to the novel, von Stroheim filmed the final scenes in 130-degree heat. He claimed that the combination of intense heat, hellish surroundings, and physical strain gave the film its proper nightmarish conclusion.

In the end, von Stroheim created a film that was ahead of its time and a commercial disaster. Studio executives (Mayer and Thalberg), ever conscious of box-office realities, demanded that severe cuts be made to reduce the film's length. They also found the film lacking in star quality. Von Stroheim, unlike most Hollywood directors, rejected the star system then in vogue. Instead, he chose his actors primarily from screen comedies. He reasoned that such actors would not be burdened with artificial dramatic mannerisms that would detract from their human qualities.

Critics found the film to be unsparingly intense (because of the severe editing, one dramatic scene follows another almost without respite) and too pessimistic (major and minor characters appear helpless against larger forces). Viewers found the contrast between innocence and degeneracy repellent and the emphasis on the tragic state of human existence too bleak. In short, the film was out of touch with the marketing realities of Hollywood and out of step with the popular culture of the 1920's and 1930's. To the post-World War II generation of film critics and film viewers, however, the film's reception appeared to indicate the public's and the critics' failure to confront the ugly side of life and to recognize the directional genius of von Stroheim. More contemporary observers have come to realize the tremendous impact *Greed* had and continues to have on the overall development of realism on the screen during the era of sound. Most modern critical viewers marvel at von Stroheim's authenticity, his sophisticated development of character, his innovative production techniques, and his visionary direction.

—*Steven L. Piott*

FURTHER READING

Curtiss, Thomas Quinn. *Von Stroheim.* New York: Farrar, Straus and Giroux, 1971. Biography written by a close friend of von Stroheim records events much as von Stroheim would have wanted. Includes a long chapter on *Greed* as well as Idwal Jones's account of the original screening of the film. Jones, the drama critic for the *San Francisco Daily News*, was one of perhaps only a dozen individuals ever to see the original, nine-hour-plus version of *Greed*.

Finler, Joel W. *Stroheim.* Berkeley: University of California Press, 1968. Brief volume focuses primarily on *Greed*. Valuable for its comparisons of Norris's novel with von Stroheim's film.

_____, ed. *"Greed": A Film by Erich von Stroheim.* New York: Simon & Schuster, 1972. Contains von Stroheim's original shooting script for *Greed* and includes brief but useful articles from Finler and from Herman G. Weinberg. Also included are valuable recollections concerning the making of *Greed* from actor Jean Hersholt, cameraman William Daniels, and von Stroheim himself.

Henry, Nora. *Ethics and Social Criticism in the Hollywood Films of Erich von Stroheim, Ernst Lubitsch, and Billy Wilder.* New York: Praeger, 2000. Examines how these three directors commented on and influenced American culture through their filmmaking. Includes brief biographies of the directors, bibliography, and index.

Koszarski, Richard. *Von: The Life and Films of Erich Von Stroheim.* Rev. ed. Portland, Oreg.: Amadeus Press, 2001. Expanded and heavily revised version of an earlier biography titled *The Man You Loved to Hate: Erich von Stroheim and Hollywood*, which was published in 1983. Provides one of the most useful syntheses available on von Stroheim's life. Includes a long chapter on *Greed*.

Noble, Peter. *Hollywood Scapegoat: The Biography of Erich von Stroheim.* Reprint. New York: Arno Press, 1972. This biography, first published in 1950, was written with the cooperation of von Stroheim. The short chapter on *Greed* is composed largely of excerpts from correspondence between the author and the director. Includes a lengthy appendix that contains a selection of critical essays.

Weinberg, Herman G. *The Complete "Greed."* New York: E. P. Dutton, 1973. An attempt to reconstruct the complete *Greed* with more than four hundred photos that remain from the original production. Scenes cut from the final film are marked, and a description or a fragment of dialogue accompanies each photo. Includes a brief but informative introduction.

Whittemore, Don, and Philip Alan Cecchettini, eds.

Passport to Hollywood: Film Immigrants. New York: McGraw-Hill, 1976. An anthology of works about important film directors, including von Stroheim. Several essays about the director describe his career and his major films.

SEE ALSO: Fall, 1903: *The Great Train Robbery* Introduces New Editing Techniques; Mar. 3, 1915: Griffith Releases *The Birth of a Nation*; 1920: Premiere of The Cabinet of Dr. Caligari; 1923: *The Ten Commandments* Advances American Film Spectacle; 1925: Eisenstein's *Potemkin* Introduces New Film Editing Techniques; 1925-1927: Gance's *Napoléon* Revolutionizes Filmmaking Techniques; 1927: Lang Expands the Limits of Filmmaking with *Metropolis*.

December 10, 1924
HOOVER BECOMES THE DIRECTOR OF THE U.S. BUREAU OF INVESTIGATION

J. Edgar Hoover transformed an ineffective and inefficient government bureau into the best-known national crime-fighting organization. Among his other accomplishments, Hoover oversaw agents' rigorous training and established scientific procedures and laboratories.

ALSO KNOWN AS: Federal Bureau of Investigation
LOCALE: Washington, D.C.
CATEGORIES: Crime and scandal; government and politics; organizations and institutions

KEY FIGURES

J. Edgar Hoover (1895-1972), director of the Federal Bureau of Investigation, 1924-1972
William J. Burns (1861-1932), Hoover's predecessor as head of the Bureau of Investigation, 1921-1924
Harry M. Daugherty (1860-1941), U.S. attorney general, 1921-1924
Calvin Coolidge (1872-1933), president of the United States, 1923-1929
Harlan Fiske Stone (1872-1946), U.S. attorney general, 1924-1925
A. Mitchell Palmer (1872-1936), U.S. attorney general, 1919-1921

SUMMARY OF EVENT

When J. Edgar Hoover became director of the Bureau of Investigation (renamed the Federal Bureau of Investigation, or FBI, on July 1, 1935), the organization was recovering from inefficiency and scandal. Hoover had been an assistant director under President Warren G. Harding's administration, and he was appointed by Harry M. Daugherty, who chose legendary detective William J. Burns as director. Burns was the personification of the independent crime-fighter romanticized in western and detective novels and films: He had first gained national attention as a Secret Service detective before he established the Burns International Detective Agency. After he accepted Daugherty's invitation to return to government work, Burns was caught in the scandals that became known after Harding's death in 1923. In particular, the Teapot Dome scandal—which involved the leasing of oil fields not subject to rules of competitive bidding—gave further credence to charges that had been leveled since Daugherty's appointment as attorney general. Daugherty was accused of corruption, and investigators specifically questioned his hiring of unsuitable personnel for the Justice Department and his inappropriate involvement in enforcement of Prohibition-related regulations. President Calvin Coolidge fired Daugherty in March of 1924, and Burns was forced to resign.

Coolidge and his new attorney general, Harlan Fiske Stone, later chief justice of the Supreme Court, were committed to restoring public faith in the integrity of government. To that end, J. Edgar Hoover seemed a logical appointment. Unlike Burns, Hoover was highly educated; he had received both his B.A. and law degrees from George Washington University while working at the Library of Congress. Hoover's family had a history of government service, and, like many Americans, Hoover feared the new waves of immigrants and growing political dissent in the country, sentiments he would zealously maintain long after the culture around him had changed. Hoover, unlike Burns, had excellent organizational abilities; until he became director of the Bureau of Investigation, his greatest source of pride was his leadership of a high school military cadet unit at the elite Central High School in Washington, D.C.

Hoover joined the U.S. Department of Justice on July 26, 1917, and quickly became known for his efficient, detail-oriented style of leadership. By the end of World War I, when the communist revolution in Russia had suc-

1924

ceeded and communists worldwide believed that revolution was at hand, Hoover shared the sense of horror expressed by many middle-class Americans. As director of the Radical Division (created by Attorney General A. Mitchell Palmer on August 1, 1919, and renamed the General Intelligence Division in 1920), Hoover was responsible for organizing the arrest and attempting the deportation of thousands of alleged subversives. The sweeping arrests—which were often based on little or no evidence—and the brutal conditions under which many were housed produced a backlash that ruined Palmer's political career. Hoover, however, was not blamed; most people believed that he had simply been obeying orders.

Hoover was named acting director of the Bureau of Investigation on May 10, 1924, and after a brief probationary period he was named director on December 10, 1924. In an attempt to terminate the bureau's surveillance of both political radicals and the violations of "conventional morality" described in the White-Slave Traffic Act (1910), Stone had ordered that the bureau's personnel be reduced and that investigations be limited to actual violations of law. Hoover used Stone's call as an opportunity to remove the bureau from the influence of party politics and the taint of corruption. Political appointees were terminated, and a merit system was established. Hoover wanted to choose future employees from candidates who had been trained either in law or accounting, although he was forced to make some exceptions for a few applicants who were better versed than their college-educated counterparts in practical matters of investigation.

During Prohibition, the bureau had been significantly hampered by its loose organization and by the lack of surveillance over Prohibition agents, and corruption had become widespread at all levels. In response, Hoover began to reorganize the bureau at its most fundamental levels. He strengthened the chain of command from Washington, from the commanders of field offices (special agents in charge, or SACs) down to individual agents. Efficiency became the sole criterion for promotion, and Hoover graded SAC performances himself using a strict system of merits and demerits. An inspection team ensured that this system was implemented.

Hoover quickly standardized reporting so that federal prosecutors could quickly ascertain whether a case could be taken to court. This was an especially important change in policy because in the past many cases could not be prosecuted because of inadequate reporting. To avoid even the appearance of corruption, Hoover attempted to standardize every aspect of an agent's life by

J. Edgar Hoover. (Library of Congress)

creating rules about dress and conduct. During Prohibition, for example, an agent's consumption of alcohol, even off duty, could result in immediate dismissal. In 1927, Hoover began to distribute loose-leaf notebooks that explicitly described procedures for investigation and reporting, and other strict rules followed. Later, these rules demoralized many agents and handicapped others in their work, but they were initially necessary to change the public's perception of federal law enforcement as corrupt.

A believer in the value of science and education, Hoover also wanted to make the Bureau of Investigation into a law-enforcement agency that would provide models, services, and education for police departments across the country. The invention of the automobile and the freedom it gave criminals who wanted to cross state lines pointed to the need for centralizing certain activities and regularizing police training and procedures. The trend toward centralization had begun long before Hoover became director, however: In 1904, the International Association of Chiefs of Police (IACP) had realized the value of the fingerprint system of identification, and in 1923, Attorney General Daugherty ordered the federal fingerprint system at Leavenworth and the IACP system to be housed and administered by the Bureau of Investigation. Hoover was in charge of implementing this change, which would allow local and state police to identify criminals from other parts of the country. The IACP had begun to collect crime statistics in 1922, and both the organization of these statistics and police training programs were also centralized. In 1925, Hoover established a training school for agents in New York, but funding eventually became a problem for the relatively small New York office.

SIGNIFICANCE

Hoover's centralization projects required time and congressional appropriations. To enhance the image of police professionalism in the United States, Hoover moved the officers' training school to Washington in 1928; in 1972, it became the FBI Academy located in Quantico, Virginia. In 1935, police training was expanded to include local and state police officers, and the Police Training School was renamed the FBI National Police Academy in 1937 and the FBI National Academy in 1945. In June of 1930, Congress authorized the FBI's establishment of the Division of Identification and Information, which housed fingerprinting and similar functions. On November 24, 1932, Hoover established a Technical Lab, and this office became the preeminent crime laboratory in the United States. Eventually, it housed forensic scientists, handwriting analysts, and other specialists.

Hoover made sure that national crime statistics were reported and available through the *Uniform Crime Reports*, which were first published in 1930. To counteract the widespread demoralization caused by the Depression, he courted publicity as the FBI pursued and captured or killed high-profile criminals such as John Dillinger. Hoover also worked with writers and Hollywood filmmakers to publicize these cases, creating the image of the FBI as an effective, efficient, and incorruptible force that led the country's fight against crime and provided facilities and training beyond the scope of any individual police force. As such, the agency was popularly perceived as a force for social stability in a time of national danger. Despite continual criticism by civil libertarians and by social activists, the image would remain relatively intact long after Hoover's death.

—*Betty Richardson*

FURTHER READING

Burrough, Bryan. *Public Enemies: America's Greatest Crime Wave and the Birth of the FBI, 1933-34*. New York: Penguin Books, 2004. Contrasts actual events with their portrayals by the FBI and popular media.

Gentry, Curt. *J. Edgar Hoover: The Man and the Secrets*. New York: W. W. Norton, 1991. Extensively uses interviews, research materials, and previously classified government documents to show how Hoover created the image of an uncorrupted FBI while abusing his power.

Hack, Richard. *Puppetmaster: The Secret Life of J. Edgar Hoover*. Beverly Hills, Calif.: New Millennium Press, 2004. Readable personal biography.

Hunt, Willam R. *Front-Page Detective: William J. Burns and the Detective Profession, 1880-1930*. Bowling Green, Ohio: Bowling Green State University Popular Press, 1990. Serious study of the legendary detective's strengths and weaknesses.

Kessler, Ronald. *The Bureau: The Secret History of the FBI*. New York: St. Martin's Press, 2002. A readable study of the FBI from the beginning; an epilogue for the 2003 paperback edition covers the investigations that followed the terrorist attacks of 2001.

Powers, Richard Gid. *Broken: The Troubled Past and Uncertain Future of the FBI*. New York: Free Press, 2004. Focuses on procedures and problems in the past that led to failure of the FBI to anticipate the September 11, 2001, terrorist attack on the United States.

_____. *Secrecy and Power: The Life of J. Edgar Hoover*. New York: Free Press, 1987. Balanced, well-documented study emphasizing the social and historical forces that shaped Hoover's thought and actions.

Theoharis, Athan. *The FBI and American Democracy: A Brief Critical History*. Lawrence: University Press of Kansas, 2004. Readable, short history of the FBI from the formation of the Secret Service through the terrorist attacks on New York City and Washington, D.C., in 2001.

SEE ALSO: July 26, 1908: Bureau of Investigation Begins Operation; June 15, 1917, and May 16, 1918: Espionage and Sedition Acts; Aug., 1919-May, 1920: Red Scare; Jan. 16, 1920-Dec. 5, 1933: Prohibition; Jan. 19, 1920: American Civil Liberties Union Is Founded; May 23, 1934: Police Apprehend Bonnie and Clyde; May 26, 1938: HUAC Is Established.

1924

1925

THE CITY INITIATES THE STUDY OF URBAN ECOLOGY

The City, *one of the most important urban studies of its time, helped propel the Chicago school of sociology to national prominence.*

LOCALE: Chicago, Illinois
CATEGORIES: Sociology; publishing and journalism; anthropology

KEY FIGURES
Robert E. Park (1864-1944), American sociologist
Ernest W. Burgess (1886-1966), American sociologist
Roderick D. McKenzie (1885-1940), American sociologist
Georg Simmel (1858-1918), German sociologist
John Dewey (1859-1952), American philosopher and educator
George Herbert Mead (1863-1931), American social psychologist and philosopher
Homer Hoyt (c. 1895-1984), American real estate economist
Chauncy D. Harris (1914-2003), American geographer

SUMMARY OF EVENT

The U.S. Census Bureau's 1925 revelation that the United States had become predominantly urban coincided with publication of *The City* by sociologist Robert E. Park, with contributions by Ernest W. Burgess and Roderick D. McKenzie. Park and Burgess had already written *An Introduction to the Science of Sociology* (1921), which proved to be the first truly influential sociology text published in the United States. That volume and *The City* helped to propel the Chicago school of sociology—that is, the University of Chicago's sociology department—to national prominence during the 1920's and 1930's, principally because of the school's novel emphasis on urban ecology. As the university's leading urban ecologists, Park, Burgess, and McKenzie theorized that urban environments are shaped chiefly by two forms of human behavior: dominance and competition.

Typically, according to Park, people with similar interests tend to congregate in particular portions of a city and eventually to dominate those areas. The city center, or downtown, in an American city was invariably dominated by principal businesses and government offices: banks, the leading shops or department stores, hotels, the main post office, courts, and other federal, state, and county offices. Immediately beyond downtown, a ring of wholesale firms or light manufacturing establishments

dominated, which in turn were ringed by working-class residential districts. Beyond these lower-class neighborhoods there developed rings of middle-class residences that gave way farther out to upper-class residences. Farther yet from the center, heavy manufacturing industries could be found that gave way to outlying business districts, residential suburbs, industrial suburbs, and finally commuter zones.

Thus, in Park's analysis, the spatial and functional structure of an average American city could be diagrammed as a series of concentric circles. Dominance within these circles over time was not necessarily static. Competition of the lower classes, for example, for middle-class housing, or of middle-class residents for upper-class residences, or the expansion of manufacturing districts into residential or into business districts could change the dominant elements within the circles. The general pattern, however, remained the same, because social status and social class, in Park's view, are closely related to the population's spatial distribution.

Park's concentric-circle theory was not formulated as an exercise in geography. Rather, it was an effort to comprehend the drama of community and the human interactions within it. To Park, the city, most particularly Chicago, was a collection of closely interacting organisms forming a community. Consequently, Park adapted to his own investigative purposes concepts that were already employed by plant and animal ecologists in order to explain the processes by which plant and animal communities develop and change. Although other explanations of urban life emerged to rival or supplant Park's theory by 1940—notably those of Homer Hoyt and of Chauncy D. Harris and Edward Ullman—Park's own ecological approach to urban community life and its interrelationships served as the chief theoretical framework for the research of his own numerous students as well as for other urban ecologists in the United States for another decade. His influence left a permanent impression on sociology.

One of the most significant of all urban ecologists, Park possessed a background different from that of most academic sociologists. Born in Harleyville, Pennsylvania, in 1864, he attended the University of Michigan, where he was influenced by philosopher John Dewey. Like Dewey, Park had a lifelong passion for social reform. He started his career as a journalist, observing and writing about city life in vivid detail. When journalism proved an insufficient challenge, he enrolled in Harvard

University's philosophy department, but he remained only for a year. He then moved to Germany, which at the time was regarded as a principal center of world intellectual life. In Berlin, he met Georg Simmel, a Jewish sociologist of broad interests who was making a brilliant, if precarious, career on the margins of the German academic establishment. Eventually, Simmel would become best known for his small-group research as well as for his theories of symbolic interactionism and exchange.

Simmel's lectures provided Park with his only formal training in sociology and exerted a profound influence over both Park and another later notable Chicago colleague, Albion Small. Completing his doctorate at the University of Heidelberg in 1904, Park refused a job at the University of Chicago, opting instead to work for

---

HUMAN NATURE AND THE CITY

Robert E. Park's opening chapter in The City *introduces the concept of human ecology:*

The city . . . is something more than a congeries of individual men and of social conveniences—streets, buildings, electric lights, tramways, and telephones, etc.; something more, also, than a mere constellation of institutions and administrative devices—courts, hospitals, schools, police, and civil functionaries of various sorts. The city is, rather, a state of mind, a body of customs and traditions, and of the organized attitudes and sentiments that inhere in these customs and are transmitted with this tradition. The city is not, in other words, merely a physical mechanism and an artificial construction. It is involved in the vital processes of the people who compose it; it is a product of nature, and particularly of human nature. . . .

The city has been studied, in recent times, from the point of view of its geography, and still more recently from the point of view of its ecology. There are forces at work within the limits of the urban community—within the limits of any natural area of human habitation, in fact—which tend to bring about an orderly and typical grouping of its population and institutions. The science which seeks to isolate these factors and to describe the typical constellations of persons and institutions which the co-operation of these forces produce, is what we call human, as distinguished from plant and animal, ecology.

Source: Robert E. Park and Edward W. Burgess, with R. D. McKenzie, *The City* (Chicago: University of Chicago Press, 1925).

---

the Congo Reform Association and then, later, joining Booker T. Washington to help African Americans, especially through the activities of Alabama's Tuskegee Institute. He remained devoted to minority education throughout his life.

By the early 1920's, Park had become president of the American Sociological Society and had secured a full-time faculty appointment at the University of Chicago, a post he held for more than twenty years. During these years, his dedication to social reform, particularly to race relations, his conversion of his beloved Chicago into a laboratory for sociological research, and his interest in symbolic interactionism left an indelible mark on Chicago sociology.

SIGNIFICANCE

Robert Park, in company with Ernest Burgess, Roderick McKenzie, Albion Small, and William I. Thomas and their students, swiftly created a sociology department at the University of Chicago that for a time was the most significant one in the country: the Chicago school. As a department, its chief characteristics were its strong religious convictions—Small has been quoted as declaring that "sociology must be essentially Christian"—and its collective view that sociological research must be conducted both scientifically and with an interest in social reform, first and foremost in Chicago. Park's career reflected all these characteristics.

Aside from his intellectual contributions, which were considerable even though he was not a prolific writer, Park was a leading sociologist for several reasons. He became the salient figure in his own department, and his department, in turn, became the most significant one in the nation, a position it held into the 1930's. In addition, Park's European studies—his association with Simmel, for example—allowed him to introduce the theories of famous European sociologists to his Chicago colleagues. Simmel's ideas, notably his theory of symbolic interactionism, helped shape the Chicago school's own theoretical bent. Of equal importance, Park had become aware of the critical nature of urban problems firsthand as a journalist, and he was convinced that sociological research and the data underpinning it had to be collected in the field—primarily in Chicago—through personal observations. It was this perspective that gave rise to the Chicago school's dedication to urban ecology, to the city as a social laboratory.

The insights that Park, among others, drew from symbolic social interactionism were initially rooted in American pragmatism, aspects of which Park had first imbibed from John Dewey at the University of Michigan. To this were added other influences from the psychological behaviorism often identified with the radical-behaviorist studies of John B. Watson, whose disciples at Chicago included Park's philosophical and sociological colleagues George Herbert Mead, Charles Horton Cooley, and William I. Thomas.

The basic theory of symbolic interactionism states that human beings are endowed with thought, the capacity for which is shaped by social interaction. Through social interaction, people acquire an understanding of meanings and symbols that in turn allow them to conduct distinctive human relationships. These meanings and symbols can be modified or changed on the basis of people's individual interpretations of situations, much as pragmatists suggested was true of the real world. Such changes or alterations occur because individuals cannot interact with themselves. Social interaction allows the individual to examine the advantages or disadvantages of particular courses of social action and to choose among them. Taken together, all these patterns of interactions make up groups and whole societies. The meanings, symbols, and interactions that went into composing specific Chicago groups and societies were the principal objects of the research conducted by Park, his colleagues, and their students.

The effect of Park's work was the initiation of a fresh research process that sought to unravel the meanings, symbols, and interactions that distinguished the peoples of urban communities. Park's efforts in making the city a focus of research had greater long-term significance than did his concentric-circle theory. In this regard, other scholars swiftly discovered that not every city displayed Chicago's peculiar characteristics. In the late 1930's, for example, Homer Hoyt, on the basis of investigations of San Francisco and Minneapolis, developed the sector theory to explain the spatial and functional configurations of these cities. Hoyt agreed with Park that cities grow outward from distinguishable centers, but in Hoyt's view, they could be diagrammed as evolving in wedge-shaped sectors that grew, among other ways, by ribbon development along railroads, main thoroughfares, or highways. These sectors had somewhat different social connotations in regard to where the rich and the poor lived or where businesses or industries were located.

Similarly, by the 1940's, both the concentric-circle theory and the sector theory had again been modified by the studies of Harris and Ullman. Unlike either Park or Hoyt, Harris and Ullman rejected the notion that cities had all grown outward from a single discernible center. On the contrary, their evidence indicated that some communities had developed around a number of discrete centers, or multiple nuclei. Nearly all these scholars agreed, however, that their theories applied only to American cities, for the social evolution of European cities, among others, clearly had been quite different.

Although specific aspects of Park's work have been modified or rejected, his pioneering role in helping to found urban ecology as a major sociological field of inquiry has had lasting influence. He was largely instrumental in directing sociologists and social psychologists to the organic groups and societies of cities as vital areas of scholarly investigation. He and his students, for example, published a series of studies on such topics as urban gangs, racial and ethnic groups, neighborhoods, ghettos, criminals and marginal populations, the urban moral order, urban social mobility, and the urban temperament and environment. Park stands as a classic example of a scholar who raised questions of enduring social and professional relevance.

—*Clifton K. Yearley*

FURTHER READING
Harris, Chauncy D., and Edward Ullman. "The Nature of Cities." *Annals of the American Academy of Political and Social Science* 242 (1945): 7-17. Introduces the multiple-nuclei theory of urban development in nontechnical language. Provides an interesting comparison with Park's theory. Includes footnotes and select bibliography.

Hoyt, Homer. *The Structure and Growth of Residential Neighborhoods in American Cities*. Washington, D.C.: Government Printing Office, 1939. Report on a federal study presents Hoyt's sector theory, which represented the initial challenge to Park's theory, with particular application to San Francisco and Minneapolis. Not easy reading, but rewarding for serious scholars. Includes graphs and bibliographic notes.

Lindner, Rolf. *The Reportage of Urban Culture: Robert Park and the Chicago School*. New York: Cambridge University Press, 1996. Unique study relates Park's research methods to those of urban journalism in the early twentieth century. Includes bibliography and indexes.

Mumford, Lewis. *The Culture of Cities*. 1938. Reprint. New York: Harvest Books, 1970. Brilliant exercise in urban ecology with deep as well as comprehensive historical range. The author shares many of Park's views, including that the city is a vital but neglected area of research and that the correct approach to cities is an ecological one. Focuses on New York City. Includes many photographs, extensive annotated bibliography, and index.

Park, Robert E. *Human Communities*. Glencoe, Ill.: Free Press, 1952. Scholarly volume deals with the city and human ecology. Clearly written and straightforward. Includes notes and indexes.

Park, Robert E., and Edward W. Burgess, with R. D. McKenzie. *The City*. 1925. Reprint. Chicago: University of Chicago Press, 1967. Presents Park's principles, his objectives, and his major sociological theory. Although Burgess and McKenzie contributed chapters, the major essays and chief influence are Park's.

Ritzer, George, and Douglas J. Goodman. *Sociological Theory*. 6th ed. New York: McGraw-Hill, 2003. Superb nontechnical survey of the subject. Provides an excellent treatment of the Chicago school and an ex-

tensive analysis of Park's ideas along with valuable biographical information. Includes photographs, biographical sketches, references, and indexes.

Sennett, Richard, ed. *Classic Essays on the Culture of Cities*. Englewood Cliffs, N.J.: Prentice-Hall, 1969. Collection of essays lives up to its title. Features ten thought-provoking essays by seven distinguished sociologists, an anthropologist, and Sennett, a major urban scholar. Fine introductory essay briefly reviews the development of urban sociology, including urban ecology.

SEE ALSO: 1910's: Garbage Industry Introduces Reforms; 1910: *Euthenics* Calls for Pollution Control; 1916: Dewey Applies Pragmatism to Education; July, 1916: New York City Institutes a Comprehensive Zoning Law; Nov. 1, 1939: Rockefeller Center Is Completed.

1925
CRANBROOK ACADEMY PROMOTES THE ARTS AND CRAFTS MOVEMENT

Although the Cranbrook Academy was founded as a model nineteenth century Arts and Crafts movement educational community, its faculty and students had major influence in shaping twentieth century design.

LOCALE: Cranbrook, Michigan

CATEGORIES: Fashion and design; organizations and institutions

KEY FIGURES

George Booth (1864-1949), American newspaper publisher and patron of the arts

Eliel Saarinen (1873-1950), Finnish architect

Eero Saarinen (1910-1961), student at the Cranbrook Academy who became an influential American architect and designer

Charles Eames (1907-1978), student at the Cranbrook Academy who became an influential American designer

SUMMARY OF EVENT

In a style typical of upwardly mobile and upper-class Victorian businessmen, George Booth became something of a patron of the arts after his marriage to Ellen Warren Scripps in 1887 and upon his assumption of a managerial position at the *Detroit Evening News*, the

flagship of his father-in-law's publishing empire. Between 1900 and 1920, Booth was actively involved in the promotion of arts and crafts at the local, state, and national levels. His interest in the Arts and Crafts movement of the nineteenth century may be traced to his roots: Both his great-grandfather and his grandfather had been English coppersmiths.

The importance of the Arts and Crafts movement to the quality of life in his own community was of particular importance to Booth. As the automobile industry in Detroit began to expand and dominate the local economy, Booth felt that he might make real contributions to the city by emphasizing the importance of good design and art education. He was a significant patron of the Detroit Museum of Art, acted as president of the Detroit Society of Arts and Crafts, and helped to found the Detroit School of Design.

By the early 1920's, however, Booth was dissatisfied with the results of his yeoman efforts. He began to consider projects over which he could have more personal and complete control. Booth spent several years traveling and researching museums and art academies in Europe, and he decided to create his own experimental art education community on his suburban farm estate, twenty miles from Detroit. In 1924, he asked the Finnish architect Eliel Saarinen, who was a visiting professor at the University of Michigan at the time, to create a master building plan for the site and to act as a consultant for the proposed academy's educational program. The Cranbrook Foundation was organized in 1927, although the Cranbrook Academy of Art, with Saarinen as its first president, was not formally established until 1932.

Booth believed the community's physical plant should be given first priority, and Saarinen immediately began to plan the Cranbrook Academy of Art. Building was dependent on the availability of funding and so took place over a fairly extended period. The first academy building was begun in 1925. Designed by George Booth and J. Robert F. Swanson, it housed an architectural office, library, and museum. The first Arts and Crafts building was finished in 1929. The Academy of Art projects, constructed between 1925 and 1963, include seven studio buildings, seven residences (including the Saarinen House), three dormitories, a foundry, a garage, and a museum and library. The Cranbrook School for Boys was built on the site of the original farm and is made up of twenty-five structures constructed between 1925 and 1979, including several remodeled farm buildings, a hockey rink, and a fire station. The Cranbrook Institute of Science is a complex of five buildings, including a revised version of George Booth's original 1930 design, a planetarium, and a nature center. Kingswood School Cranbrook, for girls, is made up of seven buildings constructed between 1930 and 1973. Brookside School Cranbrook is housed in the meetinghouse that George Booth designed in 1918 to provide his father with a pulpit. Several additions, a gymnasium, and two residences complete the Brookside facilities. The original estate, including Cranbrook House (designed in 1907 by Albert Kahn to contain Booth's sizable Arts and Crafts collection and library), a Greek-style theater built in 1915, a greenhouse, and a number of cottages, has also been preserved.

The architectural development of the community was seen as a symbolic and practical emblem of the educational program and goals of the academy. Following the model of the American Academy of Art in Rome, Cranbrook's educational plan was loosely organized. Ideally, there was to be no formal curriculum, and students and scholars would be encouraged to interact informally. Originally, Booth wanted to invite "master artists" to Cranbrook with the understanding that, in addition to working on their own projects, they would contribute to the physical and educational environment of the academy. Residences, studios, and honoraria

would be provided, and each "master" would supervise a select group of "fellows," who would also receive payment for work done in cooperation with their teachers. In this spirit, and because costs were high, in 1930 Booth established a gradual self-sufficiency plan for the craft studios.

For Saarinen, this organizational scheme was uncomfortably reminiscent of medieval guilds, and he attempted, not altogether successfully, to guide the school toward a more organic model of the relationship between art and life. Despite a fuzzy theoretical orientation and administrative difficulties (the school did not grant degrees until 1942), beginning in the 1930's, Cranbrook was able to provide a unique educational setting in which students were expected to learn by doing. Personal projects, individual interests, and experimentation were the norm, and the diversity of the professional experiences and backgrounds of both students and faculty made Cranbrook a rich laboratory of design ideas and practices. As a center for advanced study in nine areas—architecture, design, metalwork, photography, sculpture, printmaking, painting, textiles, and ceramics—the Cranbrook Academy of Art made major contributions to the forms, practice, and production of arts and crafts around the world.

SIGNIFICANCE

George Booth founded the Cranbrook Academy in the early 1920's as a utopian community that would focus its energies on returning art and craftsmanship to a primary place in the commercial and industrial arenas of American design. For Booth, the development of social utopia was dependent on aesthetic reform. Booth's ideas for Cranbrook place art and craftsmanship squarely in the center of a number of "reform" movements of importance to American culture: the ideal of the dedicated community that has influenced Americans since the time of the Puritans; the Arts and Crafts movement, which reached its peak in the United States between 1890 and 1910; and later attempts to define an aesthetic that would unite new technologies with moral values and social purposes.

Cranbrook was meant to be a special place, devoted to the integration of labor and leisure, life and art. Contentious British philosophers and artists such as John Ruskin and William Morris argued that industrialization debased both design and production and, by extension, culture itself; redemption, they claimed, lay in a return to "arts and crafts." In the United States, reformers in the nineteenth century Arts and Crafts movement were disillusioned with urban society. In response, they attempted to revive handcraftsmanship, to promote simplicity and traditionalism of design and lifestyle through unification of the applied and fine arts, and to celebrate nativist culture.

Eliel Saarinen, Cranbrook's master planner and guiding hand until his resignation in 1946, embodied both the social and aesthetic components of Booth's vision of reform. Like his contemporary Frank Lloyd Wright, Saarinen was interested in an expansive universe of creative design, from city planning to carpets. His architectural works influenced the stream of modernism that focused on the importance of the environment as a physical and emotional center of meaning. Saarinen's presence as an instructor made Cranbrook a central testing site for early experiments in American modernism, particularly in the decorative arts. By the late 1930's, the interaction of Cranbrook's first generation of European teachers with a second, younger generation of American instructors and students produced works that had a tremendous influence on post-World War II design. Much of the work of Cranbrook students and faculty from the 1920's on reveals how an ideal of the Arts and Crafts movement—the elevation of the applied arts to the level of fine arts—affected the ways modern designers searched for an integration of artistic style and lifestyle.

Under Saarinen's direction, faculty and students were encouraged to experiment and collaborate. As the academy had no established curriculum, national and international competitions often provided the impetus for exploration of new concepts. For example, four designs by Cranbrook students won prizes at the "Organic Design for Home Furnishings Competition" sponsored by the Museum of Modern Art in 1940 and 1941. Students Charles Eames and Eero Saarinen (Eliel Saarinen's son), both of whom had backgrounds in architecture, collaborated to create a group of chairs, modular storage units, tables, and a sectional sofa that won two first prizes. Benjamin Baldwin and Harry Weese also won prizes in multiple categories of the competition; their most significant entries were for outdoor furniture and lighting fixtures. The competition generated designs that were influential in shaping American furniture between 1950 and 1975 and helped to establish Eames and Saarinen as leaders of American design.

Florence Knoll, who had attended Kingswood School Cranbrook, gained a reputation as an important interior designer and entrepreneur. She domesticated the European International Style for American homes and offices and designed elegant hospital, bank, university, and ho-

tel interiors from the 1940's to the 1960's. Along with her husband, Hans, in 1951 she formed Knoll Associates, a company that drew on the best talent in Europe and the United States to design furniture, textiles, and graphics.

The worlds of modern architecture, furniture, and interior design were not the only beneficiaries of the Cranbrook Academy. Booth's interest in traditional craftsmanship remained a steady influence on study and practice at Cranbrook. Although the Cranbrook Press, which he founded in 1900, was a short-lived experiment, his efforts on behalf of metalworking, textiles, and ceramics continue to be central to Cranbrook's importance as an American educational institution. In the early twenty-first century, Cranbrook is one of the few U.S. institutions to offer instruction in fine metalworking in an educational environment. Eliel Saarinen was very active in metalworking, and a number of his designs grace the Cranbrook campus. Harry Bertoia revived the metal shop in the late 1930's, first as a student and then as an instructor, and his work there in jewelry, precious and nonprecious metals, and sculpture was a remarkable mixture of technique and technology. After World War II, Richard Thomas began the first teaching department in metalwork at Cranbrook.

Cranbrook's contributions to the crafts of textiles and ceramics also began in the 1920's. In the early years, Eliel Saarinen's wife, Loja, established her weaving studio at Cranbrook, and a weaving department and shops soon followed. Many of the carpets, curtains, wall hangings, and decorative textiles for community buildings were produced under Loja Saarinen's supervision. The best known of Cranbrook's textiles students is, no doubt, Jack Lenor Larsen, a practicing weaver whose international corporation gained fame in the mid-twentieth century for mass-produced fabrics with handwoven characteristics.

Booth intended that ceramics be one of the first arts taught at Cranbrook, although the ceramics department was small and undistinguished until the late 1930's, when Maija Grotell joined the faculty. Under her guidance, the department became a center of individual creative activity at Cranbrook, and Grotell's students have made significant contributions to modern American ceramics.

In attempting to create a community that illustrated the positive relationship between aesthetics and social life, George Booth laid a foundation for the transformation of education and production. Such a spirit characterized the modernist agenda of the twentieth century, and it remains at the heart of Cranbrook's impact on American design. Despite the passage of time and changes in technology, society, and aesthetics, this spirit continues to influence the work of the graduates, faculty, and students of the Cranbrook Academy of Art.

—*J. R. Donath*

FURTHER READING

Becker, Howard. "Arts and Crafts." *American Journal of Sociology* 83 (January, 1978): 862-868. An information-packed introduction to the crafts revival movement by an insightful sociologist of art.

Clark, Robert Judson, et al. *Design in America: The Cranbrook Vision, 1925-1950.* New York: Harry N. Abrams, 1983. Profuse and beautiful illustrations characterize this excellent volume of essays, which served as the catalog for an exhibition organized by the Detroit Institute of Fine Arts. Includes biographies of artists, chronology, notes, and index.

Design Quarterly 98 (1975). Special issue titled "Nelson/Eames/Gerard/Propst: The Design Process at Herman Miller" discusses the work of four important American designers. Excellent introduction to postwar American design. Well illustrated.

Kaplan, Wendy. *"The Art That Is Life": The Arts and Crafts Movement in America, 1875-1920.* Boston: Little, Brown, 1987. Well-illustrated, articulate cata-

log, with fine introductory essays, created to accompany an exhibition at the Boston Museum of Fine Arts. Includes index.

Lecuyer, Annette. "Cranbrook Continuum." *Architectural Review*, November, 1997, 76-77. Article focuses on architectural and other design projects completed at the Cranbrook Academy from the late 1980's to 1997, connecting this work to the institution's tradition of excellence.

Noyes, Eliot F. *Organic Design in Home Furnishings.* New York: Museum of Modern Art, 1941. Monograph designed to accompany an exhibit illustrates various entries and winners. Includes black-and-white photographs.

Sparke, Penny. *An Introduction to Design and Culture: 1900 to the Present.* 2d ed. New York: Routledge, 2004. History of the development of modern design includes discussion of the work of many people associated with the Cranbrook Academy. Features illustrations, bibliography, and index.

SEE ALSO: 1902-1913: Tiffany Leads the Art Nouveau Movement in the United States; 1903: Hoffmann and Moser Found the Wiener Werkstätte; Oct., 1907: Deutscher Werkbund Is Founded; 1937-1938: Aalto Designs Villa Mairea.

1925
EISENSTEIN'S *POTEMKIN* INTRODUCES NEW FILM EDITING TECHNIQUES

Sergei Eisenstein created his masterpiece by splicing segments of film shot at many locations, an approach that many film directors subsequently adopted.

LOCALE: Soviet Union
CATEGORY: Motion pictures

KEY FIGURES

Sergei Eisenstein (1898-1948), Soviet film director
Éduard Tissé (1897-1961), Russian motion-picture cameraman
Vladimir Ilich Lenin (Vladimir Ilich Ulyanov; 1870-1924), leader of the Soviet Union
Lev Vladimirovich Kuleshov (1899-1970), Soviet film director

SUMMARY OF EVENT

After the successful Bolshevik Revolution of 1917, the leaders of the Communist Party (especially Vladimir

Ilich Lenin) launched a massive propaganda effort to win support for their new government from all segments of Soviet society. Lenin saw motion pictures as potentially the most effective tool not only for gaining public acceptance for Communist rule but also for convincing citizens to make the sacrifices necessary to build a socialist economic system. Accordingly, he authorized the creation of a government bureau to commission the making of "agitprop" (agitational propaganda) films to elicit the desired responses from the public. Lenin's action set in motion a chain of events that eventually led to the production of a motion picture titled *Bronenosets Potyomkin* (1925; *Potemkin*) that revolutionized filmmaking around the world.

Early in 1925, the Soviet government issued an order for the production of an agitprop film commemorating the twentieth anniversary of the unsuccessful Revolution of 1905. To direct the film, government officials chose twenty-six-year-old Sergei Eisenstein, who had already directed several very effective films. Eisenstein, educated as a civil engineer, had joined the Communist Party early and had worked diligently for its success during the revolution. After the revolution, he became interested in theater and joined the Prolitkult Theater (an official government agency, as were all groups involved in the arts). He rapidly became disenchanted with theater because small stages limited his ideas of dramatic productions, and he subsequently turned to the relatively new medium of motion pictures.

After working with Lev Vladimirovich Kuleshov (who had been involved in filmmaking since its introduction in czarist Russia) for several years, in 1924 Eisenstein received permission to direct an agitprop film titled *Stracha* (1925; *Strike*), which enjoyed great success. The effectiveness of his first project resulted in his being chosen to direct the commemorative film, which was tentatively titled *1905*. The government apparently envisioned a film that would re-create the entire yearlong revolt against the czarist government in 1904 and 1905.

Eisenstein, in collaboration with several writers, created a hundred-page script for the film, detailing dozens of events to be filmed at more than thirty locations from Leningrad to the Black Sea. He and his crew began filming in Leningrad on March 31, 1925. When, in August, cloudy weather made filming in Leningrad difficult, Eisenstein and his crew moved to the Black Sea port of Odessa. Even before the move, Eisenstein had concluded that the original script was much too ambitious in scope. When he saw the massive marble steps leading from Odessa down to the seashore, he resolved to discard the film already shot and to concentrate instead on one event that would epitomize the entire revolution: the mutiny of the sailors aboard the battleship *Potemkin*.

In making the film, Eisenstein introduced two innovations that have profoundly influenced the making of motion pictures ever since. The first was the use of "typage" in choosing actors, and the second was the use of montage editing techniques to heighten the emotional impact of the film.

According to Eisenstein's theory of typage, a director

Sergei Eisenstein. (Hulton Archive/Getty Images)

should study each character in the script and determine what physical and mental traits might be found in the character's "type." The director should then employ a person who exhibits those traits to play the character rather than depend on professional actors. The character of an Orthodox priest who figures prominently in *Potemkin* was in reality a gardener whom Eisenstein concluded displayed all the traits usually associated with a priest.

The montage editing techniques that Eisenstein perfected for his motion picture undoubtedly became his most important contribution to the evolution of filmmaking. "Montage" refers to the splicing together of segments of film to heighten dramatic effect. One of the most powerful scenes in *Potemkin* occurs during the massacre on the marble steps (arguably the most famous sequence in motion-picture history), when an old woman wearing pince-nez asks the Cossacks to stop the slaughter. Eisenstein shows a close-up of the Cossack swinging his sword, followed by another close-up of the woman with her glasses broken, blood spurting from her eye. The film never shows the sword striking the woman, but because of the placement of the shots, the audience is left in no doubt as to what has happened.

In several scenes, Eisenstein introduced a technique subsequently adopted by many directors called "breaking from real time." In one particular sequence, the audience sees a sailor, disgusted with the food he is forced to eat, break the plate of one of his officers. In real time, this action would have taken only a second. Eisenstein filmed the breaking of the plate from nine different angles, spliced the shots together, and created a four-second sequence that produced a greatly enhanced effect on the audience.

Finally, Eisenstein also introduced several innovative camera techniques during the making of *Potemkin* that were widely copied by most subsequent filmmakers. In collaboration with cameraman Éduard Tissé, he constructed a trolley for the camera that enabled the cameraman to descend the Odessa steps with the actors. He ordered another camera to be strapped to the waist of a circus acrobat to capture the movement as the acrobat ran, jumped, and fell down the steps.

The film that ultimately emerged from Eisenstein's tremendous burst of creativity did not entirely please the Communist leadership, although its propaganda effect was undeniable. Outside the Soviet Union, however, motion-picture critics hailed *Potemkin* as a masterpiece.

SIGNIFICANCE

When *Potemkin* debuted in Moscow in January, 1926, it stirred immediate controversy in the ranks of the Communist Party and the Soviet artistic community. Many of Eisenstein's rivals in cinematic production accused him of putting art before propaganda. Some of his enemies in the party hierarchy dismissed the film as a decadent bourgeois documentary. Eisenstein's relationship with the Soviet bureaucracy became strained, and his reputation never fully recovered. Although he continued to direct films in the Soviet Union, the government declined to distribute many of them.

In Western Europe and the United States, *Potemkin* won instant acclaim. American film stars Douglas Fairbanks and Mary Pickford traveled to Moscow in July, 1926, to view the film. Fairbanks, in a widely quoted interview after seeing the film, declared that Eisenstein's film had at last mastered the science of motion. Some months later, Fairbanks, along with German actor Emil Jannings and producer Max Reinhardt, endorsed *Potemkin* as the greatest motion picture made to that time.

Fairbanks's praise heightened American audiences' anticipation of the film, which finally premiered in New York City at the Biltmore Theater on December 5, 1926.

Film viewers in the United States were enthusiastic about Eisenstein's film, and American film critics even more so. One critic writing for the *Christian Science Monitor* correctly predicted that *Potemkin* would make motion-picture history as a model of how films should be made. The National Board of Review of the motion-picture industry chose the film as the best of the year and identified it as a perfect re-creation of a historical event. Ironically, this last bit of praise was totally undeserved. No slaughter of innocents occurred on the Odessa steps in 1905, as depicted in the film's most famous scene; the director fabricated the entire event. The mutiny aboard the *Potemkin* was not an expression of revolutionary ideology, as Eisenstein portrayed it; rather, it was a protest against deplorable conditions. Eisenstein continued a trend that has only rarely been reversed in filmmaking, that of creating history rather than re-creating it.

Potemkin's reception in the West somewhat rejuvenated Eisenstein's standing with Soviet officials. They allowed him to direct the agitprop films *Octyabr* (1927; *October: Or, Ten Days That Shook the World*) and *Generalnaya Linya* (1929; *The General Line*), both of which employed many of the techniques pioneered in *Potemkin*. In 1929, Paramount Pictures brought Eisenstein to Hollywood but ultimately rejected the scripts he submitted for two proposed films, *Sutter's Gold* and *An American Tragedy*. American novelist Upton Sinclair then arranged for Eisenstein to make an epic motion picture about the Mexican revolution, but Soviet officials recalled him to Moscow before he completed the film. An American studio released some of the footage from the Mexican venture as *Thunder over Mexico* in 1933. This film also employed many of the techniques pioneered in *Potemkin* and, judging from the wide adoption of such techniques by American directors, heavily influenced the evolution of U.S. cinema.

Eisenstein's masterpiece confirmed motion-picture making as a true art form. Although Eisenstein never received the acclaim in the Soviet Union that his work merited, *Potemkin* vindicated Lenin's view of motion pictures as potentially the most effective medium for molding a particular point of view among the masses. The film evokes powerful emotions even among modern viewers: revulsion at the deplorable conditions among the lower classes depicted in the film's scenes; disgust with the arrogant and ruthless officers, czarist officials, and priests; moral outrage at the massacre of civilians on the Odessa steps. Eisenstein achieved this tremendous emotional impact by pioneering techniques that continue to dominate filmmaking.

— *Paul Madden*

FURTHER READING

Cook, David A. *A History of Narrative Film*. 4th ed. New York: W. W. Norton, 2004. Identifies *Potemkin* as an epochal event in motion-picture history. Describes Eisenstein's innovative techniques in language lay readers can understand and locates the film in its proper place from the perspective of world cinema history.

Eisenstein, Sergei M. "The Composition of *Potemkin*." In *The Emergence of Film Art*, edited by Lewis Jacobs. New York: Hopkinson and Blake, 1969. Eisenstein's explanation in his own words of the thought process and chance happenings that resulted in his masterpiece. Invaluable to those who wish to understand *Potemkin*.

_____. *Potemkin*. Translated by Gillon R. Aitken. New York: Simon & Schuster, 1968. The complete script of the film, annotated by Eisenstein himself. Difficult reading, but worthwhile to those seeking in-depth knowledge about the famous film.

Fabe, Marilyn. *Closely Watched Films: An Introduction to the Art of Narrative Film Technique*. Berkeley: University of California Press, 2004. Presents analytic tools for understanding the narrative structure of films. Chapter 2 is devoted to examination of Eisenstein's use of montage in *Potemkin*. Includes illustrations, glossary, bibliography, and index.

Kauffman, Stanley. "*Potemkin*." In *Great Film Directors: A Critical Anthology*, edited by Leo Braudy and Morris Dickstein. New York: Oxford University Press, 1978. Identifies Eisenstein as perhaps the most important director of his era because of his perfection of montage in *Potemkin*. Provides informative explanations of Eisenstein's techniques.

Lawder, Standish D. "Eisenstein and Constructivism." In *Great Film Directors: A Critical Anthology*, edited by Leo Braudy and Morris Dickstein. New York: Oxford University Press, 1978. Attempts to show that Eisenstein's films, especially *Potemkin*, were heavily influenced by a banned artistic movement in the Soviet Union called constructivism.

Leyda, Jay. *Kino: A History of the Russian and Soviet Film*. 3d ed. Princeton, N.J.: Princeton University Press, 1983. Shows that Eisenstein's genius did not appear out of a vacuum but instead drew heavily on the work of Russian filmmakers who preceded him, especially his mentor, Kuleshov. Also clearly demonstrates the influence that Eisenstein had on subsequent Soviet directors.

Macdonald, Dwight. "Eisenstein, Pudovkin, and Others." In *The Emergence of Film Art*, edited by Lewis Jacobs. New York: Hopkinson and Blake, 1969. Portrays Eisenstein as an important member of a trend in Soviet filmmaking, but not as an epochal genius, as many other critics have seen him.

Murray, Edward. *Ten Film Classics: A Re-Viewing*. New York: Frederick Ungar, 1978. Maintains that the true greatness of a film lies in its ability to communicate with audiences far removed from its original place and time. Concludes that *Potemkin* possesses that rare quality and thus must be considered a true masterpiece of cinematic art.

Nizhny, Vladimir. *Lessons with Eisenstein*. Edited and translated by Ivor Montagu and Jay Leyda. 1962. Reprint. New York: Hill & Wang, 2000. Extremely thorough examination of the innovations that appeared in Eisenstein's films, especially *Potemkin*. Some readers may be put off by the overt Marxist-Leninist philosophy expounded by the author.

SEE ALSO: Fall, 1903: *The Great Train Robbery* Introduces New Editing Techniques; Mar. 3, 1915: Griffith Releases *The Birth of a Nation*; 1920: Premiere of *The Cabinet of Dr. Caligari*; 1923: *The Ten Commandments* Advances American Film Spectacle; Dec. 4, 1924: Von Stroheim's Silent Masterpiece *Greed* Premieres; 1925-1927: Gance's *Napoléon* Revolutionizes Filmmaking Techniques; 1927: Kuleshov and Pudovkin Introduce Montage to Filmmaking; 1927: Lang Expands the Limits of Filmmaking with *Metropolis*.

1925
GIDE'S *THE COUNTERFEITERS* QUESTIONS MORAL ABSOLUTES

André Gide's questioning of absolutes paralleled societal doubts about the validity of established authorities and reflected the increasing importance of individual conscience in determining ethics and self-authenticity.

LOCALE: France
CATEGORY: Literature

KEY FIGURE
André Gide (1869-1951), French writer

SUMMARY OF EVENT

André Gide's questioning of absolutes reflected the trends and temper of early twentieth century cultural and intellectual life. As the French celebrated the arrival of a new century, inventions such as the electric light, the automobile, and film enriched life; however, France's defeat by Germany in the Franco-Prussian War in 1871 undermined the French public's confidence in traditional beliefs and recognized institutions. For Gide, the ideals and truths that had shaped principles and practices conflicted with individual aspirations and differing perspectives. In his works, human beings confront confusion and crisis.

Gide presented in *Les Faux-monnayeurs* (1925; *The Counterfeiters*, 1927) an anguish that results from the tensions between the ineffectiveness of authoritative institutions and the significance of individual responsibility. The novel reworks an incident recorded in 1906. Like the historical counterfeiters on which the story is based, the characters Léon Ghéridanisol, Georges Molinier, and Philippe Adamanti pass illegal coins and, although discovered, escape prosecution. Recalling the images of specious currency, they project, along with other characters, appearances that reflect reality but do not disclose all its aspects. Uncertain and ambiguous knowledge forms the basis of actions that, derived from illusions, weaken credibility, induce individualism, and end in conflicts. Nevertheless, personal perspectives determined by relative circumstances can combine to reveal truth. By juxtaposing opposing views, Gide, through the character of Édouard, examines the ambivalence of illusion and enables the reader to reconcile varying visions into a coherent concept. Such a privileged position, however, is more apparent than real, and Gide's characters experience misunderstanding, frustration, disappointment, and dejection.

In the novel, human perception of reality assumes a truth that, ultimately invalid, controls behavior and influences subsequent artistic and literary representations. Bernard, the illegitimate son of Édouard, the book's narrator, leaves home to seek freedom and authenticity. By responding to individual impulses, he enjoys independence and thereby defeats inner disturbances and social repression. In replacing his family with other communities, however, Bernard recognizes the contradictions between the incontrovertibility of biological fact and the shifting perceptions of self-identity. Incapable of achieving total detachment, he acknowledges the necessity of participating in society; upon returning home, he attempts to forge the illegitimacy of birthright with the legitimacy of human interaction.

Like Bernard and other characters in the novel, Boris, a schoolboy, suffers an entrapment that fuses fiction and truth, morality and immorality, autonomy and interdependence. His self-identification proceeds from interaction with others; winning acceptance among his schoolmates requires that he play the dangerous game of Russian roulette, and Boris shoots himself. Man teeters between the futilities of human endeavor and the nothingness of death; however, the certainty of human persistence and pain remains. Like the specious coins that are tangible but worthless, human beings are biologically real but spiritually counterfeit.

Gide develops in his novel themes presented in earlier writings. Like such Symbolist poets as Charles Baudelaire, Arthur Rimbaud, and Stéphane Mallarmé, he reacted initially against the realistic and naturalistic objectivities of Gustave Flaubert and Émile Zola. Through the use of archetypes and myths, he dramatized the contentions between realities of fragmentation and ideals of integration. In Gide's *Les Cahiers d'André Walter* (1891; *The Notebooks of André Walter*, 1968), Angel, or spiritual aspiration, contests for the human soul against Beast, or earthly attractions. Revolt against societal values leads to impotence and, in *Paludes* (1895; *Marshlands*, 1953), to self-destruction. Man is imprisoned in a cosmic game, which in *Le Prométhée mal enchaîné* (1899; *Prometheus Misbound*, 1953) Gide narratively conveys as a battle between Zeus's erratic and amoral purposes and Prometheus's resolute and useless yearnings.

When endorsing these views in subsequent works, Gide emphasized ethical implications. His artistry moved from a description of images and self-imaginings to accounts of actions and character portrayals. In shifting from personal confession to fictional narrative, he described the anguish of dilemmas and the ambivalent interpretation of actions. Gidean personages strive to reconcile oppositions through conscious and self-determined acts. Like their Nietzschean and Dostoevskian counterparts, they demonstrate an individualism that attacks and denies moral certainties. Yet the exuberance evolving from questioning and rebellion is transitory and elusive and results in the substitution of one authority for another. Michel in *L'Immoraliste* (1902; *The Immoralist*, 1930) and Lafcadio in *Les Caves du Vatican* (1914; *The Vatican Swindle*, 1925; better known as *Lafcadio's Adventures*, 1925) pursue deliverance from moral responsibilities. Michel's defiance of ethical codes and Lafcadio's murder without motive, however, lead, respectively, to the sadness of solitude and the necessity of human interaction. Through submission to inner impulses, protagonists in *La Porte étroite* (1909; *Strait Is the Gate*, 1924) and *La Symphonie pastorale* (1919; *The Pastoral Symphony*, 1931) reject Protestant ethics, but changes of circumstances rob them of the opportunity to reconcile internal consciousness with external realities. Contradictions persist, and characters experience delusion, displacement, and dejection.

By situating personal perplexities and individual dilemmas within the framework of a social drama, in *The Counterfeiters* Gide adapted previous philosophical and psychological themes to objective reality. Like Flaubert, he entrapped his characters in tangles of amorous relationships. Love requires interpretation and interaction, and personal perceptions deceive but direct destiny, culminating, in Flaubert's work, in Emma Bovary's suicide and, in *The Counterfeiters*, in Boris's self-destruction. Moreover, Gide, like Marcel Proust, expanded the scope of social realism and, in depicting the dynamics of bourgeois life, described the difficulties of man's search for self-understanding and meaningful values. Moral questions elicited by the Dreyfus affair and World War I compelled thinkers and artists to examine external realities in order to reform society.

Like Anatole France and Romain Rolland, Gide attacked social and political practices; however, in constructing numerous credible, interrelated episodes that detail man's futile search for absolutes in a relative, changing world, he universalized the historical and particular. Inner crises characterize a social setting where varying, limited perspectives evolve into the single certainty of despair and death. Authenticity and dignity are based on absolutes. Yet in questioning authorities and values, Gidean characters become imprisoned by doubt and frustration. As Bernard returns home, the novel concludes at the beginning, and the new story of Caloub Molinier continues the circular narrative of man's disappointments and displacements in a delusionary world.

André Gide. (The Nobel Foundation)

SIGNIFICANCE

In his journal, Gide described *The Counterfeiters* as a failure. His stress on concision and his abandonment of accepted narrative structures made the book a departure from the engaging novels of Honoré de Balzac, Gustave Flaubert, Charles Dickens, and Thomas Hardy. In 1952, one year after Gide's death, the Roman Catholic Church prohibited the reading of his works on moral grounds. Nevertheless, this reserved reception of his fiction contrasts with the important impact of his ethical thought and novelistic theory on contemporary and subsequent writers. As founding editor of the highly regarded periodical *La Nouvelle Revue française*, moreover, Gide welcomed and advanced innovative and controversial ideas on ideology and style. *The Counterfeiters* reflected much of his thinking and novelistic practice, and it shaped the direction of attitudes toward later developments in ethics and aesthetics.

Like Gide, proponents of Surrealism and its precursor Dadaism reacted against the values and authorities that had brought about the atrocities of World War I. Dadaism, initiated in Zurich in 1916, denounced arbitrary absolutes that denied individual thought and reduced human worth. The nihilism expressed in verse by poets such as André Breton, Paul Éluard, and Louis Aragon reflected an empty and disturbing vision of the human situation. Humanity, according to Breton, confronts the conflicts of opposing absolutes; however, through internal images derived from observed realities, humans translate physical phenomena into inner truths that, in Breton's novel *Nadja* (1928; English translation, 1960), become indicators of external beauty.

Gide did not participate in the Surrealist movement, but his themes of human aspirations, anxieties, exuberance, and futility reinforced the Surrealist call to reject established values. During the 1930's, the failure of the League of Nations, the economic deprivations of global depression, and the rise of totalitarian governments shattered illusions of humanity's ability to reform ethics and to attain economic security and social equality within existing orders.

Like Bernard, the characters created by Georges Bernanos contend against falsity; but, instead of enjoying momentary exhilarations, they discover, through moral and physical torments, an inner redemption and spiritual nobility. Gide's skepticism of moral absolutes also assumed the form of revolution in André Malraux's *La Condition humaine* (1933; *Man's Fate*, 1934), in which images of war reflect the need to destroy existing authorities. In Malraux's work, however, unlike in *The Counterfeiters*, a fraternity among the revolutionaries permits an integration of spiritual affiliations.

After the defeat of France in 1940, Jean-Paul Sartre and Albert Camus addressed the validity of absolutes. Sartre saw humans as defined by external realities and inner recognitions; in assuming imposed values, Sartre asserted, humans falsify their true nature and suffer anguish. Rather, Sartre argued, humankind must resist artificial restrictions and assert self-authenticity. Camus, in *L'Étranger* (1942; *The Stranger*, 1946), reaffirms Gide's vision of man who, guided by impulses and checked by absolutes, endures the confusions of absur-

dity. The hero of Camus's work, Meursault, like Gide's Bernard, finds freedom through rebellion and, in declaring his self-worth, experiences a deliverance.

Stylistically and structurally, *The Counterfeiters* advanced and foreshadowed later developments in novelistic techniques. Gide's use of a direct, classical simplicity paralleled styles adopted by François Mauriac, Camus, and T. S. Eliot. The portrayal of diverse characters, moreover, necessitated the use of multiple perspectives. Édouard's journal and comments synthesize views, recalling the scattered but unified perceptions recorded by omniscient narrators in the novels of Marcel Proust or Virginia Woolf. Further, like Roger Martin du Gard, John Galsworthy, and Thomas Mann, Gide presented a social panorama. Yet his emphasis on individual perspectives also suggests techniques characterizing the French New Novel. Michel Butor and Alain Robbe-Grillet, in particular, similarly combined conflicting images that, individually observed, denoted the apparent chaos of existence and the uselessness of human aspirations. Indeed, the close relationship between denial of absolutes and the emergence of brutal absolutist regimes that in turn denied traditional ethical restraints produced a century of horrific murder on a scale previously unknown, an unattractive fruit of the philosophical nihilism of the age.

Gide's moral skepticism led to an individualism shared by subsequent thinkers and fiction writers. In assuming a detached, reportorial stance, however, Gide contented himself with describing situations and thereby resisted personal commentary. Through doubts and disappointments, his characters mature in self-understanding and suffer the frustrations of human existence. In fact, by foreshadowing Samuel Beckett's representations of misunderstanding and Jean Genet's dramatizations of meaninglessness, Gide depicted the painful paradox of ideals that inevitably end in misinterpretation, disintegration, and death.

—*Donald Gilman*

FURTHER READING

Brée, Germaine. *Gide*. 1963. Reprint. Westport, Conn.: Greenwood Press, 1985. An enlarged revision of a French study published in 1953, this intelligent, insightful analysis of Gide's works emphasizes novelistic techniques that facilitate the expression of intellectual and ethical themes.

Brennan, Joseph G. *Three Philosophical Novelists: James Joyce, André Gide, Thomas Mann*. New York: Macmillan, 1964. Places Gide's works within the contexts of Nietzschean and Bergsonian philosophies to demonstrate Gide's interpretation of intellectual currents.

Conner, Tom, ed. *André Gide's Politics: Rebellion and Ambivalence*. New York: Palgrave Macmillan, 2001. Collection of essays focuses on Gide's growing commitment to a number of literary and social issues from the 1920's to 1936. Includes index.

Cordle, Thomas. *André Gide*. Rev. ed. Boston: Twayne, 1992. A superb reading of Gide's attempts to resolve oppositions that reflect Symbolist expression, Romantic idealism, and realistic objectivity. Includes annotated bibliography.

Falk, Eugene H. *Types of Thematic Structure: The Nature and Function of Motifs in Gide, Camus, and Sartre*. Chicago: University of Chicago Press, 1967. Systematically and rigorously elucidates Gide's uses of plot, characterization, and imagery through a reading of Gide's *The Pastoral Symphony*. Contrasts Gide's themes and techniques with those employed in Camus's *The Stranger* and Sartre's *La Nausée* (1938; *Nausea*, 1949).

Guerard, Albert J. *André Gide*. 2d ed. Cambridge, Mass.: Harvard University Press, 1969. Reading of Gide's works explores personal tensions between ascetic and amorous impulses, spiritual self-accounts, novelistic techniques, and possible influences. Slightly dated, this intelligent, perceptive study nevertheless provides an indispensable introduction to Gide's works.

Holdheim, W. Wolfgang. *Theory and Practice of the Novel: A Study on André Gide*. Geneva: Droz, 1968. A comprehensive, meticulous study of Gide's novelistic theory and techniques. Examines Gide's creative works in the light of his journal, suggesting parallels between Gide's style and structure and those of earlier novelists.

Hytier, Jean. *André Gide*. Translated by Richard Howard. Garden City, N.Y.: Doubleday, 1962. Originally published as a series of lectures (1938), this first aesthetic survey of Gide's works includes a detailed plot summary of *The Counterfeiters* and offers interesting insights into the themes of doubt and reform.

Ireland, G. W. *André Gide: A Study of His Creative Writings*. Oxford, England: Clarendon Press, 1970. Although lacking in defined methodology and single focus, presents intelligent, perceptive readings that provide a useful commentary on Gide's works.

Rossi, Vinio. *André Gide: The Evolution of an Aesthetic*. New Brunswick, N.J.: Rutgers University Press, 1967. Traces Gide's transition from the use of image to the development of narrative in describing the novelist's artistic growth.

Sheridan, Alan. *André Gide: A Life in the Present*. Cambridge, Mass.: Harvard University Press, 1999. Literary biography places Gide's works within the context of the time in which he lived and relates them to the events of his life. Includes family trees, bibliography, and index.

SEE ALSO: 1911-1923: Rilke's *Duino Elegies* Redefines Poetics; 1913: Apollinaire Defines Cubism; 1913-1927: Proust Publishes *Remembrance of Things Past*; Oct. 18, 1923: Stravinsky Completes His Wind Octet; 1924: Mann's *The Magic Mountain* Reflects European Crisis.

1925
HAMILTON PUBLISHES *INDUSTRIAL POISONS IN THE UNITED STATES*

In Industrial Poisons in the United States, *Alice Hamilton summarized decades of research and opened the way to later legislation to control health hazards in the workplace.*

LOCALE: United States
CATEGORIES: Environmental issues; business and labor; publishing and journalism

KEY FIGURES
Alice Hamilton (1869-1970), American physician
Jane Addams (1860-1935), American social reformer
Florence Kelley (1859-1932), American social worker
Julia C. Lathrop (1858-1932), American social reformer

SUMMARY OF EVENT

Alice Hamilton's *Industrial Poisons in the United States* (1925) was the summation of research that she began in the 1890's at Hull House, a Chicago settlement house opened in 1889 by Jane Addams. At its peak, the Hull House complex hosted activities for nine thousand nearby residents each week. Rooms were available for professional men and women who, while earning their living at other occupations, were committed to life and volunteer work among the immigrants who made up approximately three-quarters of Chicago's population. The lives of many of these immigrants were marked by unsanitary and unsafe housing and working conditions, a high child mortality rate, and a death rate from contagious diseases disproportionate to the rate among the general population.

Hamilton earned her medical degree from the University of Michigan in 1893. After postgraduate years at The Johns Hopkins University and elsewhere (she studied bacteriology and pathology at the Universities of Leipzig and Munich), in 1897 she was appointed professor of pathology at the Women's Medical School of Northwestern University in Chicago. When the school closed in 1902, she became a bacteriologist at the New Memorial Institute for Infectious Diseases. Living at Hull House, she joined a group of women who shared intellectual companionship and emotional support to a degree rarely experienced by educated women at that time. With no formal training in social work available to them, they created a methodology based on scrupulous accuracy and shared successful techniques.

Hamilton credited Florence Kelley with her political education; she learned from Julia C. Lathrop her highly successful, nonconfrontational techniques for eliciting in-

formation and cooperation in hostile environments. Together, these women became a significant force for change. They exercised considerable political influence, even though women in the United States did not receive the vote until 1920. Addams, for example, seconded Theodore Roosevelt's nomination for president at the 1912 convention of the Progressive Party, and Hull House reformers had developed many of the principles of that party's platform. Addams, who in 1931 became the first woman to win the Nobel Peace Prize, remained at the center of most Hull House activities, which usually originated as group projects. Lathrop became a specialist in institutional care, and in 1899, she joined with Kelley in the National Consumers League to fight industrial abuses. Kelley led investigations of sweatshop conditions.

Hamilton discovered her own specialization in 1902, when Addams encouraged her to investigate a typhoid epidemic. The Hull House area had the highest death rate in the city. Although her conclusions were wrong (she did not discover a leakage of raw sewage into the water supply), she developed the methodology she would use later, directly examining tenement buildings with illegal

Alice Hamilton. (Library of Congress)

A DOCTOR'S INTEREST IN INDUSTRIAL DISEASE

In her 1943 autobiography, Alice Hamilton related why she started investigating the medical hazards of the workplace:

It was . . . my experience at Hull-House that aroused my interest in industrial diseases. Living in a working-class quarter, coming in contact with laborers and their wives, I could not fail to hear tales of the dangers that workingmen faced, of cases of carbon-monoxide gassing in the great steel mills, of painters disabled by lead palsy, of pneumonia and rheumatism among the men in the stockyards. Illinois then had no legislation providing compensation for accident or disease caused by occupation. (There is something strange in speaking of "accident and sickness compensation." What could "compensate" anyone for an amputated leg or a paralyzed arm, or even an attack of lead colic, to say nothing of the loss of a husband or son?) There was a striking occurrence about this time in Chicago which brought vividly before me the unprotected, helpless state of workingmen who were held responsible for their own safety.

A group of men were sent out in a tug to one of Chicago's pumping stations in Lake Michigan and left there while the tug returned to shore. A fire broke out on the tiny island and could not be controlled, the men had the choice between burning to death and drowning, and before rescue could arrive most of them were drowned. The contracting company, which employed them, generously paid the funeral expenses, and nobody expected them to do more. Widows and orphans must turn to the County Agent or private charity—

that was the accepted way, back in the dark ages of the early twentieth century. William Hard, then a young college graduate living at Northwestern Settlement, wrote of this incident with a fiery pen, contrasting the treatment of the wives and children of these men whose death was caused by negligence with the treatment they would have received in Germany. His article and a copy of Sir Thomas Oliver's *Dangerous Trades*, which came into my hands just then, sent me to the Crerar Library to read everything I could find on the dangers to industrial workers, and what could be done to protect them. But it was all German, or British, Austrian, Dutch, Swiss, even Italian or Spanish—everything but American. In those countries industrial medicine was a recognized branch of the medical sciences; in my own country it did not exist. When I talked to my medical friends about the strange silence on this subject in American medical magazines and textbooks, I gained the impression that here was a subject tainted with Socialism or with feminine sentimentality for the poor. The American Medical Association had never had a meeting devoted to this subject, and except for a few surgeons attached to large companies operating steel mills, or railways, or coal mines, there were no medical men in Illinois who specialized in the field of industrial medicine.

Source: Alice Hamilton, *Exploring the Dangerous Trades: The Autobiography of Alice Hamilton, M.D.* (Boston: Little, Brown, 1943).

outdoor toilets, inadequate indoor facilities, and yards overflowing with rainwater and sewage; later, she would walk narrow catwalks over dangerous machinery and explore the depths of mines. In 1903, she began to examine the relationship between the unsanitary conditions of work among the poor, the long and irregular hours, and the prevalence of tuberculosis in the Hull House area; Addams and Hamilton presented a paper on the subject at the International Congress of Tuberculosis in 1908. Her reading of Sir Thomas Oliver's *Dangerous Trades* (1907) introduced her to a large body of European literature on occupational diseases. Germany and England, in fact, had instituted factory inspection. She found no similar research in the United States.

In 1908, Hamilton was appointed to an Illinois commission on occupational diseases. The commission's 1911 report included Hamilton's research into the dangers of painting, smelting, refining, and the manufacture of storage batteries, among other subjects. She discov-

ered seventy-seven industrial processes that exposed workers to lead poisoning and identified 358 unquestionable cases of workplace-related lead poisoning; her research was among the first to correlate hospital and pharmacy records with particular occupations. In 1912, she published *Plumbism in the Industries of the Middle West.*

In 1911, Hamilton was asked to undertake a national investigation for the U.S. Bureau of Labor (later the Department of Labor). Visiting all but three of the twenty-five white lead factories in the United States, she found that the United States had higher rates of lead poisoning than did European industry. She had no power to obtain admission into factories, and the U.S. government had no power of enforcement, but she persuaded owners and managers to allow her access, interviewed workers at their homes or saloons when she suspected illnesses were being hidden, and concluded that, next to tuberculosis, lead poisoning was the principal danger to the U.S. working classes. In 1914, she published *Lead Poisoning in the*

Smelting and Refining of Lead, a bulletin for the U.S. Bureau of Labor Statistics. She was so effective in communicating with hostile industry owners and managers that she was often asked back to inspect workplaces after reforms were put in place as a result of her recommendations.

By 1915, Hamilton had become the foremost U.S. authority on industrial diseases. In 1919, she accepted a part-time appointment as professor of industrial medicine at the Harvard Medical School (after 1925, in the School of Public Health). She was the first woman professor there in any discipline; at that time, Harvard did not even admit women into its medical program.

SIGNIFICANCE

Industrial Poisons in the United States was a textbook primarily addressed to physicians, who in the early twentieth century had little training or interest in the diagnosis of occupation-related diseases. In the book, Hamilton explained, in terms comprehensible to a layperson, the connection between occupation and disease, especially lead poisoning, and refuted the common argument that such diseases were caused by the unhygienic habits of ignorant immigrants. She was among the first to observe the effect of lead poisoning on the reproductive capabilities of both sexes. The publication not only firmly established Hamilton as the authority in the field but also opened the way to systematic academic and medical study of the subject. She followed the book with *Industrial Toxicology* in 1934, which was revised with Harriet L. Hardy and reissued in 1949.

Hamilton became a member of or consultant to many organizations, including labor organizations. In 1924, she was appointed to the Health Committee of the League of Nations, the forerunner of the World Health Organization of the United Nations. Her appointment was in part the result of her work, with Addams, to publicize the disease and starvation she found in Europe after World War I. By then, Hamilton had long been a consultant to General Electric. Working with that corporation from the 1920's to the 1930's, she investigated less direct hazards than those she had studied earlier, opening the way to later research into the effect on workers of improper seating, poor lighting, and excessive fatigue. She persuaded the U.S. surgeon general to call two national conferences on industrial health hazards, one on tetraethyl lead in 1925 and the other on radium in 1928.

Working with labor groups, Hamilton was instrumental in obtaining the first labor contracts that prohibited the use of benzene in certain occupations. Largely because of her leadership, by 1935 fifteen states had legislated workers' compensation for industrial diseases. Such legislation made the improvement of working conditions inevitable. Employers insured against claims that might be made against them under the new legislation; insurance companies protected themselves by insisting that the causes of claims be removed.

A controversial figure from the beginning, Hamilton provided a model for future reformers who might face similar condemnation and even censorship. As the Progressive Era gave way to conservative backlash after World War I, she was criticized as a socialist or communist, although, like most other Hull House workers, she favored improving the existing system rather than replacing it. Known for her outspoken defense of freedom of speech, she also worked extensively in the postwar years through organizations then considered controversial, including the League of Women Voters, the Women's Trade Union League, and the National Consumers League; she also assisted the Worker's Health Bureau, a group founded by radical women, during the 1920's. She visited the Soviet Union and Nazi Germany and was alarmed by their repression of individual freedom, but she continued to criticize the United States for failing to join other nations in outlawing poison gas and germ warfare. Her advocacy of birth control also brought criticism. In a 1909 study of working-class families, immigrant and native-born, she had shown a relationship between the number of children and child health and mortality; she joined various committees to discuss the subject and spoke in 1925 at the Sixth International Neo-Malthusian and Birth Control Conference, organized by birth control advocate Margaret Sanger.

In 1932, Hamilton withstood efforts to censor *Industrial Poisons in the United States*. Five companies manufacturing fire extinguishers brought pressure on her publisher to remove the book from circulation and recall known copies, on the grounds that the book contained false material damaging to those marketing fire extinguishers of the carbon tetrachloride type. Hamilton stood her ground and the censorship failed, but her outspokenness and the controversy that swirled around her placed her on various lists of subversives until the 1960's. The Federal Bureau of Investigation continued to keep records on her when she was in her nineties.

Asked to retire from Harvard in 1935, apparently because of age, she became a medical consultant to the Division of Labor Standards, formed the previous year by working-class advocate Frances Perkins, the secretary of labor and the first woman to hold a U.S. cabinet post. Hamilton continued her investigations until 1940, when her final report was published as a bulletin titled *Occupational Poisoning in the Viscose Rayon Industry*. She regularly lectured at colleges and universities, including Bryn Mawr, Tufts, the University of Pennsylvania, Harvard, and Connecticut College for Women. In 1944, she became president of the National Consumers League.

She died at her Connecticut home on September 22, 1970, at the age of 101. Three months later, Congress passed the Occupational Safety and Health Act (OSHA), which first gave the government power to enforce safe conditions in the workplace. The law authorized on-site inspection, regulation, and enforcement; the related National Institute of Occupational Safety and Health established standards for chemical, dust, and toxic exposure. Unquestionably, Hamilton's work had led the way to that legislation.

—Betty Richardson

FURTHER READING

Addams, Jane. *My Friend Julia Lathrop*. New York: Macmillan, 1935. Primarily a discussion of Lathrop's public service. Revised by Hamilton after Addams's death, describes the work and background of several Hull House reformers and shows the obstacles they faced in seeking environmental reform.

_____. *Twenty Years at Hull-House*. New York: Macmillan, 1910. Reprint. Urbana: University of Illinois Press, 1990. The classic work about the most famous U.S. settlement house. Contains little about any specific reformer, but chapters 10-16 and chapter 18 provide essential background for an understanding of working-class conditions at the beginning of the twentieth century and of Hull House and its pioneering social and reform work.

Gottlieb, Robert. "Urban and Industrial Roots." In *Forcing the Spring: The Transformation of the American Environmental Movement*. Rev. ed. Washington, D.C.: Island Press, 2005. General history presents an exceptionally complete discussion of women's contributions. Includes a summary of Hamilton's research and an excellent, if brief, discussion of the political forces that enabled the work of the Hull House reformers to gain national importance.

Grant, Madeleine P. *Alice Hamilton: Pioneer Doctor in Industrial Medicine*. London: Abelard-Schuman, 1967. A good, simply written summary of Hamilton's work, completed before Hamilton's death, although it is heavily dependent on Hamilton's autobiography (cited below) and adds little to it.

Hamilton, Alice. *Exploring the Dangerous Trades: The Autobiography of Alice Hamilton, M.D.* Boston: Little, Brown, 1943. Reprint. Boston: Northeastern University Press, 1985. Presents a readable, sometimes anecdotal, account of the obstacles and adventures Hamilton encountered in pursuing her research. Includes little serious discussion of her research or publications and practically nothing about her personal life or the difficulties she encountered as a pioneering woman scientist.

Rosner, David, and Gerald Markowitz, eds. *Dying for Work: Workers' Safety and Health in Twentieth-Century America*. Bloomington: Indiana University Press, 1987. Of particular interest are the editors' introduction and their essay "Safety and Health as a Class Issue: The Workers' Health Bureau of America During the 1920s." Also helpful for an understanding of Hamilton's work is Ruth Heifetz's "Women, Lead, and Reproductive Hazards: Defining a New Risk."

Sellers, Christopher C. *Hazards of the Job: From Industrial Disease to Environmental Health Science*. Chapel Hill: University of North Carolina Press, 1997. Study of the development of industrial medicine includes discussion of Alice Hamilton's contributions. Features notes and index.

Sicherman, Barbara. *Alice Hamilton: A Life in Letters*. 1984. Reprint. Champaign: University of Illinois Press, 2003. Excellent study of Hamilton and her work combines scholarly understanding with fluent writing. Makes excellent use of family letters and records not accessible to earlier writers.

Wertheimer, Barbara Mayer. *We Were There: The Story of Working Women in America*. New York: Pantheon, 1977. Includes little discussion of the Hull House reformers but much about the groups through which they worked, such as the National Consumers League. One of the best studies available concerning the conditions that gave rise to the Hull House reformers and their work.

SEE ALSO: 1910: *Euthenics* Calls for Pollution Control; 1910: Steinmetz Warns of Pollution in "The Future of Electricity"; Apr. 28-May 1, 1915: International Congress of Women; Jan., 1922: Izaak Walton League Is Formed; 1930's: Wolman Begins Investigating Water and Sewage Systems; Mar. 31, 1930-1931: Hawk's Nest Tunnel Construction Leads to Disaster; Apr. 15, 1935: Arbitration Affirms National Responsibility for Pollution.

1925
MCKINSEY FOUNDS A MANAGEMENT CONSULTING FIRM

James Oscar McKinsey, a noted certified public accountant in Chicago, established in 1925 what was to become the world's largest management consulting firm.

LOCALE: Chicago, Illinois
CATEGORIES: Business and labor; organizations and institutions

KEY FIGURES
James Oscar McKinsey (1889-1937), American certified public accountant, university professor, and management consultant
George E. Frazer (1889-1972), American university professor

SUMMARY OF EVENT
James Oscar McKinsey was a certified public accountant (CPA) and professor of accounting at the University of Chicago when, in 1925, he established a CPA firm that was to become McKinsey & Company, the largest management consulting firm in the world. Management accounting intrigued McKinsey. He wrote the first textbook on management accounting (*Managerial Accounting*, 1924) and the first book on the subject of budgeting (*Budgetary Control*, 1922). Both were the products of early consulting engagements. Before McKinsey, educators in accounting largely neglected the users of accounting information. Only through years of experience could an accountant master the knowledge needed to use accounting information profitably.

McKinsey was born near Mexico, Missouri, in 1889. In 1912 he received a bachelor of pedagogy degree from the State Teacher's College in Warrensburg, Missouri, and a year later he received a law degree from the University of Arkansas. McKinsey's penchant for business education was noted even by his law student colleagues at Arkansas, whose "class prophecy" predicted that McKinsey would someday buy out Draughon's Business College (a large chain of proprietary business schools) and change the name to McKinsey's Business College.

McKinsey's accounting career began in 1914 at St. Louis University, where he studied and taught bookkeeping. Although he already had a bachelor's degree and a law degree, he decided to enter the School of Commerce at the University of Chicago, where he subsequently earned both bachelor's and master's degrees. He received his master's degree in 1919, the same year he

passed the CPA examination. Before he had finished his degree at Chicago, he was asked to join the accounting faculty. This was a typical experience for McKinsey: He claimed that he was hired to teach in every school he attended even before he had attained his degree there.

It was during 1919 that McKinsey began his prolific writing career, which led to his being viewed as having the expertise to be a management consultant. Although much of his work was of a pragmatic nature for management use, he also wrote for accounting students. McKinsey applied a pioneering philosophy to accounting education through his emphasis on principles over techniques. Unlike other authors of the time, he required students to view accounting from the position of a manager rather than from that of a bookkeeper. Consequently, he emphasized the uses of accounting data. He believed that most firms had adequate accounting systems, partly as a result of requirements of the 1913 income tax law; the only problem that many firms faced was how to use the accounting information that was available.

Perhaps the real root of McKinsey & Company was the publication of McKinsey's *Budgetary Control* in 1922. This book provided impetus for the spread of industrial budgeting. World War I and the resultant emphasis on efficiency provided stimulus for acceptance of McKinsey's work, which summarized all experimentation to date in a complete budgetary program. McKinsey's was the first book on budgeting and the first attempt to cover the entire budgetary program. Before *Budgetary Control* was published, budgeting was not even considered applicable to business operations; only government units used it. The book was a compilation of several articles that McKinsey had published over the two preceding years. Although these articles had appeared primarily in *Administration* magazine, some were also published in such journals as *American Fertilizer* and *Cost Accountant*. The book was heavily based on McKinsey's early consulting work and included numerous illustrations of real situations.

McKinsey noted in the preface of *Budgetary Control* that he was indebted to his mentor at the University of Chicago, George E. Frazer, for counsel and assistance. As McKinsey's professor, his department chairman at Chicago, and later his CPA firm partner, Frazer was the source of many of the ideas published in McKinsey's book. Frazer was reportedly pleased with *Budgetary*

Control because it followed outlines used in his seminar at the University of Chicago in 1917 and 1918.

In the book, McKinsey stressed the fact that budgeting is a dynamic field in which all the answers are not known. Despite the fact that the book was a pioneering effort, it covered most of the budgeting aspects used today. In 1945, *Budgetary Control* was included on a list of twelve indispensable books in the field of management. The author of that 1945 critique apologized for including such an old book on the list but argued that McKinsey's work had lost none of its value with the passage of time.

Although McKinsey's first managerial accounting textbook was not published until 1924, he publicly espoused his philosophy of managerial accounting education in a 1919 article that appeared in the *Journal of Political Economy*. McKinsey's philosophy was that accounting was something that should serve as a basis of functional control in a business. In the preface of *Managerial Accounting*, he stated that it was time to organize the business curriculum into one coherent whole:

> If the accountant is to be of most service to the business executive, he must understand the latter's point of view, and be able to present data of such nature and in such form that the executive can use it in the solution of his daily problems. Unfortunately the accountant and the business executive often do not appreciate each other's point of view or understand each other's problem.

McKinsey pioneered an approach that emphasized teaching students how to use accounting data. Even the problems at the end of each chapter of his textbook were unusual, in that a student could not answer them by memorizing the text material. Instead, the problems required the application of the material in the text to new situations. Unfortunately, McKinsey's philosophy did not catch on soon enough for him to sell many books—a second edition never appeared. Another of his books was very successful, however. In 1929, South-Western Publishing Company published McKinsey's *Accounting Principles*, which became one of the best-selling books in the field of accounting for decades.

The year 1924 marked a turning point in McKinsey's career, as his interest began to shift from accounting and budgeting to managerial accounting. He was later to move further away from accounting as he developed his interest in management. After 1927, he taught only business policy courses and devoted the remainder of his time to his consulting work, to the exclusion of research and other faculty activities.

McKinsey is best remembered as the founder of what was to become the largest management consulting firm in the world. In 1925, he started his own accounting and consulting firm, McKinsey & Company. One of his former students later recalled how impressed students were with McKinsey's success. McKinsey would have his chauffeur drive him to class and carry his briefcase into the classroom. Following the class, the chauffeur would reappear to erase the blackboard and take McKinsey downtown to his office.

The success of McKinsey's firm was as much attributable to perspiration as to inspiration. McKinsey worked seven days a week and expected his staff to do the same. Staff members could never accept social engagements or even promise their wives that they would be home at night, because McKinsey might decide on the spur of the moment that they were needed in some distant city. He even made his secretary work on Christmas Day, because the client always had to come first.

SIGNIFICANCE

McKinsey's contributions can still be found in accounting and business education in the fields of budgeting, managerial accounting, accounting principles, business policy, managerial finance, and management consulting. McKinsey was fortunate to be affiliated with the School of Commerce and Administration at the University of Chicago at a time when that school was experimenting with a comprehensive approach to business education. He worked within the confines of that experiment and developed programs for both industry and education that are still in use today.

McKinsey's consulting firm was immediately successful. Even in the 1920's he charged $500 per day for his services, and he still received more requests than he could handle. McKinsey's consulting philosophy hinged on three elements: unquestioned respectability, a reputation for expertise in an area of some concern to top management, and professional exposure. He established the element of respectability through his academic connections, used his writings to establish his expertise, and gained professional exposure through his officer roles in such professional organizations as the American Accounting Association and the American Management Association, both of which he served as president. He was also active in community organizations such as the Red Cross and various charities because he wanted to be known as a good citizen. He gave speeches to various groups most nights.

McKinsey claimed that he ate more than half of his

meals, including breakfasts, with potential clients. At such a meal, McKinsey would probe the mind of his guest to learn what problems the individual was facing. He would then either offer a solution or return to his office and enlist his staff in coming up with the solution. McKinsey would then write the guest a letter full of free advice. Consequently, the guest would think of McKinsey as a person who could help solve problems; many such guests became clients.

McKinsey's affiliation with the University of Chicago provided status to his consulting firm, but his educational background helped in another way as well. McKinsey's teaching experience contributed to the success of the firm in that he was always teaching younger staff members. Even within the firm, he thought of himself as a teacher. Staff members never went out on a job without the proper training and the shared expertise of their leader. McKinsey's emphasis on individual coaching did have its downside, in that he did not hesitate to point out a person's mistakes and frequently suggested to staff members and partners how they could improve themselves. This style meant that McKinsey was never really loved by his coworkers, but he was always respected.

Another element of the firm's success was McKinsey's interpersonal style with clients. McKinsey would begin by establishing rapport with interviewees and then start asking questions rather than giving answers. After listening to an individual, he would diagnose the problem. Finally, he would make suggestions as to how the problem could be solved.

In 1935, McKinsey's firm was hired to conduct a study of Marshall Field and Company, the Chicago department store. The company's directors were so impressed that they offered McKinsey the position of chairman of the board. Because Marshall Field was still hurting from the Great Depression, McKinsey thought the job would be a challenge. He had long been telling others how to manage their businesses; now he would have a chance to prove himself. In addition, a position as chairman of the board and chief operating officer at the largest store in the world would fulfill McKinsey's desire for prestige and status. McKinsey severed his ties with the University of Chicago and decided to take a temporary leave from his consulting firm. He soon turned Marshall Field's red ink into profit by making drastic cuts in departments and personnel; in fact, he received several death threats as a result of the personnel cuts. The job of cleaning up Marshall Field was accomplished at the cost of his health, however. McKinsey died of pneumonia on November 30, 1937.

At the time he became chairman of Marshall Field, McKinsey was approached by about a dozen firms that wanted to acquire his consulting firm. Although he planned to return to consulting as soon as he had solved Marshall Field's problems, he agreed to merge his firm. A merger was accomplished with the CPA firm of Scovell, Wellington & Company to form McKinsey, Wellington & Company. Following McKinsey's death, the firm split into two separate consulting firms, with McKinsey & Company having offices in New York and Boston, and McKinsey, Kearney & Company keeping the Chicago office. Subsequently, McKinsey, Kearney & Company changed its name to A. T. Kearney & Company because McKinsey & Company grew into a national firm and moved into Chicago.

Under later leaders, McKinsey & Company became the largest management consulting firm in the world. In addition, the American Management Association, a professional organization that McKinsey helped found and served as second president, became the world's largest professional management organization.

James Oscar McKinsey operated at the frontiers of business research. To some, it might be surprising that the author of the first managerial accounting book and the first budgeting book is best remembered as a management consultant, but perhaps that is appropriate. McKinsey always stressed how information could be used by managers.

—Dale L. Flesher

FURTHER READING

Flesher, Tonya K., and Dale L. Flesher. "James O. McKinsey." *Accounting Historians Journal* 12 (Fall, 1985): 117-128. Summarizes McKinsey's contributions to managerial accounting and accountancy education. Includes analyses of several books authored by McKinsey.

Hopf, H. A. "Soundings in the Literature of Management: Some Classic Contributions to Professional Management." In *Historical Perspectives*. Vol. 2. New York: General Electric, 1956. Describes McKinsey's contributions to the profession of management.

McKinsey, James O. *Budgetary Control*. New York: Ronald Press, 1922. The first book on business budgeting, containing virtually everything on the subject of budgeting, is still useful today. In 1945, this book was ranked as one of the twelve greatest business books ever written.

_____. *Managerial Accounting*. Chicago: University of Chicago Press, 1924. Reprint. New York: Ayer,

1980. The first book on the subject of managerial accounting. Although not a big seller, its legacy can be traced to the most popular managerial accounting books of the present.

Wendt, Lloyd, and Herman Kogan. *Give the Lady What She Wants! The Story of Marshall Field and Company.* 1952. Reprint. Chicago: Rand McNally, 1997. Discusses McKinsey's role at the Chicago department store.

Wolf, William B. *Management and Consulting: An Introduction to James O. McKinsey.* Ithaca: Cornell University, New York State School of Industrial and Labor Relations, 1978. Excellent work includes not only a biography of McKinsey but also an analysis of his perspectives and strategies. Describes McKinsey's diagnostic approach to business problems, including his general survey outline.

SEE ALSO: 1914: U.S. Government Begins Using Cost-Plus Contracts; Sept. 19, 1916: American Institute of Accountants Is Founded; Oct. 3, 1917: U.S. Congress Imposes a Wartime Excess-Profits Tax; 1931: *Ultramares* Case Establishes Liability for Auditors.

1925
NEW OBJECTIVITY MOVEMENT IS INTRODUCED

New Objectivity, an artistic and literary trend in Germany that repudiated abstraction, succeeded expressionism in the 1920's and lasted until 1932. Its artists often produced bleak, satirical works that reflected the tensions of the times.

ALSO KNOWN AS: *Neue Sachlichkeit*
LOCALE: Mannheim, Germany
CATEGORY: Arts

KEY FIGURES

Otto Dix (1891-1969), painter and graphic artist who was one of the leading exponents of the veristic wing of New Objectivity

George Grosz (1893-1959), painter and graphic artist whose socially conscious pictures exemplified the work of the veristic wing of New Objectivity

Max Beckmann (1884-1950), painter and graphic artist whose work has some affinities with New Objectivity

Georg Scholz (1890-1945), socially committed artist whose work was included in the 1925 Mannheim exhibition

Georg Schrimpf (1889-1938), painter in New Objectivity's magic realist wing whose work reveals many neoclassical influences

Alexander Kanoldt (1881-1939), painter known mainly for his clearly rendered, airless still lifes and landscapes

SUMMARY OF EVENT

In 1923, Gustav Hartlaub, the newly appointed director of the Mannheim museum, planned an exhibition to chart the realistic trend in postwar painting. The exhibition, titled *New Objectivity: German Painting Since Expressionism*, however, did not take place until 1925. Hartlaub used the term *Neue Sachlichkeit* (New Objectivity) to differentiate this style from the subjective and abstract tendencies of expressionism. His aim was to exhibit the works of "those artists who have remained—or who have once more become—avowedly faithful to positive, tangible reality." Among the artists most fully represented in the 1925 Mannheim show were Otto Dix, George Grosz, Max Beckmann, Alexander Kanoldt, Georg Scholz, and Georg Schrimpf. The art historian Franz Roh also noted the return to representational painting in his influential book *Nach-Expressionismus, magischer Realismus: Probleme der neuesten Europäischen Malerei* (1925; postexpressionism, magic realism: problems of the newest European painting). Roh used the term "magic realism" to distinguish the new realism from the earlier, nineteenth century style of realism exhibited by the artists Hans Thoma and Wilhelm Leibl. For Roh, magic realism also suggested a connection with French Surrealism and with the work of the Italian artist Giorgio De Chirico, whose precisely rendered paintings of vacuous mannequins in ambiguous spatial settings evoked a sense of mystery.

Hartlaub noted that there were two different aspects of the realist trend and divided the movement into two wings. He assigned the artists Dix, Grosz, Beckmann, and Scholz to a socially critical wing that he called verism, and the Italianate-inspired German artists such as Kanoldt and Schrimpf to a neoclassical wing. Although Hartlaub included some of Scholz's work in the verist wing, the artist's work is more often representative of magic realism. The phrases "New Objectivity" and "magic realism" essentially denoted the same thing: After expressionism, artists moved away from abstraction to realism. Although these terms were initially interchangeable, "New Objectivity" became more commonly used.

Both wings of New Objectivity shared some common characteristics. The artists all emphasized visual clarity, sobriety, and unemotional detachment in their work. They concentrated on depicting ordinary people and seemingly insignificant scenes from everyday life, and they painted in rigid, tightly compressed compositions. Their preference for static compositions and fidelity to the outlines of objects differed from the dynamic and generalizing manner of the expressionists. Some of the New Objectivity artists did, however, retain expressionistic devices such as distortion, exaggeration of detail, and alteration of reality in their work. The New Objectivity artists eschewed utopian illusions, and they scrutinized the cold, hard, often ugly facts of life as Germany struggled to recover from the harsh effects of World War I. During the 1920's, Germans faced economic hardships, runaway inflation, political unrest, uncertainty, and fear; shattered, insecure, corrupt, empty, and banal lives became common subjects for several leading exponents of the movement, especially Dix, Grosz, and Beckmann.

Dix volunteered for military service during World War I and later became a staunch opponent of war. In his paintings and graphics, he became a satirist and exposed the indecencies of postwar life. Motivated by ethical issues, his work was devoted to depictions of people, especially representations of dismembered ex-soldiers, repulsive, greedy prostitutes, and suffering victims. He frequently employed collagelike elements in his paintings to emphasize the fragmented, irrational, inhumane atmosphere of postwar Germany. Dix used these devices in his painting *Streichholzhändler* (1920; *The Matchseller*), which portrays a mutilated male victim of the war as mere rubbish sitting on an urban street. As the blind, quadriplegic matchseller attempts to sell his wares to people hurrying by, a dog lifts its leg and urinates on him. Much of Dix's work centered on the lack of human values and protests against social injustices.

Grosz volunteered for military service in 1914, but he later became disillusioned with the war and became a pacifist. His style was initially influenced by expressionism, and before his association with New Objectivity, he was a member of the most radical and politicized faction of Berlin Dada. In the 1920's, Grosz was frequently charged with blasphemy for his irreverent depictions of German militarism. Harboring a deep hatred for both militarism and bourgeois complacency, he developed a grim, satirical style that portrayed society as morally bankrupt. Grosz unleashed his anger against the social decay in the Weimar Republic and produced numerous images of grisly sex murderers, fat bureaucrats, and power-hungry, duplicitous generals. Many of his paintings, such as *Sonnenfirsternis* (1926; *Eclipse of the Sun*), lampoon wealthy, empty-headed bureaucrats who conspire with generals. For Grosz, these despised figures epitomized corruption, power, and cruelty. A consummate social critic, Grosz used his analytic and detached style to develop De Chirico's Surrealist mannequin figures into dehumanized, mutilated, robotlike representations of people reveling in their own banality. Grosz's precisely rendered painting *Republikanische Automaten* (1920; *Republican Automatons*) depicts faceless, maimed mannequins as symbols of people's lost identities in postwar German society.

Beckmann, along with Dix and Grosz, was perceived to be one of the most important representatives of the verist wing of New Objectivity. Beckmann's work, however, is difficult to assign to a particular style. Although he eschewed abstraction and remained aloof from expressionism, his style had many affinities with the artists of the movement know as Die Brücke (the bridge), especially the use of distortion and exaggeration of detail. During World War I, Beckmann volunteered for military duty and briefly served as a medical orderly on the front. His horrific war experiences resulted in a nervous breakdown, and he was discharged from the military in 1915. He was permanently affected by the war: His style was transformed, and humanity's inhumanity became its general theme. Beckmann's painting *The Night* (1919) shows a family being robbed and physically violated in their garret by a gang of thugs. In the center of this spatially compressed composition, a woman, naked and splayed, is about to be raped. Beckmann's stark, heavily outlined figures retain the expressionist device of distortion, but the somber mood and theme of social injustice anticipates New Objectivity. In this matter-of-fact portrayal of mutilation and physical and mental torture, Beckmann's angular use of line and exaggeration of detail heighten the effect of polar opposites: weak against strong, good against evil. Much of his work centered on the themes of temptation and cruelty, human exploitation and degradation, and Beckmann sought to show that goodness does not always triumph over evil. Dix, Grosz, and Beckmann, unlike the members of the magic realist wing of New Objectivity, all shared the common aesthetic of disillusionment.

Scholz, Kanoldt, and Schrimpf were minor artists in comparison to Dix, Grosz, and Beckmann, whose verist works epitomized and dominated New Objectivity. Hartlaub included some of Scholz's work in the veristic wing of the 1925 Mannheim exhibition, but though Scholz painted some socially critical works in the style of Grosz, he is better known for his disquieting still lifes and landscapes that juxtapose industrialized technology with nature or idealized objects from the past. Kanoldt and Schrimpf initially worked in Munich, the center of the magic realist wing of New Objectivity, and they looked toward Italy, not contemporary Germany, for inspiration. They assimilated aspects of De Chirico's metaphysical paintings, which presented a timeless, inanimate, and disquieting world, and they incorporated these qualities into their own clearly rendered, tightly ordered compositions. The magic realists created gentle, neoclassic images of simple, monumental forms that were smoothly painted and carefully modeled. Their rigid reconstructions of reality were far removed from the concerns of the veristic wing of New Objectivity.

SIGNIFICANCE

When Adolf Hitler came to power in the early 1930's, the New Objectivity movement quickly dissipated. By 1933, Hitler had initiated cultural purges to cleanse the nation of modernism. Museums and galleries were emptied of offending examples of modern art. Hitler outlawed modernism and imposed an official style, a realistic naturalism; Dix, Grosz, Beckmann, Scholz, Schrimpf, and Kanoldt were forbidden to paint, and their works were defamed. For the next twelve years, Nazi policy dominated the arts in Germany, and illusionistic painting prevailed. After World War II, German artists who survived the war and Nazi defamation resumed their work. At first, postwar painting in Germany continued to be largely illusionistic, but gradually abstract art and semi-abstract painting became popular.

The impact of New Objectivity remained a chiefly German phenomenon. In the 1960's, a new group of German artists known as critical realists merged the stylistic characteristics of New Objectivity with the formal elements of pop art and Socialist Realism in an attempt to revive the critical social commentary of Dix and Grosz. In the late 1970's, a group of German artists sharing some unified stylistic affinities exhibited together in a Berlin show focusing on "ugly realism"; artists featured in the exhibit included Salomé (Wolfgang Cilarz), Helmut Middendorf, Rainer Fetting, and Bernd Zimmer. Their raw, abrasive images of sexual and political brutal-

ity were stylistic and thematic mixtures of the verist wing of New Objectivity and the brashness of American pop art. Yet, unlike the New Objectivity artists, who primarily depicted social outcasts (prostitutes, beggars, mutilated individuals) as the victims of society, these Berlin artists demonstrate in their work their conviction that everyone is a political victim in modern society.

—Carmen Stonge

FURTHER READING

Barton, Brigid S. *Otto Dix and Die Neue Sachlichkeit, 1918-1925.* Ann Arbor, Mich.: UMI Research Press, 1981. One of the few good studies in English on Dix. Provides an excellent overview of the artist and discusses his role in the emergence of the New Objectivity movement. Well researched and thoroughly documented. Contains good bibliography and numerous reproductions of Dix's work.

Beckmann, Max. *Max Beckmann: Retrospective.* Edited by Carla Schultz-Hoffmann and Judith C. Weiss. Munich: Prestel-Verlag, 1984. Compilation of essays provides a solid overview of Beckmann's work, style, and career, but, unfortunately, does not discuss his role in the New Objectivity movement. Profusely illustrated with excellent color reproductions of the artist's paintings and numerous examples of his graphics. Good bibliography.

Eberle, Matthias. *World War I and the Weimar Artists: Dix, Grosz, Beckmann, Schlemmer.* Translated by John Gabriel. New Haven, Conn.: Yale University Press, 1985. Small book discussing the work and biographical backgrounds of four artists whose styles were fundamentally formed by their experiences during World War I. Specifically focuses on how these artists, except for Oskar Schlemmer, were actively involved in political events that they assimilated into their art. Useful source for the general public and students.

Grosz, George. *George Grosz: An Autobiography.* Translated by Nora Hodges. New York: Macmillan, 1983. The artist's lively and provocative account of his life in the 1920's as well as of the art of the period. Presents a fusion of Grosz's art and politics during the Weimar Republic. Contains numerous illustrations, including thirty-seven reproductions of Grosz's major artworks.

Hayward Gallery. *Neue Sachlichkeit and German Realism in the Twenties.* Translated by David Britt and John Whitford. London: Arts Council of Great Britain, 1978. Contains two excellent essays defining and examining this artistic phenomenon during the Weimar Republic. Discusses both New Objectivity's painters and its photographers. One of the best sources in English on the topic. Includes a good, annotated bibliography and many illustrations.

Joachimides, Christos M., Norman Rosenthal, and Wieland Schmied, eds. *German Art in the Twentieth Century: Painting and Sculpture, 1905-1985*. Munich: Prestel-Verlag, 1985. Presents a broad survey of German art with a compilation of excellent essays, including two on Dix and Beckmann. Profusely illustrated with numerous color reproductions and an extensive, useful bibliography. Contains short biographical annotations on the major German artists. Recommended for both students and the general reader.

Laqueur, Walter. *Weimar: A Cultural History, 1918-1933*. New York: G. P. Putnam's Sons, 1974. An insightful survey of Weimar culture that explores the rise and decline of the avant-garde in Germany. Highly readable and interesting. Contains some photographs and a few illustrations of artists' works. Good bibliography.

Lewis, Beth Irwin. *George Grosz: Art and Politics in the Weimar Republic*. Madison: University of Wisconsin Press, 1971. In-depth study of Grosz examining his relationship between art and politics. Provides an excellent understanding of the artist as well as insight into the Weimar Republic. Includes many black-and-white reproductions of the artist's line drawings.

Lloyd, Jill, and Michael Peppiatt. *Christian Schad and the Neue Sachlichkeit*. New York: W. W. Norton, 2003. An important but little-known artist, Schad has been associated with both realists and Dadists. This volume includes 140 full-color images and an in-depth discussion of the general nature of the New Objectivity movement.

McGreevy, Linda F. *The Life and Works of Otto Dix: German Critical Realist*. Ann Arbor, Mich.: UMI Research Press, 1981. Scholarly endeavor that focuses on Dix as a social critic by examining his graphic work of the 1920's. Only one chapter on Dix's work and his role in New Objectivity in Germany. Some black-and-white reproductions and an extensive bibliography. Good source for Dix's biography.

Michalski, Sergiusz. *New Objectivity*. Los Angeles: Taschen, 2001. A meticulously researched history of the movement. Essential reading for any art student, this book places New Objectivity in its historical and political contexts, examines the movement's general philosophy, and then studies its influence in specific regions in and outside Germany.

Schrader, Bärbel, and Jürgen Schebera. *The Golden Twenties: Art and Literature in the Weimar Republic*. Translated by Katherin Vanovitch. New Haven, Conn.: Yale University Press, 1990. A good, broad survey of Weimar culture. The authors examine the opera, street entertainment, popular music, films, literature, art, and architecture to demonstrate that the Weimar Republic's cultural life was as troubled as its politics. Numerous photographs and illustrations.

SEE ALSO: Summer, 1905: Avant-Garde Artists Form Die Brücke; 1912: Kandinsky Publishes His Theory of Abstract Art; 1917: *De Stijl* Advocates Mondrian's Neoplasticism; July 17, 1927: Brecht and Weill Collaborate on the *Mahagonny Songspiel*; 1928: Buñuel and Dalí Champion Surrealism in *An Andalusian Dog*; 1930's: Hindemith Advances Music as a Social Activity; July 19-Nov. 30, 1937: Nazi Germany Hosts the *Degenerate Art Exhibition*.

1925
SEARS, ROEBUCK OPENS ITS FIRST RETAIL OUTLET

The opening of retail stores catapulted Sears into the position of the largest retail chain in the United States.

LOCALE: Chicago, Illinois
CATEGORIES: Trade and commerce; organizations and institutions

KEY FIGURES
Richard W. Sears (1863-1914), founder of Sears
Alvah C. Roebuck (1864-1948), American watchmaker who became the partner of Richard W. Sears
Robert E. Wood (1879-1969), vice president of Sears when the first retail outlet opened
Julius Rosenwald (1862-1932), partner of Richard W. Sears under whom Sears became a catalog empire

SUMMARY OF EVENT
In 1925, Robert E. Wood, then vice president of Sears, Roebuck and Company, was responsible for the company's entering retailing. In 1906, Richard W. Sears wrote that his company did little business in cities and that he believed that cities were not the company's territory. Nineteen years later, Wood proved that cities were part of Sears territory.

In the 1800's, the population of the United States was widely scattered, with many living in isolated areas. When Sears established his mail-order business, agriculture was a principal source of wealth and income. Sears's success was based largely on his understanding of the American farmer.

In the 1920's, the complexion of the United States was changing. With cars and modern roads, rural customers were no longer limited to shopping by catalog, as they had with Sears. They could drive to towns, where growing retail chains offered more and better merchandise. In 1914, about 24,000 chain stores were operating in the United States; by 1920, more than 150,000 were in business. In 1900, the rural population outnumbered the urban population; by 1920, the situation was reversed. Wood believed that city people were not good catalog customers, as they shopped in city stores. Unless Sears opened stores, it faced a shrinking market. Wood experimented with one store, located in the company's Chicago mail-order plant, and it was an immediate success.

The principal credit for the stature and growth of Sears goes to three executives: founder Richard W. Sears, Julius Rosenwald, and Robert E. Wood. Sears was born in Minnesota in 1863. He was working for the Minneapolis and

St. Louis Railroad when the turning point in his life came, in 1886. A local jeweler refused to accept a shipment of watches, and Sears made a deal with the shipper for the watches. In six months, Sears made enough money selling the watches to start the R. W. Sears Watch Company. He advertised for a watchmaker and hired Alvah C. Roebuck, a tall, thin, nonaggressive man. Sears expanded into jewelry sales and published the first Sears catalog in 1887, offering his famous money-back guarantee. Sears was adept at describing the shape of a young nation's material dreams; it was said that he could sell a breath of air.

In 1895, Julius Rosenwald, a clothing supplier for Sears, invested in the company. He was to become known as the architect of Sears. Rosenwald was convinced that the mail-order business could have a profitable future only if Sears would refrain from using daring promotional campaigns and operate in a more businesslike manner. In 1924, Rosenwald hired Wood, who was then the merchandising vice president at Montgomery Ward and had been a brigadier general in World War I. In 1928, Wood became president of Sears. Under Wood's leadership, the company entered a prolonged period of growth and profitability.

As early as 1920, Wood realized that the only way to reach a broader mass market in rapidly urbanizing America was through a system of retail stores. Within several months of joining Sears, he used the mail-order business as a base for retailing and opened the first Sears retail store in the company's Chicago mail-order plant. Before the year was out, he opened 7 more outlets. By the end of 1927, he had 27 stores in operation, and by 1932 there were 324. In 1931, the volume of retail store sales surpassed that of catalog sales.

All but one of the first stores were in relatively large cities but situated outside established downtown shopping areas to take advantage of lower land values, taxes, and rents. Each store also had ample parking. Eventually Sears moved into smaller towns that could not support full-line stores, prompting the question of which departments to stock. Gradually a classification system of A, B, and C stores emerged as Sears balanced stock with town size and clearly defined the stores' public image. As a town's population grew, service at its Sears store was upgraded to the next level.

Sears buying began to change in the late 1920's. Some mail-order merchandise already was being sold under Sears trade names. With the opening of retail stores, volume increased in these lines, which included the labels of Kenmore and Craftsman.

Catalog sales desks were installed in retail stores, allowing customers to purchase items not on display. In the 1930's, telephone sales offices were established. Eventually, catalog sales offices were opened in towns too small to support retail stores.

The integration of mail-order and retail operations was not always smooth. Wood believed that only by combining the two operations would the company realize economies of scale, and therefore savings. Mail-order branches served jobbing functions for the retail stores, receiving bulk shipments and distributing goods to stores. Mail-order branches ran the stores in their area, using them to unload unsold merchandise. As mail-order buyers were not accustomed to buying for city populations, which differed from the largely rural catalog customers, many buying mistakes occurred. Retail executives wanted separation from mail-order departments.

In time, retail stores were given more autonomy to meet the individual needs of their territories. Stores were allowed to have their own buyers and department managers, people who had the management and product expertise needed for the urban retail environment. This began the decentralization of Sears.

Store planning also emerged. Early stores were built as quickly as possible. In 1932, Sears established a store planning and display department. Previously, merchandise had been fit into buildings; now, buildings were built around merchandise. The Glendale, California, store, which opened in 1935, used this concept. Space requirements for different product lines, customer flow, and width of aisles were considered in the planning of store space.

Promotion of personnel from within became common practice at Sears. This was considered the best way to serve the company's needs and essential for long-term survival.

Although Wood had begun with little experience in retailing, by 1935 his vision and learning experience from the catalog business had solidly established Sears in meeting the needs of a changing United States. By the time of his retirement in 1954, sales had risen from $200 million in 1924 to $3 billion. Sears had become the largest general merchandise distributor in the world and one of the nation's largest employers.

SIGNIFICANCE

The establishment of Sears retail stores is important not only because of the company's size but also because of

its methods. For years, the firm was the most successful retailer in the United States. One immediate impact of the opening of Sears retail stores was the opening of Montgomery Ward stores. Although initially opposed to the idea, Ward's president in 1926 established "display stores" to exhibit goods carried in Montgomery Ward catalogs. Customers quickly insisted on buying the goods immediately rather than waiting for delivery. Ward opened stores across the country in response. In comparison with Sears, Montgomery Ward opened smaller stores in smaller towns but opened more of them. The orientation of Sears to larger cities and Ward to smaller ones continued.

The longer-term impacts of the Sears venture into retail stores came from the type of organization built by Wood and its influences on communities and other retailers. Sears provided merchandise for a rapidly urbanizing mass market. It developed a buying strategy that integrated mass production with mass distribution. Finally, it fashioned a uniquely effective body of policies in organization (such as decentralization), personnel and employee relations (such as promotion from within and excellent benefits), and public responsibility. By the 1960's, Sears was a superpower referred to as the "colossus of American retailing."

During the time of the early store openings, national demographic shifts were dramatic. People were moving from farms to cities; they had rising personal incomes, increased education, increased leisure, and increased rates of home ownership, and many were moving up the social scale. Information was transferred more quickly and new ideas were accepted more readily. Advertising was increasingly important in generating consumer preferences. All of these factors resulted in changing needs and diversified tastes.

Wood was one of the first to see clearly the changes in American life symbolized by the completion of highways and the increasing numbers of automobiles. The Sears practice of locating stores outside major downtown shopping areas was based on the ease of transportation the automobile represented. Other retailers, including large department stores, rushed to establish branches outside downtown areas. After World War II, the rapid development of suburban shopping centers radically changed urban America. The automobile also spurred growth areas for Sears. Wood drew up specifications for an improved tire and contracted with Goodyear to make it. The tire was marketed under the Allstate brand, which Sears subsequently applied to other automobile supplies and automobile insurance.

The merchandise mix at Sears stores was different from that of the typical department store of the times, which carried food, clothing, household necessities, and some luxuries, with women as the prime customers. The Sears mail-order business served the needs of farms and farm families, as did the Sears retail stores. Sears promoted shopping as a family affair. Merchandise reflected the trend toward families owning their own homes. Home maintenance and repairs increased, generating a need for paint, building materials, and other supplies that Sears met through its stock. Wood fashioned Sears to respond to the changes occurring in the United States. The necessities of life as well as luxuries were brought to the mass population instead of only to the elite, strengthening local economies. Wood was one of the first business leaders to think of social responsibility in terms of customers, employees, stockholders, and sources of merchandise supply.

As Sears grew, the importance of the company's ability to influence public policy became evident, as small business attempted to restrict the growth of large chains. Sears strengthened its markets, made influential friends, and gained a broad base of public support. One example involves the banking industry, which was affected by the presence of Sears stores. Initially, Sears used local banks only for short-term deposit of daily receipts, which were then transferred to a central location. This transfer of business angered local banks. Sears could see that goodwill, especially from the banking industry, an influential political force, was important in combating the antichain movements under way in the 1920's. Instead of borrowing from a few large banks, Sears began sharing loan activity with local small banks. Sears managers became integral parts of their communities, unlike the "absentee owners" of the other chains. As they sat on boards and became community leaders, it was hard for local businessmen to turn against them in the fight against the chains.

A Sears outlet often was the largest store in a community. It could attract customers from a wide trading area, benefiting other nearby merchants. This lessened hostility toward the growing company. From the beginning, Sears supported activities to improve local economies and the national economy. Rosenwald helped strengthen the agricultural economy, for example, by offering grants to train farmers in efficient practices. Sears grants became an integral part of national agriculture policy.

In 1927, Sears established a public relations department that became involved in addressing social needs. As the population of the American South expanded and

the agriculture of the area suffered, Sears encouraged its suppliers to expand to the South, to strengthen the region's economy. In addition, Sears supported 4-H clubs and contests to encourage agricultural efforts beyond the problematic one-crop formula in the South. The company tailored similar agriculture programs to the needs of different parts of the country, including the needs of future homemakers as well as future farmers. Sears also created a scholarship program that became an important component of the company's public activities. Such social programs left a lasting imprint on American life and earned Sears a unique place among American businesses. Wood's legacy to Sears and to business as a whole was his demonstration that human and economic values are not necessarily in conflict. He created a corporate policy based on human and democratic values that may well be unique in American business history.

—*Nancy J. Rabolt*

FURTHER READING

Asher, Louise E., and Edith Heal. *Send No Money*. Chicago: Argus Books, 1942. Asher worked with Richard Sears as general manager in a period that witnessed the transition of Sears, Roebuck into a firmly established catalog business. This book is Asher's attempt to set the record straight regarding the early days of Sears. Includes prophecies of changes to come.

Cohen, David L. *The Good Old Days*. New York: Simon & Schuster, 1940. A history of American home life, morals, and manners as seen through Sears, Roebuck catalogs from 1905 to 1935. Discusses the "largest store in the world" and includes copies of letters from customers.

Emmet, Boris, and John E. Jeuck. *Catalogues and Counters*. Chicago: University of Chicago Press, 1950. In-depth work presents the history of Sears in great detail, describing how the company's managers met internal problems and adjusted their business approach to meet the demands raised by external developments.

Katz, Donald R. *The Big Store: Inside the Crisis and Revolution at Sears*. New York: Viking Penguin, 1987. Analysis of the Sears corporation in the late twentieth century against the background of the glory years of Sears.

Mahoney, Tom, and Leonard Sloane. *The Great Merchants*. Rev. ed. New York: Harper & Row, 1974. Detailed accounts of twenty-six American retail institutions and the merchants who built them. Includes discussion of the largest department store, specialty shop, mail-order house, variety chain, apparel chain, and drugstore.

Martinez, Arthur C. *The Hard Road to the Softer Side: Lessons from the Transformation of Sears.* New York: Crown Business Books, 2001. Account of a troubled period in Sears history near the end of the twentieth century, as related by the executive who is credited with saving the company.

Michman, Ronald D., and Alan J. Greco. *Retailing Triumphs and Blunders.* Westport, Conn.: Quorum Books, 1995. Describes how retailers of various kinds have responded to changes in U.S. society and the marketplace. Includes discussion of Sears and other department stores.

Werner, Morris R. *Julius Rosenwald: The Life of a Practical Humanitarian.* New York: Harper & Brothers, 1939. Describes Rosenwald's philanthropic activities in an era of laissez-faire economics, when social con-sciousness was new. Presents an account of the changes occurring at Sears and Rosenwald's ability to lead the company profitably into the future.

Worthy, James. *Shaping an American Institution: Robert E. Wood and Sears, Roebuck.* Urbana: University of Illinois Press, 1984. History of Sears under the leadership of Wood and others, written by a former employee of the company. Presents analyses of policies and strategies, including decentralization and reliance on individual initiative. Many accounts of events come from observation and personal documentation.

SEE ALSO: 1913: Fuller Brush Company Is Incorporated; Sept. 11, 1916: First Self-Service Grocery Store Opens; July, 1920: Procter & Gamble Announces Plans to Sell Directly to Retailers; 1922: First Major U.S. Shopping Center Opens; 1930's: Invention of the Slug Rejector Spreads Use of Vending Machines.

1925
WHIPPLE DISCOVERS IMPORTANCE OF IRON FOR RED BLOOD CELLS

George Hoyt Whipple discovered that liver/meat diets are effective treatments for anemia and that iron is an essential dietary ingredient.

LOCALE: School of Medicine and Dentistry, University of Rochester, New York

CATEGORIES: Science and technology; biology; health and medicine

KEY FIGURES

George Hoyt Whipple (1878-1976), American surgeon and pathologist

Frieda S. Robscheit-Robbins (b. 1895), American pathologist

George Richards Minot (1885-1950), American physician

William Parry Murphy (1892-1987), American physician

SUMMARY OF EVENT

Pernicious anemia is one of several forms of anemia in which there is a severe reduction in the number of red blood cells (erythrocytes) in the affected individual's bloodstream. Accompanying this severe reduction of red blood cells is a decreased level of blood hemoglobin, the most important protein found in blood cells and blood plasma. Hemoglobin is a tetrameric (that is, four-sub-unit) protein that transports oxygen from an individual's lungs throughout the bloodstream to every cell in the body, where it is used to drive the production of energy molecules (that is, adenosine triphosphate—ATP) via the Krebs cycle. Hemoglobin carries waste carbon dioxide back to the lungs via the bloodstream for exhalation. If a person has a low red blood cell count (anemia), then his or her body will not be producing enough hemoglobin to transport oxygen to all the cells in the body. Consequently, these cells will be incapable of producing enough energy for the chemical reactions needed to survive. Many cells will die, and often the affected individual will die as well.

In 1905, George Hoyt Whipple received his medical degree from The Johns Hopkins Medical School in Baltimore, Maryland, and continued researching blood and liver disorders. He and a colleague, John H. King, studied liver necrosis (decay) in dogs exposed to chloroform and discovered that the dogs' livers regenerated rapidly after being damaged by this chemical. Whipple became very interested in the interrelationship between the liver and the bloodstream. He and King subsequently concentrated on the disease obstructive jaundice (icterus), where liver damage results in the release of yellowish bile pigments that concentrate in the victim's skin. They demonstrated that obstructive jaundice was caused by the escape of bile pigments into the bloodstream and not into the lymphatic system.

The liver, the largest organ in the body, has numerous functions essential for survival, including bile production, hemoglobin recycling, sugar storage (as the carbohydrate glycogen), protein and carbohydrate metabolism, blood filtering and detoxification, and storage of essential vitamins and minerals. All these functions are closely interrelated, and the liver's storage of vitamins and minerals is of special importance. Many of the body's enzymes—proteins that control the rate of cellular chemical reactions—require the assistance of minerals (for example, iron, copper, molybdenum) and vitamins (for example, vitamins A, B$_{12}$, C, D, niacin). For example, hemoglobin requires iron in order to transport oxygen.

In 1914, Whipple continued his studies of icterus with Charles W. Hooper at the University of California in San Francisco. After they discovered that the liver filters hemoglobin from the blood and recycles the protein as a bile pigment called bilirubin, Whipple and Hooper considered the possibility that the liver may be involved in certain types of anemia, including pernicious anemia. Their experiments were performed on dogs obtained from local pounds and involved changing diets as well as periodic bleeding to induce anemia. The goal of their experiments was to determine how the dogs' bodies responded to conditions of artificially induced anemia. Despite the fact that these experiments were performed humanely and the dogs usually survived, Whipple and his colleagues were criticized heavily by the general public, politicians, and animal rights groups, and they were forced to battle these groups legislatively for several years to defend their research.

Whipple and Hooper periodically bled dogs to maintain artificially induced anemia. These dogs had low red blood cell and hemoglobin counts as a result. Whipple and Hooper attempted several techniques at rapidly increasing hemoglobin production in these animals—rates faster than the body would normally recover on its own. They varied the dogs' diets and found different degrees of success. A diet composed of carbohydrates (for example, bread and milk) was ineffective, requiring one to five months for hemoglobin regeneration. A diet of rice and potatoes was somewhat more effective; meat-rich diets were very effective. Diets composed of liver, lean scrap meat, and beef heart stimulated complete hemoglobin regeneration within two to four weeks.

Whipple and Hooper developed liver and meat extracts that produced the same dramatic results in artificially anemic dogs. In 1918, Hooper was the first physician to administer a liver extract to human victims of pernicious anemia. The three anemic patients' conditions improved considerably. Nevertheless, various clinical doctors ridiculed Hooper and his treatment. As a result, Hooper discontinued his research. Seven years would pass before the Harvard University physicians George Richards Minot and William Parry Murphy would use virtually the same treatment, save many lives, and subsequently receive a Nobel Prize.

Whipple continued his liver extract work with Frieda S. Robscheit-Robbins at the new School of Medicine and Dentistry at Rochester University in New York. From 1923 to 1929, they performed an extensive and elaborate series of dietary administration experiments on artificially anemic dogs. During these years, Whipple and Robscheit-Robbins defined the necessary dietary constraints for treating pernicious anemia. They tested various substances isolated from liver and muscle extracts of cow, pig, and chicken. They developed new extracts

George Hoyt Whipple. (The Nobel Foundation)

that, in conjunction with products from Minot's group at Harvard University and the Eli Lilly Pharmaceutical Company of Indianapolis, Indiana, became effective treatments for human patients suffering from pernicious anemia. Thousands of lives were saved by these extracts.

In 1925, Whipple and Robscheit-Robbins discovered that the most effective mineral found in beef and liver extract that would stimulate hemoglobin regeneration was iron. They reported their results in an article titled "Blood Regeneration in Severe Anemia: III. Iron Reaction Favorable—Arsenic and Germanium Dioxide Almost Inert," which appeared with three additional articles in volume 72 of the *American Journal of Physiology*. They found that iron by itself is a very effective hemoglobin regenerator, which is not surprising given that iron is the central active portion of each hemoglobin protein subunit. They also discovered that beef liver was the most effective dietary treatment, causing hemoglobin and red blood cell regeneration from one-third of normal to normal in as little time as two weeks. Other effective dietary supplements included chicken gizzard smooth muscle, pig kidney, and beef kidney. They also discovered that the liver recycles hemoglobin into bile pigments (for example, bilirubin) and bile pigments into hemoglobin. Whipple and Robscheit-Robbins continued this research into the 1930's and 1940's.

Although iron is an essential component of the pernicious anemia meat/liver extracts, vitamin B_{12} was later shown to be equally as important. In 1949, vitamin B_{12} was isolated from liver extracts by the American biochemist Karl Folkers and the English biochemist Alexander Todd. Diets of iron and vitamin B_{12} are modern treatments for individuals suffering from pernicious anemia.

Whipple shared the 1934 Nobel Prize in Physiology or Medicine with Minot and Murphy. Minot and Murphy had applied Whipple's beef/liver extracts to treating human pernicious anemia patients beginning in 1925.

SIGNIFICANCE

George Hoyt Whipple's contributions to medicine and to biology are multifold: First, Whipple discovered a treatment for pernicious anemia, thereby saving countless thousands of lives. Second, he discovered that the mineral iron, stored in the liver, is essential for hemoglobin regeneration. Third, he unraveled several basic recycling enzymatic pathways within the mammalian body, including the recycling of hemoglobin and bile pigments. Finally, he improved the understanding of human liver and blood physiology, breaking new ground in the study

of blood disorders. The 1934 Nobel Prize in Physiology or Medicine, along with other awards, demonstrated the importance of his lifesaving work.

The use of liver extracts to treat human victims of pernicious anemia saved countless individuals from a disease that many scientists had thought to be untreatable. It is regrettable that Whipple and Hooper's 1918 treatment of patients had been ridiculed; many lives might have been spared during the seven-year interval between this event and its ultimate acceptance by the medical community. The liver extracts led eventually to the isolation of the important active ingredients for hemoglobin regeneration, including the mineral iron and vitamin B_{12}.

Iron is one of many minerals stored by the liver for later use in the body's cells. Iron serves as a cofactor, or helper substance, in the active centers of protein enzymes—the cellular molecules that control essential life chemical reactions in cells. Iron is essential for proper functioning of the protein hemoglobin, a molecule that is mass produced by red blood cells for the transport of oxygen to the cells of the body to drive cellular energy production reactions. Hemoglobin is nonfunctional without iron. The phrase "iron-poor blood" indicates a semianemic physical state. Whipple showed that iron can regenerate hemoglobin rapidly in only a few weeks. Hemoglobin is regenerated in the liver, one of the few body tissues capable of regeneration when it is not too severely damaged. This regenerative capacity of liver could be caused somehow by the fact that the liver is a storage center for virtually every type of material needed by the body. The liver controls the buildup and breakdown of the body's food reserves according to the body's needs. The liver can split hemoglobin into two sections: a heme component, which is iron, and the precursor of a bile pigment, bilirubin. The second section is a globin component, which is protein. The globin is recycled back into the body's protein metabolism; the heme is used to construct bile, a substance released from the liver into the small intestine to emulsify fat, thereby allowing the body to absorb the essential fat-soluble vitamins A, D, E, and K. Bile pigments can be reabsorbed back into the blood, returned to the liver, and used to construct the heme component of hemoglobin or more bile.

Whipple's achievements greatly improved the understanding of organisms as intricately interconnected organ systems. His work demonstrated the interplay between the liver, blood, and digestive systems. His studies would pioneer later research into other types of anemia, including the inherited thalassemia and sickle-cell anemia.

—*David Wason Hollar, Jr.*

FURTHER READING

Alberts, Bruce, et al. *Molecular Biology of the Cell.* 4th ed. New York: Garland, 2002. Comprehensive introductory molecular biology textbook for undergraduate biology majors offers a theoretical survey of cell biology by several leading scientists. Features excellent photographs, diagrams, and reference lists. Includes a good discussion of liver function and its regenerative capacity.

Corner, George W. *George Hoyt Whipple and His Friends: The Life of a Nobel Prize Pathologist.* Philadelphia: J. B. Lippincott, 1963. A touching portrait of not only a great scientist and physician but also a wonderful man by a close friend and colleague. Provides a detailed and enjoyable summary of both the scientific and private sides of Whipple's life.

Garrison, Fielding H. *An Introduction to the History of Medicine.* 4th ed. Philadelphia: W. B. Saunders, 1963. Comprehensive history of medical research from ancient times up to 1928. Includes a year-by-year chronology and extensive references. Notes the contributions of Whipple, Minot, Murphy, and other twentieth century pathologists.

Goldman, Lee, and Dennis Ausiello, eds. *Cecil Textbook of Medicine.* 22d ed. Philadelphia: W. B. Saunders, 2003. Enormous medical reference work is a tremendously informative source on anatomy, physiology, pathology, hematology, and more. Features detailed graphs, tables, and diagrams as well as an extensive reference list. Provides considerable information on all types of anemia.

Nobelstiftelsen. *Nobel: The Man and His Prizes.* 3d ed. New York: Elsevier, 1972. An excellent history of the Nobel Prize, beginning with Alfred Nobel and including the Nobel laureates in all fields up through the 1960's. Discusses each laureate's work within the context of the history of his or her own field.

Whipple, George H. "Autobiographical Sketch." *Perspectives in Biology and Medicine* 2 (Spring, 1959): 253-289. Brief autobiography presents a personal summary of Whipple's life and his thoughts about science, academia, and his colleagues. Emphasizes his undergraduate and medical school days as well as his experiences in supervising two medical schools and makes clear his love for teaching and research.

SEE ALSO: 1901: Discovery of Human Blood Groups; Dec., 1905: Crile Performs the First Direct Blood Transfusion; 1912-1914: Abel Develops the First Artificial Kidney; 1921-1922: Banting and Best Isolate the Hormone Insulin; Fall, 1934-May 6, 1953: Gibbon Develops the Heart-Lung Machine.

1925
WOOLF'S *MRS. DALLOWAY* EXPLORES WOMEN'S CONSCIOUSNESS

Virginia Woolf, already recognized as having made a stylistic break with the past, made a powerful statement about how women perceive themselves and society in her 1925 novel Mrs. Dalloway.

LOCALE: London, England
CATEGORY: Literature

KEY FIGURES
Virginia Woolf (1882-1941), English novelist
Leonard S. Woolf (1880-1969), English writer and Virginia Woolf's husband
George Duckworth (1868-1934), Virginia Woolf's half brother
Vanessa Bell (1879-1961), Virginia Woolf's sister

SUMMARY OF EVENT
Virginia Woolf was born into a family noted for its literary achievements. Her father, Leslie Stephen, is best known as the editor of the *Dictionary of National Biography*, the standard against which biographical dictionaries have long been measured. The Stephens have often been cited as the model Victorian family, with the loving if gruff father and the doting mother providing a supportive home environment. The appearance of such a family situation was almost entirely a facade. Leslie Stephen not only disassociated himself from the problems of his children (his parental concern was mostly expressed in letters to his wife) but also demanded an exaggerated level of attention for himself.

Virginia's mother was Leslie's second wife, Julia (née Jackson) Duckworth. They were married March 26, 1878, and had between them five children from their former marriages. They were to have four of their own as well, of which Virginia was the third. By the time Virginia was old enough to be aware of her surroundings, Laura, Leslie's daughter from his first marriage, had been confined to a separate section of the house because of her emotional problems. Although Laura may have been of less-than-normal intelligence, it appears that her real crime was willfulness—completely unacceptable in a Victorian daughter and to be curbed by virtually any level of force needed. Laura's fate was a powerful message about the importance of conformity for the other daughters in the Stephen family.

Worse emotional traumas were to follow. Virginia's half sister Stella Duckworth was not protected from the exuberant courtship of J. W. "Jack" Hills, and although the young woman was certainly frightened and possibly raped, Hills was not excluded from the house. No child could feel protected. Further, after the death of Julia Stephen in 1895, Stella was forced into the role of wife and mother and was expected to run the house and tend to the needs of Leslie and the children. There are hints, although no hard evidence, that her wifely functions included sex with her stepfather. She eventually married Hills in 1897 only to die of peritonitis shortly after returning from her honeymoon. It is quite possible that her illness was the result of an injury that occurred during sexual intercourse.

Nor were Leslie and Julia's own children safe and secure. Both Virginia and her elder sister Vanessa were sexually abused by their half brothers George and Herbert Duckworth. In an autobiographical fragment, Virginia recalls the first incident: She was about six, and George Duckworth put her up on a shelf outside the family's dining room and felt her genitalia. The abuse expanded in nature and continued through her teenage years. It is not surprising, then, that Virginia never found much pleasure in heterosexual activity or that she suffered from bouts of depression throughout her life. During her teenage years, these resulted in periods of reduced activity and reductions—which she resented bitterly—in the already limited education the daughter of a Victorian was allowed.

After the death of Leslie Stephen early in 1904, the Stephen children were left to fend for themselves. They eventually settled in the Bloomsbury section of London, where a literary circle formed around the family. This loose association, often called the Bloomsbury Group, included Clive Bell (eventually Vanessa's husband), Lytton Strachey, E. M. Forster, and Saxon Sydney-Turner. Bloomsbury, which came to include a number of other intellectuals such as Roger Fry and John Maynard Keynes, was known for a bohemian lifestyle and

sexual freedom. It was as part of this group that Virginia began to write—she needed money—and met her husband, Leonard S. Woolf, who had spent a number of years as a colonial administrator in India. The wedding occurred in 1912.

Virginia Woolf's first novel, *The Voyage Out*, did not appear until 1915. Although she had already begun to make a name for herself as a critic and reviewer, the tension of waiting for reviews and the desire for success took an emotional toll. Her husband, who had not been prepared for the intensity of his bride's emotional storms, got her the necessary medical help and saw to it that she had several months of rest until she recovered her equilibrium. This sort of breakdown, although not always as serious, accompanied the publication of most of her novels. Clarissa Dalloway, the protagonist of Woolf's 1925 novel, makes a brief appearance in *The Voyage Out*.

A WOMAN'S CONSCIOUSNESS

In the opening paragraphs of Mrs. Dalloway, *Virginia Woolf immediately places the reader within the stream of thoughts going through the title character's mind:*

Mrs. Dalloway said she would buy the flowers herself.

For Lucy had her work cut out for her. The doors would be taken off their hinges; Rumpelmayer's men were coming. And then, thought Clarissa Dalloway, what a morning—fresh as if issued to children on a beach.

What a lark! What a plunge! For so it had always seemed to her when, with a little squeak of the hinges, which she could hear now, she had burst open the French windows and plunged at Bourton into the open air. How fresh, how calm, stiller than this of course, the air was in the early morning; like the flap of a wave; the kiss of a wave; chill and sharp and yet (for a girl of eighteen as she then was) solemn, feeling as she did, standing there at the open window, that something awful was about to happen; looking at the flowers, at the trees with the smoke winding off them and the rooks rising, falling; standing and looking until Peter Walsh said, "Musing among the vegetables?"—was that it?—"I prefer men to cauliflowers"—was that it? He must have said it at breakfast one morning when she had gone out on to the terrace—Peter Walsh. He would be back from India one of these days, June or July, she forgot which, for his letters were awfully dull; it was his sayings one remembered; his eyes, his pocket-knife, his smile, his grumpiness and, when millions of things had utterly vanished—how strange it was!—a few sayings like this about cabbages.

Source: Virginia Woolf, *Mrs. Dalloway* (London: Hogarth Press, 1925).

The success of her first book started Woolf on a career as a novelist. She began to develop a new style of novel that rejected the past, which she saw as represented by the works of Arnold Bennett, John Galsworthy, and H. G. Wells. Her novels were about everyday life, but they added layer after layer of symbolism and meaning. She wrote the essay "Mr. Bennett and Mrs. Brown" (1924) to set forth her ideas about what fiction should be.

Meanwhile, in 1922 she had decided to write two books at the same time—a novel and a book of criticism. These became *The Common Reader: First Series* (1925) and *Mrs. Dalloway*. She hoped that this approach would help ameliorate the emotional disturbance that publishing a novel produced. Her expectation of critical comment about *Jacob's Room* (1922) had caused her significant difficulty. Although the projects were not connected, her reading of Greek classics for an essay titled "Not Knowing Greek"—she resented the lack of education for girls—clearly influenced the psychological symbolism in *Mrs. Dalloway*.

The character Clarissa Dalloway has been associated with Kitty Maxse, whose death in a fall in 1922 Woolf attributed to suicide. Woolf intended to write of the realities of English life: "I want to give life and death, sanity and insanity; I want to criticise the social system and to show it at work, at its most intense." As is always the case in Virginia Woolf's fiction, many symbols and meanings can be found in *Mrs. Dalloway*, but one theme in the book is Clarissa Dalloway's effort to give her life meaning.

SIGNIFICANCE

Mrs. Dalloway was met with significant critical approval when it was published. Although the book was not as widely regarded as a work of genius as *To the Lighthouse* (1927) and especially *A Room of One's Own* (1929) would later be, it left few serious critics with doubt that Virginia Woolf was a major figure in modern literature. It was also, for a serious novel, a popular success as measured by sales. It further marked, perhaps coincidentally, the beginning of one of the longest periods of stability and happiness in Woolf's life.

Superficially, the novel is the story of a day in Clarissa Dalloway's life. She is planning one of her famous parties—giving parties is her only talent—and preparations bring her into contact with a number of friends and acquaintances. The unexpected arrival of an old flame, Peter Walsh, brings some complications and memories of youth. Woolf is brilliant in her ability to weave past and present into a seamless picture. Other than Mrs. Dal-

loway and her friends, the only significant character is Septimus Warren Smith, a shell-shocked World War I veteran who is slipping into madness because of what he describes as an inability to feel, though his plight might be better described as feeling too much and too intensely. Smith's friend Evans was killed at the end of the war, and in confusion and pain Smith married in search of comfort and support. He is unable to satisfy his wife's demands for love and children, he is haunted by visions of Evans, and he feels guilt for being alive when his friend is dead. Ultimately, Smith kills himself.

On first reading, there might seem to be little comment about feminism in the novel. Clarissa, however, has found a way to escape some of the limitations placed on women in her society. In her parties, she brings together people from a variety of walks of life, even across class lines. Clarissa's parties are experiments in communication, much as Virginia Woolf's novels were for her. Clarissa has a consciousness of the potential for a unity in life in which divisions created by gender, class, and wealth disappear.

Freedom, as far as Woolf was concerned, came from successfully coping with the barriers one faced and from finding a vision such as Clarissa Dalloway's. Miss Kilman, the teacher of Clarissa's daughter, is the novel's representative modern woman. She has a profession and much integrity—she lost her standing by refusing to condemn German friends as monsters during the war. Her consciousness of facts and logic leaves her, however, narrow and unfulfilled. Unlike Clarissa, she has no sense of transcendence. She is unhappy and unloved. Clearly, Woolf did not see the triumph of women as simply a matter of moving into the sphere that in the 1920's was still regarded as that of the male; women could and had to be more than that.

Regrettably, but hardly surprisingly given her experiences, Woolf's male characters do not fare particularly well. With one exception, they are inept at life and love. Richard Dalloway, Clarissa's husband, upon hearing that Peter Walsh has returned, resolves to take his wife some flowers and tell her that he loves her. He manages only the flowers. Walsh, who has had trouble with women all of his life, is so governed by his passions that, although he follows a pretty girl around the city, he can never bring himself to approach her; he must be satisfied with his fantasies. The only admirable male character, Septimus Smith, is mad. He has a sense of transcendence, but unlike Clarissa, who remembers with longing the time another woman kissed her on the lips, he cannot cope with his homoerotic feelings. Ultimately, only

Clarissa—who does not regret her almost total lack of education or her lack of productive employment and who has only the gift of party giving—has a sense of completeness.

It is easy to see in Virginia Woolf's background the elements of life portrayed in *Mrs. Dalloway*. The sexual abuse had to leave her with a jaundiced view of men and heterosexual activity and must have produced feelings much like those described by Septimus. Woolf, unmoved by heterosexuality, found lesbian relations more fulfilling. Just as she was writing *Mrs. Dalloway*, she was developing a relationship with Vita Sackville-West that seems to have been the most sexually fulfilling of her life. Woolf never escaped the traumas of her childhood, and if, like Clarissa, she knew transcendence, like Septimus, she found it hurt too much to survive. In 1941, Virginia Woolf put a stone in her pocket and walked into the River Ouse to drown.

—*Fred R. van Hartesveldt*

FURTHER READING

Bell, Quentin. *Virginia Woolf: A Biography*. New York: Harcourt Brace Jovanovich, 1972. Written by Woolf's nephew, this book is filled with facts, some probably known only to the family. It should be noted that Bell tends to dismiss the traumas of Woolf's childhood as of little importance. An important source, but should not be used without consulting the work of Louise DeSalvo (see below).

Bloom, Harold, ed. *Clarissa Dalloway*. New York: Chelsea House, 1990. A collection of critical writings focusing on the character of Clarissa Dalloway. Brings together a variety of critical commentary from seven decades.

DeSalvo, Louise. *Virginia Woolf: The Impact of Childhood Sexual Abuse on Her Life and Work*. Boston: Beacon Press, 1989. Depends on inference and comparison of Woolf's comments about her life and problems with those of women who have chosen to speak openly of their experience of sexual abuse, but presents a powerful and convincing logic. No student of Woolf or her fiction can reasonably avoid reading this volume.

Kelley, Alice van Buren. *The Novels of Virginia Woolf: Fact and Vision*. Chicago: University of Chicago Press, 1973. Focuses on Woolf's recurrent theme of transcendence versus logic as a defining characteristic of personality. Well-written work of criticism provides important insights into Woolf's understanding of consciousness. Includes a chapter about *Mrs. Dalloway*.

Rosenfeld, Natania. *Outsiders Together: Virginia and Leonard Woolf*. Princeton, N.J.: Princeton University Press, 2000. Examines Virginia and Leonard Woolf's life together and its influence on the writings of both partners. Includes notes and index.

Woolf, Virginia. *The "Mrs. Dalloway" Reader*. Edited by Francine Prose. Orlando, Fla.: Harcourt, 2003. Includes the complete text of *Mrs. Dalloway* as well as the earlier short work *Mrs. Dalloway's Party*, copies of journal entries and letters written by Woolf related to *Mrs. Dalloway*, and essays and commentary on the novel by critics and other authors.

_____. *Three Guineas*. 1938. Reprint (annotated). New York: Harvest Books, 2006. This work, written less than three years before the author's suicide, is a statement of her views and anger about the mistreatment of women. One of the book's working titles gives a sense of Woolf's feelings: "On Being Despised." Useful for anyone seeking to understand Woolf's ideas about women and life.

SEE ALSO: Nov., 1903: Henry James's *The Ambassadors* Is Published; 1922: Eliot Publishes *The Waste Land*; 1925: Gide's *The Counterfeiters* Questions Moral Absolutes.

1925-1926
MUSSOLINI SEIZES DICTATORIAL POWERS IN ITALY

Benito Mussolini's seizure of power in the 1920's led to a dictatorship that destroyed political freedom in Italy and threatened international peace and stability during the 1930's.

LOCALE: Italy
CATEGORIES: Government and politics; civil rights and liberties

KEY FIGURES

Benito Mussolini (1883-1945), founder and leader of the National Fascist Party
Victor Emmanuel III (1869-1947), king of Italy, r. 1900-1946
Giacomo Matteotti (1885-1924), attorney and Socialist representative in the Italian parliament

SUMMARY OF EVENT

Italy made slow but notable progress in human rights during the first decades of the twentieth century. Under a constitutional monarchy, Italians shaped a limited parliamentary democracy similar to those of other Western European nations. By the early 1900's, the working class had won the right to organize and strike. Socialist labor unions vigorously advanced both economic and political goals. A lively, diverse press gave voice to a wide range of political opinion, although the more radical publications were often restrained by government censorship and the moral condemnation of the Roman Catholic Church. Universal male suffrage, enacted in 1913, underscored the nation's political progress. Women, although denied the vote, acquired important legal and property rights in 1919. The emergence of mass political parties after World War I heralded the prospects for democratic reform.

The post-World War I years offered new opportunities to create a more equitable, democratic society. The war also jeopardized Italy's progress by creating grave economic and political instability. Conservative government leaders, businesspeople, and landowners feared a communist revolution similar to the one that took place in Russia in 1917. Benito Mussolini's National Fascist Party compounded the political crisis with its revolutionary program and its violence against political opponents. Mussolini, a former Socialist Party leader and newspaper editor, had founded the Fascist movement immediately after the war. His virulent nationalism, anticommunism, antidemocratic politics, and appeal to violence attracted a large following of war veterans and political malcontents. Fascist paramilitary units, known as *squadristi*, carried out "punitive expeditions" against their rivals, primarily the Socialist Party and labor unions. Their brutal assaults and destruction of property, often unopposed by local government authorities, brought the country to the brink of civil war in the early 1920's.

The political crisis in Italy culminated in October, 1922, with the "March on Rome." Benito Mussolini orchestrated this threat to occupy the nation's capital with his party's paramilitary forces. While threatening armed conflict, he negotiated with influential business and political leaders and pressured King Victor Emmanuel III to invite him to form a new government. Mussolini assumed the position of prime minister and organized a coalition cabinet, filling the ministerial posts with members of his own and other conservative parties. Although the Fascists were a minority party, they achieved political dominance in the parliament following the elections of April, 1924. Under a new election law, the party receiving the most votes was given two-thirds of the seats in the Chamber of Deputies.

Mussolini's new government contended with a large, but divided, parliamentary opposition on the political left—democrats, socialists, and communists. One of his most persistent and outspoken adversaries was Giacomo Matteotti, leader of the reformist Socialist Party and a member of parliament. Matteotti gained a reputation as Mussolini's most dangerous critic by carefully documenting specific cases of abuse and corruption in the government. His report on the 1924 elections revealed widespread election fraud and violence by the Fascist Party. Despite personal threats from Fascist leaders, including Mussolini, Matteotti continued to denounce the government from his seat in parliament and to collect information about financial improprieties of government officials.

Matteotti's disappearance on June 10 immediately raised allegations of government involvement, and several witnesses later verified his kidnapping by Fascist *squadristi*. Although Matteotti's body was not discovered until mid-August, most of the public assumed that his abduction and murder had been sanctioned at the highest level of Fascist Party leadership, perhaps by Mussolini himself. The Matteotti affair provoked a spontaneous outpouring of popular protest against the government. Labor unions organized political strikes and

Benito Mussolini. (NARA)

public demonstrations. More than one hundred deputies from opposition parties refused to participate in parliamentary proceedings, declaring that Mussolini had lost all moral and political right to govern. The "Aventine Secession"—alluding to similar protests during the ancient Roman Republic—gave the outward appearance of solidarity on the political left. Even leading conservatives, who had previously supported Mussolini's government, now called for his resignation.

The overwhelming protest initially paralyzed Mussolini, belying his reputation as a man of action. He attempted to mollify the political right—the king, influential businesspeople, and senators—by reshuffling his cabinet and replacing Fascist ministers with well-respected conservatives. This compromising outraged Fascist militants, especially the local party leaders, who demanded a "second wave" of violence to destroy the remnants of political opposition and the pretense of par-

liamentary government. They confronted Musolini and threatened him personally in several heated party meetings. Defiance to his authority within the Fascist Party as well as in the government compelled him to take action.

On January 3, 1925, Mussolini made a dramatic speech in the Chamber of Deputies in which he assumed complete responsibility for the violence committed by the Fascists, including the murder of Matteotti. He challenged the members of the parliament to impeach him, and with a threatening overtone he announced that the situation would be "cleared up all along the line" in the following forty-eight hours. This speech marked the beginning of Mussolini's dictatorship. Within hours, local authorities began closing down the meeting halls of opposition groups and suppressing antigovernment publications. More than one hundred political dissidents were arrested. The *squadristi* unleashed a "second wave" of violence, destroying opposition presses and using intimidation and physical assaults to silence protest. The anti-Fascist opposition, contentious, divided, and unable to agree on a course of action, offered little effective resistance to Mussolini's seizure of power.

Mussolini's personal dictatorship gradually took shape over the next two years. He established his authoritarian rule through rigorous enforcement of existing laws, new restrictive legislation, and special executive decrees. After several unsuccessful assassination attempts against Mussolini in 1925 and 1926, the government passed a series of "exceptional decrees" that formally outlawed all political parties, banned anti-Fascist organizations and publications, and canceled all passports. The participants in the Aventine Secession were stripped of their parliamentary immunity and barred from taking their seats in the Chamber of Deputies. Local elected governments were eliminated and replaced by state-appointed administrators.

The exceptional decrees created the Special Tribunal for the Defense of the State, a military court that functioned outside the normal judicial process and allowed the arbitrary arrest and imprisonment of more than five thousand government opponents. The death penalty, which had been abolished in 1890, was reintroduced. Giovanni Amendola, Piero Gobetti, Antonio Gramsci, and several other prominent anti-Fascists died as a result of street beatings or lengthy prison terms. Hundreds of others fled the country in order to escape the *squadristi* violence or imprisonment.

The government decrees sanctioned the operations of a secret state police, identified by the sinister, but apparently meaningless, acronym OVRA. Under the efficient direction of Arturo Bocchini, the police monitored antigovernment activity and used their authority to place individuals under house arrest or send them into "internal exile" in remote villages or on coastal islands. Mandatory identity cards allowed the police to control personal movement, employment, and access to public services. By 1927, Mussolini's regime had eliminated most vestiges of political freedom in Italy. Discarding the parliamentary designation of prime minister, he referred to his position as "head of state" and adopted the title *Il Duce*— the Leader. Through his dictatorship, he sought to fulfill his own maxim: "Everything in the State, nothing outside the State, nothing against the State."

SIGNIFICANCE

Mussolini's seizure of power marked a disturbing political development in the modern world. It repudiated more than a century of European progress toward greater political democracy and individual liberty and introduced the term "totalitarian" into modern political vocabulary. Although Mussolini's regime never achieved the totalitarianism of Adolf Hitler's Germany or Joseph Stalin's Soviet Union, the results of Mussolini's dictatorial rule proved devastating to a free society. The ban on political parties and elections destroyed democratic politics, the abolition of labor organizations stripped workers of their right to seek economic redress, and the purging of the state bureaucracy and the courts ensured total government acquiescence to Mussolini's authority.

The establishment of the Special Tribunal allowed the regime to bypass regular judicial procedures and arrest, imprison, or exile thousands. Many Italians defied the government by leaving the country on their own accord. During the 1920's and 1930's, Italy lost some of its most talented citizens to emigration, including the nuclear physicist Enrico Fermi and the renowned orchestral conductor Arturo Toscanini. The elimination of a free press, strict control of the media and education, and the use of secret police to stifle political dissent further eroded individual freedoms.

The goal of creating a totalitarian state represented an unprecedented degree of government intrusion into the daily lives of citizens. Even organized sports, recreational programs, youth groups, artistic activities, and professional associations fell under government supervision. Only the conservative institutions that lent timely support to Mussolini in his first years—the military, the monarchy, and the Roman Catholic Church—retained a large degree of autonomy under the Fascist regime.

Mussolini's success in Italy inspired similar "fascist" movements in several European countries. Each had its own identity, but they all shared an affinity for political violence and an abiding contempt for democracy and individual civil rights. In Germany, the Nazis imitated and refined the methods of the Italian Fascists. Their success brought Adolf Hitler to power in 1933 and marked the beginning of an unparalleled disaster for human rights and international peace.

Mussolini's belligerent foreign policy effectively destabilized international relations at a time when most nations were seeking ways to ensure peace. In the years following World War I, European diplomats had worked diligently to limit armed conflict through the newly founded League of Nations, naval disarmament treaties, and collective security agreements. With his invasion of Ethiopia in 1935, Mussolini challenged the League of Nations and revealed its impotence against military aggression. He defied the Geneva Convention's ban on poison gas and used it with devastating results against Ethiopian troops. His military assistance to Francisco Franco in the Spanish Civil War helped destroy democratic government in Spain and install a dictatorial regime that remained in power for more than thirty-five years. Mussolini's military success in Africa encouraged Hitler's ambitious plans for German territorial expansion. With the Pact of Steel in 1939, the two men cemented a military alliance that brought on the greatest human catastrophe in modern history, World War II.

—Michael F. Hembree

FURTHER READING

Bosworth, R. J. B. *The Italian Dictatorship: Problems and Perspectives in the Interpretation of Mussolini and Fascism.* New York: Arnold, 1998. Places fascism within the broader context of the social and cultural times in which it developed. Written by an authority on Italy's history.

_____. *Mussolini.* New York: Arnold, 2002. Lauded as a definitive new biography of the life of the infamous leader. Detailed, exhaustive study includes footnotes and bibliography.

Cannistraro, Philip V., ed. *Historical Dictionary of Fascist Italy.* Westport, Conn.: Greenwood Press, 1982. The standard reference for individuals, institutions, and events in Italy under Fascist rule. Includes informative entries on the anti-Fascist movement. Features an appendix that contains a complete listing of government ministers who served in the Fascist government.

Lyttelton, Adrian. *The Seizure of Power in Italy, 1919-*

1929. 2d ed. London: Weidenfeld & Nicolson, 1987. Brilliant study is one of the best works available in any language on Mussolini's seizure of power. Focuses on the intricate personal and institutional relationships that brought Mussolini to power and maintained his dictatorship for almost twenty years.

Mack Smith, Denis. *Mussolini*. New York: Alfred A. Knopf, 1982. One of the best of several modern biographies available in English. Thoroughly researched from a wide range of archival and secondary sources. The author's highly critical, even derisive, assessment of Mussolini strips away the mythology of *Il Duce* and Fascist revolution to reveal a corrupt, unscrupulous, and often inept political leader.

Matteotti, Giacomo. *The Fascisti Exposed: A Year of Fascist Domination*. New York: Howard Fertig, 1969. First published clandestinely in 1923, this report documents in detail the terrorism of the *squadristi*, the complicity of government authorities in the Fascist violence, and the political corruption during Mussolini's first year in power. This impressive exposé established Matteotti's reputation as Mussolini's most dangerous critic and eventually led to his murder by Fascist agents.

Salvemini, Gaetano. *The Fascist Dictatorship in Italy*. New York: Howard Fertig, 1967. First published in 1927 by one of the most important anti-Fascist historians. Weaves pointed commentary with extracts from contemporary documents (some taken from Matteotti's exposé) to underscore the criminality of the Fascist movement and its leadership.

_____. *The Origins of Fascism in Italy*. New York: Harper & Row, 1973. Written in 1942 and based on Salvemini's lectures at Harvard University, this book remained unpublished until after the author's death. Goes beyond the author's earlier polemic against the Fascist regime and explores the conditions in Italy that made Fascism possible. Chapter 26 provides a good summary of the political infringements that resulted from the creation of Mussolini's totalitarian state.

Seton-Watson, Christopher. *Italy from Liberalism to Fascism, 1870-1925*. London: Methuen, 1967. Although somewhat dated, this remains among the best surveys of modern Italy up to the Fascist period. Traces the triumph of Fascism to the failure of liberalism during the post-World War I political crisis. Includes an annotated bibliography and a helpful listing of the many Italian governments and their cabinet ministers during the years 1871-1925.

SEE ALSO: Oct. 24-30, 1922: Mussolini's "March on Rome"; Aug. 27-Sept. 29, 1923: Corfu Crisis; Feb. 11, 1929: Lateran Treaty; Jan. 23, 1933: Italy Creates the Industrial Reconstruction Institute; Oct. 11, 1935-July 15, 1936: League of Nations Applies Economic Sanctions Against Italy; Mar. 7, 1936: German Troops March into the Rhineland; Nov. 9-10, 1938: Kristallnacht; Apr. 7, 1939: Italy Invades and Annexes Albania; Sept. 1, 1939: Germany Invades Poland; Aug. 3, 1940-Mar., 1941: Italy Invades British Somaliland.

1925-1927
GANCE'S *NAPOLÉON* REVOLUTIONIZES FILMMAKING TECHNIQUES

Filmmaker Abel Gance revolutionized the epic motion picture and expanded the horizons of world cinema by employing new techniques for his innovative treatment of the French national hero Napoleon Bonaparte.

LOCALE: France
CATEGORY: Motion pictures

KEY FIGURES
Abel Gance (1889-1981), French filmmaker
André Debrie (1891-1967), French inventor and manufacturer of film equipment
Léonce-Henry Burel (1892-1977), French cameraman
Ricciotto Canudo (1879-1923), French journalist and editor
Élie Faure (1873-1937), French art critic and historian
Jean Epstein (1897-1953), Russian French filmmaker
Kevin Brownlow (b. 1938), English film archivist, historian, and film editor

SUMMARY OF EVENT
By the early 1920's, Abel Gance had made twenty-three films, including *J'Accuse!* (1919) and *La Roue* (1923), and had established himself as France's most innovative avant-garde filmmaker, particularly in his rapid editing technique and camera movement in the melodrama *La Roue*. By 1923, he had started the screenplay for his monumental French epic *Napoléon*, a project that would take four years to complete. Gance completed the script in 1925, originally intending to make six massive films to capture the epic sweep of the life of Emperor Napoleon I. Each film was intended to run about ninety minutes, but in June, 1925, Gance's major financier for the series withdrew his support. Eventually, Gance found new backers, but they were willing to fund only the first film of the series, which Gance then expanded to include as much of the original project as possible.

What Gance produced became a monument of the silent cinema and surely one of the most impressive and innovative biographical features ever made. The completed version, which premiered at the Paris Opera House on April 7, 1927, was epic in scope and length and traced Napoleon's life from his childhood in Corsica through the turmoil of the French Revolution and the Reign of Terror, and concluded with Napoleon's Italian campaign and his rise to power. The film was released about the time the new technology of talking pictures came into prominence and fell into obscurity during the

sound period. Thanks to the dedicated efforts of film historian and archivist Kevin Brownlow, who collected whatever materials he could locate, the film was eventually restored during the 1970's and 1980's, partly under Gance's supervision, to a version that ran to nearly six hours.

The achievement of the film is partly a matter of technical innovation but is mainly a consequence of Gance's personal vision of what the cinema might become. Gance's ideas in this regard were influenced by a number of artists and intellectuals with whom he was associated, particularly the journalist and editor Ricciotto Canudo. Other artists in this circle included the novelist Blaise Cendrars, who would eventually write more than twenty books; the avant-garde filmmaker Jean Epstein, who employed inventive visual techniques; and the art critic and historian Élie Faure, who influenced Gance's belief in the power of the cinema as a collective and unifying art form that could create "visual symphonies." Canudo and the others helped to shape Gance's belief that the primary function of the cinema was to create dazzling spectacles, "cathedrals of light," that would surprise, stun, and elevate the consciousness of the spectator as no other art form could do. In *Napoléon*, Gance attempted to put those notions to the test; his challenge was to find technicians who could help him to realize the vision.

A key talent who assisted Gance in expanding the horizons of the cinema was the inventor André Debrie, who, over his lifetime, personally patented nearly fifty cinema-related inventions, including the Parvo camera, the Matipo printer, an ultrahigh-speed camera developed during the mid-1920's, and, perhaps most important for the achievement of *Napoléon*, the means of interlocking three synchronized cameras to create a panoramic triple-screen projection through the use of three projectors. The approach was both creative and innovative, permitting a cinema spectacle unlike any ever seen before, but it was also complicated and expensive, given that specially equipped theaters were needed to demonstrate the effect. The Gance-Debrie creation was in fact a precursor of what was later called Cinerama, but it represented the invention of a technology that proved to be ahead of its time. Sound was the novelty of choice at the time Gance's film was released.

Most of Gance's film, apart from location footage shot at Nice, Toulon, and Corsica, was made at the Billancourt Studio outside Paris. Gance recruited an army of technicians for the project, including seven cameramen, led by Léonce-Henry Burel and Jules Kruger, and six gifted assistant directors: Alexandre Volkoff, Victor Tourjansky, Henry Krauss, Henri Andréani, Marius Nalpas, and Anatole Litvak.

According to the French critic Léon Moussinac, Gance's original ideas "enlarged the resources of cinematography" and the release of *Napoléon* marked a significant date "in the history of the technological development of the cinema." Gance's assistant director Alexandre Volkoff later remembered Gance as being obsessed by the idea of "surpassing himself and all others."

Gance was determined to liberate the camera in ways that had never been tried before with a demonstration of visual pyrotechnics that would astonish the viewer. A sequence concerning the young hero's time at school experimented with camera movement for subjective effect. Gance, for example, instructed cameraman Jules Kruger to use a camera strapped to his chest, enabling the cameraman to run into the action of a snowball fight in which the young Napoleon marshals his forces to win the day. Kruger also mounted the camera on a sled that could be pushed into the fray. In a later sequence that begins with Napoleon's escape from Corsica in a small boat, the camera was mounted on the boat to capture the turbulence at sea. In the chase to the sea, it was mounted on horseback. Intercut with Napoleon's escape at sea are dramatized scenes of turmoil at the Convention Hall in Paris as the revolution takes a violent turn. Here, Gance mounted the camera on a pendulum that could be swung down and over the crowd.

The film became famous for its multiplication, manipulation, and orchestration of images. Gance had already experimented effectively with the use of rapid montage for emotional effect in *La Roue*; in *Napoléon*, Gance carried this sort of experimentation to new levels of achievement. In places, the editing is so rapid that the effect is nearly subliminal. In addition to using this highly subjective montage technique, Gance experimented with layered, superimposed images, piling one image on top of another with up to sixteen overlays. Gance later remarked in Nelly Kaplan's documentary film *Abel Gance: Yesterday and Tomorrow* (1964) that, as no single viewer could sort out all the images of a single, multilayered frame, no two people would "see" exactly the same action when viewing these overlays. Gance also experimented with a split-screen technique that divided the screen into four panels, then into six, then into nine, and superimposed full-frame images over the split screen. Used to show the young Napoleon engaged in a pillow fight, the technique created a perfect emblem of boyhood frenzy.

The film's most impressive innovation, however, was its use of the triple-screen effect (in the drastically cut version of the film that was originally released in the United States, this effect was largely lost). The triple-screen projection is sometimes used to create a panoramic effect as Napoleon moves his army into Italy; at other times, three separate images are projected, the center screen carrying the main action and the outside screens framing it with ancillary action. In a final burst of patriotism, the three screens are tinted to present the image of the French tricolor flag over images of Napoleon at the height of his authority. The conclusion of *Napoléon* has not been surpassed in visual effect by any other film.

SIGNIFICANCE

Few films in the history of cinema have had the impact of *Napoléon*. D. W. Griffith's *The Birth of a Nation* (1915) first served to make the cinema an art form to be taken seriously. Gance's achievements came a few years after Griffith's epic landmark and a few years before Sergei Eisenstein's groundbreaking work in the Soviet Union. Gance's vision was perhaps even larger than Griffith's (the two men did meet in the early 1920's in New York); Gance's intellectual sophistication surpassed Griffith's, and his film techniques tended to advance rather than duplicate those of the American master. In the Soviet Union, Eisenstein had studied Gance's earlier montage techniques, which influenced Eisenstein's montage work in *Strike* (1925) and *Potemkin* (1925). When *Napoléon* was released in 1927, however, it served to demonstrate as no other film had done the full potential of a thoroughly cinematic spectacle. When it was rediscovered and revived fifty years later, *Napoléon* still had the power to astonish spectators in London, Paris, Washington, and New York. Cinema historians invariably would mention the film as an important technological landmark, but the original film was eclipsed by the novelty of sound and was unseen for decades.

It is surprising, however, that *Napoléon*, despite its achievements, was destined to lie dormant for more than half a century and become a nearly lost and forgotten masterpiece. This was partly a consequence of economics and popular taste. Gance's film made demands on audiences because of its length, and it was also costly to mount properly in theaters, which had to be specially equipped to handle its triple-screen spectacle. The film also tended to be overlooked because of the craze for talking pictures.

Gance, however, was also a pioneer in developing sound film technology in France. In 1929, he patented his Perspective Sound technique, and he directed the first French talking feature, *La Fin du monde* (1931). In 1934, he completed a shortened, synchronized sound version of his masterpiece titled *Napoléon Bonaparte*. In later life, he would return repeatedly to the Napoleon project, reworking its content and its technology. In 1956, he developed an experimental program called "Magirama," which used sequences from his earlier films. Gance's Magirama spectacle in Paris paralleled the Cinemascope craze in the United States and was intended to demonstrate the potential of what Gance called "Polyvision."

In his later years, Gance set about remaking *Napoléon* in collaboration with filmmaker Claude Lelouch. The result of their work was released in 1972 under the title *Bonaparte et la révolution* and was grandly billed as "the masterpiece of masterpieces, the greatest film of the history of the cinema, four hours and thirty-five minutes in length, forty-five years in the making." In fact, however, the Gance-Lelouch version is inferior in every way to the original masterpiece of 1927, which was being quietly restored by the British historian, archivist, and filmmaker Kevin Brownlow, who had devoted a lifetime to restoring *Napoléon* to an approximation of its original length.

In 1973, the Brownlow reconstruction, running to nearly five hours, was screened with the triple-screen triptych finale at the American Film Institute Theater in Washington, D.C., but the Brownlow reconstruction was blocked from wider distribution because of the Gance-Lelouch remake. Six years later, an expanded Brownlow version was screened at the Telluride Film Festival in Colorado in August of 1979. Gance himself, more than ninety years old and in failing health, flew to Colorado to accept an award for his achievements on August 31. The film was also screened the next year at the London Film Festival of 1980 at the Empire Cinema, accompanied by music arranged by Carl Davis and played by a forty-three-piece orchestra. By that point, it had also been screened at the Pacific Film Archive and at the Walker Arts Center in Minneapolis.

In the United States, filmmaker Francis Ford Coppola joined forces with film distributor Robert A. Harris to organize a *Napoléon* revival at Radio City Music Hall in New York. The film was well presented, accompanied by the sixty-piece American Symphony Orchestra under the baton of Maestro Carmine Coppola, who composed more than three and a half hours of original music for the premiere on January 23, 1981. Because of union regulations and financial considerations, the film was compromised, as the Radio City presentation was not to exceed four hours in running time. Among purists, this abridgment of the Coppola version raised questions about exactly whose *Napoléon* was being shown.

Despite Coppola's shortening of the film, the Radio City premiere was a huge critical and financial success, playing to a packed house of six thousand people. The original screenings set for January 23 through January 25 quickly sold out, and additional performances were scheduled during the following weeks. The initial showing at Radio City was the first premiere of a silent film in New York City in more than fifty years, and it was treated as an unusual, spectacular, and newsworthy event, covered by network television news shows, by *Time* and *Newsweek* magazines, and by major newspapers in cities as distant as Toronto and Washington.

Napoléon was destined to become the media event of the year. The film then went on a national tour, playing other major American cities from coast to coast. The immediate impact of the film was that other talents imitated its inventions and technology. The ultimate impact was to come some fifty years after its original release, as *Napoléon* became recognized as the ultimate demonstration of the power and achievement of the silent cinema.

—*James M. Welsh*

FURTHER READING

Abel, Richard. *The French Cinema: The First Wave, 1915-1929*. Princeton, N.J.: Princeton University Press, 1984. Meticulously researched survey of French silent cinema covers Gance's career through the period and includes a substantial treatment of *Napoléon*.

Brownlow, Kevin. *"Napoleon": Abel Gance's Classic Film*. 1983. Reprint. London: British Film Institute, 2005. Invaluable, definitive treatment of the film, written by the filmmaker and archivist responsible for its later reconstruction and revival, in collaboration with Gance himself. Expands on Brownlow's earlier published research on the film.

_____. *The Parade's Gone By. . . .* New York: Alfred A. Knopf, 1968. Beautifully produced book on the silent cinema, dedicated to Gance. Offers a substantial chapter on *Napoléon* based on interviews with Gance and other research culled from French sources; one of the best brief introductions to the film. Brownlow writes from the perspective of an informed enthusiast and collector who went on to become a filmmaker and cinema historian.

Gance, Abel. *Napoleon*. Translated by Moya Hassan, edited by Bambi Ballard. London: Faber, 1990. Presents Gance's script, started in 1923, painstakingly edited to indicate scenes cut from extant prints of the film. Includes Gance's comments to spectators written when the film was released in 1927, a list of cast and credits, and an introduction by Kevin Brownlow.

King, Norman. *Abel Gance: A Politics of Spectacle*. London: British Film Institute, 1984. Follows the response of left-wing critics who objected to *Napoléon*'s alleged "fascistic representation of Bonaparte as restorer of order in the midst of chaos." Aims "to reinsert the political" into the discussion of Gance's aesthetic and finds a polarity between "progressive form" and "reactionary content." Includes filmography.

_____. "History and Actuality: Abel Gance's *Napoléon vu par Abel Gance*." In *French Film: Texts and Contexts*, edited by Susan Hayward and Ginette Vincendeau. London: Routledge & Kegan Paul, 1990. Aptly calls *Napoléon* a "filmic *chanson de geste*" and asserts that it is a film "of and for its own time." Admits that the film is innovative but argues that it is also authoritarian.

Kramer, Steven Philip, and James Michael Welsh. *Abel Gance*. Boston: Twayne, 1978. First book-length study of Gance's life and career published in English attempts to place Gance within his cultural context. Includes a chapter on *Napoléon* as well as a reprint of an interview with Gance. Features chronology, selected bibliography, and filmography.

Lanzoni, Rémi Fournier. *French Cinema: From Its Beginnings to the Present*. New York: Continuum International, 2002. History of French filmmaking places Gance's work within its larger social and cultural context. Includes photographs.

SEE ALSO: Aug., 1902: *A Trip to the Moon* Introduces Special Effects; Fall, 1903: *The Great Train Robbery* Introduces New Editing Techniques; Mar. 3, 1915: Griffith Releases *The Birth of a Nation*; 1920: Premiere of *The Cabinet of Dr. Caligari*; 1923: *The Ten Commandments* Advances American Film Spectacle; Dec. 4, 1924: Von Stroheim's Silent Masterpiece *Greed* Premieres; 1925: Eisenstein's *Potemkin* Introduces New Film Editing Techniques; 1927: Kuleshov and Pudovkin Introduce Montage to Filmmaking; 1927: Lang Expands the Limits of Filmmaking with *Metropolis*.

1925-1935
WOMEN'S RIGHTS IN INDIA UNDERGO A DECADE OF CHANGE

During the period 1925-1935, the status of women in traditional Indian society underwent substantial change as a result of specific legislative measures as well as growing social consciousness.

LOCALE: India
CATEGORIES: Laws, acts, and legal history; social issues and reform; human rights; women's issues

KEY FIGURES
Ram Mohun Roy (1772-1833), Indian social reformer
William Bentinck (1774-1839), governor-general of India, 1833-1835
Mahatma Gandhi (1869-1948), leader of the Indian nationalist movement and social reformer

SUMMARY OF EVENT
Before the twentieth century, the status of women in India traditionally had been defined by the patrilineal structure of society. Religion and custom provided the guidelines for restricting women's rights and prescribing their

conduct. Hindu and Muslim women were equally affected by these factors, although in somewhat different ways. Muslim women were subject to many strictures, the most visible being segregation of female children and adults and the practice of *purdah* (curtain), which required Muslim women to be veiled when in public. This custom eventually spread to upper-class Hindu women in northern India. Hindu women were governed by the tenets of their religion, which restricted their rights regarding inheritance, possession of property, and divorce, among others.

By the nineteenth century, the cruel suppression of women's fundamental rights was accepted as a norm of society in India rather than a cause for concern. The vast majority of women had no control over their destinies. Women had no choice in selecting their husbands; this was done by their families or their communities, often at birth. Child marriage was widely practiced, and polygamy was prevalent among several groups. Marriages were governed by caste and community restrictions, and intercaste marriages were not recognized. A particularly abused custom was that of dowry and its attendant assumption that the bride's family would pay for a lavish wedding. The birth of several daughters was a financial liability, and female infanticide was not unknown. Many tragic incidents resulted from the inability of some families to meet these often unreasonable expenses. The practices of dowry payment and extravagant weddings drew public attention and protest when the press reported an incident in 1914 in which a young Bengali girl committed suicide. Upon learning that her father had mortgaged his home in order to provide for her dowry, the young woman set fire to herself. The popular indignation aroused by this story led to a short-lived trend of refusing dowries; however, in the absence of specific legislation to outlaw the practice, the custom continued as before.

The practice of *sati* (widow burning) continued in many northern communities despite the 1829 legislation declaring it to be illegal. The condition of widows in society reflected the inhumanity of custom. Even if a widow was allowed to survive her husband's death, she was treated as a menial in the household and denied adequate food and simple pleasures such as new clothing, ornaments, and entertainment. The practice of shaving off a widow's hair was part of this denial of life. A widow thus had the choice of literally dying with her spouse or enduring a living death. This was the logical outcome of a system in which the wife's dependence on her husband was so complete that his death left her no alternative means of survival.

Efforts to change this state of affairs intensified during the nineteenth century, when the spirit of social reform gained momentum along with a rise in public consciousness. During this period, the energies of several individuals and organizations were directed toward the improvement of conditions of society in general and the lot of women in particular. Many significant changes occurred during this period, partly as a result of the promotion of social causes by various reform organizations and partly as a result of the passage of specific legislation that made some of the inhumane practices illegal and punishable. The change in public opinion toward women's rights far outpaced the actual legislation that was passed. The growing involvement of women of all social classes in the freedom struggle also gave impetus to the forces of reform in Indian society.

Many of the legislative measures that were proposed failed to pass or were postponed for later consideration, but enough legislation did pass to set a trend in equalizing the status of women with that of men. Even the un-

successful measures reflected a variety and scope that ranged from Viththalbhai Patel's bill to recognize intercaste marriage (1918) to the civil marriage legislation (1911, 1922) that was eventually passed in modified form in 1923. Monogamy and divorce bills introduced at this time also failed initially, with opposition to reform coming from conservative elements of society. The cause of women's education had been greatly enhanced by the government's resolution on educational policy in 1904. Commenting on the lack of encouragement and limited opportunities for educational and professional training of girls, the report cited the noticeably small proportion of females—less than 10 percent of enrollment—in public schools. The pace of change in this area was slow. The percentage of girls attending educational institutions had risen only slightly, from 1.58 percent in 1886 to 2.49 percent in 1901. The founding of Lady Hardinge Medical College in Delhi and the Women's University in Poona in 1916 initiated a new phase in the opportunities available to women.

A number of other progressive measures contributed to the currents of change. These included a law restricting dowries (1916), the establishment of several children's homes following the lead taken by the Indian Women's Association (1923), and the founding of the Birth Control League (1924) to address issues of population control. Equally important was a 1925 measure aimed at curbing the prostitution that flourished under the shelter of *Devadasi*, the traditional institution of temple service. Muslim women took a decisive step when they decided to abolish *purdah* by a resolution adopted at the All India Women's Congress in 1928.

Two acts of legislative reform stand out in the decade of change from 1925 to 1935. The first was the Sarda Act of 1929, which tackled the issue of child marriage. It applied equally to all religious and caste groups and expressly forbade the marriage of girls under the age of fourteen and boys under the age of eighteen. Child marriage was made an offense punishable by imprisonment, a substantial fine, or sometimes both. Anyone identified as performing, directing, or in any way encouraging child marriage was subject to severe penalties. This included parents and any male over the age of twenty-one who was a party to the marriage. This represented a tremendous achievement in the struggle for women's emancipation.

The Government of India Act of 1935 was the second measure that resulted in significant gains for Indian women. Several provisions of the act served to extend the political rights of women. A number of seats were allocated specifically for women in the federal and provincial assemblies and the Federal Council of State. A total of forty-one seats were set aside in the assemblies of eleven provinces. In addition, nine seats were allocated for women in the Federal Assembly and six seats in the Federal Council of State. These numbers may not appear to be large, but their symbolic value was substantial, as an acknowledgment of women's right to represent others and to be represented in government. Women could at last participate in the decision-making process themselves rather than rely on the efforts of male legislators. A further gain was achieved through the amendment of qualifications for exercising the franchise. This enabled more than six million women to exercise their political prerogatives.

SIGNIFICANCE

The immediate impact of these changes was to free women from the confines of religious codes and traditional custom. Through a process of steady consolidation, some of the objectives of the social reformers of the nineteenth century were finally realized. The decade of change represented one significant phase in an ongoing process of social change. The most valuable gain was a recognition that a new social order could not be established while a large proportion of the population continued to occupy a subordinate status. The value of women as a human resource was being acknowledged by enlightened individuals, both British and Indian. Women themselves, through their organizations and through their active participation in the civil disobedience movement for independence, demonstrated their ability to help their own cause. Women of all social classes and religious persuasions set aside their traditional roles to participate in the freedom struggle alongside men, endured imprisonment, and simultaneously continued to organize themselves to deal with women's issues. The role of women in the freedom struggle was both a consequence of and an impetus for social change.

In order to achieve equality, women had to challenge some of the fundamental assumptions underlying the social order as it had functioned for centuries. The patrilineal structure and caste system had drawn their legitimacy from ascribed status. This created closed groups that were ranked in a specific hierarchy and maintained through rules for permissible marriages. Most of these assumptions were challenged by the reforms relating to the position of women in society, as these reforms introduced the validity of achieved status in a traditional culture. This, in turn, presaged the weakening of the caste

system over time. Even the "untouchables" could look to the position taken by women as precedent for change.

The groups that benefited the most were the educated, the urban dwellers, and the upper classes. The poor, the rural inhabitants, and the uneducated continued to lag behind. The success of the reforms cannot therefore be stated in easily measurable terms. Public attitudes and practices far outweighed the specific acts of legislation that were passed. This explains the persistence of some customs despite statutes declaring them to be illegal, and it also explains why women could play an active role in the freedom struggle despite the presence of traditional barriers. Attitudes varied according to social class and education. While the upper and middle classes pressed ahead with reforms, many of the less advantaged required the inspired leadership of individuals such as Mahatma Gandhi. The seeds had already been sown by earlier reformers such as Ram Mohun Roy, founder of the reformist organization the Brahmo Samaj, and Sir William Bentinck, whose anguish at the practice of customs such as *sati* set them apart from their contemporaries. The decade of change saw the realization of their efforts. As a result, some Indian women could aspire to be educators, physicians, scientists, and even prime ministers. Women could reasonably aspire to equal rights in society, but an occasional instance of *sati* was still possible. Social reforms continued to be an important concern.

—*Sai Felicia Krishna-Hensel*

FURTHER READING

Brown, Judith M. *Modern India: The Origins of an Asian Democracy*. 2d ed. Delhi, India: Oxford University Press, 1994. Astute analysis of the foundations of Indian society is helpful in illuminating the background of social reform. Valuable general source.

Forbes, Geraldine. *Women in Modern India*. New York: Cambridge University Press, 1996. Examines the history of women in India from the nineteenth century to after Indian independence. Shows the effects of changes through the accounts of Indian women. Includes illustrations, bibliographic essay, and index.

Majumdar, R. C., ed. *Struggle for Freedom*. Vol. 11 in *The History and Culture of the Indian People*. Mumbai, India: Bharatiya Vidya Bhavan, 1978. One of the most detailed sources available on the history of the freedom struggle from the Indian perspective. Provides comprehensive coverage of social reform in general and women's issues in particular. An invaluable resource for the specialist as well as the general reader.

Majumdar, R. C., H. C. Raychaudhuri, and Kalikinkar Datta. *An Advanced History of India*. London: Macmillan, 1951. One of the best general histories of India, with a level of detail not often found in works of this breadth. Written from the indigenous perspective.

Panikkar, K. M. *The Foundations of New India*. London: Allen & Unwin, 1963. An eminently readable account of the course of modernization in India. Written for the general reader.

Philips, C. H., ed. *The Evolution of India and Pakistan, 1858 to 1947*. Vol. 4 in *Select Documents on the History of India and Pakistan*. London: Oxford University Press, 1962. A well-chosen collection of source materials relating to the formative period in the history of the modern nations of India and Pakistan. A useful reference source for both specialists and interested general readers.

Sarkar, Sumit. *Modern India, 1885-1947*. 8th ed. New York: Macmillan, 2002. History of India includes coverage of changes in women's status.

Spear, Percival. *The Oxford History of Modern India, 1740-1947*. Oxford, England: Oxford University Press, 1978. A fully revised and rewritten version of part 3 of the third edition of the *Oxford History of India* (1958). Concentrates on the process of social change in a modernizing nation. Brilliantly traces the interaction of Western influences and Indian forces as they transformed Indian society.

SEE ALSO: Apr. 28-May 1, 1915: International Congress of Women; Sept. 20, 1917: Canadian Women Gain the Vote; Feb. 6, 1918: British Women Gain the Vote; 1920-1922: Gandhi Leads a Noncooperation Movement; Aug. 26, 1920: U.S. Women Gain the Right to Vote; Mar. 12-Apr. 5, 1930: Gandhi Leads the Salt March; Mar. 5, 1931: India Signs the Delhi Pact.

1925-1979
PAHLAVI SHAHS ATTEMPT TO MODERNIZE IRAN

The numerous social and economic reforms instituted by the modernizing Pahlavi shahs over a period of more than forty years were imposed at the expense of political freedom and social justice.

LOCALE: Iran
CATEGORIES: Civil rights and liberties; human rights; social issues and reform; government and politics

KEY FIGURES

Reza Shah Pahlavi (1878-1944), first ruler of the Pahlavi Dynasty in Iran, r. 1926-1941
Mohammad Reza Shah Pahlavi (1919-1980), shah of Iran, r. 1941-1979
John F. Kennedy (1917-1963), president of the United States, 1961-1963

SUMMARY OF EVENT

On February 21, 1921, General Reza Khan led a coup d'état in Iran, effectively ending the rule of the Qājār Dynasty. By the time of his coronation, in 1926, as the first ruler of the Pahlavi Dynasty, his reform program was well under way. Both Reza Shah Pahlavi (he gave himself the title of shah) and his son, Mohammad Reza Shah Pahlavi, who succeeded him in 1941, believed that Iran should become part of the modern world as quickly as possible. Although Reza Shah repeatedly emphasized the need for Iran to be rid of foreign influence, even rejecting foreign loans, the Pahlavi shahs were convinced that modernization meant Westernization.

The challenges of modernization were great. Iran had experienced little economic development before 1925, and the country was on the verge of bankruptcy when Reza Khan ascended to the throne. There was little centralization of services; a small, ineffective army was trying to keep order; the Muslim clergy's influence was pervasive; and only slightly more than half of the population was educated. The Pahlavi shahs turned Iran around through their policies of nationalism, industrialization, centralization, secularization, and emancipation of women.

One of Reza Shah's first reforms was to establish a centralized bureaucracy. This centralization was further expanded under Mohammad Reza, so that by the mid-1970's, Iran had nineteen ministries with 560,000 civil servants whose authority reached out to all aspects of Iranian life.

Until 1920, there was no national army in Iran. To keep internal order and fend off foreign invasion, Reza Shah created a large army equipped with modern weapons. Mohammad Reza was even more obsessed than his father with having a large, well-equipped army. The Iranian army grew from a force of 23,000 in 1920 to

410,000 in 1977. Mohammad Reza built his regime around the army and used the army to suppress opposition to his regime.

In order to accomplish his goal of creating a unified state, Reza Shah emphasized the importance of the Persian language. Non-Persian languages were forbidden, and schools and printing presses using other languages were closed. Ethnic differences were to be eradicated through the creation of a genuine Iranian identity (modeled on the West). Consequently, the Iranian parliament (Majles) passed the Uniform Dress Law, which made the wearing of Western clothes compulsory. In 1928, Reza Shah ordered every adult male in Iran, with the exception of the clergy, to wear the rounded, peaked Pahlavi cap. Eight years later, he decreed that all men must replace their Pahlavi caps with European felt hats. This law created great opposition among devout Muslims, who found it impossible to pray with the European-style hats on their heads. When Muslims defied the order, troops were dispatched to make sure they obeyed.

Closely related to nationalism were Reza Shah's policies toward the tribes. He considered nomadic tribes, a key group in rural Iran, to be a serious impediment to the creation of a modern state. At the beginning of the twentieth century, Iran's nomadic tribes accounted for almost one-fourth of the total population. Tribal leaders were very powerful and posed a threat to the shah's one-man rule. Consequently, in 1933, Reza Shah embarked on a policy of settling the nomadic tribes in order to bring them under control of the central government. This policy was continued under Mohammad Reza, so that by 1979, the tribal population had dwindled to 1 percent of the total population. Under the policy of forced sedentarization, grazing lands were confiscated, so that tribes were deprived of a means of support, and tribal leaders were often imprisoned and executed.

Reza Shah opened up society to Iranian women. Traditionally, women had been confined to the home, married off at an early age, and rarely given an education. Both shahs are credited with increasing women's opportunities for education, although the benefits of higher education accrued most often to middle- and upper-middle-class urban women.

In 1936, Reza Shah banned women's wearing of the chador (a head-to-foot black cloth covering everything but the face). This law was often implemented mercilessly. Women wearing the chador were not permitted in movie theaters or in public baths, and taxi and bus drivers could be fined for transporting veiled women in their conveyances. After 1935, government officials who re-fused to bring their wives, unveiled, to office parties could be dismissed from their positions. There were even recorded instances of police forcibly ripping off the chadors of women who defied the order.

In 1963, women were permitted to vote and to hold public office, and in 1967 important reforms were made in marriage and divorce law under the Family Protection Law. These changes were violently opposed by the clergy.

The reigns of both shahs were weakened and strained by their relations with the Muslim clergy. Both shahs endeavored to break the power of the religious hierarchy, which often resisted their reforms. From the onset, Reza Shah's policies emphasized creating an Iranian nationalism distinct from Islam. From 1925 to 1928, he replaced sharia (the religious law of Islam) with civil codes modeled on French law. State courts were created, weakening the power of religious courts. The educational system and registration of documents, formerly the province of the clergy, were turned over to secular authorities, depriving many clerics of jobs. General restrictions on religious observance were instituted. Public demonstrations on certain religious holidays were forbidden. Exit visas were denied for those wishing to make religious pilgrimages. The economic strength of the clergy was weakened when the government seized control over the administration of the *vaqfs* (large religious endowments).

When the secular reforms were greeted with violent opposition by the clergy, the shah's army units did not hesitate to use force. Reza Shah himself once entered the shrine at Qom without removing his boots and personally flogged the *mujtahid* (religious leader), who had dared to criticize the queen for removing her veil. Mohammad Reza continued the antagonization of religious authorities begun by his father, seizing control of virtually all religious education, cutting subsidies to the clergy, and replacing the Islamic calendar with a royal calendar.

The bazaars (clusters of small shops, sometimes numbering in the thousands, in particular sections of urban areas, where merchants, moneylenders, and commodity producers do business) played a crucial role in Iran's economy, but Mohammad Reza claimed the bazaars were relics of the past and obstacles to modernization. In actuality, he felt threatened by their independence from the state and their close alliance with the religious elements. With the creation of new companies, the proliferation of modern financial institutions, and the invasion of foreign consumer goods sold in modern supermarkets, the monopoly the bazaars had over the economy was gradually weakened.

Bazaar merchants began to speak out against rapid modernization, infuriating the shah. He embarked on an antiprofiteering campaign to scapegoat bazaars for inflation, and the government planned to build a superhighway right through the Tehran bazaar. To weaken bazaar wholesalers and retailers further, the government created state purchasing corporations for such essentials as wheat, meat, and sugar. Many neighborhood shops were replaced with supermarkets that received cheap bank credit. When economic pressures on the bazaars failed to eliminate them, the government took more drastic steps. During the antiprofiteering campaign of 1975, forty thousand shops were closed and more than eighty thousand bazaar shopkeepers were imprisoned or exiled.

With the creation of new industries, growth exceeded expectations. From 1925 to 1976, Iran's gross national product multiplied seven hundred times, per-capita income two hundred times, and imports almost one thousand times. Although industrial development was important to Iran's modernization, it often led to exploitation of workers under both shahs. Under Mohammad Reza, the state supported workers' demands for higher wages but kept them from creating independent unions. Workers were allowed to enter only state-created labor unions. Savak, an intelligence agency, set up branches in factories to harass workers and suppress strikes, using violence if necessary.

Although Reza Shah pursued a vigorous industrialization policy, his agricultural policy continued traditional practice. Large landlords were allowed to remain in possession of their lands and wealth. By 1941, Reza Shah, who did not have any property before coming to power, possessed 2,670 villages. At the end of his reign, Iran remained basically a semifeudal agricultural system.

It fell to Mohammad Reza to break up the traditional landholding system. In 1963, acting under pressure from U.S. president John F. Kennedy, the shah issued an ambitious program of reforms known as the White Revolution. Particularly noteworthy was the land reform program, through which Mohammad Reza hoped to destroy the influence of the landlords, improve agricultural output, and create a base of support for his regime among the peasants and the working class.

Before land reform, less than 1 percent of the total population owned close to 60 percent of the land under cultivation, and the vast majority of tenants lived at subsistence level. Under the land reform policy, landlords' holdings were cut to a single village. All other holdings were to be sold to farmers who were already tilling the soil. Approximately eight thousand villages, or one-seventh of the total number, were affected by the reforms. Under later phases, farmers were given leasing options and agricultural corporations were established to improve farming methods.

SIGNIFICANCE

The Pahlavi shahs' reforms radically transformed Iran within a relatively short time from a backward Middle Eastern outpost into a thriving modern country. Although the oil flowed, bringing great wealth, and state-of-the-art weapons poured in, the impact of too-rapid modernization eventually tore Iranian society apart and was partially responsible for the revolution in 1979 that overthrew the Pahlavi regime and established an Islamic republic.

The land reform program was a dismal failure. The best land in the country was chopped up into inefficient small pieces, and productivity declined. In the end, only

Mohammad Reza Shah Pahlavi (left) with President Franklin D. Roosevelt in 1943. (Library of Congress)

1925

a small group of peasants benefited from land distribution. Two-thirds of the peasants did not acquire land or received minuscule plots. The majority of the peasants who gained land later lost it because they could not obtain enough credit or because they could not keep up with the rising cost of agricultural production. Peasants were forced to join cooperatives in which they were excluded from making decisions by government bureaucrats who had in fact assumed the role of the former landlords. Richer peasants were soon buying out poorer peasants and creating a new small landlord class. Millions of peasants left the farms and flocked to the cities to become discontented laborers for the new agribusinesses, often living in shantytowns of cheap houses lacking electricity, water, and gas.

Although economic growth was impressive, the political apparatus of the state continued to be underdeveloped and unable to serve the needs of a modern society. The drive for modernization lacked a wide base of support and a prominent ideology. The newly emancipated modern middle class demanded political rights and institutions to channel its views. The shahs refused to grant these, and those who were foolish enough to speak out against the shahs' reforms were brutally suppressed. As alienation to the regime increased, Mohammad Reza began to rely more and more on repression and foreign support. Like his father, Mohammad Reza instituted reforms under a dictatorship backed up by the army and Savak.

The shah's internal policies widened the existing cleavages in society. As some scholars have pointed out, the rapid modernization from above and secularization created two cultures. The upper class and new middle classes became increasingly Westernized and unwilling to understand the traditional and religious values of the peasants and traders in the bazaars. As the pace of social change accelerated and traditional values were frowned upon, the family and ethical values began to disintegrate.

The campaign against the religious authorities begun under the first shah intensified during the latter part of his son's reign. The increasing Westernization and secularization of society, along with suppression of the clerical class and expropriation of clerics' lands, increased the hostility of this group toward the regime and resulted in its alliance with other alienated groups in society to undermine the shah's rule. The shah had failed to realize that the majority of Iranians were attached to the Islamic part of Iranian culture.

The shahs' emphasis on nationalism was contradicted by their dependence on Western values and advisers. As more and more of Western culture was imported, Irani-

ans became increasingly alienated from their roots. Resentment built against the shahs' foreign consultants, who took away jobs, caused rents to soar, and often displayed an acute insensitivity to traditional Iranian cultural mores and religious beliefs. Demands on the government intensified. In the end, by resorting to political repression and overly rapid modernization, Mohammad Reza could not deliver the better life he had promised. He succumbed to a revolution headed by Islamic leader Ayatollah Khomeini and fled Iran in 1979.

—Renée Taft

FURTHER READING

Abrahamian, Ervand. *Iran Between Two Revolutions.* Princeton, N.J.: Princeton University Press, 1982. Analysis of the social bases of politics in Iran focuses on how socioeconomic development gradually transformed the shape of Iranian politics from the late nineteenth century to 1979.

Arjomand, Said Amir. *The Turban for the Crown: The Islamic Revolution in Iran.* New York: Oxford University Press, 1988. Provides an excellent chronology of significant events in Iranian history. Chapters deal with the rise of the modern state, constitutional revolution, formation of a modern bureaucratic state, and the Islamic Revolution. Excellent appendix including tables and charts showing Iranian institutions and economic sectors before and after reforms.

Banani, Amin. *The Modernization of Iran, 1921-1941.* Stanford, Calif.: Stanford University Press, 1961. Examines the reforms instituted by Reza Shah and evaluates the consequences of Westernization in Iran in general. Based primarily on Persian sources.

Cronin, Stephanie, ed. *The Making of Modern Iran: State and Society Under Riza Shah, 1921-1941.* New York: Routledge, 2003. Collection of essays by various scholars reflects the recent revival of interest in the years of Pahlavi rule in Iran. Includes illustrations.

Keddie, Nikki R. *Modern Iran: Roots and Results of Revolution.* New Haven, Conn.: Yale University Press, 2003. Updated and revised version of *Roots of Revolution* (1981) provides an in-depth study of the tensions in Iran between the secularized middle and upper classes and the religiously oriented bazaar class as well as coverage of the aftermath of the revolution. Includes illustrations, select bibliography, and index.

Lenczowski, George, ed. *Iran Under the Pahlavis.* Stanford, Calif.: Hoover Institution Press, 1978. Compilation of articles by a team of international scholars describes and evaluates the changes that occurred in Iran after the Pahlavi Dynasty came to power. The authors are generally favorable to the shahs and conclude that the Pahlavis brought a real revolution.

Reza Shah Pahlavi. *Mission for My Country*. New York: McGraw-Hill, 1961. Autobiography includes the shah's life story and discussion of Iran's social and political problems as well as his views on various issues such as land reform, education, the role of women, and modernization.

SEE ALSO: Oct., 1906-Oct., 1907: Persia Adopts a Constitution; May 26, 1908: Oil Is Discovered in Persia; Apr. 26, 1920: Great Britain and France Sign the San Remo Agreement.

January 1, 1925
BELL LABS IS FORMED

The American Telephone and Telegraph Company's consolidation of the research and development arms of its telephone companies created one of the world's most important and successful industrial laboratories.

LOCALE: New York, New York

CATEGORIES: Organizations and institutions; science and technology

KEY FIGURES

Theodore Newton Vail (1845-1920), American businessman

John J. Carty (1861-1932), American electrical engineer

Harold D. Arnold (1883-1933), American physicist

Frank B. Jewett (1879-1949), American engineer and first president of Bell Labs

Edward B. Craft (1881-1929), American engineer

SUMMARY OF EVENT

The Bell Telephone Company, which was established in July, 1877, was formed around Alexander Graham Bell's valuable patents and was intended to finance his experiments. The company's emphasis on research and development began as soon as the first spoken words were transmitted along a wire. It was clear that telephone transmission could be significantly improved and would have to be improved if it was to become a commercial proposition. The large number of inventors who entered the field of telephonic communication brought instant competition. The industry was dependent on technological innovation.

The telephone business was soon divided between local operating companies and companies that manufactured equipment. The latter usually had the facilities to experiment and test. The first individual to be given the right to make telephones was Charles Williams, in whose machine shop Bell had constructed his first experimental telephones with the assistance of Thomas A. Watson, who was a machinist employed by Williams. As demand for telephones grew, Bell Telephone looked for a larger and better-organized manufacturing arm to replace the several individual manufacturers licensed to make telephones. It approached the Western Electric Manufacturing Company of Chicago, which was formed in 1872 as a manufacturer of telegraphs and had become a major supplier of telephones to competing companies. In 1881, the Bell company bought controlling interest in Western Electric, creating a partnership that was to last for much of the twentieth century. Bell operated the service, and Western Electric made the equipment.

By 1900, Western Electric was carrying out much of the technical development of telephone service. It had departments that carried out testing and tried to solve problems that arose in operations. It had a department devoted to designing new equipment and improving old machines. This still did not constitute industrial research, as defined by pioneers such as General Electric and the Du Pont companies, which set out to investigate new technologies in the hope of finding new products.

The forces that pushed the telephone companies into industrial research were primarily competitive. Although telecommunications is a natural monopoly—that is, service provision is most efficient when there is only one system—there was no hope of this happening in the United States until one system was so technically superior to all the others that it dominated communications. When Bell's central patents began to expire after the turn of the century, competitors entered the telephone business. The strategy adopted to overcome the independent companies was for the Bell organization to dominate the long-distance telephone networks. This goal could be achieved only through a massive influx of capital and the development of a new technology of amplifying and switching telephone messages.

American Telephone and Telegraph (AT&T) was the vehicle for this grand plan. It began as a subsidiary of the original Bell company, but in 1889 the latter transferred all of its assets to AT&T to provide a better base to raise capital. With the support of financier J. P. Morgan, AT&T pursued the policies of experimenting to improve service while buying out independent telephone companies. Theodore Newton Vail was made president of the company in 1907. He energetically pursued the twin goals of universal service and a coast-to-coast telephone network. Vail was committed to research and development, and his tenure as president marked a significant increase in the resources devoted to industrial research.

AT&T had its own research organization, the Engineering Department, which looked into problems connected with telephone transmission, such as sound quality and interference from power lines. Western Electric's Engineering Department was charged with improving the equipment used in the telephone system.

Vail consolidated many of these functions at one large Western Electric laboratory in New York City. He placed the facility under the command of chief engineer John J. Carty, whose major task was to find a method of extending the distance of telephone communications. The Western Electric Engineering Department was provided with the scientists and funds to develop a transcontinental telephone system in time for the Panama-Pacific International Exposition, which was scheduled for 1914.

After examining magnetic and electromagnetic devices, the Western Electric laboratory decided to investigate the potential of the newly invented vacuum tube as a means of amplifying telephone messages. AT&T had purchased the rights to Lee de Forest's "audion" vacuum tube, which was the basis of the experiments. A team of about twenty-five researchers, under the direction of physicist Harold D. Arnold, produced a vastly improved "triode" vacuum tube, which was responsible for the success of the transcontinental telephone service introduced in January, 1915. This work put AT&T on the leading edge of electronic technology and gave it a dominant position in the later exploitation of the many uses of vacuum tubes, including radio receivers and control devices.

On the eve of World War I, the Western Electric Engineering Department was one of the largest industrial research organizations in the world. It had a staff of more than one hundred formally trained scientists and engineers. Its policy of recruiting graduates from the leading universities and technical institutes brought it some of the finest young minds in the country. This policy also represented an investment in basic scientific knowledge

that was to pay dividends in the years to come.

In 1925, AT&T consolidated its research activities through an amalgamation of Western Electric's and AT&T's engineering departments into Bell Telephone Laboratories, commonly known as Bell Labs. Frank B. Jewett, who had worked for Carty on the transcontinental telephone project, was made president of the laboratories. As the name implies, Bell Labs was never concentrated in one place but consisted of several research laboratories working in different parts of the country.

SIGNIFICANCE

The creation of Bell Labs did not change the research activities undertaken by its two parts, nor did it change the location or function of its principal personnel. The research teams stayed in the same laboratories and continued with the projects assigned to them. Several elements of AT&T's Development and Research Laboratory were not incorporated into Bell Labs until the 1930's. AT&T and Western Electric shared ownership of the new organization. What the founding of 1925 achieved was a consolidation of research and development, making it more responsive to corporate control. Formation of a single research entity also provided a greater public profile to this activity. AT&T exploited this profile in advertising and public relations; Bell Labs was soon known around the world as the epitome of industrial research. More than any other laboratory, Bell Labs represented the application of pure science to commercial ends. Every triumph of innovation and Nobel Prize awarded to a researcher served to underline the importance of basic research to the business community.

Bell Labs did not confine its attention to telephone service; it also exploited technological opportunities in other areas. In 1925, it introduced a system of electrical recording of sounds, a technology that was successfully diffused to record companies and to motion-picture studios. This proved that the modern industrial laboratory was a means to develop entirely new products and create new industries.

Bell Labs had undertaken a study of the characteristics of human speech to provide a basis for its research on telephony. Its scientists needed a method to save sound as part of their recording of experiments. Telephone engineers also needed samples of messages for testing. The existing system of sound recording was the acoustical method invented by Thomas Edison in 1877, the phonograph. A team of experimenters under the direction of Joseph Maxfield worked to devise an electrical version of this system, using a microphone invented by another Bell

Labs scientist, E. C. Wente, and the amplification units developed by Arnold.

Maxfield's system of electrical recording was successfully demonstrated to representatives of the record and talking machine industry and soon became standard in recording studios. The project had been initiated by Edward B. Craft, who was second in command under Jewett. Craft persuaded the upper management of AT&T that this technology had applications in the motion-picture industry and received permission to develop a system of talking pictures. Another research team was assigned the task of synchronizing the electrical recording machine with a film camera. The results were first shown to the public in 1926. The opening of *The Jazz Singer* in 1927 marked not only the beginning of the "talkies" but also the entry of the telephone company into the vastly profitable film business. The Western Electric logo seen on numerous old films is a testament to the universal use of this sound recording system.

During the 1930's, Bell Labs undertook a wide range of research in telephone and radio communications, sound recording, electronic switching, amplification, and a host of other subjects. Some of this research had immediate practical applications; some had potential for future use, such as the system of stereo sound recording demonstrated in 1933; and some was basic scientific research with no commercial application, such as the investigation of the conducting properties of certain types of silicon materials. That project was the foundation of the transistor research of the 1940's.

The focus of Bell Labs was widened to cover all aspects of communications. It investigated the possibilities of transmitting images as well as telephone messages, including the transmission of photographs along the wires. It was also one of the first laboratories to experiment with television pictures. This was part of AT&T's strategy to provide video telephone service, through which customers could see as well as hear one another.

During World War II, Bell Labs was devoted to war work, including the development of radar, the pioneer guidance systems for guns and missiles, and synthetic substances to replace strategic materials, such as the rubber substitute polymer microgel. The staff of Bell Labs had grown to about six thousand, all of whom were exempt from military service because of the importance of their contribution to the war effort. In 1941, the Murray Hill, New Jersey, facility was opened; this would become the headquarters of Bell Laboratories.

The postwar years saw Bell Labs' greatest and most publicized success—the invention of the transistor. This was again the work of teams of scientists and the consequence of pathbreaking basic research. John Bardeen and Walter H. Brattain had begun their research into semiconductors as part of a larger project to find a better method of amplification that might replace the fragile and expensive vacuum tube. Their invention of the first point-contact transistor in 1947 was the first step in a long process of forming semiconductors into the switches, amplifiers, and receivers later at the heart of most electronic equipment. Bardeen and Brattain were awarded the Nobel Prize for their work, along with William Shockley, who led the team and produced the first junction transistor in 1951.

Much of the groundwork for these famous inventions had been done in the 1930's and early 1940's. The same could be said for the digital revolution of the 1980's: Bell Labs was a pioneer in the transformation of electrical information into digital codes. The goal was to increase the carrying capacity of telephone wires and reduce crosstalk between messages along the wires, but the applications spread to many other functions and produced many important new products. The combination of basic scientific research and practical engineering produced technology with wide commercial applications and gave the telephone companies an important competitive edge in a new field. Bell Labs continued to work on the frontiers of scientific knowledge with the goal of improving telephone communications.

—*Andre Millard*

Further Reading

Bell Telephone Laboratories. *Facts About Bell Laboratories*. 12th ed. Murray Hill, N.J.: Author, 1982. Brief volume describes the variety of work undertaken by Bell Labs. An essential reference source for any study of the laboratories. Intended for general readers.

Bernstein, Jeremy. *Three Degrees Above Zero: Bell Labs in the Information Age*. New York: Charles Scribner's Sons, 1984. Brief account by a leading science writer provides a clear and easily understood picture of the work of Bell Labs and describes some of its most important research projects.

Brooks, John. *Telephone: The First Hundred Years*. New York: Harper & Row, 1976. Excellent single-volume history of the telephone provides an introduction to the technological development of telephone systems.

Mabon, Prescott C. *Mission Communications: The Story of Bell Laboratories*. Murray Hill, N.J.: Bell Telephone Laboratories, 1975. Provides a good overview of the work of Bell Labs. Written to commemorate the fiftieth anniversary of the founding of Bell Labs, and has a self-congratulatory tone throughout.

McMaster, Susan E. *The Telecommunications Industry.* Westport, Conn.: Greenwood Press, 2002. History of the rise of telecommunications in the United States includes discussion of the roles played by AT&T and Bell Labs. Features glossary, bibliography, and index.

Reich, Leonard S. *The Making of American Industrial Research: Science and Business at GE and Bell, 1876-1926.* 1985. Reprint. New York: Cambridge

University Press, 2002. Scholarly and meticulous account of the early research carried out by the telephone companies. Covers the period up to the formation of Bell Labs. Provides an understanding of the motivation and style of industrial research in the communications industry.

SEE ALSO: 1902: Johnson Duplicates Disc Recordings; Jan. 25, 1915: First Transcontinental Telephone Call Is Made; May 11, 1928: Sound Technology Revolutionizes the Motion-Picture Industry.

January 5, 1925
FIRST FEMALE GOVERNOR IN THE UNITED STATES

With Nellie Tayloe Ross's inauguration, Wyoming became the first U.S. state to have a female governor.

LOCALE: Wyoming
CATEGORIES: Government and politics; women's issues

KEY FIGURES
Nellie Tayloe Ross (1876-1977), governor of Wyoming, 1925-1927
William Bradford Ross (1873-1924), governor of Wyoming, 1922-1924
Eugene J. Sullivan (fl. early twentieth century), American attorney and politician

SUMMARY OF EVENT
The unexpected death of Governor William Bradford Ross on October 2, 1924, provided the opportunity for his wife, Nellie Tayloe Ross, to establish her place in the history of Wyoming and the United States. William Ross, a Democrat, had been elected to a four-year term as governor of Wyoming in November, 1922. His victory resulted from a split in the state's dominant Republican Party between liberals and conservatives. The liberal Republicans decided to support Ross, and thus a Democrat was elected governor of a state where nearly 70 percent of the voters considered themselves to be Republicans. Ross saw himself as a political progressive, but he focused heavily on such traditional Wyoming interests as farm policies and law and order. Although he confronted a solidly Republican state legislature, Ross was a popular governor when he was stricken with appendicitis in late September, 1924. Surgeons removed his appendix, but the surgery brought about a secondary infection that

caused his death on October 2, 1924. Ross's death came as a shock to Wyoming citizens, who poured out their sympathy to Ross's widow. It was primarily this sympathy, and the Democratic Party's wish to take advantage of it, that brought Nellie Tayloe Ross to the nation's attention.

Within days of her husband's funeral, Nellie Ross was beseeched by state Democratic leaders to consider

Nellie Tayloe Ross. (Library of Congress)

fulfilling the remainder of her husband's term. The state's attorney general had ruled that a new governor would need to be elected at the next scheduled general election, which was less than five weeks away. Although she expressed doubts about her ability to carry out the duties of a governor, Ross made no attempt to stop her nomination by the state Democratic convention on October 14.

Nellie Davis Tayloe was born in St. Joseph, Missouri, to parents of considerable wealth and station. She was educated as a kindergarten teacher and taught for a brief time in Omaha, Nebraska, before meeting William Bradford Ross while on a visit to her father's family in Tennessee. A romance quickly developed, and they were married in Omaha in 1902. The new Mrs. Ross then surrendered her teaching position and moved to Wyoming with her politically ambitious husband. As William Ross's career moved forward, Nellie Ross devoted herself to rearing three children (a fourth child died at the age of ten months). She once said that until her husband died the thought of a vocation outside the home never entered her mind.

What Nellie Ross knew about politics came through years of observing her husband's political career. She admitted that she was bereft of political experience, but she believed that she had "unconsciously absorbed" knowledge of what it meant to be chief executive of a state government. Nevertheless, Ross was reluctant to test her understanding of politics in the crucible of an election campaign. She chose instead to remain at home during the days prior to the November 4 election. She was confident that the voters of Wyoming would pay tribute to her husband's memory by electing her. It was left to other Democratic Party leaders to explain that Ross intended to follow the policies initiated by her husband.

The Republican nominee, Eugene J. Sullivan, was a New Hampshire-born attorney. He found it very difficult to campaign against a candidate who was in mourning and who refused to leave her house. Sullivan had close ties with major oil companies, and Democrats repeatedly suggested that whereas Ross would continue her husband's practice of fighting for the "little fellow," Sullivan would support big business interests.

During the three-week campaign, Democrats worked to capitalize on the fact that Wyoming could make history by being the first state to have a female governor. This, they argued, would be in keeping with Wyoming's reputation for granting political rights to women. In 1869, the first legislature of the Wyoming Territory had given women the right to vote and to hold office. (Two

male suffragists had convinced the tiny legislature that providing rights for women would attract more females to the West.) Ross's supporters also used the slogan "Beat Texas to It," a reference to the campaign of Miriam A. "Ma" Ferguson, who was expected to win the election for governor in Texas. Ferguson was elected in Texas (she was also campaigning for an office left vacant by her husband's death), but the inauguration there was scheduled for three weeks later than Wyoming's.

In the last days of the campaign, it was apparent that Ross held the advantage. The Republicans were hurt by Sullivan's association with big business and by the continuing sympathy for Ross generated by her husband's death. Many Republicans joined with Democrats in placing newspaper advertisements supporting Ross. On the eve of the election, an editorial in the *Wyoming Labor Journal* noted that tea parties in the state capitol certainly would be preferable to "Teapot Dome" parties.

The results of the election showed Nellie Tayloe Ross winning handily. She reacted to her victory by pointing out that a peculiarly tragic turn of events had made her governor. Ross reiterated that she would never have sought the governor's office of her own volition. She had taken on the challenge because so many friends had told her that only she could guarantee the attainment of her husband's legislative programs.

Nellie Tayloe Ross served out the remaining two years of William Ross's term and then was defeated in an attempt to gain reelection. Her two years as governor were undistinguished. She found it nearly impossible to work with the Republican-dominated legislature. During the course of the 1926 campaign, in which Ross did take to the stump, she discovered that the sympathy votes she had had in 1924 were no longer there. Women's rights advocates complained that while she was governor Ross had shown no interest in advancing their cause, a charge that Ross did not deny. Republicans who had supported her during her first campaign now gave their votes to their own party's candidate.

Her defeat in 1926 did not end Ross's involvement in politics. The two years in the state capitol had convinced her to become an activist on behalf of the Democratic Party. In 1928, she was vice chair of the Democratic National Convention and seconded the nomination of Alfred Smith for president. In that same year, she moved to Washington, D.C., and directed the national efforts of Democratic women. She was especially prominent in the campaign of Franklin D. Roosevelt in 1932. As a reward for her efforts, Roosevelt appointed her the first female director of the U.S. Mint, a post she held until 1953.

When her duties permitted, Ross wrote political articles for a variety of women's magazines and supervised a large tobacco farm she had purchased in Maryland. Although she had much success as a businesswoman and as a government officeholder, Ross never spoke out forcefully for more opportunities for women.

SIGNIFICANCE

The election of Ross, along with that of Ferguson in Texas, created a stir in the nation's press. Most of the commentary was far from positive. It was widely reported that Ross had achieved election on the basis of sentiment and that she had no political expertise in her own right. There were doubts that Ross or Ferguson would ever carry out anything more constructive than baking a pie or making a bed. A writer for the Consolidated Press Association hoped that Ross would "keep house" for the state by following the "homely virtues of rigid economy, neatness, orderliness, and efficiency." On the other hand, some observers noted that both women had been freely elected and that this had to mean an improved image for women in politics.

Wyoming citizens seemed proud of the fact that the first female governor had been inaugurated in their state; they especially enjoyed the attention Wyoming received in the eastern press. It seemed to confirm that Wyoming really was the "Equality State," an appellation given to Wyoming as a result of the women's suffrage bill passed by the territory's first legislature in 1869. That bill, in fact, gained more favorable interest from feminists across the country than did Ross's election.

The long-range impact of Ross's election on the course of the women's rights movement appears to have been negligible. As T. A. Larson notes in his bicentennial history of Wyoming, the state consistently lagged behind even neighboring states in granting opportunities to women. In the 1970's, the federal government pressured Wyoming to move more swiftly to diminish sexual discrimination. Ross's election to the governor's office did not change basic attitudes toward women in male-dominated Wyoming.

On a national level, there is no way to gauge the effect of Ross's election. Surely her victory showed that in very special circumstances women could be elected to high office. This may well have encouraged other women to pursue political ambitions. The fact remained, however, that even at the end of the twentieth century it was still considered unusual for a woman to be voted into high political office in the United States.

—*Ronald K. Huch*

FURTHER READING

Brown, Dorothy M. *Setting a Course: American Women in the 1920s.* Boston: Twayne, 1987. Comprehensive study by a professor of history at Georgetown University discusses the wide variety of experience among American women in the 1920's, including in the areas of church, politics, education, and work. Features endnotes and index.

Flexner, Eleanor, and Ellen Fitzpatrick. *Century of Struggle: The Woman's Rights Movement in the United States.* Enlarged ed. Cambridge, Mass.: Belknap Press, 1996. Breakthrough book in the study of women's history in the United States recounts the efforts of women to extend their rights and opportunities and especially to gain the franchise. Includes discussion of the considerable achievement of black women under adverse circumstances and gives some attention to Wyoming's role in opening the door to female voters while placing this event in perspective. Includes bibliographical summary, notes, and index.

Gillmore, Inez Haynes. *Angels and Amazons: A Hundred Years of American Women.* Garden City, N.Y.: Doubleday, 1934. A pioneering study, written in a lively style, of the progress of women in the United States from 1833 to 1933. Discusses the struggle for opportunities for women in education, politics, and the workplace, with especially strong coverage of the many organizations formed to advance the cause of women. Perhaps places more importance on Wyoming's extension of suffrage to females in 1869 than is justified. Includes appendix and index.

Gould, Lewis J. *Wyoming: A Political History, 1868-1896.* New Haven, Conn.: Yale University Press, 1968. Well-researched and well-written account of early politics in Wyoming. Discusses the territorial legislature that startled the country by allowing women to vote and to hold office.

Larson, T. A. *Wyoming: A Bicentennial History.* New York: W. W. Norton, 1977. One of the best general histories of Wyoming's politics and culture available. Puts into perspective Wyoming's claim to be the "Equality State." Includes brief but useful discussion of Ross's election.

Marshall, Brenda DeVore, and Molly A. Mayhead, eds. *Navigating Boundaries: The Rhetoric of Women Governors.* New York: Praeger, 2000. Collection of essays examines how women governors in the United States have used discourse to navigate political boundaries. Chapter 3 is devoted to discussion of Ross.

Scheer, Teva J. *Governor Lady: The Life and Times of Nellie Tayloe Ross.* Columbia: University of Missouri Press, 2005. Biography places Ross's political life in the context of her times. Includes bibliography and index.

SEE ALSO: June 12, 1902: Australia Extends Suffrage to Women; Nov. 7, 1916: First Woman Is Elected to the U.S. Congress; 1917: National Woman's Party Is Founded; Sept. 20, 1917: Canadian Women Gain the Vote; Feb. 6, 1918: British Women Gain the Vote; Feb. 14, 1920: League of Women Voters Is Founded; Aug. 26, 1920: U.S. Women Gain the Right to Vote; Feb. 28, 1933: Perkins Becomes First Woman Secretary of Labor.

February 2, 1925
U.S. CONGRESS AUTHORIZES PRIVATE CARRIERS FOR AIRMAIL

By authorizing the awarding of contracts to private operators for airmail carriage, the Kelly Act and its amendments provided the impetus for development of the airline industry in the United States.

ALSO KNOWN AS: Air Mail Act; Kelly Act
LOCALE: Washington, D.C.
CATEGORIES: Laws, acts, and legal history; transportation; trade and commerce; space and aviation

KEY FIGURES

M. Clyde Kelly (1883-1935), U.S. congressman from Pennsylvania
Harry S. New (1858-1937), U.S. postmaster general during Calvin Coolidge's presidential administration
Otto Praeger (1871-1948), second assistant U.S. postmaster general during Woodrow Wilson's presidential administration
Paul Henderson (1884-1951), second assistant U.S. postmaster general during Calvin Coolidge's presidential administration

SUMMARY OF EVENT

From the inception of airmail service in the United States in 1918 until the Air Mail Act of 1925, all aspects of the service, including pilots, airplanes, and facilities, were solely the responsibility of the U.S. Post Office Department, in accordance with that agency's historical support of improvements in the carriage of mail. Even then, the Post Office Department publicly acknowledged that at some point this responsibility should be shifted to the private sector. Postal officials repeatedly stated that the government was not an operating agency and that there never had been any intention on the part of the department to remain in the transportation business.

The success of the Post Office Department's airmail operation created an environment that made it possible for Congress, responding to a strong recommendation from the Post Office Department, to consider the feasibility of relinquishing operational control of airmail service to private carriers. Congressman M. Clyde Kelly, a Republican from Pennsylvania, became convinced that contract service would provide advantages over continued Post Office Department operation. In late 1924, Kelly introduced legislation that called for private bidding for existing airmail routes then being operated by the department.

Kelly's original legislation, the Air Mail Act of 1925, also known as the Kelly Act, authorized the postmaster general to contract with any individual, firm, or corporation for the carriage of airmail by aircraft between points designated by the postmaster general at a rate not to exceed four-fifths of the postage revenues derived. Kelly included this 80 percent provision as a compromise to offset resistance to what some members of Congress perceived as government subsidization.

Following the act's passage, Paul Henderson, then second assistant U.S. postmaster general, indicated that funds would be made available on July 1, at the beginning of the new fiscal year. He added that only those routes that could be operated without loss to the contractors would be awarded.

Bids were advertised in mid-1925, and within three months seventeen bids from ten companies had been received for eight specified routes. Three of the original bidders were removed from consideration because of lack of proof of adequate financial resources. Only five routes were awarded immediately, but by early 1926 the number of awards had risen to twelve. All were feeder routes that linked with the Post Office Department's own transcontinental route. Ford Air Transport, Henry Ford's venture into aviation, became the first private carrier to begin operating when it initiated service on the route between Detroit and Chicago on February 15, 1926. By mid-June, seven more routes were being flown by the new contract carriers, but it was not until April 21 of the following year that the last of the original twelve route awards was activated.

During the first year of contract service, the basis for payment to carriers created recurring operational problems. Because the private operators were paid a percentage of the postal revenues that were derived from the mail they actually carried, the pieces of mail had to be counted individually at each mail bag's point of origination so that the postage totals could be determined and the correct apportionment of funds made to the operators.

The Air Mail Act's first amendment, made in June, 1926, eliminated this problem by revising the payment rate to a per-pound basis. Even more important, the amendment's provisions ended the requirement to relate the carriers' rates of payment to actual postage revenues from mail carried. In essence, Congress no longer required the Post Office Department to guarantee that the service operate on at least a break-even basis. As a result, compensation to private operators could legally exceed postage amounts, and the fledgling industry very quietly began to be subsidized by the government in much the same manner as railroads and steamship lines.

The second amendment, in June, 1928, permitted periodic renegotiation of each carrier's right to operate over its prescribed routes for a period not to exceed ten years. More important, the amendment lowered the airmail postage rate from ten cents per half ounce to five cents per ounce. This rate reduction served to increase significantly not only the total volume of airmail but also the number of users of the service. The primary goal of the Post Office Department in seeking a lower rate was to increase the number of users. The critical first stage of development of commercial air transportation in the United States was now complete. The airline industry had been born and was ready to begin moving out of its infancy.

SIGNIFICANCE

Although the Kelly Act and its two amendments created conditions that enabled commercial air transportation to take hold and develop, it was the Post Office Department that, in 1918, initially set in motion the original attempt at scheduled airmail service, using army pilots and airplanes to fly mail from and to New York City, Philadelphia, and Washington, D.C. Airmail service's subsequent development was made possible by Post Office Department efforts and congressional support through continuing appropriations. Development of airmail service was in keeping with the department's philosophy of providing assistance to new modes of transportation that could be expected to improve the nation's mail service.

At a 1926 Senate subcommittee hearing on postal rate changes, Paul Henderson, who had resigned his position as second assistant postmaster general in 1925 to head the newly formed National Air Transport, one of the original group of Kelly Act contract recipients, suggested that as the government had encouraged railroad building and maintenance of the nation's waterways, it should extend like assistance to aviation. Given this history, it was not surprising that the Post Office Department decided to pioneer the development of airmail service. Otto Praeger, second assistant postmaster general during Woodrow Wilson's presidential administration, was the guiding force behind the development and growth of the Post Office Department's airmail service. As airmail routes gradually were expanded under Praeger's leadership, Congress became interested enough in the benefits and potential that airmail service offered to provide an annual appropriation to support the developing service. Two separate appropriation line items, to support both transcontinental airmail service and expanding night operations, were contained in the Post Office Department's annual budget in the years 1921 to 1927, averaging a combined annual total of approximately $2.5 million.

Although surplus U.S. Army airplanes were made available to the Post Office Department for use in the airmail service, their use was restricted because of virtual obsolescence. Needs of the airmail service began to dictate that aircraft manufacturers, particularly after the Kelly Act's first amendment, begin concentrating their efforts on developing airplanes that could carry a few passengers in addition to mail. This, too, was in keeping with the expressed view of Postmaster General Harry S. New that the contract carriers should begin emphasizing passenger service in order to improve their financial outlook.

Virtually overnight, the Kelly Act created a new industry, that of private airmail operators. Most of the carriers involved in the original twelve route awards, through mergers and acquisitions, eventually formed some of the larger airlines. Colonial Airlines, recipient of Contract Air Mail Route One (CAM 1, New York to Boston), merged with Robertson Aircraft to become the foundation of what would one day be American Airlines. National Air Transport, Varney Air Lines, and Pacific Air Transport eventually joined forces and became

United Air Lines. Western Air Express, recipient of two of the original twelve routes, eventually merged with Transcontinental Air Transport and Maddux Air Lines to form Transcontinental and Western, the forerunner of Trans World Airlines. Florida Airways Corporation grew into Eastern Airlines, and the beginnings of Northwest Airlines can be traced to Charles Dickenson's three-plane operation between Minneapolis and Chicago.

The need for larger and more reliable airplanes stimulated the manufacturing segment of the industry, and it was during this time that first Boeing and later Douglas began to take the lead in aircraft design and manufacture. Within two years after the Kelly Act took effect, a few contract operators were using airplanes capable of carrying two passengers in addition to mail. One year later, three aircraft manufacturers, responding to the increased demand for passenger capacity, were producing trimotor transports capable of carrying eight to ten passengers. The Post Office Department encouraged passenger service growth, the rationale being that more passenger revenue would translate into less subsidization.

Compensation for the contract carrier began to increase markedly as more routes were relinquished by the Post Office Department. For fiscal year 1926-1927, Congress appropriated $2 million for the transport of airmail by contract carriers. For the following year, during which there was major divestment of routes by the Post Office Department, the appropriation jumped to $13.3 million, attributable directly to the provision in the Kelly Act's first amendment that changed the basis of payment to weight rather than number of items and eliminated the requirement of relating compensation payments to actual postage revenues. Annual payments to air carriers continued to increase over the next few years as the public's use of airmail became more commonplace. This increased use resulted directly from the lower postage rate approved by Congress as part of the Kelly Act's second amendment in 1928.

Together, the two amendments accelerated the developmental pace of the new industry. The Kelly Act's first amendment provided that airmail compensation payments be set at a rate not to exceed three dollars per pound of airmail for the first one thousand miles and thirty cents per pound for each one hundred miles beyond the first thousand. Given that the weight of mail carried was now the basis for payment, it followed that the private operators would seek larger aircraft in which to carry the anticipated heavier mail loads. The other important provision of the first amendment eliminated the relationship between compensation and postage, allow-

ing subsidization of the new industry. This ultimately made possible the financing of larger aircraft, which in turn hastened the growth of passenger service. It was during this period that aircraft design and performance technology caught up with the new airlines' needs, with each seeming to spur the other's rapid development.

Both Congress and the Post Office Department believed that further action, including a reduction in the airmail postage rate, could be expected to increase airmail volume even more rapidly, thereby improving the new industry's overall financial outlook. Calvin Coolidge's postmaster general, Harry S. New, already was on record as advocating increased emphasis on passenger service so that marginal operators could become profitable, but this added dimension would require a heavy financial outlay by the private carriers for a new generation of aircraft.

The amendment's changing of payments to a weight basis led to some enterprising activities by some of the carriers. For example, equipment and spare parts, normally shipped by carriers on their own aircraft when space was available and airplanes could take the extra weight, now were mailed to their destinations. The airlines were being paid to carry their own freight. The second amendment did not change the basis for payment, but it did allow for periodic renegotiation of contracted rates and the extension of route authorities for up to ten years.

Neither of these provisions was as important to the air carriers as the airmail postage rate reduction. Airmail had become a bargain, and public use of the service grew rapidly, so much so that some carriers were forced to curtail passenger service temporarily to accommodate burgeoning airmail loads. In the first month of operation under the lower rate, airmail volume increased 95 percent.

Through 1926 and 1927, the Post Office Department continued the orderly and gradual process of relinquishing its remaining airmail routes, the last of which was flown by the department on September 9, 1927. The purpose of the Kelly Act had been fulfilled.

—*James D. Matthews*

FURTHER READING

Christy, J., and L. R. Cook. *American Aviation: An Illustrated History.* 2d ed. Blue Ridge Summit, Pa.: TAB Books, 1994. Offers a panoramic view of the evolution of American aviation. Focuses primarily on the military but contains some interesting material on early airmail service and the beginnings of the airline system. Includes many photographs.

Johnson, Robert E. *Airway One*. Chicago: Lakeside Press, 1974. Interesting corporate narrative authored by a member of top management at United Airlines (1929-1972). Includes a fascinating look at United's developmental years, together with its predecessors that began operating after passage of the Kelly Act.

Kane, Robert M. *Air Transportation*. 14th ed. Dubuque, Iowa: Kendall/Hunt, 2002. Undergraduate textbook provides a section on history that includes excellent coverage of the early airmail days and the Kelly Act's ramifications. Material on subsequent aviation legislation nicely supplements earlier coverage.

Loening, Grover. *Takeoff into Greatness*. New York: G. P. Putnam's Sons, 1968. Fascinating autobiography by one of the Wright brothers' pupils, who established himself as one of the leaders in aircraft design and manufacture during the 1920's. Includes interesting recollections of early airmail operations, with details, some technical, on the first group of private airmail carriers.

Wells, Alexander T., and John G. Wensveen. *Air Transportation: A Management Perspective*. 5th ed. Monterey, Calif.: Brooks/Cole, 2003. Textbook aimed at undergraduates includes a brief but thorough discussion of contract airmail service and the original twelve contract airmail routes. Presents interesting information on the competition in the early 1930's between Douglas, with its DC-2, and Boeing, with its B-247.

SEE ALSO: Dec. 17, 1903: Wright Brothers' First Flight; July 25, 1909: First Airplane Flight Across the English Channel; Sept. 8, 1920: U.S. Post Office Begins Transcontinental Airmail Delivery; Nov. 20, 1920: Formation of Qantas Airlines; May 20, 1926: Air Commerce Act Creates a Federal Airways System; June 25, 1936: The DC-3 Opens a New Era of Air Travel; June 30, 1940: Congress Centralizes Regulation of U.S. Commercial Air Traffic.

February 21, 1925
ROSS FOUNDS *THE NEW YORKER*

The New Yorker set standards of style for other literary magazines, helped to advance the careers of many significant American authors, and powerfully affected American literature in the twentieth century.

LOCALE: New York, New York
CATEGORIES: Publishing and journalism; literature

KEY FIGURES
Harold W. Ross (1892-1951), American journalist and editor
Jane Grant (1895-1972), American journalist and wife of Harold W. Ross
Peter Arno (1904-1968), American cartoonist
E. B. White (1899-1985), American essayist
James Thurber (1894-1961), American cartoonist and writer
Katharine Sergeant White (1892-1977), literary editor and later managing editor of *The New Yorker*

SUMMARY OF EVENT
On February 21, 1925, a new magazine of reporting, humor, fiction, and criticism hit the newsstands of New York. Initially unimpressive, *The New Yorker* seemed destined to be stillborn. Few could have guessed that it would soon attract a large, sophisticated readership, publish the work of some of the most talented authors in the United States, and significantly influence the nation's literary standards and tastes.

The eventual success of *The New Yorker* was in large part the result of the work of its founder and first editor, Harold W. Ross. Ross was born in 1892 in Aspen, Colorado, and moved with his parents to Salt Lake City when he was seven years old. After quitting high school to take a job with the *Salt Lake City Tribune*, Ross worked for newspapers in Sacramento, Atlanta, Panama City, New Orleans, and San Francisco. During World War I, he edited *Stars and Stripes*, a newspaper published in Paris for American servicemen.

After the war ended, Ross successively edited three different magazines in New York City: *Home Sector* (a stateside version of *Stars and Stripes*), the house organ of the American Legion, and the humor magazine *Judge*. In 1920, Ross married journalist Jane Grant, and during the early years of their marriage they frequently discussed ideas for various kinds of new magazines.

The publication of *Yank Talk*, a collection of jokes from *Stars and Stripes*, had provided the Rosses with twenty-five thousand dollars to invest in a new magazine. Believing that such a venture would require at least fifty thousand dollars, Harold Ross appealed to Raoul Fleischmann, the heir to a yeast and baking fortune whom Ross knew from their mutual association with the so-called Algonquin Round Table, a group of prominent New York literati. Arguing that the older humor magazines attempted to reach too broad an audience, Ross proposed to create a magazine for a sophisticated and educated urban elite, primarily in New York City. Looking for a creative outlet, Fleischmann agreed to help finance the project, an investment that by 1928 grew to more than half a million dollars.

Ross's prospectus explained that the magazine would be "a reflection in word and picture of metropolitan life" that would not appeal to "the old lady in Dubuque." To be characterized by "wit and satire," *The New Yorker* would be "entertaining and informative." The magazine would cover contemporary events, people of interest, amusements, and arts. It would include reviews of books, films, and plays, prose and verse, editorials, caricatures, sketches, cartoons, and humorous drawings. Ross planned to employ the best features of earlier "smart" magazines such as *Smart Set* and *Vanity Fair* and of the humor weeklies, but he resolved to avoid their weaknesses, such as stale jokes and dreary visual formats.

Although this prospectus was an accurate description of what *The New Yorker* would soon become, the issues produced during the first year were not of high quality. Fifteen thousand readers paid fifteen cents per copy to read the original issue, which appeared on February 21, 1925. Its thirty-six pages included six pages of ads; two pages of short news items about life in New York; brief analyses of music, books, and films; a profile of an opera impresario; sketches; satirical drawings; and cartoons. By April of 1925, the magazine's circulation had dropped to eight thousand an issue, and the enterprise was losing eight thousand dollars a week. Some ridiculed the magazine; most simply ignored it. Contrary to Ross's expectations, his friends from the Algonquin Round Table initially provided little material, and Ross, who could not write original copy, struggled to attract publishable work and to develop a winning formula. He scoured the city for talent, placing notices on bulletin boards, examining other publications, and calling everyone he knew. In May, Ross, Fleischmann, and two advisers met at the Princeton Club. Discouraged by the magazine's lack of success and his financial losses, Fleischmann almost decided to pull the plug on the venture, but at the last moment he relented.

By the fall of 1925, advertising revenues had increased slightly, but the magazine's existence was still precarious. An article titled "Why We Go to Cabarets," by Ellin Mackay, appeared in the November 28, 1925, issue and helped *The New Yorker* turn the corner. Although the article was poorly written, its thesis was rather shocking: New York debutantes went to cabarets to meet men who interested them because the men they met at high-society functions were boring. Discussed by *The New York Times*, the article stirred considerable controversy and brought *The New Yorker* to the attention of the Park Avenue set. By the end of 1925, both the advertising revenues and circulation of the magazine had risen substantially. Although *The New Yorker* did not earn a profit until 1928, its survival had been assured.

Although hundreds of artists, writers, and editors passed through the magazine's editorial offices during its early years, several individuals played key roles. The artwork, primarily because of the direction of Rea Irvin and the drawings of Peter Arno, was superior to the writing in the magazine. The most important writers to join *The New Yorker* in its formative period were E. B. White and James Thurber. Through his clear, precise, graceful prose, White helped to establish the style of the magazine, and he wrote two of its major departments, "The Talk of the Town" and "News and Comments." Thurber's comic writing and his cartoons (filled with strange dogs, amused seals, frustrated men, and predatory women) set a new standard for magazine humor. As a literary editor and then as managing editor, Katharine Sergeant White did much to promote staff harmony and to produce a well-written magazine.

SIGNIFICANCE

The New Yorker emerged after 1930 as the leading American magazine of literature, humor, and cultural analysis. Its refined, literate style of writing was widely applauded, admired, and imitated. Many prominent American authors and artists furthered their careers through the magazine's pages. *The New Yorker* elevated the character of American humor, developed a new approach to magazine biography, and followed high standards of investigative reporting. The style of *The New Yorker* was especially evident in its compelling short stories and beautifully polished essays. In all these ways, the magazine significantly influenced American journalism.

The New Yorker owed its success primarily to Harold Ross's outstanding editorial ability and leadership. Ross did not seem to possess either the background or the personality needed to create or direct an urbane, witty, sophisticated literary magazine intended for New York's upper crust. Lacking formal education, ignorant about many important facts, an explosive man who frequently lost his temper and used profanity, Ross was arrogant, aloof, tactless, and rude. Moreover, he could not write

THURBER ON ROSS

In his memoir about his years working with Harold W. Ross at The New Yorker, *James Thurber discusses the editor's famous concern for accuracy:*

The carelessness and confusion of the first two years . . . are undoubtedly responsible for Ross's later intense dedication to precision, order, and system. He studied the New York Telephone Company's system of verifying names and numbers in its directories, and used to say that, despite the company's careful checking, it had never got out a phone book with fewer than three mistakes. He found out about the *Saturday Evening Post*'s checking department, which he said consisted of seven women who checked in turn every fact, name, and date. He must have set up a dozen different systems, during my years with him, for keeping track of manuscripts and verifying facts. If the slightest thing went wrong, he would bawl, "The system's fallen down!"

He lived always in the wistful hope of getting out a magazine each week without a single mistake. His checking department became famous, in the trade, for a precision that sometimes leaned over backward. A checker once said to me, "If you mention the Empire State Building in a Talk piece, Ross isn't satisfied it's still there until we call up and verify it." When Robert Coates, in a book review, said that [William] Faulkner sometimes seemed to write about the woodland of Weir instead of the American South, checkers ransacked postal guides, maps, and other sources looking for the Weir that existed only in the imagination of Edgar Allan Poe.

Source: James Thurber, *The Years with Ross* (Boston: Little, Brown, 1959).

---

as diverse as Nicholas Murray Butler, W. C. Fields, Henry R. Luce, Cecil B. DeMille, Jimmy Walker, and Carl Sandburg.

Another of Ross's contributions was his recognition that the best way to attract advertising dollars was to have a well-defined audience that could be easily targeted. *The New Yorker* gained large revenues from advertising and pioneered in advertising craftsmanship. The magazine's advertisements have often been read with as much care and pleasure as have its commentaries and articles.

In addition, Ross's painstaking editorial method helped to produce *The New Yorker*'s lucid, suave, informative, and humorous prose style. He meticulously edited all the contents of each issue, demanding factual accuracy and complete clarity. Ross's passion for precision led him to organize a checking system that closely examined all facts printed in the magazine. Often his notes, complaints, questions, and directions were as long as the printer's galleys themselves. William Shawn, Ross's successor, who served as editor of the magazine from 1952 until 1987, has written that Ross's editorial queries "influenced writers and other editors, set technical and literary standards, established a canon of taste, and laid the basis for a tradition of good writing." Ross's editorial style was somewhat overbearing, but he knew how to sift wheat from chaff, and he was willing to give way when he knew that others were better informed than he was.

Many of the best American writers, humorists, and artists have worked for *The New Yorker* since its founding. Among the literary greats who have written for the publication are Sherwood Anderson, James Baldwin, Rachel Carson, John Cheever, F. Scott Fitzgerald, Ernest Hemingway, Lewis Mumford, Irwin Shaw, John Updike, Rebecca West, and Edmund Wilson. Truman Capote, John O'Hara, and J. D. Salinger each had more than one hundred pieces published in the magazine. By the 1930's, most of the leading humorists in the United States were contributing to *The New Yorker*, including Ring Lardner, Robert Benchley, Ogden Nash, Dorothy Parker, Frank Sullivan, Clarence Day, and H. L. Mencken. The magazine also originated the one-line cartoon. Drawn by such artists as Gardner Rea, Gluyas Williams, Helen Hokinson, Whitey Darrow, Jr., and Charles Addams, these witty cartoons focused on business, the sexes, politics, and the pretensions of the upper middle class.

copy, but he shaped the character of *The New Yorker*, established its basic policies and principles, assembled a talented team of writers, artists, and contributors, guided the magazine through its formative years, and meticulously edited it for twenty-seven years.

Ross also continually experimented with the magazine's format until he found the best blend of layout, fiction, commentary, reviews, and art. The centerpiece of the magazine became its regular departments, especially "Goings on About Town," a thorough guide to the city's sports, films, shows, concerts, museums, and nightclubs; "On and Off the Avenue," a shopper's guide; and "The Talk of the Town," a collection of narratives, anecdotes, essays, and quips. Profiles also became an important aspect of *The New Yorker*. Over the years, these biographical sketches of industrial leaders, writers, actors, politicians, and other interesting personalities featured people

Since the mid-1930's, *The New Yorker* has been, in the words of George H. Douglas, "the quintessential American smart magazine, the one against which, today, all the others are judged." Skillful editing, careful planning, and graceful writing combined to make *The New Yorker* instructive, amusing, and entertaining. In 1985, the Fleischmann family, which had owned *The New Yorker* since its inception, sold it to the Newhouse media empire, but the magazine continued to serve as the nation's leading arbiter of literary taste. In the early twenty-first century, American college students are taught to emulate the writing style of *The New Yorker*; aspiring writers look to it for inspiration. As Douglas notes, the magazine "has enjoyed a long and enviable history and an enduring popularity and mystique that are probably unequaled among American magazines."

—*Gary Scott Smith*

FURTHER READING

Bryan, J., III. *Merry Gentlemen (and One Lady)*. New York: Atheneum, 1985. Memoir presents humorous profiles of fourteen writers who were connected in one way or another with the Algonquin Round Table and with *The New Yorker* in its early years. Among those profiled are Robert Benchley, Finis Farr, Dorothy Parker, and S. J. Perelman.

Douglas, George H. *The Smart Magazines*. Hamden, Conn.: Archon Books, 1991. Analysis of various magazines of literature, culture, and humor, including *Vanity Fair*, *Smart Set*, *Life*, and *Judge*. Provides an excellent brief account of the early history of *The New Yorker*; describes the context in which the magazine arose, matured, and achieved greatness as well as the personality, style, and contribution of its founder.

Gill, Brendan. *Here at "The New Yorker."* 1975. Reprint. New York: Da Capo Press, 1997. Illuminating account of the magazine by a writer who had spent almost forty years on its staff at the time this book was first published. Insider's view of colleagues, artists, and contributors discusses their idiosyncrasies and their attitudes about fame, literature, money, and one another. Filled with funny stories. Compares and contrasts the long-running regimes of the magazine's two most influential editors, Harold Ross and William Shawn.

Grant, Jane. *Ross, "The New Yorker," and Me*. New York: Reynal, 1968. Memoir by Ross's wife provides more information on New York literati and the flavor of the 1920's than it does on Ross's editorship of *The New Yorker*.

Kramer, Dale. *Ross and "The New Yorker."* Garden City, N.Y.: Doubleday, 1951. One of the best sources of information about Ross's founding and editing of the magazine. Presents a detailed and at times entertaining account of the history and policies of *The New Yorker*, filled with amusing anecdotes and interesting facts.

Kunkel, Thomas. *Genius in Disguise: Harold Ross of "The New Yorker."* New York: Random House, 1995. Comprehensive biography of Ross also describes the history of *The New Yorker*. Includes photographs, selected bibliography, and index.

_____, ed. *Letters from the Editor: "The New Yorker"'s Harold Ross*. New York: Modern Library, 2000. Collection of Ross's letters reveals his personality while providing information unavailable elsewhere regarding the founding and nurturing of *The New Yorker*. Includes index.

Mahon, Gigi. *The Last Days of "The New Yorker."* New York: McGraw-Hill, 1988. An account of events leading to the sale of the magazine to S. I. Newhouse in 1985. Concludes that the sale represented the triumph of business interests over editorial integrity. Focuses primarily on events of the 1980's but includes a brief description of the magazine's founding and early days.

Thurber, James. *The Years with Ross*. 1959. Reprint. New York: Harper Perennial, 2001. Personal, highly anecdotal account of Ross's character and editorial style based on Thurber's own memory, letters, and contributions from colleagues at *The New Yorker*. Discusses the tensions and feuds between Ross and his staff.

SEE ALSO: Nov. 7, 1914: Lippmann Helps to Establish *The New Republic*; Sept. 15, 1917: *Forbes* Magazine Is Founded; Feb., 1922: *Reader's Digest* Is Founded; Mar. 3, 1923: Luce Founds *Time* Magazine; Feb., 1930: Luce Founds *Fortune* Magazine; Nov. 23, 1936: Luce Launches *Life* Magazine.

February 28, 1925

CORRUPT PRACTICES ACT LIMITS POLITICAL CONTRIBUTIONS

The Federal Corrupt Practices Act of 1925 served a symbolic purpose but proved to be inadequate in regulating political financing in the United States.

LOCALE: Washington, D.C.

CATEGORIES: Business and labor; laws, acts, and legal history; government and politics

KEY FIGURES

Theodore Roosevelt (1858-1919), president of the United States, 1901-1909

Marcus A. Hanna (1837-1904), American industrial and political leader

Boies Penrose (1860-1921), American politician

Henry Ford (1863-1947), American industrial leader

Truman Handy Newberry (1864-1945), American politician

Carl A. Hatch (1889-1963), U.S. senator from New Mexico

SUMMARY OF EVENT

Political parties are generally credited with making the U.S. democracy work. Democracy entails parties' competition for an ever-increasing number of offices by selecting candidates and then aiding their campaigns. At no time in the American past, however, has the general electorate been prepared to pay for the privilege of nominally belonging to or voting for a political party. The competition for political offices, however, almost year by year has become more expensive for parties and their candidates. Consequently, combinations of ingenuity and loosely defined corruption persistently marked attempts by parties and politicians to pay for the very party mechanisms that made democracy a viable form of governance. One price paid for this has been widespread public cynicism and periodic public condemnations of party and campaign financing.

Until after the Civil War, political candidates usually were men of sufficient means to contribute in one fashion or another to their own and to their party's struggles at the polls. By the 1930's, as the "spoils system" began to characterize office seeking, officeholders, whether elected or appointed, were expected to have their salaries "taxed" by party leaders to finance party operations.

America's spectacular leap to world preeminence in industry in the half century after 1865 was marked by the rise of the corporation. Corporate influence quickly penetrated the realm of politics, where it served its interests by funding candidates and parties. On the local level, men such as New York City politician William Marcy "Boss" Tweed not only looted the treasuries with an entrepreneurial panache entirely their own but also allied themselves with business interests. The phenomenon was national. Pennsylvania's Boies Penrose, the state's political boss for years, was famed for encouraging business and corporate leaders to pay the toll for his party's candidates and elections. Businessmen who did not cooperate faced "sandbag" legislation that would cost them heavily. Inevitably, the crude couplings of politics and business emerged as a factor in congressional and presidential elections. Ohio's Marcus A. Hanna, a wealthy industrialist in his own right, converted much of the corporate world into a money machine for an always money-hungry Republican Party. His fund-raising in William McKinley's presidential campaign against William Jennings Bryan was a landmark in American political financing.

A few years later, although it ran contrary to his principles, President Theodore Roosevelt was accurately accused of receiving secret corporate funds to aid his election. By way of mitigation, Roosevelt called for the public funding of elections. In 1907, Congress passed the Tillman Act, which had been under consideration since 1902. The act made it unlawful for corporations or national banks to make political contributions to candidates for any federal office.

With Progressive reformism in full flood, Congress enacted the Federal Corrupt Practices Act of 1910, requiring every political committee that in two or more states attempted to influence or influenced the results of elections to the House of Representatives to file names of contributors and recipients with the clerk of the House. In 1911, similar legislation was extended to Senate elections, and candidates for all congressional seats were obliged to file financial reports. In addition, limitations were placed on candidates' spending for House and Senate seats.

The scandals tainting the administration of President Warren G. Harding, Teapot Dome prominent among them, encouraged Congress to enact the Federal Corrupt Practices Act of 1925 (FCPA). Until passage of the Federal Election Campaign Act (FECA) of 1971, the FCPA operated as the country's basic statute on political financing.

Seeking to regulate campaign spending and calling for disclosures of receipts and expenditures by congressional candidates, the FCPA also revised existing ceilings on expenditures. Bans on political contributions by national banks and by corporations, a major feature of the 1907 Tillman Act, were also embodied in the new legislation. So, too, were prohibitions against candidates or parties soliciting campaign funds from federal employees. Barring states prescribing lower ceilings, Senate candidates were allowed to spend $10,000 and House candidates $5,000 on their campaigns. Reports on campaign financing were required in addition, and giving or taking money for anyone's vote was made illegal. Such restrictions were limited to general election campaigns, as congressional power to regulate the fairly new practice of primary elections had not yet been tested in the courts. Few historians, even of the 1920's, mentioned the 1925 act, for good reason. As campaign costs were rising rapidly at all levels and just as the new medium of radio presented candidates with novel opportunities for campaigning, the costs of running parties and political campaigns had begun to soar. Law and political reality were thus starkly juxtaposed.

SIGNIFICANCE

Experts commenting on the FCPA have consistently drawn attention to its numerous deficiencies. On its face, the FCPA was a sop to public opinion rather than a serious attempt to reform party and campaign election spending. It was riddled with loopholes and contained no enforcement provisions. It also left reportage of spending by candidates and by parties incomplete and indicative only. Finance reports did not have to be presented publicly, and the act included no mandates for reviewing them for accuracy. Contributions or expenditures in the critical instances of presidential and congressional primary campaigns, as well as spending intended to fuel presidential nominations, did not fall within the act.

Excluded by the act as well was money contributed to or spent by political committees whose activities were confined solely to one state and committees that were not literal affiliates of parties. Thus political committees were free to solicit and spend campaign contributions at will. These committees were relatively innocuous during the 1920's and 1930's, but after the 1940's, in the form of political action committees (PACs), they became extremely important, even integral, parts of election financing. The activities of PACs allowed candidates to disavow "knowledge and consent" of committees' fund-raising machinations in their behalf. Candidates evaded spending limitations imposed by the FCPA by having PACs spend for them.

Because of the importance of primary elections, particularly after passage of the Seventeenth Amendment (1913), which called for popular election of U.S. senators, the exclusion of primaries from the FCPA proved to be a major deficiency. In this regard, the defect was attributable not to Congress but to the U.S. Supreme Court. The matter had come to issue in 1921 as the result of an election contest between one of America's folk heroes and leading industrialists, Henry Ford, and Truman Handy Newberry. Ford lost to Republican Newberry in the general election for U.S. senator in 1918. Newberry proceeded to take his Senate seat. Ford, however, charged Newberry with having exceeded the $10,000 spending limit set by 1911 amendments to the Tillman Act. Initially, Newberry was convicted, but in 1921, on appeal, a divided Supreme Court ruled the primaries were not "elections" as construed by the Tillman Act. The decision obscured Congress's right to regulate primary nominations and in fact was one of the factors that motivated Congress to enact the FCPA in 1925.

Nevertheless, with the Court ruling in mind, Congress shied away from the regulation of primary financing by not requiring accounts either of receipts or of expenditures. In many states, however, a candidate's victory in the primary was tantamount to election. Not surprisingly, no House or Senate candidate was ever prosecuted for violations of the FCPA, despite, as experts have noted, general knowledge that campaign contributions and expenditures wildly exceeded legal limits.

After a special Senate Committee on Privileges and Elections reviewed the campaign finances of two senators-elect in 1927, the men were refused their Senate seats. In one instance, the Senate Committee discovered that proponents of Philadelphia's Republican political boss, William Vare, in seeking to win a Republican factional fight for nomination to a Senate seat, had spent $785,000, or $760,000 over the legal limit. In the other case, Republican William B. McKinley had expended $500,000 in a primary renomination effort, while his ultimately successful challenger, Republican Frank L. Smith, had spent $450,000 to win. Smith's democratic opponent, on the other hand, had not exceeded the $25,000 limit. Smith was not prosecuted, but his Democratic opponent was not declared a victor.

The Vare and Smith cases were distinguished only in that they revealed the commonplace. Politicians faced rising campaign costs in all quadrants, and their hunger for funds was endless. Veteran political reporters such as Frank R. Kent of the *Baltimore Sun* recorded that no law effectively regulating campaign fund-raising or expenditures "has been enacted through which politicians cannot drive a four-horse team." Implicit was the belief that such a law never would be enacted. Wealthy contributors along with Prohibition-enriched gangsters such as Al Capone ignored the FCPA. So, too, did special interests such as the Anti-Saloon League and the Methodist-backed Southern Anti-Smith Democrats, in company with hundreds of other cause-oriented groups.

Several changes, some observers believed for the better, occurred during the 1930's and 1940's. The Supreme Court ruled in January, 1934, in *Burroughs and Cannon v. United States,* that the FCPA did apply to elections of presidential electors, thereby implicitly acknowledging that federal regulation of the financing of congressional elections was also permissible. To that degree, the Court had overruled its 1927 decision in *Newberry v. United States.* Furthermore, in 1939, the Clean Politics Act sponsored by New Mexico's Senator Carl A. Hatch (frequently known as the Hatch Act) amended campaign finance laws with several new restrictions. The Hatch Act barred federal employees from participation in national politics and further prohibited the collection of political contributions from anyone receiving federal (Depression-related) relief funds.

Amendments to the Hatch Act in 1940 further barred federal contractors, whether individuals or companies, from contributing to any political committees, including PACs, or to any candidates. In addition, the amended act asserted Congress's authority over regulation of primary elections of candidates for federal office, limiting financial contributions to federal candidates or political committees to $5,000 per year. A ceiling of $3 million, moreover, was placed over the annual expenditures of political committees operating in two or more states.

Well-intentioned law, however, effected little positive change. In 1967, President Lyndon B. Johnson, his own political career revealing countless examples of dubious and unlawful campaign financing, described the FCPA, the Hatch Act, and similar legislation as inadequate in scope, obsolete from the outset, and more loophole than law. Only in 1971, with congressional passage of the Federal Election Campaign Act, were serious attempts renewed to rectify the endemic and epidemic illegalities associated with political financing. As experts noted, although money did not invariably win elections, the costs of democracy were high and the morality involved was low. New legislation, however, breeds new means of controverting the spirit of the law, and the growth of soft-money contributions by political groups led to the passage of the Bipartisan Campaign Reform Act of 2002 (also known as the McCain-Feingold Act). This act actually did little to stop the resurgence of soft money, given the loophole created for 527 organizations, such as unions, which could continue to raise large sums for issue-oriented advertising by groups technically unconnected to any party or to any candidate's official campaign. Another reform measure bowed before the logic of expensive and often bitter political contests.

—*Clifton K. Yearley*

FURTHER READING

Alexander, Herbert E. *Money in Politics.* Washington, D.C.: Public Affairs Press, 1972. Clear, authoritative account by a former director of the Citizens' Research Foundation and executive director of President John F. Kennedy's committee on campaign costs. Chapter 12 deals with reform efforts.

Drew, Elizabeth. *Politics and Money.* New York: Macmillan, 1983. Briefly and incisively traces the road to corruption paved by political financing. Drawn from the author's pithy columns on the Washington scene in *The New Yorker.* Keen, accurate, impressionistic reporting.

Gierzynski, Anthony. *Money Rules: Financing Elections in America.* Boulder, Colo.: Westview Press, 2000. Provides a brief history of attempts to regulate campaign financing in the United States and discusses the long-term impacts of the failure of lawmakers to establish any real limits on campaign spending. Includes glossary, references, and index.

Heard, Alexander. *The Costs of Democracy.* Chapel Hill: University of North Carolina Press, 1960. Classic work provides a reminder of the price Americans pay for political spectacle.

Malbin, Michael J., ed. *Parties, Interest Groups, and Campaign Finance Laws.* Washington, D.C.: American Enterprise Institute for Public Policy Research, 1980. Collection of symposium essays and discussion by many experts in the field of political financing. Updates materials on the FCPA. Valuable source of information on PACs since the 1940's.

Mutch, Robert E. *Campaigns, Congress, and Courts.* New York: Praeger, 1988. One of the best works in the field; informed and clearly presented. Provides fresh perspectives and reflections not only on the FCPA but also on American experiences with political financing.

Smith, Bradley. *Unfree Speech: The Folly of Campaign Finance Reform.* Princeton, N.J.: Princeton University Press, 2001. Argues for repeal of all campaign finance regulations, asserting that they violate free-speech rights and are in any case doomed to failure. Chapter 2 presents a brief discussion of the history of attempts to regulate campaign financing. Includes bibliography and index.

Sorauf, Frank J. *Money in American Elections.* Glenview, Ill.: Scott, Foresman/Little, Brown College Division, 1988. Excellent, clearly written work by a political scientist. The approach is historical, with emphasis on the period after the 1960's. Covers state as well as federal law.

Thayer, George. *Who Shakes the Money Tree?* New York: Simon & Schuster, 1973. A breezy, enjoyable review of American campaign financing practices from 1789 to the early 1970's. Provides colorful details while maintaining a high standard of accuracy.

SEE ALSO: Sept. 14, 1901: Theodore Roosevelt Becomes U.S. President; May 12-Oct. 23, 1902: Anthracite Coal Strike; Aug.-Dec., 1905: Armstrong Committee Examines the Insurance Industry; Nov. 5, 1918-Nov. 2, 1920: Republican Resurgence Ends America's Progressive Era.

Spring, 1925
PAULI FORMULATES THE EXCLUSION PRINCIPLE

Wolfgang Pauli significantly advanced the understanding of the structure of the atom by establishing the principle that electrons are elementary particles of the "antisocial" type.

LOCALE: Hamburg, Germany
CATEGORIES: Science and technology; physics

KEY FIGURES

Wolfgang Pauli (1900-1958), Austrian theoretical physicist
Pieter Zeeman (1865-1943), Dutch physicist
Arnold Sommerfeld (1868-1951), German theoretical physicist
Niels Bohr (1885-1962), Danish theoretical physicist
Johannes Robert Rydberg (1854-1919), Swedish physicist
Alfred Landé (1888-1975), German American physicist
Edmund C. Stoner (1899-1968), English physicist

SUMMARY OF EVENT

Niels Bohr's pioneering quantum model of the atom explained the spectral systems of the hydrogen atom. Logically, physicists, including Bohr, directed their efforts toward extending the theoretical success to more complex atoms. From chemical study, it was concluded that every chemical element corresponds to one type of atom, and all the elements display their chemical properties regularly in the periodic table, beginning with the lightest and simplest: the hydrogen atom. Therefore, one task of atomic physicists of the 1910's and 1920's was to explain the periodic table of elements—the orderly array and the increasing complexity of the atoms. Another task

was to explain the phenomena of atomic spectra. Bohr's quantum postulates were found inadequate for more complex atoms or for atoms in an external force field such as a magnetic field. Between about 1915 and 1925, European physicists searched intently for new principles and guidelines for the construction of atomic models that would consistently account for chemical phenomena: the periodic table, physical phenomena, and spectral data.

That these phenomena would come together to reveal the structure of the atom became increasingly clear for a number of scientists, although it also became clear that the phenomena would be difficult to solve. In this regard, Wolfgang Pauli stated that it was the famous Swedish spectroscopist Johannes Robert Rydberg who noticed that the lengths of the periods in the periodic table—2, 8, 18, 32, and so on—can be expressed simply as "two times n squared" if n takes on all integer values. Atomic physicists were fascinated by these integers and incorporated them into their atomic models.

When Pauli was beginning his serious study of atomic structure, Bohr had already published his explanation of the periodic table with the *Aufbauprinzip*, which included two important ideas: The state of an electron in an atom is specified by three quantum numbers (the principal, the angular, and the magnetic), and atomic electrons form "shells" that are filled up and closed with specific numbers of electrons. In a sense, the idea of electron shells and their closing anticipated the Pauli exclusion principle. Bohr was applying a basic axiom without much awareness about it. In doing so, among other things, he left a fundamental physical problem unanswered: why all electrons of an atom in its ground state are not bound in the innermost shell. (A physical principle believed to be universally true is that a stable physical system tends to stay in the state of minimum potential energy.) Bohr wrote in his paper, "Going from Neon to Sodium, we must expect that the eleventh electron goes into the third shell." Pauli, however, was very conscious of the necessity of logic and evidence. He wrote in the margin of Bohr's paper near the quoted passage: "How do you know this? You only get it from the very spectra you want to explain!" Pauli was on the verge of explaining the difficult spectral phenomena, especially the so-called anomalous Zeeman effect, which was the magnetic splitting of the spectral lines discovered by Pieter Zeeman.

Alfred Landé had already succeeded in summarizing the spectroscopic data of the anomalous Zeeman effect into simple laws. His true innovation was the introduction of half integers as quantum numbers to explain the doublet spectra of the alkali metals. Although Pauli generalized Landé's result to account for the so-called Paschen-Back effect—a special case of the anomalous Zeeman effect discovered by Ernst Back and Friedrich Paschen—Pauli was still very puzzled by the "problem of the closing of the electronic shells."

In order to explain the doublet structure of the alkali spectra, Bohr and others hypothesized that the atomic core had an "angular momentum"—that is, it rotated. Now, after much hard thinking, Pauli realized that he had to eliminate this hypothesis and attribute a new quantum theoretic property to the electron. At that time, he called it a "two-valuedness not describable classically." This would be the electron's fourth degree of freedom, requiring a fourth quantum number to specify it. This question of the physical meaning of this "two-valuedness" was answered in 1925 by George Eugene Uhlenbeck and Samuel A. Goudsmit, who realized the idea of the spin of the electron. According to them, the electron has an intrinsic angular momentum that can assume two values that are of the same magnitude but opposite directions.

In October, 1924, an English physicist, Edmund C. Stoner, published "The Distribution of Electrons Among Atomic Levels." Whenever Pauli talked about the history of the exclusion principle, he would state that it was Stoner's paper that finally helped him to solve the problem of the closing of the electronic shells. Pauli particularly liked to quote an essential remark made by Stoner: "The number of energy levels of a single electron in the alkali metal spectra for a given value of the principle quantum number in an external magnetic field is the same as the number of electrons in the closed shells of the rare gases which corresponds to this principal quantum number." In the periodic table, the alkali metals are

Wolfgang Pauli. (The Nobel Foundation)

neighbors of the rare gases. The former are chemically active, whereas the latter are completely inactive. Essentially, Stoner was solving this causal problem: The rare gases have their electron shells closed, whereas each of the alkalis has one electron in an otherwise empty shell; thus this electron is "chemically active."

Finally showing true loyalty to physical phenomena, Pauli made a trip to Tubingen to use the spectroscopic data assembled there. He was obliged to verify some conclusions of the exclusion principle concerning the anomalous Zeeman effect of more complicated atoms. In the spring of 1925, Pauli published the exclusion principle, which can be formulated as follows: The state of every electron in an atom is specified by four quantum numbers; no two or more electrons in an atom can be at the same time in the same state—in other words, they can never assume simultaneously identical sets of the values of the four quantum numbers.

The formulation of the exclusion principle was made

at the same time other fundamental principles of quantum mechanics were being established: Louis de Broglie's paper was published in 1925, Werner Heisenberg's in 1925, and Erwin Schrödinger's in 1926. In pursuing the structure of the atom, like his mentor Arnold Sommerfeld, Pauli adhered to physical phenomena closely. De Broglie, Heisenberg, and Schrödinger were more fascinated by classic quantum correspondence in terms of mathematical formalism. It is an inexplicable historical irony that they became the true founders of quantum mechanics, whereas Pauli, then a "true" physicist, did not.

SIGNIFICANCE

With the foundation of quantum mechanics laid, it was concluded that quantum mechanics implies a statistical (probabilistic or indeterministic) nature for microcosmic configurations and processes. Combining such understanding with the Pauli exclusion principle, Heisenberg, in 1926, pointed out that in comparison with classical physics, quantum mechanics leads to conclusions for particles of the same kind (for example, for electrons, protons, neutrons, or others) that are qualitatively different from conclusions for particles of different kinds (for example, mixed systems of electrons and other particles). In fact, to reflect the fundamental distinction, quantum mechanics needs an independent principle, which can be called the principle of absolute identity.

In both classical and quantum physics, particles of the same kind are supposed to be physically indistinguishable, but classical and quantum physics differ in that the principle of absolute identity does not apply to the former. In classical physics, one can always assume that each of the particles of the same kind is given a (nonphysical) sign—a number or a name—and, from then on, these particles are distinguishable by their signs. Quantum particles of the same kind, however, are absolutely indistinguishable from one another; they cannot even be assigned numbers or any other nonphysical signs. Assigning numbers to particles of the same kind is a meaningful act in "classical" physics because the trajectory of every particle is traceable, at least in principle. Assigning numbers to particles of the same kind is a meaningless act in "quantum" physics because particles are not exactly particles; they do not follow trajectories. The numbers assigned to particles at any moment automatically "drop" at any subsequent moment.

From this principle, it was easily derived that quantum systems of the same kind of particles are either "symmetrical" or "antisymmetrical." The antisymmet-

rical particles, called fermions, obey the Pauli exclusion principle. Like electrons, these particles are "antisocial"; they can never stay in the same quantum state described by the same set of quantum numbers. In contrast, the symmetrical particles, called bosons, are "sociable." In fact, these particles tend to gather in the same quantum state. The behavior of a system of the same fermions is decided by the so-called Fermi-Dirac statistics; the behavior of a system of the same bosons is decided by the so-called Bose-Einstein statistics.

After his discovery of the exclusion principle, Pauli was still dissatisfied with its theoretical understanding. In 1940, he succeeded in developing a relativistic quantum theory with which he could prove a necessary connection between spin and statistics: Particles with half-integer spin must be fermions (or fulfill the exclusion principle); those with integer spin must be bosons.

When Paul Adrien Maurice Dirac pioneered in developing "quantum electrodynamics," he applied the exclusion principle to predict the existence of the positrons. Later, in 1932, Dirac's prediction was verified by Carl David Anderson, who found positrons, the first particles of antimatter. Because the inside of metals is actually an electron gas, and the inside of the atomic nuclei is an assembly of the fermionic nucleons, the Pauli exclusion principle plays an important role in both solid-state physics and nuclear physics.

—Wen-yuan Qian

FURTHER READING

Boorse, Henry A., and Lloyd Motz, eds. *The World of the Atom.* Vol. 2. New York: Basic Books, 1966. Collection of clear and informative essays on the nature of atoms. Chapter 59, "The Exclusion Principle," includes three parts: the editors' introductory commentary, Edward U. Condon and J. E. Mack's paper "An Interpretation of Pauli's Exclusion Principle" (originally published in 1930), and Pauli's Nobel lecture.

Born, Max. "Quantum Mechanics." In *My Life: Recollections of a Nobel Laureate.* New York: Charles Scribner's Sons, 1975. In the founding of quantum mechanics, Pauli's contribution was great, but not vital. This chapter describes Pauli's early, somehow misguided attitude toward the physical interpretation and mathematical formalisms of quantum mechanics.

Cropper, William H. *Great Physicists: The Life and Times of Leading Physicists from Galileo to Hawking.* New York: Oxford University Press, 2001. Presents portraits of the lives and accomplishments of important physicists and shows how they influenced one another with their work. Chapter 17 is devoted to Wolfgang Pauli. Includes glossary and index.

Gamow, George. *Biography of Physics*. New York: Harper & Row, 1961. Informative, interesting history of mostly modern physics. Discusses the Pauli exclusion principle as well as the so-called second Pauli principle in the context of Dirac's developing relativistic quantum mechanics.

_____. *Matter, Earth, and Sky*. 2d ed. Englewood Cliffs, N.J.: Prentice-Hall, 1965. Excellent popular science volume explains electron shells and period systems as well as Pauli's exclusion principle in chapter 13.

Gamow, George, and Russell Stannard. *The New World of Mr. Tompkins*. Cambridge, England: Cambridge University Press, 2001. Revised and updated (by Stannard) edition of *Mr. Tompkins in Paperback*, a 1965 volume that combined Gamow's two classic popular science books, *Mr. Tompkins in Wonderland* (1940) and *Mr. Tompkins Explores the Atom* (1945). Provides an excellent introduction to many scientific concepts for lay readers, including Pauli's exclusion principle.

Polkinghorne, John. *Quantum Theory: A Very Short Introduction*. New York: Oxford University Press, 2002. Aims to make quantum theory accessible to the general reader. Among the concepts discussed are uncertainty, probabilistic physics, and the exclusion principle. Includes mathematical appendix and index.

SEE ALSO: 1914: Rutherford Discovers the Proton; 1918: Noether Shows the Equivalence of Symmetry and Conservation; Feb.-Mar., 1927: Heisenberg Articulates the Uncertainty Principle; Summer, 1928: Gamow Explains Radioactive Alpha Decay with Quantum Tunneling; Nov.-Dec., 1933: Fermi Proposes the Neutrino Theory of Beta Decay.

April, 1925-May, 1927
GERMAN EXPEDITION DISCOVERS THE MID-ATLANTIC RIDGE

Using a newly developed echo sounder, the Meteor, *a refitted German gunboat, made the first transoceanic crossing with closely spaced soundings, leading to the discovery of the Mid-Atlantic Ridge.*

LOCALE: Southern and equatorial Atlantic Ocean
CATEGORIES: Science and technology; earth science; geography

KEY FIGURES
Alfred Merz (1880-1925), German geographer
Fritz Haber (1868-1934), German chemist
Georg Wüst (1890-1977), German oceanographer and student of Merz

SUMMARY OF EVENT
The initial purpose of the German *Meteor* expedition was economic. In 1872, E. Sonstadt reported that the oceans contained a gold concentration of 65 milligrams per metric ton of seawater. The Treaty of Versailles (1919), which ended World War I, required that Germany repay its enormous war debt in gold, and Fritz Haber, a German chemist, proposed that gold extracted from the international seas might solve the problem.

The Treaty of Versailles prohibited the German navy from sending ships to foreign ports; however, in 1919, a member of the German admiralty, Captain Nippe, persuaded authorities to allow a German vessel to be outfitted and sent on a major peacetime oceanographic expedition. The *Meteor*, a class C gunboat, was selected for the study. Alfred Merz, an adviser to the German navy, was named the chief scientist of the *Meteor*. After Merz's death, Georg Wüst took over leadership of the oceanographic data and study, which was to take place in the Atlantic Ocean.

The *Meteor* was to be equipped with the newly developed echo sounder, a device used to find the distance and direction of objects under or partially under the water. An echo sounder works by measuring the time it takes a sonic or ultrasonic pulse emitted by the sounder to reach the object below and then return to the sounder. The time intervals and other data are then converted into numerical reference points of distance and direction. The navies of the world use echo sounding to chart the positions of foreign ships and submarines. During peacetime, echo sounders are used to locate sunken ships, find schools of fish, and map the profile of the seafloor.

The *Meteor* expedition marked the first use of echo sounders to map the profile of the deep seafloor. With the exception of the *Meteor*, no such detailed maps were available before World War II. The profiles aboard the *Meteor* were closely spaced echo soundings taken by extremely diligent workers, which only made the recordings that much more accurate and detailed. Moreover, a new anchor system had been developed that enabled the ship to anchor in deep waters.

On April 26, 1925, the *Meteor* left for Buenos Aires, Argentina, to start work on the planned sections in the South Atlantic. Actual surveys began on June 3, 1925. Merz was in charge in spite of his illness; however, by the time the vessel arrived at the fifth hydrographic station, his condition had worsened to the point that the captain ordered the ship to return to Buenos Aires so that Merz could receive medical attention. Merz then turned the leadership of the scientific part of the expedition over to the captain. In reviewing the work along the first section, the captain found that the acoustic depth sounder had revealed that much of the bottom had been incorrectly charted.

After completing the thirteenth traverse in the equatorial Atlantic Ocean, the *Meteor* sailed for Germany, arriving home on May 29, 1927. In two years, the *Meteor* had traveled more than 41,943 miles (67,500 kilometers), had collected data at 310 hydrographic stations, had anchored ten times in deep ocean, and had made approximately 70,000 soundings of ocean depths. As a result, the expedition was the first to reveal the true ruggedness of the ocean floor.

The significant discovery of the *Meteor* was that a continuous ridge (the Walvis Ridge) runs in a southwesterly direction from the vicinity of Walvis Bay, southwest Africa. (A ridge is a long, narrow elevation on the sea-floor.) This in turn led to the discovery of the Mid-Atlantic Ridge. It runs along the north-south axis of the Atlantic and is basically a long, curving zone of mountains, volcanoes, and fractured plateaus. This ridge's now-familiar herringbone pattern was first suggested in 1935 by Wüst and Theodor Stocks.

SIGNIFICANCE

The *Meteor* expedition's discovery of the Mid-Atlantic Ridge was a significant event. Unfortunately, this finding was not recognized widely at the time as being enough to support the theory of continental drift. That theory had continued to generate controversy and debate among scientists ever since 1912, the year it was first proposed by the German geophysicist and meteorologist Alfred Wegener. Wegener's theory stated that the earth was once made up of one large ocean and one large landmass. Gradually, this supercontinent split into two parts. Additional separations and "drift" continued to occur across many millions of years, eventually resulting in the seven continents as they have come to be known.

As modern science now recognizes, these massive continental "plates" tend to drift apart at divergent boundaries. These boundaries may be seen as the mid-oceanic ridges such as the Mid-Atlantic Ridge. Such rending of the earth's crust brings with it great earthquakes and great flows of volcanic materials that, as they pile up in the "cracks," slowly create ridges.

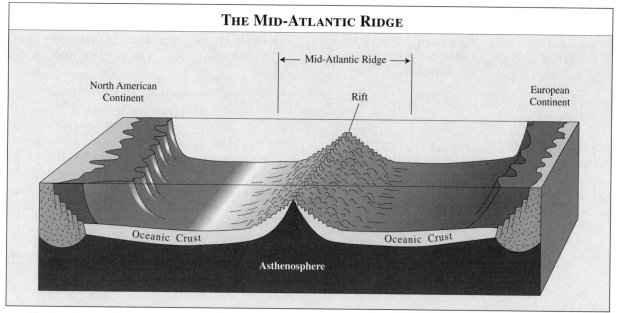

THE MID-ATLANTIC RIDGE

The Mid-Atlantic Ridge is a major site of seafloor spreading, where the North American and European plates pull apart.

In the 1950's, a new generation of equipment and instruments was introduced that led to an explosion of data supporting the theory of continental drift, or "plate tectonics," as it is now called. Continuously recording echo sounders, magnetometers, temperature probes, explosion seismometers, piston corers, dredgers, and deep-sea submersibles were used not only to discover additional evidence to support the theory of continental movement but also to add to the sum of knowledge about deep-sea activity.

The *Meteor*'s discovery was a midpoint during the development of the proposed theory of continental drift in 1912 and the concept of plate tectonics that became widely accepted in 1968. Earth scientists realize now that the positions of landmasses are not fixed. The separation of continental plates has resulted in the formation of new ocean basins, and older segments of the seafloor are being recycled continually in areas where deep-ocean trenches are found. This profound reversal of scientific opinion has been described as a scientific revolution, one in which the *Meteor* expedition played a pioneering role.

—Earl G. Hoover

FURTHER READING

Idyll, C. P. *Exploring the Ocean World: A History of Oceanography*. New York: Thomas Y. Crowell, 1969. Comprehensive overview for high school and college students. Includes photographs, graphs, charts, a chronology of oceanographic developments, and individual chapter bibliographies.

Medwin, Herman, et al. *Sounds in the Sea: From Ocean Acoustics to Acoustical Oceanography*. New York: Cambridge University Press, 2005. Textbook aimed at students in oceanography, engineering, and physics describes the tools scientists use to examine the characteristics of physical and biological bodies in the oceans.

Menard, H. W. *The Ocean of Truth: A Personal History of Global Tectonics*. Princeton, N.J.: Princeton University Press, 1986. A volume ideally suited for high school and college readers who would like an overall view of the topic without technical language. Very informative.

Pickard, George L. *Descriptive Physical Oceanography: An Introduction*. 5th ed. Elmsford, N.Y.: Pergamon Press, 1990. A nontechnical introduction to oceanography for undergraduates in the sciences and advanced high school students who wish to learn something of the aims and achievements of this field of study. Includes bibliography and index.

Sears, M., and D. Merriman, eds. *Oceanography: The Past*. New York: Springer-Verlag, 1980. Collection of papers from the Third International Congress on the History of Oceanography. An excellent reference source for graduate students and researchers, as most chapters include numerous notes and references. Few illustrations.

Thurman, Harold V., and Alan P. Trujillo. *Introductory Oceanography*. 10th ed. Upper Saddle River, N.J.: Prentice Hall, 2003. College-level introductory text is extensively illustrated and provides a very good general survey of the topic. Each chapter concludes with a glossary and references.

SEE ALSO: 1906-1910: Oldham and Mohorovičić Determine the Earth's Interior Structure; Jan., 1912: Wegener Proposes the Theory of Continental Drift; Oct., 1915-Mar., 1917: Langevin Develops Active Sonar.

April 10, 1925
FITZGERALD CAPTURES THE ROARING TWENTIES IN *THE GREAT GATSBY*

In The Great Gatsby, *F. Scott Fitzgerald both reflected the glitter of the Roaring Twenties and warned of the potential destructiveness of pursuing the American Dream at any cost.*

LOCALE: United States
CATEGORY: Literature

KEY FIGURES

F. Scott Fitzgerald (1896-1940), American writer
Zelda Fitzgerald (1900-1948), American writer and
    wife of F. Scott Fitzgerald
Ernest Hemingway (1899-1961), American writer
Edmund Wilson (1895-1972), American literary editor

SUMMARY OF EVENT

By the time *The Great Gatsby* was published on April 10, 1925, F. Scott Fitzgerald had established himself with a string of impressive moneymaking stories and had gained some attention from critics who pointed to his occasional flashes of literary genius. He had already published the novels *This Side of Paradise* (1920) and *The Beautiful and Damned* (1922), collections of short stories including *Flappers and Philosophers* (1920) and *Tales of the Jazz Age* (1922), and a play, *The Vegetable: Or, From President to Postman* (1923).

Fitzgerald was successful because he wrote with great gusto about the young post-World War I generation—its bashing of traditional values, its search for wealth, its rebelliousness, and its unorthodox behavior. His stories embodied a high degree of wish fulfillment for readers, pitching them into living vicariously among the smart set of the 1920's, with their wild parties, sporty automobiles, and pleasure-seeking adventures.

Fitzgerald—whether in France, New York, or Hollywood—always used his own personal experiences and observations as the basis for his stories. So it was with *The Great Gatsby*, which presented fictional versions of his painful social rejections, his thwarted loves, his excesses with drink, and his search for success and money. Moreover, his wife, Zelda Fitzgerald, served as the model for the novel's Daisy Buchanan, a quicksilver beauty representing the unattainable.

For *The Great Gatsby*, Fitzgerald drew on the lavish Long Island parties he had attended, populating his story with a mix of intellectuals, frauds, bootleggers, gangsters, madcap flappers, and sad, naïve young men such as

Nick Carraway, the book's narrator. Carraway retrospectively narrates the events of the summer of 1922 that led up to the death of Jay Gatsby. Visiting his distant cousin Daisy Buchanan and her husband, Tom, in West Egg, Long Island, New York, Nick learns that the Buchanans are unhappily married and that Tom is unfaithful and having an affair with plump Myrtle Wilson, the wife of a local garage owner.

Through a series of dinner parties, lunches, and drinking sprees, Nick becomes acquainted with the mysterious, wealthy Jay Gatsby, who lives on a nearby estate where he throws fabulous parties for speakeasy society. Nick is alternately repelled and fascinated by Gatsby, a thirty-year-old with adolescent romantic dreams, fictitious upper-class parentage to hide the reality of his impoverished farm background, and bad taste in whatever he buys.

Nick learns that Gatsby is a self-made man. Years before, a poor Gatsby had fallen hard for the dazzling Daisy before he went overseas to fight in World War I. She, however, spurned him for the arrogant Tom Buchanan, a rich and eligible socialite. Four years later, Gatsby, still pursuing his idealistic love for Daisy, has made a fortune partly from bootlegging liquor, has purchased a garish mansion across the harbor from the Buchanans, and yearns to reclaim his lost love.

Because Nick is related to Daisy, Gatsby asks Nick to arrange a tea at Nick's house for the purpose of staging a reunion between Gatsby and Daisy. The reunion results in the Buchanans' inviting Gatsby, Nick, and friends to a party at a New York hotel. Events turn ugly when a drunken Tom accuses Gatsby of being a swindler and of trying to steal Daisy. An angry Daisy leaves with Gatsby for the return drive home.

During Tom and Nick's return car trip to West Egg, they stop to investigate a fatal accident and discover that Myrtle Wilson (Tom's mistress) has been killed by a hit-and-run driver in a car similar to one owned by Gatsby. Nick learns later that Daisy, not Gatsby, was driving the car. Gatsby, however, gallantly offers to shoulder the blame.

Through the connivance of Tom Buchanan, Myrtle Wilson's husband becomes convinced that Gatsby is the cause of his wife's death. A few hours later, an enraged Wilson shoots Gatsby in an act of revenge and then turns the gun on himself. Nick arranges for Gatsby's funeral, but no one comes except for one former guest and Gatsby's father, who believes his son to have been a great man. At the end, Nick breaks off his friendship with the corrupt Buchanans and returns to the Midwest.

The novel's plot outline sounds like material fit for sensational tabloids and pulp magazines. As scholars and critics have observed, plots were never Fitzgerald's forte. What elevates *The Great Gatsby* and makes it memorable is Fitzgerald's handling of these melodramatic events.

At the time the book was published, reactions among critics were generally favorable. Many praised the spare style of the short (fifty-thousand-word) novel. Commentators were especially impressed by Fitzgerald's compressed details that make scenes blaze with life, his po-

etic imagery, his framing of complex characters and universal themes in ironic terms, and his use of a sophisticated first-person narrative.

Unhappily, the book's sales were modest. Only about twenty-four thousand copies were printed, and it was not reprinted by Fitzgerald's publisher during his lifetime. The reading public seemed put off by the unpleasant characters—each a moral failure—the downbeat ending, and the sophisticated writing techniques so highly praised by critics. Although Fitzgerald made little money from sales of the book, he did earn close to thirty thousand dollars from stage and film rights.

One result of the lukewarm popular reception of *The Great Gatsby* was that Fitzgerald turned to writing profitable short stories and Hollywood scripts. He faced financial crises caused by his family's expensive living style. Zelda's increasing mental problems required her institutionalization, and Fitzgerald's own increasing alcohol problems, self-doubts, declining health, and inability to write a new novel commensurate with the quality of *The Great Gatsby* made his life a troubled one.

Even his good friend Ernest Hemingway took Fitzgerald to task for betraying his craft and writing for easy money. The two had been on intimate terms since *The Great Gatsby* appeared, with Fitzgerald—then at the top of his powers—championing the fledgling Hemingway. Over the next few years, the two authors counseled each other, but as Hemingway's star rose and Fitzgerald's declined, they drifted apart by the 1930's. Hemingway wanted Fitzgerald to discipline his art and to write simply, but Fitzgerald would not.

SIGNIFICANCE

The Great Gatsby was the watershed of Fitzgerald's own rise and decline as a writer. Both his career and his life paralleled America's fortunes, riding the crest of the prosperity wave of the 1920's and tailing off during the Depression years of the 1930's. Fitzgerald died in obscurity in 1940 as a Hollywood hack writer.

Fitzgerald's novels were largely ignored and unread from the 1930's until the 1950's. Two factors led to the revival of the novelist's reputation: renewed interest

F. Scott Fitzgerald with his wife, Zelda, and their daughter, Scottie, in their apartment in Paris in 1925. (AP/Wide World Photos)

in the personal and artistic tragedy of Fitzgerald himself and academic interest in the unique way Fitzgerald structured his art.

The interest in Fitzgerald's life and its excesses began with Edmund Wilson, the author's longtime confidant. Wilson edited *The Crack-Up* (1945), a collection of Fitzgerald's essays, notebooks, and letters revealing the emotional bankruptcy and disillusionments in Fitzgerald's life. The essays not only detailed the extravagant lifestyle of the Fitzgeralds but also chronicled the devastating effects of the Great Depression on their lives and on his art.

Interest in Fitzgerald's life intensified with the popular success of Budd Schulberg's *The Disenchanted* (1950), a fictionalized account of Fitzgerald's drunken sprees, his fistfights with and insults of friends, and his declining ability to write during his Hollywood years. Arthur Mizener fueled further interest with *The Far Side of Paradise: A Biography of F. Scott Fitzgerald* (1951).

The academic community also helped revive interest in Fitzgerald. The New Criticism, a method of scrutinizing the form and texture of literary works, was in vogue during the 1950's, and *The Great Gatsby* was made for such close textual analysis. A spate of academic commentary poured forth, focusing in particular on Fitzgerald's brilliant handling of the novel's first-person retrospective point of view. Nick Carraway does not merely narrate the tale; he observes, participates, and evaluates. The narrative structure thus allows Fitzgerald to work simultaneously within and outside the scenes and to be both immersed immediately in and psychologically distanced from the action. Not since Joseph Conrad had an author been able to pull off such a double-vision feat as Fitzgerald did in *The Great Gatsby*.

In addition, the New Critics wrestled with the ambiguities of Nick Carraway as a reliable narrator and the probability of his moral and ethical development. They disagreed in their interpretations of the shadowy character of Gatsby: Was he a tragic, noble figure in the Shakespearean sense? Was he a Christlike martyr, an Antichrist figure, or perhaps a knight-errant seeking the Grail and idealizing his lady? Or was Gatsby just an unlucky racketeer gunned down in a bizarre twist of fate? In addition, the New Critics charted the complex chronology of the novel, with its sudden shifts of past and present, and traced the imagery clusters found in it, such as the ironic contrasts between the stately mansions of Long Island and the nearby valley of ashes where the poor live.

A number of critics found the scenes of the valley of ashes in *The Great Gatsby* to be the American counter-

---

GATSBY'S FIRST APPEARANCE

In The Great Gatsby, *the reader gets a first glimpse of the mysterious title character through the eyes of the novel's narrator, Nick Carraway:*

Already it was deep summer on roadhouse roofs and in front of wayside garages where new red gas-pumps sat out in pools of light, and when I reached my estate at West Egg I ran the car under its shed and sat for a while on an abandoned grass roller in the yard. The wind had blown off, leaving a loud bright night with wings beating in the trees and a persistent organ sound as the full bellows of the earth blew the frogs full of life. The silhouette of a moving cat wavered across the moonlight and turning my head to watch it I saw that I was not alone—fifty feet away a figure had emerged from the shadow of my neighbor's mansion and was standing with his hands in his pockets regarding the silver pepper of the stars. Something in his leisurely movements and the secure position of his feet upon the lawn suggested that it was Mr. Gatsby himself, come out to determine what share was his of our local heavens.

I decided to call to him. Miss Baker had mentioned him at dinner, and that would do for an introduction. But I didn't call to him for he gave a sudden intimation that he was content to be alone—he stretched out his arms toward the dark water in a curious way, and far as I was from him I could have sworn he was trembling. Involuntarily I glanced seaward—and distinguished nothing except a single green light, minute and far away, that might have been the end of a dock. When I looked once more for Gatsby he had vanished, and I was alone again in the unquiet darkness.

Source: F. Scott Fitzgerald, *The Great Gatsby* (New York: Charles Scribner's Sons, 1925).

---

part of the British vision in T. S. Eliot's 1922 poem *The Waste Land*. Both authors described intense disillusionments, the results of radical changes in the postwar era. The rich, the middle class, and the lower class were equally portrayed as culturally empty, entrapped in sterile, purposeless lives. Both Fitzgerald and Eliot conceived of the world as coming apart because no moral principle was holding it together.

In addition, the New Critics scrutinized the novel's use of color images (especially greens), eye and vision cues, careening speedboats and cars, and the changing seasons. They also paid tribute to the animated phrasing and sentence structures Fitzgerald used to achieve the novel's rhetorical brilliance and lyric energy.

Later literary criticism focused on Fitzgerald as a social commentator, as the issues and values clashes of the 1920's depicted in the novel were confronted by succeeding generations pursuing the American Dream. Fitzgerald thus was seen as more than a keen-eyed chronicler of the Roaring Twenties; he became a prophet warning oncoming generations of the terrible price to be paid for pursuing illusive dreams.

Aside from being a cultural and historical allegory, the novel presented universal themes of human yearnings. An example is the book's theme of social class: Fitzgerald shows the careless rich victimizing their lessers because of the empty values of the upper class. The initiation theme shows a naïve Nick Carraway learning that wealth and power do not necessarily beget happiness; the book's frontier theme implies that the Midwest is morally superior to the corrupt, materialistic East Coast.

In essence, Fitzgerald's *The Great Gatsby* goes beyond capturing the frantic atmosphere of the Roaring Twenties. It is a novel for all ages. Gertrude Stein, writing, ironically, in the early 1930's, when Fitzgerald's reputation was fading, prophesied that "Fitzgerald will be read when many of his well-known contemporaries are forgotten." Time has proven Stein's judgment correct.

—*Richard Whitworth*

FURTHER READING

Bruccoli, Matthew J. *Some Sort of Epic Grandeur: The Life of F. Scott Fitzgerald.* 2d rev. ed. Columbia: University of South Carolina Press, 2002. Comprehensive, detailed biography covers all of Fitzgerald's life and career. Includes illustrations, chronology, and index.

＿＿＿＿, ed. *F. Scott Fitzgerald's "The Great Gatsby": A Literary Reference.* New York: Carroll & Graf, 2002. Companion to the novel provides information on Fitzgerald's writing process as well as on celebrities, events, crazes, and other aspects of the times in which the book is set to aid contemporary readers' understanding. Includes a brief biography of Fitzgerald, illustrations, chronology, and index.

Bruccoli, Matthew J., and Jackson R. Bryer, eds. *F. Scott Fitzgerald in His Own Times: A Miscellany.* Kent, Ohio: Kent State University Press, 1971. A delightful potpourri, ranging from early writings of Fitzgerald to his obituary notices. Provides glimpses of his acerbic wit and astute perceptions along with original reviews of *The Great Gatsby.*

Eble, Kenneth E., ed. *F. Scott Fitzgerald: A Collection of Criticism.* New York: McGraw-Hill, 1973. Highly readable commentary by critics who share their insights on the craft and art of Fitzgerald. The essays on *The Great Gatsby* are a must for potential writers.

Lehan, Richard. *"The Great Gatsby": The Limits of Wonder.* Boston: Twayne, 1990. Useful historical background about Fitzgerald and the novel, including a chronology of Fitzgerald's life and works. Also provides a series of critical interpretations of the major characters in the novel.

Mellow, James R. *Invented Lives: F. Scott and Zelda Fitzgerald.* Boston: Houghton Mifflin, 1984. Presents fascinating details of the Fitzgeralds' glamorous lives and their stormy relationships with well-known contemporaries. Basic theme is that the Fitzgeralds actually created their own legend, "acting out their stories in real life." Somewhat moralistic in tone.

Mizener, Arthur. *The Far Side of Paradise: A Biography of F. Scott Fitzgerald.* Boston: Houghton Mifflin, 1951. Chronicles the rise and fall of F. Scott Fitzgerald as a person and literary artist in dramatic terms. Includes photos of Fitzgerald at various stages of his career and appendixes on his method of revision.

SEE ALSO: Fall, 1905: Stein Holds Her First Paris Salons; 1919: Founding of the World Christian Fundamentals Association; 1922: Eliot Publishes *The Waste Land*; Feb. 21, 1925: Ross Founds *The New Yorker*; Oct. 22, 1926: Hemingway's *The Sun Also Rises* Speaks for the Lost Generation; Winter, 1932: Huxley's *Brave New World* Forecasts Technological Totalitarianism.

May-June, 1925
PARIS EXHIBITION DEFINES ART DECO

When Paris hosted a large invitational applied arts exhibition seeking the best in contemporary design, designers came to terms with modernism.

LOCALE: Paris, France
CATEGORIES: Fashion and design; architecture

KEY FIGURES
Pierre Patout (1879-1965), French architect
Émile-Jacques Ruhlmann (1879-1933), French cabinetmaker
Louis Süe (1875-1968), French interior designer
André Mare (1885-1932), French interior designer

SUMMARY OF EVENT

Art Deco was a major decorative arts style of the 1920's that survived in altered forms through the 1930's and into the early 1940's. During those decades, it also was called Art Moderne. It was in part a compromised modern style, but its association with the modern style caused much confusion in the reassessments made at the end of the twentieth century. The now nearly universal term "Art Deco" did not appear until the late 1960's, when a revival of interest in 1920's and 1930's interior design and decorative arts occurred. That revival gained tremendous momentum for at least the next twenty years. The term "Art Deco" is derived from the name of an invitational exhibition of decorative and industrial arts that was held in Paris, France, in 1925. The goal of the style was to adapt design to the needs of mass production. Items thus incorporated straight lines instead of curves and symmetry rather than asymmetry, as forms of this type were easier to produce with machines. Art Deco also attempted to incorporate manufactured, rather than natural, materials.

The Exposition Internationale des Arts Décoratifs et Industriels Modernes occupied the same central Parisian site as the World's Fair of 1900, a fair that introduced Art Nouveau to an international audience. The area of the Esplanade des Invalides was smaller than the area used twenty-five years earlier, reflecting the 1925 exhibition's major focus on just the decorative arts. The Grand Palais, immediately adjacent, was serviceable and quickly was transformed for display use.

Approximately seventy-five pavilions and other structures graced the grounds. As in past fairs, most were intended to be temporary. Individual pavilions were composed of wood frames covered with plaster, a style similar to the so-called staff architecture of the "White

City" of the World's Columbian Exhibition in Chicago in 1893. Temporary construction or not, the exterior surfaces of the pliable structures seemed to encourage widespread decorative relief sculpture, often a hallmark of Art Deco design. Otherwise, all the pavilions respected established ordinances for low heights and gardenlike settings, taking care to utilize existing trees. Altogether there were about 130 buildings and thirteen entrances, four of which were major, in addition to a good number of intervening gardens and fountains.

Architecturally speaking, the fair buildings ranged from neoclassical constraints to bold cubist experimentations and novelties. Said to be among the best designs were the pavilions of the department stores Au Printemps, Au Bon Marche, Grands Magasins du Louvre, and Galéries Lafayette. Collectively they embodied grandiosity, with faceted planes, rich decorative surfaces, and prominent use of metal and glass. Another structure that has been singled out for the excellence of its design was the Pavilion of a Rich Collector, by architect Pierre Patout. This closely resembled a home Patout had produced for Émile-Jacques Ruhlmann, a gifted furniture designer in the Art Deco style. In turn, Ruhlmann and his design team were responsible for most of the interior design and contents of Patout's pavilion, which was also known as the Ruhlmann Townhouse.

Regardless of building styles, the buildings' interiors received the most attention, as they promoted changes in contemporary lifestyles and sought to showcase the best of the new decorative arts. Redesigned family spaces included living rooms, dining rooms, specialized bedrooms for gentlemen and ladies, libraries, smoking rooms, and studies, in addition to accommodations for live plants and flowers in volume. The decorative appointments for these rooms suggested high ideals, as unrestricted patronage was the rule. That resulted in items of high craftsmanship but occasionally of dubious practicality. For example, furniture was generally sumptuous and surface-oriented, with a preference for rare and imported woods. It was often large or exhibition-oriented, even pompous and overly finished. When less hybrid in style, however, it was civilized, striking, and comfortable. Legs on Art Deco furniture at this fair were often tapered or minimized by a platform for a chair or chaise, adding a sense of importance. Key designers in 1925 included Ruhlmann, André Groult, Pierre Chareau, and partners Louis Süe and André Mare.

Lighting in the interiors was more scientific, at least in

theory, than it was at the 1900 Paris World's Fair. Illumination was more logical than the Tiffany lamps used twenty-five years earlier. Indirect lighting diffused and softened the glow of electric lamps, which had become affordable. Table lamps and chandeliers, however, often incorporated the French passion for exotic materials, forms, and surface treatment.

The Paris fair of 1925 was a study in contrasts, contradictions, and crosscurrents. Rising architect Le Corbusier (Charles-Édouard Jeanneret) observed that the fair was a turning point away from antiques and handcraft and toward machined solutions, as well as an expression of a keen interest in newness and experimentation. Caught in the middle of this flux was a major ornamental design style, Art Deco.

SIGNIFICANCE

Europe seemed to be more affected by the decorative arts of the 1925 Paris fair than by the fair's architecture. The exhibition focused almost exclusively on applied art, and almost all the exhibitors were Europeans.

Careers were launched immediately for some designers, and the reputations of others were solidified. The furniture design partnership of Süe and Mare, critically successful at the fair, continued in a firm called the French Art Company until it was purchased in the late 1920's by the Maison Fontaine. The exposure of Süe and Mare's work at the 1925 exhibition surely helped the partners land major commissions for the luxury-class cabins of the steamship *Paris* and decorative schemes for the grand salon of the ocean liner *Ile de France*.

The success of Süe and Mare, whose workshop was relatively large, was repeated by smaller design studios, although Art Deco furniture was popularized by aggressive Parisian department stores more than by designers' showrooms or the annual salons. For example, the Grands Magasins du Louvre produced designs for a wide variety of household items in the Art Deco style without extravagant decoration, manufactured them, and subsequently introduced a large public to an affordable range of Art Deco items.

In the fields of art glass and utilitarian glass, René Lalique's fortunes following the 1925 exhibition are legendary. By 1900, he was the leading Art Nouveau jewelry designer in Europe and could have rested comfortably on that reputation and retired. Instead, he embarked on a serious exploration of both art and production glass and mastered them by the 1925 exhibition. By then, he was well past sixty years of age. Within a few years of the fair, his production had become exceptionally varied.

His company was prolific, producing items ranging from ashtrays to clock cases, from decanters to perfume vaporizers. Lalique became the leading Art Deco glass designer of the 1920's and 1930's. His firm survived the German occupation of World War II and was perpetuated by a son and grandson. To the examples of Süe and Mare and of Lalique can be added dozens more in the media of metalwork, graphic design, sculpture, ceramics, textiles, painting, and silver.

The designers of Art Deco responded to changes in life and society, both of which had become more urban and faster paced. Products reflecting this new life, including automobiles, cigarette cases, cocktail shakers, radios, electric lamps, and posters, were created in Art Deco style. In addition, those items were produced in new ways, often incorporating new materials or experimental combinations of existing ones. Likewise, themes and imagery reflecting a changing society were explored well into the 1930's in the media of sculpture, glass, painting, and lighting. These themes included flight, the emancipation of women, the machine, modern art movements, non-Western cultures, dance, and jazz.

The 1925 Paris fair was influential in introducing Art Deco to a broad public. One wish or dream of the fair organizers, however, was not realized. The 1925 Paris fair showcased both decorative and industrial arts, as the full title of the exhibition stated. Its organizers hoped that artists, designers, manufacturers, and capitalists would collaborate in the design, production, and marketing of domestic items of high design but realistic prices. The hoped-for collaboration saw few projects by the fair's opening or even after it closed, as manufacturers generally were wary of expensive-sounding proposals of doubtful financial success.

Collaboration did occur between designers and teams of designers for complete interiors, both at the fair and elsewhere, but that was a different development. The creation of a more affordable or more popular Art Deco occurred primarily in the United States, with its much larger middle class and its advanced marketing, advertising, and capitalist potential.

Thousands of visitors from the United States traveled to the 1925 exhibition. Many may have wanted to visit an American pavilion, but there was none, as President Herbert Hoover had declined the invitation to have the United States represented. Among the throngs of Americans in attendance were members of numerous professional design organizations who provided detailed reports on the pavilions and their contents to their respective design groups back home. These reports translated into a major impact on architecture and design in the United States for the next fifteen years.

Within a year of the 1925 Paris fair, selections from the exhibition toured the United States, being placed on view at the Metropolitan Museum of Art in New York City and at other major sites. Two years later, the fashionable New York City store Lord and Taylor hosted an exhibition of furniture by Émile-Jacques Ruhlmann and Francis Jourdain. Their strain of Art Deco design, combining a respectful classicism with ornamentally elegant surfaces, found favor among Americans as something both old and contemporary. That kind of thinking in turn encouraged the rise of a major architectural style, American Art Deco. The result was a compromised modernism. It was both decorative and functional, new but not shocking, and it appealed to corporate image makers and real estate developers who were somewhat frightened by the international style of modernism.

The 1925 Paris exhibition's most noticeable impact on the United States took the form of Art Deco architecture. The movement was primarily surface-oriented, with design motifs or relief sculpture at the cresting and at the bases of buildings and their lobbies. New York City saw the construction of the largest number of Art Deco buildings in a single urban space, including the highly emblematic and even spectacular Chrysler Building, designed by William Van Alen; the Empire State Building, by the firm of Shreve, Lamb, and Harmon; and the Fuller Building, by A. Stewart Walker and Leon Gillette.

World War II interrupted the Art Deco episode in architecture and the decorative arts. People seemed ready to forget it during the 1950's, but from the 1970's onward an amazing revival occurred. Museum-quality decorative arts items began to fetch tremendous prices in galleries devoted to Art Deco and at auction. Since that time, many major Art Deco buildings have been restored. In Miami, Florida, four hundred or so "Tropical Deco" buildings have been protected as the largest architectural historic district in the United States, and many have been renovated and restored. Postmodern architecture of the 1980's and 1990's, reflecting a hunger for ornamentation and inclusion of past styles, incorporated aspects of Art Deco, as did the fine-art media of painting and sculpture.

—*Tom Dewey II*

FURTHER READING

Arwas, Victor. *Art Deco*. Rev. ed. New York: Harry N. Abrams, 1998. Introduction to Art Deco in its original European setting; includes information on sources, major designers, and their seminal works. Devotes a chapter to the 1925 exposition, with special emphasis on pavilions and their contents' designers.

Bouillon, Jean-Paul. *Art Deco, 1900-1940*. Translated by Michael Heron. New York: Rizzoli, 1989. Tracks avant-garde design and ornament from 1900 to the eve of World War II, weaving in a subtheme of sumptuous materials and anthropomorphic decorative motifs versus taut abstract patterns. Includes perceptive commentary on relationships between major art movements and corresponding developments in interior design and decorative art.

Duncan, Alastair. *American Art Deco*. 1986. Reprint. New York: Thames and Hudson, 1999. Discusses architecture, interiors, and decorative arts created in the United States by both European immigrants and American-born designers. Stresses two formative international design tendencies: the German-Austrian emphasis on logic, geometry, and function applicable to mass production, and the colorful, ornamental, and playful French tendencies.

Hillier, Bevis, and Stephen Escritt. *Art Deco Style*. London: Phaidon Press, 1997. Opens with a chapter on the 1925 Paris exhibition and then traces manifestations of Art Deco design around the world. Includes many illustrations, brief biographies of notable designers, and bibliography.

McClinton, Katherine M. *Art Deco: A Guide for Collectors*. New York: C. N. Potter, 1972. Important, informative work by a knowledgeable professional who visited the 1925 exposition. Preface and first two chapters offer helpful descriptions of major emblematic features of the style.

Morgan, Sarah. *Art Deco: The European Style*. Greenwich, Conn.: Dorset Press, 1990. A general study aimed at collectors and connoisseurs of the style. Presents a dutiful account of the 1925 Paris exhibition followed by fourteen chapters showcasing major divisions of decorative arts.

SEE ALSO: 1903: Hoffmann and Moser Found the Wiener Werkstätte; 1920's: Chanel Defines Modern Women's Fashion; 1927: Lang Expands the Limits of Filmmaking with *Metropolis*; May 1, 1931: Empire State Building Opens; May 27, 1937: Golden Gate Bridge Opens; Nov. 1, 1939: Rockefeller Center Is Completed.

May 1, 1925
CYPRUS BECOMES A BRITISH CROWN COLONY

Originally leased by the British from the Ottoman Empire in 1878 and annexed in 1914, Cyprus was granted Crown Colony status in 1925.

LOCALE: Cyprus; London, England
CATEGORIES: Colonialism and occupation; government and politics; diplomacy and international relations

KEY FIGURES

Sir Malcolm Stevenson (1878-1927), high commissioner and subsequently governor of Cyprus
L. S. Amery (1873-1955), British secretary of state for colonies
Cyril III (d. 1933), Greek Orthodox archbishop of Cyprus

SUMMARY OF EVENT

Great Britain proclaimed the island of Cyprus a Crown Colony on May 1, 1925. Britain had directly administered the island for a number of years, but the proclamation formalized and regularized British rule there. However, since the change in legal status failed to lead to any immediate reforms in British administration and did not solve any of the island's long-term problems, most Cypriots regarded the change as unimportant.

At 3,572 square miles (9,251 square kilometers) Cyprus is the third largest island in the Mediterranean Sea and lies only forty miles south of the great Turkish peninsula historically known as Asia Minor. Cyprus's strategic location led to its invasion and rule by a succession of powers, including the Ottoman Empire, which came to power in 1571. By the end of the nineteenth century, however, Russia was attempting to increase its influence in the eastern Mediterranean at the expense of the languishing Ottoman Empire, which was widely regarded as the "sick man of Europe." After agreeing to protect the Ottomans from Russian aggression, Great Britain leased Cyprus on June 4, 1878, under the terms of the Cyprus Convention.

At the time of the lease, the Britain Empire stretched around the world, and as a territory, Cyprus was at first something of an anomaly in Britain's vast assemblage of possessions. As a result, the British were uncertain about how to treat the colony; for example, an early plan to use the island as a site for a large military base never came to fruition. The leased territory was initially administered by the British Foreign Office but passed to the supervision of the Colonial Office on December 6, 1880.

According to a British census taken soon after the Cyprus Convention, more than three-fourths of the island's residents were Greek and Christian, while most of the remainder were Turkish and Muslim. After years of Ottoman corruption, both groups welcomed British rule, particularly the Greeks, who hoped that the British would give them control of the island. Since the Cypriots remained Ottoman subjects under the terms of the convention, however, it was more convenient for Britain to ignore the Cypriots' larger political aspirations. This pattern would persist despite changes in the island's status.

The most dramatic change in Cyprus's status took place during the opening phases of World War I, when the Ottoman Empire sided with Germany against Great Britain. On November 5, 1914, the British announced that the Ottomans' actions annulled the Cyprus Convention and that Great Britain was adopting the island as a colony. Questions about the legality of this move would be resolved on July 24, 1923, when the new nation of Turkey, created from the core of the dismembered Ottoman Empire, signed the Treaty of Lausanne, recognizing Britain's actions.

With the island's annexation by the British, the attitudes of the citizens of Cyprus intensified. Greek Cypriots saw the move as yet another prelude to unification with Greece, a step referred to as "enosis" and routinely supported by the archbishops of the Cypriot Orthodox Church. Most Turkish Cypriots were receptive toward the idea of annexation, but they were mindful of the reprisals taken against the Turkish population of Crete when that island became part of Greece in 1908. As a result, Turkish Cypriots came to favor *taksim*, the partition of Cyprus between the two ethnic and religious groups. Britain actually offered to cede Cyprus to Greece in 1915 as a reward for entering the war on the side of the Allies, but Greece remained neutral and Britain retained the island.

Compared to the annexation of 1914, Britain's conferral of Crown Colony status on Cyprus in 1925 was anticlimactic. To the British, a Crown Colony was simply an overseas possession under its direct control. A Crown Colony's primary administrator was British and was appointed by the British monarch on the recommendation of the secretary of state for colonies. Depending on the colony's level of development, it might have a legislative council of elected and appointed members (usually civil servants), from which the administrator could choose an

CYPRUS

it to war loans on which the Ottomans had defaulted during the Crimean War (1853-1856). This situation that did not change with annexation, and it was a constant source of frustration to the Cypriots.

SIGNIFICANCE

Great Britain's designation of Cyprus as a Crown Colony was more significant for what it did not do than for what it did. The step formalized a legal and constitutional situation that had existed for years, but Britain's reluctance to address the issue of tax reform and its autocratic refusal to grant a greater degree of freedom to its Cypriot subjects undermined the goodwill that the Cypriots once felt toward the colonial power. Britain did gradually undertake improvements in health and sanitation, education, forest conservation, and the preservation of antiquities, but British parsimony led observers to call Cyprus the "Cinderella colony," a reference to the ill-treated fairy-tale character.

advisory executive council. Cyprus had essentially been ruled in this manner from its earliest years as a leased territory.

The changes enacted on May 1, 1925, were almost all formal in nature. High Commissioner Sir Malcolm Stevenson became governor, and the number of members of the legislative assembly was increased from twenty-one to twenty-four. As before, however, the seats were divided among Greeks, Turks, and appointees in such a way that votes routinely ended in a tie, which allowed the governor to cast the deciding vote (a power he had often similarly exercised as high commissioner). When the Cypriots appealed for greater control over their affairs, Secretary of State for Colonies L. S. Amery turned down the request, asserting that Cyprus had not yet reached an appropriate level of political development.

Predictably, the 1925 conferral provided Cyril III, Cyprus's orthodox archbishop, with another occasion to lobby publicly and emphatically for enosis. Turkish Cypriot leaders pressed the case against enosis, and Secretary Amery rejected the idea. The conferral of Crown Colony status also failed to remedy the issue of the tax known as the Cyprus tribute. Under the terms of the Cyprus Convention, the British had been obligated to turn over excess taxes collected on Cyprus to the Ottoman Empire, but in practice they kept the money and applied

Most seriously of all, conferral of Crown Colony status did nothing to mollify the contradictory but deeply held attitudes of Cyprus's divided citizenry. Greek Cypriots saw, or at least pretended to see, the move as another prelude to enosis, which Turkish Cypriots feared as emphatically as Greek Cypriots supported. Admittedly, there was no easy solution to this situation, but Britain's reluctance to disturb the status quo would lead to increasingly serious outbreaks of violence in the decades ahead.

—*Grove Koger*

FURTHER READING

Boatswain, Tim. *A Traveler's History of Cyprus*. New York: Interlink, 2005. Readable survey with a chapter devoted to the years of British rule, a chronology, and a list of British governors.

Hill, George Francis. *The Ottoman Province, the British Colony, 1571-1948*. Vol. 4 in *A History of Cyprus*. Cambridge, England: Cambridge University Press, 1972. This volume of the standard history discusses the period in considerable detail. Lists of orthodox archbishops, British high commissioners, and British governors.

1925

Holland, R. F., and Diana Weston Markides. *Britain and the Hellenes: Struggles for Mastery in the Eastern Mediterranean, 1850-1960.* Oxford, England: Oxford University Press, 2006. Chapter 7, "The Peculiarity of Cyprus, 1878-1931," deals with Cyprus during the periods leading up to and following the conferral of Crown Colony status.

McHenry, James A. *The Uneasy Partnership on Cyprus, 1919-1939: The Political and Diplomatic Interaction Between Great Britain, Turkey, and the Turkish Cypriot Community.* New York: Garland, 1987. Emphasizes Britain's interactions with Turkey and the Turkish Cypriot minority. Includes guides to key British and Turkish figures.

Purcell, Hugh Dominic. *Cyprus.* New York: Praeger, 1969. Chapter 6, "The British Period," covers all aspects of British control.

Solsten, Eric, ed. *Cyprus: A Country Study.* 4th ed. Washington, D.C.: Federal Research Division, Library of Congress, 1993. Authoritative volume in the Area Handbook series; includes a balanced discussion of British rule.

SEE ALSO: July 24, 1908: Young Turks Stage a Coup in the Ottoman Empire; Nov. 5, 1914: British Mount a Second Front Against the Ottomans; Apr. 24, 1915: Armenian Genocide Begins; May 19, 1919-Sept. 11, 1922: Greco-Turkish War; July 18, 1926: Treaty of Ankara; Dec. 11, 1931: Formation of the British Commonwealth of Nations.

May 5, 1925
JAPAN INTRODUCES SUFFRAGE FOR MEN

The extension of suffrage to all males over the age of twenty-five was a significant aspect of democratic development during the Taisho period in Japan.

ALSO KNOWN AS: Universal Manhood Suffrage Act
LOCALE: Tokyo, Japan
CATEGORIES: Civil rights and liberties; laws, acts, and legal history

KEY FIGURES
Kiyoura Keigo (1850-1942), nonparty Japanese prime minister, January-May, 1924
Yamamoto Gonnohyōe (1852-1933), nonparty Japanese prime minister, September, 1923-January, 1924
Katō Tomosaburō (1861-1923), nonparty Japanese prime minister, June, 1922-August, 1923
Hara Takashi (1856-1921), Seiyukai party leader and Japanese prime minister, 1918-1921
Katō Takaaki (1860-1926), Kenseikai party leader and Japanese prime minister, 1924-1926
Takahashi Korekiyo (1854-1936), Seikukai party leader, 1921-1925

SUMMARY OF EVENT
Universal male suffrage was established in Japan in 1925, at the end of the Taisho period (1912-1926). It stands as one of the high points of an expansion of freedoms often called the Taisho democracy. Democratic government in Japan began under the Meiji constitution of 1889, which created an elected House of Representatives. Initially, only males over the age of twenty-five who paid annual national taxes of fifteen yen or more could vote for their representatives, but this meant that voting rights were held by only approximately 1 percent of the population. Over time, the tax qualification was gradually lowered—to ten yen in 1900 and to three yen in 1919—so that in 1919 the number of eligible voters had risen to include slightly more than 5 percent of the national population.

The idea of extending voting rights to all male voters was first introduced in the House of Representatives in 1902, and a bill to accomplish this was actually passed in that body in 1911, only to be unanimously defeated the same year in the House of Peers, the upper, nonelected legislative body. The issue was temporarily set aside in the often volatile political climate of the period that followed, and the major parties during those years made the question a matter of party loyalty: Members were prohibited from voting for any bill that was not officially sanctioned by the party.

The topic did not surface again until 1919, when legislators began to debate lowering the tax qualification. The Seiyukai Party, the majority party led by the country's prime minister, Hara Takashi, supported the bill (requiring that voters pay at least three yen in taxes) that was eventually enacted. The Seiyukai were opposed by the Kenseikai, who supported lowering the requirement to two yen. In response to public demonstrations arguing for the complete elimination of the tax qualification, some members of the Kenseikai and some independent members reintroduced the question of universal male suffrage. Among this group of Kenseikai was Kurosu Ryutaro, who introduced a proposal to this end in October of 1918. He was joined by Imai Yoshiyuki, who was not affiliated with either party but was sometimes called "Mister Universal Suffrage" because he published a magazine article supporting the idea in January of 1919. Some members of the Seiyukai Party also argued for the policy change, most notably Saito Takao, who sought ways to extend the vote beyond the official position taken by his party even though he did not support full male suffrage.

Following passage of the 1919 bill, the debate over universal male suffrage continued, particularly within the Kenseikai Party. The issue carried a great deal of political risk. On the positive side, support for the motion would strengthen the party's position among urban voters, who had benefited less from the 1919 bill than had their rural counterparts. Politicians also believed that passage might mitigate growing political unrest in the country. On the negative side, however, was the fear that universal suffrage might alienate conservative interests both inside and outside the party and could even lead to a split within the party.

After some initial uncertainty, Katō Takaaki, the Kenseikai leader, eventually gave his support to the idea, and the party gave formal approval to a proposal favoring universal male suffrage at a meeting held in December of 1919. In the meantime, the party in power, the Seikukai, stuck with the newly enacted three-yen tax-qualification bill; Hara saw universal male suffrage as a matter for later consideration. Things remained in this state until Hara's assassination by a student with right-wing ties in November, 1921.

Following Hara's assassination, his successor, Takahashi Korekiyo, lost control of the party (although he continued as its leader until 1925). A series of nonparty governments were appointed by the genro, the powerful behind-the-scenes group that advised the emperor. These included the governments of Admiral Katō Tomosaburō, Admiral Yamamoto Gonnohyōe, and Viscount Kiyoura Keigo. The first two took some modest steps toward suffrage. Admiral Katō established a committee to study the question, and in June of 1923 the committee issued a report in favor of further lowering of the tax qualification. After Katō's death in August of that year, his successor, Admiral Yamamoto, came out in support of universal male suffrage. Unfortunately, Yamamoto's January,

1924, resignation created another hurdle in the move toward suffrage. Ironically, it was the third of the nonparty governments that contributed the most—albeit unintentionally—to the growth of the suffrage movement.

The Kiyoura government offered the strongest support of any of the nonparty cabinets for expanding voting rights. In fact, a bill supporting universal male suffrage was approved by cabinet members in January of 1924. From its inception, however, the government encountered strong opposition from the parties of the lower house. The administration's close connections to the nonelected House of Peers caused it to be viewed by many as a throwback to an earlier era of privilege and hereditary control. As a result, a united, anti-Kiyoura movement began to emerge, and it eventually included both the Seiyukai and the Kenseikai.

The question of universal male suffrage presented the greatest stumbling block as the two parties formed a united front, but in the end, opposition to the Kiyoura government overrode differences over suffrage. In an election held on May 10, 1924, the Kiyoura cabinet was defeated by an alliance of the Seiyukai, the Kenseikai, and a group known as the Reform Club. A coalition government was formed with Kenseikai leader Katō Takaaki as its head, and universal male suffrage became one of the new movement's primary goals.

With both of the major parties now supporting the issue, acceptance by the House of Peers and the Privy Council (the more formal advisory group to the emperor) remained the final steps to enactment. The inclusion of an independent-living clause in the bill became a sticking point: This idea, which would give the vote only to males over the age of twenty-five who were financially self-sufficient, actually dated back to the bill approved by the Kenseikai in December of 1919. The provision had been removed from later Kenseikai versions of the bill, but it was now reinserted, with slightly different wording, by both the upper house and the Privy Council.

The matter was hotly debated, but in the end a compromise led to the bill's acceptance with some rewording of the independent-living clause. The bill passed both houses at the end of March, was approved by the Privy Council a month later, and was officially promulgated in the name of the emperor on May 5, 1925. On May 7, the Katō government took steps to ensure that local officials would interpret the law in such a way that much of the independent-living requirement was lost. For all practical purposes, universal male suffrage had been fully implemented in Japan.

SIGNIFICANCE

Both the establishment of universal male suffrage and the active roles political parties played in its passage offer clear evidence of a growth of democracy in Japan. Unfortunately, 1925 also saw the passage of the Peace Preservation Law, which gave the government power to limit political dissent and helped set the stage for the militarism of the 1930's. This period undercut the development of democracy and led Japan along the road to territorial expansion and war. Nevertheless, from a long-term perspective, the democratic developments of the Taisho period provided a foundation for Japan's postwar move toward democracy and led to the establishment of suffrage for Japanese women in 1945.

—*Scott Wright*

FURTHER READING

Duus, Peter. *Party Rivalry and Political Change in Taisho Japan.* Cambridge, Mass.: Harvard University Press, 1968. A good source of information about the movement relationship to the larger Taisho political background.

Griffith, Edward G. "The Universal Suffrage Issue in Japanese Politics, 1918-25." *Journal of Asian Studies* 31, no. 2 (February, 1972): 275-290. The most detailed treatment of the subject in English.

Sims, Richard. *Japanese Political History Since the Meiji Renovation, 1868-2000.* New York: Palgrave, 2001. For the broader historical and political context.

Wray, Harry, and Hilary Conroy, eds. *Japan Examined: Perspectives on Modern Japanese History.* Honolulu: University of Hawaii Press, 1983. Scholarly essays by Stephen S. Large, David A. Titus, and Henry D. Smith II on the subject of Taisho democracy.

SEE ALSO: Jan. 7, 1932: Stimson Doctrine; Feb. 24, 1933: Japan Withdraws from the League of Nations; Dec. 29, 1934: Japan Renounces Disarmament Treaties; Aug., 1940: Japan Announces the Greater East Asia Coprosperity Sphere.

May 17, 1925
THÉRÈSE OF LISIEUX IS CANONIZED

After waiving the fifty-year waiting period required by canon law, Pope Pius XI proclaimed Thérèse Martin a saint of the Roman Catholic Church less than twenty-eight years after her death.

ALSO KNOWN AS: Thérèse of the Child Jesus and of the Holy Face; Little Flower of Jesus
LOCALE: The Vatican, Rome, Italy
CATEGORY: Religion, theology, and ethics

KEY FIGURES

Thérèse Martin (1873-1897), French Carmelite nun who became one of the most popular saints of the twentieth century
Pius XI (Ambrogio Damiano Achille Ratti; 1857-1939), Roman Catholic pope, 1922-1939, who canonized Thérèse
Benedict XV (Giacomo della Chiesa; 1854-1922), Roman Catholic pope, 1914-1922, who declared Thérèse Martin's practice of virtue "heroic"
Pius X (Giuseppe Melchiorre Sarto; 1835-1914), Roman Catholic pope, 1903-1914, who formally began Thérèse Martin's beatification process
Pauline Martin (1861-1951), also known as Mother Agnes of Jesus, the first of the Martin sisters to become a Carmelite nun

Marie de Gonzague (1834-1904), Mother Agnes's successor as prioress
Marie Martin (1860-1940), Thérèse Martin's godmother and a Carmelite nun and who later testified for her sister's canonization as Marie of the Sacred Heart

SUMMARY OF EVENT

The abbreviated life of Thérèse Martin is marked by one pivotal paradox: Somehow, this obscure Carmelite nun, who did nothing extraordinary in her Normandy convent, became, according to popes, bishops, and millions of Catholics, the greatest saint of the modern world. In an attempt to explain this paradox, some scholars have offered a concomitance of fortuitous events, such as the exemplarily devout family in which she, as the youngest of five daughters, was treated as the favorite. Others have pointed to her special linguistic gift: In her spiritual autobiography, she was able to express her religious insights in a naïve simplicity that eventually touched the lives of millions in many countries. Through what she called her "little way," she helped to revive Jesus Christ's ideal of holiness, in which a person becomes a saint not through great words or deeds but through faithfulness to the will of God in one's vocation, however humble. Particularly during her final eighteen months, when tuberculosis caused her a great deal of suffering, she was able, despite occasional thoughts of suicide, to achieve the self-renunciation that led to her ultimate liberation. One writer compared her journey to that of a "perfected butterfly" emerging from the chrysalis of her torturned soul.

Thérèse's fellow nuns were deeply affected by Thérèse's death and by her promise to do good on earth from heaven. Pauline Martin, who was both Thérèse's biological sister and the prioress of Thérèse's convent (where she was known as Mother Agnes of Jesus) began the process of canonization by circulating Thérèse's writings to Carmelite convents. Twenty-one months before she died, Thérèse, at the request of Mother Agnes, began writing down her childhood memories in a notebook. In 1896, at the request of her godmother, Marie of the Sacred Heart, Thérèse analyzed her vocation, and a few months before her death, Thérèse complied with a request from Marie de Gonzague (Mother Agnes's successor as prioress) that Thérèse complete the recollections of her life at Carmel.

The unification of these notebooks with other material was largely the work of Mother Agnes, although Marie de Gonzague insisted on having Thérèse's reminiscences directed to her. On September 30, 1898, a year after Thérèse's death, two thousand copies of Thérèse's *L'Histoire d'une âme* (1898; *The Story of a Soul: The Autobiography of Saint Thérèse of Lisieux*, 1952) were printed. During the early decades of the twentieth century, the demand for this book increased so quickly that by the time of Thérèse's canonization, more than a million copies of the French edition had been sold. Within three years of the book's publication, the convent was receiving reports of cures in Thérèse's name, and by the date of her canonization, the convent's collection of cures, answered prayers, and other favors contained more than three thousand pages.

The formal process of making a saint usually begins at the diocesan level, and early in the twentieth century evidence of Thérèse's holiness was collected and tested. Testimonials to her sanctity were also given. For example, Thérèse's sister Pauline's testimonial recounted Thérèse's courage during her final illness, and Pauline also stated that most of the nuns who entered Carmel after 1897 did so because of Thérèse. Thérèse's sister Marie provided letters received by the convent, as many as a hundred a day, thanking Thérèse for favors, cures, and conversions. By 1910, church officials had become convinced that Thérèse had lived a heroically virtuous life, and they bestowed on her the traditional title of venerable.

In response to the requests of many bishops and religious superiors, Pius X signed a decree initiating the process of Thérèse's beatification in June of 1914. This process was entrusted to the postulator-general of the Discalced Carmelites. Consultors and theological experts in the Congregation for the Causes of Saints began to assess the accumulated evidence, especially the miracles attributed to the Venerable Thérèse's intercession. By August of 1921, Benedict XV, convinced that Thérèse had exhibited extraordinary valor in her practice of the theological and cardinal virtues, gave an address on her "way of spiritual childhood." On March 6, 1923, Cardinal Vico, the prefect of the Sacred Congregation of Rites, formally declared (with the unanimous agreement of the doctors who had examined the cures) that two of the miracles attributed to Thérèse's intercession were genuine and that her beatification could be safely undertaken. Pope Pius XI then issued a brief for the ceremony, which took place at St. Peter's Basilica on April 29, 1923. The papal mass and beatification ritual were very well attended.

On July 27, 1923, the pope commissioned the Sacred Congregation of Rites to continue the investigations that would lead to Thérèse's canonization. The promoter of the faith, popularly known as the "devil's advocate," raised objections against Thérèse's cause, including her emphasis on God's mercy to the neglect of justice. Medical doctors were appointed to examine miraculous cures, and theologians studied Thérèse's writings, which were much more extensive than generally recognized. In addition to her spiritual autobiography, she wrote 266 letters and 54 poems, many of which concerned the mystery of God's love in her life and in the lives of others. She also composed prayers and little plays. Contained in these writings were more than a thousand biblical quotations.

On March 17, 1925, after hearing from Cardinal Vico and other cardinals and consultors, Pius XI solemnly proclaimed that the two new cures attributed to Thérèse's intercession were "certainly miraculous." Thérèse's canonization could therefore proceed, and the pope convoked a secret consistory of cardinals on March 30, 1925, to seek their advice on the question of this canonization, which met with their unanimous and enthusiastic approval. At a public consistory held on April 2, all the cardinals present encouraged the pope to decide in favor of Thérèse's sanctity. The pope then sought the opinions of patriarchs, archbishops, and bishops from around the world, and he found that they also were united in favor of this canonization, which the pope decided to celebrate on May 17 in St. Peter's.

In a canonization ceremony, a person previously beatified is publicly recognized as a saint who has entered into eternal glory. Vatican officials received more than 200,000 applications for the 50,000 available seats in St. Peter's. When the day of Thérèse's canonization arrived, more than half a million people celebrated the event in Rome, and millions more celebrated in other countries. In the papal mass, Pius XI, who considered Thérèse "the star of his pontificate," chose as the theme of his homily Jesus Christ's admonition that "unless you become as little children, you shall not enter into the Kingdom of Heaven." In his bull of canonization, the pope noted that Thérèse had achieved sanctity "without going beyond the common order of things." Her "little way" was one of trust and total surrender to God's will. She believed that the chief architect of her perfection was not herself but God. Like her, Pius said, Christians must abandon themselves, like infants, to the arms of a caring God—an appropriate sentiment for a nun who chose to call herself "Thérèse of the Child Jesus."

SIGNIFICANCE

In the years after her canonization, Thérèse's influence in and outside of the Catholic Church expanded and deepened. Her writings were translated into more than fifty languages, and hundreds of biographies were published. To accommodate the many pilgrims visiting Lisieux, a large basilica was erected in her honor in the 1920's. In 1927, Pius XI, in response to the requests of many bishops, proclaimed Thérèse copatron of missions with St. Francis Xavier. She was later named copatron of France, along with St. Joan of Arc, whom Thérèse had deeply admired. She was also named patron saint of florists, aviators, and those suffering from AIDS.

Thérèse was contemplative—her struggles with atheism touched on issues that concerned the French existentialists—but her message also appealed to such social activists as Dorothy Day, who was converted from atheism to Catholicism by reading *The Story of a Soul.*

Surprisingly, Thérèse also influenced several modern writers. In his *Journal d'un curé de campagne* (1936; *The Diary of a Country Priest,* 1937), Georges Bernanos placed several of Thérèse's sayings in the mouth of his anguished curé. In Graham Greene's *How Father Quixote Became a Monsignor* (1980), Thérèse is the "Dulcinea" of the quixotic priest. Jack Kerouac, the quintessential Beat generation writer, was fascinated by this nun's poems, prayers, and passion for holiness. Jewish philosopher Henri Bergson beieved that Thérèse was a greater mystic than Saint Teresa of Avila, and Mother Teresa of

Calcutta joyfully informed people that she had taken her religious name not from the great Teresa of Avila but from the "Little Flower," Thérèse of Lisieux. Thérèse was also beloved by important churchmen. While he was nuncio in Paris, Cardinal Angelo Giuseppe Roncalli, the future Pope John XXIII, often visited Lisieux. When Pope John Paul II, on the hundredth anniversary of Thérèse's death, named her a doctor of the universal church, she joined the ranks of such spiritual giants as Saint Catherine of Siena, Saint Teresa of Avila, Saint Augustine, and Saint Thomas Aquinas.

—*Robert J. Paradowski*

FURTHER READING

Balthasar, Hans Urs von. *Two Sisters in the Spirit: Thérèse of Lisieux and Elizabeth of the Trinity.* San Francisco: Ignatius Press, 1992. The famous Swiss theologian has reworked spiritual biographies published on these two holy Carmelites in 1950 and 1953 to emphasize their comparable mission to "open up the treasures of God's Word to ordinary believers." Chronologies, but no index.

Goerres, Ida Friedericke. *The Hidden Face: A Study of St. Thérèse of Lisieux.* New York: Pantheon, 1959. This English translation of the eighth revised edition of a very successful book originally published in German represents the author's attempt to discover the "true Thérèse" based on her writings (before they were edited). Selected bibliography and index.

Harrison, Kathryn. *Saint Thérèse of Lisieux: A Penguin Life.* New York: Viking Press, 2003. This brief account by a novelist emphasizes psychological analysis rather than the saint's rootedness in scripture and the truths of the Catholic faith.

Martin, Thérèse. *Autobiography of a Saint.* London: Fount, 1960. This translation by Ronald Knox from the facsimile of Thérèse Martin's manuscripts made the unedited versions of her notebooks available to English readers for the first time.

Ulanov, Barry. *The Making of a Modern Saint: A Biographical Study of Thérèse of Lisieux.* 1966. Reprint. Springfield, Ill.: Templegate, 2004. An astute analysis of Thérèse's oeuvre by a writer who had published more than forty books by the time of his death in 2000. He admired this saint's ability to find dignity in the smallness and pain of everyday life.

SEE ALSO: May 16, 1920: Canonization of Joan of Arc; Dec. 8, 1933: Canonization of Bernadette Soubirous; Oct. 5, 1938: Death of Maria Faustina Kowalska.

June 17, 1925
GENEVA PROTOCOL IS SIGNED

Representatives from several nations, including most of the Great Powers, signed a protocol banning the use of poison gas and bacteriological weapons in war.

LOCALE: Geneva, Switzerland

CATEGORIES: Diplomacy and international relations; health and medicine

KEY FIGURES

Theodore E. Burton (1851-1929), U.S. congressman from Ohio and representative of the United States at Geneva

Calvin Coolidge (1872-1933), president of the United States, 1923-1929

Gerald R. Ford (1913-2006), president of the United States, 1974-1977

SUMMARY OF EVENT

On June 17, 1925, representatives from several nations met in Geneva, Switzerland, and signed a protocol to prohibit "the use in war of asphyxiating, poisonous or other gases, and of all analogous liquids, materials or devices," and further consented to extend this prohibition to bacteriological methods of warfare as well. This relatively brief document acknowledged that gas warfare had been condemned by civilized opinion and expressed the hope that the accord would one day become an accepted part of international law. The swiftness with which the agreement was reached was a tribute to the negotiating skills of the U.S. representative in Geneva, Theodore E. Burton, and also to the strong support that President Calvin Coolidge gave to the project.

The protocol was a response to the widespread use of poison gas in World War I. Poison gas was first used at the Battle of Ypres in April, 1915, when the Germans released clouds of chlorine gas against French positions. Other nations, including Great Britain, France, and eventually the United States, either conducted extensive research or actually used poison gas in battle. Each year of the war witnessed an increase in use of this nefarious weapon. There is no consensus on the actual number of people affected, but after the war, the figures of one million casualties and 100,000 deaths were frequently cited. Although these numbers were undoubtedly an exaggeration, they were readily accepted by the general public. When these statistics were combined with graphic accounts of gas attacks in antiwar poems and novels and with photographs depicting pathetic columns of soldiers

with bandages covering their eyes or hideous blisters marring their bodies, the effect on public opinion was dramatic. A significant body of opinion soon began to call for an end to gas warfare.

By the time the delegates gathered in Geneva in 1925, there were already three international agreements on the subject. Even before World War I, several nations had signed the 1899 Hague Declaration, promising to abstain from using "projectiles" to deliver poison gas. Advances in technology, however, later made it possible to disperse gas from cylinders or from aerial bombs. After the war, the victorious Allied governments inserted Clause 171 into the Treaty of Versailles, which prohibited Germany from possessing, manufacturing, or importing chemical weapons. A more extensive agreement was reached at the Washington Disarmament Conference in 1921 and 1922, when the Five Powers (the United States, Great Britain, Japan, Italy, and France) adopted Article 5, which banned the use of poison gas in war. All five countries signed the agreement, but it never came into force because France subsequently refused to ratify it over a dispute concerning submarines.

The Geneva Protocol was in many respects an unexpected and unplanned success. Originally, the delegates had a rather narrow mandate: to regulate the international arms trade. Although the issue was not on the agenda, Burton suggested that chemical weapons be included in the discussions. Smaller nations did not like the idea of a ban on the export of chemical weapons, because such a ban would help to perpetuate the substantial gap that already existed between the arsenals of the Great Powers and those of the lesser ones. Moreover, enforcement of such a law would have been complicated by the difficulty of distinguishing between chemicals destined for legitimate use and those intended to be converted into poison gas; such uses often overlapped. Finally, some delegates feared that regulating the trade in poison gas would in effect legitimate gas as a weapon by placing it on the same level with conventional weapons.

Responding to these concerns, Burton therefore proposed a total ban on the use of chemical weapons in war, not simply a ban on trade. About the same time, President Coolidge stated that if the delegates in Geneva failed to agree to a ban on use, he would invite them to Washington for a conference in order to achieve that objective. Burton's proposal was warmly received, however, and the U.S. delegation readily accepted a friendly amendment from the Polish delegate that the prohibition be extended to bacteriological warfare. Initially, some two dozen nations signed the protocol, but several nations, including the United States, had to have their national legislatures ratify it to give it the force of law.

Ironically, the United States, the nation given credit for negotiating the agreement, failed to ratify it. Because the protocol was a treaty, it needed to be approved by a two-thirds majority in the U.S. Senate. The protocol had the support of Coolidge, the U.S. Navy, and the War Department and the personal backing of General John J. Pershing, who had been commander in chief of the U.S. forces in World War I. Nevertheless, the military establishments in many countries, including the United States, did not wish to give up the new weapon. Moreover, there were powerful voices that asserted that chemical weapons designed to incapacitate or immobilize were less horrible than other weaponry designed to kill or maim. A particularly telling statistic often quoted by opponents of the protocol was that 25 percent of the soldiers hit by artillery shells died, compared with only 3 percent of gas casualties. In addition, influential organizations such as the American Legion, the Veterans of Foreign Wars, the Association of Military Surgeons, and the prestigious American Chemical Society were opposed to ratification. The protocol was deliberated for only one day on the Senate floor before being withdrawn by its supporters, who feared certain defeat. Despite this failure, the protocol came into force in 1928. By the outbreak of World War II, more than thirty countries had ratified it, including all of the Great Powers save the United States and Japan.

SIGNIFICANCE

Over the decades, there has been a tendency for the public to expect too much of the Geneva Protocol, mainly as a result of several misunderstandings. The agreement did not ban further research, manufacture, or importation of chemical weapons, only their use in war. Significantly, it included neither provisions for verification nor penalties for noncompliance. The wording of the protocol obligated the signees only with respect to those nations that also signed the pact; in other words, it was permissible for a signee to use poison gas against an enemy that was not a signatory. Furthermore, many nations that ratified the protocol did so with the reservation that they would be at liberty to retaliate if an enemy first employed chemical methods of warfare. Many observers have pointed out that this meant the protocol was tantamount to an agreement renouncing first use of chemical weapons, nothing more.

Moreover, diplomats, scholars, and jurists skilled in international law have found some disturbing ambiguities in the agreement. It was unclear whether the protocol banned all chemical agents or only those that were clearly intended to kill, wound, or seriously maim. It was also unclear whether the agreement applied only to international wars or to all wars, including civil wars and undeclared wars such as the U.S. conflict in Vietnam. Some scientists wondered whether references to bacteria should be interpreted narrowly or broadly, as some highly toxic substances exist (for example, among viruses and fungi) that technically are not bacteria.

The Geneva Protocol did not stop the practice of chemical warfare. The first nation to breach the agreement was Italy, which unleashed poison gas against Ethiopia in 1935 and 1936. Japan used gas against China beginning in the late 1930's. After World War II, the United Arab Republic employed chemical weapons in Yemen's civil war in 1967; the United States used nonlethal chemicals, such as riot-control agents, herbicides, and defoliants, in the Vietnam conflict during the late 1960's; and Iraq employed both mustard and nerve gas in the Gulf War with Iran in 1983. During the 1980's, the Soviet Union was suspected of using chemical weapons in Afghanistan, and Vietnam was alleged to have used chemical agents in Laos and Kampuchea. These allegations, although widely believed, were never authenticated. Such a list of violations may appear formidable, but in the context of a century that produced literally hundreds of wars and atrocities, the use of poison gas and chemical warfare has been remarkably restrained.

Most notably, chemical weapons were not employed in World War II. Most scholars believe that a universal fear of retaliation prevented such use. Nazi Germany was alarmed by the prospect of chemical warfare, fearing that its enemies were much better prepared defensively and offensively. German chancellor Adolf Hitler, who was himself gassed in World War I, reportedly believed this form of warfare to be especially barbaric. In turn, France, Great Britain, and the Soviet Union had a healthy respect for Germany's chemical industry and its scientists and confidently believed that Germany would retaliate with full fury and effectiveness if so attacked. Japan never used gas against European troops in the Asian theater, assuming that U.S. industrial might and technical genius would wreak a terrible vengeance with similar weapons against Japan's crowded cities.

Most of the belligerents in the war were not adequately prepared, offensively or defensively, for chemical warfare. Stocks of chemical weapons were insufficient for continuous and effective use, and there had been little training of elite military units in the techniques of delivering gas attacks. Finally, much of the war saw the application of blitzkrieg tactics. In a war of mobility, the effectiveness of poison gas was limited, because it worked best on a stable front.

After World War II, fears of chemical warfare partially receded. The atomic bomb replaced poison gas as the "doomsday" weapon. In addition, the major powers shrouded much of their research into new biological and toxic agents in secrecy, thus temporarily allaying the public's apprehension. The protocol, however, was not forgotten. In 1966, the United Nations General Assembly voted unanimously to observe the principles and objectives of the Geneva Protocol. By 1970, the number of signatories to the treaty had reached eighty-four; the United States remained a significant exception.

On November 25, 1969, however, President Richard Nixon reaffirmed U.S. support for the Geneva Protocol and renounced first use of lethal chemical weapons. Nixon also renounced the use of all biological weapons, even in retaliation, and stated that the Department of Defense had been ordered to dispose of existing stocks of such weapons. The following year, Nixon submitted the Geneva Protocol to the Senate for consent to ratification, where it ran into opposition from liberal senators. The Republican Nixon administration made it clear that it believed the protocol did not prohibit the use of nonlethal chemical agents. Democrats, however, were upset that the United States was using nonlethal herbicides, defoliants, and riot-control agents in Vietnam; many liberal senators argued that the protocol banned all chemical weapons, not only lethal chemicals.

The stalemate was finally resolved during the presidency of Gerald R. Ford. Senate opposition was stilled when Fred Icke, director of the U.S. Arms Control and Disarmament Agency, promised that nonlethal chemicals would be used in the future only under stringent limitations. The Senate gave its consent to the protocol by a vote of ninety to zero, and on January 22, 1975, President Ford signed the agreement, fifty years after it had been negotiated. On the day the Senate approved the protocol, it also unanimously approved the Convention on the Prohibition of Bacteriological and Toxin Weapons (1972). This agreement, negotiated principally by the Soviet Union and the United States but open to other countries, was an attempt to update the Geneva Protocol by including scientific advances made over the years and providing for some measure of verification and compliance—two essential components missing from the protocol.

Most diplomatic activity since 1975 has revolved around this newer instrument.

The Geneva Protocol has had a mixed history. It did not prevent the use of chemical agents in some conflicts, nor did it prevent research into and production of such weapons. It was, however, taken seriously by most nations. Countries cited the protocol when other nations violated the letter or the spirit of the agreement, and it proved a useful tool with which to embarrass other powers in the propaganda battles of the Cold War. Smaller nations believed that the protocol afforded some modest legal protection against weapons that they neither had nor wished to develop. It became, in the words of Hubert Humphrey, the Democratic senator and vice president, "the basic building block for all efforts to control chemical and biological warfare." As of 2006, the treaty had 133 signatories, attesting to its vitality and endurance.

—David C. Lukowitz

FURTHER READING

Adams, Valerie. *Chemical Warfare, Chemical Disarmament*. Bloomington: Indiana University Press, 1990. Brief and readable survey of the subject includes little discussion of the protocol but addresses its impact on later developments. Features extensive bibliography.

Brown, Frederick J. *Chemical Warfare: A Study in Restraints*. 1968. Reprint. New Brunswick, N.J.: Transaction, 2005. Account of the history of the use of chemical weapons and attempts to restrain use by legal measures. Also discusses the "humanity" of chemical warfare. Includes important material about chemical warfare and chemical arms control that is difficult to find elsewhere.

Coleman, Kim. *A History of Chemical Warfare*. New York: Palgrave Macmillan, 2005. Describes the development and use of chemical weapons from 700 B.C.E. to the beginning of the twenty-first century, with extensive discussion of World War I. Also assesses current attempts to control the use and proliferation of such weapons and analyzes their potential use by terrorist groups.

Croddy, Eric, with Clarisa Perez-Armendariz and John Hart. *Chemical and Biological Warfare: A Comprehensive Survey for the Concerned Citizen*. New York: Springer-Verlag, 2002. Provides in-depth information on all aspects of chemical and biological warfare and weapons. Chapter 6 includes discussion of the Geneva Protocol. Features selected bibliography and index.

Friedman, Leon, ed. *The Law of War: A Documentary History*. Vol. 1. New York: Random House, 1972. A respected collection of the original texts of treaties dealing with the origins, development, and enforcement of the laws of war, including the names of original signatories.

Haber, L. F. *The Poisonous Cloud: Chemical Warfare in the First World War*. Oxford, England: Clarendon Press, 1986. Excellent work on how poison gas affected soldiers, governments, military doctrine, and the chemical industry during and after World War I. Meticulously documented, with an excellent bibliography.

Spiers, Edward. *Chemical Warfare*. Urbana: University of Illinois Press, 1986. Excellent historical survey of the topic by an authority in the field. Focuses on how nations have simultaneously relied on deterrence and disarmament negotiations in order to avoid chemical

warfare. Includes copious footnotes and a fine bibliography.

Thomas, Ann Van Wynen, and A. J. Thomas, Jr. *Legal Limits on the Use of Chemical and Biological Weapons*. Dallas: Southern Methodist University Press, 1970. Impressive study of the development and status of international law as it relates to chemical and biological warfare. Contains a brief but excellent section on the ambiguities and limitations of the protocol. For the advanced student.

SEE ALSO: Oct. 18, 1907: Second Hague Peace Conference; June 28, 1914-Nov. 11, 1918: World War I; Apr. 22-27, 1915: Germany Uses Poison Gas Against Allied Troops; Apr. 28-May 1, 1915: International Congress of Women; 1925-1926: Mussolini Seizes Dictatorial Powers in Italy.

June 26, 1925
CHAPLIN PRODUCES HIS MASTERPIECE *THE GOLD RUSH*

With its characteristic combination of humor and pathos, The Gold Rush *became a landmark film both for Charles Chaplin's career and for the history of motion-picture comedy.*

LOCALE: United States
CATEGORY: Motion pictures

KEY FIGURES
Charles Chaplin (1889-1977), English film actor and filmmaker
Georgia Hale (1906-1985), American film actor
Mack Swain (1876-1935), American film actor
Lita Grey Chaplin (1908-1995), American film actor

SUMMARY OF EVENT
Charles Chaplin's place in film history was already assured long before the release of *The Gold Rush* in 1925. Within two years of his film debut in the two-reel comedy *Making a Living* (1914), Chaplin had become the most popular performer in motion pictures. His "Little Tramp" character was an internationally recognized figure, well on its way to becoming a cinematic icon so powerful that it remains one of the few images capable by itself of evoking the idea of Hollywood moviemaking.

Charlie Chaplin's career began while he was still a child. Abandoned by his father, who died when Chaplin was twelve, and with his mother often a patient in mental

asylums, Chaplin, along with his older brother Sydney, was forced to make his own way in the world from the age of nine. He gained experience as an actor, dancer, and comedian on England's music-hall stages, finally joining the popular Fred Karno Company—which also included a young Stan Laurel—in 1908.

At the close of an American tour by the group in 1913, Chaplin chose to remain in the United States to embark on a career in motion pictures. Under contract to Keystone Studios, he made thirty-five comedy shorts during the next year; his Tramp character appeared for the first time in his second film, *Kid Auto Races in Venice* (1914). Chaplin described the character's creation in his 1964 autobiography:

> I thought I would dress in baggy pants, big shoes, a cane and a derby hat. . . . I added a small mustache . . . the moment I was dressed, the clothes and the make-up made me feel the person he was. I began to know him, and by the time I walked onto the stage he was fully born.

Before the year was through, Chaplin was directing as well as starring in his films, and he had already begun to achieve a remarkable degree of popularity among motion-picture audiences across the country. The character of the Tramp—down on his luck but always resourceful, agile, and quick-witted—struck a chord with audiences and soon emerged as a creation of such complexity and durability that Chaplin would continue to develop and refine him for more than two decades. After leaving Keystone for the Essanay Studios, Chaplin began to explore the character's potential in more depth, experimenting for the first time in *The Tramp* (1915) with the combination of comedy and pathos that would become his trademark. The film ends with the Tramp losing the girl he loves and setting off down the road alone, his back to the camera.

The introduction of pathos into Chaplin's films gave the Tramp a vulnerability that marked him as more than merely a comic figure, and it won for Chaplin a measure of artistic respect beyond that already accorded him as a comedian. In films such as *The Vagabond* (1916), *The Immigrant* (1917), and *A Dog's Life* (1918), Chaplin demonstrated a style of comic filmmaking that combines both slapstick and subtlety while at the same time incorporating a potent measure of heartfelt human emotion. Chaplin's decision to allow his essentially comic character to experience pain, loss, and disappointment—and to end some of his films on that note—is almost unique in the annals of film comedy. That he did so at a time when the medium was still in its infancy is especially remarkable.

In 1920, Chaplin released his first feature-length film featuring the Tramp. *The Kid* costarred Jackie Coogan as the abandoned boy the Tramp adopts and then nearly loses, and the film demonstrated Chaplin's ability to sustain his character's appeal in a format longer than the short comedies in which he had previously appeared. The film was a great success, and although Chaplin would make two more short films and one four-reel comedy in the years that followed, *The Kid* marked the beginning of his career as a feature filmmaker.

In 1924, Chaplin began work on *The Gold Rush*. Inspired by his interest in the tragedy of the Donner Party, a group of settlers who resorted to cannibalism while snowbound in the Sierras, the film is the story of the Tramp's adventures as a gold prospector in turn-of-the-century Alaska: his run-ins with the villainous Black Larson (portrayed by Tom Murray), his near starvation in a snowbound cabin with his partner, Big Jim (Henry Bergman), and his love for Georgia (Georgia Hale), a beautiful dance-hall girl. The film contains two of Chaplin's best-known comic scenes: his attempts to cook and eat his boot and the famous "Oceana Roll" sequence, in which he manipulates a pair of bread rolls on forks as if they are dancing feet. *The Gold Rush* also features scenes of great poignancy, particularly the sequence in which the Tramp waits forlornly for Georgia and her friends to arrive for a dinner he has prepared—an invitation she has forgotten.

Chaplin always worked slowly on features, and *The Gold Rush* was a year and a half in the making. The period would prove to be a tumultuous one in Chaplin's life. His original costar was to be a fifteen-year-old girl named Lita Grey, who had appeared briefly in two earlier Chaplin films. By the fall of 1924, however, Lita was expecting Chaplin's child, and their subsequent marriage—and divorce two years later—was the source of a scandal that haunted Chaplin for many years to come. Lita was replaced in the film by Georgia Hale, and shooting resumed in early 1925.

The Gold Rush opened to tremendous critical acclaim, with *The New York Times* terming it "the outstanding gem of all Chaplin's pictures" and the *New York Daily News* calling it "the funniest and saddest of all comedies." The film is a masterpiece of silent comedy,

Charles Chaplin in character as the Little Tramp. (Hulton Archive/Getty Images)

drawing on all of Chaplin's skills in pantomime, comic timing, and the careful construction of sight gags. Its story is tailor-made for the Tramp's particular blend of plucky resourcefulness and vulnerability, and Chaplin succeeds behind the camera in telling an engaging story that brilliantly showcases his talents onscreen.

After *The Gold Rush*, Chaplin devoted himself exclusively to feature-length productions. He would make only eight more films during the next fifty years, with *City Lights* (1931) and *Modern Times* (1936) joining *The Gold Rush* in the ranks of his acclaimed masterpieces and *The Circus* (1928) winning for its creator a special Oscar at the first Academy Awards ceremony in 1929.

SIGNIFICANCE

Comedy has been an important component of theater since its earliest incarnation, with Aristophanes' work surviving into the modern age alongside that of Euripides and Aeschylus. The strong link between theater and film, therefore, led quite naturally to a position of similar importance for comedy in the medium of film. That early films were silent made them particularly well suited to visual comedy, in which a minimum of dialogue is needed to convey the story; as the medium grew in popularity, its comedians quickly emerged as favorites with audiences. Founded in 1912, the Keystone Studios produced one split-reel comedy a week and introduced Mabel Normand, Roscoe "Fatty" Arbuckle, director Mack Sennett and his Bathing Beauties, and the Keystone Kops to the screen. When Chaplin joined their ranks two years later, the studio had already established itself as a leading force in Hollywood by tapping into the universal language of laughter and adapting it to the new technology of film.

Chaplin's training in the acrobatic style of English music-hall comedy had prepared him well for the physical nature of silent film comedy. The early shorts produced by the Keystone Studios relied primarily on sight gags and actors' talent for comic pantomime. Chaplin excelled at the physical agility needed for such routines, and his skill at mimicry and wordless self-expression remains unsurpassed. The specific nature of silent comedy would also lend itself brilliantly to the deadpan comedy of Buster Keaton and the boyish enthusiasm of Harold Lloyd, both of whom successfully tailored their talent for physical comedy to the requirements of the screen.

One of those requirements arose from the camera's ability to bring a viewer closer to the action taking place than is possible for a stage theater audience. That factor, coupled with the exaggerated size that figures projected on a screen assume, made it necessary for film comedians to master subtle gestures and expressions in addition to slapstick. The best silent comedians soon learned that a laugh could be achieved not only through a pratfall or a well-aimed pie but also with a raised eyebrow or deadpan stare. Chaplin, Keaton, and Lloyd all excelled at combining slapstick with subtlety, but only Chaplin used this skill to move his screen persona into the realm of pathos. With his expressive dark eyes and mobile face, the Tramp could evoke sorrow as readily as humor with a shrug or a glance.

Chaplin's extraordinary combination of popular and critical acclaim made him the yardstick against which other comedians were measured, often to their detriment. So great was Chaplin's fame during the years of silent comedy that he in many ways unfairly overshadowed the work of his contemporaries. Indeed, both Buster Keaton and Harold Lloyd have grown in critical stature in the years since their best work was done. Keaton, in particular, has achieved well-deserved cult status among silent comedy aficionados—a welcome development that does not detract from Chaplin's own mastery of the field, but rather enhances the field itself by recognizing the depth of talent it contained. The era that produced *The Gold Rush* also produced such comic masterpieces as Keaton's *The Navigator* (1924) and *The General* (1927) and Lloyd's *Safety Last* (1923) and *The Freshman* (1925).

Ironically, however, the release of these films marked not only the pinnacle of silent film comedy but also the beginning of the end of the silent era. In 1927, two years after *The Gold Rush*—and the same year as *The General*—*The Jazz Singer* introduced sound to motion pictures and changed the medium forever. Chaplin resisted the change longer than his contemporaries; *City Lights*, released in 1931, contains sound effects but no spoken dialogue, and *Modern Times* (1936) confines its spoken lines to a character using a loudspeaker and a nonsense song sung by the Tramp near the film's close. Despite these few concessions, both remain silent films in spirit.

Although the introduction of sound changed filmmaking irrevocably, the techniques perfected by Chaplin and his contemporaries continued to influence film comedy. The screwball comedies of the 1930's and the films of Preston Sturges in the 1940's effectively combined physical comedy with witty dialogue. In films such as *Bringing Up Baby* (1938) and *The Lady Eve* (1941) slapstick is an integral part of the humor, and the actors in these films, such as Cary Grant, Katharine Hepburn, Henry Fonda, and Barbara Stanwyck, rely on the same pratfalls and elaborate sight gags that were the highlights of silent comedies. During the 1950's and 1960's, French director Jacques Tati drew heavily on the silent comedy tradition in such films as *Les Vacances de Monsieur Hulot* (*Mr. Hulot's Holiday*, 1953) and *Playtime* (1968), in which he created a screen persona who rarely spoke in films that relied almost entirely on visual humor.

The work of filmmakers Mel Brooks and Woody Allen also owes a debt to Chaplin and silent comedy. Allen's earlier films, in particular, combine verbal and physical humor and feature central characters who are outsiders and hapless "little guys" thrust into situations larger than themselves. Brooks's films have long made use of slapstick humor, a debt he acknowledged in the film *Silent Movie* (1976), which contains only one word of dialogue. Indeed, physical comedy in any visual medium, whether it be film, television, or live theater, continues to draw on the brilliant comic technique of Chaplin and his contemporaries.

Yet Chaplin's contribution to motion pictures does not end with comedy. In his hands, comedy was transformed into art at a time when the relatively new medium of film was struggling to gain credibility as more than simple entertainment. Chaplin's role in achieving this was recognized by the Academy of Motion Picture Arts and Sciences in the special Oscar he received in 1971. The award was presented to the eighty-three-year-old Chaplin for "the incalculable effect he has had in making motion pictures the art form of the century."

—*Janet Lorenz*

FURTHER READING

Brownlow, Kevin. *The Parade's Gone By. . . .* Berkeley: University of California Press, 1968. One of the best books available on the history of silent film, thoughtfully conceived and exceptionally well written and researched. Offers an engrossing look at Hollywood's early years, drawing extensively on interviews that bring the material to life. A highly recommended source for anyone with an interest in film history.

Chaplin, Charles. *My Autobiography.* 1964. Reprint. New York: Plume Books, 1992. Chaplin's life and career in his own words. Early portions relate in vivid detail Chaplin's harrowing, Dickensian childhood in the slums of Victorian London. Also interesting for behind-the-scenes reminiscences on Chaplin's life and films and his assessments of his own work.

Hayes, Kevin J., ed. *Charlie Chaplin: Interviews.* Jackson: University Press of Mississippi, 2005. Collection of interviews Chaplin gave to various reporters and others from 1915 to 1967 provides insights into his views on filmmaking and comedy. Includes chronology, filmography, and index.

Huff, Theodore. *Charlie Chaplin.* New York: Henry Schuman, 1951. The first, and for many years the only, in-depth study of Chaplin and his work. Contains the first complete (up to that time) Chaplin filmography. Weakest where Chaplin's autobiography is at its best—his childhood years—devoting only five pages to the first twenty-four years of Chaplin's life.

McCabe, John. *Charlie Chaplin.* Garden City, N.Y.: Doubleday, 1978. Thorough, well-researched biography includes an extensive bibliography and a filmography with credits. Draws on many interviews with Stan Laurel for unique insights into Chaplin's career. Informative and well written.

McCaffrey, Donald W., ed. *Focus on Chaplin.* Englewood Cliffs, N.J.: Prentice-Hall, 1971. Excellent compilation of essays and reviews of Chaplin's work. Contributors include George Jean Nathan, Louis Delluc, Gerald Mast, Walter Kerr, Winston Churchill, and Chaplin himself. Also features scenario extracts from three of Chaplin's films: *Shoulder Arms* (1918), *The Kid,* and *Modern Times.*

McDonald, Gerald D., Michael Conway, and Mark Ricci, eds. *The Complete Films of Charlie Chaplin.* Secaucus, N.J.: Citadel Press, 1988. Brief introductory essays followed by chronologically ordered entries on all of Chaplin's films. Each entry contains credits, plot synopsis, photographs, and excerpts from reviews of the film in question. A useful reference, although the credits do not include character names.

Manvell, Roger. *Chaplin.* Boston: Little, Brown, 1974. Well-written, well-researched biography offers an absorbing account of Chaplin's life and work. One of the better entries in the vast array of literature on the comedian. Includes a limited bibliography and suggestions for further reading.

Mast, Gerald. *A Short History of the Movies.* 3d ed. Indianapolis: Bobbs-Merrill, 1981. One of the best comprehensive overviews of film history offers a context for Chaplin's work. In addition to a general outline of Chaplin's career, provides a comparison of *The Gold Rush* and Keaton's *The General.* A valuable addition to any film library.

Robinson, David. *Chaplin: His Life and Art.* 1985. Reprint. New York: Da Capo Press, 1994. Excellent comprehensive examination of Chaplin's life and work is vividly written, exhaustively researched, and thoroughly annotated. Offers not only a detailed retelling of Chaplin's life but also a look at his work that includes numerous interviews with colleagues and contemporaries. Contains a useful chronology of the major events in Chaplin's life, appendixes chronicling his early theatrical career, scenarios from three Keystone shorts, an excellent filmography, and a "who's who" of people who figured prominently in Chaplin's life and career.

Vance, Jeffrey. *Chaplin: Genius of the Cinema.* New York: Harry N. Abrams, 2003. Comprehensive biography uses some five hundred photographs, many never before published, to illustrate Chaplin's life and his creative process.

SEE ALSO: Fall, 1903: *The Great Train Robbery* Introduces New Editing Techniques; 1909-1929: Pickford Reigns as "America's Sweetheart"; Aug., 1912: Sennett Defines Slapstick Comedy; Mar. 3, 1915: Griffith Releases *The Birth of a Nation*; 1920: Premiere of *The Cabinet of Dr. Caligari*; 1923: *The Ten Commandments* Advances American Film Spectacle; Dec. 4, 1924: Von Stroheim's Silent Masterpiece *Greed* Premieres; 1925: Eisenstein's *Potemkin* Introduces New Film Editing Techniques; Dec., 1926: Keaton's *The General* Is Released.

July 10-21, 1925
SCOPES TRIAL

The Scopes trial constituted a legal test of one U.S. state's prohibition of the teaching of the theory of evolution in the public schools, underscoring the concept of the separation of church and state.

ALSO KNOWN AS: *Tennessee v. John Thomas Scopes*; monkey trial

LOCALE: Dayton, Tennessee

CATEGORIES: Education; civil rights and liberties; publishing and journalism; laws, acts, and legal history

KEY FIGURES

John T. Scopes (1900-1970), American schoolteacher
William Jennings Bryan (1860-1925), American attorney and politician
Clarence Darrow (1857-1938), American attorney
Arthur Garfield Hays (1881-1954), American attorney
Dudley Field Malone (1882-1950), American attorney
H. L. Mencken (1880-1956), American journalist
John T. Raulston (1868-1956), American jurist
A. T. Stewart (1892-1972), district attorney for the Eighteenth Circuit

SUMMARY OF EVENT

In July, 1925, one of the most widely publicized and bizarre legal cases in U.S. history, *Tennessee v. John Thomas Scopes*, better known as the "monkey trial," was tried in Dayton, Tennessee. Scopes, a football coach and science teacher at Dayton's Rhea County High School, was charged with violating the Butler Act, a state law passed in January, 1925, that made it illegal to teach in public schools any theories that denied the story of creation as found in the Bible's book of Genesis. The Butler Act was a reaction to the increasing alarm of many fundamentalist Christians who feared the challenge that science and evolutionary theory presented to a literal interpretation of the Bible. From 1921 through 1929, thirty-seven similar bills opposing the teaching of evolution were introduced in twenty U.S. states.

Shortly after the passage of the Butler Act, the American Civil Liberties Union (ACLU) offered to provide legal services to any teacher in Tennessee who would test the constitutionality of the act. George Rappleyea, a local mining engineer, learned of the ACLU's offer and discussed the possibility of a test case with Scopes, even though Scopes himself was not teaching biology that year. Because the principal of the school, who actually taught the class, had a family who stood to suffer from the attention that such a trial would invite, Scopes volunteered to be the defendant. With the reluctant consent of the chairman of the school board and the county superintendent of schools, Scopes was arrested for teaching evolution in his biology class and bound over to the grand jury. The ACLU was immediately notified.

Within a few days, William Jennings Bryan, three-time Democratic presidential candidate and a well-known religious fundamentalist, announced that he would aid District Attorney A. T. Stewart in the prosecution of the case. Bryan, a populist who had been one of the nation's most progressive politicians, advocating woman suffrage, railroad regulation, campaign fund disclosure, and abolition of the death penalty, was obsessed with the social implications of the theory of evolution. He was especially outraged by social Darwinism, an un-

Defendant John T. Scopes (seated behind table, in white shirt, with arms folded) and his defense team, including Clarence Darrow (leaning on table), during the trial proceedings. (Library of Congress)

scientific extension of Charles Darwin's theory of natural selection that some used to rationalize neglect of society's poor and weak members. Darwin had never intended his theory to be used as justification for such attitudes, but social Darwinism had become popularized along with the theory of biological evolution. The idea of "survival of the fittest" went against Bryan's populism and smacked of an elitism he had been fighting all his life.

The lawyers for the defense in the Scopes trial were led by Clarence Darrow, a well-known agnostic and the most famous trial lawyer in the United States. Darrow had not been interested in the case until he learned that Bryan was to be part of the prosecution. The journalist H. L. Mencken happened to be in Richmond with Darrow when word came about Bryan's participation, and Mencken persuaded his friend to join the defense. Both Darrow and Mencken considered the trial an opportunity to confront obscurantism, which they saw incarnate in Bryan and the South. Darrow later said of his par-

ticipation: "For the first, the last, and the only time in my life, I volunteered my services in a case. I did it because I really wanted to take part in it." Other noteworthy attorneys on the defense team were Dudley Field Malone, a well-known divorce lawyer, and Arthur Garfield Hays, perhaps the most outstanding civil liberties attorney of the time.

Because of the dramatic nature of the trial and the fame of the opposing attorneys, Dayton became the center of national and even international attention. Mencken was the most prominent journalist present, but many others were also there; the country's major newspapers flooded the small town with reporters. All the wire services had reporters there, and millions of readers followed the case daily in both the United States and Europe. Telegraph wires were run into the courthouse, and the *Chicago Tribune* installed radio equipment; the trial was the first to be broadcast in American history. The town of Dayton took on a carnival-like atmosphere as the local inhabitants began to prepare for the expected crush

---

DAY 7 OF THE SCOPES TRIAL

Prosecuting attorney William Jennings Bryan made the mistake of allowing defense attorney Clarence Darrow to get him on the stand. Darrow relentlessly grilled Bryan on his beliefs, making Bryan look like a fool. Many have speculated on whether this episode contributed to the death of the "Great Commoner" a mere five days later.

DARROW: You have given considerable study to the Bible, haven't you, Mr. Bryan?

BRYAN: Yes, sir, I have tried to. . . .

DARROW: You claim that everything in the Bible should be literally interpreted?

BRYAN: I believe everything in the Bible should be accepted as it is given there: some of the Bible is given illustratively. For instance: "Ye are the salt of the earth." I would not insist that man was actually salt, or that he had flesh of salt, but it is used in the sense of salt as saving God's people. . . .

DARROW: Now, Mr. Bryan, have you ever pondered what would have happened to the earth if it had stood still?

BRYAN: No.

DARROW: You have not?

BRYAN: No; the God I believe in could have taken care of that, Mr. Darrow.

DARROW: I see. Have you ever pondered what would naturally happen to the earth if it stood still suddenly?

BRYAN: No.

DARROW: Don't you know it would have been converted into molten mass of matter?

BRYAN: You testify to that when you get on the stand, I will give you a chance.

DARROW: Don't you believe it?

BRYAN: I would want to hear expert testimony on that.

DARROW: You have never investigated that subject?

BRYAN: I don't think I have ever had the question asked.

DARROW: Or ever thought of it?

BRYAN: I have been too busy on things that I thought were of more importance than that.

DARROW: You believe the story of the flood to be a literal interpretation?

BRYAN: Yes, sir.

DARROW: When was that Flood?

BRYAN: I would not attempt to fix the date. The date is fixed, as suggested this morning.

DARROW: About 4004 B.C.?

BRYAN: That has been the estimate of a man that is accepted today. I would not say it is accurate.

DARROW: That estimate is printed in the Bible?

BRYAN: Everybody knows, at least, I think most of the people know, that was the estimate given.

DARROW: But what do you think that the Bible, itself says? Don't you know how it was arrived at?

BRYAN: I never made a calculation.

DARROW: A calculation from what?

BRYAN: I could not say.

DARROW: From the generations of man?

BRYAN: I would not want to say that.

DARROW: What do you think?

BRYAN: I do not think about things I don't think about.

DARROW: Do you think about things you do think about?

BRYAN: Well, sometimes.

---

of visitors. Stands were built to sell soft drinks and sandwiches; hotels and boardinghouses were quickly filled. One Daytonian later described the scene: "One was hard put to it on the tenth of July to know whether Dayton was holding a camp meeting, a Chautauqua, a street fair, a carnival or belated Fourth of July celebration. Literally it was drunk with religious excitement."

On Friday, July 10, Judge John T. Raulston had the trial opened with a prayer, to which Darrow objected and was overruled. The jury was selected and the trial began. The state's case as it was presented was simple: Three schoolboys testified that Scopes had taught evolution in the science class and the prosecution rested.

From the beginning it was the defense's goal to put the Butler Act, rather than Scopes, on trial. Darrow wanted to prove that the theory of evolution was neither contrary to the Bible nor nonreligious, and therefore the Butler Act was unconstitutional and violated the civil rights of all Tennessee teachers. The first controversy surrounded the question of admitting the testimony of "experts" (scientists) who had been assembled by Darrow and Malone for the defense. Each of the experts was both an evolutionist and a Christian whose testimony was intended to prove that there is no conflict between science and religion. When the first expert was called, Stewart objected on the grounds that any interpretation of evolution or the Bible, whether by an expert or not, would be opinion rather than fact and should therefore not be admissible as evidence. Further, said Stewart, such testimony would have nothing to do with the case at hand, which was to ascertain whether or not Scopes had taught material that conflicted with the law. At this point, the judge excused the jury until he could rule on whether or not scientific testimony was admissible. He admonished the jurors not to stand around in the courthouse grounds, where they might hear the trial in progress over the public-address system that was broadcasting to the crowd outside.

On Friday, July 17, Judge Raulston, agreeing with the prosecution, refused to permit the scientists to testify, declaring that the only relevant question for the court to decide was whether Scopes had actually taught the theory of evolution. This ruling destroyed the defense's case because it prevented the testing of the questions of the constitutionality of the law and the violation of the defendant's civil liberties, as well as the truthfulness of the doctrine of evolution.

The trial probably would have ended there, for the defense did not deny that Scopes had taught evolution, had not Bryan made the mistake of allowing Darrow to get him on the stand as an "expert" on the Bible. Darrow bore down hard on Bryan's fundamentalist beliefs, and in a grueling and sarcastic hour and a half of cross-examination made a shambles of the man often called the "Great Commoner," eliciting an admission from Bryan that he did not really believe in a literal interpretation of the Bible. This admission shocked many of Bryan's fundamentalist followers. Darrow's cross-examination had a shattering effect on Bryan himself as well, and many think that it caused his death, which occurred five days later in Dayton.

Bryan had prepared a long oration to deliver when he summed up the prosecution's case. He hoped to regain his lost stature by overwhelming the crowd with his oratory, but he never got the chance. Darrow and Malone did not make a final summation for the defense; therefore, none was allowed for the prosecution. Indeed, the defense attorneys asked the jury to find their client guilty so that they could appeal the verdict to a higher court.

On July 21, Scopes was found guilty and fined one hundred dollars. The defense appealed the verdict to the Tennessee State Court of Appeals, and in 1927 Scopes was cleared on a technicality—the appeals court found that the lower court had exceeded its authority in fining Scopes.

SIGNIFICANCE

By throwing out Scopes's conviction, the Tennessee Court of Appeals effectively destroyed Darrow's case. His whole plan had been to take the issue all the way to the federal courts in order to get the Butler Act declared unconstitutional. The case never made it to the federal courts, and the law remained on the books until 1967.

Initially, many journalists and educators assumed that the spectacle of the Scopes trial had dealt a death blow to the influence of religious fundamentalism in the public schools. On the contrary, however, many school boards across the United States reacted by taking evolution out of their high school curricula. Textbooks were revised quietly to avoid controversy. Tennessee, for example, stopped using high school biology textbooks that included discussion of evolution. Like dozens of other states, Tennessee allowed no such textbooks to be used until several decades later. It was only in the late 1950's, with the Soviet Union's launch of the first human-made satellite, *Sputnik*, that American school boards made a concerted attempt to strengthen science textbooks, which included reinstating information on evolution. Debates concerning how American public schools should approach the teaching of the theory of evolution and the subject of creationism did not end there, however; they continued into the twenty-first century, further complicated by the introduction of the concept of "intelligent design."

—*John H. DeBerry and Daniel Brown*

FURTHER READING

Bird, Wendell. *The Origin of Species Revisited: The Theories of Evolution and of Abrupt Appearance.* New York: Philosophical Library, 1989. Idiosyncratic study of the legal and religious issues involved in the debate about evolution.

Ginger, Ray. *Six Days or Forever: Tennessee v. John Thomas Scopes.* Chicago: Quadrangle Books, 1969. A highly readable, accurate account of the trial.

Larson, Edward J. *Summer for the Gods: The Scopes Trial and America's Continuing Debate over Science and Religion.* New York: Basic Books, 1997. Offers analysis of the trial and its impacts from cultural, historical, and legal perspectives. Draws on previously unavailable archival materials.

_____. *Trial and Error: The American Controversy over Creation and Evolution.* 3d ed. Oxford, England: Oxford University Press, 2003. Provides a careful assessment of the legal, cultural, and religious issues involved in the debate.

Olasky, Marvin, and John Perry. *Monkey Business: The True Story of the Scopes Trial.* Nashville: Broadman & Holman, 2005. Argues that slanted newspaper coverage of the trial and later accounts of the trial by historians failed to depict the events and their importance accurately. Examines the trial from a creationist viewpoint.

Scopes, John Thomas, and James Pressley. *Center of the Storm: Memoirs of John T. Scopes*. New York: Holt, Rinehart and Winston, 1967. Reminiscences about the trial from the central figure after a long passage of time.

Wills, Garry. *Under God: Religion and American Politics*. New York: Simon & Schuster, 1990. Presents a

penetrating examination and analysis of American religious history. Chapters 8, 9, and 10 address the issues raised in the Scopes trial.

SEE ALSO: 1919: Founding of the World Christian Fundamentals Association; Jan. 19, 1920: American Civil Liberties Union Is Founded; 1928: Smith-Hoover Campaign.

July 18, 1925-December 11, 1926
MEIN KAMPF OUTLINES NAZI THOUGHT

Adolf Hitler, the future Nazi dictator of Germany, published a heavily edited and ponderous political statement that was slow to sell until Hitler's rise to power in 1933, when sales figures jumped significantly. The racist and militaristic nature of the work provided a chilling window into Nazi thought.

LOCALE: Bavaria, Germany
CATEGORIES: Government and politics; publishing and journalism

KEY FIGURES
Adolf Hitler (1889-1945), dictator of Germany, 1933-1945
Rudolf Hess (1894-1987), Hitler's secretary and later deputy
Max Amman (1891-1957), head of the Nazi Party's publishing house

SUMMARY OF EVENT
In the so-called Beer Hall Putsch of November, 1923, Adolf Hitler and his Nazi followers attempted to seize power in Munich, the capital of Bavaria. After the movement's failure, Hitler was tried and found guilty of high treason, and he spent a year in Landsberg Prison. While there, he began writing the first volume of his political manifesto, *Mein Kampf* (1925-1926; English translation, 1939). Hitler used the book, the title of which means "my struggle," to set down his life story and political views.

During his year of enforced idleness, Hitler dictated a mass of thoughts and reminiscences, much of which was taken down by his close companion Rudolf Hess. After his release from prison, Hitler turned the manuscript over to Max Amman, the Nazi Party's publisher, who found it in need of major editing. With the help of Hess and a few others, Amman put the work into publishable form. Hitler had wanted to title it *Four and a Half Years of Struggle Against Lies, Stupidity, and Cowardice*, but Amman

gave it the shorter title of *Mein Kampf*. From 1924 to 1927, the German government banned Hitler from speaking, and so after the publication of the first volume on July 18, 1925, Hitler quickly set to work on a second volume, which was published on December 11, 1926.

Dust jacket that appeared on Adolf Hitler's Mein Kampf. *(Library of Congress)*

Although Hitler believed that world events occur not by writing but by speaking, he seemed to have had little trouble becoming a writer.

Mein Kampf is a mixture of autobiography and political ideology that both reveals and hides a great deal about Hitler. The author described himself as a seeker of truth who spent a pleasant childhood in his native Austria despite his father's harsh discipline. His mother's death in 1907 came as a crushing blow, and Hitler moved to Vienna, where he had his first real exposure to Jews and to anti-Semitic doctrine. Life in Vienna intensified his dislike for the Austro-Hungarian Empire, and Hitler came to believe that Germany was the only true home of German culture. In 1912, Hitler moved to Munich, a city he found truly German, and in 1914 the coming of World War I allowed him to experience the life of a soldier. For Hitler, military service was a crowning educational achievement and the inspiration for his career as a speaker. Recalling the heroic deeds of the German army, Hitler blamed the Jews and Marxists for the country's collapse at war's end, the establishment of a weak democratic government, and the punitive treatment of Germany by its enemies. He promised readers that Germany would rearm and assume its rightful role as a world power.

Race dominates the ideology on display in *Mein Kampf*. Hitler was convinced that every race should preserve its purity or face decline, and he was especially distraught that the Aryan race (whose nature he never precisely defined), especially German Aryans, seemed to have failed in this effort. He believed that if the German race could be kept pure—that is, if its most Aryan elements could be increased through careful breeding—Germany could achieve world domination. The greatest threat to Germany in Hitler's eyes were the Jews, whom he compared to parasites, and he promised that the score against the Jews would soon be settled. To Hitler, the

---

FROM *MEIN KAMPF*

Mein Kampf describes Adolf Hitler's racist beliefs in alarming detail, as this excerpt illustrates.

The Jewish domination in the State seems now so fully assured that not only can he now afford to call himself a Jew once again, but he even acknowledges freely and openly what his ideas are on racial and political questions. A section of the Jews avows itself quite openly as an alien people, but even here there is another falsehood. When the Zionists try to make the rest of the world believe that the new national consciousness of the Jews will be satisfied by the establishment of a Jewish State in Palestine, the Jews thereby adopt another means to dupe the simple-minded Gentile. They have not the slightest intention of building up a Jewish State in Palestine so as to live in it. What they really are aiming at is to establish a central organization for their international swindling and cheating. As a sovereign State, this cannot be controlled by any of the other States. Therefore it can serve as a refuge for swindlers who have been found out and at the same time a high-school for the training of other swindlers.

As a sign of their growing presumption and sense of security, a certain section of them openly and impudently proclaim their Jewish nationality while another section hypocritically pretend that they are German, French or English as the case may be. Their blatant behaviour in their relations with other people shows how clearly they envisage their day of triumph in the near future.

The black-haired Jewish youth lies in wait for hours on end, satanically glaring at and spying on the unsuspicious girl whom he plans to seduce, adulterating her blood and removing her from the bosom of her own people. The Jew uses every possible means to undermine the racial foundations of a subjugated people. In his systematic efforts to ruin girls and women he strives to break down the last barriers of discrimination between him and other peoples. The Jews were responsible for bringing negroes into the Rhineland, with the ultimate idea of bastardizing the white race which they hate and thus lowering its cultural and political level so that the Jew might dominate. For as long as a people remain racially pure and are conscious of the treasure of their blood, they can never be overcome by the Jew. Never in this world can the Jew become master of any people except a bastardized people.

That is why the Jew systematically endeavours to lower the racial quality of a people by permanently adulterating the blood of the individuals who make up that people.

Source: Adolf Hitler, *My Struggle*, translated by James Murphy (London: Hurst & Blackett, 1939).

---

serve its purity or face decline, and he was especially distraught that the Aryan race (whose nature he never precisely defined), especially German Aryans, seemed to have failed in this effort. He believed that if the German race could be kept pure—that is, if its most Aryan elements could be increased through careful breeding—Germany could achieve world domination. The greatest threat to Germany in Hitler's eyes were the Jews, whom he compared to parasites, and he promised that the score against the Jews would soon be settled. To Hitler, the

state was the means to a more important end: racial self-preservation. He saw Germany's mission as one that would secure the land required by future Aryan populations, which Hitler believed would number 250 million in a hundred years. The only alternative plan, as Hitler saw it, was to secure "living space" (*Lebensraum*) for Germans in Russia.

Hitler saw himself as Germany's political savior and the Nazi Party as the source of the force necessary to prevail in a racial and political struggle against Jews and

Marxists. One man, he insisted, had to step forward to lead, and he clearly saw himself in that role: *Mein Kampf* referred to the "strong man" who is "mightiest alone" and whose ideas are so revolutionary that they may not be accepted in his lifetime. Hitler was known to be a great admirer of Benito Mussolini, the Fascist dictator who had ruled Italy since 1919, but he mentioned Mussolini by name only once in *Mein Kampf*, leaving the implication that he wanted to avoid sharing history's heroic role.

Given that Hitler had served as propaganda chief of the Nazi Party, it is not surprising that *Mein Kampf* offered a lengthy commentary on propaganda. In an early chapter on war propaganda, Hitler wrote scornfully of Germany's weak and ineffective efforts during World War I. In Hitler's view, war propaganda was a means to German victory, and to accomplish this the government needed to appeal to the psychology of the masses. In Hitler's view, British and American propaganda succeeded, especially in their portrayals of Germans as barbarians and in their observation of the principle that propaganda must be simple and repetitious.

Hitler also stressed the superiority of oratory to the written word. He took pride in his own prowess as a speaker and asserted that speaking was the most effective way to capitalize on the emotions (rather than the intellect), which would propel audience members to action. In a later chapter, Hitler described the distinct roles played by propaganda and organization, saying that propaganda was best used as a tool to recruit a movement's core members and that organization was needed to ensure that only the most valuable followers were made members.

The publication of *Mein Kampf* yielded Hitler a steady income, one that was initially modest but tripled after the Nazis made gains in the 1930 elections. The book's royalties became truly significant after Hitler became chancellor in 1933, and it also sold well in Italy, where Mussolini took a personal interest in having it published. By 1945, sales had reached ten million in Germany alone, and the book had been translated into sixteen foreign languages. After World War II, its sale was banned in Germany, but it continued to sell in many parts of the world. In the Middle East, a former Nazi functionary translated it into Arabic, and in Latin America an Argentine publisher put out German and Spanish editions. Many of Hitler's imitators have attributed their conversion to Nazism to reading *Mein Kampf*, including George Lincoln Rockwell, the founder of the American Nazi Party.

SIGNIFICANCE

Mein Kampf has little to offer connoisseurs of literature, and as political science it is too full of crackpot ideas to be taken seriously. Still, Nazism without *Mein Kampf* would be like Marxism without *Manifest der Kommunistischen Partei* (1848; *The Communist Manifesto*, 1850). Beyond offering Hitler's version of the events that preceded his rise to power, the book provided an outline of the Nazi Party's goals, and it became obligatory reading material for many Germans. It also sounded a warning to the world that went largely unheeded. Historical events such as the German invasion of Russia in 1941 and the forced sterilization of hundreds of thousands of Germans are clearly predicted in its pages, and even the Nazi slaughter of millions is not surprising given the unbridled hatred that Hitler expressed toward Jews and others whom he considered unworthy. The most lasting legacy of *Mein Kampf*, however, is that it preserved Hitler's ideas beyond his own lifetime.

—*Lawrence W. Haapanen*

FURTHER READING

Bracher, Karl Dietrich. *The German Dictatorship: The Origins, Structure, and Effects of National Socialism.* New York: Praeger, 1970. Definitive work on Nazi Germany contains chapters concerning the origins of Hitler's ideology, the writing of and meaning of the ideas expressed in *Mein Kampf*, and the effects of those ideas in practice. Offers insights into the nature of Nazism and into Hitler's personality not available in other works. Includes extensive bibliography.

Hamann, Brigitte. *Hitler's Vienna: A Dictator's Apprenticeship.* New York: Oxford University Press, 1999. Focuses on Hitler's years in Vienna and how his experiences there influenced him. Includes photographs, select bibliography, and index.

Hauner, Milan. *Hitler: A Chronology of His Life and Time.* New York: St. Martin's Press, 1983. Very detailed chronology of the major events in Hitler's life and the rise and fall of Nazism in Germany. Quotes extensively from *Mein Kampf* and from Hitler's speeches to illuminate the ideological underpinnings of many of the otherwise enigmatic policies adopted by Hitler and the Nazis. Includes bibliography (with mostly German-language sources) and index.

Hilberg, Raul. *The Destruction of the European Jews.* 3d ed. New Haven, Conn.: Yale University Press, 2003. Comprehensive account of the Nazi treatment of the Jews of Germany and Nazi-occupied Europe. Graphically illustrates how the ideas Hitler expressed in

Mein Kampf led directly to unspeakable suffering for millions of people. Includes excellent bibliography and index.

Hitler, Adolf. *Mein Kampf.* New York: Reynal & Hitchcock, 1939. This is the first complete and unabridged English translation. It includes copious annotations.

_____. *Mein Kampf.* Translated by Ralph Manheim. Reprint. New York: Mariner Books, 1998. No commentary can illustrate Hitler's ideas as well as *Mein Kampf* itself. Hitler's clumsy and often pompous prose does not prevent the reader from understanding that his program called for the destruction of many basic human rights, including freedom of the press, freedom of speech, freedom of association, free enterprise, and sexual freedom. Manheim's translation is among the best available.

_____. *The Speeches of Adolf Hitler, April 1922-August 1939.* Edited by Norman H. Baynes. New York: H. Fertig, 1969. Includes translations of all Hitler's important speeches from 1922 to the outbreak of World War II. The various speeches, many of them very long, elaborate and expand on the topics emphasized in *Mein Kampf* in language often much more graphic than the turgid prose of the book. Editor's commentary is perceptive and illuminating.

Kershaw, Ian. *Hitler, 1889-1936: Hubris.* New York: W. W. Norton, 1999. A comprehensive and well-documented examination of Hitler's rise to power.

Lee, Martin A. *The Beast Reawakens.* Boston: Little, Brown, 1997. Reviews Hitler's legacy after World War II.

Lukacs, John. *The Hitler of History.* New York: Alfred A. Knopf, 1998. Critical survey of the historical and biographical works on Hitler.

Maser, Werner. *Hitler's "Mein Kampf": An Analysis.* London: Heinemann, 1974. Shows that many of the autobiographical details in Hitler's account of his early life are inaccurate and misleading. Tries (often unconvincingly) to explain many of the obscure references in Hitler's book and to extrapolate the sources of some of the ideas expressed there. Includes bibliography (with mostly German-language sources) and index.

Pulzer, Peter G. *The Rise of Political Anti-Semitism in Germany and Austria.* Rev. ed. Cambridge, Mass.: Harvard University Press, 1988. Examines the origins and evolution of anti-Jewish feeling in Germany immediately before and during Hitler's formative years. Shows that the ideas concerning Jews in *Mein Kampf* were by no means unique to Hitler, and in fact were widely shared, and analyzes the reasons judeophobia became so widespread in Germany and Austria. Includes bibliography and index.

Shirer, William L. *The Rise and Fall of the Third Reich: A History of Nazi Germany.* 30th anniversary ed. New York: Ballantine, 1991. Classic work recounts Hitler's career from the perspective of a journalist who spent years reporting from Germany.

Stuadinger, Hans. *The Inner Nazi: A Critical Analysis of "Mein Kampf."* Baton Rouge: Louisiana State University Press, 1981. A study by a scholar who fled Germany in 1933.

Toland, John. *Adolf Hitler.* 1976. Reprint. New York: Anchor Books, 1992. One of the most accurate, most comprehensive, and most objective biographies of Hitler available. Devotes many pages to analyzing the ideas Hitler expressed in *Mein Kampf* and echoed in his speeches. Includes exhaustive bibliography and excellent index.

SEE ALSO: 1919-1933: Racist Theories Aid Nazi Rise to Political Power; Nov. 8, 1923: Beer Hall Putsch; Jan. 30, 1933: Hitler Comes to Power in Germany; Feb. 27, 1933: Reichstag Fire; Mar., 1933: Nazi Concentration Camps Begin Operating; June 30-July 2, 1934: Great Blood Purge; Mar. 7, 1936: German Troops March into the Rhineland; Nov. 25, 1936: Germany and Japan Sign the Anti-Comintern Pact; Feb. 12-Apr. 10, 1938: The Anschluss; Nov. 9-10, 1938: Kristallnacht; 1939-1945: Nazi Extermination of the Jews; Sept. 1, 1939: Germany Invades Poland.

August 7, 1925
WEST AFRICAN STUDENT UNION IS FOUNDED

In response to racial discrimination, West African students living in the United Kingdom formed the community-based West African Student Union (WASU) to provide support and information for Africans and to promote anticolonial activism in their quest for an independent homeland. WASU members also participated in the larger pan-African movement and Pan-African Congresses, which trained future African leaders.

LOCALE: London, England; Africa
CATEGORIES: Civil rights and liberties; colonialism and occupation; indigenous peoples' rights; organizations and institutions

KEY FIGURES
Lapido Solanke (1884-1958), creator of the Nigerian Progress Union in 1924 and cofounder of the West African Student Union
Marcus Garvey (1887-1940), Jamaican activist who organized the Universal Negro Improvement Association
Kwame Nkrumah (1909-1972), early proponent of pan-Africanism and prime minister of Ghana, 1957-1966
Joseph Emmanuel Appiah (1918-1990), early proponent of pan-Africanism

SUMMARY OF EVENT
In the 1920's, many West African students living in London and in other large British cities gathered to address numerous grievances, such as constant racial discrimination, and to draft an agenda for political change in the British colonies in Africa. As a result of these meetings, on August 7, 1925, twenty-one West African law students studying in Britain formed the West African Student Union (WASU) at the University of London. The word *wasu* means "to preach" in the Yoruba language, although the term is often mistaken for a direct acronym of the name West African Student Union.

The organization provided room and board for West Africans in London, but it also served as a space for political discussion and action. Led by Lapido Solanke, a Nigerian (Yoruba) law student, and Herbert Bankole Bright, a doctor from Sierra Leone, WASU opened a hostel for West Africans in Camden Town (part of London) in 1933. The hostel also served as an information and resource center on Africa for all who needed it. Gradually,

WASU spread throughout West Africa, and as it did the link between Great Britain and the African continent became essential to anticolonial activism. Much of the funding for WASU's activities was raised by Solanke on trips to West Africa and elsewhere.

WASU sought to raise awareness about the plight of African people, to educate and mobilize Africans on civil rights issues, and to work against the colonial regime when necessary. To accomplish these tasks, WASU members traveled in Africa and Europe to garner support for their efforts. They also formed youth organizations all over Africa, and these groups held regular meetings that provided opportunities for community discussions and consultations with British political officials. WASU members also utilized various media to inform people about their activities, and they created a regularly published magazine called *WASU* in 1926. The magazine included articles by prominent union members and supporters from the United States such as the noted scholar Alain Locke; it also featured news, information, and fund-raising appeals from the branches of WASU in Great Britain, West Africa, and the Caribbean. The periodical was essentially a public relations tool used to establish the movement's voice and to spread the gospel of liberation.

Despite the communication barrier created by the diversity of African languages, WASU members organized and inspired followers, rallying them around their shared goals: a vision of an independent Africa and a feeling of urgency about addressing colonial Africa's problems. During the 1920's, students such as Lapido Solanke, Kusimo Soluanda, Olatunde Vincent, Ekuudayo Williams, M. A. Sorinola Siffre, W. Davidson Carrol, B. J. Farreira (from Nigeria), J. B. Danquah (from Ghana), Otto Oyekan-During (from Sierra Leone), and Kushida Roberts (from Gambia) wanted to create the United States of Africa.

Like these students, many West Africans, particularly those from the British colonies of Ghana (formerly the Gold Coast), Nigeria, Sierra Leone, and Gambia, had been living in the United Kingdom, and the numbers of promising young (and typically male) students arriving from West Africa grew significantly during the late nineteenth century. Wealthy West African families sent their children to Britain to be educated, but the limited number of scholarship opportunities meant that few Africans were admitted to British universities. Those admitted were courted by the British Colonial Office, which hoped to obtain the sympathies of these future agitators and leaders. Ironically, the students' stay in London only facilitated their development as activists.

WASU's cause was furthered when Lapido Solanke and Marcus Garvey met in London in 1928, when Garvey was working with the local branch of the United Negro Improvement Association (UNIA). Garvey (who would later be deported) offered financial support for WASU, and he and Solanke began a lengthy correspondence. Garvey allowed WASU to locate its original headquarters in a recently vacated UNIA building, and this house became a base for WASU's expanding intellectual and militant activities. Between 1928 and 1930, WASU's branches in Africa included eleven in Nigeria, five in Ghana, and two in Sierra Leone, all of which were founded while Solanke was on a fund-raising trip in West Africa. Because many of the educated West African elite, such as Kwame Nkrumah, future president of Ghana, were active in WASU, economic support for the organization was relatively easy to find.

During World War II, WASU continued its anti-colonial activities and consulted with the British government on its colonial policies. WASU supported the Allied Powers in the belief that British colonial rule was better than German or Italian. Meanwhile, however, the organization remained focused on achieving independence and on promoting Africans' self-determination. Toward that end, in 1945 WASU played a significant role in the Pan-African Congress held in Manchester, England. Following the war, a Labour government came to power in Britain, and it was much more sympathetic to WASU. As a result, WASU enjoyed greater access to political officials and more influence on the policy-making process.

Also important to the organization was the work of Nkrumah, who was active in WASU from his arrival in London in 1945. He participated in study groups on key issues and in discussions with prominent Labour politicians, including Clement Attlee (who would later become prime minister in the United Kingdom). Nkrumah also founded the Circle, a revolutionary subgroup within WASU that agitated for political independence. While he remained closely connected with WASU, Nkrumah also formed connections with other organizations such as the Pan-African Federation and the World Federation of Trade Unions. Nkrumah was also closely involved with the 1945 Pan-African Congress in Manchester, England.

He collaborated with Joseph Appiah, a WASU member from the Gold Coast. Appiah served as the union's president for a time, and like Nkrumah, he was a key player in nation-building efforts after Ghanaian independence. For both Appiah and Nkrumah, WASU was a crucial training ground for future work.

SIGNIFICANCE

Although ethnic and religious differences within WASU became increasingly salient and the group found it difficult to speak with one voice, WASU's efforts effected significant social change by influencing a shift in the British political climate toward colonial Africa. Once independence for the British colonies seemed inevitable, the political work of WASU lost its urgency. As a direct result of the group's work, however, West African governments appointed officials to protect the interests of their students in Britain. At the same time, the achievement of Ghanaian independence in 1957 and the subsequent independence of other West African colonies meant that many of WASU's initial goals had been fulfilled. While the organization continued to exist, it evolved into a minor group for foreign students rather than a major source of continued support and political action for West Africans. Nonetheless, its history serves as a model for leadership, unity, and organization in the face of huge geographic, economic, and linguistic challenges.

—*Kathleen M. Bartlett*

FURTHER READING

Adi, Hakim. *West Africans in Britain, 1900-1960: Nationalism, Pan-Africanism and Communism*. London: Lawrence & Wishart, 1998. Traces the history of the movement and identifies leaders and issues.

Olusanya, G. O. *The West African Students' Union and the Politics of Decolonisation, 1925-1958*. Ibadan, Nigeria: Daystar Press, 1982. Explores the influence of WASU in colonial and postcolonial Africa.

Sherwood, Marike. *Kwame Nkrumah: The Years Abroad, 1935-1947*. Legon, Ghana: Freedom, 1996. Provides the biographical chronology of this militant member of WASU's work in London and Europe.

SEE ALSO: 1910-1930: Great Northern Migration; May 31, 1910: Formation of the Union of South Africa; Jan. 8, 1912: South African Native National Congress Meets; May, 1917: Universal Negro Improvement Association Establishes a U.S. Chapter.

August 14, 1925
NORWAY ANNEXES SVALBARD

After years of international indecision, Norway was allowed to annex the distant northern archipelago of Svalbard under the terms of a unique and far-reaching agreement.

ALSO KNOWN AS: Svalbard Act
LOCALE: Oslo, Norway; Svalbard
CATEGORIES: Expansion and land acquisition; diplomacy and international relations; government and politics

KEY FIGURES

Fredrik Hartvig Herman Wedel-Jarlsberg (1855-1942), Norwegian diplomat
Robert Lansing (1864-1928), American statesman
Fredrik Stang (1867-1941), Norwegian professor
Paal Berg (1873-1978), Norwegian jurist
Johannes Gerckens Bassøe (1878-1962), Norwegian civil servant

SUMMARY OF EVENT

Under provisions of the Svalbard Treaty of 1920, Norway took possession of the Svalbard archipelago on August 14, 1925. The treaty had been signed at the Paris Peace Conference by representatives of nine nations—Denmark, France, Great Britain, Italy, Japan, the Netherlands, Norway, Sweden, and the United States—and represented an unusual but practical solution to a complex and long-standing international problem. While Norway assumed control of the archipelago, the economic right of citizens of other nations to operate within the islands was recognized and guaranteed.

Mountainous and forbidding Svalbard, the northernmost territory in Europe, lies in the Arctic Ocean about halfway between Norway's North Cape and the North Pole. Its area is 23,951 square miles (62,033 square kilometers), nearly two-thirds of which is occupied by the island of Spitsbergen, a name sometimes applied to the entire group. The archipelago had no permanent inhabitants until the early twentieth century and had been legally regarded as *terra nullius* (Latin for "no-man's-land"). However, the pressure of commercial and scientific attention from a range of nations made this status increasingly difficult to maintain as the nineteenth century drew to a close.

Svalbard's position far above the Arctic Circle means that the area has a harsh climate, but its commercial potential has been recognized for centuries. Whale and seal hunters from Denmark, England, Germany, the Netherlands, and Norway were active in the group as early as the seventeenth century, while the Pomor peoples of Russia established several short-lived settlements during the early eighteenth century. Early hunters had discovered coal, but it was only in 1899 that a Norwegian entrepreneur made the first commercial coal mining venture. Several other Norwegians followed suit, and within a few years companies representing American, English, Soviet, and Swedish interests also established claims. Scientific expeditions from several countries had also begun a series of visits in the late eighteenth century; in Svalbard they found a living laboratory in which to study extreme geological and meteorological conditions.

In the early years of the twentieth century, several conferences were held to settle Svalbard's status, but none of them was successful. At the end of World War I, Norway again raised the issue by submitting the question to the Paris Peace Conference, which had been established to negotiate treaties ending the war. On July 7, 1919, the conference created the Spitsbergen Commission, which consisted of representatives from France, Italy, Great Britain, Japan, and the United States. This commission considered three choices: declaring the islands an international territory with a multinational administration, giving Norway a mandate over the islands under the supervision of the newly created League of Nations, or simply conferring sovereignty on Norway.

In the past, Norway had advocated preservation of Svalbard's *terra nullius* status, but it had recently come to regard that solution as unworkable. Now the country campaigned for Norwegian sovereignty, a position advanced by the influential Norwegian ambassador to France, Baron Fredrik Herman Wedel-Jarlsberg. In addition, the Norwegian coal company Store Norske had appointed a committee, headed by Fredrik Stang, to draft a treaty that reflected Norwegian commercial interests. Wedel-Jarlsberg presented this document to the commission on July 24, 1919.

The United States also favored Norwegian control, a solution prompted in part by the sale of American mines to a Norwegian banking syndicate in 1916 and publicly espoused by American secretary of state Robert Lansing the following year. The eventual decision of the Spitsbergen Commission, ratified on February 9, 1920, as the Svalbard Treaty, favored Norway's annexation with several reservations, some of which had been anticipated by Stang's committee.

The groundwork for Svalbard's incorporation into Norway was laid in a piece of internal Norwegian legislation, the Svalbard Act of July 17, 1925, and Norway assumed actual sovereignty over the archipelago on August 14, 1925. Norwegian minister of justice Paal Berg traveled to the Svalbard settlement of Longyearbyen (whose name means "long year city") to make the official declaration. His country thus became responsible for defending Svalbard, for maintaining its relations with the rest of the world, and for overseeing legislation and administration within the archipelago. A *sysselmann*, or governor, who also functioned as chief of police and judge when necessary, headed the archipelago's minuscule government. Edvard Lassen acted briefly in this position until an official *sysselmann*, Johannes Gerckens Bassøe, was appointed on September 4, 1925.

Although Svalbard had become an integral part of Norway, several provisions of the Svalbard Act placed limitations on the country's administration. The first of these required Norway to grant full economic and commercial rights to citizens of the signatory countries. Norway was also required to establish a code to regulate mining activities, and this code was subject to the approval of all the treaty's signatories. Should any nation object, the matter was to be referred to a committee made up of representatives of the signatories. In order to facilitate the process, Norway worked closely and quickly with the other nations to develop this code, and it was adopted as part of Norwegian law on August 7, 1925.

Under terms of the treaty, Norway was forbidden to tax the export of minerals at more than 1 percent, which ensured that mining activities of other countries could continue unhindered. In general, Norway was not to levy taxes in excess of what was needed for direct administration of the archipelago. Another important provision of the treaty stipulated that although Norway bore responsibility for the archipelago's defense, the area was to remain demilitarized: The construction of naval bases and fortifications was forbidden, as was the commencement of war on or from the archipelago. Initially, Norwegian annexation made little difference in the slow and difficult pace of life in Svalbard, because Norway was inclined to take a laissez-faire approach to almost all affairs in the islands. So little construction had taken place at the time of annexation that Bassøe had to spend his first uneventful winter as *sysselmann* living at a radio station in the tiny settlement of Green Harbour.

SIGNIFICANCE

Norway's annexation of Svalbard represented the first expansion of Norwegian territory in centuries, and the step led to a surge of national pride, strengthened, perhaps, by the fact that Norway had separated from a union with Sweden only in 1905. It also meant that for the first time, Norway had within its own borders a plentiful supply of coal, the lack of which had become a matter of serious national concern during World War I.

On the international scene, the grant of Norwegian sovereignty avoided the inherent complications of an international administration. At the same time, retention of aspects of Svalbard's *terra nullius* status and the guarantee of its demilitarization relieved international pressures that might well have led to armed conflict. Although American mining interests had sold their operations to their Norwegian counterparts in 1916, the Soviet Union (which signed the Svalbard Treaty in 1935) had maintained active coal mines since the early years of the twentieth century. Svalbard's strategic location between the Arctic and North Atlantic oceans would become increasingly significant as the Soviet Union developed an enormous concentration of naval power near the Kola Peninsula.

—Grove Koger

FURTHER READING

Derry, Thomas Kingston. *A Short History of Norway: 1814-1972*. London: George Allen & Unwin, 1957. First authoritative survey by an English author, supplemented with a chronology and an excellent bibliography of works in English.

Humlum, Ole. "Svalbard." In *Encyclopedia of the Arctic*, edited by Mark Nuttall. New York: Routledge, 2005. Excellent summary covering all aspects of the archipelago's geography, history, and development.

Peters, Jochen. "Svalbard Treaty." In *Encyclopedia of the Arctic*, edited by Mark Nuttall. New York: Routledge, 2005. Summary of the treaty, its background, and its structure.

Singh, Elen C. *The Spitsbergen (Svalbard) Question: United States Foreign Policy, 1907-1935*. Oslo, Norway: Universitetsforlaget, 1980. Survey of American policies and attitudes toward Svalbard in light of the country's changing commercial interests. Includes maps, a substantial bibliography, and the text of the 1920 treaty.

Ulfstein, Geir. *The Svalbard Treaty: From Terra Nullius to Norwegian Sovereignty*. Oslo, Norway: Scandinavian University Press, 1995. Extremely detailed consideration of Norwegian administration, nondiscriminatory requirements, military prohibitions, and mining regulations. Includes maps and the text of the treaty.

Umbreit, Andreas. *Spitsbergen: Svalbard—Franz Josef Land—Jan Mayen.* 3d ed. Chalfont St. Peter, Buckinghamshire, England: Bradt Travel Guides, 2004. One of the few publications devoted to the archipel-

ago and its island neighbors written for the general reader. Maps, color illustrations.

SEE ALSO: Oct. 26, 1905: Norway Becomes Independent; Jan. 19-21, 1919: Paris Peace Conference Addresses Protection for Minorities; June 28, 1919: Treaty of Versailles; Apr. 9, 1940: Germany Invades Norway.

September 30, 1925
CHESTERTON CRITIQUES MODERNISM AND DEFENDS CHRISTIANITY

Responding to secular biological, anthropological, economic, and historical explanations for human existence and behavior, G. K. Chesterton's The Everlasting Man *reaffirmed arguments for humanity's sacred, nontemporal origins. Divided into two parts, the book featured the sudden appearance of humanity on earth and the equally sudden birth of Christ as unique events outside the normal or predictable progression of time.*

ALSO KNOWN AS: *The Everlasting Man*
LOCALE: New York, New York; England
CATEGORIES: Religion, theology, and ethics; philosophy; publishing and journalism

KEY FIGURES

G. K. Chesterton (1874-1936), English journalist, novelist, and Christian apologist
Charles Darwin (1809-1882), English theorist of biological evolution
Sigmund Freud (1856-1939), Austrian founder of psychoanalysis
Herbert Spencer (1820-1903), English philosopher
Sir James George Frazer (1854-1941), Scottish founder of modern anthropology
H. G. Wells (1866-1946), English novelist and social critic

SUMMARY OF EVENT

The Everlasting Man (1925) was G. K. Chesterton's attempt to refute the cultural authority of modernist thought. He criticized the modernist conception of humanity, which saw humans as creatures beholden to animal instincts that would always be determined by natural forces beyond understanding or control. Chesterton was especially aware of Charles Darwin's *On the Origin of Species by Means of Natural Selection: Or, The Preser-*

vation of Favoured Races in the Struggle for Life (1859) and *The Descent of Man and Selection in Relation to Sex* (1871), books about evolution that had an enormous impact on the modernist understanding of humanity's animal origins.

Chesterton also knew that modernist thought endorsed Sigmund Freud's challenge to human dignity and his studies of human will, which theorized the existence of unconscious influences that governed individual actions. In addition, Chesterton did not ignore Herbert Spencer's evolution-based explanation of the most advanced social developments in human civilization (including the formation of organized churches) or the findings of Sir James George Frazer. Frazer's *The Golden Bough* (1890, 1911-1915) undercut the cultural status of Christianity and other religions by positioning Christianity's foundations in ancient social or religious myths.

In *The Everlasting Man*, Chesterton referred to these findings, particularly in relation to H. G. Wells's bestselling *The Outline of History: Being a Plain History of Life and Mankind* (1920), which Chesterton targeted as a compendium of mistaken modernist concepts. In Wells's thoroughly secular version of history, people were fundamentally defined and limited by their biological makeup. Moreover, according to Wells, in the course of humanity's messy but steady advancement, progress toward higher modes of self-understanding and social organization was hampered by various political and religious powers. Human salvation, Wells contended, would be possible only after an intellectual liberation from these detrimental authorities, which would allow for the creation of a paradise on earth rather than an imaginary heaven outside of time.

Chesterton wanted to counter this modernist rejection of Christianity's authority, but first he had to contest Wells's materialist definition of humanity as an organ-

G. K. Chesterton. (Library of Congress)

ism limited to its biology. He reminded Wells and other modernists that their fashionable emphasis on scientific rationalism misrepresented the full range of human experience, and that the modernist point of view particularly ignored the long history of humanity's mystical perception. Modernists, Chesterton insisted, had lost touch with their innate sense of wonder. This intuitive sense, stirred by creation's fundamentally mysterious nature, could not be satisfied by exclusively scientific or fact-based explanations of life because these explanations failed to dispel the sense that humans were less the kin of animals than strangers from somewhere other than earth.

Chesterton highlighted the appearance of the human race and the birth of Christ as two especially inexplicable events. These two occasions were not, as modernists asserted, merely logical historical developments; humanity did not evolve from animals, Chesterton continued, and Christianity did not evolve from pagan myths. On the contrary, the creation of humanity and the birth of Christ were amazing interruptions of history. As unique events, Chesterton contended, they revealed a sacred history more plausible than modernist versions of secular history.

To argue his case, Chesterton pointed to art and laughter as exclusively human characteristics that demonstrated an extraordinary difference between hu-

---

FROM *THE EVERLASTING MAN*

As this excerpt from the book's introduction illustrates, G. K. Chesterton's great wit is evident throughout The Everlasting Man.

The point of this book . . . is that the next best thing to being really inside Christendom is to be really outside it. And a particular point of it is that the popular critics of Christianity are not really outside it. They are on a debatable ground, in every sense of the term. They are doubtful in their very doubts. Their criticism has taken on a curious tone; as of a random and illiterate heckling. Thus they make current and anti-clerical cant as a sort of small-talk. They will complain of parsons dressing like parsons; as if we should be any more free if all the police who shadowed or collared us were plain clothes detectives. Or they will complain that a sermon cannot be interrupted, and call a pulpit a coward's castle; though they do not call an editor's office a coward's castle. It would be unjust both to journalists and priests; but it would be much truer of journalists. The clergyman appears in person and could easily be kicked as he came out of church; the journalist conceals even his name so that nobody can kick him. They write wild and pointless articles and letters in the press about why the churches are empty, without even going there to find out if they are empty, or which of them are empty. Their suggestions are more vapid and vacant than the most insipid curate in a three-act farce, and move us to comfort him after the manner of the curate in the Bab Ballads; "Your mind is not so blank as that of Hopley Porter." So we may truly say to the very feeblest cleric: "Your mind is not so blank as that of Indignant Layman or Plain Man or Man in the Street, or any of your critics in the newspapers; for they have not the most shadowy notion of what they want themselves. Let alone of what you ought to give them." They will suddenly turn round and revile the Church for not having prevented the War, which they themselves did not want to prevent; and which nobody had ever professed to be able to prevent, except some of that very school of progressive and cosmopolitan sceptics who are the chief enemies of the Church. It was the anti-clerical and agnostic world that was always prophesying the advent of universal peace; it is that world that was, or should have been, abashed and confounded by the advent of universal war. As for the general view that the Church was discredited by the War—they might as well say that the Ark was discredited by the Flood. When the world goes wrong, it proves rather that the Church is right. The Church is justified, not because her children do not sin, but because they do.

Source: G. K. Chesterton, *The Everlasting Man* (London: Hodder & Stoughton, 1925).

mans and animals. Since art and laughter were without animal precedent but had been present since the beginning of the human race, these faculties could not be the result of evolution. Their lack of evolutionary antecedent, then, suggested that humanity could not have derived from animals. Instead, Chesterton argued, the ability to laugh and appreciate art implied that human existence stemmed from a source outside the material world.

Chesterton valued art as a sign of humanity's exceptional distinction from the rest of nature, and much of his argument in *The Everlasting Man* was advanced through the art of rhetoric. His favorite rhetorical device was the analogy, and his were effortlessly constructed, humorous, and based in common sense. For example, in response to the modernist claim that economic pressures explain the emergence of moral standards, Chesterton replied that such a notion was akin to saying that because we walk on two legs, we walk only for the purpose of purchasing shoes.

In addition to his pointed analogies, Chesterton employed clever rhetorical inversions of modernist contentions. He observed, for instance, that the modernists' trust in their own rational objectivity was undercut by their philosophical conviction that personal points of view determined individual beliefs. Given this conviction about the relativity of perspective, Chesterton argued, the materialist accounts of humanity cannot be understood as anything other than a subjective interpretation.

Modernists were half right about human subjectivity, Chesterton maintained, but they needed to appreciate and value the emotions informing subjectivity. He continued, saying that humans' deepest emotions—such as a sense of wonder—surpass reason's way of knowing; emotional truths trump rational thought as a source for understanding the history of the sacred. Chesterton pointed to the appeal of myth and fiction, which can paradoxically be truer than materialist histories like Wells's, and he also discussed art, which he saw as a unique and mysterious creation that further demonstrated the modernists' error in relying on objective material facts to explain human existence.

Chesterton extended his investigation of art by asserting that its appeal to the imagination pointed to the superiority of imagination over reason as a tool for understanding being: Only imagination could be capable of intuiting an explanation for such unlikely events as the origin of humanity and the birth of Christ. Chesterton compared this intuitive knowing to a child's way of seeing, an idea inherited from nineteenth century Roman-

tics. This idea proposed that children know more than they can say and feel more of the subtle texture of being than they can understand; in short, they have a keener sense of the sacred and magical. Chesterton urged the recovery of this intuitive sense of wonder as an antidote to the modernists' dehumanizing scientific rationalism.

This sense of wonder was a crucial part of Chesterton's argument in the second half of *The Everlasting Man*. There he spoke of Christ's birth as a true story that read like a myth. The coming of Christ into the world seemed strange, Chesterton acknowledged, because it involved a paradox beyond reason's historical understanding: Christ was not merely a physical man but a paradoxical union of the divine and the human. By reversing the implications of materialist interpretations of Christ that required him to be either a historical or imaginary figure, Chesterton avoided taking a stand on Christ's divine nature. Instead, he was able to argue that the sheer plentitude of modern interpretations of Christ resulted from the wonder and profound mystery that this figure engendered. Christ's miraculous birth was as extraordinary and unique as humanity's own peculiar appearance on Earth, and the church founded on Christ's teachings, Chesterton insisted, did not evolve from the decay of the Roman Empire any more than humanity descended from animals.

SIGNIFICANCE

Like Wells's *Outline of History*, *The Everlasting Man* affected readers across the social spectrum. Some readers considered it Chesterton's masterpiece, whereas others saw it as second to *Orthodoxy* (1908), Chesterton's autobiographical account of his conversion to Christianity. If *The Everlasting Man* was less influential than *Orthodoxy*, its alternative version of history—particularly of the rise of Christianity—had a significant impact on many people. Detective-fiction writer Dorothy L. Sayers, for example, thought *The Everlasting Man* was an act of Christian liberation, and C. S. Lewis, author of the seven popular novels comprising *The Chronicles of Narnia* (1950-1956), converted to Christianity after reading Chesterton's book.

For those not predisposed to Chesterton's point of view, his argument seemed more a matter of style than of substance. They found his commonsense humor and rhetorical artistry to be entertaining but finally unconvincing compared to the methods used by modernist science and history. Some critics complained that Chesterton needed to know more about what he was critiquing. In marked contrast to *Orthodoxy*, *The Everlasting Man* received more bad reviews than good ones, and it sold poorly. Even so, the book has remained in print, and Chesterton devotees continue to celebrate it as a cogent reply to agnostic and materialist interpretations of human existence.

—*William J. Scheick*

FURTHER READING

Corrin, Jay P. *G. K. Chesterton and Hilaire Belloc: The Battle Against Modernity.* Athens: Ohio University Press, 1981. Considers *The Everlasting Man* only briefly but is a useful guide to modernist issues addressed by Chesterton throughout his career.

Dale, Alzina Stone. *The Outline of Sanity: A Life of G. K. Chesterton.* Grand Rapids, Mich.: William F. Eerd-

mans, 1982. A sympathetic biography with part of a chapter devoted to *The Everlasting Man.*

Sheed, Wilford. "On Chesterton." In *G. K. Chesterton: A Half Century of Views,* edited by D. J. Conlon. 1958. Reprint. Oxford, England: Oxford University Press, 1987. Provides an insightful, succinct review of Chesterton's strengths and weakness as a critic of modernism.

SEE ALSO: 1902: James Proposes a Rational Basis for Religious Experience; 1923: Buber Breaks New Ground in Religious Philosophy; 1932: Gilson's *Spirit of Medieval Philosophy* Reassesses Christian Thought; Oct., 1937: *The Diary of a Country Priest* Inspires American Readers.

October, 1925
GERMANY ATTEMPTS TO RESTRUCTURE THE VERSAILLES TREATY

Germany initiated the Locarno Conference to reduce the German debt, offering reassurances of security for France in exchange.

LOCALE: Locarno, Switzerland

CATEGORIES: Diplomacy and international relations; economics; civil rights and liberties

KEY FIGURES

Gustav Stresemann (1878-1929), foreign minister of Germany

Aristide Briand (1862-1932), foreign minister of France

Charles G. Dawes (1865-1951), vice president of the United States, 1925-1929

Austen Chamberlain (1863-1937), British foreign secretary

SUMMARY OF EVENT

The Treaty of Versailles, which concluded World War I, left Europe in an uneasy state. France and Great Britain had, with American backing, imposed on Germany an immense war indemnity. The German people felt grievously and unjustly persecuted, and the French dreaded Germany's recovery and possible vengeance.

This was the situation addressed when delegates from Germany, France, Great Britain, Italy, Belgium, Poland, and Czechoslovakia met in Locarno, Switzerland, on October 5, 1925. On October 16, seven treaties were signed. The principal document was the Treaty of Mutual Guarantee signed by France, Great Britain, Belgium,

Italy, and Germany. Also called the Rhineland Security Pact, it guaranteed that the fifty-kilometer zone in Germany east of the Rhine would remain demilitarized and that Germany would honor its Belgian and French frontiers. By two separate treaties, Germany pledged not to make war on Belgium or France except in legitimate defense or in a League of Nations action and to settle disputes by arbitration. In the east, however, German foreign minister Gustav Stresemann refused to pledge the same boundary guarantees as in the west. Rather, Germany signed treaties of arbitration with Poland and with Czechoslovakia. France also signed treaties with Poland and Czechoslovakia against the possibility of German aggression. The treaties were formally signed in London on December 1, 1925, effective as soon as Germany entered the League of Nations (September 8, 1926). For the first time since World War I, Germany was treated as a friendly nation.

In order to appreciate fully the meaning of the Locarno Treaties of 1925, it is necessary to understand the events that led to World War I and the Treaty of Versailles of 1919. According to one interpretation, the major impetus to war was the aggressive posture of Germany, unified as a nation only in 1870 and impatient to gain respect and territory on a par with its well-established and prestigious neighbors, Great Britain and France. This interpretation, which became operative after the victory of Britain and France in World War I, is not by any means clear and unambiguous fact.

Animosities between England and Germany did play

their part in establishing a general war mood. Eager to catch up, Germany embarked at the turn of the century on a program of rapid naval construction, including thirty-eight battleships. This was perceived in world opinion as a challenge to traditional British supremacy on the high seas, but in Germany it was seen as a security measure appropriate for a full-fledged nation.

Another area of Anglo-German rivalry was Germany's expansion as a colonial power in Africa, the South Pacific, and especially the Middle East. The contract of the Deutsche Bank with the Turkish government (November 27, 1898) to construct a railroad from Istanbul to Baghdad was initially favored by Great Britain, which hoped to use Germany as a foil to Russian expansionism in Turkey. British public opinion discouraged British banks

from accepting a German request to finance the project jointly. As the railway subsequently resulted in a nearly monopolistic German influence in the economic and political life of Turkey, Great Britain came to view it as a threat to its lifelines in Egypt and India.

Franco-German relations had long been strained. Since the humiliation of France in the Franco-Prussian War of 1870, the French nationalist press had demanded a war of revenge. A spirit of resentment toward Germany persisted in France. At the same time, the French felt alarmed and threatened by Germany's already superior numbers and the rapid growth of its naval power.

The June 28, 1914, assassination in Sarajevo of the heir to the throne of Habsburg Austria, Archduke Francis Ferdinand, and his wife, by a Serbian citizen, Gavrilo Princip,

Representatives of European nations gather in London to sign the Locarno Treaties on December 1, 1925. (Library of Congress)

was only the trigger that set in motion a series of responses culminating in the war. Princip's deed was the final event in a history of small Eastern European wars and of a dangerous animosity between Serbia and Austria.

The South Slavic peoples residing in the Austro-Hungarian Empire in the nineteenth century had long agitated for independence, with moral support from czarist Russia. In 1867, Hungary had satisfied its nationalist aims through the creation of a new national entity, Austria-Hungary. Both Serbia and Montenegro achieved a landlocked independence from Turkey at the 1878 Congress of Berlin, but concurrently the South Slavs of Bosnia and Herzegovina were annexed by Austria. Serbia claimed a right to rule these formerly Turkish provinces based on their ethnic relationship and, in anticipation of Russian support, gradually prepared for a possible war with Austria. In deference to a German demand, however, Russia officially, at least, ceased support of Serbia and recognized Austria's possession of Bosnia and Herzegovina in 1909.

The two Balkan Wars in 1912 and 1913 added fuel to Serbia's animosity toward Austria-Hungary. Victorious in the second of these wars, Serbia gained parts of Macedonia, but Austria-Hungary fiercely opposed acquisition of lands bordering on the Adriatic that would allow Serbian access to the sea. That corridor was filled by Albania, newly created by the Great Powers by means of the 1913 Treaty of London.

Opinions differ about the rush of events after the assassination of the Habsburg heir. One question was whether Serbian leadership sponsored the assassination, or knew of it in advance. Austria demanded satisfaction, as if there had been official Serbian complicity. Although involvement of the Serbian leaders remains questionable, Serbia acceded to nearly all the Austrian demands. Austria rejected the Serbian response as unsatisfactory. Russia was committed to defense of Serbia. Germany, it was clear to all, would support fellow Germans in Austria.

Germany was thus, by some accounts, no more guilty as a cause of World War I than any other European state. Nevertheless, Article 231 of the Versailles treaty proclaimed that defeated Germany accepted guilt for the war. Other articles outlined the exorbitantly high indemnity that the new Weimar government of Germany acknowledged it must pay. Aggravating this not clearly deserved war debt, Germany was deprived of a nation's normal means of generating revenue, natural energy resources and overseas possessions as markets and sources of raw materials. Germany had to cede the rich coal-producing Saar basin to France and return other disputed lands won by Germany in the Franco-Prussian War of 1870. Article 119 of the Versailles treaty took away all of Germany's overseas possessions.

After the war, Emperor William II of Germany had fled to Holland. The Weimar regime's acquiescence to the stipulations of the Versailles treaty exposed it to criticism. No doubt the new republican government anticipated actual reparations to be lenient, given that it had had no part in Germany's role in the war. That was not the case, however. Much discussion has been devoted to the question of whether the Allies' lack of consideration for the Weimar democracy promoted the German nationalism of the 1930's.

In the years that followed the Treaty of Versailles, the Allies sensed the extent to which it had been excessively harsh and that the Germans must in time seek satisfaction. British foreign secretary Lord Arthur Balfour announced in 1922 that if the United States, which had claimed no part of Germany's reparations payments, would cancel European debts, then Great Britain would discontinue demanding German payments. The United States, however, viewed reparations and inter-Allied debts as entirely separate problems. Britain then offered a unilateral cessation of its claims. France, with a debt to Britain much less than its anticipated reparations from Germany, refused to grant a moratorium.

British goodwill toward Germany left the French government feeling increasingly isolated and insecure. The solution of French prime minister Raymond Poincaré was to maintain and even increase the obstacles to German growth. Thus in 1923 France occupied Germany's mineral-rich Ruhr basin on the pretext that Germany had become delinquent in deliveries of timber. The response of the Weimar government, now even more profoundly prevented from generating the wealth with which to make payment, was "passive resistance." This took the form of issuing worthless paper marks for the purpose of making the requisite payments.

The French, British, and American governments, banks, and private speculators worsened the situation by purchasing German marks at current low exchange rates, planning to sell them back when the mark stabilized at its normal higher value. Instead, the resultant flood of marks into the money market led to the collapse of the German monetary system in 1923. By then, the mark was worth as little as 4.2 trillion to the dollar, less than the paper it was printed on. A disastrous general European inflation had set in, and a worldwide financial collapse seemed imminent.

The 1923-1925 period saw massive efforts to rectify matters. Stresemann designed a plan to convert old German marks into strongly backed Rentenmarks at a rate of a trillion to one. This was the major step in alleviating the world's general inflation. In 1924, the Dawes Plan, proposed by Charles G. Dawes, who subsequently became the U.S. vice president, provided for a large Allied loan to help stabilize the mark and regulate the amounts of reparations required. Finally, a British-sponsored Geneva Protocol attempted to define aggression and provide for peaceful settlement of international disputes. Although never implemented, it established a spirit for Locarno.

France sought to contain Germany by preponderant force while Britain worked at conciliation, removing the causes of German dissatisfaction. Britain constantly tried to keep France from provoking Germany. The French could charge that Germany's resentment was the result of Britain destroying Germany as a world power, taking its colonies, dismantling its navy, and seizing its capital holdings abroad. It was unfair, said the French, of Britain to ask France, Poland, and other continental powers to make concessions while Britain made none.

SIGNIFICANCE

In February, 1925, Stresemann had expressed to France his government's desire to guarantee the Franco-German Rhine frontiers as established by the Versailles treaty. The Germans regarded as great sacrifices their acknowledgment of French possession of Alsace-Lorraine and their promise not to use force in Eastern Europe. Perhaps these sacrifices would alleviate France's fear of its more populous neighbor, assure France of Germany's peaceful stance, and thereby meet the French need for security. If successful, Germany could hope in return for a reduction of its war indemnity and possibly, in time, even a dismantling of other provisions of the Versailles treaty.

Locarno was regarded as marking the start of an era of goodwill and as the reconciliation of former enemies of World War I. The high hopes of the moment were reflected in the Nobel Peace Prize awarded to Aristide Briand of France, Austen Chamberlain of Great Britain, and Gustav Stresemann of Germany. One assessment regards Locarno as the true end of World War I.

What precisely did the Locarno Conference do, and how did it affect the sense of security of the peoples of Europe and the world? After a war that had surpassed all fears, and after an inflation that had destroyed the savings and economic security of countless middle-class families, the world was sorely in need of good news. The Locarno Treaties offered hope of a peaceful future.

The Locarno Treaties have also received a negative interpretation, which to some extent may reflect the true state of affairs. Such an interpretation came only after the treaties were known to have failed to bring permanent peace and after Stresemann's private papers had been published. Was Locarno a screen behind which Stresemann actually supervised German rearmament? Did Stresemann's trade and nonaggression pacts with the Soviet Union after Locarno prove Germany's hypocrisy?

Disillusionment exists even regarding the motivations of the Allies. It is argued that Locarno reflected Great Britain's desire to keep continental commitments at a minimum. Great Britain's unwillingness to concern itself with Eastern Europe seemed to be a portent of its attitude in 1938, and was so assessed by Adolf Hitler. The West, through the Locarno Treaties, may simply have been protecting itself by turning German ambitions eastward against the Bolsheviks. The Soviet Union did in fact see the treaties as a hostile scheme against it, as Germany's eastern frontiers were not guaranteed. Finally, in both Germany and France nationalists attacked the treaties.

For ten years, Locarno represented a ray of hope. Hope proved illusory, however, when Hitler violated the pacts in March, 1936. A week later, the other powers voted to condemn Germany but took no punitive action.

—*Daniel C. Scavone*

FURTHER READING

Borsody, C. Stephen. *The Triumph of Tyranny*. New York: Macmillan, 1960. Argues that the Allied purpose at Locarno was to keep Germany and the Soviet Union apart and that, perceiving this, the Soviets viewed it as portentous of a new European war.

Eyck, Erich. *A History of the Weimar Republic*. 2 vols. New York: John Wiley & Sons, 1967. One of the best general histories of the Weimar period available. Volume 2 includes extensive and incisive detailed material on Locarno.

Jacobson, Jon. *Locarno Diplomacy: Germany and the West, 1925-1929*. Princeton, N.J.: Princeton University Press, 1972. Explores the personalities and diplomacy of the Locarno era and offers an interpretation by means of newly released American, British, and German state documents and contemporary private documents, including Stresemann's private papers. Jacobson views Locarno as a sinister diplomatic duel between Briand and Stresemann. Includes an extensive bibliography.

Marks, Sally. *The Illusion of Peace: International Relations in Europe, 1918-1933*. 2d ed. New York: Palgrave Macmillan, 2003. Views the period as extremely unstable and inevitably explosive because the Versailles treaty was so unfair to Germany. Provides a useful chronology of important events from 1915 to 1937.

Nicholls, A. J. *Weimar and the Rise of Hitler*. 4th ed. New York: St. Martin's Press, 2000. Analysis of the failure of the Weimar government. Regarding Locarno, presents Stresemann's argument that the eastern arrangements left Germany free to resort to war there. Stresemann believed Locarno would forestall a bilateral Anglo-French treaty and saw it as the beginning of the dismantling of the whole Versailles treaty. Includes chronological table, bibliography, and index.

Taylor, A. J. P. *The Origins of the Second World War*. 1961. Reprint. New York: Touchstone, 1996. Praises Stresemann and Briton Ramsay MacDonald for their peacekeeping roles between the wars. Stresemann's posthumous papers prove that he wanted to destroy the Versailles treaty. It had to be revised, by peace or war; Stresemann sought peace.

Wolfers, Arnold. *Britain and France Between Two Wars*. New York: Harcourt, Brace, 1940. Good general introduction to the diplomacy of the period after World War I. Points up the high level of friction that developed between the two allies with reference to Germany.

SEE ALSO: Apr. 28, 1919: League of Nations Is Established; June 28, 1919: Treaty of Versailles; Apr. 16, 1922: Treaty of Rapallo; Jan. 11, 1923-Aug. 16, 1924: France Occupies the Ruhr; Sept. 1, 1924: Dawes Plan; Jan. 30, 1933: Hitler Comes to Power in Germany; Mar. 7, 1936: German Troops March into the Rhineland; Feb. 12-Apr. 10, 1938: The Anschluss.

October-December, 1925
BAKER DANCES IN *LA REVUE NÈGRE*

Parisian café society was spellbound by exotic dancer Josephine Baker, who would soon change how Europe viewed modern dance.

LOCALE: Paris, France
CATEGORY: Dance

KEY FIGURES

Josephine Baker (1906-1975), American dancer who became a symbol of expressive, exotic performing in Europe during the 1920's

André Daven (fl. early twentieth century), director of the Théâtre des Champs-Élysées during the showing of *La Revue nègre*

Rolf de Mare (1888-1964), manager of the Théâtre des Champs-Élysées during the showing of *La Revue nègre*

Paul Colin (1892-1985), amateur painter responsible for designing the cover of the program and the poster for *La Revue nègre*

Caroline Dudley (fl. early twentieth century), chief organizer in New York City of the black song-and-dance show that sailed to Paris to perform at the Théâtre des Champs-Élysées

Jacques Charles (fl. early twentieth century), producer at the Moulin Rouge who helped with the production of *La Revue nègre*

SUMMARY OF EVENT

By the age of nineteen, Josephine Baker had risen from her poverty-stricken background in East St. Louis to the endless possibilities of New York City show business. In 1921, she first made her name known in Noble Sissle and Eubie Blake's show *Shuffle Along*. She later appeared in their show *Chocolate Dandies*. Both of these all-black Broadway shows are remembered for their role in helping to introduce black entertainment to the stages of New York City. Baker's clowning, comical style helped to get her noticed during rehearsals and auditions, but she appeared in these productions only briefly, as a dancer or a "walk-on." Her well-known ragamuffin period was labeled as such because of her popular cross-eyed and knees-turned-in dance position that eventually helped her break into entertainment. However, Baker's stage appearances were not due to her dancing ability or beautiful body. On the contrary, Baker was perceived as an ugly tomboy and was clad in big shoes and tattered clothes.

In the summer of 1925, show coordinator Caroline Dudley organized a black song-and-dance troupe at the request of the French theater director André Daven. Dudley and Daven believed that if anything would help save Paris's Théâtre des Champs-Élysées from hard economic postwar times, it would be a real African American show. The theater was very large for such a small production, but the directors hoped to move the show into smaller dance halls later. Baker was one of the twenty-four musicians, singers, and dancers to travel across the Atlantic Ocean and perform in what is one of the best-known American productions of the 1920's, *La Revue nègre* (the black revue).

Baker arrived in Paris dumbfounded and ready to return to the United States immediately after the show was completed. Her attitude would soon change, however. *La Revue nègre* was developed to give the European audience an idea of how black Americans danced. When the opening night of *La Revue nègre* finally came, Paris was caught by surprise. A popular comment from the audience was that the show had the most black people they had ever seen on a stage at one time. To Parisian café society, the popular class of people involved in the city life of downtown Paris, this was a part of the world they knew little about.

Before *La Revue nègre* was ready for its preview showing at the Théâtre des Champs-Élysées, director Daven and producer Rolf de Mare had to make significant changes to the format and content of the show, which had been presented in Britain and across Europe as *Blackbirds*. They thought the show was too noisy, too long, inelegant, and not black enough. Jacques Charles, a producer at the well-known Moulin Rouge, rearranged the dancers and put more focus on Baker. She was given the spotlight in one particularly exotic dance, the "Danse sauvage," which was strategically placed at the end of the show to create a shocking finale. Baker and her partner appeared in bare skin and feathers, and they raced around the stage to upbeat African music. Baker's part in the "Danse sauvage" was the foundation of her exotic dance period. Interestingly, Baker was not originally scheduled to star in the show. When Maud de Forrest, the original lead singer, could no longer handle the pressure of performing in *La Revue nègre*, she was dismissed from the show. Baker took her place as the leading lady, and a star was born.

When the show was ready for opening night, journalists and celebrities were given an exclusive preview showing. An enormous amount of publicity appeared in the French tabloids and newspapers. What mattered was not whether the reviews were good or bad, but that the show had become the most talked-about production in Paris. Almost immediately after opening night, Baker became a well-known success. Surrounded by handsome men, publicity people, and artists, her impression of Paris quickly changed, and she became accustomed to the European lifestyle. France would soon become her new home, and she became part of France's growing obsession with black entertainment.

An artist by the name of Paul Colin was partly responsible for Baker's fame in *La Revue nègre*. Colin was called in to draw the publicity program cover and poster. As the posters covered walls throughout Paris, positive reviews continued to flourish, and more and more Parisians came to see the show. *La Revue nègre* had created a celebrity and proved to Paris that black is beautiful. Artists soon drowned Baker with requests to photograph or paint her in the nude. She was at first too modest but soon realized that nude portrayals were going to become common.

Although Baker was said not to have liked *La Revue nègre*, she would not have become a dance celebrity without it. Colin's posters made her recognizable long before the public knew her by name. *La Revue nègre* played for three months, from October to December of 1925. As the directors of the Théâtre des Champs-Élysées had predicted, *La Revue nègre* was able to continue its run by moving into smaller theaters. The show traveled from Paris to Brussels and then to the Nelson Theatre in Berlin. Although it was not a long-running show, by the end of 1925 it had made Baker one of the most famous dancers in Europe.

From Baker and *La Revue nègre*, European society gained a knowledge and understanding of a dance culture that was previously all but unknown to it. Credit for this discovery must be given not only to Charles, Daven, de Mare, and the other show organizers, but to Baker and her unique talent. Her dance was not regarded immediately as artistically valuable. On the opening night of *La Revue nègre*, Baker was pleased to hear what she thought were whistles of approval coming from the audience. She soon found out, however, that in Paris whistling signaled rejection and dislike. Baker was in disbelief. In the weeks after opening night, the whistling came to be drowned out by chants of "Josephine" and calls for more wonderful dance. Parties were thrown for the singers and dancers night after night.

La Revue nègre certainly left an impression on Jacques-Émile Blanche, a renowned French portrait painter. He had been searching for a "manifestation of the modern spirit" in the Art Deco Show but found it instead in *La Revue nègre*. This led other people to look at the show in that manner. The numerous reviews became Baker's texts for learning the French language. Whether good or bad, the critiques of *La Revue nègre* educated Baker and the public. One critic compared the dance movements in the show to St. Vitus's Dance, a nervous disorder that makes the body tremble. Another labeled Baker a "Black Venus."

A particularly harsh critic of Baker was distinguished dance critic Andre Levinson. He referred at first to black dance as primitive and prehuman, saying that black dancers turned their bodies into percussion instruments. He gave *La Revue nègre* a favorable although somewhat condescending review and later was persuaded of the validity of black dance and jazz music. Librettist and playwright Robert de Flers referred to *La Revue nègre* as "the most direct assault ever perpetrated against French taste." It is difficult to assess the widely differing opinions of Baker and the show. Unfortunately, there are no film recordings of *La Revue nègre*, only photographs and stories told by Baker's friends and family.

The fame Baker received from *La Revue nègre* was only a fraction of what was to come. In 1926, she was asked to join productions of the Folies-Bergère, a major tourist attraction in the Paris theater district. In 1927, she performed at the Folies-Bergère with two live cheetahs, wearing nothing but a short skirt made of imitation bananas. Ironically, Baker was not received as well when she returned to the United States to appear in *Ziegfeld Follies of 1936*. After that, it would be fifteen years before she would return to her native country again. Baker joined the French Women's Air Force at the outbreak of World War II and later joined the French Resistance; for this work she was awarded the Croix de Guerre with Palm, among other decorations. When she did return to the United States in 1951, she refused to appear in clubs that did not allow black patrons. Her stand convinced the Copa City Club in Miami, Florida, to change its discriminatory policies, and other clubs began to follow the trend.

Baker's performances included singing as well as dancing, but it was her dancing that made her famous. She performed all over the world in various shows and eventually went on a solo world tour. Baker visited the United States on her tours and, in later years, said that she thought of it once again as her home. With the stamina of a twenty-year-old, Baker performed into the final days of her life, appearing in *Josephine*, a show commemorating her fifty years in show business, five days before she died on April 12, 1975, in Paris. Her funeral was publicized throughout the country. Starting at the church of the Madeleine, the procession went by the theaters at which she had performed. Eulogies recognized her civil and military achievements as well as her artistic ability. Baker is remembered as one of the most famous female performers, responsible in large part for bringing new dance forms to Europe, beginning with her performance in *La Revue nègre*.

SIGNIFICANCE

When *La Revue nègre* opened at the Théâtre des Champs-Élysées, the French had no idea what impact Baker would have on the history of dance. European audiences were enchanted immediately when Baker stepped out on stage and became a beautiful, flowing piece of art. Because so little was known about African dance, Baker became even more of a celebrated creature. When she danced, her somewhat-disproportionate body became unexplicably beautiful and perfect, moving in ways no one knew were possible. Baker danced so exotically that the audience was mesmerized just by watching her move. Her dancing was said to have been on the verge of being obscene.

Many different events illustrate how African dance was regarded after the popularity of *La Revue nègre*. According to the average Parisian audience member, black dancers were instinctive and incapable of discipline. When on stage, they were thought of as indecent, primitive, and savage. Because Baker's dance moves were so unconventional and so different from those of Caucasian dancers, it was easy to understand why these thoughts were prevalent. *La Revue nègre* came to symbolize postwar modernism, bringing to Europe the spirit of Americanized Africa. The dance culture was left refreshed and more dynamic, with unconventional forms more accepted. Baker helped introduce popular American dances to Europe, including the Charleston and the Black Bottom. Her dancing also helped to popularize the jazz music that accompanied it. Critic Andre Levinson wrote about jazz, "The music is born from the dance, and what a dance!" The impact Baker had on the European culture was strong, and Baker's style became an institution in French society. Restaurateurs and club owners named their establishments after her. Fashion designers followed the advice of Baker and eventually designed dresses in her name, such as Robe Josephine.

—*David Francis*

FURTHER READING

Baker, Josephine, and Jo Boullion. *Josephine*. Translated by Mariana Fitzpatrick. New York: Harper & Row, 1977. Biography written by Baker and her former husband, with many interviews with her associates. Because of Boullion's relationship to Baker, the information is very accurate. Baker reveals personal thoughts and stories that do not appear in other biographies. Portions of the book tend to include Boullion excessively, but the reader can overlook these excerpts. Good index and small section of photographs.

Bennetta, Jules Rosette. *Two Loves: Josephine Baker in Art and Life*. Urbana: University of Illinois Press, 2006. A thorough and carefully researched biography that provides a particularly interesting discussion of Baker's experiences as an African American. Bibliography and index.

Hammond, Bryan. *Josephine Baker*. London: Jonathan Cape, 1988. Complete photographic biography of Baker's performing life. Extraordinary photographs of Baker on stage, at home, and in various publicity pieces. Complete discography and index. The text is very brief, but this book is a good visual aid to other Baker biographies.

Haney, Lynn. *Naked at the Feast: A Biography of Josephine Baker*. New York: Dodd, Mead, 1981. A good basic reference concerning Baker's dance career. Haney is thorough and accurate in her accounts of which theaters, directors, and other celebrities were involved at each stage of Baker's performing life. A large part of the book is devoted to Baker's problems with her husbands and children.

Lahs-Gonzales, Olivia, Bennetta Jules Rosette, and Tyler Stovall. *Josephine Baker: Image and Icon*. St. Louis, Mo.: Reedy Press, 2006. This generously illustrated volume was created to commemorate the one hundredth anniversary of Baker's birth. In addition to its many images, it contains two substantial biographical essays.

Rose, Phyllis. *Jazz Cleopatra*. New York: Vintage Books, 1989. Excellent biography in a story format. The book is separated into three sections, of which the first, covering 1925 and 1926, is the most complete. Only one chapter on *La Revue nègre*, but the "Danse sauvage" is covered extensively. Numerous photographs show Baker's diverse phases.

Wiser, William. "Josephine Baker, 1906-1975." In *The Great Good Place: American Expatriate Women in Paris*. New York: W. W. Norton, 1991. Wiser offers a succinct but lively account of the dancer's life. He paints a picture of a 1920's Paris so jaded that almost nothing could shock it—except Baker's energetic, seminude dancing.

SEE ALSO: Dec. 26, 1904: Duncan Interprets Chopin in Her Russian Debut; May 19, 1909: Diaghilev's Ballets Russes Astounds Paris; May 29, 1912: *L'Après-midi d'un faune* Scandalizes Parisian Audiences; May 29, 1913: *The Rite of Spring* Stuns Audiences; Summer, 1915: Denishawn School of Dance Opens; July 3, 1932: Jooss's Antiwar Dance *The Green Table* Premieres.

October 23, 1925
GREECE INVADES BULGARIA

A frontier incident between Greece and Bulgaria resulted in a brief invasion of southwestern Bulgaria by Greece. The League of Nations intervened to resolve the conflict.

LOCALE: Bulgaria; Greece; Geneva, Switzerland
CATEGORIES: Diplomacy and international relations; wars, uprisings, and civil unrest

KEY FIGURES

Aristide Briand (1862-1932), French diplomat and politician and president of the Council of the League of Nations in 1925

Theodoros Pangalos (1878-1952), Greek military and authoritarian political figure and initiator of the 1925 invasion

SUMMARY OF EVENT

In October of 1925, a violent but minor frontier incident between Bulgaria and Greece caused the Greek government to respond with a medium-sized military action against Bulgaria. The Bulgarian government in Sofia appealed to the League of Nations for support in the conflict, and the League engineered a cease-fire, conducted an investigation, and had issued its findings by December of 1925. The lion's share of blame for the violations of sovereignty, deaths, and material destruction belonged to Greece, which was then forced to pay a hefty fine.

The roots of this conflict lay in the tangled domestic political situations in both Greece and Bulgaria. To some degree, however, the incidents also reflected the unresolved national question that had plagued Greco-Bulgarian relations for more than a decade. The cause of the conflict was not, it should be noted, related to any of the so-called ancient ethnic hatreds between the Balkan peoples.

In the period 1912-1913, a Balkan League—consisting of Montenegro, Bulgaria, Serbia, and Greece—had, with Russian backing, overrun most of the Ottoman Empire's remaining (and ethnically diverse) territories in Europe. This First Balkan War (October, 1912-May, 1913), was a forerunner of World War I, which began in 1914; it was also a cruel variety of intra-European imperialism, practiced not by the major world powers like Britain and France overseas but closer to home, by four states that claimed to be "liberating" their own historical or ethnic territories. The feeding frenzy among the four brought them into conflict with each other and with the diverse populations they now ruled. The Second Balkan War (1913) ensued, and in it Bulgaria was humiliated by a number of states whose leaders thought Bulgaria had seized an unacceptable amount of land in Macedonia and Thrace.

A final key element behind the Greek invasion of Bulgaria was the revolutionary nationalist organization known as the Internal Macedonian Revolutionary Organization (IMRO), which had originally been founded in the 1890's and then split into several factions. The Mihailovists, an IMRO fraction, wanted to annex the large region of Macedonia bordering Bulgaria. In 1925, both Serbia (which became part of Yugoslavia in 1918) and Greece held large portions of Macedonia, so their governments and populations were targeted by IMRO operatives. The Bulgarian government was unable to dismantle the terrorist group, much to the anger of its neighbors. Meanwhile, in Greece, nationalist sentiments were also running high, and the irresponsible military leader, General Theodoros Pangalos, was presented with a tempting opportunity to both mobilize the public and satisfy his urge for personal glory. The area around the southern Bulgarian border town of Petric became a center of operations for the Mihailovists' aims within Bulgaria. They also used Petric as a base from which to launch attacks into the disputed border areas of nearby Greece and Yugoslavia. Several such forays into Greece had already been made.

It was in the exceedingly tense atmosphere of this cross-border terrorism—which Athens accused Sofia of being unwilling to stop—that the frontier incident that triggered the invasion occurred between Greek and Bulgarian troops. On October 19, 1925, the Bulgarian border forces killed one Greek officer and one soldier near Demir Hissár, and Greek outrage was immediate and thunderous, particularly because some Greeks had also recently been killed in Bulgaria. Bulgaria's neighbors also feared that the *komitadjis*, as the Bulgarian underground fighters were called, were being supported by the Soviet Union in order to advance a communist agenda.

The ensuing conflict became front-page news around the world. Before resorting to military means, the Greeks first demanded satisfaction within forty-eight hours in the form of an indemnity of two million gold francs (more than eighty thousand dollars), an official apology, and the punishment of the responsible Bulgarian parties. When these demands were not met, more than a thousand Greek troops, accompanied by air and artillery units, crossed the border and moved toward the city of Petric. The incursion began on October 23, and Bulgaria contacted the League of Nations in Geneva on the same day. Led by the French foreign minister Aristide Briand, the League Council, a subgroup of both permanent and nonpermanent members, agreed to meet on October 26 to consider the issue. The League quickly demanded that the two countries agree to accept its decision and that the

BULGARIA, 1925

ROMANIA
★ Bucharest
YUGOSLAVIA
Sofia ★
BULGARIA
Black Sea
Struma River
MACEDONIA
Petrich
BELASITSA MOUNTAINS
Demir Hissár
THRACE
Istanbul
Thessaloniki
GREECE
Aegean Sea
TURKEY

fighting cease and troops returned to their respective territories before any adjudication would take place, and Greece and Bulgaria agreed to these conditions.

Over a period of two days, the Greeks advanced about eight kilometers inside Bulgaria along a front that was roughly thirty kilometers wide. A number of Bulgarian homes and fields were destroyed or plundered, and refugees fled. Some accounts give the number of Bulgarian soldiers and civilians killed as fifty, and many others were wounded. Greek casualty figures are not available, but Bulgarian resistance had stiffened as the invaders approached Petric, and there were reports of Bulgarian sniper activity.

When the Greeks heard of President Briand's demand, attacks ceased, and Greek troops quickly withdrew. The League first sent the military attachés from nearby British, French, and Italian legations to conduct a preliminary report, which was followed by a commission of inquiry. This special commission presented its findings in a report on December 3, 1925. It found that Bulgaria had been at fault for the original incident, but that Greece's culpability in using aggression instead of the good offices of the League was much greater; the penalty to be paid by Greece, adjusted downward for the indemnity owed by Bulgaria, was set at £45,000, or about $219,000. Greece paid the sanction in February of 1926. Bulgaria had based its appeal for the League to safeguard the peace on Article 11 of the Covenant, the constitution-like founding document of the League's principles and procedures. The League considered economic sanctions or a military show of force under Article 16, but these were not necessary.

Bulgaria was predisposed to rely on the League to help resolve this dispute because of a number of dealings that already linked Sofia and Geneva. The League had helped raise reconstruction loans for Bulgaria to repair damage from World War I. Bulgaria's appeal to the League makes sense, then, given its functional relationship with that body as a defeated belligerent attempting to regain international acceptance. Greece's grudging acceptance of the League's intervention—penalties imposed on it by its former allies in the recent world war—indicates the momentum of the Locarno Pact of 1925, which prepared a rehabilitated Germany for a new international role, had given the League considerable authority. When the League was not hindered by internal bickering or budget constraints, it could be quite effective.

SIGNIFICANCE

One of the most important outcomes of the 1925 Greco-Bulgarian conflict was the demonstration of the effectiveness of the League of Nations. Diplomats within the League came to view Article 11 as justification for earlier intervention in nascent conflicts than previously allowed by an emphasis on Article 16, which referred to full-blown cases of war. A second key result was that the importance of irredenta (an area culturally connected to one nation but politically controlled by another) in the Balkans was still important. Elite and popular preoccupation with these "unredeemed lands"—one country's territory claimed by another on the basis of historical or strategic rights or of current national or ethnic composition—served to skew the domestic political scene of Greece, Bulgaria, and their neighbors. Perceived foreign threats to conationals or to a culture's place of origin allowed more constructive, concrete agendas to be relegated to the political sidelines.

With the military, intelligence and secret police services, and underground political groups playing key roles in the framing of political discourse, common developmental needs and historical similarities among the Balkan peoples were minimized; similarly, state budgets for education, the health system, industrial investment in nonmilitary branches, and the all-important agricultural industry were kept anemic. In addition, the continued cultivation of these frontier disputes helped make the Balkan states vulnerable to manipulation at the hands of the Nazis and, to a lesser degree, the Italian fascists.

A final effect was pressure from inside Greece for the ouster of General Pangalos, who had initiated the assault on Bulgaria. As one of Greece's many antimonarchical but decidedly militaristic strongmen of the period 1924-1935, he held power for fourteen months, and his failed foreign policy adventurism helped bring his government's downfall. This shift in power was an echo of the tumultuous time in which King George II had abdicated after losing the Greek regions of Asia Minor to the new Turkish state in 1923.

—*John K. Cox*

FURTHER READING

Clogg, Richard. *A Concise History of Greece*. 2d ed. New York: Cambridge University Press, 2002. An excellent concise history of the country that emphasizes the political instability of the interwar years.

Crampton, R. J. *A Concise History of Bulgaria*. New York: Cambridge University Press, 1997. A model of historical scholarship for narrative histories of small countries. Full of salient comparisons of Bulgarian policies and ideas with those of Europe in general.

Stavrianos, Leften. *The Balkans Since 1453*. New York:

New York University Press, 2000. The magisterial work on nearly all aspects of Balkan history by touching on its political, diplomatic, intellectual, and economic, and even to some degree military and social histories.

Walters, F. P. *A History of the League of Nations*. New York: Oxford University Press, 1967. A well-documented source for information on and analysis of individual League projects that lays to rest stereotypes about the League's supposedly universal ineffectiveness. Also contains biographical information on ma-

jor diplomats and blow-by-blow accounts, based on diplomatic and newspaper sources, of conflicts and developmental problems that garnered the League's attention.

SEE ALSO: Aug. 2-Sept., 1903: Ilinden Uprising in Macedonia; Oct. 7, 1908: Austria Annexes Bosnia and Herzegovina; Oct. 18, 1912-Aug. 10, 1913: Balkan Wars; Apr. 28, 1919: League of Nations Is Established; Dec. 13, 1920: Permanent Court of International Justice Is Established; Aug. 27-Sept. 29, 1923: Corfu Crisis.

November, 1925
ARMSTRONG RECORDS WITH THE HOT FIVE

Louis Armstrong's Hot Five recording sessions between 1925 and 1928 led to recognition of Armstrong as the father of modern jazz music.

LOCALE: Chicago, Illinois
CATEGORY: Music

KEY FIGURES
Louis Armstrong (1901-1971), American jazz musician
Fletcher "Smack" Henderson (1897-1952), American bandleader
Bessie Smith (1894-1937), American blues singer
Fatha Hines (1905-1983), American jazz pianist
King Oliver (1885-1938), American jazz musician and bandleader

SUMMARY OF EVENT
On November 12, 1925, Louis Armstrong and his Hot Five band recorded three songs for the OKeh Record Company in Chicago. These were the first of more than fifty records made by the group that changed the course of jazz music. In addition to Armstrong, the original Hot Five included Johnny Dodds on clarinet, Kid Ory on trombone, Lillian Hardin Armstrong (Armstrong's second wife) on piano, and Johnny St. Cyr on banjo. Except for one or two isolated public appearances, these musicians performed together only in the OKeh studios. From 1925 to 1928, the Hot Five, also known by a variety of other names during this period, recorded on twenty-two occasions; those sessions reflect a musical growth that has caused music critics to conclude that the Hot Five, and especially Armstrong, had a major influence on the evolution of twentieth century American popular music.

Armstrong had established himself as a popular

showman and musician prior to the Chicago recording session in 1925. He performed as a soloist in cabarets, as an accompanist for other jazz musicians, and in various jazz bands. Audiences already knew him as the "World's Greatest Trumpet Player," and they came by the hundreds to hear him. Reared in New Orleans from his birth until he left in 1922, Armstrong naturally adopted the loose ensemble style of music common in that city.

Between 1922, when he first arrived in Chicago, and 1925, Armstrong was a member of King Oliver's band and also a member of Fletcher "Smack" Henderson's East Coast-based jazz band. Oliver established a dominant relationship with Armstrong, and, although Armstrong did not learn much about the cornet from Oliver, he did learn something about responsibility. Henderson's band was easily the best jazz band of the early 1920's, and Armstrong profited from his years (1922-1924) in Henderson's group. During these years, Armstrong gradually broke away from the New Orleans ensemble style. When not playing with a band, he made public appearances that emphasized his singular virtuosity with the horn.

In some ways, the Hot Five recordings, especially the early ones, were a return for Armstrong to the more relaxed New Orleans music. Armstrong and others in the Hot Five group viewed the Chicago recording sessions as a holiday in their rigorous schedule of performances. Many critics argue that this informal attitude is what made the sessions so successful. The composition of Armstrong's group changed frequently between 1925 and 1928, and with each change, Armstrong advanced his improvisation without disrupting the casual New Orleans rhythm. The group's 1927 recording of "Potato

The original Hot Five in 1925 (from left): Louis Armstrong, Johnny St. Cyr, Johnny Dodds, Kid Ory, and Lillian Hardin Armstrong. (Hulton Archive/Getty Images)

Head Blues" is generally considered a breakthrough for Armstrong and for jazz music in general. In the recording, Armstrong improvised two solos that set a standard for future musicians. Earlier, in 1925, he had revealed his potential for improvisation in a remarkable recording session with the great blues singer Bessie Smith.

By the time he left Chicago in 1929, Armstrong was just short of star status. His recordings brought him thousands of new followers, and his personal appearances attracted both musicians and the general public. Near the end of the Hot Five sessions in 1928, Armstrong began to sing regularly on the recordings, and singing gradually became a more important part of Armstrong's music. He began by singing in a tenor voice similar to the "crooners" of his time, but he soon developed the gravelly, rasping style for which he became famous.

The Depression years were rough for Armstrong. His record sales and bookings declined, his second marriage ended, and he was arrested for smoking marijuana in California. Things soon turned around for him, however,

and he extended his horizons as a popular and commercial performer in the 1930's and 1940's. He began to tour Europe on a regular basis, and he acquired a hard-driving, well-connected agent, Joe Glaser, who demanded that he smile as broadly as possible and use facial expressions to endear himself to audiences. Some black musicians and critics objected to this "jolly darky" routine, but most who knew Armstrong agreed that his onstage antics were merely extensions of his joyous personality. He was now often referred to as "Satchmo," an appellation of uncertain origins.

As his commercial star ascended, Armstrong's cornet playing declined. A recording contract with Decca in 1935 required him to play and sing innocuous popular songs, songs that were suitable for radio listeners in the comfort of their living rooms. The big bands were all the rage, and Armstrong fell into line by leading a number of mediocre groups during this era. There was also a serious problem with Armstrong's lips. Throughout his career, he suffered from split lips, which forced him to rest for long periods of time. The scar tissue hampered his ability to play with clarity. His singing, however, was not affected. One of his 1930's songs, "A Kiss to Build a Dream On," clearly demonstrates his brilliant application of jazz phrasing to an otherwise ordinary lyric.

Armstrong reached the peak of his popularity in the 1950's and 1960's. Although he had been almost completely deserted by jazz enthusiasts, the general public responded to his many film appearances and to his singing. His hit records included "Blueberry Hill," "Mack the Knife," and "Hello, Dolly!" The latter song was such a smash that it became number one on the charts in May, 1964. It also led to a much-heralded appearance in the movie of the same name and to many television bookings. This success marked a high point in Armstrong's show business career. Shortly thereafter, his health began to fail, and he died on July 7, 1971. Armstrong had fulfilled the promise of the Hot Five sessions, but not quite in the way jazz musicians had expected or would have preferred.

SIGNIFICANCE

Biographer James Lincoln Collier has written that Armstrong "struck the first two generations of jazz musicians with the force of a sledgehammer." This is not an exaggeration. Most jazz writers and musicians without hesitation cite Armstrong as the father of modern jazz or as the "Bach of Jazz." He was truly a creator, for there was almost no musician who influenced him. He learned something from King Oliver, but what he learned was related more to presentation than to the music itself. Armstrong displayed technical and imaginative talent that astounded and inspired Roy Eldridge, Dizzy Gillespie, Benny Goodman, Humphrey Lyttelton, and a legion of other jazz musicians. The clarity of Armstrong's horn, his sharp attacks, and his ability to play effectively in the highest register startled those who heard him for the first time in the 1920's. His imagination appeared boundless in those early days; he could create melodies of grace and power almost instantly. The most cherished of Armstrong's attributes, however, and the one that had the greatest impact on future musicians, was his ability to lift all around him, musicians and audiences alike, by the sheer joy and energy he brought to his music. He taught American musicians how to "swing," how to give even simple music verve and excitement. It certainly helped if one had the virtuosity possessed by Armstrong, but lesser musicians could at least emulate his enthusiasm.

The Hot Five recordings, particularly "Potato Head Blues" and "Weather Bird," convinced musicians to be more independent and to eschew jazz orchestras, in which they sat in sections and played notes, for the delight of improvisation, the opportunity to soar. Armstrong had, in effect, given all musicians the opportunity to use their creative talent to the fullest. Whether a musician played the clarinet, the piano, the bass, or the cornet, Armstrong was the model. His 1928 recording of "Weather Bird" (which he and King Oliver wrote in 1923) with pianist Fatha Hines was so spectacularly successful that such collaborations became standard for jazz musicians from that time onward.

Although Armstrong's major contribution was to the future of jazz, Armstrong's influence can also be traced in rhythm and blues, rock and roll, country music, and all forms of popular singing. Even when he ceased to produce great creative music after the early 1930's, his impact persisted. The Beatles, Collier points out, played as an "extra" for a jazz band in England that emulated the Hot Five numbers. Jimmie Rodgers, one of the original country singers, had Armstrong as an accompanist on his recording of "Blue Yodel No. 9," and Rodgers's singing always had a jazz flavor. Bing Crosby, a regular at Armstrong's Chicago appearances, undoubtedly profited from observing Armstrong's impeccable understanding of lyrics. Crosby once said he learned to swing from watching Armstrong.

No summary of Armstrong's impact can be complete without some mention of his effect on those who listened to his recordings, watched him in movies, or saw him in person. There was the Armstrong who influenced musicians, and there was the Armstrong who taught the general public how to enjoy the music. Although his impact was greatest with black audiences early in his career, in the later years, most in his audiences were white. White crowds found joy in his very appearance on stage, but not all the reasons for this were positive. As the Civil Rights movement in the United States intensified in the 1960's, many blacks found Armstrong's wide smile, rolling eyes, and general mugging increasingly grating. To some, he seemed to be pushing the happy-go-lucky image a little far. Many whites, however, found comfort in Armstrong, especially in an era of racial stress. By his rise from abject poverty and rejection to the heights of success, he seemed to prove that the American Dream did apply to blacks. In a time of growing anger and strident demands, Armstrong continued to play and sing and look happy. He offered marvelous reassurance, and the popularity of his 1964 hit record "Hello, Dolly!" said as much about the political and social circumstances in the United States as it did about Armstrong's singing.

The reaction to Armstrong was the same throughout

the world. When he first appeared on screen in the 1969 film *Hello, Dolly!* the huge gathering in a London cinema burst into sustained cheering and applause. The response was not so much for Armstrong's great musical contributions since the Hot Five days, but rather a recognition of the warmth that emanated from his horn, his voice, and his entire being.

—*Ronald K. Huch*

FURTHER READING

Bradbury, David. *Armstrong*. London: Haus, 2003. Brief biography serves as an introduction to Armstrong's life and his music. Includes notes, chronology, and index.

Collier, James Lincoln. *Louis Armstrong: An American Genius*. New York: Oxford University Press, 1983. Superb biography, filled with insights, provides strong coverage on all phases of Armstrong's life and music. Highly recommended for both casual and serious students of Armstrong. Includes notes, photographs, discography, and index.

Jones, LeRoi. *Blues People: The Negro Experience in White America*. 1963. Reprint. New York: William Morrow, 1999. Examines how blues and jazz evolved in white America, including valuable discussion of Armstrong's work. Generally an important and useful study. Includes index.

Jones, Max, and John Chilton. *The Louis Armstrong Story, 1900-1971*. Boston: Little, Brown, 1971.

Written by two British critics, this biography was rushed into print shortly after Armstrong's death. Anecdotal and filled with reminiscences.

Lyttelton, Humphrey. *The Best of Jazz: Basin Street to Harlem*. New York: Taplinger, 1978. Excellent collection of essays on the great names in jazz history by a well-known British jazz musician. Two essays dealing with Armstrong contain explanations for his musical influence. Strongly recommended. Includes select bibliography, discography, and index.

Priestley, Brian. *Jazz on Record: A History*. London: Elm Tree Books, 1988. Impressive history of jazz recordings from the 1920's to the 1980's features a useful record guide. Includes photographs, brief bibliography, and index.

Southern, Eileen. *The Music of Black Americans: A History*. 3rd ed. New York: W. W. Norton, 1997. Excellent scholarly account of the subject provides both background and important detail. Includes critical bibliography and discography as well as numerous selections from scores and an extensive index.

SEE ALSO: 1910's: Handy Ushers in the Commercial Blues Era; 1920's: Harlem Renaissance; Feb. 15, 1923: Bessie Smith Records "Downhearted Blues"; Dec. 4, 1927: Ellington Begins Performing at the Cotton Club; 1933: Billie Holiday Begins Her Recording Career.

November 28, 1925
WSM LAUNCHES *THE GRAND OLE OPRY*

With the start of its barn dance show, soon to be known as The Grand Ole Opry, *radio station WSM brought country music to millions and helped to build Nashville into a major recording center.*

LOCALE: Nashville, Tennessee
CATEGORIES: Music; entertainment; radio and television

KEY FIGURES

George D. Hay (1895-1968), American radio personality and first master of ceremonies for *The Grand Ole Opry*
Uncle Jimmy Thompson (1848-1931), American fiddle player
Uncle Dave Macon (1870-1952), American singer and banjo player
Roy Acuff (1903-1992), American singer

SUMMARY OF EVENT

On November 28, 1925, WSM, a Nashville, Tennessee, radio station that was barely a month old, launched a music show that would help to revolutionize American tastes, mold a huge industry, and stimulate a sleepy southern city to become a national center for the recording of popular music. WSM had hired nationally famous radio announcer George D. Hay as program director; Hay had been successful on radio in Memphis and with WLS-Chicago's *The National Barn Dance* old-time music program, which had been inaugurated in 1924. Lured to Nashville, Hay wanted to set up a show similar to the one at WLS so that WSM, broadcast throughout the South, could tap the region's rich tradition of folk song.

Hay did not have to look far for talent for that first night. The Nashville region was rich in performers of old-time and folk music: fiddlers, banjo players, har-

A large group of country musicians pose on the stage from which The Grand Ole Opry *was broadcast in the early 1930's.* (Hulton Archive/Getty Images)

monica players, and an assortment of string bands made up of part-time musicians eager to be heard over the airwaves, although they were paid nothing. Hay seized on a seventy-seven-year-old champion fiddler named Uncle Jimmy Thompson. After setting Thompson down before a single microphone, Hay let him play some of the hundreds of tunes he knew for two hours. The response was swift; phone calls and telegrams poured in, and Uncle Jimmy was back the next week.

By December, Hay had decided to expand the program with more old-time and folk musicians. *The National Barn Dance* had already been successful with this kind of music, although it favored some pop music in the mix. Other radio stations, such as WSB in Atlanta, had experimented with broadcasting old-time tunes and had succeeded. Old-time music—also to be called "hillbilly" and, later, "country" music—had first drawn the attention of recording company executives in 1923 and now was selling well in rural areas. New radio stations (the first had opened only in 1920) were eager to give their audiences what they liked.

Although Hay wanted to develop a full-scale show with all kinds of performers, many executives at WSM remained skeptical. The National Life and Accident In-

surance Company, which owned the station, had sophisticated leaders who largely did not know this kind of music, and an insurance company putting down roots in the "Athens of the South" could hardly afford to appear too backwoodsy. After all, Nashville had an upper class that was proud of the city's historic origins and of its many schools, colleges, churches, and financial institutions. Indeed, even late into the twentieth century, the city's social and cultural leaders remained aloof from, and often disdainful of, its most famous product—country music.

Hay persisted, however, and the response continued to grow. People even came to the studio, in the fifth floor of the majestic stone building that housed National Life, to gaze at the performers through the broadcast booth's window. Nothing succeeds like success; even the skeptics reconsidered. By 1928, National Life decided that by offering low-cost insurance policies to the rural poor and by having its salesmen introduce themselves as from the station that broadcast *The Grand Ole Opry*, they had a gold mine.

In 1925 and 1926, however, Hay still had a long way to go before the show would achieve an identity and workable format. By early 1926, with the program still known as *The WSM Barn Dance*, Hay started to add the variety of performers with which *The National Barn Dance* had succeeded. The talent was easy to find locally. Next to Uncle Jimmy Thompson in popularity were Uncle Dave Macon and the harmonica player DeFord Bailey. Although Thompson died in 1931, Bailey stayed on until the late 1930's, and Macon remained a favorite until his death in 1952.

Hay started to format the show into fifteen- and thirty-minute segments, and it was expanded from two hours to three and, eventually, four hours each Saturday night. The curious who flocked to the building were soon better accommodated in a larger studio. Soon the show would have to respond to the crowds by moving to several theaters in Nashville, where the program would be done as a remote broadcast. The show moved to its most famous home, the downtown Ryman Auditorium, around 1941. There it generally hosted crowds of several thousand until its move to Opryland in 1974.

In 1927, the station hooked up with the new National Broadcasting Company (NBC) radio network. On Saturday nights immediately before the barn dance show, WSM carried a program of classical and grand opera music from New York. On one such Saturday, Hay got a bright idea for a catchy name for the barn dance. As the listeners had just heard an hour of grand opera music, now they could hear music of the "Grand Ole Opry." The name stuck.

In the early years and on into the 1930's, *The National Barn Dance* from Chicago dominated among radio's barn dance formats. Starting in 1924, it held the edge until the late 1930's, when *The Grand Ole Opry* caught and surpassed it. Several explanations for the *Opry*'s eventual leadership have been suggested. Certainly, Hay's ability to spot talent in a region rich in it was one factor in the show's success. Chicago did not have so rich a talent pool of folk musicians in the area; in addition, *The National Barn Dance* tended to mix more pop music into its format than the *Opry* did. Yet with stars such as Gene Autry, *The National Barn Dance* gave the *Opry* stiff competition in the early 1930's.

SIGNIFICANCE

During the Great Depression, *The Grand Ole Opry* changed from its initial studio-bound format to a combination radio and live-audience entertainment variety show. Show business values began to alter things. Hay costumed his performers for visual excitement; pseudo-rustic wear became a norm. Rustic comedians were added to provide visual humor suited to the crowds in attendance. An artists' bureau was instituted to help *Opry*

acts tour the region and to travel into other regions where the clear-channel WSM could reach. WSM expanded from 1,000 to 50,000 watts in 1932, giving it an enormous reach across most of the country.

The greatest change in the *Opry*'s direction, however, was the shift to a singing star system. Roy Acuff's arrival as a member of the *Opry* cast in 1938 signaled the change dramatically. With his intense and piercing East Tennessee mountain voice, Acuff quickly took over as the *Opry*'s greatest favorite. His repertoire of love songs, old ballads, and hymns was delivered with great emotion and sincerity. Still performing on the *Opry* as he neared ninety, Acuff became known as the "king of country music." He was joined in 1939 by another seminal figure, Bill Monroe from Kentucky. Monroe also sang with great intensity and, like Acuff, wrote songs and arranged old folk songs. In addition, he was an accomplished mandolin player, and he developed a style of hard-driven string-band music later to be called bluegrass. With bands such as Pee Wee King's western-flavored group also added to the *Opry*, a new era opened.

By the time of World War II, recordings began to dominate musical performers' careers. Nashville became a recording and publishing center in its own right, in large part because of *The Grand Ole Opry*'s contingent of singers, musicians, and support personnel. In the late 1940's and into the 1950's, Nashville became the center of the growing country music industry.

With the arrival of Texan Ernest Tubb on the *Opry* in 1943, another historic shift occurred. Tubb became the leading exponent of "honky-tonk," or hard country, music. Songs of failed love and marriages, adultery, divorce, and hard times soon became the norm for country music. Tubb's use of an electric lead guitar in his band—and his later use of a steel guitar with prominent string bass and drums—set the pattern for modern country music.

When Hank Williams joined the *Opry* in 1949, the show in a sense reached its artistic peak. This enormously talented singer and songwriter was a member of the *Opry* only until late 1952, and he died at the age of thirty in January, 1953, but his legacy of songs still haunts country music. No one has ever rivaled his intense style, inspired by Acuff and Tubb but influenced by his rural roots in the pinewoods of south Alabama.

After Williams's death, the *Opry* took on honky-tonk singers who began to put the older styles in the shadows. Rock and roll offered a threat, too. By the early 1960's, the *Opry* started to feel the pinch, and audiences declined. With the new interstates and touring buses, stars could make more money touring than by playing the *Opry*, with its minimum pay scale and its rule that performers appear twenty-six Saturday nights in a year. Those performers who could succeed on the basis of record sales, concert dates, and syndicated country shows on television either quit the *Opry* after a short membership or found they could bypass it entirely.

New female superstars such as Loretta Lynn and Dolly Parton were members of the *Opry* cast for a time in the 1960's and 1970's, but the field had grown so large and diverse that the *Opry* simply ceased being the "only show in town." Furthermore, the recording studios in Nashville met the challenge of rock and roll by developing the "Nashville sound," which reached out toward pop music audiences with smooth choral and string arrangements and by eschewing fiddles and steel guitars. It was a manufactured sound, and the *Opry* as a live show could hardly duplicate it. The *Opry* had to move from the increasingly archaic Ryman to more modern and technically sophisticated quarters.

In 1974, the program moved to the Opryland complex twenty miles outside downtown Nashville. The new Opry House, which seats 4,400, was a marvel of modern entertainment technology, and its location on the same site as the Opryland theme park gave the show access to tourists who might have avoided the old downtown location of the show, which was in an increasingly seedy area of Nashville. In one sense, the *Opry* had indeed gone "uptown" to the suburbs.

It took a while for it all to come together, but in the 1980's *The Grand Ole Opry* witnessed a rebirth. Young, fresh performers, male and female, managed by the early 1990's to put country music on the popular music charts in an unprecedented way. The *Opry* was quick to make many of these singers cast members.

Perhaps just as significant in the revitalization of the *Opry* was the formation of The Nashville Network (TNN) cable television operation in 1983. Located on the grounds of Opryland, the network began broadcasting half an hour of the Saturday night *Opry* show live and featured *Opry* stars on its other live shows. TNN and the *Opry* showcased live country music through various channels of communication, including the Internet and the always-popular radio vehicles, until TNN's corporate owner changed the network's programming and its name in the early 2000's.

—*Frederick E. Danker*

FURTHER READING

Daniel, Wayne W. *Pickin' on Peachtree: A History of Country Music in Atlanta, Georgia*. Urbana: University of Illinois Press, 1990. A good introduction to country radio and its relation to local talent and tradition.

Evans, James F. *Prairie Farmer and WLS: The Burridge D. Butler Years*. Urbana: University of Illinois Press, 1969. Study of the context for barn dance shows explains well the commercial and business aspects of these programs. Includes discussion of *The National Barn Dance* as well as of its different focus in comparison with *The Grand Ole Opry*.

Hagan, Chet. *Grand Ole Opry*. New York: Henry Holt, 1989. A full history of the show, generously illustrated with informative captions.

Malone, Bill C. *Country Music, U.S.A.* 2d rev. ed. Austin: University of Texas Press, 2002. Excellent history puts the barn dance shows in context succinctly and accurately. Includes a few illustrations, bibliography, and indexes.

Malone, Bill C., and Judith McCulloh, eds. *Stars of Country Music*. Urbana: University of Illinois Press, 1975. Collection of essays on early country music pioneers includes discussion of several key members of the *Opry* cast. Features individual chapter bibliographies and index.

Wolfe, Charles K. *A Good-Natured Riot: The Birth of "The Grand Ole Opry."* Nashville: Vanderbilt University Press, 1999. Comprehensive history covers all the program's ups and downs and offers interesting portraits of many cast members. Includes many photographs, discography, and index.

SEE ALSO: 1920's: Radio Develops as a Mass Broadcast Medium; Aug. 20-Nov. 2, 1920: Radio Broadcasting Begins; Sept. 9, 1926: National Broadcasting Company Is Founded; 1930's: Americans Embrace Radio Entertainment; 1939-1949: Bill Monroe and the Blue Grass Boys Define Bluegrass Music.

December 14, 1925
BERG'S *WOZZECK* PREMIERES IN BERLIN

Alban Berg's opera Wozzeck *demonstrated that it was possible to write an effective opera that utilized both a modern story and nontraditional compositional techniques.*

LOCALE: Berlin, Germany
CATEGORIES: Music; theater

KEY FIGURES
Alban Berg (1885-1935), Austrian composer
Arnold Schoenberg (1874-1951), Austrian-born
    American composer
Georg Büchner (1813-1837), German dramatist

SUMMARY OF EVENT
The beginning of the twentieth century was a time of tremendous upheaval in politics, science, technology, philosophy, and the arts. The first two decades of the century would see, among many dramatic events, the horrifying carnage of World War I; the fall of the Russian czars and the birth of the Soviet Union; Albert Einstein's development of the special theory of relativity, which would change the way humanity viewed the universe; and the work of Sigmund Freud, which would change the way humanity viewed itself.

In the arts, the work of such masters as Wassily Kandinsky, Pablo Picasso, Igor Stravinsky, Kazimir Malevich, Franz Kafka, and Sergei Diaghilev was challenging artistic traditions. Not even Vienna, a city that had long been known both as a center of the arts and as a bastion of conservatism, was immune to the changes sweeping the world. Indeed, it was a brilliant, self-taught Viennese composer, Arnold Schoenberg, who would develop a compositional approach that would change music forever.

Schoenberg's primary contribution to composition was his championship of atonality, a compositional style that does not adhere to a single musical key, or tonal center. (The commonly used term "atonality" implies the rejection of tonality, but Schoenberg actually preferred the term "pantonality," which implies the acceptance of all tonalities.) Ultimately, Schoenberg developed the "twelve-tone system," also called serialism, which involved using all twelve tones of the chromatic scale (that is, all the notes in the Western system of music) in a single predetermined order as the basis for composition.

It is ironic that, although Schoenberg was the architect of a new style of composition, his compositions in that style would never be as artistically successful as those of his two greatest students, the Viennese composers Anton von Webern and Alban Berg. Both Webern and Berg developed their remarkable musical gifts rapidly under the stern tutelage of Schoenberg, who was intolerant of those who did not agree with him in all things. To his credit, however, he insisted from the very beginning that his pupils express their own personalities in their music, and their later achievements testify to his ability as a teacher.

In spite of the ability of Schoenberg, Webern, and Berg, the infrequent performances of their works in Vienna met with little success; in fact, whenever their works were performed, they met with furious reactions from conservative musicians, critics, and listeners who could not understand or appreciate what they were doing musically. It was not until 1925, when Berg's opera *Wozzeck* premiered, that an atonal work met with a significant measure of acceptance and success.

On May 5, 1914, Berg attended the premiere in Vienna of *Woyzeck*, a play written in 1836 by Georg Büchner, a German dramatist who had died in 1837. (Because Büchner's manuscript was extremely difficult to decipher, the name *Woyzeck* was misread by the compiler of Büchner's collected works, and the play was first published as *Wozzeck*, the title that Berg gave to his opera.) In spite of the fact that the play had been written more than seventy years earlier, its undiluted, bitter realism had a powerful effect on the audiences of Berg's time.

Woyzeck, which was based on an actual event, tells the story of a soldier who is destroyed by his times and by his station in life. Taunted by his superior officer and victimized by a sadistic doctor who pays him a small amount of money to adhere to a series of extreme and unhealthy diets, Woyzeck, the protagonist, drifts further and further into madness. Ultimately, he murders his mistress, Marie, after she is seduced by a drum major, and then drowns while trying to wash off the blood in which he imagines he is covered. The unrelenting horror of the story and the work's condemnation of an unjust society were a tonic to audiences who were accustomed to stylized, genteel works. Berg was overwhelmed by the power of the play, and he determined at once to use it as the basis for an opera.

Although he was ultimately rejected as unfit for active military duty because of his chronic asthma and general poor health, Berg was called into military service in 1914, when World War I broke out, and it was not until 1922 that he completed *Wozzeck*. Berg not only wrote the music but also composed the libretto, which was quite faithful to Büchner's play.

Berg took the twenty-six scenes in Büchner's play and reduced them to fifteen. He was able to use much of the material in the deleted scenes in the scenes that he retained. In that way, he was able to use most of Büchner's material without producing a dramatic structure that would have been too long to function as an effective opera. The final form of *Wozzeck* consisted of three acts of five scenes each.

Although *Wozzeck* is an atonal work, Berg was extremely conscious of tradition—particularly the musical tradition of his beloved Vienna—and it is characteristic of Berg's approach to composition that he used traditional musical structures as vehicles for his extremely modern music. In addition, Berg sometimes used atonality in ways that suggested tonality, which occasionally led Schoenberg to criticize him but also enabled him to combine the best aspects of tonality and atonality in a way that Schoenberg himself was never able to achieve.

Wozzeck was not performed immediately after Berg completed it, but one of Berg's friends suggested that Berg take selections from the opera and create a concert cycle that could be performed more easily than could the entire opera. Berg did so, and on June 15, 1924, the *Wozzeck* cycle was performed at a festival in Frankfurt, Germany. Berg was pleased with the performance, and the cycle became the hit of the festival. Meanwhile, Berg had asked a pianist he knew to play the score of the opera for Erich Kleiber, who was the conductor of the Berlin State Opera. Kleiber was impressed by the work, and he is reported to have said: "It's settled! I am going to do the opera in Berlin, even if it costs me my job!"

Kleiber's willingness to perform the opera was a stroke of luck for Berg, particularly because Kleiber made every effort to ensure that the work would be exhaustively rehearsed and well performed. In fact, the rehearsal schedule consisted of an unheard-of thirty-four full orchestral rehearsals and fourteen ensemble rehearsals—far more rehearsals than are customary for even the longest and most complicated works.

When *Wozzeck* received its premiere performance on December 14, 1925, it became an immediate sensation. Although, as everyone had expected, some critics attacked the exceedingly modern opera in the most virulent way, many others recognized the work for the tremendous achievement that it was. In spite of its unusual

compositional techniques, *Wozzeck* won over audiences and critics with its emotional power and with the effective way in which the music not only reflected but also enhanced the physical and psychological action of the play. Subsequent performances of the opera in Prague and Leningrad were also extremely successful, although they, too, were marked by attacks on the modern style of *Wozzeck*. With the success of his atonal opera, Berg achieved international renown.

SIGNIFICANCE

It is remarkable that Berg broke completely with the traditional approach to opera—both dramatically, in his choice of story, and musically, in his use of atonality—and still produced an effective dramatic work that has been accepted as part of the operatic tradition. *Wozzeck* is regularly performed as part of the operatic repertoire, in spite of its avant-garde nature, and it is one of the few twentieth century operas that are regularly performed. It is interesting to note that other modern operas, such as Schoenberg's *Moses und Aron* (begun in 1930 but never completed), are rarely staged. Berg's *Wozzeck* is simply a particularly effective work that has found favor with musicians, audiences, and critics alike.

Structurally, *Wozzeck* is unlike any opera that preceded it. After Berg had settled on the dramatic structure of his work—three acts of five scenes each—he sought

---

BERG ON *WOZZECK*

Although Alban Berg sometimes questioned his achievement in composing Wozzeck, *two years after the opera's premiere he wrote an article about it for a music journal in which he concluded:*

What I do consider my particular accomplishment is this. No one in the audience, no matter how aware he may be of the musical forms contained in the framework of the opera, of the precision and logic with which it has been worked out, no one, from the moment the curtain parts until it closes for the last time, pays any attention to the various fugues, inventions, suites, sonata movements, variations, and passacaglias about which so much has been written. No one gives heed to anything but the vast social implications of the work which by far transcend the personal destiny of Wozzeck. This, I believe, is my achievement.

Source: Alban Berg, "A Word About *Wozzeck*," *Modern Music* (November/December, 1927).

out particular musical forms that he believed would best express the essence of each scene. He found the forms he needed in the traditional forms of music, but the forms he chose were not, traditionally, part of opera.

The first act of *Wozzeck* consists of five scenes that introduce the opera's primary characters and indicate the kind of relationship that Wozzeck has with each of them. Berg selected musical forms that would serve those functions for each scene: a suite (a form made up of a number of separate movements), a rhapsody (a kind of fantasy), a military march and a lullaby, a passacaglia (a baroque form in a triple, or waltz, meter), and an andante affetuoso (a slow form played warmly, or affectionately).

The second act is, strangely enough, cast in the form of a symphony in five movements. The first scene is in the classic sonata form, the second scene consists of a fantasia (fantasy) and fugue (a form in which a theme is played at different times by different instruments), the third scene is a largo (slow) movement, the fourth scene is a scherzo (a fast, rhythmic movement), and the fifth scene utilizes a rondo (a strictly organized form often used to end symphonies).

The third act is made up of five inventions, which consist of creative explorations of counterpoint (counterpoint consists of multiple melodic lines played simultaneously). These five are an invention on a melodic theme, an invention on a note, an invention on a rhythm, an invention on a chord, and an invention on a movement in eighth notes. It is interesting that, between the fourth and fifth inventions in this atonal piece, Berg inserted an orchestral interlude that is an invention on a tonality.

It should also be mentioned that Berg provided, in all three acts, connecting music that heightened the drama of the opera and united the individual scenes into a coherent whole. Berg also ended all three acts on the same chord, thereby enhancing the unity of the three acts.

The structure of the opera is noted both to demonstrate its complexity and to emphasize the care that Berg took in selecting the forms that he thought would best express the nature of the action that took place in each scene. The danger of using such a complex structure is that it is difficult to write moving music in so many forms. In the hands of a lesser artist, this structure might have been nothing more than a fascinating exercise. The fact that the complex and unusual musical structure of the opera is not apparent when *Wozzeck* is performed but is instead seamlessly merged with the dramatic action is evidence of Berg's tremendous talent and skill.

It is even more significant that the music of *Wozzeck* explores the psychological aspect of the action that takes place on the stage. The music not only supports the action that takes place but also extends the range of meaning of that action. It is the combined effect of the drama and the music that gives the opera its undeniable power. At a time when Sigmund Freud was becoming famous for opening up the field of psychology, Berg—like Freud, a Viennese—scored an unprecedented success for atonal music by demonstrating the power of music to explore the psychological realm of operatic drama.

Berg was, to some extent, gratified by the success of *Wozzeck*, particularly because it earned for him a measure of respect throughout the world that was never extended to him in his native Vienna. He was never quite comfortable with the acclaim, however, because he doubted the good judgment of the listening public. In fact, he wondered at times whether he had failed in composing *Wozzeck*, whether he had unconsciously pandered to the public in his most accepted work.

Berg went on to compose another superb opera, *Lulu* (1937), which used the twelve-tone system devised by Schoenberg, and a violin concerto that is one of the most beautiful works composed in the twentieth century. Berg's primary goal was to create music of great beauty, and he demonstrated conclusively that atonality could be used to achieve that goal.

—Shawn Woodyard

FURTHER READING

Carner, Mosco. *Alban Berg: The Man and the Work.* London: Duckworth, 1975. An excellent examination of Berg's life and music. Perhaps the best place to begin a study of Berg.

Headlam, Dave. *The Music of Alban Berg.* New Haven, Conn.: Yale University Press, 1996. Examines the development of Berg's music from late Romantic tonality to atonality. Includes notes, bibliography, and index.

Jarman, Douglas. *Alban Berg: "Wozzeck."* Cambridge, England: Cambridge University Press, 1989. In-depth analysis of Berg's first opera includes background information about Büchner and his play *Woyzeck*, musical analysis, information about the opera's premiere and subsequent performances, reviews (both favorable and unfavorable), and writings by Berg himself.

Perle, George. *Wozzeck.* Vol. 1 in *The Operas of Alban Berg.* Berkeley: University of California Press, 1980. Excellent, detailed study includes much useful background information. Also presents a careful musical analysis intended for readers with background in music.

Redlich, H. F. *Alban Berg: The Man and His Music*. New York: Abelard-Schuman, 1957. Fine volume on Berg is divided into four parts: The first discusses the Second Viennese School and "the problem of tonality," the second examines Berg's music in detail, the third presents a brief biography of Berg, and the fourth consists of appendixes that include Berg's lecture on *Wozzeck* and Schoenberg's brief reminiscences of Berg.

Reich, Willi. *Alban Berg*. 1965. Reprint. New York: Vienna House, 1974. An insightful biographical and musical study that is all the more interesting for having been written by a man who knew Berg well. Personal reminiscences and insights make this book extremely useful.

Simms, Bryan R., ed. *Schoenberg, Berg, and Webern: A Companion to the Second Viennese School*. Westport, Conn.: Greenwood Press, 1999. Examines the works of these composers in the context of earlier Viennese musical developments and compares the modernism in their music with that in the nonmusical arts in Vienna during the same period. Includes bibliography and index.

SEE ALSO: 1908-1909: Schoenberg Breaks with Tonality; Mar. 31, 1913: Webern's Six Pieces for Large Orchestra Premieres; 1921-1923: Schoenberg Develops His Twelve-Tone System; June 2, 1937: Berg's *Lulu* Opens in Zurich.

1926

1926
VERNADSKY PUBLISHES *THE BIOSPHERE*

Vladimir Vernadsky's publication of The Biosphere *inspired imaginative investigations and speculations about humankind's role in shaping the world's environment.*

ALSO KNOWN AS: *La Biosphère*
LOCALE: Soviet Union
CATEGORIES: Environmental issues; biology; earth science; publishing and journalism

KEY FIGURES

Vladimir Vernadsky (1863-1945), Russian professor of mineralogy, crystallography, and biogeochemistry
George Vernadsky (1887-1973), Russian American historian
A. E. Fersman (1883-1945), student of Vladimir Vernadsky
Vasily Vasilyevich Dokuchayev (1846-1903), Russian pioneer of landscape geochemistry
Alfred Lotka (1880-1949), American biologist
V. M. Goldschmidt (1888-1947), German mineralogist
James Lovelock (b. 1919), British American biologist and inventor
G. Evelyn Hutchinson (1903-1991), British limnologist and ecologist

SUMMARY OF EVENT

A pioneer in the field of biogeochemistry, Vladimir Vernadsky was given professional direction early in his life. An older cousin who was a retired army officer and an independent man of extensive reading remarked to Vernadsky that "the world is a living organism." Profoundly impressed with this concept, Vernadsky within a few years began his scholarly studies of the earth's physiology—the ways in which its matter and biota, including humankind, interact and affect one another and their common planetary environment.

Vernadsky graduated from St. Petersburg University in 1885 and earned his Ph.D. from the University of Moscow in 1897. He was professor of crystallography and mineralogy at Moscow University from 1890 until 1911. After the 1917 Russian Revolution, he spent three years at the Sorbonne University in Paris, where he wrote extensively on the subjects of geochemistry and biochemistry, crystallography and mineralogy, geochemical activity, marine chemistry, the evolution of life, and futurology, displaying all the signs of a polymath. From 1926 until 1938, he directed the State Radium Institute in Leningrad (now St. Petersburg); he was among the earliest scientists to recognize the tremendous importance of radioactivity as a source of thermal energy. He established the first Soviet national scientific academy, the Ukrainian Academy of Science, in 1928, serving simultaneously as its president and as the director of the Academy of Science's Leningrad biogeochemistry laboratory. Vernadsky founded the field of biogeochemistry, and it was the principal one in which he gradually gained international distinction.

A man of broad scholarly talents and mastery of several scientific specialties, Vernadsky became best known outside the Soviet Union for his publication of *La Biosphère* in 1926 (*The Biosphere*, 1929), a study in which he elaborated on his theory of the biosphere. Vernadsky borrowed the term "biosphere" from Eduard Suess (1831-1914), a Viennese professor of structural geology and eminent scholar who suggested the existence of an ancient supercontinent. Suess—who had first used the word at the end of a monograph about the Alps—and Vernadsky used the word "biosphere" to refer to the total mass of living organisms that process and recycle the energy and nutrients available in the earth's environment. This activity occurs inside a thin veneer of life that circles the globe.

Vernadsky was concerned that the importance of life in the entire structure of the earth's crust had been underestimated—when it was not ignored altogether—by his scientific colleagues. For most scientists of the late nineteenth and early twentieth centuries, the investigation of possible interactions between living organisms—human beings included—and the "dead" earth lay beyond the pale of narrow specializations. Biologists studied live organisms, for example, and geologists studied inert rocks; there was little inquiry into interrelationships between the "live" and the "dead." Vernadsky, however, had measured both the distribution and the migration of chemical elements and isotopes in the earth's crust, and he became convinced that the earth exists within a crustal layer permeated with life—life that continuously interacts chemically with dead matter in reshaping a common environment.

Vernadsky did not accept the loose, generalized notions of his day that suggested that the earth itself is a living organism—a proposition he found to be overstated. He elaborated on an imaginative theory that, like the lithosphere, the atmosphere, the hydrosphere, and the sphere of fire—the earth's reliance on the Sun—the biosphere forms another of the concentric circles enveloping the earth.

Vernadsky pursued his curiosities relentlessly, a pursuit enhanced by his enormous capacity for work. In the early 1940's, toward the end of his life, having fixed the word "biosphere" in the scientific lexicon, he added another word and therefore still another concept: that of the "noosphere." *Noös* is the Greek word for "mind"; Vernadsky believed that the "sphere of the mind" represented a new power altering the face of the earth. Defined precisely in the manner of science, the noosphere is neither a sphere, like the atmosphere or lithosphere, nor a physical phenomenon, yet it has physical consequences, for the human mind, in Vernadsky's words, had become, for the first time, "a large-scale geological force" that was reshaping the planet.

SIGNIFICANCE

Vernadsky enjoyed a lofty reputation in the Soviet Union and in Europe well before American scientists became familiar with his work. Just as the United States was emerging as a center of international scientific thought during the 1940's, Vernadsky's data and interpretations were introduced to the U.S. scientific community. Vernadsky's son, George Vernadsky, had emigrated to the United States to join the Yale University faculty as a historian, and he and another member of the Yale faculty, G. Evelyn Hutchinson, a well-respected English-born limnologist and ecologist, arranged for the elder Vernadsky's major studies to be published in English. The first of these translations, a seminal work on biogeochemistry, appeared in the *Transactions of the Connecticut Academy of Sciences* in 1944. A second contribution, summarizing Vernadsky's conceptions of the biosphere and noosphere, was published in the *American Scientist* in 1945.

As scholars familiar with Vernadsky's scientific achievements have noted, Vernadsky's imaginative conceptions of the biosphere and noosphere predated James Lovelock's inspired Gaia hypothesis and paralleled some fundamental ideas integral to it. Late in his life, for example, Vernadsky, like later Gaia theorists, contradicted prevailing scientific perspectives on the relationships between human beings and nature. According to Vernadsky, all but a few historians, students of the humanities, and even biologists had failed to comprehend the laws of the biosphere, "the only terrestrial envelope in which life can exist." Although human beings spoke confidently about individual freedom and had amassed a history independent of natural laws, the fate of the human race, Vernadsky observed, is inseparable from the natural laws of the biosphere. Humankind is geologically tied to these laws and to their material and energetic structures. As a consequence, none of the earth's organisms can live in a state of freedom. All organisms are connected "indissolubly and uninterruptedly" through nutrition and respiration as well as through their surrounding material and its energetic medium. For Vernadsky, life of every kind, preeminently human life, constitutes a geological force within a global web that links all of nature. Thus Vernadsky's studies and the intellectual constructs that flowed from them—the concepts of the biosphere and the noosphere—are closely related to later conceptions of an ecosystem. One general characteristic of an ecosystem, for example, is that every natural zone composes a regular, natural complex in which living organisms and nonliving matter are inextricably bound together by their interactions.

Vernadsky, enticed by the specifics of his research, was not alone in grasping the realities informing this perception. Vasily Vasilyevich Dokuchayev, the founder of landscape geochemistry and a pioneer in the Soviet school of soil science, for example, shared this view, even though the substance of his research differed from Vernadsky's. V. M. Goldschmidt, a German mineralogist, stressed the interrelationships of geochemical cycles. Similar conclusions emerged from the work of Vernadsky's student A. E. Fersman, who devised methods for mapping geochemical provinces, thereby providing a spatial component to his mentor's studies.

Analogous investigations were also being pursued during the 1930's and 1940's by such figures as the biologist Alfred Lotka, a pioneer in physical chemistry who viewed the earth as a single system driven by solar energy, and the limnologist, biomineralogist, and biogeochemist G. Evelyn Hutchinson. As students of the meteorological, biological, mineralogical, chemical, and other processes interacting in freshwater lakes, limnologists, like biochemists, often appeared in the forefront of ecological theorizing after the 1930's.

The American "discovery" of Vernadsky's work was recognized soon after his death as having contributed both a partial history of and an intellectual foundation for the development of the Gaia hypothesis. The English-born American James Lovelock, who first expounded the Gaia hypothesis in 1972 and published further specifics during the 1980's, fully acknowledged Vernadsky's importance to his work. Lovelock, indeed, described Vernadsky as "our most illustrious predecessor." Lovelock, moreover, was the first to publish a review of *The Biosphere* in an American scientific journal. Praise for Vernadsky's work also came from Lynn Margulis, another major scholarly contributor to Gaia studies.

Although Soviet Marxist-Leninist ideology was antithetical to most Americans during much of the twentieth century, recognition of the significance of Vernadsky's work facilitated the further recognition that Soviet scientific thought, whatever its limitations in some areas, nevertheless offered Western science fresh perspectives. Although great advances had accrued to Western, particularly American, science through the development of specializations and subspecializations, these advances were accompanied by a loss of communication and understanding among many specialists, which tended to discourage the creation of syntheses and of comprehensive, or holistic, perspectives. The formulation of holistic theory was no more appealing to Soviet authorities, chiefly because it smacked of religion, than it was to

many scientific specialists in the United States. Vernadsky, in fact, was snubbed by Soviet officialdom. It was not until many years after Vernadsky's death that Soviet general secretary Mikhail Gorbachev revived the scientist's reputation in the Soviet Union by quoting him—and then made his own contribution to *The Gaia Peace Atlas* (1988).

Vernadsky's explanations of the interplay between the environment and living organisms at a time when such concepts were unfamiliar to all but a few Western scientists also encouraged subsequent reevaluations of Darwinian and neo-Darwinian ideas about the nature of evolution. Darwinian and neo-Darwinian thought, although accurate about many fundamental aspects of evolution, emphasized competition among and between organisms as the principal mechanism of selection for survival. Because Darwinians tended to ignore chemical interactions between living organisms and their environments, however, a number of leading scientists after the 1970's believed that Darwinian explanations of evolution were significantly incomplete. Theorists such as Lovelock and Margulis insisted that, as a result of "academic apartheid," many scientists were largely ignorant of discoveries such as those of Vernadsky in biogeochemistry, geology, and ecology. They argued that Darwinians were consequently unable to account for the impacts that the evolution of life has had on planet Earth.

Placed in historical context, Vernadsky's research and his detailed conceptualization of the biosphere and the noosphere were perceived by the close of the twentieth century to constitute important additions to scientific understanding of the environment as well as to add important components to ecological studies. In these respects, Vernadsky joined the ranks of Gaia theorists and others such as the paleontologist-philosopher Pierre Teilhard de Chardin and author-philosopher Édouard Le Roy. The writings of these two Frenchmen not only acknowledged the reality of Vernadsky's biosphere and noosphere but also emphasized that humankind, as the planet's dominant geological force, had introduced a new geological era that could be described as "psychozoic," "anthropozoic," or "mental." A few worried that this might be the planet's last geological era.

—*Clifton K. Yearley*

FURTHER READING

Balandin, Rudolf K. *Vladimir Vernadsky: Outstanding Soviet Scientist*. Moscow: Mir Publishing, 1982. Presents a clear, competent, and balanced discussion

1926

of Vernadsky's life and scientific career. Includes endnotes and index.

Golley, Frank Benjamin. *A History of the Ecosystem Concept in Ecology: More than the Sum of the Parts*. New Haven, Conn.: Yale University Press, 1993. A fine and lucid history, chronologically arranged, on the evolution of a little-understood seminal idea. Chapter 3 places Vernadsky in historical context. Includes extensive bibliography and index.

Grinevald, J. "A History of the Idea of a Biosphere." In *Gaia: The Thesis, the Mechanisms, and the Implications: Proceedings of the First Annual Camelford Convention on the Implications of the Gaia Thesis*, edited by P. Bunyard and B. Goldsmith. Wadebridge, Cornwall, England: Quintrell, 1988. Invaluable survey of the concept of the biosphere, clearly presented and well documented. Includes notes and references.

Joseph, Lawrence. *Gaia: The Growth of an Idea*. New York: St. Martin's Press, 1990. Nontechnical survey of the subject includes discussion of Vernadsky's importance, particularly in chapter 10. Includes index.

Lovelock, James E. "Geophysiology: The Science of Gaia." In *Scientists on Gaia*, edited by Stephen H. Schneider and Penelope J. Boston. Cambridge, Mass.: MIT Press, 1991. Brilliant and clearly presented exposition of the Gaia hypothesis by its chief theorist. Pays tribute to Vernadsky's work at the outset. Includes graphs and bibliographic notes.

Margulis, Lynn, and Gregory Hinkle. "The Biota and Gaia." In *Scientists on Gaia*, edited by Stephen H. Schneider and Penelope J. Boston. Cambridge, Mass.: MIT Press, 1991. Aims at securing financial support for Gaia scientists, but much of the substance is an exposition of the science behind Gaia (Margulis was almost a cocreator of the Gaia theory along with Lovelock). Explains Vernadsky's work favorably. Includes graphs and bibliographic notes.

Schneider, Stephen H., James R. Miller, Eileen Crist, and Penelope J. Boston, eds. *Scientists Debate Gaia: The Next Century*. Cambridge, Mass.: MIT Press, 2004. Collection of essays reexamines the Gaia hypothesis from the perspectives of numerous scientific disciplines.

Vernadsky, Vladimir I. *The Biosphere*. Translated by David B. Langmuir. New York: Springer-Verlag, 1998. First translation into English of the entire text of Vernadsky's original work, with extremely helpful annotation by Mark A. A. McMenamin. Includes a foreword by Lynn Margulis, bibliography, and index.

Weiner, Jonathan. *The Next One Hundred Years*. New York: Bantam Books, 1990. Clearly written and at times fascinating account of forces shaping the face of the earth. Cites Vernadsky's biosphere and noosphere as significant concepts. Includes notes and index.

SEE ALSO: Feb. 1, 1919: Lenin Approves the First Soviet Nature Preserve; May 20, 1919: National Parks and Conservation Association Is Founded; 1924: Soviets Establish a Society for the Protection of Nature.

1926-1927
MAIL-ORDER CLUBS REVOLUTIONIZE BOOK SALES

Sales strategies used by the Book-of-the-Month Club and Literary Guild of America revolutionized the publishing, sales, distribution, and reading of books in the United States.

ALSO KNOWN AS: Book-of-the-Month Club; Literary Guild of America
LOCALE: United States
CATEGORIES: Publishing and journalism; organizations and institutions; marketing and advertising

KEY FIGURES
Harry Scherman (1887-1969), force behind the founding and success of the Book-of-the-Month Club
Maxwell Sackheim (1890-1982), advertising copywriter specializing in mail-order sales and cofounder of the Book-of-the-Month Club
Robert K. Haas (1890?-1964), founding partner of the Book-of-the-Month Club and its first president
Henry Seidel Canby (1878-1961), well-known literary critic and first chair of the board of judges that chose Book-of-the-Month Club selections
Samuel W. Craig (1874-1960), cofounder of the Literary Guild of America
Harold Kleinert Guinzburg (1900-1961), cofounder of Viking Press, Craig's partner in founding the Literary Guild
Nelson Doubleday (1889-1949), publishing executive who brought the Literary Guild into the Doubleday publishing empire in 1934

SUMMARY OF EVENT

The antecedents of book clubs can be traced to the subscription library that Benjamin Franklin organized in 1731. Before the Civil War, the American Tract Society introduced a "tract-of-the-month" plan, which described its publications and sold them in a monthly magazine. Book guilds established in post-World War I Germany, which sold low-priced reprints of classic works, were more immediate forerunners. Modern book clubs emerged in the United States during the 1920's, when prosperity favored leisure activities and the businesses that supported them. The shortened workweek gave at least some segments of the population more leisure time. Even more important was the dramatic increase in the size of the reading public, which resulted from the rapid expansion of high school and college enrollments. At the same time, there were few bookstores outside large metropolitan centers. Growth in the number of titles published meant that readers needed, or at least wanted, guidance in choosing books to read. Readers who did not have ready access to bookstores became a large new market for both books and advice on selecting them.

Harry Scherman is generally acknowledged as the father of the modern book club. After a stint as a newspaperman, in 1913 Scherman took a job with the newly established advertising agency Ruthrauff and Ryan, writing copy for direct-mail sales campaigns. The following year, he was hired by the direct-mail department of the J. Walter Thompson advertising agency. In 1916, he joined with brothers Charles and Albert Boni in launching the Little Leather Library, a series of low-priced reprints of classic books. The Bonis later sold their interest to Scherman and Maxwell Sackheim, an advertising copywriter who had worked with Scherman at J. Walter Thompson. When sales through retail stores began to fall off, Scherman and Sackheim decided to shift the focus of their sales effort to mail order. Thanks to the aggressive promotion campaign of Robert K. Haas, another alumnus of J. Walter Thompson's mail-order department, sales of the Little Leather Library books reached forty-eight million copies by 1925.

Scherman predicted that the market for classics would become saturated. He reasoned that as millions of Americans had been persuaded to buy classics through the mail, they could be persuaded to buy current books the same way. The Book-of-the-Month Club (BOMC) tested this reasoning. It was founded in February, 1926, with an initial investment of $40,000. Haas put up half this amount and was president of the new corporation;

Scherman and Sackheim each put up $10,000. The BOMC founders recognized that the key to a successful mail-order business was finding a gimmick to generate repeat sales. They applied the magazine subscription model to book sales: Subscribers would agree to buy one new book per month for a year at full retail price (plus postage). The most important innovation was the BOMC selection committee, or editorial board, composed of experts and celebrities who chose club selections. The board was promised a free hand in choosing the "book of the month" without any interference by management; the only limitation was that the price could not exceed three dollars. The first selection, Sylvia Townsend Warner's *Lolly Willowes: Or, The Loving Huntsman* (1926), was sent out to 4,750 members in April, 1926. By the end of the year, club membership had climbed above 46,000.

The BOMC's main source of competition was the Literary Guild of America, which began operation early in 1927. The Literary Guild was the brainchild of Samuel W. Craig, who claimed that he envisioned the plan for his club as early as 1922 but could not attract the required capital to begin it as a business. Heartened by reports of the success of German book guilds, Craig revived his plan. He joined with the cofounder of Viking Press, Harold Kleinert Guinzburg, and incorporated the Literary Guild of America late in 1926. Like Scherman, Craig arranged for a jury of experts to make selections for the club. Guild subscribers, like BOMC subscribers, would receive twelve books a year. The Literary Guild offered lower cost, at $18 per year (later raised to $21 a year, including delivery). The guild's first selection, sent in March, 1927, was Heywood Broun and Margaret Leech's *Anthony Comstock: Roundsman of the Lord* (1927), a biography critical of the antivice crusader. The turning point in the guild's fortunes was its June, 1927, selection of what became a runaway best-seller, *Trader Horn* (1927), by Alfred Aloysius Horn. The guild's monthly sales reached nearly twenty thousand copies by September, 1927.

SIGNIFICANCE

At the beginning, the BOMC sent out its monthly selection to each subscriber along with a report on the book written by one of the editorial board members. The BOMC adopted a variant of the return guarantee that had been adopted by big mail-order firms to deal with customers who were unhappy with a selection. Subscribers could return an unwanted book in a carton provided for that purpose and choose another from a list of supplementary books in the monthly newsletter. In 1929, the Literary Guild adopted a similar exchange policy: Selections could be returned and the charge canceled or used as a credit against any book in print. Subscribers paid the difference between $1.75 (one-twelfth of the $21 yearly subscription) and the price of the new book. As returns began to mount up, the BOMC replaced the exchange policy with the practice of allowing subscribers to refuse a selection or order an alternate selection in advance of the shipping date. The monthly selection was sent to members who did not reply by a deadline. This prenotification or automatic shipment plan became the standard method of operation for book clubs.

The BOMC began by purchasing regular edition copies of its selections from publishers at a discount. The Literary Guild similarly had the publisher do the manufacturing, but with special binding and title page. The pressure of competition—first from the Literary Guild, then from new low-priced publishers' lines spawned by the Great Depression—led the BOMC to make policy changes in the late 1920's and early 1930's that became standard for book clubs. The subscription contract was modified to require the purchase of only four books a year. A free book was given as an introductory offer to attract new members. At first occasionally, then more regularly, the prices of selections were reduced below list. To cut its costs, in 1930 the BOMC instituted the practice of giving publishers flat payments for the printing plates to run off its own editions of books. The savings from large print runs were so great that the BOMC in 1931 started a book dividend plan for distribution of special editions of books free to members as a reward for making purchases. As of 1945, the BOMC was giving away seventy-five cents in free books for every dollar taken in but still made a handsome profit.

Although the lures of free introductory books, book dividends, and discounted prices contributed to the BOMC's success, BOMC advertising placed its heaviest emphasis on the expertise of its board of judges in culling out the best titles from the hundreds that were published. As a contemporary reporter perceptively observed, the BOMC's board "carried the stamp of culture without being too frighteningly high brow." Its first chairman, the most influential member until his retirement in 1955, was the founder-editor of the *Saturday Review of Literature*, Henry Seidel Canby. Second to Canby in influence on selection decisions was popular novelist Dorothy Canfield Fisher, who served until 1950. The others making up the board were novelist Christopher Morley (who would become best known for his 1939 novel *Kitty*

Foyle: The Natural History of a Woman) and two of the most famous journalists in the United States, Heywood Broun and William Allen White. The BOMC's target audience was the relatively well-off college-educated segment of the population, or at least members of that segment living in smaller cities and towns having few or no retail bookstores. The BOMC promised to deliver conveniently the important current books that a knowledgeable person would choose. Its advertising simultaneously underlined the social benefits that members would gain by staying up to date with the latest in the world of culture.

In 1928, Sackheim sold his quarter interest in the BOMC to Scherman for $150,000 and left publishing to become vice president of a wire and fence company that sold directly to farmers through mail order. He later returned to advertising in New York and was responsible for the Literary Guild's advertising from 1944 to 1960, during its period of most rapid growth. In 1931, Haas left the BOMC to study economics at Columbia University; he would later return to publishing as a partner in Random House. Scherman took over as BOMC president, retaining that position until he became chairman of the board in 1950. He was succeeded as president by his longtime associate Meredith Wood. The BOMC went public with its stock in 1946, but Scherman and members of his family continued to hold a majority of the shares. This continuity in top management was matched by continuity in the membership of the board of judges. Broun died in 1939 but was not immediately replaced. Only after White died in 1944 were novelist John P. Marquand and literary critic and anthologizer Clifton Fadiman named to fill the two openings. Later replacements included drama critic John Mason Brown, Columbia University classics professor Gilbert Highet, and Basil Davenport.

The Literary Guild made its major selling point the financial savings received by members. Craig left the guild shortly after its founding because of a dispute over policy, leaving Guinzburg in full charge. Seeing that its members were attracted more by the low price of its books than by the jury method of selection, in 1929, the guild began to deemphasize the jury selection feature in its advertising. That same year, Nelson Doubleday, the president of Doubleday, Doran, and Company, bought a 49 percent interest in the Literary Guild with the idea of taking advantage of its mailing list for the Doubleday firm's mail-sales subsidiary. In 1934, he bought the rest of the stock and began to screen publishers' submissions for the jury. Three years later, the guild abandoned the jury method of selection. Under Doubleday's control, the guild specialized in the mass marketing of light, escapist fiction.

Although the BOMC continued to grow even through the Depression, its most rapid expansion occurred during and after World War II. The Literary Guild, which appealed to what appeared to be a less sophisticated audience, surpassed the BOMC in membership. By 1946, the two boasted a combined membership of 3.5 million. That year, they distributed approximately 75 million books, paid copies, dividends, and bonuses, or one book for every two Americans. In 1948, the Federal Trade Commission charged that the book clubs' use of the word "free" in their advertising was "false, misleading, and deceptive." The BOMC challenged the ruling in federal court, but no final decision was handed down before the FTC reversed itself in 1953 and dropped its complaint.

The success of the BOMC and the Literary Guild stimulated imitation. By mid-1928, there were nine active clubs, including such long-lived survivors as the Religious Book Club, the Catholic Book Club, and the Crime Club. The most successful of the new entrants were those directed to specialized niches in the market. In response, the general-audience book clubs—the largest of which remained the BOMC and Literary Guild—were driven to multiply the number of their alternate selections to appeal to broader ranges of interests and tastes.

At first, most booksellers and some publishers were hostile to the clubs and accused them of unfair competition. Publishers could not, however, resist the financial rewards of selection by a club. Booksellers came to accept that selection by a major book club boosted a title's sales through retail stores. By the early 1970's, book clubs had an estimated membership of 7 million and accounted for approximately 8.5 percent of total book sales in the United States. The general-audience clubs faced difficulties because of the paperback revolution, the expansion of retail book outlets, rising postal rates, and the heavy expense of the advertising required to attract new members. Member turnover remained high. With the rise of Internet technology, online book clubs started forming in the 1990's, and they gave members the opportunity to enter into discussions with others of similar reading tastes from all over the globe.

The formula pioneered by the book clubs was eventually extended to the sale of many other kinds of goods. The most successful extension was to phonograph records. In 1955, the Columbia Records Division of the Co-

lumbia Broadcasting System launched the Columbia Record Club, and the success of that venture forced RCA Victor to follow with its own club. Other "of the month" undertakings included Barton's Sweet-of-the-Month Club; Beer-of-the-Month Club, Inc.; Cheese-of-the-Month; Dessert-of-the-Month; Fad-of-the-Month Club; Flowers-of-the-Month; Plant-of-the-Month Club; Toy-of-the-Month; and even Kosher Salami-of-the-Month Club.

—*John Braeman*

FURTHER READING

Epstein, Jason. *Book Business: Publishing Past, Present, and Future*. New York: W. W. Norton, 2001. Epstein, a giant in the publishing industry, gives a lively account of publishing's recent history and discusses the trend toward corporatization, which in many respects began with the BOMC.

Lee, Charles. *The Hidden Public: The Story of the Book-of-the-Month Club*. Garden City, N.Y.: Doubleday, 1958. A gushingly admiring account written in cooperation with BOMC officials. Indispensable because of its information about the inner operations of the BOMC.

Lupoff, Richard A. *The Great American Paperback: An Illustrated Tribute to the Legends of the Book*. Portland, Oreg.: Collectors Press, 2001. A more general history of paperback books that focuses more on their seamy side. Valuable for understanding the degree to which Penguin broadened the notion of the paperback book and its readership.

Madison, Charles A. *Book Publishing in America*. New York: McGraw-Hill, 1966. A handy brief survey that deals only sketchily with the book clubs but that shows the larger context of the commercialization of literature.

Radway, Janice. "The Scandal of the Middlebrow: The Book-of-the-Month Club, Class Fracture, and Cultural Authority." *South Atlantic Quarterly* 89 (Fall, 1990): 707-736. An illuminating examination of the attacks on the BOMC by intellectuals for its supposed pandering to "common" tastes.

Rubin, Joan Shelley. *The Making of Middlebrow Culture*. Chapel Hill: University of North Carolina Press, 1992. Includes an examination of the role played by the BOMC in the emergence of what has been termed American "middlebrow" culture. Features analyses of the themes emphasized by BOMC advertising and the standards and values influencing book selection by BOMC judges.

1926

Sackheim, Maxwell. *My First Sixty Years in Advertising.* Englewood Cliffs, N.J.: Prentice-Hall, 1970. Autobiographical recollections combined with suggestions about techniques of mail-order advertising by one of the founders of the BOMC.

Tebbel, John. *A History of Book Publishing in the United States.* 4 vols. New York: R. R. Bowker, 1972-1981. Intended as the authoritative history, these volumes have much information not readily available in other accounts. Unfortunately, the work is also a nearly unreadable mass of ill-digested facts. Treatment of the founding and later history of the book clubs is found in volume 3 (covering 1920-1940) and volume 4 (covering 1940 to 1980).

SEE ALSO: 1903: Scott Publishes *The Theory of Advertising*; 1913: Fuller Brush Company Is Incorporated; Sept. 11, 1916: First Self-Service Grocery Store Opens; June, 1917: First Pulitzer Prizes Are Awarded; July, 1920: Procter & Gamble Announces Plans to Sell Directly to Retailers; Feb., 1922: *Reader's Digest* Is Founded; Mar. 3, 1923: Luce Founds *Time* Magazine; 1935: Penguin Develops a Line of Paperback Books; Nov. 23, 1936: Luce Launches *Life* Magazine.

1926-1949
CHINESE CIVIL WAR

In 1926, the Chinese Nationalist Party (also called the Kuomintang) broke with the Chinese Communist Party. The nationalists pushed the Communists into remote sanctuaries until Japan's invasion of China in 1937 forced an uneasy truce in the civil war. After Japan's surrender in August of 1945, hopes for a Chinese coalition government were dashed when the Kuomintang and the Communists resumed their conflict. Fighting ended in late 1949, when the Communists conquered mainland China and the Kuomintang fled to Taiwan.

ALSO KNOWN AS: Fall of the Kuomintang
LOCALE: China
CATEGORIES: Wars, uprisings, and civil unrest; government and politics

KEY FIGURES
Chiang Kai-shek (1887-1975), leader of the Kuomintang, president of China, 1948-1949, and president of the Republic of China (Taiwan), 1950-1975
Mao Zedong (Mao Tse-tung; 1893-1976), chairman of the Chinese Communist Party, 1949-1976
Lin Biao (Lin Piao; 1907-1971), Communist general who captured Manchuria
Zhou Enlai (Chou En-lai; 1888-1976), Communist leader
Zhang Xueliang (Chang Hsüeh-liang; 1901-2001), Manchurian warlord
George C. Marshall (1880-1959), American general who was largely responsible for the success of the U.S. Army during World War II

SUMMARY OF EVENT
The Chinese revolution of 1912 established the Republic of China, but it did not give rise to a stable government. To unify China, in early 1923 the revolutionary leader Sun Yixian (also known as Sun Yat-sen) allied his Nationalist Party, or Kuomintang, with the Soviet Union and the tiny Chinese Communist Party. In September of 1924, Sun's Soviet-advised forces defeated northern Chinese warlords. However, Sun died of liver cancer in Beijing on March 12, 1925.

Without Sun, the Communist-Kuomintang alliance began to break under the weight of different ideological positions. On March 20, 1926, the new Kuomintang leader, Chiang Kai-shek, suspected that the captain of a Communist gunboat planned to kidnap him, and Chiang had him arrested. He and the Soviets agreed to limit Communist influence and continued their military alliance.

After capturing Shanghai from a warlord in March of 1927, Chiang Kai-shek moved against the Communists. On April 12, Kuomintang-controlled gangsters attacked the city's union members, killing and arresting many, and the next day, Kuomintang troops fired on protestors, killing about one hundred. Chiang Kai-shek set up a rival Nationalist government in Nanjing on April 18 and purged it of all Communists.

Soviet leader Joseph Stalin instructed the Chinese Communists to fight Chiang's government. On August 1, 1927, Communist troops under Zhou Enlai seized Nanchang in Jiangxi Province, but they were defeated and fled east to the coast and then into the mountains. Mao Zedong proposed a Communist uprising in Hunan, but it failed. A Communist uprising in Guangzhou, in

December of 1927, was suppressed with equal brutality. By 1928, the Communists were surviving in remote rural sanctuaries while Chiang destroyed the warlord's powers either through military victory or political alliance. His Kuomintang formed a new national government on October 10, 1928.

Chiang Kai-shek's efforts to annihilate the Communists were thwarted by two forces: the Japanese army and the Kuomintang's unstable alliances with warlords. In September of 1931, the Japanese moved into Manchuria and annexed Chinese land to form the country of Manchukuo in February of 1932. Chiang's policy was to avoid fighting Japan while trying to destroy Communist strongholds such as Mao's Jiangxi Soviet area, a tactic that alienated many Chinese.

Chiang launched an attack on the Jiangxi Soviet in late 1934. Mao engineered a prominent role for himself on the Communists' Long March to northern Yan'an in Shaanxi Province, and he was officially recognized as chairman of the Chinese Communist Party in 1935. He firmly established his rule once the surviving Communists reached Yan'an in late October of 1935.

The Communists appealed to the Kuomintang in hopes of forming a common front against the Japanese. On a visit to troops designated to attack the Communists, on December 12, 1936, Chiang Kai-shek was kidnapped by Manchurian warlord Zhang Xueliang, who wanted to resurrect the Communist alliance. The Chinese public and Joseph Stalin objected to killing Chiang, and he was released on December 25 after promising to establish a truce. Zhang accompanied Chiang to his jail cell in Nanjing.

Negotiations dragged on between the Kuomintang and the Communists until incidents in Beijing on July 7, 1937, and Shanghai on August 13 provoked a Japanese attack. On August 21, China and the Soviet Union signed a treaty allying their nations, and Stalin sent military supplies, piloted aircraft, and advisers. As Chiang's best armies were destroyed in late 1937 and 1938, the Communists held back most of their troops.

Chiang Kai-shek moved the Nationalist government to Chongqing, in Sichuan Province, in October of 1938.

CHINESE CIVIL WAR

For a time, the Japanese held on to the territory they had conquered in China, and the Kuomintang and Communists avoided fighting each other. A major clash, however, occurred in January of 1941, when the Kuomintang destroyed a Communist force south of the Chang (also called the Yangtze) River. Chinese people protested the Kuomintang's attack, and the shaky alliance between Kuomintang and Communists survived.

When Germany attacked the Soviet Union on June 22, 1941, the Chinese Communists lost an important source of support; the Soviets were too distracted with defending their own nation to help China. Japan's attack on Pearl Harbor on December 7, 1941, however, brought the Western Allies into the war in China. Western support generally went to Chiang, who faced the Japanese in a long stalemate. While Mao consolidated his power through terror and permitted the use of guerrilla tactics against the Japanese, the Kuomintang faced severe economic difficulties. In the meantime, in 1944 Japan's Ichi-Go offensive destroyed vast Kuomintang armies and gave some Americans the feeling that the Communists were worth supporting.

Before Japan gave its unconditional surrender on September 2, 1945, the United States tried to produce a Kuomintang-Communist coalition, but the desire for unity could not overcome the two Chinese factions' mutual hatred. Instead of joining sides, both the Kuomintang and the Communists raced to occupy as much territory as possible. While the Americans transported Kuomintang troops into Manchuria to prevent a Communist takeover in late 1945, American General George Marshall desperately tried to negotiate a compromise. By early 1946, however, it was clear that both Chinese parties preferred civil war. General Marshall asked Chiang Kai-shek on May 31 to stop warfare in Manchuria, and Chiang, dependent on American support, agreed to a temporary truce.

After the truce, Kuomintang troops advanced in Manchuria but could not defeat the Communists led by Lin Biao. The United States grew weary of the Kuomintang and objected to its intensely corrupt adminstration. When the Kuomintang promulgated a new constitution for China on January 1, 1947, the Communists ended negotiations. Lin Biao continued guerrilla warfare in Manchuria, and the Communists brutally enforced land reform in their areas. Meanwhile, the Kuomintang faced severe inflation and a loss of public trust.

The Communists had several major victories in 1948. Leadership by the Kuomintang's generals was so bad that some historians suggested that some of their generals were Communist moles. In northeastern China, Communist armies solidified their position, won major battles, and captured Jinan, in Shandong Province, on September 24. Lin Biao's army triumphed in Manchuria, where it encircled Kuomintang troops in the key cities it had been ordered to hold and won decisive defeats. On October 17, Shenyang, the capital of Liaoning Province, fell after a brutal siege, and Changchun followed on October 20. After terrible civilian losses, Communist control over Manchuria was finally secured.

On January 10, 1949, Mao's general Zhu De won the Battle of Xuzhou, and on January 21, Chiang Kai-shek resigned as president of China. Although he was succeeded by Li Zongren, Chiang still wielded considerable power. On February 23, Beijing surrendered to the Communists, who controlled China north of the Chang River. Communist terms for peace proved too harsh for the Kuomintang to accept, but the United States had decided on a policy of neutrality. In April, the Communists launched their final offensive, and they captured Nanjing on April 24 and Shanghai on May 25. In Beijing, on October 1, 1949, Mao Zedong established the People's Republic of China. Remaining Kuomintang forces were in disarray and were easily defeated, and the Communists took the last cities in mainland China in October and November. On December 10, 1949, Chiang Kai-shek flew from Chengdu to Taiwan, ending organized Kuomintang presence on mainland China.

SIGNIFICANCE

The Communist victory in China's civil war effectively placed the people of mainland China under Mao Zedong's power and added the world's most populous nation to the Communist camp. China was exhausted and suffering by the end of the civil war, and the Communists used the people's desire for peace and stability to erect an iron rule. Because of their decisive military victory, the Communists enjoyed virtually unlimited power in mainland China, and they were able to unify the area, which had been divided since 1912.

By using propaganda to glorify the Communists' role in the civil war and by maintaining complete control over Chinese society, Mao and the Communists had virtually free rein, although their actions often had catastrophic consequences. Victory in the civil war, however, ensured the Communist Party's political dominance into the twenty-first century, even as the economy was liberalized. Stunned Westerners realized that the Communists blamed them for their earlier support of the Kuomintang, and the People's Republic of China conducted a strong anti-Western foreign policy until 1972.

In the United States, Americans laid the blame for the loss of China on politicians who had supported neutrality toward Chiang Kai-shek, and the Communist victory in China further hardened Western resolve in the Cold War. Chiang Kai-shek and his successors managed to hold on to the Taiwan-based Republic of China, which prevented China's complete reunification. Increased democratization in Taiwan continued to be viewed with utter suspicion by the People's Republic, as was any attempt to establish a Taiwan formally independent from China.

—*R. C. Lutz*

FURTHER READING

Chang, Jung, and Jon Halliday. *Mao: The Unknown Story*. New York: Alfred A. Knopf, 2005. Stunning historical deconstruction of Mao's Communist propaganda that proposes a radical new look at the history of the event. Controversial but based on thorough research, this book has opened fresh historical debate about the facts of the event. Illustrated, maps, notes, bibliography, index (generally uses Pinyin to romanize text).

Spence, Jonathan. *The Search for Modern China*. Rev. ed. New York: W. W. Norton, 2001. Detailed, accessible and generally balanced presentation of the event. Maps, illustrations, notes, glossary, bibliography, index (uses Pinyin).

Westad, Odd Arne. *Decisive Encounters: The Chinese Civil War, 1946-1950.* Stanford, Calif.: Stanford University Press, 2003. Covers the final years of the civil war with references to its origin and earlier development. Strong focus on Communist side. Maps, bibliography, index, notes.

SEE ALSO: 1901-1911: China Allows Some Western Reforms; Oct. 10, 1911: Sun Yixian Overthrows the Qing Dynasty; May 4, 1919: May Fourth Movement; Oct. 16, 1934-Oct. 18, 1935: Mao's Long March; July 7, 1937: China Declares War on Japan; Dec., 1937-Feb., 1938: Rape of Nanjing.

March 16, 1926
LAUNCHING OF THE FIRST LIQUID-FUELED ROCKET

The development of a liquid propellant made rocketry, and thus space exploration, possible.

LOCALE: Auburn, Massachusetts
CATEGORIES: Science and technology; physics; space and aviation

KEY FIGURES
Robert H. Goddard (1882-1945), American physicist
Konstantin Tsiolkovsky (1857-1935), Russian scientist

SUMMARY OF EVENT

On a cold winter day in March, 1926, three men and a woman in heavy coats gathered around a small launching stand built of pipes that had been set up in the snow in a field near Auburn, Massachusetts. Held in place on the stand, which resembled a large metal ladder, was a ten-foot-long rocket. It consisted of a two-foot-long motor at the front, connected by long, slender tubes to two tanks in the rear that contained gasoline and liquid oxygen. The individuals gathered in the field were Robert H. Goddard, a physics professor at Clark University who had designed and built the rocket; his wife, Esther Kisk Goddard; P. M. Roope, also of Clark's physics department; and Henry Sachs, the university's instrument maker. The rocket they were about to launch was the product of nearly ten years of research in Goddard's shop and laboratory. Its most unusual feature was its propellant—a combination of gasoline and liquid oxygen fed into the combustion chamber by separate tubes. Up to that time, rockets usually had been fueled with black powder that was stored and ignited in the combustion chamber.

In a few minutes, all was in readiness to begin the test. Esther Goddard started her motion-picture camera, and Robert Goddard touched a blowtorch to an opening near the top of the rocket. There was a steady roar, and a few seconds later, the rocket rose slowly from the launch frame and then shot into the air. It flew 184 feet at a maximum altitude of 41 feet while achieving a speed of 60 miles an hour. Then it curved sharply to the left and descended, plowing into the ice and snow as it hit the ground at high speed. The flight had lasted less than three seconds. There were no speeches and no interviews, and no newspaper reported the event, yet the rocket's brief flight marked a giant advance toward the exploration of space.

Goddard had received a bachelor of science degree from Worcester Polytechnic Institute in 1908 and a master of arts and a doctorate from Clark University in 1910 and 1911, respectively. He had a lifelong interest in rocketry, and despite a lack of government support, he had continued the research he began in the basement of Worcester Polytechnic Institute in 1907 when he fired a powder-fueled rocket.

Goddard's early work came out of his interest in high-altitude weather research. The limitations on balloons led him to the development of mathematical theories of rocketry as well as to two patents, one for a liquid-fueled rocket and the other for a multistage rocket. To prove that rockets could function in the vacuum of space, Goddard had to overcome popular misconceptions of Newton's third law: For every action there is an equal and opposite reaction. His research proved that a rocket engine could deliver propulsion in the vacuum of space.

After initial experiments with solid fuels, in 1921, Goddard switched to the more efficient and cheaper liquid hydrogen and oxygen rocket propellants. By 1924, he had a working engine. Until that year, Goddard had not flown a rocket. Problems with pumps and the size of the combustion chamber needed to be overcome before a flight would be feasible. His work also focused on separating the combustion chamber from fuel storage and changing the exhaust nozzles to increase the velocity.

At the time Goddard performed his experiment, rockets had been known for several centuries. They were mentioned in Chinese writings as far back as the eleventh century, and they had been used as artillery weapons by European armies at various times between the fifteenth and early nineteenth centuries, until they finally became outmoded with the advent of modern long-range artillery. Then, in 1918, Goddard developed and tested the bazooka. Even though it came too late for use then, he continued his work, and the bazooka became an important weapon during World War II. Until that time, however, the chief use of rockets seems to have been in staging elaborate fireworks displays.

When interest in space travel first began early in the seventeenth century, few people thought of the rocket

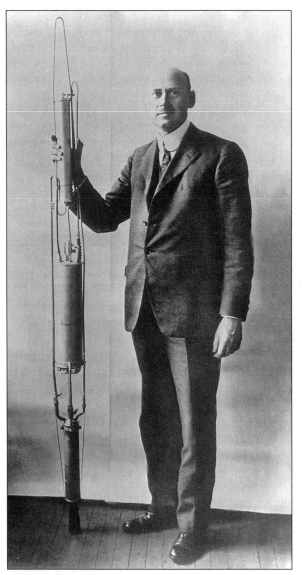

Robert H. Goddard with a 1926 rocket. (Library of Congress)

as the most suitable vehicle for the purpose. In Jules Verne's celebrated 1865 novel *De la terre à la lune* (*From the Earth to the Moon*, 1873), space explorers reach the Moon by riding inside a projectile shot out of a gigantic cannon on Earth. In 1903, however, a little-known Russian scientist, Konstantin Tsiolkovsky, conclusively demonstrated in a series of articles that the rocket would have to be the vehicle of space exploration. As Tsiolkovsky saw it, the rocket had several peculiar properties that made it the only vehicle capable of carrying a payload into outer space. First, a rocket engine could develop more thrust, or push, than any other engine of the same weight; second, because a rocket is a self-contained system carrying its own oxygen supply, it could operate anywhere, even in airless space; and third, because a rocket gradually loses weight as its fuel supply is exhausted, its maximum speed comes at the end of its powered flight.

While Tsiolkovsky was developing his ideas, Goddard, unaware of the Russian scientist's work, was reaching the same conclusions. Goddard was interested in designing a vehicle that could be used to carry instruments high into the upper atmosphere for purposes of research. In January, 1920, he published a paper in the *Smithsonian Institution Reports* titled "A Method of Reaching Extreme Altitudes" in which he summed up the conclusions he had reached in the previous ten years regarding the unique suitability of rockets for high-altitude research. In this paper, Goddard demonstrated that it was theoretically possible to design a rocket that would weigh less than ten tons and attain a great enough velocity to reach the Moon. The paper would have gone unnoticed had it not been for Goddard's suggestion that a rocket fired at the Moon should contain flash powder that would ignite on impact, thus marking the landing site for observers on Earth and proving that the rocket actually had reached its destination.

Goddard was not only a theoretician; he actually designed and built several rockets. At the time of his experiments, the only rockets he could obtain used the same type of propellant used in the Chinese rockets of the eleventh century, which was black powder. This kind of rocket clearly was unsuitable for the high-altitude flights Goddard had in mind. A high-altitude rocket had to accelerate slowly and at a fairly uniform rate, so that its maximum speed would be reached when it was several miles above Earth, where there is less air resistance. A black-powder rocket exerted its greatest thrust immediately after ignition and then slowed down as its fuel was exhausted.

Some means needed to be found to feed the fuel into the rocket's combustion chamber at a constant and predictable rate, so that the rocket's acceleration would be constant and predetermined. As this was impractical with solid (powder) fuels, Goddard hit upon the idea of using liquid fuels, such as ether or gasoline, which also would give the rocket a greater exhaust velocity. Because gasoline and similar liquid fuels do not contain oxygen, the rocket also would have to carry its own oxygen supply. Goddard's Auburn rocket contained two separate tanks, one for the gasoline and another for the liquid oxygen. Fuels from both tanks were piped into the combustion chamber.

SIGNIFICANCE

Having demonstrated the feasibility of the liquid-fueled rocket as a high-altitude vehicle with the Auburn test firing, Goddard went on to conduct successful experiments with other liquid-fueled rockets during the next twenty years. One of his rockets eventually reached a height of seventy-five hundred feet. With another, Goddard achieved the first successful controlled flight of a rocket. His tiny 1926 rocket and the larger ones he built during the 1930's are the direct ancestors of the German V-2's, which in turn were the precursors to the U.S. and Russian rockets that carried the first payloads into Earth orbit.

Despite his many accomplishments, including the first U.S. patent for a multiple-stage rocket and the development of vanes for guidance and gyro control devices, Goddard's work went unrecognized during his lifetime. He published little for two reasons: First, he was an intensely shy individual, and second, he feared the German scientists, with their emphasis on race superiority, and did not want to encourage their work. Today, however, Goddard is recognized as the father of modern rocket technology. In his early work, he theorized the means of landing humans on other celestial bodies. This ability to combine practical research with a vision of spaceflight and rocketry represents his great contribution.

—Ronald N. Spector and Duncan R. Jamieson

FURTHER READING

Arnold, H. J. P., ed. *Man in Space: An Illustrated History of Space Flight*. New York: Smithmark, 1993. Examines humankind's progress in space travel. Focuses more on the results of Goddard's pioneering work than on the work itself.

Braun, Wernher von, and Frederick I. Ordway III. *Space Travel: A History*. 4th ed. New York: Harper & Row, 1985. One of the best single-volume histories on human beings' conquest of space. Chapter titled "The Pioneers of Space Travel" provides thorough discussion of the scientific and technical contributions of Konstantin Tsiolkovsky, Hermann Oberth, and Goddard. Includes many remarkable photographs, an extensive time line, and an excellent bibliography.

Clary, David A. *Rocket Man: Robert H. Goddard and the Birth of the Space Age*. New York: Hyperion, 2003. First full-scale biography of Goddard in more than forty years places his accomplishments within the context of the times and reveals more about his personality and private life than previous works. Includes chronology, bibliography, and index.

Goddard, Robert H. *The Papers of Robert H. Goddard*. Edited by Esther C. Goddard. 3 vols. New York: McGraw-Hill, 1970. Invaluable resource for any serious student of Goddard and the history of rocketry. Edited papers contain summaries of Goddard's diary entries, reprints of noteworthy technical papers, and relevant correspondence among important members within the scientific community. Provides an intimate glimpse into the world of the distinguished scientist, clearly and chronologically outlining the evolution of his ideas and techniques.

_____. *Rocket Development*. New York: Prentice-Hall, 1948. A selection of Goddard's research notes from 1929-1941, published posthumously.

_____. *Rockets*. New York: American Rocket Society, 1946. Includes Goddard's two most important published papers, "A Method of Reaching Extreme Altitudes" and "Liquid-Propellant Rocket Development."

Gruntman, Mike. *Blazing the Trail: The Early History of Spacecraft and Rocketry*. Reston, Va.: American Institute of Aeronautics and Astronautics, 2004. Relates the events that paved the way for human beings to begin exploring space. Describes the early work in rocketry science of Tsiolkovsky, Goddard, and others.

Hacker, Barton C. "Robert H. Goddard and the Origins of Space Flight." In *Technology in America: A History of Individuals and Ideas*, edited by Carroll W. Pursell, Jr. 2d ed. Cambridge, Mass.: MIT Press, 1990. Brief essay traces Goddard's career and characterizes the institutional context within which he worked. Despite popular notions of Goddard as a solitary, persevering scientific figure, the Smithsonian Institution, the Guggenheim Foundation, and the U.S. military played crucial roles in his ultimate success.

Lehman, Milton. *This High Man: The Life of Robert H. Goddard*. New York: Farrar, Straus and Giroux, 1963. Readable biography exhaustively covers God-

1926

dard's life from youth to World War II. Includes many details, but Goddard's personality and social relationships remain somewhat unexplored.

Pendray, G. Edward. "Pioneer Rocket Development in the United States." In *The History of Rocket Technology: Essays on Research, Development, and Utility*, edited by Eugene M. Emme. Detroit: Wayne State University Press, 1964. Essay by a pioneer in the development of rockets in the United States who had intimate knowledge of Goddard's scientific and technical work succinctly sketches Goddard's ma-

jor accomplishments in astronautics.

Williams, Beryl, and Samuel Epstein. *The Rocket Pioneers: On the Road to Space*. New York: Julian Messner, 1958. Historical study includes chapters on Sir William Congreve, Konstantin Tsiolkovsky, Hermann Oberth, and Goddard. Clearly describes Goddard's key technological innovations within the context of his lengthy scientific career. Well researched and well written.

SEE ALSO: 1903: Tsiolkovsky Proposes Using Liquid Oxygen for Space Travel.

May, 1926
DURANT PUBLISHES *THE STORY OF PHILOSOPHY*

Will Durant's The Story of Philosophy *was one in a series of publications written to make materials that had previously been available only through college-level texts available to the wider public. Durant sought to bring the field of philosophical inquiry to the increasing numbers of people who had not had the opportunity for higher education but wanted to educate themselves for personal and cultural reasons.*

LOCALE: New York, New York
CATEGORIES: Philosophy; publishing and journalism

KEY FIGURES
Will Durant (1885-1981), author, public speaker, and scholar
Richard L. Simon (1899-1960), businessman and publisher
Max Lincoln Schuster (1897-1970), publisher
Emanuel Haldeman-Julius (1889-1951), publisher of Little Blue Books and the series Life and Letters

SUMMARY OF EVENT
The publication of Will Durant's *The Story of Philosophy* was the result of several events, one of which was the popular realization that owning certain books gave the impression of belonging to the culturally elite. In the autobiographical work that he coauthored with his wife Ariel Durant, *A Dual Autobiography* (1977), Durant reflected on the unprecedented demand for *The Story of Philosophy*, stating, "My book became a social necessity; every proper family felt obliged to display it on the table or the shelf." Another, more significant reason was the increasing public desire for education beyond that provided in secondary schools, which led to the popular-

ity of "outlines" of particular subjects. As Durant stated, "The 'outlines' came because a million voices called for them." Durant's book drew on the success of H. G. Wells's *The Outline of History: Being a Plain History of Life and Mankind* (1920), a summary of world history that contained many volumes on a variety of subjects and was written in a readable, unpretentious style that clearly summarized important ideas. Hendrik Willem Van Loon's *The Story of Mankind* (1921) had been second in nonfiction sales to Wells's history, but *The Story of Philosophy* sold 100,000 copies in its first year. The public was eager to understand philosophical concepts that had been hidden from them by languages such as Greek and German, the complexity of ideas developed by the philosophers, and in some instances, the desire of academics to protect their territory.

Will Durant made it his life's work to disseminate Western culture to those unable to attend university. An academic who earned a Ph.D. in philosophy from Columbia in 1917, Durant wished to make knowledge accessible to all. Consequently, he began to lecture to adult workers at New York's Labor Temple. His initial course in 1914 was on the history of philosophy from Socrates to French philosopher Henri Bergson. Soon, in addition to teaching at the Labor Temple and taking courses for his degree at Columbia, Durant started a career as a public lecturer outside of New York City.

He also began producing a series of guides to philosophy for the publisher Emanuel Haldeman-Julius. From 1922 to 1925, Durant wrote eleven essays on philosophers from Plato to John Dewey. Some of these were first printed in Haldeman-Julius's Life and Letters series, and all were issued as Little Blue Books. These small books (which, at roughly fifteen hundred words each, were actually more like pamphlets) were designed to make culture "seem both manageable and disposable." They were bought to be read, rather than displayed, and cost five cents each. Haldeman-Julius also changed the titles from "guides" to "stories," making them appear more accessible. Durant's "little books" sold an average of twenty-seven thousand copies annually.

The success of Durant's books led Haldeman-Julius to propose that the pamphlets be bound together and sold as a single volume. The firm asked Durant to provide some text that would unify the different books and suggested that Durant offer the publication to the new publishing house of Simon & Schuster. The new firm was touting itself as a democratized publisher, and as such it was in tune with Durant's desire to popularize knowledge. Richard L. Simon and Max Lincoln Schuster believed that their mission as publishers was to widen the readership for fine literature, and they planned to publish "better books for more and more people, at lower prices." Consequently, they embarked on a vigorous advertising campaign that depicted Durant's book as a painless form of liberal education. The campaign included special incentives for bookstores that sold more than their sales quotas, direct-mail solicitation of Labor Temple students, and eventually a money-back guarantee. Advertisements, which at first were relatively small in size, grew into one- and two-page spreads that quoted from prepublication reviews. A full-page advertisement on the back cover of *Saturday Review* extolled the book as "the outstanding best seller that discriminating people are talking about" and focused on people's desire to become one of the cultural elite.

When *The Story of Philosophy* was published in May of 1926, it was priced at five dollars. It was almost six hundred pages long, and the chapters were basically copies of the versions published in the Little Blue Books. By the end of the year, the work was the best-selling nonfiction book in the United States. Durant offered access to what most people believed was beyond their understanding: the great philosophers and their ideas. The subtitle of the book, *The Lives and Opinions of the Greater Philosophers*, made the book more human by focusing on a biographical approach and putting the difficult concepts into language people could understand. Durant made it clear that the book was not a complete history, and he interjected himself (using the first person plural) as a congenial guide through the stories of philosophers Plato, Aristotle, Francis Bacon, Baruch Spinoza, Voltaire, Immanuel Kant, Arthur Schopenhauer, Herbert Spencer, Friedrich Nietzsche, Henri Bergson, Benedetto Croce, Bertrand Russell, George Santayana, William James, and John Dewey. The style and tone of the volume helped Durant show that the study of philosophy could be a source of pleasure: He included chatty speculations, witty asides, and lively anecdotes to keep the reader engaged. By directly addressing the reader as well as asking rhetorical questions, Durant forced the reader to become engaged with the book. The book was selected as a Book-of-the-Month

1926

FROM *THE STORY OF PHILOSOPHY*

In his introduction to The Story of Philosophy, *Durant defines the difference between science and philosophy:*

Science is analytical description, philosophy is synthetic interpretation. Science wishes to resolve the whole into parts, the organism into organs, the obscure into the known. It does not inquire into the values and ideal possibilities of things, nor into their total and final significance; it is content to show their present actuality and operation, it narrows its gaze resolutely to the nature and process of things as they are. The scientist is as impartial as Nature in Turgenev's poem: he is as interested in the leg of a flea as in the creative throes of a genius. But the philosopher is not content to describe the fact; he wishes to ascertain its relation to experience in general, and thereby to get at its meaning and its worth; he combines things in interpretive synthesis; he tries to put together, better than before, that great universe-watch which the inquisitive scientist has analytically taken apart. Science tells us how to heal and how to kill; it reduces the death rate in retail and then kills us wholesale in war; but only wisdom—desire coordinated in the light of all experience—can tell us when to heal and when to kill. To observe processes and to construct means is science; to criticize and coordinate ends is philosophy: and because in these days our means and instruments have multiplied beyond our interpretation and synthesis of ideals and ends, our life is full of sound and fury, signifying nothing. For a fact is nothing except in relation to desire; it is not complete except in relation to a purpose and a whole. Science without philosophy, facts without perspective and valuation, cannot save us from havoc and despair. Science gives us knowledge, but only philosophy can give us wisdom.

Source: Will Durant, *The Story of Philosophy: The Lives and Opinions of the Great Philosophers* (New York: Simon & Schuster, 1926).

choice, which was the ultimate stamp of approval for many readers.

Although the public loved the book, many critics did not. Academics found fault with Durant's failure to include selection principles, and others did not like his chatty approach to such a serious subject. Mortimer Adler, in a September 29, 1926, review in *The Nation* titled "Sleight of Hand," began by stating that the book "is probably no worse than its fellow outlines," but then goes on to deplore the "vaudevillian character" in which Durant handles the "ponderous problems" inherent in philosophy. "The worst sin of all," according to Durant himself, "was the omission of Chinese and Hindu philosophy."

SIGNIFICANCE

Durant's former professor at Columbia and philosopher John Dewey hailed the book as "thoroughly scholarly, thoroughly useful, human, and readable." In his foreword to the book, Dewey stated that Durant had "humanized rather than merely popularized the story of philosophy." The review in *The New York Times*, titled "Even Philosophy May Now Be Comprehended," praised the book, stating that Durant presented knowledge, "even the most abstruse, in a manner and with a lucidity that conveys to ordinary mortals the convictions that it originates with human beings."

Sales of the Modern Library's philosophy titles in 1926 increased, suggesting that Durant's summaries motivated readers to read the work of the philosophers discussed in *The Story of Philosophy*. The sales of philosophical classics increased 200 percent, and a librarian at the New York Public Library reported that since the publication of *The Story of Philosophy* there had been "a wide and increasing demand" for the philosophical classics.

Publications such as *The Story of Philosophy* made self-education possible for those who yearned for more education, but were unable to attend a university. Durant's book, written in accessible language and focused on key concepts, amazed readers who discovered relevance in the thinking of the philosophers to issues in their own life, and the American Philosophical Association noted that many people chose to become philosophers after reading the book.

—*Marcia B. Dinneen*

FURTHER READING

Adler, Mortimer J. "Sleight of Hand." *The Nation*, September 29, 1926, 298-299. In his lengthy, negative review of *The Story of Philosophy*, Adler deplores Durant's "chatty" style.

Benton, Megan. "'Too Many Books': Book Ownership and Cultural Identity in the 1920's." *American Quarterly* 49, no. 2 (1997): 268-297. A discussion of book ownership as an indication of belonging to the "cultural elite."

Cotkin, George. "Middle-Ground Pragmatists: The Popularization of Philosophy in American Culture." *Journal of the History of Ideas* 55, no. 2 (April, 1994): 283-302. Cotkin discusses how philosophy was "popularized" and integrated into American intellectual and culture life during the interwar period.

Durant, Will. Preface to *The Story of Philosophy*. 2d ed. New York: Simon & Schuster, 1961. Durant defends his outlines as a viable way to learn and responds to his critics. His describes his book as "an introduction and an invitation" to the world of philosophy.

Durant, Will, and Ariel Durant. *A Dual Autobiography*. New York: Simon & Schuster, 1977. Durant and his wife reflect on their lives and provide background information on *The Story of Philosophy*.

Forman, Henry James. "Even Philosophy May Now Be Comprehended." *The New York Times*, June 20, 1926. A lengthy and positive review of *The Story of Philosophy*.

Rubin, Joan Shelley. *The Making of Middlebrow Culture*. Chapel Hill: University of North Carolina Press, 1992. A detailed study covering the impact of Durant's book.

Sherman, Stuart. "Philosophy and the Average Man's Adult Education." *New York Herald Tribune*, June 20, 1926. Positive review of Durant's book shows how it provides a response to people's hunger for education.

SEE ALSO: June 16, 1902: Russell Discovers the "Great Paradox"; 1907: Publication of James's *Pragmatism*; 1927: Heidegger Publishes *Being and Time*; 1935: Penguin Develops a Line of Paperback Books.

May 3-12, 1926
BRITISH WORKERS LAUNCH GENERAL STRIKE

Despite the support of most major labor unions, the General Strike failed to win concessions for miners in their dispute with mine owners.

LOCALE: Great Britain
CATEGORIES: Business and labor; government and politics; social issues and reform

KEY FIGURES
Stanley Baldwin (1867-1947), prime minister of Great Britain, 1923-1929 and 1935-1937
Herbert Smith (1862-1938), president of the Miners' Federation of Great Britain, 1921-1938
Ernest Bevin (1881-1951), British labor leader and member of the General Council of the Trades Union Congress, 1921-1940
Herbert Samuel (1870-1963), chair of the Royal Commission on the Coal Industry, 1925-1926

SUMMARY OF EVENT
The General Strike of 1926 in Great Britain was the largest effort up until that time to win more favorable contract terms for workers through the support of sympathy strikes. Its object was to put pressure on the government to support the wage demands of the miners against the owners, if necessary by the promise of a government subsidy for the industry. Failure of the strike ensured that collective bargaining would take place only between management and labor, with government providing mediation services at most. It led ultimately, however, to the nationalization of the mining industry when the Labour Party won political dominance after World War II.

Prior to World War I, the British coal mining industry had experienced steady growth in output and profitability. The island nation produced nearly as much coal as did the United States, but much of the market for the coal lay outside Great Britain. There was a widespread tendency throughout Europe to regard the conditions prevailing before the war as "normalcy." It was believed that once the fighting came to an end, things would return to normal and the British coal mining industry would continue on its upward trend of profits and wages.

Many of these expectations were reinforced by the war. The pressing need for coal, as bunker fuel for cargo and naval vessels and as power for the munitions industry, led the government to support nearly all the wage demands made by miners through their union, the Miners' Federation of Great Britain (MFGB). The justification

advanced for a steady increase in wages was the inflation that occurred during the war, with the cost of living doubling between 1914 and 1918. In 1917, in order to avert continued wage conflicts, the government took control of the industry, guaranteeing the owners a minimum level of profits. During this period, the government subsidized the industry in order to keep the domestic price of coal down for the benefit of consumers.

After the war, the government decided that it wished to withdraw from the operation of the coal mining industry and return the management, including responsibility for profits and wages, to the owners. In the immediate postwar period, this posed no great problem, because the British industry was able to export large quantities of coal to Europe, and profits remained substantial. Beginning with the postwar depression of 1920, however, the export market for British coal began to decline. It continued on a downward path, with brief intermissions when political developments interrupted European coal production, throughout the interwar period. Profits declined dramatically, and owners of the mines maintained that only with a sharp reduction in wages could costs be brought sufficiently under control that the industry as a whole could operate at a profit.

Meanwhile, the British organized labor movement had won increasing support from workers, so that by the 1920's the unions were a force to be reckoned with. The Miners' Federation of Great Britain had grown from about 600,000 members in 1910 to nearly a million in 1920. It had long since won the right to negotiate wage agreements with the mine owners and during the war had won a long-sought goal, the right to negotiate national minimum wages. Most wage agreements took the form of a specified percentage above the minimum wage.

By 1921, the market for British coal in Europe had declined drastically. The government wished to withdraw definitively from control of the industry. The owners' position was that, in view of the weak export market, the industry could be profitable only if a drastic reduction in wages took place. Meanwhile, the miners' union, the MFGB, had concluded a "triple alliance" with the National Union of Railwaymen (NUR) and the Transport and General Workers' Union (TGWU). The three unions agreed to strike together should one of them be faced with a refusal of management to concede to labor's terms.

When the government announced that it would termi-

An armored car escorts a convoy of bee wagons through Aldgate on its way from the docks of London to Hyde Park depot during the General Strike. (Hulton Archive/Getty Images)

nate its control of the coal mining industry on March 31, 1921, mine owners and miners began their battle. The owners offered wages drastically below the level the miners had been earning, in some cases as much as 50 percent lower. They insisted that henceforth wage agreements be negotiated on a regional basis. The MFGB refused these terms, insisting on a national minimum wage. The owners announced that unless an agreement was reached, they would lock out the miners on April 1, 1921. The miners called for help from their allies in the triple alliance, and the two other unions promised to strike in sympathy. Intervention by the government, offering a limited renewal of the subsidy, was used as justification by the two other unions, the NUR and the TGWU, to withdraw their strike threat. The withdrawal occurred on Friday, April 15, a day that came to be remembered with much bitterness in labor ranks as Black Friday.

The miners continued their strike until July, when they were forced to settle. A limited government subsidy was provided, profits from the sale of coal were pooled so as to provide support for unprofitable mines, and a relatively short-lived recovery in the European coal market brought relative peace back to the mining districts.

By 1925, however, conditions in the European export market had worsened again. A threat of a strike in the summer of 1925, and the renewed possibility of a sympathy strike, led to another government intervention. The government promised a temporary subsidy until May 1, 1926, and in the meantime to sponsor another investigation into conditions in the industry. The miners viewed the government concession as a victory. It was announced on Friday, July 31, which became known as Red Friday. The investigation was headed by Sir Herbert Samuel, and its report was known as the Samuel Report. The Samuel Report acknowledged the need for some wage reductions but in addition urged extensive consolidation of the large number of firms in the industry as a means of reducing costs.

The owners as well as the miners rejected the Samuel Report. The owners refused to consider consolidation, especially if forced by governmental action; the miners refused to accept any wage reduction, on the grounds that the existing wage was not a "living wage." The owners announced that if there were no wage agreements in place on May 1, they would institute a lockout.

Meanwhile, anticipating a deadlock, the miners' leaders had turned to the General Council of the Trades Union Congress, the executive organ of the federation of almost all the unions of Great Britain. Organization of a sympathy strike fell to the General Council and to various working groups within it. Ernest Bevin, general secretary of the TGWU, was the chief organizer. The miners, maintaining that they would never consent to a wage reduction or enter into negotiations based on the Samuel Report, which envisaged some reduction, began their strike on May 1. Although Prime Minister Stanley Baldwin made repeated efforts to find some basis for negotiation before the lockout and strike began, he failed.

On May 3, the General Strike itself began. Railway workers and transport workers went out on strike. The General Council believed that the cessation of transport would be a weapon that would compel the government to intervene and jump-start negotiations, if necessary with a renewal of the subsidy. Successively, other unions were called on to join the strike. Electrical workers, engineers, and printers followed transport workers. Streetcars, railroads, and heavy truck traffic were affected. The greatest concern of the government was that food shipments should not be so curtailed that anyone went hungry.

Although initially the strike appeared to be a success, as time wore on it became apparent that it was likely to fail in its objective, which was to force the government once again to intervene, as it had done in 1925. Sir Herbert Samuel attempted to mediate, but with little effect. The miners steadfastly refused even to negotiate unless their prime demand was conceded at the outset, namely, that there would be no reduction in wages. Meanwhile, an emergency effort by the government kept basic supplies moving. The government astutely had begun planning for such an emergency in 1925. Prime Minister Baldwin effectively used radio broadcasts to ensure that the public remained calm.

The General Council of the Trades Union Congress, realizing that neither government nor the mine owners would concede the miners' condition for negotiation of no reduction in wages, desperately sought a way out. The

council agreed to call off the strike on May 12 if the government would force the owners to negotiate on the terms provided in the Samuel Report. By withdrawing the support of the other unions, the General Council in effect forced the miners to negotiate on the basis of the Samuel Report.

Although workers in other fields returned to their jobs, the miners continued to strike. They did not return to work until November, 1926, and then substantially on the owners' terms.

SIGNIFICANCE

A general strike had always been the threat the labor movement held in reserve, to be applied only when conditions of work became intolerable. The concept came out of the syndicalist movement, which saw a general strike as the revolutionary event that would overthrow capitalism because if all workers refused to work, society would come to a halt. The General Strike as applied in Great Britain in 1926, however, differed in important respects from the syndicalist notion.

First of all, the General Strike was not truly a general strike. The General Council referred to it as the "national strike," and it involved only a portion of the organized labor movement. The motives of the General Council in organizing the strike were several. The experience of Red Friday, when the mere threat of a general strike had forced the government to renew the subsidy to the coal mining industry, gave the General Council hope for a quick victory. The council also feared reproach from the workers on the line if it gave in, as had happened in 1921 on Black Friday. The council was certainly pushed by the intransigence of Herbert Smith, leader of the miners, who continued to maintain that any reduction would bring miners' wages down to a level at which no man could live.

Nevertheless, the men who made up the General Council, the leaders of the trade union movement, had serious doubts about the potential of the General Strike as it developed. First, it depended entirely on feelings of solidarity with the miners. No other worker had anything at stake in the disagreement between the miners and mine owners. Second, resources were simply not at hand to support a prolonged strike. If the strike did not achieve its aims within a week, it was unlikely to achieve them at all. In fact, after a week, men were beginning to drift back to work. Even though the miners were protected from legal action by the mine owners—they had, after all, been locked out for refusing to agree to reduced wages on May 1—the other unions had no such excuse and were therefore at risk for suits for breach of their own contracts. As the terms of settlement were worked out, one of the main concerns of the union leaders was to avoid retribution from the government or from management.

In an important sense, the concept behind the General Strike of 1926 was flawed. It assumed that society would not be able to function if the railways did not run and if shipments of food at the docks were not unloaded, and that these things would happen if the existing work forces in those industries refused to work. The government, however, had been anticipating just such a stoppage as occurred. Since the Conservatives had returned to power in 1925, they had been organizing emergency response teams to keep essential services going. Most trains did not run, but some did. The electrical power stations continued to operate with emergency personnel. An army of trucks was enlisted so that goods that could not move by rail could move by road.

The existence of a substantial number of unemployed workers enabled the government to recruit unskilled labor for the movement of supplies. The determination of the government not to be blackmailed in 1926 as it had been in 1925 was a major factor in the defeat of the strike. Although there were some clashes between picketers and those who came in to fill the places of the striking workers, on the whole violence was kept to a minimum.

The miners' strike was eventually settled largely along the lines of the Samuel Report. The structural problem of the industry, overproduction, was gradually addressed in the years following the strike as uneconomic mines were closed. Unfortunately for the miners, however, they were working in an industry that was to a substantial degree obsolete. Gas and oil were gradually replacing coal as the fuel of choice.

Nevertheless, the General Strike left a residue of bitter feeling on both sides that was to have long-range effects. The miners and leaders of the trade union movement realized that collective action in pursuit of purely industrial ends would not work. What would work, they realized, was political organization, with labor eventually strong enough politically to take over the government. The result of this realization was the extensive nationalization of industry when the Labour Party achieved victory at the polls in 1945.

Although the mine owners believed that they had defended capitalism and the right of management to operate without government interference, it was a Pyrrhic victory. The inescapable consequences of worldwide overproduction of coal forced many mines to close in the years following the General Strike; many that did not

close voluntarily were forced to do so under government pressure. Instead of competition, mine owners tried cooperation, in the form of a variety of cooperative marketing schemes. The decline of coal as a source of power in the end defeated the owners.

—Nancy M. Gordon

FURTHER READING

Boyce, Robert. *British Capitalism at the Crossroads, 1919-1932*. New York: Cambridge University Press, 1988. Provides excellent background on the economic policies leading up to and following the General Strike, along with a perceptive analysis of the strike itself.

Farman, Christopher. *The General Strike, May 1926*. London: Rupert Hart-Davis, 1972. Straightforward and readable account of the strike attempts to tell the story without ideological bias. Focuses on personalities and the political conflict involved. Includes illustrations.

Florey, R. A. *The General Strike of 1926: The Economic, Political, and Social Causes of That Class War*. New York: Riverrun Press, 1987. Presents in-depth analysis of the strike from the perspective of the working class.

Graves, Robert, and Alan Hodge. *The Long Week-End: A Social History of Great Britain, 1918-1939*. 1940. Reprint. New York: W. W. Norton, 2001. Fascinating account of daily social life in Great Britain between the world wars. Focuses on fads, controversies of the day, fashions, entertainment, sports, and other activities that ordinary people think important but that historians sometimes miss. Chapter on the General Strike emphasizes how the events affected people's daily lives.

Kirby, M. W. *The British Coalmining Industry, 1870-1946*. Hamden, Conn.: Archon Books, 1977. Scholarly and impartial account is essential background to an understanding of the industry and why the problems of the miners were so intractable.

Morris, Margaret. *The General Strike*. Harmondsworth, Middlesex, England: Penguin Books, 1976. Comprehensive treatment of the General Strike examines its causes, main events, and significance and provides numerous details of the strike's local effects. Written with much sympathy for the striking workers.

Noel, Gerard. *The Great Lock-Out of 1926*. London: Constable, 1976. Account focuses on the social issues underlying the strike.

Phillips, G. A. *The General Strike*. London: Weidenfeld

& Nicolson, 1976. Broad-based and impartial account provides a wealth of details. Includes a list of the important figures in the strike as well as a brief bibliography.

Pugh, Martin. *The Making of Modern British Politics, 1867-1945*. 3d ed. Oxford, England: Blackwell, 2002. Sophisticated account of British political history from the 1860's to the outbreak of World War II. Includes discussion of the General Strike and its impacts on British politics.

_____. *State and Society: A Social and Political History of Britain 1870-1997*. 2d ed. London: Arnold, 2000. Analyzes social policy and political developments in Great Britain from the last part of the nineteenth century onward. Features illustrations, figures, tables, and index.

Renshaw, Patrick. *Nine Days That Shook Britain: The 1926 General Strike*. Garden City, N.Y.: Anchor Press, 1976. Readable survey of the General Strike's background, course, and consequences, placed in the context of the history of coal mining. Includes a chronology of events and a comprehensive and useful bibliography.

Symons, Julian. *The General Strike: A Historical Portrait*. 1957. Reprint. Thirsk, North Yorkshire, England: House of Stratus, 2001. Landmark study, written as narrative history, captures the spirit of the strike.

Taylor, A. J. P. *English History, 1914-1945*. 1965. Reprint. New York: Oxford University Press, 2001. Indispensable source of background information on the period in which the General Strike took place. Deals with social and economic developments as well as with political history. Includes bibliography, list of cabinets, and maps.

1926

SEE ALSO: Feb. 12, 1906: Establishment of the British Labour Party; Jan. 1, 1927: British Broadcasting Corporation Is Chartered; Winter, 1932: Huxley's *Brave New World* Forecasts Technological Totalitarianism.

May 12-15, 1926
PIŁSUDSKI SEIZES POWER IN POLAND

*Incapable of sharing power, Polish political parties fought bitter campaigns from 1919 until 1926, when a coup orchestrated by Józef Piłsudski ended right-left conflicts, instituted the "*sanacja *regime," and shaped Poland until the nation's second partition at the start of World War II.*

ALSO KNOWN AS: Piłsudski's coup d'état; May Coup
LOCALE: Warsaw, Poland
CATEGORIES: Government and politics; wars, uprisings, and civil unrest

KEY FIGURES
Józef Piłsudski (1867-1935), Polish revolutionary, politician, and military leader
Roman Dmowski (1864-1939), Polish nationalist and politician
Wincenty Witos (1874-1945), prime minister of Poland, 1920-1921, 1923, 1926

SUMMARY OF EVENT
"Turmoil" might serve as a good one-word synonym for interwar Poland. Starting in 1914 as a critical theater of World War I and continuing through the Polish-Soviet War (1919-1921; also known as the Russo-Polish War),

the nation suffered tremendous human and financial losses. Although foreign conflict ended in 1921, the newly created Second Republic did not enjoy peace. Rather, five years of intense political struggles split Poles into contentious factions that were unwilling to compromise on any issue. The end result was the May Coup of 1926, which ended this turmoil and shaped Polish politics for the next thirteen years.

The coup's antecedents date back to the early twentieth century, when stateless Poles argued how best to regain their independence. Of the many who raised their voices, two shouted louder than the rest: Józef Piłsudski and Roman Dmowski. These men were polar opposites. The former, a charismatic revolutionary, admired Poland's past as a multiethnic federation and socialism as a political force to unite his people. The latter dismissed Polish history for role models and advanced modern nationalism, with its undercurrent of racism, as the proper tool for building a new Poland. Piłsudski and Dmowski could avoid each other during the war years of 1914-1921, when the possibility of any kind of Polish state was very much in the balance. When the fighting ended, however, and both were viewed as key players in the rebirth of Poland, they initiated a bitter political struggle.

Piłsudski, promoted to marshal for his success in creating a Polish army and leading it to victory over Soviet invaders at the Battle of Warsaw (1920), at first seemed the more powerful. His revolutionary past, however, was centered more in conspiracy than in politics, and he was unable to dominate the constituent Sejm (parliament) that designed the constitution of March 17, 1921.

Dmowski, a consummate politician, influenced the Sejm through his National Democrats. Often referred to as Endecs (an acronym derived from the group's Polish name, Narodowa Demokracja), they were Polish chauvinists, very Catholic, and often fascistic. National Democrats tended to distrust Piłsudski for his previous support of socialism and his willingness to work with minority groups. Piłsudski dismissed Endecs as small-minded bigots who were incapable of protecting Poland's newly gained independence.

Piłsudski had already shown a strong interest in becoming Poland's president. He intended to use that position to direct a transformation of the Polish army and prepare the nation for future conflicts. Fearing his already powerful hold over Polish soldiers, Endecs and other anti-Piłsudski forces tailored the new constitution to make this unlikely. Article 46 of the constitution prohibited the president from serving as commander in chief of the armed forces during wartime. Given Piłsudski's strong interest in military affairs, this was seen as a means of keeping him out of the government.

As expected, Piłsudski refused to run for office. Instead, he supported the campaign of an old friend, Gabriel Narutowicz, who managed to win election by a very small margin in December, 1921. As Narutowicz gained office with the support of Piłsudski and minority political parties, Endec extremists claimed he was "president of the Jews." This started a campaign of lies and slander that culminated in Narutowicz's assassination in January, 1922.

Saddened by the death of his friend, Piłsudski blamed Endec leaders but maintained his position as Poland's leading military man and worked to reorganize the armed forces. He believed that a future war with the Soviet Union or Germany was very likely, and Poland's military needed the ability to make rapid decisions in case of friction with these powerful neighbors.

Neither Piłsudski nor his army reorganization was ever accepted by the right-center coalitions that governed Poland in the early 1920's. When Endecs combined with the Peasant Party to form yet another cabinet in 1923, Piłsudski refused to serve the men he held responsible for the murder of Narutowicz, and he resigned. Control of the military went to his old rivals, mainly veterans of the Austrian army such as General Stanisław Szeptycki and General Józef Haller de Hallenburg—dull men with lackluster records, but politically acceptable to the right.

With Piłsudski went his reorganization scheme, which opponents claimed was a vehicle through which he intended to dominate the government. This was countered by his allies, who argued that he was the only logical choice as Poland's military leader, and as such should be allowed to establish a personally acceptable command structure. Although unable to implement his plans, Piłsudski had enough political influence to keep any alternative system in limbo. He maintained his military and political contacts, and through newspaper articles and his own publications, he skirmished with what he called the "Viennese War Academy"—men

Józef Piłsudski (center). (Library of Congress)

like Szeptycki and Haller de Hallenburg—claiming that it was mismanaging Poland's defenses. To a public very aware of Piłsudski's considerable qualifications for making such claims, these were unsettling accusations.

Poles also worried about their struggling republic. From 1921 to 1926, unstable coalitions created ten different cabinets. In addition to a rapid turnover of ministers, these governments produced scandals that easily rivaled the early 1920's Teapot Dome scandal in the United States. Simultaneously, Poland went through a period of hyperinflation during which its currency, the mark, which exchanged nine to one U.S. dollar in 1919, reached an all-time low of fifteen million to one U.S. dollar in 1923.

Many Poles viewed the government as incapable of defending the new nation, managing the economy, or creating much-needed stability. Piłsudski watched from the sidelines, publishing arguments for change, maintaining contact with an extensive network of serving military officers, and reconnecting with some of his old leftwing political allies of pre-World War I days. He made no secret of his complete disgust with Polish politics, referring to the Sejm as a "house of prostitutes" and as a "locomotive pulling a pin."

A showdown started on May 10, 1926, with a new alliance between Endecs and the Peasant Party. Their combined strength made Wincenty Witos prime minister and allowed for the appointment of General Juliusz Malezewski as minister of war. An archrival of Piłsudski, the general made it clear that he would purge the army of all officers supporting the marshal.

On the same day, Piłsudski told newspaper reporters he was ready to fight the new government. On May 11, the Warsaw garrison was placed on alert as surrounding military units began an unauthorized concentration near the suburb of Rembertow. There, under the direction of Piłsudski, Polish soldiers were preparing to overthrow the government.

Piłsudski's coup started on May 12 as rebel forces captured bridges across the Vistula River and Witos declared a state of emergency. A last-minute meeting between Piłsudski and President Stanisław Wojciechowski brought no concessions from either side, and fighting started that evening. It continued for two days and included artillery and even aerial bombardment.

Although Piłsudski was in command of some of the best local forces, government reinforcements could have tipped the balance. This became less likely after May 14, however, when socialists came out in favor of the coup and ordered a general strike, effectively shutting down

the rail system. This critical delay convinced Witos and Wojciechowski that they could not prevail, and both resigned. The fighting ended on May 15. In all, 390 had died and another 900 had been wounded.

SIGNIFICANCE

The May Coup allowed Piłsudski to create his "*sanacja* regime," which would rule Poland until October 1939. *Sanacja* was defined as a "return to political health"—thus reminding everyone of the venal officials who had controlled government agencies before the coup. Piłsudski's political opponents countered that *sanacja* "blended the philosophies of Nietzsche and Kant"; in Warsovian slang, *nietzsche* implied rubbish and *kant* meant swindle.

Although a new government formed under Prime Minister Kazimierz Bartel, with Piłsudski as minister of military affairs, the divisive nature of Polish politics continued, and what Piłsudski himself first saw as a corrective effort for better government soon evolved into an authoritarian regime. After Piłsudski's death in 1935, *sanacja* perpetuated itself through his lieutenants—the triumvirate of Ignacy Mościcki as president, Józef Beck as foreign minister, and Edward Rydz-Smigły as commander of the armed forces.

The Polish armed forces were directly affected by the May Coup. Piłsudski pushed rapidly for the re-creation of the military committees he had established before 1923. Adding refinements to the old ideas, he introduced the complex "two-track system" of command and control. His reorganization of the Polish high command brought much-needed stability to the army. Hand in hand with the creation of the new command system, however, came a purge of army officers who had sided with the government during the May Coup. These men were either removed from the military (*zmajowany*, or "Mayed") or not considered for promotions. This reduced the talent pool from which the armed forces could draw and helped to continue political divisions right up to the time of the Nazi invasion of September 1, 1939, which ended Poland's Second Republic.

—*John P. Dunn*

FURTHER READING

Garlicki, Andrej. *Jozef Piłsudski, 1867-1935*. London: Scolar Press, 1995. Important biography of a complex man. Condensed translation from the original Polish.

Jachymek, Jan, and Waldemar Paruch. *More than Independence: Polish Political Thought, 1918-1939*. Lublin, Poland: Marie Curie-Sklodowska University Press, 2003. Useful look at the ideologies, methods,

1926

and goals of the political right, center, and left in inter-war Poland.

Rothschild, Joseph. *Piłsudski's Coup d'État*. New York: Columbia University Press, 1966. One of the best scholarly works on the May Coup in any language.

SEE ALSO: 1917-1920: Ukrainian Nationalists Struggle for Independence; Feb. 24, 1918-Aug. 11, 1920: Baltic States Gain Independence; Mar. 18, 1921: Poland Secures Independence; Mar. 20, 1921: Plebiscite Splits Upper Silesia Between Poland and Germany.

May 20, 1926
AIR COMMERCE ACT CREATES A FEDERAL AIRWAYS SYSTEM

Through the Air Commerce Act of 1926, the U.S. government moved to develop air commerce, giving a mandate to operate and maintain the airways system and related aids to air navigation.

LOCALE: Washington, D.C.
CATEGORIES: Space and aviation; transportation; trade and commerce

KEY FIGURES
Benjamin Franklin (1706-1790), founder of the American postal service
Orville Wright (1871-1948), American aviation pioneer
Dwight D. Eisenhower (1890-1969), president of the United States, 1953-1961

SUMMARY OF EVENT
The U.S. Post Office Department, through its development of an airmail distribution system, was directly responsible for the development of commercial air transportation and, subsequently, the airline industry. Many credit the Post Office Department with being the progenitor of the American commercial air transportation system. Benjamin Franklin, by establishing the postal service at the birth of the nation, recognized the importance of such postal service and communication systems at large. His policy for the postal service focused on its role in assisting and developing all new forms of transportation, which would in turn provide better mail delivery. Early subsidies were paid to stagecoach lines, and the Pony Express was established solely because of the lucrative mail payments given to the contractors involved. Likewise, federal policy provided government assistance to early railroads, including loans for equipment and land grants. Such a policy thrust also involved the Post Office Department in airmail service development.

By 1925, the Post Office Department had conducted airmail service long enough to prove the practicality of

this commercial nonmilitary use of the airplane. Throughout the initial period of the department's support for airmail operations, it was firmly understood that government investment and control would be temporary, with a move by the mid-1920's to involve private industry in airmail operations. Through the involvement of private firms in airmail, attention was given to the growth of the commercial airline industry.

The last direct flight of the Post Office Department operation took place on September 9, 1927. Beginning in June of that year, department pilots were released as newly formed airlines took over various airmail routes. There had been more than forty pilots involved in the postal airmail service and more than six hundred employees in ground jobs. These employees had contributed to the more than twelve million airmail miles flown.

From the beginning of U.S. government airmail service in 1918 until the last flight in 1927, the entire cost totaled $17.5 million, with more than $5 million in airmail postage sold. The balance cannot be counted as a loss, given that it led to the establishment of commercial air transportation and the entirety of the U.S. airline industry. It should instead be counted as an investment.

Civilian air transportation largely began in the United States with the passage of the Air Mail Act, also known as the Kelly Act, on February 2, 1925. The act made possible the awarding of contracts to private contractors for the transport of airmail and, hence, led to the development of private airmail contractors. The act held that the amount of compensation paid to an air carrier would not be more than 80 percent of the revenue derived from the sale of airmail postage for such mail.

In the middle of 1925, the postmaster general advertised for bids on eight airmail routes. Only five routes were immediately awarded, but by the beginning of 1926 twelve contract airmail routes had been awarded. The awards went to entrepreneurs of various backgrounds, many of them pioneers in commercial operations in the United States. The routes all focused on feeder lines branching off into the main transcontinental routes. Bids were accepted on main routes beginning in 1927, and contracts were written for major as well as feeder routes throughout that year.

Subsequent amendments to the Kelly Act abandoned difficult methods of apportioning payments for letters carried and, over time, reduced airmail postage, leading to a substantial increase in airmail traffic. The young airlines, entrepreneurs, and inventors involved in airline service benefited through the adjustments and the growth in the market, which led to substantial progress in the establishment of commercial aviation.

Although the Kelly Act and Post Office Department policy provided that airlines could carry airmail, it became clear that airlines were not financially stable or large enough to provide for the maintenance and operation of the airways system organized for the postal service's operation. Therefore, the U.S. Congress passed another major piece of legislation known as the Air Commerce Act of 1926, the purpose of which was to promote air commerce. The law charged the federal government with the development, operation, and maintenance of the airways system and all aids to air navigation. It also charged the federal government with providing safety in air commerce generally through a system of regulation. Air transportation presented new and serious safety issues for the federal government to consider. Unlike many forms of surface transportation, it involved such speed and distance from the surface of the earth that it pointed to potentially hazardous safety situations. Any failures in maintenance, construction, or operation could lead to serious problems of efficiency and safety. The initiative of the 1926 act gave rise also to a complex, continuing structure of safety regulation.

The 1926 act was unlike other legislation dealing with airmail, leaving no hesitancy or reluctance in the belief that the federal government was strongly in the picture of growth and development of aviation by way of its aid and encouragement. The function of safety regulation was to be carried out by the Department of Commerce, and that agency established a department of air commerce. Among the earliest safety regulations provided were requirements of registration and licensing of aircraft and the certification and medical examination of pilots. Civil penalties were allowed in the enforcement of these regulations. This structure was the foundation of what later became the Civil Aeronautics Administration (in 1940) and still later the Federal Aviation Administration (in 1966), when the new Department of Transportation was established and the FAA moved to it from the Depart-

ment of Commerce. The Air Commerce Act of 1926, along with the Kelly Act, provided a firm foundation for the development of civilian air transportation in the United States.

SIGNIFICANCE

The Air Commerce Act of 1926 had several impacts. First, it reinforced the movement of aviation into the civilian or private sector, beginning with the handling of airmail operations. Second, it brought the firm recognition of a new and different role for the government by virtue of government provision of support for infrastructure development and operating assistance in that industry. From the act grew considerable investment in the development of a usable and progressive air traffic control system (largely federally funded and developed), considerable investment in airport expansion and maintenance, and subsidies for airlines. Finally, it established the precursors of regulation in the industry by focusing federal attention on safety mandates for craft and pilots.

The act of 1926 can be viewed as a foundation of government promotion of industry. In its reaction to transportation systems, government normally gives attention to regulation and promotion. Regulation targets itself to monitoring the safety and economic performance of regulated carriers. Statutes mandate inspections and provide guidelines for the acquisition of operating rights and the provision of published fares or rates. Promotion, on the other hand, recognizes the opportunity and responsibility of government to support the development and maintenance of large-scale transport systems. Government can promote transportation through the provision of infrastructure such as highways, airports, and ocean ports; through regulation that adds stability and limits destructive competition; through the allocation of government business that becomes a solid base of financial support; and through assistance in the areas of both military and nonmilitary research and development, the offshoots of which may be advances in the commercial sector of the industry. The 1926 act established solid directions in these areas.

From the act have grown the intricate system of air traffic control as well as myriad standards for the use of air and ground transportation systems. Just as traffic controls, signals, and patrols govern the operation of surface transport systems, an intricate air transportation control system governs the maintenance of the nation's airways. This system continues to be a marvel in terms of the number and variety of aircraft handled. Despite new threats posed by congestion around major hub cities, the system

1926

continues to perform amazingly well. Such development has fostered the growth of the world's most far-flung and significant air cargo and passenger system. It also has given rise to further interest in the expansion of transportation resources. Orville Wright gave testimony in 1925 before the House of Representatives, arguing that the greatest drawback to the use of aircraft for civilian purposes was the lack of suitable airports. The provision of such airports became a continuing concern of the federal government. Passage of the act of 1926 spurred the development of commercial civil aviation, putting new stress on expanding the outreach of the nation's airways. Such expansion could not be encouraged solely by expanding the revenue base of the airlines, requiring in addition considerable infrastructure improvements. Subsequent acts provided for considerable investment in the development of airports in the continental United States.

The country continues to enjoy the availability of one of the world's finest airport and air traffic control systems. Prior to 1946, airports were operated by state, county, or municipal governments, and because of this, development of the system was slow. The Federal Airport Act of 1946 brought about a comprehensive national system of airports, administered by the Civil Aeronautics Administration. Congress appropriated $520 million over a seven-year period to aid in the development of airport systems. During the administration of President Dwight D. Eisenhower, the act was extended and expanded to encompass operational facilities such as runways as well as public buildings or terminals related to the operational facilities. The administration of funds gave rise to the development of a national airport plan and to extensive local and regional planning in airport design. Funds devoted to the program continued to be expanded throughout the 1950's and 1960's, leading to massive construction of airport facilities. The Airport and Airway Development Act passed in 1970 furthered the development of related facilities for airports. It further enhanced the move, as well, to national planning for airports. In the same time frame, various devices were instituted by way of taxes and charges to ensure that users and beneficiaries of the airport system paid, at least in part, for governmental investment in development and maintenance of the system.

The regulatory activities initiated by the act of 1926 gave rise in 1966 to the work of the Federal Aviation Administration in evaluating the equipment operating characteristics and the personnel involved in commercial aviation. Considerable concern was focused on the safe operation of the transportation system and on participants in such operation. The FAA continued to be actively involved in safety issues in the field. Although the agency expanded and altered certain of its techniques and structures, it maintained concern for adequate testing and certification of operators and for construction and operating standards for the nation's airways. The FAA underwent several reorganizations over the decades, culminating in the formation by Congress, after the terrorist attacks on New York City and Washington, D.C., on September 11, 2001, of the Transportation Security Administration, which succeeded the FAA as the principal body responsible for civil aviation security, although the FAA continued to function in all its other capacities.

The Air Commerce Act of 1926 recognized the essential movement of air carrier operations from a government-sponsored airmail focus to general passenger and freight, at first built around airmail contracts. With the act came incentives for the expansion of the nation's commercial aviation system. The system saw heavy military use in World War II, following which domestic airways were freed for considerable expansion. Airways came to pose a considerable threat to surface forms of passenger and freight transportation. By 1950, the airlines were a permanent fixture and the carrier of choice in a number of long-haul markets. This role continued to grow. Expansion of air transport would likely not have occurred at such speed or depth in the absence of government provision of infrastructure development as called for in the Air Commerce Act of 1926.

—Theodore O. Wallin

FURTHER READING

Davis, Grant M. *Transportation Regulation: A Pragmatic Assessment.* Danville, Ill.: Interstate Printers & Publishers, 1976. Examines the U.S. government's efforts to regulate various transportation industries.

Dilger, Robert Jay. *American Transportation Policy.* New York: Praeger, 2002. Examines the development of transportation policy in the United States since the nation's founding, including regulation of the civilian air transport system. Features bibliography and index.

Fair, Marvin L., and John Guandolo. *Transportation Regulation.* 8th ed. Dubuque, Iowa: William C. Brown, 1979. Comprehensive basic text on transportation regulation provides some details on the state of transportation in the early twentieth century.

Harper, Donald V. *Transportation in America: Users, Carriers, Government.* 2d ed. Englewood Cliffs, N.J.:

Prentice-Hall, 1982. Discusses provision of transportation services and markets for those services, along with government regulation of transportation markets.

Hazard, John L. *Transportation: Management, Economics, Policy.* Cambridge, Md.: Cornell Maritime Press, 1977. Discusses the foundations of the economics of transportation and provides references to a whole panorama of regulatory actions in this area.

Kane, Robert M., and Allan D. Vose. *Air Transportation.* 14th ed. Dubuque, Iowa: Kendall/Hunt, 2002. Comprehensive coverage of the history of air transportation and its regulation. A good reference for readers interested in the development of the aviation industry.

Locklin, D. Philip. *Economics of Transportation.* 7th ed.

Homewood, Ill.: Richard D. Irwin, 1972. Introductory textbook provides background on the regulation of air transportation.

SEE ALSO: July 25, 1909: First Airplane Flight Across the English Channel; Sept. 8, 1920: U.S. Post Office Begins Transcontinental Airmail Delivery; Nov. 20, 1920: Formation of Qantas Airlines; 1924-1976: Howard Hughes Builds a Business Empire; Feb. 2, 1925: U.S. Congress Authorizes Private Carriers for Airmail; May 20, 1927: Lindbergh Makes the First Nonstop Transatlantic Flight; June 25, 1936: The DC-3 Opens a New Era of Air Travel; June 30, 1940: Congress Centralizes Regulation of U.S. Commercial Air Traffic.

1926

May 20, 1926
RAILWAY LABOR ACT PROVIDES FOR MEDIATION OF LABOR DISPUTES

The 1926 Railway Labor Act set up mechanisms for mediating labor disputes acceptable both to organized labor and to the railroad companies, in the process guaranteeing the right to collective bargaining for workers.

LOCALE: Washington, D.C.

CATEGORIES: Business and labor; laws, acts, and legal history

KEY FIGURES

Calvin Coolidge (1872-1933), president of the United States, 1923-1929

Harry M. Daugherty (1860-1941), U.S. attorney general, 1921-1924

Warren G. Harding (1865-1923), president of the United States, 1921-1923

Herbert Hoover (1874-1964), U.S. secretary of commerce, 1921-1929

Donald Randall Richberg (1881-1960), American attorney

SUMMARY OF EVENT

The 1926 Railway Labor Act brought peace to an industry plagued by strikes and violence. It created machinery acceptable to the railroad carriers and labor to mediate their disputes while guaranteeing labor's long-sought goal of collective bargaining. The carriers submitted to these terms in exchange for excluding specific bargaining agents (unions) for labor from the act. This enabled the railroads to maintain their company unions, despite the intent of the act.

The origins of the Railway Labor Act lie in a fiercely contested strike in 1922. That action stemmed from wage cuts ordered by the Railroad Labor Board (RLB), an agency charged by the 1920 Transportation Act with monitoring and regulating wages and rates in the railroad industry. Staffed by appointees of President Warren G. Harding, who held strong antilabor views, the RLB rescinded wage increases granted in 1920. This action hit hardest the shopcraft and other workers not directly included in operating the railroads. At the same time, the RLB tolerated the Pennsylvania Railroad's defiance of the RLB's orders that carriers restore union contracts that they had unilaterally abrogated and that the carriers also dismantle recently established company unions. Fearing for their long-term survival, the shopcraft and nonoperating unions struck the railroad carriers on July 1, 1922, primarily over the issues of wages and hours. Hurt least by the reductions and conciliated by the RLB's promise of no further wage cuts, the operating employees remained on the job.

Soon the strike took a new turn, as the carriers demanded an end to seniority rights, the very heart of union strength. In order to sustain operations, the companies recruited scores of strikebreakers to fill the positions held by striking workers. By eliminating seniority, the carriers eased their task of rehiring strikers and, as the unions asserted, created a massive surplus of railroad workers.

By this measure, the railroad companies had raised the stakes from mere wages to union survival. The unions complained bitterly about the RLB's decision to urge the carriers to try to break the strike and to allow the companies to broach the seniority issue.

Working behind the scenes, Secretary of Commerce Herbert Hoover proved unable to persuade the carriers to negotiate. The refusal angered Harding. By the fall of 1922, Harding had reversed his earlier stand. Frustrated by the unions' continued rejection of the RLB demands for wage cuts, the president placed the blame for the prolonged strike squarely on the shoulders of organized labor. By the late summer, he had embraced Attorney General Harry M. Daugherty's position of the strike's illegality and agreed that only drastic action could prevent the country's transportation system from grinding to a halt. With presidential backing, Daugherty used a sweeping injunction to end the strike action, forcing compliance with the RLB wage cuts. The injunction, issued by Judge James Wilkerson of the District Court of Chicago on September 1, 1922, exceeded past judicial orders by prohibiting picketing and even minimal communications among the strikers and their supporters. The measure outraged many moderate Republicans such as Hoover, who had advocated a cooperative rather than confrontational solution to the strike.

Faced with a hostile government and determined carriers, the unions had no choice but to return to work. Most unions followed the Baltimore & Ohio plan suggested by Hoover ally Daniel Willard, president of that railroad. The plan entailed negotiating with the companies on a separate basis in exchange for salvaging their seniority rights.

In the wake of this massive confrontation, union members and moderate Republicans agreed that the industry needed a new mechanism to cope with grievances and disputes. The Special Committee Representing Railroad Labor Organizations prepared an initial report that outlined labor's objectives in its relationships with the carriers. Union representatives turned this document over to Donald Randall Richberg, who had earned a reputation as the leading labor attorney for his work in the 1922 strike. Charged with resolving the problems inherent in the carrier-union relationship, Richberg integrated these recommendations into his proposed legislation aimed at establishing new negotiating procedures.

Richberg's early drafts inevitably sparked controversy. The original proposal, known as the Howell-Barkley Bill, contained a provision that the carriers found particularly objectionable. It designated sixteen railroad labor organizations as specific bargaining agents for the rail employees. Acceptance of this condition would acknowledge carrier recognition of the unions, a position the railroad companies fiercely resisted. The two parties worked out a compromise, which President Calvin Coolidge signed on May 20, 1926.

The final version of the act disbanded the RLB and substituted new procedures for settling disputes. As a first step, these included conferences between the two parties to iron out differences on wages, hours, and other items in the contract. If the parties remained deadlocked, an adjustment board, which would handle disputes over interpretation of the terms of a contract, assumed jurisdiction. The act was vague as to whether a national board (favoring the unions) or a systemwide board (implicitly allowing for company unions) would hear the grievances. The carriers seized on the ambiguity of the act to maintain their employee representation schemes and bring grievances to systemwide boards. As late as 1933, 147 of the 233 largest carriers still maintained company unions that predated the 1926 law. The law included neither the means to enforce decisions nor the power to inflict penalties on guilty parties, therefore emboldening the railroad carriers. The weaker shopcraft and nonoperating workers proved most vulnerable to the company union strategy.

The National Mediation Board was to intervene in disputes involving changes in a contract. The act required either party to provide a thirty-day prior notice before such changes went into effect. Once that period elapsed, the board would step in to negotiate a settlement. Arbitration stood as the absolute last choice of the board and occurred only if both parties agreed. If the mediation board perceived that the dispute endangered the transportation system, it could so inform the president, who could appoint an emergency board to deal with the crisis. The emergency board lacked enforcement power. The National Mediation Board's course of moderation and accommodation contrasted sharply with the aggressive and hostile character of the RLB.

The Railway Labor Act of 1926 established industrial peace throughout the railroad industry and acted as a model for other industries seeking accommodation between company owners and union advocates. Its recognition of collective bargaining as an employee right opened alternatives for workers throughout the economy who had no access to any form of bargaining procedure.

SIGNIFICANCE

The 1926 Railway Labor Act marked an important turning point in organized labor's drive for recognition and the right to collective bargaining. It drew on earlier legislation such as the Erdman and Newlands Acts and played a critical role in the formulation of the 1933 Bankruptcy Act, the 1934 amendments to the Railway Labor Act, and the 1935 Wagner Act.

The Erdman Act of 1898 attempted to restore equality to the bargaining process between the railroad carriers and organized labor. The act applied only to operating employees—specifically, engineers, firemen, conductors, and trainmen—yet it moved toward establishing mediation procedures that dealt fairly with unions. It banned the "yellow-dog contract," which threatened workers engaged in union activity with dismissal. The act also outlawed blacklisting, which permanently barred union supporters from employment through a system of files that carriers maintained on dissidents. A court test struck down these last two provisions. The 1913 Newlands Act sought to keep alive the negotiation process by setting up the U.S. Board of Mediation and Conciliation, which again dealt only with the operating workers.

World War I created an atmosphere more favorable to union demands. The urgency of continued production, the need for industrial peace, and the government's desire to placate unions sparked administrative and legislative decisions that favored organized labor. Even before the declaration of war, the railroad unions had won the eight-hour day with the passage of the Adamson Act in 1916. During the conflict, the federal government assumed control of the nation's rail system. The government promoted standard wages and hours, long favored by the rail unions, and ensured that union members remained free of discriminatory practices by the carriers.

The unions found federal control far more in tune with their interests than was private ownership. The end of the war and the specter of company interests reclaiming control worried the unions. Quickly, their representatives brought forth the Plumb Plan, which outlined a scenario in which the unions, the bondholders, and the shippers exercised administrative control of the industry. Organized labor clearly wished to hold on to the gains made during the war and to sustain what the workers perceived as favorable conditions.

The war's end proved disappointing to organized labor. Collective bargaining faced a sustained assault by carriers. Railroads pushed for open shops, in which workers did not have to belong to unions, and workers saw a resurgence of yellow-dog contracts. The passage of the Railway Labor Act transformed the hostile environment that menaced the very existence of unions. The act salvaged the union goals first articulated in the

Erdman Act and pursued through World War I. It revived collective bargaining and ended yellow-dog contracts in the rail industry while guaranteeing the long-term survival of unions. Its success provided a model that greatly influenced subsequent legislation regarding labor relations through the mid-1930's and acted as a beacon for pro-union forces in the economy.

The revision of the 1890 Bankruptcy Law in June of 1933 demonstrated the continued influence of the Railway Labor Act. The Great Depression forced many railroads to the brink of ruin. Bankruptcy offered one alternative for troubled companies. It also opened the possibility of companies' suspension of all union contracts. To prevent such an action, the unions insisted on amendments that enabled the terms of the Railway Labor Act to prevail despite economic contingencies and secured the right to self-organization free from carrier intrusion. The Emergency Railroad Transportation Act of 1933, with a one-year life, reiterated these provisions. Designed to promote efficiencies and reduce waste in the industry, that act ensured that no workers would lose their jobs as a result of measures enacted under this law.

In 1934, the unions sought permanent legislation to create a more stable workplace. Specifically, they intended to change the conditions that allowed company unions to persist in more than half the carriers. The 1934 amendments to the Railway Labor Act guaranteed employees the right to organize independent of carrier influence. The act also established the National Board of Adjustment, which acknowledged the unions as bargaining agents for the workers and created a new board of national mediation. The act gave the president the power to appoint members to this board, subject to congressional confirmation. The mediation board also exercised the authority to certify representatives from either side, a measure that preserved the autonomy of the unions. Equally as important, workers had the right to select their representatives through secret ballots, which isolated them from company pressures.

The success of the rail workers was illustrated most prominently in the formulation of the Wagner Act of 1935, which was the culmination of a drive for collective bargaining throughout the economy. Already the National Industrial Recovery Act (NIRA) had incorporated boards of mediation and arbitration that had assumed a central role in the rail industry. Donald Richberg, who oversaw the writing of the Railway Labor Act, also participated in the preparation of the NIRA, so it is not surprising that there are similarities between the 1926 measure and the NIRA.

1926

The Wagner Act, or National Labor Relations Act, replaced the NIRA, which was found to be unconstitutional. It repeated many of the staples of the Railway Labor Act and its 1934 revisions. Company unions and yellow-dog contracts fell by the wayside, and the law recognized the right of workers to organize, free of company interference, throughout all industries. Collective bargaining assumed a central role in labor-company relations. The Wagner Act, unlike the Railway Labor Act, acknowledged closed shops, in which workers had to belong to the union before beginning work, but these were subsequently outlawed in the Taft-Hartley Act of 1947. By the mid-1930's, the unions had achieved their long-sought autonomy.

—Edward J. Davies II

FURTHER READING

Babson, Steve. *The Unfinished Struggle: Turning Points in American Labor, 1877-Present.* Lanham, Md.: Rowman & Littlefield, 1999. Concise and comprehensive history of the American labor movement. Includes notes and index.

Bernstein, Irving. *The Lean Years: A History of the American Worker, 1920-1933.* 1960. Reprint. New York: Da Capo Press, 1983. One of the most thorough accounts of labor's activities in the 1920's and early 1930's. Provides a complete account of the railway union-carrier relationship and explains the positions of the participants in the 1926 legislation. Contains one of the best and most detailed descriptions available of the various parts of the Railway Labor Act.

_____. *Turbulent Years: A History of the American Worker, 1933-1941.* Boston: Houghton Mifflin, 1970. Chapters 5 and 7 discuss the amendments to the Railway Labor Act and the Wagner Act, pinpointing the influence of the original legislation in the formulation of national labor policy. One of the most thorough accounts available on the labor-company debates of the 1930's.

Breen, W. J. *Labor Market Politics and the Great War: The Department of Labor, the States, and the First U.S. Employment Service, 1907-1933.* Kent, Ohio: Kent State University Press, 1997. History of the federal government's involvement in labor issues through the critical period from before World War I through the early years of the Great Depression. Includes lengthy bibliography and index.

Fleming, R. W. "The Significance of the Wagner Act." In *Labor and the New Deal*, edited by Milton Derber and Edwin Young. New York: Da Capo Press, 1972. Provides a concise description of the various influences on preparation of the NIRA and the Wagner Act. Serves as a useful introduction to the debates of the era.

Foner, Philip S. *On the Eve of America's Entrance into World War I, 1915-1916.* Vol. 6 in *History of the Labor Movement in the United States.* New York: International Publishers, 1982. Provides a systematic description of labor conditions in the United States just prior to the nation's participation in World War I. Includes a succinct description of the legislative history of labor relations in the rail industry from the Erdman Act of 1898 through the Adamson Act of 1916.

Jacoby, Daniel. *Laboring for Freedom: A New Look at the History of Labor in America.* Armonk, N.Y.: M. E. Sharpe, 1998. Examines opposed ideas concerning freedom as manifested in labor history in the United States. Includes bibliography and index.

Keller, Morton. *Regulating a New Economy: Public and Economic Change in America, 1900-1930.* Cambridge, Mass.: Harvard University Press, 1990. Chapter 3 contains a brief discussion of the development of the federal government's transportation policies from the beginning of the twentieth century through the 1920's. Stresses the complexity of the rail industry, which is subject to multiple influences. Indispensable source for readers seeking to understand the importance of regulation throughout society.

Locklin, D. Philip. *Economics of Transportation.* 3d ed. Chicago: Richard D. Irwin, 1947. Chapter 12 lists all the relevant railroad legislation for the period, outlining each act in a concise fashion and providing a clear guide to its legal history. The description of the Railway Labor Act does not address the ambiguity of the law that enabled carriers to maintain their company unions.

Montgomery, David. *The Fall of the House of Labor: The Workplace, the State, and American Labor Activism, 1865-1925.* New York: Cambridge University Press, 1987. One of the most analytic and detailed descriptions available of labor relations in general. Includes much information on the rail industry, particularly the activities of the operating unions and their role in the debates on national transportation policy both before and after World War I.

Tomlins, Christopher L. *The State and the Unions: Labor Relations, Law, and the Organized Labor Movement in America, 1889-1930.* New York: Cambridge University Press, 1985. Chapter 4 traces the legal origins of collective bargaining, including brief descriptions of legislation in the rail industry.

Vadney, Thomas E. *The Wayward Liberal: A Political Biography of Donald Richberg*. Lexington: University of Kentucky Press, 1970. Chapter 3 explains in detail Richberg's role in the formation of pro-union railroad legislation. Provides a thorough account of Richberg's motivations.

Zieger, Robert H. *Republicans and Labor, 1919-1929*. Lexington: University of Kentucky Press, 1969. Excellent analysis of the influence of the Republican Party in shaping labor's position in its relationship with the carriers. Particularly effective in explaining the reversal of the Republican Party from hostility to-

ward the rail unions under President Harding and Attorney General Daugherty to the cooperative spirit promoted by Herbert Hoover under President Coolidge and embodied in the Railway Labor Act.

SEE ALSO: Feb. 14, 1903: Creation of the U.S. Department of Commerce and Labor; Jan. 27, 1908: U.S. Supreme Court Ruling Allows Yellow-Dog Contracts; Oct. 15, 1914: Labor Unions Win Exemption from Antitrust Laws; Mar. 23, 1932: Norris-La Guardia Act Strengthens Labor Organizations; July 5, 1935: Wagner Act.

1926

July, 1926
EDDINGTON PUBLISHES *THE INTERNAL CONSTITUTION OF THE STARS*

Arthur Stanley Eddington's pioneering contribution to astronomy and astrophysics, set forth in The Internal Constitution of the Stars, *spanned the most important aspects of stellar structure constitution and evolution.*

LOCALE: Cambridge, England
CATEGORIES: Science and technology; astronomy

KEY FIGURES

Arthur Stanley Eddington (1882-1944), English astronomer and physicist
Walter Sydney Adams (1876-1956), an American astronomer
Ralph H. Fowler (1889-1944), English astrophysicist
Francis Gladheim Pease (1881-1938), American astronomer
John August Anderson (1876-1959), American astronomer
Hendrik Anthony Kramers (1894-1952), Dutch physicist
Hans Albrecht Bethe (1906-2005), German American physicist and astrophysicist

SUMMARY OF EVENT

At the beginning of the twentieth century, astrophysical knowledge was at best only rudimentary. The source of stellar energy had not yet been discovered. Although scientists understood the proper motions of the stars—that is, the sum of radial and transverse velocities—William Herschel's assumption of their randomness relative to the Sun had been abandoned by Jacobus Cornelius Kapteyn on the basis of his pioneering study of the subject. At this stage, Karl Schwarzschild attempted to rep-

resent the radial velocity vectors of the stars as forming an ellipsoid. Kapteyn, however, noted that they formed, instead, a double-lobed curve.

In 1906, Sir Arthur Stanley Eddington, investigating proper motions of stars, was able to isolate two star streams, or drifts. He confirmed the above-mentioned facts through a statistical analysis of the proper motion data. During these early years, Eddington studied problems associated with the distribution of stars of different spectral class, planetary nebulas, open clusters, and the dynamics of globular clusters.

Eddington's pioneering work in astrophysics began in 1916. A decade earlier, Ralph Allen Sampson had pointed out the importance of radiation pressure in the physics of stars, and Schwarzschild later developed a theory of radiative equilibrium for the stellar atmospheres. Eddington, realizing the important role the radiation pressure played in maintaining the equilibrium in massive stars, extended Schwarzschild's theory all the way to the stellar core. Utilizing Robert Emden's differential equation for a polytropic sphere with index $n = 3$, assuming that the materials of a giant star behave like a perfect gas, and accounting for gravitational force, gas pressure, and radiation pressure, he developed the well-known equation of radiative equilibrium. Known as Eddington's model of a star, it was found to be applicable to white dwarfs as well.

It was known that matter inside a star would be highly ionized because of extreme temperature. Incorporating this fact into his theory of stellar equilibrium, Eddington showed that high ionization reduced the molecular weight of a gas by two for all elements except hydrogen.

Radiation pressure was found to increase rapidly with rising stellar mass, resulting in instabilities; hence Eddington concluded that the number of stars in excess of ten solar masses would be rare.

The derivation of mass-luminosity relation of a star requires knowledge of fundamental processes contributing to stellar opacity. After the photoelectric absorption process, regarded as dominant, met with criticism, Eddington, employing Hendrik Anthony Kramers's theory of absorption coefficients and introducing his so-called guillotine factor, obtained the important mass-luminosity relationship. Moreover, having realized that electron scattering is the major source of stellar opacity, he was able to derive an upper limit to luminosity for a given mass—"Eddington's limit"—which plays an important role in the investigation of X-ray sources and accretion discs around black holes. Based on the fact that the observed luminosity data fit well with his theoretical computation, Eddington concluded that both giant and dwarf stars were gaseous, even though the latter had exceedingly high density.

Eddington's computation on the basis of his theory of stellar constitution of angular diameters of several giant stars—including Betelgeuse, Antares, and Aldebaran—was confirmed observationally by Francis Gladheim Pease and John August Anderson at Mount Wilson Observatory in California. Applying his theory to the dwarf star Sirius B, Eddington noted to his astonishment that the mass density of the star was 50 million kilograms (approximately 55,116 tons) per cubic meter. He realized that such a dense star should exhibit measurable gravitational redshift in accordance with Einstein's relativity theory, and he had Walter Sydney Adams at Mount Wilson successfully verify this effect. Having established the diameter of Sirius B to be 38 million meters (about 23,612 miles), comparable to that of Earth, Eddington found its density to be 53 million kilograms (58,422 tons) per cubic meter. Ralph H. Fowler, employing Erwin Schrödinger's wave mechanics, formulated the theory of degenerate dense matter found in stars such as Sirius B.

A problem of great complexity that resulted in Eddington's interest in the internal constitution of stars and occupied his attention for a long time is associated with the Cepheid variable. Luminosities of these bright F and G stars vary with a periodicity ranging from a day to several weeks. After generalizing Johann Wilhelm Ritter's analysis of the adiabatic pulsation of a gaseous star in convective equilibrium to the case of a star in radiative equilibrium, Eddington was able to combine the result with the mass-luminosity formulism, so as generally to obtain period-luminosity relations of Cepheids. Although these earlier attempts did not agree with correct phase relations among the observed variables such as brightness and temperature, Eddington realized that one had to examine the problem of energy transfer more thoroughly and returned to it several times. He was able to establish that the longer the periodicity of a star, the lower its surface temperature. With his pulsation theory, Eddington laid the foundation for future work on the Cepheids.

In addition to covering his research for a time span of ten years, beginning in 1916, Eddington's *The Internal Constitution of the Stars* also contains chapters devoted to stellar surface, chromosphere, atmosphere, and abundance of elements. His speculative prediction about the source of stellar energy appears in one of his papers. Twenty years later, Hans Albrecht Bethe showed that within the dense, hot core of a star, four protons would combine to form a helium atom via the carbon-nitrogen-carbon cycle so that a small fraction of the mass would be converted into radiant energy. This is one of the possible sources of stellar energy. Eddington was keenly aware that the source of the star's energy must be deep within the core.

While involved with the major projects, Eddington investigated the problem of cosmic abundance of hydrogen and the central temperature and density of stars. His theory of absorption lines of stellar atmosphere made it possible to interpret many observed spectral line intensities. His theory concerning the temperature, density, and composition of interstellar matter and its emission and absorption properties of light provided an independent rough measurement of distances.

SIGNIFICANCE

Eddington wrote more than 150 scientific articles and more than a dozen books. His profound knowledge of mathematics, deep intuitive insight into natural problems, and unrelenting drive enabled him to delve into a wide range of topics. His pioneering contributions to astronomy and astrophysics are distilled in his classic masterpiece *The Internal Constitution of the Stars*. It would not be an overstatement to say that the publication of his work opened up a new and exciting vista of astronomy and astrophysics. Even while Eddington's research work was being published, the stimulus it provided was evident from the immediate and long-lived controversy it generated among leading researchers in the field of astrophysics, such as James Hopwood Jeans and Edward Arthur Milne.

The publication of *The Internal Constitution of the*

Stars established Eddington firmly as the founder of modern theoretical astrophysics and provided pathways to the study of structure, constitution, and evolution of stars. Several aspects of investigations of stellar structure—pioneered by Eddington and treated in his book—were pursued by others, leading to successful conclusions. Eddington's search for a theory to explain the periodicity of Cepheid variables, one of his earliest research interests, occupied him for a substantial period of his life. The problem of the Cepheids was ultimately solved by Martin Schwarzschild, Paul Ledoux, and Robert Frederick Christy. His speculations and predictions in regard to stellar energy turned out to be an important initial step, leading Bethe and others to elegant solutions. Eddington's study of the effects of reflection in binaries for determining their masses served later as a prototype solution to problems of diffuse reflection and transmission of light.

Eddington's investigation of interstellar absorption of lines led to dual results: determination of relative abundance of elements by the method of the "curve of growth," developed by Albrecht Otto, Johannes Unsold, and Marcel Gilles Minnaert, as well as prediction of radial velocities and, hence, approximation of distances, confirmed by Otto Struve and John Stanley Plaskett. Eddington's deduction of the size and ultrahigh density of dwarf stars, followed by Fowler's theory of degenerate matter, later led Subrahmanyan Chandrasekhar to deduce an upper limit to masses of such stars, which is known as the Chandrasekhar limit. Eddington's contributions to astrophysics thus spanned the most important aspects of stellar structure. As Milne noted in 1945, Eddington "brought it all to life, infusing it with his sense of real physics and endowing it with aspects of splendid beauty. . . . Eddington will always be our incomparable pioneer."

— *V. L. Madhyastha*

FURTHER READING

Chandrasekhar, Subrahmanyan. *Eddington: The Most Distinguished Astrophysicist of His Time*. Cambridge, England: Cambridge University Press, 1983. Presents two Sir Arthur Stanley Eddington Centenary Lectures delivered by Chandrasekhar at Trinity College, the University of Cambridge, in late 1982. Valuable source offers a cameo view of the life and achievements of Eddington by a great astrophysicist of modern times.

Douglas, A. Vibert. *The Life of Arthur Stanley Eddington*. London: Thomas Nelson & Sons, 1957. This biography includes a complete list of Eddington's scientific papers and books, in addition to a genealogical table. The volume reads like a novel and is comprehensive in every respect, embodying all aspects of Eddington's life and scientific achievements. The text may serve even as an excellent primer for stellar structure, relativity, and the philosophy of science.

Eddington, Arthur Stanley. *The Internal Constitution of the Stars*. 1926. Reprint. Mineola, N.Y.: Dover, 1959. Eddington's celebrated work is written in a style accessible to general readers. Many of the arguments presented are easy to understand; readers with some college-level background in astronomy should be able to absorb the work in its entirety. Includes references.

_____. *Stellar Movements and the Structure of the Universe*. London: Macmillan, 1914. Presents Eddington's statistical analysis of data on the proper motion of stars, distribution of stars based on their spectral class, planetary nebulas, and star clusters, published in about fifteen papers, in addition to the cosmological knowledge of the period. Aimed at general readers of scientific literature. Provides a background for understanding Eddington's later work on stellar structure.

Miller, Arthur I. *Empire of the Stars: Obsession, Friendship, and Betrayal in the Quest for Black Holes*. Boston: Houghton Mifflin, 2005. Provides background on the history of the idea of black holes and describes the debate between Chandrasekhar and Eddington concerning the nature of black holes as well as the implications of that debate for twentieth century science.

Motz, Lloyd, and Jefferson Hane Weaver. *The Story of Astronomy*. New York: Plenum, 1995. Presents the history of astronomy from ancient times to the end of the twentieth century. Chapter 15 discusses Eddington's work in the context of the beginnings of astrophysics. Includes bibliography and index.

Struve, Otto, and Velta Zebergs. *Astronomy of the Twentieth Century*. New York: Macmillan, 1962. Excellent survey for the general reader includes discussion of stellar properties and mass determination for binary stars. Features drawings, black-and-white photographs, and diagrams as well as glossary and bibliography.

SEE ALSO: Nov. 6, 1919: Einstein's Theory of Gravitation Is Confirmed over Newton's Theory; Dec. 13, 1920: Michelson Measures the Diameter of a Star; Mar., 1924: Eddington Formulates the Mass-Luminosity Law for Stars.

July 18, 1926
TREATY OF ANKARA

The contentious Mosul question involved the issue of whether the oil-rich region of northern Iraq should return to Turkish sovereignty or be transferred permanently to British-mandated Iraq after World War I.

LOCALE: Mosul, Iraq; Ankara, Turkey
CATEGORIES: Diplomacy and international relations; expansion and land acquisition

KEY FIGURES

Tevfik Rüştü Aras (1883-1972), Turkish foreign minister, 1925-1937, ambassador to Great Britain, 1939-1942, and Turkish representative to the United Nations Palestine Conciliation Commission, 1950-1952

Maḥmūd Barzanjī (1881-1956), alternately British-appointed governor of Mosul and self-proclaimed king of Kurdistan

Sir Percy Zachariah Cox (1864-1937), British high commissioner in Iraq, 1920-1923, and British plenipotentiary for negotiating the Turkish-Iraqi border in 1924

Sir Ronald Charles Lindsay (1877-1945), Britain's ambassador to Turkey

Nūrī al-Saʿīd (1888-1958), acting Iraqi minister of national defense

SUMMARY OF EVENT

Following the victorious Allies' armistice agreement with the defeated Ottoman Empire at Moudros on October 30, 1918, and the stillborn Treaty of Sèvres of August 10, 1920, the amending Treaty of Lausanne of July 24, 1923, with the Turkish Republic failed to set a definitive, internationally agreed-upon border between Turkey and the new, League of Nations-approved, British-mandated territory of Iraq. The latter was created from three former Ottoman provinces in Mesopotamia, including the northern province of Mosul. However, when the Treaty of Lausanne was ratified on August 6, 1924, it left open the possibility of referring the border issue to the League of Nations if Britain and Turkey could not find an amicable settlement to the matter within nine months.

The two parties were unable to agree on the border's placement at Lausanne because the Turkish representatives repeatedly claimed sovereignty over Mosul from 1923 through 1926. They based their claims on geographic, demographic, ethnographic, historic, economic, and other issues, including the alleged political wishes of the province's Turkish and Kurdish speakers, whose numbers and ethnicities could not be accurately determined. The Turks demanded that the border (and thus the sovereignty) issue be settled by plebiscite among the approximately 700,000 inhabitants of the province, who were anchored primarily around the cities of Mosul, Kirkuk, Arbīl, and as-Sulaymānīyah and the surrounding countryside. For its part, Britain claimed priority for the right of conquest, which the Turks characterized as an outdated principle of international law and mandatory power that they refused to recognize.

Following an inconclusive conference in Constantinople in May of 1924, an armed clash between the two confronting armies in Mosul became a real possibility. The British submitted the issue to the Council of the League of Nations in September of 1924, and the League established a commission of inquiry composed of Af de Wirsén of Sweden (a neutral country), the committee's chairman; Count Paul Teleki of Hungary, previously aligned with the Central Powers and the Ottoman Empire; and Colonel A. Paulis of Belgium (an Allied country). After visiting London and Ankara, the commission went to Baghdad and Mosul, where members conducted numerous interviews and surveys. The three-member commission then presented its report to the League of Nations.

Although the report was ambiguous in many respects—it often wavered between favoring Turkish sovereignty and favoring British sovereignty—the Commission finally awarded control to British-mandated Iraq. Accordingly, the League of Nations Council granted Mosul Province to Iraq on October 29, 1924. The Turks, however, challenged the binding nature of the League Council's determination of the so-called Brussels line, the provisional border that awarded Mosul to Iraq. In response, the Council sought the advice of the Permanent Court of International Justice, which opined that the award was indeed arbitral rather than mediational or recommendatory so long as the League Council's decision, ignoring the self-interested British and Turkish votes, was unanimous. The League Council thus endorsed the award of Mosul to Iraq on December 16, 1925.

Turkey reluctantly assented to the decision on June 5, 1926, through the Treaty of Ankara, which was ratified on July 18, 1926. As a sop to Turkish nationalist sensitivities, the British-advised Iraqi government committed itself to paying Turkey 10 percent of all royalties from the Turkish Petroleum Company (which had obtained the conces-

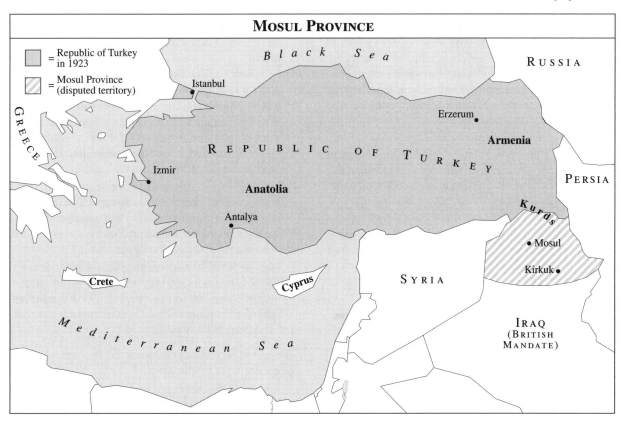

MOSUL PROVINCE

= Republic of Turkey in 1923

= Mosul Province (disputed territory)

Black Sea

RUSSIA

Istanbul

Erzerum

Armenia

R E P U B L I C   O F   T U R K E Y

Izmir

Anatolia

PERSIA

Antalya

Kurds

Mosul

Kirkuk

SYRIA

Crete

Cyprus

IRAQ (BRITISH MANDATE)

M e d i t e r r a n e a n   S e a

1926

sion for all oil operations in Mosul on March 14, 1925) for a period of twenty-five years. On that basis, Turkey eventually collected 3,685,536 Iraqi dinars between 1931 and 1951, when the provision expired. Meanwhile, as the Turkish-British dispute was unfolding, a heated rivalry grew among various Kurdish tribal leaders for ascendancy and power. These Kurds came to oppose the British presence, and one of them, Sheikh Maḥmūd Barzanjī, alternated between supporting the British and opposing them after declaring himself king of Kurdistan.

The reluctant Turks accepted the League Council's decision without engaging in battle for several reasons. First, the new Turkish Republic wished to consolidate its internal power after termination of the Ottoman sultanate and caliphate. Second, the Turks were weary following their bloody 1919-1923 war with Greece, in which the Greeks invaded Anatolia in the hope of collecting the reward promised to them by the Allies during World War I. At the time, there was uncertainty about promised Soviet aid to Turkey. Finally, and perhaps most important, Turkish diplomats such as Foreign Minister Tevfik Rüştü Aras realized that the balance of power in the League Council lay with the victorious Allied members,

who were broadly represented, in contrast to the defeated ones (such as Turkey), who were not.

The British, encouraged by Sir Percy Zachariah Cox, a senior British negotiator, were not about to give up their controlling interest in much of the oil discovered in Mosul. Accordingly, when the Treaty of Ankara was signed by Sir Ronald Charles Lindsay, Britain's ambassador to Turkey; Colonel Nūrī al-Saʿīd, acting Iraqi minister of national defense; and Tevfik Rüştü Aras, the signatories confirmed the border adopted by the League of Nations at its session of October 29, 1924—the Brussels line—with minor modifications to be recommended by a boundary commission to be established soon after the treaty's signature.

SIGNIFICANCE

Long after the "definitive" settlement of the Mosul question by the Treaty of Ankara of June 5, 1926, the delineation of Mosul's border with Turkey—like Iraq's other artificial borders, which were remnants of its colonial rule—continued to cause conflict. The League's neglect of Kurdish aspirations to national self-determination (which the Kurds had expected to achieve under U.S.

president Woodrow Wilson's Fourteen Points) resurfaced after the first Persian Gulf War in 1991.

Kurds in Mosul, who lived in semiautonomy after the defeat of Iraqi president Saddam Hussein's central government in 1991, started to infiltrate the porous Turkish border to support their Kurdish brethren's insurgency against the Ankara government. Some thirty-five thousand Turkish troops crossed into northern Iraq in hot pursuit of the Kurdish fighters of the militant Kurdish Workers Party—the PKK—in May of 1995. On that occasion, Turkish president Süleyman Demirel and some of the media suggested that the border between the two countries should be redrawn. While the subsequent outcry muted those demands, the Kurds in Iraq, fearing strong Turkish opposition to the creation of an independent Kurdistan in Mosul, started to consider the possibility of a Kurdish-Turkish federation. Possibilities for this type of federation increased as some Kurds questioned whether they could find a niche within the new Iraqi regime after the ouster of Saddam Hussein in 2003. Under this scenario, Mosul would revert to Turkey, giving the Turks a strong bargaining chip—namely, non-Arab Mosul oil—in seeking admission into the European Union.

—*Peter B. Heller*

FURTHER READING

Hurewitz, J. C., ed. *The Middle East and North Africa in World Politics: A Documentary Record*. 2d ed. Vol. 2. New Haven, Conn.: Yale University Press, 1979. Includes the texts of the Treaty of Lausanne of 1923 and the Treaty of Ankara of 1926. Contains introductory blurbs.

Pipes, Daniel. "Hot Spot: Turkey, Iraq, and Mosul." *Middle East Quarterly* 2, no. 3 (September, 1995): 65-68. Highlights how the contentious post-World War I delineation of the northern Iraqi border with Turkey had repercussions following Operation Desert Storm in 1991 and the loosening of Baghdad's control over the Kurds.

Polk, William R. *Understanding Iraq*. New York: HarperCollins, 2005. In his sweep of Iraqi history, this former American official and scholar evidences the ill-advised, imperialistically driven post-World War I settlements involving Iraq.

Tripp, Charles. *A History of Iraq*. 2d ed. Cambridge, England: Cambridge University Press, 2002. Of particular interest is the section headed "The Mosul Question: Territory and Oil" in the extensive chapter titled "The British Mandate."

SEE ALSO: July 24, 1908: Young Turks Stage a Coup in the Ottoman Empire; Nov. 5, 1914: British Mount a Second Front Against the Ottomans; Apr. 26, 1920: Great Britain and France Sign the San Remo Agreement; May-Nov., 1920: Great Iraqi Revolt; Dec. 13, 1920: Permanent Court of International Justice Is Established; Aug. 11-13, 1933: Iraqi Army Slaughters Assyrian Christians.

August, 1926-September, 1928
WARNER BROS. INTRODUCES TALKING MOTION PICTURES

Warner Bros. innovated talkies, films with sound, giving rise to the Golden Age of the Hollywood film.

LOCALE: United States
CATEGORIES: Motion pictures; communications and media; entertainment; science and technology; inventions

KEY FIGURES

Harry Warner (1881-1958), American motion-picture executive

Albert Warner (1884-1967), American motion-picture executive

Sam Warner (1887-1927), American motion-picture executive

Jack Warner (1892-1978), American motion-picture executive

SUMMARY OF EVENT

When shown in theaters, silent films were accompanied by live sound, featuring music and sound effects. Five-hundred-seat neighborhood theaters made do with a piano and violin; four-thousand-seat picture palaces in New York and Chicago maintained resident orchestras with more than seventy members. What the silent cinema lacked was prerecorded, synchronized sound. During the late 1920's, the Warner Bros. studio led the American film industry first to motion pictures with sounds recorded on synchronized records and added on the film beside the images.

The ideas that led to the coming of sound were the products of corporate-sponsored research by American Telephone and Telegraph Company (AT&T) and the Radio Corporation of America (RCA). Both improved sound recording and playback to help their design of long-distance telephone equipment and improvement of radio sets. Neither company could or would enter filmmaking, however. It took Warner Bros. to prove to the predecessors of today's Paramount Pictures, Twentieth Century Fox, Metro-Goldwyn-Mayer (MGM), Universal Pictures, and Columbia Pictures that motion pictures with synchronized sound should be made standard in the film industry.

Warner Bros. pioneered sound in motion pictures with a plan formulated by brothers Harry and Sam Warner. In 1924, Warner Bros. (the studio's official spelling, to cut the cost of printing "Brothers") was a prosperous, albeit small, corporation that produced films needing financing. That year, Harry Warner approached the important Wall Street investment banking house of Goldman, Sachs and secured the help he needed. In

1925, Warner Bros. purchased Vitagraph, a pioneer film producer and distributor, an action that doubled the company's production capacity and provided a worldwide network to market its films. Thus, in 1925, before Warner Bros. even considered the new sound technology, astute film industry watchers began to notice the rise of the company.

As part of this initial wave of expansion, Warner Bros. acquired a Los Angeles radio station in order to publicize its films. Through this deal, the four Warner brothers—Harry, Sam, Albert, and Jack—learned of the new technology the radio and telephone industries had developed to record sound. During the spring of 1925, the brothers devised a plan to use the new recording technology to help with their corporate expansion. Warner Bros. could record the most popular musical artists on film and then offer these short films as added attractions

1926

Crowds outside Warners' Theatre in New York for the 1926 opening of Don Juan, *a silent film with recorded synchronized musical accompaniment.* (NARA)

PROMOTING VITAPHONE

The following is an excerpt from an "open letter" signed by Harry Warner that appeared on the front page of the July 24, 1926, issue of the film exhibitors' newsletter Brass Tacks, *published by Warner Bros.:*

A new era in motion picture presentation has arrived. It will thrill and startle the world. The marvelous Vitaphone process, which will have its first public presentation at the Warner Theater on August 6, will revolutionize the industry. It will make it possible for small town theaters to have the same musical accompaniment as that enjoyed in the biggest theaters the world over. Small town exhibitors will become big time showmen. They can rent music and they can rent film. . . .

The greatest artists of the operatic and musical field can be heard in the smallest theaters as well as the largest. Millions of people will be educated to a finer appreciation of the best music that has ever been written by the foremost composers.

Imagine! The wonderful New York Philharmonic Orchestra . . . 107 pieces . . . Henry Hadley, the great musical director, directing. . . . In a small town! The synchronization of music and motion pictures is an established fact, and on August 6 the great invention will be heard by the public. . . .

Spread the great message, and deliver it to the exhibitors of the world!

to theaters that booked its features. (Albert Warner was instrumental in getting Warner Bros. films into theaters.) As a bonus, Warner Bros. could add recorded orchestral music to the studio's feature films and offer it to those theaters that relied on small musical ensembles. Brothers Sam and Jack Warner would handle the actual filmmaking.

The innovation of sound did not come easily for Warner Bros. For example, it contracted for necessary equipment from AT&T. The telephone company would have rather dealt with a more important Hollywood corporation, but Paramount and the other major Hollywood companies of the day did not want to risk their sizable profit positions by junking silent films. The giants of the film industry were doing fine with what they had; they did not want to switch to something that had not been proved.

On August 6, 1926, Warner Bros. premiered its new technology, which it labeled Vitaphone. The first package consisted of a traditional silent film (*Don Juan*) with

a recorded musical accompaniment, plus six recordings of musical talent that were highlighted by the most famous opera tenor of the day, Giovanni Martinelli, doing his specialty from *I Pagliacci*. These recordings were made in New York, before almost all filmmaking moved to Hollywood in 1927.

From the fall of 1926 through the spring of 1927—during the prime moviegoing season in those days, before theaters had air-conditioning—Warner Bros. developed several packages consisting of a silent film with recorded orchestral music plus six shorts of noted musical talent. As this policy evolved, the shorts became more "pop" and less classical. Al Jolson, for example, appeared before the Warner cameras and recorded two of his most famous hits. Warner Bros. concentrated on these so-called vaudeville shorts. By April, 1927, the company had recorded all the popular stars of the day.

Warner Bros. soon ran out of musical stars to record and had to devise something new. The company began to add Vitaphone segments to feature films. The reasoning was that if Jolson did so well in a short subject, a feature film designed and written especially for him would likely be even more successful. The film would be silent as the necessary narrative moved along, but as soon as the Jolson character was required to break into song, the sound technology would be utilized. This strategy, merging the new with the old, was designed to avoid offending dedicated silent filmgoers while attracting new patrons to theaters throughout the United States.

The first such Vitaphone feature was *The Jazz Singer*, which premiered early in the fall of 1927. Over the summer months, Warner Bros. had convinced enough theater owners to install the required sound equipment to make the investment in the part-talkie feature film a financial success. During the summer of 1927, Warner salespersons performed a masterful job of selling skeptical exhibitors on the idea, and the Vitaphone projection equipment began to appear in picture palaces throughout the United States.

The Jazz Singer premiered as scheduled in October, 1927. From the opening it was a hit. (Sadly, Sam Warner did not live to see and hear it; he died shortly before the premiere.) *The Jazz Singer* package (including its accompanying shorts with sound) forced theaters in cities that rarely held films over for more than a single week to ask to have the package stay for two, three, and sometimes four straight weeks. (One week was considered normal in the 1920's; two weeks' duration usually set a house record.)

The Jazz Singer did well at the box office, but it failed

to better records set by such silent film blockbusters as *Four Horsemen of the Apocalypse* (1921), *Ben-Hur* (1925), and *The Big Parade* (1925). Skeptics questioned the staying power of talkies. If sound was so great, they wondered why *The Jazz Singer* did not move to the top of the all-time box-office list. That would come a year later with *The Singing Fool*, also starring Al Jolson. From that film's opening day (September 20, 1928), reviewers from *The New York Times* to the cynics writing for *Variety* tracked the greatest motion-picture hit of its day. *The Singing Fool* cost an estimated $200,000 to make and returned $5 million. By Thanksgiving Day of 1928, the Warner brothers knew that *The Singing Fool* was inexorably climbing to become the new Hollywood box-office champion. In New York City, *The Singing Fool* registered the heaviest business in Broadway history, with an advance sale that exceeded more than $100,000.

Warner Bros. pioneered the use of sound in motion pictures and thus functioned as the innovator of this important new feature. The Fox Film Corporation (predecessor of the later Twentieth Century-Fox) came second. Once it was shown that talkies could make money, the other major Hollywood movie corporations soon followed.

SIGNIFICANCE

The coming of sound transformed filmmaking in its day as did other later changes in motion-picture technology, such as the coming of color, wide-screen images, and stereo sound. Indeed, film history is segmented by this monumental change. The addition of sound led to major shifts in the economic, aesthetic, and social power of films.

Through its innovation with sound, Warner Bros. changed the American film industry in a fundamental manner. Hollywood was transformed from a competitive environment to a tight oligopoly of eight companies. Those eight companies (except for Radio Keith Orpheum—RKO—which dropped out in the 1950's, and MGM and United Artists, which merged) remained dominant in the industry for decades. As a single company, Warner Bros. was the sole small competitor of the early 1920's to succeed in the Hollywood elite, producing films for consumption throughout the world and for presentation in the more than eight hundred theaters the company owned throughout the Mid-Atlantic region of the United States in the 1930's and 1940's. This transformation led to what is known as the Golden Age of Hollywood, the period of the 1930's and 1940's. Hollywood, with its images of multimillion-dollar deals, film stars,

and press agents, became a symbol of the film as a popular cultural force throughout the world. By 1930, for example, more reporters were stationed in the filmmaking capital of the world reporting on the images and sounds of the new talkies than were found in any capital of Europe or Asia.

In particular, through *The Singing Fool*, Warner Bros. taught the film industry how to spill over into other popular entertainment markets through what came to be called spin-offs. Warner Bros. created the first talkie sequel: *Say It with Songs*, released at the beginning of the 1929-1930 movie season. (Like many a future sequel, *Say It with Songs* failed to match the box-office take of its predecessor.) Two tunes from the film, "Sonny Boy" and "There's a Rainbow 'Round My Shoulder," went on to make up the first million-selling phonograph record of the talkie era. Thereafter, popular films would prove to be a gold mine for creating new hit tunes.

Filmmakers had a new standard by which to fashion future classics of the cinematic art. No longer were films presented with different sounds from theater to theater. The sound track became one of the features controlled by the filmmaker. Indeed, sound became a vital part of the filmmaker's art. A musical score, in particular, could make or break a film.

Finally, the coming of sound made films the dominant medium of mass culture in the United States and throughout the world, increasing their influence on fashion, design, and slang. Many cultural observers had not viewed the silent cinema as important, but with the coming of the talkies there was no longer any question of the power of films. The talkies gave birth to a means of expression that affected all aspects of society. This is reflected in the fact that soon after the coming of sound, the notorious Hays Code of prior restraint on film content went into effect. Talking films were so powerful it was deemed necessary to prevent filmmakers from presenting many realistic images and sounds.

—Douglas Gomery

FURTHER READING

Bordwell, David, Janet Staiger, and Kristin Thompson. *The Classical Hollywood Cinema: Film Style and Mode of Production to 1960*. New York: Columbia University Press, 1985. Massive tome includes analysis of the implications of the coming of sound for the making of films and the Hollywood production process. Argues, surprisingly, that the addition of sound changed little in the look and style of the Hollywood film.

Eyman, Scott. *The Speed of Sound: Hollywood and the Talkie Revolution, 1926-1930*. New York: Simon & Schuster, 1997. Comprehensive history of the period in Hollywood filmmaking when silents gave way to sound. Includes photographs and index.

Geduld, Harry M. *The Birth of the Talkies: From Edison to Jolson*. Bloomington: Indiana University Press, 1975. Pioneering study details the creation of the inventions that were necessary to make talkies technologically possible. Includes substantial material on the film industry's relations with the phonograph and radio industries.

Gomery, Douglas. "The Coming of Sound: Technological Change in the American Film Industry." In *The American Film Industry: A History Anthology of Readings*, edited by Tino Balio. Rev. ed. Madison: University of Wisconsin Press, 1985. Discusses the coming of sound and the important role this technological change played in the transformation and development of the American film industry.

_____. "Warner Bros. Innovates Sound: A Business History." In *The Movies in Our Midst*, edited by Gerald Mast. Chicago: University of Chicago Press, 1982. A history, based on corporate files, of the rise of a major movie company through its success in innovating sound films. Argues that the innovation was based on business, not artistic, factors.

_____. "The Warner-Vitaphone Peril: The American Film Industry Reacts to the Innovation of Sound." In *The American Movie Industry: A Case Study Approach*, edited by Gorham Kindem. Carbondale: Southern Illinois University Press, 1982. Previous film historians argued that the film industry happened into sound in a chaotic manner. Gomery argues, based on company records, that Warner Bros. slowly and systematically innovated talkies.

Higham, Charles. *Warner Brothers*. New York: Charles Scribner's Sons, 1975. Examines the history of the family and the company that pioneered the coming of sound and operated a major studio into the 1950's.

Sarris, Andrew. *"You Ain't Heard Nothin' Yet": The American Talking Film—History and Memory, 1927-1949*. New York: Oxford University Press, 1998. Comprehensive history of American cinema since *The Jazz Singer* by one of the most respected American writers on film. Opens with a chapter on the Hollywood studios that includes discussion of Warner Bros. Features an index of films and an index of names.

Shindler, Colin. *Hollywood in Crisis: Cinema and American Society, 1929-1939*. New York: Routledge, 1996. Describes the state of American cinema in the decade immediately following the advent of sound, the years of the Great Depression, during which Warner Bros. produced a number of radical films. Includes filmography, bibliography, and index.

Walker, Alexander. *The Shattered Silents: How the Talkies Came to Stay*. New York: William Morrow, 1979. History of the innovation of sound in films, by Warner Bros. and others, based solely on a close reading of the trade paper *Variety*. Interesting but limited.

SEE ALSO: 1913: Edison Shows the First Talking Pictures; Oct. 6, 1927: *The Jazz Singer* Premieres as the First "Talkie"; May 11, 1928: Sound Technology Revolutionizes the Motion-Picture Industry; 1930's: Hollywood Enters Its Golden Age.

August 6, 1926
EDERLE SWIMS THE ENGLISH CHANNEL

Gertrude Ederle's athletic achievement made it clear that women were capable of the vigorous, extended physical activities often associated only with males despite public opinion and media reports that often dismissed women's athletic potential and were disapproving of females who participated in sports.

LOCALE: Cape Gris-Nez, France; English Channel; Kingsdown, England

CATEGORIES: Sports; women's issues

KEY FIGURES

Gertrude Ederle (1906-2003), American distance swimmer

Charlotte Epstein (1884-1938), founder of the Women's Swimming Association of New York and U.S. Olympic coach

Jabez Wolffe (c. 1877-1943), English distance swimmer and trainer

Thomas William Burgess (1872-1957), English distance swimmer and trainer

Clare Belle Barrett (b. 1891), American distance swimmer and high school swimming coach

Amelia Gade Corson (c. 1899), Danish American distance swimmer

Ernst Vierkoetter (c. 1901-1967), German distance swimmer

SUMMARY OF EVENT

As a child, Gertrude Ederle learned to swim in the Shrewsbury River near her family's vacation home in New Jersey and in the Atlantic Ocean, experiences that prepared her for distance swimming in open water. When she was thirteen, Ederle joined the Women's Swimming Association of New York, where she took lessons and used a pool to master her stroke techniques. There she met Charlotte Epstein, who became her mentor and encouraged her to develop her natural talent, build her stamina, and compete in races.

Sixteen-year-old Ederle swam the seventeen miles between Manhattan, New York, and Sandy Hook, New Jersey, in slightly more than seven hours, setting a time record and becoming the first female to achieve that feat. Ederle stunned swimming enthusiasts when she consistently defeated acclaimed international swimmers in races: She earned three medals at the 1924 Olympic Games in Paris, and her times at swimming competitions set twenty-nine American and international records by 1925.

Although Ederle valued her competitive achievements, her longtime goal was to swim across the English Channel, a goal for long-distance swimmers since the nineteenth century. Prior to Ederle's first attempt, five male swimmers had survived the twenty-one-mile feat, which usually took place in the Dover Strait between France and England. Initially, the Women's Swimming Association of New York decided to sponsor Helen Wainright, a fellow Olympian, to swim the Channel. When Wainright became injured, association leaders asked Ederle to attempt the crossing and offered to pay her expenses.

Despite her many athletic achievements, Ederle encountered criticism, particularly from journalists, that women were physically unable to cross the Channel. Eager for the challenge, she ignored negative comments and trained in the ocean, where she conditioned her body

Gertrude Ederle on a Long Island, New York, beach in 1923. (AP/Wide World Photos)

to withstand cold temperatures and became accustomed to the tug of waves and tides. Ederle had competition, however: Other American female swimmers, including Clare Belle Barrett and Amelia Gade Corson, also aspired to cross the Channel.

At dawn on August 18, 1925, Ederle began swimming at Cape Gris-Nez, France. She was accompanied by a boat that carried her trainer, Jabez Wolffe, who had attempted swimming across the Channel approximately twenty times, and other helpers. She withstood the chilly, turbulent water for nine hours. Seven miles from the English coast, Ederle was dragged into the boat by an assistant; Wolffe mistakenly thought that Ederle was choking on seawater, and his physical contact eliminated her. Ederle located another trainer, Thomas William Burgess, who in 1911 had become the second man to cross the Channel, and prepared for another attempt. She raised money, secured media sponsorships, and trained near Cape Gris-Nez.

By August 6, 1926, Ederle prepared to swim to England from Cape Gris-Nez. Greased to keep the icy water away from direct contact with her skin, she wore a silk two-piece bathing suit of her own design that would not impede her movement and enabled her to glide through water with minimal resistance. Aware that extreme sea conditions had halted steamboat traffic, Ederle placed goggles over her eyes to protect them from saltwater, covered her hair with a swimming cap, and began swimming toward England just after 7:00 A.M. Her father, her sister Margaret, Burgess, and several swimmers rode beside her in the tugboat *Alsace*. They guided her through fog, diverted her from threats such as jellyfish, and encouraged her. Journalists traveled nearby in another boat. Ederle's entourage sang patriotic songs and extended chicken, chocolate, and other sustenance to her on a pole. Burgess urged Ederle to pace herself in smooth water during the morning, but she continued her steady crawl and made quick progress.

That afternoon, a storm threatened to end Ederle's attempt. Rain pelted, and wind caused waves to surge and drag her backward. She ignored Burgess's demands that she stop. During the evening, the storm intensified, and Ederle was temporarily separated from the two boats. When her left leg cramped, she saw the tugboat but vowed to continue swimming despite Burgess's continued pleas. Determined, she surged forward, and eventually she saw boats signaling with flares and a massing of torches and searchlights on the horizon as she approached the beach at Kingsdown, England.

Ederle neared the shore at approximately 9:40 P.M. Many people went into the sea to celebrate and walk beside her in the darkness: Her swim had lasted fourteen hours and thirty-one minutes. Since the strong currents added distance to her swim, Ederle had probably swum as much as 35 miles (56 kilometers). She set a new record, completing the swim two hours faster than the male record holder. Ederle returned by tugboat to France, enjoyed celebrations in that country, and then visited her grandmother in Germany.

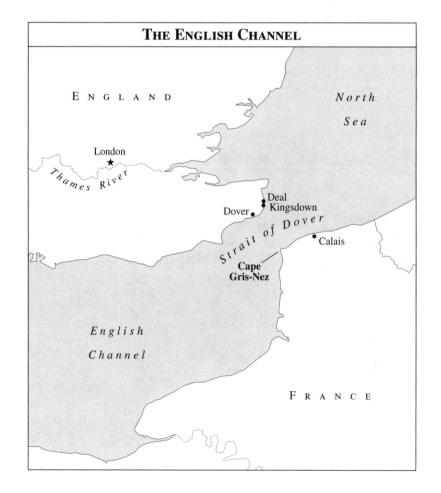

THE ENGLISH CHANNEL

Many newspapers around the world bore headlines cheering Ederle's accomplishment accompanied by stories stating that she had proved that females are capable athletes. The *London Daily News*, however, suggested she was an anomaly and emphasized that women are weaker than men. Others dismissed Ederle's endeavor as a stunt. Ederle traveled on the SS *Berengaria* to New York, where she rode in a parade attended by a crowd of approximately two million. Both U.S. president Calvin Coolidge and New York City mayor Jimmy Walker lauded Ederle's achievement.

Later that August, two other swimmers also successfully swam the Channel. Corson completed the swim with quicker times than her male predecessors, but she did not beat Ederle's record. Frustrated that she was the second woman to achieve the feat, Corson emphasized her special status as the first mother to swim across the English Channel. Two men who swam with Corson quit mid-Channel, but later Ernst Vierkoetter beat Ederle's record by almost two hours.

Ederle's celebrity equaled and even surpassed that of many male sports stars. After her swim, polls ranked her as more popular than Babe Ruth, and she considered offers from companies that wanted her to endorse their products. She starred in the 1927 silent film *Swim Girl, Swim*, had dance steps and a song named for her, and swam for vaudeville performances. She was uncomfortable with publicity, however, and did not encourage fame. She gradually faded into obscurity, especially after such feats as Charles A. Lindbergh's 1927 solo flight across the Atlantic captured media attention.

SIGNIFICANCE

Although Ederle insisted that her desire to swim the English Channel was not part of a larger agenda to become a heroine or promote feminist agendas, her accomplishment inspired women worldwide and affected public views on women's athletic abilities. Her success also represented a victory for promoters of women's rights. Ederle had endured extreme, dangerous conditions to achieve her goal, and she proved that strength and perseverance were traits that women could display without risking permanent public ostracism for being unfeminine.

Ederle also demonstrated that women were physiologically capable of competing with men in many sports without harming their health. Her accomplishment showed that physical activity was acceptable for women, although many people still criticized women's swimming attire as too provocative. As a result of Ederle's success, many women were inspired to participate in athletics for fun and competition, and swimming became a popular recreational sport. Thousands of American women subsequently earned Red Cross certificates for swimming.

Ederle's mastery of modern strokes—especially the crawl—helped her cross the Channel much more efficiently than her predecessors, who had mostly floated or paddled to cross. Ederle's success encouraged coaches and officials in several ways: Her swim promoted research into techniques to improve strokes and training as well as consultation of data on time, direction, and strength of tides. It also encouraged the holding of long-distance swims between prominent geographic sites adjacent to large bodies of water.

—*Elizabeth D. Schafer*

1926

FURTHER READING

Colwin, Cecil M. *Breakthrough Swimming*. Champaign, Ill.: Human Kinetics, 2002. Internationally renowned swimming coach discusses the pioneering roles in women's competitive swimming played by Ederle and her coaches.

Smith, Lissa, ed. *Nike Is a Goddess: The History of Women in Sports*. New York: Atlantic Monthly Press, 1998. Includes a chapter on swimming that comments on the public response to distance swimmers and on Ederle's celebrity.

Unwin, Peter. *The Narrow Sea: Barrier, Bridge, and Gateway to the World—The History of the Channel*. London: Review, 2003. Examines historic events relevant to the English Channel. Discusses swimmers' attempts to cross the Channel since the 1870's.

Wennerberg, Conrad A. *Wind, Waves, and Sunburn*. New York: A. S. Barnes, 1974. History of marathon swimming devotes a chapter to the English Channel that discusses Ederle and other swimmers. Addresses the physiology of swims across the Channel and provides a table of tides.

Woolum, Janet. *Outstanding Women Athletes: Who They Are and How They Influenced Sports in America*. 2d ed. Phoenix, Ariz.: Oryx Press, 1998. Includes a profile of Ederle. Discusses how female swimmers contributed to improved public perception of women's roles in athletics.

SEE ALSO: July 1, 1903: First Tour de France; Nov. 7, 1916: First Woman Is Elected to the U.S. Congress; Feb. 6, 1918: British Women Gain the Vote; Aug. 26, 1920: U.S. Women Gain the Right to Vote; Sept. 27, 1930: First Grand Slam of Golf; May 20-21, 1932: First Transatlantic Solo Flight by a Woman.

September 9, 1926
NATIONAL BROADCASTING COMPANY IS FOUNDED

With the founding of the National Broadcasting Company in 1926, the first permanent radio network was created.

LOCALE: New York, New York

CATEGORIES: Radio and television; communications and media; organizations and institutions

KEY FIGURES

David Sarnoff (1891-1971), founder of the National Broadcasting Company

William S. Paley (1901-1990), founder of the Columbia Broadcasting System

SUMMARY OF EVENT

The successful use of radio by the U.S. Navy in World War I and an emerging view that the national interest of the United States required the development of this new technology by strictly American hands led to the formation of the Radio Corporation of America (RCA) in 1919. The new company, formed by a combination of the industrial giants General Electric (GE), American Telephone and Telegraph (AT&T), Western Electric, and Westinghouse, was not without its problems. Patent conflicts and disagreements over commercial boundaries did much to impede the early progress of radio. In fact, forward movement was achieved only after an agreement that clearly delineated the spheres of industrial influence for each member of the new conglomerate. Under the accord, AT&T gained control over both wire and wireless telephone communications, and GE and Westinghouse received RCA patents to manufacture equipment.

Fortunately for RCA and the development of radio broadcasting, the narrow operating purview adopted early on by RCA leadership was widened through the insistent efforts and vision of David Sarnoff. Sarnoff, a commercial manager for RCA and an early intimate of Guglielmo Marconi, a pioneer in radio development, foresaw both the cultural and commercial possibilities of radio. His argument that radio sets would in time be common household items like phonographs was so persuasive that in less than a decade he would orchestrate the founding of the National Broadcasting Company (NBC) as a subsidiary of RCA. Sarnoff's case, it should also be noted, was greatly assisted by successful radio broadcasting ventures by Westinghouse and AT&T.

The Westinghouse radio enterprise was inaugurated

in 1920 when scientist and radio enthusiast Frank Conrad began broadcasting from his home on a regular basis. Conrad's programming, although limited in entertainment richness, caught on with a number of amateur radio operators. In time, these individuals and a growing number of new listeners required equipment—radios built by Westinghouse and distributed by the Joseph Horne department store in Pittsburgh, Pennsylvania. Executives from both of these organizations quickly recognized that for the radio phenomenon to grow and prosper, more professional and varied programming would be required. This was accomplished when station KDKA signed on the air. The station's broadcast of the 1920 presidential election results did much to spur the sale of sets.

From 1920 to 1921, only nine radio stations came into existence, but 1922 was a banner year for this new medium. Scores of department stores, colleges and universities, churches and religious organizations, and municipalities sought and received broadcast licenses. This flurry of activity did not go unnoticed by executives at AT&T. They theorized that significant long-term financial gains would accrue to holders of broadcast licenses. More important, short-run financial rewards were possible if broadcasts were paid by toll, just like telephone calls. Thus AT&T's radio station WEAF was open to anyone who wished to buy time and perform over the airwaves. Over time, however, toll broadcasting, unlike telephone calling, found only limited success.

A most positive approach to financing radio involved connecting radio stations in a web of broadcasting activity. A primitive technology of network transmission was available as early as 1920. A "pickup" network was tried successfully at KDKA, which broadcast remote programs such as religious, sporting, and political events by running telephone wires from the place of the event with a central transmitter and receivers. A crude distribution network with two radio stations linked by telephone wires was initiated in 1922. The linkage of WJZ in Newark, New Jersey, to WGY in Schenectady, New York, to broadcast the World Series not only attracted the attention of many sports fans but also convinced executives at the technologically superior WEAF that network broadcasting was the future for radio.

The AT&T foray into a network arrangement occurred in June, 1923, when four stations were connected to broadcast the National Electric Light Association meeting from Carnegie Hall in New York City. An effort

David Sarnoff (left), the founder of NBC, in 1938 with Arturo Toscanini, a world-famous conductor and the leader of the NBC Symphony Orchestra. (AP/Wide World Photos)

1926

networks broadcast many individual programs and special events. Programming similarities aside, however, the two networks enjoyed distinct broadcasting philosophies and unique technology. Rivalry between the networks extended to animosities among their respective staff members and performers.

It is with this background that one can imagine the dismay of WEAF employees upon learning that AT&T had decided to bow out of the radio broadcasting arena. They learned that, after negotiations with David Sarnoff, the telephone company had sold its network to RCA for one million dollars. AT&T would now do what it did most efficiently—enjoy exclusive rights to wire telephone and two-way wireless telegraphy. In turn, RCA would lease radio relay facilities from AT&T and cease using Western Union lines.

With two fiercely independent and competitive networks under its control, RCA formed the National Broadcasting Company (NBC) as a subsidiary on September 9, 1926, to organize and take control over network broadcasting. Although senior managers from both organizations were integrated to run NBC, there was no easy way to combine the stations. Thus WJZ would operate as the leader of the Blue Network and the stronger WEAF would operate as the lead station for the Red Network. This bifurcated operation would exist for nearly two decades, until the Blue Network was sold to the American Broadcasting Company (ABC) after a court ruling ordering divestment by NBC.

one month later to connect WEAF to WNAC in Boston through the use of two long-distance circuits, technologically advanced amplifiers, and special filters attracted an audience of one hundred thousand listeners and caused the press to become ecstatic over the possibilities for this new mode of communication. The WEAF broadcast of a speech by President Warren G. Harding from the St. Louis Coliseum shortly thereafter raised press and popular excitement over radio to new heights.

WEAF successes galvanized executives at Westinghouse, RCA, and GE to attempt a similar venture. Although prohibited from using telephone company lines, the competitors successfully forged a fourteen-station network broadcasting from Aeolian Hall in New York City. Despite the poor quality of transmission, stations in New York, Pennsylvania, Maryland, and Washington, D.C. were linked.

By 1925, two rival networks had formed. Although continuing to present locally oriented programs, the

SIGNIFICANCE

Network broadcasting at NBC was sporadic until early 1927, when the "national" in the company name became a reality with the addition of a number of West Coast stations to the network. What began in 1926 as a network of 19 station outlets grew until 1940, when the network was composed of 214 stations.

The early history of NBC is tied to the founding of its rival, the Columbia Broadcasting System (CBS), by

William S. Paley in 1928. Although lacking in radio experience, this young entrepreneur took control over two struggling networks and in time forged them into one of the world's premier entertainment corporations. By attempting to appeal to large audiences with jazz and comedy offerings, in contrast to NBC's more staid classical music and educational programming, CBS grew to seventy-six stations less than a decade after its founding. Shortly thereafter, it would surpass its older competitor in popular appeal.

The formation of NBC in 1926 as a network of independent radio stations linked by agreement and common interest had a dramatic effect on the way Americans are informed and entertained. The development of radio programs, the economics of broadcasting, and overarching effects on American culture can be traced to the founding of NBC and its main early rival, CBS.

During the 1920's, as radio technology advanced, commercial managers explored new ways of paying for this new medium. Radio executives discovered early in the history of radio that broadcasting public events via telephone lines was an expensive undertaking. Artists, in addition, wanted to be paid according to their talents and accomplishments. Entertainers who in the nascent days of radio would accept first-class transportation to a radio studio as payment for their performance now wanted more tangible rewards in the form of a paycheck. Creators of shows and songs wanted royalties for their copyrighted material, which radio station managers and announcers previously had used liberally.

The network concept went a long way toward providing the financial wherewithal to rectify these problems. When the networks were formed, almost all programs were developed and produced by the network or by individual stations. In the 1930's, broadcasting became a big business. By 1931, virtually all sponsored network programs were developed by advertising agencies. Sponsors typically paid two hundred to five hundred thousand dollars to produce a popular program and an additional ten thousand dollars per week to be hooked up to NBC's coast-to-coast network of about fifty stations.

"Commercial sales talks" dominated early radio broadcasting, but throughout the early years networks expanded their schedules. Sponsored programs began to share airtime with unsponsored ones and with special events, thus providing greater diversity in the broadcast schedule. In 1931, for example, the NBC network featured hundreds of special events and international programs from around the world. It broadcast twenty-eight

appearances by the president, thirty-seven by cabinet members, and seventy-one by U.S. senators and representatives. It also earned a net income of more than two million dollars.

The founding of NBC as a powerful national broadcasting network brought intensified efforts to improve radio transmission and reception. Competition between the WEAF network, controlled by AT&T, and the WJZ network, operated by RCA, had hampered the technological enrichment of radio. With conflicting cross-licensing agreements mostly resolved, network listeners could enjoy broadcasts of popular programs free of static and other local interference. Moreover, in an effort to ensure that radio technology would always stay on the cutting edge, NBC appointed a board of consulting engineers under Alfred N. Goldsmith of RCA. The board included Ernst F. W. Alexanderson of General Electric and Frank Conrad of Westinghouse.

Although radio had its early detractors, the National Broadcasting Company and its major competitors—CBS, Mutual, and the American Broadcasting Company—had a dramatic impact on American culture. The broadcast of a sporting event, a political speech, a religious talk, or a program of wide popular appeal crossed not only geographic boundaries but also cultural ones. A diverse population was connected as never before, and a national identity was forged in ways few of the pioneers of radio could have envisioned.

—S. A. Marino

FURTHER READING

Barnouw, Erik. *A Tower in Babel*. Vol. 1 in *A History of Broadcasting in the United States*. New York: Oxford University Press, 1966. Offers important insights into the social, commercial, and technological factors that influenced the development of early radio broadcasting.

Bilby, Kenneth. *The General: David Sarnoff and the Rise of the Communications Industry*. New York: Harper & Row, 1986. Biography written by a longtime associate of Sarnoff benefits from both the author's conversations with the visionary broadcasting leader and his own extensive research while at the Harvard Business School. An invaluable resource for those interested in learning how leaders such as Sarnoff and Paley helped shape the broadcasting industry.

Douglas, George H. *The Early Days of Radio Broadcasting*. 1987. Reprint. Jefferson, N.C.: McFarland, 2001. Authoritative and highly enjoyable study provides important information on such topics as news reporting, sportscasting, classical and popular music programming, and educational stations in the nascent stage of radio.

Head, Sydney W., Thomas Spann, and Michael A. McGregor. *Broadcasting in America: A Survey of Electronic Media.* 9th ed. Boston: Houghton Mifflin, 2000. The standard introduction to the institutions of radio and television in the United States.

Lewis, Thomas. *Empire of the Air: The Men Who Made Radio.* New York: HarperCollins, 1991. Exceptionally well-written and thoroughly researched chronicle of the pioneering contributions to the development of radio. Written for both the serious scholar and the general reader.

Lichty, Lawrence W., and Malachi C. Topping, comps. *American Broadcasting: A Source Book on the History of Radio and Television.* New York: Hastings House, 1975. Presents the history of broadcasting in a series of articles written by scholars, journalists, and broadcasting executives who reflected on events in the industry as they occurred. Provides extensive coverage of networks and broadcast economics. Includes statistical tables.

Lyons, Eugene. *David Sarnoff.* New York: Harper & Row, 1966. Biography provides important insights into the formation of NBC and Sarnoff's contribution to the growth and development of the television medium. An informative and entertaining work.

Sarnoff, David. *Looking Ahead: The Papers of David Sarnoff.* New York: McGraw-Hill, 1968. Presents extensive excerpts from more than one hundred documents covering Sarnoff's entire professional life, including speeches, public statements, and letters. Captures Sarnoff's passion for broadcasting, courageous leadership under adversity, and vision of the future in his own words.

Sterling, Christopher H., and John Michael Kittross. *Stay Tuned: A History of American Broadcasting.* 3d ed. Mahwah, N.J.: Lawrence Erlbaum, 2001. The standard one-volume history of radio and television in the United States. A good beginning point.

SEE ALSO: Dec. 12, 1901: First Transatlantic Telegraphic Radio Transmission; Dec. 24, 1906: Fessenden Pioneers Radio Broadcasting; Oct. 21, 1915: First Demonstration of Transatlantic Radiotelephony; 1919: Principles of Shortwave Radio Communication Are Discovered; 1920's: Radio Develops as a Mass Broadcast Medium; Aug. 20-Nov. 2, 1920: Radio Broadcasting Begins; Apr. 30, 1939: American Television Debuts at the World's Fair.

1926

September 25, 1926
LEAGUE OF NATIONS ADOPTS INTERNATIONAL SLAVERY CONVENTION

The 1926 International Slavery Convention was part of an effort begun by colonial nations a century earlier to suppress slavery in all its forms.

LOCALE: Geneva, Switzerland
CATEGORIES: Civil rights and liberties; human rights; diplomacy and international relations

KEY FIGURES

Paul Hymans (1865-1941), Belgian delegate to the League of Nations
Sir Frederick Lugard (1858-1945), British delegate on the Temporary Slavery Commission
Henry Morton Stanley (1841-1904), British writer and explorer

SUMMARY OF EVENT

Slavery has been one of the most persistent institutions of human society, existing from the dawn of history into modern times. During the Middle Ages, under the influence of Christianity in Western Europe, there were notable periods when the practice of slavery and slave trade diminished substantially, but throughout most of the world and most of human history, slavery has been regarded as either a necessary evil or an ineradicable one.

The reappearance of slavery in colonial lands discovered by Europeans saw a resurgence of the slave trade by European countries starting in the 1400's. Although opposed officially by the Church, which issued proclamations of excommunication against those engaged in slave trade, the practice continued to gain momentum in subsequent centuries. The philosophers of the American and French revolutions did much to discredit slavery by condemning it for destroying the natural liberty of human beings, although the U.S. Constitution fell short of the ideal by treating slaves for purposes of taxation and representation as only three-fifths of a person, a flaw left unremedied until the passage of the Thirteenth, Fourteenth, and Fifteenth Amendments in the wake of the American Civil War.

In the aftermath of the Napoleonic Wars, at the Congress of Vienna on February 8, 1815, the victorious nations declared their intention to suppress the slave trade. The powers with colonial possessions were advised of their obligation and duty to abolish the slave trade. However, the institution of slavery itself, in the form of plantation slavery in the British possessions and in the United States, was virtually untouched. None of the nations at the Congress of Vienna in 1815 was willing to trespass on the sovereignty of other states to end any form of domestic slavery. Nevertheless, the Congress of Vienna was a major step toward engendering an agreement among European nations to work to abolish the international traffic in slaves, especially the transatlantic trade.

Colonialism could be justified, according to Sir Frederick Lugard, who had served for many years in Africa as a colonial administrator, only if it provided mutual advantages for the colonized "natives" and for the world. Colonialism was a "school" to Christianize and civilize "savage" peoples. In return, the colony would provide European capitalists with raw materials for their industries and markets for their manufacturers.

In 1884-1885, European nations held the African Conference at Berlin. That conference called for the suppression of slavery and specifically of "the Negro slave trade," but the act passed by the conference applied only to the Congo basin. It was, however, an important development in creating a body of international law that was militantly opposed to slavery.

Explorers such as Henry Morton Stanley had discovered and publicized the existence of a vast area in Africa that was controlled by Arab slave raiders. Arab traders such as Tippu Tib actually posed a military threat to the tribes of the region and even to the Belgian military. Strong military operations were necessary in the Congo and elsewhere in Africa to defeat combative slave traders. The parties to the African Conference, in an 1886 decree, provided for penal servitude for slave traders.

Slave caravans penetrated the interior of Africa from the shores of the Mediterranean, the Red Sea, the Persian Gulf, and the Indian Ocean. The traffic in slaves encompassed the modern countries of Nigeria, Sudan, Ethiopia, Ghana, Burundi, and Democratic Republic of the Congo, among others. Slaves brought to trading centers in northern and eastern Africa were sold for local use or, as was more often the case, were sent to Turkey, Saudi Arabia, Iran, and other eastern countries. Another

decree in 1888 regarding labor contracts prohibited the enslavement of natives by nonnatives. The colonial powers were trying to abolish slavery indirectly by abolishing the slave trade.

There were difficulties connected with the outright abolition of domestic slavery (that is, slavery within a colony) and forced labor, and an international consensus did not yet exist for a frontal attack on slavery and its analogous forms. An impressive step was taken to suppress slavery at the Second Brussels Conference of 1890. The General Act of Brussels, signed on July 2, 1890, as a result of that conference, had more signatories than earlier international conventions on the suppression of slavery; it also had more enforcement requirements in its articles than did preceding conventions. The nations meeting at Brussels included all of the major European nations, as well as the United States, Turkey, Iran, and Zanzibar. The General Act of Brussels prescribed specific measures for the acceding nations to take against slave raiding and trading in the territory under European control.

The measures enacted by the antislavery alliance were designed to spur the parties to organize the administrative, judicial, and military services of government in their territories of Africa so that they could more effectively regulate the slave traffic. The General Act of Brussels required the establishment of military posts in the interior, where slave raiders collected slaves for overland transit to the coasts for shipment to eastern countries; an increase in the use of steamships manned by soldiers on navigable waterways and lakes, thus expanding the presence of the central government throughout the region; more operations by "flying columns" of soldiers to maintain contact between various military posts; and the installation of telegraphs as a means of linking isolated areas to the provincial capital to monitor movements of slave traders and to allow for a more rapid deployment of military forces.

The articles of the General Act of Brussels were meaningful in setting the foundation for more expansive efforts toward suppressing the slave trade, domestic slavery, and many of the forms of forced labor. Belgium employed military force against slave raiders to gain control of the interior and to suppress slavery. In time, with the use of native troops and modern weapons, the Belgians secured the interior from large-scale raids from outside the Congo basin, at a cost of considerable losses of Belgian soldiers. The problem of domestic slavery was left to languish. It was difficult to differentiate between slavery, according to many European apologists, as an acceptable social institution and slavery as a barbaric and cruel method of employment of individuals against their will. Domestic slavery was seen as inevitable but susceptible to gradual elimination through the "civilizing" of native peoples by European colonizers. Europeans considered the enslavement of natives by natives to be beyond the realm of their control, whereas slavery imposed by nonnatives on natives was strictly prohibited as odious to all civilized people and was punishable by law.

World War I interrupted the international efforts to stop slavery and the continuing endeavor at enforcement of the precepts of the General Act of Brussels. The victorious allies—Belgium, the United Kingdom, France, Italy, Japan, Portugal, and the United States—signed a new compact at Saint-Germain-en-Laye on September 10, 1919. The new convention was formulated to complete the work started by the General Act of Brussels.

The Saint-Germain-en-Laye Convention was short-lived. It was superseded by antislavery activities of the newly founded League of Nations. The League of Nations confirmed the previous antislavery declarations and proclaimed its own intent to achieve the complete suppression of slavery "in all of its forms and of the slave trade by land and sea."

In 1924, the League of Nations appointed a Temporary Slavery Commission of eight experts to compile information on slavery, so-called domestic slavery, slave raiding, serfdom, purchase of girls as brides, simulated adoption of children for purposes of sexual exploitation, varied forms of indenture, and compulsory labor by state and private employers. Lugard, perhaps the most influential and respected member of the Temporary Slavery Commission, helped to craft the commission's report to the Council of the League of Nations. His broad experience and practical approach to the suppression of slavery assured the report's adoption by most of the member states of the League of Nations. His suggestions moved the members to moderate positions while retaining the goal of the eventual end of de facto slavery through a process of transition and the development of new modes of employment.

Paul Hymans, the Belgian delegate to the League of Nations in 1926, personified the efforts by Belgium to establish an unambiguous posture toward the suppression of the slave trade and nonnative enslavement of natives. He was reluctant, as were most members, to grapple with the question of forced labor and domestic slavery. The Belgians were, to a good extent, successful in suppressing the slave trade in the Congo basin.

The report of the Temporary Slavery Commission stated the objectives of the commission. It defined "enslavement," made proposals for regulating and punishing persons engaged in slave raiding and the slave trade, and addressed "slave dealing" and the more controversial domestic slavery issue. In an auxiliary category, the report discussed the acquisition of girls by purchase, disguised as payment of dowry, and adoption of children "with a view to their virtual enslavement or the ultimate disposal of their persons."

The Temporary Slavery Commission was shrewdly cautious on the question of forced labor: Its abolition was desirable but not achievable given the provisions of the Covenant of the League of Nations, which prohibited intervention by member states into the domestic affairs of any state. In addition, the commission recognized a need for compulsory native labor in an environment that was inhospitable to white workers. According to the Convention on Slavery adopted on September 25, 1926, signatories recognized the need for governments to use compulsory or forced labor for public projects but noted that such use should be transitional and should end as soon as possible. Signatories were allowed to accept all or only some of the provisions of the convention, which significantly weakened its impact. It was more moral suasion than enforceable law, but it represented a goal to be striven for by many members of the League of Nations.

SIGNIFICANCE

The 1926 Slavery Convention defined slavery as "the status or condition of a person over whom any or all of the powers attaching to the right of ownership are exercised." The convention required the former colonies of Germany and the Ottoman Empire, now mandates of the League of Nations, to suppress slavery and to prepare the people of the mandates for active participation in their own political affairs.

Ethiopia was denied entry into the League of Nations until it formulated a definite plan to eliminate all forms of slavery, which it finally accomplished to a limited extent in the official abolition of slavery in 1942. Liberia, the other recalcitrant slave state, was pressured by the League of Nations to outlaw intertribal slavery and to abolish some other forms of servitude.

The most significant impacts of the 1926 Slavery Convention were on slave raiding and the de jure abolition of slavery in Ethiopia and Liberia. The mandate system also gave the League of Nations moral clout and some circumscribed political leverage in suppressing domestic slavery and specific forms of forced labor.

It was the transition from slavery to certain forms of servile labor, including debt bondage and contract labor, that undermined the effects of emancipation of slaves around the world. Two strategies emerged to replace de facto slavery. One was to entice new labor from other areas by means of indentures, or contracts to work for specific periods of time. This system often involved the accumulation of debts by the laborer. The other form, emerging in the aftermath of emancipation, was peasant bondage, which used former slaves on small landholdings and on large projects, such as road building and railroad construction. Peasant bondage was a form of virtual slavery in which workers were "paid" in the form of training or provisions. Both systems, in many variations, are indirect forms of slavery, or servitude. In the United States, servile labor took the form of sharecropping and share tenancy, in which workers paid part of their harvest as rent. In the Caribbean, it took the form of contracted labor from India and the Middle East.

The 1926 International Slavery Convention had an important impact in that it laid the foundation for continuing struggle against de jure slavery and international opposition to all forms of slavery. It did not, however, immediately end all forms of exploitative labor arrangements.

—Claude Hargrove

FURTHER READING

Barnes, Anthony J. *Captain Charles Stuart: Anglo-American Abolitionist*. Baton Rouge: Louisiana State University Press, 1986. Solid biography of a relatively obscure militant abolitionist. Stuart's attack on gradualists in the movement convinced people such as William Lloyd Garrison to take a more militant stance.

Drescher, Seymour. *Capitalism and Antislavery: British Mobilization in Comparative Perspective*. New York: Macmillan, 1986. Convincing account of black slavery in the Americas and in Africa. Presents a broad and powerfully written assessment of the historiography of slavery. Explains English law concerning slavery.

Drescher, Seymour, and Stanley L. Engerman, eds. *A Historical Guide to World Slavery*. New York: Oxford University Press, 1998. Collection of essays by noted scholars presents information on the institution of slavery from ancient times to the end of the twentieth century. Includes index.

Ennew, Judith. *Debt Bondage*. London: Anti-Slavery Society, 1981. Survey of debt bondage throughout the world in the late twentieth century shows graphically the persistence of contract labor and how little progress has been made to end it.

Koger, Larry. *Black Slaveowners: Free Black Slave Masters in South Carolina, 1790-1860*. Columbia: University of South Carolina Press, 1985. Of the several works written on free blacks owning slaves in the antebellum South, this is the first to show that free black masters behaved similarly to white slave owners, in that both exploited slaves for profit.

Ostrower, Gary B. *The League of Nations from 1919 to 1929*. Garden City Park, N.Y.: Avery, 1996. Interesting and readable volume covers the first ten years of the League of Nations. Includes illustrations, chronology, bibliography, and index.

Watson, Alan. *Roman Slave Law*. Baltimore: The Johns Hopkins University Press, 1987. Argues that in a strict sense there was scarcely any such thing as "Roman slave law"; rather, every category of the law was affected by the fact of an individual's being a slave.

SEE ALSO: May 18, 1904: International Agreement Targets White Slave Trade; Apr. 28, 1919: League of Nations Is Established; Sept. 10, 1919: Saint-Germain-en-Laye Convention Attempts to Curtail Slavery.

October 22, 1926
HEMINGWAY'S *THE SUN ALSO RISES* SPEAKS FOR THE LOST GENERATION

The novel changed forever when Ernest Hemingway evoked the lives of disillusioned "lost generation" expatriates in a novel of brilliant dialogue and understated style.

LOCALE: New York, New York; Paris, France
CATEGORY: Literature

KEY FIGURES

Ernest Hemingway (1899-1961), American journalist and novelist
Gertrude Stein (1874-1946), American author
F. Scott Fitzgerald (1896-1940), American author
Maxwell Perkins (1884-1947), American literary editor

SUMMARY OF EVENT

By October of 1925, Ernest Hemingway was identified as a rising literary star with the publication of his unified short-story collection *In Our Time*. Hemingway's collection alternated autobiographically derived stories of the Michigan woods and war-torn Europe with miniature pieces that seemed the distillation of prose fiction under the influence of the principles of the Imagist poets, who preached attention to the moment of perception and the presentation of poetic images in a minimum of words. The collection's title was taken from a line in the Book of Common Prayer: "Oh Lord, give us peace in our time." It was an impressive beginning to Hemingway's career as a popular but artistic writer, yet cementing his reputation required that he write in that most commercial but also most difficult of forms, the novel.

This would not be so easy. Hemingway had begun his literary efforts by burlesquing the sports fiction of Ring Lardner for his high school newspaper and had moved on to work as a cub reporter for the *Kansas City Star*. After being seriously wounded during a stint with the American Red Cross Ambulance Corps on the Italian front during World War I, he had written fiction unsuccessfully and then turned to journalism, becoming a foreign correspondent for the *Toronto Star* by the age of twenty-three. In the atmosphere of literary Paris, he had continued his efforts in fiction, internalizing the influences of such literary expatriates as Gertrude Stein, Ezra Pound, James Joyce, and Ford Madox Ford. Yet his pieces seemed more like sketches than stories to many editors to whom he submitted them at the time, despite the fact that he was working with Stein's emphasis on psychological insight

and the economy of language urged by the Imagist Pound. The subtlety of his achievements began to be realized in *In Our Time*, which also owed a considerable debt to American regionalist Sherwood Anderson's *Winesburg, Ohio* (1919).

Vacation trips from Paris to the religious and bullfighting fiesta in Pamplona, in the Basque Navarre region of northern Spain, provided the setting (and some of the characters) for *The Sun Also Rises*, which Hemingway began writing on or about his twenty-sixth birthday, July 21, 1925. For his participating narrator, he was indebted to the example of F. Scott Fitzgerald, whose classic short novel *The Great Gatsby* had appeared on April 10 of that year. He also would be indebted to Fitzgerald for his influential new editor, Maxwell Perkins of Scribner's, who at Fitzgerald's insistence lured Hemingway away from the publisher of *In Our Time*, Horace Liveright. Both Perkins and Fitzgerald would contribute valuable advice on the polishing of *The Sun Also Rises*. In particular, Fitzgerald counseled against a rambling, discursive introduction that attempted to explain rather than directly to present the characters and their situation; Perkins curbed Hemingway's satiric tendencies.

Like Fitzgerald's Nick Carraway, the narrator of *The Great Gatsby*, Hemingway's journalist-narrator Jake Barnes was a fairly ordinary person out of place among the fast-living set in which he traveled. Jake's sensational war wound (he has had his genitals shot away) and his thus doomed love affair with the alcoholic Lady Brett Ashley helped to assure the novel's notoriety and popular success, as did the sensational aspects of Brett's successive sexual alliances with a Jewish American novelist, a bankrupt Scottish war veteran, and a young Spanish matador, affairs that Jake Barnes witnesses and sometimes abets. That many of these characters were based on real people from Paris's colony of literary expatriates increased interest in what some critics saw as a story of meaningless drinking and fornication. An epigraph to the novel taken from Gertrude Stein, "You are all a lost generation," seemed to sum up the meaninglessness of it all. The epigraph certainly did name the rising young writers of the 1920's; they became known as the lost generation, wounded forever.

Still, the work struck a chord with readers who had experienced the war or its aftermath. It was for a time a

1926

Ernest Hemingway. (Hulton Archive/Getty Images)

scription is designed not only to set a scene but also to evoke an emotional response on the part of the reader.

A major theme of the novel involves "knowing the values." At first, this seems merely a matter of knowing how much things cost. As the novel progresses, however, it becomes clear that the characters ultimately may be judged by how well they know real values, values that might have some hope of enduring even in a modern world in which all traditional, received values have lost their force. Such a view of the novel balances the Stein epigraph with the novel's second epigraph, taken from the Book of Ecclesiastes, which emphasizes the cyclical renewal of the earth's promise: "One generation passeth away, and another generation cometh; but the earth abideth forever. . . . The sun also ariseth. . . ."

SIGNIFICANCE

The Sun Also Rises launched Hemingway's subsequent career as novelist, short-story writer, journalist, and public personage. That career took him to fame as the author of such American literary classics as *A Farewell to Arms* (1929), "The Snows of Kilimanjaro" (1936), "The Short Happy Life of Francis Macomber" (1936), *For Whom the Bell Tolls* (1940), and *The Old Man and the Sea* (1952). As a public figure, he was often somewhat misidentified as a macho man: World War I veteran, biggame hunter and deep-sea fisherman, amateur boxer, war correspondent in the Spanish Civil War and World War II, connoisseur of fine food and drink, world traveler. He was all these things, but unlike the reputation that sometimes seemed to imprison him personally as he grew older, his fiction often made clear the psychic cost of such roles to twentieth century man.

His protagonists, including Jake Barnes, usually are vulnerable men, wounded psychically if not physically. Their plight is often seen as existential in nature, a matter of discovering how to live day to day when conventional structures of meaning have lost their power to compel belief. They also are usually American innocents meeting the far from innocent world and finding they have lost the ability to return to the innocent America in which they were nurtured. Yet, over time, Hemingway continues to chart his heroes' search for meaning. Jake Barnes finds it in work. The hero of *A Farewell to Arms*, a World War I deserter, places all his belief in the woman he loves—and loses her, ending the novel wandering the streets alone. The protagonist of *For Whom the Bell Tolls* begins as a loner, a saboteur in the Spanish Civil War, yet finds by novel's end that "no man is an island" and sacrifices himself in the cause of humanity. Santiago, the impoverished

campus fad in the United States, with young men adopting Jake Barnes's stoic persona, if not his sexual incapacity, the young women copying Brett Ashley's brilliant, tense conversation.

More important, attentive readers and critics recognized that there was more to the novel than a crude summary might indicate. It was not a popular potboiler but a literary work of art. Read perceptively, it was in many ways like a prose version of T. S. Eliot's resonant long poem *The Waste Land* (1922). In Eliot's modernist poem, meaning is sought in an exploration of civilization and history, both of the East and of the West. Similarly, *The Sun Also Rises* is a quest for meaning in which the novel's main characters leave behind the modern world, broken by the world war, to travel to a seemingly more innocent, rural Spain. To these pilgrims, such sports as fishing and bullfighting marked a return to pre-Christian rituals of control and unity with the natural world. A parallel control is seen in Hemingway's prose style, in which dialogue is precisely rendered and in which de-

Cuban fisherman of *The Old Man and the Sea*, suffers months without a catch yet survives his greatest defeat with dignity and optimism. In Hemingway's work, some meaning finally is found.

In addition to describing the modern dilemma, Hemingway influenced and reshaped Americans' way of writing. Hemingway's skill in dialogue and narration (for which he admitted a debt to Mark Twain's 1884 *Adventures of Huckleberry Finn*) and his artistic integrity made him a hero and model to American writers ranging from Dorothy Parker to Norman Mailer, who wished to tell the truth without hiding behind conventional literary devices and values. Hemingway's apparently simple sentences and clarity of style influenced writers for magazines as diverse as *The New Yorker* and the pulps; hardboiled detective fiction owes him a considerable debt for its manner and subject matter. The Beat generation writers of the 1950's who went "on the road" in America and abroad in a sense were following in the footsteps of Jake

Barnes and his friends. Indeed, Hemingway's influence on modern writers, particularly in style, is so ingrained and nearly ubiquitous as to seem invisible, save to literary scholars comparing the mainstream writing that went before and that followed his work. His emphasis on the value of the ordinary person and ordinary experiences—a part of a line of influence passing through Mark Twain and Gertrude Stein—continues to have its effect as well.

—*Frederic Svoboda*

FURTHER READING

Baker, Carlos. *Ernest Hemingway: A Life Story*. New York: Charles Scribner's Sons, 1969. The standard full-length biography of Hemingway remains one of the best introductions to his life.

Bruccoli, Matthew J. *Scott and Ernest: The Fitzgerald/Hemingway Friendship*. Carbondale: Southern Illinois University Press, 1978. Pays primary attention to the personal aspects of the famous friendship, but also discusses Hemingway's literary debts to Fitzgerald, who read and commented on *The Sun Also Rises* before publication. Includes lengthy excerpts from a number of the authors' letters to each other.

Bruccoli, Matthew J., and Judith S. Baughman, eds. *The Sons of Maxwell Perkins: Letters of F. Scott Fitzgerald, Ernest Hemingway, Thomas Wolfe, and Their Editor*. Columbia: University of South Carolina Press, 2004. Collection of more than two hundred letters written by Perkins and his three famous authors to one another, in which they often discuss one another's work. Offers insight into the personalities of all four men. Includes chronology and index.

Griffin, Peter. *Less than a Treason: Hemingway in Paris*. New York: Oxford University Press, 1990. Imaginative re-creation of Hemingway's life in Paris evokes the spirit of creation in the 1920's, but, unfortunately, sometimes blurs the distinction between Hemingway's life and his writings.

Hemingway, Ernest. *A Moveable Feast*. New York: Scribner's, 1964. Published posthumously, this highly fictionalized memoir of the life of Hemingway as a young artist in 1920's Paris makes clear the dedication that he felt to his art. Accounts of his relationships with Gertrude Stein, F. Scott Fitzgerald, and others are best taken with a grain of salt so far as the facts are concerned, but their emotional resonances are revealing.

Hemingway Review 6, no. 1 (Fall, 1986). Special issue devoted to *The Sun Also Rises* includes articles addressing questions of religion, the treatment of women, and bullfighting in a reader's understanding

1926

FINE PHILOSOPHIES

In The Sun Also Rises, *the novel's main characters, broken by World War I, leave behind the modern world to travel to a seemingly more innocent, rural Spain. However, they are unable to escape a postwar world in which all traditional values seem abandoned. Hemingway's protagonist and alter ego Jake Barnes finds himself caught between his cynicism and his struggle to make sense of it all:*

I thought I had paid for everything. Not like a woman pays and pays and pays. No idea of retribution or punishment. Just exchanged of values. You gave up something and got something else. Or you worked for something. You paid some way for everything that was any good. I paid my way into enough things that I liked, so that I had a good time. Either you paid by learning about them, or by experience, or by taking chances, or by money. Enjoying living was learning to get your money's worth. The world was a good place to buy in. It seemed like a fine philosophy. In five years, I thought, it will seem just as silly as all the other fine philosophies I've had.

Perhaps that wasn't true, though. Perhaps as you went along you did learn something. I did not care what it was all about. All I wanted to know was how to live in it. Maybe if you found out how to live in it you learned from what it was all about.

Source: Ernest Hemingway, *The Sun Also Rises* (New York: Charles Scribner's Sons, 1926).

of the novel. Also gives accounts of the novel's composition, Hemingway's use of language, and the reactions of a more traditional writer, Western novelist Owen Wister, to the book's subject matter.

Reynolds, Michael. *Hemingway: The Paris Years*. New York: Basil Blackwell, 1989. Meticulous re-creation of Hemingway's life in Europe during the composition of *In Our Time* and *The Sun Also Rises*. Includes detailed maps and chronology.

_____. *"The Sun Also Rises": A Novel of the Twenties*. Boston: Twayne, 1989. Evaluation and close reading of the novel in the context of its time. Explains particularly well how to avoid common misreadings and examines many of the subtleties involved in coming to a full understanding of the novel.

Sarason, Bertram. *Hemingway and the Sun Set*. Washington, D.C.: NCR Microcard, 1972. A good guide to *The Sun Also Rises* as *roman à clef*. Discusses the novel's many sources among the real people of Paris whose characteristics Hemingway adapted in constructing his fictional characters.

Svoboda, Frederic. *Hemingway and "The Sun Also Rises": The Crafting of a Style*. Lawrence: University Press of Kansas, 1983. Analyzes the composition of the novel and the development of Hemingway's prose

style through the examination of manuscript drafts and revisions. Includes a number of facsimiles of manuscript pages as well as the text of the first chapters cut from the novel at Fitzgerald's urging.

Tyler, Lisa. *Student Companion to Ernest Hemingway*. Westport, Conn.: Greenwood Press, 2001. Presents a brief biography of the author and then addresses individual works, discussing plot, character, theme, literary devices, and social and historical context. Intended to introduce Hemingway to high school students and college undergraduates.

Wagner-Martin, Linda, ed. *New Essays on "The Sun Also Rises."* Cambridge, England: Cambridge University Press, 1987. Useful collection of commentary tends to discount the macho Hemingway reputation in favor of discovering what in his work will withstand rigorous literary scrutiny.

SEE ALSO: Fall, 1905: Stein Holds Her First Paris Salons; 1919: Founding of the World Christian Fundamentals Association; 1922: Eliot Publishes *The Waste Land*; Feb. 21, 1925: Ross Founds *The New Yorker*; Apr. 10, 1925: Fitzgerald Captures the Roaring Twenties in *The Great Gatsby*; Winter, 1932: Huxley's *Brave New World* Forecasts Technological Totalitarianism.

December, 1926
KEATON'S *THE GENERAL* IS RELEASED

At the apogee of an arc of creativity that produced ten films between 1923 and 1928, Buster Keaton directed and acted the principal role in the great silent comedy The General.

LOCALE: United States
CATEGORY: Motion pictures

KEY FIGURES
Buster Keaton (1895-1966), American film actor and director
Joseph M. Schenck (1878-1961), American film producer

SUMMARY OF EVENT
Although Buster Keaton's career as a filmmaker began with a kind of apprenticeship to Roscoe "Fatty" Arbuckle in 1917 and continued into the 1960's, the work Keaton did as an actor and director in the mid-1920's is at the core of his achievement as a film artist. Beginning

with the moderately amusing *Three Ages* in 1923, Keaton made a series of silent comedies that demonstrated the range of possibility of the medium. *Our Hospitality* (1923), *Sherlock, Jr.* (1924), *The Navigator* (1924), *Seven Chances* (1925), *Go West* (1925), *Battling Butler* (1926), and *The General* (1926) are the heart of a body of work (including *College* in 1927 and *Steamboat Bill Jr.* in 1928) that exhibits a style, philosophy, and technical proficiency achieved by only the greatest masters in any area of artistic achievement. When Keaton began work on *The General*, he had developed his skills as a director and actor in his previous films and was at a peak of energy and enthusiasm; he was also in his prime as an athlete. In addition, his relationship with his brother-in-law, producer Joseph M. Schenck, enabled him to work on a scale equal to his ambitions, and the striking authenticity of the period settings and decor of *The General* reflect Keaton's access to a production budget sufficient to his needs.

Schenck had formed a connection with the recently established United Artists distributing organization, a company designed to release the independently produced films of such notables as Charles Chaplin, D. W. Griffith, and Douglas Fairbanks, and Schenck became the company's president in 1926. The organization needed films to release, and Schenck made a commitment to Keaton to distribute his next film, guaranteeing Keaton the kind of lavish budget to which Chaplin and Fairbanks were accustomed. Keaton had completed *Battling Butler* and was considering other projects when the writer Clyde Bruckman showed him a book titled *The Great Locomotive Chase* (1868) by William Pittenger, an eyewitness account of a Civil War incident in which a small squad of Union raiders operating behind Confederate lines tried to steal a steam locomotive. The narrative had no comic qualities, but Bruckman knew the comic potential of any kind of chase, and Keaton was captivated by the idea of re-creating the appearance of the Civil War era. He was also intrigued by the chance to place a man in conjunction with a gigantic piece of machinery, one of Keaton's basic comic preoccupations. He asked Bruckman to be his assistant director and told him that he planned to spare no pains to make the film seem authentic.

Keaton and Bruckman originally intended to stage the film on its original location along the Alabama-Tennessee border, but they found no suitable railroad track left in the region and were refused permission to use the original locomotive, which was in a Chattanooga museum. Keaton then decided to make his film in Oregon, because, he later recalled, "the whole state is honeycombed with narrow-gauge railways for all the lumber mills." Keaton's chief technical assistant, Fred Gabourie, found sufficient rolling equipment to provide three locomotives and many freight cars. Keaton hired five hundred men from the Oregon National Guard to play soldiers, and seventeen railway carloads of equipment were shipped from Los Angeles. The crew was housed in tourist cars rented from the Union Pacific railroad, and the film was shot during June and July of 1926. Typically, Keaton was directly in charge of almost every aspect of the production. "Now this was my own story, my own continuity," he later commented. "I directed it, I cut it and titled it. So actually it was a pet."

Pittenger's original story was told from the Union point of view, but Keaton knew that, to make a comedy, he had to make the main character a sympathetic underdog. Keaton remarked that "you can always make villains out of the Northerners, but you cannot make a vil-

Buster Keaton. (Library of Congress)

lain out of the South." His story was centered on an engineer named Johnnie Gray—an almost generic name for an American southerner—who tries to enlist when war breaks out but is turned down because his skills are needed to operate trains during the conflict. In the midst of typical comic confusion, his prospective bride, Annabelle Lee—whose name echoes Edgar Allan Poe's poetic vision of romantic innocence—rejects him as a coward. Gray is then involved in the double tasks of trying to win her back and trying to recapture his engine, the *General*, after Union spies seize them both. The first half of the picture involves Gray's pursuit of the Union troops on another locomotive, the *Texas*; in a symmetrical turn, the second half depicts Gray and Annabelle fleeing from the Union forces on the *General* while the *Texas* gives chase. The visual climax of the film occurs when the Union commander orders the *Texas* to cross a burning bridge to prevent Gray's escape. The bridge does not support the locomotive, and in one of the most expensive single takes to that point in film history (Schenck estimated the cost at $42,000), the locomotive falls into the river below, sending steam and debris across the screen. This stunning and still-effective moment is given a dramatic emphasis by Keaton's cut to the stunned expression on the face of the commander. The film moves from beginning to end with almost no breaks in time and uses only fifty subtitles, primarily in the earlier parts of the narrative; most eight-reel silent features used more than three hundred. Keaton was very pleased with his work, and he discussed the film enthusiastically for the rest of his life.

SIGNIFICANCE

In 1977, the American Film Institute asked its members to submit lists of the fifty greatest films produced in the United States. Only five films from the silent era were chosen—D. W. Griffith's *Intolerance* (1916) and *The Birth of a Nation* (1915), Chaplin's *The Gold Rush* (1925) and *City Lights* (1931), and Keaton's *The General*. Yet acclaim for Keaton's achievement was hardly immediate. The film was released during Christmas week in 1926 in Los Angeles and then put into general release in February, 1927. Initial critical response was almost uniformly negative. Of the eleven New York newspapers that reviewed the film, eight were actively hostile, and only the *Brooklyn Daily Eagle* critic Martin Dickstein acknowledged Keaton's accomplishment. Even he felt it necessary to point out that the film would not seem funny for "lots of people," and *The New York Times* critic Mordaunt Hall found it "by no means as good as Mr. Keaton's previous efforts." Another reviewer judged it "the least funny thing Keaton has ever done," and still another called it "a pretty trite and stodgy piece of screenfare" and observed that the audience responded with "occasionally a laugh, and occasionally a yawn."

Such an assessment of viewer reaction was generally accurate, given that the film grossed $474,264, more than $300,000 less than the receipts for *Battling Butler*. The basic production costs of *The General* had exceeded $400,000, and United Artists took a considerable loss, as 1920's films did not become profitable until receipts totaled about twice the production cost. Keaton never publicly acknowledged his disappointment or even admitted that the film lost money, but he knew the figures and was under some pressure to succeed financially with his next effort. His creative freedom was curtailed by the experience, and Schenck essentially was responsible for the decision to make *College*, a film that resembled Harold Lloyd's very successful *The Freshman*, one of the most

popular films of 1925. For the first time since *The Saphead* (1920), Keaton was not listed as director or codirector, and the words "Supervised by Harry Brand" in the credits meant that there was someone present to watch the budget during production.

When Keaton signed a contract with Metro-Goldwyn-Mayer (MGM) in 1928, a proviso to the agreement indicated that although Keaton would "be consulted as to story and direction," the decision of the producer would be final. This effectively ended the brief era in which Keaton made some of the finest comic films in motion-picture history. Yet while Keaton's career continued on a downward curve through the next three decades, reaching a nadir of sorts with cameo appearances in American International films such as *How to Stuff a Wild Bikini* (1965), his reputation gradually began to move in the opposite direction. In 1953, *The General* was selected to share a place of honor with Chaplin's new film *Limelight* (1952) at the coronation of Elizabeth II of England. When the Museum of Modern Art in New York presented an exhibition of United Artists films, *The General* was the only film that had to be shown more than once because of demand for tickets. By the 1960's, serious full-length academic studies of Keaton were appearing, especially in Europe.

The turning point in the appreciation of Keaton's work can be traced to the famous essay "Comedy's Greatest Era," by James Agee, which appeared in the September 5, 1949, issue of *Life* magazine. Agee discussed Keaton, Lloyd, Chaplin, and Harry Langdon, and although he devoted only a few pages to Keaton's work, his perceptions were so accurate and his prose so compelling and lucid that no one who read the article could look at a Keaton film afterward without being struck by the truth of Agee's observations. What Agee understood and described was that Keaton's finest films were not only great comic statements but also great filmmaking and, perhaps more crucially, great American art. The striking authenticity of *The General*'s sets, props, costumes, and milieu were as instrumental as Mathew Brady's photographs in projecting a sense of reality about the Civil War. Keaton's rare combination of almost Lincolnesque nobility, daunting handsomeness, and appealing friendliness is at the heart of his visual conception of Johnnie Gray, the film's underdog hero. Gray's struggle to serve his country, win the hand of the woman he loves, overcome the forces of darkness, and amuse the audience is so engrossing that it is hard to understand how contemporary audiences in Keaton's time were not captivated. As some critics have observed, however, the film was so rich—such a mixture of comedy, adventure, suspense, and serious commentary about war—that its fusion of categories overwhelmed audiences unprepared by anything they had seen previously. Keaton had to instruct the filmgoers of the 1920's in the art of vision, and *The General* was part of a process that formed a film-literate public capable of appreciating Keaton's masterpiece.

The General displays Keaton's endless invention, his ability to link comic bits in a remarkably tight structure, his extraordinary capabilities as a physical performer, his feeling for the fascination and perplexity men and women experience in the presence of gigantic machines, his sensitivity to such cultural values as decency, modesty, resoluteness, quick wit, and courage, and ultimately, the generosity of spirit and humane qualities that are the essence of comic art. Because Keaton worked in celluloid rather than print or canvas, his accomplishments were undervalued at the time of their creation. In time, however, his genius was recognized, and his place among the giants of film history is secure.

—Leon Lewis

FURTHER READING

Agee, James. "Comedy's Greatest Era." In *Film Theory and Criticism*, edited by Gerald Mast and Marshall Cohen. New York: Oxford University Press, 1974. Landmark essay about film comedians, including Keaton, originally published in *Life* magazine in 1949, is generally credited with marking a turning point in appreciation of Keaton's work.

Benayoun, Robert. *The Look of Buster Keaton*. Translated by Randall Conrad. New York: St. Martin's Press, 1982. Glossy book combines somewhat esoteric, theoretical analysis with a wonderful collection of stills from Keaton films. Includes an excellent filmography with a biographical outline.

Blesh, Rudi. *Keaton*. New York: Collier Books, 1966. Affectionate biography by one of Keaton's friends presents considerable inside information, many anecdotes, and some critical analysis.

Dardis, Tom. *Keaton: The Man Who Wouldn't Lie Down*. 1979. Reprint. Minneapolis: University of Minnesota Press, 2002. A good complement to the Blesh biography (cited above), written from a more distant perspective and utilizing additional information and interviews with some of Keaton's contemporaries. Includes a detailed filmography and some photographs.

Keaton, Eleanor, and Jeffrey Vance. *Buster Keaton Remembered*. New York: Harry N. Abrams, 2001. Celebration of Keaton's work begun by his third wife and completed after her death by a respected film historian. Features more than two hundred photographs, filmography, bibliography, and index.

McPherson, Edward. *Buster Keaton: Tempest in a Flat Hat*. Winchester, Mass.: Faber & Faber, 2004. Discusses Keaton's life and career, focusing on the ways in which the actor and director presented comedy on the screen. Includes photographs.

Moews, Daniel. *Keaton: The Silent Features Close Up*. Berkeley: University of California Press, 1977. Contains a lucid, extremely detailed analytic chapter on *The General* as well as a useful survey of Keaton scholarship.

Rubinstein, Elliot. *Filmguide to "The General."* Bloomington: University of Indiana Press, 1973. Attempts to be descriptive as well as explanatory while concentrating on the qualities that made Keaton a screen presence and a cinematic genius.

SEE ALSO: Fall, 1903: *The Great Train Robbery* Introduces New Editing Techniques; Aug., 1912: Sennett Defines Slapstick Comedy; Mar. 3, 1915: Griffith Releases *The Birth of a Nation*; 1920: Premiere of *The Cabinet of Dr. Caligari*; 1923: *The Ten Commandments* Advances American Film Spectacle; Dec. 4, 1924: Von Stroheim's Silent Masterpiece *Greed* Premieres; 1925: Eisenstein's *Potemkin* Introduces New Film Editing Techniques; June 26, 1925: Chaplin Produces His Masterpiece *The Gold Rush*.

1926

1927
HEIDEGGER PUBLISHES *BEING AND TIME*

Martin Heidegger established himself as a major philosophical figure with the publication of Being and Time, *his most important and influential work, in which he applied Edmund Husserl's principles of phenomenology to the field of ontology.*

ALSO KNOWN AS: *Sein und Zeit*
LOCALE: Marburg, Gemany
CATEGORIES: Philosophy; publishing and journalism

KEY FIGURES
Martin Heidegger (1889-1976), German philosopher
Edmund Husserl (1859-1938), German philosopher
Wilhelm Dilthey (1833-1911), German philosopher
Henri Bergson (1859-1941), French philosopher
Friedrich Nietzsche (1844-1900), German philosopher
Søren Kierkegaard (1813-1855), Danish theologian

SUMMARY OF EVENT
In 1927, Martin Heidegger, an associate professor of philosophy at the German University of Marburg, published a long, difficult book titled *Sein und Zeit* (1927; *Being and Time*, 1962). In it he proposed to ask and answer a question that he argued had been forgotten or obscured in the Western philosophical tradition since the time of the ancient Greeks: the question of the meaning of Being. *Being and Time* is Heidegger's most important work, and its publication established him as one of the twentieth century's major philosophers.

The approach that Heidegger took to his great question was strongly influenced by the thinking of philosophers Edmund Husserl, with whom Heidegger had worked closely at Marburg, and Wilhelm Dilthey. Husserl's phenomenology focused on examination of the nature of pure human consciousness. To pursue his inquiry, Husserl found it necessary to abstract from or to bracket off the real world. It was precisely this real world, however, that Dilthey emphasized in his philosophy, stressing the historical character of human life and the lived experience that all individuals have in their social and cultural worlds. Dilthey's work embodied a critique of Husserlian phenomenology. The inquiry that Heidegger pursued was in a way a synthesis of the positions of these two thinkers.

While Husserl and Dilthey were two of the primary influences on Heidegger's thinking, Heidegger himself situated his work in the long tradition of Western philosophy stretching back to Plato and Aristotle. From the time of the great Greek thinkers, Heidegger argued, philosopher after philosopher had asked about the nature of Being, but over time the importance of the question of the meaning of Being had been obscured. Heidegger promised to restore the original power and mystery of that question. That was an extraordinary undertaking: to rethink and subvert the whole tradition of Western philosophical thinking, an audacious aim perhaps comparable only to that of the late-nineteenth century German thinker Friedrich Nietzsche.

In *Being and Time*, when Heidegger confronts the question of the meaning of Being, he argues that answering it must begin with the consideration of some *particular* being, since Being is always the being *of* something. He chooses to focus on human being, what he calls *Dasein* (being there). Heidegger devotes the whole of his great work to the phenomenological analysis of *Dasein* in all its human complexity. It is this philosophical analysis of human being that he pursues en route to the question of the meaning of Being itself.

Heidegger pursues a particular type of philosophical inquiry in *Being and Time*, which he calls ontological inquiry, as opposed to ontical inquiry. The latter would produce external descriptions of the distinctive characteristics of *Dasein*, whereas the former, Heidegger's way, seeks to enter into *Dasein*'s understanding of being to interpret it rather than to describe it. Heidegger calls this interpretive ontological inquiry "existential."

What, then, does Heidegger's inquiry reveal about *Dasein*? It reveals that *Dasein* is always involved in relations with other entities, what Heidegger characterizes as "being-in-the-world." Further, it reveals that *Dasein* is never alone in the world; rather, it is always with others, what he calls "being-with-others." The everyday world of *Dasein* is constituted within these complexes of relationships, and it is unavoidable, for *Dasein* is always embedded within them, is *thrown* there, to use Heidegger's evocative term.

Heidegger makes a distinction between two possible ways of being-in-the-world: ready-to-hand and present-to-hand. In the former, things are available for practical use; in the latter, they are encountered in a detached, observational way. (An example of this detached mode would be the modern scientific viewpoint, which for Heidegger was classically embodied in the thinking of the seventeenth century French philosopher René Descartes.) Both are ways in which *Dasein* encounters entities in the world, but Heidegger valorizes the ready-to-hand mode.

Like being-in-the-world, being-with-others is fraught with difficulties. *Dasein* is unique, but each is immersed in relationships with that larger complex of human social and cultural relations that Heidegger called *das Man* ("the One" or "They"), his term for mass society. Thus, for Heidegger, *Dasein*'s everyday life is necessarily characterized by its absorption in the world and with *das Man*; this condition he calls Fallenness. *Dasein*, however, does not choose to be in the world, to be born. It is *thrown* into the world at some point in the past. Thrownness is *Dasein*'s inheritance from the past; Fallenness is *Dasein*'s absorption in the present.

Dasein can and must, however, project different possibilities into the future. Every *Dasein* is thrown into the world at some past time, is fallen into the world of the present, but is oriented toward the future. In short, *Dasein* is historical, temporal. *Dasein* always lives in three modes of experiencing time, past, present, and future; for Heidegger, *Dasein* is always *in time*. (Husserl's ideas on the meaning and experience of time, as well as those of the French philosopher Henri Bergson, guided Heidegger's thinking about the human experience of time-embeddedness.) Since there is always a future, *Dasein* is incomplete until the final moment of existence, which is death. *Dasein* is therefore always a being-toward-death.

Dasein's Thrownness produces a deep disquiet that Heidegger, taking inspiration from the nineteenth century Danish religious thinker Søren Kierkegaard, calls angst (anxiety), a mood that can easily precipitate *Dasein* into absorption in the Fallenness of the present. To remain fixed in the present and to ignore being-toward-death is all too easy, but such an existence Heidegger calls inauthentic. For Heidegger, only living in all three temporalities—Thrownness, Fallenness, and Projection—with the recognition that *Dasein* is being-toward-death would constitute an authentic existence.

Heidegger intended a further section of *Being and Time* to move from the analysis of the being of *Dasein* to the question of Being itself and its meaning (his original question), but he did not produce that section. Nor did he ever write an intended second part, in which he had said he would critique the philosophies of Immanuel Kant, René Descartes, and Aristotle. Heidegger continued to lecture and write extensively until his death in 1976, turning increasingly to the study of art and poetry, but *Being and Time* was his greatest work.

1927

Martin Heidegger. (AP/Wide World Photos)

SIGNIFICANCE

For many, *Being and Time* became a twentieth century classic of philosophy, one that placed its author in the pantheon of Western philosophical greats from Plato to Nietzsche. For others, the book's forbidding language was impenetrable, not philosophy but obscurantism. Heidegger's reputation was tarnished by his close association with (and brief membership in) the Nazi Party in the 1930's, an association he never repudiated after World War II. However, his influence on twentieth century intellectual history was enormous. The critique of mass society by thinkers such as Karl Jaspers, the political philosophy of Heidegger's student Hannah Arendt, the existentialist philosophy of Jean-Paul Sartre, the deconstructionist program of Jacques Derrida, the structuralist psychoanalyis of Jacques Lacan, and many other of the century's most important intellectual developments bear the imprint of Heidegger's thinking in *Being and Time*.

—*Michael W. Messmer*

FURTHER READING

Guignon, Charles, ed. *The Cambridge Companion to Heidegger*. New York: Cambridge University Press, 1993. Contains a wide-ranging selection of essays on all aspects of Heidegger's thought.

Inwood, Michael. *Heidegger: A Very Short Introduction.* Oxford, England: Oxford University Press, 2000. Excellent short introduction to Heidegger that focuses on *Being and Time*.

Ree, Jonathan. *Heidegger*. New York: Routledge, 1999. Very brief but stimulating analysis of the argument of *Being and Time*.

Safranski, Rudiger. *Martin Heidegger: Between Good and Evil*. Cambridge, Mass.: Harvard University Press, 1998. Very probing intellectual biography of Heidegger; especially helpful in situating his thinking among that of his contemporaries.

Sluga, Hans. *Heidegger's Crisis: Philosophy and Politics in Nazi Germany*. Cambridge, Mass.: Harvard University Press, 1933. Provocative analysis of Heidegger's relationship with both Nazism and with broader contemporary currents of cultural critique in his era.

Steiner, George. *Heidegger*. Rev. ed. Chicago: University of Chicago Press, 1987. Stylish introduction to the breadth of Heidegger's thought by a major contemporary literary critic. Good place to begin reading about Heidegger.

SEE ALSO: 1902: James Proposes a Rational Basis for Religious Experience; 1907: Publication of James's *Pragmatism*; 1913: Husserl Advances Phenomenology; 1921: Wittgenstein Emerges as an Important Philosopher; 1922: First Meeting of the Vienna Circle; 1923: Buber Breaks New Ground in Religious Philosophy; May, 1926: Durant Publishes *The Story of Philosophy*; 1932: Gilson's *Spirit of Medieval Philosophy* Reassesses Christian Thought.

1927
KULESHOV AND PUDOVKIN INTRODUCE MONTAGE TO FILMMAKING

Lev Vladimirovich Kuleshov and his pupil Vsevolod Illarionovich Pudovkin, through their experimental work, theoretical writings, and films, brought Soviet cinema to a high level of achievement.

LOCALE: Moscow, Soviet Union (now Russia)
CATEGORY: Motion pictures

KEY FIGURES
Lev Vladimirovich Kuleshov (1899-1970), Soviet film theoretician and director
Vsevolod Illarionovich Pudovkin (1893-1953), Soviet actor, director, and film theoretician
Sergei Eisenstein (1898-1948), Soviet director and film theoretician
Dziga Vertov (1896-1954), Soviet newsreel and documentary film pioneer
Vladimir Ilich Lenin (Vladimir Ilich Ulyanov; 1870-1924), Russian revolutionary leader and first Soviet premier

SUMMARY OF EVENT

By 1927, the tenth anniversary of the Bolshevik Revolution, Soviet cinema had reached the pinnacle of international success. Filmmakers formulated basic doctrines and theories, guiding the young film industry with the support and approval of the government. Cinema, thus encouraged, developed as a singular art form, with its own principles and aesthetics, different from other art. Filmmakers rose to the challenge by creating films that were both politically pleasing and invigorated with artistic dynamism.

Ten years earlier, in March, 1917, the czar was replaced by a provisional government headed by Aleksandr Fyodorovich Kerensky. The government moved to abolish film censorship and even permitted production of anticzarist pictures. In October of that same year, the Bolsheviks, headed by Vladimir Ilich Lenin, overthrew the government, and the Soviet era began. Lenin was acutely aware of the importance of cinema in spreading the development of Communism and consolidating his power among the vast population. He declared, "Of all the arts for us the cinema is the most important." He created a formula that came to be known as "Lenin's proportion," which established a ratio of entertainment films to such educational motion pictures as travelogues, studies of cultures, and anticapitalist statements that could be played at Soviet theaters.

Although Lenin had in mind a cinema specializing in agitation and propaganda, two individuals emerged who changed the projected course of Soviet cinema. The first was Dziga Vertov, now hailed as the father of Soviet newsreel and documentary film. Born Denis Kaufman (brother of noted filmmakers Boris and Mikhail Kaufman), he took the name of Dziga Vertov, which in Russian means "spinning top," a reference to the action of winding film. His success came through clever editing and camera manipulation. Vertov gathered together and inspired a number of documentarists who believed life should be filmed as it really is, not staged with a narrative format. The group called itself Kinoki (cinema eyes). They believed fictional films were unimportant, opium for the masses.

The other seminal individual in Soviet motion pictures was Lev Vladimirovich Kuleshov. Heavily influenced and inspired by American film-editing techniques, particularly the work of D. W. Griffith, Kuleshov realized that film was a plastic art form that could be manipulated by a filmmaker. He used experiments to prove that film must be edited and constructed frame by frame. Taking Griffith's epic 1916 masterpiece *Intolerance*, with its four interlocking stories, he completely reedited the footage into very different combinations.

In one of Kuleshov's best-known film experiments, two people—a man and a woman in two separate shots—are seen walking in different districts of Moscow. In a third shot, they meet, shake hands, and look off in the distance as the man points. The fourth shot shows the American White House followed by the final shot, the couple climbing the steps of a famous Moscow cathedral. Through five different shots taken at different times and places, Kuleshov created a cinematic illusion of spatial and temporal unity. In another example, he photographed various parts of different women, then cut the film in such a way as to synthesize a new entity. Perhaps his most famous experiment involved using the expressionless face of matinee idol Ivan Mozhukin. Kuleshov intercut it with shots of a bowl of borscht, a dead woman in a coffin, and a girl playing with a toy bear. In each case, the audience raved about the power of Mozhukin's acting. He was seen as pensive in the first, sorrowful in the second, and smiling in the third. Through such experiments, Kuleshov slowly formulated the concept that became known as the Kuleshov effect. Kuleshov argued that a film shot has two values: its own photographic image of reality and what it acquires when spliced next to another shot. To Kuleshov, editing, or "montage," was the key to cinema, because it subordinated time and space and could also be used symbolically on a nonliteral level.

Kuleshov gathered into his workshop some of the Soviet cinema's brightest filmmakers: Sergei Eisenstein,

Boris Barnet, Mikhail Kalatzov, and Yakov Protazanov. The brilliant Eisenstein, in particular, although he studied only briefly with Kuleshov (and also worked briefly with Vertov), launched a remarkable film career based on montage. Kuleshov's special disciple, however, and the one most associated with and influenced by his work, was Vsevolod Illarionovich Pudovkin, who collaborated with his teacher on a number of experimental film projects. Pudovkin was six years older than his professor and had originally studied to be a chemist. His primary goal was to become an actor, but Kuleshov expected his students to learn all aspects of cinema. Pudovkin was an eager pupil and quickly assimilated Kuleshov's important concepts. He was particularly fascinated by the way a film performance could be manipulated via skillful editing.

Pudovkin's scientific training and his dramatic visual sense prompted him to become a director. He gained experience working on Kuleshov's films before embarking on his own. Pudovkin created three silent masterpieces of the 1920's, *Mother* (1926), *The End of St. Petersburg* (1927), and *The Heir to Ghengis Khan* (1928). His appeal in all three was directly to the audience's emotions, and he kept his story lines simple and powerful, in contrast to his fellow filmmaker Eisenstein, whose work seemed detached and intellectual. Kuleshov remained proud of both his pupils and found much to admire in their creative work.

SIGNIFICANCE

In 1926, Kuleshov abandoned his workshop to become involved with a project that became his most important film, *By the Law*. The film was adapted from a short story by Jack London titled "The Unexpected" and was made on one of the smallest budgets in Soviet cinema history. It was set in a one-room cabin in a desolate part of the Yukon. The story line concerns justice and how two people must try, condemn, and execute a third person who murdered their friends. *By the Law* is economical and polished in style; artistically, it implies social criticism. Kuleshov cleverly used montage to create a remarkable film that achieved international success when released in December of 1926.

The same year, Pudovkin was emerging as a self-confident artist and began the first of his three revolutionary films, *Mother*, based on a Maxim Gorky novel that takes place during the 1905 revolution. The story is about a family consisting of a poor peasant woman, her husband, a brutal drunkard, and the couple's son. Father and son come to blows over differing political views, and the father is killed. The mother naïvely betrays her son to the authorities, and he is sentenced in a rigged trial. The mother helps him to escape jail, and later the two unite and both are killed at a workers' demonstration held on May Day. Pudovkin edited the film brilliantly, creating breathtaking montage effects; the film always stays in touch with the human drama unfolding underneath the great moments of history.

Pudovkin also found time in 1926 to write two books on filmmaking that helped to clarify the Kuleshov-Pudovkin concept of montage. He restated Kuleshov's basic premise that films are not "shot" but are artistically "built" from separate strips. Both artists discovered that individual film clips become part of a larger form with intrinsic structural unity and effectiveness. Pudovkin stated that the key process was actually one of a cognitive "linkage" of frames. In his films, he intercut images in exciting new ways, arranging them on a metaphysical as well as narrative level, clearly showing his indebtedness to Kuleshov. Pudovkin stressed the story, keeping it simple and clear; his attitude was personal and emotional. He used fluid narrative editing and used shock montage effects sparingly. His handling of actors was brilliant, and his films are memorable for their performances. He excelled in using montage to contrast the horrible brutality of wars with the idealism that fuels them.

By 1927, both Kuleshov and Pudovkin, through their experiments, writings, and films employing the principle of montage, had made a decided impact on Soviet and world cinema. Their editorial concepts opened up the artistic possibilities of film. Filmmakers could now manipulate what the audience experienced, enabling them to elicit certain emotions, associations, and thoughts. Kuleshov and Pudovkin not only demonstrated theoretically their concepts of montage but also created masterpieces of early Soviet cinema.

In 1927, Pudovkin made the film that won him an international reputation, *The End of St. Petersburg*, which had the distinction of being the first Soviet film to play in New York City at Broadway's largest theater, the Roxy. Through the eyes of a peasant, the film shows the historic events that rocked Russia from 1912 to 1917, when it was transformed from czarist to Soviet rule. Pudovkin graphically showed how his hero radically changes from a bumbling youth to a mature man aware of his country's suffering. The director intercut the hysteria of the czarist stock market exchange with the hysteria found on the battlefield. When the peasant enters Leningrad, he is viewed from above the building, as though he is an ant, but by picture's end, the camera is on the ground looking up at him. One breathtaking sequence shows a midlevel bureaucrat in an elevator with a tycoon promising a great promotion. As the elevator rises, the light changes, and the toady's smile grows as he rises to the top; the scene stands as a brilliant testament to the montage theories of Kuleshov and Pudovkin.

By the end of 1927, the first decade of the Soviet Union was over. There was much to celebrate in the film industry. Soviet filmmakers, inspired by Kuleshov, were producing exciting and celebrated films. Montage was being employed in new and innovative ways. Important theoretical developments in the cinema had been established and encouraged because they played an important role in promoting the revolution. The aim was to build a glorious Communist future. Pudovkin wrote that when "the old and familiar artistic methods crumbled and collapsed. . . . Lev Kuleshov forced us to acquire visual taste and taught us the ABC of montage."

The honeymoon of state and art would not last. Joseph Stalin had assumed complete power after Lenin's death, and by the end of 1927, he was moving to consolidate his hold over the Communist Party. Stalin grew increasingly suspicious of criticism, particularly from the cinema, which was forced to eschew artistic concerns and was pressured into creating pictures for the working classes. It is no wonder, then, that neither Kuleshov nor Pudovkin ever again achieved his original level of critical success and even, along with Eisenstein, fell into political disfavor. During the mid-1920's, however, these filmmakers created a vital cinematic language that invigorated the screen and made the Soviet cinema the envy of the world.

—Terry Theodore

FURTHER READING

Birkos, Alexander S. *Soviet Cinema: Directors and Films*. Hamden, Conn.: Archon Books, 1976. Divided into two comprehensive sections focusing on Soviet cinema from 1918 to 1975. The first part examines the creative lives of the important directors; the second concerns the important films released during the period. Encyclopedic approach, with a good short introduction to the subject.

Dickinson, Thorold, and Catherine De La Roche. *Soviet Cinema*. New York: Arno Press, 1972. Brief volume pairs two essays by different critics, one on silent film and the other on film with sound. Illustrated with many photographs.

Feldman, Seth R. *Evolution of Style in the Early Work of Dziga Vertov*. New York: Arno Press, 1975. Dissertation on Vertov's pioneering work and his important place in Soviet cinema. Examines political, historic, and aesthetic concerns as they relate to Vertov's theories.

Kenez, Peter. *Cinema and Soviet Society: From the Revolution to the Death of Stalin*. New York: I. B. Tauris, 2001. History of Soviet film includes discussion of changes in cinematic content and style from before the revolution and the constraints of Socialist Realism. Features illustrations, glossary, filmography, bibliography, and index.

Kuleshov, Lev. *Kuleshov on Film: Writings by Lev Kuleshov*. Edited and translated by Ronald Levaco. Berkeley: University of California Press, 1974. Kuleshov's essays reveal him to be cinema's first aesthetic theorist. Levaco, through his essay selection, translation, and editing of Kuleshov's writings, transforms Kuleshov from a shadowy figure to a director with a unique place in Soviet cinema.

Leyda, Jay. *Kino: A History of the Russian and Soviet Film*. 3d ed. Princeton, N.J.: Princeton University Press, 1983. Classic study of Russian/Soviet cinema gives a marvelous overview, including the screening of films in 1896 through the revolution, the great achievements in the 1920's, the repressive Stalinist era, and the resurgence following Stalin's death.

Pudovkin, V. I. *Film Technique and Film Acting*. Translated by Ivor Montagu. London: Vision Press, 1954. Pudovkin's two studies on cinema are as important as any of his films and are considered classics by both filmmakers and scholars. He openly acknowledges Kuleshov as his mentor.

Schnitzer, Luda, Jean Schnitzer, and Marcel Martin, eds. *Cinema in Revolution: The Heroic Era of the Soviet Film*. 1973. Reprint. New York: Da Capo Press, 1987.

Excellent collection of twelve essays by the leading Soviet filmmakers, including Kuleshov, Vertov, Eisenstein, Pudovkin, and Alexander Dovzhenko.

Taylor, Richard. *Film Propaganda: Soviet Russia and Nazi Germany*. Rev. ed. New York: I. B. Tauris, 1998. Demonstrates the significance of propaganda in twentieth century politics and the controlled way cinema has been used. Offers only a limited look at Soviet film achievement.

Vertov, Dziga. *Kino-Eye: The Writings of Dziga Vertov*. Edited by Annette Michelson. Berkeley: University of California Press, 1984. Valuable collection of Vertov's work, gathered from his articles, public addresses, notebooks, diaries, creative projects, and proposals. Good introductory section includes Vertov's filmography.

Vorontsov, Iu, and Igor Rachuk. *The Phenomenon of the Soviet Cinema*. Translated by Doris Bradbury. Moscow: Progress, 1980. Politically correct Soviet interpretation of cinema from its origins through the 1970's. Includes chapters on Soviet audiences, films shown abroad, and a good filmography.

1927

SEE ALSO: Fall, 1903: *The Great Train Robbery* Introduces New Editing Techniques; Mar. 3, 1915: Griffith Releases *The Birth of a Nation*; 1920: Premiere of *The Cabinet of Dr. Caligari*; 1923: *The Ten Commandments* Advances American Film Spectacle; Dec. 4, 1924: Von Stroheim's Silent Masterpiece *Greed* Premieres; 1925: Eisenstein's *Potemkin* Introduces New Film Editing Techniques; 1925-1927: Gance's *Napoléon* Revolutionizes Filmmaking Techniques; 1927: Lang Expands the Limits of Filmmaking with *Metropolis*.

1927
LANG EXPANDS THE LIMITS OF FILMMAKING WITH *METROPOLIS*

In Metropolis, *Fritz Lang used boldly innovative cinematic techniques to tell a story that blended futuristic science fiction with nineteenth century melodrama and prophetic social criticism.*

LOCALE: Berlin, Germany
CATEGORY: Motion pictures

KEY FIGURES
Fritz Lang (1890-1976), Austrian filmmaker
Thea von Harbou (1888-1954), German novelist and
  screenwriter
Eugen Schüfftan (1893-1977), German American
  special-effects artist
Otto Hunte (1881-1960), German film set designer

SUMMARY OF EVENT
In 1924, Fritz Lang journeyed from Germany to the United States with the intention of touring American film studios in New York and Hollywood. Lang had already achieved critical acclaim as an innovative filmmaker with such films as the spy thriller *Dr. Mabuse der Spieler* (1922; *Dr. Mabuse the Gambler*) and the lavish, two-part *Die Nibelungen* (1924), a retelling of the Siegfried legend. Upon reaching New York, Lang was immediately struck by the city's glittering skyline of concrete, glass, and neon, a sight responsible for the germ of an idea for a new film. Lang envisioned a futuristic world where machines and efficiency are worshiped and where human compassion and sacrifice are things of the ancient past. When he returned to Germany, Lang discussed this basic concept with his wife, screenwriter and novelist Thea von Harbou, who turned the idea into a novel.

Over the next two years, Lang labored to bring his vision of the world in the year 2000 to the screen. Because of his earlier successes, Universium Film, Germany's premier film studio, agreed to finance the project. Two years later, the studio was nearly bankrupt, largely because of Lang's project. Lang shot nearly two million feet of film during a shooting schedule consisting of 310 days and 60 nights. He employed a cast of more than thirty-five thousand, built elaborate full-scale sets and intricate miniatures, developed innovative special-effects techniques, and spent close to two million dollars, making his film the most expensive European production up to that time. The result was *Metropolis*, a dazzling, sixteen-reel extravaganza, cut down to nine reels for its American premiere. The film was described in a

contemporary review as "an extraordinary motion picture, in some ways the most extraordinary ever made," and in another review by American film critic and playwright Robert E. Sherwood as "too much scenery, too many people, too much plot and too many platitudinous ideas."

Like Sherwood, many who first saw *Metropolis* were overwhelmed by its scope, its amazing visual richness, and its strange blending of the ultramodern and the mystically medieval. Many were awed by the film's innovative special effects, which showed masses of humans scurrying through towering landscapes made up of thousands of Art Deco and gothic skyscrapers and monstrous, steam-belching machines. Although contemporary reviewers praised the film for its dazzling look and innovative cinematic techniques, they also condemned its story as a confusing mishmash of politics, social commentary, Christian symbolism, and futuristic prophecy. Although the film was a commercial success, it never made enough money to save the studio that financed it.

Over the years, the film suffered more reeditings, further muddling its already confusing story line. It was not until 1984, when music producer Giorgio Moroder put together a restored version of the film based on all existing film fragments and using key stills to fill in gaps in the story line, that the public was finally able to experience *Metropolis* as Lang and his collaborators had first envisioned it. Although the restored version is still missing footage, Moroder's version clarifies the story line, making the film a much more strongly cohesive blending of astounding imagery and thought-provoking storytelling.

The film itself deals with the story of a mastermind builder, Fredersen, who has designed and now lords over a glittering city, Metropolis. Fredersen and his elite followers live in luxury far above ground while the workers who built and run the machines that power the city slave below, living in drab communal structures underground. The workers who operate the machines move in piston-like formation, as if their prolonged exposure to the giant machines has turned them, too, into soulless automatons. When Fredersen's son, Freder, encounters the spiritual leader of the workers, Maria, he begins to question the reasons for maintaining the brutal division between the slave workers and the decadent elite. Freder eventually joins the ranks of the workers and falls in love with Maria, who believes Freder can help act as a mediator—

Fritz Lang (center) prepares an actor for a scene with the Maria robot in Metropolis. (Hulton Archive/Getty Images)

1927

as the heart needed to mend the rift between the head that designed Metropolis and the hands that built it. When Fredersen learns of Maria's existence and her powerful influence over the workers, however, he persuades a mad inventor, Rotwang, to fashion the likeness of Maria onto one of Rotwang's inventions, a robot, so that Fredersen can use the Maria robot to keep the workers in line. After Rotwang kidnaps Maria and empowers his robot with her likeness, the false Maria develops an evil mind of its own and leads the workers on a rampage that destroys the city. The film's climax has Freder and Rotwang battling for the real Maria on the top of a gothic cathedral, as Fredersen and the workers watch horrified from below amid the wreckage of the city. In the end, Rotwang falls to his death, and Freder acts as the city's heart, joining its head and hands, presumably to build a more compassionate future.

SIGNIFICANCE

Even in its restored version, *Metropolis* features an extremely melodramatic story line and is marred by over-

acting, principally by Gustav Frölich, who plays the Christlike mediator Freder. What has endured and continues to awe those who see the film, however, is its overwhelmingly dazzling imagery. Lang, who studied architecture, art, and painting before becoming a filmmaker, confessed many times to his strong preference for using visual imagery to express his personal philosophical insights. In all of his films, and especially in *Metropolis*, Lang used the visual to express his ideas regarding the conflict between the divine and demonic sides of human beings. The entire film is an amazing, swirling dance of opposites, of humans acting as machines and machines acting as humans, of scientists using advanced technology and black magic to create a robotic thing that represents a perverted image of perfection, of gorgeously glittering superstructures powered by ugly, massive, soul-killing machines. In one amazing scene, the machines transform into a likeness of the cannibal god Moloch, which begins to devour the workers who march willingly into its gaping mouth.

Lang, who had been the first choice to direct another

2153

visually innovative landmark German film, *Das Kabinett des Dr. Caligari* (1920; *The Cabinet of Dr. Caligari*), and Otto Hunte, head set designer for *Metropolis*, used the earlier film's creative yet cinematically static set designs as a model for the *Metropolis* sets, but Lang then went far beyond the look of the earlier film by combining moody, expressionistic lighting with fluid camera movements. The most dynamic example of this innovative combination of lighting and camera movement occurs in the scene in which the real Maria is stalked by the scientist Rotwang through underground catacombs. As Rotwang pursues Maria, he uses a strong beam of light from an electric torch to "capture" her, propelling her forward through the catacombs. At one point, the beam crawls up Maria's body like a snake.

In other scenes depicting the city's intricate skyline, complete with towering skyscrapers, flashing neon lights, scurrying masses of people, and quaint flying machines circling above the structures, Lang and his special-effects master, Eugen Schüfftan, pioneered the "Schüfftan process," in which two cameras are used simultaneously to create the effect of live-action figures cavorting through miniature sets. Still another innovative touch was Lang's use of the robot in the scene showing Rotwang empowering his creation with the likeness of Maria. Although the concept of the robot had been created earlier, Lang took the concept to a most elaborate extreme, using dynamic lighting, electrical effects, and expressive staging to overwhelm the viewer.

At the time the film was made, Lang was interested in mysticism, and he wanted to play up the contrast between the world of soulless technological efficiency and the mysterious world of spirits and powers from beyond. Although he ultimately toned down this aspect of the film, he still managed to include an amazing scene of statues representing the seven deadly sins coming alive and dancing around a cathedral while the false Maria dances provocatively amid a leering group of rich admirers and a delirious Freder twists in bed, gripped by vivid, decadent dreams. In another scene, Lang sought to parallel the fate of Metropolis with the fate of the Tower of Babel. To do so, he created an intricate miniature tower and surrounded it with thousands of worker-extras shown to be struggling to build the decadent structure and finally rebelling against the tower's spiritually bankrupt architects.

Such scenes, elaborately (and expensively) staged, visually dynamic, cinematically innovative, yet at the same time expressing the filmmaker's personal view of the world, made *Metropolis* an enduring classic and an inspiration for a legion of filmmakers who followed. Such big-budget film spectaculars as Stanley Kubrick's *2001: A Space Odyssey* (1968), George Lucas's *Star Wars* trilogy (1977, 1980, 1983), Francis Ford Coppola's *Apocalypse Now* (1979), Steven Spielberg's *Close Encounters of the Third Kind* (1977) and *E.T. the Extra-Terrestrial* (1982), Ridley Scott's *Blade Runner* (1982), and James Cameron's *Terminator 2: Judgment Day* (1991) all owe a debt to *Metropolis* and to Lang's megalomaniacal attention to detail, innovative cinematic techniques, and personal, dynamic vision. Although Lang went on to create several more film masterpieces expressing his ideas on the spiritual and moral conflicts within each individual, *Metropolis* remains the most spectacular example of his personal vision of the soul of man.

—*Jim Kline*

FURTHER READING

Armour, Robert A. *Fritz Lang*. Boston: Twayne, 1978. Presents an overview of Lang's life, the factors that influenced his unique vision of the world, and the films he wrote and directed. Includes detailed descriptions of Lang's complete film output.

Bogdanovich, Peter. *Fritz Lang in America*. London: Studio Vista, 1968. Focuses primarily on Lang's American film period, but also includes information about his early German period, with many comments about the making of *Metropolis*. Interview format vividly captures Lang's opinionated and humorous character.

Eisner, Lotte. *Fritz Lang*. Translated by Gertrud Mander. 1976. Reprint. New York: Da Capo Press, 1986. Detailed analysis of Lang's entire film career, with many insightful comments by Lang himself, presented by a respected film critic and personal friend of Lang. Includes the text of a fragmented autobiography left uncompleted by Lang.

Gunning, Tom. *The Films of Fritz Lang: Allegories of Vision and Modernity*. London: British Film Institute, 2000. An examination of all of Lang's films by a historian and theorist of early cinema. Chapter 3 is devoted to discussion of *Metropolis*.

Jenkins, Stephen, ed. *Fritz Lang: The Image and the Look*. London: British Film Institute, 1981. Collection of essays by film authorities on various aspects of Lang's approach to filmmaking, including analyses of his cinematic themes and his methods of expressing his personal views with visual imagery.

Jensen, Paul M. *The Cinema of Fritz Lang*. New York: A. S. Barnes, 1969. Presents a concise overview of

Lang's life and a film-by-film examination of his artistic output. Includes photographs from each production.

Minden, Michael, and Holger Bachmann, eds. *Fritz Lang's "Metropolis": Cinematic Views of Technology and Fear*. Columbia, S.C.: Camden House, 2000. Collection of previously published and new essays on *Metropolis*, commentary by Lang, and other materials related to the film. Editors' introduction examines the production of the film and its reception in 1927 as well as the views of later critics.

Ott, Frederick. *The Films of Fritz Lang*. Secaucus, N.J.: Citadel Press, 1979. Profusely illustrated volume begins with a long, detailed introduction that examines

Lang's life and influences. Includes a plot synopsis of each film, some of Lang's own set and scene drawings, and insightful information on Lang's film output.

SEE ALSO: Fall, 1903: *The Great Train Robbery* Introduces New Editing Techniques; Mar. 3, 1915: Griffith Releases *The Birth of a Nation*; 1920: Premiere of *The Cabinet of Dr. Caligari*; 1923: *The Ten Commandments* Advances American Film Spectacle; Dec. 4, 1924: Von Stroheim's Silent Masterpiece *Greed* Premieres; 1925: Eisenstein's *Potemkin* Introduces New Film Editing Techniques; 1925-1927: Gance's *Napoléon* Revolutionizes Filmmaking Techniques.

1927
LEMAÎTRE PROPOSES THE BIG BANG THEORY

Georges Lemaître proposed that the universe was once a giant atom that exploded and continues to expand.

LOCALE: United States
CATEGORIES: Science and technology; astronomy; physics

KEY FIGURE
Georges Lemaître (1894-1966), Belgian cleric and astronomy and mathematics hobbyist

SUMMARY OF EVENT
In the early twentieth century, astronomers and physicists were eager for new discoveries about the macrocosm of universal life. Although these sciences often worked together, an individual did not need to have a full understanding of one field in order to contribute successfully to research or theory in the other. Often, astronomers would observe the physical world and puzzle about unknown or unexplained phenomena, and then physicists would resolve the issues raised in terms of their theories and equations. Conversely, physicists might develop new theories about the nature of the universe without having any observational data. In such cases, astronomers would proceed to seek out the projected physical realities the physicists proposed from their equations. The big bang theory is an example of this discovery method: equation first, observation second.

Georges Lemaître's formal training was theological and clerical, leading him to a career in the Catholic Church as a monsignor. Similar to other religious men

who pursued interests in science as a hobby (such as Gregor Mendel in genetics), Lemaître's interests included theoretical mathematics and astronomy. In 1923, Lemaître left Belgium for an extended time of study and travel in the United States. During this visit, Lemaître pursued his own interest in science and math instead of formal church-related matters. Lemaître stayed in Cambridge, Massachusetts, at Harvard University, where he studied astronomy as a research student. Albert Einstein's theory of gravitation, now accepted over Sir Isaac Newton's, had been confirmed four years prior to Lemaître's visit to Harvard. Edwin Powell Hubble's discovery of independent galaxies was still a year away. The following year, 1924, Lemaître, on an official trip for Harvard, went to the Mount Wilson Observatory in Southern California to observe the work in which Hubble and others were engaged. During that year, Hubble would confirm that independent galaxies did indeed exist; however, the full ramifications of that discovery and the accompanying data were not fully developed at the time of Lemaître's visit. Lemaître was therefore unable to call on these data when he first proposed the big bang theory.

During his visit to the United States, Lemaître began exploring Einstein's equations of gravitation. When Lemaître solved these equations in the simplest manner, he discovered that they described an expanding universe. The long-held view of the universe prior to Lemaître's discovery was that it was homogeneous, isotropic, and static. Although Lemaître still believed the universe to be homogeneous and isotropic, he now discarded the static view of the universe for a view of the universe as expanding. In 1927, Lemaître's first paper on the homogeneous but expanding universe was published. He affirmed his belief in a universe that is the same in all directions in terms of its physical makeup and the physical laws by which it is governed; however, he denied that it is a fixed universe. He argued that the simplest solution to Einstein's theory of gravitation demanded that the universe be expanding. At that time, there were no observational data to support Lemaître's claim. Einstein was reluctant to endorse the proposed theory until he had investigated Lemaître's solutions to the gravity equations. Unknown to most of the scientific community of the Western world, a Soviet meteorologist, Aleksandr Friedmann, had discovered the same solutions to the gravity equations and proposed the same view of an expanding universe in 1922. Both men came to the same conclusion independently and without any experimental data.

At Mount Wilson Observatory in 1929, Hubble discovered that the galaxies he was observing were moving away from Earth at incredible speeds; furthermore, those galaxies farther out in the universe were moving more rapidly than those galaxies that were closer. Hubble made his discovery unaware of Lemaître's theory of an expanding universe and rejection of the traditional static view. There now existed observational data to support Lemaître's view of expansion. In papers published in 1931 and 1933, Lemaître used Hubble's discovery to support his theory. Lemaître's argument was simple: Hubble had discovered that the galaxies in the universe are hurling themselves away from some central point at incredible speeds; therefore, if one were to "reverse the film," one would see these galaxies rushing in toward one another at some central point. Furthermore, the well-established law of entropy (an organized unit becomes more disordered as time passes) suggested that the universe, which was becoming more disorderly, must at some point have been very orderly. These two arguments led Lemaître to suggest the existence in history of some large primordial atom that contained all the matter of the universe. Lemaître's view of the universe is well described as follows: Imagine a deflated balloon covered in spots. As the balloon inflates, the spots move away from one another but continue to be the same relative distance apart. Dots far apart, such as two dots on opposite sides of the balloon, would be moving away from each other at a greater speed during the inflating than would two dots that are adjacent to each other. When the balloon is deflated, the dots rush back to a central point.

Hubble's research provided Lemaître with the observational data to support his theory, and Einstein agreed that Lemaître's solutions were indeed the best solutions to the gravitational equations. As a result of this support, scientists began to investigate Lemaître's theory, which the scientific community would label the big bang theory. For a short time, Lemaître continued to develop his ideas about the theory and its effects. He made some predictions about the effects of the big bang that should be evident if indeed that was how the universe began. These proposals suggested areas that scientists could investigate in an effort to confirm the theory. The idea most pursued was the existence of some type of background radiation that must have been given off by the primordial atom when it exploded. Lemaître was confident that some type of background radiation would be discovered. After the theory became the property of the scientific community and several research projects were undertaken to examine it, Lemaître faded from the field to pursue other studies and problems of science that intrigued him. Until his death in 1966, he was still lecturing on the theory of the origins of the universe, although he did not actively engage in the current investigations.

SIGNIFICANCE

Lemaître's bold new insight into an expanding universe sent astronomers and physicists delving into their observations and calculations, hoping to unravel the mysteries of the origin of the universe. The big bang theory brought physics and astronomy together to create a joint science known as astrophysics, which investigates the credibility of the theory and seeks an explanation of the first few minutes of universal history. Although Lemaître explained how the universe started, his theory and calculations told little about the nature of that early universe, aside from the idea of the primordial atom. The nature of that atom, the particles that constituted the atom, and the reaction of those particles in the first few minutes after the explosion were questions unanswered by Lemaître or his theory. Also unanswered were the cause and nature of the explosion that sent matter hurling through space.

The big bang theory required the examination of both the macrocosm and the microcosm. Astronomers and many physicists, focusing on the macrocosm, began to study the current universe in the light of the big bang in an effort to gather data about the first few minutes of history. Using Lemaître's idea of running the film backward from where the universe currently is to where it was, these scientists searched for clues. This search included scanning the heavens for the background radiation; such discoveries as cosmic rays and other forms of radiation resulted. In the microcosm particle, physicists began to explore the inside of the atom hoping to discover clues there that might lead back to the first few minutes of history. Their search required the building of particle accelerators in an effort to duplicate the energy of the initial explosion, which brought the scientific community into the subatomic world full of unknown particles. Lemaître's theory required scientists to fit antimatter, quarks, and other new forms of matter being discovered into the picture of early universal history.

Although Lemaître's theory is a theory of science, it had many philosophical ramifications. If it is possible to run the film backward and understand the cause-and-effect beginning of the universe, would it then be possible to project forward with certainty where the universe would be in any number of years? Did this theory then support a deterministic view of reality? How did creatures with free will fit into the picture? Another philosophical and scientific question centers on the cause of the explosion and time. Einstein proved that time is relative to space and speed, but if the universe was once contained in one large atom taking up nothing defined as space and traveling at no speed, what was the cause of the explosion? The explosion could not be the result of changing circumstances over time, because time did not exist. The search for all the answers of the early history of the universe has been successful back to the first few thousandths of a second after the explosion. What nature was like in those fractions of a second and before requires a grand theory that unifies all of physics.

—Charles Murphy

FURTHER READING

Abell, G. O., and G. Chincarini, eds. *Early Evolution of the Universe and Its Present Structure*. Boston: D. Reidel, 1983. Collection of papers presented at a symposium of the International Astronomical Union in Kolymbari, Crete. Topics include cosmology, early history of the universe, and conjecture as to where the universe could be heading. Presents a detailed discussion of the current structure of the universe and how this informs the science of the past. Includes bibliographies and indexes.

Berger, A., ed. *Big Bang and Georges Lemaître*. Boston: D. Reidel, 1984. Compilation of papers delivered at the International Symposium on Georges Lemaître represents an excellent source of biographical information, information on the development of Lemaître's theory, and an overview of work in cosmology up to 1984. Includes many equations, illustrations, and bibliographies.

Contopoulos, G., and D. Kotsakis. *Cosmology: The Structure and Evolution of the Universe*. Translated by M. Petrou and P. L. Palmer. 2d ed. New York: Springer-Verlag, 1987. Presents various explanations of the big bang theory and the implications of the differing interpretations of the theory. Includes some equations and technical diagrams, but is written for the beginning student of cosmology and provides excellent explanations of some complicated issues.

Gribbin, John. *In Search of the Big Bang: The Life and Death of the Universe*. Rev. ed. New York: Penguin Books, 1998. History of modern cosmology presents the story of the discovery of the nature of external galaxies. Intended for the general reader. Includes illustrations, bibliography, and index.

Silk, Joseph. *The Big Bang*. 3d ed. New York: W. H. Freeman, 2000. Excellent historical account of the big bang theory from Lemaître and Friedmann through Hubble's discoveries to the end of the twentieth century. Explains how the discoveries were made, their implications, and the reactions of the scientific community. Also traces the history of the universe using the big bang model. Includes glossary and index.

_____. *On the Shores of the Unknown: A Short History of the Universe*. New York: Cambridge University Press, 2005. A history of the universe and the development of humankind's knowledge about it that is accessible to lay readers. Includes illustrations and index.

Trefil, James S. *The Moment of Creation*. New York: Charles Scribner's Sons, 1983. Begins with the premise that the big bang theory is correct, so does not mention Lemaître or attempt to defend the theory. Explains how science has come to an understanding of the first few minutes of history, using examples of discovery such as Hubble's work at Mount Wilson. Also proposes what the universe might have looked like in the first few milliseconds after the explosion. Includes illustrations and bibliography.

SEE ALSO: 1903-1904: Hale Establishes Mount Wilson Observatory; 1904: Kapteyn Discovers Two Star Streams in the Galaxy; Early 1920's: Slipher Presents Evidence of Redshifts in Galactic Spectra; 1924: Hubble Determines the Distance to the Andromeda Nebula; Dec., 1924: Hubble Shows That Other Galaxies Are Independent Systems; 1929: Hubble Confirms the Expanding Universe.

1927

1927
NUMBER OF U.S. AUTOMAKERS FALLS TO FORTY-FOUR

The consolidation of the U.S. auto industry into three large firms began in the 1920's and demonstrated that only large and efficient producers could survive.

LOCALE: United States

CATEGORIES: Trade and commerce; organizations and institutions; transportation; manufacturing and industry

KEY FIGURES

William Crapo Durant (1861-1947), founder of General Motors and its president, 1915-1920

Alfred P. Sloan (1875-1966), president of General Motors, 1923-1937, and chair of the board, 1937-1956

Walter P. Chrysler (1875-1940), founder of the Chrysler Corporation and its president, 1925-1940

Henry Ford (1863-1947), founder of the Ford Motor Company

Charles E. Duryea (1861-1938), cofounder of the Duryea Motor Wagon Company

J. Frank Duryea (1869-1967), cofounder of the Duryea Motor Wagon Company

Benjamin Briscoe (1869-1945), organizer of the United States Motor Company and its president, 1910-1912

SUMMARY OF EVENT

In 1921, the number of firms actively producing automobiles in the United States was eighty-eight; by 1927, the number had declined to forty-four. Consolidation of the American automobile industry continued for decades after 1927 as a result of basic economic factors associated with motor vehicle production.

Brothers Charles E. Duryea and J. Frank Duryea built the first gasoline-powered automobile in Springfield, Massachusetts, in 1893. In 1896, they organized the Duryea Motor Wagon Company, the first American company to make automobiles powered by gasoline internal combustion engines. During the next thirty years, more than fifteen hundred firms entered the industry. These firms included builders producing automobiles powered by steam, electricity, and gasoline. The forty-four firms surviving by 1927 almost exclusively produced gasoline-powered vehicles.

Early automobile factories consisted of buildings with little machinery and were devoted mostly to the final assembly of vehicles. In 1908, the Ford Motor Company, founded by Henry Ford in 1903, began output of the Model T, which used standardized, interchangeable parts, most produced by Ford itself. These factors allowed production on a modern assembly line. In 1901, Olds Motor Works (founded in 1897 as the Olds Motor Vehicle Company) used the first crude assembly line, consisting of cars supported by rolling coasters moving along wooden platforms. Ford, however, employed a more sophisticated assembly line on a conveyor system, with complex systems to handle materials and highly specialized labor.

Mass-production techniques reduced the cost of building an automobile and therefore cut the retail price. The 1907 Ford Model K had a retail price of $2,750. The mass-produced Ford Model T retailed for a base price of $850 in 1908; by the early 1920's, the base price had fallen to $265.

The growth of Ford's production to two million cars per year by 1923 was generated internally, except for the purchase of the Lincoln Motor Company in 1922. The success of Ford indicated to other auto manufacturers that mass-production techniques were needed. To become large and compete, most firms had to undertake mergers and consolidations.

The creation of General Motors and the United States Motor Company in the early 1900's established a pattern for auto industry consolidation. In 1904, William Crapo Durant, a wagon and carriage builder from Flint, Michigan, organized a recapitalization of the Buick Motor Company, founded in 1902. Benjamin Briscoe of Maxwell-Briscoe, organized in 1904, met with Durant in early 1908 to discuss combining about twenty manufacturers. Durant rejected the idea because too many divergent interests would be involved.

Briscoe persisted in his automotive consolidation efforts and founded the United States Motor Company in 1910. It included more than 150 affiliated companies, with the Maxwell-Briscoe Company, Columbia Motor Car Company, Dayton Motor Car Company, and Brush Runabout Company forming the nucleus. The company went into receivership in 1912; the liquidation created the Maxwell Motor Company, which later reorganized as the Chrysler Motors Corporation.

In September, 1908, Durant incorporated General Motors (GM). Within one year, GM acquired Oldsmobile, Buick, Cadillac Automobile Company (founded 1902), Oakland Motor Car Company (founded 1907), Reliance Motor Truck Company (founded 1903), and the

Rapid Truck Company (founded 1902). The rapid expansion of GM caused a cash shortage. Bankers agreed to lend GM fifteen million dollars on the condition that they could name a new board of directors. As a result, Durant remained a director but was excluded from management. He continued his interest in automobiles, however, and founded the Chevrolet Motor Company in 1911 with former race driver Louis Chevrolet. Meanwhile, Durant continued to acquire General Motors stock. He was able to reassume control of GM in 1916, when Chevrolet Motor Company bought controlling shares of General Motors. In 1916, Durant also created United Motors Corporation, a combination of five parts manufacturers including Perlman Rim corporation, Dayton Engineering Laboratories, Remy Electric, New Departure Manufacturing, and Hyatt Roller Bearing Company. In 1918, United Motors became part of General Motors.

The 1920 recession caused financial problems at General Motors. After a series of moves to raise the market value of GM stock, Durant sold his GM stock to the E. I. Du Pont de Nemours Company, which assumed control of 36 percent of the common stock of GM. Durant resigned as president of GM by the end of 1920.

In 1921, Maxwell went into receivership. Walter P. Chrysler, who began his automotive career at Buick in 1911 and headed the Buick division of GM until 1920, was brought in to reorganize Maxwell. In 1924, Maxwell produced a car bearing the Chrysler name. In 1925, Chrysler completed a takeover of Maxwell and incorporated the firm as Chrysler Motors Corporation.

Chrysler needed an efficient manufacturing facility to compete with GM and Ford. In 1928, Chrysler purchased Dodge Brothers, Inc. (founded in 1914), which had a modern assembly, forge, and foundry plant and was then the third largest U.S. automobile producer. Chrysler thus became the successor to a series of consolidations that began in 1910 with the founding of United States Motor Company. The consolidations included bringing the Everitt-Metzger-Flanders Company and Chalmers Motor Company into Maxwell and the purchase of Dodge. With modern facilities available, Chrysler introduced a low-priced car called the Plymouth to compete with Ford and Chevrolet and a medium-priced car called the De Soto.

During the 1920's, the U.S. automobile industry evolved into a structure with three dominant firms—General Motors, Ford, and Chrysler. A number of important independent firms also existed, including Studebaker (founded as a wagon maker in 1852, with auto production beginning in 1904), Packard (founded 1899), Nash (founded as the Thomas B. Jeffrey Company in 1902), Hudson (founded 1909), and Willys-Overland (founded 1903).

SIGNIFICANCE

The major impact of the consolidation of the U.S. auto industry to forty-four firms by 1927 was the recognition that the production of motor vehicles requires large volumes for efficient operation and survival because of the high fixed costs of developing new vehicles and equipping plants. As of the 1980's, achieving minimum costs per unit required an annual output of about 200,000 units in auto assembly and 500,000 units in engine plants. These levels of output for efficient operation were consistent with the experience of Japanese producers—including Honda, Nissan, Toyota, Mazda, and Mitsubishi—that had built plants in the United States after 1980. The thirty-two auto assembly plants in operation in the United States in 1993 had capacity levels consistent with these estimates. The number of auto assembly plants nearly doubled in the late 1990's as non-U.S. companies built additional plants.

Consolidation of the auto industry continued from the late 1920's through the 1980's. The Great Depression of the 1930's caused the failure of several firms. U.S. auto production declined from 4.5 million in 1929 to 1.1 million in 1932, and output did not recover to the 1929 level until 1949. Industry volume was insufficient to support the number of producers in existence. Once-prominent firms such as Chandler-Cleveland, Marmon, Peerless, Auburn-Cord-Duesenberg, Hupmobile, Graham, and Pierce-Arrow exited the industry in the 1929-1941 period.

Following World War II, a series of mergers occurred among independent automobile manufacturers. In 1954, the Studebaker Corporation was purchased by the Packard Motor Car Company. The combined car and truck output of Studebaker and Packard was nearly 400,000 units in 1950. Studebaker-Packard Corporation was unable to generate sufficient sales to be efficient, however, even after consolidating automobile production into one U.S. assembly plant in 1957 from three in 1954. Output was 164,000 vehicles in 1959, but by the final year of the company's production in 1966, Studebaker-Packard built only 2,000 cars in a small Canadian plant.

In 1953, the Kaiser-Fraser Corporation, founded in 1947, merged with Willys-Overland. Kaiser-Willys ended its passenger car output in 1955 and concentrated on production of the Jeep. In 1969, Kaiser-Jeep Corporation was purchased by American Motors Corporation (AMC), which was formed in 1954 through the merger of Nash and Hudson. American Motors produced more than 400,000 cars in 1962 and 1963 but was unable to maintain sales at that level even after combining with Jeep. Renault of France bought control of AMC in the early 1980's but was unable to generate sufficient sales to achieve efficient low-cost production in the AMC facilities. Combined AMC and Jeep production in 1986 was 280,000 units.

During the 1980's, Chrysler Corporation emerged from a decade of financial problems during which it nearly entered receivership. Lee Iacocca, a former Ford executive, became president and board chair of Chrysler in 1978 and reorganized the firm to be more efficient in production and marketing strategies. In 1987, Chrysler purchased American Motors to obtain the Jeep line of vehicles, to strengthen the Chrysler product line, and to increase Chrysler volume to achieve more efficient levels of production. A consolidation beginning in 1910 with the emergence of Maxwell as a survivor of the United States Motor Company had thus led to the development of Chrysler, which now included the remnants of Hudson, Nash, Willys-Overland, and Kaiser-Fraser.

The consolidation of the U.S. auto industry into three major producers demonstrated that auto producers must be large to have the capital resources necessary to adopt lean production techniques and to gain the full advantages of large-scale production. Lean production utilizes multiskilled workers with flexible machinery to produce large numbers of vehicles efficiently. The major Japanese producers pioneered the use of lean production processes in the 1970's. In the early 1980's, Ford and Chrysler invested the capital to become lean producers. General Motors began to adopt lean production practices in the late 1980's and early 1990's.

In order to generate the production volume necessary to be an efficient producer, an automaker must offer the public a substantial product line. At General Motors, Alfred P. Sloan recognized the importance of a full line of vehicles. Sloan joined General Motors in 1918, when United Motors, which he headed, was acquired by GM. In 1923, he became president of GM and created a management and production system that became a model for industry in general. Under Sloan's leadership, GM became the largest U.S. automobile manufacturer. Sloan's product policy was that GM should produce a full line of cars covering every price field, from low-priced basic transportation to high-priced luxury cars.

GM's commitment to a full-line philosophy—low-priced Chevrolets, medium-priced Pontiacs (formerly Oaklands), Oldsmobiles, and Buicks, and high-priced Cadillacs—combined with the success of the production and financial controls instituted by Sloan, set a pattern for the industry. Chrysler recognized this trend in the industry when the Plymouth, Dodge, De Soto, and Chrysler lines were offered in the late 1920's. Chrysler achieved refinement of the full-line concept in 1987, when the acquisition of American Motors enabled the company to add the Jeep utility vehicle to its product line.

Ford initially maintained a limited product offering of low-priced Fords and a few luxury Lincolns. Introduction of the medium-priced Mercury in the late 1930's indicated that Ford now recognized the need to offer a full line of vehicles to remain competitive.

By 1927, the U.S. automobile industry had three major producers. The development of production, design, and marketing techniques over the subsequent years evolved an industry in which only those three firms became large enough to survive as U.S.-based automobile producers. Foreign firms, however, made increasingly substantial incursions into the market and established U.S. plants to augment their home production.

—*Robert R. Ebert*

FURTHER READING

American Automobile Manufacturers Association. *Automobiles of America*. 5th ed. Lakeland, Fla.: Cars & Parts, 1997. Excellent chronicle of the development of the U.S. automobile industry and the major persons involved. Features an appendix that lists all the makers of automobiles in the United States since 1893.

Edwards, Charles E. *Dynamics of the United States Automobile Industry*. Columbia: University of South Carolina Press, 1965. Provides excellent analysis of consolidation in the American auto industry following World War II. Discusses manufacturing, marketing, and management problems of independent automobile manufacturers in depth. Includes tables and graphs.

Farber, David. *Sloan Rules: Alfred P. Sloan and the Triumph of General Motors*. Chicago: University of Chicago Press, 2002. Biographical work focuses on Sloan's years at GM. Sheds light on Sloan's personality, his politics, and his motivations as a manager. Includes photographs and index.

Moritz, Michael, and Barrett Seaman. *Going for Broke: The Chrysler Story*. Garden City, N.Y.: Doubleday, 1981. Presents an analysis of the problems at Chrysler Corporation in the late 1970's. Excellent, readable history of the early years of Chrysler Corporation and its predecessor firms.

Seltzer, Lawrence H. *A Financial History of the American Automobile Industry*. 1928. Reprint. New York: A. M. Kelley, 1973. Excellent comprehensive examination of the early years of the industry. Provides insight into the consolidation of the auto industry from the perspective of an analyst writing in the 1920's. Includes useful statistical information.

Sloan, Alfred P., Jr. *My Years with General Motors*. 1963. Reprint. New York: Doubleday, 1990. Definitive, readable biographical work on Sloan, the person primarily responsible for management decisions at GM during a critical thirty-year period. Includes his analysis of policy and product development at the company.

White, Lawrence J. *The Automobile Industry Since 1945*. Cambridge, Mass.: Harvard University Press, 1971. Presents a thorough analysis of economic trends in the American auto industry following World War II. Invaluable for readers interested in the fundamental economic forces that have determined the structure of the U.S. auto industry. Includes excellent footnotes and bibliography.

Womack, James P., Daniel T. Jones, and Daniel Roos. *The Machine That Changed the World*. New York: Rawson Associates, 1990. Definitive work on the concept of lean production presents the results of a five-year study of the global automobile industry conducted by the Massachusetts Institute of Technology. Includes graphs, tables, footnotes, and bibliography.

SEE ALSO: Mar. 4, 1902: American Automobile Association Is Established; Feb. 29, 1908: Cadillac Demonstrates Interchangeable Parts; 1911: Hashimoto Founds the Nissan Motor Company; Mar. 1, 1913: Ford Assembly Line Begins Operation; Jan. 5, 1914: Ford Announces a Five-Dollar, Eight-Hour Workday; Dec. 29, 1920: General Motors Institutes a Multidivisional Structure.

1927

1927
OORT PROVES THE SPIRAL STRUCTURE OF THE MILKY WAY

Jan Hendrik Oort provided convincing evidence of the correctness of Bertil Lindblad's proposal that the Milky Way is a rotating spiral like many of the exterior galaxies.

LOCALE: Leiden, the Netherlands
CATEGORIES: Science and technology; astronomy

KEY FIGURES
Jan Hendrik Oort (1900-1992), Dutch astronomer
Bertil Lindblad (1895-1965), Swedish astronomer
John Stanley Plaskett (1865-1941), Canadian astronomer

SUMMARY OF EVENT
In 1927, Jan Hendrik Oort published data that provided dynamical proof of the proper motion of the stars near Earth. This evidence established that the observed effects were the result of differential velocities that could best be explained as the result of movement in the spiral arm of a large galaxy. He found the galactic center in the direction of Sagittarius in opposition to the direction Jacobus Cornelius Kapteyn had found, but in accord with the findings of Harlow Shapley. Oort came to this study quite naturally, as he had been a student of Kapteyn, the famous Dutch astronomer who was active in the study of the structure of the Milky Way. At the age of seventeen, Oort went to the University of Gröningen to study with Kapteyn. In his elementary lectures, Kapteyn emphasized deriving interpretation from observation rather than hypotheses or conjectures; in many ways, Oort's career followed this dictum.

After earning a degree at Gröningen, Oort studied at Yale University in the United States. He began work in 1924 at the Leiden Observatory, becoming a professor in 1935 and director of the observatory in 1945. Oort was always fascinated by the conflict between Kapteyn's star counts and Shapley's studies of the globular clusters. Oort hoped to resolve this conflict and applauded Bertil Lindblad's rather bold proposal of the solution to the problem. Lindblad was a Swedish astronomer who had suggested that a rotating model of our galaxy could explain most of the observed phenomena. Oort was aware that no globular clusters appeared near the galactic plane and surmised that gas and dust were obscuring them. It did not occur to him until 1925 that the same obscuration was causing Kapteyn to propose a much too small stellar system as well, because his assumption of uniform luminosity was not valid. This was the key to unraveling the conflict between the two systems.

Prior to Lindblad and Oort's work with the motion of

2161

the Milky Way, dynamical astronomy was almost solely the province of the solar system specialists. Oort recognized from Kapteyn's discovery of the star streams, and Karl Schwarzschild's interpretation of them as an ellipsoidal distribution of stellar motions, that there was potential for the dynamical study of our galaxy. He was also influenced by Sir Arthur Stanley Eddington and Sir James Jeans. This interest in dynamics led to his 1927 presentation and was a consistent theme throughout his varied career, extending to the dynamics of star clusters, stellar systems, galactic clusters, and finally superclusters. Oort consistently emphasized the lack of homogeneity in the distribution of galaxies, whereas Edwin Powell Hubble and others emphasized the large-scale homogeneity of the distribution of galaxies.

Oort began his research in the middle of the 1920's with a study of high-velocity stars. Other astronomers had already found a strange phenomenon, namely, that stars with radial velocities of 150 kilometers (93.2 miles) per second or higher tended toward one direction in galactic longitude. Oort studied somewhat lower-velocity stars and found a surprisingly sharp limit at 65 kilometers (40.4 miles) per second, above which all the stars were on the same side of Earth and below which the stars were uniformly distributed over all longitudes. Oort's 1926 doctoral dissertation contained a full description of the effect but an inadequate explanation, for he was still attempting to explain the phenomenon on the basis of the dynamics of a local system within Kapteyn's perception of the shape and size of the Milky Way. He noted, however, the concentration of globular clusters in the galactic plane and in only one direction. He further noted other objects with the same kind of concentration. He stated that the globular clusters had the same type of motion as the high-velocity stars and that their average velocity was about 92 kilometers (57.2 miles) per second, well above the 65-kilometer-per-second limit. The data pointed toward the strength of Shapley's contention that the universe was larger than Kapteyn perceived and that Earth was far from the center.

Within a year, however, rather than proposing a collection of swarms drifting in the large system of globular clusters—which had been Kapteyn's compromise with Shapley's evidence—Lindblad suggested that the Milky Way consisted of concentric subsystems at various velocities, with the high velocities the consequence of the faster rotation of inner stars around the galactic center far from the Sun in that direction. Oort then provided the evidence from his studies of the differential rotation of the galaxy, which conformed to Lindblad's model. He demonstrated that Kapteyn's streaming effect was caused by the inner stars catching up with the Sun while the outer stars lagged behind. This initial research could have implied concentric rings of a circular or elliptical galaxy, and his research continued seeking firmer evidence for the spiral nature of the Milky Way. He established in 1930 (allowing for Robert Julius Trumpler's discovery of dust clouds that absorbed light and made distant star clouds appear fainter and more distant than they were) that Earth's orbit of rotation was 30,000 light-years from the center of the galaxy, which was a reduction of Shapley's 50,000 light-year estimate. He found the Sun to be following a fairly circular orbit at a rate of approximately 220 kilometers (136.7 miles) per second, a velocity that would lead to orbiting the galactic center in approximately 230 million years.

Next, Oort investigated the relationship between his previous velocity distribution studies and the decrease in density of star numbers with increasing distance from the galactic center and increasing distance from the galactic plane. He determined the density of matter in the vicinity of the Sun and made estimates of density at other points toward the center for the purpose of computing the gravitational forces and reaching a comprehensive dynamical model of the distribution of the mass. He noted that the high-velocity globular clusters could not be held by a system unless it was at least two hundred times more massive than Kapteyn's universe.

By 1932, Oort had established that only about two-thirds of the mass of the Milky Way could be accounted for from the known stars and gas; he thus implied a considerable unseen mass in the galactic plane that was hidden by gas and dust. The distribution of the mass also implied the spiral nature of the galaxy.

The desire to penetrate the unseen core led Oort into radio astronomy. During World War II, while the Netherlands was occupied and observation was denied, Oort turned to theoretical work on the structure of the Milky Way and encouraged his student Hendrik Christoffell van de Hulst to study the hydrogen atom emission in radio wavelengths. In 1944, van de Hulst announced that hydrogen ought to emit at the 21-centimeter (8.3-inch) wavelength. After the war, Oort and C. A. Muller built a 21-centimeter receiver and hooked it to an 8-meter (26.2-foot) antenna owned by the Dutch Post and Telegraph Service. An unfortunate fire destroyed their experiment and before they could rebuild, Edward Mills Purcell and Harold Ewen announced observations of hydrogen emissions. Oort duplicated their effort six weeks later. Oort and Muller then mapped a halo of hydrogen around the galaxy; in the following years, they went on to study the galactic structure in the optically obscured center, mapping the distribution of gas in the galactic disk. This gas distribution, as well as the earlier research on mass distribution, supported the spiral nature of the galaxy. These studies verified rotation rates near the center and found a concentrated mass.

The variety of Oort's career interests led him to propose the existence of a comet cloud outside the planetary orbits as an explanation for the origin of comets and to conclude that the Crab nebula was the supernova of 1054 C.E. recorded by Chinese astronomers. He studied the origin and evaporation of solid particles in interstellar space with van de Hulst. His wide-ranging interests contributed to his remarkably long, active career in astronomy.

SIGNIFICANCE

Jan Hendrik Oort's work in seeking to resolve the issue of size, shape, and motion of the Milky Way was a natural consequence of his studies under Kapteyn. His primary concern was to resolve the conflict between the size of Kapteyn's "universe" and that of Shapley, which was several times larger. Significantly, he was able to blend physics, mathematics, and astronomy into a dynamical interpretation of the observed phenomena that took into account gaseous absorption of light in the galactic plane and toward the center of the galaxy. He was able to provide evidence for a rotating spiral galaxy that resolved many issues and made Shapley's view with modifications more acceptable than in its previous form.

Oort's published observational confirmation of differential galactic rotation, built on the mathematical theoretical work of Lindblad, encouraged other astronomers to search for further evidence and to continue efforts to resolve the remaining problems of scale, which were not finally completed until Walter Baade's work on the two stellar populations appeared in 1952. Oort had a great effect on John Stanley Plaskett, who spent much time studying hot blue stars (types O and B) at the Dominion Astrophysical Observatory in Victoria, British Columbia. Plaskett applied Oort's analysis to the radial velocities of faint B-type stars, which, because they are extremely bright, can be detected at great distances. His analysis reduced the relative error of their radial velocities. His independent method produced results close to Oort's value for distance and direction of the galactic center.

Oort established that Kapteyn's galaxy was too small and Shapley's too large. Plaskett's verification of Oort's results focused renewed efforts to resolve the problem of the distance scale. The problem of identifying the nature and magnitude of absorption of light by gas and dust continued into the 1930's. Trumpler's work provided the first definitive proof of an absorbing medium that Oort had insisted was present. Those who followed Trumpler were able to use the absorption he found to resolve the issues among Kapteyn's, Oort's, and Shapley's models of the galaxy and the conflict between Oort's and Shapley's distances. Oort's extremely long career allowed him to follow up his own work by moving into radio astronomy in the late 1940's and 1950's, when his research resulted in more complete confirmation of the spiral structure of the galaxy. Later studies have demonstrated that Trumpler's uniform absorbing medium is really small clouds with irregular patterns of absorption in different parts of the sky.

Oort's early work stimulated the development of better photography, faster films, shorter focal lengths, and the use of radio astronomy. Oort's many honors were well deserved, and the fertility of his astronomical efforts can only be admired. His long career spans the full development of a comprehensive view of the nature, structure, and size of our galaxy.

—*Ivan L. Zabilka*

FURTHER READING

Berendzen, Richard, Richard Hart, and Daniel Seeley. *Man Discovers the Galaxies*. New York: Columbia University Press, 1984. Excellent cosmological history includes a somewhat technical description of Lindblad's and Oort's efforts to comprehend the dynamics of the Milky Way. Notes the importance of Oort's evidence for later cosmological studies.

Ferguson, Kitty. *Measuring the Universe: Our Historic Quest to Chart the Horizons of Space and Time*. New York: Walker, 1999. Examines the history of humankind's efforts to measure and understand the size and structure of the universe. Chapter 7 includes discussion of research concerning the Milky Way, including Oort's work. Features glossary and index.

Motz, Lloyd, and Jefferson Hane Weaver. *The Story of Astronomy*. New York: Plenum, 1995. Presents the history of astronomy from ancient times to the end of the twentieth century. Chapter 17 includes discussion of Oort's work and galactic research in general. Features bibliography and index.

Oort, Jan Hendrik. "The Development of Our Insight into the Structure of the Galaxy Between 1920 and 1940." In *Education in and History of Modern Astron-*

1927

omy, edited by Richard Berendzen. New York: New York Academy of Sciences, 1972. Historical lecture delivered at the New York Academy in September, 1971, in which Oort discussed his work and its relation to that of several others active in this field.

_____. "Some Notes on My Life as an Astronomer." *Annual Review of Astronomy and Astrophysics* 19 (1981): 1-5. Brief survey of some of Oort's early accomplishments, focusing especially on his galactic studies. Indicates the influences that led him into galactic studies.

Stromgren, Bengt. "An Appreciation of Jan Hendrik Oort." In *Galaxies and the Universe*, edited by Lodewijk Woltjer. New York: Columbia University Press, 1968. Tribute to Oort by an eminent Danish astronomer provides excellent commentary on Oort's career to that point.

Whitney, Charles A. *The Discovery of Our Galaxy.*
1971. Reprint. Ames: Iowa State University Press, 1988. Includes concise and clear exposition of Oort's work. Also discusses the issue of whether the Milky Way's spiral arms lead or trail as they rotate, which was an issue between Lindblad and Hubble, with Hubble eventually able to demonstrate that they trail. Includes illustrations, glossary, and bibliography.

SEE ALSO: 1904: Kapteyn Discovers Two Star Streams in the Galaxy; 1912: Slipher Obtains the Spectrum of a Distant Galaxy; Mar. 3, 1912: Leavitt Discovers How to Measure Galactic Distances; 1913: Hertzsprung Uses Cepheid Variables to Calculate Distances to the Stars; Nov., 1917: Hooker Telescope Is Installed on Mount Wilson; Jan. 8, 1918: Shapley Proves the Sun Is Distant from the Center of Our Galaxy; Early 1920's: Slipher Presents Evidence of Redshifts in Galactic Spectra.

1927

U.S. FOOD AND DRUG ADMINISTRATION IS ESTABLISHED

With the establishment of the Food and Drug Administration, the U.S. government undertook the task of protecting consumers.

LOCALE: Washington, D.C.
CATEGORIES: Agriculture; health and medicine; organizations and institutions

KEY FIGURES
Walter Gilbert Campbell (1877-1963), head of the Food and Drug Administration, 1927-1944
George P. Larrick (1901-1968), commissioner of the Food and Drug Administration, 1954-1965
Harvey W. Wiley (1844-1930), first head of the U.S. Bureau of Chemistry

SUMMARY OF EVENT

The establishment of the U.S. Food and Drug Administration (FDA) grew out of a need to enforce regulations intended to protect the nation's food and drug supplies. The push for regulating food and drugs began soon after the United States was founded, when Massachusetts enacted a general food law in 1785. The first federal protection legislation came in 1848, when Congress passed the Drug Importation Act, which enabled U.S. customs inspectors to stop adulterated drugs from entering the country. During the second half of the nineteenth century, many new drugs appeared on the market containing unknown and questionable substances, including highly addicting ones such as morphine, heroin, and cocaine. Congress tried, unsuccessfully, to respond to the problem by introducing more than 190 bills between 1879 and 1906 to regulate food and drugs.

At the turn of the century, however, came renewed public interest in the conditions under which food was produced. As a result of Upton Sinclair's *The Jungle* (1906), which exposed conditions in the meatpacking industry, Congress passed the Pure Food and Drug Act in June, 1906. Enforced by the Bureau of Chemistry within the U.S. Department of Agriculture (USDA), the act made the interstate commerce of mislabeled or adulterated food, drinks, and drugs a federal crime. The act defined food as all substances used for food, drink, or seasoning for human or animal consumption; adulteration was defined as adding substances to reduce the quality or strength, hiding damaged conditions, or using filthy or diseased animals in production. Harvey W. Wiley, the USDA chief chemist who was also known as the father of the pure food movement, led the Bureau of Chemistry's efforts to enforce the 1906 act, although the act gave him no power to invoke fines or penalties.

Frustrated with the limitations of the 1906 act, Wiley retired from the Bureau of Chemistry in 1912 and was succeeded by Carl Alsberg. During the 1910's, the bureau struggled to enforce the law. Several cases reached the U.S. Supreme Court, including one in 1914 in which the Court ruled that the government needed merely to show that a substance might affect public health in order to declare it illegal. In 1921, attorney Walter Gilbert Campbell, who had been chief inspector of the Bureau of Chemistry since 1907, took over as the bureau's head.

Aware of the bureau's struggles to enforce the 1906 law, Congress began to consider creating a separate law-enforcement agency charged with administering the country's food and drug laws. With the creation of the Food, Drug, and Insecticide Administration (FDIA) in 1927, the country had its first regulatory agency dedicated to enforcing public health laws specifically related to food and drugs. Established as a separate agency under the Department of Agriculture, the FDIA became the Food and Drug Administration in 1930. Under Campbell's direction, the agency addressed many problems in the food and drug industries and began to educate the public on nutrition and health.

In 1933, the New Deal policies of President Franklin D. Roosevelt led the FDA to recommend a complete revision of the 1906 law. Roosevelt demanded consumer protection for the millions of Americans struggling during the Depression and looked to the FDA to end questionable practices within the food and drug industries. Unfortunately, it took a major public health threat to prompt Congress to enact a revised food and drug law. In 1937, the S. E. Massengill Company manufactured, without proper testing, a product called Elixir of Sulfanilamide for the treatment of sore throats. Almost twelve gallons were distributed before the FDA received notice of deaths attributed to the elixir. Upon testing, the FDA found the product to contain a highly toxic solvent related to radiator antifreeze. Under the 1906 law, the FDA could do little, and more than one hundred people, mostly children, died.

This incident dramatized the desperate need for change, and strong prompting by the FDA led Congress to pass the Federal Food, Drug, and Cosmetic Act in 1938. With more than forty provisions, this act served as the nation's basic food law and as the basis for the FDA's actions. The law set food standards, placed cosmetics under regulation for the first time, and required that all new drugs be tested for safety. Moreover, the law gave the FDA the power to inspect factories and to seek the penalty of court injunctions. (The power to inspect without prior consent was added in 1953.) It was on the basis of this law and future amendments that the FDA established firm regulations to protect the country's consumers.

In 1940, the FDA moved from the Department of Agriculture to the Federal Security Agency, and Walter Campbell was named the first commissioner of the Food and Drug Administration. The FDA made two other moves over the next thirty years—to the Department of Health, Education, and Welfare in 1953 and to the Public Health Service under the Department of Health and Human Services in 1968. By the early 2000's, the agency had nine thousand employees working at offices or inspection posts in nearly 170 cities. FDA personnel conducted about sixteen thousand visits annually to facilities under its oversight.

In 1988, the Food and Drug Administration Act officially established the FDA as an agency of the Department of Health and Human Services, with a commissioner appointed by the president with the advice and consent of the Senate. This act also broadly listed the responsibilities for the commissioner in four major areas: research, enforcement, education, and information. All responsibilities were related to the primary goal of protecting the country's food and drug supplies.

SIGNIFICANCE

The FDA's multitude of responsibilities were geared toward protecting the food, drugs, and cosmetics available to U.S. consumers. By establishing quality standards and conducting periodic inspections, the agency helped companies comply with the complicated regulations governing food, drug, and cosmetic production. Every substance that went into a product—from pesticides used to control insect problems in the food industry to color additives in cosmetics—came under FDA control. The FDA also worked to ensure that foreign products sold in the United States were produced under sanitary conditions. In addition, the FDA served as an information resource for American consumers regarding the quality of thousands of products. Through consumer consultants and publications such as *FDA Consumer* and *FDA Drug Bulletin*, the agency brought information as well as warnings to the public's attention. The FDA also used the media to prevent illness from widespread contaminations such as those that often follow natural disasters.

Even after the 1938 law provided increased options for the FDA, the agency continued to be hampered by limitations. FDA regulation applied only to interstate commerce; food prices, advertising, and mailed food products did not fall under FDA control, and meat and poultry were controlled by another agency. After 1938, once a violation was determined to have been committed, several options were available to the agency, includ-

1927

ing recalls, seizures, fines, and injunctions. Until 1985, the maximum fine was $1,000 for misdemeanor violations and $10,000 for felony violations. After federal revisions, the maximum fine was raised to $100,000 per offense and $250,000 for a felonious offense or one that resulted in death. Corporations faced fines twice as high. Noting an increase in criminal violations in the late 1980's, the FDA opened the Office of Criminal Investigations to deal with criminal offenses.

Passage of the 1938 Food and Drug Act received little public attention. After World War II brought several technological advances that companies wanted to carry over into consumer use, however, many products and substances needed FDA approval. Under Commissioner George P. Larrick, the FDA worked to set strict regulations and research guidelines to protect consumers. In the 1950's, the agency increased its regulation of food production. In 1954, Congress passed the Pesticide Amendment, which gave the FDA the power to set and enforce pesticide tolerances in foods. (The newly created Environmental Protection Agency took over this area in 1970.) The Food Additives Amendment in 1958 charged the FDA with establishing the proven safety of all chemical additives before they were used in food. One year later, the "Generally Recognized as Safe," or GRAS, list appeared, which included the most common substances used in food production—including salt, pepper, sugar, and vinegar—that were permissible and excluded from testing. That same year, the Delaney Clause to the 1938 act prohibited the use of substances if they were proven to be carcinogenic in animals. With the addition of the Color Additives Amendment in 1960, no substance could be put into the U.S. food supply without first being determined safe. The responsibility to prove safety fell on the producers, and the responsibility for policing the producers fell on the FDA. During the 1960's, several problems with the manufacture of baby food and infant formula showed that companies could not be relied upon to police themselves. As a result of these problems, the FDA pushed for the 1980 Infant Formula Act and its 1986 amendment, which strengthened quality standards and established recall procedures.

In addition to developing strict guidelines for approving substances for use in food, the FDA also recalled some products after they had been approved. In response to new medical information regarding cancer, the FDA removed such products as cyclamates and saccharin from the food supply. When necessary, the agency also responded to concerns about contaminated seafood and other products.

The FDA also worked to educate the public about good nutrition. The labeling of food proved to be an integral part of raising public awareness. Food labels had been under federal control since 1906, but they became more important in the 1980's. Increased public attention to fitness caused the FDA to lower the recommended diet to 2,000 calories per day in 1980. In addition, the FDA and the Department of Agriculture revised the recommended diet from the "basic four" food groups to the "food pyramid" of the 1990's. The 1990's also brought new FDA guidelines that required uniform labels on all food products and defined such food-related terms as "lower," "light," and "free."

The FDA provided consumers and doctors with the security that drugs were safe and uniform. With the emergence of a number of chemicals during World War II, pharmacology became a vital field of medicine and one that relied on the resources of the FDA. Antibiotics appeared as a direct result of World War II, and the FDA responded by requiring the certification of five different antibiotics by 1949, including penicillin and streptomycin. Manufacturers were required to test for efficacy and to keep distribution records so that entire batches could be recalled if necessary. Soon after, companies were required to keep distribution records of all drugs. The importance of this policy was demonstrated in 1982, when the pain reliever Tylenol was linked to several poisoning cases and had to be recalled. Safety also came into play in the early 1960's when the drug thalidomide, which had been widely used in Europe throughout the 1950's as a supposedly safe sedative and antinausea treatment for pregnant women, came to the FDA for approval. Frances Kelsey, who was assigned to review the drug, learned of an association between the use of thalidomide and deformed babies and was instrumental in keeping the drug off the U.S. market.

The FDA also controlled the distribution of drugs by determining which products would be available by prescription only—after 1952, these carried the warning "Caution: Federal law prohibits dispensing without prescription"—and which would be available over the counter. Several drugs previously available only by prescription started appearing in over-the-counter versions when the FDA established new guidelines in the 1970's. The 1980's also saw a dramatic increase in the availability of generic drugs, for which the FDA provided strict guidelines.

Despite all the FDA's efforts to monitor the drug industry, problems throughout the 1940's and 1950's pointed to a loophole in the 1938 law. Although manufacturers were required to prove safety, they were not required to prove effectiveness. Many "safe" products were consequently approved even though they were not effective. Congress investigated the issue in the early 1960's, and in 1962, reforms were passed that required all new drugs to prove both safety and effectiveness. The reforms also called for manufacturers to report the benefits and risks of their products to the FDA and medical professionals, and the FDA was charged with evaluating the drugs approved between 1938 and 1962 for effectiveness.

In the 1980's and early 1990's, two unrelated issues, acquired immunodeficiency syndrome (AIDS) and breast implants, brought increased pressures on the FDA. Throughout the 1980's, critics and AIDS activists charged the FDA with being too slow to test and release drugs. The FDA did not approve an AIDS test for blood until 1985. Frustrated with the delayed approvals, AIDS sufferers often turned to fraudulent "cures" and highly unpredictable experimental procedures available in other countries. The FDA also came under fire for problems with silicone breast implants. The Medical Device Amendments of 1976 had provided the same guidelines for these devices as for drugs; another measure in 1990 compelled hospitals and other medical facilities to report any problems with medical devices that resulted in serious illness, injury, or death. These amendments came under heavy criticism when silicone breast implants were found to be dangerous in the early 1990's. Many again thought that the FDA had moved too slowly in response to the issue.

The FDA has unquestionably had a tremendous effect on American life. Protecting the products that account for more than 25 percent of a consumer's budget, the FDA has worked to ensure that those products are safe and of the highest quality. Once it had been given power to enforce the country's food and drug laws, the agency made significant advances in ending questionable practices that could harm public health.

—Jennifer Davis

FURTHER READING

Hawthorne, Fran. *Inside the FDA: The Business and Politics Behind the Drugs We Take and the Food We Eat.* New York: John Wiley & Sons, 2005. Examines the inner workings of the powerful agency, including how it makes decisions while under pressure from industry, agriculture, politicians, and consumers. Features notes, bibliography, and index.

Hilts, Philip J. *Protecting America's Health: The FDA, Business, and One Hundred Years of Regulation.* New York: Alfred A. Knopf, 2003. Documents the history of the U.S. Food and Drug Administration from its establishment during Theodore Roosevelt's presidency to the beginning of the twenty-first century. Emphasizes the FDA's regulatory role and its battles against entrenched business interests.

Mintz, Morton. *By Prescription Only.* Boston: Beacon Press, 1967. Covers the role of the FDA in regulating the drug industry. Discusses the problems of drug testing and regulation as well as the role of advertising and the media in promoting new drugs.

Patrick, Bill. *The Food and Drug Administration.* New York: Chelsea House, 1988. Covers the history and influence of the FDA on the food and drug industries. Also discusses the societal impact of the agency's work.

Young, James Harvey. *American Health Quackery: Collected Essays.* Princeton, N.J.: Princeton University Press, 1992. Discusses the scams that have pervaded medical practice in the United States and how the FDA has responded to false claims and misinformation.

SEE ALSO: Feb., 1906: Sinclair Publishes *The Jungle*; June 30, 1906: Pure Food and Drug Act and Meat Inspection Act; Aug., 1913: Advertisers Adopt a Truth-in-Advertising Code; 1933: Kallet and Schlink Publish *100,000,000 Guinea Pigs*; June 25, 1938: Federal Food, Drug, and Cosmetic Act.

1927

January 1, 1927
BRITISH BROADCASTING CORPORATION IS CHARTERED

The British Broadcasting Corporation, a public institution rather than a privately owned company, set the world's standards for quality production in radio and television.

LOCALE: London, England

CATEGORIES: Radio and television; communications and media; organizations and institutions

KEY FIGURES

John Charles Walsham Reith (1889-1971), first director-general of the British Broadcasting Corporation

Stanley Baldwin (1867-1947), prime minister of Great Britain, 1923-1924, 1924-1929, and 1935-1937

Godfrey Isaacs (1867-1925), managing director of the Marconi Wireless Telegraph Company

Peter Eckersley (1892-1963), chief engineer of the British Broadcasting Corporation

Joseph Albert Pease (First Baron Gainford; 1860-1943), first chairman of the British Broadcasting Corporation

SUMMARY OF EVENT

After several years of evolution and development, the British Broadcasting Company, Ltd., a private company, was rechartered in late 1926 as the British Broadcasting Corporation (BBC). On January 1, 1927, the new entity officially came into being. The new BBC, however, was not a radical departure from what had previously existed. Rather, the new public corporation was a logical outcome of various social, cultural, institutional, and political developments established long before the founding of the private company in 1922.

The development of the transmission of sound by "wireless" broadcasting instead of through telegraphic wire methods began in the nineteenth century. Numerous scientists and inventors, particularly Guglielmo Marconi, provided the theory and the technology. Electronic wave transmission also coincided with other fundamental changes in media communication. In Great Britain, Alfred Harmsworth (later Lord Northcliffe) revolutionized print journalism with his newspaper the *Daily Mail*, a development paralleled by the accomplishments of Joseph Pulitzer and William Randolph Hearst in the United States, and motion pictures started to affect society as early as the 1890's. Even the possibility of television was

predicted before the end of the century. Wireless development was not unique.

World War I added to the interest and application of wireless technology. When the war ended in 1918, however, the wireless, or radio, was still primarily a technology pursued on an amateur level. In Great Britain, the General Post Office had been given responsibility for transmitting telegrams in 1869 and for licensing various wireless stations in 1904. Unlike in the United States, where government involvement in influencing the direction and content of radio broadcasting was initially minimal, in the United Kingdom the government played a much larger role. The leading British radio company was the Marconi Wireless Telegraph Company, headed by its managing director, Godfrey Isaacs, who was not alone in seeing the possibilities inherent in radio. On June 15, 1920, Lord Northcliffe's *Daily Mail* sponsored a radio concert by the famous singer Dame Nellie Melba, and the concert was heard all over Europe. Nothing in radio history up to that time had so captured the public's attention.

The Marconi Company was the largest but not the only private radio company in Great Britain. In many quarters, however, there was a fear of excessive competition and chaotic rivalry, and in May, 1922, the General Post Office took the lead in bringing together the Marconi Company and the other wireless companies in an attempt to bring order and comprehensiveness to radio service in Great Britain. The Marconi Company probably could have provided adequate service itself, but both its business rivals and most politicians, fearful of a private monopoly, were opposed to such a development. On the other hand, Post Office officials were reluctant to assume day-to-day operational control of the new technology. The result, after long negotiations, was the establishment of the British Broadcasting Company, Ltd., in October, 1922. The new company represented two potentially conflicting aspects of radio broadcasting: The interests of private business were essentially economic, but it was also argued that there was a broader public interest that had to be served. The company's shares were owned by the British manufacturers of wireless equipment. No advertising would be accepted as a means of financing radio; instead, a small fee would be collected by the Post Office from each individual owning a wireless receiver, or radio. Half of such fees would then be given to the company.

There were issues other than advertising that had to be resolved. Newspaper proprietors feared the wireless as a news competitor; thus, initially, the BBC was forbidden to have its own news service. Also, despite discussion of a second broadcasting company during the negotiations, the decision in 1922 was to give the British Broadcasting Company a monopoly. Finally, there was a concern that the BBC might present shows that were too controversial, particularly in regard to political, social, and economic issues such as birth control and socialism.

The first chairman of the BBC was Joseph Albert Pease, First Baron Gainford, who remained on the BBC's board until 1932. The key figure in the years that followed was John Charles Walsham Reith, a Scotsman who had been injured and disfigured in the war; Reith had had business experience, but he had not worked in radio. Nevertheless, in late 1922 he applied for the position of the BBC's general manager and was accepted. By the following November, he had become managing director, and by the end of 1923, he was the recognized head of the BBC. Reith, whose father was a Presbyterian minister, believed that the function of the BBC should be primarily to educate rather than to entertain the public. In his offi-

cial capacity, he gave the BBC both the substance and image of quality and public service, a reputation that continued long after he left the BBC.

The company grew rapidly. When the BBC was founded, it had only four employees; by December, 1923, the staff numbered almost four hundred. By the end of 1923, there were more than half a million privately owned receiver sets, and a year later the number had increased to more than a million. Such growth would undoubtedly have occurred even if Reith had not been the driving force of the BBC, but it was Reith more than anyone else who transformed the private company operating through a Post Office license into a public corporation. Of course, he was not the only figure committed to the public possibilities of the wireless, but it was his vision and leadership that led the way. In May, 1925, Great Britain's postmaster general announced the appointment of a committee to examine the status of the BBC. Chaired by Lord Crawford, the committee ultimately accepted Reith's argument that broadcasting must be for public service and should not merely be the province of private

1927

John Charles Walsham Reith (front row, center) with staff outside the BBC's headquarters in London in 1924. (Hulton Archive/Getty Images)

business interests. In Reith's opinion, the British Broadcasting Company was a threat to the fulfillment of what the wireless could and should accomplish for the betterment of society. The Post Office had already arrived at a similar conclusion. In July, 1926, the postmaster general accepted the recommendations of the Crawford Committee and announced that a public corporation, the British Broadcasting Corporation, established by royal charter, would supersede the private British Broadcasting Company. In spite of dire predictions of socialism, bureaucracy, and monopoly, on January 1, 1927, the era of the British Broadcasting Corporation officially began.

SIGNIFICANCE

The first chairman of the newly constituted BBC was Lord Clarendon, whose selection did not meet with Reith's approval; he preferred Gainford. Reith was given a knighthood and named director-general. The corporation was chartered for ten years, and the chairman and the other four governors, including Gainford, served five-year terms. During Reith's reign, his influence was paramount; he generally got his way with the chairman and the other governors, and it was his vision of the BBC that continued to govern the direction of radio broadcasting in Great Britain.

Wireless in the United Kingdom had been strongly influenced by the development of radio in the United States in the years after World War I. In 1919, the private Radio Corporation of America (RCA) was created under the leadership of David Sarnoff. A competitor, Westinghouse, led the way in regular broadcasting beginning in 1921. By 1924, there were more than five hundred radio stations in the United States, and in spite of opposition to the practice, the American stations accepted advertising. British observers, including Godfrey Isaacs and Frank James Brown, an assistant secretary at the Post Office, although impressed by the business acuity of the American radio industry, predicted chaos in Great Britain if the same unregulated growth transpired. There was also agreement that advertising had no place on British radio. Monopoly rather than competition and licensing fees instead of advertising had been adopted when the British Broadcasting Company was founded in 1922, and the policy continued after the British Broadcasting Corporation began operation in 1927. Because licensing fees were paid through the General Post Office, the British government retained its ultimate hold on the BBC. Governmental oversight of, and possible interference with, radio broadcasts thus always existed.

The early restrictions on discussing controversial issues on the radio and on the BBC's having its own news service were only gradually relaxed. Reith attempted to have the BBC provide live coverage of parliamentary debates, but he was rebuffed by the politicians of the day. The company did, however, broadcast a speech by King George V in April, 1924, that was heard by ten million people. Reith's emphasis on public service saw him establish a number of advisory committees on religion, music, and education in order to give the proper tone and substance to radio programs. When newspaper publishers threatened to charge the BBC a fee for printing program announcements, Reith established *Radio Times*, which provided information on programs and developments. Founded in 1923, by the end of 1927 *Radio Times* was selling more than a million copies an issue; by the eve of World War II in 1939, it had a circulation of three million. By 1935, 98 percent of the British population had access to the programs of the BBC.

One of the challenges for the BBC both before and after the creation of the public corporation in 1927 was the difficulty of being relevant and significant and yet at the same time noncontroversial. Reith hoped to have political issues seriously discussed on the radio by major politicians, but most only very reluctantly made use of the new technology. The 1920's leaders of both the Liberal and Labour Parties, David Lloyd George and Ramsay MacDonald, were failures in the use of radio. The most successful politician to use the wireless in the 1920's was Stanley Baldwin, prime minister in 1923 and then again from 1924 to 1929. Baldwin's relaxed and conversational style in his 1924 campaign address anticipated the "fireside chats" of U.S. president Franklin D. Roosevelt in the 1930's.

Baldwin was the central figure in the most severe challenge to the BBC's educative objectivity during the interwar years. In May, 1926, a general strike broke out in Great Britain, and the subsequent walkout by most British union workers seemed to some to threaten both representative government and the capitalist economic system. Winston Churchill, Baldwin's Chancellor of the Exchequer, wished the BBC to become a mouthpiece for the government, but Reith refused, arguing that the BBC should remain objective in its reporting of events. A number of leading politicians spoke on the radio during the days of the strike, but none more effectively than Baldwin, whose calming words were widely credited with keeping the strike both peaceful and short. Years later, during World War II, Churchill's own oratory, often carried on the BBC, inspired Great Britain and the world against the evils of Nazism.

Reith and the BBC's attempt to uplift, to educate, and to be objective was generally, but not universally, approved. Churchill was not the only dissenter from Reith's approach to broadcasting. From the founding of the company through the establishment of the corporation and beyond, many listeners desired more entertainment and less education, more popular and dance music and less classical music, more humor and less serious discussion. Some objected to the domination of the BBC by London, demanding more programs reflecting the various regions of Great Britain. Although compromises were made and more entertainment programs were presented, the belief and practice that the BBC should level society up rather than down predominated. Both speech and dress standards were imposed on announcers, who were not identifiable personalities, as in American radio, but simply gentlemen of culture. The BBC's standard speaking style, sometimes called "BBC English," perhaps did help break down some of the regional and class divisions among the British. Announcers were required to wear formal dress, including dinner jackets, when speaking over the radio. Moral uplift was even carried over to the private lives of BBC employees; Peter Eckersley, an important radio figure even before the company was founded in 1922 and the BBC's chief engineer from 1923 until 1929, was forced to resign because of his involvement in a divorce.

Nevertheless, the path established by the early founders of the BBC continued even after Reith's own resignation in 1938. Pure entertainment was secondary to education and societal improvement, quality was paramount, and the primary goal remained public service. The BBC retained its monopoly position in British broadcasting until long after World War II ended, still financed by licensing fees rather than through advertising. The precedents set during the early radio era were carried over when the BBC began television transmission in 1936. The monument created in the 1920's by Reith and others continued to cast its influential shadow over Great Britain and the world decades later.

—Eugene Larson

FURTHER READING

Boyle, Andrew. *Only the Wind Will Listen: Reith of the BBC.* London: Hutchinson, 1972. Unconventional biography focuses only on Reith's years at the BBC. Adopts a psychological approach, emphasizing the puritanical and depressive side of Reith's personality. Fascinating reading.

Briggs, Asa. *The BBC: The First Fifty Years.* Oxford, England: Oxford University Press, 1985. Excellent introduction to the BBC by a distinguished British scholar. Includes useful list of significant dates and a fine bibliography.

_____. *The Birth of Broadcasting, 1896-1927.* Vol. 1 in *The History of Broadcasting in the United Kingdom.* 1961. Reprint. New York: Oxford University Press, 1995. Presents the story of the beginnings of the BBC, up to its transformation into a public corporation in 1927. Features illustrations and index.

Cain, John. *The BBC: Seventy Years of Broadcasting.* London: British Broadcasting Corporation, 1996. Lively, entertaining, and informative volume provides an ideal introduction to the history of BBC radio and television. Includes numerous photographs, including some depicting early television sets and transmitting apparatus.

Crisell, Andrew. *An Introductory History of British Broadcasting.* 2d ed. New York: Routledge, 2002. Comprehensive history of British radio and television discusses the beginnings of BBC television in chapter 4. Includes time line, bibliography, and index.

Middlemas, Keith, and John Barnes. *Baldwin: A Biography.* New York: Macmillan, 1970. Excellent study of Baldwin and his times. Includes an informative discussion of the General Strike of 1926 and provides insights into why Baldwin was so successful at communicating on the radio.

Paulu, Burton. *Television and Radio in the United Kingdom.* Minneapolis: University of Minnesota Press, 1981. Scholarly work by a noted authority on European television details the structure of the BBC, including finances, personnel, programming, and legal status.

Smith, Anthony, ed. *Television: An International History.* 2d ed. New York: Oxford University Press, 1998. Collection of essays on the history of television around the world includes discussion of the BBC and its impacts. Features a list of television museums and archives.

SEE ALSO: 1920's: Radio Develops as a Mass Broadcast Medium; Aug. 20-Nov. 2, 1920: Radio Broadcasting Begins; Sept. 9, 1926: National Broadcasting Company Is Founded; 1930's: Americans Embrace Radio Entertainment; Nov. 5, 1935: Armstrong Demonstrates FM Radio Broadcasting; Nov. 2, 1936: BBC Airs the First High-Definition Television Program.

February-March, 1927
HEISENBERG ARTICULATES THE UNCERTAINTY PRINCIPLE

With his uncertainty principle, Werner Heisenberg asserted that there are definite limits to precise knowledge of atomic processes, a theory that has become a cornerstone of modern physics.

LOCALE: Copenhagen, Denmark
CATEGORIES: Science and technology; physics

KEY FIGURES
Werner Heisenberg (1901-1976), German physicist
Niels Bohr (1885-1962), Danish physicist
Albert Einstein (1879-1955), German physicist

SUMMARY OF EVENT
At the beginning of the nineteenth century, Sir Isaac Newton's laws of physics, first published in 1687, were enjoying such enormous success, particularly regarding their power to predict the movements of heavenly bodies, that thinkers such as the French mathematician and astronomer Pierre-Simon Laplace began to extend these laws to the universe as a whole. Laplace argued that complete knowledge of the locations and speeds of the Sun and planets at one point in time would allow scientists, using Newton's laws, to determine the state of the solar system at any other time. Therefore, if a superhuman intelligence could once know fully the state of every bit of matter and the forces acting on them, such an intelligence could determine precisely the state of the universe at any past or future time. The universe and everything in it was thought to function with the precision and regularity of clockwork—the state of the mechanism at one moment determining completely the future course of events.

The notion of universal determinism—the idea that the present and future are totally bound by the past—was the guiding spirit of much scientific inquiry throughout the nineteenth century. Many scientists rejected the idea, saying that it left no room for the elements of chance, choice, and creativity. Certain philosophers, such as Charles Sanders Peirce, argued that strict determinism cannot account for the phenomena of growth and evolution. Nevertheless, determinism continued to reign supreme within the scientific community, particularly in physics, which was considered the most basic example of a precise, predictable science.

It is against this background of classical physics that the significance of Werner Heisenberg's principle of uncertainty, or indeterminacy, is most easily seen. In attempting to predict the exact future state of any sort of physical system—from solar to subatomic—it is necessary that one be able to measure precisely the qualities and coordinates of the parts of the system at a given point in time. The belief in universal determinism and absolute predictability held by many nineteenth century physicists was based largely on the assumption that such precision of measurement is theoretically unlimited. Heisenberg's uncertainty principle dealt a fatal blow to this assumption and shook the supremacy of strict causality, or determinism. Heisenberg stated simply that it is impossible to measure simultaneously both the exact position and the exact momentum of a subatomic particle.

Heisenberg used the example of the gamma-ray microscope to demonstrate the validity of the uncertainty principle, proposing that concepts such as position and momentum can have meaning only if one specifies how they are to be measured. In this hypothetical experiment, one measures the location and speed of a particle such as an electron by shining a tiny ray of light, as little as one photon, on the particle. This light will be scattered by the particle and will then enter the microscope and make a mark on a photographic plate; the particle's position and momentum can be calculated from this mark. The accuracy of the calculations, however, depends on the distance between the crests in the light waves used to make the observation. To obtain an exact measurement of the particle's position, one would need to use light of very short wavelength. Such high-frequency light, however, contains much energy, and when the light is directed toward the particle, it will alter the particle's momentum. By using light of longer wavelength and lower energy, on the other hand, one could obtain a precise measure of the particle's speed, but uncertainty would then creep in with regard to its location. Therefore, the more one closes in on the position, the less accurately one can know the momentum, and vice versa. In the realm of microphysics, as the exact state of an atomic system can apparently never be fully open to view, physical processes at this level cannot be precisely predicted.

Heisenberg formulated his uncertainty principle early in 1927, the year after he became an assistant to Niels Bohr at Bohr's research institute in Copenhagen. The two scientists engaged in almost daily dialogue on the foundations of quantum theory and the nature of physical reality. Near the end of February, 1927, there was a brief, but rather deliberate break when Bohr left to take a skiing vacation in Norway. During this time, Heisenberg con-

Werner Heisenberg. (The Nobel Foundation)

ceptualized the gamma-ray microscope experiment and decided that the indeterminacy evident in the measurement of subatomic particles had to be considered a fundamental principle of quantum theory. When Bohr returned to Copenhagen, he realized that Heisenberg's thinking was at variance with the ideas he had been pursuing. Bohr, who was also searching for basic principles, had been trying to understand the fact, established in part by Albert Einstein's study of the photoelectric effect, that light, as well as matter, displays wavelike properties under some conditions and particle-like properties under other conditions. Physicists had been trying to understand the nature of the wave-particle duality for years.

Bohr realized that, as the property that appears depends on the type of experiment or observing apparatus one is using, one simply cannot describe microphysical phenomena as either particle-like or wavelike without also referring to the method of observation. The observer does not merely observe these properties, they are

evoked. Bohr formulated the principle of complementarity as a way of understanding the wave-particle paradox: that the wave aspect and the particle aspect are mutually exclusive but complementary, and emphasizing that both aspects must be included in any complete picture of microphysical phenomena.

Bohr was convinced that the principle of complementarity revealed a basic fact about the possibilities and limitations of the knowledge of microphysics. Heisenberg believed that the principle of uncertainty expressed a similarly fundamental fact. The apparent disparity between these two principles was the focus of long and sometimes heated discussions between Bohr and Heisenberg. In the end, however, they were able to agree that uncertainty and complementarity were compatible, with Heisenberg's principle understood as a particular mathematical formulation of the more general principle of complementarity. These two principles, together with Max Born's probabilistic interpretation of electron waves, combined to form what has become known as the Copenhagen interpretation of quantum theory.

The basic issue at stake in the interface between the different but related principles of Heisenberg and Bohr concerns the appropriateness of using concepts familiar to classical physics and everyday life in understanding the realm of the atom. Heisenberg believed that concepts such as position and momentum, or particle and wave, are of limited applicability in this domain because of the limitations involved in their measurement. He thought that a clear and consistent theory could be expressed only in abstract mathematical terms. Bohr, on the other hand, maintained his strong conviction that concepts rooted in the everyday world of objects and events can, and indeed must, be used to describe microphysical phenomena, but that only one aspect of a complementary pair of concepts will be appropriate in a given experimental situation. Heisenberg recognized the great philosophical importance of Bohr's approach and added to his famous 1927 paper enunciating the uncertainty principle a postscript in which he said that Bohr would present a related principle that would deepen and extend the meaning of the uncertainty principle. Bohr introduced the principle of complementarity in September of 1927, likewise acknowledging Heisenberg's groundbreaking work.

SIGNIFICANCE

In the new brand of physics ushered in by Heisenberg, abstract mathematics played a much greater role than in any previous form of physics. Quantum physics thus became a very powerful and influential mathematical tool

1927

that has been used to forge new theoretical developments in other fields of science such as chemistry and biology and to fashion a variety of technological innovations such as transistors, lasers, and microchips. All of this scientific and technological activity can be carried out with little concern for the profound philosophical questions posed by the uncertainty principle. Many scientists who, like Einstein, have been deeply concerned with the meaning of science for human life as a whole have given much thought to these issues.

Soon after Heisenberg and Bohr presented their principles of uncertainty and complementarity in 1927, the Copenhagen interpretation became established as the generally accepted foundation for quantum theory. A number of major physicists, including Einstein, challenged the conceptual cornerstones on which this version of the theory was built. The debate centered on the questions of objectivity and indeterminism. If the principle of uncertainty is taken as truly fundamental, then the state of a particle when it is not being observed should be considered. One would have to conclude that an unobserved particle has no definite characteristics. Actually, it could not be called a particle, or a wave, nor does it have any real position or momentum. As Heisenberg stated, "What we observe is not nature in itself, but nature exposed to our method of questioning."

Einstein believed that any theory of physics that does not include physical reality cannot be considered a complete theory of nature. From 1927 to 1935, Einstein formulated a number of hypothetical experiments designed to discredit the uncertainty principle, but Bohr was able to refute each of these arguments. The Copenhagen interpretation maintained its sovereignty in the theoretical and practical work of the majority of physicists.

The controversy sparked by the uncertainty principle did not diminish. During the 1980's, it emerged again as a lively topic of discussion, partially as a result of new experimental findings. Certain physicists and philosophers, notably David Bohm, continued in the spirit of Einstein to explore the possibility of formulating an expanded interpretation of quantum theory.

It is important to understand that although the uncertainty principle revolutionized microphysics and led indirectly to numerous technological developments, it had little impact on the physics of familiar objects. In the realm of everyday, easily perceived and measured objects and events, the determinism of classical physics still provides quite satisfactory predictions and explanations. Heisenberg's uncertainty principle has been quite effective in shaking the assumptions and assurances of

universal determinism that had guided the thinking of many people—scientists and nonscientists alike—since Laplace proposed the idea in the early nineteenth century.

Something that both advocates and opponents of the Copenhagen interpretation would certainly agree on is that the uncertainty principle has helped to reveal the perhaps unsuspected richness of reality, a wealth of patterns and potentialities too great to be grasped in a single observation or to be exhausted by a given experimental or conceptual structure. Heisenberg helped to push the search for an understanding of nature to a new level, to the point where matter meets mind and physics meets philosophy.

—Gordon L. Miller

FURTHER READING

Bohm, David. *Causality and Chance in Modern Physics.* 1957. Reprint. New York: Routledge, 1997. Reprint edition features a preface that refers to developments in Bohm's sustained efforts to formulate an interpretation of quantum theory capable of encompassing both classical determinism and the indeterminism of the Copenhagen interpretation in a broader understanding of the laws of nature. A clearly articulated, searching, and sophisticated philosophical inquiry by a contemporary physicist.

Bohr, Niels. *Atomic Physics and Human Knowledge.* New York: John Wiley & Sons, 1958. A collection of mostly short essays exploring the implications of research in atomic physics for various other fields, such as biology, anthropology, and philosophy.

Cline, Barbara Lovett. *Men Who Made a New Physics.* 1965. Reprint. Chicago: University of Chicago Press, 1987. An interesting narrative, written for a general audience, of the lives, theories, and interrelationships of the physicists, primarily Einstein, Bohr, and Heisenberg, but also the earlier Ernest Rutherford and Max Planck, who between 1900 and 1930 created quantum theory. Includes illustrations, bibliography, and index.

Crease, Robert P., and Charles C. Mann. *The Second Creation: Makers of the Revolution in Twentieth-Century Physics.* Rev. ed. New Brunswick, N.J.: Rutgers University Press, 1996. Readable volume follows the development of physics from its nineteenth century roots to the mysteries of the late twentieth century. Examines characters and personalities as well as the issues of physics. Includes discussion of Heisenberg's work.

Cropper, William H. *Great Physicists: The Life and Times of Leading Physicists from Galileo to Haw-*

king. New York: Oxford University Press, 2001. Presents portraits of the lives and accomplishments of important physicists and shows how they influenced one another with their work. Chapter 18 is devoted to Heisenberg. Includes glossary and index.

Guillemin, Victor. *The Story of Quantum Mechanics.* 1968. Reprint. Mineola, N.Y.: Dover, 2003. Places quantum theory in the context of the history of physics and discusses the philosophical and religious implications of the new physics. Includes glossary of scientific terms, annotated bibliography, and index.

Heisenberg, Werner. *Physics and Beyond.* Translated by Arnold J. Pomerans. New York: Harper & Row, 1971. Writing for a wide audience, Heisenberg demonstrates his belief that "science is rooted in conversations." Gives a firsthand account of some of the conversations that have shaped modern physics and, in important ways, the modern world. Chapter 6 details the events surrounding the creation of the uncertainty principle.

_____. *Physics and Philosophy: The Revolution in Modern Science.* 1958. Reprint. Amherst, N.Y.: Pro-

metheus Books, 1999. Discusses in largely nontechnical terms a variety of topics, including the history of quantum theory, the Copenhagen interpretation and some of its critics, and the role of modern physics.

Pagels, Heinz R. *The Cosmic Code: Quantum Physics as the Language of Nature.* New York: Simon & Schuster, 1982. A theoretical physicist's popular, readable, and reliable account of the development of relativity and quantum theory, research into elementary particles, and the nature of the scientific investigation of the physical world. Provides interesting insights into the personalities involved and includes many illuminating examples and illustrations of the major issues. Includes bibliography and detailed index.

SEE ALSO: 1914: Rutherford Discovers the Proton; 1923: Discovery of the Compton Effect; Spring, 1925: Pauli Formulates the Exclusion Principle; Summer, 1928: Gamow Explains Radioactive Alpha Decay with Quantum Tunneling; Sept., 1932: Anderson Discovers the Positron; Nov., 1934: Yukawa Proposes the Existence of Mesons.

1927

February 21, 1927
EASTMAN KODAK IS FOUND TO BE IN VIOLATION OF THE SHERMAN ACT

In one of many antitrust suits brought against the Eastman Kodak Company, the U.S. Supreme Court found the firm guilty of enforcing exclusive contracts.

LOCALE: Washington, D.C.; Rochester, New York
CATEGORIES: Trade and commerce; laws, acts, and legal history

KEY FIGURES

George Eastman (1854-1932), American inventor, industrialist, and philanthropist
Hannibal W. Goodwin (1822-1900), American clergyman and inventor
Thomas Alva Edison (1847-1931), American inventor

SUMMARY OF EVENT

Passage of the federal Sherman Antitrust Act in 1890 coincided with American industry's increasing resort to combination, that is, to organization as mergers, amalgamations, conglomerates, and trusts. The structuring of businesses along these lines was most notable among firms with capitalizations in excess of one million dol-

lars. Of the roughly 220 such combinations effected between 1890 and 1900, an important minority were trusts. A trust puts the stocks of various companies into a central pool, to be controlled by a board of trustees. The companies then act in concert for their mutual benefit rather than competing. The rate of trust formation slackened after 1900, but this type of combination continued on a large scale until 1904. Trusts were epitomized by United States Steel (the world's first billion-dollar corporation) as well as by the original trust, Standard Oil, in company with American Tobacco, Du Pont, Northern Securities, and International Harvester. Their names translated as "monopolies" in public and in political parlance. These were also chief among the organizations whose sheer size or practices gave impetus to the first serious Sherman Act prosecutions, which were begun during the presidency of Theodore Roosevelt and increased through the administrations of William Howard Taft and Woodrow Wilson.

There were some modestly capitalized trusts that

seemed less menacing in the eyes of reformers, muckrakers, and the public. Their degrees of market power nevertheless often equaled or exceeded those of their more prominent and notorious counterparts. Reorganized as a trust in 1901 with a capitalization of about twenty-seven million dollars, the Eastman Kodak Company was one of these smaller trusts. The astuteness of its leader, its innovative edge, its control over patents, and its exclusionary marketing strategies allowed it to control nearly 90 percent of its market, a higher proportion than U.S. Steel, American Tobacco, or International Harvester controlled of their respective markets and about equal to the market power exercised by Du Pont, Pullman, and Singer. Moreover, the Eastman Kodak Company attained this measure of power within just a few years after its restructuring as a trust. A conjunction of inventiveness, scientific curiosity, artistic imagination, risk taking, business acumen, public interest, and ready markets contributed to making this ascendancy over the photographic industry possible.

By the last quarter of the nineteenth century, photography had evolved in many of its dimensions beyond the seminal contributions made earlier by Louis Jacques Mandé Daguerre, William Henry Fox Talbot, and scores of ingenious chemists, opticians, physicists, and amateur photographers. Because of the weight, bulk, awkwardness, and fragility of the glass plates on which photography relied as a base for its light-sensitive materials, the international search for improvements from the 1860's onward centered on contriving an unbreakable, lightweight, flexible, and still sensitive film. Experimentation in the United States and Western Europe initially involved various wet collodion processes as well as the gelatinous silver bromide dry process. Uses of celluloid soon showed great promise, thanks to the work of John Hyatt in the late 1860's and, two decades later, to discoveries by John Carbutt and Hannibal W. Goodwin. Goodwin, a Newark, New Jersey, Episcopal clergyman and amateur photographer, was in 1887 the first American to apply for a patent for the production of flexible, transparent film, in the form of light-sensitive, celluloid-like, collodion strips. The patent was not granted until 1898. It covered an area in which George Eastman, who was also working assiduously on the manufacture of films and roll films, was to be credited with pioneering advances.

Eastman was born in a small town in northern New York in 1854 and at the age of six moved with his family to Rochester, where his father established a commercial school. His father's death forced fourteen-year-old George to leave school to help his mother. At the age of twenty, believing he had been cheated out of a promotion, he left a well-paying bank job to devote himself to photography, formerly a hobby.

After several years of experiments informed by his studies of photography advances reported in American, British, and European journals and by later consultative journeys to England, he began manufacturing dry plates, first at home and then in a small factory. By 1879, he had devised a dependable formula for producing emulsions for coating glass plates. He soon patented a machine that performed this task. Having solicited the financial backing of investor Henry A. Strong and the camera-making expertise of William H. Walker, Eastman founded the Rochester-based Dry Plate & Film Company in 1884 for the manufacturer of a hand camera with roll film. Eastman heavily advertised his handy box camera, featuring a roll holder and stripping film combined within it. He trademarked his product "Kodak," a nonsense word, in 1888. Improvements in the quality and varieties of film as well as in the camera itself thereafter were patented swiftly by Eastman and his chemist, Henry Reichenbach. Low price and simplicity paved the way for the Kodak's immense commercial success.

Eastman guarded his firm's novelties and quality in many ways. He helped block the patent application filed by Goodwin, securing similar patents under his and Reichenbach's names. Goodwin subsequently sued after his own film and camera company came under control of the Ansco Company. Years later, the courts ordered Eastman to pay millions of dollars in damages to Ansco, thus acknowledging Goodwin's invention of the celluloid base for roll films. Eastman also licensed important patents and eventually bought some of them outright. Eastman produced Thomas Alva Edison's "first motion-picture camera" and manufactured most projection film then used by the rapidly growing motion-picture industry. Eastman joined leaders of that fledgling industry in crowding out competitors.

By 1913, the Eastman Kodak Company had fallen foul of the Sherman Act. Federal courts alleged that it enjoyed a monopoly of the manufacture, sale, and distribution of photographic supplies, that it had bought out a score of competitors, and that it had acquired sole rights to sell domestic and foreign-made paper suitable for photography. Further, the government contended that Eastman had engaged in price fixing and had entered exclusive dealings arrangements. All of these activities were deemed harmful to competition. The company was ordered to dissolve its monopoly. The litigious affair of consents and decrees dragged on until 1935.

In the meantime, a small Georgia wholesaler that had dealt in Eastman products for many years, Southern Photo Materials, won its case against Kodak before the U.S. Supreme Court, which handed down its decision on February 21, 1927. The case arose when Kodak sought to purchase all competing wholesalers in Georgia, Southern Photo Materials included. That company refused the offer. Eastman then cut off sales to it except at retail prices. At the time, Kodak manufactured more than nine-tenths of American motion-picture film. By entering agreements with its customers through an association of laboratories making motion-picture prints, it also prevented firms such as Southern Photo Materials from purchasing imported film.

Having already been deemed an illegal combination in 1916, and under federal decrees to present plans for its dissolution in 1916, 1921, and 1926, Eastman Kodak in 1927 was found guilty before the U.S. Supreme Court of exclusionary practices, discrimination, and the "forward integration" of competitors, or buying up customers of its products to avoid having to compete to sell to them and to final customers for its products.

SIGNIFICANCE

For nearly half a century following its initial conviction under the Sherman Act in 1913, and for more than twenty years after its 1927 conviction by the Supreme Court, the Eastman Kodak Company maintained an estimated 90 percent share of its market, with no measurable change. It remained America's largest manufacturer of cameras, photographic and motion-picture film, and supplies. Its branches were international. If antitrust prosecutions had any effect on it, they were most discernible in what experts defined as the medium ease of entry by others into Eastman's fields of enterprise. By most criteria, Eastman's advantages were enormous, muted only by litigation.

Irrespective of its business practices, Eastman Kodak in major respects ranked as one of the world's most enlightened and progressive firms, exactly as George Eastman intended. His employees were made shareholders in the company and were recipients of generous welfare, benefit, promotion, and pension plans. Eastman, who never married, treated Rochester and other communities as beneficiaries of his wealth, favoring education, the arts, and propagation of the music he loved. Before his unusual suicide in 1932—it was simply the rational decision of a satisfied man—he disposed of nearly all his wealth, contributing to philanthropies almost one billion dollars as measured in 1990 purchasing power.

Carl Ackerman, Eastman's definitive biographer, notes that Eastman was disciplined and temperate. He was deservedly liked and was accorded respect by his associates, scientists, employees, and the communities with which he dealt. Before his retirement in 1929, he had stamped his organization with his own admirable personality. Neither Eastman nor his organization conformed with the popular stereotypes of his day of "robber barons," tycoons, or captains of industry. From the perspective of the 1990's, business consultant Peter F. Drucker cited Eastman Kodak as one of a handful of "long-pull performers," successful because of its concentration on a single market and single technology.

Whatever the internal organizational excellence of Eastman Kodak and the wisdom of its business strategies, the company again found itself challenged when its performance was assessed by federal authorities. In the 1950's, depicted as an aggressive near monopoly in its dealings with competitors, inventors, and consumers alike, it was again charged by the Antitrust Division of the Department of Justice with violations of sections 1, 2, and 3 of the Sherman Act.

Eastman Kodak, according to the complaint, had sold its Kodachrome and Kodacolor films on the understanding that it obtain all processing business connected with the films. It therefore marketed Kodachrome and Kodacolor at prices that included Eastman's subsequent processing charges. In so doing, Eastman foreclosed competitive processing. Moreover, as consumers generally expected the film developer to develop at least one set of prints, Eastman was charged further with illegally tying its sale of film to the making of Kodacolor prints. In addition, it was alleged that Eastman illegally fixed the resale price of these films beyond "fair trade" price exemptions to the Sherman Act as set by other federal statutes.

The consent judgment entered against Eastman Kodak required the company to cancel its fair trade contracts relative to the resale price maintenance (setting a minimum price that all sellers would charge) of Kodachrome and Kodacolor products and to abstain from entering into similar contracts for controlling the price of its color films. Amateur users of Eastman's color film were also freed thereafter to obtain the benefits of open competition for the film's processing.

Federal authority further compelled Eastman Kodak to grant reasonable royalty licenses for numerous related patents and to distribute manuals describing its commercial color film processing technology, with annual supplements for seven years. The company was also ordered

1927

2177

to provide the services of a technical representative to any recipient of these manuals who needed further instruction. If necessary, Eastman Kodak's major eastern processing plants were to be opened to these recipients to observe and learn the technology employed. Finally, within seven years the company was to divest itself of any facilities in excess of 50 percent of the current domestic capacity for processing its color film.

Operating in a legally complex field, Eastman Kodak and the U.S. attorney general agreed, immediately upon filing of the government's consent judgment, to negotiate a settlement. The parties resolved their difficulties over the bargaining table rather than in court. Unlike its previous experiences in bringing an end to antitrust proceedings against Eastman Kodak, federal authorities, at modest expense, procured what they described as an equitable judgment achieved by reasonable cooperation between business and government.

Dominating much of the technology of its industry, Eastman Kodak traditionally had wielded its edge in the market until competitors' or consumers' complaints snarled it in the often illusory web of antitrust technicalities. Many American businesses had pursued similar courses. Beginning in 1947, Edwin H. Land, inventor of the Polaroid instant camera, had also seized and maintained his market advantage while he could, exclusive of competition. Polaroid, Eastman Kodak, and other manufacturers understood that when antitrust laws were invoked against them they faced a Justice Department that was politically vulnerable, understaffed, and otherwise short of the resources for lengthy legal battles. Rational settlements with which all parties could live, that opened the marketplace somewhat and arguably redounded to the public good, were justifications enough for America's singular antitrust tradition.

—Clifton K. Yearley

FURTHER READING

Ackerman, Carl W. *George Eastman*. London: Constable, 1930. Well-written and exhaustive biography places both Eastman and his firm in specific context. Includes notes, bibliography, and index.

Coe, Brian. *George Eastman and the Early Photographers*. London: Priory Press, 1973. Essay with excellent photos places Eastman in the tradition of his hobby and craft. Focuses on his work, not on his business practices. Includes chronology, glossary, bibliography, and index.

Eder, Josef Maria. *History of Photography*. New York: Columbia University Press, 1945. Massive, scholarly history includes discussion of Eastman's interests, career, and contributions in chapters 47 through 49. Dense but invaluable. Includes notes and index.

Gernsheim, Helmut, and Alison Gernsheim. *The History of Photography*. 2d ed. London: Thames and Hudson, 1969. Less exhaustive and more readable than Eder's book (cited above) and a supplement to it for the post-1945 period. A fine work with good perspective on Eastman's main contributions. Includes interesting photos, notes, bibliography, and index.

Peritz, Rudolph J., Jr. *Competition Policy in America, 1888-1992: History, Rhetoric, Law*. Rev. ed. New York: Oxford University Press, 2001. A history of federal government policies relating to antitrust issues. Includes a substantial bibliography and index.

Sandler, Martin W. *Photography: An Illustrated History*. New York: Oxford University Press, 2002. Presents a chronological overview of the major figures in the history of photography and their artistic and technical contributions. Includes many photographs as well as a chronology, a bibliography, and a list of photography museums around the world and Web sites devoted to photography.

Shepherd, William G. *The Treatment of Market Power: Antitrust, Regulation, and Public Enterprise*. New York: Columbia University Press, 1975. Written by a former U.S. Justice Department antitrust expert, this is a novel clinical diagnosis of market power into which Eastman Kodak has been fit. Excellent discussion of the difficulties of applying antitrust policies. Includes notes, graphs, charts, tables, appendixes, and index.

SEE ALSO: Mar. 14, 1904: U.S. Supreme Court Rules Against Northern Securities; Jan. 30, 1905: U.S. Supreme Court Upholds Prosecution of the Beef Trust; May 15, 1911: U.S. Supreme Court Establishes the "Rule of Reason"; May 29, 1911: U.S. Supreme Court Breaks Up the American Tobacco Company; Oct. 15, 1914: Clayton Antitrust Act; Mar. 1, 1920: *United States v. United States Steel Corporation*; 1924: U.S. Government Loses Its Suit Against Alcoa; Nov., 1932: Antitrust Prosecution Forces RCA to Restructure.

February 25, 1927

MCFADDEN ACT REGULATES BRANCH BANKING

The McFadden Act granted national banks in the United States the right to open branches in their head-office cities in order to reduce the comparative disadvantages they had suffered and to retain government control over banking and monetary policies.

LOCALE: Washington, D.C.

CATEGORIES: Banking and finance; laws, acts, and legal history

KEY FIGURES

Louis Thomas McFadden (1876-1936), chairman of the Banking and Currency Committee of the U.S. House of Representatives, 1920-1931

Daniel Richard Crissinger (1860-1942), chairman of the Office of the Comptroller of the Currency, 1920-1923, and a governor of the Federal Reserve Board, 1923-1927

Herbert Hoover (1874-1964), president of the United States, 1929-1933

SUMMARY OF EVENT

The main provisions of the McFadden Act, which became law on February 25, 1927, permitted branch banking by federally chartered banks (national banks) that were located in states in which laws granted such authority to state-chartered banks (state banks). The act was intended to remove some of the handicaps under which national banks had been competing with state banks.

The Federal Reserve Act of 1913 prohibited national banks from branching; each could operate from only one full-service office. State banks, however, were often allowed to branch within their head-office cities or counties, or even statewide. The purpose of this differential regulation was to protect small (state) banks from competition from branches of large (national) banks. This disadvantage to national banks in competing with state banks caused many banks to convert to state charters. During the 1920's, 127 large national banks (with total assets of five million dollars or more at that time) converted to state charters.

Unlike national banks, state banks were not required to be members of the Federal Reserve system and were not subject to the reserve requirements set by the Federal Reserve, under which banks had to keep certain percentages of deposits available as reserves to meet demands for withdrawals. Therefore, the Federal Reserve's ability to maintain direct control over banking policies and the money supply was weakened as national banks converted to state charters.

To alleviate this problem, Daniel Richard Crissinger, chairman of the Office of the Comptroller of the Currency, in 1921 authorized national banks (in states that permitted state banks to branch) to open teller windows that would accept only deposits and cash checks. These acted as limited-service branches. The problem of conversion to state charters nevertheless continued. Between 1924 and 1927, the issue of branch banking was extensively debated in the banking industry, in state governments, and in Congress.

The McFadden Act allowed national banks to open full-service branches. Under the McFadden Act, national banks were allowed to branch within the cities or towns in which they were located, provided that state banks had the same privilege. State banks were permitted to retain all branches established prior to the McFadden Act but were forbidden to establish new branches outside their head-office cities.

The purpose of the McFadden Act was to reduce the comparative disadvantage suffered by national banks thereby reducing the incentive to abandon federal charters in favor of state charters. The bill was designed to slow defections from the national banking system. The disadvantage to national banks remained, however, in states in which state banks had already established branches outside their head-office cities, because the branching of national banks was limited to the cities in which they were located.

According to Louis Thomas McFadden, it was not the purpose of his act to encourage branch banking in the broadest sense. The act was in fact an "anti-branch banking bill" that cut the number of bank branches per capita by about half between 1920 and 1930. The reduction came about because of the restrictions on branching by state banks.

On June 16, 1933, the Glass-Steagall Act was passed, amending the McFadden Act by extending the branching privilege of national banks to outside their head-office cities if state law permitted state banks this freedom. Under this bill, national banks and state banks had the same branching rights. Branching authority for both national and state banks was subject to state branching laws. Bank branching can be classified into three categories. First, unit-banking states permitted only single-office banks.

1927

Second, limited-branching states allowed state banks to branch within a city, county, or portion of the state. Third, statewide-branching states allowed banks to open branches anywhere within the state.

Branch banking began on a large scale after passage of the Glass-Steagall Act. National banks took advantage of the right to branch outside their head-office cities. For example, the number of branches of Bank of America increased to five hundred by 1946 and to more than a thousand by 1976, with at least one branch in every county in California. During the period from 1933 to 1951, three-fourths of new branches created were outside head-office cities.

Although banks were granted more freedom to branch intrastate, neither national nor state banks were allowed to branch across state lines. The purpose of this interstate branching restriction was to prevent monopolistic tendencies in the banking system. That is, the restriction was intended to prevent development of a monopolistic bank that would have control over loan and deposit markets in the entire nation. In addition, the interstate branching restriction was believed to prevent banks from draining funds from one state to lend in another state. Local banks were believed to be more likely to commit to serving local businesses and investments within the state. In supporting this argument, President Herbert Hoover stated in 1929 that the American credit system should be subject to the restraint of local interest.

Some banks were interested in branching beyond their intrastate branching rights. These banks evaded the interstate branching restriction by setting up holding company organizations to acquire banks in other states. Up until the 1950's, the multibank holding company was frequently used as a mechanism to expand across state lines. Forty-seven bank holding companies existed in 1960.

This loophole in the McFadden Act was closed on May 9, 1956, by the Douglas Amendment to the Bank Holding Company Act, which prohibited bank holding companies from acquiring banks in other states. Those bank holding companies that had already acquired bank subsidiaries in other states were allowed to keep them and operate them. The Douglas Amendment effectively prohibited banks from branching across state lines unless specifically authorized to do so by state authorities.

The Bank Holding Company Act of 1956 was amended in 1970 to define a bank as an institution that accepts deposits that can be withdrawn on demand and also makes commercial loans. A branch office that did not provide one of these services would not satisfy the definition of a full-service bank. These branch offices were called "nonbank banks" and were not regulated by the Federal Reserve system. Some banks evaded the interstate branching restriction by opening nonbank banks in other states as a way to expand across state lines. The Competitive Banking Equality Act of 1987 closed this loophole by defining a bank as any institution insured by the Federal Deposit Insurance Corporation (FDIC), but it exempted nonbank banks established before March 5, 1986.

Branch liberalization within states (intrastate branching) continued as more and more states converted from unit banking to statewide banking. For example, New Jersey and New York converted to statewide branching in 1973 and 1975, respectively. Florida converted from unit banking to countywide branching in 1977, and then to statewide branching in 1980. By the end of 1990, forty-two states had statewide branching, and Colorado was the only unit-banking state in the nation.

SIGNIFICANCE

More important than allowing national banks to branch within their head-office cities, the McFadden Act imposed interstate branching restrictions for both national and state banks, one of the most important restrictions on the nation's banking industry. All banks were prohibited from branching across state lines in order to prevent monopolistic tendencies in the banking system. This interstate branching law had an unintended effect. In addition to tampering with the degree of competition in the banking industry, the law imposed restrictions on banks' ability to diversify geographically, as banks were not able to open branches in other states to diversify their loan and investment portfolios.

The limitation on geographic diversification increased bank risks. An economic downturn in a state could have a disastrous effect on banks with business concentrated in the state and cause a chain of bank failures in that state. For example, First Republic Bank of Texas, the fourteenth largest bank in the nation at the time, went bankrupt in the late 1980's, as did several other Texas banks. Problems in the oil industry and real estate in Texas caused the failures, which used up a large part of the FDIC insurance fund.

As the number of bank failures increased dramatically in the 1980's, the FDIC attempted to minimize depositor losses and resulting communitywide or nationwide disruption by arranging for troubled banks to be merged with healthy ones, with FDIC financial assistance. This policy was applied particularly to large banks, which regulators considered to be too big to be allowed to fail because of the disruptions that would result from failure. The FDIC sometimes had a difficult time finding a healthy bank within the same state to acquire a troubled bank, as problems in a state tended to affect all the state's banks.

The Garn-St. Germain Depository Institutions Act was passed on October 15, 1982, to affirm the power of the FDIC to arrange interstate mergers if an acquirer from the same state was not found. For example, First Republic Bank of Texas was acquired by the North Carolina National Bank (NCNB) in July, 1988, under an FDIC emergency rescue program. The FDIC emergency rescue program helped to promote nationwide banking and improve geographic diversification in the U.S. banking system.

In addition, starting in the early 1980's, states began to pass laws that would allow out-of-state banks to enter under specified circumstances. Some states required a reciprocal arrangement that allowed banks and bank holding companies from other states to enter by acquiring existing banks within their borders only if the home state of an entering bank granted similar privileges to banks headquartered in the state being entered. By the end of 1992, the only four states that did not allow out-of-state banks to enter were Hawaii, Kansas, Montana, and North Dakota. The trend appeared to be toward nationwide banking, which would help to reduce banks' vulnerability to regional economic downturns.

Aside from the issue of geographic diversification, it has also been argued that the interstate branching restriction imposed by the McFadden Act reduced cost efficiencies in the banking system. Small banks are generally likely to be handicapped by higher costs relative to large banks. Banks could obtain economics of scale by expanding nationwide. Some analysts argued that banks did not necessarily have to expand across state lines to be large enough to realize economies of scale. Whether U.S. banks could become more efficient by branching across state lines remains an issue that will have to be decided by experience. Cost efficiency studies for commercial banks have provided mixed results. The fact that branching was being allowed on a larger scale showed that regulators were swayed by cost considerations and were less concerned with potential monopoly power.

Nationwide banking as opposed to branching has also been a topic for debate since the late 1980's. Under state branching laws, such as reciprocal arrangements, and the FDIC emergency rescue program under the

Garn-St. Germain Depository Institutions Act, banks are allowed to acquire existing banks in other states and operate them as bank subsidiaries. This improves the geographic diversification of bank holding companies, but it may not significantly reduce the rate of bank failures if profits and losses are not pooled among bank subsidiaries. That is, diversified bank holding companies may choose to let their troubled bank subsidiaries fail and continue to impose potential liabilities on the FDIC insurance fund. In 1994, passage of the Riegle-Neal Interstate Banking and Branching Efficiency Act gave banks much greater ability to operate interstate branches. The impacts of this change in banking law are still being debated.

—Julapa Jagtiani

FURTHER READING

Burns, Helen M. *The American Banking Community and New Deal Banking Reforms, 1933-1935*. Westport, Conn.: Greenwood Press, 1974. Discusses the development of banking reforms and presents interesting statistics on bank branching by both state and national banks during the period 1900-1935. Unlike many books on regulatory reforms in the 1930's era, this one was written long after the events, allowing the author to relate important issues in the 1930's to more recent regulatory development.

Calomiris, Charles W. *U.S. Bank Deregulation in Historical Perspective*. New York: Cambridge University Press, 2000. Offers historical background on U.S. banking laws to explain the changes in the banking industry in the last two decades of the twentieth century. Briefly discusses the McFadden Act.

Chapman, John M., and Ray Westerfield. *Branch Banking*. New York: Harper & Brothers, 1942. Useful for information on the history and theory of branch banking, both in the United States and abroad. Provides statistics about branch banking.

Frieder, Larry A. *Commercial Banking and Interstate Expansion: Issues, Prospects, and Strategies*. Ann Arbor, Mich.: UMI Research Press, 1985. Provides detailed arguments for and against interstate banking. Discusses issues such as geographic diversification, cost efficiency, effects on competition, and the safety and soundness of the banking system. Examines Florida's regulation of interstate banking in detail. Well written, but perhaps too technical for readers with no special background in finance or economics.

Johnson, Richard B., ed. *The Bank Holding Company,*

1927

1973. Dallas: Southern Methodist University Press, 1973. Collection of conference papers devoted to issues related to bank holding companies, with a focus on regulatory issues. Intended for readers with background in banking and finance.

Klebaner, Benjamin J. *American Commercial Banking: A History*. Boston: Twayne, 1990. Well organized history, easy to understand even for readers without background in finance and economics. Provides a chronology of important events from 1781 to 1989.

Matasar, Ann B., and Joseph N. Heiney. *The Impact of Geographic Deregulation on the American Banking Industry*. Westport, Conn.: Quorum Books, 2002. Addresses the changes in American banking since the passage of the Glass-Steagall Act in 1933. Intended for readers with some background in banking and finance. Includes an appendix containing the text of the McFadden Act, bibliography, and index.

Ostrolenk, Bernhard. *The Economics of Branch Banking*. New York: Harper & Brothers, 1930. Discusses the development of and reasons for branch and chain banking. Chapters 8-10 examine the history of branch banking in the United Kingdom, Canada, and California.

SEE ALSO: Apr. 5, 1910: First Morris Plan Bank Opens; Dec. 23, 1913: Federal Reserve Act; Nov. 4, 1924: Coolidge Is Elected U.S. President; Dec. 11, 1930: Bank of United States Fails; June 16, 1933: Banking Act of 1933 Reorganizes the American Banking System; Aug. 23, 1935: Banking Act of 1935 Centralizes U.S. Monetary Control.

May, 1927
INDIANA DUNES ARE PRESERVED AS A STATE PARK

The struggle to preserve the unique Indiana Dunes landscape, which provides a classic model for ecological studies, spanned decades and presented formidable challenges for environmentalists.

LOCALE: Northwestern Indiana
CATEGORIES: Environmental issues; government and politics; natural resources

KEY FIGURES
Henry C. Cowles (1869-1939), American botanist and university professor
Stephen T. Mather (1867-1930), founder and first director of the U.S. National Park Service
Paul H. Douglas (1892-1976), U.S. senator from Illinois
Dorothy Buell (1886-1977), founder of the Save the Dunes Council

SUMMARY OF EVENT
The Indiana Dunes State Park has long been recognized for its unique landscape and for the five plant communities that inhabit it. The area contains several dune types in various stages of development as well as bogs, marshes, prairies, and forests. Nearly fifteen hundred species of plants populate the dunes. Among major parks in the United States, only the Great Smokies and the Grand Canyon have more native species, and yet the Indiana Dunes park encompasses only fourteen thousand acres,
far less than either of the other two. Preservation of the dunelands is critical, not only for the survival of the distinctive plant life but also for the benefit of the many people who wish to study and explore the area.

Preservation of the Indiana Dunes has been a struggle since the early part of the twentieth century. The urbanization and growth of industry around the southern shore of Lake Michigan provided a formidable challenge to conservation efforts, but the spirit of local and regional environmentally minded citizens and politicians has prevailed. Little by little, parts of the Indiana Dunes have been acquired for preservation, first as an Indiana state park and much later as an expanded national park. Preservation of the dunes was greatly enhanced by the efforts of Henry C. Cowles, whose studies of dune plant communities made the Indiana Dunes internationally famous.

The dry hills and wet lowlands of the Indiana Dunes were unsuitable for settlement. Native Americans used the area for hunting grounds and for gathering berries and the abundant wild rice that grew in the wetlands. French and British fur traders inhabited the area in the mid- to late 1700's. A few homesteads were built in the 1800's, but no successful settlement was established until railroads reached the area in the 1850's. In the late 1800's, serious development of the southern Lake Michigan shoreline began. Pine and cedar trees in the dunes area were cut to supply expanding Chicago with lumber and firewood. In 1869, George Hammond built a meatpacking plant on the Grand Calumet River, and by 1887, East Chicago was being promoted as a choice industrial site. Many large dunes were mined away by the trainload to supply sand for fill so that Chicago could expand into Lake Michigan; the dunes also supplied sand for construction projects and glass industries. By 1920, the dunes area contained the world's largest power plant as well as a steel mill, a chemical plant, a cement plant, and an oil refinery.

At the same time, scientific studies were being conducted by Cowles, a professor at the University of Chicago. Cowles came to Chicago with a fellowship in 1895 to study geology. He visited the dunes for the first time in 1896 and became enthralled with the vegetation distributions there. He began a systematic study of the vegetation and its relationship with the dune environment and promoted the idea of a relationship between vegetation patterns and changing dune environments. Cowles's work marked the first application of the principles of ecology in the United States. He patterned his work after that of Eugenius Warming, who had conducted studies of dune vegetation in coastal Denmark. Cowles published three classic articles that declared the Indiana Dunes to be the ideal model for the study of changing landforms and the response of vegetation to those changes. He pointed out the importance of climatic influences on the cycles he was observing, and he noted that the area's vegetation was unique because the region was a meeting point of northern and southern species as well as of eastern forests and western prairies. After he presented his third paper at a conference in Europe, Cowles organized the 1913 International Phytogeography Excursion. He polled the European scientists who participated and found that they were most interested in visiting four American natural landmarks: the Grand Canyon, Yosemite, Yellowstone, and the Indiana Dunes. Cowles and others often used this expression of international interest in the dunes to illustrate the value of the area; Cowles's work thus formed the cornerstone of the dunes preservation movement.

In the early 1900's, local conservationists became increasingly alarmed by the encroaching industrial development. In response, the Playground Association of Chicago began a successful program of Saturday afternoon walks in the dunes area to encourage local interest. By 1911, this group had evolved into the famed Prairie Club of Chicago, headed by Cowles and industrialist Stephen T. Mather. By 1913, the Prairie Club was fully engaged in major efforts to save the dunes from further de-

INDIANA DUNES STATE PARK

Lake Michigan

MICHIGAN

Chicago

■ Indiana Dunes State Park

• Valparaiso

ILLINOIS

INDIANA

OHIO

• Indianapolis

KENTUCKY

1927

velopment, and the idea of creating a national park evolved. In 1916, Cowles organized the National Dunes Park Association specifically to fight for the establishment of a national park to preserve the dunes.

Trainloads of people attended meetings at the dunes. Supporters coordinated attempts to purchase parcels of the dune land for the purpose of turning the land over to the federal government for a national park; in 1917, the Prairie Club of Chicago staged an elaborate historical pageant to promote the idea. Moreover, Mather, who had become the founder and first director of the National Park Service, tried to convince Congress to set the area aside as a national park. Many local people, however, were more interested in the jobs and the tax revenue that industry would bring to the area than they were in saving the dunes. With the onset of World War I, plans for a national park were suspended. After the war, the booming economy fostered a frenzy of industrial growth. Conservationists realized that the dunes would be con-

National Park Service director Stephen T. Mather (front left) and others on a visit to the Indiana Dunes in October, 1916. (National Park Service Historic Photograph Collection)

sumed by encroaching industry in the years that it would take to form a national park; they thus decided to seek state park status for the dunes, a process that would take less time.

In 1923, U.S. Highway 12, the "Dunes Highway" that ran directly through the area, was completed, threatening further deterioration of the dunes area. Increased pressure was applied to obtain the state park status, and later that year, the Indiana legislature provided for special tax money to be used to purchase three miles of Lake Michigan shoreline for a state park. The tax, along with contributions from Elbert Gary of U.S. Steel and Julius Rosenwald of Sears, Roebuck and Company, provided enough funding to purchase the park land in 1927. Preservation of the dunes had finally begun.

SIGNIFICANCE

The formation of the Indiana Dunes State Park represented a dramatic victory for preservationists in their struggle against industry and development interests in northern Illinois and Indiana. Cowles's scientific work was one of the keys to this success. The formation of the state park and the scientific studies in the dunes area resulted in a continuing fight for the preservation of even more land and the eventual establishment of a national park in the area. Moreover, the fight over the dunes had implications for the continued development of scientific thought about ecology.

The Great Depression and World War II caused a lull in land acquisition for the dunes, but the booming economy after the war once again created industrial development pressures for the area. Indiana's economic and political climate was not amenable to land conservation. On the contrary, there was broad support for development, and the main focus was Indiana's long-held desire for a deep-water port on its small stretch of dune-filled shoreline. In 1952, Dorothy Buell organized the Save the Dunes Council, originally a women's movement designed to educate the public, organize grassroots support, and coordinate fund-raising efforts to buy up tracts of land for preservation. The council was unable to sway Indiana legislators to its cause, however, so it approached Senator Paul H. Douglas from Illinois, who took the matter to the federal government and proposed the dune area be designated a national monument. He was unsuccessful at the time, but he continued his fight for a national park.

The John F. Kennedy administration remained neutral, supporting both a port and a park. In 1961, the purchase of the Cape Cod National Lakeshore set a precedent for the federal government to purchase natural lands for national parks. Cape Cod was one of Kennedy's favorite spots, so Douglas drew attention to the similarities between it and the Indiana Dunes in order to secure Kennedy's favor for the dunes. Kennedy's death, however, postponed further action on the park issue.

Because the Lyndon B. Johnson administration was enthusiastic about developing urban parks, interest in an Indiana Dunes National Lakeshore was revived. Finally, in 1966, authorization for an eight-thousand-acre Indiana Dunes National Lakeshore was approved. It became the first urban national park in the country, but it was a park only "on paper," for lawmakers had not appropriated any funds for additional land acquisition, staffing, or maintenance. The area could still be threatened with development. Senator Douglas's influence in Congress ended when he lost his bid for reelection, and the Save the Dunes Council assumed a custodial role in park matters. In the late 1960's there was a feeble attempt to deauthorize the park, and in the early 1970's Indiana again tried to oppose expansion of the park. The Indiana Dunes National Lakeshore was dedicated in 1972, however, and laws in 1976, 1980, and 1986 provided for additional land purchases. By the 1990's, the park consisted of nine units and covered approximately fourteen thousand acres. Interest in park expansion would continue with the Save the Dunes Council and the Izaak Walton League acting as vigilant watchdogs of the dunes.

Another effect of early dune preservation lay in the blossoming of the principles of ecology advanced by Henry Cowles. Cowles's importance to the dunes lies in three contributions: He clearly demonstrated the principles of ecology through his studies of plant succession on the Indiana Dunes and in its associated wetlands; he contributed significantly to the preservation of the dunes; and he influenced the thinking of hundreds of students, scientists, and teachers who continued his work and eventually improved it.

Shortly after Cowles demonstrated his ideas of plant ecology, Victor Shelford and, later, W. Clyde Allee applied Cowles's principles to animals, developing ideas about animal ecology. In the mid-1940's, Jerry Olson performed a sophisticated updating of Cowles's original work that led to similar work in many areas.

Cowles's work on the dunes helped to lay the groundwork for incorporation of his ideas into evolving thoughts on "ecology," a term that began to encompass not only a scientific field but also a broad social viewpoint. For example, Allee continued to develop ecological ideas of interdependence to include not only biological systems but also social and religious systems. Cowles's ideas thus carried on through the decades, reaching fruition in 1969 with the passage of the National Environmental Policy Act.

—*Diann S. Kiesel*

FURTHER READING

Cockrell, Ron. *A Signature of Time and Eternity: The Administrative History of Indiana Dunes National Lakeshore, Indiana.* Omaha, Nebr.: National Park Service, 1988. An account of the history of the Indiana Dunes from the perspective of the National Park Service.

Cook, Sarah G. *Cowles Bog, Indiana, and Henry Chandler Cowles.* Chicago: Great Lakes Heritage, 1980. A well-researched biographical account of Cowles and his work in the Indiana Dunes. Includes a useful bibliography.

Engel, J. Ronald. *Sacred Sands: The Struggle for Community in the Indiana Dunes.* Middletown, Conn.: Wesleyan University Press, 1983. Extremely thorough historical account of the Indiana Dunes. Excellent bibliography.

Engel, Joan Gibb, ed. *The Indiana Dunes Story: How Nature and People Made a Park.* 2d rev. ed. Michigan City, Ind.: Shirley Heinze Land Trust, 1997. Collection of ten essays relates the history of the Indiana Dunes preservation movement. Includes bibliography.

Franklin, Kay, and Norma Schaeffer. *Duel for the Dunes: Land Use Conflict on the Shores of Lake Michigan.* Urbana: University of Illinois Press, 1983. Detailed history of land use in the Indiana Dunes area and the struggle to preserve the dunes.

Sellars, Richard West. *Preserving Nature in the National Parks: A History.* New Haven, Conn.: Yale University Press, 1997. Critical examination of the history of resource management in the United States by a historian for the National Park Service. Includes notes and index.

1927

Waldron, Larry. *The Indiana Dunes.* New York: Eastern Acorn Press, 1983. Brief overview of the Indiana Dunes discusses Lake Michigan, formation of the dunes, and the area's vegetation. Provides a good summary of historical land use and ecological studies.

SEE ALSO: May, 1903: Roosevelt and Muir Visit Yosemite; Jan. 11, 1908: Roosevelt Withdraws the Grand Canyon from Mining Claims; Aug. 25, 1916: National Park Service Is Created; Feb. 26, 1917: Mount McKinley National Park Is Created; Oct. 19, 1934: Marshall and Leopold Form the Wilderness Society; Feb. 4, 1936: Darling Founds the National Wildlife Federation; Jan., 1937-Feb., 1940: Adams Lobbies Congress to Preserve Kings Canyon.

May 17, 1927
MONET'S *WATER LILIES* ARE SHOWN AT THE MUSÉE DE L'ORANGERIE

Painter Claude Monet's canvases depicting the water lilies of his residence at Giverny were unveiled to the public five months after Monet's death.

LOCALE: Musée de l'Orangerie des Tuileries, Paris, France
CATEGORY: Arts

KEY FIGURES
Claude Monet (1840-1926), French painter
Eugène Boudin (1824-1898), French painter
Georges Clemenceau (1841-1929), French statesman
Wassily Kandinsky (1866-1944), Russian artist

SUMMARY OF EVENT
The patriarch of Impressionism, Claude Monet, who pioneered techniques of converting observations of the effects of light and cloud clusters on textured foliage and water into lyrical brushwork, did not live to see his transient, iridescent images hung in the two specially designed galleries on the ground floor of the Musée de l'Orangerie set aside to honor his artistic vision. Five months after his death, the focal point of the exhibit—his *Décorations des Nymphéas*, the ephemeral, liquid impressions of the water lilies in the pond on the grounds of his rural home near Vernon, northwest of Paris—drew record crowds of admirers. Unaccustomed to contemporary scenes depicted under the dappled, shimmering light and indistinct leafy patterns reflected in shallow water, patrons of the arts absorbed the rich, evocative canvases and lauded the painter as one of the world's most creative and innovative artists.

The oldest son of a wealthy, iron-willed wholesaler, Monet, who was drawn to the subtleties of color and light during long hours spent on the shore at the seaport of Le Havre, began drawing in childhood. He incurred the displeasure of his father yet persevered in the development of his talent. Influenced by the work of Johan Jongkind and his mentor, Eugène Boudin, he chose Paris as the place to study. At the age of nineteen, surrounded by other young rebels defying the stuffy, proprietary conventions of academic art, he joined the admiring coterie that formed around Édouard Manet and Edgar Degas. Along with his peers, Monet rejected the emphasis on religious and historical representations and established a working relationship with the outdoors, where he studied the optic phenomena that allow the eye to separate segments of objects into patches of light.

Under the influence of photography, which was still in its infancy, Monet duplicated lifelike moments in ordinary life by breaking down each scene into a free-form chiaroscuro of light and component hues, thereby freeing perception from traditional limitations. Working from a floating deck near Argenteuil, he concentrated on riverside activities along the Seine and re-created typical scenes of strollers and boaters eating, drinking, and enjoying the outdoors. Later, through travels to the Riviera, Rouen, Normandy, Venice, Norway, and London, he expanded his repertoire to a variety of subjects, most of which emphasized the interplay of sky and water.

The first public acclaim for Monet's canvases came in 1874, at what came to be known as the *First Impressionist Exhibition.* This was a decade after Manet's humiliation by protests against his *Déjeuner sur l'herbe* (1863; luncheon on the grass), capped by the Emperor Napoleon III's description of the work as offensive to public sensibilities. Reacting with similar vitriol to Monet's departure from the static guidelines of the École des Beaux-Arts, scoffing critics, preferring the hard outlines of realistic art, evolved the pejorative term "Impressionism" to refer to the softer, less well-defined images in his work. The term, which came from the title of Monet's *Impression: Sunrise* (1872), indicated the rise of an avant-garde approach to perception that centered on the elusive optical effects of shifting flecks of light on outdoor settings. Applying a matrix of short, precise brushstrokes, Monet utilized bright colors to emulate natural scenes, often painting sequential groupings representing the same object viewed at different times of day and under varying weather conditions. The best of Monet's serial works depict haystacks, poplar trees, the Gare Saint-Lazare, and the stone facade of Rouen Cathedral.

In contrast to the vibrant, cheery subject matter of his paintings, Monet survived a somber period of poverty and public disparagement, during which his wife and chief model, Camille, the mother of his two sons, suffered from tuberculosis. After Camille's death, Monet married Alice Raingo Hoschedé, the widow of his agent, in 1879 and entered a more promising era as public response to his innovations began to mellow. As his prospects improved, Alice, an uplifting companion, helped establish local and familial ties that provided necessary emotional support for his endeavors.

Moving in 1883 from oppressive rented quarters in Poissy, the Monets settled at Giverny in the Seine Valley near the Epte River. Monet expanded the original grounds, the Clos Normand, to include a fern-edged pond, overhanging willows, footpaths, wisteria trellises, clumps of bamboo, and a gently arched Oriental bridge. To expedite his work, he erected a photographic lab, a garage, and the first of three studios. After the death of his wife in 1911 and his son Jean's death three years later, he grew more reclusive and intensified his work. For the remaining years of his life, he battled double cataracts and underwent two eye operations that were only marginally successful.

Still attuned to his earlier philosophies despite impaired vision, Monet concentrated his remaining artistic output on the lilies rising from the waters behind the flowerbeds and produced his massive *Water Lilies* cycle, which the French government commissioned in 1914. To accommodate his oversized canvases, Monet built a larger studio. He then immersed himself in the beauties of his garden while Blanche Hoschedé, his widowed stepdaughter, tended the house and kept him company. Painting primarily from memory as his eyesight deteriorated, he retreated in despair and grew discouraged with his paintings; he reworked some and burned others.

By 1920, critics drawn to Monet's unique style agreed with politician Georges Clemenceau's support for a permanent collection at the Hôtel Biron and initiated a more thorough study of his technique and point of view. Plagued by increasing bouts of depression and exhaus-

tion, Monet lost heart with his work yet continued painting. On April 12, 1922, pressed by Clemenceau for a formal agreement, Monet signed papers donating *Water Lilies* to France. The notarized statement pledged two salons in the Orangerie, where nineteen panels would be arranged in an oval. Monet did most of the work on these panels during World War I but continued to rework them. On his death in 1926, Monet was attended by Clemenceau, his longtime friend and supporter. The *Water Lilies* cycle at the Orangerie was dedicated on May 17, 1927.

SIGNIFICANCE

A profound influence on the field of art, Monet's unrestrained experimentation with chromatic abstraction led to an irrevocable break with the old order, which had been dominated by gallery critics. Most significant of his influence was the emergence of abstract art, a direct outgrowth of his limpid reflecting pools, which distorted the shapes of objects and allowed the imagination full play in viewing hard realities. Applying intense study of the complex relationship between light and object, Monet's followers evolved their own reality, which often required a leap of faith from the viewing public. Splinter movements associated with Impressionism included pointillism, the use of minute, controlled points of color to create images. Pointillist works often are unclear when viewed up close and take shape only when viewed at a distance. Pointillism is exemplified in Georges Seurat's *Un Dimanche d'eté à la Grande Jatte* (1884-1886; Sunday afternoon on the island of La Grande Jatte). Moving in the opposite direction, Vincent van Gogh's swirling, emotional, distorted expressionism, as represented in *The Starry Night* (1889), brought an ecstasy to the canvas never before seen in European art. Similarly, Paul Gauguin's Symbolist canvases—among them *Where Do We Come From? What Are We? Where Are We Going?* (1897) and *The Yellow Christ* (1889)— evolved from his sojourn in Tahiti and shocked European sensibilities with his frank assessment of island settings, nude Polynesians, and juxtaposition of Christian and pagan religious symbols.

During this same era, Auguste Renoir and Paul Cézanne returned to a closer identity with solid form. Renoir, one of Impressionism's most skilled craftsmen, extended Monet's use of patchy light with a pearly glow exuding a harmony and beneficence on his graceful subjects. In his best-loved paintings, he imparts a mature, dignified beauty to middle-class Europeans engaged in lighthearted pastimes.

1927

An even greater departure from realism, the Fauvism of Henry Matisse, Maurice Vlaminck, Raoul Dufy, and André Derain, carried Impressionism into the realm of flat planes of exotic colors. Likewise, the cubism of Georges Braque and Pablo Picasso took similar liberties with geometric forms, often viewing subjects simultaneously from several blended points of view by breaking the whole into planes and cubes. The resulting geometric treatments created greater demands on a bewildered viewing public, which was, on first exposure, repulsed by both artistic styles.

Delving deeper into the elements of perception, Russian painter Wassily Kandinsky, influenced by a viewing of Monet's haystack paintings early in his career, wrote an incisive theoretical commentary, *Concerning the Spiritual in Art, and Painting in Particular* (1912). Kandinsky's paintings, energized by swirls of color, demonstrated an intensity of geometric interest similar to the abstractions of the cubists. His disciples Paul Klee, Franz Marc, and August Macke formed the Blaue Reiter group, which exhibited at the German Bauhaus until the Bauhaus was suppressed by the Nazis in 1933.

Still viable and influential a century later, Monet's art, with its free splashes of color and emphasis on ordinary activities, undergirded a burst of enthusiasm from publishers, who met the public's demand for art with affordable photographic reproductions, prints, and art books. Completely trouncing the tyranny of elitism, followers of Monet created a market for galleries, museums, and open-air markets.

To the average patron of the arts, the post-Monet era proved baffling, as artists including painters, musicians, dancers, sculptors, writers, and architects moved further away from finite, hard-edged objectivity toward the dreamy, indistinct Impressionism of Monet's water lilies. The presentation of Monet's artistry unleashed a drive for self-expression, experimentation, and rebellion against the values inherent in the Edwardian era. Some artists, particularly Picasso, abandoned controlled brushstrokes for dots, swirls, and dollops of paint on canvas. Sculptors used found objects such as gears and tangles of wire to create free-form art, sometimes creating pictorial collages that were textural blends of painting and sculpture.

Minimalism, a direct outgrowth of Impressionism that sprouted in the 1950's, saw painting develop into colorful geometric shapes—circles, squares, chevrons, nested boxes, and grids—on oversized canvases. Like Monet, the minimalists often serialized their work, concentrating on a single theme, often producing diptychs and triptychs that critics labeled "systematic." Huge,

austere sculptures, equally pared down to modular shapes, appeared in public plazas, courtyards, and modern galleries such as New York's Guggenheim Museum.

Offshoots of minimalism produced a burst of energy in optical art and pop art, as demonstrated by the intensity of Andy Warhol's experimental canvases, including his notorious Campbell's Soup cans and Brillo boxes. Likewise, poets, dramatists, and novelists strove for the focus and freedom of the Impressionists by shutting out needless detail and concentrating on the stream of consciousness of a single character, as with the speakers in William Faulkner's *As I Lay Dying* (1930) and the absurdist dramas of Eugène Ionesco, Edward Albee, Harold Pinter, Jean Genet, and Samuel Beckett, whose *En attendant Godot* (pb. 1952; *Waiting for Godot*, 1954) served as the high-water mark of Surrealist drama. Equally unfettered were the atonal musical compositions of Charles Ives and Paul Hindemith, the daring twelve-tone works of Arnold Schoenberg, the whimsical, unpredictable tunes of Erik Satie, and the modern dance forms of Martha Graham.

Another important adjunct to Monet's twentieth century audience was the restoration of his deteriorating house and garden, which he willed to his second son, Michel. Underwritten by the Académie des Beaux-Arts, the project, begun in 1966, reestablished the public's admiration for Impressionism by providing a spot of natural beauty for recreation and relaxation. An inviting outdoor retreat and museum, Monet's Giverny ranks as one of France's most beloved tourist attractions. Its popularity inspired a review of turn-of-the-century art at a Metropolitan Museum of Art exhibit titled *Monet's Years at Giverny: Beyond Impressionism*, which featured eighty-one of his canvases dating from 1883 to 1926.

—*Mary Ellen Snodgrass*

FURTHER READING

Burchell, S. C. *The Age of Progress*. Rev. ed. New York: Time-Life Books, 1979. A compelling overview of the guiding philosophy that steered nineteenth century artists into new realms, particularly in art, music, and literature. Covers the era that gave birth to Monet and his fellow Impressionists.

Clay, Jean. *Impressionism*. New York: Putnam, 1973. Well-organized text includes an essay on prices, concise essays about each artist, and bibliography.

Herbert, Robert L. *Impressionism: Art, Leisure, and Parisian Society*. New Haven, Conn.: Yale University Press, 1988. A grand, complete study of Impressionism, including ample color plates, a list of the museums that house the paintings, notes, lengthy bibliography, and index.

Kemp, Gerald van der. *A Visit to Giverny*. Translated by Bronia Fuchs. Versailles, France: Éditions d'Art Lyc, 1980. Useful brief guide to Monet's home contrasts photographs of the original residence and grounds with later paintings and pictures after the estate's restoration. Provides a detailed grounding in Monet's Giverny period, backed by sufficient fact and commentary.

Monet, Claude. *Monet's Years at Giverny: Beyond Impressionism*. New York: Metropolitan Museum of Art, 1978. Lavish book of Monet's art features photographs of the artist in his studio and country home, a chronology, incisive essays about his work and influence, and a selected bibliography. More than the standard coffee-table book it appears to be; closer examination proves its use to the student and art historian.

Picon, Gäeton. "Impressionism." In *Modern Painting: From 1800 to the Present*. New York: Newsweek Books, 1974. Useful guide for the general reader. Contains a satisfying balance of text and illustration to define art philosophy of the late nineteenth century. Especially helpful are writings by the principal artists (including an interview with Claude Monet concerning his early training) as well as a detailed chronology and thorough index.

Sagner-Duchting, K., ed. *Monet and Modernism*. New York: Prestel, 2002. Discusses the influence of Monet's work on the artists who came after him. Beautifully illustrated, juxtaposing paintings by Monet with those of twenty-five modern artists.

Time-Life Books. *Seven Centuries of Art*. New York: Author, 1970. A useful overview of art history, setting Impressionism within its time frame, with brief commentary about its offshoots. Although too shallow for art scholars, provides an appropriate beginning for students.

Tucker, Paul Hayes, with George T. M. Shackelford and MaryAnne Stevens. *Monet in the Twentieth Century*. New Haven, Conn.: Yale University Press, 1999. Catalog for a 1998 exhibition at the Museum of Fine Arts in Boston focuses on Monet's work after 1900. Includes useful essays that place the artist within the context of the time. Features chronology, selected bibliography, and index.

SEE ALSO: 1903: Hoffmann and Moser Found the Wiener Werkstätte; Oct., 1905: Fauves Exhibit at the Salon d'Automne; 1906-1907: Artists Find Inspiration in African Tribal Art; Summer, 1908: Salon d'Automne Rejects Braque's Cubist Works; Sept., 1911: Der Blaue Reiter Abandons Representation in Art; Feb. 17-Mar. 15, 1913: Armory Show.

1927

May 20, 1927
LINDBERGH MAKES THE FIRST NONSTOP TRANSATLANTIC FLIGHT

The first nonstop transatlantic flight from New York to Paris heralded a new era of air transportation and global commerce.

LOCALE: From New York, New York, to Paris, France
CATEGORIES: Science and technology; space and aviation; transportation

KEY FIGURES
Charles A. Lindbergh (1902-1974), American aviator
Harold Bixby (1890-1965), American banker

SUMMARY OF EVENT
Charles A. Lindbergh, born in Michigan in 1902, was an adventurous child who did not like school. After barely graduating from high school, he made a failed attempt to study at the University of Wisconsin and ended up as a flying cadet in the U.S. Army. After completing the

training and joining the Missouri National Guard instead of choosing active duty, Lindbergh was appointed chief pilot of a new airmail route linking the Midwest with New York City.

Aviation in the 1920's was fairly dangerous, especially flying the mail. Pilots had to fly with little ground support and unreliable weather reports, often with visual ground contact as their only guide. Most aircraft were still unsafe in their own right as well. Because of these problems, Lindbergh and other airmail pilots were continually pushing the U.S. Post Office Department to improve the quality of air facilities. The government did begin providing ground facilities, such as beacons and emergency fields, along contract airmail routes, but it would not provide airplanes, money for their purchase, or funding for private aeronautical research. This perpetuated a fundamental problem: Few contractors could afford to provide safe aircraft for their pilots, and few lenders provided money to do so. Lindbergh himself knew that safer planes could be built, but he also felt that before money would be made available, aviation had to become a less adventurous way to travel and a more normal, accepted means of transport. He had often considered how this might be accomplished, and he was intrigued when he read of a transatlantic flying contest sponsored by millionaire Raymond Orteig.

Orteig had for several years offered a prize of twenty-five thousand dollars to anyone who could complete a nonstop flight linking New York and Paris. René Fonck, a well-known French pilot, had already tried and failed, his plane crashing at the end of his reserved New York runway before takeoff, killing several crew members. Attempting the trip in reverse, two French pilots had departed from Paris but disappeared over the Atlantic. Another group of pilots were caught in a legal entanglement and were forbidden to take off at all. Lindbergh felt that the contest was the perfect way to get aviation into the public eye, and he began preparing for an attempt.

Whereas the other pilots had placed their faith in multiengine biplanes, Lindbergh envisioned a single-engine monoplane. He also wanted to fly alone. Although Lindbergh hated soliciting for support, his plane would cost an estimated ten thousand dollars, so he had

to make the effort. He finally got help from a group of businessmen led by St. Louis banker Harold Bixby. The group produced fifteen thousand dollars to finance Lindbergh's flight, which would be billed as a St. Louis-to-Paris flight, with a stop in New York. Ryan Airlines, Inc., of California was contracted to work with Lindbergh on an aircraft meeting his own specifications. Because Bixby was from St. Louis, he suggested the plane be named *The Spirit of St. Louis*.

The Spirit of St. Louis made its maiden test flight in April, 1927, in California, but the plane would never be fully tested. Lindbergh learned that several other pilots were set to take off from New York on their transatlantic voyages. Lindbergh feared he would be too late if he waited, so despite the lack of test flights, the plane was readied. Lindbergh flew from San Diego to St. Louis and then on to Long Island, New York, where he landed on May 12, 1927.

Upon arriving on Long Island, Lindbergh had his first extensive contact with the press. The Orteig contest was current news, and reporters began calling Lindbergh the "flying fool" because he planned to use a single-engine aircraft and fly solo. He also would not carry a parachute; he needed as much fuel as the plane could carry, and he thought that if he had to bail out over the Atlantic Ocean, he would in any case perish before he could be rescued.

Despite disliking the press and considering their attention distracting, the aviator did not want to ignore the media, because he wanted public attention to focus on aviation.

Another problem was that, because Lindbergh had not expected to be in New York so soon, he had not yet cleared all of the eligibility requirements for the contest. Afraid that if he waited he would be beaten across the ocean, Lindbergh contacted his sponsors, who agreed that the flight itself was more important than the prize money. The aviator was given the green light to embark when ready. Bad weather kept Lindbergh from departing immediately, but he finally took off on Friday, May 20, despite not having slept for twenty-three straight hours.

During his solo transatlantic flight, Lindbergh's greatest danger was not inclement weather, fog, low clouds, or even a sizable storm around which he had to detour. The aviator's biggest problem was his desire for sleep. In his later writings, Lindbergh described his experience in surreal terms, with phantoms and other apparitions appearing as he drifted in and out of a state of half

LANDING AT LE BOURGET

On the evening of May 21, 1927, Charles Lindbergh became the first pilot to fly solo across the Atlantic Ocean when he landed at Paris's Le Bourget Field at 10:22 P.M. He was mobbed by the waiting crowd of thousands and instantly became a hero. The feat was no less than that of a man stepping on the Moon. Lindbergh later related that landing in his book We *(1927):*

The sun went down shortly after passing Cherbourg and soon the beacons along the Paris-London airway became visible.

I first saw the lights of Paris a little before 10 P.M., or 5 P.M., New York time, and a few minutes later I was circling the Eiffel Tower at an attitude of about four thousand feet.

The lights of Le Bourget were plainly visible, but appeared to be very close to Paris. I had understood that the field was farther from the city, so continued out to the northeast into the country for four or five miles to make sure that there was not another field farther out which might be Le Bourget. Then I returned and spiralled down closer to the lights. Presently I could make out long lines of hangars, and the roads appeared to be jammed with cars.

I flew low over the field once, then circled around into the wind and landed.

sleep. Lindbergh was able to nap briefly, for as he nodded off, the plane, which did not fly particularly smoothly, would jerk him back awake. After sixteen hours of flying, Lindbergh crossed the southwest coast of Ireland, then passed over Cornwall, England, two hours ahead of schedule and landed at Le Bourget aerodrome outside Paris after thirty-three and one-half hours in the air. Lindbergh had been so efficient in his flying that there was still enough fuel in the tanks for a flight to Rome.

SIGNIFICANCE

Later, in his autobiographical works, Lindbergh admitted that nothing could have prepared him for the commotion that followed his successful flight. He had expected to land and spend the day talking to and trading experiences with French pilots. Instead, he was suddenly the world's greatest celebrity. After nearly running over crowds of people who swarmed onto the runway, Lindbergh was literally carried off and welcomed by all manner of people, showered with awards and honors, toasted and praised. There were ceremonies, dinners, parades, meetings with French and U.S. officials, and audiences with royalty. He was no longer the "flying fool" but rather "Lucky Lindy," and he was flooded with telegrams, invitations, and business proposals. He received a similar welcome when he flew on to England, after repairing the parts of his plane that people had torn off as souvenirs.

Lindbergh was taken back to the United States by the U.S. Navy, and when he arrived in Washington, D.C., and as he traveled from there to New York City, he was busy with dinners, speeches, and receptions. At a dinner with President Calvin Coolidge, the aviator met Dwight W. Morrow, an ambitious but capable politician, and Morrow's three daughters. Lindbergh paid the daughters little attention, but one of them, Anne, would later become his wife. The aviator also was given a huge parade in New York, receiving the city's biggest welcome ever. More than four million people lined the streets, and eighteen hundred tons of ticker tape rained down on the cavalcade bearing Lindbergh.

On June 16, Lindbergh was given the Orteig Prize of twenty-five thousand dollars, despite the fact that he had never been technically eligible for the contest. Along with more than two million pieces of mail and all manner of business endorsements, Lindbergh was awarded the Medal of Honor and promoted to the rank of colonel. His later life and career would be filled with all manner of accomplishments, in and out of aviation, but he also met with considerable controversy surrounding his view of Hitler's Luftwaffe just before World War II.

Charles A. Lindbergh poses with The Spirit of St. Louis *before taking off on his solo transatlantic flight.* (AP/Wide World Photos)

1927

The first solo transatlantic flight was clearly a boost for aviation. Lindbergh's success made flying seem slightly more routine and also showed that a single-engine craft could make such a journey. The flight was also important as a watershed date in U.S. history. During the 1920's, many Americans still did not want to accept that the United States was part of a growing global community; the flight forced them to accept that fact, and it encouraged them to begin to look toward the future.

—*Wayne Ackerson*

FURTHER READING

Bilstein, Roger E. *Flight in America: From the Wrights to the Astronauts.* 3d ed. Baltimore: The Johns Hopkins University Press, 2001. A thorough history of aviation in the United States by a leading historian in the field. Chapter 2 places Lindbergh's flight in the context of its era.

Dick, Ron, and Patterson, Dan. *The Early Years.* Vol. 1 in *Aviation Century.* Erin, Ont.: Boston Mills Press,

2003. Highly illustrated history details the progress of aviation from 1900 to 1939, analyzing why developments in flight took the directions they did and presenting information on the individuals who created the world's aviation industry, including Lindbergh. Features bibliography and index.

Fife, George Buchanan. *Lindbergh, the Lone Eagle: His Life and Achievements*. New York: World Syndicate, 1927. Representative of a literary genre on Lindbergh that appeared within a year of his successful New York to Paris flight. Not only captures the phenomenal public response to the achievement but also describes with excellent detail the layout and instrumentation aboard *The Spirit of St. Louis*.

Gill, Brendan. *Lindbergh Alone*. New York: Harcourt Brace Jovanovich, 1977. Extremely well-written short biography of Lindbergh concludes with the years immediately after the 1927 transoceanic flight. Traces the "lone eagle's" life, his development as a pilot during the early 1920's, and the events that led to his transatlantic achievement. Especially of interest for its analyses of Lindbergh's claims to have seen phantoms or ghosts during the flight.

Lindbergh, Charles A. *Autobiography of Values*. 1976. Reprint. Orlando, Fla.: Harcourt Brace Jovanovich, 1992. Written near the end of his life and published posthumously, this autobiography provides a second look at Lindbergh's 1927 flight, supplementing his award-winning 1953 *The Spirit of St. Louis*. Also sheds light on Lindbergh's personality, including his concern with environmental issues and his perceptions of the dynamic relationships among science, technology, and society.

_____. *The Spirit of St. Louis*. 1953. Reprint. New York: Charles Scribner's Sons, 1998. Beautifully written account of Lindbergh's New York-Paris flight written some twenty-five years after the event. Remains the most important source for the details of Lindbergh's momentous achievement. Uses flashbacks and free association in describing the exhilaration and hazards of the flight, the scenery observed, and navigational methods employed to maintain the airplane's course.

Milton, Joyce. *Loss of Eden: A Biography of Charles and Anne Morrow Lindbergh*. New York: HarperCollins, 1993. Introduction to the lives of the Lindberghs focuses on the couple's relationship, not on specific historical events.

Mosley, Leonard. *Lindbergh: A Biography*. 1976. Reprint. Mineola, N.Y.: Dover, 2000. Examines Lindbergh's long career, paying special attention to the aviator's efforts in the late 1930's and early 1940's to prevent the United States from entering World War II. Addresses the controversial aspects of Lindbergh's life with a journalistic flair, but also perhaps with a degree of simplicity in matters of scholarship that fails to deal with the subject adequately and with total fairness.

Parfit, Michael. "Retracing Lindy's Victorious Trip Across the Country." *Smithsonian* 18 (October, 1987): 200-220. Informative article describes Lindbergh's forty-eight-state tour of 1927, following his historic flight. Asserts that Lindbergh not only kept the excitement of his achievement alive among the public but also did more in a short time to promote civil aeronautics than previous federal government attempts. Argues that Lindbergh's transatlantic flight and his subsequent tour convinced the public that flying was no longer a sport for daredevils, but that it was safe, reliable, and could be used to move precious cargo.

Ross, Walter S. *The Last Hero: Charles A. Lindbergh*. New York: Harper & Row, 1976. A balanced account of Lindbergh's life; more objective than many other works on the aviator.

Ward, John William. "Charles A. Lindbergh: His Flight and the American Ideal." In *Technology in America: A History of Individuals and Ideas*, edited by Carroll W. Pursell, Jr. Cambridge, Mass.: MIT Press, 1981. Insightful article focuses on the consequences of Lindbergh's flight. Argues that the hero worship directed at Lindbergh was the result of Americans' need to celebrate both the individual in an increasingly bureaucratic age and, paradoxically, the modern mechanical technology that made *The Spirit of St. Louis* possible. Lindbergh represented the individual pioneer, rooted in the past and untainted by the modern institutions of a new industrial order that emerged in early twentieth century America.

SEE ALSO: Dec. 17, 1903: Wright Brothers' First Flight; July 25, 1909: First Airplane Flight Across the English Channel; Sept. 8, 1920: U.S. Post Office Begins Transcontinental Airmail Delivery; 1924-1976: Howard Hughes Builds a Business Empire; May 20-21, 1932: First Transatlantic Solo Flight by a Woman; June 25, 1936: The DC-3 Opens a New Era of Air Travel.

July 17, 1927
BRECHT AND WEILL COLLABORATE ON THE *MAHAGONNY SONGSPIEL*

Bertolt Brecht and Kurt Weill collaborated in the first manifestation of "epic theater" in the Mahagonny Songspiel; *their use of* Gebrauchsmusik *in* Rise and Fall of the City of Mahagonny *and in* The Threepenny Opera *introduced "cheap" music into opera and theater.*

LOCALE: Baden-Baden, Germany
CATEGORIES: Music; theater

KEY FIGURES
Bertolt Brecht (1898-1956), German playwright
Kurt Weill (1900-1950), German composer
Lotte Lenya (1898-1981), German singer
Paul Hindemith (1895-1963), German composer
Ferruccio Busoni (1866-1924), Italian German
    composer and teacher of music composition

SUMMARY OF EVENT

The meeting in 1927 between the avant-garde composer Kurt Weill and the revolutionary playwright Bertolt Brecht and their ensuing collaboration was significant for the development of both men's careers. When Weill heard a radio production of Brecht's *Mann ist Mann* (pr. 1926; *A Man's a Man*, 1961), he responded with a highly complimentary review and subsequently asked Brecht whether he could use some of Brecht's poems for a song cycle he was preparing for the festival of new music in Baden-Baden. Brecht was interested in Weill's ideas about "gestic" music, as they corresponded to attempts he was making to popularize drama through the use of popular culture motifs from cinema and the cabaret. According to Weill, gestic music, a concept that also relates to Paul Hindemith's notion of *Gebrauchsmusik*, or functional music, instead of processing the text for purely musical ends focuses on the manner through which the words of a song communicate the gest, or social attitude, through rhythmic means, including pauses. The object was to extend the communicative quality of music in order to make social statements. Composers such as Weill sought corresponding texts with simplicity of diction and clarity of sense. Similarly, Brecht was attempting to strip drama of figurative language in order to bring out the "epic," or communicative, nature of his texts. He did this by concentrating on the message rather than the subtext in order to foreground the social rather than the psychological situations of his plays.

Brecht and Weill were not alone at this time in considering the traditional theater and opera to be out of step with an egalitarian modern society, for these were notions central to *Neue Sachlichkeit*, or New Objectivity, in the arts. In particular, Hindemith was influential in exploring applied music. He and the composers in his group rejected the purely aesthetic explorations of atonality represented by Arnold Schoenberg and others. The new music was to project an ease of execution and accessibility to the unsophisticated ear. For that reason, Hindemith and Weill, as well as composers such as Igor Stravinsky and the group known as Les Six, established a kinship with the dynamic rhythms and unsnobbish popular appeal of jazz and cabaret songs. From the outset, Brecht's songs, initially with simple tunes of his own, were central to his attempts to popularize theater. At the same time, Weill, one of the most prominent of Ferruccio Busoni's students, was the first German composer of any consequence to show an interest in setting to music texts by contemporary German writers such as Iwan Goll, Georg Kaiser, and ultimately Brecht. For that reason, the collaboration between Brecht and Weill was particularly fruitful. It gave both the opportunity to explore similar concerns regarding the relationship between popular culture and the arts.

Weill and Brecht's collaboration began with the *Mahagonny Songspiel*, sometimes known as *The Little Mahagonny*, which consisted of six songs with orchestral interludes, lasting about forty-five minutes in all. Brecht and Weill chose the English word "song" as part of the title as an obvious gesture to disassociate it from the German word *Lied*, which to them seemed to relate too strongly to the classical *Lieder* tradition. The *Mahagonny Songspiel* was produced at the Deutsche Kammermusik festival in Baden-Baden on July 17, 1927. The work can be described as a chamber opera that thematically represents the degeneration of life in a mythical American city and is set to music with a jazzy accent. Caspar Nehar, Brecht's scenic designer, produced a series of sketches for the setting with themes relating to the greed and corruption of capitalism in the symbolic American city of Mahagonny, with a location kept intentionally vague in order to project the allegorical universality of social conditions. In addition, a small boxing ring, as a metaphor for the fighting inherent in capitalistic competition, became the platform for the performance. Weill requested that his wife, Lotte Lenya, sing the leading role. Her obviously untrained, gravelly voice, with its grotesque mispronunciations of the English words of the "Alabama Song," symbolized the rejection on the part of the Brecht/Weill duo of the accepted standards of high culture. In addition, Weill, having caught Brecht's eagerness to tweak the pretensions of high culture, made good musical capital out of the glottal catch between "Ma" and "hagonny," imbuing the setting of the six poems with a musical accompaniment that brought out its comic quality and an aggressive provocative edge as well.

The audience reaction was divided: There was booing, whistling, cheering, and stomping. The singers participated, pulling whistles out of their pockets. Later that evening in the bars throughout town, however, everyone seemed to be singing lyrics from the opera. The *Mahagonny Songspiel* brought Weill popular success and also projected him into a striking new area of emphasis on "song," a development that was to endure for the remainder of his career, both in his collaboration with Brecht and later in his Broadway musicals.

SIGNIFICANCE

The immediate consequence of the attention that Weill and Brecht received in Baden-Baden was the continuation of their collaboration in *Die Dreigroschenoper* (pr. 1928; *The Threepenny Opera*, 1949), *Happy End* (pr. 1929; English translation, 1972), *Aufstieg und Fall der Stadt Mahagonny* (pb. 1929; *Rise and Fall of the City of Mahagonny*, 1957), the ballet *Die Sieben Todsünden der Kleinbürger* (pr. 1933; *The Seven Deadly Sins*, 1961), and songs for a revival of *A Man's a Man*. In particular, *The Threepenny Opera* became the rage of the season and immediately was translated into many languages, bringing Weill a reputation in the United States even before he arrived in 1935. The text for *The Threepenny Opera* was based on the eighteenth century play by John Gay called *The Beggar's Opera*. Its plot concerns Macheath, a thief of thieves, who marries Polly, daughter of his fellow crook, the entrepreneur Peachum. Peachum plans Macheath's arrest, and, although Macheath flees, he is caught through the treachery of Jenny and other whores. He is sentenced to be executed but is reprieved in a deliberately artificial happy ending. Brecht's text was cobbled together quickly from a translation of Gay's work, and Weill composed the music virtually overnight. *The Threepenny Opera* opened in the Theater am Schiffbauerdamm in Berlin on August 31, 1928. Lenya had one of the leading roles, that of the whore Jenny, and once again Weill's score infected

the public. The audience would barely allow the song "Mack the Knife" to finish before demanding an encore. Theatergoers left humming and whistling such tunes as the "Cannon Song" and "Mack the Knife." It is no exaggeration to say that the play swept across Europe. Within its first year, it was performed more than four thousand times. In addition, it was recorded by seven companies. Overnight, Weill was transformed from a serious composer to a commercial success.

A year after the premiere of *The Threepenny Opera*, its producer, hoping to capitalize on its phenomenal success, persuaded Brecht and Weill to write another play with songs. *Happy End*, which opened in Berlin in September of 1929, did not, however, justify its title and was both a critical and a popular flop. Brecht was later to repudiate writing it, but several of Weill's songs for the play, in particular "Surabaya-Johnny," belong to the general repertory of famous Weill songs. At the same time, Brecht and Weill continued working on the full-length opera *Rise and Fall of the City of Mahagonny*, first produced in Leipzig in March, 1930, then in Berlin in December, 1931, with Lenya once again singing the leading role. The political content of that opera became a source of conflict between Brecht and Weill. Brecht saw the opera as a parable of capitalism and wanted members of the cast to sing and march about the stage carrying placards as Mahagonny goes up in flames. Weill became less interested in the political view and saw the opera as a parable of greed. With the rise of Nazism, the opera was met with resistance from the public, although critics noted Weill's musical accomplishment of blending the teachings of Busoni with his popularized version of jazz.

In addition to his collaboration with Brecht, Weill also composed songs, choral numbers, and instrumental movements for Georg Kaiser's *Silbersee*, which unfortunately opened as Adolf Hitler became chancellor of Germany in January of 1933. Immediately after the burning of the Reichstag, Brecht emigrated to Prague, and performances of Weill's music were prohibited until 1945. In addition, as both Weill and Lenya were Jewish, they left Germany in March of 1933, escaping across the border to France.

Upon his arrival in the United States in September of 1935, Weill began a second career, composing for Broadway. Although his compositions were not generally known by the American public, his work was known to a number of important musicians and theater directors, and he soon was presented with a number of projects. One of the first was *Knickerbocker Holiday*, based on Washington Irving's book, which met with considerable success when it opened in October of 1938. It was not until *Lady in the Dark* (1941), however, that Weill achieved his first Broadway hit. After its premiere on January 23, 1941, the show ran for two seasons. In 1944, Paramount bought the rights to make its film version, starring Ginger Rogers and Ray Milland. *One Touch of Venus*, Weill's greatest Broadway success, followed, opening on October 7, 1943. Another popular hit was the folk opera *Street Scene*, composed in 1946.

In his adjustment to Broadway, Weill abandoned the bold and disillusioned bitterness of his musical style from the *Mahagonny Songspiel* and *The Threepenny Opera* in favor of sophisticated love songs, barbershop ballads, and mock patriotic songs. Contemporary critics point out that Weill's contributions to American music are as significant as those of his European period, because in this transition he consciously attempted to create an indigenous American operatic tradition based on the classic American themes. The impact of Weill's popularization of serious composition is apparent in the many versions of "Mack the Knife" recorded by popular singers and the recording of the "Alabama Song" by the Doors. At the same time, serious interpretations of Weill's music continue. *Rise and Fall of the City of Mahagonny* belongs to the repertoire of New York's Metropolitan Opera, and opera singer Teresa Stratas has recorded Weill's collected songs.

—*Christine Kiebuzinska*

FURTHER READING

Brecht, Bertolt. *Brecht on Theatre: The Development of an Aesthetic*. Edited and translated by John Willett. 1964. Reprint. New York: Methuen, 2003. Comprehensive collection of Brecht's writings on theater. Significant essays for an understanding of the collaboration between Brecht and Weill include "The Modern Theatre Is the Epic Theatre," "The Literarization of the Theatre" (notes to *The Threepenny Opera*), "On the Use of Music in Epic Theatre," and "On Gestic Music." Includes photographs and index.

Hirsch, Foster. *Kurt Weill on Stage: From Berlin to Broadway*. New York: Alfred A. Knopf, 2002. Biography draws on Weill's journals and personal correspondence as well as on interviews with individuals who knew him. Includes discussion of his collaboration with Brecht and his work with other writers. Features notes, bibliography, and index.

Jarman, Douglas. *Kurt Weill: An Illustrated Biography*. Bloomington: Indiana University Press, 1982. Well-researched, balanced, and informative text provides a two-part discussion focusing on Weill's life and analysis of his musical style. Assesses Weill's early instrumental and vocal music, the music that characterizes his collaboration with Brecht, and the American period of his popular Broadway productions. Includes numerous photographs, chronological list of works, discography, bibliography, notes, and index.

Kowalke, Kim. *Kurt Weill in Europe*. Ann Arbor, Mich.: UMI Research Press, 1979. Scholarly analysis of Weill's career provides a context for the development of Weill's musical style, acknowledging the influence of Ferruccio Busoni and the relevance of his period of experimentation. Illustrated by examples from Weill's scores. Intended for readers with strong background in musicology. Includes appendix with catalog of Weill's compositions (1900-1935) and annotated translations of Weill's essays, notes, bibliography, and index.

_____, ed. *A New Orpheus: Essays on Kurt Weill*. New Haven, Conn.: Yale University Press, 1986. Collection of a wide range of essays by Weill scholars covering the full spectrum of his musical career. Several contributions focus on Weill's collaboration with Brecht in creating "epic opera"; others focus on Weill in the United States and his influence on the Broadway musical. Includes illustrations, chronology of Weill's life and works, and index.

Leach, Robert. *Makers of Modern Theatre: An Introduction*. New York: Routledge, 2004. Examines the lives and work of four individuals who had significant influence on theater in the twentieth century. Chapter 4 is devoted to Brecht. Includes illustrations, notes, and index.

Sanders, Ronald. *The Days Grow Short: The Life and Music of Kurt Weill*. 1980. Reprint. Los Angeles: Silman-James Press, 1991. Comprehensive biography and analysis of Weill's musical career, accessible to the general reader. Skillfully relates the effects of Weill's personality on his individual musical style. Includes source notes, list of Weill's principal compositions, discography, and illustrations.

Willett, John. *The Theatre of Bertolt Brecht*. 1959. Reprint. New York: Methuen, 2003. Invaluable, concise introduction to Brecht's work. Brief chronology and analysis of Brecht's plays are followed by a discussion of individual aspects of Brecht's theatri-

1927

cal style, including subject matter, use of language, theatrical influences, music, theatrical practice, theory, and politics. Of particular interest concerning the collaboration between Brecht and Weill is the discussion on music. Includes illustrations, bibliography, and index.

SEE ALSO: Nov. 24, 1905: Reinhardt Becomes Director of the Deutsches Theater; Feb. 12, 1924: Gershwin's *Rhapsody in Blue* Premieres in New York; 1925: New Objectivity Movement Is Introduced; July 19-Nov. 30, 1937: Nazi Germany Hosts the *Degenerate Art Exhibition*.

August 4, 1927
RODGERS CUTS HIS FIRST RECORD FOR RCA VICTOR

Commercial country music was in its infancy when Jimmie Rodgers cut his first record for RCA Victor; he would soon become famous and influential in country and blues music.

LOCALE: Bristol, Tennessee
CATEGORY: Music

KEY FIGURES
Jimmie Rodgers (1897-1933), American singer, guitarist, and composer
Ralph S. Peer (1892-1960), American music recording industry pioneer

SUMMARY OF EVENT
In the early 1920's, the recording industry in the United States became interested in the rural market and therefore in rural music and performers, particularly in the South. "Old-time music" and "mountain music" were two of the terms often used to describe what the industry wanted, and the phrase "hillbilly music" was also coined at the time. In addition, new interest was growing in rural blues as performed by African Americans.

One of the pioneers in recording such music was Ralph S. Peer, at one time with OKeh Records but by 1927 under contract with the RCA Victor company. (It was Peer who first applied the term "hillbilly" to white country tunes.) A staunch believer in field expeditions, he set out to find and record new talent from among performers already known in their native locales. In July, 1927, Peer brought his wife, two engineers, and some new electrical recording equipment to Bristol, Tennessee. He already knew, or knew of, some of the people he planned to record, but he also welcomed walk-in performers. One of them was Jimmie Rodgers.

James Charles Rodgers was born on September 9, 1897, in Pine Springs, near Meridian, Mississippi, the son of Aaron and Eliza Rodgers. Like his father, Rodgers became a railroad worker—he would one day be billed as

the "Singing Brakeman"—but from childhood on he was fascinated by show business, and he managed to combine some professional musical performances with his railroading and other jobs. By 1925, however, ill health ruled out further railroad work; Rodgers had been suffering from tuberculosis for some time, so he committed himself entirely to the entertainment industry. He worked in vaudeville, performed dance music, and, briefly, worked for a radio show, poverty always dogging his steps, especially as he now had a small family to support.

He had already become connected with a small string band, renamed the Jimmie Rodgers Entertainers, when he heard about Ralph Peer's expedition to Bristol. The Entertainers auditioned for Peer, but the band broke up the night before their recording date. The band members' musical styles and personalities had never matched very well, and Rodgers had earlier announced his intention to leave the band, so a quarrel arose over whether they should keep the name "Jimmie Rodgers Entertainers" for recording purposes. As a result, the other band members recorded for Peer under their original name, the Tenneva Ramblers, while Rodgers showed up alone with only his guitar. It was a fortuitous development, one apparently encouraged by Peer himself. Thus it was that Rodgers cut his first record for RCA Victor on August 4, 1927.

By that time, Rodgers had absorbed influences from so many sources that it is difficult to trace them and equally difficult to categorize the result. He had been singing and playing guitar, banjo, and other instruments in a number of styles. Sometimes he sang popular music, sometimes African American blues—fragments of which he remembered from railroad and vaudeville days—and sometimes he did "old-time" sentimental tunes. He also yodeled. This was nothing new; there had long been Swiss-style and other yodeling, and even the new, commercial country music field had at least a nodding acquaintance with that genre. Rodgers's yodeling, however, was something special; it was "blue yodeling," a type unique at that time to Rodgers himself, incorporated into his white man's version of the blues.

Which of these types of music would Rodgers choose for his recording debut? Peer was anxious to record something new in the way of country music, new in the sense that it would catch the public's attention, but also new in the sense that it could be copyrighted. Rodgers, however, apparently did not feel that his blue yodeling was ready for recording; moreover, Peer was insisting on "hillbilly," or something like hillbilly—whatever that was. Rodgers may also have wanted to prove that he could sing any sort of music. In any case, he chose an old song he had reworked called "The Soldier's Sweetheart," a ballad about a World War I soldier (as Rodgers's version would have it) who died in battle, leaving his sweetheart to live a single life forever in his memory. These sentimental lyrics were put to an old Irish melody, "Where the River Shannon Flows," but the final product was new enough for copyright purposes.

The second cut was another old song, a lullaby called "Sleep, Baby, Sleep." Rodgers's version included some of his soon-to-be-famous yodeling, fine work, although it, and the whole performance, seem a bit loud for a lullaby. Still, his voice in song and yodel had a loving sound that was appropriate. Although Rodgers had apparently intended the first cut to be his showpiece, "Sleep, Baby, Sleep" has been preferred by many over the years. Peer was somewhat disappointed that "Sleep, Baby, Sleep" was uncopyrightable, but Rodgers simply did not have much else ready to go. Both songs were good enough to lead to later recording sessions and instant fame for Rodgers in 1928.

SIGNIFICANCE

The Bristol sessions are justly famous in the history of country music, not only because of Jimmie Rodgers but also for the other talented performers who recorded there, especially the Carter Family. The importance of those sessions could scarcely have been imagined at the time, however. In Rodgers's case, many months would pass before his recordings caught on with the public. It was his first blue yodel, "T for Texas," that made him a star when it was released in 1928. There would be thirteen blue yodels in all, plus other songs that featured yodeling and bluesy lyrics or tunes.

Before long, Rodgers was hard-pressed for new material, and he accepted songs from various sources, in particular from his sister-in-law, Elsie McWilliams. True to his heritage, he recorded in many different styles. In ad-

dition to the blues, with their often somewhat bawdy lyrics, he composed or accepted sentimental songs, songs of unrequited love, prison songs, quasi-cowboy songs, lullabies, a pseudo-Hawaiian tune, novelty songs, and even some semiautobiographical songs such as "T. B. Blues." Often he recorded alone with his guitar, often with side men, and sometimes with jazz orchestras; Louis Armstrong joined him on "Blue Yodel No. 9." He also did some comedy skits with the Carter Family. One type of music he hardly touched was gospel, in contrast to the practice of most hillbilly musicians such as the Carters; Rodgers was not a religious man.

Much of this product has been regarded as outstanding. Most of the blue yodels were stunningly good, as were many of his other recordings, such as "Waiting for a Train." On the other hand, a number of his records were flawed, either because he had run out of good material or because he gave indifferent performances. Some of these sides were released, it seems, only because Rodgers's death prevented the recording of better material. Much of what he produced must have sounded trite even then— such as his recording of "Desert Blues," which features a tuba—but trite lyrics and "cornball" productions in most cases simply added to his music's charm. If one sets out to produce a novelty tune such as "Desert Blues," why not go all the way and use a tuba? As for performance problems, Rodgers had scant musical training, and sometimes his guitar work was, to put it mildly, unorthodox. Again, however, the primitive nature of some of his singing and playing made him all the more authentic-sounding and therefore appealing. Rather than merely rising above his limitations, he carried them with him, making his unorthodox style part of his greatness.

In considering the impact of Rodgers's work, one must first note the lasting fame of his recordings. Although Rodgers's sales declined in the final year or so of his career, this was not a reflection of his work's true worth but a result of the deepening Great Depression in the early 1930's, which cut into sales everywhere. It was also a reflection of his own declining health. Rodgers died in New York City on May 26, 1933, shortly after exhausting himself in his final recording session, but his records continued to sell. Of his career total of some 110 sides, 25 were released after his death. Many of his songs were later reissued in 78 and 45 RPM formats, and the entire corpus of Rodgers's work was rereleased on albums in the 1950's and early 1960's; a complete edition appeared in Japan in 1973. On November 3, 1961, Rodgers was installed as the first member of the new Country Music Hall of Fame.

1927

His influence on country music in the short run is obvious. Many artists of the 1930's copied his style of singing and yodeling, new songs were written in his manner, and many of his own songs were performed by other artists in the 1930's and after. "Mule Skinner Blues," for instance, has been sung by Bill Monroe, Dolly Parton, and many other performers; "In the Jailhouse Now" is another example. One of the later giants of country music, Hank Snow, named his son after Rodgers.

In the longer term, much of what Rodgers did has not remained standard. Few modern country artists have continued the practice of recording with only an acoustic guitar for accompaniment, and the records Rodgers made with jazz orchestras did not set much of a precedent. Few white country artists have continued to sing the blues in his style since World War II, and fewer still have carried his yodeling tradition into the postwar era.

Rodgers's brief career raised a number of unanswered questions: Would much of what he made famous have caught on even without his help? "Cowboy" music, for example, predated Rodgers's career and probably did not require his work to guarantee its subsequent popularity. To what extent did Rodgers inspire young artists? To what extent did he make country music acceptable to urbanites? Such questions are perhaps unanswerable, but it is nevertheless clear that Rodgers deserves the title of "father of country music."

—*Karl G. Larew*

FURTHER READING

Malone, Bill C. *Country Music, U.S.A.* 2d rev. ed. Austin: University of Texas Press, 2002. Excellent history puts Rodgers's music in context. Includes a few illustrations, bibliography, and indexes.

_____. *Don't Get Above Your Raisin': Country Music and the Southern Working Class*. Champaign: University of Illinois Press, 2002. History of American country music focuses on the relation of the music and its performers to working-class culture in the South. Includes notes and index.

Paris, Mike, and Chris Comber. *Jimmie the Kid*. London: Eddison Press, 1977. First full-length study of Rodgers's work remains a useful source. Includes a detailed discography.

Porterfield, Nolan. *Jimmie Rodgers: The Life and Times of America's Blue Yodeler*. 1979. Reprint. Champaign: University of Illinois Press, 1992. Indispensable, balanced examination of Rodgers's life and music. Based to a large extent on original sources and interviews.

Rodgers, Carrie Cecil Williamson. *Jimmie Rodgers' Life Story (Complete)*. Nashville: Ernest Tubb Publications, 1935. Personal and somewhat romanticized account by Rodgers's widow. Valuable for insights and anecdotes.

Sanjek, Russell, and David Sanjek. *American Popular Music Business in the Twentieth Century*. New York: Oxford University Press, 1991. Comprehensive and exhaustively detailed history of the subject cowritten by an insider who was there through much of the period. Includes numerous references to Rodgers and Peer.

SEE ALSO: Nov., 1925: Armstrong Records with the Hot Five; Nov. 28, 1925: WSM Launches *The Grand Ole Opry*; 1939-1949: Bill Monroe and the Blue Grass Boys Define Bluegrass Music.

August 23, 1927
SACCO AND VANZETTI ARE EXECUTED

Anti-immigrant sentiment contributed to the sentencing and eventual execution of Nicola Sacco and Bartolomeo Vanzetti for murder. The two men's guilt remained in doubt for decades after their deaths.

LOCALE: Dedham, Massachusetts
CATEGORIES: Crime and scandal; social issues and reform

KEY FIGURES

Nicola Sacco (1891-1927), Italian immigrant and anarchist
Bartolomeo Vanzetti (1888-1927), Italian immigrant and anarchist
Webster Thayer (1857-1933), presiding trial judge
Fred H. Moore (fl. early twentieth century), chief defense counsel from November, 1920, to November, 1924
William G. Thompson (fl. early twentieth century), chief defense counsel from November, 1924, to August, 1927
Alvan T. Fuller (1878-1958), governor of Massachusetts
Celestino Madeiros (1902-1927), convicted bank robber and murderer
Mike Boda (fl. early twentieth century), Italian anarchist
Feruccio Coacci (fl. early twentieth century), Italian anarchist

SUMMARY OF EVENT

Although Nicola Sacco and Bartolomeo Vanzetti were executed in 1927, the arrest and trial of these Italian immigrants took place amid the paranoia that characterized much of American politics immediately after the end of World War I. In the war's aftermath, Europe had undergone a political shuffling that culminated in a communist revolution in Russia. As European immigrants began flooding into the United States, there was fear that this communist ideology and anarchy—the belief that compulsory government should be replaced by voluntary, self-governing groups—would also be imported. Many native-born citizens worried about secret plots to undermine the democratic structure of the country, and often anyone who appeared different or foreign was branded as a "Red."

The two events, which may or may not have been connected, that culminated in the arrest of Sacco and Vanzetti began on December 24, 1919. It was payday at the L. Q. White Shoe Company of Bridgewater, Massachusetts, and a truck carrying approximately thirty-three thousand dollars in company payroll was unsuccessfully attacked. Pinkerton Agency detectives investigated the incident, and during interviews with eyewitnesses they determined that one of the suspects appeared to be an immigrant with a dark complexion and a mustache and that he fled in a large vehicle that was probably a Hudson. The identified license plate had been stolen a few days earlier in Needham, Massachusetts, as had a Buick touring car. Thus, despite witnesses' testimony to the contrary, the detectives concluded that the Buick had likely been used in the robbery. No suspects were arrested, although tips emerged connecting the getaway car to a group of Italian anarchists.

On April 15, 1920, in nearby South Braintree, the payroll for the Slater and Morrill Shoe Factory was being escorted, on foot, from the office to the factory by two security guards, Frederick Parmenter and Alessandro Berardelli. En route, the guards were attacked, robbed, and murdered by two men who escaped in a waiting vehicle. At the inquest, twenty-three eyewitnesses testified that the assailants appeared to be Italian, but few could positively identify the men.

Police Chief Michael E. Stewart traced the lead to Feruccio Coacci, an Italian citizen scheduled for deportation, after recalling the tip about Italian anarchists storing a car in Bridgewater. Coacci revealed that the car belonged to his housemate, Mike Boda, a known anarchist, and that it was currently being repaired in a garage in West Bridgewater. A police guard was planted outside the garage to wait for Boda.

Meanwhile, as a result of the prevalent U.S. attitude against radicals and in the wake of a national roundup and arrest of aliens, Italian immigrants Nicola Sacco and Bartolomeo Vanzetti had decided it would be wise to destroy their anarchist literature. The abundance of material required transportation, and they arranged to borrow Boda's vehicle. Although the trap was laid for Boda, Sacco and Vanzetti were arrested as they attempted to claim the car. Neither man had a police record, but both were armed.

Because the men were not informed of the reason for their arrest, they assumed they were being held as anarchists. Although they were read their rights, the language barrier may have obstructed their complete understanding. They were fingerprinted, their weapons were confiscated but not tagged, and they were questioned for seven days without being charged. There was no lineup; the two were paraded in front of witnesses who were asked if they were the men involved in the holdup. On May 12, 1920, Vanzetti was charged with attempted murder and robbery at Bridgewater.

His trial began on June 22, 1920, in Plymouth, Massachusetts, with Judge Webster Thayer presiding. The initial interviews by the Pinkerton detectives were not admitted, and all witnesses for the defense were of Italian origin. After only five hours of deliberation, the jury found Vanzetti guilty of assault with intent to rob and murder. Six weeks later, he was sentenced to twelve to fifteen years in prison for intent to rob, though the attempted murder charge was dropped after it was discovered that one of the jurors had brought his own shell casings for comparison.

In September, 1920, Sacco and Vanzetti were charged with the murder of Alessandro Berardelli and Frederick Parmenter during the South Braintree robbery. Both pleaded not guilty. A committee for their defense raised enough money to hire the radical California attorney Fred H. Moore, who cited the case as an establishment attempt to victimize the working man. The trial began on May 31, 1921, in Dedham, Massachusetts. As the presiding judge in Vanzetti's first trial, Judge Thayer should have been disqualified, but instead he oversaw the second trial's administration. On June 4, the all-male jury was sworn in, and on June 6, Sacco and Vanzetti were marched, handcuffed, into the courtroom.

Throughout the trial, the prosecution presented a bounty of circumstantial evidence: testimony from witnesses whose status as eyewitnesses was questionable; a cap from the scene that was alleged to be Vanzetti's but was too small for his head; expert testimony qualified with "I am inclined to believe"; no positive identification on the getaway car; ballistic evidence that was technical and confusing; and the accusation of "consciousness of guilt," based on false statements made by the two when they thought they were being held for anarchy. Judge Thayer instructed the jury to be "true soldiers," who would display the "highest and noblest type of true American citizenship," while referring to the defendants as slackers. On July 14, after another five-hour deliberation, the jury returned a verdict of guilty of first-degree murder. The standard penalty in Massachusetts at the time was death by electric chair.

Sacco and Vanzetti remained incarcerated for six years while motions were filed for them. The presiding

judge heard all appeals, and each was weighed and denied by Judge Thayer. One motion stated Judge Thayer himself had demonstrated out-of-court prejudice against the two. However, despite growing doubts about the men's guilt, Thayer remained adamant, and his animosity toward Moore grew. On November 8, the defense committee forced Moore to resign and hired William G. Thompson.

While Thompson continued to encounter roadblocks, Sacco was slipped a note from another prisoner, Celestino Madeiros, who confessed to the crime. From the note, Thompson traced a link to the Morelli Gang, a group of Italian immigrants from Providence, Rhode Island, led by Joe Morelli and his brothers. This group had attacked the shoe factory in the past, and one member of the gang bore a resemblance to Sacco. Based on the new evidence, Thompson filed a motion for retrial, which was

---

SACCO AND VANZETTI ON TRIAL

Many of Sacco and Vanzetti's supporters argued that neither man spoke fluent English and that the defendants' inability to understand the questions asked during the trial placed them at an unfair disadvantage. This excerpt from the 1926 trial proceedings gives an indication of Nicola Sacco's familiarity with English.

The testimony of the defendant Sacco to which the remarks of the district attorney . . . referred was as follows: He was shown exhibit 43 and was asked if he knew whose cap it was. He answered, "It looks like my cap." He then was asked, "Did you have such a cap as that in your house at the time of your arrest?" and answered, "Yes, sir, something like. . . . I think it is my cap, yes." Asked to "look at it carefully," he reiterated, "Yes," and in answer to the question, "There isn't any question but what that is your cap, is there?" he answered, "No, I think it is my cap." He then was asked to try it on, and stated, "A. I don't know. That cap looks too dirty to me because I never wear dirty cap. I think I always have fifty cents to buy a cap, and I don't work with a cap on my head when I work. I always keep clean cap. Right when I go to the factory, take all my clothes off and put overalls and jump. It look to me pretty dirty and too dark. Mine I think was little more light, little more gray." He then was asked, "Is it your cap?" and stated, "I think it is. It look like, but it is probably dirt—probably dirty after."

Source: Supreme Judicial Court of Massachusetts, *Commonwealth v. Nicola Sacco & Another*, 255 Mass. 369; 151 N.E. 839 (1926).

Bartolomeo Vanzetti (left) and Nicola Sacco, manacled together and surrounded by guards and onlookers, as they approach the Massachusetts courthouse where they will be sentenced to death. (Library of Congress)

denied, and in April of 1927, Sacco and Vanzetti were sentenced to die during the week of July 10. Public outcry caused the date to be moved to August 10, and Vanzetti wrote a plea for clemency to Massachusetts governor Alvan T. Fuller. In the letter, he asked not for pardon but for a complete review of the case.

On June 1, the governor appointed a committee to review the case, but after examination of the findings, he denied a new trial. On August 10, Sacco and Vanzetti were prepared for execution. Thirty-six minutes before the execution, the governor issued a postponement pending the results of an appeal to the Supreme Court. On August 19, the U.S. Supreme Court refused to hear the case, citing a lack of authority. In Europe and South America, mobs rioted and marched on U.S. embassies. In France, Italy, and the United States, workers went on strike to protest. Five hundred extra policemen, armed with machine guns and tear gas, barricaded the crowd of thousands outside the jail. Sacco and Vanzetti were executed just after midnight on August 23, 1927.

SIGNIFICANCE

The robbery and murder case against Nicola Sacco and Bartolomeo Vanzetti, one of the most famous U.S. trials of the twentieth century, generated worldwide protests, strikes, and riots as it focused the international spotlight on the small town of Dedham, Massachusetts in 1927. Controversy over the trial and its verdict continued long after the two men were executed. Some maintained that both men were innocent and were the targets of ethnic and political discrimination, whereas others insisted that only Vanzetti was innocent. However, most scholars agreed that Sacco and Vanzetti should have been granted a second trial, and in 1977 Massachusetts governor Michael S. Dukakis released an official state document asserting that the men's guilt had not been proven.

—*Joyce Duncan*

FURTHER READING

Bortman, Eli C. *Sacco and Vanzetti.* Beverly, Mass.: Commonwealth Editions, 2005. A brief, dramatic, and evenhanded account of the trial and its circumstances.

Dickinson, Alice. *The Sacco-Vanzetti Case*. New York: Franklin Watts, 1972. An abbreviated overview of the case, including chronology and photos.

Ehrmann, Herbert. *The Case That Will Not Die: Commonwealth vs. Sacco and Vanzetti*. Boston: Little, Brown, 1969. Liberally illustrated account by the case's assistant defense attorney during the period 1926-1927. Maps, time tables, and bibliography.

Frankfurter, Marion Denman, and Gardner Jackson, eds. *The Letters of Sacco and Vanzetti*. New York: Penguin Classics, 1997. Collection of correspondence by both men written from prison, including Vanzetti's letter to the governor.

Joughin, G. L., and E. M. Morgan. *The Legacy of Sacco and Vanzetti*. New York: Harcourt, Brace, 1948.

Early work provides masterful analysis of the case.

Russell, Francis. *Tragedy in Dedham*. New York: McGraw-Hill, 1962. Illustrated chronological recitation of events, including a discussion of public temperament.

Topp, Michael M. *The Sacco and Vanzetti Case: A Brief History with Documents*. Boston: Bedford/St. Martin's, 2004. A good resource for those interested in primary-source material.

SEE ALSO: June, 1917: First Pulitzer Prizes Are Awarded; Oct. 15, 1917: France Executes Mata Hari; Aug., 1919-May, 1920: Red Scare; Jan. 19, 1920: American Civil Liberties Union Is Founded; May 26, 1924: Immigration Act of 1924; Feb. 14, 1929: Valentine's Day Massacre; May 23, 1934: Police Apprehend Bonnie and Clyde.

October 6, 1927
THE JAZZ SINGER PREMIERES AS THE FIRST "TALKIE"

The commercial success of The Jazz Singer *began the era of talking pictures and led to a restructuring of the film industry.*

LOCALE: New York, New York
CATEGORIES: Motion pictures; entertainment

KEY FIGURES
Al Jolson (1886-1950), American entertainer
Harry Warner (1881-1958), American motion-picture executive
Jack Warner (1892-1978), American motion-picture executive
Sam Warner (1887-1927), American motion-picture executive
Edward B. Craft (1881-1929), American engineer

SUMMARY OF EVENT
The opening of the film *The Jazz Singer* in New York City on October 6, 1927, represented the culmination of one in a long series of attempts to bring synchronized sound to motion pictures. Thomas Alva Edison had invented the motion-picture camera in 1891, not because he saw a great commercial future in film but because he wanted a visual accompaniment to another of his inventions, the phonograph. Edison's idea was that sight and sound should combine in one home entertainment machine. Thirty-five years later, he had failed to accomplish

that goal, as had numerous inventors who saw commercial potential in talking films. When the introduction of storefront film theaters, called nickelodeons, created a boom in the film industry beginning in 1905, more attention was devoted to improving the technology of motion pictures. Nobody, however, could solve the problem of synchronizing sound with the moving image.

The solution to this tricky technological problem was finally found in the laboratories of Western Electric, the research and manufacturing subsidiary of the American Telephone and Telegraph Company (AT&T). Western Electric's scientists had invented a system of electrical recording based on vacuum tube amplifiers, which had been perfected in their laboratories. The sound was picked up on microphones, amplified, and recorded onto disks. Loudspeakers were developed to complement the system. The first commercial application of this technology was the public-address system, introduced in 1920, which could fill a large auditorium with amplified sound. The chief engineer of the Western Electric laboratories, Edward B. Craft, saw many potential applications for this technology, and in 1922 he obtained permission from his superiors at AT&T to perfect it and begin its commercial application.

Craft demonstrated electrical recording to film producers and record companies in 1924, but without success. Both groups had large investments in existing technology, and the film industry had not forgotten the string of failures of talking-picture technology, not the least of which was Edison's disastrous and highly publicized kinetophone of 1913, which was booed off the stage in many theaters.

It was therefore left to a smaller company to see the advantages of Western Electric's system and manage its commercial introduction. The Warner brothers had started in the nickelodeon business in Newcastle, Pennsylvania, at the turn of the century. Sam ran the projection machine, Jack sang in the pit, and the oldest brother, Harry, ran the business. From these small beginnings, they moved to Hollywood and produced their first feature film in 1918, repeating a process by which many film exhibitors had moved into the production of motion pictures. The Warner Bros. film company grew steadily in the 1920's, and by 1925 it was attempting to build a distribution network of film rental services and theaters to market its growing output.

The Warner brothers' initiation into the new technology of vacuum tubes and amplification of sound came when they built a radio station to enter the broadcasting business. They recognized that this was an important new form of entertainment and that it could be used to advertise their films. Sam Warner, who managed this operation, heard about Western Electric's new technology from radio experts he consulted. His brothers saw that electrical recording could be married to Western Electric's public-address equipment of amplifiers and loudspeakers to fill theaters with recorded sound. Their business strategy was to replace the professional musicians in theaters, enabling smaller exhibitors to provide the kind of musical accompaniment that was heard in the big picture palaces. It was never the Warner brothers' intention to make synchronized sound tracks for motion pictures; all they wanted was background music of recorded sound.

Warner Bros. entered into an agreement with Western Electric in 1925 to introduce the sound-on-disk system. The brothers formed a joint company, the Vitaphone Corporation, and set about recording an orchestral accompaniment to a silent picture. Their first attempt was *Don Juan*, which was released with several Vitaphone short features in 1926. Critical and audience reaction was favorable, but none of the major film producers saw any reason to convert to sound. The Warner brothers were convinced that the future was in the "talkies," however, and they acquired a Broadway play to turn into an elaborate, full-length picture.

The studio convinced Al Jolson to play the leading role in the planned film. As one of the most popular vaudeville stars in the United States, Jolson was a major attraction, and his presence ensured that the film would not go unnoticed. *The Jazz Singer* tells the story of a young Jewish man who abandons his family and the traditional music of his religion to become a star in the world of popular entertainment, a plot that reflected Jolson's own career. It was to be another silent film with short musical interludes until Jolson ad-libbed his famous line, "Wait a minute, wait a minute, you ain't heard nothing yet!" during a rehearsal. It was therefore by accident that *The Jazz Singer* introduced synchronized speech to films. The finished film contained only a few scenes with speech and Jolson singing; the rest was silent, with the usual titles interjected to display dialogue for the audience to read.

The Jazz Singer premiered in New York City at Warner's Theater on October 6, 1927. It was not an immediate success. The audience was thrilled when Jolson spoke from the screen, but neither critics nor leading filmmakers were very impressed. In the weeks that followed the premiere, Warner Bros. mounted a national press campaign to attract attention to the innovation of sound. Despite lukewarm reviews, attendance for the film grew rapidly as it opened in theaters across the United States. In 1928, *The Jazz Singer* began to set records for the length of run, and it finally grossed the unprecedented sum of three million dollars. By the end of the year, the returns from *The Jazz Singer* and other sound films convinced Warner Bros. to shift all of its film production into "talkies." The other major filmmakers soon followed.

Western Electric pressed Warner Bros. to return its initial exclusive license and then formed Electrical Research Products Inc. (ERPI) to market the technology to the film industry. Several large film companies took out licenses from ERPI in 1928, and by the end of the year every major film producer was making talking pictures. The process of wiring up film theaters for sound moved ahead rapidly, and in a very short time about fifteen hundred of the largest theaters in the United States were equipped to show talking pictures.

In the same year that Warner Bros. released *The Jazz Singer*, William Fox demonstrated his Movietone system, which recorded sound directly onto film. There were now two competing technologies for synchronized sound. Sound on film had the advantage of being easier to operate because there were no disks to be mixed up or broken. Filmmakers could also edit talking pictures by cutting and rejoining lengths of film, a task impossible

Al Jolson performs in blackface makeup in The Jazz Singer. *(Hulton Archive/ Getty Images)*

with sound on disk. Another system of sound on film was developed by the Radio Corporation of America, which organized Radio-Keith-Orpheum (RKO) to make and show sound pictures. By 1930, all the major filmmakers had graduated to sound on film, and the technology made famous by *The Jazz Singer* was obsolete.

SIGNIFICANCE

The Jazz Singer began a transition to a new form of motion-picture technology that completely changed film production and restructured the film industry. In only three years, sound recording was incorporated into film-making, sound equipment was installed in theaters, and silent films had all but vanished. Thousands of actors and musicians lost their jobs, and only one major star of silent films, Charles Chaplin, managed to survive in the new order of the "talkies."

The five largest film studios—Loew's/ Metro-Goldwyn-Mayer (MGM), Universal, Paramount, First National, and United Artists—prudently waited until *The Jazz Singer* was a proven commercial success before they moved into sound. By that time, the Warner and Fox companies had taken the lead in applying the new technology to filmmaking. Warner Bros. followed the success of *The Jazz Singer* in 1928 with *The Singing Fool*, which also starred Al Jolson and commanded the record admission price of eleven dollars for its premiere. *The Singing Fool* was a great success and one of the highest-grossing Hollywood features of the 1930's and 1940's.

The enormous enthusiasm for talking pictures generated record levels of profits for the film industry. Warner Bros. and Fox took the lion's share of the early rewards. From 1928 to 1929, profits at Fox increased by $3.5 million, and those at Warner Bros. increased by an astounding $12 million. Both studios began to acquire theaters and other film producers at a rapid rate. Warner Bros. took over First National, and Fox temporarily took control of Loew's/MGM. The two pioneers of sound quickly became major forces in the film industry.

In 1930, the major film producers were Paramount, Loew's/MGM, Warner Bros., Fox, and RKO. The Big Five, as they were known, went on a buying spree, acquiring film theaters, buying out smaller competitors, and purchasing music publishers and record companies. Each company controlled a network of film theaters to exhibit its films. Warner Bros. became the first integrated entertainment empire, with holdings in film, radio, music publishing, and records. As one example of integration, *The Singing Fool* promoted Al Jolson's songs, which were recorded on the Brunswick record label, controlled by the Warners, and were owned by music publishing companies under Warner control. Two songs from the film, "Sonny Boy" and "There's a Rainbow 'Round My Shoulder," were the best-selling records of 1928.

Talking pictures ushered in a period of great profits for exhibitors as well. The novelty of sound captivated audiences, and the five years after the premiere of *The*

Jazz Singer saw unprecedented levels of enthusiasm for motion pictures. It has been estimated that on average every person in the United States over the age of six went to a film theater once a week during this period. The onset of the Great Depression severely damaged other entertainment industries, but the motion-picture industry appeared to be immune to depression.

The popularity of film musicals, which provided the best showcase for the new technology, made film producers the leading consumers of music in the entertainment business. They acquired the rights to numerous Broadway musicals, and a stream of songwriters and artists made their way west to work in Hollywood. The average cost of a motion picture began to rise as filmmakers indulged themselves in ambitious musical productions involving large casts and highly paid stars. Musicals such as *The King of Jazz*, made by Paramount for about $2 million in 1930, overshadowed the great epics of the silent era in terms of spectacle and set a precedent for the Hollywood musicals of the 1930's.

The transition to sound favored larger film companies, for only they could raise the money to pay for it. The complex process of putting sound on film required great amounts of capital and considerable technical expertise. Adopting the technologies of synchronized sound required a massive construction program, because new film studios had to be built to accommodate sound recording and all theaters had to be converted to reproduce film sound. Sound was an important factor in the consolidation of the film industry. A small number of fully integrated companies came to dominate both film production and theatrical exhibition. The corporate structure that emerged in reaction to the advent of sound was to define Hollywood in its Golden Age of the 1930's and 1940's.

—*Andre Millard*

FURTHER READING

Bandy, Mary Lea, ed. *The Dawn of Sound*. New York: Museum of Modern Art, 1989. Published in conjunction with an exhibition and series of films commemorating the introduction of sound to film. Contains several excellent short essays that describe the technology and its history. Includes many rare photographs.

Cameron, Evan W., ed. *Sound and the Cinema*. Pleasantville, N.Y.: Redgrave, 1980. Collection of essays by scholars and technicians on the transition to sound in film and its development as an important feature in motion pictures.

Crafton, Donald. *The Talkies: American Cinema's Tran-*

sition to Sound, 1926-1931. New York: Charles Scribner's Sons, 1997. Discusses all aspects of the shift from silent films to films with sound, including the public's reaction to talking pictures and the effects of sound on the aesthetics of filmmaking. Includes bibliography and indexes.

Eyman, Scott. *The Speed of Sound: Hollywood and the Talkie Revolution, 1926-1930*. New York: Simon & Schuster, 1997. Comprehensive history of the period in Hollywood filmmaking when silents gave way to sound. Includes photographs and index.

Freedland, Michael. *Jolson*. New York: Stein & Day, 1972. Entertaining, concise biography is short on detail in some respects, but still a first-rate telling of Jolson's story. Includes photographs.

Geduld, Harry M. *The Birth of the Talkies: From Edison to Jolson*. Bloomington: Indiana University Press, 1975. Excellent discussion of the development of sound in films. Highlights the roles of the pioneers who developed sound technology.

Goldman, Herbert G. *Jolson: The Legend Comes to Life*. New York: Oxford University Press, 1988. Classic biography, well written and detailed. Includes numerous photographs from all aspects of Jolson's life and an extensive listing of Jolson's appearances on stage, in films, and on records.

Gomery, Douglas. *Movie History: A Survey*. Belmont, Calif.: Wadsworth, 1991. History of the American film industry written by the leading authority on the conversion to sound. Provides a good introduction to the transformation of the industry following the introduction of sound. Illustrated.

Lyman, Darryl. *Great Jews on Stage and Screen*. Middle Village, N.Y.: Jonathan David, 1987. Includes a section on Al Jolson that provides an overview of the entertainer's career, including brief discussion of *The Jazz Singer*.

Sarris, Andrew. *"You Ain't Heard Nothin' Yet": The American Talking Film—History and Memory, 1927-1949*. New York: Oxford University Press, 1998. Comprehensive history of American cinema since *The Jazz Singer* by one of the most respected American writers on film. Features an index of films and an index of names.

Shipman, David. *The Story of Cinema*. New York: St. Martin's Press, 1982. Well-written history includes a chapter on the development of sound films. Features numerous photographs.

Warner, Jack, with Dean Jennings. *My First Hundred Years*. New York: Random House, 1964. Personal ac-

1927

count of the making and impact of *The Jazz Singer* by one of the Warner brothers; entertaining and full of important insights. Presents a firsthand look at the trials and tribulations of introducing a new technology into the motion-picture industry.

Weis, Elisabeth, and John Belton, eds. *Film Sound: Theory and Practice.* New York: Columbia University Press, 1985. Collection of scholarly articles addresses

every aspect of the conversion to sound and shows its effects on filmmaking and the film industry.

SEE ALSO: 1913: Edison Shows the First Talking Pictures; Aug., 1926-Sept., 1928: Warner Bros. Introduces Talking Motion Pictures; May 11, 1928: Sound Technology Revolutionizes the Motion-Picture Industry; 1930's: Hollywood Enters Its Golden Age.

December 4, 1927
ELLINGTON BEGINS PERFORMING AT THE COTTON CLUB

When Duke Ellington began a three-year engagement at Harlem's Cotton Club, he launched his career as the most important composer-arranger-leader in jazz history.

LOCALE: New York, New York
CATEGORY: Music

KEY FIGURES
Duke Ellington (1899-1974), American pianist, composer, arranger, and bandleader
Bubber Miley (James Miley; 1903-1932), American trumpeter
Tricky Sam Nanton (Joseph Nanton; 1904-1946), American trombonist
Irving Mills (1894-1985), American song publisher and promoter
Johnny Hodges (1907-1970), American alto saxophonist

SUMMARY OF EVENT

With Louis Armstrong and Charlie Parker, Duke Ellington (Edward Kennedy Ellington) is one of the greatest figures in jazz and twentieth century American music. His importance rests on his achievements as a composer, orchestrator, and pianist-leader of the remarkable orchestra he headed for almost half a century. When he and his band made their debut at New York City's Cotton Club in 1927, Ellington was still a musician with a modest if growing reputation. He already had acquired the nickname that reflected his suave good looks and courtly manner when he emerged as the leader of a small black cooperative dance band that had moved to New York City from Washington, D.C., in 1923.

Ellington's debut at the Cotton Club on December 4, 1927, is now recognized as one of the most important openings in jazz history even though the unprepared

band's first few performances there were unimpressive. The band soon mastered the demanding fifteen-act program and also played for dancing and radio broadcast. It quickly became a major attraction in itself, as Ellington used the opportunity to transform his dance-show band into a collaborative vehicle for superior artistic expression.

The Cotton Club was one of the best-known and most successful of more than a dozen Harlem establishments that catered exclusively or mainly to a white clientele. Ellington's white manager, Irving Mills, had arranged for the job at the club. Its success was based mainly on its exotic and relatively sophisticated ambience, the quality of its all-black entertainment, and the sale of illegal alcohol. The elaborate shows, which usually featured comedians, dancers, vocalists, a chorus line, and the house band, were staged by experienced Broadway show people with original music by Jimmy McHugh.

The engagement at the Cotton Club enabled Ellington to build and consolidate his all-star band. It also spurred him to create a body of distinctive compositions and orchestral arrangements that drew on the African American tradition and expanded and elevated the vocabulary of jazz. Many of the club's acts appealed to white fantasies of exotic and primitive Africa, and the muted brass growls that the Ellington band had developed were labeled and marketed as "jungle style." Compositions such as "Echoes of the Jungle" served a functional purpose at the Cotton Club; they also transcended that context and, together with other original works, made an impact when heard on records and radio.

Nationwide radio broadcasts from the Cotton Club on the fledgling Columbia Broadcasting System (CBS) network made Ellington's name and music familiar to millions. Records by Duke Ellington and His Famous Cotton Club Orchestra sold widely and were heard in

Europe, where Ellington became a celebrity before his first visit there in 1933. In 1929, Mills arranged for Ellington to lead his band in Florenz Ziegfeld's theater production of George Gershwin's *Show Girl*. The band performed with Maurice Chevalier, then traveled to Hollywood to make the film *Check and Double Check* (1930). Ellington was included in a group of important African Americans invited to the White House in 1931.

In addition to writing arrangements in the jungle style, Ellington mastered the sectional formula developed by Fletcher "Smack" Henderson for his own much-admired orchestra. Henderson's model became the basis for many big band arrangers. Ellington frequently departed from the formula, mixing instrumental voices from across the trumpet, trombone, and reed sections to produce unique and sometimes haunting blends, as in the muted trumpet, muted trombone, and clarinet sound of "Mood Indigo" (1930).

Ellington often borrowed or developed the ideas of his musicians in creating music for his band. The frequent use of unwritten "head arrangements," which gradually evolved as suggestions were incorporated, contributed to the collaborative expression of the band but sometimes made the question of authorship difficult, even though the organizing intelligence was clearly Ellington's. In his more formal and personal arrangements, Ellington sometimes used sound in much the same way as the pointillists used paint. His impressionistic compositions, skillful use of dissonance, and unusual textures led to comparisons with such modern European composers as Claude Debussy, Frederick Delius, and Maurice Ravel, of whom Ellington probably had little knowledge. In his career of more than fifty years, Ellington wrote approximately twelve hundred compositions of an amazing variety, including simple blues, popular hit songs, dance tunes, showcases for individual musicians, short

orchestral pieces, extended works designed mainly for concerts, film music, television themes, ballet and opera scores, and religious music for his "sacred concerts." Ellington's abiding inspiration was the black American community and its culture, which he sought to portray in compositions such as "Black Beauty," *Black, Brown, and Beige*, "Harlem Airshaft," and "My People."

One of Ellington's greatest achievements was the creation of an orchestra unrivaled for its stability, longevity, and number of influential musicians who stayed within

Duke Ellington (at the piano) and his band perform at the Cotton Club. (Hulton Archive/Getty Images)

1927

its ranks for prolonged periods. Throughout his life Ellington was in an almost constant state of exploration, reevaluation, and development; his music is so various that it defies classification. He kept the band together, sometimes at great personal expense, because he needed to hear his compositions and arrangements played on the instrument for which they were intended: his orchestra.

SIGNIFICANCE

The Ellington orchestra's success was in part a result of the talent of its individual members, many of whom became models for thousands of other artists. Johnny Hodges was one of the preeminent alto saxophonists in jazz, influencing almost all who came after him, even tenor saxophonists such as bandmate Ben Webster and modernist John Coltrane. Harry Carney, who was with the band from 1927 until Ellington's death in 1974, is known as the father of the baritone saxophone, which he established as an important ensemble and solo voice. Trumpeter Bubber Miley and trombonist Tricky Sam Nanton developed the plunger-mute techniques on their respective instruments that created the "jungle sounds" that were an important characteristic of the Ellington orchestral style. These expressive techniques sprang from the roots of the jazz instrumental tradition and subsequently were used by brass players everywhere. Miley's successor with Ellington, Charles "Cootie" Williams, became an influence in his own right, as did trombonist Lawrence Brown, trumpeter Clark Terry, and saxophonist Ben Webster. In his short life, Jimmy Blanton established the path followed by most jazz bass players since 1940. Ellington himself was a competent if not outstanding pianist who began by playing mainly in the "stride" style that had developed out of ragtime. He also developed an effective accompaniment style and ways of voicing chords that are widely imitated. Imitations of Ellington's influence can be heard in the work of the modernist pianist/composer Thelonious Monk, who made a piano-trio recording of Ellington compositions.

Ellington's appeal to jazz musicians has transcended periods and styles and proved timeless; there are few who have not acknowledged his influence in one way or another. Ellington's life and musical interests spanned the first seventy-five years of jazz history. He recorded and sounded comfortable with the greatest artists of every period, including Louis Armstrong, Coleman Hawkins, Dizzy Gillespie, Charles Mingus, and John Coltrane.

Because they seem so quintessentially to belong to his orchestra, Ellington's longer compositions are seldom

heard performed except on his own recordings. They are demonstrations that the American dance band can be an extremely flexible vehicle, both for popular entertainment and for high artistic expression. Although the Ellington spirit and influence permeate big band music, few arrangers (aside from his collaborator and musical alter ego, Billy Strayhorn) have been able to duplicate Ellington's unique orchestral sound. The bands of Charlie Barnet and Woody Herman at times provided rough approximations, aided by the fact that both leaders were saxophonists in the style of Johnny Hodges. The persistence of Ellington's influence as a composer and orchestrator can be heard in the modern works of Charles Mingus, Gil Evans, and Oliver Nelson.

Ellington's compositions have been played by groups large and small since the 1930's, and his legacy is perhaps most alive in the thirty or so short compositions that are still part of the working repertoire of most jazz musicians around the world. Melodies such as "Satin Doll," "In a Mellow Tone," "Solitude," and "In a Sentimental Mood"—works on a par with those of Cole Porter, George Gershwin, and Irvin Berlin—can be heard wherever jazz is played. Ellington's compositions have been recorded thousands of times by musicians ranging from traditionalists to the avant-garde and have been reinterpreted as they have been discovered by each succeeding generation.

In his many tours abroad, some under the aegis of the U.S. government, Ellington took his music and the American ideals of individuality and freedom of expression within a cooperative group context to thousands of people. In addition to his influence on musicians and leaders such as Ted Heath of Britain and Francy Boland of Belgium, Ellington absorbed and later (often with Strayhorn) transformed foreign musical influences in such works as *Far East Suite, Virgin Islands Suite*, and *Latin American Suite*.

Wynton Marsalis, one of the most impressive and influential musicians to appear in the 1980's, has stated that "Duke Ellington is what jazz is, he is the greatest jazz musician . . . because he addressed most comprehensively what jazz music actually is . . . the fundamentals of group improvisation, vocalization, and a swinging optimism." Marsalis has devoted much of his considerable talent to educating young musicians in the value of Ellington's music and in performing the composer's works with the Lincoln Center Jazz Orchestra, as on the recording *Portraits by Ellington*.

Ellington's musical achievement elevated jazz as an African American art form and brought increased acceptance and respect to its practitioners. His personal sophistication and dignity made him an important representative of the black community. Ellington's hundreds of honors and awards, including many honorary doctorates, also served to acknowledge the contributions of black people to American society and culture. On the occasion of his seventieth birthday, a celebration was held at the White House during which President Richard Nixon presented Ellington with the highest civilian award of the United States, the Presidential Medal of Freedom.

During the height of big band popularity in the 1930's and early 1940's, Ellington's band was not as commercially successful as many white bands, but his organization was often the standard against which other bands were measured, especially by musicians. Through courage, hard work, and artistry, Ellington was able to sustain his band after all but a handful of others had disappeared. When Ellington died in 1974, the leadership of his still-functioning band was taken up by his son Mercer, who continued to present his father's music to the world until his own death in 1996.

—Douglas Rollins

FURTHER READING

Collier, James Lincoln. *Duke Ellington*. New York: Oxford University Press, 1987. Well-written, scholarly, and sometimes controversial biography of Ellington sets his work within its historical, social, and musical contexts. Examines the importance and role of Ellington's musicians, both as instrumentalists and as contributors to compositions generally ascribed to their leader. Includes musical analysis, photographs, discographical note, and index.

Dance, Stanley. *The World of Duke Ellington*. 1970. Reprint. New York: Da Capo Press, 2000. Collection of articles, interviews, memorabilia, sketches of musicians, and diary entries written mainly in the 1960's by a longtime Ellington associate and observer. The whole adds up to a fascinating picture of the personalities and interrelationships of many of the most important members of the Ellington musical family. Includes photographs, selective discography, index, and chronology from 1899 to 1970 highlighting the major events in Ellington's life, band personnel changes, important compositions, and performances.

Ellington, Edward Kennedy. *Music Is My Mistress*. Garden City, N.Y.: Doubleday, 1973. Ellington's autobiography reflects his lively and at times eccentric mind, his sophistication, and his ironic sense of hu-
mor. A potpourri of straight memoir, flights of imagination, sketches of more than one hundred musicians and other associates, anecdotes, religious meditations, poems, prose poems, a libretto, and journals of various foreign tours. Rich in personal commentary but of uneven literary quality, this work reveals Ellington's love of life and passion for music, but, as always, he guards his privacy and the essential man remains elusive. Includes photographs, lists of honors and awards, list of compositions, and bibliography.

Ellington, Mercer, with Stanley Dance. *Duke Ellington in Person: An Intimate Memoir*. New York: Da Capo Press, 1978. Written after Ellington's death to supplement the autobiography and the Dance book cited above. Reveals the darker side of Ellington's personality, his love-hate relationship with his son, his amorous liaisons, and his professional and artistic struggles. Includes photographs, copyright and discographic information, and index.

Haskins, James. *The Cotton Club*. 1977. Reprint. New York: Hippocrene Books, 1994. The story of the nightclub that, between 1923 and 1940, brought Broadway-type entertainment to Harlem, although for white audiences only. The club introduced and served as a showplace for many of America's greatest black artists. Despite some inaccuracies, a good introduction to an important chapter in entertainment history. Includes photographs, notes, and bibliography.

Lawrence, A. H. *Duke Ellington and His World: A Biography*. New York: Routledge, 2001. First Ellington biography written by a jazz musician draws heavily on interviews with the composer's colleagues, friends, and family members, including his son Mercer. Features list of compositions, bibliography, and index.

Schuller, Gunther. "Duke Ellington, Master Composer." In *The Swing Era: The Development of Jazz, 1930-1945*. New York: Oxford University Press, 1989. Examines Ellington's music into the 1940's. Successfully combines historical detail with a systematic analysis of the music in terms best understood by trained musicians. Features many transcribed musical illustrations and select discography.

_____. "The Ellington Style: Its Origins and Early Development." In *Early Jazz: Its Roots and Musical Development*. 1968. Reprint. New York: Oxford University Press, 1986. Focuses on Ellington's music as recorded from 1926 through the Cotton Club period to 1931.

1927

Vail, Ken. *Duke's Diary, Part I: The Life of Duke Ellington, 1927-1950.* Metuchen, N.J.: Scarecrow Press, 2002. First of two volumes covers the period in Ellington's life when his career began to take off. Illustrates the progress of his success through photographs, newspaper articles, advertisements, reviews, and other documents from that time.

SEE ALSO: Feb. 13, 1914: ASCAP Forms to Protect Writers and Publishers of Music; 1920's: Harlem Renaissance; Feb. 15, 1923: Bessie Smith Records "Downhearted Blues"; Feb. 12, 1924: Gershwin's *Rhapsody in Blue* Premieres in New York; Nov., 1925: Armstrong Records with the Hot Five; 1933: Billie Holiday Begins Her Recording Career.

December 27, 1927
SHOW BOAT IS THE FIRST AMERICAN MUSICAL TO EMPHASIZE PLOT

Show Boat *was the first major musical theater production to make use of a strong, plotted story line.*

LOCALE: New York, New York
CATEGORIES: Theater; music; entertainment

KEY FIGURES

Jerome Kern (1885-1945), American composer
Oscar Hammerstein II (1895-1960), American librettist
Florenz Ziegfeld (1869-1932), American impresario
Edna Ferber (1885-1968), American author

SUMMARY OF EVENT

By 1927, Jerome Kern, Oscar Hammerstein II, and Florenz Ziegfeld already had made significant contributions to the world of musical theater. Ziegfeld was known primarily as an impresario whose yearly editions of the Ziegfeld Follies introduced New York City audiences to such performing talents as Fanny Brice and Bert Williams and such writing talents as Irving Berlin and the team of Richard Rodgers and Lorenz Hart. The Ziegfeld Follies were revues that featured skits, stand-up comedy, specialty acts, individual songs, and many beautiful women. Ziegfeld had made the decision to branch out into the more conventional musical comedy. He also had decided, in 1927, to open a new theater that bore his name; it was built on Sixth Avenue and Fifty-Third Street. He promised Kern and Hammerstein that their new musical would be the first production in the new theater.

Hammerstein and Kern, along with Otto Harbach, had written an earlier musical for Ziegfeld. *Sunny,* produced in 1925, featured Marilyn Miller. Hammerstein came from a theatrical family. His grandfather was an opera impresario, his father ran a vaudeville house, and his uncle produced shows on Broadway. Hammerstein had studied law at Columbia University but was soon drawn into theater. With Harbach, he teamed on the book and

lyrics (the libretto) for several musicals with a variety of composers. Kern was impressed with Hammerstein's work on *Sunny* and approached him to create the libretto for *Show Boat.*

Turning Edna Ferber's 1926 novel *Show Boat* into a musical was Kern's idea. This was not the first time Kern was involved in groundbreaking musical theater. In 1915, Kern, along with librettist Guy Bolton, wrote a musical called *Nobody Home.* This was the first of a series of musicals that have become known as the Princess Theater shows. The name comes from the theater where the shows were first performed. In an era of operetta with the libretto serving as a showcase for songs and set pieces by featured comics, usually in the setting of a lush European fantasy, the Princess Theater shows were marked by smaller productions (usually two sets), smaller casts (eight chorus members or fewer), and smaller orchestras (ten instruments or fewer).

Although the physical production of the Princess Theater shows might have been smaller, the ambitions and talents involved were quite large. The Princess Theater shows used American situations, and the songs and comedy grew out of these situations. Other musicals in the series included *Very Good Eddie* (1915), *Oh, Boy!* (1917), and *Oh, Lady! Lady!!* (1918). The last two had the added feature of the British wit of P. G. Wodehouse.

Work on *Show Boat* began during the intermission of another Kern musical, *Criss Cross* (1926). Kern had read the Ferber novel and was determined to meet with the author to discuss its musical possibilities. He approached his friend Alexander Woollcott to ask for an introduction. Conveniently, Ferber was Woollcott's guest that evening at the theater. In the lobby, during intermission, Kern broached his idea to the novelist. Ferber was no stranger to the theater. She had written a play with George S. Kaufman. In fact, it was a casual comment from Kaufman that sparked the idea for the novel *Show*

Boat. When the novel was published, it quickly became a best seller. This only added to Ferber's fame, as she had won the Pulitzer Prize for her 1924 novel *So Big*.

The idea of turning *Show Boat* into a musical at first did not appeal to Ferber. Her experience with musicals had been shows such as *Criss Cross* that featured comic routines, tap dancing, and lines of chorus girls. Kern had a different vision and was able to convince the novelist that *Show Boat* would not be a conventional musical comedy but rather a musical play.

Having won her consent, Kern approached Hammerstein to write the libretto and Ziegfeld to produce the show. Kern and Hammerstein went to work, secure with the promise from Ziegfeld that *Show Boat* would open the new Ziegfeld Theater. What they did not know was that Ziegfeld had made the same commitment to Guy Bolton and Harry Tierney, who were writing *Rio Rita*. On February 2, 1927, the theater was ready and so was *Rio Rita*. Ziegfeld was a man of business and opened his theater with a likely hit. With *Rio Rita* opening the Ziegfeld Theater, any sense of time pressure on Kern and Hammerstein to finish *Show Boat* was removed, allowing them to fine-tune their work and to introduce innovations.

Show Boat tried out in Washington, D.C., in November of 1927. The show was too long, but the audience responded well. Kern and Hammerstein continued to refine their work. The production then moved to Philadelphia, where refinements continued. On December 27, 1927, *Show Boat* opened at the Ziegfeld Theater in New York City. Although the show was still long, the response from the critics and the audience was very positive. *Show Boat* ran for two years in New York, went on a national tour, returned to New York for another run, opened a production in London, generated three film versions, and became the first Broadway musical to be part of the repertory of the New York City Opera.

SIGNIFICANCE

When *Show Boat* opened in 1927, musical theater fare was divided among revues such as Ziegfeld's Follies and George White's Scandals, European operettas, and American musical comedies such as the Princess Theater shows. Although these musical comedies represented a distinct departure in style and subject matter from the operetta, the music and comedy were the focus. This often meant that character-driven plots were sacrificed for comic situations and catchy tunes.

It would be misleading to suggest that one show, even *Show Boat*, could change all that. Such is not the nature

of art. *Show Boat* did, however, point the way for such artists as Richard Rodgers and Stephen Sondheim. This happened because of the promise Jerome Kern made to Edna Ferber. Instead of using the outline of Ferber's novel as a skeleton for songs and comic routines, Kern and Hammerstein were concerned with telling the story.

This was an ambitious task. *Show Boat* tells the story of Magnolia Hawkes, the daughter of Cap'n Andy, proprietor of the *Cotton Blossom*, a showboat. Magnolia meets and falls in love with Gaylord Ravenal, a suave riverboat gambler. They marry and have a daughter named Kim. Ravenal leaves his wife and child. Another performer with the *Cotton Blossom* company, Julie, is found to be a mulatto, and, because she is married to a Caucasian, she is charged with miscegenation and forced to leave the boat. She later turns up as an alcoholic saloon singer in Chicago. Magnolia and Kim also are in Chicago during the World's Fair, and they have a brief reunion with Ravenal. *Show Boat* is a sprawling tale that covers several decades and locales. Alcoholism, racism, and broken families are some of the issues that drive the plot. This was not the usual material for musical comedy.

Show Boat demonstrated that, if handled with skill and taste, such issues could be material for musical theater. *Carousel* (1945), by Rodgers and Hammerstein, deals with spousal abuse and dysfunctional families. *South Pacific* (1949), by the same team, uses interracial marriage as a key element. Alan Jay Lerner and Frederick Loewe told the story of King Arthur in *Camelot* (1960); several adulterous affairs are central to that story. Kern and Hammerstein first demonstrated that the American musical could deal with serious issues, breaking the ground for these later shows.

Serious issues alone did not make *Show Boat* great, however. The source material, although successful as a novel, did not guarantee a successful musical. Kern and Hammerstein had to combine their experience, their talents, and their ideas for innovation to create *Show Boat*. Many of the songs they wrote have become standards. The score includes "Only Make Believe," "Can't Help Lovin' Dat Man of Mine," and "Why Do I Love You?" Each of these shows Kern's considerable melodic gifts. They also demonstrate Hammerstein's unique lyrical turn with love songs. Instead of writing the commonplace "I love you," Hammerstein suggested that the characters "make believe" they love each other.

There is a love song in *Show Boat* with lyrics not written by Hammerstein. The song "Bill," sung by Julie, was written by Kern and P. G. Wodehouse. It was intended for *Oh, Lady! Lady!!* but had been cut. When Helen Mor-

1927

gan was cast as Julie, Kern thought that the song "Bill" would lend itself perfectly to Morgan's trademark of sitting on a piano to sing a torch song. Hammerstein was given credit so often for this song that he took pains to include a program note giving due praise to Wodehouse.

Another song, "Ol' Man River," also had a lasting effect on the musical theater. With such a sprawling story to tell, Hammerstein thought it necessary to use a song to tie the work together. Using a slowed down, inverted version of the *Cotton Blossom* theme, Hammerstein fashioned a ballad of pain, despair, and some hope based on the unceasing flow of the Mississippi River that binds all these lives together. Oddly enough, this song, which is the theme of the show, is sung by Joe, a relatively minor character.

The idea of a concept or theme tying a musical together has been used in some of the most enduring productions. In *Fiddler on the Roof* (1964), the idea of tradition, both in the family and in society, is the theme that ties the plot together. Stephen Sondheim, a protégé of Hammerstein, wrote a musical, *Company* (1970), that all but dispenses with plot and relies heavily on the themes of marriage and New York City to unite the production. *Company* has often been called the first "concept" musical. Summer theaters and opera companies make sure that *Show Boat* itself, in so many ways a pioneering show, endures.

—*William B. Kennedy*

FURTHER READING

Engel, Lehman. *The American Musical Theater.* New York: Macmillan, 1975. Evaluation of trends in musical theater history by an experienced conductor and theorist. Excellent source for any serious study of the musical theater. Chapter titled "Breakaway" includes discussion of *Show Boat*. Contains several useful appendixes.

Ewen, David. *The World of Jerome Kern.* New York: Henry Holt, 1960. Highly readable biography aimed at general readers. Kern is clearly the hero, so scholars should be wary of a lack of objectivity. Presents anecdotes and direct quotes from Kern on *Show Boat*, but only sketchy information on his work with Hammerstein. Includes photographs.

Green, Stanley. *The World of Musical Comedy.* New York: Grosset & Dunlap, 1962. One of the first major histories of the musical takes the form of a cross between chronology and studies of the writers. Includes a very good section on Kern, with valuable notes on getting *Show Boat* to the stage.

Kislan, Richard. *The Musical: A Look at the American Musical Theater.* Rev. ed. New York: Applause Books, 1995. Textbook for a general course in musical theater includes a brief but thorough history and a study of the various crafts and artists in the musical theater. Features a chapter on Kern and goes into some depth on Ziegfeld and the Princess Theater. Includes excellent photographs.

Knapp, Raymond. *The American Musical and the Formation of National Identity.* Princeton, N.J.: Princeton University Press, 2004. History of the genre focuses on how themes in American musical theater productions relate to how Americans view themselves. Chapter 8 addresses *Show Boat* within the context of a discussion of race and ethnicity. Includes useful appendixes, notes, bibliography, and index.

Smith, Cecil, and Glenn Litton. *Musical Comedy in America.* 1981. Reprint. New York: Theatre Arts Books, 1991. Excellent overall history of the musical theater provides photographs and thorough and literate text. Goes beyond the expected chronology and discusses technique. Particularly skillful at creating a sense of what the musical theater was like in the early twentieth century.

SEE ALSO: Nov. 7, 1904: Cohan's *Little Johnny Jones* Premieres; Oct. 10, 1935: Gershwin's *Porgy and Bess* Opens in New York.

1928
BUÑUEL AND DALÍ CHAMPION SURREALISM IN *AN ANDALUSIAN DOG*

The Surrealist film An Andalusian Dog *launched the directing career of Luis Buñuel and gave him a vehicle for expressing his deeply felt indignation at the moral failures of church and society.*

LOCALE: Paris, France
CATEGORY: Motion pictures

KEY FIGURES
Luis Buñuel (1900-1983), Spanish filmmaker and moralist
Salvador Dalí (1904-1989), Spanish Surrealist painter
André Breton (1896-1966), French writer and critic

SUMMARY OF EVENT
The intellectual movement that dominated the careers of both Luis Buñuel and Salvador Dalí and that drove them to produce *Un Chien andalou* (1928; *An Andalusian Dog*) was Surrealism. Along with Dadaism and expressionism, Surrealism was a revolt against representational art. Led by founder André Breton, the Surrealist movement had its first exhibition in Paris in 1925. Surrealists believed that the contents of the unconscious mind are as real as the concrete world; therefore, artistic rules that govern merely the physical world, such as those of perspective, are not sufficient as an expression of reality. Surrealist art attempted to depict objects in incongruous juxtapositions, as they might occur in a dream.

Dalí and Buñuel met in 1920 at the University of Madrid. Dalí called his friends there a "strident and revolutionary group." The first one-man exhibition of Dalí's paintings came in 1925 in Barcelona. Dalí held Jean-Auguste-Dominique Ingres and Jacques-Louis David, realist painters from the nineteenth century, in high esteem. In arguing for tradition and classical form, Dalí shocked his Spanish contemporaries, most of whom were absorbed in the post-Impressionist rejection of academic rules and traditions. Dalí's Surrealism would permit him his realism, but with unrelated objects depicted in dreamlike, infinitely receding landscapes. In 1927, he dedicated to Buñuel an essay suggesting that film could promote a new way of seeing.

After an apprenticeship from 1925 to 1928 at Jean Epstein's Académie du Cinéma in Paris, Buñuel joined Dalí in making a Surrealist film. The script was written in three days, and filming was completed in less than two weeks. The resulting short film, *An Andalusian Dog*, was shown to Breton and other Paris Surrealists, who enthu-

siastically received it and accepted the pair into their ranks.

Dalí described the aim of the film as jolting viewers. He and Buñuel wanted to make a film that "would carry . . . the audience back to the secret depths of adolescence, to the sources of dreams, destiny, and the secret of life and death, a work that would scratch away at all received ideas." Buñuel wrote that in working out the plot, every idea of a rational, aesthetic, or other preoccupation with technical matters was rejected as irrelevant. He described the aim of the film as producing instinctive reactions of attraction and repulsion. Despite the fact that both artists insisted that nothing in the film symbolizes anything, others have interpreted the film as having various meanings.

Analysts agree that the opening sequence of the twenty-minute film, in which a razor slices a human eye, was intended as a typical, if horrifying, Surrealist attack on the viewer's (and the world's) complacency in the midst of worldwide atrocities. What follows is a series of intentionally unrelated scenes that has been called "a catalog of Freudian metaphors."

A male bicyclist, dressed as a nurse and thus sexually ambiguous, arrives at a woman's apartment. To recordings of Argentine tangos alternating with Richard Wagner's *Liebestod* from *Tristan und Isolde*, the script calls for a close-up of a hand full of crawling ants. This dissolves into a close-up of the hairy armpit of a woman who is sunbathing and then to a close-up of the spines of a sea urchin.

From a window, the man and woman observe a girl being run over in the street. This sexually excites the cyclist. The woman allows his fondling but then becomes frigid. Protecting herself with a tennis racket, she too manifests a certain androgyny. Desperately trying to reach her, the man must drag two grand pianos, on which are dead and putrefying donkeys, and two priests. This grotesque comic relief may symbolize, as one critic has suggested, "the dead weight of a decaying society chaining the free expression of man's desire."

A more assertive man, the alter ego of the bicyclist, enters. The bicyclist shoots him dead, possibly symbolizing the murder of the man he might have been. Later, the woman is walking on a beach with another man, possibly another alter ego. He appears mature and confident but still unhappy. At the end, they are seen buried up to their chests in sand and being eaten alive by swarms of insects. The scene is enigmatically titled "In the Spring."

Buñuel and Dalí's collaboration ended during work on the 1930 Surrealist masterpiece *L'Âge d'or* (*The Golden Age*), Buñuel's first feature-length film at sixty-three minutes. Dalí called that film a caricature of his ideas. Perhaps Buñuel was too strident in his assault on religion and conventional morality as constraints on human freedom. This frontal attack, first signaled in *An Andalusian Dog* and powerfully extended in this film, caused *The Golden Age* to be banned widely. In the film, a documentary-like prologue shows two scorpions killing a rat. Scenes follow in Surrealist juxtaposition. Prosperous colonists arrive on an island. They recall Spain's voyages of discovery and Christianization. In a famous sequence, four lavishly attired bishops turn into skeletons. Next, a couple making love in public are arrested by scandalized society. The colonists then dedicate a stone to their new colony. A small pile of soft cement on the stone looks like excrement.

Salvador Dalí. (Library of Congress, Prints and Photographs Division, Carl Van Vechten Collection)

Polite socialites at a party barely notice an oxcart filled with drunken peasants crossing the hall, a kitchen fire, and a murder, but they are horrified at an insult and a slap in their midst. Later, at a concert, they seem oblivious to the passionate groping of the reunited lovers and unmoved by the surging crescendos of the *Liebestod*. Finally, in a sadistic orgy in a medieval castle, a duke is depicted as Christ and a cross is decorated with the heads of religiously exploited women. Buñuel's message appears to be that respectability requires society to repress its sexuality and spontaneity. A culture that does this is not alive but a fossil (the bishop/skeletons). Not only does institutional religion not serve, but it is also harmful and degrading. Such attitudes were a harbinger of the anticlerical spirit of the Spanish Civil War, which produced considerable persecution of clergy.

SIGNIFICANCE

Buñuel's next silent film had to be funded privately, but his 1932 documentary *Las Hurdes* ranks among the best ever made. Miserable in a Spanish region hostile to life in any form, the people of Las Hurdes eat only potatoes and beans, and they incestuously produce retarded children. In school, barefoot, ragged children are taught bourgeois values. Here documentary becomes editorial, indicting a morality that ignores human degradation, surrealistically juxtaposing peasant hovels and ornate churches and surveying the people's animal existence against the inspiring strains of Brahms's Fourth Symphony.

From 1932 to 1959, Buñuel learned to moderate his fervor, making sound films in the United States, France, Spain, and Mexico. His seventeen Mexican films, at first dismissed as commercial, were later recognized to be rich in veiled satire on the hypocrisy of conventional morality. The period saw his 1950 masterpiece, *Los Olvidados* (*The Young and the Damned*). Pedro, refused love by his prostitute mother, is taught to steal by Jaibo. In a Surrealist dream sequence, Pedro appeals for love, and his mother responds erotically. Jaibo comes out from under the bed. Reality and dreams are skillfully and inextricably confused. Pedro is murdered by Jaibo and, ironically, the mother becomes the lover of her son's killer.

Buñuel's pessimism was even more pronounced in *Nazarin* (1959) and *Viridiana* (1961). Both won prizes at the Cannes film festival; both are criticisms of the church, whose most sincere ministers do more harm than good in the world. The priest Nazarin symbolizes Christ's return being rejected in the modern world. *Viridiana*, Buñuel's first film shot in Spain in thirty years, was banned for its criticism of Francisco Franco.

A religious novice, Viridiana unintentionally destroys those who helped her and is nearly raped by blind and poor beggars she has helped. Values are reversed as the ungrateful poor destroy her house and eat everything, in a parody of the Last Supper. She renounces her vocation.

In 1962, Buñuel produced *El Angel exterminador* (*The Exterminating Angel*), a Surrealist masterpiece. The elegant guests at a dinner party find that, unaccountably, they cannot leave the dining room. Somehow they must adapt to their curious situation. An older man dies and frustrated lovers commit suicide. The bodies are stuffed in one closet while another closet serves as a bathroom. The prisoners engage in a variety of superstitious rituals and vices. Finally extricated, on Sunday they appear at church. Again they find themselves unable to leave.

Diary of a Chambermaid (1964) was a commentary on the social changes in France after World War I. The chambermaid Celestine openly despises her Royalist employers. Their neighbor is an insulting republican who pitches his garbage into their yard. Their game-keeper is a fascist triumphantly demonstrating in the streets of Paris for the moral rebirth of France, but he brutally rapes and murders a child and gets away with it. Celestine marries the old republican but cruelly turns him into her servant. Buñuel again provides a coldly dispassionate, even documentary, view of decadent class privilege, gross injustice, the failure of idealism, and the reversal of values.

In 1965 came *Simon of the Desert*. A fifth century hermit, Simon Stylites, spent his life atop a sixty-foot column. Buñuel shows him preaching, healing, and overcoming sometimes bizarre temptations. Later, conveyed to twentieth century New York City, he learns that for all of his virtue and self-negation, people have remained morally unchanged. In his own time he was significant, but in the modern age he has no lasting impact.

In *Belle de Jour* (1967), Buñuel so smoothly moves between fantasy or dreams and actuality that the audience often cannot tell them apart. His Surrealist message is that both realms are equally real. In *The Milky Way* (1969), Buñuel again assaulted the church. The title refers to the pilgrimage to the Spanish shrine of Santiago Campostella. The film is an allegorical journey through church history. Along the way, ordinary people discuss important theological mysteries. Nearing the shrine, two vagrant pilgrims are diverted from their quest by a prostitute. Here, as in *Simon of the Desert*, the imposing doctrines of the church appear sterile and irrelevant.

Buñuel's Surrealism overturns conventional values. Evil triumphs over good and often results from the good intentions of the innocent, who themselves become compromised. Opposites, even good and evil, do not exist but are fictions of the conscious mind. Physical beauty is no better than ugliness. Buñuel's camera sees "objects and men without blinking at deformity and without winking at a superior viewer." Poor and deformed people do not generate pity, as he depicts them as vicious and greedy.

Buñuel's audiences, conditioned to seeing morality triumph, are left bothered by the apparent moral ambiguity of a filmmaker who has been called one of the great moralists of the twentieth century. Henry Miller, who considered Buñuel a genius, wrote in 1932 that Buñuel portrays "the lunacy of civilization, the record of man's achievement after ten thousand years of refinement." In achieving this goal, however, Buñuel falsified the Surrealist denial of intentionality. After he reached the age of seventy, he produced a series of films—*Tristana* (1970), *The Discreet Charm of the Bourgeoisie* (1972), and *Cet obscur objet du desir* (1977)—that are among the greatest masterpieces of Surrealism in any medium. Buñuel's influence probably has been less over the films of other directors than over audiences and film critics, who gradually have come to better understand his art, insights, and bite.

—*Daniel C. Scavone*

FURTHER READING

Ades, Dawn. *Dalí and Surrealism*. New York: Harper and Row, 1982. Fine biography with special reference to Dalí's attachment to the Surrealist movement and chapters on his role in Surrealist cinema.

Durgnat, Raymond. *Luis Buñuel*. Rev. ed. Berkeley: University of California Press, 1977. Excellent filmography examines individual films from a moderate Marxist point of view. Copiously illustrated with stills of key scenes.

Higginbotham, Virginia. *Luis Buñuel*. Boston: Twayne, 1979. Excellent introductory biography and filmography of Buñuel. Modestly illustrated.

Hopkins, David. *Dada and Surrealism: A Very Short Introduction*. New York: Oxford University Press, 2004. Concise introduction to these art movements discusses their international nature and the range of media employed. Also addresses the debates surrounding them, including issues of quality and attitudes toward women.

Nadeau, Maurice. *The History of Surrealism*. Translated by Richard Howard. 1965. Reprint. Cambridge, Mass.: Belknap Press, 1989. Extremely detailed history of Surrealism in literature, art, and film. Contains

1928

translations of André Breton's three Surrealist manifestos and other documents of the movement.

Read, Herbert. "Introduction." In *Surrealism*. 1936. Reprint. New York: Praeger, 1971. Offers a sophisticated and clearly written definition of every nuance of Surrealism, using historical, artistic, and Freudian points of departure.

Richardson, Michael. *Surrealism and Cinema*. Oxford, England: Berg, 2006. Presents an introduction to surrealist film as well as an examination of the works of Luis Buñuel and other surrealist filmmakers from the 1920's to the beginning of the twenty-first century.

Schillaci, Peter P. "Luis Buñuel and the Death of God." In *Three European Directors*, edited by James M. Wall. Grand Rapids, Mich.: Wm. B. Eerdmans, 1973. Interpretation of Buñuel is rich in insights into the director's mind and vivid descriptions of his major films. Highly recommended.

SEE ALSO: Aug., 1902: *A Trip to the Moon* Introduces Special Effects; Oct., 1924: Surrealism Is Born; 1930-1935: Von Sternberg Makes Dietrich a Superstar; Jan., 1935: Schiaparelli's Boutique Mingles Art and Fashion.

1928
BUSH BUILDS THE FIRST DIFFERENTIAL ANALYZER

The differential analyzer developed by Vannevar Bush and his colleagues at the Massachusetts Institute of Technology was the first modern analog computer.

LOCALE: Cambridge, Massachusetts

CATEGORIES: Science and technology; inventions; mathematics; engineering; computers and computer science

KEY FIGURES

Vannevar Bush (1890-1974), American electrical engineer

Baron Kelvin (William Thomson; 1824-1907), English physicist and engineer

Charles Babbage (1791-1871), English mathematician and inventor

SUMMARY OF EVENT

Calculating equipment has developed along two distinct lines: one is digital computation and the other is analog computation. Analog machines, of which the mechanical differential analyzer is an example, operate on quantities that are capable of continuous variation. These quantities—shaft rotation, electrical voltage, and so on—are physical analogues of the problem under consideration, and the use of analog machines to simulate the behavior of actual equipment can be an important engineering tool. In addition to serving as simulators of actual physical situations such as electrical power networks, analog machines are used as equation solvers. One type of analog machine was both easily portable and in common use—the slide rule—but was replaced by electronic calculators in the 1970's. Another type, the differential ana-

lyzer, was developed to provide solutions for differential equations through a process of successive integration in a closed-loop configuration. Early mechanical differential analyzers were extremely large, composed of many different parts, and often weighed thousands of tons. In addition, these early analyzers required several days of setup before a problem or series of problems could be run.

Calculating devices are as old as humanity, but most have relied on treating variables as being counted as discrete entities. The abacus and its modern counterpart, the digital computer, both embody this assumption of counting discrete units; the analog computer does not. Instead, the analog computer measures variables along a continuous range of values in much the same way that a thermometer can measure temperature at any point or an odometer measures miles. Further, whereas digital calculators have an ancestry reaching back to antiquity, analog computers are a comparatively recent development. Because digital computers are based on counting, simple machines to aid humanity in establishing the presence or absence of discrete units were developed in a variety of places and cultures. The abacus dates from at least five thousand years ago and is still used in many countries. In 1642, Blaise Pascal, the noted French philosopher-scientist, constructed a calculating machine to assist him in computing business accounts. A few years later, a German mathematician, Gottfried Wilhelm Leibniz, built a machine that he called a "stepped reckoner."

Not until 1820, however, did a reliable calculating machine capable of addition, subtraction, multiplication, and division become commercially available. It was not until 1835, when Charles Babbage designed his "Analytical Engine," that a computer in the modern sense appeared, at least on paper. Had it been built, it would have been the first digital computer to incorporate the principles of sequential control.

The first mechanical analog computers also appeared in the nineteenth century. Baron Kelvin (Sir William Thomson, known as Lord Kelvin), an English physicist, attempted to build one of the earliest known analog computers in 1872 to serve as a tide predictor. The first modern working analog computer, however, was designed and built by a team headed by Vannevar Bush at the Massachusetts Institute of Technology (MIT) in the late 1920's. The machine was a forerunner of the specialized type of analog computers known as differential analyzers and was designed to solve a specific form of differential equation. When completed in 1928, the device could perform eighteen different functions.

When Bush joined the MIT faculty in 1919, his research focused on electrical power transmission. Calculating precisely the distribution of power within a network entailed solving large problems of simultaneous linear equations. This was a difficult and time-consuming procedure because the calculations frequently involved differential equations that were particularly intractable. Lord Kelvin had attempted to build a machine to solve such equations almost fifty years earlier but had been unsuccessful in going beyond second-order differential equations. Lord Kelvin showed that coupling together two of the integrators described by James Clerk Maxwell in the 1873 paper "Treatise on Electricity and Magnetism" would work to solve for second-order derivatives. In principle, Lord Kelvin also contended that combining Maxwell's integrators in various configurations also should allow solutions for higher-order differential equations to be found. Simple integrators, such as the one described by Maxwell, have become common in a variety of settings. Perhaps the most familiar example is household electrical meters, which measure current and voltage and integrate their product, power or kilowatts, with respect to time.

When Bush began working on a differential analyzer, he used an electrical meter as the core of the machine. Working under Bush's supervision, a graduate student completed the first simple computer, a continuous

Vannevar Bush. (Library of Congress)

integraph, in 1926. It was constructed to evaluate integrals that contained a product but was limited to the solution of first-order differentials. Having obtained both accurate and useful results from the continuous integraph, Bush and his students added a second integrating unit to the first computer. They discovered, however, that they could not use another electrical meter. Bush turned to the Kelvin device as a possible solution, as the rotation of the meter appeared ideally suited to rotate the disk of a mechanical integrator. Unfortunately, as soon as a load was placed on the moving parts of the machine, its accuracy dropped. Connecting the two integrators with a servomotor solved the problem, and a Kelvin device capable of solving for second-order derivatives became a reality. It still had limitations, however: It could not solve higher-order differential equations or systems of simultaneous differential equations. Bush decided to try to build a true differential analyzer, a machine that would connect integrator after integrator.

When he attempted to build the larger machine, Bush discovered that the servomotor provided only a partial solution. It proved difficult to set properly and oscillated

1928

wildly at times when transmitting large magnifications of turning force, or torque. In 1927, a new device appeared: the torque amplifier. Use of torque amplifiers meant there was no longer a limit to the number of integrators that could be interconnected and a true differential analyzer could be built. The first had six integrators and could be used to solve most of the differential equations engineers were likely to encounter, including systems of two or three simultaneous second-order equations.

The increase in scale and the addition of torque amplifiers required that a large room be used to house the differential analyzer with its complex mass of interconnected metal axles, gears, disks, handles, and electric motors. The six integrators consisted of glass disks on movable tables. One set of measurements determined the movement of the table, another determined the rotation of the disk, and a metal wheel on the glass disk measured a third variable by its distance from the disk. The torque amplifiers controlled all of this by permitting the wheels and shafts running the differential analyzer to move easily without slippage. In an analog computer, the physical movement of parts performs the actual computation, so all parts must move precisely. A collection of shafts and straps connected to servomotors through the torque amplifiers moved the integrators, but the differential analyzer itself was purely mechanical. Electricity was used only for powering the amplifiers, the shafts, and the printers.

SIGNIFICANCE

The differential analyzer was the first serious attempt to build a computer for use by scientists. When Bush described the differential analyzer in a paper published in 1931, other scientists and engineers immediately began to build similar machines. The differential analyzer quickly found a variety of applications in civilian and military settings, as it could be used both to simulate complex systems, such as electrical power grids, and to solve the difficult equations posed by ballistics problems.

As political conditions in Europe and the Far East deteriorated during the 1930's, the U.S. War Department became involved increasingly in both computer research and the use of computers. The U.S. Navy was particularly interested in applying the differential analyzer to solving ballistics problems and funded such research actively. This research support soon was extended to include work on digital computers, and mathematicians such as Grace Hopper, who later became known as the

inventor of COBOL, were recruited to work as programmers on these projects.

In addition to spin-offs such as an increased interest in digital computers, the successful development of an analog computer meant that scientists and engineers could perform simulations of complex technical systems at a considerable savings over the expense of actual tests of those systems. The analog computer proved to be an invaluable tool in the development of aircraft, guided missiles, automobiles, and the like. By using simulator studies, researchers could obtain large databases before trial flights or test drives commenced, and those studies also could suggest how a limited number of physical trials could be most efficiently utilized. The development of the analog computer corresponded to a number of other significant developments within the history of technology, such as research in nuclear power and the development of jet aircraft, and contributed significantly to them.

It would have been impossible to build actual working prototypes of some large technological systems, such as nuclear power plants, and to construct preliminary design models for jet aircraft, which would be prohibitively expensive if done for every proposed design change or modification. Analog computers allowed engineers and scientists to progress in the development of new technological devices and systems more economically and more quickly than they could have otherwise.

Bush's successful work with the differential analyzer may have helped to shape future science policy in the United States. Although his own research interests moved away from analog computing in the 1930's, the interest the differential analyzer aroused in the scientific community contributed to Bush's personal influence and success. As chairman of the National Research Committee and director of the Office of Scientific Research and Development during World War II, Bush helped to forge connections among the federal government, universities, and private industry that led to the priorities that were set for basic research in the physical sciences for generations. Bush's personal influence on the American scientific community will persist long after the mechanical differential analyzer has been relegated to the status of a historical curiosity.

—*Nancy Farm Mannikko*

FURTHER READING

Ashurst, F. Gareth. *Pioneers of Computing*. London: Frederick Muller, 1983. Explains differences between digital and analog computers in addition to providing biographies of John Napier, Pascal, and others.

Campbell-Kelly, Martin, and William Aspray. *Computer: A History of the Information Machine*. 2d ed. Boulder, Colo.: Westview Press, 2004. Comprehensive history begins with the work of mathematicians in the nineteenth century and covers developments through the beginning of the twenty-first century. Includes notes, bibliography, and index.

Hartley, M. G. *An Introduction to Electronic Analogue Computers*. New York: John Wiley & Sons, 1962. Provides a brief history of computers and explains the difference between analog and digital computers.

Heyn, Ernest V. *A Century of Wonders: One Hundred Years of Popular Science*. Garden City, N.Y.: Doubleday, 1972. Presents easy-to-understand explanations of the evolution of a variety of technologies, including electronic computers. Excellent illustrations.

Shurkin, Joel. *Engines of the Mind: The Evolution of the Computer from Mainframes to Microprocessors*. Updated ed. New York: W. W. Norton, 1996. General history of computers attempts to explain priority disputes without taking sides. Focuses more on the social history of computer development and the personalities of the persons involved than on the technical aspects of computing.

Williams, Raymond Wilson. *Analogue Computation: Techniques and Components*. New York: Academic Press, 1961. Provides background in both the history and theory of analog computers.

SEE ALSO: Feb., 1924: IBM Changes Its Name and Product Line; 1935-1936: Turing Invents the Universal Turing Machine.

1928
SMITH-HOOVER CAMPAIGN

A presidential election marked the emergence of northeastern, urban, first-generation Americans in a powerful new Democratic Party.

LOCALE: United States
CATEGORY: Government and politics

KEY FIGURES
Alfred E. Smith (1873-1944), Democratic presidential candidate in 1928
Herbert Hoover (1874-1964), Republican presidential candidate in 1928
H. L. Mencken (1880-1956), literary critic and satirist of American mores during the 1920's
James Cannon (1864-1944), influential bishop in the Methodist Episcopal Church South and defender of Prohibition
John Jakob Raskob (1879-1950), wealthy industrialist and campaign manager for Alfred E. Smith
Franklin D. Roosevelt (1882-1945), Democratic candidate for governor of New York in 1928 and president of the United States, 1933-1945

SUMMARY OF EVENT
During the 1920's, the United States became an urban nation. The Bureau of the Census reported that for the first time in the nation's history, most of the population resided in areas defined as urban. Statistics cannot convey the disruption that took place as the nation shifted on its cultural axis, however. There was nothing quiet or secret about this "revolt from the village."

Indeed, some of the major literary figures of the period took delight in emphasizing how out of touch with the realities of an increasingly urban nation the rural United States was becoming. Critics such as H. L. Mencken, editor of the *American Mercury*, assailed Puritanism and haughtily proclaimed the superiority of the city dwellers over the "hicks" and the fundamentalists. *The New Yorker* magazine was founded in 1925 as a weekly periodical for urban sophisticates. On the other side, rural voices cried out against the evil influences of the city. From rural newspapers and from conservative, fundamentalist religious leaders—such as Methodist bishop James Cannon, Jr., of Virginia—came warnings about the decadence of urban life. To many, the city offered a challenge to Anglo-Saxon dominance in U.S. affairs.

In 1928, these tensions permeated the presidential campaign, primarily because the Democratic candidate, Alfred E. Smith, personified the new urban forces. Al Smith had spent his entire life within the shadow of New York City's skyscrapers. Although he quit school at the age of fifteen, he became a powerful and vigorous leader because of his abilities and hard work. He was elected governor of New York four times, and in 1928 he was nominated by the Democrats to run for the presidency. In the eyes of his followers, Smith was the urban version of

1928

Alfred E. Smith waves to a crowd during his presidential campaign tour. (AP/Wide World Photos)

Abraham Lincoln; he represented the fulfillment of the American Dream. The son of an immigrant was aspiring to the highest office in the land. With his derby hat, his big cigar, his opposition to Prohibition, and his devotion to Roman Catholicism, Smith jauntily and proudly bore his urban label.

The career of Herbert Hoover, the Republican candidate, also resembled a Horatio Alger story. Hoover was born in a small town in Iowa. Initially projected into national prominence through his work as food administrator during World War I and later as a leader of postwar relief work in Europe, he served during the 1920's as secretary of commerce under two U.S. presidents, Warren G. Harding and Calvin Coolidge. When Coolidge uttered his cryptic statement about choosing not to run in 1928, Hoover was the most outstanding figure in the Republican Party, and he easily captured the nomination.

Because the substantive issues that might have distinguished the two candidates on rational grounds became blurred, the campaign soon began to focus on emotional factors. Smith's anti-Prohibition stand and his religion, both of which gained support for him in urban areas of the Northeast, were bitterly criticized in the West and

South. To some, such as Kansas editor William Allen White, Smith's candidacy presented a threat to the long-established political forces dominant in the United States.

Undue emphasis, however, should not be given to Smith's political disadvantages. Probably more decisive in the campaign were Hoover's advantages. The Republican candidate had a distinguished record in public service and was able to project the image of efficiency and industry. Furthermore, he had the overwhelming advantage of Republican prosperity behind him. Although many farmers were suffering financially in 1928, Smith failed to garner the farm vote. The election count gave Hoover twenty-one million popular and 444 electoral votes. Smith won fifteen million popular votes and only 87 electoral votes. The total popular vote in 1928 was much higher than in 1924. Smith made substantial gains in the nation's large urban centers. This "revolt of the cities" was important in the development of a Democratic majority in 1932.

SIGNIFICANCE

As the campaign of 1928 unfolded, a number of vexing problems faced a seemingly prosperous nation. American farmers had been suffering from unfavorable profit margins since 1921. The nation's policy toward Latin America had generated considerable antagonism south of the border. The excessive speculation on Wall Street was gradually becoming a source of increasing concern. Some Democrats held that Smith, who had a progressive record as governor of New York, should attack the farm program of the Republicans and promise more positive federal action in general. The more conservative elements warned that radicalism during a period of prosperity would cause the average voter to turn away from the Democratic Party. Smith decided to adopt a cautious platform. Symbolic of this decision was the appointment of John Jackob Raskob, a General Motors executive, as Democratic campaign manager.

Immediately after the election, many Catholics and Democrats complained that Smith had been the victim of a bigoted whispering campaign. Violent anti-Catholicism was exhibited in the election. In retrospect, however, factors other than religion clearly estranged many voters. Smith was a capable statesman and a spokesman for the northeastern urban areas, but for a majority of the voters he was not an acceptable national symbol. His most significant contribution in 1928 was to arouse the latent political potential of many first-generation Americans in eastern cities. It remained for Franklin D. Roosevelt to combine this element with a disenchanted farm vote—in addition to the discontent engendered by the Depression—to produce a winning Democratic coalition in 1932.

—George Q. Flynn and Michael Witkoski

FURTHER READING

Anderson, Kristi. *The Creation of a Democratic Majority, 1928-1936.* Chicago: University of Chicago Press, 1979. Examines how the election of 1928 was a turning point in American political life, one that transformed the Democratic Party into the majority party for almost half a century and had a lasting impact on the nation.

Finan, Christopher M. *Alfred E. Smith: The Happy Warrior.* New York: Hill & Wang, 2001. Although clearly

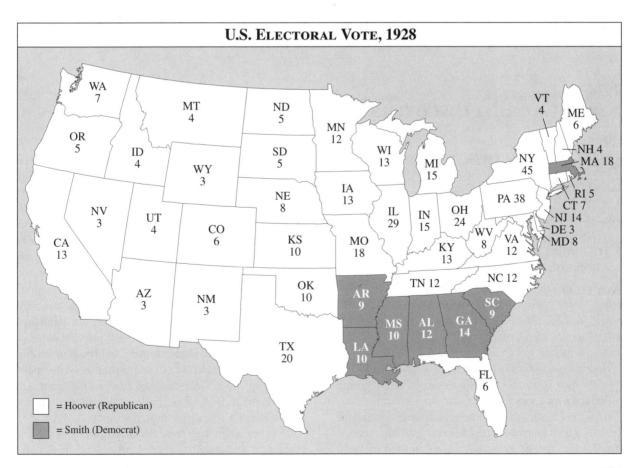

U.S. ELECTORAL VOTE, 1928

WA 7 · MT 4 · ND 5 · MN 12 · VT 4 · ME 6
OR 5 · ID 4 · SD 5 · WI 13 · MI 15 · NY 45 · NH 4 · MA 18
WY 3 · NE 8 · IA 13 · PA 38 · RI 5 · CT 7
NV 3 · UT 4 · CO 6 · IL 29 · IN 15 · OH 24 · NJ 14 · DE 3 · MD 8
CA 13 · KS 10 · MO 18 · WV 8 · VA 12
KY 13
AZ 3 · NM 3 · OK 10 · TN 12 · NC 12
TX 20 · AR 9 · SC 9
MS 10 · AL 12 · GA 14
LA 10 · FL 6

☐ = Hoover (Republican)
▧ = Smith (Democrat)

1928

2221

biased in Smith's favor, Finan's biography nonetheless provides a careful examination of the politician's career and Smith's subsequent absence from the pages of American history books.

Maisel, L. Sandy, ed. *Political Parties and Elections in the United States*. New York: Garland, 1991. An interesting and valuable review of the 1928 campaign and of the nature of Smith's candidacy. Reveals how the campaign, along with contemporary political trends, helped send the Democrats toward long-lasting victory in American electoral politics.

Reichley, A. James. *The Life of the Parties: A History of American Political Parties*. Lanham, Md.: Rowman & Littlefield, 2000. Helpful review of the role of the party machinery as it first comprehended and then articulated the public mood in the 1928 election. Asserts that Al Smith's candidacy was not an isolated phenomenon but a watershed event in American political history.

Schlesinger, Arthur M., Jr., ed. *1928-1940*. Vol. 7 in *History of American Presidential Elections*. New York: Chelsea House, 1985. The Democratic Party platform, Smith's speeches, and the relevant speeches and remarks of other figures of the time help make the

specific circumstances of the election alive and relevant for the reader.

Slayton, Robert A. *Empire Statesman: The Rise and Redemption of Al Smith*. New York: Free Press, 2001. This highly acclaimed biography provides a number of new and important details about Smith's life and delves into the difficult issue of determining what makes a "true" American.

Ward, Geoffrey C. *A First-Class Temperament: The Emergence of Franklin Roosevelt*. New York: Harper & Row, 1989. The relationship between two of the greatest Democratic politicians of the twentieth century was often stormy and ultimately tragic. This biography reveals how Smith's defeat in 1928 was, in many ways, essential for Roosevelt's victory in 1932 and the emergence of the New Deal as the shaping force in modern U.S. history.

SEE ALSO: Sept. 14, 1901: Theodore Roosevelt Becomes U.S. President; Nov. 5, 1912: Wilson Is Elected U.S. President; 1921-1923: Scandals of the Harding Administration; Nov. 4, 1924: Coolidge Is Elected U.S. President; Oct. 29, 1929-1939: Great Depression; Nov. 8, 1932: Franklin D. Roosevelt Is Elected U.S. President.

1928-1932
SZENT-GYÖRGYI DISCOVERS VITAMIN C

Albert Szent-Györgyi isolated "hexuronic acid" in England, and four years later, in Hungary, he and Joseph L. Svirbely proved that this substance was vitamin C.

LOCALE: Cambridge, England; Szeged, Hungary; Pittsburgh, Pennsylvania

CATEGORIES: Science and technology; biology; chemistry; health and medicine

KEY FIGURES

Albert Szent-Györgyi (1893-1986), Hungarian biochemist

Charles Glen King (1896-1988), American biochemist and nutritionist

Joseph L. Svirbely (b. 1906), American chemist

SUMMARY OF EVENT

Vitamin C is both a complex chemical substance and the physiological linchpin in the deficiency disease scurvy. Physicians in the Middle Ages had recognized some as-

pects of this disease, which was characterized by weakness, swollen joints, a tendency to bruise easily, bleeding from the gums, and the loss of teeth. It was not until the eighteenth century, however, that the Scottish physician James Lind recognized that these symptoms constitute a disorder caused by defective nutrition. His experiments on sailors during long ocean voyages showed that the ingestion of certain fruits and vegetables could cure the disease.

The most significant step toward the discovery of vitamin C was made in 1907, when Axel Holst, a bacteriologist, and Theodor Frölich, a pediatrician, published their discovery that, through dietary manipulations, a disease analogous to human scurvy could be generated in guinea pigs. (Like humans and unlike most animals, guinea pigs do not manufacture their own vitamin C.) When Holst and Frölich fed hay and oats (foods deficient in vitamin C) to guinea pigs, the animals developed scurvy, but when they were fed fresh fruits and vegetables, they remained healthy. In this way, Holst and

Frölich were able to measure a food's ability to prevent scurvy.

While other scientists were trying to isolate vitamin C directly, Albert Szent-Györgyi actually found the substance in the course of searching for something else. In the 1920's, his research centered on biological oxidation, that is, on how cells oxidize various foodstuffs. He was particularly entranced by the observation that some plants (apples and potatoes) turn brown after being cut and exposed to air, whereas others (oranges and lemons) experience no color change.

Szent-Györgyi suspected that a certain substance was controlling these color-change reactions, and he looked for it not only in fruits and vegetables but also in the adrenal cortex of mammals. He believed that the color change to a bronzelike skin in patients with Addison's disease (a disorder of the adrenal gland) was associated somehow with the color changes in plants. He hoped to isolate this substance, a powerful reducing agent, from the adrenal glands.

Unfortunately, his research was plagued with problems until he met the English biochemist Frederick Hopkins at a conference in Sweden in 1926. Hopkins was interested in vitamins and biological oxidation, and he invited Szent-Györgyi to the University of Cambridge to continue his research. Using many glands from oxen, Szent-Györgyi was able to separate a reducing agent from all other substances present. He also was able to obtain the same substance from orange juice and cabbage extracts, a result that his colleagues found most surprising.

Through chemical analysis, Szent-Györgyi determined that the substance contained six carbon atoms and eight hydrogen atoms and that it was a carbohydrate related to the sugars. He initially wanted to name the substance "Ignose" (from the Latin *ignosco*, meaning "I don't know," and *ose*, the designating suffix for sugars). The editor of the *Biochemical Journal* thought that the name was too flippant, however, whereupon Szent-Györgyi suggested "Godnose," which was similarly rejected. Because the substance contained six carbon atoms and was acidic, he and his editor agreed on the name "hexuronic acid." News of the discovery of this acid was published in 1928.

At the time, scientists recognized five distinct vitamins. They had failed, however, to isolate any of them successfully. For this reason, it was not clear that Szent-Györgyi's hexuronic acid and vitamin C were the same substance.

In the fall of 1931, Joseph L. Svirbely, a postdoctoral

Albert Szent-Györgyi. (The Nobel Foundation)

1928

student, arrived at Szeged, Hungary, where Szent-Györgyi had gone to continue his studies of vitamin C. Svirbely had done his doctoral studies on vitamin C under Charles Glen King at the University of Pennsylvania. King was trying, with limited success, to isolate vitamin C from lemon juice. He was testing his results with time-consuming experiments using animals.

Svirbely provided a bridge between King's work and Szent-Györgyi's. Szent-Györgyi had not previously tried to prove that hexuronic acid was identical to vitamin C because he did not enjoy working with animals. Furthermore, he was against vitamin research (he once said that vitamins were problems for the chef, not the scientist).

Nevertheless, when Svirbely mentioned that he could tell if something contained vitamin C or not, Szent-Györgyi gave him some of his hexuronic acid for experimentation. In a fifty-six-day test using guinea pigs, Svirbely established, in the fall of 1931, that the animals without hexuronic acid in their diets died with symptoms of scurvy, whereas the animals receiving hexuronic acid were healthy and free from scurvy. Further experiments in 1931-1932 proved once and for all that hexuronic acid and vitamin C are identical.

SIGNIFICANCE

The isolation of vitamin C generated widespread comment and convinced most scientists that the long-sought vitamin had been found. Vitamin C's impact was deepened and extended by Szent-Györgyi's discovery in 1933 that Hungarian red peppers contained large amounts of the vitamin. Whereas previously biochemists could make only minuscule amounts of the material with great difficulty, Szent-Györgyi now could produce the substance in great quantities. In his lectures about his work, he liked to hold up a bottle containing several kilograms of the vitamin. To scientists accustomed to thinking of vitamins solely in extremely minute amounts, this was a surprising and enlightening experience.

In the 1930's, the League of Nations set up a committee to establish international standards for the vitamin, and the committee recommended that individuals ingest at least 30 milligrams each day to prevent scurvy. The vitamin came to be known as "ascorbic acid" for its property of combating scurvy. In the period during and after World War II, some scientists suggested that dosages larger than the recommended 30 milligrams would help keep humans in the best possible health. Many people, convinced that modern food processing was destroying vitamins, began to supplement their diets with vitamin pills, and some industries began to fortify their products with vitamins.

Beginning in 1965, Nobel Prize-winning chemist Linus Pauling became interested in the megavitamin theory popularized by industrial chemist Irwin Stone in 1960. Pauling suggested that many maladies, from schizophrenia to cancer to the common cold, could be treated and prevented by large doses of vitamins. Pauling's books and articles created an ongoing controversy, guaranteeing that this fascinating substance, discovered through the efforts of Szent-Györgyi and others, will continue to provide subjects for rewarding scientific research well into the future.

—*Robert J. Paradowski*

FURTHER READING

Carpenter, Kenneth J. *The History of Scurvy and Vitamin C.* Cambridge, England: Cambridge University Press, 1986. The story of scurvy told by a professor of nutrition at the University of California, Berkeley. Makes occasional use of chemical formulas, but most of the discussions are accessible to the general reader. Illustrated with many photographs and line drawings.

Includes tables, extensive references, and detailed index.

_____. "A Short History of Nutritional Science: Part 3 (1912-1944)." *Journal of Nutrition* 133 (October, 2003): 3023-3032. Third part of a four-part series includes brief discussion of the discovery of vitamin C. Places Szent-Györgyi's work in the context of the history of nutritional science in general.

Friedrich, Wilhelm. *Vitamins.* New York: Walter de Gruyter, 1988. A systematic presentation of the historical, chemical, biological, and medical aspects of the most important vitamins. Valuable research tool for scientists as well as for students synthesizes a massive amount of material, as is particularly evident in the chapter on vitamin C. Concludes with literature supplement and extensive index.

Goldblith, Samuel A., and Maynard A. Joslyn, eds. *Milestones in Nutrition.* Westport, Conn.: AVI, 1964. Anthology of important papers in nutrition (part of a series), intended to "inspire and encourage" students to learn the chief ideas of food science through the foundational classics of the discipline. Ample section on vitamin C includes the principal papers of Szent-Györgyi, King, and others.

Leicester, Henry M. *Development of Biochemical Concepts from Ancient to Modern Times.* Cambridge, Mass.: Harvard University Press, 1974. History of biochemistry written by a biochemist with a strong interest in the history of science. Chapter on vitamins discusses the history of ascorbic acid. Includes endnotes and indexes.

Moss, Ralph W. *Free Radical: Albert Szent-Györgyi and the Battle over Vitamin C.* New York: Paragon House, 1988. Depicts Szent-Györgyi as a romantic scientist, ruled by intuition in his personal, political, and scientific lives. Takes Szent-Györgyi's side in the controversy with King over the discovery of vitamin C, and presents new information to bolster Szent-Györgyi's claim. Includes endnotes and index.

Packer, Lester, and Jürgen Fuchs, eds. *Vitamin C in Health and Disease.* New York: Marcel Dekker, 1997. Collection of scholarly papers begins with a chapter on the history of vitamin C. Includes index.

Pauling, Linus. *Vitamin C, the Common Cold, and the Flu.* San Francisco: W. H. Freeman, 1976. Updated version of *Vitamin C and the Common Cold* (1970), which was dedicated to Szent-Györgyi for his discovery of the vitamin. Argues that a proper understanding of previous research leads to the conclusion that most people would benefit from larger amounts of vitamin

C in their diets. Award-winning book, aimed at a general audience; initiated a controversy about the effectiveness of megadoses of vitamin C in preventing colds and alleviating their symptoms. Includes references and index.

Waugh, William A. "Unlocking Another Door to Nature's Secrets: Vitamin C." *Journal of Chemical Education* 11 (February, 1934): 69-72. A review of studies on the isolation and characterization of vitamin C

written by one of King's principal associates. Presents the story from King's point of view, but is objective in tone. Includes references.

SEE ALSO: 1901: Grijns Suggests the Cause of Beriberi; 1906: Hopkins Postulates the Presence of Vitamins; 1922: McCollum Names Vitamin D and Pioneers Its Use Against Rickets; 1924: Steenbock Discovers Sunlight Increases Vitamin D in Food.

January, 1928
PAPANICOLAOU DEVELOPS A TEST FOR DIAGNOSING UTERINE CANCER

George N. Papanicolaou developed a cytological technique called the Papanicolaou smear (Pap test) for diagnosing uterine cancer, the second most common type of fatal cancer in American woman.

LOCALE: Cornell Medical College, New York
CATEGORY: Health and medicine

KEY FIGURES
George N. Papanicolaou (1883-1962), Greek American physician and anatomist
Charles Stockard (1879-1939), American anatomist and chairman of Cornell Medical School's anatomy department
Herbert Traut (1894-1972), American gynecologist

SUMMARY OF EVENT
Cancer, first named by the Greek physician Hippocrates of Cos (c. 460-c. 370 B.C.E.), is one of the most painful and dreaded forms of human disease. It is known now to occur when body cells run wild and interfere with the normal activities of the body. The early diagnosis of cancer is extremely important because early detection often makes it possible to effect successful cures. The modern detection of cancer is usually done through the microscopic examination of the appearance of cells using the techniques of the area of biology called cytology.

Development of cancer cytology began in 1867, after L. S. Beale reported tumor cells in the saliva from a patient who was afflicted with cancer of the pharynx. Beale recommended the use in cancer detection of microscopic examination of cells shed or removed (exfoliated) from organs, including the digestive, urinary, and reproductive tracts. Soon, other scientists identified numerous

striking differences between normal cells from various tissues and cancers of those tissues. These differences include cell size and shape, the size of cell nuclei, and the complexity of cell nuclei.

Modern cytological detection of cancer evolved from the work of George N. Papanicolaou, a Greek physician who trained at the University of Athens Medical School. In 1913, he emigrated to the United States and began his American career as an assistant in the pathology department of New York Hospital. Papanicolaou entered the arena of cytological examination of cells when he began working, in 1917, with Charles Stockard at New York's Cornell Medical College. Stockard, chairman of the anatomy department, allowed Papanicolaou to study sex determination in guinea pigs. Papanicolaou's efforts required him to obtain ova at a precise period in their maturation cycle, a process that required an indicator of the time at which the animals ovulated. In search of this indicator, Papanicolaou designed a method that involved microscopic examination of the vaginal discharges from female guinea pigs. Initially, he sought traces of blood, such as those seen in the menstrual discharges of both primates and humans, but he found no blood in the guinea pig vaginal discharges. Instead, he saw temporal changes in the size and shape of the uterine cells shed in the discharges. The changes he noted recurred in a fifteen- to sixteen-day cycle. This cycle correlated well with associated changes of uterus and ovaries during the fifteen- to sixteen-day guinea pig menstrual cycle. The findings of Papanicolaou's research, published in 1917 in the *American Journal of Anatomy*, laid the basis for the study of the sexual cycle in laboratory animals. It also became a standard method for the identification of the effects of sex hormones in these animal species. Its use was instrumental in the first isolation of sex hormones (estrogens) by Edgar Allen and E. A. Doisy in 1923.

Papanicolaou next extended his efforts to the study of humans. His original intent was to identify whether comparable changes in the exfoliated cells of the human vagina occurred in women. His end goal was to gain an understanding of the human menstrual cycle similar to that he had obtained in the animal studies. In the course of this work, Papanicolaou observed distinctive abnormal cells in the vaginal fluid from a woman afflicted with cancer of the cervix. This led him to begin to attempt to develop a cytological method for the detection of uterine cancer, the second most common type of fatal cancer in American women of the time.

In 1928, Papanicolaou published his cytological method of cancer detection in the *Proceedings of the Third Race Betterment Conference*, held in Battle Creek, Michigan. The work was received well by the news media (for example, the January 5, 1928, *New York World* credited him with a "new cancer detection method"). Nevertheless, the publication—and others he produced over the next ten years—were not very interesting to gynecologists of the time. Rather, they preferred use of the standard methodology of uterine cancer diagnosis (cervical biopsy and curettage). As Papanicolaou said, "I failed to convince my colleagues of the practicability of the procedure." Consequently, in 1932, Papanicolaou turned his energy toward studying human reproductive endocrinology problems related to the effects of hormones on cells of the reproductive system. One example of this work was published in the *American Journal of Anatomy* (1933), where he described "the sexual cycle in the human female." Other such efforts resulted in better understanding of reproductive problems that include amenorrhea and menopause.

It was not until Papanicolaou's collaboration with gynecologist Herbert Traut (beginning in 1939), which led to the publication of *Diagnosis of Uterine Cancer by the Vaginal Smear* (1943), that clinical acceptance of the method began to develop. Their monograph documented an impressive, irrefutable group of studies of both normal and disease states that included nearly two hundred cases of cancer of the uterus. Soon, many other researchers began to confirm their findings; by 1948, the newly named American Cancer Society noted that the "Pap" smear seemed to be a very valuable tool for detecting vaginal cancer. Wide acceptance of the Pap test followed and, beginning in 1947, hundreds of physicians from all

over the world flocked to Papanicolaou's course on the subject. They learned his smear/diagnosis techniques and disseminated them around the world.

With widespread use of the Pap test came many honors for Dr. Papanicolaou. Some of them included the Cross of a Grand Commander of the Greek Royal Order of the Phoenix, the Lasker Award of the American Public Health Association, the Honor Medal of the American Cancer Society, the Bordon Award of the American Association of Medical Colleges, and the Amory Award of the American Association of Arts and Sciences. In time, Papanicolaou became one of the best-known members of the American medical profession.

At the end of 1961, he became the director of the Papanicolaou Cancer Research Institute in Miami, Florida. Unfortunately, he died shortly thereafter; however, he has not been forgotten: At the posthumous dedication of the Papanicolaou Cancer Research Institute, he was eulogized as "a giver of life—one of the elect men of earth who stand for eternity like solitary towers along the way to human betterment." This sentiment remains throughout the biomedical community.

SIGNIFICANCE

Many physicians have cited the Pap test as the most significant and useful modern discovery in the field of cancer research. One reason for its impact is that the test allows the identification of uterine cancer in a presymptomatic stage, long before any other methodology can be used. With such early diagnosis, the disease can be cured in more than 80 percent of all cases identified by Pap test. In addition, Pap testing allows the identification of cancer of the uterine cervix so early that its cure rate can be nearly 100 percent.

Another measure of the efficacy of the Pap test comes from actuarial examination of the consequences of its widespread utilization in routine cancer screening technique, beginning in the early 1950's. For example, several insurance companies reported that the 1951 death rate from uterine cancer of insured thirty-five- to forty-four-year-old women (160 per million) was halved by 1961 (80 per million). In contrast, the reduction in the death rate from cancer of all types was only about 11 percent in that time period.

Papanicolaou extended the use of the smear technique from examination of vaginal exudates to diagnosis of cancer in many other organs from which scrapings, washings, and exudates can be obtained. These tissues include the colon, the kidney, the bladder, the prostate, the lung, the breast, and the sinuses. In most cases, such examination of these tissues has made it possible to diagnose cancer much sooner than is possible by other existing methods. The smear method has thus become a keystone of cancer control in voluntary and required national health programs throughout the world.

The principal use of Pap testing has traditionally been in cancer screening. The test is utilized successfully in evaluation of the effectiveness of both cancer radiotherapy and cancer chemotherapy, and in the early detection of recurrence of cancer after surgery. Papanicolaou's 1928 prediction has come to pass: "A better understanding and more accurate analysis of the cancer problem is bound to result from use of this method. It is possible that analogous methods will be developed for the recognition of cancer in other organs."

—*Sanford S. Singer*

FURTHER READING

Berkow, Samuel G. "After Office Hours: A Visit with Dr. George N. Papanicolaou." *Obstetrics and Gynecology* 16 (1960): 248-252. Personal interview with Papanicolaou shows him both as a man and as a medical scientist. Provides insight into Papanicolaou's great contributions to endocrinology in general and to cancer research in particular. Describes the overall value of the Pap test.

Carmichael, D. Erskine. *The Pap Smear: Life of George N. Papanicolaou*. Springfield, Ill.: Charles C Thomas, 1973. Brief but thorough biography describes the life and career of Papanicolaou and chronicles his development as a man and as a scientist. Contains excellent documentation of his research efforts.

Papanicolaou, George N. "New Cancer Diagnosis." In *Proceedings of the Third Race Betterment Conference*. Battle Creek, Mich.: Race Betterment Foundation, 1928. Describes Papanicolaou's study of the existence of distinctive cells in the vaginal fluid of humans with cancer and describes a new method for diagnosing cancer of the genital tract. Suggests that a better understanding of the cancer problem will come from the use of this method.

_____. "The Sexual Cycle in the Human Female as Revealed by Vaginal Smear." *American Journal of Anatomy* 52 (1933): 519-637. Lengthy article presents a compendium of normal cytological changes seen in human vaginal discharges. Describes the use of the smear test to identify normal cytological changes in the human reproductive cycle. This report established human cytology on a firm basis.

Papanicolaou, George N., and Charles Stockard. "The Existence of a Typical Estrus Cycle in the Guinea Pig: With a Study of Its Histological and Physiological Changes." *American Journal of Anatomy* 22 (1917): 225-283. Describes a study of the vaginal fluid of guinea pigs and sets down the sequence of cytological patterns of shed cells occurring in fifteen- to sixteen-day cycles correlatable with changes in the reproductive system of the guinea pig. Establishes the technique used for the study of the sexual cycle in laboratory rodents.

Papanicolaou, George N., and Herbert F. Traut. *Diagnosis of Uterine Cancer by Vaginal Smear*. New York: Commonwealth Fund, 1943. Describes the exfoliate cytology of many normal and disease states, including the menstrual cycle, abortion, ectopic pregnancy, menopause, several vaginal and cervical infections, and cases of cancer of the uterus. This monograph was instrumental in clinicians' acceptance of the Pap test as a means for cancer diagnosis.

1928

SEE ALSO: 1910: Rous Discovers That Some Cancers Are Caused by Viruses; 1912-1914: Abel Develops the First Artificial Kidney; 1913: Salomon Develops Mammography; 1913: Schick Introduces a Test for Diphtheria; 1921: Tuberculosis Vaccine BCG Is Developed; 1923: Kahn Develops a Modified Syphilis Test; 1929-1938: Berger Studies the Human Electroencephalogram; July, 1929: Drinker and Shaw Develop a Mechanical Respirator.

March, 1928
MUSLIM BROTHERHOOD IS FOUNDED IN EGYPT

The Muslim Brotherhood was the first Islamist movement of the twentieth century, and its influence spread across the Arab world. The movement originated as a Muslim social service and educational movement, and it reflected the anticolonialism of midcentury Egypt. Its ideology survived and became a major component of the later global jihad movement.

ALSO KNOWN AS: Society of the Muslim Brothers
LOCALE: Ismailia, Egypt
CATEGORIES: Organizations and institutions; religion, theology, and ethics; colonialism and occupation

KEY FIGURES

Ḥasan al-Bannā' (1906-1949), Egyptian schoolteacher and intellectual who founded the Muslim Brotherhood

Farouk I (1920-1965), son of Fu'ād I and king of Egypt, r. 1936-1952

Gamal Abdel Nasser (1918-1970), prime minister of Egypt, 1954-1956, and president of Egypt, 1956-1970

Sayyid Quṭb (1906-1966), Egyptian educator and Islamist theoretician, dominant figure in the Brotherhood after Ḥasan al-Bannā''s death

Ismāʿīl Ṣidqi (1875-1950), prime minister of Egypt, 1930-1933, 1946

Maḥmūd Fahmī al-Nuqrāshī (1888-1948), prime minister of Egypt, 1945-1946, 1946-1948

SUMMARY OF EVENT

The Muslim Brotherhood was founded in 1928 by an Egyptian schoolteacher named Ḥasan al-Bannā', who was motivated by a sense of disarray in the Muslim world: He saw the dissolution of the caliphate in 1923 by Turkey's secular reformer Atatürk and the occupation of the Islamic heartlands by France and Britain as disastrous events. Stressing anti-imperialism and Islamic renewal, Ḥasan al-Bannā' and six followers, employees of the Suez Canal Company, founded the Society of the Muslim Brothers in Ismailia, a commercial city on the canal and the epicenter of British occupation and foreign influence. Taking an old house as headquarters, the Brotherhood then raised money to build mosques and schools. Early on, the Brothers focused on service facilities, schools, workshops, and mosques that served their lower-middle-class base. The organizational pattern that developed at Ismailia spread to other centers throughout the country.

In 1932, Ḥasan al-Bannā' moved the Brotherhood's headquarters to Cairo. He used the organization's charitable and service activities to recruit from a variety of social groups, including civil servants, students, urban laborers, and rural peasants. At first, he stayed aloof from politics, rejecting an offer of government aid from Prime Minister Ismāʿīl Ṣidqi in exchange for Ḥasan al-Bannā''s help in countering the influence of the nationalist Wafd Party. In 1933, the Brotherhood held its first general conference and established a weekly magazine as a vehicle for Ḥasan al-Bannā''s writings. The Brotherhood offered the idea of Islamic modernity as an alternative to European modernity, arguing that Islam is a complete blend of society, state, culture, and religion. Ḥasan al-Bannā''s solution to the political problems that beset Muslims at the time was an Islamic state ruled by a caliph and the implementation of Islamic law (sharia).

The Brothers' ideology had three core features: a sense of Islam as a total system complete unto itself, one that did not need Western values; a sense of Islam based on the original texts, the Qur'ān and the Hadith; and an understanding of Islam's universality, which made it applicable to all times and places. Ḥasan al-Bannā' distinguished between Westernization and modernization, however. Modern science, technology, even certain political ideas could be accepted if they were separated from corrupting Western values. Ḥasan al-Bannā' also believed that Islam had been heavily corrupted by Western values and ideologies and was in need of violent redemption. Unlike mainstream scholars, he did not hesitate to characterize as hypocrites those Muslims who professed Islam but did not adhere to its principles. He called for a purge in the ranks of Muslims in advance of a global battle against Christians and Jews. In fact, he was among the first to introduce a corrosive hatred of the Jews into modern Islamic discourse. He saw both Jews and Christians as peoples who sought to pollute Muslim values and beliefs.

In 1936, the Brotherhood became openly political. That year, Ḥasan al-Bannā' addressed a letter to Egypt's newly crowned King Farouk I, urging the king to lend his support to the Brotherhood's anti-imperialist and pro-Islamic political agenda. The Brothers were especially notable for their support of the Arab revolt in Palestine (1936-1939). While most Egyptian political organizations stayed away from this issue, the Brothers raised money and sent organizers to help the Palestinians in their struggle against Jewish settlement and British occupation. Ḥasan al-Bannāʾ appealed to King Farouk for government help in this endeavor, and the Brotherhood's support for the Arab revolt renewed the association between Islam and social justice, one that earned moral capital and would later pay dividends for the Brotherhood.

By the time World War II began, the Brotherhood had become thoroughly politicized, taking the lead in anti-British and anti-Jewish protests. Ḥasan al-Bannāʾ openly courted King Farouk's entourage and was granted an audience, and by the interwar period, the Brotherhood had become a powerful source of opposition to the left-leaning, proindependence Wafd Party, and Farouk's government found the Brothers increasingly useful in deflecting the Wafd's influence. In 1946, King Farouk consulted Ḥasan al-Bannāʾ before reappointing Ismāʿīl Ṣidqi as prime minister. As he had done in the 1930's, Ṣidqi courted the Brothers as an instrument to use against the nationalist Wafds and the Communists. This time, however, Ḥasan al-Bannāʾ accepted government financial support in exchange for his political influence.

By the late 1940's, Farouk was using the Brotherhood as a counterweight to the rising power of the secular nationalists. Politics proved a dangerous arena in the volatile postwar years, however; this period saw the Israeli declaration of independence and the humiliating First Palestine War as well as the steady rise in influence of Egypt's secular nationalists. From 1947 through 1949, violence shook the Egyptian regime, much of which was perpetrated by the Brotherhood through their secret military wing called the Specialists. After the murder of the Cairo police chief (an attack allegedly carried out by a Brother), Prime Minister Maḥmūd Fahmī al-Nuqrāshī dissolved and disbanded the Brotherhood in June of 1948. When Nuqrāshī was himself assassinated a few months later, again reportedly by a Brother, the government took more definitive action; Ḥasan al-Bannāʾ was murdered by suspected palace agents in February of 1949.

After the overthrow of King Farouk by the 1952 secular-nationalist Egyptian Revolution and the subsequent rise to power of Gamal Abdel Nasser, the Brotherhood offered to support the new, independent government. At first the Brothers embraced Nasser's movement because of its stance against imperialism and Zionism and its promise of Egyptian renewal. However, Nasser and the Brothers were divided over issues like secularism (as opposed to an Islamic state) and nationalism (as opposed to the caliphal ideal). Nasser found the Brothers' narrow vision of Islam threatening to his pluralist policies and saw their populist mass organization as a possible rival for power. After an attempt on Nasser's life in 1954 was blamed on the Brothers, the Nasser regime had the excuse it needed to crush the Brotherhood. Many of the organization's leaders were arrested, and some were hanged. The Brotherhood went into eclipse until the 1970's.

SIGNIFICANCE

The significance of the Muslim Brotherhood lies in the affiliated organizations that sprang up in neighboring Arab countries, in the teachings of its influential spokesman of the post-Ḥasan al-Bannāʾ period, Sayyid Quṭb, as well as in its role in contemporary Egyptian society. Branches of the Brotherhood sprang up in Lebanon (1936), Syria (1937), and Palestine (1946). They were founded by students from these countries who had studied and worked with the Brothers in Egypt. After these branches were formed, the Brotherhood tried to play the role of an international organization whose international representatives met in Cairo.

The society's international appeal was enhanced by the radical writings of educator and theoretician Sayyid Quṭb, who joined the Brotherhood in 1951 after returning from the United States, where he had completed a masters degree in education. Arrested in Nasser's 1954 crackdown, Quṭb wrote two major works while in prison (from 1954 to 1965) that laid out the principles of the modern Islamist agenda, including rejection of "Zionist" and "Crusader" values and subversions, denunciation of Arab "hypocrite" regimes, and glorification of the cult of martyrdom. Released from prison briefly in 1965, then rearrested and hanged the following year, Quṭb became the greatest single ideological influence on the contemporary Islamist movement. However, although Quṭb's teachings went on to animate the global jihad movement, the Muslim Brotherhood generally represented a more moderate Islamist strain. The Brotherhood became Egypt's largest political opposition group, and the organization clung to its service and charitable functions, while expanding its political base and its influence in civil society and retaining its emphasis on the imposition of Islamic law.

—*Stephen A. Harmon*

FURTHER READING

Berman, Paul. *Terror and Liberalism.* New York: W. W. Norton, 2003. Gives one of the best accounts in English of the life and teachings of Sayyid Quṭb.

Campagna, Joel. "From Accommodation to Confrontation: The Muslim Brotherhood in the Mubarak Years. *Journal of International Affairs* 50, no. 1 (1996): 278-304. Very good depiction of the contemporary Brotherhood and its role in politics and civil society.

Esposito, John L. *The Islamic Threat: Myth or Reality?* New York: Oxford University Press, 1993. Gives an extensive account of the origins and ideology of the Brotherhood, including its nineteenth century antecedents and influences.

Kepel, Gilles. *Jihad: The Trail of Political Islam.* Cambridge, Mass.: Harvard University Press, 2002. Particularly strong on the ideological formation of the Brotherhood and on its organizational structure and base.

_____. *Muslim Extremism in Egypt: Prophet and Pharaoh.* 1993. Reprint. Los Angeles: University of California Press, 2003. An excellent account of the long and complex relationship between the Brotherhood and various Egyptian governments.

Mitchell, Richard P. *The Society of the Muslim Brothers.* 1963. Reprint. New York: Oxford University Press, 1993. The best single-volume treatment of the origins and history of the Brotherhood up to the Nasser era. Relies heavily on the writings of Ḥasan al-Bannāʾ as well as on British and Egyptian archival sources.

Walsh, John. "Egypt's Muslim Brotherhood: Understanding Centrist Islam." *Harvard International Review* 24, no. 4 (2003): 32-36. Provides a good comparison of the Brotherhood's contemporary ideology with the agendas of more radical Islamists.

SEE ALSO: 1912-1929: Wahhābīism Strengthens in Saudi Arabia; May-Nov., 1920: Great Iraqi Revolt; July 24, 1922: League of Nations Establishes Mandate for Palestine; Aug. 11-13, 1933: Iraqi Army Slaughters Assyrian Christians; Apr. 15, 1936-1939: Great Uprising of Arabs in Palestine; May 26, 1937: Egypt Joins the League of Nations.

March 19, 1928
AMOS 'N' ANDY RADIO SHOW GOES ON THE AIR

Amos 'n' Andy, a pioneering radio network comedy show, greatly influenced the direction of national commercial radio and became a controversial yet integral part of American popular culture.

LOCALE: Chicago, Illinois
CATEGORIES: Radio and television; entertainment

KEY FIGURES
Charles Correll (1890-1972), American radio writer and actor
Freeman Fisher Gosden (1899-1982), American radio writer and actor
Walter White (1893-1955), executive secretary of the National Association for the Advancement of Colored People

SUMMARY OF EVENT
At ten o'clock on the evening of March 19, 1928, radio station WMAQ, broadcasting from its studio in Chicago's Merchandise Mart, aired the first episode of the *Amos 'n' Andy* comedy series, primarily for Chicago-area listeners but also for a number of smaller stations elsewhere by means of recordings. The show immediately proved to be successful and was quickly bought by the National Broadcasting Company's (NBC) Blue Network. NBC began broadcasting the show nationwide beginning on August 19, 1929. Thereafter, *Amos 'n' Andy*

was destined to become a radio legend.

The program's share of the radio audience has probably never been equaled by any other serial broadcast. It became a national mania. Estimates made between 1931 and 1932 placed the fifteen-minute show's audience at forty million, or one-third of the American population. Officials of all ranks, including presidents, made it known that they were listeners, work schedules were altered so that employers and their employees could tune in, and national conventions and local gatherings alike characteristically interrupted their proceedings so that followers among the attendees would not miss a single episode. Although the show's character and content increasingly provoked racial controversy, especially after the television adaptation began airing in 1951, its audience appeal was nearly universal, cutting across political, regional, social, ethnic, and color lines. By the time *Amos 'n' Andy* left the air on November 20, 1960, after 4,090 broadcasts, it had become an integral part of American popular culture as well as an abiding reminder of unresolved conflicts in national life.

Amos 'n' Andy was the creation of Freeman Fisher Gosden and Charles Correll. They not only conceived the comedy but also through most of the show's history wrote each of its scripts themselves and, unrehearsed, furnished the voices of its principal characters. Both men had southern backgrounds. Gosden was born in Richmond, Virginia, the son of a man who had served with the famed Confederate raider Colonel John Singleton Mosby. He was reared with African Americans as members of his household. Correll, although born the son of a skilled stonemason and construction foreman in Peoria, Illinois, also shared a strong southern heritage through his maternal grandmother. Both men pursued careers as performers, chiefly in minstrel shows and blackface comedy—entertainment traditions that predated the Civil War—before and after joining Joe Bren's Chicago theatrical company, where they met. Gosden and Correll's southern antecedents and their blackface comedy careers were vital to the creation of *Amos 'n' Andy*, for its featured characters, as well as nearly all others, were black.

Amos 'n' Andy sprang from an earlier comedy broadcast, *Sam 'n' Henry*, that also was the brainchild of Gosden and Correll. Aired initially on January 12, 1926, by the *Chicago Tribune*'s station, WGN, *Sam 'n' Henry* was radio's first serialized situation comedy. Its name derived from its two main characters, two African Americans who left Birmingham, Alabama, for Chicago. Like millions of real black migrants, they had joined what historians have since labeled the Great Migration to northern cities that began in the 1920's, seeking opportunity denied them in the South. Because WGN owned *Sam 'n' Henry*, Gosden and Correll were obliged to change the show's name to *Amos 'n' Andy* when, after 586 episodes of *Sam 'n' Henry*, their services were purchased by station WMAQ and NBC in 1928. Other changes were minor. Instead of having left Birmingham, for example, Amos Jones and Andy Brown had left Atlanta for Chicago's increasingly black, and generally poor, South Side.

Although their speech was identifiably a southern black dialect, replete with mispronunciations and other linguistic distortions, the characters of the *Amos 'n' Andy* show depended less for appeal on their blackness—and the humor attending their speech—than they did on their manifest humanity. Amos was recognizably a decent, hardworking, amiable, and lovable, if uneducated, poor man surviving in a depression-ridden and altogether strange urban

environment, thus resembling millions of his fellow Americans of all colors. Ostensibly more intelligent than Amos, Andy was pretentious, pompous, lazy, equally uneducated, and invariably engaged in using and abusing his long-suffering companion as the two tried their hands at enterprise, running their shoestring Fresh-Air Taxicab Company. In dramatic contrast to this pair, the real villain (such as anyone was) was the Kingfish (George Stevens), who slyly and crookedly presided over a fraternal lodge known as the Mystic Knights of the Sea and continually sought to exploit everyone.

The show's characters, in short, were not intended overtly to be racially demeaning. Rather, they reflected Gosden and Correll's prior show business experience with and mastery of a plausible black dialect. Otherwise, their characters and story lines could equally well have been applied (as they were by other writers and performers) to immigrant Poles, Italians, or Germans, or for that matter to any befuddled and unlettered country bumpkins. Similar stories and characters were common in earlier American comedy and vaudeville productions and in other comedy shows during the early days of radio. Gosden and Correll's version put the elements together in a way the public particularly enjoyed, and after two decades of effectively uncontroverted success, *Amos 'n' Andy* became a part of national folklore and an identifiable contribution to American culture.

1928

Charles Correll (left) and Freeman Fisher Gosden perform in blackface makeup as their popular characters Amos and Andy. (Hulton Archive/Getty Images)

SIGNIFICANCE

Amid the initial chaos of radio's early development, with more than six hundred stations vying for both audiences and sponsors, and without guidelines or precedents to indicate to broadcasters what either group wanted, the *Amos 'n' Andy* show was, in many significant ways, a pioneering experiment. As much as any other single nontechnical factor, the show was responsible for the explosive success of commercial radio. The broad human appeal of Amos, Andy, and Gosden and Correll's other characters, along with the common denominator of the easily understood troubles they encountered, drew audiences of unimagined magnitude. Sponsors previously had been reluctant to trust the repute of their products to the relatively untried advertising forum of radio. After noting Pepsodent's ballooning sales, attributable in part to its sponsorship of *Amos 'n' Andy*, they scrambled to identify themselves with any of the host of subsequent radio comedies and dramas that the show helped spawn.

The Great Depression virtually mandated that entertainment be provided at low cost, preferably within the home. Sales of radio sets increased by geometric leaps, as they provided virtually unlimited free entertainment after the initial purchase of a set. With a mass market beckoning, cheaper radios (the earlier models had been expensive console sets) were soon on the market. By 1933, one authority estimated that three-fourths of all radio sales were inexpensive table models that cost between twelve and twenty dollars. *Amos 'n' Andy* was a major contributor to this aberrant prosperity for an industry.

Amos 'n' Andy provided powerful impetus to the success of commercial radio, and also, in less quantifiable but doubtless equally significant ways, steadied the morale of millions of its listeners by supplying nightly laughter in the face of adversity. Audiences could easily identify with the plight of the show's principals. The common sense and down-home candor of the two struggling urban African Americans cut through the welter of official nostrums, pontifications, predictions, exhortations, and superficial idealism about the state of the economy, the stock market, unemployment, and the trials of disadvantaged rural folk seeking a living in an urban environment. Even their additions to the American vernacular were unpretentious, to the point, and funny. The show offered bits of wisdom, as in this remark by Andy to the members of the Mystic Knights of the Sea: "I might talk about de repression an' good times bein' around de corneh, soon as I check up wid somebody an' find out whut corneh 'tis." Although Amos and Andy sometimes voiced dour expectations about the length

and seriousness of the Depression, they, as marginal entrepreneurs, exuded optimism and by implication reaffirmed the cult of individual success and the work ethic—for which both President Herbert Hoover and President Franklin D. Roosevelt thanked the show's creators.

Although *Amos 'n' Andy*'s immense audience was drawn from all classes and races, protests against the show were raised by African Americans almost from its inception. Theresa Kennedy of St. Louis was among the first to voice complaints publicly. She admitted that she and her black neighbors were entertained by *Amos 'n' Andy* and that the show's characterizations were true to life, but, she complained, the obvious ignorance and shiftlessness of many of its characters gave a false impression of African Americans. Black newspapers during the early years of the show were divided, a majority praising it enthusiastically, as did most of the black organizations contacted by Gosden and Correll. A few were ambivalent about the show or were frankly hostile. A Chicago bishop, W. J. Walls, fell into the former category, whereas editor Robert L. Vann of the *Pittsburgh Courier* from the show's start denounced Gosden and Correll's "exploitation" of certain types of American blacks for their own gain, with a result of undermining black self-respect. In support of his position, Vann claimed to have 740,000 signatures on petitions against the show by the fall of 1931. Some black trade unionists and business organizations likewise protested that Amos, Andy, and their cohorts reflected adversely on the integrity of African American enterprise.

Over ensuing years, divisions in opinions of the show within black communities mirrored varying degrees of African American security, self-respect, and personal identity. Concerns over long-standing racial injustices and a resurgent national Civil Rights movement came to the fore in national life during the later years of the show. *Amos 'n' Andy* was launched as a television comedy in 1951, its major roles played by black actors. Leaders of the National Association for the Advancement of Colored People (NAACP), some of whom, such as Roy Wilkins, had earlier either enjoyed the radio show or tolerated it, became more vigorously opposed to it, in company with some white liberals. During Walter White's tenure as executive secretary of the NAACP, the organization made strenuous efforts first to alter the show's characters and content, and then to abolish it as a continuing harm to African Americans and a caricature of their race. No one ever accused Gosden or Correll, however, of stooping to pointed racial language, and many critics conceded that the race of the show's characters was largely incidental to their unfolding stories.

The radio show left the air in 1960. The television version was broadcast in first-run episodes from 1951 to 1953, then rerun widely on local stations. The television show remained popular in reruns and even was sold to broadcasters in Kenya and western Nigeria. After an official of Kenya's government announced that the program would be banned in his country, controversy over the show reemerged. The program was withdrawn from sale in 1966. Gosden and Correll also created an animated television show with animal characters, titled *Calvin and the Colonel*, that aired in 1961 and 1962. The animal characters had origins in the Deep South and had migrated to a large northern city; the show had obvious similarities to *Amos 'n' Andy* but avoided racial controversy through its use of animated animal characters.

Amos 'n' Andy left legacies of several types. It is remembered as the most popular radio serial of its time, and as such it was important in the development of radio as an entertainment medium. It was a pioneering effort in the emergence of serialized stories that were broadcast, both on radio and on television. More important, it indicated the effects that entertainment presentations can have on the popular consciousness and showed that art and entertainment often reflect reality and can bring attention to existing problems and conflicts. The controversy about racial presentations endured past the end of *Amos 'n' Andy*, and creators of the television shows that followed learned to evaluate their plots and characters carefully to avoid obvious insults or slurs against any group. This contributed to what some observers have called the relatively homogenized entertainment fare of the late twentieth century.

—Clifton K. Yearley

FURTHER READING

Barnouw, Erik. *A Tower in Babel*. Vol. 1 in *A History of Broadcasting in the United States*. New York: Oxford University Press, 1966. The finest history of its kind—comprehensive, authoritative, detailed, and well written. Gives great credit to *Amos 'n' Andy* for launching successful commercial radio, but is more critical of the show's racial content than many other analyses. Includes photographs, superb bibliography, detailed chronology, appendix of relevant laws, and index.

Douglas, George H. *The Early Days of Radio Broadcasting*. 1987. Reprint. Jefferson, N.C.: McFarland, 2001. Provides a good summary of *Amos 'n' Andy*'s influence as well as useful background and context. Includes photographs, splendid bibliography, notes, and excellent index.

Ely, Melvin Patrick. *The Adventures of Amos 'n' Andy: A Social History of an American Phenomenon*. 10th anniversary ed. New York: Free Press, 2001. The definitive study of the show, its context, and its influences. Detailed and scholarly, but accessible to lay readers as well as specialists. Several chapters deal with the show's racial content, problems of race, and racial opposition. Includes notes, bibliographical essay, and index.

Harmon, Jim. *The Great Radio Comedians*. Garden City, N.Y.: Doubleday, 1970. Breezy, knowledgeable survey of forty prominent radio comedy programs, including *Amos 'n' Andy*. Deals with the content of the shows rather than their place in the radio industry or history. Allows comparison of Gosden and Correll's comedy with the work of other writers. Ably researched, with humorous excerpts that afford the reader a feel for these programs. Includes photographs and index.

McLeod, Elizabeth. *The Original Amos 'n' Andy: Freeman Gosden, Charles Correll and the 1928-1943 Radio Serial*. Jefferson, N.C.: McFarland, 2005. Presents the history of the radio program in balanced fashion, discussing the innovations of its creators as well as the charges of racism against it. Examines scripts from the show's earliest version. Includes script excerpts, cast and crew information, photographs, bibliography, and index.

Wertheim, Arthur Frank. *Radio Comedy*. New York: Oxford University Press, 1979. Authoritatively traces the evolution of radio comedy (*Sam 'n' Henry* and *Amos 'n' Andy* included) and its impact on American values and society through the Great Depression and World War II. Also ties the content and character of comedy shows to traditional vernacular humor manifested earlier in vaudeville and stage comedy, highlighting radio comedy's innovations. Features many funny quotations from shows' scripts. Includes excellent photos, ample source notes, and index.

SEE ALSO: Feb. 12, 1909: National Association for the Advancement of Colored People Is Founded; Mar. 3, 1915: Griffith Releases *The Birth of a Nation*; 1929: *Hallelujah* Is the First Important Black Musical Film; 1930's: Americans Embrace Radio Entertainment.

1928

May 11, 1928
SOUND TECHNOLOGY REVOLUTIONIZES THE MOTION-PICTURE INDUSTRY

When Hollywood's major film studios signed an agreement with American Telephone and Telegraph to use AT&T technology to produce films with sound, the result was an explosion in the popularity of motion pictures.

LOCALE: United States
CATEGORIES: Motion pictures; science and technology; inventions

KEY FIGURES
Harry Warner (1881-1958), American motion-picture executive
Albert Warner (1884-1967), American motion-picture executive
Sam Warner (1887-1927), American motion-picture executive
William Fox (1879-1952), American motion-picture executive

SUMMARY OF EVENT

When Hollywood's major studios agreed in May, 1928, to incorporate sound into their films, the decision transformed the American film industry almost overnight. Attendance at theaters doubled, new talent poured into Hollywood, and "talkies" became the rage around the world. The introduction of sound to motion pictures created America's favorite midcentury leisure-time activity.

The production of the first sound films required several stages of innovation. First, scientists had to develop apparatus to record and synchronize sounds and images, complete with a quality and tone that would permit the resulting product to be shown before large audiences. Moreover, companies had to learn how to market sound films to the public, knowing the inherent risk in trying to sell something many critics said would not work. Finally, the major film companies had to decide to accept the new technology and to substitute it for the standardized silent film.

Such a transformation took place between 1926 and 1930. The silent-film era ended; Hollywood switched completely to the making of talkies. In 1925, silent filmmaking stood as the standard; a mere five years later, Hollywood produced only films with sound. The speed of the transition surprised almost everyone. Within the space of half a decade, formerly perplexing technical problems were resolved, marketing and distribution strategies were reworked, soundproof studios were constructed, and fifteen thousand theaters were wired for sound. Given that Hollywood dominated the film business throughout the world, foreign film industries were forced to follow suit, and by 1935, sound films had become the world standard.

The transformation to sound films did not begin in Hollywood. It took one of the world's largest corporations, American Telephone and Telegraph (AT&T), to overcome the frustrating technological problems involved. During the silent era, mammoth picture palaces used seventy-five-piece orchestras to provide live sound for silent films. Every two-hundred-seat neighborhood house had a hardworking piano player plunking out a musical accompaniment. Inventors, however, had long sought to develop a mechanical sound system to supply needed music and even dialogue. In the early years of the twentieth century, single inventors (including Thomas Alva Edison) failed to link phonograph technology to the silent film; they could not solve the problem of synchronizing sounds from a speaker with film of speaking actors.

During the 1910's, AT&T's scientists, working in a corporate unit that would later become known as Bell Labs, perfected an electronic sound-on-disk recording and reproducing system in order to test AT&T's then-new long-distance telephone network. As a spin-off of this telephone research, AT&T scientists invented the first true loudspeaker and sound amplifier. Combining these inventions with film technology produced a system that could record and project clear, vibrant sounds to audiences even in huge picture palaces.

In 1922, AT&T had begun trying to sell its new sound technology. Despite AT&T's formidable technical reputation and financial muscle, however, the barons of the American film industry, fully cognizant of the multitude of embarrassing failures of talkies a decade earlier, passed when initially offered the new AT&T equipment.

A minor Hollywood company, Warner Bros., took up the challenge. The brothers Warner (led by the eldest, Harry, who was assisted by his younger brothers Albert and Sam) had come a long way from their nickelodeon days in Ohio, but their company was still tiny in comparison to giants such as Famous Players-Lasky, then Hollywood's largest company. Warner Bros. sought a means

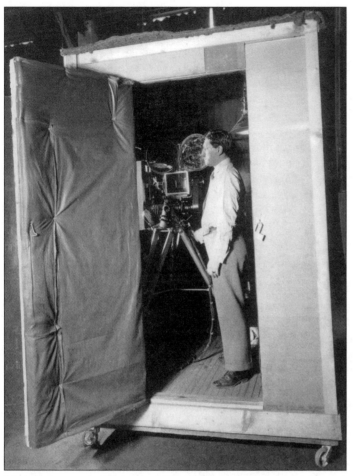

Motion-picture camera surrounded by soundproofing to prevent the camera noise from being picked up by early sound recording equipment. (Library of Congress)

by which to grow, and so in 1924, the brothers expanded into more expensive feature-film production, added offices for worldwide distribution, and bought a chain of picture palaces.

During this phase of corporate growth, Sam Warner learned of AT&T's inventions. He was immediately smitten, but he somehow had to trick the head of the family, Harry, into approving a deal. Harry saw a demonstration, and soon the brothers were working up a strategy to use sound to further build up their company. The Warner brothers decided to make sound films of vaudeville acts and offer them as novelties to exhibitors along with Warner Bros. feature-length (still silent) films. The Warner sales pitch stressed that these vaudeville sound shorts could substitute for the then-omnipresent stage shows offered by picture palaces. The very first talkies

thus were conceived as short recordings of the acts of top musical, comic, and variety talent.

In September, 1925, Warner Bros. set in motion its strategy of using vaudeville shorts to innovate sound films. It took a year to work out the technical problems, but by August, 1926, Warner Bros. was ready to premiere the marvel it called "Vitaphone." The premiere held that August allowed audiences to see and hear operatic favorites sung on film by such stars as Metropolitan Opera tenor Giovanni Martinelli. The presentation of the silent film *Don Juan* (1926), with music on a sound track replacing the usual live orchestra, followed.

As Warner Bros. developed more silent feature films with orchestral music on disk and more sound vaudeville shorts, the Warner brothers quickly realized that the public preferred recordings of popular musical acts to recordings of opera stars. Al Jolson and Elsie Janis, two of the biggest names in the pop music business during the 1920's, became the first stars of Vitaphone vaudeville shorts.

Warner Bros. soon began to insert vaudeville numbers into its features, beginning with Al Jolson in *The Jazz Singer*, which premiered in October, 1927. The enormous success of *The Jazz Singer* forced rival studios to take notice of the new sound technology.

During 1927 and the early part of 1928, Warner Bros. had only one competitor, the Fox Film Corporation, in the production of sound films. Fox had adapted a version of AT&T's pioneering technology to make newsreels with sound. Like the brothers Warner, William Fox, head of the Fox Film Corporation, did not see a future for feature-length talkies, but he reasoned that the public might prefer newsreels with sound to current silent offerings.

William Fox never made a better business decision in his career. Fox Film engineers labored to integrate sound with accepted newsreel techniques. On the final day of April, 1927, five months before the opening of *The Jazz Singer*, Fox Film presented its first sound newsreels. Less than a month later, Fox stumbled across the publicity coup of the decade when it tendered the only sound footage of the takeoff and triumphant return of aviator Charles A. Lindbergh. The enormous popularity of Lindbergh's hop across the Atlantic undoubtedly contributed heavily to Fox's success with sound newsreels.

1928

Fox newsreel cameramen soon spread to all parts of the globe in search of stories "with a voice." Theater owners queued up to wire their houses simply to be able to show Fox Movietone newsreels. To fans of the day, Movietone newsreels offered as much an attraction as any feature-length film.

The major film companies, led by Paramount, did not want to be left behind. For more than a year, a committee of experts from Paramount, Metro-Goldwyn-Mayer (MGM), First National, and United Artists met secretly to study their options. They examined AT&T's sound film technology and drew up plans to anticipate all attendant problems. After nearly six months of haggling over terms, on May 11, 1928, at AT&T's headquarters in Manhattan, these four major companies signed up with AT&T, and the rush to make talkies was on.

SIGNIFICANCE

Once the necessary contracts were signed, the diffusion of sound proceeded logically. First, Paramount, MGM, and the other major studios came out with "scored features," existing silent films with recorded music added. Theater owners immediately let go resident orchestras, freeing funds to help pay for the necessary wiring. Musicians' unions protested, but by 1930, only a handful of theaters in the largest U.S. cities still maintained house orchestras and organists. By January, 1929, less than a year after Paramount, MGM, First National, and United Artists had signed their original contracts, the majors began to distribute "100 percent talking" features, and the silent film became a thing of the past.

The widespread adoption of sound took place within the space of two years; the major Hollywood companies had too much at stake to procrastinate. Few unanticipated difficulties arose. Within the framework of the Academy of Motion Picture Arts and Sciences, the major studios cooperated to resolve any remaining problems as quickly as possible.

In short, the big studios continued to prosper. Smaller producers—save for pioneering Warner Bros. and Fox—could not afford the transition and either went out of business or were taken over by larger concerns. The Hollywood studios experienced a building boom, doubling studio space in less than two years. Several companies reopened studios near New York City to accommodate Broadway stage talent unwilling to trek to California. Paramount's Long Island City complex, a simple commute across the East River, was the largest of these. The greatest construction, however, came in California, as the modern studios came to life as filmmaking centers.

Fox had adapted a version of AT&T's pioneering technology that recorded sound on film itself. Warner's original sound-on-disk system proved ever more cumbersome, and by 1930 sound on film became the industry standard.

Theaters owned by Hollywood companies received their sound film installations first; smaller, independently owned houses had to sign up and wait, sometimes for more than a year. The major Hollywood companies could hardly keep track of the millions they were making. Warner Bros. and Fox moved to the top of the industry, and a new major company, Radio-Keith-Orpheum (RKO), was formed. In a rush to compete with AT&T, the Radio Corporation of America (RCA) developed its own version of sound on film, but RCA could not convince the major Hollywood companies to use its product, the "Photophone." To make the best of this situation, RCA founder and president David Sarnoff turned to a friend, financier Joseph P. Kennedy, the patriarch of the Kennedy political family. At the time, the elder Kennedy owned a small Hollywood studio, the Film Booking Office (FBO). During the last six months of 1928, Sarnoff and Kennedy merged RCA's sound equipment with the FBO studio and added the theaters from the Keith-Albee-Orpheum vaudeville theater empire to create RKO.

The public's infatuation with talkies set off the greatest rush to the box office in American history. At its peak in the months before the Great Depression, on average, every person over the age of six in the United States went to the movies once a week. Profits for the major Hollywood companies soared.

Mergers and takeovers became the order of the day. By 1930, there were only five major studios in Hollywood (Paramount, Loew's/MGM, Warner Bros., Fox, and RKO) and three minor studios (Columbia, Universal, and United Artists). Unlike their larger cousins, the minor studios owned no theaters. The coming of sound had set in place a corporate structure that would define the studio era of the 1930's and 1940's—the Golden Age of Hollywood.

By controlling picture palaces in all of America's downtowns, the major studios took in three-quarters of the average box-office take. Naturally, they granted their own theaters first-run privileges for top films and only then permitted smaller, independently owned theaters (found, by and large, outside downtown areas and in thousands of small towns) to scramble for remaining bookings, sometimes months, or even years, after films premiered. The major studios' regulation of the distribution and exhibition of films provided them with the power base from which they dominated American filmmaking for the next three decades.

—*Douglas Gomery*

FURTHER READING

Balio, Tino, ed. *The American Film Industry: A History Anthology of Readings*. Rev. ed. Madison: University of Wisconsin Press, 1985. Collection of essays analyzes the history and development of the American film industry, including the coming of sound. Aimed at a scholarly audience.

Crafton, Donald. *The Talkies: American Cinema's Transition to Sound, 1926-1931*. New York: Charles Scribner's Sons, 1997. Discusses all aspects of the transition from silent films to films with sound, including the public's reaction to talking pictures and the effects of sound on the aesthetics of filmmaking. Part of a ten-volume series on the history of the film industry in the United States. Includes bibliography and indexes.

Eyman, Scott. *The Speed of Sound: Hollywood and the Talkie Revolution, 1926-1930*. New York: Simon & Schuster, 1997. Comprehensive history of the period in filmmaking when silents gave way to sound. Includes photographs and index.

Geduld, Harry M. *The Birth of the Talkies: From Edison to Jolson*. Bloomington: Indiana University Press, 1975. Pioneering study details the creation of the inventions that were necessary to make talkies technologically possible. Includes substantial material on the film industry's relations with the phonograph and radio industries.

Mast, Gerald, ed. *The Movies in Our Midst*. Chicago: University of Chicago Press, 1982. Collection of essays presents a social history of the American cinema; generally readable and lively. Includes a useful introduction by the editor and comprehensive bibliography.

Sarris, Andrew. *"You Ain't Heard Nothin' Yet": The American Talking Film—History and Memory, 1927-1949*. New York: Oxford University Press, 1998. Comprehensive history of American cinema since *The Jazz Singer* by one of the most respected American writers on film. Opens with a chapter on the Hollywood studios. Features an index of films and an index of names.

Walker, Alexander. *The Shattered Silents: How the Talkies Came to Stay*. New York: William Morrow, 1979. Survey of the history of the coming of sound to motion pictures based on a close reading of the trade paper *Variety*. Interesting but limited.

Weis, Elisabeth, and John Belton, eds. *Film Sound: Theory and Practice*. New York: Columbia University Press, 1985. Collection of essays discusses the place of sound in the cinema. The first two essays address the film industry's transition to sound. Includes annotated bibliography and index.

SEE ALSO: 1913: Edison Shows the First Talking Pictures; Aug., 1926-Sept., 1928: Warner Bros. Introduces Talking Motion Pictures; Oct. 6, 1927: *The Jazz Singer* Premieres as the First "Talkie"; 1930's: Hollywood Enters Its Golden Age.

1928

May 15, 1928
AUSTRALIA BEGINS THE FLYING DOCTOR SERVICE

The advent of the first flying doctor service in Australia in 1928 opened the doors for further settlement and development of the nation's vast interior. Previously, Outback settlers rarely had access to medical treatment, and minor injuries could quickly turn deadly. Eventually armed with radios as well as airplanes, members of the flying doctor service changed the face of Australian medicine, providing what became known as a "mantle of safety" for the Outback's pioneers.

ALSO KNOWN AS: Royal Flying Doctor Service; Australian Aerial Medical Service
LOCALE: Cloncurry, Queensland, Australia
CATEGORIES: Health and medicine; transportation; space and aviation

KEY FIGURES
John Flynn (1880-1951), Presbyterian minister and founder of the Australia Inland Mission
Clifford Peel (1899-1918), Australian medical student and soldier during World War I
Alfred Traeger (1895-1980), Australian radio engineer
Jimmy Darcy (1895-1917), Western Australian stockman

SUMMARY OF EVENT
In May of 1928, the tiny Outback settlement of Cloncurry in Queensland, Australia, witnessed the birth of the country's first flying doctor service. In March of that year, the fledgling Australian airline Qantas had signed a one-year contract with the Presbyterian Church's Australian Inland Mission to carry a doctor to patients in remote Outback locations. On May 15, the Aerial Medical Service was officially established at Cloncurry, and on May 17, the Qantas airplane *Victory* made the first historic flight, taking Dr. Kenyon St. Vincent Welch from Cloncurry to Julia Creek. This marked the beginning of a yearlong experiment in which the "flying doctor" would travel more than 30,000 kilometers (18,641 miles) and treat more than 250 patients. The program's success led to a larger national cooperative effort in 1932 called the Australian Aerial Medical Service (AAMS), to which the Presbyterian Church ultimately transferred its flying doctor services in 1934. The AAMS was renamed the Flying Doctor Service in 1942, and it received a Royal Charter in 1955 that added the honorific "Royal" in front of its name.

The establishment of the flying doctor service was the realization of a dream held by the Reverend John Flynn.

Flynn was the first superintendent of the Australian Inland Mission, an organization that he created in 1912 with the help of the Australian Presbyterian Church. The purpose of the mission was to provide spiritual service, health care, education, and other assistance to the pioneering settlers who were attempting to establish a foothold in the vast Australian interior. During his work with the mission, Flynn had traveled great distances and had become familiar with the harsh and primitive conditions that Outback settlers endured. Before long, wherever Flynn went, he lobbied for the establishment of a medical-assistance network, but he had not yet figured out exactly how such a service would operate.

In 1917, the death of Jimmy Darcy, a young stockman, made national news and drew attention to the lack of medical attention in the Outback. According to the official history of the Royal Doctor Flying Service, Darcy was badly injured in a fall in rural Western Australia and was carried 50 kilometers (about 31 miles) to the nearest town, Halls Creek. The town's postmaster, Fred Tuckett, eventually reached a doctor by telegraph, but the doctor was so far away that he had to guide Tuckett through an emergency operation procedure using Morse code. Although the operation itself appeared to be successful, Darcy later died due to unrelated complications—a death that the doctor might have been able to prevent if he had been there in person.

Darcy's death motivated Flynn to press on with his efforts, and it also inspired a young Australian soldier named Clifford Peel, who was serving in Europe. Peel wrote a lengthy letter to Flynn, who reprinted it in the October, 1918, issue of the Australian Inland Mission's publication the *Inlander*. Peel, who had been a medical student before going to war, had provided cost estimates and specific suggestions for a flying doctor service. Unfortunately, Peel was killed in action in France in 1918, a full decade before his ideas would be put into practice.

It took several years of lobbying, fund-raising, and research before the flying doctor service could be started. Flynn felt strongly that connecting the inhabitants of the coastal areas and the inland was critical to Australia's future, and he eloquently argued his case. In addition, the continuing tensions in Europe contributed to a nationalistic desire to populate the country's interior. Recognizing that the success of a flying doctor service was dependent on communication, Flynn persuaded radio engineer Alfred Traeger to join him in Cloncurry to begin working on the communication issues. In the meantime, Flynn drafted the organization's guidelines and constitution. In doing so, he deliberately avoided limiting the organization's services to medical treatment.

Finally, in May of 1928, the Aerial Medical Service was ready to launch the inaugural flight that carried Qantas pilot Arthur Affleck and Dr. Kenyon St. Vincent Welch from Cloncurry to Julia Creek. Because Traeger's radio system was not yet ready, during its first year the service depended on telephone links that existed between towns and settlements and on the ability of individuals to travel to places where they could relay requests for assistance. In addition, pilots had to rely on landmarks for navigation, which was difficult considering that long stretches of Outback territory could not easily be distinguished from other parts of the region. The situation was much improved when Traeger unveiled the system he had developed: a pedal-operated radio set with a Morse typewriter keyboard that could be used by those who did not know Morse code.

In 1932, Traeger further improved the organization's communications by distributing transistorized voice sets that allowed doctors to diagnose from a distance and created a continuous communication network among Outback stations separated by wide distances. In 1942, coded medical chests for the Outback stations were introduced, and 1952 saw the development of a detailed chart of the human body that patients could use to tell doctors precisely where their injuries or pains were located. All of these innovations greatly improved the effectiveness of long-distance diagnosis and medical treatment. Gradually, the Flying Doctor Service added base stations at various locations throughout Australia so that it could reach a growing population. It continued to improve its equipment and training for personnel, which shortened the response time needed to get to any location in Australia for a medical emergency.

SIGNIFICANCE

Robert Gordon Menzies, who served as the prime minister of Australia from 1939 to 1941 and from 1949 to 1966, was widely quoted as saying that the Flying Doctor Service may have been the single most important factor in the effective settlement of the Australian Outback. Before the service was established, lack of medical treatment meant that the most minor injury could develop into a lethal condition. As the program grew, the Australia population came to revere the brave pilots and doctors who worked hard to save lives, and the organization's founder, John

Flynn, was eventually honored by having his portrait on the Australian $20 note and on a postage stamp.

The Royal Flying Doctor Service also had far-reaching implications outside the medical realm; for instance, its radio network was utilized for the School of the Air, which provided long-distance school lessons for children in the Outback. In addition, the network provided an important source of social contact for lonely settlers.

—*Amy Sisson*

FURTHER READING

Batstone, Kay. *Outback Heroes: Seventy-Five Years of the Royal Flying Doctor Service of Australia.* Melbourne, Vic.: Lothian Books, 2003. Commemorative volume that examines the origins and development of the Royal Flying Doctor Service; contains archival photographs and detailed accounts of life-saving rescue missions.

Hains, Brigid. "Antipodean Alchemist: 'Flying Doctor' Pioneer John Flynn Thought That a Vital Society Was a Humane One." *Meanjin* 63 (March, 2004): 27. In this essay, historian Hains examines some of the philosophies behind Flynn's vision, including his dislike and distrust of cities, his thoughts on race, and his belief that accessible transportation between Australia's interior and coastal areas would address not only medical needs but also the nation's mental and social health in general.

Royal Flying Doctor Service of Australia. "Our History." http://www.flyingdoctor.net/default.htm. Extensive history section on the organization's official Web site includes a time line showing when each geographic base was added to the Royal Flying Doctor Service.

Rudolph, Ivan. *John Flynn: Of Flying Doctors and Frontier Faith.* 2d ed. Rockhampton: Central Queensland University Press, 2000. Biographical account focusing on Flynn's pioneering role in founding the organization that would become the Royal Flying Doctor Service.

SEE ALSO: Jan. 1, 1901: Commonwealth of Australia Is Formed; July 25, 1909: First Airplane Flight Across the English Channel; Sept. 8, 1920: U.S. Post Office Begins Transcontinental Airmail Delivery; Nov. 20, 1920: Formation of Qantas Airlines; May 20, 1926: Air Commerce Act Creates a Federal Airways System; May 20, 1927: Lindbergh Makes the First Nonstop Transatlantic Flight; Dec. 11, 1931: Formation of the British Commonwealth of Nations; June 25, 1936: The DC-3 Opens a New Era of Air Travel.

1928

May 18, 1928
SHAKHTY CASE DEBUTS SHOW TRIALS IN MOSCOW

In a prelude to the Great Terror, a group of engineers working in the Donbas area of Ukraine were accused of sabotage and publicly tried.

LOCALE: Moscow, Soviet Union
CATEGORIES: Civil rights and liberties; government and politics; human rights

KEY FIGURES

Joseph Stalin (Joseph Vissarionovich Dzhugashvili; 1878-1953), general secretary of the Communist Party in Russia and dictator in the Soviet Union, 1929-1953

Andrey Yanuaryevich Vyshinsky (1883-1954), presiding judge during the Shakhty trials

Nikolai Vasilyevich Krylenko (1885-1938), prosecutor during the Shakhty trials

SUMMARY OF EVENT

During the First Five-Year Plan, in which the Soviet Union's entire economy was geared toward transforming itself into a modern industrial nation, the country encountered various difficulties. These ranged from small errors, such as mismatched gauges in pipes, to major catastrophes, such as the failures of boilers and furnaces, which killed thousands and put whole factories out of commission. All of these mistakes were likely caused by the huge rush toward industrialization and exacerbated by the central planning committees, and the result was that industrial growth occurred in fits and lurches rather than through an organic evolution.

No one was allowed to admit, however, that Stalin's plan could be at fault. Instead, fear of Stalin's harsh tactics caused the Soviet government to argue that its difficulties were due to the nefarious work of saboteurs sent by the capitalist nations of the West to destroy the dream of building the perfect socialist society. An opportunity to convince the Soviet people of this scheme came from a region in the North Caucasus, near Rostov-na-Donu, where a secret police informer, Yevgeny Yevdokimov, reported a supposed conspiracy to commit sabotage in the town of Shakhty. The tip was soon spun into an elaborate scenario in which Soviet and foreign engineers were accused of taking orders from Paris and attempting to bomb and destroy mining equipment throughout the Donbass region. Fifty-three defendants—an unprecedented number—were named.

The sheer size of the planned trial led Stalin to revive the Special Judicial Presence, a judicial body whose powers and jurisdictions were not specified by any legal document. To head it, Stalin chose the rector of Moscow University, Andrey Yanuaryevich Vyshinsky, a man of international stature whose reputation added further luster to both the trial and its verdict. The fact that Stalin had shared a cell in a czarist prison with Vyshinsky during

Idealized painting shows Joseph Stalin (center) leading a Central Committee meeting. (Library of Congress)

their revolutionary days only helped solidify Stalin's confidence in Vyshinsky's willingness to follow Stalin's orders. Stalin assigned the role of chief prosecutor to Nikolai Vasilyevich Krylenko, Vyshinsky's old rival. In order to make sure that there would be plenty of room for observers, including foreign correspondents, the trial was held in the famous Hall of Columns in the Trade Union House, which had been the Moscow Club of the Nobility.

Even before the trial opened, Stalin had made a speech in which he publicly declared that the defendants were guilty of sabotage. The fact that not one of the members of the Central Committee spoke up behalf of the accused was a mark of how thoroughly Stalin had already cowed Communist Party's most senior members. Even Bolshevik leader Nikolay Ivanovich Bukharin loudly called for the execution of the Shakhty engineers, perhaps because Bukharin himself was now pleading for his own life in the face of Stalin's increasing threats to have him destroyed.

The trial was noteworthy for its lack of interest in using evidence in arguments. Instead, Vyshinsky emphasized the power of wringing confessions from the accused, a theory of jurisprudence that he had been personally involved in developing. However, things did not always go smoothly. During the course of the trial, defendants repeatedly retracted their previous confessions, and several indicated that their confessions had been extracted by blackmail or by outright brutality. As a result, the confessions were often confusing and could change several times during the course of the trial.

As the trial progressed, the rivalry between Vyshinsky and Krylenko became increasingly obvious. While Krylenko taunted and ridiculed the defendants and often came across as ham-handed or boorish, Vyshinsky relied on relentless, logic-based arguments, which he delivered in a level, scholarly tone. As a result, Vyshinsky was remembered with respect, if not actual admiration, and this respect intensified when he used his authority as presiding judge to discipline Krylenko when the latter became carried away with his attacks on the defendants. It was fairly obvious, however, that Vyshinsky enjoyed the opportunity to embarrass a long-time rival at least as much as he cared about keeping the trial on track.

Over the trial's six weeks, its various problems made it the target of a fair amount of mockery in the foreign press. There were simply too many signs that the trial was a sham and that the supposed confessions were actually meaningless products of state terror. Vyshinsky gradually realized that there was no way to carry out Stalin's grand scheme without looking absurd, and so he gained permission to reduce the number of guilty ver-

dicts and death sentences. Only eleven of the eighteen originally marked as guilty were actually sentenced to death. Of those, only five sentences actually were carried out, a reduction that occurred largely as the result of international outcry against the obvious injustice.

SIGNIFICANCE

The show trials that Stalin held in 1928 were in some sense a dress rehearsal for the later, more famous Moscow show trials of 1935 and 1936, in which Stalin publicly discredited and destroyed the last of the Bolshevik leaders who had carried out the October Revolution and could have moved against him. All the major elements and themes of the later trials are evident in the Shakhty case, including the intimidation and ultimate destruction of the very people the Soviet Union most needed to lead its move toward progress and industrialization.

By 1935, Stalin's government had perfected its methods and techniques to ensure that it would not again experience the embarrassment of having defendants who refused to confess or who repeatedly changed their pleas and retracted confessions (only to later offer further confessions). If it was clear that certain defendants were likely to cause trouble in court, they were tried in secret sessions, and the public saw nothing but newspaper reports. Most notably, this method was used in the destruction of Marshal Mikhail Tukhachevsky and other notable officers of the Red Army, men of great physical courage unlikely to be cowed into submission by torture.

However, Vyshinsky would not reprise his role as the presiding judge when it came time for the Moscow show trials. Instead, he would replace Krylenko, whose performance Stalin had found crude and unsatisfactory, at the prosecutor's table. Vyshinsky's oratory would become famous, and he was especially well known for the imaginative abuse he was able to heap on defendants. Even as prosecutor, Vyshinsky continued to have a major role in the operations of the Moscow show trials, as the military judge chosen to preside over them was a lackluster figure with no real legal training—the judge was useful primarily because he could be depended upon to hand down guilty verdicts and death sentences. Krylenko would ultimately vanish into an unmarked grave, but Vyshinsky would survive the Great Terror with his reputation intact and move into diplomacy.

—Leigh Husband Kimmel

FURTHER READING

Conquest, Robert. *The Great Terror: A Reassessment.* Oxford, England: Oxford University Press, 1990. A postglasnost reissue of the most authoritative volume on the era. Includes discussion of the Shakhty trials and other preludes to the actual terror.

Medvedev, Roy. *Let History Judge: The Origins and Consequences of Stalinism*. Translated by George Shriver. New York: Columbia University Press, 1989. A glasnost-era edition of the study of Stalinism by one of the former Soviet Union's leading historians. Includes material on the Shakhty case and treats it as a prelude to the Moscow show trials.

Montefore, Simon Sebag. *Stalin: The Court of the Red Tsar*. New York: Alfred A. Knopf, 2003. Includes information on Stalin's use of henchmen (including Vyshinsky) to prepare and run the terror while deflecting attention from himself.

Rayfield, Donald. *Stalin and His Hangmen: The Tyrant and Those Who Killed for Him*. New York: Random House, 2004. Study of the relationship between Stalin and his chief lieutenants reveals Stalin's preference for staying in the background during repressions so that others could take the blame, a tactic that allowed him to preserve his image as fatherly leader.

Vaksberg, Arkady. *Stalin's Prosecutor: The Life of Andrei Vyshinsky*. New York: Grove Weidenfield, 1990. One of the few biographies of Vyshinsky available. Includes extensive information on the Shakhty trials.

SEE ALSO: 1917-1924: Russian Communists Inaugurate the Red Terror; Mar.-Nov., 1917: Lenin Leads the Russian Revolution; 1918-1921: Russian Civil War; 1921-1923: Famine in Russia Claims Millions of Lives; Oct. 1, 1928: Stalin Introduces Central Planning; Jan., 1929: Trotsky Is Sent into Exile; Dec., 1932-Spring, 1934: Great Famine Strikes the Soviet Union; Dec., 1934: Stalin Begins the Purge Trials.

Summer, 1928

GAMOW EXPLAINS RADIOACTIVE ALPHA DECAY WITH QUANTUM TUNNELING

George Gamow used the newly established quantum mechanics to explain the puzzling phenomenon of radioactive alpha decay.

LOCALE: Leningrad, Soviet Union (now St. Petersburg, Russia); Göttingen, Germany
CATEGORIES: Science and technology; physics

KEY FIGURES

George Gamow (1904-1968), Soviet American physicist
Edward U. Condon (1902-1974), American physicist
Ronald Wilfred Gurney (1898-1953), British American physicist
Ernest Rutherford (1871-1937), British physicist
Louis de Broglie (1892-1987), French physicist
Werner Heisenberg (1901-1976), German physicist
Erwin Schrödinger (1887-1961), Austrian British physicist
Max Born (1882-1970), German physicist
Hans Geiger (1882-1945), German physicist
John Mitchell Nuttall (1890-1958), British physicist

SUMMARY OF EVENT

In 1928, George Gamow provided a theoretical explanation of the phenomenon of radioactive alpha decay. The newly established quantum mechanics served as the theoretical basis for his explanation. Beginning from 1898, Ernest Rutherford and his assistants studied radioactivity most successfully. They classified the phenomenon and clarified many important phenomenological regularities. The alpha particles, the heaviest of all three types of radioactive emissions, are positively charged; in fact, they are the atomic nuclei of the inert gas helium. All atomic nuclei are not alpha radioactive, however. Only the heavy ones can emit alpha particles, which are usually of uniform kinetic energy characteristic of the parent species of nuclei. The kinetic energy of alpha particles ranges from 4 to 9.5 MeV (millions of electronvolts).

Radioactivity is a probabilistic phenomenon. All radioactive nuclei change as a result of one or more of the three types of disintegration, but when disintegration occurs to one particular nucleus, it is unpredictable. It may happen instantly, or it may occur in the remote future. Some nuclei (isotopes) disintegrate rapidly, whereas others disintegrate slowly. The probabilistic character of the phenomenon required physicists to use statistical concepts such as the "half-life" to describe and discuss them. The half-life of an isotope is the time for one-half of any given quantity of the nuclei to disintegrate. Half-lives vary vastly from one species of nuclei to another. Some isotopes are very radioactive; in one-trillionth of a second, a half of this type of atom could change its identity. Some isotopes are radioactively very stable; it may take one trillion years for half of this type of atom to change.

In 1911, two physicists in Rutherford's group, Hans Geiger and John Mitchell Nuttall, derived from experimental data a remarkable law that relates the half-life of a species of nuclei to the energy of the alpha particles emitted from them: the parent nuclei. The Geiger-Nuttall law was, in fact, a set of succinct equations. The theoretical understanding of these empirical equations, however, had to wait for the establishment of quantum mechanics, a milestone that was reached sixteen years later.

In 1927, Rutherford published his discovery of the phenomenon of alpha decay. Gamow conceived his quantum theory of tunneling from this publication. From the standpoint of classical physics, the phenomena were simply paradoxical. First, the experiment of atomic scattering made it clear that every atom has a positively charged, small, and heavy nucleus. As alpha particles are also positively charged when they approach a nucleus, because of the mutual repulsion between electricity of the same sign, they are rejected and scattered by the nuclei. Thus, for positive charges, including alpha particles, the atomic nucleus is surrounded with a barrier of potential energy.

By shooting alpha particles of different kinetic energy at various species of nuclei, Rutherford assessed the height of the potential barrier around a nucleus, which could be as high as 25 to 35 MeV, several times the kinetic energy of alpha particles. For example, uranium 238 is a radioactive species that emits alpha particles of 4.2 MeV. The scattering experiment showed that the potential barrier around the uranium 238 nucleus might be as high as 25 MeV, more than five times the kinetic energy of the alpha particle that the same nucleus sometimes emits. It was not known how a 4.2 MeV alpha particle could escape a 25 MeV barrier. Rutherford proposed an ingenious classical solution to the puzzle.

He suggested that, starting from the nucleus, each alpha particle is accompanied by two electrons that neutralize its positive charge. For this neutralized alpha particle, the potential barrier is no longer a barrier, and it has no difficulty passing the barrier zone. After sending off the alpha particle, the two electrons somehow separate from it and return into the nucleus. Gamow, however, thought this theory was too ingenious; he believed that the phenomenon was another quantum event inexplicable to classical physics.

Louis de Broglie's first step in 1925 toward the establishment of quantum mechanics was a startling suggestion. He argued, on the basis of analogy with classical physics, that every elementary particle is associated with a "matter wave." One year later, following de Broglie's

---

GEORGE GAMOW:
PHYSICIST, COSMOLOGIST, GENETICIST

Born March 4, 1904, in Odessa, Russia, George Gamow started his scientific career as a boy, when his father gave him a telescope for his thirteenth birthday. Little did his father know that his son would one day become one of the greatest scientists of the twentieth century.

After graduating from the University of Leningrad in 1926, Gamow went to Göttingen, a center for the study of the new quantum mechanics. At this time, natural radioactivity was the focus of research of many of the great physicists of the day, from the Curies to Lord Rutherford, and Gamow was particularly interested in its relationship to the atomic nucleus. In 1928, he made his first great contribution when he described quantum tunneling of alpha particles to explain the radioactive process of alpha decay. His investigation of the atomic nucleus would take him to Copenhagen, where he worked under Niels Bohr laying the theoretical groundwork for nuclear fusion and fission.

During the 1930's, Gamow taught at universities in Copenhagen, Leningrad, Cambridge, Paris, and the United States. In Washington, D.C., he and Edward Teller worked on the theory of beta decay. He also turned his attention to astrophysics and the origin of the elements. This work led to his 1948 proposal of the "big bang" theory of the universe, for which he is best known.

Gamow was more than a theoretical physicist, however: Known for his sense of humor and revered by his students, he was also devoted to education. His "Mr. Tompkins" series used science fiction to explain difficult science in a way that anyone—including Tompkins, whose attention span was notoriously short—could understand. In 1954, inspired by the Watson-Crick DNA model, he theorized that the order of the DNA molecules determined protein structure. The problem, as he saw it, was to determine how the four-letter "alphabet" of nucleic acid bases could be formed into "words." His "diamond code" paved the way for Marshall W. Nirenberg to crack the genetic code in 1961.

In 1956, Gamow settled in Boulder to teach at the University of Colorado. That year, he received UNESCO's Kalinga Prize for his popularization of science, and two years later he was married (a second time) to Barbara "Perky" Perkins, who initiated the George Gamow Lecture Series after his death, in 1968.

1928

lead, Erwin Schrödinger introduced a general "wave equation." He stated that his differential equation should solve microcosmic problems in general—such as Sir Isaac Newton's equation, the second law of motion, in classical mechanics. Werner Heisenberg formulated his version of microcosmic mechanics in 1925. Atomic spectra are sharp lines representing radiations with definite frequencies, intensities, and polarizations. One of Niels Bohr's basic ideas was that spectral lines were transitions between quantum states. As the easiest way to specify a quantum state is to assign an integer to it, the transition between two quantum states could be specified by a pair of integers. Heisenberg pursued this line of thinking and concluded that every microcosmic "observable" should be specified the same way: by a pair of integers. Consequently, Heisenberg's mechanics was formulated with matrices—that is, square arrays of numbers. This was the origin of matrix mechanics, accomplished by Heisenberg, Pascual Jordan, and Max Born. After introducing his basic equation, Schrödinger proved the mathematical equivalence between matrix mechanics and wave mechanics.

In 1927, Heisenberg and Born succeeded in arriving at important results that would clarify the physical meaning of the new quantum mechanics: Heisenberg formulated the "uncertainty principle" and Born propounded the statistical interpretation of the quantum wave function. According to Heisenberg, it is impossible, even in principle, to determine at the same time the exact position and exact velocity of a particle. Born understood that the square of the amplitude of the wave function—the solution of the Schrödinger equation—represented an opportunity of finding a microcosmic particle.

In the summer of 1928, Gamow applied these empirical and theoretical results to solve a long-standing paradox in the phenomenon of radioactivity. He followed de Broglie in using an analogue from classical physics, the relation between geometrical and wave optics, especially with regard to the issue of total reflection, which is a logical consequence of geometrical optics. According to the wave optics, however, no total reflection is total. Gamow pointed out that, according to wave mechanics, penetration into a potential barrier of a microcosmic particle, although with insufficient kinetic energy, is not impossible. Gamow solved the Schrödinger equation of this problem and showed that the wave function beyond the barrier did not vanish. Thus, according to Born's statistical interpretation of the wave function, the probability for the particle to tunnel through the barrier is not nil. Probability should depend on how large the barrier is.

The new quantum mechanics could calculate the exact dependence of the probability on the height and the width of the barrier: The higher and wider the barrier is, the smaller the probability becomes. The theory also shows that, for an ordinary baseball or tennis ball, for example, the chance of penetration, let alone tunneling through, is practically zero.

SIGNIFICANCE

It soon became evident that the quantum effect of "tunneling" also could be derived directly from Heisenberg's uncertainty principle, more specifically, from its energy-time format. This was a satisfying step that further demonstrated the inherent consistency of quantum mechanics.

Following the initial theoretical success, Gamow discussed the tunneling of potential barriers with John Douglas Cockcroft and encouraged him to bombard light nuclei with moderately accelerated protons. (Their goal was to explore the possibility of inducing artificial nuclear transmutation. Before the theory of quantum tunneling was evinced, the suggestion of using protons with insufficient kinetic energy would be rejected offhandedly.) Cockcroft performed such experiments. In the early 1930's, this preliminary achievement commenced a new stage for particle acceleration as well as artificial transmutation.

The empirical equations of alpha decay—the Geiger-Nuttall law—together with the conspicuous fact that radioactive half-lives vary in a vast range (from a trillionth of a second to trillions of years) were now given a unified quantum theoretical explanation. The great success of the new theory in a new realm of physical phenomena, and on the difficult issues of the probabilistic nature of the microcosm and the statistical character of its theory, left an immediate and dramatic impact in scientific circles.

The founding of quantum mechanics between 1925 and 1927 represented a denouement of prolonged and collective effort in explaining physical and chemical phenomena pertaining to the structure of the atom. To the practicing physicists of the time, the denouement was also a propitious beginning. The significant development showed that microcosmic phenomena needed a new type of mechanics, intrinsically different from the classical Newtonian mechanics so that it could be used to extend and refine the original crude theories of atomic and molecular structures.

The timely appearance of publications by Gamow, Ronald Wilfred Gurney, and Edward U. Condon signaled the beginning of the theoretical study of the atomic nucleus. More significant, their theory of quantum tunneling dramatically furthered the success of quantum mechanics and strengthened confidence in this new and strange theory. Quantum tunneling is not trajectory, but wavelike; it is not exact, but statistical; or, as physicists and philosophers believe, it is not deterministic, but indeterministic. The theory has to be statistical because microcosmic phenomena themselves are probabilistic.

Scientists such as Albert Einstein did not accept the statistical interpretation of the wave function. To a lesser extent, de Broglie and Schrödinger, cofounders of quantum mechanics, shared Einstein's viewpoint. The majority, however, disagreed with Einstein, de Broglie, and Schrödinger. Most theoretical and experimental physicists were won over by the indeterminism of the new microcosmic mechanics. In this serious academic debate, the theoretical success achieved by Gamow, Gurney, and Condon played a significant role. Long before any theory was proposed, radioactive phenomena had been recognized as statistical. It is very satisfying for most physicists that such phenomena are explained by a theory that is intrinsically statistical.

—Wen-yuan Qian

FURTHER READING

Boorse, Henry A., and Lloyd Motz, eds. *The World of the Atom.* Vol. 2. New York: Basic Books, 1966. Chapter 67, "The Barrier Around the Nucleus," includes two parts: an explanatory essay by the editors and an English translation of Gamow's "Quantum Theory of the Atomic Nucleus," originally published in German in 1928. The first part is accessible to readers with little scientific background.

Born, Max. *My Life: Recollection of a Nobel Laureate.* New York: Charles Scribner's Sons, 1978. A substantial volume valuable for its historical scholarship. Several chapters discuss the history of quantum mechanics. Careful readers will gain a clear picture of Born's contribution to the founding of quantum mechanics.

_____. *Physics in My Generation.* 2d rev. ed. New York: Springer-Verlag, 1969. An important work for anyone seeking to understand the history of quantum mechanics. Suitable for the general reader.

Ford, Kenneth W. *The Quantum World: Quantum Physics for Everyone.* Cambridge, Mass.: Harvard University Press, 2004. Explains the concepts of quantum physics in nontechnical language for lay readers. Illustrated.

Gamow, George. *Thirty Years That Shook Physics: The Story of Quantum Theory.* 1966. Reprint. Mineola, N.Y.: Dover, 1985. Very interesting anecdotal history of quantum mechanics. Discusses the evolution of the quantum theory of the nucleus in chapter 2.

Gamow, George, and Russell Stannard. *The New World of Mr. Tompkins.* Cambridge, England: Cambridge University Press, 2001. Revised and updated (by Stannard) edition of *Mr. Tompkins in Paperback*, a 1965 volume that combined Gamow's two classic popular science books, *Mr. Tompkins in Wonderland* (1940) and *Mr. Tompkins Explores the Atom* (1945). Provides an excellent introduction to many scientific concepts for lay readers.

Heisenberg, Werner. *Nuclear Physics.* New York: Methuen, 1953. Discusses radioactive phenomena in chapter 3, and clearly explains the tunneling theory in chapter 6. Accessible to interested lay readers.

Rutherford, Lord Ernest. *The Newer Alchemy.* 1937. Reprint. Whitefish, Mont.: Kessinger, 2003. A brief discussion of nuclear physics by a great authority. Probably still the best introduction to radioactivity for the general reader, although somewhat dated.

1928

SEE ALSO: Early 20th cent.: Elster and Geitel Study Radioactivity; Dec. 10, 1903: Becquerel Wins the Nobel Prize for Discovering Natural Radioactivity; 1905-1907: Boltwood Uses Radioactivity to Determine Ages of Rocks; Feb. 11, 1908: Geiger and Rutherford Develop a Radiation Counter; 1933-1934: First Artificial Radioactive Element Is Developed.

July 2, 1928
GREAT BRITAIN LOWERS THE VOTING AGE FOR WOMEN

The 1928 Representation of the People Act lowered the age at which British women could vote from thirty to twenty-one, thereby granting them suffrage at the same age as male voters.

ALSO KNOWN AS: Representation of the People Act
LOCALE: London, England
CATEGORIES: Laws, acts, and legal history; women's issues; social issues and reform; civil rights and liberties

KEY FIGURES
Nancy Astor (1879-1964), first female member of the House of Commons
Stanley Baldwin (1867-1947), prime minister of Great Britain, 1923-1924 and 1924-1929
Winston Churchill (1874-1965), Chancellor of the Exchequer of Great Britain
Eleanor Rathbone (1872-1946), president of the National Union of Societies for Equal Citizenship
Margaret Rhondda (1883-1958), leader of the Equal Political Rights Campaign Committee

SUMMARY OF EVENT
In 1918, Parliament passed the Representation of the People Act, which gave men in Great Britain the right to vote at age twenty-one but restricted suffrage for women to those qualified to vote in local elections and age thirty and over. This step was welcomed by women's suffrage organizations because it conceded the principle of women's suffrage, but as women remained second-class citizens, it did not fulfill their objective of equal suffrage rights. Therefore, almost immediately after celebrating their partial victory, women's suffrage organizations began preparing for a new campaign to obtain the vote on the same terms as men.

Women sought equal suffrage for a variety of reasons. Many viewed it as an insult that they should not be trusted with the vote until they reached the age of thirty, whereas men could vote at the age of twenty-one. Unequal suffrage was seen as a symbol of the wider pattern of sex-differentiated policies that hampered women's opportunities in employment and in public life in general. Jobs were generally segregated by gender, with higher-status and higher-paying positions reserved for men. Even in the few areas, such as teaching and the civil service, in which women did the same work as men, they received lower pay. In many areas, employers imposed a marriage bar that forced female employees to resign from their positions if they married. In addition, the government refused to allow doctors at public health clinics to provide married women with birth control information. Women hoped that the additional political power they would gain from equal suffrage rights would enable them to change these discriminatory policies.

The postwar campaign for equal suffrage was conducted primarily by women's organizations that had fought for woman suffrage before the war. The largest and most important of these was the National Union of Societies for Equal Citizenship (NUSEC), which was known as the National Union of Women's Suffrage Societies until 1918. Led by Eleanor Rathbone, NUSEC worked for reform by quietly lobbying political leaders rather than by using the more militant, and more public, methods associated with the prewar suffragists.

NUSEC's efforts to get a commitment from the Conservative Party to act on the issue benefited from the assistance of the first female member of the House of Commons, Lady Nancy Astor. An American who had married the wealthy British member of Parliament David Astor, Lady Astor was elected to the House of Commons as a Conservative in 1919. She viewed herself as a spokesperson for women and was taken seriously in this role by politicians seeking support from female voters. Those who find it curious that equal suffrage was eventually enacted by a Conservative government should bear in mind Lady Astor's persistent lobbying for that reform within her own party.

During the 1924 election campaign, under prodding from NUSEC and other women's groups, the Conservative Party leader, Stanley Baldwin, pledged that if his party were returned to office, it would sponsor a special parliamentary conference on the issue of equal suffrage. Many women understood this as a commitment to introduce legislation for equal suffrage, although some Conservatives who opposed that reform thought it a clever way of attracting female votes without promising to do anything more than hold a conference to discuss the issue. The Conservative government thus did not become unequivocally committed to proceed with equal suffrage until 1925, when a cabinet minister, William Joynson Hicks, pledged that the government would act on the matter before the end of the current Parliament.

When the government failed to take action during the next two years, women's groups began to fear that they

Nancy Astor. (Hulton Archive/Getty Images)

Churchill, feared that granting the vote to women at age twenty-one would be a political disaster for the Conservative Party, as he anticipated that most of the newly enfranchised women would vote for the rival Labour Party. Other Conservatives opposed reform on the ground that it meant enfranchising "flappers," a pejorative term implying immature, empty-headed females who knew nothing about politics or life and who would likely cast their votes for the most attractive male candidate. Underlying the various arguments opposing equal suffrage was an awareness that it would make women the majority of the electorate; some Conservatives feared that women would be less willing than men to vote for policies running the risk of war to protect the British Empire.

Despite the strong resistance within his party, Baldwin insisted that the government proceed with legislation. He was aware that if the Conservatives did not act, the Labour Party would make an issue of it at the next general election and might gain enough female votes to defeat the Conservatives. As a Labour government would then almost certainly introduce equal suffrage, Baldwin believed that reform was inevitable and that inaction by the Conservative government would only improve the Labour Party's election prospects. He was also convinced that a majority of the newly enfranchised women would become Conservative voters, given the party's special interest in promoting home and family life.

As a result of Baldwin's support, the government finally introduced its equal-franchise bill in 1928. It granted women the right to vote at age twenty-one on the same terms as men. Once the bill was introduced in Parliament, the outcome was never in doubt, in part because opponents feared that speaking against the bill could antagonize existing female voters. The bill was supported by the Labour and Liberal Parties, and thus the only opposition came from a handful of diehard Conservatives. The antisuffragists' dire predictions of the consequences that would follow if the bill passed seemed so outdated that they provoked laughter rather than serious discussion from the members supporting the measure. Late in March, 1928, the House of Commons voted overwhelmingly for the bill: 387 endorsed it with only 10 opposing. When a majority of the House of Lords also voted for it,

1928

had been deceived. NUSEC joined with more than forty other women's organizations on July 3, 1926, in sponsoring a march through London to Hyde Park to demonstrate the degree of support among women for equal suffrage. Although some speakers warned that there could be a revival of suffragist tactics if the government did not proceed with reform, Lady Astor privately discouraged militant action. She claimed that suffragist violence would make it impossible for the government to proceed with legislation, as it would appear that the politicians were giving in to force. Reluctantly, Lady Margaret Rhondda accepted this advice, but her dissatisfaction with NUSEC's backstage lobbying tactics led her to form a new group, the Equal Political Rights Campaign Committee, to increase pressure on the government.

The suffrage reformers were correct in believing that prominent members of the cabinet were seeking a way to avoid honoring the government's pledge on equal suffrage. The cabinet committee appointed by Baldwin to draft a bill devoted most of its time to trying to find some reason for not proceeding with it. One of the cabinet ministers most adamantly opposed to legislation, Winston the Representation of the People Act, also known as the Equal Suffrage Act, became law on July 2, 1928.

SIGNIFICANCE

The Equal Suffrage Act removed one of the most important remaining symbols of women's inferior position under British law. Baldwin described the act as the final step in granting women equal rights. Many women accepted this claim and withdrew from women's reform organizations to devote themselves to their families and private lives. Women viewed the act as the culmination of a movement for political rights begun nearly sixty years earlier. Some activists, such as Dame Millicent Garrett Fawcett, had devoted most of their adult lives to the suffrage campaign. It should not be surprising, therefore, that for many women the sense of elation was mixed with a feeling of relief that the struggle was finally over.

Although antisuffragists had predicted that equal suffrage would bring radical change to British political life, this expectation proved mistaken. About five and one-half million women gained the right to vote as a result of the act. Although the act is usually described as having granted the vote to women between the ages of twenty-one and thirty, nearly one-third of those who gained the franchise were over thirty and had been prevented from voting by the property-owning requirements of the previous electoral law. As a result of the act, women became a majority of the electorate; at the next general election, held in 1929, 52.7 percent of the voters were female.

Nevertheless, only 14 women were elected to the House of Commons in 1929, compared with 601 men. The new women members were absorbed into the existing political parties and voted as the male members of their parties did; they did not form a distinct women's group in Parliament. Women voters did not vote as a bloc but divided their votes among the three major parties much as men did. Although some claimed that the new female voters were responsible for Labour's victory in the 1929 election, this has not been proven. Most studies have shown, on the contrary, that women were slightly more likely than men to vote Conservative.

In the short term, women gained few direct benefits from equal suffrage. The newly elected Labour government was surprisingly indifferent, if not openly hostile, to women's issues. It took no steps to protect women's rights to work when rising male unemployment stimulated public criticism of women workers. Although Minister of Labour Margaret Bonfield was the first female cabinet minister, she was directly responsible for legislation that deprived many married women of their right to

unemployment benefits. The Labour government did nothing to assist the campaign for family allowances that had been so important to Labour Party women in the 1920's. Finally, the Labour government resisted women's demand that public health clinics be allowed to provide birth control information to married women and permitted this change to be introduced only when Labour-controlled city councils joined in the campaign.

One of the most important consequences of equal suffrage was women's withdrawal from active campaigning for sex equality. After 1928, the membership of the largest feminist organization in Great Britain, the National Union of Societies for Equal Citizenship, declined rapidly. By the early 1930's, it had become a much smaller and much less influential organization.

—*Harold L. Smith*

FURTHER READING

Adam, Ruth. *A Woman's Place, 1910-1975.* 1975. Reprint. London: Persephone Books, 2000. Well-written, lively history of British women for the general reader. Presents a good summary of developments affecting women in the 1920's and relates the suffrage campaign to other women's issues. Includes bibliographic endnotes and index.

Alberti, Johanna. *Beyond Suffrage: Feminists in War and Peace, 1914-1928.* New York: St. Martin's Press, 1989. Well-informed study of British feminists in the 1920's. Makes extensive use of manuscript material to add to the understanding of the women involved in the campaign. Includes an appendix with useful biographical information on the major feminists.

Harrison, Brian. *Prudent Revolutionaries: Portraits of British Feminists Between the Wars.* Oxford, England: Clarendon Press, 1987. Collection of excellent biographical studies of many of the women involved in the campaign for equal suffrage. Presents much information not previously published, especially on the women's personal lives. Includes valuable bibliographical essay and outstanding index.

Mayhall, Laura E. Nym. *The Militant Suffrage Movement: Citizenship and Resistance in Britain, 1860-1930.* New York: Oxford University Press, 2003. Discusses the use of militant tactics by the woman suffrage movement in Great Britain. Presents material from participants' private papers as well as pamphlets and newspaper articles of the time to place the suffragists' actions in context. Includes bibliography and index.

Middlemas, Keith, and John Barnes. *Baldwin: A Biogra-*

phy. London: Weidenfeld & Nicolson, 1969. One of the fullest biographies available of the prime minister responsible for the 1928 suffrage act. Includes discussion of the conflict within the Conservative Party on the issue and Baldwin's reasons for proceeding with it against the strong opposition of prominent members of his own party. Features references and index.

Smith, Harold L., ed. *British Feminism in the Twentieth Century*. Amherst: University of Massachusetts Press, 1990. Collection of original essays on various aspects of British feminism. Chapters on feminism in the 1920's and on Eleanor Rathbone provide the context for the 1920's suffrage campaign. Includes brief bibliography and index.

Strachey, Ray. *"The Cause": A Short History of the Women's Movement in Great Britain*. 1928. Reprint. London: Virago, 1978. Important study by a prominent figure in the largest women's suffrage organiza-tion, although rather bland and not as revealing as it could have been. Useful as a detailed narrative of what happened and how the women involved per-ceived the events. Includes brief bibliography (now badly dated) and index.

Vickery, Amanda, ed. *Women, Privilege, and Power: British Politics, 1750 to the Present*. Stanford, Calif.: Stanford University Press, 2001. Collection of essays addresses the various ways in which British women have exercised political power in Great Britain since the mid-eighteenth century. Includes discussion of the woman suffrage movement.

SEE ALSO: June 12, 1902: Australia Extends Suffrage to Women; July 20, 1906: Finland Grants Women Suf-frage; Sept. 20, 1917: Canadian Women Gain the Vote; Feb. 6, 1918: British Women Gain the Vote; Aug. 26, 1920: U.S. Women Gain the Right to Vote.

August, 1928
MEAD PUBLISHES *COMING OF AGE IN SAMOA*

With the publication of the very successful Coming of Age in Samoa, *Margaret Mead popularized the field of cultural anthropology.*

LOCALE: New York, New York
CATEGORIES: Anthropology; publishing and journalism

KEY FIGURES
Margaret Mead (1901-1978), American anthropologist
Franz Boas (1858-1942), German American anthropologist

SUMMARY OF EVENT

In 1911, Franz Boas, Margaret Mead's mentor, pub-lished his landmark book *The Mind of Primitive Man*, which freed anthropology from the stigma of racism. Be-fore that time, "higher" and "lower" races were consid-ered to exist, rated on a scale of intellectual capacity. Boas's book was the cornerstone of a new view of hu-mans and led to the controversy between two schools of thought in anthropology that is sometimes dubbed the "nature versus nurture" debate. Those on the side of "na-ture" contended that innate racial differences account for differences in individual intellectual abilities, whereas those on the side of "nurture" (Boas's followers) argued that the abilities of members of the human species often differ because of cultural differences in their upbringing as well as differences in their heredity. Boas believed that researchers needed to study this problem so as to deter-mine the relationship between hereditary factors and en-vironmental factors.

Margaret Mead was only twenty-three years old when she set out on her great adventure to the South Seas, where she hoped to study what remained of primitive cultures before they disappeared forever. In her autobi-ography, Mead later described her thoughts as she left for Samoa—thoughts of urgency to study and record the ways of life in remote parts of the world. She had a sense that such ways of life were vanishing before the on-slaught of modern civilization. She believed that she must be one of the scientists to record these unknown ways before they were lost forever.

Mead had been married to Luther Cressman, a theo-logical student, in September, 1923. She retained her maiden name for professional purposes, a relatively un-common practice in those days. Two years later, how-ever, she and Cressman agreed to go off on separate paths of study—he to Europe and she to Samoa. She had many misgivings about what she was setting out to do, because she really did not know much about fieldwork. Her course on methods with Boas was not about fieldwork, but about theory, how to organize material so as to refute

1928

Margaret Mead. (Library of Congress)

or support some theoretical point. She had consented to Boas's suggestion that she study the adolescent girl, but she persisted in her determination to do the study in the South Seas, against Boas's recommendation that the study be made in some safer location, such as among a group of American Indians.

On arrival in Samoa, Mead's first problem was to learn the language. She had been warned that the reports others had made were "contaminated by the ideas of European grammar," and even the recorded descriptions supposed to have been given by local chiefs were weighted by European notions about rank and status inserted by the researchers doing the recording. Therefore, she moved into the household of a "chief who enjoyed entertaining visitors." She slept with the chief's daughter on a pile of sleeping mats on a sleeping porch. Mead learned much from the family about Samoan habits and etiquette. She even had to bathe in public, in full view of crowds of children and passing adults, under the village shower. She learned to wear a saronglike garment, which she could slip off before a shower and exchange for a dry one afterward.

Mead learned enough of the Samoan language in her first six weeks to give her the confidence to look for a place to stay among the natives of the island of Tau, about 240 kilometers (149 miles) east of Pago Pago in

American Samoa. The western half of the Samoan Islands, which contains by far the greater part of the land area, is a United Nations Trust Territory, administered by New Zealand. She moved into the household of the only American family on Tau, a pharmacist's mate in the U.S. Navy, Edward Holt, his wife, and children. From November, 1925, to June, 1926, Mead lived with the Holts while she conducted interviews with a group of about fifty teenage girls and kept notes on her findings. By entertaining crowds of adolescent girls on her porch day after day, she gradually built up a census of the whole village and worked out the background of each of the girls she was studying.

In June, 1926, Mead ended her Samoan sojourn and boarded a small ship in Pago Pago bound for home by way of Sydney, Australia, and then through Ceylon, Aden, Sicily, and Marseilles, where her husband met her. They traveled to New York, where she worked as assistant curator of ethnology at the American Museum of Natural History, where she was to remain the rest of her professional life. Mead soon completed all but the last two chapters of *Coming of Age in Samoa*, which she subtitled *A Psychological Study of Primitive Youth for Western Civilization*. In the foreword she asked Boas to write for the book, he described the difficulties that beset the individual in civilization, difficulties likely to be ascribed to fundamental human traits. Boas noted his doubt about the correctness of this assumption, but said that hardly anyone had yet set out to identify him- or herself with a primitive population in sufficient depth to obtain insight into these problems. Mead had confirmed, he believed, the suspicion long held by anthropologists that "much of what we ascribe to human nature is no more than a reaction to the restraints put upon us by our civilisation."

Coming of Age in Samoa was published in August, 1928. When Mead returned from Samoa, she was asked to give lectures about her work. Audience members often asked her what the meaning was of what she had found in Samoa. She then wrote the last two chapters of her book, one comparing the lives of Samoan girls with their American counterparts and the other titled "Education for Choice." Mead soon left for the Admiralty Islands to conduct a new study, and it was months before she learned that her book had become a best seller. Mead would write many more books, but none brought her the phenomenal success of *Coming of Age in Samoa*. By 1968, the book had gone through a new edition and at least five more printings. In the early twenty-first century, *Coming of Age in Samoa* remains among the most frequently sought books in many libraries, despite some ongoing controversy about its contents.

SIGNIFICANCE

The publication of *Coming of Age in Samoa* broke new ground in anthropology, making Mead one of the most famous American scientists and bringing recognition to the science of anthropology. In 1970, Mead was honored with one of the most prestigious offices in American science, the presidency of the American Association for Advancement of Science. *The New York Times* was moved to editorialize on anthropology shortly after the book came out, in its June 4, 1929, edition, under the headline "American Race Types."

Although the book's reception was favorable for the most part, some have questioned Mead's clear support for the "nurture" side in the "nature versus nurture" controversy in anthropology. In 1983, Derek Freeman, an emeritus professor of anthropology at the Australian National University, criticized Mead in an unabashedly polemical book, *Margaret Mead and Samoa: The Making and Unmaking of an Anthropological Myth*. The debate over Freeman's book began two months before its publication, when a copy of the text brought on an editorial in *The New York Times* in January, 1983, headlined "New Samoan Book Challenges Margaret Mead's Conclusions." The controversy even made the cover of *Time* magazine. More recently, anthropological work among several New Guinea tribes has suggested that Mead inaccurately portrayed these groups as pacifistic in her book *Sex and Temperament in Three Primitive Societies* (1935), raising again the question of the reliability of her data and her descriptions of traditional societies. Supporters of Mead have responded with publications of their

own, and debates about her work continue in anthropological circles.

—*Joseph A. Schufle*

FURTHER READING

Freeman, Derek. *The Fateful Hoaxing of Margaret Mead: A Historical Analysis of Her Samoan Research*. Boulder, Colo.: Westview Press, 1998. Detailed analysis of Mead's training and her research in Samoa, written after the uproar caused among anthropologists by the author's earlier work on Mead (cited below). Argues that Mead's findings in Samoa resulted from a hoax perpetrated by some of her informants.

_____. *Margaret Mead and Samoa: The Making and*

MEAD DESCRIBES A SAMOAN MORNING

Margaret Mead opens Coming of Age in Samoa *with a vivid summary of a day in the life of a Samoan village. She begins with the morning:*

The life of the day begins at dawn, or if the moon has shown until daylight, the shouts of the young men may be heard before dawn from the hillside. Uneasy in the night, populous with ghosts, they shout lustily to one another as they hasten with their work. As the dawn begins to fall among the soft brown roofs and the slender palm trees stand out against a colourless, gleaming sea, lovers slip home from trysts beneath the palm trees or in the shadow of beached canoes, that the light may find each sleeper in his appointed place. Cocks crow, negligently, and a shrill-voiced bird cries from the breadfruit trees. The insistent roar of the reef seems muted to an undertone for the sounds of a waking village. Babies cry, a few short wails before sleepy mothers give them the breast. Restless little children roll out of their sheets and wander drowsily down to the beach to freshen their faces in the sea. Boys, bent upon an early fishing, start collecting their tackle and go to rouse their more laggard companions. Fires are lit, here and there, the white smoke hardly visible against the paleness of the dawn. The whole village, sheeted and frowsy, stirs, rubs its eyes, and stumbles toward the beach. "Talofa!" "Talofa!" "Will the journey start today?" "Is it bonito fishing your lordship is going?" Girls stop to giggle over some young ne'er-do-well who escaped during the night from an angry father's pursuit and to venture a shrewd guess that the daughter knew more about his presence than she told. The boy who is taunted by another, who has succeeded him in his sweetheart's favour, grapples with his rival, his foot slipping in the wet sand. From the other end of the village comes a long drawn-out, piercing wail. A messenger has just brought word of the death of some relative in another village. Half-clad, unhurried women, with babies at their breasts, or astride their hips, pause in their tale of Losa's outraged departure from her father's house to the greater kindness in the home of her uncle, to wonder who is dead.

Source: Margaret Mead, *Coming of Age in Samoa: A Psychological Study of Primitive Youth for Western Civilisation* (New York: William Morrow, 1928).

1928

Unmaking of an Anthropological Myth. Cambridge, Mass.: Harvard University Press, 1983. Controversial book sets out its purpose in the first paragraph: the refutation of Mead's Samoan work and her defense of cultural determinism. Written in a polemical tone.

Holmes, Lowell D. *The Quest for the Real Samoa: The Mead/Freeman Controversy and Beyond*. South Hadley, Mass.: Bergin & Garvey, 1987. Written in response to Freeman's 1983 book, cited above, by an anthropologist who began fieldwork in Samoa in 1954. Presents conclusions that, for the most part, corroborate Mead's.

Howard, Jane. *Margaret Mead: A Life*. New York: Simon & Schuster, 1984. Definitive Mead biography is complimentary for the most part but addresses some of the criticisms of her work as well. Discussion of her private life includes information about her three marriages—the first to an American clergyman, the second to a New Zealand psychologist, and the third to the father of her only daughter, Mary Catherine Bateson, who became an eminent English anthropologist.

McGee, R. Jon, and Richard L. Warms. *Anthropological Theory: An Introductory History*. 3d ed. New York: McGraw-Hill, 2003. Presents classic and contemporary readings in anthropology along with introductions and commentary to help students understand the history of theory in the field. Includes bibliography and index.

Mead, Margaret. *Blackberry Winter: My Earlier Years*. New York: William Morrow, 1972. Autobiography vividly describes Mead's fieldwork in Samoa, New Guinea, and Bali and the opposition she met and overcame as a young woman in a profession dominated by men. Mead describes herself as a child, student, wife, mother, and grandmother. Illustrated.

_____. *Coming of Age in Samoa*. 1928. Reprint. New York: Harper Perennial, 2001. The book that "put anthropology on the map." In addition to the original text, reprint edition includes a brief introductory piece by Mead's daughter and the preface to the 1973 edition.

SEE ALSO: 1911: Boas Publishes *The Mind of Primitive Man*; Sept. 30, 1925: Chesterton Critiques Modernism and Defends Christianity; 1934: Benedict Publishes *Patterns of Culture*.

August 27, 1928
KELLOGG-BRIAND PACT

Signatories to the Kellogg-Briand Pact, a multilateral treaty, pledged to renounce war as an instrument of national policy and to maintain peace by common action.

ALSO KNOWN AS: Pact of Paris; General Pact for the Renunciation of War
LOCALE: Paris, France
CATEGORY: Diplomacy and international relations

KEY FIGURES
William E. Borah (1865-1940), U.S. senator from Idaho
Aristide Briand (1862-1932), French foreign minister
Frank B. Kellogg (1856-1937), U.S. secretary of state
Salmon O. Levinson (1865-1941), American attorney

SUMMARY OF EVENT
The multilateral Kellogg-Briand Pact, also known as the Pact of Paris, held out the promise of a new era of international harmony when it was signed on August 27, 1928. The chief architects of the treaty, Aristide Briand and Frank B. Kellogg, and the other member signatories took a formal pledge "not to have recourse to war as an instrument of national policy, and to settle all disputes arising between them by peaceful means." The treaty was signed originally by fifteen countries, and by 1934 it embraced the participation of sixty-four nations, the exceptions being Argentina, Brazil, and the tiny countries of Andorra, Liechtenstein, Monaco, and San Marino.

The movement to outlaw war was initiated by Salmon O. Levinson in the United States in the aftermath of the first global war and became a worldwide movement in a few years. This movement was of great importance in bringing about the negotiation and general ratification of the Kellogg-Briand Pact. Briand proposed the idea of a definitive treaty on April 6, 1927, when he suggested the conclusion of a bilateral Pact of Perpetual Friendship between France and the United States for the renunciation of war. Briand's aim was to bind the United States—which still remained outside existing international accords, such as the League of Nations Covenant and the Locarno Treaties—to France through a separate bilateral

President Calvin Coolidge (seated at table, left) and U.S. secretary of state Frank B. Kellogg (at table, right) sign the Kellogg-Briand Pact. (Library of Congress)

1928

pact in an effort to reinforce the international movement toward world peace.

At the beginning, the French proposal was ignored completely by Kellogg and the Department of State. It was Nicholas Murray Butler, the president of Columbia University, and Professors J. T. Shotwell and Joseph P. Chamberlain who developed the implications of Briand's offer by drawing up a draft treaty celebrated as the "American Locarno." The idea had an overwhelming impact on both educated and common Americans, creating widespread support for the antiwar idea. Encouraged by these developments, Briand formally presented a "Draft Pact of Perpetual Friendship between France and the U.S." to the Department of State on June 20, 1927.

Levinson's untiring campaign to make the United States the champion of the movement to outlaw war bore

fruit. He persuaded William E. Borah, chair of the Senate Committee on Foreign Relations, to introduce a resolution in the Senate on December 27, 1927, calling for the outlawing of war. Kellogg, now responding to public enthusiasm, made a new proposition to the French minister: that "the two governments would make a more signal contribution to world peace by joining in an effort to obtain the adherence of all of the principal powers of the world to a declaration renouncing war as an instrument of national policy." There ensued a long period of complex negotiations among France, the United States, the other Great Powers except Russia, and some lesser powers.

The French did not immediately endorse the suggested alterations to their original proposal. They feared that a new multilateral agreement would conflict with the obli-

GENERAL PACT FOR THE RENUNCIATION OF WAR

The President of the German Reich, the President of the United States of America, His Majesty the King of the Belgians, the President of the French Republic, His Majesty the King of Great Britain, Ireland and the British Dominions beyond the Seas, Emperor of India, His Majesty the King of Italy, His Majesty the Emperor of Japan, the President of the Republic of Poland, the President of the Czechoslovak Republic

Deeply sensible of their solemn duty to promote the welfare of mankind;

Persuaded that the time has come when a frank renunciation of war as an instrument of national policy should be made to the end that the peaceful and friendly relations now existing between their peoples may be perpetuated

Convinced that all changes in their relations with one another should be sought only by pacific means and be the result of a peaceful and orderly process and that any signatory power which shall hereafter seek to promote its national interests by resort to war should be denied the benefits furnished by this treaty

Hopeful that, encouraged by their example, all the other nations of the world will join in this humane endeavor and by adhering to the present treaty as soon as it comes into force bring their peoples within the scope of its beneficent provisions, thus uniting the civilized nations of the world in a common renunciation of war as an instrument of their national policy;

Have decided to conclude a treaty and for that purpose have appointed as their respective plenipotentiaries [list of names] . . . who, having communicated to one another their full powers found in good and due form have agreed upon the following articles:

ARTICLE 1

The high contracting parties solemnly declare in the names of their respective peoples that they condemn recourse to war for the solution of international controversies, and renounce it as an instrument of national policy in their relations with one another.

ARTICLE 2

The high Contracting parties agree that the settlement or solution of all disputes or conflicts of whatever nature or of whatever origin they may be, which may arise among them, shall never be sought except by pacific means.

ARTICLE 3

The present treaty shall be ratified by the high contracting parties named in the preamble in accordance with their respective constitutional requirements, and shall take effect as between them as soon as all their several instruments of ratification shall have been deposited at Washington.

This treaty shall, when it has come into effect as prescribed in the preceding paragraph, remain open as long as may be necessary for adherence by all the other powers of the world. Every instrument evidencing the adherence of a power shall be deposited at Washington and the treaty shall immediately upon such deposit become effective as between the power thus adhering and the other powers parties hereto.

It shall be the duty of the Government of the United States to furnish each government named in the preamble and every government subsequently adhering to this treaty with a certified copy of the treaty and of every instrument of ratification or adherence. It shall also be the duty of the Government of the United States telegraphically to notify such governments immediately upon the deposit with it of each instrument of ratification or adherence.

In faith whereof the respective plenipotentiaries have signed this treaty in the French and English languages, both texts having equal force, and hereunto affix their seals.

Done at Paris, the twenty-seventh day of August in the year one thousand nine hundred and twenty-eight.

---

gations and machinery of sanctions embodied in the League Covenant and the Locarno Treaties. Because the United States was not a signatory to those international accords, France desired only a bilateral pact with the United States. In his reply of February 27, 1928, Kellogg allayed French fears by assuring that the multilateral pact would neither conflict with nor violate the specific obligations of the Covenant and the Locarno Treaties. Rather, it would act as an effective instrument for strengthening the foundations of world peace. On March 30, 1928, the French accepted the revised United States proposal to universalize the treaty. It is historically accurate to say

that the Briand offer formed the basis of the multilateral Kellogg-Briand Pact, and its wording, with slight modifications, became the wording of the final treaty.

On April 7, 1928, Kellogg secured an understanding with the French ambassador that both France and the United States would separately address the other four Great Powers—Great Britain, Germany, Italy, and Japan—inviting their opinions and participation. According to *The New York Times* of April 14, 1928, a copy of the U.S. draft treaty and a note were sent to those powers and to France. The note stated that the U.S. government "desires to see the institution of war abolished and stands ready to conclude with the French, British, German, Italian, and Japanese governments a single multilateral treaty open to subsequent adherence by any and all other governments binding the parties thereto not to resort to war with one another." The draft treaty contained two articles calling for the renunciation of war as an instrument of national policy and peaceful settlement of all international disputes. The French sent their draft on April 20. The French draft contained six articles, adding other clauses concerning matters such as self-defense, violation and release of obligation by others, and ratification by all before the treaty would be enforced.

The responses of the four Great Powers to both drafts were more than favorable. The only concern, expressed by the British minister, Sir Austen Chamberlain, was the restrictions that the treaty would place on British freedom of action over its far-flung empire. This fear was lessened by the sovereign right of self-defense implicit in the pact. Every sovereign state, Kellogg emphasized, possessed the inherent right to defend its territory, and wars fought to repulse aggression would be entirely legal and not a violation of the pact. On the suggestion of the British, other signatories of the Locarno Treaties—Belgium, Poland, and Czechoslovakia—were included among the principal signatories, along with India and the five British dominions of Australia, Canada, the Irish Free State, New Zealand, and South Africa. The U.S. interpretation of the treaty was sent to fourteen governments. The vital element in the fourteen replies received in July was that all the governments had agreed to sign the treaty as proposed by Kellogg.

The diplomatic exchanges thus came to a successful conclusion. This represented a personal triumph for Kellogg, who was awarded the Nobel Peace Prize in 1929. Since December 28, 1927, he had unremittingly pursued the aim of a global multilateral treaty for the renunciation of war as an instrument of national policy, and he had achieved his goal. The other great hero and the original inspiration, Briand, also was awarded the Nobel Peace Prize. He had accomplished everything that he deemed essential for France.

SIGNIFICANCE

The most important aim of the Kellogg-Briand Pact was to prevent war. The treaty linked the United States to the League of Nations as a guardian of world peace and in turn strengthened the sanctions of the Covenant. It simultaneously enhanced the feeling of security in Europe and in the rest of the world, and abetted the motive for general disarmament. The practical influence of the pact lay in the mobilization of the moral and legal conscience of humankind against aggressive militarism.

The treaty remained permanently flawed, however. Although it outlawed war, it did not codify this into a principle or rule of international law. Hence breaches of the resolution—many of which happened in subsequent years—were not tantamount to crimes or violations of international law. Italy's attack on Ethiopia in 1935 and Japanese imperialism in China in the 1930's could not be prevented, as the pact included neither moral sanctions nor any tribunals to enforce its provisions. Moreover, the blanket interpretation of self-defense allowed many nations to justify their wars of aggression. Nevertheless, the pact, although violated many times, was never officially repealed. It served as the legal basis for the Nuremberg and Tokyo war crimes trials after World War II.

—*Sudipta Das*

FURTHER READING

Ferrell, Robert H. *Peace in Their Time: The Origins of the Kellogg-Briand Pact*. New York: W. W. Norton, 1969. Essential source provides superb analyses of the U.S. State Department's stratagems with French diplomats and domestic peace activists in the shaping of the pact.

Marks, Sally. *The Illusion of Peace: International Relations in Europe, 1918-1933*. 2d ed. New York: Palgrave Macmillan, 2003. Presents general, scholarly coverage of European diplomatic events, with critical analysis of the Kellogg-Briand Pact and its ramifications. Includes chronological table, bibliography, and index.

Miller, D. H. *The Peace Pact of Paris: A Study of the Briand-Kellogg Treaty*. New York: G. P. Putnam's Sons, 1928. Detailed and objective study of the shaping and writing of the pact from both French and American perspectives. Research based on official documents and firsthand information.

Shotwell, J. T. *War as an Instrument of National Policy and Its Renunciation in the Pact of Paris*. 1928. Reprint. New York: Garland, 1974. An essential, firsthand source on the peace pact. Explains the perspective of the U.S. peace seekers.

Steiner, Zara. *The Lights That Failed: European International History 1919-1933*. New York: Oxford University Press, 2005. Comprehensive, scholarly work examines efforts to reestablish equilibrium in Europe after World War I through peace treaties and other means. Includes maps, tables, and bibliography.

Vinson, John C. *William E. Borah and the Outlawry of*

1928

War. Athens: University of Georgia Press, 1957. A major contribution to an understanding of the U.S. commitment to promote world peace. Portrays Borah as the spokesperson for the United States and highlights his role in effecting peace plans, especially the Kellogg-Briand Pact.

SEE ALSO: Oct. 18, 1907: Second Hague Peace Conference; Apr. 28, 1919: League of Nations Is Established; Nov. 12, 1921-Feb. 6, 1922: Washington Disarmament Conference; Jan. 7, 1932: Stimson Doctrine.

September, 1928
FLEMING DISCOVERS PENICILLIN IN MOLDS

Alexander Fleming's discovery of the antibiotic penicillin led to the development of a wonder drug that saved millions of lives.

LOCALE: London, England

CATEGORIES: Health and medicine; science and technology; chemistry

KEY FIGURES

Alexander Fleming (1881-1955), English bacteriologist
Ernst Boris Chain (1906-1979), German English biochemist
Baron Florey (1898-1968), Australian pathologist
Almroth Edward Wright (1861-1947), British bacteriologist

SUMMARY OF EVENT

During the early twentieth century, scientists became increasingly interested in bacteriology, or the study of infectious disease. This field has since come to be called microbiology and includes the study of viruses, protozoa, fungi, and bacteria. Early bacteriologists were able to identify the sources of diseases such as pneumonia, syphilis, meningitis, gas gangrene, and tonsillitis. Prior to the discovery of antibiotics, exposure to bacteria such as streptococci, staphylococci, pneumococci, and tubercle bacilli resulted in serious and often fatal illness. Penicillin was the first of a series of twentieth century "wonder drugs" used to treat bacterial infections. This powerful antibiotic altered the lives of millions of patients who would otherwise have fallen prey to diseases caused by bacteria.

Sir Alexander Fleming began his scientific career in 1901, when he inherited a small legacy that enabled him to enter St. Mary's Medical School in London. Fleming was a prizewinning student and a superb technician. He qualified as a doctor in 1906 and remained at St. Mary's as a junior assistant to Sir Almroth Edward Wright, a prominent pathologist and well-known proponent of inoculation. In 1909, Fleming was one of the first to use Paul Ehrlich's new arsenical compound, Salvarsan, for treatment of syphilis. He became renowned for his skilled administration of Salvarsan.

During World War I, Wright and Fleming joined the Royal Army Medical Corps and conducted wound research at a laboratory in Boulogne. Fleming was in charge of identifying the infecting bacteria by taking swabs from wounds before, during, and after surgery. His results showed that 90 percent of the samples contained *Clostridium welchii*, the anaerobic bacteria that cause gas gangrene. Although scientists could isolate the bacteria, they were uncertain as to the best method for combating diseases. Antiseptics were a known means for killing bacteria but were not always effective, especially when used in deep wounds. Wright and Fleming showed that white blood cells found in pus discharged from wounds had ingested bacteria. Fleming also demonstrated that contrary to popular opinion, when antiseptics were packed into a wound, bacteria survived in the crevasses. Antiseptics destroyed the body's own defenses (white blood cells), allowing the remaining bacteria to create serious infection unimpeded. The horrors of bacterial infection during World War I had a lasting impact on Fleming, who decided to focus his postwar research on antibiotic substances. Fleming was convinced that the ideal antiseptic or bacteria-fighting agent should be highly active against microorganisms but harmless to the body's own white blood cell defenses.

In 1921, Fleming observed the dissolving effect that a sample of his own nasal mucus had on bacteria growing in a petri dish. He isolated the antibiotic component of the mucus and named it "lysozyme." Further research showed that lysozyme was also present in human blood serum, tears, saliva, pus, and milk. Fleming had discovered a universal biological protective mechanism that kills and dissolves most of the airborne bacteria that invade exposed areas of the body. He also found that lysozyme does not interfere with the body's white blood cells. Surprisingly, the discovery of lysozyme, subsequently recognized as fundamentally important, received little attention from the scientific community. Ronald Hare, Fleming's associate and biographer, attributes the neglect of lysozyme to "Fleming's inability to express himself clearly and lucidly in either words or print." The significance of lysozyme continued to be overlooked until researchers discovered its presence in white blood cells. Despite the neglect of lysozyme, Fleming continued to focus his research on antibiotics.

In September, 1928, Fleming noticed that a mold was growing in a petri dish containing strains of staphylococci and that bacteria surrounding the mold were being destroyed. It is likely that the source of the mold spores was the laboratory below Fleming's, where mycologist C. J. La Touche was growing molds for research on allergies. Because of his interest in antibiotics, Fleming was conditioned to recognize immediately that an agent capable of dissolving staphylococci could be of great biological significance. He preserved the original culture plate and made a subculture of the mold in a tube of broth. Fleming's mold was later identified as *Penicillium notatum*. Further experiments showed that the "mould

Alexander Fleming. (The Nobel Foundation)

juice" could be produced by several strains of *Penicillium* but not by other molds. The substance was nontoxic and did not interfere with the action of white blood cells.

Fleming described his findings in a paper titled "On the Antibacterial Action of Cultures of a Penicillium, with Special Reference to Their Use in the Isolation of B. Influenzae," which appeared in the *British Journal of Experimental Pathology* in 1929. The unusual title refers to Fleming's use of penicillin to isolate bacteria that were not vulnerable to penicillin. In his paper, Fleming described the mold extract and listed the sensitive bacteria. Most important, Fleming suggested that penicillin might be used in the treatment of infection. In addition to describing his experiments, Fleming also stated that the name "penicillin" would be used to refer to the mold broth filtrate. This article on penicillin came to be regarded as one of the most important medical papers ever written.

Fleming's petri dish elicited little interest from colleagues at St. Mary's, who were familiar with his previous work and assumed that this was an example of lysozyme being produced by a mold. Fleming knew this to be untrue, as lysozyme was incapable of destroying a pathogenic organism such as staphylococcus. Once again, Fleming's limited ability as a writer and speaker left his audience content to shelve his latest discovery along with lysozyme. Even Ernst Boris Chain, who discovered Fleming's paper during a literature search in 1936, "thought that Fleming had discovered a sort of mould lysozyme which, in contrast to egg white lysozyme, acted on a wide range of . . . pathogenic bacteria."

During 1929, Fleming continued to investigate the antibiotic properties of penicillin, collecting data that clearly established the chemotherapeutic potential of penicillin. Fleming was unable to purify and concentrate penicillin adequately, and, hence, did not conduct clinical tests that could prove the effectiveness of the antibiotic in vivo. The significance of Fleming's discovery was not recognized until 1940, when Baron Florey and Chain discovered the enormous therapeutic power of penicillin.

SIGNIFICANCE

Fleming's discovery of penicillin had no immediate impact on twentieth century medicine. By 1931, Fleming had discontinued work on the antibiotic and turned to the study of sulfa drugs. In 1940, Florey and Chain succeeded in concentrating and clinically testing penicillin, after which Fleming's discovery gained enormous notoriety and he was showered with accolades and honors. In

1928

1943, he was elected to fellowship in the Royal Society; in 1944, he was knighted; and in 1945, he received the Nobel Prize in Physiology or Medicine jointly with Florey and Chain.

Penicillin achieved particular notoriety because of World War II and the demand for an antibiotic that could halt diseases such as gas gangrene, which infected the wounds of numerous soldiers during World War I. With the help of Florey and Chain's Oxford group, scientists at the U.S. Department of Agriculture's Northern Regional Research Laboratory developed a highly efficient method for producing penicillin using fermentation. An excellent cornstarch medium was developed for both surface and submerged culture of penicillium molds. After an extended search, scientists also were able to isolate a more productive penicillium strain (*Penicillium chrysogenum*). By 1945, a strain was developed that produced five hundred times more penicillin than Fleming's original mold.

During World War II, the U.S. Office of Scientific Research and Development's Committee on Medical Research conducted large-scale clinical tests of penicillin on 10,838 patients. Their results provided doctors with effective methods and dosages for use of penicillin in treatment of many diseases.

American pharmaceutical companies were galvanized by the development of an efficient production technique and positive clinical tests. Corporations such as Merck, Pfizer, Squibb, and many others built large factories to mass-produce penicillin for use by the U.S. armed forces. The War Production Board increased production by allocating supplies and equipment to twenty-two U.S. chemical companies engaged in the production of the antibiotic. Penicillin prevented many of the horrendous casualties that Fleming witnessed during World War I.

Penicillin is regarded as among the greatest medical discoveries of the twentieth century. Almost every organ in the body is vulnerable to bacteria. Before penicillin, the only antimicrobial drugs available were quinine, arsenic, and sulfa drugs. Of these, only the sulfa drugs were useful for treatment of bacterial infection, but high toxicity precluded their use in many cases. With this limited arsenal, doctors were helpless as thousands died in epidemics caused by bacteria. Diseases such as pneumonia, meningitis, and syphilis are now treated with penicillin all over the world.

Penicillin and other antibiotics also had a broad impact on medicine as major procedures such as heart surgery, organ transplants, and management of severe burns became possible once the threat of bacterial infection was minimized. Fleming's discovery brought about a revolution in medical treatment by offering an extremely effective solution to the enormous problem of infectious disease.

—*Peter Neushul*

FURTHER READING

Epstein, Samuel, and Beryl Williams. *Miracles from Microbes*. New Brunswick, N.J.: Rutgers University Press, 1946. Presents the background of the development of several antibiotics, including penicillin and streptomycin.

Fleming, Alexander. "On the Antibacterial Action of Cultures of a Penicillium, with Special Reference to Their Use in the Isolation of B. Influenzae." *British Journal of Experimental Pathology* 10 (1929): 226-236. Fleming's first description of his discovery gives valuable insight into his experimental technique and understanding of the antibiotic potential of penicillin.

Hare, Ronald. *The Birth of Penicillin, and the Disarming of Microbes*. London: George Allen & Unwin, 1970. Provides a firsthand description of Fleming's work by a scientist who worked at St. Mary's at the time of Fleming's discovery and was among those who witnessed Fleming's early work with penicillin. Presents an interesting perspective on penicillin research before 1940.

Hobby, Gladys L. *Penicillin: Meeting the Challenge*. New Haven, Conn.: Yale University Press, 1985. Presents a good overall description of the roles played by Fleming, Florey, Chain, and numerous other scientists in the discovery, development, and eventual mass production of penicillin. Includes extensive footnotes.

Lax, Eric. *The Mold in Dr. Florey's Coat: The Story of the Penicillin Miracle*. New York: Henry Holt, 2004. Relates the story of the discovery of penicillin and its development into a useful drug. Sheds light on the personalities of the scientists involved—Florey and Chain as well as Fleming. Includes bibliography and index.

Ludovici, L. J. *Fleming: Discoverer of Penicillin*. London: Andrew Dakers, 1952. Contemporary biography of Fleming reflects the fact that he was revered both by the author and by the general public.

Macfarlane, Gwyn. *Alexander Fleming: The Man and the Myth*. Cambridge, Mass.: Harvard University Press, 1984. Authoritative biography of Fleming draws on interviews as well as Fleming's own notes to dispel somewhat the "Fleming myth" that abounds in earlier biographies.

Mateles, Richard I., ed. *Penicillin: A Paradigm for Biotechnology*. Chicago: Canadida Corporation, 1998. Volume reprints *The History of Penicillin Production*, a classic work first published in 1970, along with new chapters that address advances in penicillin research since that time. Also discusses the status of penicillin and its derivatives at the end of the twentieth century.

Maurois, André. *The Life of Alexander Fleming*. New York: E. P. Dutton, 1959. Authorized biography of Fleming includes two chapters on his penicillin research.

Ryan, Frank. *The Forgotten Plague: How the Battle Against Tuberculosis Was Won—and Lost*. Boston: Little, Brown, 1993. Written for nontechnical readers, a significant portion of this volume discusses the methodology behind the discovery and testing of many major antibiotics.

Sheehan, John C. *The Enchanted Ring: The Untold Story of Penicillin*. Cambridge, Mass.: MIT Press, 1982. Definitive history of the discovery, development, and marketing of penicillin, accessible to general readers.

SEE ALSO: Nov.-Dec., 1908: Ehrlich and Metchnikoff Conduct Pioneering Immunity Research; Apr., 1910: Ehrlich Introduces Salvarsan as a Cure for Syphilis; 1913: Schick Introduces a Test for Diphtheria; 1921: Tuberculosis Vaccine BCG Is Developed; 1927: U.S. Food and Drug Administration Is Established; May, 1940: Florey and Chain Develop Penicillin as an Antibiotic.

September 17, 1928

OIL COMPANIES COOPERATE IN A CARTEL COVERING THE MIDDLE EAST

To curtail competition, American, British, and European petroleum industry executives formed an international cartel controlling production, markets, and Middle East oil exploration.

ALSO KNOWN AS: Achnacarry Agreement
LOCALE: Ostend, Belgium; Achnacarry Castle, Inverness, Scotland
CATEGORIES: Trade and commerce; energy; natural resources

KEY FIGURES

Walter Clark Teagle (1878-1962), president of Jersey Standard
Henri W. A. Deterding (1866-1939), Royal Dutch/ Shell executive
Sir John Cadman (1877-1941), leader of British Petroleum
Calouste Sarkis Gulbenkian (1869-1955), international investor powerful in the Turkish Petroleum Company
John D. Rockefeller (1839-1937), founder and leader of Standard Oil Company

SUMMARY OF EVENT

At the opening of the 1920's, the position of major U.S. petroleum companies appeared unassailable in many regards, both at home and abroad. Their ability to furnish the Allied Powers with huge supplies of American oil—80 percent of their requirements—had helped immeasurably in World War I. Profits tended to be high. Consumption, despite plateaus between peaks, grew rapidly with industry's increased mechanization, with new lifestyles dependent on oil, and with the massive influence of the automotive age. American production of crude oil from domestic fields accounted for 70 percent of the world's total, and new American oil fields were being discovered with comforting frequency.

Customarily, only surpluses of domestic petroleum were marketed abroad. Led by John D. Rockefeller's Standard Oil and, after the dissolution of Standard Oil in 1911 for federal antitrust violations, by Jersey Standard (Exxon) and Standard affiliates, American oil companies nevertheless held seemingly impregnable positions in Canada and in Central and Latin America, as well as in much of the Far East. With Russia's crude oil production curtailed by the 1917 revolution, by ensuing civil war, and then by the Soviets' impaired diplomatic relations, American oilmen seriously challenged many of their European rivals in their own domestic markets. The American companies had won these international marketing positions without the direct support of the federal government and without direct linkages to the nation's military or diplomatic objectives.

The Allied Powers' territorial division immediately following World War I and the U.S. State Department's affirmation of "open door" diplomacy on behalf of

1928

American oil interests abroad set the stage for further international expansion. The private negotiations of four oil company executives were primarily responsible for American companies, by the late 1920's, joining in the exploration and exploitation of Middle Eastern oil concessions. Three of these oilmen each guided one of the seven leading international oil companies: Henri W. A. Deterding directed Royal Dutch/Shell, Sir John Cadman led British Petroleum as well as Anglo-Persian, and Walter Clark Teagle presided over Jersey Standard. A fourth figure, Calouste Sarkis Gulbenkian, an Armenian investor in the strategically and politically well placed but much smaller Turkish Petroleum Company (TPC), was instrumental in persuading British, French, and Turkish interests to accept American participation in Middle East concessions.

Several factors explain why Deterding, Cadman, and Teagle, who had long battled one another for shares of mutually attractive markets, united to divide and cartelize the oil resources of the Middle East. Teagle, who became Jersey Standard's president at the age of thirty-three and who soon led the Rockefeller firm to unprecedented profitability, was snarled in a price war that during the 1920's threw Jersey Standard and Standard Oil of New York (Mobil) on the defensive. Profits fell, and the added threat of an oil glut loomed. Jersey Standard was the largest of these international giants. Teagle was laboring to make it a fully integrated concern. Despite marketing 23 percent of the world's refined oil outside the United States (against 16 percent for Royal Dutch/Shell and 11.5 percent for Anglo-Persian, with most of the rest coming from other companies based in the United States), Jersey Standard, unlike its competitors, enjoyed access to few overseas sources of crude oil. Its crude supplies were drawn overwhelmingly from American fields that were heavily pumped. World War I had proven a serious drain on known reserves. Domestic consumption had reached astronomical proportions, and oilmen and government officials labeled the domestic industry's future prospects as precarious.

The British government, sensitive to its navy's role in imperial defense and thus to the oil requirements of that navy, lent strong diplomatic support to Deterding (Shell) and to Cadman (Anglo-Persian) against foreign oil interests. Encouraged by such diplomatic backing, Deterding, with characteristic boldness, subsequently sought control over a substantial proportion of the world's remaining crude oil resources in Mexico, Venezuela, the Soviet Union, and even California. Standard of New York's access to Soviet supplies and its subsequent effort

to underprice Shell in India had provoked an "oil war" that spread worldwide and into the domestic markets of each company. Like all cutthroat competitions, the "war" was costly to both sides.

With State Department backing, Teagle's Jersey Standard and several other American companies began protracted negotiations with Deterding's Shell, Cadman's Anglo-Persian, France's Compagnie Française des Petroles (CFP), and Gulbenkian's Turkish Petroleum. After Turkish Petroleum struck oil in northern Persia (now Iran) in 1927, agreement among the parties came swiftly. The American companies as a group, Anglo-Persian, Shell, and CFP received equal 23.75 percent interests in Turkish Petroleum. Gulbenkian retained the remaining 5 percent. On July 31, 1928, the Americans placed all of their holdings in the Near East Development Corporation (NEDC), 25 percent of which was owned by Jersey Standard and 25 percent by Standard of New York, with equal one-sixth interests belonging individually to Atlantic, Gulf, and Doheny interests. (By 1934, these last three firms had sold their NEDC interests to Standard.) Acting in concert, these companies consented to operate solely through Turkish Petroleum, renamed Iraq Petroleum. Their territory, delineated at a meeting in Ostend, Belgium, by a "red line" drawn by Gulbenkian, encompassed most of the Ottoman Empire before its dismemberment by the victorious Allies after 1918.

To resolve the competing giants' more discrete problems, Teagle initiated a series of discussions with Cadman and Deterding that led to a meeting of the three at Achnacarry Castle in Scotland during August of 1928. The outcome, which was kept secret until 1952, was the Achnacarry Agreement (or the "As Is" Agreement), finalized on September 17, 1928. The agreement's seven principles sought to preclude further competition—and its costly disturbances—among their three companies by freezing market shares "as is" and by providing for sharing of existing facilities (at cost), cooperation on extensions of new facilities, and mutual actions to stabilize production. In order to maintain mutually acceptable prices, a "Gulf plus system" was adopted, under which prices were set at the level for oil delivered from the Gulf of Mexico, no matter what the true source of the oil. This consensus was intended to guide the future operations of local cartels.

SIGNIFICANCE

The "red line" and the Achnacarry Agreement among Jersey Standard, Royal Dutch/Shell, and Anglo-Persian were only the first of several subsequent arrangements by these dominant international oil companies. Later in 1928, for example, the giants drafted a Memorandum for European Markets (MEM) whereby quotas were allotted to each for petroleum products sold in each country. Each company could fulfill its quota and even increase it, but only at the expense of oil companies not party to the MEM. To ensure compliance, monthly meetings were to be convened for exchange of trade figures. A Draft Memorandum of Principles and its subsequent amendments instituted specific penalties for noncompliance and outlined procedures that were to be invoked when companies retired from the cartel, when they purchased new companies, or when they dealt with newer petroleum products that replaced older ones. Some interpreted the last provision as discouraging innovations.

In all these agreements and statements of principles and procedures, stress was laid on the companies' cooperation. Rules attempted to prevent members of the cartel from profiting at the expense of the others through unilateral adjustments of quotas and prices in the form of selling more than allowed by quota or at a different price from that charged by the other companies. Increasingly elaborate schemes evolved to ensure that such issues were exposed to frank discussion and that a common front was presented to independent or "outside" oil companies. Governance of the cartel was by vote, the voting power of each member being determined in proportion to its allotted quota. Dominance within the cartel therefore went to those members with the largest quotas, and it was they who set the prices that other participants were obliged to observe.

Cooperation within its ranks, stability within the oil industry and its markets, and moderation in profits were the goals by which the cartel set its course. In language reflective of American antitrust decisions, the cartel agreed that prices in all markets were to be maintained on a basis that yielded fair returns on reasonable investments. Critics at once dismissed such declarations of intent as a mask for profiteering. Nothing in cartel principles or procedures, however, suggested that the giant oil companies had issued themselves a license to gouge the consumers to whom they supplied their products. On the contrary, the cartel's agreements specifically recognized the consuming public's interests by explicitly warning cartel members against allowing prices to rise "to a point where the buying public is exploited."

Furthermore, leaders of the cartel—and, in the background, Rockefeller—were applauded by conservationists in government positions, in the ranks of the general public, and inside the oil industry for acting to curtail the obvious chaos and monumental wastefulness that had been concomitants of the petroleum industry's rapid development. Frenetic, disorganized drilling in American oil fields had prematurely exhausted some U.S. reserves and had led to the creation of the Federal Oil Conservation Board in 1924. The fact that the board had proved to be ineffectual did not deter the official drive toward some form of governmental regulation of oil production, despite critics' assertions that regulation was synonymous with keeping oil prices high. Before 1930, while denying oil companies the right to regulate production and essentially abnegating any responsibility to do so itself, the federal government left the drafting of regulatory measures to whatever compacts could be drawn by the oil-producing states. These actions on the American scene lent credibility to the self-disciplinary activities that the NEDC instituted to regulate the cartelization of Middle East concessions.

By 1930, other American oil companies, with strong support from the U.S. State Department, had made ventures of their own in Middle East oil concessions outside the NEDC's red line. Standard Oil of California (SoCal) bought Gulf Oil's options in Bahrein. After arranging to do business as a British (Canadian) subsidiary, it began operations in the Persian Gulf as the Bahrein Petroleum Company, Limited. Similarly, Gulf Oil, pending British approval, entered negotiations for concessions in Kuwait.

Taken together, these initial Middle East oil concessions laid the foundations for immense future American investments throughout this vast area. Although no oil was shipped from American wells inside NEDC territory until completion of pipeline facilities in 1934, American interests nevertheless had established a continuing presence there. The monopoly previously enjoyed by British, French, and Dutch oil companies had been broken. Moreover, of the world's seven great international oil companies—the "Seven Sisters"—five were American: Jersey Standard (Exxon), Standard Oil Company of New York (Mobil), Standard Oil of California (SoCal), Texaco, and Gulf Oil. Furthermore, regardless of where their concessions lay, the companies adhered to the NEDC's principles and procedures in evolving their own cartels.

—Clifton K. Yearley

FURTHER READING

Blair, John M. *The Control of Oil.* New York: Pantheon Books, 1976. Offers clearly written and informative coverage of the topic. Chapters 2 and 3 dis-

1928

cuss American penetration of Middle East oil fields. Stronger on companies' competition than on diplomatic efforts. Includes tables and charts, notes, and index.

Chester, Edward W. *United States Oil Policy and Diplomacy*. Westport, Conn.: Greenwood Press, 1983. Chapter 1 provides a helpful historical overview. Includes useful chronology, notes, fine bibliographical essay, and index. A valuable work for keeping track of companies' name changes over the years.

Jacoby, Neil H. *Multinational Oil: A Study in Industrial Dynamics*. New York: Macmillan, 1974. One of the first of many books on the phenomenon of multinationals. Includes individual chapter notes, bibliography, and many tables, graphs, and charts.

Nash, Gerald D. *United States Oil Policy, 1890-1964*. Pittsburgh: University of Pittsburgh Press, 1968. Scholarly work traces a theme of the U.S. government's continuous cooperation with oil companies. Chapters 2 and 3 are relevant to American penetration of the Middle East. Includes splendid bibliographical essay.

Pelletière, Stephen. *Iraq and the International Oil System: Why America Went to War in the Gulf*. New York: Praeger, 2001. As background to a discussion of American motives for waging war in the Persian Gulf, Chapters 1 and 2 present the history of the U.S. oil industry and its role in the 1928 formation of a cartel with European oil interests.

Sampson, Anthony. *The Seven Sisters: The Giant Oil Companies and the World They Shaped*. New York: Viking Press, 1975. Excellent introduction to the subject for the layperson. Offers good sources, interesting reading, and balanced perspectives. Includes a map, brief page notes, and a splendid index.

Shwadran, Benjamin. *The Middle East, Oil, and the Great Powers*. 3d rev. ed. New York: John Wiley & Sons, 1973. Scholarly work focuses on what happened to Middle Eastern countries after oil development. Includes a good introduction and a useful discussion of the phasing out of the "red line" agreement. Features many tables and charts, a map, notes, and an excellent bibliography.

Venn, Fiona. *Oil Diplomacy in the Twentieth Century*. New York: St. Martin's Press, 1986. Good source for background. Chapter 4, on the Anglo-American "oil war," is excellent. Includes ample notes, tables, and select bibliography.

Wilkins, Mira. *The Maturing of Multinational Enterprise: American Business Abroad, 1914-1970*. Cambridge, Mass.: Harvard University Press, 1974. Authoritative, scholarly work is invaluable for placing the oil business in context. Chapters 1 and 2 are most relevant to the topic of oil and the Middle East. Includes many tables, notes, bibliography, and index.

SEE ALSO: May 26, 1908: Oil Is Discovered in Persia; Apr. 26, 1920: Great Britain and France Sign the San Remo Agreement; Dec. 14, 1922: Oil Is Discovered in Venezuela; Mar. 3, 1938: Rise of Commercial Oil Industry in Saudi Arabia; Mar. 18, 1938: Mexico Nationalizes Foreign Oil Properties.

October 1, 1928
STALIN INTRODUCES CENTRAL PLANNING

By initiating the First Five-Year Plan, Stalin rejected the New Economic Policy and started large-scale industrialization and forced agricultural collectivization.

ALSO KNOWN AS: Five-Year Plan
LOCALE: Soviet Union
CATEGORIES: Social issues and reform; trade and commerce; government and politics

KEY FIGURES

Joseph Stalin (Joseph Vissarionovich Dzhugashvili; 1878-1953), Soviet leader who established a centrally planned economy
Vladimir Ilich Lenin (Vladimir Ilich Ulyanov; 1870-1924), leader of the Bolsheviks and founder of the Soviet Union
Leon Trotsky (Lev Davidovich Bronstein; 1879-1940), radical Bolshevik leader who opposed Stalin but emphasized the role of industrialization
Nikolay Ivanovich Bukharin (1888-1938), Bolshevik leader, economist, and theorist who defended the New Economic Policy and was purged by Stalin
Yevgeny Preobrazhensky (1886-1937), leading Bolshevik economist who called for massive development of heavy industry
Lev Borisovich Kamenev (1883-1936), Bolshevik leader who led the opposition against Stalin
Grigory Yevseyevich Zinovyev (Ovsel Gershon Aronov Radomyslsky; 1883-1936), Bolshevik leader who opposed Stalin
Mikhail Tomsky (1880-1936), Communist and trade union leader who opposed Stalin

SUMMARY OF EVENT

The year 1929 was one of tremendous tumult in the Soviet Union. After consolidating his power, Joseph Stalin introduced authoritarian central planning in the Soviet Union and rejected the private profits and market mechanisms allowed by Vladimir Ilich Lenin's New Economic Policy. Stalin's First Five-Year Plan was implemented on October 1, 1928. Its major goals included developing heavy industry and national defense, efforts that would be funded by extracting profits from agriculture to invest in industry. To do this, Stalin called for rapid agricultural collectivization. As a result, the end of the 1920's saw both the liquidation of the New Economic Policy and the

initiation of a radically new phase in the development of the Soviet system.

When Lenin died in 1924, he left no designated political heir. One of his last messages, however, urged the Communist Party to reject Stalin as "too rude." Stalin, however, was general secretary, and he used his position to gain control of the party's structure. He handpicked supporters for leading party positions and defeated opponents, including Lev Borisovich Kamenev, Grigory Yevseyevich Zinovyev, and Leon Trotsky by 1926. Another Stalin opponent, Nikolay Ivanovich Bukharin, attempted to continue working within the framework of the New Economic Policy. Stalin, however, was able to prevail over opposition led by Bukharin and Mikhail Tomsky in the course of a protracted struggle between July, 1928, and April, 1929. At the struggle's end, Stalin had gained firm control of both domestic and foreign policy.

In 1924, a debate had begun among Soviet economists. One of these thinkers, Yevgeny Preobrazhensky, sharpened his criticism against the slow pace of industrialization, arguing for "primitive socialist accumulation." In other words, Preobrazhensky thought that industrialization should be financed using the funds left over from exchanges of agricultural produce and consumer goods and machinery. He insisted that setting artificially low agricultural prices and/or artificially high industrial-goods prices was the politically advantageous method of accomplishing this accumulation.

Preobrazhensky was opposed by Bukharin, who was strongly against treating the peasantry as an enemy. Instead, Bukharin argued for a policy that would encourage the peasants to enrich themselves. When agriculture developed, according to Bukharin, there would be more funding for industrialization. Stalin supported the idea of rapid industrialization and forced agricultural collectivization, and he tried to justify his position by emphasizing the external threat facing the Soviet Union. He said that the country was between fifty and one hundred years behind advanced nations like Great Britain, and that if it did not catch up with these countries in about ten years, it would be crushed by foreign aggressors.

The success of Stalin's argument led to the First Five-Year Plan's focus on defense and heavy industry. In the projections, sources of energy (coal and electric power), steel, and heavy engineering were emphasized. Increases in agricultural production were expected but failed to materialize. Output of consumer goods fell below pro-

1928

jections, and much of the small-scale handicraft industry, which had served local consumer markets, was closed. The First Five-Year Plan went into operation in October, 1928, although its formal adoption did not take place until April, 1929. The objectives were stunning: Total industrial output was to increase by 250 percent, and coal's output was to jump more than 330 percent. Output of pig iron was to be nearly tripled, and electric power's output was to be more than quadrupled. Agricultural production was scheduled to increase 150 percent, and 20 percent of the peasants were to be collectivized. At first, optimism was rampant. In July, 1930, the party adopted a slogan: The Five-Year Plan in Four Years.

During 1928 and 1929, however, dramatic shifts in policy took place. At the beginning of 1928, Stalin was already committed to the continued use of coercion to secure essential supplies of grain and to an accelerated but still protracted program of voluntary collectivization. In the summer of 1929, the party launched a drive to collect more grain more rapidly than in any previous year. In November, the Soviet government called for the comprehensive collectivization of the main grain surplus areas

Joseph Stalin. (Library of Congress)

within five months. The new collective enterprises took two basic forms: the state farm and the collective farm. The state farm was the full property of the Soviet government; its manager used hired labor in accordance with the directives put forth by the Ministry of State Farms or by any other ministry to which the farm reported. In contrast, the collective farm was supposed to be a self-governing cooperative made up of peasants who voluntarily pooled their means of production and divided the proceeds.

The plan's administrators had no blueprint to follow, and the nature and principles of planning were worked out by trial and error. Stalin personally and openly identified himself with the need for harsh emergency action, and the implementation of the First Five-Year Plan marked a return to the military traditions of War Communism (1918-1921), a Bolshevik policy that tried to keep towns supplied with weapons and food. The party and government approved the plan, and it became law. Businesses that contravened any element of the plan were considered guilty of a criminal offense.

The overall Five-Year Plan gave grand targets, and their detailed application was contained in annual or quarterly operative plans. This enabled administrators to make regular revisions to the plan, which typically involved raising production quotas. Planned output was expressed in physical units, and the plan's fulfillment was achieved by producing the requisite number, size, weight, or volume of production. Compulsory procurement, which echoed War Communism, had been initiated in 1928; this policy essentially amounted to confiscation. Gradually, a system emerged: Fixed deliveries were made by collectives (and others) in return for fixed prices.

The forced collectivization of agriculture was one of the major causes for the breakdown of market relations between the regime and the peasantry in the winter of 1927-1928. When the state had difficulty obtaining enough grain from peasants in the autumn of 1927, its use of coercive measures resulted in an expedient resolution of the grain crisis. The party quickly became committed to using force against the peasants when doing so helped achieve its ambitious goals. In this way, the Soviets launched a program of rapid industrialization that would have been unachievable within the framework of the New Economic Policy.

SIGNIFICANCE

The 1917 revolution had transformed the Russian political and economic system, but the Stalinist revolution was more fundamental and far-reaching in its socioeconomic and political impact, and it dramatically transformed state-market relations. Late in 1929, the Communist Party called for the mobilization of twenty-five thousand urban workers to spearhead the agricultural collectivization drive. The kulaks (rich peasants) were to be liquidated as a class, and the expropriation of their property was sanctioned. The introduction of this policy was one of the most important additions to the legacy of authoritarian central planning, whose tightening of state control on all major aspects of the Soviet economy had profound impacts on the country's economic development.

Under central planning, heavy industry and the defense industry expanded at the cost of agriculture and consumer industry. The establishment of the Stalinist system involved not only material costs but also enormous human sacrifices. The will of the Communist Party permeated the machinery of the state, and the state controlled many aspects of citizens' lives. The party, through the state, took charge of all public affairs. The state was the only employer; all independent sources of income were eliminated. Even peasants were now subject to state supervision of production; they were allowed to retain only their garden plots.

At the end of 1932, the First Five-Year Plan was declared to have been fulfilled, but the claim had a hollow ring. Stalin contended that production of machinery and electrical equipment had risen 157 percent, but many admitted that output in heavy metallurgy had increased only 67 percent, coal output 89 percent, and consumer goods 73 percent. Even these figures are questionable. Under the impetus of the First Five-Year Plan and the industrialization drive of the 1930's, the Soviet Union imported massive quantities of advanced foreign technology, skilled workers, technicians, and engineering consultants. The Soviets went on to combine borrowing with heavy investment in their own research and training programs in science and technology.

Forced collectivization of agriculture was met with significant peasant resistance. Armed peasant uprisings against the Soviet government were ruthlessly suppressed, and many peasants chose to kill their animals rather than join collective farms. In 1933, the number of horses in the Soviet Union was less than half the 1928 figure; during the period from 1929 to 1931 alone, the number of cattle fell by 30 percent, and the number of sheep and goats fell by 50 percent. Peasants slaughtered their animals on such a scale that cattle and sheep numbers and total meat production did not reach their 1929 levels again until after World War II.

To ensure that grain would be collected and delivered to the state, machine tractor stations were established in 1933. Because grain was the most easily mechanized form of work, the state was able to solve the grain procurement problem simply by retaining the necessary grain harvested by the machine tractor stations and by paying whatever price it desired. This practice was largely effective, and by July of 1934, 71.4 percent of households were officially collectivized. By 1937, private agriculture was virtually eliminated. These achievements, however, came at significant human cost: Historians have concluded that nearly 300,000 families (averaging four members each) were exiled to distant regions during the collectivization drive, and several million people died.

Soviet figures for growth in industrial production show 19 percent growth per year in the First Five-Year Plan. Although this figure is grossly exaggerated, industrial growth during the period was impressive: From 1928 to 1932, coal production increased from 35.4 million tons to 64.4 million tons and oil from 11.7 million tons to 21.4 million tons. Consumer goods and agricultural output, however, fell far short of their targets.

The extraordinary rates of growth projected in the First Five-Year Plan period were not achieved, but industry did grow rapidly. For example, the amount of oil produced rose from 11.7 million tons in 1928 to 31.1 million tons in 1940 to 70.8 million tons in 1955; coal production rose from 35.4 million tons in 1928 to 165.0 million in 1955; steel production rose from 4.3 million tons in 1928 to 18.3 million tons in 1955; and electrical energy production rose from 5.0 billion kilowatt-hours in 1928 to 48.3 billion in 1940 to 170.2 billion in 1955.

In the 1930's, the foundation of the Soviet's centralized, administrative command economy was established, and this bureau oversaw many of the plan's campaigns. Results, however, were conflicted: Growth was uneven and unbalanced, and living standards were sacrificed. By 1937, 53.1 percent of national income (by the Soviet definition) was produced by industry, compared with 41.7 percent in 1929. Industry accounted for 77.4 percent of aggregate production and laid the foundation for defense and military production.

The agricultural sector remained large and inefficient; in 1937, 54 percent of the labor force still worked in agriculture. Terror was employed as an economic weapon: Forced labor was used in some areas for particular projects, but the appeared more often as general coercion backed up by the real threat of imprisonment or death. This system was so highly centralized that a small error

1928

could result in huge problems, and the balancing mechanisms that exist in most market economies were absent from the Soviet model. No real prices existed to indicate surpluses or shortages, and only terror and coercion could control the crises created by the demands put on the economy.

—*Guoli Liu*

FURTHER READING

Cohen, Stephen F. *Rethinking the Soviet Experience: Politics and History Since 1917*. New York: Oxford University Press, 1985. An influential revisionist study of Soviet history with emphases on change and continuity. Examines possible alternatives to the Stalinist system.

Conquest, Robert. *The Harvest of Sorrow: Soviet Collectivization and the Terror-Famine*. New York: Oxford University Press, 1986. Critically examines the collectivization of agriculture. Reveals terrible human suffering and sacrifice during Stalin's rule.

Davies, R. W. *The Socialist Offensive: The Collectivization of Soviet Agriculture, 1929-1930*. Cambridge, Mass.: Harvard University Press, 1980. The authoritative study of the collectivization of Soviet agriculture in connection with the industrialization program. Highly informative and analytic.

Fitzpatrick, Sheila. *Stalin's Peasants: Resistance and Survival in the Russian Village After Collectivization*. New York: Oxford University Press, 1994. A pioneering work on collectivization from the point of view of the peasants. Based on previously secret Soviet archives.

_____, ed. *Cultural Revolution in Russia, 1928-1931*. Bloomington: Indiana University Press, 1984. Collection of essays examines sociopolitical and cultural aspects of the dramatic transformation initiated by Stalin in 1928.

Hosking, Geoffrey. *The First Socialist Society: A History of the Soviet Union from Within*. Cambridge, Mass.: Harvard University Press, 1985. A comprehensive and interesting introduction to the history of the Soviet Union with excellent analysis of the Stalin period.

Hough, Jerry F., and Merle Fainsod. *How the Soviet Union Is Governed*. Cambridge, Mass.: Harvard University Press, 1979. A good explanation of the development of the Soviet system and its policy process. Explores how Stalin consolidated his power and established the highly centralized system.

Jasny, Naum. *Soviet Industrialization: 1928-1952*. Chicago: University of Chicago Press, 1961. A close examination of the origins, process, and characteristics of Soviet industrialization. Supported by quantitative data, although dated.

Kuromiya, Hiroaki. *Stalin's Industrial Revolution: Politics and Workers, 1928-1932*. New York: Cambridge University Press, 1988. Studies the implementation of rapid industrialization during the First Five-Year Plan and analyzes support and resistance among industrial workers.

Lewin, Moshe. *Russian Peasants and Soviet Power: A Study of Collectivization*. Translated by Irene Nove with the assistance of John Biggart. New York: W. W. Norton, 1968. Focuses on debates over economic policy within the Communist Party during the 1920's and the pivotal grain procurement crisis of 1928.

Scott, John. *Behind the Urals: An American Worker in Russia's City of Steel*. Enlarged ed. Bloomington: Indiana University Press, 1989. These memoirs by an American who worked in Magnitogorsk, a steel-producing city founded during the First Five-Year Plan, vividly describe working and living conditions.

Tucker, Robert C. *Stalin in Power: The Revolution from Above, 1928-1941*. New York: W. W. Norton, 1990. Argues that Stalin forged a new autocracy modeled on Russia's Muscovite and czarist past to carry out his revolutionary policy of state-sponsored industrial development.

Viola, Lynne. *The Best Sons of the Fatherland: Workers in the Vanguard of Soviet Collectivization*. New York: Oxford University Press, 1999. An excellent study of the campaign of the twenty-five thousand members of the Soviet industrial proletariat who were recruited to participate in agricultural collectivization.

Wolfe, Bertram. *Three Who Made a Revolution: A Biographical History of Lenin, Trotsky, and Stalin*. 1964. Reprint. New York: Cooper Square Press, 2001. One of the best histories of the Bolshevik Revolution available, a masterpiece of research and writing. The author was acquainted with several original Bolsheviks and lived for a time in Moscow.

SEE ALSO: May 18, 1928: Shakhty Case Debuts Show Trials in Moscow; Dec., 1932-Spring, 1934: Great Famine Strikes the Soviet Union; Dec., 1934: Stalin Begins the Purge Trials; Summer, 1939: Stalin Suppresses the Russian Orthodox Church.

December 10, 1928

UNDSET ACCEPTS THE NOBEL PRIZE IN LITERATURE

Sigrid Undset was awarded the Nobel Prize in Literature for her contributions to that area, notably for her multivolume historical novels set in medieval Norway. She was the first Norwegian woman to receive the award as well as only the third woman of any nationality to be so honored.

LOCALE: Stockholm, Sweden
CATEGORY: Literature

KEY FIGURES

Sigrid Undset (1882-1949), Norwegian author
Ingvald Undset (1853-1893), Undset's father, an
　archaeologist
Anders Svarstad (1913-1940), Undset's elder son
Maren Charlotte Svarstad (1915-1940), Undset's
　mentally challenged daughter
Hans Benedict Svarstad (b. 1919), Undset's younger son

SUMMARY OF EVENT

Although she was thirty-eight when the first volume of her first epic novel appeared, from the time of her birth Sigrid Undset had been accumulating the knowledge and the experience that would enable her to write the books for which her Nobel Prize was awarded. Undset was born in Denmark, but her family moved to her father's native Norway when she was two. During her childhood, Undset learned Scandinavian folktales from her mother. However, she said later that it was the influence of her father, Ingvald Undset, and his archaeological work that dominated her imagination. At the museum of antiquities, Undset was allowed to handle medieval artifacts, and she made up stories to go with the objects. She might well have become an archaeologist, as her father hoped she would, had his relatives in Trondheim not turned her attention to the saga. Her best-known works would be her prose sagas, which were set in Norway during the Middle Ages.

Undset's life experiences also prepared her to write novels that recognized women's psychological stresses while at the same time emphasizing the importance of the family and the need for moral responsibility. When Undset was eleven, her father died, leaving the family in financial difficulties. For the next ten years Undset worked in an office, painting and writing in her spare time. After she was making enough from her writing so that she could leave her secretarial job, she quit and married the painter Anders Svarstad. In 1913, they had a son,

Anders; two years later, their daughter Maren Charlotte was born, but she was severely retarded. The couple removed Svarstad's other three children from the institution where they had been living and added them to their household; one of these children also had brain damage. Undset had to find time for her writing while she managed a household of seven and took care of five children. In 1919, she and Svarstad separated, but she was already pregnant; a son, Hans, was born later that year. The marriage was later annulled.

Undset had already created a sensation with her contemporary novel *Jenny* (1911; English translation, 1921), the story of a young woman who has an affair with her fiancé's father, bears an illegitimate child, suffers through the child's death, becomes convinced that she is a failure as an artist, and commits suicide. Undset explored the same conflicts between passion and sexual fidelity and be-

Sigrid Undset. (The Nobel Foundation)

tween motherhood and the creative impulse in her trilogy *Kristin Lavransdatter* (1929), which comprised *Kransen* (1920; *The Bridal Wreath*, 1923), *Husfrue* (1921; *The Mistress of Husaby*, 1925), and *Korset* (1922; *The Cross*, 1927). However, in these novels the conflicts were played out against a medieval setting, brilliantly and accurately re-created by the author. The fact that the trilogy ends with the title character's entrance into a cloister, where just before her death she acknowledges the sovereignty of God, is another indication of the close correlation between Undset's experiences and those of her characters: In 1924, the author, who for many years had classified herself as an agnostic, converted to Catholicism.

Sin, guilt, faith, and redemption are also important themes in the tetralogy that followed, *Olav Audunssøn i Hestviken* and *Olav Audunssøn og hans børn* (1925-1927; *The Master of Hestviken*, 1928-1930), published in English as *The Axe* (1928), *The Snake Pit* (1929), *In the Wil-*

derness (1929), and *The Son Avenger* (1930). Again, these works were praised by critics as medieval epics that were both brilliant re-creations of the past and masterpieces of psychological insight. The general public was just as enthusiastic: As soon as they were translated into other languages, her novels became international best sellers. While Undset had been mentioned in previous years as a possible Nobel laureate, her reading public was limited as long as her works were available only in Norwegian, and so the Nobel Committee was hesitant to award her the prize. Her worldwide popularity meant that almost no one could object to Undset's being selected.

In the presentation speech delivered on December 10, 1928, Per Hallström, chairman of the Nobel Committee of the Swedish Academy, indicated that the award was made principally for Undset's epic novels about medieval Norway. The effectiveness of those works, he suggested, derived from the fact that by moving from contemporary settings to the distant past, Undset had been able to create characters who were motivated by abstract principles such as honor and faith even though they had the same need for erotic expression as their distant descendants. Hallström spoke of the profound vision exhibited both in *Kristin Lavransdatter* and in the *Olav Audunssøn* stories and concluded by calling Undset a genius whose works reflected her own greatness of spirit.

At the Nobel banquet held that night at the Grand Hôtel in Stockholm, Sweden, Professor Gösta Forssell compared Undset to Homer, saying that the Norwegian writer also dramatized the values on which a long-standing culture was based. Undset responded with a graceful acknowledgment of the kinship between Norway and Sweden. She concluded by bringing regards from her own people to Sweden and commenting on the beauty of Stockholm. With her usual generosity, Undset gave most of her prize money to her favorite causes, which included the Norwegian Authors' Union, aid for parents of mentally disabled children, and financial help for students at Catholic schools. In 1940, she donated her gold medal to aid the Finnish war effort.

UNDSET'S HOMAGE TO SWEDEN

In her Nobel acceptance speech, Undset chose to focus on Sweden's beauty and on the cultural and geographical links it shared with Norway:

The preceding speakers have far better expressed our gratitude for the Prizes awarded to us than I could have done, and I subscribe to their words. I write more readily than I speak and I am especially reluctant to talk about myself. Instead, I wish to offer a salute to Sweden. Before I left for Sweden, a party was given for me—that is to say, not strictly speaking for me but because I was going to leave for Sweden—and everybody, the President of the Council of Ministers of Norway as well as my personal friends, asked me to give regards to Sweden. After all, the people of our peninsula form a distinct part of the world. Our forests and our mountains run into each other and our rivers carry their waters from one country to the other. Our houses in Norway resemble those in Sweden. God be praised! We have always lived in a great number of small, private dwellings spread all over our countries. Modern technology has not yet completely intruded on the humanity of the North.

But what I wished to say here is that I have been asked to give regards to Sweden, the country we think of with joy, and to Stockholm, which we Norwegians consider the most beautiful city in the world.

Source: Sigrid Undset, "Banquet Speech," in *Nobel Lectures, Literature 1901-1967*, edited by Horst Frenz (Amsterdam: Elsevier, 1969).

SIGNIFICANCE

Sigrid Undset's selection as a Nobel laureate marked a change in literary taste from the sentimental romanticism of the nineteenth century to uncompromising realism. As the author herself commented, seen at a distance, a murder can appear interesting, even exciting, and so Undset chose to show violence close up, as the Icelandic sagas on which she modeled her own novels had done. Thus she did much to transform the genre of the historical novel. After Undset, such books were no longer mere masquerades, with cardboard characters posing in front of colorful settings, certain that they were in no real danger. Instead, books in the tradition Undset established were inhabited by real people, who sinned, agonized, dreamed, and were disappointed, fell into despair, and often died unpleasant deaths.

Undset also insisted on presenting realistic depictions of women. Some readers were shocked by her insistence on the strength of the female's biological drive, but feminists could accept that idea. What enraged the very feminists who applauded a woman's being chosen as a Nobel laureate was Undset's stated belief that motherhood was a woman's highest duty. In her emphasis on the tragic consequences that ensue when a human being denies moral responsibility, Undset was simply attempting to show life as she had experienced it. Later writers did not necessarily agree with all of Undset's ideas, but they had to recognize her importance as a writer who remained faithful to her deepest conviction: that above all, a writer must tell the truth.

—*Rosemary M. Canfield Reisman*

FURTHER READING

Bayerschmidt, Carl. *Sigrid Undset*. New York: Twayne, 1970. A standard study of the life and works. Discusses Undset's conversion at length.

Brunsdale, Mitzi. *Sigrid Undset, Chronicler of Norway*. Oxford, England: Berg, 1988. A volume in the Berg Women's Series. Includes an outline of Norwegian history and literature and a useful chronology. Illustrated.

Dunn, Margaret, Sister. *Paradigms and Paradoxes in the Life and Letters of Sigrid Undset*. Lanham, Md.: University Press of America, 1994. Relates the paradigms of St. Benedict, St. John of the Cross, and Pierre Teilhard de Chardin to Undset's paradoxical views.

Lytle, Andrew. *Kristin: A Reading*. Columbia: University of Missouri Press, 1992. An analysis of the saga by a highly respected author and critic.

Maman, Marie. *Sigrid Undset in America: An Annotated Bibliography and Research Guide*. Lanham, Md.: Scarecrow, 2000. Contains a useful chapter on autobiographical elements of Undset's works.

Page, Tim, ed. *The Unknown Sigrid Undset*. South Royalton, Vt.: Steerforth Press, 2001. Features a new translation of *Jenny* and English versions of important letters.

Whitehouse, J. C. *Vertical Man: The Human Being in the Catholic Novels of Graham Greene, Sigrid Undset, and Georges Bernanos*. London: Saint Austin Press, 1999. Shows how three major twentieth century Catholic novelists challenged prevailing attitudes.

SEE ALSO: Dec. 10, 1901: First Nobel Prizes Are Awarded; 1925: Woolf's *Mrs. Dalloway* Explores Women's Consciousness; Dec. 10, 1938: Buck Receives the Nobel Prize in Literature.

1929
BAYLOR PLAN INTRODUCES PREPAID HOSPITAL CARE

By offering a solution to the problem of high medical bills, the Baylor Plan contributed to the evolution of a unique financing scheme that preserved a medical care system based on technically advanced nonprofit hospitals.

LOCALE: Baylor University Hospital, Dallas, Texas
CATEGORIES: Health and medicine; organizations and institutions; economics

KEY FIGURES

Justin Ford Kimball (1872-1956), American lawyer, educator, and executive vice president of Baylor University

Clarence Rufus Rorem (1894-1988), American accountant and economics professor who was the first president of the Blue Cross Association

E. A. van Steenwyk (1905-1962), executive secretary of the St. Paul prepayment plan

SUMMARY OF EVENT

The plan for prepaid hospital care established in 1929 at Baylor University Hospital played a key role in the evolution of the Blue Cross Association and of voluntary health insurance in the United States. The Baylor Plan itself was a response to the financial problems resulting from the changing role of the nonprofit hospital.

For much of the nineteenth century, hospitals played the role of shelters for the sick poor. Charitable donations paid the bills. Late in the century, however, the forces that were to change that role began gathering strength. The development of anesthesia in the 1840's and the triumph of the germ theory of disease in the 1870's made surgery safer and laid the groundwork for medical laboratories. Medical technology became capital-intensive, nursing became a respected profession, and workers inched into the middle class. Hospital administrators started applying the principles of scientific management to the operation of hospitals. By 1920, hospital administrators no longer saw themselves as guardians of the sick poor; rather, they viewed themselves as managers of social capital placed in the community to protect the health of all members. To pay for the operating costs of this social capital, administrators depended less on charity and more on charges. This created problems both for families unable to pay hospital bills and for hospitals unable to collect.

Insurance companies seemed unable to solve this problem by selling policies against medical expenses. Insurance theorists considered medical expenses to be uninsurable because there was no way to set premiums. The mathematics of probability can set premiums for events beyond the control of the insured such as hurricanes, fires, and even loss of income resulting from illness. Medical expenses, however, lie somewhat within the control of the insured, who can buy a larger quantity of, or more costly, services than they would choose if they had no insurance. Insurance creates a "moral hazard" in that those who have it lose the incentive to control their expenditures. Because of this "moral hazard," insurance companies held back from issuing medical insurance.

Hospital administrators and local entrepreneurs devised their own schemes. Many failed, but a few succeeded. One that succeeded, the plan created by Baylor University in Dallas, Texas—known as the Baylor Plan—is considered to be the forerunner of the Blue Cross prepayment plans.

In 1929, Justin Ford Kimball, Baylor University's executive vice president, examined the accounts of the university hospital and noticed that teachers owed many of the bad debts. Kimball divided total hospital expenses by the number of teachers in Dallas to generate an average monthly cost of fifteen cents. He concluded that the hospital could remain solvent and the teachers could remain financially secure if the hospital offered twenty-one days of free care to anyone making a regular monthly payment of fifty cents. More than one thousand teachers enrolled in the plan.

The evolution from the Baylor Plan to a national association of regional plans started with discussions of Kimball's plan at the 1931 and 1932 meetings of the American Hospital Association. Hospital administrators were eager for new ideas. The Great Depression had cut hospital revenues by 75 percent, and investigations by

the Committee on the Cost of Medical Care (a privately funded task force) had heightened interest in broader issues. This committee had started a massive investigation of the American medical care system in 1927. Its final report, issued in 1933, advocated voluntary health insurance as a solution to the problem of financing health care for Americans.

The Baylor Plan offered a successful example of such insurance, but it restricted its benefits to a single hospital, limiting the free choice of physician. In 1932 and 1933, hospitals in Sacramento, California; Essex County, New Jersey; and St. Paul, Minnesota, organized prepayment plans that would provide free care in any community hospital that patients and their physicians might choose. The executive secretary of the St. Paul plan, E. A. van Steenwyk, embellished his letterhead stationery with a blue cross, and people began referring to "St. Paul Blue Cross."

SIGNIFICANCE

By the end of 1935, fifteen hospital prepayment plans were operating, and they were facing their first challenges. State insurance laws imposed capital reserve requirements on traditional insurance companies because they paid cash indemnities. The managers of the prepayment plans believed that because they offered service benefits, their true reserves rested in the capacities of the hospitals. They believed, therefore, that they did not need to maintain cash reserves. When challenged by insurance commissioners in New York and Ohio, the plans successfully lobbied legislatures for laws that would exempt them from the capital reserve requirements. Such challenges highlighted the need for national coordination of responses to common challenges.

The driving force behind such coordination was Clarence Rufus Rorem, a research associate with the Committee on the Cost of Medical Care. The Julius Rosenwald Fund had financed Rorem's position. In 1936, the fund's directors decided to end their support for the Committee on the Cost of Medical Care but granted Rorem $100,000 per year for the next four years to use in any way he chose. Rorem chose to organize a national association of prepayment plans. He persuaded the leaders of the American Hospital Association to sponsor the Hospital Service Association. Rorem was the executive secretary.

In 1938, the Hospital Service Association promulgated seven characteristics required for certification of a regional prepayment plan: There could be no stockholders or investments or profits for any individual; the board of directors should have representatives from hospitals, physicians, and the public; state insurance departments should supervise the plans; plans should hold low cash reserves, because their true reserves lay in the capacities of the hospitals; plans should provide service benefits, not cash indemnities; plans should not compete with one another; and all employees would be salaried, with no one working on commission. In 1941, the grant from the Julius Rosenwald Fund ended. The Hospital Service Association became the Council on Hospital Service Plans of the American Hospital Association, supported by dues from the member plans. Rorem remained secretary.

Two events during World War II influenced the evolution of Blue Cross. A War Labor Board decision allowed employers to increase fringe benefits at the rate of 5 percent per year, and the Emergency Maternity and Infant Care Program provided maternity and child-care benefits to the families of military personnel. The War Labor Board decision enabled employers to compete for scarce workers by offering benefits such as group health insurance. Many large employers had plants in the jurisdictions of different prepayment plans. These employers wanted single-package plans including hospital and physician services and applicable to all of their plants.

In 1937, a group of California physicians had organized a nonprofit indemnity insurance plan. Similar plans, under the control of local medical societies, grew into the Blue Shield organizations. Links between the organizations did not arise immediately, but the pressure for such links started from this demand for a single comprehensive package.

The Maternity and Infant Care Program operated through private providers. Its government administrators developed a reimbursement system based on the concept of "reasonable cost." Previously, plans had reimbursed hospitals on a rough per diem basis. "Reasonable cost" committed them to pay more to hospitals that provided more services.

At the end of 1946, Rorem resigned. The Blue Cross Council officially replaced the Hospital Service Council. In 1960, the Blue Cross Association would replace the Blue Cross Council, but the essential characteristics of Blue Cross were in place by 1946. It was a national organization of nonprofit, noncompeting, regional prepayment plans, offering service benefits to consumers and reimbursing hospitals on the basis of reasonable cost.

Blue Cross saved the nonprofit hospital system from bankruptcy during the Great Depression and pioneered medical care insurance. It contributed to the development of the unique health care system in the United States, which brought flexibility and technical sophisti-

cation as well as high costs and limited access.

Noting the success of the prepayment plans, traditional insurance companies began offering group health insurance on a wide basis in 1934. During World War II, health insurance of all types grew rapidly. Between 1947 and 1949, decisions by the National Labor Relations Board and the U.S. Supreme Court established health insurance as a legitimate subject for collective bargaining. Unions and employers extended health insurance until most of the middle class was covered.

The Hospital Reconstruction Act of 1946 made it illegal for hospitals to refuse care to people unable to pay. This made free care available to the poor. Hospitals could shift the cost of free care by raising charges to the Blue Cross plans and the insurance companies. Cost shifting was consistent with the nonprofit belief that a hospital is a community resource, but it was not consistent with the free market philosophy of the insurance companies. In the clash of philosophies, the Blue Cross system began to unravel. The Blue Cross plans set their premiums through a system called "community rating," charging all community members the same premium. Traditional insurance companies set their premiums through "experience rating," charging higher premiums to people using more services and lower premiums to people using fewer. As insurance theorists viewed it, community rating was unfair because it forced low-risk people to subsidize high-risk people.

A plan using community rating cannot compete with one using experience rating. Experience raters can lure a low-risk group away from a community rater by offering rebates to employers or by offering favorable rates to low-risk groups. The community raters, forced to spread the costs of a riskier remnant over a smaller population, must raise their premiums. This gives the experience raters an opening to break off a new group less risky than the average. The process continues until the community raters serve only the high-risk, high-cost part of the market. Competition forced most Blue Cross plans to abandon community rating. Blue Cross plans in some northeastern states continued to use community rating, but with subsidies from state governments.

With experience rating the rule, however, premiums rose beyond the reach of many high-risk groups, particularly the elderly. The inability of the elderly to buy insurance at affordable rates prompted the creation of Medicare, a system of government insurance for the elderly and for people with end-stage kidney disease.

Following the precedent of the 1960 Federal Employees Benefit Bill, Medicare and Medicaid allowed

1929

hospitals to choose to deal either directly with the government or through an intermediary. Most hospitals preferred to deal through Blue Cross, again expanding the role of the national Blue Cross Association.

Shortly after the passage of Medicare and Medicaid, public attention became focused on the increasing cost of health care. In 1933, the United States spent only 4 percent of its gross national product (GNP) on health care, and the Committee on the Cost of Medical Care argued that it should spend more. Beginning in 1950, that percentage began an inexorable march upward, and by the 1980's health spending had surpassed 10 percent of GNP. Many people argued that the nation should spend less.

Blue Cross and the traditional insurance companies shared the blame for rising costs. Complete coverage for hospital care, some argued, created an incentive for people to use costly hospital care when it was not really needed. Reimbursement for all reasonable costs destroyed some incentives for efficiency and cost control. Moral hazard—the tendency for insured people to seek more costly care—was mentioned again.

The emphasis on cost control strengthened alternative forms of organization. Some large companies chose to self-insure, bypassing all intermediaries. The Social Security amendments of 1972 actively encouraged the formation of health maintenance organizations. Health maintenance organizations began expanding their coverage at the expense both of traditional insurance companies and of the Blue Cross system. The Blue Cross Association remained the major administrative intermediary of the Medicare program. It sponsored major initiatives in health care research and remained a major proponent of the position that the nonprofit hospital is a form of social capital.

—*John Dennis Chasse*

FURTHER READING

Anderson, Odin W. *Blue Cross Since 1929: Accountability and the Public Trust*. Cambridge, Mass.: Ballinger, 1975. A historical treatment of the origins of the Blue Cross Association based both on interviews with the founders and on the author's wide experience as a social scientist and researcher. This work is, in part, a response to the highly critical treatment by Sylvia Law, cited below.

Cunningham, Robert, III, and Robert M. Cunningham, Jr. *The Blues: A History of the Blue Cross and Blue Shield System*. DeKalb: Northern Illinois University Press, 1997. First complete history of the oldest health insurance companies in the United States sheds light on the development of the American system of health care. Includes glossary and index.

Law, Sylvia. *Blue Cross: What Went Wrong?* New Haven, Conn.: Yale University Press, 1974. Well-researched and highly critical analysis of the role of the Blue Cross Association in the U.S. health care field. Includes a brief history of Blue Cross through the period when it became a major intermediary for the Medicare and Medicaid programs.

MacIntyre, Duncan. *Voluntary Health Insurance and Rate Making*. Ithaca, N.Y.: Cornell University Press, 1962. A very readable introduction to insurance theory and to the differences between the Blue Cross Association and traditional stock and mutual insurance companies. Includes evenhanded treatment of the experience rating versus community rating controversies.

Reagan, Michael D. *The Accidental System: Health Care Policy in America*. Boulder, Colo.: Westview Press, 1999. Examines how American health care policy has been formed over the years. Chapter 2 offers brief discussion of the origins of Blue Cross. Includes index.

Rorem, C. Rufus. *A Quest for Certainty: Essays on Health Care Economics, 1930-1970*. Ann Arbor, Mich.: Health Administration Press, 1982. Collection of articles by one of the major architects of the Blue Cross Association includes Rorem's influential 1933 article on hospital prepayment plans, a key excerpt from the report of the American Hospital Association outlining the characteristics of an acceptable plan, and a number of other articles that clarify the philosophy that grounded the actions of founders of the Blue Cross Association.

Starr, Paul. *The Social Transformation of American Medicine*. New York: Basic Books, 1982. An influential interpretive history of medical care in the United States. Focuses in particular on the methods by which the American Medical Association maintained professional control over medical care decision making until late in the twentieth century, when control shifted to professional managers and financial analysts. Places the evolution of Blue Cross and of stock and mutual health insurance within this context.

SEE ALSO: Aug. 14, 1912: U.S. Public Health Service Is Established; Aug. 14, 1935: Roosevelt Signs the Social Security Act; Jan. 1, 1936: Ford Foundation Is Established.

1929
HALLELUJAH IS THE FIRST IMPORTANT BLACK MUSICAL FILM

King Vidor sacrificed salary to direct the first serious all-black musical motion picture, successfully blending music and drama to depict southern farm life and its tragedies.

LOCALE: Metro-Goldwyn-Mayer studios, Culver City, California

CATEGORY: Motion pictures

KEY FIGURES

King Vidor (1894-1982), American film director
Daniel L. Haynes (1894-1954), American actor and minister
Nina Mae McKinney (1913-1967), American actor

SUMMARY OF EVENT

When Warner Bros. released *The Jazz Singer* in 1927, the era of silent films came to an end, but some studio heads believed sound to be a fad. Metro-Goldwyn-Mayer (MGM) did not release a sound film until 1928; its first musical was 1929's *The Broadway Melody*, a backstage story full of young women in abbreviated costumes. The studio intended to follow this film with similar money-makers, and it turned down King Vidor's proposal of an all-black musical tragedy set among impoverished farmers.

By then, however, Vidor had achieved a considerable reputation. A Galveston, Texas, native who as a boy had taught himself film techniques by watching silents, Vidor had come to California in 1915 and had taken every studio job he could get in order to learn his profession. He made his reputation with *The Turn in the Road* (1919); it was characteristic of Vidor that he convinced a group of physicians to back the film, which had a Christian Science theme. *The Turn in the Road* depicted a man's search for his personal truths, a theme that was to dominate Vidor's films.

D. W. Griffith's films taught Vidor the relationship of films to musical forms, and from Robert J. Flaherty's *Nanook of the North* (1922) he learned the dramatic value of everyday experience. His two most important silent films foreshadowed *Hallelujah* in evidencing both interests. In *The Big Parade* (1925), starring John Gilbert, he showed a common soldier, neither a hero nor a coward. In *The Crowd* (1928), Vidor showed a common office worker whose struggles were everyman's: marriage, parenthood, dead-end work, unemployment, the loss of a child, alcoholism, and periods of happiness.

Vidor used music to spectacular effect in the background for *The Big Parade*. He conceptualized the film in terms of musical movements, pacing off the troops' steps with a metronome and speeding up the beat as tension mounted. As troops marched toward the battlefront and death, the musical score ceased, and the soldiers moved only to the cadence of an ominous bass drum. Although critics attacked Vidor's use of music in *Hallelujah* as a racist depiction of black music and attacked the hero's sordid story and emotionalism, these themes were in fact set in Vidor's work before he came to *Hallelujah*. The film's hero, Zeke, is searching for his true life. He is caught between two women who represent the extremes of his own psychological needs. Music represents this conflict. Gospel songs and traditional spirituals are associated with the order and family harmony of Zeke's family's farm, whereas syncopated jazz represents the world that tempts him. (Until the end of his life, Vidor was disturbed by the studio's insistence on adding such elements as two Irving Berlin songs, "At the End of the Road" and "Swanee Shuffle," that gave the film a Tin Pan Alley air he wanted to avoid.)

Vidor's was not the first all-black musical. Earlier in 1929, Fox (later Twentieth Century-Fox) released *Hearts in Dixie*, which featured the talented actor Clarence Muse and provided the first major role for comedian Stepin Fetchit. *Hearts in Dixie*, however, focused on the happy-go-lucky life of a fictional plantation. Later in 1929, *St. Louis Blues*, released by Warner Bros., provided singer Bessie Smith her only film role, but it was not a full-length feature; it ran only seventeen minutes.

Vidor took a bigger risk. He wanted to treat his black hero as seriously as he had treated the white soldier in *The Big Parade* and the white office worker in *The Crowd*. Vidor's operational problems were staggering, with sound techniques still in their infancy, and MGM refused to make the film until Vidor donated the money due him under his MGM contract to the production.

For his cast, Vidor went to Chicago, New York, and Memphis, visiting black churches to hire his singers. For Zeke, he first wanted Paul Robeson, who was unavailable. Instead, he hired Daniel L. Haynes, the understudy for Jules Bledsoe, who sang "Ol' Man River" in the 1927 Broadway production of *Show Boat*. Nina Mae McKinney was hired from the chorus of a Broadway show. Three child musicians were hired when Vidor saw them dancing for quarters in a Memphis hotel. Vidor ap-

1929

2273

proached Harry Gray, who had been born into slavery, to play the father of the family. Musician Victoria Spivey played Missy Rose, William Fountaine played the gambler Hot Shot, and Fannie Bell McKnight was cast as the mother. All were relatively unknown.

The mood of *Hallelujah* was as somber as that of *The Crowd*. Zeke, the eldest son of a hardworking farm family, goes to town with his brother and is fascinated by Chick (McKinney), who plays a tempting Eve. He is cheated by Hot Shot; in a brawl, he accidentally shoots his brother. In atonement, he becomes a preacher, but, still fascinated by Chick, he leaves the ministry. Vidor explicitly shows Zeke's religious fervor to be an unsuccessful attempt to sublimate a sexual drive that finally conquers him. Zeke and Chick flee. Zeke ultimately kills Chick's lover, Hot Shot, and Chick dies in a symbolic fall. Zeke serves time in prison, then returns to the order and stability of his father's farm, where Missy Rose, the good girl, waits for him. They return to harvesting the earth and to the cycles of the seasons.

SIGNIFICANCE

By the end of Vidor's long life, the significance of *Hallelujah* was recognized, but its immediate reception was mixed. As Vidor recalled, the film may never have shown a profit. For the actors in the film, it was virtually a dead end, and no one at the time understood that Vidor had created a new film genre. His technical accomplishment, however, was immediately apparent.

Vidor shot the film on location near Memphis, Tennessee, and in Arkansas. Sound equipment, large and difficult to move, did not arrive, so much of the film was shot as a silent and then matched with sound tracks recorded in Hollywood, a feat so difficult that it literally drove one film cutter to a nervous breakdown.

For the scenes shot as silents, Vidor used impressionistic special effects. Perhaps the most dramatic scene shows Zeke chasing Hot Shot through a swamp. In his autobiographical *A Tree Is a Tree* (1953), Vidor recalled that "when someone stepped on a broken branch, we made it sound as if bones were breaking," and that when Hot Shot drew his foot from the sticky mud, "we made the vacuum sound strong enough to pull him down into hell." Recording a group of dock workers, Vidor for the first time used synchronous sound recording in the studio. The final print had flaws, but remarkable effects were readily evident.

Controversy, however, arose about the film's content. Although accused of racism, Vidor was unquestionably sincere; he had not intended to portray the black race as a whole but simply to show the harsh lives of the black people he had known in Galveston, where his father's lumber company had employed mostly black men and where he was taken to witness river baptisms. Although reviews in the white East Coast press were generally favorable, the black press reacted against the gambling and emotionalism of the black characters depicted in the film.

Controversy even surrounded the film's showing. In New York, the film was given dual premieres, one at the Lafayette Theater in Harlem and one downtown. Black journalists were indignant, assuming this meant that white audiences were willing to see blacks on film but were unwilling to sit next to them in audiences. In Chicago, two major theaters, the Balaban and Katz, refused to book the film for fear the black audiences would drive off white patrons. Vidor had to visit Chicago, show the film to critics, and wait for the positive reviews. Once these appeared, it was possible to convince a small independent theater to book the film. Its success at that theater forced major Chicago theaters to show it. In an attempt to get southern bookings, Vidor talked a Jacksonville, Florida, theater owner into booking the film by promising him a personal check for one thousand dollars if *Hallelujah* did not bring in more profit than whatever was currently showing. It did, and the man booked it into his theaters, but there were few other southern showings. Even in Paris, where black entertainers had received a warmer welcome than in the United States, the film's showings were restricted. In a 1932 essay in *Le Crapouillot*, Pierre Bost recalled, perhaps with some exaggeration, that he could see the film only in the early hours of the morning and in a cellar, although it was the talk of the city.

The minor actors of *Hallelujah* are virtually lost to time. Of the stars, McKinney was signed to an MGM contract, but few roles were available for black women. Her portrait of Chick, however, is said to have created the figure of the feisty vamp later acted by such stars as Dorothy Dandridge and Jean Harlow. McKinney is said to have dubbed Harlow's songs in *Reckless* (1935). She appeared in a number of major studio films and in films made by independent black companies; in England, she appeared opposite Paul Robeson in Alexander Korda's *Sanders of the River* (1935). Her final film appearance was in *Pinky* (1949). There were also few roles for black men in American films after *Hallelujah*. Haynes played in Marc Connelly's *The Green Pastures* (1930) for five years on Broadway and for almost two thousand performances on tour; he played the major figure of De Lawd in a later revival. Haynes also played secondary roles in a number of films and achieved a distinguished career as pastor of New York churches.

Vidor went on to make a series of distinguished films. *Street Scene* (1931) and *Our Daily Bread* (1934) were in many ways reminiscent of his earlier films, with their emphasis on the overlooked dramas of everyday life. Other Vidor films included *Billy the Kid* (1930), *Stella Dallas* (1937), *The Citadel* (1938), *Northwest Passage* (1940), *Duel in the Sun* (1946), *The Fountainhead* (1949), *Ruby Gentry* (1952), and the Italian-American production of *War and Peace* (1956). He directed the "Over the Rainbow" scene and other Kansas scenes for *The Wizard of Oz* (1939) when director Victor Fleming was called away.

In 1979, Vidor received a special Academy Award for career achievement. By that time, he was, among other things, recognized to have been the originator of the American folk musical film, a genre in which stories tend to be set in a mythic American past and tend to focus on domestic and traditional values. The genre's peculiar synthesis of these elements can be traced to the stage performance of *Show Boat*, which opened on Broadway in 1927, but it was in *Hallelujah* that it came to first fruition in film. After *Hallelujah* were to come such folk musicals as *Cabin in the Sky* (1942), *Meet Me in St. Louis* (1944), and *The Harvey Girls* (1946) as well as the film versions of *Oklahoma!* (1955) and *Carousel* (1956), but Vidor's seriousness of tone and fervor of purpose in *Hallelujah* were to distinguish it from all the rest.

—*Betty Richardson*

FURTHER READING

Altman, Rick. "The Folk Musical." In *The American Film Musical*. Bloomington: Indiana University Press, 1989. Provides an analysis of *Hallelujah* that is essential reading for anyone interested in the folk musical form and its development.

Bogle, Donald. *Toms, Coons, Mulattoes, Mammies, and Bucks: An Interpretive History of Blacks in American Films*. 4th ed. New York: Continuum, 2001. Extremely important book on black films and stereotypes contains a lengthy and moderately sympathetic analysis of *Hallelujah* as well as a discussion of McKinney's influence on the figure of the vamp in film.

Dowd, Nancy, and David Shepard. *King Vidor*. Metuchen, N.J.: Scarecrow Press, 1988. Lengthy interview is essential reading not only for anyone interested in Vidor and *Hallelujah* but also for students of silent and early sound films.

Knight, Arthur. *Disintegrating the Musical: Black Performance and American Musical Film*. Durham, N.C.: Duke University Press, 2002. Scholarly study examines the history of film musical representations of African Americans, focusing on early musicals with all-black casts. Includes photographs, bibliography, and index.

Mordden, Ethan. *The Hollywood Musical*. New York: St. Martin's Press, 1981. Readable, witty, and opinionated book contains several pages about *Hallelujah*. An excellent starting place for students of film musicals.

Vidor, King. *A Tree Is a Tree*. 1953. Reprint. New York: Garland, 1977. Autobiography offers fascinating insights into how the founders of film learned their trade by trial and error. Focuses on Vidor's professional life rather than on his personal life, and includes much information about the direction of silent films. Features filmography from 1918 to 1952.

SEE ALSO: Oct. 6, 1927: *The Jazz Singer* Premieres as the First "Talkie"; 1930's: Hollywood Enters Its Golden Age; 1933: *Forty-Second Street* Defines 1930's Film Musicals; 1934: Lubitsch's *The Merry Widow* Opens New Vistas for Film Musicals; Sept. 6, 1935: *Top Hat* Establishes the Astaire-Rogers Dance Team; Aug. 17, 1939: *The Wizard of Oz* Premieres.

1929

1929
HUBBLE CONFIRMS THE EXPANDING UNIVERSE

Edwin Powell Hubble established that distant galaxies are moving away from the Milky Way galaxy at speeds that are determined by their distance from the Milky Way.

LOCALE: Mount Wilson, California
CATEGORIES: Science and technology; astronomy

KEY FIGURES

Edwin Powell Hubble (1889-1953), American astronomer
Vesto Melvin Slipher (1875-1969), American astronomer
Henrietta Swan Leavitt (1868-1921), American astronomer
Georges Lemaître (1894-1966), Belgian cosmologist
Walter Baade (1893-1960), German American astronomer

SUMMARY OF EVENT

In 1929, Edwin Powell Hubble announced that the greater the distance to a given galaxy, the faster it is traveling away from the Milky Way galaxy. This discovery was of major importance because it implied that the universe was expanding; the discovery, in turn, supported a theory proposed by Georges Lemaître in 1927 that would be developed into the "big bang" theory of the creation of the universe by the American physicist George Gamow in 1948.

Hubble made his discovery by studying photographs of stellar spectra that Vesto Melvin Slipher had taken as a way of measuring the distances to those stars. The initial key in measuring the distances to the galaxies was the work of Henrietta Swan Leavitt. In 1911 and 1912, Leavitt analyzed Cepheid variables, which are stars that change their brightness according to a predictable cycle. Leavitt arranged the stars in order according to the periods (durations) of their cycles. She noticed that arranging them by period placed them in order of actual, or absolute, brightness. She developed what became known as the "period-luminosity scale," by means of which, once the period of a Cepheid was measured, the star's actual brightness could be determined and compared to its apparent brightness, which in turn would reveal its distance.

The "redshift" measurements that Slipher had begun in 1913 suggested that the farther away a galaxy was, the faster it was receding. (The phenomenon is called "redshift" because, as the galaxy moves away, the light it emits has longer wavelengths; that is, its light moves, or shifts, toward the red end of the spectrum of visible light.) Slipher had no reliable way of measuring distances, however, and thus no means of proving the relationship. It was left to Hubble to put together the redshift results with the measurements of distance, leading to what is now called "Hubble's law."

Hubble began work in 1919 with the 60-inch (152-centimeter) telescope on Mount Wilson, near Pasadena, California, when he returned from service in World War I; he then moved to the 100-inch (254-centimeter) Hooker telescope at the same location. He studied objects within the Milky Way, such as novas (exploding stars), stars associated with gaseous nebulas, and variable stars. By 1922, he had published a paper noting the differences between the gaseous nebulae and those that were suspected of being more remote.

By 1928, using Leavitt's period-luminosity scale, Hubble estimated that the Andromeda nebula was more than 900,000 light-years away (a light-year is the distance that light, moving in a vacuum, travels in one year—at the rate of 299,000 kilometers, or 185,790 miles, per second). This figure was far higher than both the Dutch astronomer Jacobus Cornelius Kapteyn's 50,000 light-year diameter for the Milky Way and the American astronomer Harlow Shapley's estimate of 200,000 light-years. Hubble later adjusted his estimate to 750,000 light-years. It is now known that Hubble's estimates were too small, because, in 1952, Walter Baade was able to demonstrate that there are two types of Cepheid variables with different absolute brightnesses. As a consequence, modern estimates of the distance to the Andromeda nebula are more than 2 million light-years. Hubble had, however, established that Andromeda is outside the Milky Way.

Later, using the Hooker telescope, Hubble was able to resolve some of the fringes of nebulae into stars. By 1929, he had measured twenty-three galaxies out to a distance of about 20 million light-years. By 1931, Hubble and Milton L. Humason had measured some forty new galactic velocities out to a distance of 100 million light-years. Their major contribution to reliable measurement had to do with the fact that twenty-six of these velocities occurred within eight clusters. Because stars in the same cluster are assumed to be moving at the same speed, measuring redshifts for different stars within the same cluster is a good way to check the accuracy of their results.

Hubble found the speed of recession to be directly proportional to distance by a factor that came to be called the "Hubble constant," which he estimated to be 170 kilometers (roughly 106 miles) per second for each million light-years of distance. The modern value is 15 kilometers (9.32 miles) per second per million light-years. His original value for the constant indicated an age for the universe of only 2 billion years, much less than the 3 or 4 billion years that geologists had derived for the age of the earth. His figure created an anomaly that persisted until Walter Baade's discovery of two stellar populations, which reduced the size of the constant and increased the estimated age of the universe. (Today, through measurements taken by the Wilkinson Microwave Anisotropy Probe the age of the universe has been measured at 13.7 billion years.)

LEAVITT, SHAPLEY, AND THE PERIOD-LUMINOSITY SCALE

In 1902, Henrietta Swan Leavitt became a permanent staff member at Harvard College Observatory. She studied variable stars, stars that change their luminosity (brightness) in a fairly predictable pattern over time. During her tenure at Harvard, Leavitt observed and photographed nearly 2,500 variable stars, measuring their luminosities over time. She was equipped with photographs of the Large and Small Magellanic Clouds collected from Harvard's Peruvian observatory. The Magellanic Clouds are very small galaxies visible in the Southern Hemisphere and close to the Milky Way. The Small Magellanic Cloud contained seventeen Cepheid variables having very predictable periods ranging from 1.25 days to 127 days. Leavitt carefully measured the brightening and dimming of the seventeen Cepheids during their respective periods. She collected photographs of other Cepheids in the Magellanic Clouds and made additional period-luminosity studies. In a circular dated March 3, 1912, she stated:

The measurement and discussion of these objects present problems of unusual difficulty, on account of the large area covered by the two regions, the extremely crowded distribution of the stars contained in them, the faintness of the variables, and the shortness of their periods. As many of them never become brighter than the fifteenth magnitude, while very few exceed the thirteenth magnitude at maximum, long exposures are necessary, and the number of available photographs is small. The determination of absolute magnitudes for widely separated sequences of comparison stars of this degree of faintness may not be satisfactorily completed for some time to come. With the adoption of an absolute scale of magnitudes for stars in the North Polar Sequence, however, the way is open for such a determination.

Ejnar Hertzsprung of the Leiden University in the Netherlands and Henry Norris Russell of the Mount Wilson Observatory in Pasadena, California, had independently discovered a relationship between a star's luminosity and its spectral class (that is, color and temperature). Together, their experimental results produced the Hertzsprung-Russell diagram of stellar luminosities, the astronomical equivalent of chemistry's periodic table. According to their classification scheme, most stars lie along the "main sequence," which ranges from extremely bright blue stars ten thousand times brighter than the Sun to very dim red stars one hundred times dimmer than the Sun. Cepheid variables fell toward the cooler, red end of the main sequence.

Leavitt carefully measured the luminosities and cyclic periods of changing luminosity for each of many Cepheid variables from the Magellanic Clouds. From her careful measurements, she graphically plotted Cepheid luminosity against Cepheid period. She noticed "a remarkable relation between the brightness of these variables and the length of their periods . . . the brighter variables have the longer periods." She had discovered that a Cepheid's apparent luminosity is directly proportional to the length of its period, or the time it takes to complete one cycle of brightening and dimming.

Harlow Shapley, an astronomer at the Mount Wilson Observatory, measured the distances of moving star clusters containing Cepheids, then related the Cepheid distances to Cepheid period-luminosity data. From these experiments, Shapley constructed a Cepheid period-absolute luminosity curve, which made it possible to plot a Cepheid variable having a specific measured period and obtain its absolute luminosity. Knowing the Cepheid's apparent and absolute luminosities, one can instantly calculate its distance and, therefore, the distances of all the stars in the star cluster containing that particular Cepheid variable.

The distances to Cepheid variables in the Milky Way and other galaxies were soon determined. Shapley used Cepheid distances to demonstrate that the center of the Milky Way is directed toward the constellation Sagittarius and that the Sun is located approximately thirty thousand light-years from the galactic center. Edwin Powell Hubble applied the technique to obtain estimates of the distances between our galaxy and others, which led to his monumental astronomical discovery that the universe is expanding.

1929

SIGNIFICANCE

The establishment of the expansion of the universe is one of the most significant achievements of twentieth century astronomy. Establishing the scale of distance was a key to understanding the nature of the universe, which has led to Hubble's being considered the founder of extragalactic astronomy.

Hubble was not the first to presume that there were objects of interest beyond the Milky Way galaxy. Many astronomers had suspected that Sir William Herschel was correct in his opinion that "nebulae," those faint patches of light scattered throughout space, were "island universes" of stars, located outside the bounds of the Milky Way. In the mid-1920's, Lemaître theorized that the universe originated from an original superdense "cosmic egg" that had expanded into the present universe; two decades later, his idea would expand into the big bang theory.

—*Ivan L. Zabilka*

FURTHER READING

Adams, Walter S. "Obituary: Dr. Edwin P. Hubble." *Observatory* 74 (February, 1954): 32-35. A short biographical sketch in which the main emphasis is the distance-redshift relationship. Reliable and interesting account of Hubble's life (although the chronology surrounding his doctoral degree and service in World War I is somewhat confusing).

Clark, David H., and Matthew D. H. Clark. *Measuring the Cosmos: How Scientists Discovered the Dimensions of the Universe.* New Brunswick, N.J.: Rutgers University Press, 2004. Relates the stories of the scientists who have contributed to current knowledge about the size, mass, and age of the universe. Chapters 4 and 5 include discussion of the work of Hubble, Slipher, and Leavitt. Features glossary, bibliography, and index.

Gribbin, John. *In Search of the Big Bang: The Life and Death of the Universe.* Rev. ed. New York: Penguin Books, 1998. Accurate and comprehensive statement of the currently accepted cosmology presents an excellent summary of Hubble's contribution. One of the most readable books on the subject for a general audience. Includes illustrations, bibliography, and index.

Hetherington, N. "Edwin Hubble: Legal Eagle." *Nature* 39 (January 16, 1986): 189-190. A fascinating short analysis of the influence of Hubble's legal training on the manner in which he presented his astronomical evidence. Also considers the way in which he conducted his conflicts with other scientists. Presents a perspective different from that found in most other sources.

Hubble, Edwin. "The Exploration of Space." In *Theories of the Universe,* edited by Milton Karl Munitz. Glencoe, Ill.: Free Press, 1957. Short discussion excerpted from Hubble's 1936 book *The Realm of the Nebulae* and from an article that appeared in *Proceedings of the American Philosophy Society.* An attractive summary and retrospect of his work that pays attention to the contributions of other astronomers working on related topics.

_____. *The Realm of the Nebulae.* 1936. Reprint. Mineola, N.Y.: Dover, 1991. Presents a comprehensive summary of Hubble's work concerning the distant galaxies. Chapters 4 and 5 contain a statement of his discovery of Hubble's law and the procedures used for determining Hubble's constant.

Mayall, N. U. "Edwin Powell Hubble." *Biographical Memoirs of the National Academy of Sciences* 41 (1970): 175-214. An extensive laudatory biography that describes each of Hubble's major accomplishments. Contains some interesting anecdotal material not found in other sources. An abbreviated version of this article appeared in *Sky and Telescope* in January, 1954.

Struve, Otto, and Velta Zebergs. *Astronomy of the Twentieth Century.* New York: Macmillan, 1962. Offers an excellent nontechnical summary of Hubble's work.

SEE ALSO: 1912: Slipher Obtains the Spectrum of a Distant Galaxy; Mar. 3, 1912: Leavitt Discovers How to Measure Galactic Distances; Early 1920's: Slipher Presents Evidence of Redshifts in Galactic Spectra; Dec. 13, 1920: Michelson Measures the Diameter of a Star; 1924: Hubble Determines the Distance to the Andromeda Nebula; Dec., 1924: Hubble Shows That Other Galaxies Are Independent Systems.

1929
LOEWY PIONEERS AMERICAN INDUSTRIAL DESIGN

With his redesign of the Gestetner duplicating machine in 1929, Raymond Fernand Loewy became a pioneer in the new profession of industrial product design in the United States.

LOCALE: New York, New York

CATEGORIES: Fashion and design; manufacturing and industry

KEY FIGURES

Raymond Fernand Loewy (1893-1986), American industrial designer

Sigmund Gestetner (1898-1956), British manufacturer

Walter Dorwin Teague (1883-1960), American industrial designer

Norman Bel Geddes (1893-1958), American theatrical stage designer and industrial designer

Henry Dreyfuss (1904-1972), American industrial designer

William T. Snaith (1908-1974), American industrial designer

SUMMARY OF EVENT

Raymond Fernand Loewy was born in Paris, France, on November 5, 1893, into an economically secure family. From childhood, he was fascinated with train locomotives and automobiles. While still a schoolboy, he invented a prizewinning model airplane powered by an elastic band. He studied engineering and, during World War I, served in the French army, rising from private to captain. In 1919, after finishing his engineering degree, he left France for New York City, where he became a freelance illustrator for fashion magazines and a window designer for stores.

In 1929, Loewy launched his own design firm. His first major commission came from Sigmund Gestetner, the head of a British company that manufactured stencil-duplicating machines. As Loewy later recalled, Gestetner came one day unexpectedly to Loewy's apartment after having read a promotional card that Loewy had written about how improving product appearance would boost sales. Gestetner reportedly insisted that the redesign of his machine would have to be done in three days, before he returned to England. Loewy agreed to do the job for two thousand dollars if Gestetner liked the result and for five hundred dollars if he did not. Loewy's solution was brilliant in its simplicity. He covered the machine in clay, shaped the clay into a shell that concealed all the mechanical parts except for the operating controls,

and mounted the whole thing on a cabinet-like base to get rid of its protruding legs. Gestetner was so pleased that he kept the Loewy design in production for forty years.

Despite his success with Gestetner, Loewy had a difficult time traveling around the country trying to sell his services to manufacturers during the Great Depression. The turning point came in 1934, when he introduced three landmark designs—the GG-1 diesel locomotive for the Pennsylvania Railroad, the Hupmobile for the Hupp Automobile Company, and the remodeled Coldspot refrigerator for Sears, Roebuck and Company. The GG-1 locomotive marked the beginning of a long and productive relationship between Loewy and the Pennsylvania Railroad, including his design of the S-1 steam locomotive (1938) and (with University of Pennsylvania architect Paul Cret) the interior of a train for the Pennsylvania Railroad (1938). The whalelike deck shape of the ferryboat *Princess Anne* that he designed for the Pennsylvania Railroad's affiliate, the Virginia Ferry Company, was so admired that commissions from other shipping lines followed. Perhaps most important, the spectacular increase in the sales of the new Coldspot refrigerator convinced American business leaders of the importance of design as a sales tool.

Those successes led to the rapid growth of the firm. By 1938, Loewy had 18 designers working for him; by 1941, he had 56. During the firm's peak years, from 1947 through the mid-1960's, it had more than 150 regular employees, with more temporarily added for special projects. When the firm was reorganized in 1944 under the name Raymond Loewy Associates, Loewy made five key associates partners with a share in the profits. The business remained wholly owned by Loewy, however, and all the finished designs were signed with his name, regardless of who had done the work.

In its early years, the firm had three divisions—transportation, product design, and packaging. Later, a corporate identity division was added. What became the largest and most profitable division, however, was the firm's Department of Architecture and Interior Design, established in 1937 under William T. Snaith (and renamed in 1944 the Department of Specialized Architecture) to handle the design and planning of retail stores. In his autobiography, Loewy recalled that "a whole new world opened up for my design organization the first day we convinced a client that a store was an implement for merchandising and not a building raised around a series of pushcarts."

The New York World's Fair that opened in 1939 transformed Loewy from a designer for corporate America into a household name. His commissions for the fair included the design of the House of Jewels, the Railroad Building, and, most important, the focal exhibit for the fair's "Transportation Zone," the Chrysler Motors Building. Loewy's imaginative animated diorama for the Chrysler Motors Building, titled "Rocketport," depicted the possibilities of space travel and became one of the fair's most popular attractions.

Other major commissions included Loewy's 1941 design of a new red-and-white package for Lucky Strike cigarettes, a corporate identity program for the International Harvester Company, and work for the Greyhound Bus Company that culminated in the 1954 creation of the Greyhound Scenicruiser bus. Loewy's most visible role during the post-World War II years was his work for the Studebaker automobile company. The three Loewy-designed Studebaker cars—the 1947 Champion, the 1953 Starliner, and the 1962 Avanti sports car—were praised at the time, and have been even more admired since, for their innovative, compact lines.

SIGNIFICANCE

Interest in industrial product design first appeared in Europe, climaxing in the 1925 Paris Exposition Internationale des Arts Décoratifs et Industriels Modernes, yet industrial design emerged as a profession first in the United States because the rise of a consumer culture occurred earlier there than in Europe. The major impetus was the pressure during the 1920's to mass-market consumer durables such as automobiles, sewing machines, refrigerators, radios, and other electric appliances. At the suggestion of their advertising agencies, manufacturers began to give more attention to the appearance of their products. No single event did more to alert business leaders to the importance of style than Henry Ford's decision in 1927 to meet the competition from General Motors by replacing the Ford Model T automobile with the new Model A. The Great Depression reinforced the attraction to product design as a merchandising tool.

Loewy became popularly identified as the founder of the new profession of industrial design. That identification was not fully accurate; he had contemporaries who were equally important. The oldest of the group was Walter Dorwin Teague. Born in 1883 in Decatur, Illinois, Teague had a successful career as an advertising illustrator before he began his second career as an industrial designer by creating, around 1930, several cameras for Eastman Kodak. He would count among his clients

such other corporate giants as the Ford Motor Company, Texaco, and Du Pont. Another midwesterner (from small-town Michigan), Norman Bel Geddes—born the same year as Loewy—moved from advertising illustration to theater stage design before going on to industrial design. His 1932 book *Horizons* did much to popularize what became known as "streamlining," and his "Futurama" exhibit for the General Motors Building at the New York World's Fair pictured a utopian future built around the automobile and the high-speed highway. The fourth of the founders of American industrial design, Henry Dreyfuss, born in New York City in 1904, moved from theatrical design to industrial design in the late 1920's. His most famous designs were Bell Telephone's standard desk telephone (1937) and the Grand Central Railroad's Twentieth-Century Limited train (1938).

Loewy did make a major—perhaps crucial—contribution to the establishment of the new discipline, however. A total of approximately five hundred designers worked for Loewy, many of whom went on to set up their own offices. In 1944, Loewy was one of the organizers of what became the Industrial Designer Society of America. In 1946, he was president of the group and was responsible for drawing up a code of professional ethics for its members. Loewy probably did more than any other person to sell industrial design through a genius for self-promotion; he seized every opportunity for media exposure.

Loewy did not share the technocratic utopianism of Teague or Geddes, who envisaged industrial design transforming the world. His major criteria for a successful design were simplicity, convenience, economy, durability, and ease of maintenance and repair. He was, however, as interested in an aesthetically pleasing result as he was with the product's utilitarian functioning. Once, when asked why he had included a particular detail in one of his designs, he bluntly replied, "Because I liked it that way." His artistic creed was "Good design keeps the user happy, the manufacturer in the black and the aesthete unoffended." Most important, he had what one of his partners termed "an unerring vulgar taste"—"vulgar" in the literal sense of appealing to large numbers of people.

In broad terms, Loewy's work belongs to the style known as "streamlining." The key to streamlining was the separation of the outer shell of a product from its internal mechanism. That outer shell typically had a smooth and flowing surface with rounded edges. Streamlining owed much to aerodynamics—the science of eliminating the friction of air resistance to a moving vehicle. Aerodynamics researchers had concluded that the teardrop was the ideal shape for a moving vehicle, and industrial designers in the 1930's extended the teardrop shape from its use in locomotives and automobiles to the design of stationary objects. Psychologists have hypothesized that the popularity of streamlining lay in its appeal to the 1930's yearning to overcome the frictions of the Great Depression.

In the post-World War II years, Loewy consciously adapted to the "planned obsolescence" approach of the corporate world. His most popular designs of the time were conceived with the potential for minor future changes in the basic models. When critics complained about the practice of annual model changes, Loewy replied pragmatically, "There is no curve so beautiful as a rising sales graph."

Perhaps Loewy's most important long-term impact on the American environment came from his collaboration with William T. Snaith in transforming retail merchandising. The Loewy-Snaith team was responsible for the first suburban branch store of a major downtown retailer, the Lord & Taylor branch at Manhasset on Long Island, outside New York City, which opened in the spring of 1941. The firm's 1945 Lucky store in San Leandro, California, became the model for the post-World War II grocery supermarket, and its new building for the Foley Brothers store in Houston, Texas, in 1947 revolutionized conventional department store operations by rearranging selling and stock areas in accord with a profit-per-square-foot calculus.

In 1956, Loewy withdrew from active management of the firm, with Snaith taking over as managing partner and, from 1961, as president of the successor business, Raymond Loewy/William Snaith, Inc. When Loewy died on July 14, 1986, he was the last of the pioneer generation of American industrial designers.

—John Braeman

FURTHER READING

Bush, Donald J. *The Streamlined Decade.* New York: George Braziller, 1975. Excellent survey of the application of streamlining during the 1930's to locomotives, automobiles, ships, airplanes, household appliances, and even buildings. Extensively illustrated.

Johnson, J. Stewart. *American Modern, 1925-1940: Design for a New Age.* New York: Harry N. Abrams, 2000. Essay on design of the period accompanies 170 photographs of items designed by Loewy, Geddes, and others. Published in conjunction with an exhibition at the Metropolitan Museum of Art. Includes glossary, bibliography, and index.

Loewy, Raymond. *Industrial Design.* Woodstock, N.Y.: Overlook Press, 1979. Includes an introductory chapter, "My Life in Design," in which Loewy answers questions from an interviewer. The bulk of the volume is a collection of photographs and drawings of designs, with Loewy's accompanying explanatory commentary.

_____. *Never Leave Well Enough Alone.* 1951. Reprint. Baltimore: The Johns Hopkins University Press, 2002. Autobiography provides one of the fullest accounts of Loewy's career available. Entertainingly written and highly readable. The 1951 French version appeared, appropriately, under the title *La Laideur se vend mal* (ugliness sells badly).

Meikle, Jeffrey L. *Twentieth Century Limited: Industrial Design in America, 1925-1939.* 2d ed. Philadelphia: Temple University Press, 2001. Excellent account of the formative years in the professionalization of industrial design. Focuses on Loewy, Walter Teague, Norman Bel Geddes, and Henry Dreyfuss and provides illuminating analyses of the concepts and values shaping their work.

Pulos, Arthur J. *The American Design Adventure, 1940-1975.* Cambridge, Mass.: MIT Press, 1988. Takes up the history of American industrial design from where Pulos's 1983 book (cited below) leaves off, with the same first-rate results.

_____. *American Design Ethic: A History of Industrial Design.* Cambridge, Mass.: MIT Press, 1983. A pathbreaking and indispensable survey of American product design from the colonial period through the 1930's. The last third of the text deals with the 1920's on, when Loewy played a major role. Includes extensive illustrations and fine bibliography.

Schönberger, Angela, ed. *Raymond Loewy: Pioneer of American Industrial Design.* Translated by Ian Robson and Eileen Martin. Munich: Prestel, 1990. This by-product of a major exhibition honoring Loewy includes excellent essays on his work and its place in the history of industrial design. Extensively illustrated. Includes a bibliography listing contemporary commentary on Loewy's work and relevant secondary works.

SEE ALSO: 1902-1913: Tiffany Leads the Art Nouveau Movement in the United States; 1903: Hoffmann and Moser Found the Wiener Werkstätte; Oct., 1907: Deutscher Werkbund Is Founded; 1917: *De Stijl* Advocates Mondrian's Neoplasticism; 1919: German Artists Found the Bauhaus; 1937: Dreyfuss Designs the Bell 300 Telephone.

1929

1929-1930
THE BEDBUG AND *THE BATHHOUSE* EXEMPLIFY REVOLUTIONARY THEATER

Vladimir Mayakovsky created a theater of spectacle in The Bedbug *and* The Bathhouse, *which laid down the principles for revolutionary theater but were banned by Soviet authorities.*

LOCALE: Moscow, Soviet Union (now Russia)
CATEGORY: Theater

KEY FIGURES
Vladimir Mayakovsky (1893-1930), Russian
    playwright and poet
Vsevolod Yemilyevich Meyerhold (1874-1940),
    Russian stage director
Aleksandr Mikhailovich Rodchenko (1891-1956),
    Soviet artist and designer
Dmitri Shostakovich (1906-1975), Russian composer

SUMMARY OF EVENT
Vladimir Mayakovsky had won accolades from Vladimir Ilich Lenin and had become the foremost poet of the Russian Revolution, but after the revolution, aspects of Western capitalism had been introduced into the Soviet Union under the New Economic Policy (NEP). This plan fell into disfavor, and Lenin's successor, Joseph Stalin, began to introduce his plan for industrializing the Soviet Union. As postrevolutionary society began to set up rigid guidelines for all forms of culture, Mayakovsky came under attack from the Soviet authorities charged with overseeing the artistic community, who advocated Socialist Realism as the proper form for theater. Socialist Realism promoted theatrical works that reflected realistic situations and emphasized psychologically rounded characters. Mayakovsky was opposed to this movement, and he joined forces with antirealist director Vsevolod Yemilyevich Meyerhold to produce two theatrical spectacles: *Klop* (1929; *The Bedbug*, 1931) and *Banya* (1930; *The Bathhouse*, 1963). On December 28, 1928, Mayakovsky read *The Bedbug* in the Meyerhold Theater. Meyerhold felt that the play would not only hold a special place in Soviet theater but would also become part of the repertoire of world theater.

The Bedbug, which opened at the Meyerhold Theater on February 13, 1929, satirized those Communist backsliders who had reverted to the crude and vulgar lifestyle of the bourgeois. Prisypkin, a worker with calluses on his hands and a union card in his pocket, is seduced into guzzling vodka, playing sentimental songs, dancing the fox-trot, and following other reactionary bourgeois pursuits. Changing his name to Pierre Skripkin and jilting his proletariat girlfriend, Zoya Berezkina, Prisypkin marries Elsevira Renaissance, a grotesque sex symbol with affected French mannerisms. Their wedding at the Renaissance beauty salon is a mixture of maudlin sentimentality, conspicuous consumption, and all-out drunken debauchery, ending in a brawl and a fire that reduces the beauty salon and everyone in it to ashes.

Prisypkin's unscathed body, buried under the ice, is then discovered in the futuristic world of 1979. The power structure in this highly organized, completely sanitized society resurrects Prisypkin, only to find that he infects their society with such bad habits as drinking vodka, engaging in modern dances, and falling in love. Finally, he is captured and put in a zoo. In desperation, Prisypkin urges the audience to join him, but his plea is dismissed as an attack of lunacy.

Mayakovsky's use of grotesque characters to satirize socialist evils set up the theater of lampooning and burlesque as a model for democratic theater. In Oleg Bayan, the effete, self-indulgent poet who teaches Prisypkin how to wiggle his behind correctly and scratch his back discreetly, Mayakovsky caricatures reactionary poets. The tawdry decor of the Renaissance beauty salon created a dismal picture of life under the NEP. No less dismal was Mayakovsky's futuristic world. It is a sterile, automated world with mechanical voting arms, mass meetings, and elaborate cleansing paraphernalia. Even worse, it is an emotionless world where love is defined as a pathological condition. Mayakovsky even had to assure the authorities that his play was not a satire on the socialist future.

The production of *The Bedbug* was a true theater spectacle. In Meyerhold's production, actors marched through the audience hawking bras and ran in all directions when the police came. Three artists who called themselves Kukrynisky designed the first half. Using clothes from Soviet shops, they designed a pop art decor with various kinds of kitsch items. The actor playing Prisypkin walked in broad strides, swaying his pot belly and bulging rear. Prisypkin came across as a thick-lipped, slit-eyed, pigeon-toed grunter and screecher. The wedding scene consisted of grotesque pantomimes and slapstick antics in which characters beat each other with fish. The futuristic scenes were designed by artist

Aleksandr Mikhailovich Rodchenko, who used large utilitarian objects, modern glasslike structures (including a glass bell-like prison for Prisypkin), and posterlike costumes in rose and light blue to add to the futuristic tone. Scientists were dressed in sterile white garb, and their scenes were bathed in a white glow. Dmitri Shostakovich wrote an original score for the production. For the wedding scene, he took a foxtrot theme and built it into a cacophonous fantasia. Bells, flashing lights, and motion-picture screens all added to the overall effect of the production. Mayakovsky had created a futuristic spectacle for the masses. Mayakovsky's critics, however, attacked the play for creating posterlike caricatures without psychological depth. They found that his attack on bourgeois socialists allowed him to pick an easy target and to avoid criticizing more menacing enemies of socialism.

In *The Bathhouse*, Mayakovsky and Meyerhold fought back and again created a futuristic spectacle. From the start, the play created controversy. First, Mayakovsky was unable to get the script approved by censors without making changes. When he finally got approval, he was attacked in the press before the play opened. Vladimir Ermilov, an important member of the Russian Association of Proletarian Writers, criticized Mayakovsky for his exaggerated art. Ermilov's criticism was reprinted in *Pravda* on March 9, 1930. When the play opened on March 16, Mayakovsky attacked Ermilov in one of the banners in the theater. Ermilov demanded that the banner be removed, and Mayakovsky complied.

The Bathhouse is a vicious attack on Soviet bureaucracy. Pobedonosikov, a paper-shuffling, cliché-mouthing, indifferent bureaucrat surrounded by bootlickers and incompetents, is too busy to deal with the problems of ordinary people. So when Chudakov, an inventor, gets caught in red tape and bureaucratic shuffles while trying to get a patent for his time machine, he sneaks the machine into Pobedonosikov's apartment. The machine is accidentally triggered into action, producing the Phosphorescent Woman, a Communist prototype from the year 2030. She paints a picture of a glorious Communist future and promises to take all qualified Communists there. Only Pobedonosikov and his cohorts are left behind, because they are "not needed for communism."

In *The Bathhouse*, Mayakovsky again attacks the theater of his day. In a Pirandelloesque third act, Pobedonosikov becomes a character watching a play about himself. He complains that he has been presented in a bad light and that the caricature of him is unnatural and not lifelike. He and his cohorts demand a drama of "poeticized reality." In this clever piece of metatheater,

Mayakovsky attacked the realistic school of the Moscow Art Theater as well as the Russian ballet theater, which tried to poeticize life. He also reduced the objects of his satire to grotesque types, broke with fourth-wall realism, and tried to jar his audience into action. Again, he wanted to create a theater of spectacle so that he could "transform the boards of the stage into a rostrum."

The Bathhouse, however, was Mayakovsky's theatrical downfall. It not only flopped, closing after three performances, but also outraged Mayakovsky's enemies, who accused him of writing abstract dramas for coterie audiences and of failing to create heroic workers who would overcome the bureaucracy. Shortly after the failure of *The Bathhouse*, on April 14, 1930, Mayakovsky shot himself. In his suicide note, he expressed regret at having given in to the critic Ermilov.

SIGNIFICANCE

Mayakovsky's plays were banned in the Soviet Union, and their impact was not immediately felt, but Mayakovsky set the tone for revolutionary theater not only in Russia but also throughout the West. Mayakovsky broke with bourgeois realism to fight for a democratic art that would allow the free word of the creative personality to be "written on the walls, fences, and streets of our cities." He eschewed notions of absolute value and eternal beauty and created a theater for the masses—a theater that produced poetic and scenic devices that were based on their ability to propagandize. Mayakovsky, along with Meyerhold, wanted to create utopian art that "would not only pose the problems of today but would project decades into the future." Mayakovsky also tried to move theater away from dreary slice-of-life realism. Realizing that the stage was "only one-third of the auditorium," Mayakovsky brought the action of drama into the audience. Instead of creating believable characters hidden behind a proscenium arch and seen against a background of decorative scenery, he created grotesque figures—slapstick clowns bouncing across constructivist sets composed of ropes, grids, and platforms. Mayakovsky turned the stage into a soapbox and used satire to effect political change.

As Stalinist repression started to ease off, the time was right for the return of Mayakovsky to the Soviet theater. In December, 1953, Victor Pluchek, a disciple of Meyerhold, successfully produced *The Bathhouse* at the Moscow Theater of Satire. Pluchek followed this production with *The Bedbug* and other Mayakovsky plays, and he toured Mayakovsky's plays from Leningrad to the Urals. By 1958, the Theater of Satire had performed *The Bathhouse* two hundred times and *The Bedbug* five hun-

1929

dred times. In 1957, the Theater of Satire took first prize at the All Union Festival of Drama for its productions of Mayakovsky's plays. Soon, Mayakovsky's works were being produced throughout the Soviet Union and its satellite countries.

In the 1960's, Mayakovsky's brand of theatricalism returned to the Soviet theater. Dissident playwright Andrei Remezov's *Yest-li zhizn na Marse?* (1961; Is there life on Mars?) begins with spectators who come to witness life on Mars. The Martian society is an anti-utopian world reminiscent of the futuristic automatons in *The Bedbug*. Robotlike characters live in a nightmarish world where one government minister has to look up the word "principle" because he does not know its meaning. Remezov's play falls directly in line with Mayakovsky's brand of fantastic satire.

Basing his views partially on Mayakovsky, writer Andrei Sinyavsky called for the end of Socialist Realism and wanted a "phantasmagoric art" in which writers could "teach us to be truthful with the aid of the absurd and the fantastic." Yuri Lyubimov took up the banner of Mayakovsky and Meyerhold. Serving as the director of the Taganka Theater from 1964 to 1984, he rebelled against the sterile realism of the Moscow Art Theater. Like Mayakovsky, he tried to create a theater of imagination and metaphor. His productions were epic and carnivalesque. He combined the sublime and the ridiculous and mixed social commentary with theatrical art. He even did a production based on Mayakovsky's poetry.

Mayakovsky's influence soon began to be felt in revolutionary theater outside the Soviet Union. Italian theater artist Dario Fo was especially influenced by Mayakovsky. Fo's leftist dramas combine mime, circus antics, and brutal satire in an attempt to arouse the working class. Fo's *L'operaio conosce trecento parole, il padrone mille: Per questo lui è il padrone* (pr. 1969; *The Worker Knows Three Hundred Words, the Boss Knows a Thousand: That's Why He's the Boss*, 1983) is a mixture of the fantastic and the grotesque. The play features a self-important bureaucrat styled right out of *The Bathhouse* and has Mayakovsky's girlfriend present a futuristic ballet incorporating Mayakovsky's own techniques of mime and dance to convey a political message. Mayakovsky is seen, like Fo himself, as a man outside of the party, playing directly to the people.

In the 1960's, the Mayakovsky/Meyerhold brand of theatricalism became prevalent in American avant-garde theater. Politically oriented theater groups such as the Living Theatre and the Performance Group used visible lighting, performed with house lights on, and featured acrobatics, clowning, and choral chants. They made extensive use of mime and extended the action of the drama into the audience. In dramas such as *Frankenstein* (1965), the Living Theatre presented futuristic spectacles on raised platforms. In *Prometheus* (1978), Julian Beck, the founder of the Living Theatre, like Fo, introduced Mayakovsky as a character. In *Prometheus*, a scene from a Mayakovsky play is enacted in gymnastic style before Mayakovsky commits suicide.

Many of the radical popular theaters that arose in the 1960's, such as the San Francisco Mime Troupe, employed Mayakovsky's methods. They appealed directly to working people, played in noise-filled rooms and open areas, used clowning and popular music, encouraged contact between actors and audience, and tried to raise political awareness through satire. Like Mayakovsky, these groups used satire not to amuse but to arouse anger. Their dramas, like his, did not offer comic resolutions; rather, they left open endings or produced fantastic resolutions. Although his impacts were somewhat delayed, Mayakovsky helped to set down the techniques that became the framework for revolutionary theater in the 1960's and 1970's. Many of these techniques have now been incorporated into mainstream theater.

—Paul Rosefeldt

FURTHER READING

Brown, Edward J. *Mayakovsky: A Poet in the Revolution.* 1973. Reprint. New York: Paragon House, 1988. The first major critical biography of Mayakovsky in English. Shows a close connection between Mayakovsky's life and his works. Provides close readings of Mayakovsky's major and minor works and even addresses his didactic verse.

Leach, Robert. *Makers of Modern Theatre: An Introduction.* New York: Routledge, 2004. Examines the lives and work of four individuals who had significant influence on theater in the twentieth century. Chapter 2, which is devoted to Meyerhold's work, includes discussion of Mayakovsky. Features illustrations, notes, and index.

Mayakovsky, Vladimir. *Mayakovsky: Plays.* Translated by Guy Daniels. Evanston, Ill.: Northwestern University Press, 1995. Collection includes *The Bedbug* and *The Bathhouse* as well as two other works.

Shklovskii, Viktor Borisovich. *Mayakovsky and His Circle.* Edited and translated by Lily Feiler. New York: Dodd, Mead, 1972. A tribute to Mayakovsky by a close associate and intimate friend. Covers not only the relationship between Shklovskii and Mayakovsky but also other figures in the Futurist movement in Russia. Promotes Shklovskii's formalist bias, but is nevertheless a good firsthand account of Mayakovsky's development as a poet as well as a history of the artistic revolutions in Russia from 1910 to 1930.

Terras, Victor. *Vladimir Mayakovsky*. Boston: Twayne, 1983. Excellent critical introduction to Mayakovsky provides a well-organized biographical sketch of Mayakovsky's life followed by a close analysis of his major works. Defines critical terms, traces the history of artistic movements, and provides a clear critical assessment of Mayakovsky's works.

Woroszylski, Wiktor. *The Life of Mayakovsky*. Trans-lated by Boleslav Taborski. New York: Orion Press, 1970. Translation of a 1966 work by a Polish poet is an encyclopedic compendium of documentary sources on Mayakovsky's life and work. A good reference work for primary source material, but does not present a clear perspective for readers who are unfamiliar with Mayakovsky's work.

SEE ALSO: Jan. 21, 1908: *The Ghost Sonata* Influences Modern Theater and Drama; Feb. 20, 1909: Marinetti Issues the Futurist Manifesto; May 10, 1921: Pirandello's *Six Characters in Search of an Author* Premieres; Apr. 23, 1932-Aug., 1934: Socialist Realism Is Mandated in Soviet Literature.

1929-1938
BERGER STUDIES THE HUMAN ELECTROENCEPHALOGRAM

Hans Berger devised a system of electrodes, the electroencephalograph, to produce an electroencephalogram—a chart measuring brainwave patterns—of the human brain. The EEG heralded an entirely new era of neurophysiology.

LOCALE: Jena, Weimar Republic (now in Germany)
CATEGORIES: Inventions; health and medicine; science and technology

KEY FIGURES
Hans Berger (1873-1941), German psychiatrist and research scientist
Richard Caton (1842-1926), English physiologist and surgeon
Edgar Douglas Adrian (1889-1977), English neurophysiologist
Brian Harold Cabot Matthews (1906-1986), English neurophysiologist

SUMMARY OF EVENT
By the latter part of the nineteenth century, the field of psychophysiology had fallen into disrepute among neurologists and psychiatrists. Two new approaches had become fashionable: the neoanatomical approach of Bernhard Friedrich A. Gudden, Theodor H. Meynert, Paul E. Flechsig, Auguste Henri Forel, and Constantin von Monakow and the functional approach exemplified by the work of Emil Kraepelin, Eugen Bleuler, Sigmund Freud, Max Adler, and Carl Jung. Hans Berger, however, was not attracted by either of these two avenues of research. The former was not functional enough to satisfy his psychophysiological interests, and the latter, in his opinion, lacked a firm foundation in the natural sciences, which he regarded as indispensable to the understanding of brain function and its relation to mental processes. From the outset of his career, Berger chose the difficult position of the outsider, a position in which he was to remain.

As a scientist, Berger's search for the human electroencephalogram, or EEG (English physiologist Richard Caton described the electroencephalogram, or "brain wave," in rabbits and monkeys in 1875), was motivated by his desire to find a physiological method that might be applied successfully to the study of the long-standing problem of the relationship between the mind and the brain. His scientific career, therefore, was directed toward the elucidation of the psychophysical relationship in terms of principles that would be rooted firmly in the natural sciences and would not have to rely on vague philosophical or mystical ideas.

During his early career, Berger attempted to study psychophysical relationships by plethysmographic measurements of changes in the brain circulation of patients with skull defects. In plethysmography, an instrument is used to indicate and record by tracings the variations in size of a part of the body. Later, Berger investigated temperature changes occurring in the human brain during mental activity and the action of psychoactive drugs. He became disillusioned, however, by his inability to generate meaningful psychophysical understanding through these investigations.

Next, Berger studied the electrical activity of the

brain and, in the 1920's, set out to search for the human electroencephalogram. He believed that the EEG would finally provide him with a physiological method capable of furnishing insight into mental functions and their disturbances. In 1920, Berger made his first unsuccessful attempt at recording the electrical activity of the brain from the scalp of a bald medical student. At that time, he modified his methods of research and attempted to stimulate the cortex of patients with skull defects by applying an electrical current to the skin covering the defect. The main purpose of these stimulation experiments was to elicit subjective sensations. Berger hoped that eliciting these sensations might give him some clue about the nature of the relationship between the physiochemical events produced by the electrical stimulus and the mental processes revealed by the patients' subjective experience. According to his diaries, the availability of many patients with skull defects—in whom the pulsating surface of the brain was separated from the stimulating electrodes by only a few millimeters of tissue—reactivated Berger's interest in recording the brain's electrical activity.

At the time of these experiments, Berger had very little electrophysiological experience, and his knowledge of physics and instrumentation was limited. In addition, the instruments available to him were not well suited to the research he was contemplating. Nevertheless, he conducted his first electrical recordings from skull defects in 1924 by using the large Edelmann string galvanometer, an instrument that had been designed to record electrocardiograms, or electrical charts measuring heart activity. In 1926, he acquired the new Siemens coil galvanometer, an apparatus that also was used in electrocardiography.

In 1932, the Siemens Company constructed an oscillograph with an amplifier for Berger. This instrument had adequate gain and, in contrast to the earlier galvanometers, was a voltage-measuring, rather than a current-measuring, device. All of these instruments were used in conjunction with an optical recording system in which electrical oscillations caused a mirror to deflect a projected beam of light beam. The deflections of the light beam were proportional to the magnitude of the electrical signals. The movement of the spot of the light beam was recorded on photographic paper moving at a speed of three centimeters per second; occasionally, slower speeds were used. The paper width was twelve centimeters, and the lengths of the records varied between about three and eight meters.

During his investigations, Berger remained faithful to his old recording instruments, even when better methods

and equipment—such as cathode-ray oscillography or Tönnies's ink-writing oscillograph—became available. In the 1930's, Berger hoped that Siemens would provide him with a multiple oscillograph system, but this hope remained unfulfilled. Thus, to the end of his career, whenever he wished to record with more than one channel at a time, he was forced to use the Siemens oscillograph and the coil galvanometer simultaneously. A major problem with this method, however, was that the gains of the two instruments were very different; thus it was difficult to place the light spots of the two systems in precise vertical alignment. Therefore, many of Berger's double recordings appear rather idiosyncratic and unsatisfactory from a technical point of view, a fact of which he was well aware.

In July, 1924, Berger observed small, tremulous movements of the galvanometer string while recording from the skin overlying a bone defect in a seventeen-year-old patient (who had been a subject for his earlier cortical stimulation experiments and who had been operated on earlier because he was suspected of having a brain tumor). In his first paper on the electroencephalogram, Berger briefly described this case as his first successful recording of an EEG. Nevertheless, from his experimental protocol, it is known that he did not fully trust this observation, although he was greatly encouraged by it. At the time of these early studies, Berger already had used the term "electroencephalogram" in his diary, yet for several years he had doubts about the cerebral origin of the electrical oscillations he recorded. As late as 1928, he almost abandoned his electrical recording studies.

Berger's first paper on the human encephalogram was published in 1929 as "Über das Elektrenkephalogramm des Menschen" ("On the Electroencephalograph of Man," 1969) in the *Journal für Psychologie und Neurologie*, but it had little immediate impact on the scientific world. Indeed, the paper was either ignored or regarded with open disbelief. Even Berger himself was not yet completely free of doubts about the validity of his findings, but he continued his work. He published additional contributions to the study of the electroencephalogram in a series of fourteen papers. As his research progressed, Berger became increasingly confident and convinced of the significance of his discovery.

In his studies on the human encephalogram, Berger repeatedly touched on basic neurophysiological and neuropharmacological problems; he also commented on the characteristics and importance of EEG changes in a variety of pathological states. He approached these questions exclusively from the point of view of his own personal interest in psychophysiology, and it is clear that he was not interested primarily in the basic neurophysiology, neuropharmacology, or clinical pathology of the EEG. Nevertheless, he was the first to make many perceptive observations in these areas and to develop some theoretical concepts about the origin and the regulation of the EEG in normal and pathological states.

There were many reasons for Berger's lack of immediate recognition and the widespread initial skepticism regarding his work on the EEG of humans. One source of the resistance was to be found among neurophysiologists. Those who conducted research on the axons and their action potentials simply could not believe that regular oscillations of quasi-sinusoidal form could represent the electrical activity of an organ as complex as the human brain and that such activity could be recorded from the scalp.

The situation changed in 1934, when Edgar Douglas Adrian and Brian Harold Cabot Matthews published a paper on the "Berger rhythm." The two neurophysiologists admitted that, initially, they had been skeptical about the validity of Berger's work. This skepticism was reinforced by the common assumption that Berger, a psychiatrist, was an unlikely person to make such a striking discovery. However, Adrian, whose competence as a neurophysiologist could not be questioned, fully confirmed Berger's observations and thus put the seal of scientific respectability on Berger's work. Soon, interest in the EEG spread throughout all the countries of the Western world—except for Germany. Ironically, soon after the international scientific community finally had accepted Berger into their ranks, he was removed from his post by the Nazis in 1937. Shortly thereafter, his laboratory was dismantled.

SIGNIFICANCE

The long-range impact of Berger's work is incontestable. When Berger published his last paper on the human encephalogram in 1938, the new approach to the study of brain function that he inaugurated in 1929 had already gathered momentum in many centers, both in Europe and in the United States. As a result of his pioneering work, a new diagnostic method had been introduced into medicine; physiology had acquired a new investigative tool. Clinical neurophysiology had been liberated from its exclusive dependence on the functional anatomical approach, and electrophysiological exploration of complex functions of the central nervous system in the neurophysiological laboratories had received major impetus. Berger's work had finally received its well-deserved rec-

ognition. Many of those who undertook the study of the electroencephalogram were able to bring a far greater technical knowledge of neurophysiology to bear on the problems of the electrical activity of the brain than Berger was ever able to, yet the community of neurological scientists has not ceased to look with respect to the founder of electroencephalography. Despite overwhelming odds and isolation, Berger initiated a new era of neurophysiology.

—*Genevieve Slomski*

FURTHER READING

Berger, Hans. "Hans Berger on the EEG of Man." Translated by Pierre Gloor. *Electroencephalography and Clinical Neurophysiology*, supp. 28 (1969). An excellent translation of Berger's fourteen reports (1929 to 1939) on the electroencephalograph of humans. The introduction is the most useful and thorough piece of writing on the history and development of Berger's work on the EEG. Places Berger's work in a historical context; provides firsthand documentation on the discovery from Berger's own diaries. Includes graphs, charts, extensive notes, and an index.

Cooper, R., et al. *EEG Technology*. 3d ed. Boston: Butterworths, 1980. In the first chapter, titled "Origins of the Encephalogram," Berger's work is cited in its historical context. Although aimed at the EEG technician, the book gives a useful overview of the advances in EEG technology since its inception. Contains appendixes; references follow each chapter.

Gale, Anthony, and John A. Edwards. *Physiological Correlates of Human Behavior*. Vol. 2 in *Attention and Performance*. New York: Academic Press, 1983. A section devoted to the EEG and human behavior describes the pioneers and popularizers of electrical brain-wave recording devices—Caton and Berger in particular. Describes advances in the understanding of brain function from these pioneers to the 1980's. Contains extensive references and an index.

Kooi, Kenneth A., et al. *Fundamentals of Electroencephalography*. 2d ed. New York: Harper & Row, 1978. A compact source of information about human electroencephalography aimed at both the student and technician. Discusses the basic concepts, principles, and clinical information necessary to evaluate EEGs; gives a brief history of the development of the phenomenon. Contains graphs, illustrations, and extensive references after each chapter.

Nunez, Paul L., and Ramesh Srinivasan. *Electric Fields of the Brain: The Neurophysics of EEG*. 2d ed. New

1929

York: Oxford University Press, 2006. Detailed study of the electrophysiology of the brain, the science of electroencephalography (the recording and analysis of the brain's electrical activity), and the applications of that science. Bibliographic references and index.

Scott, Donald. *Understanding the EEG*. Philadelphia: J. B. Lippincott, 1975. Explains, in simple language, what an EEG is, what diagnostic information it can provide, and what deductions can be made from it. Appeals to those interested in brain activity and its significance—students and practitioners alike. Discusses Berger's work in a brief historical section. Contains a glossary of terms, bibliography, and an index.

Zani, Alberto, and Alice Mado Proverbio, eds. *The Cognitive Electrophysiology of Mind and Brain*. Boston: Academic Press, 2003. An analysis of the relationship between the brain and the mind, using electrophysiological studies of cognitition to bridge the gap. Bibliographic references and index.

SEE ALSO: 1905: Einthoven Begins Clinical Studies with Electrocardiography; 1912-1914: Abel Develops the First Artificial Kidney; July, 1929: Drinker and Shaw Develop a Mechanical Respirator; Fall, 1934-May 6, 1953: Gibbon Develops the Heart-Lung Machine.

1929-1940
MAGINOT LINE IS BUILT

The Maginot line was built to defend France from a German invasion. The line itself was effective, but the French strategy failed as a result of the German Blitzkrieg strategy, which allowed the Germans to advance through Belgium and outflank the wall before the French forces could stop them.

LOCALE: French-German border
CATEGORIES: Engineering; military history; World War II; wars, uprisings, and civil unrest

KEY FIGURES

André Maginot (1877-1932), French minister of war, 1922-1924, 1929-1932
Paul Painlevé (1863-1933), French minister of war, 1925-1929
Édouard Daladier (1884-1970), premier of France, 1933, 1934, 1938-1940
Charles de Gaulle (1890-1970), French undersecretary of state for national defense, 1940, and leader of the Free French government, 1940-1945
Philippe Pétain (1856-1951), commander in chief of the French armies after World War I and minister of war, 1934-1935
Joseph-Jacques-Césaire Joffre (1852-1931), commander in chief of the French armies during World War I

SUMMARY OF EVENT
The Maginot line was created in the aftermath of the carnage of World War I, but its designers failed to take into account the technical advances of 1918 that had made it obsolete long before construction began. After November 11, 1918, France began to explore different means of defense against a possibly resurgent Germany. Having lost more young men per capita than any other nation in the war just ended, the French were convinced that without an adequate system of security, they would lose to Germany if war should break out again.

The French based their plan on three aims. First, they sought a defensive alliance with Great Britain against Germany. England, however, perceived France as the strongest nation in Western Europe and therefore refused to commit to a Continental ally in the interest of a balance of power. Second, France concluded treaties with nations on Germany's eastern border including Poland, Czechoslovakia, Yugoslavia, Romania, and—in 1934—the Soviet Union, in order to replace the security of the prewar Franco-Russian alliance. Finally, as a deterrent to Germany, the French signed a defensive alliance with Belgium and then began to construct a system of fortifications along their border with Germany that became known as the Maginot line.

The construction of the Maginot line had its genesis in the experience of World War I. Following their defeat in the Franco-Prussian War (1870-1871), the French had sought as their national goal the reconquest of Alsace and Lorraine from the German Empire. The country's only strategy for success in 1914 depended on a sustained offensive. As Allied casualties mounted, both British and French trenches were designed to be as uncomfortable as possible to encourage troops to attack. By contrast, the Germans attempted to create both strong and relatively

MAGINOT LINE

attack France. The suggestions were taken up by the two men who served as ministers of war in the 1920's, André Maginot and Paul Painlevé.

A sergeant who was wounded in World War I and who served as a member of the National Assembly, Maginot was primarily concerned with helping veterans obtain benefits. After he oversaw the occupation of the Ruhr in 1923, however, Maginot became convinced that a fortified line was needed to protect France. During the last nine years of his life, he worked to convince the French legislature to vote funds for its construction using the double themes of jobs and patriotism. After Maginot's death, successive ministers of war continued his work and had the fortifications named in his honor in recognition of his interest and determination.

In 1930, the Chamber of Deputies approved the expenditure of 2.9 billion francs over four years for frontier defenses, but the undertaking proved so immense that by 1940 its cost had doubled. Finished shortly before the start of World War II, the Maginot line was a continuous system of advance posts, casemates, and ourages,

comfortable positions that could be easily held. After French mutinies in 1917, the French military commanders, Marshal Joseph-Jacques-Césaire Joffre and Marshal Philippe Pétain, drew the conclusion that switching to a defensive posture would significantly reduce losses. They failed, however, to take into consideration the fact that new offensive techniques using tanks and mobile infantry ultimately overcame Germany's well-constructed defenses. Instead, the French concluded that a future war should find France maintaining a defensive position against an offensive Germany; only then would the odds be in France's favor.

After World War I, Joffre was appointed head of a special commission to plan the military defense of France. Both he and Pétain suggested that a system of fortifications be constructed along the Franco-German border. These fortresses would be so impenetrable that the Germans would face great losses if they attempted to

holding between two hundred and twelve hundred men, running from Switzerland to Belgium along the entire length of the Franco-German border. Vast underground bunkers, cannons that could be raised automatically, and the most modern equipment were installed. The government made public the existence of the Maginot line, but not the details of its armaments, in the hope of convincing the Germans that it would be folly to assault it.

As a result of the advertisement of its presence, a myth was established about the Maginot line. Most citizens of the republic believed that it ran the entire length of France's eastern border, passing through Belgium to the English Channel. At the time of the fortification's construction, Belgium was a friendly nation with its own defenses on the German border. Pétain foresaw that in the event of war with Germany, the French troops stationed on the Maginot line would be able to hold the border, while the bulk of the mobile French forces would move

1929

Workers plow the earth in preparation for the construction of the Maginot line along France's eastern border with Germany. (NARA)

into Belgium to help that country hold its lines against the Germans. In 1914, the British had joined France to protect Belgium, and the French believed that the need to do so again might be the only means to gain England's support in the future. The Maginot line's strength, it was believed, would invite such a German attack on Belgium. When Belgium signed a pact with Germany in 1939, France's northern flank became exposed, but few foresaw the weakness that a static defense now posed.

In 1940, the Germans both outflanked the Maginot line and split the Allied forces by launching a mobile attack through the Ardennes Forest. Although many Germans marched through France as their fathers had done in 1914, dramatic penetrations were made by Panzer tank units. The success of such an attack had been envisioned as early as 1922 by Major General J. F. C. Fuller and Captain Basil Liddell Hart of Great Britain and warned against by Charles de Gaulle. Much to de Gaulle's frustration and the country's detriment, the General Staff failed to take his arguments seriously.

After the French garrisons surrendered on June 25,

1940, the Germans made an in-depth study of the Maginot line. Impressed by the small amount of damage wrought by their aerial bombardment, the army used French construction techniques and many of the guns it had seized in the construction of the Atlantic Wall. The Germans converted much of the Maginot line to storage or factory space until the Allied liberation of Europe in June, 1944. At this stage, part of the fortifications at Faulquemont and Wittring were rearmed and successfully slowed the advance of General George S. Patton's Third U.S. Army. Following the war, the French military began a reconstruction of the line that continued until 1964, when the fortifications were abandoned for defense and parts were opened to tourists and historians.

SIGNIFICANCE

The Maginot line has entered popular lore—along with the Trojan Horse and the invasions of Russia by Napoleon I and Adolf Hitler—as one of the great blunders of military history. The line itself, however, did not fail, nor were the French wrong in predicting that the Germans would storm Belgium and attack France through its Belgian border. The strategy broke down simply because the French had not foreseen the ability of the Germans to advance their tanks so quickly through the Ardennes Forest, which most cartographers and military strategists believed to form a natural defense. The German Blitzkrieg (literally, lightning war) strategy, in which armored divisions advanced as quickly as possible, seizing territory before defenders could forestall them, proved effective: It enabled the German army to get around the line before the French could stop them. Once in the country, moreover, the German troops had a clear path to Paris. Most of France's mobile forces were in Belgium or on the Belgian border, without an opportunity to place themselves between the invaders and the French capital.

—José M. Sánchez and Edmund Dickenson Potter

FURTHER READING

Chapman, Guy. *Why France Fell: The Defeat of the French Army in 1940*. New York: Henry Holt, 1968. Chapman examines the fall of France by first studying the victory of 1918 and the mistakes that were made outside the political front involving the military.

De Gaulle, Charles. *War Memoirs, Vol. I: The Call to Honour, 1940-1942*. Translated by Jonathan Griffin. London: Collins, 1955. As the champion of mobile warfare in France before 1940, de Gaulle uses his autobiography to contradict the notion that the Maginot line and a policy of defense were created without protest.

Fuller, General J. F. C. *The Second World War, 1939-1945*. London: Eyre & Spottiswoode, 1948. As an early theorist on mobile warfare and the use of the tank, Fuller brings a unique perspective to the study of the war.

Hughes, Judith M. *To the Maginot Line: The Politics of French Military Preparation in the 1920's*. Cambridge, Mass.: Harvard University Press, 1971. Hughes addresses how the debate between peace and security created an atmosphere from which the Maginot line was born.

Joseph-Maginot, Marguerite. *Maginot: He Might Have Saved France*. Translated by Allan Updegraff. New York: Doubleday, 1941. This work not only provides a contemporary biography of Maginot but also includes not-so-subtle recriminations for the fall of France shortly after it took place.

Kaufmann, J. E., and H. W. Kaufmann. *Fortress France: The Maginot Line and French Defenses in World War II*. Westport, Conn.: Praeger Security International, 2006. Study of the state of French defenses at the beginning of World War II and their failure to defend against the German invasion. Bibliographic references and index.

Kemp, Anthony. *The Maginot Line: Myth and Reality*. New York: Stein & Day, 1982. Kemp provides not only the history of the fortifications construction but also diagrams and photographs that illustrate the immense nature of the project. Further, he follows the history of the Maginot line through the German occupation into the Cold War when France and her neighbor became allies.

Rowe, Vivian. *The Great Wall of France*. New York: G. P. Putnam's Sons, 1961. Provides detailed accounts of the battles around the Maginot line and suggests that it was the best defense for France at the time.

Weinberg, Gerald L. *A World at Arms: A Global History of World War II*. New York: Cambridge University Press, 1994. This comprehensive work addresses the world war chronologically rather than thematically.

SEE ALSO: Mar. 7, 1936: German Troops March into the Rhineland; Sept. 1, 1939: Germany Invades Poland; Apr. 9, 1940: Germany Invades Norway; May 10-June 22, 1940: Collapse of France.

1929

January, 1929

ALL QUIET ON THE WESTERN FRONT STRESSES THE FUTILITY OF WAR

Written by a participant in World War I, All Quiet on the Western Front, *with its vivid descriptions of the horror and waste of armed conflict as well as of the humanity and comradeship of the combatants, became a powerful antiwar statement.*

LOCALE: Berlin, Germany
CATEGORY: Literature

KEY FIGURES

Erich Maria Remarque (1898-1970), German author
Joseph Goebbels (1897-1945), chief propagandist for the Nazi Party in Germany
Cyrill Soschka (fl. early twentieth century), German publishing company production manager
Jutta Ilse Zambona (1901-1975), German actor and Remarque's wife

SUMMARY OF EVENT

In August, 1914, after the longest period of uninterrupted peace in European history up to that time (forty-three years), Germany plunged the world into war. Four years of slaughter brought unheard-of human and material loss. Of all the nations involved, Germany, with 1.8 million dead, suffered the greatest number of casualties.

After the war's end, two general currents of thought emerged in German life and literature. The first promoted militaristic, belligerent, authoritarian beliefs. The second, profoundly pacifistic, denounced militarism and war.

A full decade after World War I ended, Erich Maria Remarque, who was destined to become a leading figure of pacifism, published an influential, controversial, and successful novel about trench warfare, written from a German perspective. *Im Westen nichts Neues* (1929; *All Quiet on the Western Front,* 1929) is semiautobiographical, recounting many of the author's experiences as a World War I infantryman.

Although christened Erich Paul Remark in 1898, the author changed his name over the years, first substituting his mother's middle name for his own a year after her death in 1917. In 1920, he published a novel so poorly received that the embarrassment caused him to adopt his great-grandfather's spelling of the family name.

In 1916, when Remarque was an eighteen-year-old student at a teacher's college, he was drafted; he received military training at the Westerberg barracks in Osnabrück (the "Klosterberg" of *All Quiet on the Western Front*). In June, 1917, he was assigned to a trench unit

near the western front and was devastated when a friend whom he had rescued on the battlefield died of head wounds (an incident reflected in the death of the character named Stanislaus Katczinsky in the novel). After another daring rescue, Remarque himself was severely injured by grenade splinters and spent almost a year recuperating.

The war changed Remarque forever. He gained an appreciation for the value and fragility of life, saw the futility and destructiveness of war, and became disillusioned with patriotism and the glorification of battle. Against the background of the horrors of combat, civilian life seemed trivial. These attitudes and beliefs were translated into the messages of *All Quiet on the Western Front*.

For the next few years following the war (amid shortages, inflation, unemployment, and extremist politics), Remarque had a difficult time, as did many. He ridiculed the war, wandered from job to job, married, became a

Erich Maria Remarque. (Library of Congress)

regular in Berlin society, and finally took a job as an associate editor of a sports magazine. In 1927, Remarque began to publish a number of pieces that reflected his love of cars and motor racing. During the latter part of that year, over a six-week period, *All Quiet on the Western Front* was written. The manuscript, however, remained in Remarque's desk for six months before he submitted it for publication.

At first, publishers were not interested. Finally, Cyril Soschka, manager of the production department of Ullstein Publishers, read the book and believed that it would be successful. In fact, Soschka threatened to establish his own firm just to publish Remarque's novel if no one else would.

The new war novel was first serialized in a German newspaper owned by Ullstein, *Vossische Zeitung*, between November 10 and December 9, 1928. The novel appeared in book form in January, 1929, and was translated into English that same year. The overnight success of the book astonished everyone, including Remarque himself, and irrevocably altered the course of his life. The previously unknown journalist became a wealthy, world-famous author.

Remarque claimed that he had not set out to write a best seller but had written instead to rid himself of the bleak moods that he and his friends were still experiencing as a result of the war. He said that the shadow of war had continued to hang over them, especially when they tried to shut their minds to it. Thus, as a kind of cathartic enterprise, the novel tells the story of a generation of young men who were destroyed by World War I—even if they survived the fighting. Remarque narrates the tale through the main character, Paul Bäumer.

Although the book was instantly popular, it generated such tremendous controversy in some circles that Remarque was accused of writing solely to shock and to sell. Others believed the book was nothing more than sentimentalism or pacifistic drivel.

Ignoring it as a work of literature, the Nazis regarded the book as an insult to and an attack on the greatness of the Germany they wanted to control. Remarque's ideas were antithetical to the Nazis' ideology and intended

---

FROM *ALL QUIET ON THE WESTERN FRONT*

The narrator expresses the relentlessness of battle in this excerpt from Erich Maria Remarque's All Quiet on the Western Front:

Is it nothing that regiment after regiment returns again and again to the ever more hopeless struggle, that attack follows attack along the weakening, retreating, crumbling line?

From a mockery the tanks have become a terrible weapon. Armoured they come rolling on in long lines, and more than anything else embody for us the horror of war.

We do not see the guns that bombard us; the attacking lines of the enemy infantry are men like ourselves; but these tanks are machines, their caterpillars run on as endless as the war, they are annihilation, they roll without feeling into the craters, and climb up again without stopping, a fleet of roaring, smoke-belching armour-clads, invulnerable steel beasts squashing the dead and the wounded—we shrivel up in our thin skin before them, against their colossal weight our arms are sticks of straw, and our hand-grenades matches.

Shells, gas clouds, and flotillas of tanks—shattering, starvation, death.

Dysentery, influenza, typhus—murder, burning, death.

Trenches, hospitals, the common grave—there are no other possibilities.

Source: Erich Maria Remarque, *All Quiet on the Western Front*, translated by A. W. Wheen (Boston: Little, Brown, 1929).

---

course of action. To the Nazis, the novel seemed to symbolize the beliefs of men who had stabbed Germany in the back by conceding defeat in a war the Nazis claimed their country should have won.

The Nazis tried to undermine Remarque's popularity by spreading rumors about his credibility, claiming that he was, among other things, a French Jew (apparently the worst combination of traits the Nazis could imagine) or an old man who had never seen battle. Leading the attack was Joseph Goebbels, the Nazi Party's chief propagandist.

In 1931, Remarque published a sequel to *All Quiet on the Western Front* based on his and his friends' experiences after they returned from the front. Titled *Der Weg zurück* (*The Road Back*, 1931), it further angered the Nazis. During this period, the author and his first wife, Jutta Ilse Zambona, a young actor, lived in Berlin. After Nazi persecution forced Remarque to leave in 1931, the couple divorced in 1932. (They later remarried, but they divorced again in 1951.) Remarque emigrated to Switzerland, bought a villa at Porto Ronco on Lake Maggiore, and began filling it with valuable antiques; he also spent a great deal of time in France and the United States, both before and after World War II.

Remarque's fame spread as he pursued a glamorous lifestyle. He hobnobbed with Hollywood stars and

1929

American authors, enjoyed fine food and expensive clothes, received awards and honors, became an American citizen, married another actor (Paulette Goddard), and even acted in *A Time to Love and a Time to Die*, the 1958 film version of one of his novels. Through it all, he continued to write, producing eleven novels altogether. Each was written in German but simultaneously translated and published in English, and each developed themes first introduced in *All Quiet on the Western Front*.

SIGNIFICANCE

The significance of *All Quiet on the Western Front* lies, first, in the influence it had on European and American thought and, second, in the reaction it generated among the new Nazi leaders of Germany. The novel deeply moved people on both sides of the Atlantic. It was, and still is, a powerful condemnation of war. It touched the hearts and minds of readers, not so much through its literary quality as through the force of its conviction that war is unmitigated waste—a conviction that grew out of Remarque's experience as a witness to horrible suffering.

In the United States, for example, magazine and newspaper reviews immediately hailed Remarque's work as an updated version of Stephen Crane's *The Red Badge of Courage: An Episode of the American Civil War* (1895). *All Quiet on the Western Front* taught its readers that World War I was one of the most terrible catastrophes of all time. At best, World War I reduced the lives of its participants to the level of simple survival. At worst, it reduced human beings to the level of animals.

Although some decried the book's scenes as horrible, it was precisely this graphic realism that made the novel sell. In the first year of publication, German readers alone bought more than one million copies. British, French, and American audiences purchased many hundreds of thousands more. By 1932, the book had been translated into twenty-nine languages. The edition in Afrikaans inspired a flood of "war diaries" about the Second Boer War.

The new war novel also made an important impact on the world when it was made into an American motion picture starring Lew Ayres and Lew Wolheim. One of the first films produced after the introduction of sound technology, it became a classic. In 1930, however, the film was banned by the Nazis in Berlin, and that event signaled the start of intense persecution directed at Remarque.

Remarque was not the only member of his family to suffer at the hands of the Nazis. *All Quiet on the Western Front* had so poisoned the Nazis against anyone or anything associated with Remarque that in 1943, the author's younger sister, Elfriede Scholz, was beheaded for spreading subversive propaganda. Reference was made to Remarque during his sister's trial, and Remarque himself acknowledged that the mere fact that Scholz was his sister had something to do with the verdict. Twenty-five years after Scholz's death, a street on the outskirts of Osnabrück was named after her. In 1971, one year after the author died, authorities of Osnabrück named a section of road along the town walls the Erich Maria Remarque Ring.

In 1933, when the Nazis had taken full control of Germany, both *All Quiet on the Western Front* and its sequel, *The Road Back*, were burned by the new regime in the notorious book-burning ceremony in Berlin. (Even before that episode, the two works had been placed on the Nazi index of prohibited literature.)

The two novels continued to arouse the ire of totalitarian regimes in the twentieth century; Remarque's works were banned by the Soviet Union and other Eastern Bloc nations in 1949. Soviet authorities feared that the antiwar sentiment of the books might adversely affect Communist youth. Although the Eastern Bloc countries removed the ban on the books in 1962, Remarque's works were still seen as a powerful argument against the assertion that unquestioned service to the state is the highest aim in life.

Latent disapproval of *All Quiet on the Western Front* by some in Germany finally manifested itself after Remarque's death in 1970. The weekly journal *Der Spiegel* published an obituary that managed to omit any mention of Remarque as ever having written a profoundly influential World War I novel. Nevertheless, the public had not forgotten Remarque's work. By the time of his death, millions of copies of *All Quiet on the Western Front* had been sold, and many more have been sold since. The continuing widespread popularity of the novel testifies to the timelessness of its message, and the book's depiction of the horror and futility of war has continued to exert a powerful impact on readers.

—*Andrew C. Skinner*

FURTHER READING

Barker, Christine R., and R. W. Last. *Erich Maria Remarque*. London: Oswald Wolff, 1979. Offers a thorough yet concise history of the man and his work. Places his novels in historical context and devotes special attention to Remarque's first major success.

Fussell, Paul. *The Great War and Modern Memory*. 25th anniversary ed. New York: Oxford University Press,

2000. Prizewinning book explores the literary sources and means by which the British experience on the western front has been remembered. Contains only a few explicit references to Remarque's work, but helps to place it in the context of the whole literary culture that centered on World War I and allows readers to compare the experiences of different nationalities in the trenches.

O'Neill, Terry, ed. *Readings on "All Quiet on the Western Front."* San Diego, Calif.: Greenhaven Press, 1999. Collection of essays by various authors provides a number of different perspectives on Remarque's novel. Intended to help students understand the work more fully.

Owen, C. R. *Erich Maria Remarque: A Critical Bio-Bibliography*. Amsterdam: Rodopi, 1984. Each chapter of this informative biography is accompanied by an annotated bibliography of books and articles about Remarque and all of his published writings. Represents one of the most complete bibliographies available. Most titles are in German, but the annotations are in English. An essential tool for scholarly research.

Schwarz, Wilhelm J. *War and the Mind of Germany*. Frankfurt: Peter Lang, 1975. A collection of five short scholarly essays, three of which discuss the life and work of Remarque. Presents comparisons between Remarque's World War I novel and the writings of German authors Ernst Junger and Theodor Plievier. One essay discusses Remarque's World War II novels.

Tims, Hilton. *Erich Maria Remarque: The Last Romantic*. New York: Carroll & Graf, 2003. Biography details Remarque's literary career but in large part focuses on his life in the United States after 1939, when he was romantically involved with a number of film stars. Includes photographs, bibliography, and index.

Wagener, Hans. *Understanding Erich Maria Remarque*. Columbia: University of South Carolina Press, 1991. Useful introduction to Remarque's works includes analyses of his major novels, a chronology of his life, and an annotated bibliography.

SEE ALSO: June 28, 1914-Nov. 11, 1918: World War I; Sept. 5-9, 1914: First Battle of the Marne; 1921-1923: Hašek's *The Good Soldier Švejk* Reflects Postwar Disillusionment.

January, 1929
TROTSKY IS SENT INTO EXILE

Leon Trotsky was sent into exile, putting an end to significant opposition within the Soviet Communist Party to Joseph Stalin's personal rule and his establishment of a totalitarian state.

LOCALE: Moscow, Soviet Union (now Russia)
CATEGORY: Government and politics

KEY FIGURES

Leon Trotsky (Lev Davidovich Bronstein; 1879-1940), Russian revolutionary leader and Soviet politician

Joseph Stalin (Joseph Vissarionovich Dzhugashvili; 1878-1953), general secretary of the Central Committee of the Communist Party of the Soviet Union, 1922-1953

Vladimir Ilich Lenin (Vladimir Ilich Ulyanov; 1870-1924), Russian revolutionary leader and creator and first leader of the Communist Party

Lev Borisovich Kamenev (Lev Borisovich Rosenfeld; 1883-1936), Bolshevik leader

Grigory Yevseyevich Zinovyev (Ovsel Gershon Aronov Radomyslsky; 1883-1936), Bolshevik leader

SUMMARY OF EVENT

Both Leon Trotsky and Vladimir Ilich Lenin played important parts in the Bolshevik seizure of power in Russia. Like Lenin, Trotsky may have been indispensable. No one agitated more effectively among the working classes to bring them to the side of the Bolsheviks and no one showed more skill and determination in organizing them into a military force capable of winning power in Petrograd in 1917. No one stood more steadfastly beside Lenin in the crucial days of October, when several of the leading Bolsheviks opposed the leader's decision to try to seize power. In the summer and fall of 1917, the special talents that Trotsky possessed—energy, determination, ruthlessness, and flaming oratory—found a situation in which they could be most effective.

In the hard days of the civil war (1918-1921), Trotsky's abilities and courage once again served the Bolsheviks well. It was he who, as people's commissar of war, organized and directed the Red Army. In less than one year, by the force of his will and intelligence, he transformed an undisciplined group of youthful enthusi-

1929

PERMANENT REVOLUTION

In a 1932 speech delivered from exile in Copenhagen, "In Defense of October," Trotsky reached a visionary conclusion:

Only a powerful increase in productive force and a sound, planned, that is, socialist organisation of production and distribution can assure humanity—all humanity—of a decent standard of life and at the same time give it the precious feeling of freedom with respect to its own economy.

Freedom in two senses—first of all man will no longer be compelled to devote the greater part of his life to physical toil. Second, he will no longer be dependent on the laws of the market, that is, on the blind and obscure forces which work behind his back. . . .

Man calls himself the crown of creation. He has a certain right to that aim. But who has asserted that present day man is the last and highest representative of the species Homo Sapiens? No, physically as well as spiritually he is very far from perfection, prematurely born biologically, with feeble thought, and has not produced any new organic equilibrium.

It is true that humanity has more than once brought forth giants of thought and action, who tower over their contemporaries like summits in a chain of mountains. The human race has a right to be proud of its Aristotle, Shakespeare, Darwin, Beethoven, Goethe, Marx, Edison and Lenin. But why are they so rare?

Above all, because almost without exception they came out of the middle and upper classes. Apart from rare exceptions, the sparks of genius in the suppressed depths of the people are choked before they can burst into flame.

But also because the processes of creating, developing and educating a human being have been and remain essentially a matter of chance, not illuminated by theory and practice, not subjected to consciousness and will. . . .

Once he has done with the anarchic forces of his own society man will set to work on himself, in the pestle and retort of the chemist. For the first time mankind will regard itself as raw material, or at best as a physical and psychic semi-finished product. Socialism will mean a leap from the realm of necessity into the realm of freedom in this sense also, that the man of today, with all his contradictions and lack of harmony, will open the road for a new and happier race.

a traitor to the revolution rather than one of its principal leaders.

After the death of Lenin in 1924, Trotsky lost the struggle for power in a personality clash with Stalin in which fateful aspects of Soviet Communist policy were thrashed out. Should the party continue the semicapitalistic New Economic Policy (NEP) within the Soviet Union? Should it govern democratically or dictatorially? Should it stake all on the victory of world revolution, or should it try to consolidate "socialism" in the Soviet Union? These were the policy questions intertwined with the struggle for personal power. Between 1923 and 1925, Trotsky tried to turn the party away from the NEP to a policy of collectivization of the peasants and massive industrialization. Stalin, with the help of important Bolsheviks, such as Lev Borisovich Kamenev and Grigory Yevseyevich Zinovyev, and with overwhelming support among the mass of party members, brought about Trotsky's defeat on this issue in the Party Congresses of 1923 and 1924. Feeling against Trotsky ran so high that Kamenev and Zinovyev at a Central Committee meeting in January, 1925, demanded his expulsion from the party, but Stalin, still unsure of himself, rejected their proposal. Trotsky was merely forced to give up his post as people's commissar of war.

By mid-1925, however, Kamenev and Zinovyev became alarmed at Stalin's demonstrated strength in the rank and file. They now saw him as a greater threat to their positions in the party than Trotsky, whom they, like many others, had suspected of a dictatorial tendency. Moreover, they had come to believe that it was time to abandon the NEP. Accordingly, they joined forces with Trotsky as he once again called for a rapid beginning of collectivization and industrialization. They also fought for the restoration of democracy in the party, which Stalin—as head of the Orgburo, which made party personnel decisions, and of the Secretariat, which controlled the party's records and conducted all correspondence between Moscow and local party organizations—had transformed into a centrally directed, bureaucratic

asts into an organized, disciplined army. He also tirelessly and ruthlessly directed that army in its struggle to the death against both the White Russians' counterrevolution and foreign intervention. The Bolsheviks might not have survived the civil war and the Red regime might have been merely a passing phenomenon in world history without Trotsky, but only ten short years later he became an outcast, exiled from his native land by the Communist Party he had done so much to defend and perpetuate. His victorious rival, Joseph Stalin, rewrote history to conceal Trotsky's important role in the Bolshevik seizure of power and victory in the civil war. Trotsky virtually became an "unperson" in the Soviet Union, remembered only for the false charge that he was machine. They also fought for an active Communist role in international affairs against Stalin's doctrine of "Socialism in one country." At the Party Congress in December, 1925, Stalin and his supporters easily overcame this opposition group.

Defeated in the higher echelons of the party, Trotsky returned to the fray in 1926 and 1927, but in a different way. He tried to reach the rank and file by speeches, articles, and pamphlets and by the surreptitious organization of an opposition faction. Such oppositional activity had been banned by the Tenth Party Congress in March, 1921. Trotsky's violation of the rule against factions led in October, 1926, to Trotsky's expulsion from the Politburo, the leading policy-making organ of the party, the last bastion of his strength after his defeats in the Party Congresses of 1923-1925. His acts ran counter to the party's deep need and desire for unity and eroded rather than increased his strength.

Trotsky's last attempt to regain power came in October, 1927, on the anniversary of the revolution. He mounted public parades and demonstrations against Stalin and the party leadership. These pathetic efforts were easily crushed by Stalin's loyal followers, and in December, 1927, at the Fifteenth Party Congress, Trotsky, Kamenev, Zinovyev, and seventy-five of their most prominent followers were expelled from the party. In a prophetic act, Stalin allowed the "guilty" to return to the womb of the party if they would publicly recant their errors. Kamenev, Zinovyev, and numerous others did so. Trotsky refused, and he was exiled, first to Alma Ata in Kazakhstan, and then—in January of 1929—out of the Soviet Union altogether.

SIGNIFICANCE

Trotsky lived on in exile, the center of forces opposing Stalin in world Communism, and the source of many polemical writings against the regime. Not content with the physical expulsion of Trotsky from the Soviet Union, Stalin sought to erase all memory of Trotsky's vital role in the Russian Revolution and Russian Civil War. Soviet history books were rewritten to misrepresent the roles of both Trotsky and Stalin. Trotsky was falsely accused of opposing Lenin in 1917 and of secretly working for the defeat of Communism in the civil war, while Stalin was given credit for Trotsky's achievements. This falsification of history reached its height in Stalin's Great Purge of 1936-1938, when thousands of Stalin's former opponents, including Zinovyev and Kamenev, were imprisoned or executed on trumped-up charges of trying to sabotage the building of socialism in Russia in collaboration with Trotsky. The exiled Trotsky was hounded by Soviet agents until 1940, when Stalin's assassins killed him.

—George F. Putnam and Richard D. King

FURTHER READING

Carr, E. H. *Socialism in One Country, 1924-1926.* 3 vols. New York: Macmillan, 1958-1964. A detailed investigation of the personal and policy struggles in the period following Lenin's death.

Deutscher, Isaac. *The Prophet Unarmed: Trotsky, 1921-1929.* New York: Verso, 2003. The second volume of a sympathetic three-volume biography, this book recounts the power struggles of the 1920's.

Fitzpatrick, Sheila. *The Russian Revolution.* 2d ed. New York: Oxford University Press, 1994. An introduction to the first two decades of Soviet history that effectively brings out Stalin's and Trotsky's different programs for building socialism.

Knei-Paz, Baruch. *The Social and Political Thought of Leon Trotsky.* Oxford, England: Clarendon Press, 1978. A comprehensive analysis of Trotsky's writings, with particular emphasis on Trotsky's interpretation of Stalinism.

Renton, Dave. *Trotsky.* London: Haus, 2004. Short monograph on the life, work, and politics of Trotsky and his effects on Soviet history.

Leon Trotsky. (NARA)

1929

Trotsky, Leon. *My Life: An Attempt at Autobiography.* Magnolia, Mass.: Peter Smith, 1930. Trotsky wrote this autobiography, which has been reissued several times, immediately after his exile from the Soviet Union in 1929.

Tucker, Robert C. *Stalin as Revolutionary, 1879-1929: A Study in History and Personality.* New York: W. W. Norton, 1973. This study of Stalin's rise to power offers a psychological interpretation of his rivalry with Trotsky.

Volkogonov, Dmitri. *Trotsky: The Eternal Revolutionary.* Translated and edited by Harold Shukman. New York: Free Press, 1996. Written by a retired Soviet general who has also published books on Lenin and Stalin, this is the first biography of Trotsky based on access to Soviet as well as Western archives.

SEE ALSO: Oct. 30, 1905: October Manifesto; Oct. 3, 1908: First Issue of *Pravda* Appears; 1917-1924: Russian Communists Inaugurate the Red Terror; Mar.-Nov., 1917: Lenin Leads the Russian Revolution; Nov. 6-7, 1917: Bolsheviks Mount the October Revolution; Mar. 2-6, 1919: Lenin Establishes the Comintern; Mar., 1921: Lenin Announces the New Economic Policy; Dec., 1934: Stalin Begins the Purge Trials.

February 11, 1929
LATERAN TREATY

The Lateran Treaty settled the question of the relationship between the Vatican and the government of Italy, which had seized the formerly independent Papal States in 1870. The treaty made Vatican City a sovereign state separate from Italy, and it instituted Roman Catholicism as the Italian state religion.

ALSO KNOWN AS: Lateran treaties; Lateran Pact of 1929; Lateran Pacts of 1929; Lateran Accords

LOCALE: Rome, Italy

CATEGORIES: Diplomacy and international relations; expansion and land acquisition; religion, theology, and ethics

KEY FIGURES

Benito Mussolini (1883-1945), Fascist premier of Italy, 1922-1943

Pietro Gasparri (1852-1934), Roman Catholic cardinal, 1907-1934, and papal secretary of state, 1914-1930

Pius XI (Ambrogio Damiano Achille Ratti; 1857-1939), Roman Catholic pope, 1922-1939

Victor Emmanuel III (1869-1947), king of Italy, r. 1900-1946

Domenico Barone (fl. early twentieth century), Italian diplomat

Francesco Pacelli (fl. early twentieth century), papal diplomat

SUMMARY OF EVENT

When the army of the new Italian state took the city of Rome from the papacy in 1870, Pope Pius IX retreated to the Vatican palace and proclaimed himself "prisoner of the Vatican." Alleging that the Italian government had usurped lands that were the heritage of the Roman Catholic Church, he condemned the government and refused to have anything to do with it. The pope hoped that his condemnation would rally pro-papal forces to overthrow the Italian state and restore him to his temporal possessions. He furthermore prohibited Catholics, by threat of excommunication, from running or holding office in the national government or voting in state parliamentary elections, hoping that their abstention would also weaken the government.

Instead, the Italian government flourished and, in the absence of Catholic deputies, passed anticlerical legislation. Successive governments, however, respected papal possession of the Vatican palace and Saint Peter's Basilica and offered the papacy a Law of Guarantees, guaranteeing the pope residence at the Vatican and a large sum of money. The pope rejected this offer because acceptance would mean the Vatican would exist as charity of the state and imply that the pope served under allegiance to the state.

After 1870, despite official unwillingness on both sides to solve the so-called Roman Question—an expression referring to the politico-religious conflict between the papacy and the kingdom of Italy—a tacit understanding was worked out between the papacy and the state. Neither interfered in the other's affairs, but the underlying conflict between church and state still existed as a constant strain to the whole country in a time that witnessed political unrest throughout the world and the

VATICAN CITY, 1929

SWITZERLAND

AUSTRIA

HUNGARY

SLOVENIA

CROATIA

SERBIA

Milan

Turin

Venice

Genoa

BOSNIA-
HERZEGOVINA

Bologna

Ravenna

SAN
MARINO

Pisa

Leghorn

Florence

Ligurian Sea

MONTE-
NEGRO

ITALY

*Adriatic
Sea*

CORSICA
(FRANCE)

Rome

**VATICAN
CITY**

Naples

Bari

*Tyrrhenian
Sea*

Sardinia

FRANCE

*Ionian
Sea*

Palermo

ALGERIA

Strait of Sicily

Sicily

TUNISIA

win them over to his side. He maintained the monarchy, assuring King Victor Emmanuel III that he had no intention of overthrowing the Italian royal house. In order to gain the support of both the papacy and the Catholics, he announced his desire to settle the Roman Question. Mussolini's seizure of power coincided with the election of Pius XI as pope. When Mussolini made public his desire to work with the papacy, Pius cautiously proceeded to cooperate with Mussolini in an effort to ward off a mutual foe of the Vatican and Mussolini: communism.

In 1926, the two leaders made secret preliminary contacts for negotiation of the problem. The pope selected Francesco Pacelli, brother of the future Pope Pius XII, as his envoy, and Mussolini directed the Italian diplomat Domenico Barone to represent him in the talks. Early in 1929, agreement was reached, and the Lateran Treaty was officially signed on February 11, 1929, by Mussolini and the papal secretary of state, Cardinal Pietro Gasparri.

The Lateran Treaty contained three separate sections (and is therefore sometimes referred to as the Lateran treaties, or the Lateran Pacts): a treaty, a financial agreement, and a concordat. The first was an agreement between the Italian state and the Vatican. By its terms, Italy recognized the Vatican as a separate and sovereign state with all the attributes of an independent nation. Italy, furthermore, recognized its usurpation of papal lands in 1870 by compensating the papacy for its loss of temporal possessions. A cash settlement of forty million dollars was paid to the pope along with another fifty-two million dollars of interest-bearing Italian government bonds. In return, the Vatican recognized the Italian government.

Under the terms of the concordat between the Italian state and the Holy See, the anticlerical laws were formally revoked. The Catholic religion was to be taught in all state schools, and Catholicism was proclaimed the official religion of the state. The clergy were given a generally favorable position in civil law. In return, the Italian

threat of communism at Italy's border. With the exception of extreme clericals, both sides wanted to effect a compromise settlement of the Roman Question, but it was a matter of prestige that neither side be the first to give in.

Early in the twentieth century, the papacy began to lift the ban on Catholic participation in national political life. In 1919, it was completely removed to allow the formation of the Catholic-oriented Popular Party, led by Sicilian priest Don Luigi Sturzo. The Popular Party originated with the hope of propagating faith in the Church among the Italian people, for the pope knew that no answer to the Roman Question could be settled by treaty alone.

In 1922, Benito Mussolini, leader of the Fascist Party, was named prime minister, and he set out to establish a dictatorship. In the process, Mussolini was anxious to reconcile with conservative groups and institutions to

Benito Mussolini (center) and other Italian government officials pay their first state visit to Vatican City after the signing of the Lateran Treaty. (NARA)

government obtained the privilege of nominating candidates for the higher clerical positions in Italy.

SIGNIFICANCE

The announcement of the signing of the treaty immediately raised Mussolini's prestige both in Italy and throughout the Catholic world. Hailed for having solved one of the world's outstanding diplomatic problems, Mussolini transformed his international image from that of a violent Blackshirt to a wise and compassionate statesman. Pius also garnered prestige for recognizing that the necessity of papal temporal possessions did not require large amounts of territory: Vatican City was one of the smallest nations in history.

The Lateran Treaty was, however, the prelude to further disagreement between the pope and Mussolini. The concordat had specifically guaranteed Catholic lay organizations freedom to function in Italy. One of these societies, the Italian Catholic Action, soon became a refuge for anti-Fascist elements, who used the organization to criticize the regime. Mussolini sent his Blackshirts to break up Catholic Action meetings, and the pope responded in 1931 by condemning Fascism in the encyclical *Non abbiamo bisogno*. After threats and counterthreats, the state and the papacy reached a tacit agreement: Catholic Action would no longer criticize the regime, and in return it would be allowed full freedom to operate outside this restriction. The pope thereafter maintained a discreet caution toward Mussolini, and when he died in

1939, Pius was considerably disenchanted with the Fascist regime.

Not even all initial reactions to the signing of the treaty were positive. Anti-Laterans were as strongly opposed to the treaty as supporters highly exalted Pius and Mussolini. The issue of equality between the pope and the state was called into question by Americans and Europeans who viewed the treaty as an opportunistic maneuver by Mussolini and believed that the pope lost prestige for the Church by compromising with a political power whose beliefs were opposed to human rights and religious devotion. Opponents of the Lateran agreements, then, hated the implied surrender to Fascism that the treaty invoked rather than the settlement itself.

Although the Lateran Treaty dealt primarily with the sovereign relations of the Holy See with the government of Italy, it was consistent with an effort by the Church to restore its rights to minister to the faithful through a series of agreements and concordats with the anticlerical governments of European countries that had been hostile to Roman Catholicism. The Lateran Treaty was essentially respected by the various governments of the Italian state throughout the confusion of the war years: In 1948, it was officially incorporated into the constitution of the new Italian Republic and remained in force until 1984, when Catholicism ceased to be the state religion of Italy. With regard to peace and mutual understanding, however, the treaty barely survived its birth in 1929.

—*José M. Sánchez and Diane Lise Hendrix*

FURTHER READING

Brendon, Piers. "The Duce and the Pope." In *The Dark Valley: A Panorama of the 1930's*. London: Jonathan Cape, 2000. Discussion of the Lateran Treaty and the relationship between Mussolini and Pius XI; part of a massive volume surveying the international socio-economic and political situation and developments of the 1930's. Bibliographic references and index.

DeGrand, Alexander J. "Cracks in the Facade: The Failure of Fascist Totalitarianism in Italy 1935-1939." *European History Quarterly* 21, no. 4 (1991): 515-535. Describes weaknesses in Benito Mussolini's Fascist reign that made it impossible for totalitarianism to survive.

Drake, Richard. "Julius Evola, Radical Fascism, and the Lateran Accords." *Catholic Historical Review* 74, no. 3 (1988): 403-419. A profile of anti-Lateran Julius Evola that critiques the Catholic Church and discusses the complexity of Fascism.

Knee, Stuart E. "The Strange Alliance: Mussolini, Pope Pius XI, and the Lateran Treaty." *Mediterranean Historical Review* 5, no. 2 (1990): 183-206. The Lateran Accords sought to end antagonism between the Italian state and the papacy. Optimism following the agreement did not last long. Discussion of Fascist and papal motivations behind the Vatican Treaty.

O'Brien, Albert C. "Italian Youth in Conflict: Catholic Action and Fascist Italy, 1929-1931." *Catholic Historical Review* 68, no. 4 (1982): 624-635. Discusses the conflict and competition between the Catholic Church and Italian Fascists for control of Italian youth.

Rhodes, Anthony. *The Vatican in the Age of the Dictators, 1922-1945.* New York: Holt, Rinehart and Winston, 1973. An in-depth look at the motivations behind initiation of the Vatican Treaty and the consequences for church and state after signing the treaty.

SEE ALSO: Aug. 9, 1903: Pius X Becomes Pope; Mar. 19, 1907-Apr., 1914: Publication of *The Catholic Encyclopedia*; May 16, 1920: Canonization of Joan of Arc; 1925-1926: Mussolini Seizes Dictatorial Powers in Italy; May 17, 1925: Thérèse of Lisieux Is Canonized; Dec. 8, 1933: Canonization of Bernadette Soubirous; Mar. 2, 1939: Pius XII Becomes Pope.

February 14, 1929
VALENTINE'S DAY MASSACRE

When George "Bugs" Moran's gang was executed by a group of men dressed as police officers in a garage in North Chicago, Al Capone was believed to be behind the hit, and the event marked the beginning of the end of Capone's reign as Chicago crime czar. The massacre sparked a wave of reforms that helped to dismantle Capone's empire.

ALSO KNOWN AS: St. Valentine's Day Massacre
LOCALE: Chicago, Illinois
CATEGORIES: Crime and scandal; social issues and reform

KEY FIGURES
Al Capone (1899-1947), leader of Chicago's South Side gang
George Moran (1893-1957), leader of Chicago's North Side gang
Jack McGurn (1905-1936), Chicago gangster and lieutenant to Moran
Frank Gusenberg (1893-1929), Chicago gangster and lieutenant to Moran
Pete Gusenberg (1889-1929), Chicago gangster and lieutenant to Moran
Adam Heyer (1889-1929), Chicago gangster and lieutenant to Moran
John May (1894-1929), Chicago gangster and lieutenant to Moran
Al Weinshank (1893-1929), Chicago gangster and lieutenant to Moran

Albert Kachellek (1890-1929), Chicago gangster and Moran's brother-in-law
Dean O'Banion (1892-1924), leader of Chicago's North Side gang
Abe Bernstein (d. 1968), leader of Detroit's Purple Gang

SUMMARY OF EVENT
During Prohibition, Chicago's Beer Wars were at the forefront of the national imagination. For years the city had been turned into a battleground. Dean O'Banion ruled the North Side, and Al "Scarface" Capone and Johnny Torrio had the South Side. O'Banion was killed in 1924 by Frankie Yale, John Scalise, and Albert Anselmi, gunners for Capone, and Torrio was killed the following year by North Siders Earl "Hymie" Weiss, Vincent "The Schemer" Drucci, and George "Bugs" Moran. Soon after, Weiss, Drucci, and Moran made an attempt on Capone's life. They failed, and Weiss later died at the hands of two Capone gunmen; Drucci was killed by a young cop. Eventually, Moran was the only one of O'Banion's men left, and he took over the North Side operation. Moran swore an eternal vendetta against Capone, who had long been desperate to have control of the North Side as well as the South Side. While on vacation at his home in Palm Island, Florida, in early 1929, Capone received word that Moran's gunners had killed several of his top lieutenants.

What happened next would become the source of a great deal of speculation. Capone was the logical person

1929

on whom to pin any attack against the North Siders, and many believed that he had ordered a hit on Moran's entire gang. According to this theory, Capone made contact from Florida with Abe Bernstein, leader of Detroit's Purple Gang. Capone and Bernstein concocted an elaborate scheme that involved placing a call to Bugs Moran. Bernstein probably placed the call—according to reports, he had somehow worked his way into Moran's good graces—and reported that a recently hijacked shipment of bonded whiskey was being sold at a cheap price. Moran jumped at the chance to get hold of the whiskey and told the caller to have the shipment delivered to his headquarters—a garage on Chicago's North Side—the next day.

On the morning of February 14, 1929, the day after the alleged call was placed to Moran, Moran's gangsters assembled at his headquarters. The garage, which was located at 2122 North Clark Street and owned by Moran stooge Adam "Frank" Heyer, was a front and had a phony sign in the window that said "S.M.C. Cartage Company." There were seven men present at the garage: Heyer; Frank and Pete Gusenberg, Moran's top gunners; safe blower John May; speakeasy owner Albert Wein-

Al Capone. (Library of Congress)

shank; bank robber Albert Kachellek (also known as James Clarke); and Dr. Reinhardt Schwimmer, an optometrist who liked to hang around with gangsters for excitement and probably used his business as a cover for criminal activities. The men were anxiously awaiting the arrival of Bugs Moran, who was traveling with two other members of the gang, Willie Marks and Ted Newbury, and was late. When Moran, Marks, and Newbury arrived at the garage, they saw a black Cadillac—the type that detectives used at the time—pulled up to the curb. Figuring that the cops had been tipped to the shipment of whiskey, Moran, Marks, and Newbury retreated to a nearby coffee shop.

Inside the garage, men dressed as police officers lined the seven members of Moran's gang up against the wall and shot them to death. Neighbors heard the racket, but minutes later those who had come outside to see what was happening witnessed two cops putting two men in plainclothes into the back of the Cadillac. Relieved because they believed the police were already there, none of the neighbors called the police. What they did not realize, of course, was that the men they had seen were not real cops.

John May's dog had been left howling in the garage, and a landlady from a nearby building, annoyed by the dog's whining, sent one of her boarders to investigate. The boarder found the dead men and called the police, who were surprised to find the dead men's large rolls of cash intact. The motive, then, was clearly slaughter. All but one of the men—Frank Gusenberg—died on the spot. Gusenberg was taken to a nearby hospital, where he obeyed the gangster's code of silence and refused to say who had shot him. Different reports indicate that his dying words were either "Nobody shot me" or "I'm not gonna talk."

It was assumed that Capone had ordered the hit in retaliation for Moran's strike against his gang. Moran, disobeying the same code of silence that Frank Gusenberg had upheld, openly pinned the massacre on Capone. Out-of-town gunman Fred "Killer" Burke and John Scalise, Albert Anselmi, and Jack "Machine Gun" McGurn, top Capone hit men, were popularly regarded as part of the extermination posse but were never convicted of the crime. Capone denied any involvement in the hit and played on Moran's comments, suggesting that only Moran himself would commit those types of murders.

Reports varied widely, but certain versions of the story recount that two of the killers were identified by a teenager walking past Moran's headquarters on the morning of the shooting. Supposedly, the teen identified

McGurn and Burke, but no one was convicted. In any case, after all the attention that the slaughter had drawn to Capone and his gang, McGurn faded from the public eye. Capone insisted that he stay out of sight, and McGurn was killed in 1936, on the eve of the anniversary of the Valentine's Day Massacre. He was shot to death with machine guns in a bowling alley by two men who, legend has it, were all that was left of Bugs Moran's gang.

Of course, much of the information surrounding the Valentine's Day Massacre was speculative, and conjecture about the issues often became legend. Later information, however, suggested that Capone's gang may not have committed the carnage. In their 2004 book titled *The St. Valentine's Day Massacre: The Untold Story of the Gangland Bloodbath That Brought Down Al Capone*, William J. Helmer and Arthur J. Bilek assert that much of the evidence points to a crew from St. Louis, known to Capone's Italian mob as the American Boys, as the perpetrators of the massacre.

SIGNIFICANCE

It is believed that Al Capone ordered the death of five hundred men in Chicago and that more than a thousand people died in his bootleg wars, but there was never enough evidence to convince authorities that he was behind the Valentine's Day Massacre. In 1934, Capone went to prison for tax evasion; the public, convinced that he had been responsible for the massacre, had long called for his imprisonment. Paroled in 1939, Capone lived out his final years at his Palm Island estate off the coast of Miami, although by this time he was a mental and physical wreck. His body was ravaged by syphilis, which he had contracted years before, and he died in 1947 at the age of forty-eight.

No matter who was behind it, the Valentine's Day Massacre certainly signaled the beginning of the end of Capone's reign as Chicago's crime czar. The event also

---

SCARFACE AND FREE ENTERPRISE

Al Capone once proudly said,

> I make my money by supplying a public demand. If I break the law, my customers, who number hundreds of the best people in Chicago, are as guilty as I am. The only difference is that I sell and they buy. Everybody calls me a racketeer. I call myself a businessman.

In 1930, British journalist Claud Cockburn interviewed Capone. Cockburn asked what Capone would have done if he had not become a gangster and related Capone's reply:

"[S]elling newspapers barefoot on the street in Brooklyn." He stood up as he spoke, cooling his finger-tips in the rose bowl in front of him. He sat down again, brooding and sighing. Despite the ham-and-corn, what he said was quite probably true and I said so, sympathetically. A little bit too sympathetically, as immediately emerged, for as I spoke I saw him looking at me suspiciously, not to say censoriously. My remarks about the harsh way the world treats barefoot boys in Brooklyn were interrupted by an urgent angry waggle of his podgy hand. "Listen," he said, "don't get the idea I'm one of these goddam radicals. Don't get the idea I'm knocking the American system. The American system. . . ." As though an invisible chairman had called upon him for a few words, he broke into an oration upon the theme. He praised freedom, enterprise, and the pioneers. He spoke of "our heritage." He referred with contemptuous disgust to Socialism and Anarchism. "My rackets," he repeated several times, "are run on strictly American lines and they're going to stay that way."

His vision of the American system began to excite him profoundly and now he was on his feet again, leaning across the desk like the chairman of a board meeting, his fingers plunged in the rose bowls.

"This American system of ours," he shouted, "call it Americanism, call it Capitalism, call it what you like, gives to each and every one of us a great opportunity if we only seize it with both hands and make the most of it." He held out his hand towards me, the fingers dripping a little, and stared at me sternly for a few seconds before reseating himself.

Source: Claud Cockburn, *In Time of Trouble: An Autobiography* (London: Rupert Hart-Davis, 1956).

---

ushered in a wave of violence in the Midwest that carried on well into the years of the Great Depression. Ultimately, the popular image of the public enemy was largely drawn from Capone, and the massacre at Moran's North Side headquarters clearly showed how gangsters dealt with one another. Like so many gangster stories, the tale of what happened at the garage on Clark Street continued to capture the public imagination.

—*William Boyle*

FURTHER READING

Helmer, William J., and Arthur J. Bilek. *The St. Valentine's Day Massacre: The Untold Story of the Gang-*

land *Bloodbath That Brought Down Al Capone*. Nashville: Cumberland House, 2004. Challenges the assumption that Al Capone ordered the annihilation of Moran's gang.

Keefe, Rose. *The Man Who Got Away: The Bugs Moran Story—A Biography*. Nashville: Cumberland House, 2005. In-depth look at the life of North Side gang leader Moran. Tells about the decline of Moran's gangland power after his top men were killed in the Valentine's Day Massacre.

Ruth, David E. *Inventing the Public Enemy: The Gangster in American Culture, 1918-1934*. Chicago: University of Chicago Press, 1996. Looks at Al Capone and other "invented" gangsters of the 1920's and

1930's and explores the role that they play in the American imagination.

Schoenberg, Robert J. *Mr. Capone*. New York: HarperCollins, 1992. Biography of Al Capone that traces his life from his boyhood in Brooklyn, New York, through his years as leader of the Chicago underworld, his imprisonment on charges of tax evasion, and his early death from syphilis.

SEE ALSO: Jan. 16, 1920-Dec. 5, 1933: Prohibition; Feb. 28, 1925: Corrupt Practices Act Limits Political Contributions; 1931-1932: Gangster Films Become Popular; May 23, 1934: Police Apprehend Bonnie and Clyde.

February 17, 1929
LEAGUE OF UNITED LATIN AMERICAN CITIZENS IS FOUNDED

One of the oldest Hispanic advocacy organizations joined different Latino groups in a cohesive front, creating the League of United Latin American Citizens. The group stressed acculturation and working to gain acceptance for Hispanics in the United States, and it worked especially hard to raise the level of education of the Hispanic community.

ALSO KNOWN AS: LULAC
LOCALE: Corpus Christi, Texas
CATEGORIES: Civil rights and liberties; education; organizations and institutions

KEY FIGURES
Ben Garza (1892-1937), leader of the Sons of America
Alonso S. Perales (1899-1960), leader of the League of Latin American Citizens
José de la Luz Sáenz (1888-1953), delegate to the first LULAC convention
Juan B. Lozano (fl. early twentieth century), delegate to the first LULAC convention
José Tomás Canales (1877-1976), member of the League of Latin American Citizens

SUMMARY OF EVENT
The League of United Latin American Citizens (LULAC) was formed in order to unite all Latin American organizations in the United States under one title. In 1927, the main Latin American groups were the Sons of America, the Knights of America, and the League of Latin American Citizens; other, less well known, groups existed as

well. The Sons of America had councils in Sommerset, Pearsall, Corpus Christi, and San Antonio, Texas; the Knights of America had a council in San Antonio; the League of Latin American Citizens had councils in Harlingen, Brownsville, Laredo, Peñitas, La Grulla, McAllen, and Gulf, Texas.

As more Anglo-Americans moved into Texas, persons of Spanish or Mexican descent experienced open discrimination and segregation that placed them in the position of second-class citizens. They had been under the rule of six different countries before Texas entered the Union. Most had continued to live and work as they always had, without being assertive about their rights. As time progressed, however, many Hispanics found that prejudice and discrimination were becoming less tolerable. Groups began to form to give more weight to requests that these practices cease. The Sons of America Council No. 4 in Corpus Christi, led by Ben Garza, originated a unification plan, believing that if all Hispanic organizations would regroup into one strong, unified, and vocal organization, more attention would be brought to the plight of those who were being discriminated against.

On August 14, 1927, delegates from the Sons of America, the Knights of America, and smaller groups met in Harlingen, Texas, to form LULAC. The resolution that was presented was adopted by those in the meeting. It was expected that the leaders of the major groups—Alonso S. Perales, José de la Luz Sáenz, José Tomás Canales, and Juan B. Lozano of the Rio Grande Valley of south Texas—would be invited by the president general of the Sons of America to begin the unification process. In response to concerns about the merger expressed by some members, Council No. 4 of the Sons of America drafted an agreement between itself and the Knights of America to unite. These two groups waited a year for the merger to be completed. Perales, president general of the Latin American League, stayed in close contact with Garza to maintain interest in the merger among the three main groups. However, the president general of the Sons of America never called the convention. After a long wait, Council No. 4 withdrew from the Sons of America on February 7, 1929. Participants at this meeting again voted to have a general convention for the purpose of unification. Invitations were sent to all the groups to meet in Corpus Christi, Texas, to vote on the merger on February 17, 1929.

Along with interested members of the Hispanic groups, Douglas Weeks, a professor at the University of Texas, attended not only to study the merger but also to open the convention as a nonaligned attendee. Ben Garza was elected chairman pro tem. His popularity as an energetic and fair civic leader made him a good spokesperson for the new group. The assembly had to choose a chairman, plan a single constitution, and select a name that would encompass the goals of the previously separate groups. The committee chosen to select a name included Juan Solis and Mauro Machado of the Knights of America, Perales and Canales of the Latin American League, E. N. Marin and A. de Luna of Corpus Christi, and Fortunio Treviño of Alice, Texas. Machado, of the Knights of America, proposed "United Latin American Citizens." This was amended to read "League of United Latin American Citizens," which was seconded by Canales. On February 17, 1929, LULAC formally came into being at Corpus Christi, Texas.

The naming committee undertook other proposals before coming back to the general convention. Canales proposed the motto "All for one and one for all" as a reminder of the purpose of the groups in uniting and as a basis for their future activities. The committee also set some basic rules to guide the league until a constitutional convention could be held. This convention was called for May 18 and 19, 1929, with an executive committee made up of Garza, M. C. Gonzales as secretary, and Canales and Sáenz as members at large. On May 18, the first meeting under the new title was called. The constitution proposed by Canales was adopted, and new officers were elected. The officers were Garza, president general; Gonzales, vice president general; de Luna, secretary-general; and Louis C. Wilmot of Corpus Christi, trea-

surer general. George Washington's prayer was adopted from the ritual of the Sons of America, and the U.S. flag was adopted as the group's official flag.

SIGNIFICANCE

The new group set about working to remove injustices that had been building for many years. LULAC was chartered in 1931 under the laws of the state of Texas and later in New Mexico, Arizona, California, and Colorado, as other councils were formed. LULAC began issuing *LULAC Notes*, but in August, 1931, the first issue of *LULAC News* was published.

In the formative years, auxiliaries were started by women whose husbands were active LULAC members. Between 1937 and 1938, junior LULAC councils were formed under the sponsorship of adult councils. In 1940, LULAC councils peaked, but with the beginning of World War II, the councils weakened with the departure of the men to military service. In 1945 and 1946, LULAC began to make great strides, as educated, trained men returned from service. Prestigious positions were filled by Hispanics, and discrimination lessened. Non-Hispanics joined as well, and LULAC moved toward achieving its objectives.

When the Civil Rights movement of the 1960's began, other Hispanic groups with a more militant response to discrimination began to form. Leaders such as the charismatic preacher Reies López Tijerina in New Mexico and Rodolfo Gonzalez in Denver marched in protest of the treatment Hispanics were receiving. César Chávez led farmworker groups in California on peaceful marches that frequently erupted into violent confrontations as the numbers of militant members rose. LULAC did not totally support all these movements. Its members preferred mediation to resolve serious disagreements and education for all Hispanics as better ways of blending peacefully into the U.S. mainstream.

LULAC evolved to stress education especially. Parents were encouraged to prepare their children well to enter school. English was encouraged as the primary language, Spanish as the second language. As students matured, they were encouraged to finish high school and enter college. For those who aspired to higher learning, LULAC sponsored many scholarships; it also offered other forms of financial aid and counseling. LULAC Education Centers, located in urban centers, provided this help. With corporate and federal aid, these centers made it possible for disadvantaged Hispanic American youth to become productive members of their American communities.

—Norma Crews

1929

FURTHER READING

De la Garza, Rodolfo O., ed. *Ignored Voices: Public Opinion Polls and the Latino Community*. Austin: Center for Mexican American Studies, University of Texas at Austin Press, 1987. Argues that the opinions of Hispanic people were virtually ignored, politically and otherwise, except in heavily Hispanic communities.

Garcia, F. Chris, ed. *Latinos and the Political System*. Notre Dame, Ind.: University of Notre Dame Press, 1988. Discusses some of the political problems that prompted the formation of organizations such as LULAC.

Garcia, Mario T. *Mexican-Americans: Leadership, Ideology, and Identity, 1930-1960*. New Haven, Conn.: Yale University Press, 1989. A thorough treatise on Hispanic assimilation into the mainstream of U.S. business and community.

Kaplowitz, Craig A. *LULAC, Mexican Americans, and National Policy*. College Station: Texas A&M University Press, 2005. A study of the history of LULAC in relation to the larger history of Mexian American advocacy and activism in the twentieth century. Bibliographic references and index.

Mirande, Alfredo. *The Chicano Experience: An Alternative Perspective*. Notre Dame, Ind.: University of Notre Dame Press, 1985. A view into the life of the less accepted Hispanic, the Chicano. Gives information on La Raza, a more militant group representing Hispanics of the 1960's and 1970's.

Shorris, Earl. *Latinos: A Biography of the People*. New York: W. W. Norton, 1992. A collection of information on Hispanics in the United States, and a general overview of those Hispanics who immigrated and settled during the 1900's.

SEE ALSO: May 19, 1921: Emergency Quota Act; May 28, 1924: U.S. Congress Establishes the Border Patrol; Early 1930's: Mass Deportations of Mexicans; Mar. 4, 1933-1945: Good Neighbor Policy.

May 16, 1929
FIRST ACADEMY AWARDS HONOR FILM ACHIEVEMENT

The first Academy Awards celebration was an anticlimactic if gala affair, as the winners in the twelve categories had been announced three months earlier. Over time, however, the event expanded, the winners were kept secret in advance, and the awards themselves became the most prestigious honors in Hollywood.

ALSO KNOWN AS: Oscars
LOCALE: Hollywood, California
CATEGORIES: Motion pictures; organizations and institutions

KEY FIGURES
Douglas Fairbanks, Sr. (1883-1939), American actor and founding president of the Academy of Motion Picture Arts and Sciences, 1927-1929
Louis B. Mayer (1885-1957), American studio owner
Conrad Nagel (1897-1970), American actor and Academy president, 1932-1933
Fred Niblo (1874-1948), American director and Academy founding vice president
Fred Beetson (1879-1953), American film producer
William C. deMille (1878-1955), American writer, producer, director, and Academy president, 1929-1931

M. C. Levee (1891-1972), American film producer, Academy founding treasurer, and later Academy president, 1931-1932
Frank Woods (c. 1860-1939), American screenwriter and Academy founding secretary

SUMMARY OF EVENT
On May 16, 1929, the first Academy Awards presentation was held in the Blossom Room of the Roosevelt Hollywood Hotel in Hollywood, California. From a simple banquet affair, the tribute would grow to gigantic proportions. The annual Academy Awards ceremony, sponsored by the Academy of Motion Picture Arts and Sciences, has become an important international event. Millions of people worldwide watch the televised event each spring. To many, the Academy Award, or Oscar, symbolizes the highest achievement in film and is seen as the film industry's most important honor.

The presentation of awards for artistic merit was largely an afterthought by the founding members of the Academy. The originally stated goals of the Academy, published in 1927, were mostly idealistic and self-serving. The Academy planned to take aggressive action in meeting outside attacks that were unjust and to promote harmony and solidarity among its membership and among the different branches, reconciling internal differences that might exist or arise. It intended to further the welfare and protect the honor and good repute of the profession of filmmaking and to encourage the improvement and advancement of the arts and sciences of professional filmmakers, through exchange of constructive ideas and by awards of merit for distinctive achievements. The Academy thus intended to do for the motion-picture professions what other national and international bodies had done for other arts, sciences, and industries.

In order better to understand the background and beginnings of the first Academy Awards ceremony, it is necessary to examine the formation of the Academy itself. Its genesis occurred in early January, 1927. Louis B. Mayer, powerful studio boss of Metro-Goldwyn-Mayer (MGM), invited four of his studio personnel to a Sunday dinner. They were Conrad Nagel, Fred Niblo, Fred Beetson, and William C. deMille. Mayer wanted to form an organization that could speak for the film industry, arbitrate labor disputes, help solve technological problems, and police screen content. The five men planned a dinner to be attended by representatives of the various creative professions involved in film production to discuss membership in the proposed organization. On January 11, at the Ambassador Hotel in Los Angeles, thirty-six people heard the proposals and enthusiastically supported the idea. The International (this word was later dropped) Academy of Motion Picture Arts and Sciences was formed. Douglas Fairbanks, Sr., was named as president, Fred Niblo as vice president, M. C. Levee as treasurer, and Frank Woods as secretary.

On May 4, 1927, the Academy was granted a charter by the state of California as a nonprofit corporation. One week later, an organizational banquet took place at the Biltmore Hotel in Los Angeles, with more than 300 guests in attendance. Speaking to the gathered assembly, Fairbanks convinced 231 of them to join and pay $100 each for membership. In his comments, Fairbanks mentioned that the new organization would bestow certain awards of merit for distinctive achievement. Days later, the Committee for the Awards of Merit was formed.

The following year, in July, 1928, the awards committee developed a voting system. Each member of the Academy would cast one vote in his or her branch. Nominees for awards would be selected from films released in the Los Angeles area between April 1, 1927, and July 31, 1928. The deadline for selection was set as August 15, 1928. A board of judges would tabulate the results, determine the top ten nominees, and narrow the field to three

contestants. Lastly, the Central Board of Judges, comprising five individuals representing each of the five divisions of the Academy—producers, actors, directors, writers, and technicians—would select the winners in twelve achievement categories.

The winners of the first awards were selected at an Academy gathering on Friday, February 15, 1929, six months after the submission deadline. The press and the winners quickly were notified. Three months later, the awards were officially presented at a glittering black-tie dinner dance. Chairman of the evening William C. deMille welcomed the assembled guests and introduced Fairbanks, who then explained the voting rules, suggested that acceptance speeches be kept short, and called up the winners to receive their trophies.

The first Academy Awards could be given for a single achievement, multiple achievements, or a body of work. Twenty additional certificates of honorable mention were given to runners-up. The winners that first evening were as follows: most outstanding production, *Wings* (1927); most unique or artistic production, *Sunrise* (1927); achievement by an actor, Emil Jannings; achievement by an actress, Janet Gaynor; achievement in dramatic directing, Frank Borzage; achievement in comedy directing, Lewis Milestone; achievement in cinematography, Charles Rosher and Karl Struss; achievement in art directing, William Cameron Menzies; achievement in engineering effects, Roy Pomeroy; achievement in original story writing, Ben Hecht; achievement in writing adaptation, Benjamin Glazer; and achievement in title writing, Joseph Farnham. The categories were revised the following year: Awards for most artistic or unique production and achievement in engineering effects were dropped, and the dramatic and comedy directing awards were combined, as were those for achievement in original story writing, writing adaptation, and title writing.

Each winner at the first Academy Awards ceremony received a solid bronze statuette slightly more than a foot high. It had been designed by Cedric Gibbons, art director at MGM, and sculpted by George Stanley. The same model of statuette was given in subsequent years, but its composition was changed from bronze to plaster and later from plaster to gold-plated britannium. The figure is of a knight holding a crusader's sword, standing on a reel of film. The statuette got its nickname of Oscar in the 1930's, possibly following a comment by Academy librarian Margaret Herrick that the figure reminded her of her uncle Oscar.

Special Academy Awards were also presented to Charles Chaplin for his work acting in, writing, produc-

1929

BEST PICTURE AWARDS, 1928-1940

The early winners of the most coveted of the Academy's awards, "Best Picture" (known as "Best Production" until 1931) are listed below.

Year	Film	Production Company (Producer)
1928	*Wings*	Paramount Famous Lasky (Lucien Hubbard)
1929	*The Broadway Melody*	Metro-Goldwyn-Mayer (Harry Rapt)
1930	*All Quiet on the Western Front*	Universal (Carl Laemmle, Jr.)
1931	*Cimarron*	RKO Radio (William LeBaron)
1932	*Grand Hotel*	Metro-Goldwyn-Mayer (Irving Thalberg)
1933	*Cavalcade*	Fox (Winfield Sheehan)
1934	*It Happened One Night*	Columbia (Harry Cohn)
1935	*Mutiny on the Bounty*	Metro-Goldwyn-Mayer (Irving Thalberg with Albert Lewin)
1936	*The Great Ziegfeld*	Metro-Goldwyn-Mayer (Hunt Stromberg)
1937	*The Life of Emile Zola*	Warner Bros. (Henry Blanke)
1938	*You Can't Take It with You*	Columbia (Frank Capra)
1939	*Gone with the Wind*	Selznick, Metro-Goldwyn-Mayer (David O. Selznick)
1940	*Rebecca*	Selznick, United Artists (David O. Selznick)

ing, and directing *The Circus* (1928) and to Warner Bros. for producing *The Jazz Singer* (1927). Only Jannings and Chaplin were not present to accept their statuettes. Speeches by Hollywood celebrities—including Mary Pickford, Louis B. Mayer, and Cecil B. DeMille—followed the awards. Entertainer Al Jolson, star of the just-honored *The Jazz Singer*, brought the festivities to a close. The first Academy Awards presentation was a quiet success.

SIGNIFICANCE

None of the founding members of the Academy could have foreseen the impact the first Academy Awards would have not only on the Hollywood community but also on the world. The awards, at the beginning, were a secondary consideration. Concern about the myriad changes taking place within the motion picture industry was the main reason for formation of the Academy. Hollywood's financial success had led to calls by spiritual leaders and government figures to control the film industry unless it could police itself. The founding of the Academy was meant to do that, and the Academy Awards were to be used to promote the organization and deflect public criticism by focusing on and showcasing Hollywood's past achievements.

Without realizing it, the first Academy members established one of the earliest, and certainly the most coveted, prizes in cinema. The tradition begun in 1929 continued uninterrupted.

During the 1920's, a series of technological and cultural breakthroughs occurred, particularly in the area of mass communication. The second Academy Awards ceremony thus took on greater importance to the media. There was full newspaper coverage, and Los Angeles radio station KNX broadcast the entire event. The Academy Awards had arrived as a media event and would never again have the intimacy of the first presentation. Over the years, especially after the awards ceremony began to be televised in 1953, the audience grew to more than one billion viewers worldwide.

Over time, the award ceremony and its importance changed. The number of nominees for each regular merit award became standardized to five, and nominations were for single achievements. From its humble origins in 1929, the reputation of the Academy Award rivaled that of awards given in other fields, such as the Emmy, the Tony, and the Grammy. An Oscar is considered to represent a higher level of recognition than are awards bestowed by critics and trade associations. Internationally, the Oscar is considered to be one of the most important film prizes, surpassing prizes offered by other countries. It is accepted as cinema's most prestigious award.

—*Terry Theodore*

FURTHER READING

Levy, Emmanuel. *All About Oscar: The History and Politics of the Academy Awards.* New York: Continuum, 2003. Excellent study dealing less with winners and losers than with the preeminence of the Academy Award, its meaning, the nomination system, the voting process, and the place occupied by the Oscar in American culture.

Likeness, George C. *The Oscar People: From "Wings" to "My Fair Lady."* Mendota, Ill.: Wayside Press, 1965. Good introductory work. Detailed biographies of performers as well as film summaries give an in-depth look at Oscar winners. Includes chapters on the supporting players and craftsmen.

Osborne, Robert. *Seventy-five Years of the Oscar: The Official History of the Academy Awards.* New York: Abbeville Press, 2003. An official history of the Oscars, licensed by the Academy to commemorate the seventy-fifth anniversary of the awards. Index.

Pond, Steve. *The Big Show: High Times and Dirty Dealings Backstage at the Academy Awards.* New York: Faber & Faber, 2005. Behind-the-scenes look at fifteen years of Oscar history, encompassing the 1990's and the early twenty-first century, including analysis of the function of the Oscars in American culture and of what they can tell us about American culture as a whole. Index.

Shale, Richard. *Academy Awards: An Ungar Reference Index.* New York: Frederick Ungar, 1978. An excellent fact book about the Academy and its origins, purpose, and activities. Details the first fifty years of films by various categories and features a short introduction, useful appendixes, select bibliography, and index. The study is well organized.

SEE ALSO: June 26, 1925: Chaplin Produces His Masterpiece *The Gold Rush*; 1929: *Hallelujah* Is the First Important Black Musical Film; 1930-1935: Von Sternberg Makes Dietrich a Superstar; 1934-1938: Production Code Gives Birth to Screwball Comedy; Feb. 27, 1935: Temple Receives a Special Academy Award; Sept. 6, 1935: *Top Hat* Establishes the Astaire-Rogers Dance Team; Dec. 21, 1937: Disney Releases *Snow White and the Seven Dwarfs*; 1939: Ford Defines the Western in *Stagecoach*; Aug. 17, 1939: *The Wizard of Oz* Premieres; Dec. 15, 1939: *Gone with the Wind* Premieres.

June 3-August 28, 1929
TACNA-ARICA COMPROMISE

The end of the War of the Pacific, involving Chile, Bolivia, and Peru, left unsettled the final disposition of the provinces of Tacna and Arica. Dispute over these regions led to ongoing feuding that was ultimately resolved after mediation by the United States.

ALSO KNOWN AS: Treaty of Santiago; Treaty of 1929
LOCALE: United States; Chile; Peru; Bolivia
CATEGORY: Diplomacy and international relations

KEY FIGURES

Frank B. Kellogg (1856-1937), U.S. secretary of state, 1925-1929, and winner of the Nobel Peace Prize
Carlos Ibáñez del Campo (1877-1960), president of Chile, 1927-1931 and 1952-1958
Augusto Bernardino Leguía y Salcedo (1863-1932), president of Peru, 1908-1912 and 1919-1930
Herbert Hoover (1874-1964), president of the United States, 1929-1933

SUMMARY OF EVENT

As the result of a long-lasting border dispute with Peru and Bolivia and competition over nitrate and other natural resources, port access, and tax issues, Chile declared war on the two countries in April, 1879. The War of the Pacific featured many bloody battles, including one in Tacna in 1880 that left five thousand casualties. The Treaty of Ancón ended the war on October 23, 1883, and resulted in temporary Chilean control over the regions of Tacna and Arica. The treaty gave Chile ownership over the region of Tarapacá, which included sections of the Pacific coastline known as Tacna and Arica. The treaty held that the ownership was to last ten years, after which a plebiscite would be held to decide which nation would permanently retain the territories. The plebiscite was not held, however. Meanwhile, the territories provided the stimulus for much of Chile's economic growth: The annexation increased Chilean land by more than a third and significantly benefited the country's economic status by providing increased port space on the Pacific. More important, however, the territories held significant amounts of sodium nitrate, a resource used to make ammunition and building materials, which were especially valuable commodities during World War I.

The United States made many concerted but unsuccessful efforts to assist in arbitration over the territory's final ownership. Finally, in 1928, with help from the ad-

1929

ministration of President Calvin Coolidge, diplomatic relations between Chile and Peru resumed, and in 1929, President Herbert Hoover was able to help broker a compromise. Chile grew substantially during the time in which the Tacna-Arica region was in dispute. More factories were founded in the decade of the 1880's than had existed in the entire country before the War of the Pacific. Tax revenues from nitrate companies, which ballooned after the beginning of World War I, helped bring industrialization, built the Chilean military, and allowed Chile to take a larger role in global politics and trade. As a result, Chile was reluctant to hold the planned plebiscite, in which residents of the regions would decide whether to remain Chilean or return to Peruvian control. Despite repeated attempts by the United States, especially under the administrations of presidents Coolidge and Hoover (whose efforts were led by Secretary of State Frank B. Kellogg), Peru, Bolivia, and Chile remained at odds for more than forty years. Peru and Bolivia faced civil war and unrest during this time, and their leaders and people remained bitter about the war, which had resulted in the annexation of the two regions and had deprived Bolivia of its access to the Pacific Ocean. Resolution was made even more difficult by the reluctance of the United States to become involved in the dispute until commercial relations among the three nations became so difficult that the countries themselves requested increased U.S. involvement.

In 1928, the Sixth Inter-American Conference was held in Havana, Cuba. During this conference, Chile proposed a settlement. Secretary of State Kellogg seized this opportunity to begin talks; he was eager to resolve the issue, which had been a source of great concern during his entire term in office. By early December of 1928, Chile had agreed to major concessions, including the surrender of Tacna and abandonment of its investments there. When Hoover took office as president of the United States in 1929, he asked Kellogg to stay on as secretary of state until the Tacna-Arica dispute was resolved. Kellogg worked even harder to help the countries find a solution. His efforts resulted in negotiations among the Chilean president, Carlos Ibáñez del Campo, the Peruvian president, Augusto Bernardino Leguía y Salcedo, and Kellogg, out of which came the text of the Treaty of Santiago (also known as the Treaty of 1929), which featured thirteen articles that delineated concessions. This agreement stipulated that Chile would retain Arica and that the region of Tacna, north of the Arica-La Paz railroad, and all its Chilean-owned real estate would return to Peruvian control, a division that remained into the twenty-first century. The treaty also established that Chile would pay six million dollars to Peru and that Chile would construct a landing pier in Arica (including a customs agency and railway station) where Peru could maintain a free port.

In order to facilitate the acceptance of this agreement, the presidents of Peru and Chile presented the plan as the recommendation for settlement of President Hoover. On May 15 and 16, Peru and Chile accepted the proposals made by Hoover, and the solution was announced. The treaty was signed in Lima on June 3, 1929, by Chilean ambassador Emiliano Figueroa Larraín and Peruvian chancellor Pedro José Rada y Gamio. Final ratifications to the agreement were made in Santiago, Chile, on July 28, and the resolution of the controversy culminated on August 28, 1929, when Peruvian civil administrators assumed the business of the town and province of Tacna.

SIGNIFICANCE

While the Tacna-Arica region remained in dispute, Chile's wealth and influence skyrocketed. The area's nitrate-rich soil largely sustained the Chilean economy and propelled the nation into the age of industrialization. Although the Great Depression and the discovery of synthetic substitutes that could replace nitrate in ammunition brought a downturn to Chile's economy, nitrate mining remained an important element in Chile's economy. (Later, copper mining and the export of wine and fruit became major industries.) The dispute's settlement presented the greatest challenge to Bolivia, whose status as a landlocked country became permanent. For the United States, mediation in the dispute stood out in an era of isolationist policies and foreshadowed the nation's increasing involvement in Latin American politics and economic affairs.

—Georgie Donovan

FURTHER READING

Coller, Simon, and William F. Sater. *A History of Chile, 1808-1994.* New York: Cambridge University Press, 1996. Traces politics, economics, social development, and culture, with special attention to its growth into an industrialized nation.

Dennis, William Jefferson. *Documentary History of the Tacna-Arica Dispute.* Port Washington, N.Y.: Kennikat Press, 1971. A series of documents related to the causes of the War of the Pacific, postwar proposals for peace, and the consequences of the Treaty of Ancón. Includes maps, memoranda, newspaper editorials, reports, and letters.

_____. *Tacna and Arica: An Account of the Chile-*

Peru Boundary Dispute and of the Arbitrations by the United States. New Haven, Conn.: Yale University Press, 1931. Written directly after the settlement of the boundary dispute. Tells the story of the settlement attempts with special attention to the efforts of the United States.

Granier, Jorge Gumicio. *United States and the Bolivian Seacoast*. La Paz, Bolivia: Ministerio de Relaciones Exteriores y Culto, 1988. Excellent overview of the settlement attempts and final treaty to resolve the Tacna-Arica dispute. Written from a Bolivian perspective; considers Bolivia's attempts to secure a seacoast.

Loveman, Brian. *Chile: The Legacy of Hispanic Capital-*

ism. New York: Oxford University Press, 2001. Noted as an excellent primer to Chilean history, the book covers the development of Chile's economy and of Hispanic capitalism and then focuses on unique aspects of politics and democracy in the country.

Wilson, Joe F. *The United States, Chile, and Peru in the Tacna and Arica Plebiscite*. Washington, D.C.: University Press of America, 1979. Chronological development and settlement of the Tacna-Arica question.

SEE ALSO: Aug. 27, 1928: Kellogg-Briand Pact; Mar. 4, 1933-1945: Good Neighbor Policy; Feb. 17, 1936: Corporatism Comes to Paraguay; Dec., 1936: Inter-American Conference for the Maintenance of Peace.

June 15, 1929
AGRICULTURAL MARKETING ACT

The Agricultural Marketing Act of 1929 established the Federal Farm Board to make loans to farm cooperatives and to control surpluses of farm commodities.

LOCALE: Washington, D.C.
CATEGORIES: Laws, acts, and legal history; agriculture; trade and commerce

KEY FIGURES
Herbert Hoover (1874-1964), president of the United States, 1929-1933
Alexander Legge (1866-1933), American businessman and first chairman of the Federal Farm Board
Arthur M. Hyde (1877-1947), U.S. secretary of agriculture
Charles L. McNary (1874-1944), U.S. senator from Oregon
Gilbert N. Haugen (1859-1933), U.S. congressman from Iowa

SUMMARY OF EVENT
In order to understand the impact of the Agricultural Marketing Act of 1929, it is necessary to understand what happened to the American farm sector early in the twentieth century. The second decade of the twentieth century was a good one for farmers. The world had experienced rapid industrial expansion, causing incomes and spending to rise. Demand for agricultural commodities had expanded, giving farmers high prices for their crops. Farmers in the United States were producing large crops

and exporting large parts of them to foreign markets. A fixed quantity of good agricultural land caused land prices to go up, making farmers feel wealthier. It appeared that this prosperity would continue indefinitely.

Things began to change in 1919, however. European farmers were producing more as they recovered from World War I, and prices started to fall. In 1921, wheat and cotton were selling for half their 1920 prices, and American farmers realized that hard times had returned. By 1923, agricultural commodity prices had started to rise slowly, and farm conditions began to improve. Things were getting better, but conditions for farmers still were unfavorable. Mechanization of farm work promised to help farmers by cutting production costs but was soon to contribute to problems of overproduction.

Agriculture was an important sector in the U.S. economy in the early 1920's, and Congress believed that help was needed for farmers, even though farm prices were edging up after the drastic drop in the early 1920's. A major attempt to help was embodied in the five bills introduced in Congress from 1924 to 1928 by Senator Charles L. McNary of Oregon and Congressman Gilbert N. Haugen of Iowa. The McNary-Haugen bills called for an export corporation that would purchase agricultural crops in amounts large enough to keep their prices at acceptably high levels. These purchases were not to be sold domestically but were to be sold in foreign markets. The bills also called for an import tariff to discourage foreign farmers from sending agricultural goods to the United States to compete with domestic products. The first three

McNary-Haugen bills did not pass Congress. The last two bills passed Congress but were vetoed by President Calvin Coolidge. Herbert Hoover, Coolidge's secretary of commerce, was influential in advising Coolidge to veto the bills.

The Agricultural Marketing Act of 1929 differed from these bills in that it focused on improved marketing as a means of aiding farmers. The government, under this act, would encourage formation of national cooperative marketing organizations but would not run them.

As director of the Food Administration and as secretary of commerce, Hoover had participated in the many agricultural policy debates of the late 1910's and the 1920's. In 1928, he campaigned for president, promising to call a special session of Congress to deal with farm problems. Hoover had grown up on an Iowa farm and believed that an improved marketing process was the solution to the farm problem. Despite his strong feelings about the issue, once in the office of president he sent no specific legislation of his own to Congress, not wanting to interfere with Congress's legislative prerogative. Even so, Congress had a good idea what Hoover wanted. It passed the Agricultural Marketing Act, which became law on June 15, 1929.

The overall goal of the act was to put agriculture on an equal footing with other business sectors in the country. The objectives specified to carry this out were to decrease agricultural surpluses, stabilize prices for agricultural commodities and thereby cut down on speculation, and provide help in marketing of agricultural commodities. The act called for the establishment of the Federal Farm Board, which was to have a budget of $500 million.

The Federal Farm Board was directed to set up national farmer cooperatives as a means of achieving its goals. These cooperatives were to be controlled by farmers and were to be used primarily to improve the marketing of crops. It was believed that the coming together of farmers into a comprehensive organization that could bargain on behalf of farmers would give farmers the power to prevent drastic price declines. The Federal Farm Board was authorized to make loans to the cooperatives to increase their size and efficiency. These loans could be used to build new facilities or for expenses of marketing agricultural crops. Farmers could obtain loans at low rates of interest.

President Hoover persuaded Alexander Legge to leave his $100,000-per-year job as chairman of International Harvester to become the first chairman of the Federal Farm Board. Seven other board members were appointed, representing the major farm commodities.

Arthur M. Hyde, as Hoover's secretary of agriculture, was an ex officio member.

By October of 1929, the Federal Farm Board had succeeded in setting up the Farmers National Grain Associations, which were stock companies in each of the major commodities. Stock in the associations was owned by the larger local grain cooperatives. The goal of each of these corporations was to become a large, centralized organization to facilitate marketing for the particular commodity it represented. It was hoped that their sheer size and the coordination of the marketing process they offered would increase the efficiency of marketing agricultural crops, thus stabilizing prices at the desired high levels. The National Grain Associations were also supposed to control agricultural surpluses. Unfortunately, the government also had in place county extension agents, whose job was to help increase production. Getting farmers to control production was difficult, and the Federal Farm Board never succeeded in this task. The government thus, to some extent, operated at cross-purposes, trying to keep prices high while also encouraging production.

SIGNIFICANCE

In 1930, the Federal Farm Board decided that its efforts were not succeeding. A surplus of major commodities kept agricultural prices low. Several factors contributed to the surpluses. The United States and Europe had had a few years of abundant harvests, and other countries were restricting imports from the United States and imposing tariffs in retaliation for the Hawley-Smoot Tariff of 1930. Farmers were particularly hurt by these retaliatory tariffs because they had long used exports as a means for eliminating agricultural surpluses. Finally, the Great Depression caused everyone to suffer. Low incomes meant that people were buying less of everything, including farm products.

The surplus in wheat was particularly troubling. Wheat prices fell dramatically, and in response the Federal Farm Board set up Grain Stabilization Boards in February of 1930. These boards hoped to control grain prices by encouraging farmers to reduce their output. Chairman Legge of the Federal Farm Board and Secretary of Agriculture Hyde toured the country trying to get farmers to participate in the production control process. They were unsuccessful in getting farmers to cooperate with these programs, so the Grain Stabilization Boards started buying surplus wheat. The purchase program was intended to be temporary, as no one recognized that the Great Depression was going to last for many years. Grain prices continued to fall, and by 1931 farm incomes were at the lowest levels of the century. The Federal Farm Board decided that it could no longer afford to buy grain or to store the grain it had already purchased. Fearing that the grain already purchased would rot in storage, the Federal Farm Board began to sell the grain it owned. This had a further dampening effect on prices and enraged farmers. The public outcry against the sale was so large that Legge resigned as chair of the Federal Farm Board.

The national cooperatives never emerged as the force that Hoover had hoped they would be. They were poorly managed and suffered from the same inefficiencies as the rest of the agricultural sector. They had little lasting effect on American agriculture, and most of them did not survive to the end of the 1930's.

The price stabilization portion of the Federal Farm Board's efforts fared no better than did the national cooperatives. The Federal Farm Board found that it could not stop the slide in agricultural prices by buying surplus grains, as illustrated by the case of wheat. Not only did it fail to keep prices from going down, it spent $400 million in taxpayers' money and disrupted commodity markets. Stabilization was a relatively new idea that was to be used in later legislation; some credit needs to be given to the Federal Farm Board for innovative thinking.

Production controls similarly failed. Hoover thought that if farmers voluntarily cut back on production, surpluses could be eliminated. Legge and Hyde toured the country to try to get farmers to cooperate with this plan. Primarily because the plan was voluntary, farmers did not participate in it. The Federal Farm Board made a special report to Congress in late 1932 in which it stressed that farm policy should include a system that would control the acreage planted. Future farm legislation made this recommendation part of production control programs.

Hoover did not recognize immediately that his farm plans were not working, so no adjustments to the plans were made during his presidential administration. His top farm advisers, Legge and Hyde, shared Hoover's vision of how to help the farmers and so did not offer alternative plans. In Hoover's defense, it is likely that the McNary-Haugen plans introduced in the 1920's would not have fared much better. The onset of the Great Depression, coinciding with increased production made possible by the mechanization of farm production, made the Federal Farm Board's goals nearly impossible to achieve.

Hoover had high hopes for solving farm problems with voluntary participation by farmers. He had seen what had happened to farmers in the Soviet Union and did not want the government to intervene on such a large scale. Farmers did not choose to participate in Hoover's

plans, however, and even if they had, the low budgets available to the Federal Farm Board doomed the stabilization plans to failure.

Congress became disenchanted with the Federal Farm Board and cut its 1932-1933 budget by 60 percent. Hoover lost the 1932 presidential election to Franklin D. Roosevelt, who had his own ideas about what should happen in the farm sector. Roosevelt abolished the Federal Farm Board in 1933, effectively ending the influence of the Agricultural Marketing Act of 1929. In 1933, Congress passed the Agricultural Adjustment Act, which was the New Deal's attempt to help farmers.

By 1935, farm income was 50 percent higher than it had been in 1932. Key elements of the 1933 act were declared unconstitutional in January, 1936, and later that year, new farm legislation was passed. As was suggested by the Federal Farm Board, production controls were a key element in the new plans.

—Eric Elder

FURTHER READING

Benedict, Murray. *Farm Policies of the United States, 1790-1950.* New York: Twentieth Century Fund, 1953. Provides a detailed discussion of American farm policy, starting during the period when the United States was primarily an agricultural country.

Davis, Joseph S. *On Agricultural Policy, 1926-1938.* Stanford, Calif.: Food Research Institute, 1939. A collection of presentations and articles written during this time period. Not a systematic presentation, but interesting because of when it was written and because Davis was a Federal Farm Board economist.

Hamilton, David. *From New Day to New Deal.* Chapel Hill: University of North Carolina Press, 1991. Focuses on the farm policies of the Hoover and Roosevelt administrations. Attributes the failure of Hoover's policies to the Depression as well as to misconceptions about the nature of the farm problem.

Kirkendall, Richard. *Social Scientists and Farm Politics in the Age of Roosevelt.* Ames: Iowa State University Press, 1982. Shows how the events of the 1920's, including the Agricultural Marketing Act of 1929, led to the farm policies of the Roosevelt administration.

Nourse, Edwin G. *Marketing Agreements Under the AAA.* Washington, D.C.: Brookings Institution, 1935. Provides a short summary of the Agricultural Marketing Act of 1929 and goes on to show how the Agricultural Adjustment Act, the legislation that replaced the 1929 act, resembled legislation of the early 1920's.

Rasmussen, Wayne, and Gladys Baker. "A Short History

1929

of Price Support and Adjustment Legislation and Programs for Agriculture, 1933-65." *Agriculture Economics Research* 18 (1966): 68-79. Brief, insightful, nontechnical discussion of the Agricultural Marketing Act of 1929 and the agriculture programs that followed it.

Tweeten, Luther. *Foundations of Farm Policy.* 2d rev. ed. Lincoln: University of Nebraska Press, 1979. Ba-

sic introduction to farm policy includes only brief discussion of the Agricultural Marketing Act of 1929 but places the act in the context of agricultural policy in general.

SEE ALSO: Nov. 4, 1924: Coolidge Is Elected U.S. President; Oct. 29, 1929-1939: Great Depression; Oct. 18, 1933: Roosevelt Creates the Commodity Credit Corporation.

July, 1929
DRINKER AND SHAW DEVELOP A MECHANICAL RESPIRATOR

Philip Drinker and Louis Shaw developed the mechanical respirator known as the iron lung, a lifesaving device for victims of poliomyelitis that led to the development of other lifesaving respiratory care.

ALSO KNOWN AS: Iron lung
LOCALE: Harvard University, Massachusetts
CATEGORIES: Health and medicine; inventions

KEY FIGURES
Philip Drinker (1894-1972), American engineer
Louis Shaw (1886-1940), American respiratory physiologist

SUMMARY OF EVENT

Poliomyelitis (polio, or infantile paralysis) is an infectious viral disease that damages the central nervous system, causing paralysis in many serious cases. Its effects result from the destruction of neurons (nerve cells) in the spinal cord. In many cases, the disease produces crippled limbs and the wasting of muscles. In others, "anterior" polio results in the fatal paralysis of the respiratory muscles. Since the 1950's, use of the Salk and Sabin vaccines has virtually eradicated polio, but in the 1920's, it was a terrifying disease. Its most feared, untreatable outcome was the paralysis of the respiratory muscles, which caused rapid death by suffocation, often only a few hours after the first signs of respiratory distress appeared.

In 1929, Philip Drinker and Louis Shaw, both of Harvard University, published an article in the *Journal of Clinical Investigation* in which they reported on their development of a mechanical respirator that would keep those afflicted with the disease alive for indefinite periods of time. This device, soon nicknamed the "iron lung," provided essential life support for thousands of people who suffered from respiratory paralysis as a result of polio or other diseases. It was used for many years, but

as John A. Meyer, a thoracic surgeon, noted in a 1990 article, iron lungs are now primarily "fascinating relics, reminders of high tech medicine of an earlier day." This comment is corroborated by the fact that as of 1986, a survey found that only three hundred iron lungs remained in use in the United States.

Development of the iron lung arose after Drinker, then an assistant professor in Harvard's Department of Industrial Hygiene, was appointed to a Rockefeller Institute commission formed to develop improved methods for resuscitating victims of electric shock and illuminating gas poisoning. The best-known use of the iron lung—treatment of polio—was a result of numerous epidemics of the disease that occurred from 1898 until the 1920's, each leaving thousands of Americans paralyzed. The concept of the mechanical respirator reportedly arose from Drinker's observation of physiological experiments carried out by Shaw and Drinker's brother, Cecil. Those experiments were components of an effort to design artificial respiration methods that would enhance a patient's survival after surgery.

The experiments involved the placement of a cat inside an airtight box—a body plethysmograph—with the cat's head protruding from an airtight collar. Shaw and Cecil Drinker then measured the volume changes in the plethysmograph to identify normal breathing parameters. Philip Drinker placed cats paralyzed by curare inside plethysmographs and showed that they could be kept breathing artificially by use of air from a hypodermic syringe connected to the device. Next, they proceeded to build a human-sized plethysmograph-like machine, using a five-hundred-dollar grant from the New York Consolidated Gas Company. The device's construction was carried out by a tinsmith and the Harvard Medical School machine shop.

The prototype machine was tested on Drinker and

Shaw, and after they made several modifications, a workable iron lung was available for clinical use. It consisted of a metal cylinder large enough to accommodate a patient. One end of the cylinder, which contained a rubber collar, slid out on casters along with a stretcher on which the patient reclined. Once the patient was in position and the collar was fitted around the patient's neck, the stretcher was pushed back into the cylinder and louvers were secured to make the iron lung airtight. The iron lung then "breathed" for the patient by using an electric blower to remove and replace air alternately.

In the human chest, inhalation occurs when the diaphragm contracts and powerful muscles expand the rib cage. This lowers the air pressure in the lungs and allows inhalation to occur. In exhalation, the diaphragm and chest muscles relax, and air is expelled as the chest cavity reduces again in size. In a case of respiratory paralysis treated with an iron lung, intake of air into and expulsion of air from the iron lung alternately compress the patient's chest, producing artificial exhalation, and allow it to expand so that it can fill with air. In this way, the iron lung "breathes" for the patient.

Careful examination of each patient was required to allow optimum adjustment of the rate of operation of the machine. The device also included a cooling system and ports for drainage lines, intravenous lines, and other apparatus needed to maintain a wide variety of patients.

The first person treated in an iron lung was an eight-year-old girl afflicted with respiratory paralysis resulting from polio. The iron lung kept her alive for five days. Unfortunately, she died from cardiac failure as a result of pneumonia. The next iron lung patient, a Harvard University student, was confined to the machine for several weeks and later recovered enough to resume a normal life. Use of the iron lung thereafter rapidly entered hospital practice. As Meyer described in 1990, "Treatment facilities tended to concentrate at university and city-county hospitals, each with its Respirator Center, where long lines of Drinker tank respirators were lined up side by side."

As James H. Maxwell pointed out in a 1986 article, one problem that limited maximum use of the iron lung came from physicians' fears that their patients would be "forever tethered to the lung." Such fears often led to inappropriate delays before patients were placed in the respirators, although in fact only a small percentage of patients became chronically dependent on the machines.

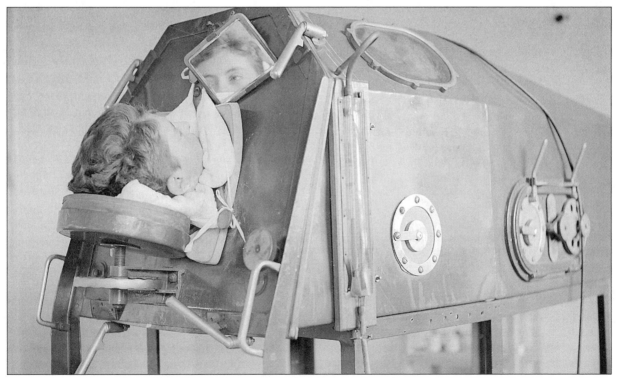

A patient lies in an iron lung in 1938. (Hulton Archive/Getty Images)

1929

SIGNIFICANCE

Soon after the iron lung, also known as the Drinker respirator, came into use in 1929, the device came to be considered indispensable. Until the Salk vaccine became available in the 1950's, iron lungs saved the lives of countless victims of polio as well as other diseases. As Meyer noted in 1990, "no satisfactory mechanical respirator existed before" the iron lung, and for a quarter of a century it was the sole reliable machine of its kind, "a lifeline for thousands of patients afflicted with respiratory failure caused by poliomyelitis."

Drinker received a number of honors for his development of the iron lung, including Philadelphia's John Scott Medal (shared with Louis Shaw, in 1931), the Charles Chapin Memorial Award (1948), and the Cummings Memorial Award of the American Industrial Hygiene Association in 1950. He was also made an honorary member of England's Royal Society of Health and the Finnish Industrial Medical Society. He was elected president of the American Industrial Hygiene Association in 1942, and he also became chairman of Harvard's Department of Industrial Hygiene.

It is generally acknowledged that the medical community's acceptance and use of the iron lung played a critical role in the development of modern respiratory care. For one thing, as Maxwell has noted, "use of the iron lung proved that large numbers of patients could actually be kept alive with mechanical support." Not all assessments are in agreement as to the device's importance, however. For example, H. H. Bendixen, an anesthesiologist, suggested in a 1982 article that the iron lung "must be called a technological detour, despite the fact that it has had life-saving clinical use." He also asserted that although the iron lung "became the mainstay of poliomyelitis treatment" until the 1950's, "the mortality rate remained high and was not significantly reduced" until combined intermittent positive pressure breathing was combined with the use of the iron lung.

—*Sanford S. Singer*

FURTHER READING

Bendixen, H. H. "Respirators and Respiratory Care." *Acta Anaesthesia Scandinavica* 102 (1982): 279-286. Review article by an anesthesiologist traces "intellectual and technical roots of respirators and respiratory care," identifies the role of polio in these developments, and addresses the roles of respirators and anesthesiology in modern respiratory care.

Black, Kathryn. *In the Shadow of Polio: A Personal and Social History*. New York: Perseus Books, 1996. Memoir relates the author's mother's two-year battle with polio, much of which she spent confined to an iron lung. Also provides information on efforts to combat the disease before a vaccine was available.

Drinker, Philip, and Charles F. McKhann, III. "The Iron Lung, First Practical Means of Respiratory Support." *Journal of the American Medical Association* 255 (1986): 1476-1480. Article written by the son of Philip Drinker and one of his major medical collaborators summarizes Drinker's development of the machine, comments on earlier respiratory devices, describes use of the iron lung in polio epidemics, and identifies later evolution of respiratory care. Provides useful insight into Drinker's life. Includes photographs of activated iron lungs.

Drinker, Philip, and Louis Shaw. "An Apparatus for the Prolonged Administration of Artificial Respiration." *Journal of Clinical Investigation* 7 (1929): 229-247. Describes in depth the development and first uses of the iron lung. Enumerates the theoretical and practical aspects of the respirator's design as well as the developers' hopes for its future use.

Maxwell, James H. "The Iron Lung: Halfway Technology or Necessary Step?" *Milbank Quarterly* 64 (1986): 3-28. Describes the history and development of the iron lung, examines its clinical utility and cost, the strengths and weaknesses of its use, and its role in the evolution of respirators and respiratory care. Includes references.

Meyer, John A. "A Practical Mechanical Respirator, 1929: The 'Iron Lung.'" *Annals of Thoracic Surgery* 50 (1990): 490-493. Describes the iron lung and discusses its development as a valuable therapeutic possibility and its use in polio epidemics. Concludes that, although the iron lung was cumbersome, "it supported patients over the long term with fewer complications than do the respirators of today."

"Philip Drinker." In *The National Cyclopedia of American Biography*. Vol. 57. Clifton, N.J.: James T. White, 1977. Brief biographical sketch is one of the only readily available sources of information on Drinker's life and work. Includes aspects of his early life as well as his education, career, and accomplishments.

SEE ALSO: 1912-1914: Abel Develops the First Artificial Kidney; Fall, 1934-May 6, 1953: Gibbon Develops the Heart-Lung Machine.

July, 1929-July, 1931
GÖDEL PROVES INCOMPLETENESS-INCONSISTENCY FOR FORMAL SYSTEMS

Kurt Gödel derived incompleteness-inconsistency theorems for any formal system strong enough to include the laws of arithmetic.

LOCALE: University of Vienna, Austria
CATEGORY: Mathematics

KEY FIGURE
Kurt Gödel (1906-1978), Austrian mathematician and logician

SUMMARY OF EVENT

Partly in response to the appearance of logical and set theoretic contradictions following David Hilbert's *Grundlagen der Geometrie* (1899; *The Foundations of Geometry*, 1902), a number of redoubled efforts focused on extending or reducing mathematics and logic to remove or resolve these difficulties. First published in 1899, Georg Cantor's paradox states that if S is the set of all sets and T is the set of all subsets of S, then because T corresponds one-by-one to itself as a subset of S, it cannot have a greater cardinal than S, yet, by Cantor's theorem, it must. In addition to Cantor's paradox, and Bertrand Russell's proof that Gottlob Frege's system was contradictory, several other paradoxes with impacts on both mathematics and logic arose during this period. These include Burali-Forti's paradox of the greatest ordinal number, Berry's paradox of the least integer not nameable in less than nineteen syllables, Richard's paradox of the class of all decimal numbers definable in a finite number of words, and symbolic forms of the Cretan-Liar conundrum.

The varying approaches of Russell and Hilbert called for the axiomatization, and then formalization, of a suitable portion of existing logic and/or mathematics, including "ideal" statements that did not have identifiable elementary intuitive meanings, to include the new system of (paradox-free) mathematics. In a formal system, all combinatory methods of constructing formulas to express mathematical propositions, and all mathematical assumptions and principles of logic used in proving theorems, are to be governed by a finite set of stated rules. An essential requirement of Hilbert's original (finitistic) program was that all demonstrations of the formal consistency of a mathematical system involve only procedures that make no reference to an infinite number of properties or operations with mathematical formulas.

Second, these proofs were to be undertaken only by "safe" methods such that the resulting formal system of axioms be entirely consistent, interpreted by Hilbert to mean that no two configurations should exist that constitute proofs in the system of a formula A and its negation $-A$.

In his 1904 lecture on the foundations of logic and arithmetic at the University of Heidelberg, Hilbert for the first time observed that, although it is possible to prove the consistency of geometry by an arithmetic interpretation, for the consistency of arithmetic itself, the appeal to some other more fundamental discipline seems illegitimate. Hilbert, for example, required use of the principle of mathematical induction to justify his definitions of whole numbers, yet had no proof of the consistency of this principle or its resulting definitions. Hilbert, nevertheless, initially suggested building up logic and arithmetic simultaneously, as well as translating these proofs completely into the language of symbolic logic to turn the proof of consistency into a problem of elementary manipulations in arithmetic. Hilbert did not return to foundational studies until his 1917 Zurich lecture on axiomatic thinking, in which he praised the axiomatization of logic by Russell and Alfred North Whitehead as the crowning of all work in efforts at completely translating all of mathematics into a self-contained symbolic language.

It was only after 1920 that Hilbert, in collaboration with Paul Bernays and in opposition to Hermann Weyl and L. E. J. Brouwer, began to focus explicitly on proof theory. In this approach, description of a formal axiomatic system must enable clear decision as to whether any given formula is an axiom and is a permissible inference from other axioms. This is considered a decision procedure for whether a given finite list of formulas constitutes a proof in any given system, yet a decision procedure is not provided as to whether a given formula is itself provable. The problem of finding a decision procedure has been called the decision problem for formal systems, first recognized as a problem for logic by Ernst Schröder in 1895, and in mathematics by Leopold Löwenheim in 1917 and Thoralf Albert Skolem in 1922. A decision procedure for a formal system embracing a segment of mathematics such as arithmetic would, in principle, make automatic the solution to any problem in that segment. Because of historically intractable problems such as whether Pierre de Fermat's last theorem is true, pointed out by Brouwer and others, a decision procedure in this case would mean that the infinitely many arithmetical problems require only a finite number of solutions.

By 1928, it was widely believed that the consistency of number theory and arithmetic had finally been nearly achieved by the finitist method of Hilbert and Bernays. As reported in Hilbert's September, 1928, lecture "On the Problems of the Foundations of Mathematics" in Bologna, Italy, Hilbert announced that his students Wilhelm Ackermann and John von Neumann had completed consistency proofs for almost the entire field of arithmetic. Hilbert then listed four of twenty-eight as-yet unresolved problems: a finite consistency proof of mathematical analysis, an extension of this proof to higher-order analysis and functional calculus, the completeness of the axiom systems for number theory and analysis, and the

completeness of the system of logical rules (first-order logic).

From the Austrian philosopher and logician Rudolf Carnap's diaries and letters to associates, it can be determined that Kurt Gödel was first stimulated to foundational problems by his reading of the text of Hilbert's lecture and by his attendance at Brouwer's Vienna lecture in March, 1928, on mathematics, science, and language. From Gödel's collected papers, it is clear that he was strongly impressed by the intuitionist claim that all of mathematics would never be completely formalizable or preplanned a priori. In 1928, Gödel read the first edition of Hilbert and Ackermann's *Grundzüge der theoretischen Logik* (foundations of theoretical logic), in which the completeness of the restricted form of Hilbert's operational first-level predicate calculus was formulated and posed as an open problem for further study.

Albert Einstein (left) presents the first Albert Einstein Award for achievement in the natural sciences to Kurt Gödel (second from right) and Julian Seymour Schwinger (right) in 1951. (AP/Wide World Photos)

A major obstacle to the general solution of Hilbert's formal decision problem was the lack of a clear and accepted concept of decidability and computability. By decision procedure or decidability for a given formalized theory is meant a method permitting one to decide in any given case whether a specific proposition formulated in the theory's symbolism can be proven exclusively by means of the axioms and techniques available to the theory itself. Gödel decided to focus explicitly on this problem and wrote the results as his doctoral dissertation in September, 1929, proving the completeness of first-order logic. In the summer of 1930, however, Gödel began to study the problem of proving the consistency of formal analysis itself (including higher arithmetic, logical analysis, and set theory), doubting the feasibility of Hilbert's wish to prove consistency directly by finitist methods Gödel instead believed that the difficulties encountered by Ackermann and von Neumann could be lessened by dividing the total problem into different stages or levels. In this case, he sought to prove the consistency of number theory by finitist number theory and then to prove the consistency of analysis by number theory, assuming the latter's truth as well as consistency.

The technical details of Gödel's proofs are practically impossible to recapitulate in nontechnical nonmathematical language. In terms of mathematical technique, Gödel's proof employed what has since been known as the arithmetizing of a formalism, in terms of a one-to-one mapping between every proposition in a given theory and the natural numbers of arithmetic. Gödel then extended to general mathematical expressions, such as variables, formulas, propositions, and logical axioms and operations, a similar higher-order arithmetical representation using various recursive functions. (A set of relations is recursive if there is a mechanical method or algorithm permitting one to decide automatically in a particular set whether a given relation does or does not belong to that set.) Gödel ran into several of the paradoxes connected with truth and definability. He realized that "truth" in number theory cannot be defined within number theory itself and that, therefore, his original plan of proving the relative consistency of analysis could not work. Although Gödel realized that these paradoxes did not, strictly speaking, apply to the precisely specified formal analysis of axiomatic systems, he realized that analogous nonlogical analogues could be carried out by substituting the notion of provability for truth.

Pursuing this approach, Gödel concluded that any formal system in which a certain amount of theoretical arithmetic can be developed (according to Giuseppe Peano's symbolic system) and that satisfies certain minimal consistency conditions is necessarily incomplete in Hilbert's sense. Gödel, therefore, proceeded to draw the conclusion that in suitably strong systems such as that of Whitehead and Russell's *Principia Mathematica* (1910-1913) and Ernst Zennelo's set theory, there are formally undecidable propositions. This means that for number and set theory, there can be no absolute consistency proof of any of these systems formalizable within these systems. Using Hilbert's own methods and formalism, Gödel showed that in any formal system with arithmetic, there exist elementary arithmetic propositions that are "intuitively" obvious, yet undeducible, within the system, and that any proof expressing the consistency of the formal system is not deducible within the system. Hence Gödel had not only settled Hilbert's first three problems in the negative but also refuted Hilbert's underlying general belief in there always being a finitist consistency proof. In Gödel's interpretation, this meant that the formal axiomatization of systems of formal mathematics cannot simplify only these systems through logical combinatorics, but introduces inescapable and insoluble problems. Gödel hinted further that the limits of mathematical formalization operate such that every concept in a mathematical theory is meaningful and legitimate, except for certain "singular" points or regions, beyond which the set- and logical-theory paradoxes appear, as something analogous to division by zero. In Weyl's view, Gödel established that what is provable by intuition and what is provable by deduction, respectively, overlap but are not mutually reducible or expressible.

SIGNIFICANCE

Whereas Brouwer's verbally expressed intuitionist convictions on the inexhaustibility and unprovability of mathematics were impressive predominantly to those of affine philosophic outlook, Gödel's precise formal arguments were more convincing (if less accessible) to mathematicians and logicians of all outlooks. Gödel's famous first paper was written as part one of a double publication; he planned to give full background and details of his second theorem's proof in his concluding paper. Unfortunately, this second exposition was never published because, as Gödel admitted, his introductory proof sketch was generally accepted even by those antagonized by his results. As noted by several authors, although many reexaminations have been attempted, no simpler proofs other than Gödel's originals have, as yet, been developed.

Gödel continued to pursue what he saw as the underlying problems of mathematical evidence and intuition.

1929

In 1941, Gödel found an interpretation of Brouwer's intuitionist number theory using primitive recursive functions of his own origination. This result was jointly regarded as an extension of both Hilbert's formalism and Brouwer's intuitionism. The further development of recursive function theory by, for example, Alonzo Church and Alan Mathison Turing, in the context of other problems that could not be decided formally with axiomatic systems, made possible a large number of results about general decision procedures.

There are as many philosophical reactions to and interpretations of Gödel's recondite conclusions as there are philosophers, including those of Ludwig Wittgenstein, Russell, and Jean Cavaillès. Both Russell and Wittgenstein, using differing arguments like Brouwer, basically acknowledged the correctness of Gödel's result as part of formal axiomatic arithmetic, but denied any wider application of Gödel's theorems to cases of "uncertainty" and "incompleteness" in mathematics, science, and language at large. Diametrically opposed responses were published by Cavaillès in *Sur la logique et la théorie de la science* (1947; on the theory of science). In his own essay on Russell's mathematical logic, Gödel wrote that he did not consider the incompletability of formal systems (such as Whitehead and Russell's *Principia Mathematica*) as encompassing a final argument against a neoplatonistic conceptually realistic interpretation of mathematics, but rather as indicating an essential limitation on the expressive power of abstract formal symbolisms considered apart from their field of application. For Gödel, the unexceptional everyday agreement in accepting a mathematical proof reveals a kind of universality and objectivity in mathematics that goes beyond the intersubjective agreement envisioned by Brouwer. Conceptual realism, according to Gödel, requires not only objective concepts but also that to which mathematical concepts are applied, that is, mathematical objects. In his largely unpublished manuscripts, Gödel speaks in a unique idiom about the "perception" and "intuition" of mathematical objects as the common denominator in learning and applying mathematics within mathematics, as well as in the physical and engineering sciences. These are still areas of much continuing debate.

—*Gerardo G. Tango*

FURTHER READING

Bulloff, J. J., T. C. Holyoke, and S. W. Hahn. *Foundations of Mathematics: Symposium Papers Commemorating the Sixtieth Birthday of Kurt Gödel*. New York: Springer-Verlag, 1969. Collection includes several valuable essays by both mathematicians and philosophers that underscore and examine the philosophical assumptions that Gödel held but never fully published.

Feferman, S., J. W. Dawson, and S. C. Kleene, eds. *Kurt Gödel: Collected Works*. 2 vols. New York: Oxford University Press, 1986-1990. Presents English translations of unpublished notes as well as technical journal and conference publications by Gödel. Includes a complete bibliography on Gödel.

Goldstein, Rebecca. *Incompleteness: The Proof and Paradox of Kurt Gödel*. New York: W. W. Norton, 2005. Examines the philosophy of Gödel's mathematics and discusses his theorem of incompleteness as well as various misinterpretations of the theorem. Includes list of suggested reading and index.

Nagel, Ernest, and James R. Newman. *Gödel's Proof*. Rev. ed. New York: New York University Press, 2002. Reasonably accessible and complete semitechnical account of the recursive functional symbolism and its motivations in a simplified reconstruction of Gödel's incompleteness proof.

Shanker, S. G., ed. *Gödel's Theorem in Focus*. New York: Croom Helm, 1988. Valuable collection of interpretations, principally by philosophers of mathematics, about the conceptual origins and implications of Gödel's theorems. Written in readable style.

Van Heijenoort, Jean, comp. *From Frege to Gödel: A Source Book on Mathematical Logic, 1879-1931*. 1967. Reprint. Cambridge, Mass.: Harvard University Press, 2002. Underscores the historical progression of the "problem of mathematical foundations." Includes bibliography.

Wang, Hao. *Reflections on Kurt Gödel*. Cambridge, Mass.: MIT Press, 1987. Offers very extensive and detailed biographical information and a painstakingly constructed detailed chronology of Gödel's readings, course work, lectures, and associations, from his diaries, collected and unpublished letters and manuscripts, and original and untranslated publications.

SEE ALSO: 1902: Levi Recognizes the Axiom of Choice in Set Theory; June 16, 1902: Russell Discovers the "Great Paradox"; 1904-1907: Brouwer Develops Intuitionist Foundations of Mathematics; 1904-1908: Zermelo Undertakes Comprehensive Axiomatization of Set Theory; 1906: Fréchet Introduces the Concept of Abstract Space; 1939: Bourbaki Group Publishes *Éléments de mathématique*.

August 23, 1929
WESTERN WALL RIOTS

Following a decade of relative calm under the British mandate, a religious dispute concerning prayers at the Western Wall of the ancient Jerusalem temple turned political. A yearlong disagreement over use of religious space brought demonstrations and counterdemonstrations, diplomatic intervention, and failed opportunities for negotiation. The chaos finally erupted in a day of violence that left several hundred Jews and Arabs dead, and the British were forced to begin reevaluating their policies toward the two peoples.

ALSO KNOWN AS: Wailing Wall riots

LOCALE: Jerusalem, Hebron (now in Jordan), Zefat (now in Israel), and Jaffa (now in Israel), Palestine

CATEGORIES: Wars, uprisings, and civil unrest; civil rights and liberties; religion, theology, and ethics; colonialism and occupation

KEY FIGURES

Sir John Chancellor (1870-1952), British high commissioner

Sir Harry Charles Luke (1884-1969), senior British official, acting high commissioner

Douglas Duff (1901-1978), police constable of Jerusalem

Amīn al-Ḥusaynī (c. 1895-1974), mufti of Jerusalem and head of the Supreme Muslim Council

Vladimir Jabotinsky (1880-1940), head of the Zionist Revisionist Party

Abraham Isaac Kook (1865-1935), chief rabbi of Jerusalem

Chaim Weizmann (1874-1952), head of the World Zionist Congress

Sir Walter Shaw (1864-1937), head of the 1929-1930 Shaw Commission

SUMMARY OF EVENT

On Yom Kippur in September, 1928, Jews erected a portable screen to separate the men and women who prayed at the Western Wall. The narrow, eleven-foot passageway between Muslim houses and the two-thousand-year-old retaining wall for Jerusalem's ancient temple had become increasingly crowded as new waves of Jewish immigrants arrived under the British mandate. The wall was also sacred to Muslims: The site was the foundation for Al-Aqsa Mosque, and Muslims believed that Muḥammad had tethered his horse to the wall on his night journey to paradise. Muslims protested the screen's installation, and the Brit-

ish responded, but an overzealous constable, Douglas Duff, roughed up a number of Jews while removing the screen. As a result, both Jews and Arabs found themselves offended by a seemingly minor incident, and they became increasingly sensitive to threats about their own safety.

Over the next months, both sides engaged in a war of words. Jewish leaders raised the issue of purchasing the Western Wall, some called for the building of a new temple, and Chaim Weizmann, head of the World Zionist Conference, wrote a public letter stating that the only solution was for European Jews to pour into Palestine. Vladimir Jabotinsky, leader of the Zionist Revolutionary Party, took a more extreme position: He helped organize a group of young men to confront Arabs in demonstrations. The group's name, Betar, was a reference to the Bar Kokhba Revolt (132-135 C.E.), in which the Romans defeated the Jews, whose army withdrew to the fortress at Betar. Jerusalem mufti Amīn al-Ḥusaynī established a committee to defend the wall and appealed for limits on Jewish immigration.

British high commissioner Sir John Chancellor was aware of the dispute and met with representatives of both sides, but tempers rose again in July of 1929, when the Arabs began a building project near the wall. On the evening of August 14, the ninth of Ab in the Jewish calendar (the day commemorating the destruction of Jerusalem's temple in 70 C.E.), crowds of Jews gathered at the wall, and they were joined the following day by Betar youth. The two groups turned a religious commemoration into a political rally, raising the Zionist flag and singing the "Hatikva," the Zionist national anthem. On the next day, a Friday, a group of Muslims left their prayers to march to the wall, where they beat Jews and burned prayer notes left in the wall.

The following Wednesday, a young Jewish teen, Avraham Mizrahi, was murdered while chasing a stray soccer ball. In retaliation, a young Arab was clubbed in the head. The Mizrahi funeral turned into a demonstration in which Constable Duff and the British police tried to keep control, but their actions resulted in charges of police brutality. On August 22, with Chancellor out of the country, his deputy Sir Harry Charles Luke tried to use dialogue to defuse the situation. Meeting first with the mufti and then with Abraham Isaac Kook, Luke appealed for calm. Later, he invited three Muslim community representatives and three Jewish community representatives to his home for a long afternoon of dialogue. Eventually, the group came up with a statement recognizing the shared nature of the wall, but they were hesitant to release the statement until after the weekend. By then, unfortunately, it was too late.

On Friday, August 23, the situation escalated out of control. Rumors spread that Jewish groups planned to attack Al-Aqsa Mosque. In response, al-Ḥusaynī appealed to Muslims to defend the holy places. Since it was a Friday, the day for Muslim prayers, crowds of worshippers poured into Jerusalem from outlying areas, but this time they came with sticks and knives. At 11:00 A.M., before prayers began, shots rang out from the area around Al-Aqsa Mosque. The mufti called for peace, but other speakers riled up the crowds. A Muslim mob left the platform area and flooded into the streets to attack passing Jews. At the same time, reports from the Jewish neighborhood of Mea She'arim stated that several Arabs had been murdered there.

The British police were unable to control the violence. Years of relative calm had created the attitude that a small police force was sufficient, and so there were only 150 British police officers and 1,500 local forces for the whole country. Jewish immigrants had organized the Haganah defensive force, and by nightfall, eight Jews and five Arabs had been killed, and several dozen people were injured on both sides of the conflict. Jewish residents of outlying areas such as Talpiot were evacuated.

The worst of the violence occurred not in Jerusalem but in Hebron, where Orthodox Jews were unarmed and the police force was small. Jews were outnumbered in the city: There were approximately six hundred Jews and approximately twenty thousand Arabs. Word had reached Hebron of the troubles in Jerusalem, but the situation in Hebron had remained calm throughout most of the day. However, at 4:00 P.M., Arabs gathered near the Jewish yeshiva and began throwing stones. When the only student present attempted to leave, he was stabbed to death.

It was not until Saturday morning that things got out of hand in Hebron. At first it seemed as though this southern town might be spared, as carloads of young men left to join the fray in Jerusalem. However, groups of Arabs began to gather outside Jewish homes. At the Heichal residence, two young men were killed while running toward a policeman for safety. Because it was the Sabbath, some had gathered at their rabbi's house for prayers, but rioters broke down the doors with hatchets and proceeded to slaughter nearly everyone inside. In a matter of two hours, sixty-four Jews had been killed. Reports of atrocities were gruesome—for instance, two elderly rabbis were castrated, and a young child was decapitated.

The situation would have been much worse if many of Hebron's Muslim families had not sheltered Jews in their own homes. As it was, the rioters dispersed only when the previously unarmed police retreated to arm themselves with rifles and began shooting into the crowds.

Jerusalem remained a focal point throughout the riots, and violence continued that day until reinforcements could arrive from Amman and Cairo. Jews in Safed suffered a fate similar to those in Hebron, and in Jaffa, Zionist forces attacked a mosque, where they killed a religious leader and six others. In the end, there were 249 fatalities—133 Jewish and 116 Arab—and 600 wounded.

SIGNIFICANCE

The British responded to the riots with a commission, headed by Sir Walter Shaw, that investigated the riots' causes and made recommendations on ways to avoid such problems. While public opinion had condemned al-Ḥusaynī for inciting the riots, the commission cleared him of direct responsibility. Instead, it focused on more general issues, such as the creation of a landless class of Palestinian peasants following increased Jewish immigration and land purchases. It also recommended that Jewish immigration be limited, that restrictions be placed on land purchases, and that the Balfour Declaration—Britain's 1917 promise for the creation of a Jewish homeland—be removed as a justification for the mandate. British high commissioner Chancellor agreed with the findings of the Shaw Commission, but lobbying efforts in London convinced British prime minister Ramsay MacDonald to ignore the findings.

The riots inspired Palestinian leaders to increase efforts to create political unity within the generally fragmented Arab population. Al-Ḥusaynī began to seek the support of other Arab leaders of the Middle East, and he invested his own money in building the new Palace Hotel outside the Jaffa Gate of Jerusalem so that foreign dignitaries could gather to discuss the Palestinian cause. A change in strategy soon emerged, however, as Arabs began to focus their energies on the British rather than on the Jews. For Zionist leaders, the immediate need was to expand the Haganah as a defense force. They also resolved to continue land purchases and to increase Jewish immigration, especially after the Jews of Hebron had to be evacuated, an act that left that city without a Jewish community.

—Fred Strickert

FURTHER READING

Morris, Benni. *Righteous Victims: A History of the Zionist-Arab Conflict, 1881-1999.* New York: Alfred A. Knopf, 1999. A reevaluation of the history of the period using original sources.

Pappe, Ilan. *A History of Modern Palestine: One Land, Two Peoples.* Cambridge, England: Cambridge University Press, 2004. Concerned that Israelis and Palestinians have separate histories shaped by their own ideologies, Pappe writes an interwoven story that focuses on the lives of the victims, not the powerful.

Segev, Tom. *One Palestine, Complete: Jews and Arabs Under the British Mandate.* Translated by Haim Watzman. New York: Metropolitan, 1999. The author, a columnist for *Ha'aretz* newspaper, compiles a comprehensive journal of the three decades of the British mandate. Drawing upon personal letters and diaries as well as official reports, he presents a thorough report of the 1929 riots.

Sherman, A. J. *Mandate Days: British Lives in Palestine, 1918-1948.* Baltimore: The Johns Hopkins University Press, 1997. Looks at the period from a British perspective.

Smith, Charles D. *Palestine and the Arab-Israeli Conflict.* 2d ed. New York: St. Martin's Press, 1992. Designed as a textbook for undergraduate college classes; gives a balanced introduction to the conflict.

SEE ALSO: 1909: First Kibbutz Is Established in Palestine; Nov. 2, 1917: Balfour Declaration Supports a Jewish Homeland in Palestine; July 24, 1922: League of Nations Establishes Mandate for Palestine; Apr. 15, 1936-1939: Great Uprising of Arabs in Palestine.

September, 1929-January, 1930
THE MALTESE FALCON INTRODUCES THE HARD-BOILED DETECTIVE NOVEL

Dashiell Hammett's masterpiece of detective fiction, The Maltese Falcon, *established a distinctively American alternative to the classic British mystery and raised the genre to the level of literature.*

LOCALE: United States
CATEGORY: Literature

KEY FIGURES
Dashiell Hammett (1894-1961), American author
Lillian Hellman (1905-1984), American playwright, screenwriter, and essayist

SUMMARY OF EVENT

Dashiell Hammett brought a new realism to detective fiction and introduced the tough, cynical private eye into American popular mythology. His best-known work, *The Maltese Falcon*, was first published in five serial installments from September, 1929, to January, 1930, with publication in book form in February, 1930. The book was an immediate popular success and was reprinted seven times in its first year. Critics were equally impressed, acclaiming it as an important novel and not simply another mystery story. Three film versions were made in the next decade; in the third, the John Huston film of 1941, Humphrey Bogart crystallized the image of Sam Spade for American audiences.

Hammett left school at the age of fourteen, and he held several different jobs for short periods of time until 1915, when he became an operative for the Pinkerton National Detective Agency. His experience with Pinkerton provided him with the background for the writing of his realistic detective fiction. When pulmonary tuberculosis ended his career as a detective in 1921, Hammett began publishing short fiction in *Black Mask*, the pulp magazine that would publish his first four novels in serial form. The appearance of his first two novels, *Red Harvest* and *The Dain Curse*, in book form in 1929 made him a successful writer, and the next two, *The Maltese Falcon* and *The Glass Key* (1931), made him internationally famous. It was then, at the height of his fame, that he met Lillian Hellman, with whom he had a close relationship until his death.

Hellman was near the beginning of her distinguished career as a writer, which would be aided considerably by Hammett's expertise as an editor and critic; Hammett, however, would publish only one more novel, *The Thin Man*, in 1934. Although he stopped writing, he still received royalties from his books and from a series of sixteen popular films, three weekly radio shows, and a daily comic strip based on his characters and stories. In 1954, his income from these various sources was more than eighty thousand dollars, an enormous sum for the time and an indication of how popular his work had become. The reasons that Hammett suddenly stopped writing are unknown, but speculation has centered on his involvement in left-wing politics, a dangerous commitment given the national temper of that time. In 1951, Hammett

INTRODUCING SAM SPADE

In the opening paragraphs of The Maltese Falcon, *Dashiell Hammett immediately sets the novel's distinctive tone:*

Samuel Spade's jaw was long and bony, his chin a jutting v under the more flexible v of his mouth. His nostrils curved back to make another, smaller, v. His yellow-grey eyes were horizontal. The v *motif* was picked up again by thickish brows rising outward from twin creases above a hooked nose, and his pale brown hair grew down—from high flat temples—in a point on his forehead. He looked rather pleasantly like a blond satan.

He said to Effie Perine: "Yes, sweetheart?"

She was a lanky sunburned girl whose tan dress of thin woolen stuff clung to her with an effect of dampness. Her eyes were brown and playful in a shiny boyish face. She finished shutting the door behind her, leaned against it, and said: "There's a girl wants to see you. Her name's Wonderly."

"A customer?"

"I guess so. You'll want to see her anyway: she's a knockout."

"Shoo her in, darling," said Spade. "Shoo her in."

Source: Dashiell Hammett, *The Maltese Falcon* (New York: Alfred A. Knopf, 1930).

---

received a six-month sentence in federal prison for refusing to answer questions about a civil rights group. As a result, he was branded a Communist, his books went out of print, his radio shows were taken off the air, and his income was attached by the Internal Revenue Service. In a word, he was blacklisted, and the year before his death his reported income was thirty dollars. Ironically, Hammett, as a veteran of two wars, was buried as a hero in Arlington National Cemetery.

Red Harvest, Hammett's first novel, is now generally regarded as one of his best, although also one of his darkest and most violent. The corruption that permeates the book eventually contaminates even the nameless protagonist, the Continental Op (an operative for the Continental Detective Agency). Hammett creates suspense by developing a technique of severely restricted first-person narration to tell the story; the reader sees and hears only as much as the Op does, and knows far less, as the protagonist seldom reveals his thoughts. At the book's close, most of the major characters have been murdered, and the ending suggests that things will continue relatively unchanged; corruption is the norm, not the aberration. Many critics have found early evidence of Hammett's Marxist views in this implicit critique of capitalist society. After a second Op novel, *The Dain Curse*, Hammett turned to a rigorously objective third-person narration for *The Maltese Falcon*

and *The Glass Key*, describing details of gesture and expression from the outside, as from a camera-eye point of view, but never revealing characters' thoughts or motives. This shift removes even the few traces of interpretation that had been provided by the taciturn Op and makes the analysis of the character of the detective himself a central concern. The question that readers of *The Maltese Falcon* must resolve is not Who committed the crime? but What sort of man is Sam Spade?

The story begins when a woman hires Spade and his partner, Miles Archer, to follow a man named Floyd Thursby. Archer and Thursby are both murdered that night, and the woman, Brigid O'Shaughnessy, turns out to be involved in a plot to steal a priceless jeweled statue of a falcon; Thursby is revealed to have been her accomplice. Other parties pursuing the falcon include Joel Cairo, one of the first homosexual characters portrayed in an American novel, and Caspar Gutman, the "Fat Man" who is the mastermind behind the quest. Unlike Hammett's first two novels, *The Maltese Falcon* contains little violence; the emphasis is on Spade's gradual uncovering of the complex relations among the various criminals and on the efforts of the criminals and police to determine Spade's own motives and intentions. Hammett's objective narration limits the reader's own knowledge to the same set of lies and half-truths that the characters must sift through.

In the novel's dramatic conclusion, Spade turns Brigid O'Shaughnessy, who has become his lover, over to the police as Archer's murderer. The reasoning that leads Spade to solve the crime is based on clues available from the start, suggesting that he may have known of her guilt all along. The question remains open as to whether he has really fallen in love but is forced by his rigid personal code of ethics to turn her in or whether he has been cold-bloodedly manipulating her throughout in order to solve the case. Both hypotheses may be partially true, and ultimately the mystery of the novel resides more in understanding the character of the protagonist than in resolving the plot. As Ross Macdonald put it, "Hammett was the first American writer to use the detective-story for the purposes of a major novelist." This interest in exploring character is extended in Hammett's fourth novel, *The Glass Key*, which is as much a psychological novel as a mystery. Hammett's fifth and final novel, *The Thin Man*, is unique in its light comic tone, which fitted it for popular adaptation in a series of films. The centerpiece of the book is the relationship between the worldly and jaded detective Nick Charles and his young and enthusiastic wife, Nora. The Charles's happy marriage, one of the few depicted in modern fiction, is clearly based on the relationship between Hammett and Lillian Hellman, to whom the book is dedicated.

SIGNIFICANCE

Before Hammett laid the foundation of the modern realistic detective novel, virtually all detective fiction had been designed on the pattern established by Edgar Allan Poe in three short stories written between 1841 and 1844: "The Murders in the Rue Morgue," "The Mystery of Marie Roget," and "The Purloined Letter." The basic ingredients of the formula were simple: a brilliant but eccentric amateur detective, his loyal but somewhat pedestrian companion and chronicler, an even more pedestrian police force, and a bizarre crime. The solution of the mystery called for a complex series of logical deductions drawn by the scientific detective on the basis of an equally complex series of subtle clues. These clues were generally available to the detective's companion, who was also the narrator, and through him to the reader, who would derive interest and pleasure from the attempt to beat the detective to the solution. The canonical popular version of

Dashiell Hammett. (Library of Congress)

this classical tradition of the mystery as a puzzle to be solved is of course the British writer Arthur Conan Doyle's Sherlock Holmes series, the success of which paved the way for similar work by other British writers such as Agatha Christie. Although this classical model was invented by the American Poe and practiced by several American mystery writers, its popularity with British writers has led to its being labeled the English school, in opposition to a more realistic type of mystery being written in the 1920's by a small group of American writers.

Hammett proved to be the master of the new kind of detective story written in reaction against the English model. Raymond Chandler made the point that "Hammett gave murder back to the kind of people that commit it for reasons, not just to provide a corpse; and with the means at hand, not hand-wrought dueling pistols, curare and tropical fish." Rather than serving as the vehicle for a bewildering set of clues and an often implausible solution, the realistic story of detection emphasized characterization, action, and rapid-fire and colloquial dialogue—as opposed to the often flat characters, slow pace, and stilted set speeches of the classical school. The essentials of the realistic model are found complete in Hammett's earliest work, almost from the first of his thirty-five stories featuring the Continental Op, just as the entire classical formula was complete in Poe's earliest stories.

Hammett's familiarity with the classical paradigm is established in the seventy-three reviews of detective novels he wrote for the *Saturday Review of Literature* and the *New York Evening Post* between 1927 and 1930, and his rejection of it is thorough. He specifically contrasted his theory of the detective with that of Doyle in describing Sam Spade: "For your private detective does not . . . want to be an erudite solver of riddles in the Sherlock Holmes manner; he wants to be a hard and shifty fellow, able to take care of himself in any situation, able to get the best of anybody he comes in contact with, whether criminal, innocent by-stander, or client." Hammett underscored the difference in methods in a 1924 short story, "The Tenth Clew," which parodies the classical detective plot with a set of nine bewildering clues, including a victim missing his left shoe and collar buttons, a mysterious list of names, a bizarre murder weapon (the victim was beaten to death with a typewriter), and so on. The solution, of course, the "tenth clue," is to ignore all nine of the earlier clues and to use standard methods such as the surveillance of suspects to find the killer.

Just as the detective is different in Hammett's work, so are the crimes and criminals. The world of the traditional mystery is one of regularity disrupted temporarily by the

1929

aberrant event of the crime. Once the detective solves the crime through the application of reason, normalcy is restored. The worldview implicit in this plot was comforting for a largely middle-class English readership at the beginning of the twentieth century, but it was remote from the experience of the generation of American readers who had just survived World War I. The world of the hard-boiled detective, as conceived by an author who had been through the horrors of that war, is one in which criminal behavior is the norm rather than the exception. There are usually several crimes and several criminals, and the society is not an orderly one temporarily disrupted but a deeply corrupt one that will not be redeemed after the particular set of crimes being investigated is solved.

Raymond Chandler observed that Dashiell Hammett "took murder out of the Venetian vase and dropped it into the alley." The two main ingredients of his breakthrough are the creation of the hard-boiled detective, a ruthless and often violent man who is bound only by his own rigid and private code of ethics, and the perfection of an almost entirely objective narrative style, restricted to terse descriptions and crisp, idiomatic dialogue, revealing the characters' thoughts and emotions only between the lines. Hammett's objective technique laid the foundations for similar stylistic experiments by Ernest Hemingway and, later, the French New Novelists of the 1950's. Moreover, his creation of the hard-boiled detective provided the inspiration for his most noteworthy successors in the mystery field, Raymond Chandler and Ross Macdonald, and introduced the tough, cynical private eye into American popular mythology.

—*William Nelles*

FURTHER READING

Chandler, Raymond. "The Simple Art of Murder." *The Atlantic Monthly*, December, 1944, 53-59. Important essay by one of Hammett's most distinguished successors analyzes Hammett's decisive role in the development of detective fiction.

Dooley, Dennis. *Dashiell Hammett*. New York: Frederick Ungar, 1984. A survey of Hammett's work for the general reader. Considers some of the better-known short fiction in more detail than do many such surveys. Includes bibliography and index.

Gregory, Sinda. *Private Investigations: The Novels of Dashiell Hammett*. Carbondale: Southern Illinois University Press, 1985. Full-length study of Hammett's major novels provides insightful close readings of individual passages but breaks little new interpretive ground. Includes bibliography and index.

Hammett, Jo. *Dashiell Hammett: A Daughter Remembers*. Edited by Richard Layman with Julie M. Rivett. New York: Carroll & Graf, 2001. Memoir by Hammett's daughter focuses on the personal side of Hammett's life. Includes many photographs.

Layman, Richard. *Shadow Man: The Life of Dashiell Hammett*. New York: Harcourt Brace Jovanovich, 1981. One of the most scholarly and reliable Hammett biographies available; objective, readable, and carefully researched and documented. An indispensable source. Contains the full text of the testimony that sent Hammett to prison. Includes photographs, bibliography, and index.

Marling, William. *Dashiell Hammett*. Boston: Twayne, 1983. Concise and well-informed survey combines a biographical framework with a unified overview of Hammett's short fiction and novels. Includes lightly annotated bibliography and index.

Nolan, William F. *Dashiell Hammett: A Casebook*. Santa Barbara, Calif.: McNally & Loftin, 1969. First book-length study of Hammett's life and work, now somewhat dated, features an extensive listing of Hammett's work in various fields, including newspapers and radio. Includes bibliography and index.

_____. *Hammett: A Life at the Edge*. New York: Congdon & Weed, 1983. Thoroughly researched work, but often subjective and personal, offering detailed interpretations of the information covered rather than letting the data speak for themselves. Includes photographs, select bibliography, and index.

Panek, Leroy Lad. *Reading Early Hammett: A Critical Study of the Fiction Prior to "The Maltese Falcon."* Jefferson, N.C.: McFarland, 2004. Examines Hammett's early works and the development of his technique leading up to *The Maltese Falcon*. Includes chronology of works, bibliography, and index.

Symons, Julian. *Dashiell Hammett*. San Diego: Harcourt Brace Jovanovich, 1985. General survey of Hammett's life and work aimed at a popular audience. Includes excellent photographs, bibliography, and index.

Wolfe, Peter. *Beams Falling: The Art of Dashiell Hammett*. Bowling Green, Ohio: Bowling Green University Popular Press, 1980. Presents close critical analyses of Hammett's novels and short fiction. Provides some valuable information, although the readings are not always convincing.

SEE ALSO: 1920: *The Mysterious Affair at Styles* Introduces Hercule Poirot; 1935: Penguin Develops a Line of Paperback Books.

October 7, 1929
THE SOUND AND THE FURY LAUNCHES FAULKNER'S CAREER

Although not widely appreciated at the time of its publication, The Sound and the Fury *was William Faulkner's breakthrough novel, launching both his own career and modernist fiction in the United States.*

LOCALE: New York, New York
CATEGORY: Literature

KEY FIGURES
William Faulkner (1897-1962), American author
Harrison Smith (1888-1971), American book editor
  and publisher

SUMMARY OF EVENT
In 1928, when he completed *The Sound and the Fury*, William Faulkner was a struggling, relatively unsuccessful writer working at odd jobs in Oxford, Mississippi, his hometown. Although his first novels, *Soldiers' Pay* (1926) and *Mosquitoes* (1927), had been well received in literary circles, they had not sold well, and Faulkner was unable to support himself by writing, as he wished to do. Publishers continued to reject his short stories and what he believed his best novel, *Flags in the Dust*, the manuscript title for what became *Sartoris* (1929). *Flags in the Dust* was finally published uncut in 1973.

Faulkner later stated in interviews that he had composed *The Sound and the Fury* in a mood of despair. Doubting that he would have a successful publishing career, he felt freed to write what was closest to his heart in the way that seemed best to him. He often said this novel was his favorite, calling it his "most splendid failure." In the book, he tried to capture those things that were most important to him personally, culturally, and artistically. In a 1933 introduction to the novel, Faulkner indicated that being able to write without the objects of publishing and selling led him to discover what became fundamental to him in storytelling and led to his thinking himself worthy to be among the writers he considered great: "The writing of it as it now stands taught me both how to write and how to read, and even more: It taught me what I had already read, because on completing it I discovered, in a series of repercussions like summer thunder, the Flauberts and Conrads and Turgenievs which as much as ten years before I had consumed whole and without assimilating at all, as a moth or a goat might."

When *The Sound and the Fury* was completed, Faulkner was complexly involved with two publishers, Horace Liveright and Harcourt Brace. Faulkner's friend Harri-son Smith was an editor for Harcourt Brace and had offered the manuscript to that publishing house, which was bringing out *Sartoris*. Harcourt Brace showed little interest in this strange, almost incomprehensible book, however. Although there are hints in Faulkner's earlier work of what he would do in *The Sound and the Fury*, it breaks decisively with the readability of his previous novels. *Sartoris* was the first novel to make full use of Yoknapatawpha County, a fictional version of northwest Mississippi, the "postage stamp of native soil" that became the setting of Faulkner's great series of novels. *The Sound and the Fury*, set in Jefferson, a fictionalized Oxford, Mississippi, presents a composite portrait of a decayed aristocratic family in the latter stages of its destruction, of a southern culture in the painful throes of transition from the Victorian era to the modern age, and of an American society undergoing a parallel, if more diffused, transition. What makes the novel seem unreadable is the unusual mode of representation that most visibly identifies Faulkner as a modernist writer.

The novel developed as a series of experiments to capture in a moving way the reaction of the family of Caddy Compson, a daughter, sister, and mother who makes a modern woman's choices at the beginning of the twentieth century. Caddy struggles to liberate herself from family and male domination. In doing so, she removes herself from a family so heavily dependent on her that the suffering proves unbearable. Her pregnancy leads to a forced marriage that ends in divorce. Unable to make her way easily, she abandons her daughter to her family's care. Faulkner finally chose to tell the story mainly from the points of view of Caddy's brothers, who feel abandoned and betrayed by her. One brother, Benjy, is developmentally disabled, his mental growth arrested before he learned speech. His section of "narration" opens the novel, plunging the reader into perceptions of a character who cannot make judgments, who can feel but who cannot comprehend or explain the loss of the one person who has mothered him. Nearly as difficult to read as Benjy's section, the next part shows brother Quentin's activities and thoughts on the day he commits suicide. Quentin is a sensitive and disturbed young man who finds that the values he wants to use to order his world and keep Caddy with him—values inherited from his family—repeatedly betray him into paradox and helplessness. The third section presents the internal monologue of Jason, a violently angry materialist who be-

1929

lieves his sister's divorce has ruined his chances for wealth and power. The final section tells about Dilsey, the black servant who becomes mother to the family after Caddy departs. This section and Jason's give indirect expression to the point of view of Caddy's daughter, also named Quentin, who has been abandoned to a painful life in the suffering and vindictive family.

Although the story is comprehensible with patience and considerable rereading, it clearly was not, in 1929, the sort of novel to be accepted easily by a commercial publisher. Harcourt Brace was glad to be able to turn it over to Cape and Smith Publishers. Upon the book's publication, the initial reviews were very positive, especially among academics and intellectuals. During the two decades after its publication, a fairly steady trickle of highly laudatory reviews identified *The Sound and the Fury* as a great novel. During this period, Faulkner produced the series of novels that extended his literary experimentation and his presentation of Yoknapatawpha

County as a microcosm of the modern world. Among his great novels of this period are *As I Lay Dying* (1930), *Light in August* (1932), *Absalom, Absalom!* (1936), and *Go Down, Moses* (1942). This series, which begins with *The Sound and the Fury*, constitutes the accomplishment for which Faulkner was awarded the 1949 Nobel Prize in Literature.

SIGNIFICANCE

The immediate impact of the publication of *The Sound and the Fury* is difficult to measure. For the general reading public, the novel was not accessible and thus not widely read; the book sold fewer than two thousand copies in the first two years after it appeared. Sales were not helped by the stock market crash that occurred two weeks after publication and the Great Depression that followed. For general readers, the more significant event was Faulkner's 1931 publication of *Sanctuary*, with its treatment of the sensational subjects of flappers, rape, and gangsters. *Sanctuary* tended to define the general view of Faulkner until after his Nobel Prize, bringing him the notoriety that allowed him to earn a living writing Hollywood screenplays.

The more important immediate impacts of *The Sound and the Fury* were on Faulkner's own conception of his writing career and on the literary and artistic intelligentsia who became his admirers and who followed his career. These readers tended to ensure that Faulkner's works would continue to be published, that he would receive prizes and honors, that his works would be translated, especially into French, and that they would be studied and read in colleges and universities. In this way, Faulkner's literary reputation was sustained until a complex series of events, beginning perhaps with Malcolm Cowley's publication of *The Viking Portable Faulkner* (1946) and the Nobel Prize, established Faulkner as a world author.

Faulkner's career can be seen as one flowering of the literary tradition of modernism. Modernism may be defined as the Western world's attempt to create a culture viable in the face of almost universal disbelief in traditional Christianity among intellectuals and a parallel secular, commercial materialism in popular culture. Faulkner's novels embody many of the problems and conflicts that result from this attempt to re-create culture in an age of religious doubt. That he was aware of himself as involved in this project is clear in his Nobel Prize acceptance speech, in which he affirms that humanity as a whole possesses a soul, as evidenced by the human capacity for love, compassion, sacrifice, endurance, and

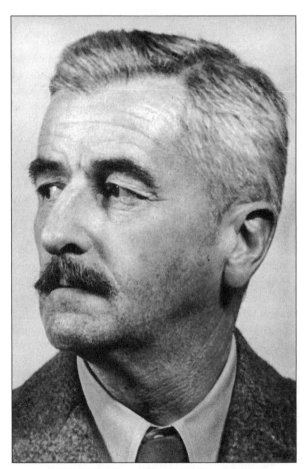

William Faulkner. (The Nobel Foundation)

FROM *THE SOUND AND THE FURY*

The first section of William Faulkner's The Sound and the Fury *is narrated by Benjy, the developmentally disabled brother of the central character, Caddy Compson. As this excerpt from the novel's first few pages shows, the reader is quickly plunged into a confusion of perceptions through a character who cannot comprehend the meanings of the actions of others and whose thoughts skip around in time.*

We went along the fence and came to the garden fence, where our shadows were. My shadow was higher than Luster's on the fence. We came to the broken place and went through it.

"Wait a minute." Luster said. "You snagged on that nail again. Cant you never crawl through here without snagging on that nail."

Caddy uncaught me and we crawled through. Uncle Maury said not to let anybody see us, so we better stoop over, Caddy said. Stoop over, Benjy. Like this, see. We stooped over and crossed the garden, where the flowers rasped and rattled against us. The ground was hard. We climbed the fence, where the pigs were grunting and snuffing. I expect they're sorry because one of them got killed today, Caddy said. The ground was hard, churned and knotted.

Keep your hands in your pockets, Caddy said. Or they'll get froze. You dont want your hands froze on Christmas, do you.

"Its too cold out there." Versh said. "You dont want to go out doors."

"What is it now." Mother said.

"He want to go out doors." Versh said.

"Let him go." Uncle Maury said.

"It's too cold." Mother said. "He'd better stay in. Benjamin. Stop that now."

"It wont hurt him." Uncle Maury said.

"You, Benjamin." Mother said. "If you dont be good, you'll have to go to the kitchen."

Source: William Faulkner, *The Sound and the Fury* (New York: Random House, 1929).

---

community of humanity that he sees in the struggles of the human heart for communion and love. The central theme of the novel is loss, and although it centers on family breakup as a cause of loss, larger causes of the family's disintegration are shown in the shift from the Old South, with its emphasis on traditional, Christian values, to a New South, with an emphasis on secular and commercial values. The novel's attitude toward this shift is ambivalent; much of good and evil is lost, and much is gained. A meaningful and moral life is not easy in either world. In worldview, technique, and theme, Faulkner illustrates a modernist point of view, bringing to completion in American fiction the influences of his great precursors and contemporaries in Europe, including Joyce and Marcel Proust.

The influence of *The Sound and the Fury* and of Faulkner's whole career pervades modern culture, not only in the English-speaking world but also in Europe, Japan, and Latin America. Like Mark Twain, Willa Cather, and other important American writers, Faulkner made a microcosm of his home region and wrote to a world audience from that base. Thus he helped to inspire writers such as Richard Wright, Ralph Ellison, and Flannery O'Connor. Jean-Paul Sartre was among the European writers to express admiration for Faulkner. Among Latin American writers in Spanish, Gabriel García Márquez is only one of many to name Faulkner as an important influence. The continued study of Faulkner in colleges helps to prepare readers for difficult modernist and postmodernist fiction and helps them to develop the intellectual and emotional tools for understanding and dealing with the complexity of contemporary Western culture.

—*Terry Heller*

FURTHER READING

Bassett, John Earl. *William Faulkner: An Annotated Checklist of Criticism.* New York: David Lewis, 1972. Excellent tool for surveying published responses to Faulkner's work and career, arranged by subject and

other "universal truths of the heart." He also asserts that literature is among the activities that can fill some of the former roles of religion, by lifting people's hearts and by reminding them about the soul's needs and yearnings, so that "the poet's voice . . . can be one of the props, the pillars" to help humanity "endure and prevail."

Modernism appears in almost every aspect of *The Sound and the Fury.* The worldview of *The Sound and the Fury* echoes, sometimes in direct paraphrase, T. S. Eliot's *The Waste Land* (1922), with its vision of the modern West as a spiritual desert. Faulkner follows Henry James, Joseph Conrad, and James Joyce in the use of complex subjective points of view and stream-of-consciousness techniques to render the sense of being imprisoned in a culture no longer able to believe in an objective reality that possesses absolute truth. Faulkner's main answer to this sense of isolation is his belief in the

1929

then chronologically within subjects. Includes brief summaries of and quotations from most of what was written about *The Sound and the Fury* from 1929 to 1971.

_____. *William Faulkner: An Annotated Checklist of Recent Criticism*. Kent, Ohio: Kent State University Press, 1983. Supplement to Bassett's earlier volume, cited above.

Bleikasten, André. *The Most Splendid Failure: Faulkner's "The Sound and the Fury."* Bloomington: Indiana University Press, 1976. Provocative study of the novel examines Faulkner's writing before *The Sound and the Fury* and discusses each character and each section of the novel in detail, offering structuralist and psychoanalytic interpretations of Caddy, Benjy, Quentin, Jason, and Dilsey. Includes bibliography and index.

_____, ed. *William Faulkner's "The Sound and the Fury": A Critical Casebook*. New York: Garland, 1982. Gathers selections from Faulkner's own commentary on the novel and adds eight interpretive essays on subjects such as Faulkner's composition process and the structure of the novel. Special emphasis on recent literary theory. Includes bibliography.

Blotner, Joseph. *Faulkner: A Biography*. 2 vols. New York: Random House, 1974. Massive, highly detailed account of Faulkner's life and works. Somewhat reticent about the less savory aspects of Faulkner's life out of deference to Faulkner's family; presents the facts but does not interpret them. Includes many photographs, chronology of Faulkner's life, genealogical chart, and index.

Faulkner, William. *The Sound and the Fury*. Norton Critical Editions. Edited by David Minter. 2d ed. New York: W. W. Norton, 2003. "Authoritative text" presents the full novel along with background materials (including Faulkner correspondence), essays that pro-

vide cultural and historical context, and critical essays on the novel from a wide variety of authors.

Kinney, Arthur, ed. *Critical Essays on William Faulkner: The Compson Family*. Boston: G. K. Hall, 1982. Contains twenty-three critical essays, selections from early reviews, and related materials by Faulkner. Deals with all of Faulkner's fiction about the Compson family, and so sheds light on *The Sound and the Fury* from several interesting directions.

Matthews, John T. *"The Sound and the Fury": Faulkner and the Lost Cause*. Boston: Twayne, 1991. A solid and useful interpretation for those familiar with the novel. Includes a brief presentation of the literary and historical context followed by careful studies of the main characters, the setting, the technical aspects of the novel, and the various commentaries, including the appendix, that Faulkner constructed for the book. Also includes annotated bibliography and index.

Minter, David. *William Faulkner: His Life and Work*. 2d ed. Baltimore: The Johns Hopkins University Press, 1997. Biography useful for general readers wishing to examine how Faulkner's life is reflected in his work, especially his major novels. Provides especially good analyses of the novels. Includes genealogy, chronology, map of Yoknapatawpha County, and index.

Parini, Jay. *One Matchless Time: A Life of William Faulkner*. New York: HarperCollins, 2004. Draws on materials unavailable to earlier biographers and on interviews with Faulkner's daughter and some of his lovers to place Faulkner's work in the context of his life and times. Includes photographs, bibliography, and index.

SEE ALSO: Nov., 1903: Henry James's *The Ambassadors* Is Published; 1918: Cather's *My Ántonia* Promotes Regional Literature; Feb. 2, 1922: Joyce's *Ulysses* Redefines Modern Fiction.

October 24-29, 1929
U.S. STOCK MARKET CRASHES

The economic boom of the 1920's ended in a dramatic crash of the stock market that was partly caused and exacerbated by the practice of buying stock "on margin" (that is, with other people's money). The crash signaled the beginning of the Great Depression of the 1930's.

ALSO KNOWN AS: Black Tuesday
LOCALE: New York, New York
CATEGORIES: Banking and finance; trade and commerce; economics

KEY FIGURES
Herbert Hoover (1874-1964), president of the United States, 1929-1933
Roger W. Babson (1875-1967), American economist
Irving Fisher (1867-1947), American economics professor
Charles E. Mitchell (1877-1955), president of the National City Bank
Thomas William Lamont (1870-1948), senior partner at J. P. Morgan & Company
Richard Whitney (1888-1974), vice president of the New York Stock Exchange
Charles E. Merrill (1885-1956), founder of Merrill Lynch & Company securities brokerage

SUMMARY OF EVENT
October 29, 1929, "Black Tuesday," is remembered as the most devastating day in American stock market history. Stock prices fell in a selling frenzy that began the moment the opening bell sounded. When the trading day was over, the Dow Jones Industrial Average had dropped more than thirty points, with some leading stocks plummeting $30-$60 a share. Billions of dollars of fortunes and the life savings of many small investors were wiped out as the decline of the market, which had begun in September, culminated on Black Tuesday. Few people had foreseen the coming of the Great Crash. The country had been riding on the boom of the 1920's.

The decade of the 1920's is often called the "Roaring Twenties." The American economy remained strong after World War I. Technological advances and mass production brought conveniences and a sense of prosperity to the average American family. With the advent of a new financial arrangement called the "installment plan," the public could easily buy on credit such luxury items as automobiles, radios, vacuum cleaners, and electric ice-boxes, all of which were just coming into widespread use. In his presidential campaign in 1928, Herbert Hoover promised "a chicken in every pot and two cars in every garage" and won the election in a landslide. Growing optimism and a sense of prosperity were reflected in the stock market.

The 1920's saw a growth in the participation of ordinary people in the stock market. As the glamorous lives of some successful stock speculators were publicized, many people became infected with the desire to make a quick fortune. Buying stocks was made easy by brokerage firms, which allowed customers to buy stocks "on margin," paying a fraction of the total value in cash and borrowing the rest from the broker. As long as the stock price rose, this speculation was safe. If the price fell, however, an investor could get a "margin call," meaning that more cash had to be put up to cover any further losses. If the money was not paid, the broker would sell the stock at the prevailing market price. Because stock prices were rising steadily in the 1920's, many investors thought that buying stocks on margin was safe speculation. Many ordinary people who had little knowledge about investments became investors in the stock market.

Overall, however, the stock market of the 1920's was dominated by a few powerful, wealthy investors. Some of them engaged in manipulation of stock prices, often using inside information. They would first artificially inflate the price of a target stock, then, when other unsuspecting investors hopped on the bandwagon, sell the stock at a profit. Michael J. Meehan, for example, successfully manipulated the stock of Radio Corporation of America (RCA) in March, 1929, making $100 million in a week. In many cases, the surge in stock prices had to do with speculative momentum rather than with company profits. In fact, there were ominous signs in the American economy in 1929. The credit burden on consumers was heavy. Automobile sales were down. Steel production was falling. Few people were worried about these signs amid the increasing optimism, although some were concerned about the nation's inflated stock investment. Economist Roger W. Babson, for example, predicted the coming of a crash in the stock market.

Stock prices reached a record high on September 3, 1929, following a decade of steady increase. There was no sign of pessimism in the air. Few investors suspected that the day marked the peak of the bull market and that from then on stock prices would steadily decline, col-

1929

lapsing in October. The market began a long slide. Stock prices fell slowly but relatively steadily during the month of September. Tumbles in prices were often followed by small rallies. By the end of the month, the stock index hit its lowest mark for the year up to that point. This decline continued through the month of October. Fear and apprehension began to mount among both large and small investors, amid confusion and uncertainty. As margin calls went out, more and more investors had to scramble to cover their losses, often drawing from their life savings. Sales of stock when margin calls could not be met put further downward pressure on prices. Still, investors were consoled by sporadic upward movements in stock prices. There were some optimistic analysts as well. For example, Irving Fisher, a respected economics professor, dismissed the selling trend of the market as a "shaking out of the lunatic fringe." He implied that eliminating marginal speculators would bring stability to the market. Stock prices, however, continued to decline.

The stock market began to crash in heavy liquidation beginning on October 23. The price of General Electric stock, for example, fell $20 from the previous day, and Auburn Auto's stock lost $77. By now, brokers and investors began openly to express their pessimism. Fear and anxiety prevailed. Few had any idea of what the next day, "Black Thursday," would bring. Prices began to plummet at the opening bell on October 24. Thousands of investors had received margin calls the night before and had no choice but to sell their shares to cover their debts. The stock ticker carrying current stock price information began to run behind as the frenzied selling continued. Furthermore, price quotations printed on the ticker were confusing, as prices were tumbling in the double digits, while the ticker tape showed only one-digit changes. Frustrated brokers scrambled to carry out their clients' sell orders but were often unable to find buyers.

At lunchtime, Thomas William Lamont, the acting head of J. P. Morgan & Company, called several bankers in an attempt to control the situation. This so-called bankers' pool met and agreed to pour a large sum of money into the market to support stock prices in an attempt to avoid catastrophe. In the early afternoon, Richard Whitney, the vice president of the New York Stock Exchange, walked onto the exchange floor and in a loud voice began to place buy orders at prices higher than actual selling prices. He and other brokers representing the bankers continued this, going from post to post. The prices of major stocks immediately began to recover. In fact, by the time the market closed, many stocks had recouped some of their earlier losses. RCA stock, for ex-

ample, closed at 58 $\frac{1}{4}$, well above the lowest level of the day, recorded at 44 $\frac{1}{2}$. The Dow Jones Industrial Average fell 6.3 points on a record trading volume of more than twelve million shares. The situation could have been much worse if the bankers had not supported stock prices.

The market remained relatively calm on Friday and Saturday. Some prices rose slightly on Friday, and the Dow Jones Industrial Average was down only a few points in Saturday morning's trading. Over the weekend, however, fear and anxiety built again among investors. When the market opened on Monday, October 28, prices began to drop at an accelerating speed. This time, there was no support from the bankers. The Dow Jones Industrial Average lost more than 38 points on a trading volume of more than nine million shares. The panic continued the next day, Black Tuesday, when the bottom fell out of the market. The great bull market of the 1920's had crashed. The crash would continue until mid-November of 1929. For the next two and a half years, stock prices would continue to slide.

SIGNIFICANCE

The stock market crash of 1929 was followed by the Great Depression of the 1930's. Investors suffered massive losses. Many businesses and banks that had invested heavily in the stock market failed as a result of losses. The collapse in stock prices was followed by the banking panic of 1931. The crash was a harbinger of economic malaise that lasted through the 1930's. National output plunged by 30 percent between 1929 and 1933, and the nation's unemployment rate climbed to more than 24 percent.

Although some have argued that the crash was a prime cause of the Depression, that claim is widely disputed. The Great Crash and the Great Depression may be only tangentially related. It is generally accepted, however, that the crash was caused in part by various abusive practices in the securities markets in the 1920's, including manipulation of securities prices, extensive speculation made possible by purchases on margin, trading by company officials using inside information, and the selling of risky securities while withholding important information about them.

The crash triggered a series of reforms in securities markets. At first, the Hoover administration was reluctant to add federal regulations to the already existing state rules for the securities exchanges. Some people, particularly in the financial circle, feared that such measures would jeopardize the capitalistic mechanism in the financial markets. President Hoover hoped that Wall Street would reform itself in order to prevent future disasters. Many people argued, however, that strict measures to safeguard investors were necessary.

In late 1931, the Senate voted to begin a major investigation of the securities markets in an attempt to unearth the manipulative practices in securities trading that were believed to have caused the crash. The hearings conducted by the Senate Committee on Banking and Currency lasted for two years and produced thousands of pages of testimony. The inquiry gave an impetus for Congress to pass several legislative measures to regulate the securities market on the federal level. When President Franklin D. Roosevelt took office in 1933, he closed the banks in an attempt to restore order in banking. The Emergency Banking Act of March 9, 1933, declared a bank holiday, and a program to reopen the banks was initiated. As part of the bank holiday, the New York Stock Exchange was closed from March 6 to March 14.

The Securities Act of 1933 was based on the idea that the securities markets needed to be regulated by the fed-eral government in order to protect investors. Underwriters of various securities were required to register new issues with the Federal Trade Commission before they could be offered to the public. The Banking Act of 1933, also called the Glass-Steagall Act, gave more power to the Federal Reserve in controlling member banks' speculative activities. Furthermore, the act mandated that commercial banks separate themselves from investment functions in order to prevent them from using depositors' funds for speculation. As a result, commercial banks were detached from the stock market by the mid-1930's. The Federal Deposit Insurance Corporation was established to safeguard depositors and to avoid widespread bank failures.

In 1934, Congress went one step further to regulate the securities markets. The Securities Exchange Act of 1934 established a federal agency called the Securities and Exchange Commission (SEC) to oversee the securities markets and to enforce provisions designed to guard against manipulations and fraud. This legislation was much broader in scope than was the Securities Act of

Crowds fill Wall Street after the crash of the stock market. (NARA)

1929

1933, in that the Securities and Exchange Act regulated securities trading at any time, even after initial distribution, whereas the Securities Act dealt only with stocks and bonds at their initial offering stages. Every aspect of securities trading was addressed. The SEC began to enforce the margin rules set by the Federal Reserve in order to regulate the buying of securities on credit. Broad provisions were established for the collection and transmission of information and for investigation of securities. Penalties for violators were also established.

These new legislative measures brought sweeping changes in Wall Street practices, ensuring better market safeguards and procedures. Regulations prohibited stock manipulation using pool operations, or the combined powers of two or more operators. More stringent requirements were established for buying stock on margin. Underwriters of securities were obliged to disclose all important information about their issues. Limits were placed on the amount of speculation allowed by insiders in the stocks and bonds of their own companies. These and other measures helped the securities markets to recover in the years to come.

—Daniel Y. Lee

FURTHER READING

Beaudreau, Bernard. *Mass Production, the Stock Market Crash, and the Great Depression: The Macroeconomics of Electrification*. Westport, Conn.: Greenwood Press, 1996. Deals with the unintended consequences of electrification, arguing that the Great Crash and the Great Depression were two of them.

Bierman, Harold, Jr. *The Causes of the 1929 Stock Market Crash: A Speculative Orgy or a New Era?* Westport, Conn.: Greenwood Press, 1998. Reconsiders the causes and effects of the Great Crash, arguing that it marked the advent of a new kind of investing. Bibliographic references and index.

Eichengreen, Barry. *Golden Fetters: The Gold Standard and the Great Depression*. New York: Oxford University Press, 1992. Although primarily concerned with the role of the gold standard in causing the international recessions that started in 1928, the author also asserts that Federal Reserve policy caused abrupt changes in purchases of commodities that would have been reflected on Wall Street.

Friedman, Milton, and Anna J. Schwartz. *A Monetary History of the United States, 1867-1960*. Princeton, N.J.: Princeton University Press, 1963. A seminal work that identifies Federal Reserve Board mistakes as causing both the stock market crash and the banking crisis of 1930-1933.

Galbraith, John K. *The Great Crash, 1929*. Boston: Houghton Mifflin, 1955. An engaging book that interprets the stock market crash as resulting from speculation, market flaws, and criminal behavior.

Hiebert, Ray, and Roselyn Hiebert. *The Stock Market Crash, 1929: Panic on Wall Street Ends the Jazz Age*. New York: Franklin Watts, 1970. This book recounts events of September through November, 1929, in and around the New York Stock Exchange. Accessible to a general audience.

Patterson, Robert T. *The Great Boom and Panic, 1921-1929*. Chicago: Henry Regnery, 1965. This book describes various aspects of the boom of the 1920's and the stock market collapse. Human aspects of the crash and the Great Depression are also discussed. Accessible to a general audience.

White, Eugene N. *The Regulation and Reform of the American Banking System, 1900-1929*. Princeton, N.J.: Princeton University Press, 1983. Significant sections on banks and their securities affliates. Shows that those banks involved in stock market lending were less likely to fail than banks not involved in such activities.

_____. "When the Ticker Ran Late: The Stock Market Boom and Crash of 1929." In *Crashes and Panics: The Lessons from History*. Homewood, Ill.: Dow Jones-Irwin, 1990. Relates the bull market to the expectation that companies would continue paying high dividends; asserts, therefore, that the stock market crash was related to changing expectations, not to Federal Reserve Board policy.

Wigmore, Barrie A. *The Crash and Its Aftermath: A History of Securities Markets in the United States, 1929-1933*. Westport, Conn.: Greenwood Press, 1985. A detailed history of the stock and bond markets between 1929 and 1933. Political and economic influences on the securities markets are analyzed. Accessible to a general audience.

SEE ALSO: Nov. 4, 1924: Coolidge Is Elected U.S. President; Oct. 29, 1929-1939: Great Depression; Sept. 8, 1930: Canada Enacts Depression-Era Relief Legislation; Dec. 11, 1930: Bank of United States Fails; Jan. 22, 1932: Reconstruction Finance Corporation Is Created; Aug. 23, 1935: Banking Act of 1935 Centralizes U.S. Monetary Control.

October 29, 1929-1939
GREAT DEPRESSION

The years of the Great Depression marked the worst period of poverty and hardship in the twentieth century, both in North America and abroad.

LOCALE: North America
CATEGORIES: Business and labor; economics; trade and commerce; manufacturing and industry

KEY FIGURES
Herbert Hoover (1874-1964), president of the United States, 1929-1933
Cordell Hull (1871-1955), U.S. congressman and senator from Tennessee, later U.S. secretary of state
Hugh S. Johnson (1882-1942), head of the National Recovery Administration
Frances Perkins (1880-1965), U.S. secretary of labor
Franklin D. Roosevelt (1882-1945), president of the United States, 1933-1945
Francis E. Townsend (1867-1960), California physician who led a movement to give a monthly pension to retired elderly persons
Walter W. Waters (1898-?), World War I veteran and head of the Bonus Army

SUMMARY OF EVENT
Beginning in the summer of 1929, the U.S. economy began a contraction that continued, with minor interruptions, until March of 1933 and from which the nation did not fully recover until 1939. The value of the nation's output of goods and services, or gross national product (GNP), fell from $104 billion in 1929 to $55 billion in 1933, causing a 30 percent decline in the quantity of output and interrupting for more than a decade the historical trend toward increase in per capita production. Industrial production declined 51 percent before reviving slightly in 1932.

Unemployment statistics poignantly revealed the impact of the Great Depression on Americans. In 1929, the Labor Department reported 1,499,000 jobless persons, or 3.1 percent of all employables. After the stock market crash, the figure soared. At its peak in 1933, unemployment stood at 12,634,000, more than 1 of every 4 people in the labor force. Some estimates placed unemployment as high as 16 million. By 1933, the annual national income had shrunk from $87.8 billion to $40.2 billion. Farmers, perhaps the hardest-hit economic group, saw their income decline from $11.9 billion to $5.3 billion.

The Depression resulted from a severe decline in ag-

gregate demand. One contributing factor was a massive wave of bank failures. As banks failed, the public withdrew large sums of currency, forcing the banks to call in loans and reducing the money supply. Decreased spending drove down prices and wages. Farmers, home buyers, and many business firms found the burden of their debts greatly increased, so bankruptcies and property foreclosures were widespread. The Depression was not limited to North America: It spread across the world, each country buying less from the others. In Germany, for example, the Depression struck sooner and went deeper than it did in the United States.

Political pressures to relieve distress and promote recovery were strong everywhere. For the first two years of the Depression, President Herbert Hoover relied on the voluntary cooperation of business and labor to maintain payrolls and production. In 1929, the government created the Federal Farm Board and gave it authority to make crop loans, which helped keep products off the market and thereby limit price declines. In 1930, Congress adopted the Hawley-Smoot Tariff Act, which drastically increased U.S. import restrictions, dragging other countries further into the deflationary process. As the crisis deepened, Hoover took positive steps to stop the spread of economic collapse. In 1932, the government established the Reconstruction Finance Corporation (RFC), a loan agency designed to aid distressed firms such as banks, insurance companies, and railroads. This approach to economic recovery was based on Hoover's belief that such government loans would halt deflation, ultimately restoring industry's ability to create jobs, increase the number of wage earners, and thereby increase consumption.

On the relief issue, the president and Congress fought a running battle for months. The Democrats wanted the federal government to assume responsibility for direct relief and to spend heavily on public works. Hoover was willing to see public works spending increase, but he insisted on a massive tax increase in 1932 to pay for it. He argued that unemployment relief was properly the province of local resources, not an appropriate federal activity:

> The proposals of our opponents will endanger or destroy our system. . . . I especially emphasize that promise to promote "employment for all surplus labor at all times." . . . At first I could not believe that anyone would

1929

be so cruel as to hold out a hope so absolutely impossible of realization. . . . And I protest against such frivolous promises being held out to a suffering people. If it were possible to give this employment to 10,000,000 people by the Government, it would cost upwards of $9,000,000,000 a year. . . . It would pull down the employment of those who are still at work by the high taxes and the demoralization of credit upon which their employment is dependent.

After a partisan fight, Hoover did, however, sign the Relief and Construction Act, which expanded the RFC's power to extend loans to states and for the creation of public works projects. Other bills passed in 1932 include the Glass-Steagall Act, which expanded credit to industry and business, and the Federal Home Loan Bank Act, which was designed to limit foreclosures by establishing a series of banks capitalized at $125 million to provide for home construction and long-term mortgages payable in installments.

Despite these efforts, by the end of Hoover's term, the nation's banking system had virtually collapsed, and the economic machinery of the nation was grinding to a halt. Tired and haggard, Hoover left office with a reputation as a do-nothing president, although he had gone far beyond his predecessors in supporting expanded federal responsibilities—even paving the way for the New Deal. His profound belief that promoting government jobs for the unemployed would break the backs of taxpayers, however, had not allowed him to do enough.

What happened to the economy after 1929 left most people baffled and bewildered. The physical structure of business was still intact, undamaged by war or natural disaster. People wanted to go to work, but plants stood dark and idle. Prolonged unemployment created a new class of superfluous people. The jobless sold apples on street corners. They queued up in breadlines and outside soup kitchens. Many lived in "Hoovervilles," shantytowns on the outskirts of large cities. Thousands of unemployed men and boys took to the road in search of work, and the

Unemployed people line up in subzero weather for a meal at a New York City relief kitchen in January, 1934. (AP/Wide World Photos)

Great Depression

gas station became a meeting place for men "on the bum." In 1932, a crowd of fifty men fought over a barrel of garbage outside the back door of a Chicago restaurant. In northern Alabama, poor families exchanged a dozen eggs, which they sorely needed, for a box of matches.

Despite such mass suffering, there was little violence or support for radical political movements. Farmers suffering from drastic price declines tried to reduce the flow of products to market. In August, 1932, for example, Iowa farmers began dumping milk bound for Sioux City. To dramatize their plight, Milo Reno, former president of the Iowa Farmers Union, organized a strike on the northern plains and cut off all agricultural products from urban markets until prices rose. Several farm states passed moratorium laws preventing the foreclosure of farms for debt. Drought aggravated the problems of farm families in the plains states, where the Dust Bowl made life so difficult that whole families packed up and left for the West Coast. Such "Okies" (named for the state where many originated) flooded into California to take jobs as migrant farm workers, as John Steinbeck vividly depicted in his 1939 novel *The Grapes of Wrath*.

In the summer of 1932, twenty-five thousand World War I veterans, known as the Bonus Army, led by former sergeant Walter W. Waters, staged an organized protest by marching on Washington, D.C., to demand immediate payment of a bonus that was not due until 1945. Congress refused, and Hoover sent troops to disperse the riot that ensued at Anacostia Flats, where the veterans were encamped.

Hoover was resoundingly defeated by Franklin D. Roosevelt in the presidential election of 1932, as the political pendulum swung strongly toward the Democratic Party. Roosevelt's New Deal drastically increased the economic role of the federal government. Roosevelt instituted several major policy innovations. For example, the dollar was devalued internationally when the price of gold was raised from $20.67 to $35 per ounce. This measure opened the way for a large flow of gold from Europe to the United States, raising bank reserves and increasing the money supply. In addition, a "bank holiday" in March, 1933, closed all banks for a few days, then reopened most of them under conditions that restored public confidence in the banking system. Federal insurance of bank deposits was established.

Roosevelt also instituted a series of relief programs that provided direct transfer payments to the needy. The system evolved from direct handouts under the Federal Emergency Relief Administration to work relief under the Civil Works Administration and the Works Progress Administration (WPA). On the business side, the National Recovery Administration (NRA) was established in 1933 under General Hugh S. Johnson. The NRA attempted to promote industrial recovery by encouraging firms in individual industries and trade groups to get together to formulate "codes of fair competition," which usually tended to reduce competition. For farmers, the Agricultural Adjustment Administration (AAA), also created in 1933, provided a system of production restrictions and price supports for agricultural products that became a permanent part of national policy. The Reciprocal Trade Agreements Act of 1934 enabled Secretary of State Cordell Hull to begin negotiations with other countries to agree on measures to liberalize international trade, beginning another permanent element of national policy. Finally, several measures promoted the establishment and power of labor unions, notably the National Labor Relations Act of 1935. Federal regulation of wages and hours began in 1938, with the Fair Labor Standards Act. Roosevelt appointed the first woman cabinet member in U.S. history when he chose Frances Perkins to head the Department of Labor.

Federal government intervention in the economy soared with these measures. For a time, this trend was resisted by the U.S. Supreme Court, which on May 27, 1935, rejected the AAA and the NRA as unconstitutional; the date of the ruling became known as Black Monday. However, after Roosevelt's landslide reelection in 1936, the Court ceased most of its opposition. The New Deal programs brought a rapid increase in government spending. Although tax rates were frequently increased, toleration of federal deficits became a normal financial policy.

In 1935, Francis E. Townsend, a California physician, popularized a proposal to help needy aged persons and stimulate economic recovery by having the government pay a pension of two hundred dollars per month to each person over sixty years of age who agreed to retire. In response, the government developed a comprehensive program of social insurance, adopted in August, 1935, as the Social Security Act. It included a program of unemployment compensation, a separate program of old-age pensions, and a third program of means-tested relief for needy aged, blind, and families with dependent children. With this, the U.S. welfare system of transfer payments came into existence.

SIGNIFICANCE

The Great Depression was a crisis of the American mind as much as it was an economic disaster. Many people be-

1929

ROOSEVELT REASSURES THE NATION

FDR was elected to an unprecedented four terms as U.S. president, serving during two of the nation's greatest crises, the Great Depression and World War II. In his first inaugural address, delivered on Saturday, March 4, 1933, he immediately addressed the first order of business: to bolster a people breaking under the burdens of the Depression:

I am certain that my fellow Americans expect that on my induction into the Presidency I will address them with a candor and a decision which the present situation of our Nation impels. This is preeminently the time to speak the truth, the whole truth, frankly and boldly. Nor need we shrink from honestly facing conditions in our country today. This great Nation will endure as it has endured, will revive and will prosper. So, first of all, let me assert my firm belief that the only thing we have to fear is fear itself—nameless, unreasoning, unjustified terror which paralyzes needed efforts to convert retreat into advance. In every dark hour of our national life a leadership of frankness and vigor has met with that understanding and support of the people themselves which is essential to victory. I am convinced that you will again give that support to leadership in these critical days.

In such a spirit on my part and on yours we face our common difficulties. They concern, thank God, only material things. Values have shrunken to fantastic levels; taxes have risen; our ability to pay has fallen; government of all kinds is faced by serious curtailment of income; the means of exchange are frozen in the currents of trade; the withered leaves of industrial enterprise lie on every side; farmers find no markets for their produce; the savings of many years in thousands of families are gone.

More important, a host of unemployed citizens face the grim problem of existence, and an equally great number toil with little return. Only a foolish optimist can deny the dark realities of the moment.

Yet our distress comes from no failure of substance. We are stricken by no plague of locusts. Compared with the perils which our forefathers conquered because they believed and were not afraid, we have still much to be thankful for. . . . The money changers have fled from their high seats in the temple of our civilization. We may now restore that temple to the ancient truths. The measure of the restoration lies in the extent to which we apply social values more noble than mere monetary profit. . . . Restoration calls, however, not for changes in ethics alone. This Nation asks for action, and action now.

Our greatest primary task is to put people to work. . . .

Hand in hand with this we must frankly recognize the overbalance of population in our industrial centers and, by engaging on a national scale in a redistribution, endeavor to provide a better use of the land. . . .

Finally, in our progress toward a resumption of work we require two safeguards against a return of the evils of the old order; there must be a strict supervision of all banking and credits and investments; there must be an end to speculation with other people's money, and there must be provision for an adequate but sound currency.

There are the lines of attack. I shall presently urge upon a new Congress in special session detailed measures for their fulfillment, and I shall seek the immediate assistance of the several States. . . .

If I read the temper of our people correctly, we now realize as we have never realized before our interdependence on each other; that we can not merely take but we must give as well; that if we are to go forward, we must move as a trained and loyal army willing to sacrifice for the good of a common discipline, because without such discipline no progress is made, no leadership becomes effective. We are, I know, ready and willing to submit our lives and property to such discipline, because it makes possible a leadership which aims at a larger good. This I propose to offer, pledging that the larger purposes will bind upon us all as a sacred obligation with a unity of duty hitherto evoked only in time of armed strife.

With this pledge taken, I assume unhesitatingly the leadership of this great army of our people dedicated to a disciplined attack upon our common problems. . . .

We do not distrust the future of essential democracy. The people of the United States have not failed. In their need they have registered a mandate that they want direct, vigorous action. They have asked for discipline and direction under leadership. They have made me the present instrument of their wishes. In the spirit of the gift I take it.

In this dedication of a Nation we humbly ask the blessing of God. May He protect each and every one of us. May He guide me in the days to come.

---

lieved that the country had reached all its frontiers and faced a future of limited opportunity. A slowdown in rates of marriages and births expressed this pessimism. The Depression smashed the old verities of the value of rugged individualism, the sanctity of business, and the American preference for limited government. Utopian movements found eager followings. In addition to Townsend's call for an old-age pension system, Father Charles Coughlin, a priest and radio personality in Royal Oak, Michigan, advocated the nationalization of banks, utilities, and natural resources. Senator Huey Long of Louisiana led a movement advocating a redistribution of wealth. All these movements tapped a broad vein of discontent among those who felt that they had been left out of the New Deal.

Slowly, however, Americans regained their sense of optimism. The New Deal revived the old faith that the nation could meet any challenge and control its own destiny. Even many intellectuals who had debunked American life in the 1920's began to revise their opinions. By 1936, there were signs of recovery, and by 1937, business indexes were up, some near 1929 levels. The New Deal had eased much of the acute distress, although unemployment remained at around 7.5 million. Although in 1938 the economy again went into a sharp recession, conditions improved by mid-1938. Still, the Depression did not end until the government launched the massive defense spending prompted by World War II.

—Donald Holley and Paul B. Trescott

FURTHER READING

Allen, Frederick Lewis. *Since Yesterday: The Nineteen-Thirties in America, September 3, 1929-September 3, 1939.* 1940. Reprint. New York: Harper Perennial, 1986. Classic social history provides a vivid picture of Americans' lives in the 1930's.

Bernstein, Irving. *The Lean Years: A History of the American Worker, 1920-1933.* Baltimore: Penguin Books, 1966.

_____. *Turbulent Years: A History of the American Worker, 1933-1941.* Boston: Houghton Mifflin, 1970. These two volumes provide readable and dramatic accounts of employment conditions and the transformation of the labor union movement during the Depression.

Chandler, Lester V. *America's Greatest Depression, 1929-1941.* New York: Harper & Row, 1970. A professional economist explains the quantitative dimensions of the Depression.

Journal of Economic Perspectives 7, no. 2 (Spring, 1993). Symposium on the Great Depression presents articles by four economic historians. Each includes analysis and bibliography.

Kyvig, David E. *Daily Life in the United States, 1920-1940: How Americans Lived During the Roaring Twenties and the Great Depression.* Chicago: Ivan R. Dee, 2004. Shows how the day-to-day experiences of average Americans changed from the 1920's through the decade of the Depression. Includes photographs.

Mitchell, Broadus. *Depression Decade: From New Era Through New Deal, 1929-1941.* 1947. Reprint. Armonk, N.Y.: M. E. Sharpe, 1989. Economic history blends data with description of the human dimension of the events of the Depression.

Shannon, David A., ed. *The Great Depression.* 1960. Reprint. Lexington, Mass.: Peter Smith, 1980. Collection of descriptive materials about the impact of the Depression reprinted from newspaper and magazine accounts of the time.

Watkins, T. H. *The Hungry Years: A Narrative History of the Great Depression in America.* New York: Henry Holt, 1999. Draws on oral histories as well as memoirs and other documents of the time to present a picture of the lives of Americans during the Depression. Includes index.

SEE ALSO: Oct. 24-29, 1929: U.S. Stock Market Crashes; Early 1930's: Mass Deportations of Mexicans; 1930's: Guthrie's Populist Songs Reflect the Depression-Era United States; Sept. 8, 1930: Canada Enacts Depression-Era Relief Legislation; Dec. 11, 1930: Bank of United States Fails; Jan. 22, 1932: Reconstruction Finance Corporation Is Created; July 21-Aug. 21, 1932: Ottawa Agreements; Aug. 1, 1932: Canada's First Major Socialist Movement; Nov. 8, 1932: Franklin D. Roosevelt Is Elected U.S. President.

1929

November 8, 1929

NEW YORK'S MUSEUM OF MODERN ART OPENS TO THE PUBLIC

The scholarship and passion of Alfred H. Barr, Jr., backed by Rockefeller money and prestige, put previously despised radical art at the center of American culture.

LOCALE: New York, New York
CATEGORIES: Arts; organizations and institutions

KEY FIGURES

Alfred H. Barr, Jr. (1902-1981), American art historian
Abby Aldrich Rockefeller (1874-1948), American heiress, philanthropist, and art collector
Conger Goodyear (1877-1964), American industrialist and art collector
Paul Sachs (1878-1965), American professor of art history

SUMMARY OF EVENT

Americans were first exposed to radical art, from post-Impressionism to cubism to expressionism, at the famous independent exhibition held in New York's Sixty-ninth Street Armory in 1913 (known as the Armory Show). Only a few independent collectors appreciated the new styles, however, and American artists who adopted them had next to no support. In the 1920's, American museums and the American rich collected European old-master art as a counterweight of "culture" to the disturbing forces that were transforming American society. European art after Impressionism was almost impossible to find in the United States, and only a few zealots collected the most innovative work being done in Europe. Even Vincent van Gogh and Pablo Picasso were dismissed as frauds or madmen.

The idea for the Museum of Modern Art (MOMA) came from three women who collected post-Impressionist art and who wished to spread appreciation for it in the United States. Abby Aldrich Rockefeller, the wife of John D. Rockefeller, Jr., was concerned that American interest in art after 1880 was entirely private and that her children's generation would have no chance to experience an art appropriate to their own time. Lizzie P. Bliss, heiress to a textile fortune, had been guided to modern art by Arthur B. Davies, one of the organizers of the Armory Show. Mary Sullivan was a former design teacher and a collector of work by such avant-garde figurative artists as Picasso, van Gogh, Paul Cézanne, and Georges Braque. The women knew that in Europe, such state-run museums as the Tate Gallery in London and the Luxem-

bourg in Paris showed advanced art of the recent past and the present, from which the best works might be chosen for official government collections. The position of modern art in the United States, they believed, would be much more secure if an American museum existed to give modern art the imprimatur of accepted taste.

Rockefeller, Bliss, and Sullivan began to discuss backing a museum devoted to such art in the winter of 1928-1929. They would lend the museum art until its director could set a firm course and begin a collection. In May, 1929, they asked wealthy industrialist and art collector Conger Goodyear to chair a committee to establish the museum. Goodyear had recently been forced out of the presidency of the Albright Gallery in Buffalo because he had spent five thousand dollars of the museum's money on a painting by Picasso. He quickly assembled a panel of art patrons and historians. In June, on the advice of committee member Paul Sachs, a professor of art history at Harvard University, the backers approached Sachs's former Harvard student Alfred H. Barr, Jr., to direct the museum.

Barr was the most brilliant and impassioned of the museum professionals whom Sachs steered toward modern art. The son of a Presbyterian minister, Barr studied art history at Princeton University and Harvard University. He was one of the first American historians to visit the Bauhaus in Germany and the Soviet Union's art academies. Believing in a liberal, forward-looking idea of historical evolution, he was convinced that the greatest radical art of his day was as inevitable an expression of the modern world as the Gothic cathedral had been of the Middle Ages.

Sachs made Barr view modernism in the art historian's usual terms of value: connoisseurship, the description of how particular artists made their works beautiful, and the evolutionary idea that styles were created along a time line of direct influences. This view put Barr in line with the conservative, art-appreciation outlook of Rockefeller and her friends. Barr, however, loved much more radical art than Sachs did and was willing to look for examples of the creative spirit outside painting (in architecture, product design, and films). He became convinced that his real mission was to make modernism popular among tomorrow's millionaire art buyers—the students Barr taught at Harvard and at Wellesley College. Only in that way could modernism get its full due as a cultural expression.

Barr's ambition of making modernism popular matched the hopes of Rockefeller, Bliss, and Sullivan that their own tastes could be shared with the public. Despite Barr's youth and scholarly unworldliness, Rockefeller accepted him as the new museum's director in July, 1929. His first exhibition for the museum, titled *Cézanne, Gauguin, Seurat, and van Gogh*, was made up of paintings loaned by the founders and other supporters. None of the shown work was abstract—indeed, all the artists had died before the emergence of cubism—and such works were already being collected by Francophiles in the American upper class. The works displayed, however, broke sharply with old-master definitions of art prevalent in the United States. Although conservative by Barr's standards, the display of works by "the founders of modern painting" would be a springboard from which he could launch shows of the more demanding art that followed them. The museum's exhibitions would serve as an education in the development of modernism.

When the Museum of Modern Art opened in rented space in a New York office building on November 8, 1929, it marked a milestone in respectability for avant-garde art. Forty-seven thousand people visited the exhibition during its month on display. Newspapers and art journals announced that the paintings shown had "converted" antimodernists by their beauty. The social exclusiveness of the museum's backers reassured viewers that a taste for the modern was an acceptable thing. Most important, the works of artists whose place in art history was beyond question but who had been kept from American audiences by museums' reactionary attitudes were finally presented to a starved public.

SIGNIFICANCE

Barr and Rockefeller's new museum quickly developed along the lines both had hoped. Barr went to Europe and convinced museums, collectors, and artists to lend to the institution. He mounted shows of increasing scope and artistic daringness, notably *Vincent van Gogh* (1935), *Cubism and Abstract Art* and *Fantastic Art, Dada, and Surrealism* (both 1936), and *Picasso: Forty Years of His Art* (1939). Lizzie Bliss's bequest of her collection and other trustee gifts in 1931 made possible Rockefeller's ambition to build a permanent public collection of the work she loved best. At the same time, Barr mounted shows devoted to, and began collections of, aspects of art in genres other than painting. These included modern architecture (1932), industrial design (1934), classic films (1935), and photography (1940). The museum moved into its own building in 1934 and acquired a new, radi-

cally modern headquarters on former Rockefeller property in 1939.

Barr intended his museum to be a teaching institution first and foremost. The erudite catalogs that accompanied his shows explained how the radical works on display had developed naturally from the art that had preceded them. Even a form as incomprehensible as abstraction had a pedigree, and its artists were as accountable to the connoisseur's taste as any old master. Such an approach reassured viewers without making the art itself any less revolutionary. Barr's personal charisma attracted young, well-placed academics and art lovers, including Philip Johnson, Edward Warburg, Dorothy Miller, and Beaumont Newhall, to the museum's staff. The publicity department's handling of exhibitions of van Gogh's paintings and of James McNeill Whistler's "Mother" added to the museum's reputation for shocking, brilliant innovation.

Because of the high social status of MOMA's backers, affiliation with the museum could be a strategy of social advancement. A taste for avant-garde art became fashionable in New York, and MOMA's shows of modern architecture and design changed the upper class's idea of what its homes were supposed to look like. Barr himself was instrumental in helping the radical German architects Walter Gropius and Ludwig Mies van der Rohe find teaching posts in the United States after Adolf Hitler came to power. By the 1940's, for MOMA's audience, radical style became what Barr believed modern art itself was: a sign of liberal (but not destructive) historical progress.

The museum's impact on artists themselves, and thus on the nature of art, was more ambiguous. American painters were offended that the first show had featured French art. Barr himself always tried to show American work, but he was constrained by the trustees' preferences and by his own feeling that the future lay with European abstraction. Barr's background in art history, which led him to judge art based on stylistic development and formal beauty, tended to discourage him from looking at art as a means of social change. The uproar that occurred when the museum showed politically radical murals in 1932 (some pillorying MOMA's own backers as capitalist oppressors) made it act more cautiously. Moreover, the institution could always be faulted for conservatism when it showed potentially subversive art, such as Soviet films or Bauhaus product designs, as works of beauty without regard to their social import.

The new audience for modernism created by MOMA led to new dealerships and galleries for avant-garde art, a

1929

development that exposed American painters to new inspiration and gave them more outlets for their works. The museum's importance in the art world, however, led to fears that MOMA, its backers, and the dealers were colluding to push certain styles on the art market. MOMA, after all, set itself up as the halfway house where modern art would be judged for its lasting merit and consequently its sale value. While doing so, MOMA was often dependent on the personal purchases of the trustees, who were building up the museum's small permanent collection. Accordingly, American artists of all stylistic persuasions distrusted the museum as much as they learned from it.

Alfred Barr's museum was transformed by the success he brought to it. By 1939, Barr had created a complex bureaucracy of scholars, publicists, and business administrators. His painstaking scholarship (which put him behind schedule and over budget) and roving interest in all the modern arts came to be seen as a hindrance to the museum's mission and stability, and, in 1943, Barr was removed as director of the institution. After an interim period, he was given the new, less powerful post of director of collections. Although his influence on MOMA's taste remained great, his idea of a free-ranging educational museum was slowed by institutional realities.

Although the Museum of Modern Art became a museum in the more conventional sense, conserving the aesthetic values of a particular institution, its example forced other museums to take contemporary art seriously. New York's Metropolitan Museum itself began buying newer art (some from MOMA's overstock) and eventually joined the bidding war for new talent that hit museums after World War II. The scholarship of Barr and his MOMA staff showed historians and curators how to write about radical art responsibly. The great role that museums came to play in the creation of art would not have been possible without the Museum of Modern Art.

—*M. David Samson*

FURTHER READING

Barr, Alfred. *Defining Modern Art*. Edited by Irving Sandler and Amy Newman. New York: Harry N. Abrams, 1978. A collection of Barr's catalog prefaces and other Museum of Modern Art publications. Together, these pieces make a laconic, somewhat repetitive argument for the historical inevitability and aesthetic merit of most branches of modern art. Includes chronology and index.

Bee, Harriet S., and Michelle Elligott, eds. *Art in Our Time: A Chronicle of the Museum of Modern Art*. New York: Museum of Modern Art, 2004. Presents his-torical photographs and documents, many of which have never been published before, to tell the story of the establishment of the museum and its growth since that time. Published on the occasion of the museum's seventy-fifth anniversary. Includes a chronology.

Chase, Mary Ellen. *Abby Aldrich Rockefeller*. New York: Macmillan, 1950. Biography of the woman who led the effort to create the Museum of Modern Art. Respectful and conventional treatment discusses the museum in the context of Rockefeller's philanthropy and love of art. Includes index.

Kantor, Sybil Gordon. *Alfred H. Barr, Jr.: The Intellectual Origins of the Museum of Modern Art*. Cambridge, Mass.: MIT Press, 2001. Combines biography with institutional history in examining Barr's career and his vision for the museum. Draws on interviews as well as Barr's personal correspondence.

Lynes, Russell. *Good Old Modern: An Intimate Portrait of the Museum of Modern Art*. New York: Atheneum, 1973. One of the best accounts of the museum up to 1970, solidly based on research and interviews. Emphasizes social status as an aspect of the museum's appeal. Discursive style makes timing of events somewhat hard to follow, but includes a chronology of museum exhibitions as well as an index.

Marquis, Alice Goldfarb. *Alfred H. Barr, Jr.: Missionary for the Modern*. Chicago: Contemporary Books, 1989. Accounts for Barr's devotion to modernism and traces his relations with museum backers and staff more fully than does Lynes's account (cited above), but otherwise follows Lynes's interpretation closely. Overworks the idea that Barr followed in his father's footsteps as a kind of preacher. Includes endnotes and index.

Meyer, Karl E. *The Art Museum: Power, Money, Ethics*. New York: William Morrow, 1979. Provides valuable background on the kinds of institutional pressures faced by MOMA in its maturing years, although dated as investigative reporting. Includes bibliography and index.

SEE ALSO: Sept., 1911: Der Blaue Reiter Abandons Representation in Art; 1912: Kandinsky Publishes His Theory of Abstract Art; Feb. 17-Mar. 15, 1913: Armory Show; Mar. 31, 1924: Formation of the Blue Four Advances Abstract Painting; Nov. 17, 1931: Whitney Museum of American Art Opens in New York; 1934: Soviet Union Bans Abstract Art; Feb. 12, 1935: Exhibition of American Abstract Painting Opens in New York; July 19-Nov. 30, 1937: Nazi Germany Hosts the *Degenerate Art Exhibition*.

November 19, 1929
SERENGETI GAME RESERVE IS CREATED

The Tanganyika government proclaimed part of the Serengeti Plains a game reserve to save one of Africa's finest wildlife herds from extinction. Twenty-two years later, the reserve would become a national park.

LOCALE: Serengeti Plains, Tanganyika (now in Tanzania)

CATEGORIES: Environmental issues; government and politics

KEY FIGURES

Donald Cameron (fl. early twentieth century), governor of Tanganyika, 1924-1931

Marcuswell Maxwell (fl. early twentieth century), British professional photographer

Edward F. Twining (fl. early twentieth century), governor of Tanganyika, 1949-1958

SUMMARY OF EVENT

The 1929 establishment by the government of Tanganyika (modern Tanzania) of a game reserve in the Serengeti Plains was the first important step in creating the world-famous wildlife sanctuary Serengeti National Park. This 5,600-square-mile park now in north-central Tanzania extends east from the shores of Lake Victoria. Within its borders there exists the greatest and most spectacular concentration of game animals found anywhere in the world. Most of the park comprises vast grassland plains that support huge herds of wildebeests, zebras, and gazelles. The Serengeti National Park is also renowned for its lion and leopard populations, as well as for its wealth of bird life.

Tanganyika officially came under British rule on July 22, 1922, when the League of Nations agreed that this territory in equatorial Africa, formerly known as German East Africa, would be administered by the British crown. In 1926, a critical period of Tanganyikan political development began, when Donald Cameron, the territorial governor, introduced the concept of "indirect rule." Under this system, the major internal and external affairs of the territory were controlled by the colonial administrative staff in conjunction with the British home government, and local administration was placed in the hands of traditional native rulers.

The Serengeti Plains covered a large area in the northeast of Tanganyika Territory adjoining the Kenya border. There were very few inhabitants, either African or European, but the plains abounded in game of many kinds, including zebras, wildebeests, gazelles, buffalos, impalas, and lions. Zoologists estimate that the plains support more than half a million large animals, the most remarkable concentration of big game in Africa or anywhere else on earth. Indeed, the biological productivity of the Serengeti's perennial grasslands is displayed in the seemingly infinite number and variety of wild animals that they support. Most of the Serengeti is grassy savanna, an open plain that provides the perfect niche for the great grazing herds, the stalking cats that prey on them, and the ravenous dogs and vultures that perform scavenging tasks. The plains are broken at places by rocky outcrops, acacia and savanna woodlands, forested rivers, and occasional swamps and lakes that add character to the landscape. In altitude, the Serengeti varies from three thousand to six thousand feet, which gives it a moderate subtropical climate despite its equatorial location.

The vegetation of the savanna, known as sward, is a palatable mixture of grasses and herbs, of which red oat grass predominates. The knee-high grass is the main food of the grazing herds, of which the most abundant are of wildebeests, zebras, hartebeests, and Thompson's gazelles. To reduce competition and increase the utilization of food resources, the grazing animals have evolved a sequential feeding strategy. Zebras eat the coarse top of the herb layer, wildebeests eat the leafy center, and gazelles eat the seeds and young shoots at ground level. Less numerous grazers and browsers include such species as topi, oribi, and warthog (which also roots in the ground for bulbs and tubers), African elephant, buffalo, Grant's gazelle, impala, steinbok, eland, giraffe, and black rhinoceros. All the major African predators are found on the Serengeti grasslands, as well as many of the smaller predators such as the serval, bat-eared fox, civet, and mongoose. It is not unusual for a visitor to the current Serengeti National Park to see forty or more lions in a single day. Many scavengers—chiefly hyena, jackal, and several species of vulture—are in constant attendance with the predators.

By the late 1920's, unchecked poaching by African gangs and indiscriminate shooting of animals from motorized vehicles threatened the big-game populations of the Serengeti. Parties in automobiles entered the plains, usually crossing the border from Kenya, and slaughtered the big game from their vehicles. This practice, although strictly forbidden by the existing game laws of Tanganyika, had continued because the territory had only a few

SERENGETI GAME RESERVE

= Serengeti Game Reserve

also strengthened the game laws by amendments intended to provide closer control over the use of motorized vehicles and rifles. The provisions included the confiscation of vehicles owned by those convicted of unauthorized shooting of game.

SIGNIFICANCE

The creation of the Serengeti Game Reserve began the process of ending poaching and the senseless killing of game in the Serengeti. The process would continue two decades later, under the leadership of Governor Edward Twining. The entire Serengeti Game Reserve was made a closed preserve in 1950, and in 1951, it was chartered as the first national park under the National Park Board of Tanganyika. Serengeti National Park was one of the first thirty national parks to be formed anywhere in the world, and it is the world's twelfth largest.

The park originally included the large areas surrounding Ngorongoro Crater, Olduvai Gorge, and the Salei Plains. In 1959, when Sir Richard Turnbull was governor, these three areas, which constituted approximately half of the original area of the park, were removed from the park despite the objections of prominent zoologists, who claimed that the areas encompassed essential migration routes of game herds. The eliminated areas were replaced by areas of nearly equal size on the Togoro Plains and the headwaters of the Duma River; these areas, however, were less important to animal migration.

In 1961, full internal self-government was granted to Tanganyika, and Julius Nyerere was selected as the first prime minister. In 1962, Tanganyika became a republic, with Nyerere as its president. Two years later, it united with Zanzibar to form the nation of Tanzania. During Nyerere's tenure in office, which continued after the unification, the trustees of the National Parks Board in 1966 established the Serengeti Research Institute at Seronera. The institute, formed to conserve wildlife, is considered the most advanced center for the study of ecology in Africa.

The park is the only place in Africa where visitors can see vast animal migrations. At the start of the dry season

game wardens. As a result of the indiscriminate killing of wildlife, in July, 1929, a game warden was sent by the Tanganyikan authorities to Serengeti specifically to protect the wild animals.

Worldwide pressure from conservationists and scientists, spurred by editorials and dramatic photographs in *The Times* of London, focused attention on this jeopardized resource. Numerous articles condemned the indiscriminate shooting of animals, and books of African big-game photographs were published by Marcuswell Maxwell. These publications testified to the worldwide interest in the preservation of the Serengeti's fauna. A common theme of the articles was that animals were so "tame" that parties in automobiles could approach lions, rhinoceroses, and antelope to within a few yards and that people intent on preservation rather than destruction could obtain remarkable photographs of wild animals in their natural state. In 1929, the Tanganyika Executive Council and Governor Cameron supported the formation of a game reserve in the central part of Serengeti Plains in what is now Serengeti National Park.

On November 19, 1929, the Tanganyika government created the Serengeti Game Reserve. The government

(May or early June), a mass migration of the park's wildlife takes place along a corridor leading west that follows the rivers that feed Lake Victoria. The migration, chiefly of zebra and wildebeest, is away from the herds' usual haunts on the central plains and into the corridor. The animals converge and then move westward, six to ten abreast, in winding columns several miles long. This movement has its following of carnivorous animals (lions, leopards, cheetahs, and hyenas) ready to dispose of stragglers and weaklings.

Serengeti National Park is perhaps the most famous game preserve in the world. The dedicated game wardens, park administrators, and wildlife scientists, through their antipoaching and antisettlement campaigns, have allowed the park to continue as one of the few natural sanctuaries for African wildlife. The management of this park has served as an inspiration and model for game reserves in other African countries. The Serengeti Research Institute has contributed greatly to knowledge of Africa's animals. The theme of studies at the institute is ecology, particularly the interactions of big game animals with their environment. Scientists have examined the veterinary problems affecting the coexistence of humans, wild animals, and domestic stock and the productivity of soils and vegetation over long periods of time. Host-parasite relationships between certain wild animals and the transmission of diseases have been determined. The creation of Serengeti National Park has thus contributed to general biological knowledge, in addition to preserving large numbers of wild animals for future generations.
— *Charles E. Herdendorf*

FURTHER READING

Austen, Ralph A. *Northwest Tanzania Under German and British Rule: Colonial Policy and Tribal Politics, 1889-1939*. New Haven, Conn.: Yale University Press, 1968. This readable monograph discusses the governorship of Sir Donald Cameron and the political climate of Tanganyika in the late 1920's that made the creation of a game reserve on the Serengeti Plains possible. Cameron's policy of "indirect rule," in which native institutions controlled local affairs, is explained.

Grzimek, Bernhard, and Michael Grzimek. *Serengeti Shall Not Die*. New York: E. P. Dutton, 1961. With magnificent illustrations and firsthand accounts that trace the migration of wild herds in the Serengeti, the authors provide a significant contribution to the knowledge surrounding big game in Africa. The controversy surrounding the coexistence of wildlife and Masai tribesmen is explored. Contains a census of big-game populations.

A topi, a type of antelope, leaps across a grassy plain watched by a hyena in a Kenyan game reserve on the Serengeti Plains. (AP/Wide World Photos)

1929

Hayes, Harold T. P. *The Last Place on Earth*. New York: Stein & Day, 1977. This book discusses the natural history of the Serengeti Plains in a readable, nontechnical narrative. The research contributions of Bernhard Grzimek are treated in a lively fashion.

Huxley, Julian, ed. *The Atlas of World Wildlife*. London: Portland House, 1988. Provides a comprehensive review of the world's animals from an ecological perspective. Contains a section on national parks and reserves, with location maps for more than seven hundred sites. The grassland of Serengeti National Park is given special attention.

Kurtz, Laura S. *Historical Dictionary of Tanzania*. London: Scarecrow Press, 1978. Documents the historical setting and the political climate in Tanganyika during the creation of the early game reserves in the 1920's and the establishment of national parks in the 1950's. This book's encyclopedic format and extensive bibliography make it particularly useful for historical and anthropological research.

Leakey, Louis S. B. *The Wild Realm: Animals of East Africa*. Washington, D.C.: National Geographic Society, 1969. Depicts the wild animals of Kenya, Tanzania, and Uganda with lucid text and startling color illustrations. Presents a table of average sizes and weights for all the animals in the book. The animals of the Serengeti National Park are prominently discussed and illustrated.

Linblad, Lisa, and Sven-Olof Linblad. *The Serengeti: Land of Endless Space*. New York: Rizzoli, 1989. This lavishly illustrated book carried on the early photographic work of Marcuswell Maxwell, whose work is now difficult to find in libraries. The large-size color photographs are excellent, but the descriptive text is limited.

Mari, Carlo, and Harvey Croze. *The Serengeti's Great Migration*. New York: Abbeville Press, 2000. Photographic essay on the migration of animals in the Serengeti, filled with stunning photographs of the creatures and their habitat. Includes a map of the region.

Martin, David. *Serengeti: Land, People, History*. Harare, Zimbabwe: African Publishing Group, 1997. Brief overview of the Serengeti region, including its human and nonhuman inhabitants and the environment they share. Bibliographic references and index.

Shetler, Jan Bender, ed. *Telling Our Own Stories: Local Histories from South Mara, Tanzania*. Boston: Brill, 2003. Oral histories of the Serengeti region collected from the area's traditional native African inhabitants. Bibliography and index.

Turner, Myles. *My Serengeti Years: The Memoirs of an African Game Warden*. New York: W. W. Norton, 1987. Traces the evolution of Serengeti National Park from a largely untouched and unexplored wilderness to Africa's finest wildlife sanctuary. Discusses the poaching problem that once threatened to destroy the animals the park was created to protect. Noteworthy researchers, scientists, filmmakers, and celebrities who have enhanced the reputation of the park are documented.

SEE ALSO: Mar. 14, 1903: First U.S. National Wildlife Refuge Is Established; Aug. 25, 1916: National Park Service Is Created; Feb. 26, 1917: Mount McKinley National Park Is Created; Feb. 1, 1919: Lenin Approves the First Soviet Nature Preserve; May 20, 1919: National Parks and Conservation Association Is Founded; June 3, 1924: Gila Wilderness Area Is Designated; May, 1927: Indiana Dunes Are Preserved as a State Park; May 30, 1930: Canadian National Parks Act; Feb. 4, 1936: Darling Founds the National Wildlife Federation.

Winter, 1929-1930
SCHMIDT INVENTS THE CORRECTOR FOR THE SCHMIDT CAMERA AND TELESCOPE

Bernhard Voldemar Schmidt extended both astronomy and astrophotography when he designed a special lens to correct a fundamental defect in images formed by spherical mirrors.

LOCALE: Bergedorf, Germany
CATEGORIES: Science and technology; astronomy; inventions

KEY FIGURES

Bernhard Voldemar Schmidt (1879-1935), Estonian optical instrument maker
Richard Schorr (1867-1951), German astronomer
Walter Baade (1893-1960), German-born American astronomer
Karl Schwarzschild (1873-1916), German astronomer and theoretical physicist

SUMMARY OF EVENT

The first telescope, invented by a Dutch spectacle maker in the early seventeenth century, was a simple combination of two lenses in a tube. Because this type of telescope employs refraction, in which light obliquely entering glass from air undergoes a change in direction, it is often termed a refractor. Although Galileo did not invent the telescope, he pioneered its astronomical use, discovering sunspots, craters on Earth's moon, the phases of Venus, and the four large moons of Jupiter, now called the Galilean moons in his honor.

Even today, many amateur astronomers use refractors; however, inescapable technical difficulties with such telescopes became evident as astronomy progressed. A lens, for example, can be supported only around its rim without obscuring the light path; therefore, large lenses may sag under their own weight and distort the image produced. Furthermore, a lens focuses red and blue lights at different places, a fault called chromatic aberration, causing colored rings around the images.

By 1897, when the Yerkes Observatory (the site of the world's largest refractor) was completed on the shores of Lake Geneva, Wisconsin, it was clear that the future of giant telescopes lay along a different path. This involved a completely new optical system called the reflector, in which the primary light gatherer is a mirror rather than a lens. In 1668, Sir Isaac Newton constructed the first working reflector: a concave mirror that was supported from behind and reflected all colors similarly, eliminat-

ing chromatic aberration. Although Newton's mirror was made from metal, subsequent telescope makers preferred to form the mirror from glass covered with a thin reflective layer of metal. Glass of high optical quality was not necessary, because light never entered it. In addition, lens makers needed to grind, or "figure," only one side of the glass, obviously saving time and cost over figuring the two sides of a lens of the same diameter.

Reflectors, on the other hand, are not without their own problems, and by the early twentieth century, one of the most troublesome of these problems was still unresolved: Would the optimum shape of the concave mirror be spherical or parabolic? A spherical one is easier to construct, but inherent in all such mirrors is a flaw called spherical aberration, in which light that does not strike the surface of the mirror along its axis of symmetry is not brought to an exact focus. Similarly, parabolic mirrors produce sharp images only for light entering from or nearly from the center of the telescope's field of view. The image formed by all other light suffers from "coma," in which fuzziness and cometlike tails appear. Stopping the aperture of either type of mirror to admit less light will sharpen the image but, unfortunately, prolongs photographic exposure times. In any case, the largest reflectors of the early twentieth century afforded a very narrow field of view, and a photographic survey of the entire sky with any of them would have required millions of separate pictures of small segments of the heavens.

The resolution to this impasse came from Bernhard Voldemar Schmidt, a highly skilled optical instrument maker. Born on the Estonian island of Naissaar in the Gulf of Finland, he was fascinated with scientific investigation in general and stars in particular. Despite the loss of much of his right arm to a boyhood experiment with gunpowder, Schmidt taught himself to grind lenses and mirrors. Hoping for better astronomical and astrophotographic equipment than he could afford, he wrote a letter in 1904 to Karl Schwarzschild, director of the Potsdam Astrophysical Observatory in Germany, offering to make a large mirror. Thus began ten years of successful cooperation in which Schmidt ground precise mirrors for Schwarzschild. The outbreak of World War I disrupted this collaboration; in addition, Schwarzschild's brilliant career was aborted in 1916 by his death from service in the war.

1929

In 1916, Schmidt contacted Richard Schorr, director of the Hamburg Observatory in Bergedorf. Even though Schorr was impressed with Schmidt's photographs, post-war financial constraints unfortunately prevented Schorr from hiring Schmidt. Depressed with the state of his career, Schmidt wrote in 1925, "I'm ready to turn my whole stock into junk and sell it for old iron and charcoal, and then take up something new." The following year, Schorr was at last able to offer Schmidt a position at the Hamburg Observatory. Schorr supplied the reclusive Schmidt with housing, unfettered use of a basement workshop, and a salary; for once, Schmidt enjoyed financial stability, access to the facilities of a large observatory, and steady encouragement. In this fertile environment grew the idea for what subsequent generations now call the Schmidt telescope and the Schmidt camera.

At Hamburg Observatory, Schmidt met Walter Baade, a staff astronomer who reached prominence at Mount Wilson Observatory and Palomar Observatory. In 1929, Schmidt confided to Baade that he was confident he could produce a telescope with both a wide field of view and a large aperture for increased light collecting. From the details he gave Baade at the time, Schmidt apparently had been pondering this approach for some time, but he characteristically left no documentation of the process whereby he had attained the breakthrough.

Schmidt's great contribution to optics was a marriage of lenses and mirrors, the prototype of catadioptric telescope designs, which include Schmidt-Cassegrain and Maksutov telescopes. In addition to a spherical mirror, Schmidt used a "corrector plate," a lens thickest in the center, not so thick near the edges, and thinnest in between. It succeeded at its primary purpose: to correct almost completely the mirror's spherical aberration by refracting the incoming light before it struck the mirror. (Strictly, the lens can exactly correct spherical aberration for only one wavelength of light.) The corrector also afforded several incidental benefits, one of which would be evident to anyone who has ever cleaned eyeglasses or contact lenses. Any optical surface open to the air will collect dust and require cleaning. Cleaning a large reflector, however, may jeopardize the thin metal coating on the mirror. By sealing the telescope tube, Schmidt's corrector plate extended vastly the operational lifetime of its associated mirror.

On the other hand, there were drawbacks to Schmidt's design. Although none has proved a serious obstacle to worldwide implementation of his idea, four might be mentioned. First, the corrector lens will introduce some small chromatic aberration (as the corrector plate is actu-

ally almost flat, this is relatively insignificant). Second, optical considerations dictate that a Schmidt telescope be longer than a comparable simple reflector. Third, the corrector plate is difficult to grind properly. Fourth, a photograph made by film inside a Schmidt telescope, thus functioning as a Schmidt camera, will be distorted unless the film itself is spherical.

With the encouragement of Baade and Schorr, Schmidt built the original Schmidt telescope in 1930; the Hamburg Observatory placed the first Schmidt camera in operation the following year. Revolutionary photographs quickly followed, but the skepticism of prospective customers, combined with international politicoeconomic considerations—including Adolf Hitler's rise to power—prevented Schmidt from selling even one Schmidt camera outside of Hamburg before his death in 1935.

SIGNIFICANCE

The Schmidt telescope, as historian of science Barbara Land has noted, "sees far and wide at the same time." Furthermore, it sees quickly. To appreciate why in each case, one must understand the concepts of angular size and f-number. The width of a fist at the end of an extended arm covers about 10 degrees of the observer's sky. In order to see faint objects, astronomers need large telescopes for their large light-gathering power. On the other hand, the field of view of the largest reflectors is minuscule. As Richard Learner has observed, the 100-inch (254-centimeter) Hooker telescope at the Mount Wilson Observatory would take at least fifty plates to photograph the full Moon, which is about half a degree across but "covers an area that is only a few millionths of the whole sky. A complete survey with such a telescope would take about 10,000 years." In contrast, the first Schmidt telescope had a field of view more than 15 degrees wide.

The focal length of a lens or mirror is the distance from the component to the point where incoming parallel light is focused. A stronger component thus has a smaller focal length. The f-number of a lens or mirror is its focal length divided by its diameter; the smaller the f-number, the shorter the time required for a given amount of light to be collected, as for a photograph. Schmidt's work can be viewed as inventing a succession of lower and lower f-numbers, culminating in f/1.75 for the 1931 Schmidt telescope. The Schmidt telescope is therefore well suited for either visual or photographic sky surveys, because it produces a wide and sensitive view of the sky with minimal distortion even out to the edges of the image or photograph.

During his life, Schmidt had jealously guarded details of the corrector plate and the curved film. In 1936, the year after Schmidt's death, Schorr revealed these details to the world. In only six years, more than twenty Schmidt telescopes with mirror diameters of more than 24 centimeters (about 9.5 inches) were produced. A mere three years after Schmidt's death, Baade and others persuaded the Rockefeller Foundation to fund an instrument that became known as the "Big Schmidt." Delayed by World War II, this telescope with a 72-inch (180-centimeter) mirror and a 48-inch (120-centimeter) corrector plate was put into operation in 1948 as an indispensable companion for the giant 200-inch (508-centimeter) Hale telescope located at the Palomar Observatory in Southern California. The Big Schmidt telescope remained in use through the early twenty-first century, operated robotically. In 1987, it was named the Samuel Oschin telescope.

With a field of view of more than three hundred times that of the Hale telescope, the Big Schmidt became the ultimate "spotter scope." Far more important, however, is its epochal survey of the northern two thirds of the sky during the 1950's, capturing objects down to one-half-millionth as bright as the dimmest naked-eye star. Each photographic plate covers an area approximately 6 degrees square and may show up to a million stars. Some two decades later, two Schmidt cameras (at the United Kingdom Siding Spring Observatory in Australia and the European Southern Observatory in Chile) cooperatively surveyed the southern third of the heavens.

Astronomical progress is ongoing, and better surveys are certain to be completed as technology improves. With these pioneering surveys, however, Schmidt cameras have already provided invaluable information in recording conditions at the time of the survey, furnishing an inventory of objects surveyed, and allowing better identification of previously observed objects.

—*Clyde J. Smith*

FURTHER READING

Asimov, Isaac. *Eyes on the Universe: A History of the Telescope*. Boston: Houghton Mifflin, 1975. Provides helpful informal background on observational astronomy, starting in prehistory. Briefly discusses Schmidt and his telescopes.

Capaccioli, Massimo, ed. *Astronomy with Schmidt-Type Telescopes*. Boston: D. Reidel, 1984. Presents the proceedings of a colloquium of the International Astronomical Union. Many contributions are highly technical, but interested readers will find this a useful overview of the diversity of applications of Schmidt's work by major-league astronomers.

King, Henry C. *The History of the Telescope*. 1955. Reprint. Mineola, N.Y.: Dover, 2003. Presents drawings, diagrams, and technical details on the mounting and optics of various kinds of telescopes. Includes photographs.

Land, Barbara. *The Telescope Makers: From Galileo to the Space Age*. New York: Thomas Y. Crowell, 1968. Simple and lucid account of the history of astrophotography up to Schmidt's time. Chapter 8 is devoted to Schmidt.

Miczaika, G. R., and William M. Sinton. *Tools of the Astronomer*. Cambridge, Mass.: Harvard University Press, 1961. Presents a moderately technical discussion of telescope optics. Serves as an excellent primer for most general readers.

Silverman, Milton. "The Eye That Exposes Secrets." *Saturday Evening Post* 222 (April 22, 1950): 28-29. Article on the Big Schmidt at the outset of its sky survey presents a delightful interview with Baade and tantalizing views of other applications of Schmidt's corrector plate. Highlights Schmidt's personality.

Wachmann, A. A. "From the Life of Bernhard Schmidt." *Sky and Telescope* 15 (November, 1955): 4-9. Excellent source of primary information on Schmidt and his work, written by a colleague of Schmidt on the occasion of the installation of a new Schmidt telescope at the Hamburg Observatory. Provides priceless glimpses of Schmidt in both prose and photographs.

Watson, Fred. *Stargazer: The Life and Times of the Telescope*. New York: Da Capo Press, 2005. History of the telescope's development includes discussion of the impacts on society of the discoveries the instrument has made possible. Presents the stories of the astronomers and other scientists responsible for advances in telescope technology, including Schmidt.

Zirker, J. B. *An Acre of Glass: A History and Forecast of the Telescope*. Baltimore: The Johns Hopkins University Press, 2005. Describes the building of telescopes in the past and present and speculates about how they will be built in the future. Includes glossary and index.

SEE ALSO: 1903-1904: Hale Establishes Mount Wilson Observatory; Nov., 1917: Hooker Telescope Is Installed on Mount Wilson.

1929

Early 1930's
MASS DEPORTATIONS OF MEXICANS

Massive unemployment in the United States during the Great Depression prompted the deportation of immigrant workers.

LOCALE: Los Angeles, California
CATEGORIES: Business and labor; economics; immigration, emigration, and relocation

KEY FIGURES
William N. Doak (1882-1933), U.S. secretary of labor, 1930-1933
Charles P. Visel (fl. 1930's), chairman of the Los Angeles Citizens Committee on Coordination of Unemployment Relief

SUMMARY OF EVENT
In the early decades of the twentieth century, immigration of Mexican nationals into the United States was a growing phenomenon. It was not viewed as a problem, however, because cheap labor was welcomed, particularly on farms and ranches. U.S. immigration laws generally were enforced selectively with regard to Mexicans. During World War I (1914-1918), at the request of U.S. businesses, the provisions of the Immigration Act of 1917 that required immigrants to pay an eight-dollar "head tax" and prove literacy were waived for Mexican laborers. This special departmental order legitimated U.S. dependence on cheap Mexican labor and institutionalized Mexico's special status.

At the end of World War I, the order was not rescinded; in fact, U.S. companies intensified their recruitment of Mexican farmworkers. Industrial companies in the Northeast and Midwest, such as steel mills and automobile manufacturers, also began recruiting Mexicans from the Southwest, resulting in an expanding migration in terms of both numbers of immigrants and their geographic spread. The Emergency Immigration Act of 1921 and the National Origins Act (Immigration Act of 1924) had each limited immigration from Europe, but no restrictions were imposed on the number of immigrants from countries in the Western Hemisphere. A large and growing population of Mexican immigrants was thus established in the United States in the first decades of the twentieth century.

In the 1920's, the U.S. government's attitude toward Mexican immigrants gradually changed from lax enforcement to severe restrictions. As social and economic conditions deteriorated on a global scale, the great pool of cheap Mexican labor was increasingly resented by unemployed U.S. citizens. Despite pressure from businesses, laws restricting entry—that is, the head tax and literacy test—began to be strictly enforced against Mexicans by immigration authorities. Two new laws also were passed that had a further chilling effect on Mexican immigration to the United States: the Deportation Act of March 4, 1929, which made entering the United States illegally a misdemeanor punishable by a year in prison or a fine of as much as one thousand dollars, followed by a May 4, 1929, law making it a felony for a deported alien to reenter the United States illegally. These laws, followed within months by the stock market crash that marked the onset of the Great Depression, set the stage for a period of repressive measures against Mexican nationals in the United States.

As the Depression caused more unemployment, the caseloads of social welfare agencies increased. By 1931, as the pool of unemployed immigrants requiring assistance grew, local agencies intensified their efforts to force repatriation; on the federal level, calls to deport immigrants increased also. President Herbert Hoover endorsed the aggressive efforts to expel aliens, restrict legal immigration, and curtail illegal entry. William N. Doak, who took office as Hoover's secretary of labor in December, 1930, proposed that any alien holding a job be deported. The Bureau of Immigration, at that time a part of the Department of Labor, began an aggressive campaign of rooting out illegal aliens, with the objective of reducing unemployment and thus hastening the end of the Great Depression. Many of the aliens deported under this program, however, were already unemployed.

SIGNIFICANCE
Although Mexicans were not specifically targeted by the immigration authorities, they were the group most affected numerically. The responses of the Mexican government to the problem varied. At times, land reform programs were established for repatriating Mexican citizens; at other times, Mexico feared the addition of more unemployed citizens to its labor surplus. Opportunities for Mexican Americans to obtain land in Mexico usually required money to be invested, although occasionally programs offered land to destitute repatriates.

In the southwestern U.S. states, particularly, immigration officials aggressively sought deportable Mexicans, and social service agencies encouraged Mexicans to volunteer for repatriation. The most ambitious of these programs was undertaken in Los Angeles County, California, but cities such as Chicago and Detroit, where Mexicans had been recruited by industry in the early 1920's, also were actively attempting to get even legal Mexican residents to leave in the 1930's.

The Los Angeles Citizens Committee on Coordination of Unemployment Relief, headed by Charles P. Visel, had been charged with assisting the unemployed residents of the city, especially through creation of jobs, for which longtime local residents would be given preference. Inspired by Labor Secretary Doak's earlier pronouncements that some four hundred thousand deportable aliens were believed to be in the country, Visel set out to identify and deport as many illegal aliens from the city of Los Angeles as possible. Visel contacted Doak and requested that a sufficient number of immigration agents be deployed in Los Angeles to create a hostile environment, from which he hoped aliens would flee voluntarily. Visel planned to open his campaign with press releases and a few well-publicized arrests.

Although the plan was not aimed specifically at Mexicans, some statements made by Visel did mention Mexicans as a group to be targeted. The Spanish-language newspapers in Southern California stirred up the Mexican community, both in Los Angeles and in Mexico, by publishing inaccurate stories that virtually all Mexicans were being targeted for deportation. In the first three weeks of February, 1931, immigration agents had investigated several thousand people, of whom only about two hundred were determined to be subject to deportation. Figures released by Visel's committee in March, 1931, indicated that 70 percent of the persons deported up to that time in the Los Angeles campaign were Mexicans. According to the Mexican Chamber of Commerce, which estimated that ten thousand of the more than two hundred thousand Mexicans thought to be living in Los Angeles prior to 1931 had left, many of the repatriates owned businesses and homes in Southern California. It should be noted, however, that the Chamber of Commerce would be more likely to have contact with the more prosperous members of the population than with the unemployed or laborers.

Concurrent with the federal and local campaigns to deport illegal aliens, Los Angeles County officials began attempting to repatriate destitute Mexicans. Many Mexican nationals had entered the United States at a time when penalties for illegal entry were nonexistent or seldom enforced against Mexicans, so their legal status was uncertain. Because it was unlikely that unemployed

Mexicans would find employment in the United States, welfare officials were beginning to put pressure on alien relief recipients to return to Mexico, at times leading them to believe that if they did not leave voluntarily, they would be cut off from aid immediately.

Frank Shaw, a member of the Los Angeles County Board of Supervisors, was the first area official to propose paying the cost of transporting families back to Mexico by train. Three hundred fifty Mexicans signed up for the first trip, in March, 1931. Many more trips were made, but statistics concerning repatriation under the county program are clouded by the fact that the same trains that carried county-aided Mexicans also carried deportees and Mexicans who had made their own arrangements to leave, and accurate records were not kept. Overall, the various efforts to reduce the number of immigrants in Southern California in the early 1930's caused a noticeable, but temporary, reduction of the Mexican population in the area.

Mexican immigration to the United States continued to be driven in subsequent decades by economic factors and employment trends. For instance, during World War II, when Texas and other southwestern states saw a reduction in the male workforce owing to enlistment in the armed forces, the bracero program was initiated to encourage Mexican immigration. When the soldiers came home after the war, the situation reversed. Throughout the twentieth century, as job realities shifted and changed, the United States relied on Mexican and other immigrant populations, whether legal or illegal in status, as a labor pool.

—Irene Struthers

FURTHER READING

Cardoso, Lawrence A. "The Great Depression: Emigration Halts and Repatriation Begins." In *Mexican Emigration to the United States, 1897-1931*. Tucson: University of Arizona Press, 1980. Brief discussion of federal deportation efforts and local repatriation efforts in the early 1930's. Includes the lyrics of *corridos* (ballads) written by returning Mexicans lamenting their plight.

Daniels, Roger. *Coming to America: A History of Immigration and Ethnicity in American Life*. 2d ed. New York: HarperCollins, 2002. Chapters 11 and 12 discuss immigration from Mexico before, during, and after the Depression. Includes tables, maps, and charts.

Ehrlich, Paul R., Loy Bilderback, and Anne H. Ehrlich. *The Golden Door: International Migration, Mexico, and the United States*. New York: Ballantine, 1978. Introductory chapters cover migration in general and

1930

European and Asian immigration into the United States. Remaining chapters cover Mexican immigration into the United States until the 1970's. Includes notes, list of recommended readings, and index.

Hoffman, Abraham. *Unwanted Americans in the Great Depression: Repatriation Pressures, 1929-1939.* Tucson: University of Arizona Press, 1974. Well-researched, comprehensive look at the deportation and repatriation of Mexicans, particularly from Los Angeles County, in the 1930's. Includes notes, extensive bibliography, and index.

Meier, Matt S., and Feliciano Ribera. *Mexican Americans and American Mexicans: From Conquistadors to Chicanos.* Rev. ed. New York: Farrar, Straus and Giroux, 1993. Comprehensive history of the Mexican presence in the United States includes discussion of deportation and repatriation in the 1930's. Features glossary, suggestions for further reading, and index.

Samora, Julian. *"Los Mojados": The Wetback Story.* Notre Dame, Ind.: University of Notre Dame Press, 1971. Discusses illegal immigration from Mexico in the twentieth century, including a chapter by an individual who attempted to enter the country illegally. Features bibliography and index.

Tichenor, Daniel J. *Dividing Lines: The Politics of Immigration Control in America.* Princeton, N.J.: Princeton University Press, 2002. Examines the history of immigration policy in the United States since the nation's founding, focusing on the factors that have influenced attitudes toward immigration and immigrants. Includes tables, figures, and index.

SEE ALSO: Feb. 5, 1917: Immigration Act of 1917; May 19, 1921: Emergency Quota Act; May 26, 1924: Immigration Act of 1924; May 28, 1924: U.S. Congress Establishes the Border Patrol.

1930's
AMERICANS EMBRACE RADIO ENTERTAINMENT

In the 1930's, radio broadcasts of music, comedy, drama, news, and sports came to pervade Americans' daily lives.

LOCALE: United States
CATEGORIES: Radio and television; entertainment

KEY FIGURES
Franklin D. Roosevelt (1882-1945), president of the United States, 1933-1945
Rudy Vallee (1901-1986), American singer
Fred Allen (1894-1956), American comic actor
George Burns (1896-1996), American comedian who teamed with his wife, Gracie Allen
Eddie Cantor (1892-1964), American comic actor
Bob Hope (1903-2003), American comedian and actor
Bing Crosby (1903-1977), American singer and actor

SUMMARY OF EVENT

The inauguration of radio networking and broadcasting after 1926 and the increasing sale of airtime for advertisements by the close of the 1920's further opened the door for the radio industry's exploration of entertainments capable of attracting and holding mass audiences. The remarkable profits earned from such efforts were a powerful underpinning to radio's phenomenally successful insertion of its messages, programs, and person-

alities into American life. Radio held sway as the reigning entertainment medium until the 1950's, when its regency was in some respects usurped by the dissemination and public embrace of television.

The "golden age" of radio was a result of outside events as much as it was a bonus from the scramble for profits. The onslaught of the Great Depression, the most massive peacetime crisis in American history, forced the leisure of tens of millions of ordinary folk, through economic necessity, back into the home. The manifestations of the Depression, including unemployment, debt, evaporating profits, a collapse of effective government, folk migrations, labor strife, and, by the late 1930's, the awareness of a distintegrating international order and impending war, created a popular hunger for morale boosting, optimism, diversion, escapism, and a sense of brotherhood and belonging. Confirmation of the extent to which radio met these wants and needs came in many ways. Social workers noted in the mid-1930's that needy families surrendered nearly all of their possessions when necessary but insisted on retaining their radios, and President Franklin D. Roosevelt, the first chief executive to use radio effectively, tried to encourage optimism and weld the nation together, beginning in March, 1933, with his series of broadcast "fireside chats."

The vastness of radio's potential audience was re-

The first U.S. president to understand the power of radio communication, Franklin D. Roosevelt won public support for his New Deal programs through a series of "fireside chats" broadcast over the radio networks. (FDR Library)

show could keep up. More serious, novel, and educational were the spontaneous interviews of notable personalities offered eventually by *The Mary Margaret McBride Show* on the Columbia Broadcasting System (CBS).

Early afternoons posed difficulties for network broadcasters, who aired a few soap operas during those hours. A number of what proved to be long-running "kids' shows" successfully blocked out late afternoons. WOR-New York's *Uncle Don*, one of the most beloved of these shows, featured original stories, personal announcements, words of caution and advice, and piano tunes and songs. Other shows that became household favorites were *The Singing Story Lady, Let's Pretend*, and, especially for school-age boys, *Jack Armstrong, All-American Boy*. For younger children, there were numerous "uncle and aunt" broadcasts such as WLS-Chicago's *Lullaby Twins*. Also important but hardly central to network broadcasting were educational shows such as conductor Walter Damrosch's *Music Appreciation Hour*, a precursor of Leonard Bernstein's later, similar, and justly famed television music series for children that reportedly reached millions of schoolchildren.

By the mid-1930's, the evening hours had become "prime time." Sponsors discovered the large potential audiences available during these hours and competed for these audiences with shows featuring constellations of stars, many of whom survived as household names into the television era. Radio's stellar personalities, who included Eddie Cantor, Fred Allen, Ed Wynn, Edgar Bergen (and Charlie McCarthy), Bing Crosby, George Burns and Gracie Allen, Jim and Marion Jordan (*Fibber McGee and Molly*), Will Rogers, Major Edward Bowes, Fanny Brice, Bob Hope, and Al Jolson, often accompanied by almost equally notable announcers and bandleaders, preempted Americans' prime leisure time with their own buoyant styles of music, wisecracks, nonsense, silliness, humor, and wit. Radio personalities became the intimates of nearly every family in the country, with popularity matching that of Hollywood's film stars.

Although serious drama played a modest role in the broadcast day and was almost nonexistent in prime time, a niche for it was carved out after the mid-1930's. Writers, poets, and dramatists such as Archibald Mac-

vealed by the reception of Freeman Fisher Gosden and Charles Correll's series *Amos 'n' Andy*, eventually a claimant to having been the most popular show ever presented by any of the media. Lesser, but still substantial, success attended broadcast of *The Rudy Vallee Show*. The program, hosted by crooner Vallee, established a format for variety shows and introduced dozens of vaudeville's greatest talents, including Eddie Cantor, Alice Faye, Milton Berle, Joe Penner, Bob Burns, and Bing Crosby, among others who were soon to host their own shows.

Programming hours were filled quickly. Morning broadcasts continued, as they had in the 1920's, with "wake-up" shows and home, health, and happiness presentations aimed primarily at female audiences. In rural areas, morning shows were sometimes augmented with livestock prices. Soap operas—so named because soap companies were early sponsors—appeared by 1932. Some of these had been "evening light" romances of the late 1920's, including *The Smith Family, The Rise of the Goldbergs*, and *True Story Hour*. To these were added *Ma Perkins, The Romance of Helen Trent*, and *Myrt and Marge*, all serials that aired for years and had audiences so caught up that some newspapers printed synopses of each day's adventures so that listeners forced to miss a

CALLS FOR SOCIALISM

During the 1930's, the radio was the Internet of its day, dominating the media and commanding the attention of Americans like nothing before. Its rise coincided with the years of the Great Depression, during Franklin D. Roosevelt's first administration, when he used it to deliver his reassuring "fireside chats." Radio also attracted charismatic (some thought dangerous) activists such as priest and radio personality Charles Coughlin. Speaking for those who felt left out of Roosevelt's New Deal, Father Coughlin advocated the nationalization of banks, utilities, and natural resources, listing his tenets in a broadcast on November 11, 1934:

1. I believe in liberty of conscience and liberty of education, not permitting the state to dictate either my worship to my God or my chosen avocation in life.
2. I believe that every citizen willing to work and capable of working shall receive a just, living, annual wage which will enable him both to maintain and educate his family according to the standards of American decency.
3. I believe in nationalizing those public resources which by their very nature are too important to be held in the control of private individuals.
4. I believe in private ownership of all other property.
5. I believe in upholding the right to private property but in controlling it for the public good.
6. I believe in the abolition of the privately owned Federal Reserve Banking system and in the establishment of a Government owned Central Bank.
7. I believe in rescuing from the hands of private owners the right to coin and regulate the value of money, which right must be restored to Congress, where it belongs.
8. I believe that one of the chief duties of this government owned Central Bank is to maintain the cost of living on an even keel, and arrange for the repayment of dollar debts with equal value dollars.
9. I believe in the cost of production plus a fair profit for the farmer.
10. I believe not only in the right of the laboring man to organize in unions but also in the duty of the Government, which that laboring man supports, to protect these organizations against the vested interests of wealth and of intellect.
11. I believe in the recall of all non-productive bonds and therefore in the alleviation of taxation.
12. I believe in the abolition of tax-exempt bonds.
13. I believe in broadening the base of taxation according to the principles of ownership and the capacity to pay.
14. I believe in the simplification of government and the further lifting of crushing taxation from the slender revenues of the laboring class.
15. I believe that, in the event of a war for the defense of our nation and its liberties, there shall be a conscription of wealth as well as a conscription of men.
16. I believe in preferring the sanctity of human rights to the sanctity of property rights; for the chief concern of government shall be for the poor because, as it is witnessed, the rich have ample means of their own to care for themselves.

Leish, Arthur Miller, Norman Rosten, Norman Corwin, Arch Obler, and Orson Welles, in company with notable actors such as John Houseman, Agnes Moorehead, Maurice Evans, John Barrymore, and Welles, created stirring dramas. Welles became famous for his terrifying adaptation of H. G. Wells's 1898 novel *The War of the Worlds* in 1938. Another niche was found for news, despite a dearth of sponsors and low ratings. News programs gained popularity after the mid-1930's, as dictatorial regimes in Europe and Asia dismantled the peace. American listeners wanted current news of these events. CBS's William S. Paley pioneered radio news, building a superior cadre of newsmen, among them Edward R. Murrow, William L. Shirer, David Schoenbrun, Richard Hottelet, and, a bit later, Charles Collingwood and Howard K. Smith. Several of them gained fame as news reporters in their own right.

SIGNIFICANCE

During the 1930's, radio network broadcasting dominated the leisure and preempted the daily attention of Americans as no other communications medium ever had. Its myriad sounds, music, and voices, heard in homes, factories, shops, and cars, became an integral part of the daily environment. Franklin D. Roosevelt, along with lesser politicians, embraced radio as a prime instrument of communication. New York's mayor, Fiorello Henry La Guardia, read the newspaper comics pages to his constituents over the radio; demagogues such as Huey Long and Father Charles Coughlin used radio's power to broadcast their values. Leaders in all types of fields, including the arts, politics, education, and religion, were dazzled by radio's possibilities and dismayed by the purported abuses of the medium.

The pervasive influences of radio on daily life during the 1930's were measurable in a narrow sense; audience samplings produced estimates of programs' comparative popularity. The radio industry's influence on the business world could be measured by profits, which were almost invariably high. The losses that occurred usually were on a relatively small scale, pertaining to specific sponsorships, shows, or stations.

Radio's more massive and profound influences, although certain, remain less precisely calculable. One of these, ephemeral as it may have been, was radio's provision of solace, diversion, escape, and the perceived companionship of a vast audible support group to those who were the actual or prospective economic casualties of the Great Depression. Radio thus helped keep a healthy edge on national morale and made valuable contributions to a sense of national unity, a fact on which political, business, and military leaders were able to capitalize. Leaders from all fields, but particularly politicians, quickly discovered that radio had the dual capacity to exalt and enhance them, as it did with Roosevelt and Winston Churchill, or to leave the public disenchanted, as it did with the twangings of President Calvin Coolidge and the nervous deliveries of President Herbert Hoover.

For more ordinary folk, the medium, by virtue of announcers and performers whose American English was soon divested of regionalisms and dialects, set new standards of clarity for speech, a judgment already being made by educators by the mid-1930's. Coast-to-coast broadcasting, while doing little to banish dialects within their home territories, further eroded the country's historic localism and sectionalism, something that the automobile and films were also accomplishing along other lines. Americans were becoming aware of wider worlds through their exposure to film and radio, and they could more readily travel to those worlds with automobiles. Radio reinforced the power of the spoken word. It likewise introduced a measure of intimacy unmatched by any other medium either in its availability or in its pervasiveness. Radio invited performers directly into listeners' homes and lives, and radio listeners worldwide learned to be entertained by outsiders on a daily basis rather than finding pastimes that were more active and in their own communities.

Radio helped create a unified national culture in the United States. This was particularly true for music. Radio could introduce new music and songs to the nation as a whole. Jazz and "race music" became available to the general public in the 1930's through radio. Presentations of jazz musicians, most of them black, as well as the songs of black singers, such as the legendary Bessie Smith, were still confined largely to nightclubs in large cities and to controlled recordings and sales by record companies. Radio, far more than the more timid motion

picture industry, changed that, making jazz respectable and giving it a wider audience. The same effect occurred with transmission of traditional country music. Because of the immediacy of radio, with programming decisions made on a daily basis, innovations could be disseminated far more swiftly and flexibly than in other media. Although radio created a national culture, it also allowed cultural elements to spread more quickly from local roots.

Before the close of the 1930's, radio broadcasting had become one of the most formidable informal educational forces in American life. The uniquely intimate medium of broadcast radio influenced American speech, manners, forms of humor, and opinions on virtually every topic. The accessibility of educational programs, popular culture, discussions of personal problems, and, increasingly by the end of the decade, floods of hard information on an unprecedented scale about the state of the country and the world helped move Americans into a more urbane, cosmopolitan, and sophisticated state. Radio programming continued its strong influence on American culture throughout the 1940's before beginning to wane with the advent of television.

—Clifton K. Yearley

FURTHER READING

Barnouw, Erik. *The Golden Web: 1933 to 1953*. Vol. 2 in *A History of Broadcasting in the United States*. New York: Oxford University Press, 1968. Part of one of the most comprehensive and authoritative scholarly histories of American broadcasting; clearly written, spare, and fascinating. Covers network battles as well as shows and radio personalities. Includes photographs, bibliography, and index.

Buxton, Frank, and Bill Owen. *Radio's Golden Age: The Programs and the Personalities*. Ansonia Station, N.Y.: Easton Valley Press, 1966. Presents many anecdotes about radio shows and personalities and provides glimpses of the early transitions of vaudevillians to radio. Includes photographs.

Douglas, George H. *The Early Days of Radio Broadcasting*. 1987. Reprint. Jefferson, N.C.: McFarland, 2001. Provides excellent coverage of the start of networking and the rise of announcers, news, and sportscasting. An admiring and sympathetic although not uncritical view of the subjects. Includes photographs, bibliography, and index.

Douglas, Susan J. *Listening In: Radio and the American Imagination*. New York: Crown, 1999. Focuses on the effects of radio listening on Americans' social, political, and economic attitudes and beliefs. Covers the

1930

period from radio's golden age in the 1930's to the end of the twentieth century.

Ely, Melvin Patrick. *The Adventures of Amos 'n' Andy: A Social History of an American Phenomenon.* 10th anniversary ed. New York: Free Press, 2001. Scholarly, readable detailed account of the radio show that was at one time the nation's most popular. Discusses the program's racial content and impact. Includes many photographs, bibliographical essay, and index.

Harmon, Jim. *The Great Radio Comedians.* Garden City, N.Y.: Doubleday, 1970. Insider's view of 1930's comedians provides interesting insights and anecdotes. Includes photographs and index.

Sterling, Christopher H., and John Michael Kittross. *Stay Tuned: A History of American Broadcasting.* 3d ed. Mahwah, N.J.: Lawrence Erlbaum, 2001. The standard one-volume history of radio and television in the United States. A good beginning point.

Wertheim, Arthur Frank. *Radio Comedy.* New York: Oxford University Press, 1979. Authoritative work, written with obvious joy, provides excellent coverage of radio's "golden age." Chapters on the war years and on radio comics' sometimes sad transition to television are particularly interesting. Includes many photographs and index.

SEE ALSO: 1920's: Radio Develops as a Mass Broadcast Medium; Aug. 20-Nov. 2, 1920: Radio Broadcasting Begins; Nov. 28, 1925: WSM Launches *The Grand Ole Opry*; Sept. 9, 1926: National Broadcasting Company Is Founded; Jan. 1, 1927: British Broadcasting Corporation Is Chartered; Mar. 19, 1928: *Amos 'n' Andy* Radio Show Goes on the Air; Dec. 1, 1934: Goodman Begins His *Let's Dance* Broadcasts; Oct. 30, 1938: Welles Broadcasts *The War of the Worlds*.

1930's
GUTHRIE'S POPULIST SONGS REFLECT THE DEPRESSION-ERA UNITED STATES

An authentic frontier balladeer, Woody Guthrie expanded the appeal of traditional American folk music by writing protest songs about poverty and social injustice. He inspired generations of politically informed folk and rock musicians, including the Weavers, Joan Baez, Bob Dylan, Bruce Springsteen, and U2.

LOCALE: United States
CATEGORIES: Music; social issues and reform

KEY FIGURES
Woody Guthrie (1912-1967), American folksinger, songwriter, and poet of social protest
Alan Lomax (1915-2002), American folklorist and recorder for the Library of Congress
Leadbelly (Huddie Ledbetter; 1885?-1949), American folk and blues muscian
Pete Seeger (b. 1919), American folk and protest singer and composer

SUMMARY OF EVENT
Before the Great Depression, the diverse regions composing the American South lagged far behind the rest of the United States in nearly every regard. From the close of the Civil War through Reconstruction and into the

1950's, the South remained distinctively and overwhelmingly rural. Its economy was tied to a few staples, principally cotton, tobacco, corn, and sugar beets. Farms tended to be small and tenant run; worse, they were enmeshed in the perpetual indebtedness characterizing the sharecrop and crop-lien systems. Labor was cheap and drew subsistence wages. Unions were considered anathema. Internal racial relations steadily, if legally, deteriorated after the close of the nineteenth century, and southerners remained under the dominance of a conservative Democratic Party.

The South's generally decrepit educational institutions were only one manifestation of the region's backward social structure. President Franklin D. Roosevelt's declaration that one-third of Americans in the 1930's were ill clad, ill housed, and ill fed perfectly described the American South—which, Roosevelt added, constituted the nation's number-one economic problem. Such was the cultural plight of Okemah, Oklahoma, where Woodrow Wilson "Woody" Guthrie was born, and of Pampa, Texas, where he was reared.

Guthrie's upbringing, like his region, was sad. His mother steadily declined under the inroads of Huntington's chorea, an incurable, inherited degenerative disease that would eventually claim Woody and other members of his family as well. His father, although at times on the make as a small-town political worthy, seldom managed to match his luck and competencies with his dreams. It appears likely that Woody's mother set fire to and killed Woody's sister and later attempted the same thing with her husband. The family lived poorly, at times being thrown individually or collectively on the sufferance of relatives. Woody wandered away from all of them as soon as he could.

A small, wiry man with fine features and a distinguishing mop of unruly hair, Guthrie was humorous, optimistic, gregarious, generous, infectiously engaging, and immensely talented. He was an omnivorous reader with wide-ranging interests. He was also a self-taught cartoonist, versifier, poet, cornball humorist, and explosively undisciplined writer. He had an amazingly eclectic bent, heedlessly putting his own words to tunes written by others, notably those of famed hymnists and of the great Virginia folksinging Carter Family. Unlike his later friends Huddie "Leadbelly" Ledbetter and the musically well-trained Pete Seeger, Guthrie was a mediocre guitarist. His nasal voice was untrained except by experience. Although he married three times and had many children, he was lovingly lazy, feckless, adulterous, frequently drunken, and an irresponsible family man. He was the quintessential free spirit—the "ramblin' man" of song and story.

From his early days in Pampa, Guthrie's real family was made up of the marginally employed and the dispossessed: oil-field roughnecks and roustabouts, Okies—southwestern farmers of the nation's Dust Bowl who were evicted from their lands and who migrated to California by the tens of thousands—railroad tramps, hoboes, dockers, seamen, the remaining Wobblies (members of the Industrial Workers of the World), "Reds," migratory workers, and unskilled laborers. It was for audiences of these people that Guthrie began singing and songwriting with hillbilly bands in Texas and thereafter on radio and in public appearances from Los Angeles to New York City. He sought to give the beleaguered masses relief and to shore up their dignity and sense of purpose. It was through their appreciation of him that he persistently sought a place in the public domain, using his untrained but authentic folk voice to carry his populist messages.

Guthrie first gained prominence with his "old-time hill-country songs" on the Los Angeles radio station KFVD in 1936 before an audience largely composed of Dust Bowl migrants. He augmented his reputation when he moved to New York City—in the 1930's the nation's radical capital—joining union, Communist, and Popular Front political causes and accepting welcome as a folk hero. There, in 1940, he began writing his Columbia River and Grand Coulee Dam songs—"Roll on Columbia," "Pastures of Plenty," "Jack Hammer John," "Hard Traveling," and, in a different context, "So Long, It's Been Good to Know You," "Those Oklahoma Hills," and "This Land Is Your Land." Typically, Guthrie attempted to use his music as a vehicle in the class struggle. While Guthrie was in New York, Pete Seeger persuaded him to join the Almanac Singers, whose political purposes appeared identical to Guthrie's and with whom he wrote and sang many more songs.

Thanks to the genius of folklorist Alan Lomax (later a close friend), Guthrie was interviewed and recorded for the Library of Congress on March 21, 22, and 27, 1940.

Woody Guthrie in 1943. (Library of Congress)

In the recordings, he presented his landmark protest songs, among them "Tom Joad," "Dust Can't Kill Me," "I Ain't Got No Home," "Talking Dust Bowl Blues," "Do Re Mi," "Blowin' Down This Road," and "Dust Pneumonia Blues." In the meantime, he continued writing and singing union songs at picket lines, rallies, and fund-raisers. His compositions included prolabor songs such as "Union Maid" and others equally political in nature such as "Pretty Boy Floyd" and "Plane Wreck at Los Gatos (Deportee)."

Guthrie, fully at home with the American proletariat and already a folk hero by the close of the 1930's, believed that the oppressed, individually and collectively, had both the right and the responsibility to sing their protests in the face of injustice. Unlike some intellectuals and academicians of his day, he was a populist by tradition and a communist of a sort by experience. He was a utopian, largely uninterested in accumulating money and even less interested in power or political position for himself. Rather, Guthrie used his heartfelt folk renditions to ensure himself a place in the public memory. It was fame that he sought—and managed to achieve.

SIGNIFICANCE

Philosophically, Guthrie identified the spirit and content of his songs and writings with those of Robert Burns, Walt Whitman, and Alexander Pushkin (just as he identified his politics with those of Jesus, Abraham Lincoln, Andrew Jackson, and Karl Marx), all of whom spread their messages by speaking, writing, and rhyming in the vernacular. The immediate tradition on which Guthrie drew, however—the tradition that he would elaborate and help to expand—was nourished by his southern environment. Protest songs were commonplace in the repertoires of southern blues and country (or "hillbilly") singers, as well as among some of the region's gospel singers, by the 1920's.

Union organizing efforts among southern laborers and tenant farmers, successions of strikes in the Piedmont textile towns, and lockouts, strikes, and open warfare between capital and labor in the eastern Kentucky and Cumberland coalfields from the late 1920's through the mid-1930's yielded substantial crops of revolutionary lyrics. These were partly inspired and augmented by the Communist-led National Miners' Union, National Textile Workers' Union, and Southern Tenant Farmers' Union, but they also grew from the almost endless erosions of hard times. Songs written by a young Gastonia, North Carolina, mother and textile worker, Ella May Wiggins, who was murdered in 1929 by antiunion thugs,

not only lifted the morale of her fellow workers but also advertised their cause. Similarly, in Kentucky's coal mining Harlan County, Florence Reece's "Which Side Are You On?" aimed at brutal company-paid deputy sheriffs and became one of labor's most beloved ballads. Elsewhere in Kentucky, similar anticapitalist balladeers sprang forth, including Aunt Molly Jackson ("I Am a Union Woman"), Sara Ogan ("I Hate the Capitalist System"), and Jim Garland ("I Don't Want Your Millions Mister"). Scores of other southern protest singers and their songs have been described by such folklorist-historians as R. Serge Denisoff, John Greenway, Archie Green, and Lawrence Gellert.

Guthrie's reputation and influence surmounted them all by the close of the 1930's. Ironically, too, like his fellow southern protesters, his songs and character became as well known in northern liberal circles as they were generally throughout the South. In New York, particularly, Guthrie became a rallying point for other expatriate southern musicians such as Lee Hays, Sonny Terry, Josh White, Brownie McGhee, Aunt Molly Jackson, Sis Cunningham, and the inimitable Leadbelly; many of these performers sang or appeared with the Almanac Singers or with Seeger's legendary folk band, the Weavers. Within a national context, however, even in the 1930's, Guthrie and his fellow protest singers enjoyed only limited visibility, and the significance of their music went largely unnoticed.

Even so, Guthrie's songs and social messages directly influenced many country singers and songwriters in the 1930's and 1940's, and many of these musicians won national celebrity during the protests of civil rights advocates, college and university students, feminists, and peace activists during the late 1950's and the 1960's. Among the most prominent was Seeger, a responsible, cultivated, musically trained, and disciplined Harvard University dropout who not only worked closely with Guthrie—and regarded him as a mentor—but also continued Guthrie's commitment to folk protest songs as weapons against social injustice. With the commercialization of folk music in the late 1950's and the 1960's, the Guthrie cult that Seeger stimulated placed Seeger himself in the forefront of the urban folk music revival. Other Guthrie disciples who gained prominence just before and immediately after Guthrie's death were his devoted imitator Ramblin' Jack Elliot and Guthrie's dear friend Cisco Houston.

Guthrie's work began to receive renewed attention in the late 1950's, when such folk-oriented bands as the Kingston Trio attained national prominence. Soon, popular folk groups including the Limelighters, the Chad Mitchell Trio, the Brothers Four, and Peter, Paul, and Mary, in company with solo artists such as Joan Baez, Tom Paxton, Odetta, and Judy Collins, were playing and recording Guthrie material and giving added currency to his work.

It was Robert Zimmerman, a fanatical devotee of Guthrie's music, who, as Bob Dylan, caught the wave of radical folk music in the early 1960's and carried Guthrie's style to new aesthetic and popular heights. Much of the best of the material on his first album, *Bob Dylan*, both in substance and style is classic Guthrie. Although the immensely creative and productive Dylan subsequently moved through at least half a dozen stylistic phases, it was in the person of a Guthrie-style balladeer that he became a popular national folk-protest phenomenon. In so doing, he ensured the longevity of Guthrie's strain of music in the nation's popular culture.

—*Clifton K. Yearley*

FURTHER READING

Cray, Ed. *Ramblin' Man: The Life and Times of Woody Guthrie*. New York : W. W. Norton, 2004. Comprehensive biography of Guthrie, beginning with his Oklahoma ancestors and concluding with his children. Bibliographic references, discography, and index.

Denisoff, R. Serge. *Great Day Coming: Folk Music and the American Left*. Urbana: University of Illinois Press, 1971. An excellent discussion of southern protest singers, including Guthrie, their connections with northern radicals, and the effects of this affiliation on the development of urban folk music. Notes, good bibliography, and index.

Guthrie, Woody. *Art Works*. Edited by Nora Guthrie and Steven Brower, with contributions from Billy Bragg and Jeff Tweedy. New York: Rizzoli, 2005. When Guthrie first set out for California, he planned to make his living as an artist and cartoonist, not a singer. This first-ever comprehensive collection of his art, journals, and sketchbooks provides a vital glimpse into the young Guthrie and the lesser-known visual side of his talents. Bibliographic references.

_____. *Born to Win*. Edited by Robert Shelton. New York: Macmillan, 1965. A collection of Guthrie's essays, poems, notes, lyrics, and letters. Conveys the spirit of a man whose often sad life might have made him a loser, but did not. Filled with Guthrie's wonderfully humorous, sometimes biting, cartoons and sketches, as well as with verses, lyrics, and rhymes.

Hampton, Wayne. *Guerilla Minstrels*. Knoxville: University of Tennessee Press, 1986. A fine study of the protest tradition through analysis of four individuals: Joe Hill, John Lennon, Guthrie, and Dylan. Engagingly written. Although sympathetic to each of these protest singers, the author maintains critical objectivity. Very informative on Guthrie-Dylan linkages. There are a few photos, page notes, a splendid select bibliography for each singer, discographies, and an excellent double-columned index. Essential reading.

Klein, Joe. *Woody Guthrie: A Life*. New York: Alfred A. Knopf, 1980. An important nonacademic study of Guthrie's character rather than an analysis of his music or its impact. A comprehensive, easy to read, matter-of-fact, and objective biography. Among the several biographies of Guthrie, this is in many ways the best. Many photos, annotated chapter notes in place of bibliography, and excellent double-columned index. Must reading.

Malone, Bill C. *Southern Music, American Music*. Lexington: University Press of Kentucky, 1979. A well-written, scholarly survey of the subject. Excellent for placing Guthrie in a broad context, and more important for underlining the powerful influences of varieties of southern music on the national musical culture. No illustrations, but an outstanding bibliographical essay, and a useful index. A very informative work.

Marsh, Dave, and Harold Leventhal, eds. *Pastures of Plenty: A Self-Portrait, Woody Guthrie*. New York: HarperCollins, 1990. Posthumous editing of Guthrie's scrapbooks and other personal sources recapitulates Guthrie's life in his own words. Provides an intimate chronological view of his life until illness overwhelmed him in 1952. Includes explanatory introductions by the editors, many photos, and many of Guthrie's wonderful cartoons and sketches.

Partridge, Elizabeth. *This Land Was Made for You and Me: The Life and Songs of Woody Guthrie*. New York: Viking, 2002. Biography of Guthrie and analysis of his songs. Bibliographic references and index.

SEE ALSO: 1903-1957: Vaughan Williams Composes His Nine Symphonies; 1904-1905: Bartók and Kodály Collect Hungarian Folk Songs; 1906: Publication of *The English Hymnal*; Nov. 28, 1925: WSM Launches *The Grand Ole Opry*; Sept. 8, 1933: Work Begins on the Grand Coulee Dam; 1934-1939: Dust Bowl Devastates the Great Plains.

1930

1930's
HINDEMITH ADVANCES MUSIC AS A SOCIAL ACTIVITY

Paul Hindemith emphasized a new trend toward music as a social activity through his concepts of Gebrauchsmusik *(music for use) and* Hausmusik *(music to be performed at home).*

ALSO KNOWN AS: *Gebrauchsmusik*; *Hausmusik*
LOCALE: Germany
CATEGORY: Music

KEY FIGURES
Paul Hindemith (1895-1963), German composer
Carl Orff (1895-1982), German composer
Matthias Grünewald (c. 1475-1528), German painter
Wilhelm Furtwängler (1886-1954), German conductor

SUMMARY OF EVENT

Paul Hindemith began his composing career as an expressionist, exploring musical territory opened up by Arnold Schoenberg and Béla Bartók. His 1919 setting of dramatist Oskar Kokoschka's *Mörder, Hoffnung der Frauen* (pr. 1909; *Murderer, the Women's Hope*, pb. 1963) is an example of his use of dissonance with an extremely shocking text.

Hindemith's early creative years coincided with the Weimar Republic, which governed Germany in the wake of World War I after Emperor William II abdicated in defeat and was replaced by a democratic regime. The culture of the Weimar Republic was the first self-consciously modern one and saw striking advances in literature, drama, art, architecture, and film as well as in music. Although the republic's early years were characterized by foreign occupation, strikes, attempted putsches (including one by Adolf Hitler in 1923), and drastic inflation, Germany after 1924 settled into a period of stability and economic growth that was abruptly terminated by the Great Depression that began in 1929. The high levels of support for the arts were curtailed by the economic stringencies, which also resulted in the polarization of the German population between Nazis and Communists. When Hitler was voted into power early in 1933, the Weimar Republic was over, and many of its leading figures emigrated.

Beginning in 1922 and for most of the remainder of the decade, Hindemith associated with a movement known as New Objectivity (*Neue Sachlichkeit*), a repudiation of both Romanticism and expressionism. In literature, New Objectivists sought to be detached and unemotionally matter-of-fact and to focus on objective reality

and ordinary people. The movement's music renounced the nineteenth century past by being unemotional and concentrating on everyday life. Elements of popular music and even jazz were included in New Objectivist music, but such elements were treated with satire and parody.

Hindemith's piano suite of 1922 clearly shows elements of both expressionism and New Objectivity. The harmonic texture is extremely dissonant, but the individual movements have parodistic subtitles: The opening march is a circus, not a military march, and is treated parodically. Such popular dances as the shimmy and the Boston (a kind of waltz) and even ragtime are included in the suite. The ragtime movement bears directions that tell the performer to forget skills learned in piano lessons and to treat the piano as an interesting kind of percussion instrument.

The opera *Neues vom Tage* (news of the day), which Hindemith completed in 1929, is an excellent example of New Objectivity. The opera, which focuses on the marital problems of a couple, includes offices, a hotel room, a jail cell, and a nightclub in its stage settings and contains many elements of popular music, which are often used in a parodic style. The opera mocks the legal system, bureaucracy, the commercialization of daily life, and the power of the news media, especially tabloid journalism. Musical effects include a chorus of typists, an operatic aria sung in a bathtub, and a cabaret revue featuring a chorus line.

Hindemith's rise in the 1920's was meteoric. He developed a style that, in its spare lines and linear writing, can be compared to the contemporaneous architecture of the German Bauhaus school. In 1927, he was appointed professor of composition at the Berlin Staatliche Hochschule für Musik despite his lack of formal academic training and his activity as a practical musician, writing music for his own performances (he was one of the world's foremost violists) as well as concertos and solo pieces for others. He received prestigious commissions, including one to produce concert music for the fiftieth anniversary of the Boston Symphony in 1930. He felt, however, that much modern music was becoming too isolated from its audience; in 1929, he wrote an article in which he stated that the old music public was dying out and that a new one would have to be created. Here lay the roots of a musical philosophy called, for want of a better name, *Gebrauchsmusik*, or "music for use."

The term itself derived from the work of musical historians who wrote about the dance suite of the early sev-

Paul Hindemith conducts the Berlin Philharmonic Orchestra in a rehearsal in 1949. (AP/Wide World Photos)

enteenth century; these scholars made distinctions between music written to accompany actual dancing and dancelike music written for artistic performances. In its strictest sense, *Gebrauchsmusik* has no independent value in itself but serves a special use, especially for radio or film, and is the opposite of art or concert music. Hindemith was later to repudiate this term, saying that it sounds as ugly in German as it does in English. His goal, rather, was the creation of community music (*Gemeinschaftsmusik*), with the idea that the young public he was striving to educate should be making music themselves rather than listening to compositions in a concert hall or on records.

Hindemith's model in this effort was *Hausmusik*, works of music from the fifteenth through the eighteenth centuries that were written for performances in the home. Examples are the *Glogauer Liederbuch*, a set of vocal and instrumental pieces by mostly unnamed composers written in the late fifteenth century, and various collections of ensemble pieces by German composers of the sixteenth and seventeenth centuries. Franz Joseph Haydn's early string quartets, for example, were written for mostly amateur performers.

A good example of Hindemith's community music is the *Plöner Musiktag* (day of music at Plon), written in 1932 for a daylong music festival at a boarding school that culminated in a concert in which all the students were participants. Another notable work is the children's operetta *Wir bauen eine Stadt* (we build a city), written, as Hindemith explained, for the instruction and practice of children rather than for the entertainment of adult observers. In both works, the style is simple without being naïve, dissonances are employed sparingly, and the children are treated with respect; as Hindemith explained, there should be some difficulties to be solved by the performers, even if they are children.

1930

At the same time, Hindemith was changing his musical style. Characteristic of much Weimar culture during the early 1930's was an artistic conservatism marked by the use of older forms and structures; Hindemith followed this trend by reviving older musical forms, such as the sonata, the fugue, and the passacaglia (a repeated melodic pattern in the bass over which new and increasingly elaborate designs are contrived).

SIGNIFICANCE

When the Nazi Party took power in Germany in the 1930's, the party's leaders stressed the need for community—but in a restricted ethnic and racist sense that was unlike the universal community Hindemith had in mind for his music. When the Nazis attacked Hindemith's music as degenerate, it was for the music of his New Objectivity period, his parodies of marches, and his association with Jewish musicians such as Kurt Weill and Otto Klemperer. Nazi propaganda minister Joseph Goebbels attacked *Neues vom Tage* as obscene and sensational.

Hindemith's major work of these years was his opera *Mathis der Maler* (1934), based on the life and career of the medieval painter Matthias Grünewald. The concert symphony taken from the opera, one of Hindemith's most enduring compositions, reveals the basic features of his mature musical style: finely arched melodies harmonized by sturdy chords in a carefully arranged system of tension and release; energetic rhythms; dramatic climaxes reinforced with powerful chords; and the idea of a musical continuity from the Middle Ages to the present emphasized by the use of musical techniques and even quotations from earlier periods.

Mathis der Maler received its long-delayed premiere under the conductor Wilhelm Furtwängler in 1938. Furtwängler had championed Hindemith's music; he had conducted the premiere of the symphony drawn from the opera in 1934 and had gotten in trouble with the Nazis for doing so. Hindemith had been given an extended leave of absence from the Berlin Hochschule, during which he toured and even advised the Turkish government on music education. He visited the United States for the first time in 1937, and he gladly accepted a position on the faculty at Yale University in 1940.

At Yale, he taught theory and composition for thirteen years and also organized and directed the Collegium Musicum, a group organized to perform early music from the Middle Ages through the time of Johann Sebastian Bach. A strict teacher who granted only twelve graduate degrees in composition during this period, he influenced a number of musicians and, despite a heavy teaching load, continued to compose.

His attitude toward community music and music for use revealed itself in a variety of ways. Foremost are the sonatas he wrote for virtually every instrument, not only those with a substantial repertoire but also those, such as the English horn, tuba, double bass, trombone, or viola, for which there were few worthwhile compositions. His trumpet sonata particularly set the standard for all subsequent extended compositions for the instrument. Despite their difficult and sometimes thickly written piano parts, these sonatas remain Hindemith's most frequently performed compositions.

Second are his orchestral showpieces, beginning with the 1930 concert music written for the Boston Symphony. Among the most popular of his orchestral works are his *Symphonic Metamorphoses of Themes by Carl Maria von Weber* (1943), arrangements of piano pieces originally intended as a ballet. His numerous concertos for various instruments are scored counterparts to his sonatas. His Symphony in B-flat, written in 1951 for the U.S. Army band, set a high standard for concert-band music.

Hindemith's most American work, the *Requiem: For Those We Love* of 1946, is a setting for soloists, chorus, and orchestra of Walt Whitman's 1865 poem "When Lilacs Last in the Dooryard Bloom'd." Whitman's poem was written as an elegy for Abraham Lincoln and the dead of the Civil War; Hindemith regarded it as a fitting text for his work, which was written to commemorate Franklin D. Roosevelt and the dead of World War II. The piece was composed for performance by a high-quality amateur chorus and professional orchestra, but since 1946 it has been presented by many university music schools.

Finally, Hindemith codified his musical ideas and techniques in a series of treatises. His *Unterweisung im Tonsatz* (1937-1939; *The Craft of Musical Composition*, 1941) consisted of a theoretical explanation followed by various exercises in part writing. In his book *A Composer's World: Horizons and Limitations* (1952), a collection of lectures originally delivered at Harvard University, Hindemith stated his musical philosophy for the general reader, reaffirmed the importance of tonality (which he compared with gravity and artistic perspective) and the continuity of musical tradition, and proclaimed the moral imperative of music, arguing that it is a form of communication between author and listener. Practical music, he claimed, should be the basis of musical instruction (he expected his composition students in

Berlin to learn the instruments for which they were writing). Although he favored open admission to schools of music instruction, he believed that such a policy should be complemented by a well-functioning weeding system to remove the presumptuous and the untalented. His enthusiasm for community music did not wane; he felt that composers should write music that amateurs could play and sing.

Hindemith's musical style was so individual that he could not develop a school of composers. His idea of educational music was effectively continued by Carl Orff, whose *Schulwerk* was written for children to perform and featured drums and tuned percussion as the principal instruments. Orff's methods were brought to North America early in the 1960's and have since become a favored way of introducing children to music.

Hindemith resigned from Yale in 1953 to accept an appointment at the University of Zurich, from which he retired two years later. He had been actively teaching for more than twenty-five years and wanted to devote himself to conducting. His interests had also turned to vocal music; his last composition, finished two months before his death, was a setting of the Mass written for a virtuoso choir. An octet Hindemith wrote in 1958 is an excellent illustration of his post-American style, combining lyricism with humor, Baroque contrapuntal techniques with old-fashioned dances such as the waltz, polka, and galop. Igor Stravinsky's and Hindemith's octets can very well serve as the framing works for a neoclassical style in twentieth century music.

—*R. M. Longyear*

FURTHER READING

Austin, William. *Music in the Twentieth Century*. New York: W. W. Norton, 1966. Discussion of twentieth century music includes a chapter on Hindemith that provides an excellent capsule introduction to his music and musical philosophy.

Burns, Rob, ed. *German Cultural Studies: An Introduction*. New York: Oxford University Press, 1995. Collection of scholarly essays on German culture and society since 1871 includes a chapter on the "birth of modernism" in the Weimar Republic.

Cook, Susan C. *Opera for a New Republic*. Ann Arbor: UMI Research Press, 1988. Study of German opera during the 1920's emphasizes works by Hindemith. Also includes chapters on New Objectivity and on the effect of jazz on European music.

Hindemith, Paul. *A Composer's World: Horizons and Limitations*. Cambridge, Mass.: Harvard University Press, 1952. Collection of the lectures that Hindemith gave at Harvard during the 1949-1950 academic year. States his musical philosophy for the general reader and emphasizes his moral and ethical view of the art.

Hinton, Stephen. *The Idea of Gebrauchsmusik*. New York: Garland, 1989. Useful source of information on the origins and cultural background of the concept of *Gebrauchsmusik*. The musical information provided is directed toward specialists.

Kater, Michael H. *Composers of the Nazi Era: Eight Portraits*. New York: Oxford University Press, 1999. Examines the careers of eight German composers who were working, whether in Germany or as exiles, during the time the Nazis were in power. Chapter 2 is devoted to Hindemith. Includes endnotes and index.

Laqueur, Walter. *Weimar: 1918-1933*. 1974. Reprint. London: Phoenix Press, 2002. One of the best studies available in English of the Weimar Republic and its variegated cultural life. Discusses both art and music.

Noss, Luther. *Paul Hindemith in the United States*. Urbana: University of Illinois Press, 1989. Describes the composer's life and activities in the United States, mostly between 1937 and 1953, with brief discussion of his later years. Includes bibliography and indexes.

SEE ALSO: Mar. 15, 1911: Scriabin's *Prometheus* Premieres in Moscow; 1919: German Artists Found the Bauhaus; Feb. 12, 1924: Gershwin's *Rhapsody in Blue* Premieres in New York; July 17, 1927: Brecht and Weill Collaborate on the *Mahagonny Songspiel*.

1930

1930's
HOLLYWOOD ENTERS ITS GOLDEN AGE

Over the course of the 1930's, the motion-picture studios—already extremely successful commercial and artistic enterprises—developed the new medium of the "talking picture" into a popular art form at least equal to its silent forebear. By the end of the decade, Hollywood had reached the height of its powers, creating films of lasting cultural and artistic power, featuring movie stars as famous as world leaders.

LOCALE: Hollywood, California

CATEGORIES: Motion pictures; manufacturing and industry; trade and commerce

KEY FIGURES

Frank Capra (1897-1991), American film director

Claudette Colbert (1903-1996), French-born American film actor

Clark Gable (1901-1960), American film actor

Greta Garbo (1905-1990), Swedish film actor

Chico Marx (1887-1961), American comedic film actor

Groucho Marx (1890-1977), American comedic film actor

Harpo Marx (1888-1964), American comedic film actor

Zeppo Marx (1901-1979), American comedic film actor

Louis B. Mayer (1885-1957), American film studio owner

SUMMARY OF EVENT

In the same decade that the Great Depression wracked the world's economy, the film industry of the United States enjoyed its golden age. The Hollywood studios achieved an extremely efficient level of organization, employing actors, writers, directors, and technical crew members under exclusive contracts that resulted in each studio enjoying continuous access to a specific pool of talent from which to assemble the crews of specific motion pictures. This talent realized technical innovations that captivated audiences at the same time that individual stars such as Clark Gable, Greta Garbo, and the Marx Brothers achieved a public following that was the envy of political and business leaders.

The introduction of synchronized sound to motion pictures was one of the most revolutionary changes in the history of the film industry, and, like most revolutions, it was accompanied by uncertainty, confusion, and excite-

ment. The Warner Bros. studio was pleased by the enthusiastic response to the 1927 premiere of *The Jazz Singer*, the first full-length film with synchronized sound, but the technology of "talking movies" remained experimental for several years. In *The Jazz Singer*, vaudevillian Al Jolson was shown speaking and singing a few words through the use of a recorded disc system that was synchronized with his image on the screen. This disc system and its rivals had their flaws; silent-screen stars faced the challenge of speaking into equipment that was often unmerciful to the human voice. By the early 1930's, however, this technology had improved considerably, as sound came to be encoded optically on a track that was part of the film itself. By 1932, nearly all Hollywood productions were "all talking"; the era of the silent screen had passed.

Although improved sound systems became common in motion pictures during the decade, high-quality special effects were rare. *King Kong* (1933), therefore, was a remarkable film. An adventure tale in which a greedy entrepreneur captured a giant ape became a vehicle for the creative genius of a team of directors and technicians. The real stars were neither human nor ape; the film's miniature animal figures, made from latex rubber over metal skeletons, the huge mechanized face and upper torso of the ape, and the painstaking stop-motion and rear-projection photography instead stole the show. Radio-Keith-Orpheum (RKO) directors Merian Cooper and Ernest B. Schoesdack turned to Willis O'Brien for special effects and Marcel Delgado for the construction of the animated models. In addition to the giant ape, dinosaurs inhabited the screen and held audiences in awe with displays of savage combat.

The use of color also reached a critical phase in the 1930's. The Technicolor Corporation devised a system of color photography and projection as early as 1915, but its complexity and expense delayed its successful commercial exploitation. The Technicolor system evolved into the "three-strip" process, in which chemical treatment added color to the film. In 1935, director Rouben Mamoulian's *Becky Sharp* appeared in vibrant—perhaps overdone—color. By 1939, this problem had disappeared, and producer David O. Selznick and director Victor Fleming brought *Gone with the Wind* to the screen with an improved Technicolor process.

The attraction of Hollywood films went far beyond innovations in technology. The most powerful phenomenon, stardom, was also the most nebulous. Film stars had a national and even international status that rivaled that of political and business leaders of the day. Although numerous stars had large and devoted followings, two stood out: the tall, dark, mustachioed Clark Gable and the svelte, blond, stunning Greta Garbo. Both achieved acclaim at Metro-Goldwyn-Mayer (MGM), where performers had to submit to the rules and expectations of powerful studio bosses, yet both projected qualities into their screen appearances that went beyond what executives and directors could control. Gable's and Garbo's individual films came to mean less than did their personal appeal to the mass audience.

Gable and Garbo manifested different qualities on the screen. Gable was the rough, sometimes brash American male who generally had his way with women and with life. Garbo was often the victim of circumstances, the fallen woman or the self-sacrificing lover who somehow suffered through her anguish with subdued resolve. Gable's image was that of the pragmatic, bullish, determined American hero; Garbo's was that of the disdainful, worldly cosmopolitan. Fan magazines and gossip columnists relished tidbits of information from their private lives but seldom grasped their personal responses to stardom. Gable was surprised and even amused by his celebrity, but Garbo, whose reclusive nature created an air of mystery, rarely revealed her inner feelings.

The Marx Brothers achieved another type of stardom as they cavorted through a series of uproarious, chaotic comedies. Their quick minds and lack of inhibition pushed comedy beyond traditional boundaries. Veterans of vaudeville and the stage who broke into films when sound allowed for the spoken joke, Groucho, Chico, Harpo, and Zeppo used the new medium to improvise and improve on old tricks. Double entendres, painful puns, manic chases, and risible pantomimes conveyed their sometimes whimsical, often cynical views of institutions ranging from real estate brokerage to university administrations to the national government. Their wild antics matched spoken humor with visual comedy in a balance suited for talking pictures.

Frank Capra, a young, relatively unknown director for financially embattled Columbia, emerged in the 1930's as one of Hollywood's major filmmakers. Working with a small budget and barely a month to complete shooting, Capra brought together Claudette Colbert and Clark Gable (on loan from MGM to Columbia as punishment for standing up to MGM boss Louis B. Mayer) to form one of the screen's most electric duos in 1934's *It Happened One Night*. Colbert played a New York socialite opposite Gable's pushy journalist. At first on the trail of a news story about the idle rich, Gable took a personal interest in Colbert and, after some brisk exchanges in risque situations, the two forgot their class differences to become enamored of each other. This unlikely matching of a daughter of the social elite and a hardworking journalist bridged the barriers of status and, during the Great Depression, represented an unorthodox reconciliation between haves and have-nots. This prototypical "screwball comedy" set a much-imitated formula and made Capra an influential director.

Gable and Colbert's characters had broken the barriers between great wealth and middling income, but such differences were not always so gracefully overcome. In the early 1930's, Warner Bros. released a series of gangster films in which the protagonists were hard-bitten, vi-

Clark Gable and Claudette Colbert in a scene from the 1934 film It Happened One Night. *(AP/Wide World Photos)*

1930

2365

olent products of urban mean streets. Edward G. Robinson's "Rico" was gunned down at the end of 1931's *Little Caesar*, but he left an unforgettable impression as to how an aggressive, unscrupulous individual could grab wealth and power, at least for a short time. Reflecting headlines in the daily press, gangster films such as *Little Caesar*, *The Public Enemy* (1931) with James Cagney, and Paul Muni's evocation of Chicago's Al Capone in *Scarface* (1932) remain as a lasting legacy of a turbulent era in which criminal activity took on disturbing proportions.

Social structure and cultural values were unstable in many films of the 1930's, but only rarely did studio executives allow their motion pictures to slash respected institutions to the core. The Marx Brothers, however, did just that. In five films made for Paramount between 1929 and 1933, they called into question the rationality and legitimacy of some of the basic components of American national life. *The Cocoanuts* (1929) ridiculed the Florida real estate industry at a time when the country was beginning to skid into depression. The culmination of their anarchistic comedy was *Duck Soup* (1933), which portrayed political leaders as demagogues, government as their pernicious plaything, and war as a result of scoundrel-dominated diplomacy.

The biting humor of the Marx Brothers was at times too much for 1930's film audiences, who often sought relief from the bleak reality of Depression life. Audiences found escape in films of glamour and excitement that featured stars who approximated a kind of royalty in the public mind. Although the lustre of her image would fade over the years following her unexpected retirement in 1941, Garbo's presence in motion pictures went far beyond sex appeal and skillful acting to construct a persona that held fascination for the public. She combined an air of sophistication with a tinge of sadness at lost opportunities; in many of her films, Garbo did not live happily every after. *Anna Christie* (1930), *Anna Karenina* (1935), and *Camille* (1937) defined the image of this reclusive and enigmatic star. Entangled in a contract with MGM's autocratic Louis B. Mayer, Garbo played redundant roles for the sake of the box office. Only in *Ninotchka* (1939), a comedic tour de force that starred Garbo as a bland, low-key Soviet agent whose personal liberation offered commentary on the pretensions of ideological purity, was Garbo able to break loose from such typecasting. Ironically, the adoring public that found escape in her films ensured her entrapment in roles that limited her development as an actor.

Whereas Garbo's magnetism stemmed from her aloofness and subtlety, Clark Gable built his star image by projecting an aggressive directness. He and Garbo costarred in *Susan Lenox*, a 1931 MGM production for Mayer. Garbo, the fallen woman, pursued engineer Gable as her last hope for the good life. Many female fans, too, pursued Gable throughout the decade. His work in *It Happened One Night* confirmed his position at the top of Hollywood's list of stars, and *Gone with the Wind* gave him the quintessential male role of the decade as the charming Rhett Butler, a cool realist who used his wits to survive the Civil War but who never found happiness with the mercurial Scarlett O'Hara. His parting thrust at her—"Frankly, my dear, I don't give a damn"—remains one of the best-known lines in film history. Unlike Garbo, Gable remained active in films all of his life, but the roots of his public persona and much of his film legacy are contained in his work of the 1930's.

SIGNIFICANCE

The launching of new technologies and the luster of the stars helped the Hollywood studios weather the storms of the Great Depression. Indeed, the output of Hollywood during the Depression has come to symbolize escapist entertainment at its best. The term "escapist" is often used in a pejorative sense, but the image of downtrodden masses enjoying momentary respites from their problems in the darkness of the nation's movie theaters has been used to counteract the term's negative connotations. The image has been used by Hollywood itself, in fact: It represents the climax of Preston Sturges's *Sullivan's Travels* (1941), in which the title character discovers that it may do greater good to produce an escapist comedy for the enjoyment of the poor and suffering than it would be to produce a weighty social tragedy dramatizing their plight.

MGM, Warner Bros., and RKO led the way during the Depression years, but Fox, Paramount, Universal, Columbia, and United Artists also survived the nation's worst economic crisis. Established as the world's center of commercial film production, Hollywood was a major contributor to popular culture, an occasional contributor to high culture, and a dynamic, if unsteady, force in the nation's economy. The essential vocabulary and conventions particular to mainstream Hollywood filmmaking had been well established even before the advent of sound. Over the course of the 1930's, the studios incorporated the new technology into their films, as they learned how best to modify the conventions of the silent era to accomodate synchronized speech and sound tracks. By the end of the decade, Hollywood's version of the cinematic art had reached its apex, as most later critics would list the years from 1939 to 1941 as the greatest in the history of classical Hollywood cinema.

—*John A. Britton*

FURTHER READING

Balio, Tino, ed. *Grand Design: Hollywood as a Modern Business Enterprise, 1930-1939*. Berkeley: University of California Press, 1995. Comprehensive survey of all aspects of Hollywood's output during the 1930's. Part of a decade-by-decade series on the history of American cinema. Bibliographic references and index.

Bergman, Andrew. *We're in the Money: Depression America and Its Films*. New York: New York University Press, 1971. General overview of film and society in the 1930's, with brief but insightful discussions of the Marx Brothers, women's roles in film, and Frank Capra's contributions to the screwball comedy and political dramas.

Capra, Frank. *The Name Above the Title*. New York: Macmillan, 1971. Lengthy, detailed, unusually frank autobiography that covers Capra's life, from his beginnings among Sicilian peasantry through his ascension to the top of Hollywood's motion-picture elite in the 1930's to his decline after World War II. Fast-paced writing, with numerous quotations from reviews.

Currell, Susan. *The March of Spare Time: The Problem and Promise of Leisure in the Great Depression*. Philadelphia: University of Pennsylvania Press, 2005. Detailed study of leisure-time activities during the Depression, including a chapter on motion pictures and music halls. Places Hollywood's role in Depression-era culture in the context of other cultural activities and products of the same period.

Dooley, Roger. *From Scarface to Scarlett: American Films in the 1930's*. New York: Harcourt Brace Jovanovich, 1981. Discusses a wide selection of films, organized in thematic sections. For example, "Continental Style" places Garbo and several of her films in the context of Hollywood's image of European history and culture.

Gabler, Neal. *An Empire of Their Own: How the Jews Invented Hollywood*. New York: Crown, 1988. Interesting biographical sketches of studio executives. The author is more sympathetic to Louis B. Mayer than are most students of the era.

Gronowicz, Antoni. *Garbo: Her Story*. New York: Simon & Schuster, 1990. Fascinating but controversial perspective on Garbo's life, ostensibly from Garbo's point of view. Too valuable to ignore in any study of her career, but readers should use with awareness of its subjectivity. Richard Schickel's afterword is a model of carefully considered judgment on the strengths and weaknesses of Garbo's work in Hollywood.

Marx, Groucho. *Groucho and Me*. New York: Bernard Geis, 1959. Rambling, autobiographical reminiscence replete with anecdotes, wisecracks, and some valuable observations on the Marx Brothers' rise from vaudeville to Hollywood stardom.

Tornabene, Lyn. *Long Live the King: A Biography of Clark Gable*. New York: Putnam, 1976. Traces Gable's rise to stardom, with more attention to his personal life than to his screen performances. Emphasizes the insecurities of stardom, Gable's combative personality, and his troubled relationship with Louis B. Mayer.

Weales, Gerald. *Canned Goods as Caviar: American Film Comedy of the 1930's*. Chicago: University of Chicago Press, 1985. A critical analysis of a dozen comedies, including a challenging critique of *Duck Soup*.

SEE ALSO: May 16, 1929: First Academy Awards Honor Film Achievement; 1930's-1940's: Studio System Dominates Hollywood Filmmaking; 1931: Karloff and Lugosi Become Kings of Horror; 1931-1932: Gangster Films Become Popular; 1933: *Forty-Second Street* Defines 1930's Film Musicals; 1934: Lubitsch's *The Merry Widow* Opens New Vistas for Film Musicals; 1934-1935: Hitchcock Becomes Synonymous with Suspense; 1934-1938: Production Code Gives Birth to Screwball Comedy; Sept. 6, 1935: *Top Hat* Establishes the Astaire-Rogers Dance Team; 1939: Ford Defines the Western in *Stagecoach*; Aug. 17, 1939: *The Wizard of Oz* Premieres; Dec. 15, 1939: *Gone with the Wind* Premieres.

1930

1930's
INVENTION OF THE SLUG REJECTOR SPREADS USE OF VENDING MACHINES

With the invention of the slug rejector, it became much more difficult to "fool" vending machines into dispensing products for free. As a result, the machines became more widely deployed, were used to sell a wider array of goods and services, and became important tools in the marketing and distribution of commodities.

LOCALE: United States
CATEGORIES: Inventions; trade and commerce; science and technology; marketing and advertising

KEY FIGURES
Thomas Adams, Jr. (1846-1926), founder of the Adams Gum Company
Frederick C. Lynde (fl. early twentieth century), English inventor
Nathaniel Leverone (1884-1969), cofounder of the Automatic Canteen Company of America
Louis E. Leverone (1880-1957), Nathaniel's brother and cofounder of the Automatic Canteen Company of America

SUMMARY OF EVENT
Following World War II, vending machines became a significant factor in the U.S. economy. The growth in the popularity of these machines among product manufacturers and distributors was driven largely by the invention in the 1930's of the slug rejector, which made them a more reliable source of income than they had been previously. Indeed, following the invention and perfection of the slug rejector, vending machines became commonplace as a means of marketing gum and candy. By the 1960's, almost every building had machines that sold soft drinks and coffee. Street corners featured machines that dispensed newspapers, and post offices even used vending machines to sell stamps. Occasionally, someone fishing in the back woods could find a vending machine next to a favorite fishing hole that dispensed cans of fishing worms.

The primary advantage offered by vending machines was their convenience. Unlike people, machines could provide goods and services around the clock, with no charge for labor. Before World War II, the major products stocked by vending machines were cigarettes, candy, gum, and soft drinks. Beginning in the 1950's, the inventory of commodities available in such machines expanded significantly.

The first recognized vending machine in history was invented in the third century B.C.E. by the mathematician Hero. This first machine was a coin-activated device that dispensed sacrificial water in an Egyptian temple. It was not until 1615 C.E. that another vending machine was recorded. In that year, snuff and tobacco vending boxes began appearing in English pubs and taverns. These tobacco boxes were less sophisticated machines than was Hero's, as they left much to the honesty of the customer. Insertion of a coin opened the box; once it was open, the customer could take out as much tobacco as desired. One of the first U.S. patents on a vending machine was issued in 1886 to Frederick C. Lynde, an English-born inventor. That machine was used to sell postcards.

If any one person can be considered the father of vending machines in the United States, however, it would probably be Thomas Adams, Jr., the founder of the Adams Gum Company. Adams began the first successful vending operation in the United States in 1888, when he placed gum machines on train platforms in New York City. Other early vending machines included scales (which sold a service rather than a product), photograph machines, strength testers, beer machines, and hot water vendors (to supply poor people who had no other source of hot water). These were followed, around 1900, by complete automatic restaurants in Germany, cigar vending machines in Chicago, perfume machines in Paris, and an automatic divorce machine in Utah.

Soft drink vending machines got their start just prior to the beginning of the twentieth century. By 1906, improved models of these machines could dispense up to ten different flavors of soda pop. The drinks were dispensed into a drinking glass or tin cup that was placed near the machine (there was usually only one glass or cup to a machine, as paper cups had not yet been invented). Public health officials became concerned that everyone was drinking from the same cup. At that point, someone came up with the idea of setting a bucket of water next to the machine so that each customer could rinse off the cup before drinking from it. The year 1909 witnessed one of the monumental inventions in the history of vending machines, the pay toilet.

Also around 1900 came the introduction of coin-operated gambling machines. These "slot machines" were typically differentiated from normal vending machines. The vending machine industry did not consider gambling machines to be a part of the vending industry, because they did not vend merchandise. Neverthless, it was the gambling machines and the dishonesty of some of their clientele that induced the industry to research slug rejection.

Early machines could be cheated by the simple ploy of tying a string to a coin and pulling the coin back out of the machine once it had dispensed its product or service. They could also be tricked into accepting crude counterfeit coins called "slugs." In the 1930's, the slug rejector was perfected, allowing machines to test the coins inserted into them to make sure they were genuine currency. The invention of this slug rejection device gave vendors more confidence that they would receive payment for products or services sold by vending machine.

SIGNIFICANCE

Slug rejectors were the most important improvement to vending machines in the 1930's, but they were not the only such improvement. Change-making machines were also instituted, and a few machines would even say "thank you" after a coin was deposited. These improved machines led many marketers to experiment with automatic vending. Coin-operated washing machines were one of the new applications of the 1930's. During the Great Depression, many appliance dealers attached coin metering devices to washing machines, allowing the user to accumulate money to make monthly payments to the dealer by using the appliance. This was a form of forced saving. It was not long before some enterprising appliance dealer got the idea of placing washing machines in apartment house basements. This idea was soon followed by stores full of coin-operated laundry machines, giving rise to a new kind of automatic vending business.

Following World War II, there was a surge of innovation in the vending machine industry. Much of that surge resulted from the discovery of vending machines by industrial management. Prior to the war, the managements of most factories had been tolerant of vending machines. Following the war, managers discovered that the machines could be an inexpensive means of keeping workers happy. They became aware that worker productivity could be increased by access to candy bars or soft drinks. As a result, the demand for machines increased, exceeding the supply offered by the industry during the late 1940's.

Vending machines have had a surprising effect on the total retail sales of the U.S. economy. In 1946, sales through vending machines totaled $600 million. By 1960, that figure had increased to $2.5 billion. The 1950's began with isolated individual machines that would dispense cigarettes, candy, gum, coffee, and soft drinks. By the end of that decade, it was much more common to see vending machines in groups. The combination of machines in a group could, in many cases, meet the requirements to assemble a complete meal.

There are limitations to the use of vending machines. Primary among these are mechanical failure and vandalism of machines. Another limitation often mentioned is that not every product can be sold by machine. There are several factors that make some goods more vendable than others. National advertising and wide consumer acceptance help. A product must have a high turnover in order to justify the cost of a machine and the cost of servicing it. A third factor in measuring the potential success of an item is where it will be consumed or used. The most successful products are used within a short distance of the machine; consumers must be made willing to pay the usually higher prices of machine-bought products by the convenience of machine location.

Merchandise is the most commonly sold type of commodity dispensed by vending machines, but the vending of services is also an important part of the industry. The largest percentage of service vending comes from coin laundries. Other types of services are vended by weighing machines, parcel lockers, and pay toilets. There are also shoe-shine machines, and some motels feature coin-operated massaging beds. Even the ubiquitous parking meter is an example of a vending machine that dispenses a service. Coin-operated photocopy machines also account for a large portion of service vending.

Vending machines have become a permanent fixture of capitalist society, and they have only scratched the surface of the potential markets. Although the machines have a long history, their popularization resulted most directly from innovations of the 1930's, particularly the slug rejector. Once they could rely on receiving payments in exchange for goods or services, marketing managers came to recognize that vending machine sales were more than a mere sideline. Increasingly, firms established separate departments to handle sales through vending machines, as vending machines became such an important marketing channel that failing to deploy them could damage a company's bottom line.

—*Dale L. Flesher*

1930

FURTHER READING

Amann, Fred. "Automated Cashless Services: A Trilogy." *Vend* (March 15, 1970): 19-20. Discusses the role of ITT Canteen Corporation in popularizing vending machines that accepted credit cards in 1967.

Diehl, Lorraine B., and Marianne Hardart. *The Automat.* New York: Clarkson Potter, 2002. A study of the most famous automated restaurant in the United States, which became an icon of New York City in the early twentieth century. Bibliographic references and index.

Latimer, Bob. "A New Breed of Bulk Vending." *Vend* (May 1, 1968): 27-28. Discusses the role of vending service companies in the proliferation of vending machines in the late 1960's.

"Machines Are Selling Everything from Peanuts to Panties." *Sales Management* 84 (June 3, 1960): 38-42, 116-118. Gives highlights in the history of vending machines and includes an extensive discussion of products being sold through vending machines in the late 1950's.

Manning, W. J., Jr. "Automatic Selling: A Business in Billions." *The Management Review* 49 (October, 1960): 14-22. A good history of the vending machine

industry dating back to 1886. Emphasizes the technological breakthroughs of the 1930's.

Molinari, Gianfranco. "Latest Developments in Automatic Retailing in Europe." *Journal of Marketing* 28 (October, 1964): 5-9. Describes developments of the early 1960's in European vending operations. Emphasizes the technical, marketing, and psychological factors that influence the success of a vending operation.

Schreiber, G. R. *Automatic Selling.* New York: John Wiley & Sons, 1954. An earlier and longer version of the book listed below. Focuses on vending machines as a sales tool.

_____. *A Concise History of Vending in the U.S.A.* Chicago: Vend, 1961. Very brief history of vending machines, published by the leading journal in the industry.

SEE ALSO: 1913: Fuller Brush Company Is Incorporated; Sept. 11, 1916: First Self-Service Grocery Store Opens; July, 1920: Procter & Gamble Announces Plans to Sell Directly to Retailers.

1930's
JUNG DEVELOPS ANALYTICAL PSYCHOLOGY

The psychiatrist Carl Jung established in the early twentieth century a very influential school of psychological analysis, now known as analytical psychology, that contrasted in many respects with Sigmund Freud's program. Not least among the differences was Jung's stress on the spiritual or religious dimension in the treatment of mental illness.

LOCALE: Switzerland
CATEGORIES: Psychology and psychiatry; health and medicine; religion, theology, and ethics; publishing and journalism

KEY FIGURES
Carl Jung (1875-1961), Swiss psychologist
Sigmund Freud (1856-1939), Austrian psychologist
Alfred Adler (1870-1937), Austrian psychologist

SUMMARY OF EVENT

In 1900, psychiatry—a branch of medicine that specialized in the examination and treatment of mental illness—was still in its infancy. Most physicians still regarded psychiatry as a kind of stepchild of the medical profession, suspect largely because its focus on the human

mind seemed inherently too subjective to fit within the parameters of the objective scientific method. Early in the twentieth century, however, three brilliant young psychiatrists appeared in Europe, and their work would change this situation dramatically. Of the three, the Austrian psychologist Sigmund Freud was already making the biggest mark in the field. However, two younger colleagues, Alfred Adler and Carl Jung, would soon rival him in their creative contributions to psychiatric theory and practice.

Carl Jung was born near Zurich, Switzerland, in 1875. As the son of a clergyman, Jung was expected eventually to take up the profession. He was a lonely child and was given to private fantasies, especially because he found his parents emotionally distant and unhappy. Later, during his undergraduate years at the University of Basel, Jung read widely, especially in science, philosophy, theology, and mythology. He decided not to follow in his father's footsteps and instead chose a career in medicine; he completed his M.D. in 1900. By then he had decided to specialize in the new discipline of psychiatric medicine because of its exciting potential.

After seeing some of Jung's early research conducted

in his medical practice at a Zurich mental hospital, Sigmund Freud invited him to Vienna to collaborate in Freud's prestigious psychoanalysis program. From 1907 to 1912, Jung assisted Freud in a number of his psychoanalytic investigations. Freud regarded Jung as his eventual successor in the program, and he managed to have Jung elected as the first president of the newly formed International Psychoanalysis Association. Jung, however, was becoming increasingly alarmed at Freud's unshakable conviction that a repressed sexual instinct was the sole explanation for human neuroses. To Jung, such a doctrinaire position contradicted the very concept of psychiatry as a science.

Meanwhile, Alfred Adler, the other luminary in the new psychology movement, had determined that the basic source of mental illness lay in a misguided will to power. Jung concluded that both Freud and Adler were wrong to reduce so complex a problem as mental illness to any single factor. His extensive reading and clinical experience in Zurich prompted him to consider a much broader range of causes for mental pathologies, including a spiritual dimension ignored by his more rationalist and material-minded colleagues.

Relations between Freud and Jung cooled, and then the publication of Jung's *Wandlungen und Symbole der Libido* (1912; *The Psychology of the Unconscious*, 1915) made the breach permanent. In the book, which was later revised as *Symbole der Wandlung* (1952; *Symbols of Transformation*, 1967), Jung directly challenged Freud's contention that repressed sexual desires could be the sole explanation for the disturbed dreams and fantasies of the mentally ill. Instead, Jung maintained that these phenomena could be better explained by a number of nonsexual factors. Each thinker went his separate way, although Jung was devastated. He felt professionally isolated and scorned, especially since many saw his book as a deliberate betrayal of Freud's trust. Jung had to resign both as president of the psychiatric association and as editor of the foremost journal in the field. In the meantime, his marriage was also in serious difficulty.

Jung continued his private practice in Zurich but produced very little from 1913 to 1919. During these troubled years, he continually grappled with a deep psychological depression and a sense of hopeless alienation. At times, he felt on the verge of madness. In final desperation, he applied several of his own psychiatric theories and techniques to his condition and gradually found his way out of the abyss, as evidenced by the publication of his major book *Psychologische Typen* (1921; *Psychological Types*, 1923).

The appearance of *Modern Man in Search of a Soul* in 1933 proved that Jung had fully recovered. This slender volume, written in a clear, nontechnical style for a larger lay audience, set forth virtually all the main themes and methods that constituted Jung's analytic psychology, some of which had benefited his understanding of his own mental illness. Not least among the themes was the idea of a midlife crisis, which Jung found afflicted many (including himself) as they approached middle age. He also described in detail the techniques of dream analysis essential to a patient's diagnosis and therapy.

Next, in his theory of psychological types, Jung divided the human race into two basic, biologically determined orientations: an other-directed extrovert and an inner-directed introvert. Each person had one of these orientations dominant in the conscious self, while the other was recessive in the unconscious. If not consciously confronted, Jung believed, the suppressed element could acquire a destructive power. In order to achieve psychic harmony, some reconciliation or adjustment of the extrovert-introvert opposition had to occur within the individual.

A cornerstone of Jung's psychiatric system was his novel theory regarding the "archetypes of the collective unconscious." The idea of a collective unconscious, distinct from the conventional personal unconscious unique to each individual, was Jung's construct to explain the striking similarity of mental patterns and images (archetypes) evident in the dreams and fantasies of the world's cultures and expressed in myths, folklore, and art. Through his clinical work, reading, and wide travels, Jung had discovered many common recurring images and symbols in various cultures, and he noted that certain innate images were shared by all humans. Among the most frequent archetypal images included the masculine and feminine figures, "the wise old man" or guru figure, and the "shadow figure of the dark side," often used to signify evil. The "shadow" within the unconscious had to be consciously acknowledged in order to neutralize its baneful opposition. Such archetypes needed to be identified in a patient by a therapist to bring about a healing of the tensions between the conscious and unconscious sides of the self.

Finally, in his essay on the relationship of psychology and religion, Jung related how his extensive work with the mentally ill had convinced him that the feelings of despair and anguish he so often encountered were invariably associated with a loss of religious faith or a lack of any spiritual meaning to life. Whereas Sigmund Freud regarded religion as a superstitious abomination that

1930

should be eliminated from society, Jung concluded that a psychiatrist had to respond to human experience in all its aspects, including the spiritual. According to Jung, who was himself a pantheist, religious belief could confer an essential purpose and dignity to human life. The addition of a transcendent spiritual dimension lifted the human race beyond the level of mere biological necessity. *Modern Man in Search of a Soul* made Jung renowned far beyond the limited circle of his fellow psychiatrists. For the rest of his life, Jung continued to elaborate the main elements of his psychic model, and his popularity seemed at times to overshadow that of Freud himself. Just before his death in 1961, Jung professed himself at peace with himself and with the world.

SIGNIFICANCE

Carl Jung's school of psychological analysis came to have a major impact on the psychiatric profession in the twentieth century. In contrast to his rival Sigmund Freud's essentially mechanistic and rationalist approach to mental illness, Jung sought to dramatically widen the purview of psychiatric theory and practice. To better understand the patient's plight, Jung adapted whatever sources or perspectives promised to illuminate the problem. In addition to his own clinical observations, Jung drew freely from the annals of mythology, folklore, art, religion, and even the occult. In his view, psychiatrists needed to be proficient in the humanities and the esoteric arts as well as in medical science.

Further, Jung believed that the psyche was as real as any physical matter that existed in time or space. Convinced that science and its methodology could not penetrate the mysterious inner realms of the human mind, Jung advocated a "psychology of the spirit" that included a significant role for religion not found in the work of Freud and Alder. Jung had observed that religious belief could, among other things, give a sense of meaning and

purpose to life, and not only for the despairing and the alienated. Finally, Jung challenged his profession by devising a number of intriguing hypotheses to account for the great variety and complexity of psychic phenomena. Prime among these ideas were his "archetypes of the collective unconscious," the "midlife crisis," and his psychological types. Jung's message and methods continue to be heard and practiced in centers of Jungian analysis across Europe and North America.

—*Donald Sullivan*

FURTHER READING

Jung, C. G. *Memories, Dreams, Reflections. Recorded and Selected by Aniela Jaffe*. Rev. ed. New York: Pantheon Books, 1963. A fascinating, highly revealing autobiographical account unlike anything Jung had previously done.

_____. *Modern Man in Search of a Soul*. 1933. Reprint. Translated by W. S. Dell and Cary F. Baynes. London: Routledge, 2001. The lectures here collected demonstrate the remarkable range of Jung's thought and point forward to his research agenda over the nearly three decades to come.

McLynn, Frank. *Carl Gustav Jung: A Biography*. New York: St. Martin's Press, 1997. A controversial but thoroughly researched examination of Jung's analytical psychology. Quite critical of Jung's personal life.

Stevens, Anthony. *Jung*. New York: Oxford University Press, 1994. The best brief introduction in English to Jungian psychology.

SEE ALSO: 1902: James Proposes a Rational Basis for Religious Experience; 1904: Freud Advances the Psychoanalytic Method; 1912: Jung Publishes *The Psychology of the Unconscious*; Apr., 1938: Cerletti and Bini Use Electroshock to Treat Schizophrenia.

1930's
WOLMAN BEGINS INVESTIGATING WATER AND SEWAGE SYSTEMS

Abel Wolman's scientific investigations exposed the dangers of municipal water and sewage pollution and contributed significantly to modernizing water management, both throughout the United States and globally.

LOCALE: Eastern United States
CATEGORIES: Environmental issues; health and medicine

KEY FIGURES
Abel Wolman (1892-1989), American sanitary engineer
George C. Whipple (fl. early twentieth century), American authority on municipal water supplies
William Thompson Sedgwick (1855-1921), American bacteriologist and Massachusetts public health official
Ira Remsen (1846-1927), American chemist
William Henry Welch (1850-1934), American pathologist and educator

SUMMARY OF EVENT
Prior to his death in 1989, Abel Wolman had long been recognized as one of the most distinguished sanitary engineers in the United States and an authority on water standards, water pollution, and water management. His major contributions to these fields of expertise—the introduction of scientific methods of chlorination, the fluoridation of water supplies, the design of improved water- and sewage-treatment facilities, the scientific analysis of water resources, and the initiation of research into national water resources—were nearly all introduced or refined between the 1930's and the late 1950's.

Because of the profound changes affecting the nation's infrastructure during these years, sanitary engineers—quite aside from effects of the Great Depression, the massive industrialization of World War II, and the unprecedented affluence that marked the country's growth beginning in the 1950's—were presented with a sequence of novel problems. Principal among these challenges were the enormous growth in the U.S. population, the shift from a predominantly rural to an overwhelmingly urban society, the physical expansion of cities through rapid suburbanization, the wastage of water resources, and increases in the amounts and kinds of water pollution.

These problems had arisen despite the progress made by Wolman's predecessors. Wolman, indeed, was foremost in acknowledging the strides taken by engineers and sanitarians, particularly during the late nineteenth century and early twentieth century, in improving the quality of water supplies and the treatment of sewage. Still earlier, a general recognition of water's critical role in "public health" (an expression coined in the nineteenth century) and in economic growth had been broadened dramatically when deadly epidemics of cholera, typhoid, and malaria were directly correlated with impure water. Behind this discovery lay sanitation movements initiated primarily in London and Paris between 1832 and the 1880's by such people as Edwin Chadwick, John Simon, John Snow, Florence Nightingale, A. J. B. Parent Du Chatelet, and Eugene Belgrand.

Wolman took more immediate instruction, however, from men who, as he entered his profession, dominated the fields of water quality and sewage treatment and the applications of those fields to public health. The distinguished bacteriologist William Thompson Sedgwick, who modernized the public health services of Massachusetts, was one of Wolman's mentors. George C. Whipple, who had closely studied the taste and odors of the municipal water supplies of Boston and New York City, was another, as was Ira Remsen, a world-class chemist who likewise made contributions to water analysis. Sedgwick, Whipple, and Remsen, in company with William Henry Welch, were associated at one time with The Johns Hopkins University, Wolman's alma mater. These men were among the influences that led to the founding of the American Water Works Association, an organization that Wolman would lead beginning in 1942.

Wolman's career commenced with his studies of stream pollution in 1913. Thereafter, he combined research with practical applications of his knowledge until the early 1970's, when advancing age curtailed—although it did not end—his commitments. Even before the peak of his activities from the 1930's until the mid-1960's, he effected significant changes in several important areas of concern to the sanitary engineer. For example, in 1917 he introduced the rational loading of water-filter plants to improve the removal of bacteria. The following year, his studies on chlorine absoption provided the basis for subsequent chlorination practice in municipal filtration plants, a procedure that until then had been haphazard and unscientific. Experts noted that this accomplishment alone had a more profound effect

1930

on public health than any other single improvement in water management.

Although Wolman's professional operations took him variously to Boston, New York City, Richmond, Kansas City, Portland, Seattle, and Washington, D.C., his base of operations was in Baltimore. As a Johns Hopkins graduate, he spent more than forty years, first as lecturer, then as professor, in the university's School of Public Health and Hygiene, but in no sense was he narrowly academic. During the 1920's and early 1930's, for example, he assumed the editorships of three of his profession's leading journals: the *Journal of the American Waterworks Association*, the *American Journal of Public Health*, and the *Manual of Water Works Practice*. Almost simultaneously, he chaired the Public Health Engineering Section of the American Public Health Association, the Potomac River Flood Control Committee, the Conference of State Sanitary Engineers, and the Maryland State Planning Commissions. In addition, he served privately as consulting engineer to the Baltimore County Metropolitan District, the state of New Jersey (in regard to a U.S. Supreme Court case), and the city of Baltimore (in regard to water supply, sewerage, and refuse disposal). By 1934, Wolman officially directed ten major state and national commissions or committees engaged in resolving water-supply problems.

In the 1930's, Wolman continued to do excellent work in a broad range of areas, among them water resources, water quality and treatment, water planning and policy, and comprehensive planning for improvements to the human environment. Specific examples of his contributions across these fields are legion. From 1931 until 1970, as consulting engineer to the Baltimore City Department of Works, he helped make that city's water supply one of the purest and most palatable in the country, and the Montebello Waterworks became an international showpiece.

In addition, from 1940 to 1964, Wolman was called to serve the Bethlehem Steel Corporation's huge Sparrows Point steelworks and shipbuilding facilities, given their immense capacities for polluting the lower Baltimore Harbor, the Patapsco River, and the Chesapeake Bay. For industrial and domestic purposes—Bethlehem employed thirty thousand people, many of whom lived in a company community—the corporation used 185 million gallons of water per day, much of it drawn through wells from underground aquifers. With increasing use by Baltimore's growing population and by its expanding industries, these aquifers were becoming dangerously depleted, as well as polluted. Because Bethlehem, like most industrial water

users, had no easily defined standards for the water it used, Wolman undertook to determine such standards while searching for new sources of supply.

Wolman's analysis indicated that both local and distant underground substitutes were inadequate for Bethlehem's requirements, as were Baltimore's own potable and raw water supplies. In the circumstances, his solution was a novel one. He ascertained that Baltimore's Back Bay Sewage Treatment plant yielded effluent of between 85 and 165 million gallons a day. The effluent, moreover, served no useful purposes and produced no revenue. Not least, it was inexpensive and was within easy transmission distance of Bethlehem's facilities. On Wolman's recommendation, therefore, Bethlehem contracted with the city of Baltimore to receive a maximum of 50 million gallons daily (subsequently raised to 100 million gallons daily) of the city's treated effluent. Bethlehem likewise absorbed all the costs of building, maintaining, and operating the works essential to handling this supply.

The solution of this one problem led Wolman into investigations of related problems. The treated sewage effluent being provided by the city of Baltimore to Bethlehem Steel contained a high—and, for Bethlehem's purposes, harmful—chloride concentration. Consequently, an additional year of study was focused on the entire Baltimore sewer system in order to locate the sources of chloride pollution, a subject about which little was known in the early 1940's. Wolman's investigations finally traced the infusions of chloride to Baltimore's industrial sections, where there were firms engaged in meat pickling, meat packing, and the salt pickling of hides. Additional pollutants were traced to saltwater discharges from water-softening plants and, not least, to the infiltration of harbor waters into sewer breaks in low-lying areas. Having previously upgraded Baltimore's own water supply to conditions of excellence, Wolman thus had further instigated a review of the city's sewer system and had established an effective, early method for locating sources of pollution.

As a participant in the first meetings of the Federation of Sewage Works Association in 1940, Wolman alerted this constituency to the increasing dangers of pollution, particularly in the nation's rivers and streams, and to the wide and dangerous variations in the application of water standards that seemed justified both by science and by law. To address this problem, he proposed a search for answers to a series of questions about the quantitative bases for water standards promulgated in the United States, about what principles should dominate policy in regard to these standards, about whether universal standards for effluents were desirable, about the results of the installation of sewage-treatment plants on stream cleanliness, and about the epidemiological aspects of sewage treatment.

In large part because of Wolman, all these questions would occupy the agendas of thousands of communities—including a dozen major American cities that he would help directly—over the next decades. These questions would also later inform Wolman's influential 1962 *Report to the National Academy of Sciences: Water Resources*, as well as water planning and policy decisions in numerous countries where he served as a consultant, among them Israel, Ceylon, and many Latin American cities and states.

SIGNIFICANCE

Wolman's engineering tasks, research, and accomplishments encompassed nearly every aspect of water management. He revised standards for the performance of mechanical filtration plants, improved water-quality tests, made analyses of the degree and nature of bacterial removal in filtration plants, evaluated the effects of water storage in open reservoirs, applied statistical methods to the evaluation of water-supply quality, suggested improvements for sandbed filtration, eradicated unpleasant tastes and odors from water in various districts, defined sewage pollution in several bays and rivers, warned of the continuing menace of typhoid in water, and constantly urged funding for water research and the training of sanitary and hydraulic engineers. A dozen cities, half a dozen states, and several major agencies of the federal government drew heavily on his expertise from the Great Depression and World War II through the 1970's. He published continuously, in reports and papers usually readable by laypersons as well as by professionals. Much as Gifford Pinchot popularized the cause of conservation in the United States, Wolman educated public leaders in the vital and manifold importance of water and environmental sanitation to life and good health.

—*Clifton K. Yearley*

FURTHER READING

Briggs, Peter. *Water: The Vital Essence.* New York: Harper & Row, 1967. A clear survey that provides sound background for understanding the importance of coping with water pollution. Emphasis is on the United States, but Briggs also deals with the condition of the worldwide water supply. Chapter notes and index.

Cech, Thomas V. *Principles of Water Resources: History, Development, Management, and Policy.* 2d ed. Hoboken, N.J.: John Wiley & Sons, 2005. Compre-

hensive handbook detailing the history of water management policy. Bibliographic references and index.

Duffy, John. *A History of Public Health in New York City, 1625-1866.* New York: Russell Sage Foundation, 1968. A splendid scholarly study that is rich in essential nineteenth century background on urban sanitary conditions and their relationship to health. Wolman's immediate predecessors, as well as Wolman himself, were still trying to alleviate many of the generic sanitary-public health problems relating to water supply. Clearly written and essential for comprehending both specific and general problems that were still mounting a century later. Ample notes and useful bibliography and index.

Melosi, Martin V. *Garbage in the Cities: Refuse and Reform, 1880-1980.* College Station: Texas A&M Press, 1981. Although the concentration in this study is on the politics of cleansing cities, there are ample discussions of sanitary engineers such as Wolman. Useful for covering much background of the period during which Wolman was active. Chapter notes, bibliography, and index.

_____. *Pollution and Reform in American Cities, 1870-1930.* Austin: University of Texas Press, 1980. A well-written analysis of the subject. Substantially updates Duffy's work in regard to relevant water-pollution problems that Wolman was to encounter when he worked in many U.S. cities. Good chapter notes, bibliography, and index.

Nesson, Fern L. *Great Waters: A History of Boston's Water Supply.* Hanover, N.H.: University Press of New England for Brandeis University, 1983. An excellent analysis of the importance of engineers in devising politically acceptable solutions to complex water problems. Good notes, bibliography, and index.

Nobile, Philip, and John Deedy, eds. *The Complete Ecology Handbook.* Garden City, N.Y.: Doubleday, 1972. Clearly written and useful as an introduction to general pollution problems. Chapter 2 deals with water pollution in rivers, lakes, and streams. Useful bibliographies, glossary, and index.

Weidner, Charles H. *Water for the City.* New Brunswick, N.J.: Rutgers University Press, 1974. An extensive history of New York City's water problems from the city's origins until the 1940's. Wolman was an important influence on many aspects of the city's water quality and water planning problems, so this book illuminates interesting aspects of his career.

White, Gilbert, ed. *Water, Health, and Society.* Bloomington: Indiana University Press, 1969. An extensive

1930

collection of Wolman's papers that covers his life and work through 1969. Provides a detailed summary of Wolman's busy career as well as a chronological list of his published works. Indispensable for grasping Wolman's intellectual abilities and his influences.

Wolman, Abel. "The Metabolism of Cities." In *Cities*. New York: Alfred A. Knopf, 1966. Part of a collection of *Scientific American* articles, this is an excellent summation of Wolman's views on urban pollution, including water and sewage problems. Charts and graphs.

SEE ALSO: 1906: Cottrell Invents the Electrostatic Precipitation Process; June 27-29, 1906: International Association for the Prevention of Smoke Is Founded; 1908: Chlorination of the U.S. Water Supply Begins; 1910's: Garbage Industry Introduces Reforms; 1910: *Euthenics* Calls for Pollution Control; 1910: Steinmetz Warns of Pollution in "The Future of Electricity"; Nov. 5, 1913: Completion of the Los Angeles Aqueduct; Mar., 1937: Delaware River Project Begins.

1930's-1940's
STUDIO SYSTEM DOMINATES HOLLYWOOD FILMMAKING

Motion-picture production changed profoundly during the Great Depression and World War II, as studio executives exercised control over much of the creative process of filmmaking.

LOCALE: Hollywood, California
CATEGORIES: Motion pictures; trade and commerce

KEY FIGURES
Frank Capra (1897-1991), American film director
Carl Laemmle (1867-1939), American film studio executive
Cecil B. DeMille (1881-1959), American film producer and director
Louis B. Mayer (1885-1957), American film studio executive
Irving Thalberg (1899-1936), American film studio executive
Jack Warner (1892-1978), American film studio executive

SUMMARY OF EVENT
Motion-picture fans often fail to appreciate that Hollywood film production began as a form of private enterprise. Vigorously competitive since the early years of the twentieth century, the companies that made Hollywood famous were locked in intense competition during the Depression-ridden 1930's and the war-torn 1940's. These trying times witnessed the emergence of the studio system, which consisted of five major corporations—Metro-Goldwyn-Mayer (MGM), Paramount, Radio-Keith-Orpheum (RKO), Warner Bros., and Twentieth Century-Fox—and the three smaller organizations Universal, Columbia, and United Artists. Studio executives consolidated their operations through "vertical integra-

tion," which gave them control of the entire process from film production to exhibition in theaters. These eight studios accounted for 95 percent of U.S. film rentals by the late 1930's. Internal centralization of studio operations meant that executives often personally supervised actual film production. For many screenwriters, directors, and performers, this extension of executive authority was an intrusion into the creative process. For management, it was a necessary means to reduce costs and increase production. In spite of this and other conflicts, the studio system left a lasting imprint on American popular culture.

Not only did the studios confront rivals in Hollywood, they also faced other challenges, such as the growth of modern home entertainment with the rise of radio in the 1930's and the advent of television in the 1940's. The catastrophe of the period, however, was the Great Depression. By 1932, the unemployment rate in the United States was at least 25 percent. Public attendance at movie theaters declined sharply from 1930 to 1933, and studio profits plummeted. The prosperity of the 1920's had encouraged heavy investments in new theaters, sound equipment for talking pictures, and new studios. In the 1930's, Hollywood staggered under the burden of these debts and became increasingly dependent on New York bankers.

MGM rode out the Depression with the least difficulty, but the reasons for its success are difficult to pinpoint. The paternalistic, flamboyant studio boss Louis B. Mayer was certainly no model of efficient management. One obvious MGM strength, however, was the brief but brilliant tenure of executive producer Irving Thalberg, whose sickly physique contained a dynamo of energy. He pushed the studio while he drove himself to an early death. Thalberg supervised production, from the hiring of screenwriters to the final editing of the film. At a time when other studios cut their budgets, MGM maintained an expensive payroll. The results were impressive, and the studio provided audiences with relief from the doldrums of the Depression through its popular, lavish productions.

In contrast to MGM, both Paramount and RKO stumbled through the 1930's in financial disarray. Paramount's legendary chief, Adolph Zukor, lost control of his company's finances as box-office receipts declined. Banks and investment companies removed Zukor as Paramount slipped into bankruptcy. An extensive housecleaning followed. Paramount survived under new management, with a trimmed-down structure that could support only a few major productions each year. RKO fared little better. Frequent changes in management and a few box-office successes such as 1933's *King Kong* were not enough to solve basic financial weaknesses. In the 1940's, both Paramount and RKO continued to struggle and were backed by increasingly skeptical investors.

Warner Bros. was closest to MGM's profit levels. Jack Warner, a somewhat heavy-handed version of Irving Thalberg, assumed control of studio operations and intervened at various stages of production. Unlike Thalberg, who was concerned with quality, Warner pressed for quick, efficient production. He held down costs to the point of personally switching off lights in studio bathrooms. Although Warner was the subject of surreptitious humor among writers, directors, and actors, his notorious cost-control methods seemed to work. The studio clung to a respectable prosperity in the 1930's.

Twentieth Century-Fox gambled on new sound equipment and a large theater chain in the late 1920's, but the studio's timing was disastrous. Studio head William Fox borrowed heavily just before the initial shocks of the Depression hit. Rights to the Fox sound system became entangled in a legal battle, and the payments on the studio's immense debt overwhelmed its income. Corporate restructuring removed Fox, and the studio survived on a narrow margin.

The "little three" of the Hollywood studios also experienced rough times. Universal was an industry leader in the 1920's under founder and patriarch Carl Laemmle, but he was forced to sell his interests in 1936. Like Columbia and United Artists, Universal struggled through the Depression. All three small studios enjoyed momentary box-office successes with the work of certain directors or stars, but the general trends were reduced income and corporate retrenchment.

World War II provided relief from financial troubles, but only temporarily. Hollywood turned out a series of morale-boosting films that pleased politicians in Washington, bankers in New York, and theater audiences across the country. The basic problems, however, were uncertain income and rising production costs. Shortages of lumber made set construction more expensive. Technicians, writers, and performers commanded higher salaries. The most devastating blow, however, came from the courts in the Paramount case (1940-1949). Federal judges ordered Paramount to sell its theater chain on the grounds that control of both production and exhibition facilities constituted unfair competition against local theaters. This decision eventually changed the structure of the film industry. Pressed by the expansion of television and rising costs, the studios faced a dim future.

SIGNIFICANCE

Economic problems shifted the artistic force behind motion pictures from the individual director—the focus of film production before 1930—to the studios themselves and to the producers and directors entrusted with the task of converting budgets directly to screen images. Each studio emphasized certain popular themes to find formulas for success at the box office. Although restricted budgets, tight schedules, and intrusive bosses generally suffocated the creative impulses in filmmaking, some strong-willed producers and directors managed to achieve high-quality productions. Studio heads, whether the autocratic Louis B. Mayer or short-term executives chosen by East Coast bankers, were quick to identify themselves and their corporations with the style and success of producers and directors who could attract large audiences and occasionally please the critics.

Two of the most solvent studios offered a striking contrast in the types of films that brought them profits. MGM used elegance and glamour to provide audiences with escapism, whereas Warner Bros. turned to films of social and political relevance. Hyperkinetic Irving Thalberg left his personal imprint on many of MGM's expensive productions, including the South Seas saga *Mutiny on the Bounty* (1935) and the Victorian romance *The Barretts of Wimpole Street* (1934). After Thalberg's death in 1936, MGM continued to attract large audiences. Director Victor Fleming worked with independent producer David O. Selznick on 1939's immensely popular *Gone with the Wind*. The studio shared in the profits, and, in 1944, MGM purchased sole rights to the long-term moneymaker.

Warner Bros. did not attempt to match MGM's gran-

1930

deur, but Jack Warner used his limited resources well. Organized in 1923 by four brothers who were outcasts in Hollywood's movie-mogul society, the studio took a large risk on sound films in the 1920's and vaulted to the forefront in the 1930's. Warner Bros. pushed directors for fast-paced, low-cost productions. Mervyn LeRoy responded by pioneering the gangster film; he directed a strong performance from Edward G. Robinson in the title role of *Little Caesar* (1931) and then worked with Paul Muni as the victim of a corrupt judicial system in the powerful *I Am a Fugitive from a Chain Gang* (1932). William Wellman directed James Cagney to stardom in *The Public Enemy*, a 1931 gangster film. Director John Huston's 1941 version of *The Maltese Falcon* created a grim world of ambiguity and betrayal, and *The Treasure of the Sierra Madre* (1948) dramatized moral degeneration through greed. World War II elicited the studio's patriotism, as reflected in *Casablanca* (1942), a potent combination of romance, character study, and propaganda. The production methods employed by Warner Bros. were exemplified in *Casablanca*, as director Michael Curtiz made the most of inexpensive sets and screenwriters completed the sharp, literate script while the film was being shot.

Hard-pressed RKO had a remarkable string of much-admired films. *King Kong* astounded audiences with its innovative special effects, and in 1937 the studio began to distribute the inventive products of cartoon genius Walt Disney, bringing adults and children alike into theaters. Orson Welles's *Citizen Kane* (1941) was a powerful and controversial film but drew small audiences. Val Lewton produced eleven low-budget, highly impressive horror classics, led by *Cat People* (1942). Producer Adrian Scott, director Edward Dmytryk, and screenwriter John Paxton collaborated on *Murder, My Sweet* (1944), a dark, moody detective story punctuated by witty dialogue adapted from Raymond Chandler's novel. This film and the work of Welles and Lewton were typical of RKO's stylish, literate productions that, somehow, never solved the company's financial woes.

Paramount and Twentieth Century-Fox also floundered financially but, thanks to skillful directors, both studios produced some superior films. Veteran producer-director Cecil B. DeMille brought out a series of historical dramas, including *Cleopatra* (1934) and *Union Pacific* (1939). Billy Wilder directed and cowrote two taut stories about contemporary life: *Double Indemnity* (1944) featured murder, and *The Lost Weekend* (1945) took a somber look at alcoholism. Twentieth Century-Fox survived with help from John Ford's 1940

film version of John Steinbeck's 1939 novel *The Grapes of Wrath*, which was perhaps the epitome of topicality as it sympathetically portrayed the migration of a dispossessed farm family from Oklahoma to California. The commercial mainstay of Fox, however, was child star Shirley Temple, who acted, sang, and danced her way through a series of box-office hits.

Carl Laemmle turned over Universal to his twenty-one-year-old son, Carl, Jr., in 1929. The younger Laemmle supervised the production of *All Quiet on the Western Front* (1930), a provocative antiwar film, and then innovated in the horror genre with Bela Lugosi's *Dracula* (1931) and Boris Karloff's *Frankenstein* (1931). These creative thrusts fell victim to bad timing, however. Audiences were too small in the Depression years, and Universal soon faced a fiscal crisis. The Laemmles sold their interest in the studio, which worked its way back to solvency through B-pictures, serials, and the popularity of teen star Deanna Durbin. By the 1940's, Universal had achieved a modest prosperity.

The two remaining minor studios relied heavily on talented directors. Frank Capra carried Columbia with films of social and political relevance, including *It Happened One Night* (1934), in which romance overcame class barriers, and highly charged populist films such as *Meet John Doe* (1941). Robert Rossen's 1949 exposé of the perils of demagoguery, *All the King's Men*, marked Columbia's return to solvency. United Artists turned to the legendary comic actor Charles Chaplin, who poked fun at industrial society in *Modern Times* (1936) and ridiculed authoritarian leaders in *The Great Dictator* (1940). Director John Ford brought maturity to the Western in his popular United Artists release *Stagecoach* (1939).

This colorful, turbulent era contained major contradictions. The period's forceful, profit-seeking executives undercut the creative process but left an impressive list of popular, critically acclaimed films, including *The Grapes of Wrath, Casablanca,* and *Gone with the Wind.* The drive to boost profits, however, ultimately failed. The growth of television, rising production costs, and adverse court decisions meant the decline and ultimate demise of the studio system in the 1950's and 1960's. The Hollywood film industry, for all its power, notoriety, and many contributions to American popular culture, had a short life span.

—John A. Britton

FURTHER READING

Bergman, Andrew. *We're in the Money: Depression America and Its Films.* 1971. Reprint. Chicago: Ivan

R. Dee, 1992. Brief interpretive study of the connection between films and American society in the 1930's. Offers especially interesting discussion of gangster and "shyster" lawyer films of the early part of the decade. Includes bibliography and index.

Dick, Bernard. *The Star-Spangled Screen: The American World War II Film*. 1985. Reprint. Lexington: University Press of Kentucky, 1996. Presents wide-ranging analysis that includes film content and historical accuracy. Features bibliographical essay, film index, and subject index.

Dooley, Roger. *From Scarface to Scarlett: American Films in the 1930's*. New York: Harcourt Brace Jovanovich, 1981. Provides extensive coverage of Hollywood films, organized by thematic chapters. Useful for thematic discussions and as a reference on individual films.

Gabler, Neal. *An Empire of Their Own: How the Jews Invented Hollywood*. New York: Anchor, 1988. Social history enlivened by biographical portraits of the generation of studio executives who led the motion-picture industry through the 1930's and 1940's. Includes discussion of Laemmle, Mayer, and Jack and Harry Warner.

Kindem, Gorham, ed. *The American Movie Industry: The Business of Motion Pictures*. Carbondale: Southern Illinois University Press, 1982. Collection of eighteen specialized essays on business aspects of film, including the rise of the studio system and competition with television.

Koppes, Clayton R., and Gregory D. Black. *Hollywood Goes to War: How Politics, Profits, and Propaganda Shaped World War II Movies*. New York: Free Press, 1987. Carefully researched account of the film industry and its relations with the government and the war effort in general. Focuses on the Office of War Information and its influence on the propagandistic content of Hollywood's World War II films.

McElvaine, Robert. *The Great Depression*. New York: Times Books, 1984. Social, economic, and political history of the United States in the 1930's focuses on the causes and consequences of the Depression. Discusses Hollywood films as a reflection of culture and values of the era, especially the public's ambivalence toward individualism and collectivism.

Shindler, Colin. *Hollywood in Crisis: Cinema and American Society, 1929-1939*. New York: Routledge, 1996. Describes the state of the American motion-picture industry during the years of the Great Depression. Includes filmography, bibliography, and index.

Sklar, Robert. *Movie-Made America: A Cultural History of American Movies*. Rev. ed. New York: Vintage Books, 1994. Historical survey connects trends in Hollywood motion pictures with broad economic and social forces in the United States. Chapters covering the 1930's and 1940's include much useful information on the rise and fall of the studio system.

Stanley, Robert. *The Celluloid Empire*. New York: Hastings House, 1978. Readable study on the business side of the film industry. Provides succinct analysis of the eight studios that dominated Hollywood from the Depression to the end of the 1940's.

See also: Aug., 1926-Sept., 1928: Warner Bros. Introduces Talking Motion Pictures; May 11, 1928: Sound Technology Revolutionizes the Motion-Picture Industry; May 16, 1929: First Academy Awards Honor Film Achievement; 1930's: Hollywood Enters Its Golden Age; Feb. 27, 1935: Temple Receives a Special Academy Award; Sept. 6, 1935: *Top Hat* Establishes the Astaire-Rogers Dance Team; Aug. 17, 1939: *The Wizard of Oz* Premieres; Dec. 15, 1939: *Gone with the Wind* Premieres.

1930

1930
DUTCH ELM DISEASE ARRIVES IN THE UNITED STATES

When Dutch elm disease was introduced into the United States by wood imported from Europe, the devastating infestation stripped city streets and parks across the nation.

LOCALE: Eastern United States
CATEGORIES: Environmental issues; natural resources

KEY FIGURES
William Middleton (fl. early twentieth century),
　American entomologist
Rachel Carson (1907-1964), American
　environmentalist, marine biologist, and author
William D. Ruckelshaus (b. 1932), first head of the
　U.S. Environmental Protection Agency

SUMMARY OF EVENT
Dutch elm disease has been the most destructive shade-tree disease ever seen in the United States. The infection was first described by Marie Beatrice Schwartz in the Netherlands in 1921 and thus became known as Dutch elm disease; there is no tree called the Dutch elm. In 1930, the disease was brought into the United States in elm logs imported from Europe for making veneer. At least four ports of entry were involved; initially, the infestation was limited to areas near New York City.

The logs were being shipped in partial payment of World War I debts. These particular logs were valued because they had burls—hard, woody growths on the sides of trees that are usually the results of entwined clusters of buds. Burls produce unusual and often attractive grain patterns that are considered valuable in wood used to make furniture. Wooden crates containing dishes from Europe were also found to contain the disease.

The range of the American elm (*Ulmus americana*) is the largest of any tree in North America. It includes the eastern United States and southern Canada and extends as far west as central Texas, North Dakota, and eastern Saskatchewan. Other elms are found in smaller ranges within the same area. Most elms, including the slippery or red elm (*Ulmus rubra*) and the rock elm (*Ulmus masii*), are susceptible to the disease. The Siberian elm (*Ulmus pumila*) and the Japanese elm (*Ulmus davidiana japonica*) show resistance to Dutch elm disease.

A major factor in the spread of the disease in the United States was that the American elm had been planted both in large numbers and close together. Urban planners in the early 1900's lined city streets with them.

New neighborhoods were often crowded with houses, and streets were narrow; with the American elm's graceful shape, the mature trees arched across the streets to form a cathedral-like roof. The result was beautiful and redeeming in the cramped neighborhoods but devastating to the elms; their proximity to one another rendered them more vulnerable to the spread of the disease. The Dutch elm infection, which had previously infested Europe, spread in the United States and killed millions of elm trees, stripping city streets and parks of their shade trees. Every year, local governments and individuals spent many millions of dollars cutting down dead and dying trees.

The disease is caused by the fungus *Ceratocystis ulmi*. Technically, the fungus is a parasite while the tree is alive and continues as a saprophyte after the tree dies. In both cases, the fungus releases enzymes that digest the cells of the tree. This digestion occurs outside the cells of the fungus, and the degraded material is then absorbed as food by the fungus. The fungus is a member of the sac fungi, so named because they produce a sac (ascus) containing reproductive cells called spores.

The spores allow the fungus to spread from tree to tree. Agents that carry the spores and transmit the infection are called vectors. The principal vectors for Dutch elm disease are the elm bark beetles that tunnel under the bark. When the beetles are under the bark, the spores from the fungus stick to them. When the beetles fly to healthy trees to feed on tender twigs, they carry spores. In 1934, U.S. Department of Agriculture entomologist William Middleton was the first to report that spores are deposited on the feeding wounds as the beetles eat. The spores germinate and grow into the conductive tissues of the tree. Birds, water, and wind can also act as vectors. Bark beetles, however, are the main culprits.

Two species of small bark beetles act as vectors. The European elm bark beetle (*Scolytus multistriatus*) is another immigrant from Europe. In 1904, this insect was found and identified near Boston. It was not considered a problem until the subsequent arrival of the fungus, for which the beetle became the major vector. A native species (*Hylurgopinus rufipes*) also helps in spreading the disease. Without the beetles, the fungus would not present much of a threat.

The growing fungus not only kills and digests tree cells but also plugs the vital conductive tissues (especially the xylem) and cuts off areas of living sapwood.

The conductive tissues form a ring of vertical tubing just under the bark. The center of a tree does not conduct water; two types of tissue allow water to travel: Xylem takes water up to the leaves, and phloem takes water and the products of photosynthesis down. The first sign of trouble in the conductive tissue is when the upper branches of the elm wilt and curl because they are not getting enough water. Leaves then yellow and fall as the chlorophyll breaks down, and branches die. The conductive tissue may also carry spores internally to start new infections in other parts of the tree. Trees may take several years to die or may die in the same season in which they are infected.

Bark beetles generally produce two broods of young each year in large numbers. As many as twenty-five thousand beetles can emerge from one square foot of bark. The first brood spreads more of the fungus than the second. When they leave a tree with fungus in order to feed on new growth, the beetles are likely to carry spores. After feeding, they fly to dead or dying elms to find breeding places for the next brood, which emerges in August. The closely planted trees helped the beetles to multiply rapidly.

The federal government limited its response to Dutch elm disease to research and did not involve itself in direct efforts to stop the spread of the disease; hence programs to save elms were local and uncoordinated. Some communities concluded that the loss of the elm was inevitable and decided to do nothing. Some control measures were undertaken, but they met with limited success.

The treatment of plant disease is usually focused on the survival of the crop, or the whole species or genus. Only occasionally is an attempt made to save older or especially valued trees.

Control efforts included the cutting and quick burning of infected trees to prevent spread of the fungus. Not only did the beetle take the fungus from tree to tree, but the fungus also was found to spread when roots of an infected tree touched another tree's roots. In such a case, a root graft is formed, allowing the spores to cross over.

A dead elm tree shows the ravages of Dutch elm disease. (AP/Wide World Photos)

1930

For a time, it seemed that the spread of the disease might be stopped by the use of dichloro-diphenyl-trichloroethane (DDT), an insecticide that proved effective against the beetles. It soon became clear, however, that widespread DDT use had unacceptable side effects. For example, Rachel Carson's classic book *Silent Spring* (1962) argued that if the spraying of DDT continued, the price would be the devastation of bird populations, with damaging effects on entire ecosystems. She also cited cases in which spraying lost its effectiveness as a result of weather conditions that favored the beetles. In 1972, out of concern for the wider effects of DDT, William D. Ruckelshaus, the head of the Environmental Protection Agency (EPA), announced a ban on the domestic use of the chemical. A less effective insecticide, methoxychlor, was substituted in many communities.

Numerous research efforts using chemotherapy (injection of chemicals) were unsuccessful and costly. Individual prized trees were drilled at the base, and fungicides were introduced into the conductive tissue; nevertheless, many such trees were eventually lost. Some success was reported with the use of the fungicide benomyl.

The infestation that was introduced in the 1930's became an epidemic in the 1950's and peaked by the 1970's. Many cities that had planted only elms were left barren.

SIGNIFICANCE

The Dutch elm infestation stripped the city and park landscapes in thirty-one U.S. states. No tree had a wider range across the nation. Whole cities and neighborhoods that had invested in massive elm plantings were changed. Often, every elm on a street was lost. Nevertheless, none of the affected elm species went extinct as a result of the disease, because the reproductive rate of these species is high. The major impact of the infestation was the realization that careful planning was required to create and protect urban forests.

Scientists warn that the practice of monoculturing, the extensive cultivation of a single crop, is hazardous. What happened to the elm populations in the United States is a lesson in how overplanting one species or related species allows infestations to spread quickly and prosper. Some planners responded only by switching from the use of elms to the use of another species, such as ash, but any species planted in high concentration is more vulnerable to infestation than are more diverse groupings.

Moreover, the epidemic vividly illustrated the dangers involved in the importation of exotic plants, animals, and even fungi. Such introduced species may have no natural enemies. Under new conditions, they may be able to prosper at the expense of native species and displace them. The case of the Dutch elm infestation demonstrates how a previously harmless exotic such as the European bark beetle may become harmful when it is combined with another species.

Another issue that surfaced during the infestation was the tendency to rely solely on modern technology as a solution. Rachel Carson convincingly argued that chemical spraying was not the answer to Dutch elm disease; nevertheless, chemical use continued. The relative amounts of chemicals sprayed on household lawns in the 1990's to maintain monocultures exceeded that used to produce food. Golf courses tend to use even more chemicals, averaging seven times the amount that farmers use on each acre. Such use requires care and understanding that are often lacking.

Any widespread loss of trees is cause for regret. Trees restore the air by making oxygen. By taking carbon dioxide out of the air, they reduce the greenhouse effect. Trees hold large amounts of water and prevent erosion and flooding. They slow the wind; they shade and cool homes. Trees are required as hosts for much animal life. The beauty of trees restores the spirit and makes the land livable. Nevertheless, they do not need to be monocultured to be beautiful, nor do they need to be planted closely in rows. One of the effects of the loss of the elm monocultures was to call into question the nature of beauty in horticulture.

Hundreds of thousands of elms were lost each year when the infestation was at its peak. Now that many of the elms are gone, the beetles and fungus have also been reduced in number. The trend has been to replant about one tree for every four that were lost in the cities. The Dutch elm infestation showed that such replanting requires careful planning. Researchers continue to study resistant strains and genetically engineered varieties of elm for urban use. Most important to the recovery of affected areas, however, is the recognition that the problems of the past can be avoided through careful planning, the use of native species, and the preservation of diversity.

—*Paul R. Boehlke*

FURTHER READING

Carson, Rachel. "And No Birds Sing." In *Silent Spring*. Boston: Houghton Mifflin, 1962. Chapter in Carson's classic attack on chemical spraying deals with efforts to save the elms. The individual cases that Carson cites to support her argument are fascinating.

Lucas, George B., C. Lee Campbell, and Leon T. Lucas.

Introduction to Plant Diseases: Identification and Management. 2d ed. New York: Springer, 1998. General reference on plant infestations presents thorough information on identification of diseases and the fundamentals of disease management. Good for gardeners or anyone interested in plants. Includes glossary, list of suggested readings, and index.

Strobel, Gary A., and Gerald N. Lanier. "Dutch Elm Disease." *Scientific American* 245 (August, 1981): 56-66. Presents good illustrations of the infestation and the bark beetles. Includes a map with dates showing the progress of the epidemic.

Tippo, Oswald, and William Louis Stern. *Humanistic Botany*. New York: W. W. Norton, 1977. Unique

book focuses on the interactions of plants and humankind. The chapter on fungi includes a useful section on plant pathology.

Wilson, Edward O. *The Diversity of Life*. Rev. ed. Cambridge, Mass.: Belknap Press, 1999. Outstanding book for the general reader. Does not directly address the problem of Dutch elm disease but presents eloquent arguments regarding the value of each species and explains why the reduction of biodiversity should be avoided. Includes glossary and index.

SEE ALSO: 1917: American Farmers Increase Insecticide Use; June 25, 1938: Federal Food, Drug, and Cosmetic Act; 1939: Müller Discovers the Insecticidal Properties of DDT.

1930

LYOT'S CORONAGRAPH ALLOWS OBSERVATION OF THE SUN'S OUTER ATMOSPHERE

When Bernard Lyot created the coronagraphic telescope, he enabled the first extended observations of the Sun's outer atmosphere without the necessity of a natural solar eclipse.

LOCALE: Meudon (Paris), France
CATEGORIES: Science and technology; astronomy; inventions

KEY FIGURE
Bernard Lyot (1897-1952), French astronomer

SUMMARY OF EVENT
Although the chromosphere and corona represent only a very small part of the Sun's total atmosphere, they have long been astronomically interesting yet difficult to access. The subdivisions of the chromosphere and corona together encompass the Sun's outer atmosphere as inferred from both visual and telescopic observation, photometrically showing only 0.5×10^{-6} the brightness of the total Sun. During the total stage of a solar eclipse, the Sun's corona appears as an asymmetric halo, the apparent brightness of which generally decreases from the Sun's limb (outer edge of the disk) outward. With an overall increase in solar activity every eleven years, additional radial streamers, or rays, can appear outward from the corona. In a period of minimal solar activity, there is simply a diffuse distribution of visible radiation, with minimum intensity at the solar poles and maximum intensity at the equator. The corona's shape also shows

minimum ellipticity every three years prior to a sunspot cycle maximum. Normally, the much greater intensity of the halo, or aureole, of scattered light surrounding the Sun's disk hides the corona. Observed visually at sea level, the average sky further scatters coronal light to about one one-thousandth of this amount. Only rare locations, such as high mountaintops, offer the chance to observe the corona unaided even during an eclipse.

Research questions concerning the origins and behavior of the corona are important for stellar as well as solar astrophysics. From a planetary solar system perspective, the corona is effectively a transition zone between the solar surface and the interplanetary medium (for example, solar wind). From an astrophysical viewpoint, the conditions that exist in the solar corona are of great interest in determining the laws governing magnetohydrodynamic gases, spectral emissions from highly ionized atoms, and the like. Some of the important questions about the corona concern the temperature implications of the greatly increased spectral emissions above the solar limb and whether the chromosphere and corona are wholly or partly a collection of turbulent gas streams or a more uniform atmosphere.

Until about 1930, the solar corona had been observed astronomically only during total eclipses of the Sun, meaning only a few minutes per year of measurements, often under hurried and less than optimum conditions, with a total observation time from 1630 to 1930 of less than one hour. Spectroheliographs are special solar tele-

1930

scopes that can make observations at any wavelength, but they are slow and unsuited to accurate observations of short-lived eclipse and flare phenomena. Various attempts by astronomers such as Alexander Hale to take spectroheliographs to mountaintops for coronal observation were failures. The first recorded spectrum of the corona was recorded by Georges Rayet in 1868. Since the late 1890's, many (unsuccessful) attempts were made at telescopically detecting the Sun's corona outside eclipse conditions, including George Ellery Hale's single absorption-line spectroscopy in 1900 and Henri-Alexandre Deslandres's use of infrared band radiation in 1904. In 1906, Karl Schwarzschild recorded the first simultaneous spectra from both the Sun's center and inner corona, using a neutral diffusing filter and spectrophotometer. In 1931, W. Grotrian published results from the 1926 eclipse, recorded by modifying Schwarzschild's instrument.

As scientists eventually realized, ordinary reflector or refractor telescopes further scattered solar light from the already weakened and scattered visual appearance. The details of designing and building a special lens and some kind of shielding disk for noneclipse coronal observation required reduction of unwanted scattered light by a factor of more than 100,000. In response to these requirements, Bernard Lyot of the Meudon Observatory conceived, and in 1930 designed and constructed, a new optical telescope in which the diffusion of light inside the lens and telescope tube was minimized to these standards. In Lyot's original coronagraph, the Sun's disk is eclipsed artificially, or occulted, by a polished metal cone. The direct image of the remaining (corona) Sun is formed on a black screen slightly larger than the disk's image. The shiny cone also reflects back the Sun's light to the side, preventing it from falling back on the main objective lens. Nevertheless, it was further necessary to prevent the solar light diffracted by the main objective from getting into the second, middle objective lens. Lyot accomplished this by placing an aperture stop at the point where the light from the main lens is imaged by the final field lens. A further refinement was to place another opaque disk at the center of the second objective to catch and multiply reflected light from the primary lens and from the occulting cone.

In this chromatically aberrant design, the occulting disk is in focus only for single wavelengths. It is possible to compensate for the overcorrection of the secondary lens so that the final image is aberration-free. To minimize scattering from even microscopic defects of the tube and dust particles, all inner surfaces were smeared with thick oil, thus reducing thermal air currents. The coronagraph requires special care and environmental conditions. All lenses must be kept as clean as possible at all times from dust and aerosol particles. Atmospheric scattering, as noted, is a severe limit, but this is reduced notably for altitudes above a few kilometers, thus most coronal observatories have been constructed at heights above 1,800 meters (about 5,900 feet) and generally above 3,000 meters (9,840 feet) if possible. Winter frequently provides the best observing times; Lyot discovered optimal conditions immediately after heavy snowfalls had cleared the air of atmospheric dust particles.

SIGNIFICANCE

Wider use of the coronagraph, from 1932 on, provided vastly increased opportunities for coronal observation. Because it is not limited by the brevity of a solar eclipse, Lyot's coronagraph permitted far more precise measurements of the comparative intensities of different spectral lines vital to astrophysical theories of stellar composition and dynamics. Observations using Lyot's coronagraph—supplementing observations made during eclipses between 1893 and 1936—showed that the maximum equatorial elongation of the corona occurs 0.7 year before the minimum of solar prominences at higher solar latitudes. Coronal "rays" were shown also to be gas bodies of higher temperature forming above solar faculae, analogous to auroral polar lights insofar as both take the shape of the prevailing magnetic lines of force. Coronagraphic measurements permitted the first rigorous estimates of the temperature, lifetime, luminosity, and characteristic length and height of solar prominences. On the basis of coronagraph and eclipse data, Bengt Edlén in 1939 first identified the coronal lines of highly ionized atoms associated with electron temperatures of 10^6 Kelvins. Lyot showed that corona emission lines are very wide, confirming hypotheses by Edlén and others that Doppler broadening because of extremely high kinematic temperature is a common solar feature.

Despite his success, Lyot was not satisfied with his coronagraph's performance, suspecting that there was a need to reduce further or compensate for residual thermal diffusion within the coronagraph itself. Continuing his experiments, Lyot combined his coronagraph with a spectroheliograph, minimizing the heat leak problem. With this combination, in 1937 he succeeded in photographing the two brightest spectral lines in the green and red regions of the corona's spectrum over the entire solar disk. Lyot and other solar astronomers wanted to be able to observe simultaneously solar prominences over the chromosphere as well as the corona. Lyot's original dissertation research, from 1923 to 1930, concerned polarization of light reflected from planetary surfaces. In 1938, Lyot devised his quartz-polaroid monochromatic interference filter system. The principle of this filter is the passage of solar light through a series of polarizing layers having their planes of polarization parallel to one another. These filters are separated by thin plates of quartz glass whose thicknesses are calculated to produce optical interference fringes. The combination of the appropriate number and thickness of polarizers permitted a transmission band of only one angstrom in width, allowing rapid observations over the entire Sun using the well-known hydrogen alpha spectral line. In 1940, Lyot added to his filter another special optical arrangement, which permitted him to isolate different wavelengths and take 16-millimeter moving films of them.

Lyot's final innovation was the coronagraphic photometer, which enabled tracing of weak spectral lines even with ordinary refractor telescopes at sea level. Because of the technical difficulties in making the main lens and meeting all environmental conditions, coronagraphs typically are not large instruments. Among the largest are the 40-centimeter (15.7-inch) coronagraphs of the Sacramento Peak Observatory in Sunspot, New Mexico, and the High Altitude Observatory in Boulder, Colorado. Other coronagraphs are located at Pic du Midi, France; Mt. Norikura, Japan; Freiburg, Germany; and Capri, Italy. As of 2004, the largest coronagraph to date was installed at the Maui Space Surveillance System, an observatory on Mount Haleakala in Hawaii.

To avoid atmospheric scatter, brightness, and fluctuations, from May, 1973, to January, 1974, the Apollo Telescope on the Skylab space station included a special white-light coronagraph. From the thermospheric altitudes of an orbiting spacecraft, the sky is completely black overhead, and coronagraphic observations nearly match those of a total eclipse. Skylab recorded more than one thousand hours of coronagraph data, leading to the discovery of the phenomenon of coronal transients: huge

shock waves of ionized gas following a flare or prominence that propagate outward through the corona.

Many researchers consider the period from 1930 to 1947 the watershed between the era of fortuitous uncalibrated coronal observations of opportunity and detailed controlled observations. Bernard Lyot succeeded in accomplishing what many predecessors had tried but failed to do: observe coronal details without an eclipse.

—Gerardo G. Tango

FURTHER READING

Beer, Arthur, ed. *Vistas in Astronomy*. New York: Pergamon Press, 1955. Technical but accessible volume presents valuable information on spectroheliograph and coronagraph technologies and results.

Dyson, Frank, and Richard van der Riet Woolley. *Eclipses of the Sun and Moon*. Oxford, England: Clarendon Press, 1937. Reports noncoronagraphic observing methods and results.

Evans, John W., ed. *The Solar Corona*. New York: Academic Press, 1963. Intermediate advanced-level text gives important summaries of empirical and theoretical understanding of the Sun's corona.

Golub, Leon, and Jay M. Pasachoff. *The Solar Corona*. New York: Cambridge University Press, 1997. Reviews the information gleaned from observations of the solar corona since the mid-twentieth century. Chapter 5 includes discussion of the coronagraph. Intended for advanced students and researchers.

King, Henry C. *The History of the Telescope*. 1955. Reprint. Mineola, N.Y.: Dover, 2003. Excellent overall history of telescopes and attachments presents some material on the coronagraph. Includes photographs.

Stix, Michael. *The Sun: An Introduction*. 2d ed. New York: Springer-Verlag, 2002. Introductory technical treatment of solar observations and structure. Includes illustrations.

SEE ALSO: 1903-1904: Hale Establishes Mount Wilson Observatory; June 26, 1908: Hale Discovers Strong Magnetic Fields in Sunspots.

1930

1930
ZINSSER DEVELOPS AN IMMUNIZATION AGAINST TYPHUS

Hans Zinsser demonstrated clinical differences in forms of typhus and developed an effective vaccine against the disease.

LOCALE: Harvard University, Cambridge, Massachusetts

CATEGORIES: Science and technology; biology; health and medicine

KEY FIGURES

Hans Zinsser (1878-1940), American bacteriologist and immunologist

Howard T. Ricketts (1871-1910), American bacteriologist

John Franklin Enders (1897-1985), American immunologist

SUMMARY OF EVENT

As a bacteriologist and immunologist, Hans Zinsser was interested in the epidemiology of infectious diseases. During an outbreak of typhus in Serbia in 1915, he traveled with a Red Cross team in order to study the clinical and pathological aspects of the disease. He made subsequent trips to the Soviet Union in 1923, Mexico in 1931, and China in 1938. His observations supported the commonly held belief that typhus was caused by an organism, the rickettsia, isolated and named by Henrique da Rocha-Lima in 1916 for Howard T. Ricketts. The organism was known to be borne by a louse or a rat flea and transmitted to humans by way of a bite. The unsanitary living conditions resulting from poverty and overcrowding provided an atmosphere conducive for the spread of the disease.

The rickettsia are microorganisms whose shapes range from rod to sphere. Within the carrier's body, the rickettsia stimulate the cells of endothelial tissue to use phagocytosis (that is, to eat) so that the microorganism can enter and live in the cytoplasm of the endothelial cells, which line the gut of the insect. The rickettsia multiply within the tissue and pass from the insect body with the feces. Because the internal cells of the insect are destroyed, the insect dies within three weeks of becoming infected with the microorganisms.

As the flea or louse feeds on a human, it causes an itch; scratching of the itch may result in a break in the skin. This, in turn, provides an opportunity for the rickettsia-laden feces to enter the body. Dried, airborne feces can be inhaled. Once within the human host, the rickettsia invades endothelial cells associated with blood vessels and causes an inflammation of the blood vessels. The resulting cell death leads to tissue death. In a few days, the infected host exhibits symptoms such as a rash, severe and sudden headache, rise in temperature, photophobia (visual intolerance to light), vertigo, tinnitus (ringing in the ears), deafness, and an altered mental state, which gives the disease its name, typhus (from the Greek meaning cloudy or misty). Left untreated, the patient dies within nine to eighteen days.

Typhus was first described in Europe in the fifteenth century. It is among the oldest diseases known to be caused by the rickettsia. Medical science now recognizes three clinical forms: the epidemic louse-borne form, the Brill-Zinsser form, and the murine, or rodent-related, form. The epidemic louse-borne or classical form is the severest manifestation of the disease. *Rickettsia prowazekii* is the causative agent and is carried by the human body louse *Pediculus humanus*. The Brill-Zinsser form

Hans Zinsser. (National Academy of Sciences)

presents symptoms similar to but milder than the epidemic type. It involves the re-activation of the organism within the host cells, indicating that the host had encountered the epidemic form earlier. The murine form is caused by *Rickettsia typhi* (previously called *Rickettsia mooseri*), which is borne by a rat flea. This variety also presents symptoms that are milder than the epidemic type. The pathology of murine typhus closely resembles that of Rocky Mountain spotted fever, which is caused by *Rickettsia rickettsii*.

When Zinsser began his work on typhus, the information that existed concerning the disease was in a chaotic state. Zinsser sought to organize the information and bring order to the study of the disease. Zinsser and his colleagues, including John Franklin Enders, Hermann Mooser, and M. Ruiz Castañeda, sought to establish the relation of one form of typhus to the others. In 1898, an endemic form of typhus prevalent among immigrants in New York City had been described. The endemic form was called Brill's disease. Mooser, in the late 1920's, proved that the causative agent of Brill's disease was *Rickettsia mooseri* and that the organism was carried by the rat flea. The endemic form became known as the murine form, and the causative agent was later renamed as *Rickettsia typhi*.

In the 1930's, Zinsser suggested that there were actually two forms of the disease being described by Brill: one that was associated with rodents (murine form) and another that had its own causative agent and was a reactivation of an organism picked up at an earlier time when the patient was exposed to the epidemic disease present in many European countries at that time. He demonstrated that *Rickettsia prowazekii* was the agent involved in both the European epidemic version and the reactivated version, which was known as Brill's disease. As a result of Zinsser's effort to distinguish the two types of typhus disease, it was renamed Brill-Zinsser disease.

Because he had analyzed the mechanism of the Weil-Feliz diagnostic test for rickettsial diseases, Zinsser was aware that the disease-causing organism had an antigenic component, most likely a polysaccharide. In 1932, Zinsser and Castañeda identified agglutinins, or antibodies, in the blood serum of typhus-infected patients with the murine and the classical forms. Although earlier attempts at preventing typhus by means of passive immunity were not satisfactory, Zinsser saw immunity as a viable solution to the problem of typhus. He determined that a large number of dead microorganisms was neces-

---

PITY THE POOR LOUSE

In his book Rats, Lice, and History, *Hans Zinsser tells the story of his work against typhus. This excerpt illustrates why the book is considered a classic of popular science writing.*

The louse is foremost among the many important and dignified things that are made the subjects of raucous humor by the ribald. Despite the immense influence of this not unattractive insect upon the history of mankind, it is given in the Encyclopædia Britannica two thirds of a column—half as much as is devoted to "Louth, a maritime county in the province of Loinster," one fifth as much as is allowed for Louisville, Kentucky. This creature, which has carried the pestilence that has devastated cities, driven populations into exile, turned conquering armies into panic-stricken rabbles is briefly dismissed as "a wingless insect, parasitic upon birds and mammals, and belonging, strictly speaking, to the order of *Anoplura*."

The louse shares with us the misfortune of being prey to the typhus virus. If lice can dread, the nightmare of their lives is the fear of someday inhabiting an infected rat or human being. For the host may survive; but the ill-starred louse that sticks his *haustellum* through an infected skin, and imbibes the loathsome virus with his nourishment, is doomed beyond succor. In eight days, he sickens, in ten days he is *in extremis*, on the eleventh or twelfth his tiny body turns red with blood extravasated from his bowel, and he gives up his little ghost.

Man is too prone to look upon all nature through his egocentric eyes. To the louse, we are the dreaded emissaries of death. He leads a relatively harmless life—the result of centuries of adaptations; then, out of the blue, an epidemic occurs; his host sickens, and the only world he has ever known becomes pestilential and deadly; and if, as a result of circumstances not under his control, his stricken body is transferred to another host whom he, in turn, infects, he does so without guile, from the uncontrollable need for nourishment, with death already in his own entrails. If only for his fellowship with us in suffering, he should command a degree of sympathetic consideration.

The louse was not always the dependent, parasitic creature that cannot live away from its host. There were once free and liberty-loving lice, who could look other insects in their multifaceted eyes and bid them smile when they called them "louse." But this was even longer ago than the Declaration of Independence, for it took the louse many centuries to yield up its individualism.

Source: Hans Zinsser, *Rats, Lice, and History* (Boston: Little, Brown, 1935).

sary to induce an immunity that would be effective. He and his colleagues set out to develop a method of growing organisms in large quantities by using tissue culture. The method started by infecting chick embryo yolk sac tissue with rickettsia. The infected tissue was used to inoculate large quantities of normal chick tissue. The infected tissue was then grown on the surface of agar in flasks. This provided Zinsser and his team with the quantities of microorganisms needed to produce the desired vaccine. The type of immunization Zinsser was proposing is known as passive immunity. The infecting organisms have markers on their cell surfaces known as antigens. The antigens are capable of eliciting an immune reaction regardless of whether the cell is living, weakened, or dead. The reaction involves recognition of the antigen by cells called macrophages and cells called B cells. The B cells produce antibodies that are capable of destroying the invading organism directly or attracting more macrophages to the area so that they can destroy the organism. B cells also produce "memory cells," which remain in the blood in order to trigger a rapid second response if there is a subsequent infection. Because the vaccine contains weakened or dead organisms, the person experiences a mild reaction to the vaccine but is not at risk of contracting the disease.

SIGNIFICANCE

Typhus is still prevalent in many areas of the world. Where it does persist, the disease is nurtured by poverty and overcrowded, unsanitary living conditions. Many countries that have experienced severe drought report high incidences of typhus. Epidemic typhus has not been reported in many countries for some time. The last report of the epidemic in the United States was in 1921. Endemic or murine typhus occurs more frequently. The incidence in the United States is low, with about fifty cases per year being reported. Because the organism is susceptible to antibiotics, such as tetracycline and chloramphenicol, reported cases can be treated; therefore, the mortality rate is low.

Zinsser's work on the treatment and prevention of the disease had important impacts. By creating an orderly classification of the typhus diseases and identifying causative agents and vectors, Zinsser and his coworkers contributed significantly to the understanding of the disease, which in turn enabled attempts to discover a cure and establish preventive measures. Louse and rodent control and improved sanitation helped to prevent the spread of the disease.

Zinsser's idea to grow large quantities of the rickettsia

to make a vaccine led him to investigate tissue culture as a quick and reliable method of securing a good yield of the desired microorganism. The attention focused on the tissue culture method and inspired researchers to modify and improve the technique so that now the use of tissue culture is a standard effective laboratory procedure.

Zinsser's greatest contribution to medicine was the development of a vaccine for typhus. This disease has a place not only in the history of medicine but also in the history of the world. Battles and wars were lost because louse-infected armies fell victim to typhus. Invading armies carried the disease across national boundaries; Europe witnessed an uninterrupted series of epidemics throughout the eighteenth and nineteenth centuries. The vaccine that Zinsser and his team developed ensured that even if wars continued and armies were subjected to undesirable living conditions, the possibility of contracting typhus would be greatly reduced. The vaccine also provided a safeguard for the poor in crowded cities. People who were forced by financial circumstances to live in densely packed housing, where they might easily become infected by lice or rat fleas, gained protection against typhus once the vaccine became available.

Because Zinsser looked to immunology for protection against typhus, he also had an impact on the growing science of immunology and its application to medicine. Vaccines have been developed against many pathogenic organisms, and their use has obliterated many diseases that were once commonplace. Zinsser was one of the pioneers in applying the principles of immunity to health care.

Zinsser was also an inspiring teacher whose students and associates appreciated his approach to science and his concern for the human condition. Unfortunately, he died before he had a chance to see all the benefits that accrued from the production of his vaccine against typhus. Today, the incidence of typhus is negligible, although small outbreaks of Q fever have been reported in the United States and Australia, and Rocky Mountain spotted fever has been reported in the United States.

—Rosemary Scheirer

FURTHER READING

Duma, Richard J., et al. "Epidemic Typhus in the United States Associated with Flying Squirrels." *Journal of the American Medical Association* 245 (June 12, 1981): 2318-2323. Flying squirrels have been added to the list of rickettsia vectors. Suggests that most cases of typhus in the United States involve contact with squirrels.

Joklik, Wolfgang K., Hilda P. Willet, and D. Bernard Amos, eds. *Zinsser's Microbiology.* 20th ed. East Norwalk, Conn.: Appleton & Lange, 1995. Presents excellent descriptions of the rickettsia organism and typhus disease. Highlights Zinsser's contributions to the immunology of the disease.

Olitsky, Peter K. "Hans Zinsser and His Studies on Typhus Fever." *Journal of the American Medical Association* 116 (January 8, 1941): 907-912. Comprehensive recitation of the highlights of Zinsser's life and career. Describes Zinsser as a humanist and philosopher as well as a scientist. Includes a summary of the typhus research available when Zinsser began his work in 1930.

Strong, Richard P. "Obituary: Hans Zinsser." *Science* 92 (September 27, 1940): 276-279. Written by a great admirer of Zinsser. Lauds the nonscientist side of Zinsser's life, including his publication of poetry and other literary works under a pseudonym. Reveals the deep feelings of admiration many of Zinsser's students and colleagues had for him.

Zinsser, Hans. *Rats, Lice, and History.* 1935. Reprint. New York: Black Dog & Leventhal, 1996. Classic volume presents what Zinsser calls a biography of a disease. Begins with his views on science and its relation to art and then provides a detailed account of epidemics and their influence on history. The last five chapters address the history of typhus. Highly readable; a must for anyone interested in history as well as science.

Zinsser, Hans, Harry Plotz, and John F. Enders. "Scientific Apparatus and Laboratory Methods: Mass Production of Vaccine Against Typhus Fever of the European Type." *Science* 91 (January 12, 1940): 51-52. A firsthand account of the problems encountered and the modifications made in the development of a method to grow organisms in large quantities. Clearly written and accessible to nonscientists.

SEE ALSO: 1908: Chlorination of the U.S. Water Supply Begins; 1913: Schick Introduces a Test for Diphtheria; 1921: Tuberculosis Vaccine BCG Is Developed; June, 1937: Theiler Develops a Treatment for Yellow Fever; 1939: Müller Discovers the Insecticidal Properties of DDT.

1930-1931
PAULING DEVELOPS HIS THEORY OF THE CHEMICAL BOND

Through his ingenious use of quantum mechanics, Linus Pauling developed a theory of the chemical bond that strongly influenced the fields of chemistry, physics, biology, and mineralogy.

LOCALE: Pasadena, California
CATEGORIES: Chemistry; physics

KEY FIGURES

Linus Pauling (1901-1994), American physical chemist
Gilbert N. Lewis (1875-1946), American chemist
John C. Slater (1900-1976), American physicist
Walter Heinrich Heitler (1904-1981), German theoretical physicist
Fritz Wolfgang London (1900-1954), German physicist

SUMMARY OF EVENT

When interviewers asked Linus Pauling to name what he considered to be his most important discovery, he often responded that he was extremely pleased by his work on the nature of the chemical bond. His series of papers on this topic in the early 1930's and his book *The Nature of the Chemical Bond and the Structure of Molecules and Crystals* (1939) clarified large areas of chemistry and contributed to important advances in such fields as biochemistry, mineralogy, and medicine. Pauling's work grew out of the contributions of his predecessors, and in several ways he was able to recapitulate the thinking of scientists who had lived many years before him. The idea of an atom's definite combining power had been developed in the nineteenth century, and it formed the theoretical backbone of a dynamic structural theory that was able, under the insightful tutelage of the Dutch physical chemist Jacobus Henricus van't Hoff (1852-1911), to reveal how the four valence bonds of certain carbon compounds are directed toward the corners of a regular tetrahedron, thus accounting for the right- and left-handed forms of particular organic molecules.

With the discovery of the electron by Sir Joseph John Thomson in 1897 and the discovery of the nucleus by Ernest Rutherford in 1911, theories about how atoms are linked together in compounds became more dependent on a physical model of the atom, especially how electrons are arranged around the nucleus. Pauling became

1930

fascinated by the ideas of Gilbert N. Lewis, who had proposed a theory of the inner structure of the atom. In Lewis's model, electrons occupy the space around the nucleus in certain patterns that are responsible for an element's specific properties, including its bonding properties. Lewis pictured the atom as a series of concentric cubes whose corners could be occupied by electrons. He used this "cubical atom" to explain the formation of chemical bonds by the transfer of electrons from one atom to another. Lewis proposed that electrons could be shared between atoms in forming a covalent bond. The idea of this covalent (or shared electron-pair) bond had a great impact on Pauling.

As a graduate student at the California Institute of Technology, Pauling made use of Niels Bohr's quantum theory of the atom in his own theoretical speculations. Bohr had been successful in applying the quantum idea to the hydrogen atom, showing how its lone electron could exist solely in specific orbits (or quantized states) around its nuclear proton. Bohr's theory, however, was not very successful in accounting for the electronic structures of complex atoms or for the combinations of atoms in molecules. Pauling tried to use Arnold Sommerfeld's version (with elliptical rather than circular orbits) of Bohr's atomic model to explain the structure and properties of benzene, a ring compound of six carbon atoms, but the old quantum theory was simply too weak to enable Pauling or any other scientist to develop a satisfactory theory of chemical structures.

With the development of quantum mechanics in the mid-1920's, a tool was now available to resolve many of the deficiencies of the old theory. Pauling was influenced principally by Erwin Schrödinger's formulation of wave mechanics and was able to use the new quantum mechanics to predict the properties of various ions and to develop a perspicacious picture of the ionic bond (an interatomic link in which one of the atoms has a disproportionate share of the electronic charge). One of the ideas on which wave mechanics was built is the wave nature of the electron. Using his wave equation, Schrödinger was able to reveal many advantages in treating the electron as a wave rather than as a particle in a strictly defined orbit. In one interpretation of Schrödinger's equation, electrons occupy orbitals, often represented by such shaded geometric figures as spheres or somewhat distorted dumbbells, the intensity of the shading corresponding to the relative probability of finding an electron in this particular region. Although Schrödinger's treatment made it difficult to speak of atoms as rigid mechanical structures, it permitted a new view of chemical bonding, particularly in the hands of Walter Heinrich Heitler and Fritz Wolfgang London.

While in Munich, Pauling met Heitler, who was working toward his doctoral degree. In the summer of 1927, Pauling discussed quantum mechanics with Heitler and met London, who had a Rockefeller Foundation grant to work with Schrödinger. After Pauling returned to the United States, Heitler and London published a paper on the quantum mechanics of the chemical bond that Pauling once called "the greatest single contribution to the clarification of the chemist's concept of valence." In the paper, Heitler and London made use of the idea of resonance, which had been introduced by Werner Heisenberg in 1926, to explain how two hydrogen atoms could bond when brought near to each other. In the resonance phenomenon, an interchange in position of the two electrons reduces the system's energy and causes the formation of a bond. Heitler and London supplied a quantum mechanical justification for Lewis's electron-pair idea. Their quantum mechanical method allowed them to calculate approximate values for various properties of the hydrogen molecule, for example, how much energy it would take to split the molecule into its component atoms.

In the fall of 1927, Pauling began a period of intense scientific creativity. He developed a theory for predicting the structures of crystals. He refined his wave mechanical treatment of the hydrogen molecule-ion (a hydrogen molecule with one rather than two electrons). Most important, he enunciated for the first time what later came to be called the hybridization of atomic orbitals. The idea of hybrid orbitals grew out of his chemical intuition. To physicists, it seemed strange that carbon, with two different types of orbitals (the spherical $2s$ and the dumbbell-shaped $2p$), should generate, in its chemical compounds, four identical bonds that were directed to the corners of a tetrahedron. To Pauling, it seemed strange that such tetrahedral compounds of carbon as methane (CH_4) could not be explained by atomic orbitals. A physicist would regard it as a very serious error to mix s and p orbitals, but Pauling recognized that the energy separation between the two orbital states was small, compared with the energy of the bond formed. For him, the ability to make the best possible bond was the most important consideration. In 1928, he published a short paper in which he reported that he had used quantum mechanical resonance to derive the four equivalent orbitals used in bonding by the carbon atom. Furthermore, these orbitals, which he also referred to as hybrid orbitals, are directed toward the corners of a regular tetrahedron.

Linus Pauling. (The Nobel Foundation)

Pauling had difficulties in translating his insight into a mathematical treatment that would be convincing to most scientists. When he was unable to solve the complex mathematical expressions, he set the matter aside. Meanwhile, in 1929, John C. Slater became interested in the quantum mechanics of the chemical bond. He had developed a method for interpreting the complex spectra of certain atoms, and when he applied his methods to molecules, he derived information about the valence and directional properties of these molecules. He first described his results in an informal talk at the Washington meeting of the American Physical Society in April, 1930. He published a paper in 1931 in the *Physical Review*, suggesting that the dumbbell-shaped charge clouds of certain orbitals were responsible for the directional properties of many chemical compounds. He also introduced the criterion of maximum overlapping of orbitals for bond strength, and he made extensive use of resonance. Further, he discussed the directional bonds formed in molecules with many atoms, and he even attempted to explain why the four valences of carbon have tetrahedral symmetry.

Slater's work stimulated Pauling to return to the problem he had set aside in 1928. In December, 1930, while he was doing some calculations, he had an idea about making an assumption to simplify the quantum mechanical equations describing the bonding orbitals of carbon so that they could be solved in an approximate way. The quantum mechanical equations describing the orbitals with which he was concerned have radial and angular parts, and given that the radial part of the 2*s* wave function of the carbon atom (from which the orbital can be readily derived) is not very different from the radial part of the three 2*p* functions, Pauling concluded that little error would be introduced if he ignored the radial factor in the *p* function. This facilitated his calculations of various hybrid orbitals, for example, the tetrahedral hybrids, called *sp*3 because they involve a combination of the 2*s* and the three 2*p* orbitals. His semiquantitative approach to the chemical bond proved so successful that he went on to develop the implications of his ideas. He was able to give explanations from the kinked structure of the water molecule to the transition from covalent to ionic bonding.

In January and February, 1931, Pauling continued to make refinements and extend their application. His most famous paper, titled "The Nature of the Chemical Bond: Applications of Results Obtained from the Quantum Mechanics and from a Theory of Paramagnetic Susceptibility to the Structure of Molecules," appeared in the *Journal of the American Chemical Society* on April 6, 1931. With this work Pauling established a framework for understanding the electronic and geometric structures of molecules and ions in terms of hybrid bond orbitals. Also, the framework permitted him to use the magnetic properties of molecules to distinguish between ionic and covalent bonding. Pauling explained how the energy barrier between *s* and *p* orbitals can be broken when strong bonds are formed. Because a large orbital overlap is associated with the formation of a strong bond, he was able to relate bond strength to the nature of the orbitals from which the bond is formed. He used the ideas of resonance and hybridization to explain the tetrahedral, square, and octahedral configurations of certain molecules.

From 1931 to 1933, Pauling published a series of papers on the nature of the chemical bond, in which he used the concepts of hybridization of bond orbitals and the resonance of molecules among two or more alternative structures to elucidate many basic chemical phenomena. For example, he was able to use hybrid orbitals and resonance to explain the properties of the benzene molecule, the carbon-to-carbon bond lengths, planar structure, hex-

1930

agonal symmetry, and great stability of which had puzzled chemists for generations. He was able to formulate an electronegativity scale of the elements, which proved to be extremely useful to chemists. Electronegativity is the tendency of an element in a compound to attract electrons to itself, and Pauling found a way to assign numbers to the elements to represent this power of attracting electrons.

Pauling's papers were so successful that, by 1935, he believed that he had a complete understanding of the nature of the chemical bond. He was able to give form to this understanding in the late 1930's, when he served as a professor of chemistry at Cornell University. Out of his lectures came a book, *The Nature of the Chemical Bond and the Structure of Molecules and Crystals*, the first edition of which was published in 1939. The book was received enthusiastically, with one reviewer calling it "epochmaking." It was an excellent summation of Pauling's decade of studies on the nature of the chemical bond.

SIGNIFICANCE

Pauling's theory of the chemical bond was a milestone in the development of modern chemistry. Chemists were deeply impressed by the power of Pauling's methods to unify a vast amount of previously unintegrated data. They were also impressed by the large amount of experimental data Pauling had collected, tabulated, and rationalized. Pauling's papers and book on the chemical bond accumulated thousands of citations in the 1930's and 1940's. Physicists, biochemists, molecular biologists, and mineralogists used his data and ideas to solve many problems in their disciplines. It is interesting to note that James D. Watson and Francis Crick made extensive use of Pauling's book while they were trying to figure out the structure of deoxyribonucleic acid (DNA).

Despite the great success of Pauling's work on the chemical bond, it shared the contingencies of all scientific achievement. Because of the many approximations involved in his approach, it had a number of limitations, which critics soon pointed out. Charles A. Coulson, for example, asserted that although Pauling's comparison of bond length and orbital overlap is very useful in a qualitative sense, it is not adequate for the quantitative determination of bond energies for certain hybrid orbitals. Nevil Sidgwick also argued that Pauling's theory of the chemical bond should be "received with a certain reserve" because of its lack of mathematical rigor. Other scientists developed a theory—often called the molecular orbital (MO) method or theory—that rivaled Pauling's. Pauling and Slater's method was a natural outgrowth of the work of Heitler and London; therefore, this

approach, which viewed the chemical bond from the perspective of two separate atoms coming together, was sometimes called the Heitler-London-Slater-Pauling (HLSP) method, but it is known most often as the valence bond (VB) method or theory. Other names given to the theory, the "method of localized pairs" and the "method of the directed valence bond," are not used often.

In the molecular orbital method, the problem of the chemical bond is attacked from the viewpoint of the single molecule produced by the coalescence of the atoms. During the late 1940's and through the 1950's, the MO method began to find favor with a number of chemists, and Pauling's VB theory came increasingly under attack. Some European and American scientists pointed out that the VB theory was encountering difficulties in explaining the excited states of molecules, whereas the MO method was successful in its quantitative discussions of these excited states. During this same period, Pauling's theory came under attack on ideological grounds. Certain Soviet critics found Pauling's notion of resonance irrational, because it went against some of the basic tenets of dialectical materialism. Essentially, certain Soviet chemists criticized Pauling, whom they called a "decadent bourgeois scientist," for his attributing reality to his formal equations and models (for these Soviet critics, resonance structures were human-made, not real). In place of Pauling's theory, the Soviet chemists preferred to turn to the Soviet chemist Aleksandr Mikhailovich Butlerov, whose theory of the mutual influence of atoms in molecules they found both scientifically and ideologically acceptable. It is ironic that Pauling, who shared with many Soviet philosophers and scientists a deterministic and realistic interpretation of quantum mechanics, should have encountered such animosity toward his theory of resonance, especially given that he admitted that his resonance descriptions bore a close resemblance to the actual molecular structures. A further irony is that at the same time Soviet chemists were attacking him for his resonance theory, American politicians were criticizing him for his attitude toward the Soviet Union.

Despite these criticisms from the East and the West, Pauling's theory of the chemical bond proved to be useful for scientists for three decades. When the VB theory began to be replaced by the MO theory in the 1960's, Pauling continued to retain a deep loyalty to his views of the chemical bond. This was characteristic of his approach to science. When he was convinced of the value of a scientific idea, he clung to it tenaciously and used it boldly. Resonance was such an idea. Early in his career, Pauling became convinced of its power and efficacy.

Continued success in applying this idea to a great variety of chemical problems confirmed this attitude. Because of the strength of the resonance concept, he was less attracted to the new ideas about chemical bonding that came on the scene. Confronted with new problems, he tended to solve them in terms that he understood. This tenacity, which had a negative side, was also a part of his genius. Without his championing of the VB theory, modern structural chemistry's great successes, such as the determinations of the structures of DNA and proteins, would have been significantly delayed. It is thus impossible to understand the evolution of modern structural chemistry without taking account of Pauling's theories.

—*Robert J. Paradowski*

FURTHER READING

Coulson, Charles A. *Valence*. 3d ed. London: Oxford University Press, 1985. Volume by an Oxford professor of mathematics who became a distinguished theoretical chemist discusses how wave mechanics transformed valence theory. Includes some use of mathematical formulas, but the treatment is mostly qualitative. Intended for "the novice chemist with few mathematical attainments." Features author, substance, and subject indexes.

Hager, Thomas. *Force of Nature: The Life of Linus Pauling*. New York: Simon & Schuster, 1995. In-depth biography places Pauling's scientific work within the context of his long life and many wide-ranging interests.

Lagowski, J. J. *The Chemical Bond*. Boston: Houghton Mifflin, 1966. Uses the words of scientists to re-create for students the exciting process of discovery. Approach is historical and accessible to both students of science and readers taking chemistry for the first time. Contains several helpful tables and diagrams and includes lists of suggested readings.

Lewis, Gilbert Newton. *Valence and the Structure of Atoms and Molecules*. 1923. Reprint. New York: Dover, 1966. Although written before the development of quantum mechanics, this interesting account is still valuable for the light it sheds on the ideas of Lewis and other scientists. Includes an introduction by Kenneth Pitzer, illustrations, references, and index.

Mead, Clifford, and Thomas Hager, eds. *Linus Pauling: Scientist and Peacemaker*. Corvallis: Oregon State University Press, 2001. Collection of essays both by Pauling and about him is divided into sections on the man, the science, and Pauling's work as a peace activist. Includes photographs, reproductions of original Pauling manuscripts, and a bibliography of Pauling's works.

Palmer, William G. *A History of the Concept of Valency to 1930*. Cambridge, England: Cambridge University Press, 1965. Uses the theme of the increasingly fertile cooperation between physics and chemistry to explain how the idea of chemical valence was established and how the modern theory of the chemical bond evolved from it. Valuable source of information on both the early history of valence theories and the later development of electronic theories.

Pauling, Linus. *The Architecture of Molecules*. San Francisco: W. H. Freeman, 1964. Demonstrates Pauling's excellent ability to communicate clearly his understanding of molecules. Illustrator Roger Hayward captures Pauling's structural imagination in beautifully drawn and colored plates. Intended for young people who are beginning to develop an interest in science, but valuable for anyone with a curiosity about the natural world. Includes a periodic table of the elements and some tables of atomic radii.

_____. *The Nature of the Chemical Bond and the Structure of Molecules and Crystals: An Introduction to Modern Structural Chemistry*. 3d ed. Ithaca, N.Y.: Cornell University Press, 1960. Pauling's magnum opus. Because his approach is structural rather than mathematical, the book is accessible to readers with modest backgrounds in chemistry, physics, and mathematics. More difficult material appears in twelve appendixes. Includes author and subject indexes.

Russell, C. A. *The History of Valency*. Leicester, England: Leicester University Press, 1971. Detailed, coherently organized study of the history of physical and chemical bonding ideas. Treats controversial material in a balanced and insightful way. Includes indexes.

Servos, John W. *Physical Chemistry from Ostwald to Pauling: The Making of a Science in America*. Princeton, N.J.: Princeton University Press, 1990. Explores the evolution of physical chemistry in the United States through an analysis of the key institutions and scientists who made the discipline into a fertile source of innovative ideas. Includes endnotes and index.

SEE ALSO: 1912-1915: X-Ray Crystallography Is Developed by the Braggs; May 14, 1913: Rockefeller Foundation Is Founded; 1928-1932: Szent-Györgyi Discovers Vitamin C.

1930

1930-1932
JANSKY'S EXPERIMENTS LEAD TO RADIO ASTRONOMY

An antenna set up to determine the causes of interference with radio transmission detected the first radio signals recognized as coming from outside the solar system.

LOCALE: Cliffwood, New Jersey
CATEGORIES: Science and technology; astronomy

KEY FIGURES
Karl G. Jansky (1905-1950), American radio engineer
Albert Melvin Skellett (b. 1901), American radio
    technician and astronomer
Grote Reber (1911-2002), American radio engineer

SUMMARY OF EVENT
In 1928, Karl G. Jansky was hired as a radio engineer by Bell Telephone Laboratories. His first assignment was to investigate the causes of interference with transatlantic radiotelephone transmissions. This investigation required a sensitive antenna whose frequency response and sensitivity were very stable—ideal characteristics of any radio telescope. The device Jansky built, which was called a "Bruce array," consisted of two parallel frameworks of brass tubing; one frame was connected to a receiver, and the other acted as a signal reflector. The antenna was mounted on four wheels from a Model T Ford and rotated every twenty minutes on a circular track. The antenna, which was about 66 feet (20 meters) long and 13 feet (4 meters) in width and height, was nicknamed the "merry-go-round."

Jansky discovered that his instrument could detect three kinds of signals. Nearby thunderstorms created infrequent but powerful radio bursts. Distant thunderstorms created weak but steady signals as their radio signals were reflected off the ionosphere, an electrically conducting layer in the upper atmosphere. The third signal, which created a steady hiss in receivers, was at first a mystery. Even though this signal was not a serious problem for radio reception, Jansky continued his efforts to identify the source. The signal varied in intensity in a daily cycle, and Jansky initially suspected that it might originate with the Sun. The problem with this theory was that the signals reached their highest point a few minutes earlier each day.

Jansky, who was unfamiliar with astronomy, did not appreciate the significance of this observation, but a friend of his, Albert Melvin Skellett, did. The planet Earth takes 23 hours and 56 minutes to complete one rotation with respect to the stars. Because Earth moves in its orbit by about one degree per day, it takes an extra 4 minutes to complete a rotation with respect to the Sun. The signals were following sidereal (star) time; that is, they came from a source that was fixed with respect to the stars. In 1933, after a full year of observations, Jansky published his estimate of the source's location: in the southern part of the Milky Way galaxy in the direction of Sagittarius. In 1935, after additional analysis, Jansky reported that signals originated from all along the Milky Way.

Once Jansky understood the nature of the cosmic signals, he found that he was completely unable to detect the Sun, which he found quite puzzling. Jansky happened to be observing at a time of minimal sunspot activity. If he had observed at a time of great sunspot activity (at "sunspot maximum"), his equipment should have detected solar radio emissions. Had he observed at sunspot maximum, however, the upper atmosphere would have been nearly opaque at the wavelengths he studied, and he probably would not have detected radio waves from the Milky Way. Jansky realized that if he could not detect the Sun, the signals from the Milky Way were not likely to originate in the stars. He suggested that the radio signals originated from interstellar dust and gas instead, a suspicion that has proved to be correct.

Jansky's observations were described in a front-page article in *The New York Times* on May 5, 1933, and a national radio program broadcast a few seconds of cosmic radio noise. Nevertheless, the discovery had little significance for practical communications. Jansky proposed the construction of a 98-foot (30-meter) dish antenna to study the cosmic signals in greater detail, but his employers, believing that such investigations were more appropriate for academic researchers, turned down the proposal. Jansky went on to other areas of communications research and received a commendation for his work on radio direction finders during World War II. He had always been in poor health, and he died in 1950 at the age of forty-four, just as radio astronomy was beginning to flourish.

One of the few people who had sufficient knowledge of both astronomy and radio to take advantage of Jansky's work was Grote Reber, who realized that investigating celestial radio sources would require completely different equipment from that Jansky had used. In 1937, Reber built a parabolic reflecting antenna with a diameter of 32.8 feet (10 meters), which was used to make maps of the sky by aiming the parabolic dish at different elevations and letting Earth's rotation sweep the antenna across the field of view.

SIGNIFICANCE

The discovery of cosmic radio signals led to the field of radio astronomy—the first time astronomers used any part of the electromagnetic spectrum other than the range of frequencies containing visible and infrared light. This new tool allowed astronomers for the first time to investigate the universe without having to depend on optical telescopes: Because radio waves penetrate cosmic dust and gas clouds, which block visible light, these radio waves could be used to map the structure of the Milky Way galaxy. In the years after Jansky and Reber's work, radio astronomy discovered great explosive bursts in other galaxies, some of which emitted so much energy that their causes became the focus of scientific investigation. Radio astronomy also discovered pulsars as well as the faint background radiation that most astronomers

consider to be the echo of the big bang. Astronomers were unprepared for the discovery that the universe could look so different at radio wavelengths.

Perhaps the most important effect of radio astronomy was to teach astronomers that every part of the electromagnetic spectrum reveals new phenomena and new types of celestial objects. The result was the opening up of new areas of investigation, including X-ray and ultraviolet astronomy.

—*Steven I. Dutch*

FURTHER READING

Burke, Bernard F., and Francis Graham-Smith. *An Introduction to Radio Astronomy*. 2d ed. New York: Cambridge University Press, 2002. Authoritative graduate-level text provides an introduction to radio telescopes as well as an overview of radio astronomy. Includes references, index, and an appendix on the origins of radio astronomy.

The Goldstone Deep Space Communication Complex in the Mojave Desert of California, one of three complexes that make up the National Aeronautics and Space Administration's Deep Space Network (DSN). The DSN provides radio communications for all of NASA's interplanetary spacecraft and is also utilized for radio astronomy and radar observations of the solar system and the universe. (NASA)

Hey, J. S. *The Evolution of Radio Astronomy*. New York: Science History Publications, 1973. History of radio astronomy concentrates mostly on the period after World War II but also provides some details regarding Jansky's work.

Reber, Grote. "Radio Astronomy." *Scientific American* 181 (September, 1949): 34-41. Written by the first radio astronomer at the dawn of radio astronomy, this article shows some of the first published radio maps of the heavens and makes a number of conjectures (later proven correct) about the causes of some cosmic radio signals.

Spradley, Joseph L. "The First True Radio Telescope." *Sky and Telescope* 76 (July, 1988): 28-30. An account of the telescope of Grote Reber, who for more than a decade was the only scientist to pursue Jansky's discoveries. Clearly describes Reber's construction and early attempts to detect cosmic radio signals and reproduces some of his first radio maps of the heavens.

Sullivan, Woodruff T., III. "A New Look at Karl Jansky's Original Data." *Sky and Telescope* 56 (August, 1978): 101-105. Summarizes the events that led to Jansky's discovery of extraterrestrial radio sources. Includes a reproduction of Jansky's original chart data and a reexamination of his data in the light of modern discoveries. The language is moderately technical, appropriate to an introductory college science course.

_____. "Radio Astronomy's Golden Anniversary." *Sky and Telescope* 64 (December, 1982): 544-550. A pictorial review of early radio astronomy from Jansky's initial discovery through 1967. Illustrations include photos of major historical figures as well as depictions of equipment and significant data recordings.

_____, ed. *The Early Years of Radio Astronomy: Reflections Fifty Years After Jansky's Discovery*. 1984. Reprint. New York: Cambridge University Press, 2005. Collected recollections of many of the pioneers in the field place the birth and early era of radio astronomy in societal and scientific context. Includes many historical photographs.

Verschuur, Gerrit L. *The Invisible Universe Revealed: The Story of Radio Astronomy*. 2d ed. New York: Springer-Verlag, 1987. Written by a leading radio astronomer, this book summarizes the history of radio astronomy and surveys the major types of celestial radio phenomena.

SEE ALSO: Mar. and June, 1902: Kennelly and Heaviside Theorize Existence of the Ionosphere; 1919: Principles of Shortwave Radio Communication Are Discovered; 1927: Oort Proves the Spiral Structure of the Milky Way; 1934-1945: Radar Is Developed; 1935: Chapman Determines the Lunar Atmospheric Tide at Moderate Latitudes; June-Sept., 1937: Reber Builds the First Intentional Radio Telescope.

1930-1935
VON STERNBERG MAKES DIETRICH A SUPERSTAR

In a series of seven films from 1930 to 1935, film director Josef von Sternberg created a hauntingly ambiguous myth of womanhood, using Marlene Dietrich as Galatea to his Pygmalion.

LOCALE: Hollywood, California
CATEGORY: Motion pictures

KEY FIGURES
Josef von Sternberg (1894-1969), Austrian American film director and cameraman
Marlene Dietrich (1901-1992), German American film and theater actor and singer
Travis Banton (1894-1958), American film costume designer
Lee Garmes (1898-1978), American cinematographer

SUMMARY OF EVENT
In the fall of 1929, Josef von Sternberg was in Germany to film *Der blaue Engel* (1930; *The Blue Angel*). His involvement in this project, which was under the aegis of the famous Universarium Film studios in Berlin, derived from his earlier collaboration in the United States with the famous German actor Emil Jannings. He had directed Jannings in the 1928 film *The Last Command*, and Jannings was sufficiently impressed to ask for von Sternberg to direct the first German sound film to be made for Universarium with Eric Pommer as producer. Von Sternberg agreed, as his career in Hollywood was on the slide; as usual, however, he insisted on having complete control of the project. That control extended to the selection of the female lead to play opposite Jannings. Both Jannings and Pommer supported the casting of either

Trude Hesterberg or Lucie Mannheim for the part, but von Sternberg had a specific idea of character, and neither of those women fit his idea. The woman he wanted was someone akin to the woman who comes to the poet in Percy Bysshe Shelley's *Alastor* as he sleeps. She is the vision of his own soul, her voice speaking "knowledge and truth and virtue." Von Sternberg found this woman in Marlene Dietrich.

Dietrich became for von Sternberg a summation of the Romantic beauty, the fatal woman whose effect on men is simultaneously liberating and imprisoning. Richly complex, this woman exists as metaphor for the male desire forever frustrated, yet she also represents the woman as Other, as necessarily lonely because the world cannot accommodate such independence and erotic power. She is a fetish, the object of the male gaze and the objectification of his desire. Even Dietrich's name, "Marlene"— a contraction of her given names Maria and Magdalene—indicates her ambiguity. In his memoir, *Fun in a Chinese Laundry* (1965), von Sternberg indicated his interest in this fatal woman, especially in her decadent, late nineteenth century form, when he noted that the specifications for the woman he wanted for his film "had been drawn up by Felicien Rops," a Belgian artist who was popular in the late 1880's. In Rops's work, the woman is polymorphously erotic; in her, innocence and experience come together. While attending the theater one night, von Sternberg found the woman he had imagined.

Dietrich, it seems, was reluctant to play the character, Lola-Lola; she thought she was not attractive enough for the part. Indeed, she was, in the words of Herman Weinberg, a "plump, pretty dumpling," and she conducted herself lethargically at the first interview she had with the film's director. Von Sternberg, however, persevered, and soon "she behaved as if she were there as my servant. . . . Not the slightest resistance was offered to my domination of her performance." In her autobiography, *Marlene* (1989), Dietrich substantiated this, noting that von Sternberg set out to "Pygmalionize" her; she credited him with having "breathed life into this nothingness. . . . I was nothing but pliable material on the infinitely rich palette of his ideas and imaginative faculties."

Before *The Blue Angel* was released in the United States, American audiences saw Dietrich in *Morocco* (1930). For that film, she had shed thirty pounds, and her face had begun to take on a mysteriously contoured look,

Marlene Dietrich. (AP/Wide World Photos)

as von Sternberg's camera and lighting played over it with effective shadows. As she had in *The Blue Angel*, Dietrich played a cabaret singer. In *Morocco*, she is Amy Jolly, a woman with a past who has traveled to Morocco, the end of the line for her, it seems. Two men seek her affections, the rangy legionnaire Tom Brown (Gary Cooper) and the suave and wealthy Frenchman LeBressiere (Adolphe Menjou). The plot is simple, even melodramatic: Offered wealth and security by LeBressiere, Amy Jolly turns her back on community and follows her soldier into the desert. More important than the melodramatic plot are the play of light and shadow on the screen and the ambiguous sexuality of Dietrich. In her first appearance in the cabaret, she wears a man's top hat and tails; in one famous scene, she leans over and plants a kiss on the lips of a giggling girl in the audience.

Dietrich and von Sternberg followed *Morocco* with a spy thriller, *Dishonored* (1931), in which Dietrich plays a prostitute turned spy known as "X-27." The story is von Sternberg's. As Amy Jolly sacrifices a life of leisure and comfort for her man, so too does X-27 sacrifice her life for her lover, Lieutenant Kranau (Victor McLaglen). In this film, von Sternberg extended the range of Dietrich's character portrayal and her costumes. Cinematographer

1930

Lee Garmes made her look like Greta Garbo, like a country maid, and like the Dietrich who would become legendary. Costume designer Travis Banton arrayed her in all sorts of outfits. The film reaches its high point as X-27 faces the firing squad. She takes a blindfold from the young officer who offers it to her, wipes a tear from his eye, then adjusts her makeup and straightens her stockings. Before the sound of the guns, von Sternberg cuts quickly to a close-up of X-27's enigmatic smile. America's Depression-era audiences loved it.

After *Dishonored*, however, Von Sternberg felt that further collaboration would be harmful to both himself and his star. Dietrich disagreed. She refused to work with another director, and Paramount brought the two of them together for *Shanghai Express* (1932). The opening of this film is remarkable for von Sternberg's masterful recreation of Beijing (then known in the West as Peking), the claustrophobia of its streets echoed in the claustrophobia of train compartments and corridors. Again, Dietrich appears as a woman of questionable behavior. She is Shanghai Lily: "It took more than one man to change my name to Shanghai Lily," she tells Donald Harvey (Clive Brook). Unlike Lola-Lola but like the characters in her American films with von Sternberg, the Dietrich character in *Shanghai Express* may be fallen, but she is not without honor and loyalty. She appears ready to sacrifice herself for her lover, although here von Sternberg is less forthright than in the earlier films. Perhaps more than any other of the von Sternberg-Dietrich films, *Shanghai Express* captures the mysterious beauty of Dietrich. Garmes won an Oscar for the film's cinematography, and both the film itself and its director received Academy Award nominations.

As much as von Sternberg's visual style captures the viewer, especially as it affects the appearance of Dietrich, his use of sound is equally significant. Unlike many in Hollywood who feared the coming of sound to the film industry, von Sternberg welcomed it as another element in the aesthetic effect of film. He avoided the use of background music; instead, he incorporated natural sound into the filmic effect. For example, in *Morocco* he used no music; instead, the drums of the legionnaires punctuate the action and intensify the emotional effect of the scene in which Amy hears them approach and realizes she must seek out her true lover. In *The Blue Angel*, sound articulates place: the classroom, the cabaret, the dressing room. The guns that fire to execute X-27 in *Dishonored* reverberate in the airplane hangar von Sternberg used to film the sequence. In *Shanghai Express*, the actors speak in monotone to complement the sound of the train. Similarly, the thudding tempo of Dietrich's "Hot Voodoo" number in *Blonde Venus* (1932) accentuates the soap-opera emotionalism of the story.

Blonde Venus is generally taken to be the most autobiographical of von Sternberg's films with Dietrich. Once again, however, the surface is the thing to catch the eye and interest of the audience. The film shimmers with light right from the opening sequence, in which Dietrich bathes nude in a glittering forest lake. The subtleties of light and shade are once again a cue to the film's interest in style, and the conventional ending with Dietrich—the film's Venus—returning to her son and husband is a perfunctory addition. Von Sternberg's great strength is to present on film both reality and the fantasy world lying deep within his audience. Much of the play with light and shade and enclosed space evokes a dreamworld, but not the dreamworld of Hollywood musicals or comedies. Von Sternberg's dreamworld is that of the unconscious. He was fascinated with mental aberration, the depths of desire, anxiety, fear, and the urge to violence.

All of this comes together in a baroque manner in the penultimate film von Sternberg made with Dietrich, *The Scarlet Empress* (1934). Ostensibly the story of Catherine the Great of Russia, *The Scarlet Empress* shows von Sternberg at his most excessive: Camera angles, sets, costumes, cutting, and other film techniques draw attention to themselves in every frame. Much of the film offers a shot-by-shot rhythm of frames that alternate between light and dark. The sets are large in scale; gargoyles and grotesque sculptures leer at the viewer from the screen. Dietrich herself is nearly lost in furs or amid sculptures, candles, fog, or smoke. Von Sternberg called the film "a relentless excursion into style."

After *The Scarlet Empress*, one film remained in the pair's collaboration; von Sternberg had done all he could with his Galatea. He would complete only seven films in the next thirty-five years of his life. For her part, Dietrich was also ready to move on. An intelligent and gifted actor and performer, she would have a brilliant career in film and on stage. First, however, the two consummated their artistic relationship with *The Devil Is a Woman* (1935). Once again the costumes were varied and chic. Parades, festivals, confetti, and balloons decorated the screen. Aluminum paint was sprayed onto dresses and backgrounds to give von Sternberg complete control over light. The film is a fitting conclusion to the years of collaboration between von Sternberg and Dietrich. She called the film their "crowning achievement" and "the most beautiful film that was ever made."

SIGNIFICANCE

It is easy to see the influence of von Sternberg's silent gangster film *Underworld* (1927); what is less clear is the influence of the seven films he made with Dietrich. Indeed, these films are strange genre pieces. Later films continued to exploit these familiar genres: the Foreign Legion film, the spy thriller, the journey through dangerous territory, the domestic tragedy, the historical romance. No one else who made such films, however, dismissed plot with such insistence as von Sternberg. Luis Buñuel comes to mind as a director who used formula plots for ideological purposes, but his art was more directly social than von Sternberg's. For von Sternberg, emotion was style. Perhaps the closest parallel of the time was Busby Berkeley, whose 1930's musicals dispensed with plot in order to present a choreography of camera, costume, and design.

Von Sternberg's high-key lighting shows up in many films of the 1930's, including Rouben Mamoulian's *The Song of Songs* (1933), with Dietrich; John Ford's *Mary of Scotland* (1936), with Katharine Hepburn; and Howard Hawks's *Barbary Coast* (1935), with Miriam Hopkins. In the 1940's, the lighting effects von Sternberg used were seen in such Michael Curtiz films as *Casablanca* (1942), with Ingrid Bergman, and *Mildred Pierce* (1945), with Joan Crawford; in Alfred Hitchcock's *Notorious* (1946), with Bergman; and in Orson Welles's *The Lady from Shanghai* (1948), with Rita Hayworth. Bob Fosse's *Cabaret* (1972), with Liza Minnelli, also echoes the costumes and ambience of *The Blue Angel*. On a more technical level, von Sternberg's tendency to avoid cutting within scenes, his use of lighting and angles to create mood, and his use of natural sound anticipated the work of Michelangelo Antonioni.

The woman fashioned by von Sternberg continued to serve Dietrich well in many roles, from Frank Borzage's *Desire* (1936) to Billy Wilder's *Witness for the Prosecution* (1957). Many echoes of her beauty have appeared on the screen, from Joan Crawford to Anouk Aimee.

—*Roderick McGillis*

FURTHER READING

Baxter, John. *The Cinema of Josef von Sternberg*. New York: A. S. Barnes, 1971. Provides cogent readings of all von Sternberg's films. Shows how the stylish aspects of the films make sense thematically. Nicely points out the irony of von Sternberg's obsession: The woman he fashioned becomes his undoing. Includes select bibliography and filmography.

Baxter, Peter, ed. *Sternberg*. London: British Film Institute, 1980. Collection of seventeen articles on von Sternberg's work dating from 1930 to 1980. Includes the famous essay by Aeneas MacKenzie, "Leonardo of the Lenses," and essays by Rudolph Arnheim, Siegfried Kracauer, Barry Salt, and von Sternberg himself. The essay on *Morocco* by the editorial staff of *Cahiers du Cinema* offers a detailed analysis of the film's social milieu.

Dietrich, Marlene. *Marlene*. Translated by Salvator Attanasio. New York: Grove Press, 1989. Covers much of the same ground as von Sternberg's *Fun in a Chinese Laundry* (cited below). Dietrich's admiration for von Sternberg is unbounded, and she has perceptive things to say about lighting and camera work. Opinionated, idiosyncratic, and delightfully candid.

Sarris, Andrew. *The Films of Josef von Sternberg*. Garden City, N.Y.: Doubleday, 1966. Brief, readable survey of von Sternberg's films includes interesting observations regarding Dietrich's performances. Accepts von Sternberg's evaluation of himself as a poet and addresses these films as dream poems to be appreciated for their visual delights.

Spoto, Donald. *Falling in Love Again: Marlene Dietrich*. Boston: Little, Brown, 1985. Presents a brief and useful survey of the years of collaboration between von Sternberg and Dietrich. Includes many exquisite photographs.

Von Sternberg, Josef. *Fun in a Chinese Laundry*. New York: Collier Books, 1965. Meandering, eccentric, and fascinating account of the author's life and theory of filmmaking. Not always accurate, but always provocative. With regard to Dietrich, he notes: "I gave her nothing that she did not already have."

Weinberg, Herman G. *Josef von Sternberg: A Critical Study*. New York: E. P. Dutton, 1967. Valuable for an interview with von Sternberg, a few excerpts from his correspondence, passages from the shooting scripts of *Shanghai Express* and *The Saga of Anatahan* (1953), and a good selection of early reviews of von Sternberg's work. Includes filmography and bibliography.

SEE ALSO: 1909-1929: Pickford Reigns as "America's Sweetheart"; Aug., 1926-Sept., 1928: Warner Bros. Introduces Talking Motion Pictures; May 11, 1928: Sound Technology Revolutionizes the Motion-Picture Industry; 1930's: Hollywood Enters Its Golden Age; 1930's-1940's: Studio System Dominates Hollywood Filmmaking.

1930

February, 1930
CRANE PUBLISHES *THE BRIDGE*

Hart Crane's dauntingly ambitious and difficult modernist poem The Bridge *was characteristic of the author's effort to see modern urban America in mythological terms.*

LOCALE: New York, New York
CATEGORY: Literature

KEY FIGURES
Hart Crane (1899-1932), American poet
T. S. Eliot (1888-1965), American poet
James Joyce (1882-1941), Irish novelist
Walt Whitman (1819-1892), American poet

SUMMARY OF EVENT

Hart Crane began work on his long poem *The Bridge* in 1923. He conceived this epic work as a rejoinder to the pessimism and sense of apocalyptic decline expressed in T. S. Eliot's epochal poem *The Waste Land*, which had been published in 1922. Although Crane much admired Eliot, he felt *The Waste Land*, with its representation of the sterility of civilization after World War I, had not done justice to the energy and excitement of the modern urban and industrial era. Hence Crane began, slowly and methodically, to put together an idiomatically American synthesis of the twentieth century machine age.

Crane's work on the poem through the 1920's was fitful and was interrupted by bouts of alcoholism, depression, and foreign travel, as well as by numerous homosexual affairs. His most productive period came in 1926, the year that also saw the publication of *White Buildings*, a collection of his shorter lyric pieces. During the late 1920's, Crane's epic endeavor attracted the private sponsorship of Otto H. Kahn, a wealthy banker, and it was Kahn's support that helped Crane to complete the poem. *The Bridge* finally appeared in a special edition printed by the Black Sun Press in February, 1930, before being published in the United States by Liveright in April of the same year.

The Bridge is made up of nine sections. It starts with the introductory "Proem: To Brooklyn Bridge," set in 1920's Manhattan, which hails Brooklyn Bridge as a modern-day deity mysteriously empowered to "lend a myth" to the capitalist affairs of Wall Street. This is followed by "Ave Maria," which features Christopher Columbus in mid-Atlantic narrating the story of his discovery of America as he returns home to Spain. Section 2 of *The Bridge* is titled "Powhatan's Daughter" and encom-

passes five distinct shorter poems that recount the history of Native American life. With section 3, "Cutty Sark," the reader returns to a saloon in lower Manhattan, where old sailors recall their seafaring adventures; section 4, "Cape Hatteras," then focuses on epic exploits of the air, notably the aviation experiments conducted in 1903 by Wilbur and Orville Wright off the coast of North Carolina. Section 5, "Three Songs," again brings the reader back to the world of twentieth century New York; one of the section's three shorter poems, "National Winter Garden," takes its title from a burlesque theater in Greenwich Village that Crane had frequented. Section 6, "Quaker Hill," proceeds to cast a jaundiced eye at golf courses in suburban Connecticut. Section 7, "The Tunnel," describes an infernal and nightmarish subway ride from Manhattan to Flatbush, passing under the East River and so beneath the Brooklyn Bridge; the final section, "Atlantis," circles back to the poem's first image of the deified bridge, a construction now found to be illuminated with an intense mythological splendor.

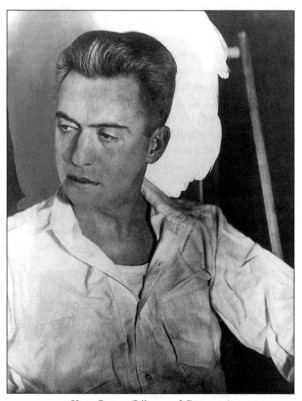

Hart Crane. (Library of Congress)

No simple narrative description of *The Bridge*, however, can capture the full extent of Crane's artistic ambitions in this work. He aspired to invent an aesthetic design of multiple interlocking strands, so as to bring to light—and into an idealistic harmony—suppressed analogies between different geographic areas and historical eras in American life. Crane's goal was indeed to evoke a series of conceptual bridges: the railway bridging the American continent, the Wright brothers' bridging of land and air, bridges between the white man and the Indian, between childhood and adulthood, between fifteenth century Christopher Columbus and twentieth century Columbus Circle in New York City. Thus each section of *The Bridge* anticipates and echoes all the other sections. As Crane himself said in a 1926 letter, his poetic technique can be seen as "symphonic in including the convergence of all the strands" introduced separately within the narrative structure of the poem.

On one level, then, Crane was reinventing the kind of mythic version of the United States that Walt Whitman had promulgated during the nineteenth century. Indeed, Crane explicitly pays tribute to Whitman in "Cape Hatteras," saluting the great "Saunterer" as a pioneer who sought to impose a mythic form on the most unpromising and inchoate American materials. Crane's own style, however, should be understood as Whitman crossed with Eliot and James Joyce, for Crane believed Whitman's language of bluff, colloquial Romanticism to be no longer adequate to address the complexities and dislocations of modern life. Instead, Crane, like Eliot and Joyce, used a dense and complicated mixture of verbal allusion and wordplay to convey his sense of the fragmented and radically unstable landscape of technological society. Crane was very interested in the first installments of Joyce's *Finnegans Wake* (1939)—then known as "Work in Progress"—which were being published during the late 1920's in the Parisian magazine *transition*, and Joyce's elaboration of punning as a narrative principle in that work was something Crane also chose to pursue, working with the idea of the pun as a bridge between disparate meanings.

Crane himself visited Paris in 1929 while putting the final touches to *The Bridge*. At the time, the French capital was home not only to Joyce but also to the Surrealist movement in art and literature, and throughout his career, Crane was conversant with the self-reflexive strategies of Surrealists such as Marcel Duchamp and Man Ray, whose perception of art as an ingenious but ultimately nihilistic game also came to influence certain aspects of the American poet's work. *The Bridge*, in fact, is shot through with moments of black humor in which its visionary idyll seems knowingly to collapse into self-parodic or burlesque forms. There is in Crane's poem an element of deliberate buffoonery, a dark self-mockery that does not altogether cancel the poem's mythological idealism but that holds it in an ambiguous suspension. It was not by chance that Crane fixed upon the image of a suspension bridge to convey his sense of how mythological transformation might (or might not) operate within the hardheaded business world of Manhattan.

SIGNIFICANCE

Immediate reaction to publication of *The Bridge* was disappointing. Crane's poem finally appeared only a few months after the Wall Street crash, and the literary climate of the early 1930's was no longer favorable to the poem's dense and cryptic style of high modernism. *The Bridge* materialized at the moment when American writing was developing methods of journalistic realism that had more direct social and political relevance to the Great Depression era; within that context, Crane's ornate rhetoric appeared uncomfortably inward-looking and self-indulgent. Even intellectuals such as Allen Tate and Yvor Winters, who had both encouraged Crane when he was writing the poem, were lukewarm in their response to the final product. In part, this happened because Crane's idiosyncratic brand of hyperbolic wordplay did not conform to any definition of "myth" sanctioned by the classical learning Tate and Winters admired. Crane was depressed at these responses, but he spent time in Mexico on a Guggenheim Fellowship during 1931 and 1932, and he began to plan another epic poem, this one centered on Hernán Cortés's conquest of Mexico. He completed only a few fragments of that work, however; gray-haired and exhausted by his emotional traumas and intellectual travails, Crane took his own life on April 27, 1932, by jumping into the Caribbean Sea from the SS *Orizaba* as he was returning home from Mexico to New York.

The most obvious long-term effect of *The Bridge* was its validation of American urban life as a fit subject for poetry. As Crane wrote in his "Modern Poetry," his intention was to ensure that the environment of the machine could form "as spontaneous a terminology of poetic reference as the bucolic world of pasture, plow, and barn." The Beat poets of the 1950's were to build on this idea of a visionary quality implicit within everyday urban life, as was another Manhattan poet of that period, Frank O'Hara. In fact, *The Bridge* helped to redress a long-standing imbalance in the American poetic tradi-

1930

tion, which up until Crane's time had been weighted heavily toward the rural and pastoral mode.

For thirty years after Crane's death, however, the most common reaction to *The Bridge* was that the poem represented a heroic but ultimately pathetic failure. It was held to be a frustrated attempt to invent a grandiose myth of America, a myth that could not be sustained either by the mundane, lapsed environment of the twentieth century or by the erratic lyric gifts at Crane's disposal. Philip Horton's 1937 biography of Crane characterized the poet as a lost romantic soul, helping to reinforce this image of noble self-immolation, which lasted for more than a quarter of a century. During the 1950's, for example, Allen Ginsberg in several poems invoked Crane as a doomed victim of corporate America, a homosexual iconoclast and visionary whose genius had been crushed by the impersonal weight of the nation's unfeeling commercial culture. Robert Lowell's poem "Words for Hart Crane," published in his 1959 collection *Life Studies*, paints a similar picture of Crane as a tortured poet, "the Shelley of my age." At this time, the legend of Crane's short and robustious life was still overshadowing the legacy of his poetic achievement, and it was not until the 1960's that critics began paying more attention to the intricacies and achievements of Crane's texts themselves.

Gradually, however, the aesthetic impact of *The Bridge* began to be felt. Several fine close readings during the 1960's and 1970's were supported by the publication of John Unterecker's massive biography, *Voyager: A Life of Hart Crane,* in 1969. After that time, interest in Crane's work continued to grow. In the 1980's, a new generation of critics such as Lee Edelman and Thomas E. Yingling wrote of Crane as having developed a radical style of gay poetics, an elliptical series of rhetorical tropes that in failing to acquiesce to the orthodox conventions of language could be seen as mirroring Crane's own ambivalent stance toward the dominant ideologies of American society. It is also significant that postmodernist writers of long poems such as Richard Howard and Alfred Corn acknowledged a greater debt to Crane than to the "concrete" poets of midcentury such as Charles Olson. Whereas Olson's style of clear-eyed realism could be seen as antithetical to Crane's thrusting rhetoric, Corn's narrative poem *Notes from a Child of Paradise* (1984) conjoins epic and mock epic in a way very reminiscent of Crane's edgy tone in *The Bridge*. Corn wrote an admiring critical essay on *The Bridge*, and these two long poems also resemble each other in their uneasy juxtaposition of public concerns with private identities,

their teasing affiliation between objective myth and subjective romance, and their knowing interrogation of how precisely one side of this equation depends on the other.

For many years, *The Bridge* was seen as something of a white elephant in American literary history: an ambitious and impressive work, but also a strange, puzzling, and ultimately perturbing one. Yet what in the 1930's was generally perceived as a weakness—Crane's refusal to adopt any standard intellectual formula for his mythic endeavor—was later viewed by many critics as an unexpected source of strength. Because the poet enjoyed an oblique relationship with the aesthetic conventions of American modernism, *The Bridge* managed subsequently to keep its distance from the various large-scale theories about a misplaced mythopoeic idealism that is sometimes said to constitute the "failure of modernism." Crane was never emotionally or intellectually wedded to utopian ideals in the manner of T. S. Eliot or Ezra Pound; rather, the ubiquitous element of mythic gamesmanship in *The Bridge* distinguishes it as a work touched more by the Surrealist mode. From this perspective, the poem's quirky humor and self-mocking wordplay lend it an elusive quality that the more solemn epic works of Eliot and Pound tend to lack. With its wry mixture of romanticism and subversive comedy, its delicate balance between sentimentalism and irony, *The Bridge* is a poem that continues to offer challenges and surprises to the reader.

—*Paul Giles*

FURTHER READING

Corn, Alfred. *The Metamorphoses of Metaphor: Essays in Poetry and Fiction.* New York: Viking Press, 1987. Considers the final section of *The Bridge* in relation to Crane's revision of utopian legends. Notes connections with Dante and T. S. Eliot. Of special interest in the light of artistic parallels between *The Bridge* and Corn's own poetry.

Crane, Hart. *The Complete Poems of Hart Crane.* Edited by Marc Simon. New York: Liveright, 2001. One of the most complete editions of Crane's poetry. Includes *The Bridge* and all other published works, plus unpublished poems, incomplete works, and fragments.

_____. *Letters, 1916-1932.* Edited by Brom Weber. Berkeley: University of California Press, 1965. Excellent collection of Crane's letters to his friends, relatives, and publishers. Provides a sense of the range of Crane's interests. Marred by some editorial bowdlerizing.

Edelman, Lee. *Transmemberment of Song: Hart Crane's Anatomies of Rhetoric and Desire.* Stanford, Calif.:

Stanford University Press, 1987. Presents a general discussion of stylistic issues in Crane's work followed by close attention to particular poems, including *The Bridge*. Provides especially perceptive psychoanalytic readings of Crane's poetry.

Fisher, Clive. *Hart Crane: A Life*. New Haven, Conn.: Yale University Press, 2002. Biography examines Crane's personal life in greater detail than earlier works on the author and places his work in the context of his life and times. Includes photographs.

Giles, Paul. *Hart Crane: The Contexts of "The Bridge."* New York: Cambridge University Press, 1986. Relates *The Bridge* to a series of historical and conceptual contexts, such as relativity, capitalism, burlesque theater, and European Surrealism. Places *The Bridge* within a particular historical framework, showing links between Crane's work and that of his artistic contemporaries.

Unterecker, John. *Voyager: A Life of Hart Crane*. 1969.

Reprint. New York: W. W. Norton, 1987. Comprehensive biography includes anything about Crane that the author thought might possibly be of significance. Difficult to read from cover to cover, but indispensable for tracing particular aspects of Crane's life.

Yingling, Thomas E. *Hart Crane and the Homosexual Text: New Thresholds, New Anatomies*. Chicago: University of Chicago Press, 1990. Concentrates on the development of Crane's poetic style in terms of a specifically homosexual aesthetic. Connects some of the alleged obscurity in Crane's work with a general reluctance on the part of critics to engage with Crane's radical subject matter. Somewhat narrow in approach but presents many perceptive readings.

SEE ALSO: Oct., 1912: Harriet Monroe Founds *Poetry* Magazine; 1917-1970: Pound's *Cantos* Is Published; 1922: Eliot Publishes *The Waste Land*; Oct., 1924: Surrealism Is Born.

February, 1930
LUCE FOUNDS *FORTUNE* MAGAZINE

Fortune magazine provided the elite in the 1930's with a chronicle of American business and keen insights about the close connections among business, society, and government.

LOCALE: New York, New York
CATEGORIES: Publishing and journalism; organizations and institutions

KEY FIGURES

Henry R. Luce (1898-1967), American founder of a magazine empire that included *Time*, *Life*, and *Fortune*

Dwight Macdonald (1906-1982), American writer and critic

Archibald MacLeish (1892-1982), American poet

Eric Hodgins (1899-1971), managing editor of *Fortune* in the early 1930's and later publisher of *Fortune*, 1937-1941

SUMMARY OF EVENT

The first issue of *Fortune* came out in February, 1930, seven years after the founding of the increasingly successful *Time* magazine, owned by the same corporation. The first issue was impressive, with a black-and-bronze cover depicting a wheel of fortune. *Fortune* was con-

ceived and designed by Henry R. Luce, cofounder of *Time*, who reportedly thought of the name while on a New York City subway. Luce believed that *Time* and other general newsmagazines devoted less space to business information than its importance warranted. The leading business magazines of the period—*Dun's Review*, *Barron's*, and *Forbes*—all concentrated on corporate finance and investment securities, and none was either stylish or well written. Luce considered the other, more broadly based, business magazines to be banal or worse, full of blatant puffery of individual businesspeople and corporations.

Luce believed that the exciting panorama of American business in the late 1920's offered more than enough promising material for a well-written and lavishly produced monthly. The prepublication advertising prospectus for *Fortune* stated that no other magazine "succeeds in conveying a sustained sense of the challenging personalities, significant trends and high excitements of this vastly stirring Civilization of Business." The prospectus promised that *Fortune* would do this, a commitment that Luce kept.

The first issue, in February, 1930, included about a dozen articles on such disparate but business-related subjects as freezing foods, glass in manufacturing, commercial orchid growing, hog farming, the Rothschilds, and the Radio Corporation of America (RCA). The RCA article was an early example of the "corporation story," a distinct *Fortune* innovation in business journalism. Such stories included detailed analysis of the policies, problems, structure, finances, and key people of a single corporation. Later, similar articles would become a feature of such business magazines as *Forbes* and *BusinessWeek*. Although the articles during *Fortune*'s first two years were confined largely to business, by the mid-1930's *Fortune* included thoughtful examinations of government and social issues in general, with an eye to their effect on business.

The July, 1935, issue of *Fortune* contained, for example, seven feature articles. Only two could be described as corporate stories, one a richly illustrated feature on Anheuser-Busch and the other on U.S. Smelting and Refining. *Fortune* pointed out that each of these companies had been helped by policies of the Franklin D. Roosevelt administration: Anheuser-Busch by the end of Prohibition, and U.S. Smelting and Refining by the June, 1934, Purchase of Silver Act. The remaining five articles included a piece on cotton that heavily emphasized the effect of Henry A. Wallace's government-funded crop-reduction program; a fifteen-thousand-word portrait of Harry Hopkins, a close adviser to Roosevelt and administrator of the controversial Federal Emergency Relief Act; a lengthy article, including a number of specially commissioned paintings by a noted artist, on the restoration of colonial Williamsburg; and the first of a ground-breaking series of three articles on "women of business" that discussed in detail what was described as the "feminization of the American office." This account of the women's movement was remarkably prescient, reading much like something that could have been written decades later.

It was also in the July, 1935, issue that *Fortune* introduced what is generally credited as being the first published public opinion poll. *Fortune*'s managing editor, Eric Hodgins, decided that the use of surveys to discover consumer preferences could be extended to help illuminate public opinion on political, social, and general economic matters. The first publication of Elmo Roper's *Fortune Survey* was touted as a "journalistic service" to business. The first survey issue examined public opinion concerning Senator Huey Long's "Share the Wealth" program, various kinds of cigarette and automobile preferences, and beliefs about proposed new utility taxes.

When Luce and his associates planned *Fortune* in 1928, they could not know that the economy would soon be sliding into a deep depression. Otherwise, Briton

Hadden, Luce's chief partner in Time Inc., may not have agreed to put up $160,000 in seed money from Time Inc.'s treasury. By the summer of 1929, a dummy copy had been prepared. It was used, along with a money-back guarantee, to entice quality advertisers for the first issue. *Fortune* was not inexpensive for advertisers or subscribers. Its newsstand price was one dollar, compared with five or ten cents for typical magazines of the 1930's. Its advertising space rate was also high. A dollar's worth of advertising in *Fortune* reached about 90 readers, fewer than the 140 reached with a dollar of advertising in *The New Yorker* or more than 280 for advertisements in *Time*.

Nevertheless, selling advertising space in *Fortune* proved to be relatively easy in spite of the Depression. Some 779 pages of advertising were sold during 1930, with this figure rising to 1,253 pages by 1934. The exceptional composition of *Fortune*'s readership accounted for its commercial success. As a 1934 advertising sales brochure pointed out, *Fortune*'s ninety thousand subscribers included more than half of the Americans with family incomes above $25,000. The combined income of its subscribers was said to surpass the total for all the income earned by taxpayers in thirty-three of the forty-eight states.

Because *Fortune* reached the nation's business elite, it attracted two types of advertising. Its primary subscribers represented a key industrial market for machinery, advertising agencies, and office equipment. Business leaders also took the beautiful magazine issues home, as indicated by one estimate that each issue was read by ten people. The families of *Fortune* subscribers provided a top market for luxurious consumer goods and services. Ads for fine jewelry, Packard and Pierce-Arrow automobiles, expensive liquors, and yachts filled each issue.

Fortune's artistic magnificence as a periodical was unparalleled and obviously appealed to America's elite. Striking photographs, portraits, maps, and drawings richly illustrated the text. Its cover, printed on boldly textured paper stock, was so heavy that the first issue weighed almost two pounds. Among the famous artists commissioned to provide paintings and etchings for *Fortune*'s covers and inside pages were Rockwell Kent, Edward Wilson, and Diego Rivera, who illustrated a feature story in the October, 1938, issue on the ongoing Mexican revolution. *Fortune* also became famous for its innovative photography. Margaret Bourke-White, a well-known industrial photographer, and Erich Solomon, who coined the phrase "candid camera," provided action-oriented pictures of industrial enterprise, from assembly lines to boardrooms.

Fortune also achieved its promise of high literary standards. In assembling the writing staff of *Fortune*, Luce decided to hire, as at *Time*, young writers fresh from Harvard, Yale, and Princeton. Luce believed that broadly educated and talented writers made better business journalists than did those trained in commerce. The senior writing and editorial staff of the 1930's included such literary luminaries as Archibald MacLeish, Dwight Macdonald, James Gould Cozzens, James Agee, and poet Russell Davenport. *Fortune* also broke ground by hiring top women's college graduates for its staff research positions.

This extraordinary publication enjoyed great success, with both its circulation and its advertising revenues rising during the 1930's. During its first year of publication, *Fortune* averaged 34,000 subscribers and had ad revenue of $354,000. It was operating at a profit by the end of 1930. By 1937, the average circulation was 143,000, with more than $1,726,000 in ad revenue. Moreover, with profits from *Time* going into the development of the new mass-circulation *Life*, the earnings from *Fortune* in the late 1930's probably saved Luce's empire from going into the red.

SIGNIFICANCE

Fortune represented, in many ways, an entirely new kind of business periodical. In depicting what it called the "business civilization" of the United States, *Fortune* pioneered the "corporation story," which provided a story, illustrations, and in-depth analysis of an individual corporation, with emphasis on the human drama inevitably involved. Sometimes such stories resulted in much more being publicly revealed than management wanted to be known about corporate matters. *Fortune* generally kept its prepublication promise not to flatter important individuals or defend business in all matters.

Luce believed that the public interest was invested in large corporations. As a result, *Fortune*'s editorial policies successfully challenged the business journalistic tradition that a public corporation's internal workings were private. Even when subjecting its corporate subjects to a critical eye, *Fortune* was relatively sympathetic to the purposes of American business. Castigated by some corporate chiefs as well as by certain radical spokesmen, *Fortune* managed to occupy a middle ground between the banal business puffery of much business journalism and the radical publications whose antibusiness voices were increasingly shrill.

In marked contrast to most business journalism during the difficult Depression years, *Fortune* adjusted well to the changing times and the New Deal. Articles during *Fortune*'s first two years were confined largely to business operations and products and to individual corporations, businesspeople, and prominent families. *Fortune*'s contents after 1932 shifted to a much heavier emphasis on social and political movements and to the New Deal. Most issues in the middle and late 1930's included stories on the personalities of Roosevelt's "Brain Trust" and the new agencies, public works projects, and other features of the New Deal. Given the well-documented liberal or even radical bias of many of *Fortune*'s writers, such features were often pro-New Deal. Luce was, at best, lukewarm to Roosevelt, but he gave his writers latitude in expressing their own opinions.

An important and enduring symbol of *Fortune*'s recognition of the increasingly close relationships among business, society, and government is the *Fortune Survey*. The first *Fortune* surveys of public opinion in 1935 indicated general public support for the New Deal socioeconomic changes taking place. A large majority of respondents, for example, believed that the government should guarantee that every man who wanted to work had a job. President Roosevelt became a regular follower of the Roper *Fortune Survey* and always tried to obtain the results in advance of their publication.

Fortune not only claimed to understand the new impacts of government on business but also, in some cases, welcomed it. In a notable 1938 series about the struggle between business and government, the consistent theme was "reconciliation, an end to the sterile and unnecessary warfare between American business and the New Deal." These editorials were widely reprinted and commented on nationwide. Some corporate leaders, such as Alfred P. Sloan, Jr., chairman of General Motors, found much to commend in the series.

The highly influential *Fortune* generally supported rapprochement between the Roosevelt administration and big business in the late 1930's. Perhaps the most valuable legacy of its influence would be the cooperation that took place between government and business during World War II. As a senior *Fortune* staffer wrote, the business and government series did much to pave the way for the collaboration soon to be required by the war effort. During World War II, *Fortune* did its part by scaling back on its lavish graphics and increasing its coverage of military-related industries beginning in 1940.

Fortune in the 1930's not only was beautiful and profitable but also became increasingly influential in the highest levels of American society and government. It was, as Archibald MacLeish wrote in a book of recollec-

1930

tions of *Fortune* staffers published in 1980, "a paradox from the start. Its first issue appeared in the worst depression of modern history, and the magazine was saved from disaster only by altering its fundamental assumption about the world." John A. Davenport, another *Fortune* writer from the period, also recalled in the 1980 book that "Henry Luce's boldest assumption in founding *Fortune* was that American business was more fascinating than stock and bond quotations and carloading statistics, the stock in trade of most previous financial journalism."

—*Anthony D. Branch*

FURTHER READING

Augspurger, Michael. *An Economy of Abundant Beauty: "Fortune" Magazine and Depression America.* Ithaca, N.Y.: Cornell University Press, 2004. Discusses the philosophy behind *Fortune* in its early years and the magazine's influence on American culture. Includes endnotes and index.

Baughman, James L. *Henry R. Luce and the Rise of the American News Media.* 1987. Reprint. Baltimore: The Johns Hopkins University Press, 2001. Provides an excellent review and analysis of the unique roles of *Time*, *Fortune*, and later *Life* within American society and Luce's marked influence on these publications. Includes bibliography and index.

Elson, Robert T. *Time Inc.: The Intimate History of a Publishing Enterprise.* 3 vols. New York: Atheneum, 1968-1986. Outstanding institutional history of Time Inc. In volume 1, chapter 12 presents a perceptive view of the founding and first years of *Fortune*.

Lubar, Robert, et al. *Writing for "Fortune": Nineteen Authors Remember Life on the Staff of a Remarkable Magazine.* New York: Time Inc., 1980. Collection of brief essays by former *Fortune* staff researchers, writers, and editors addresses subjects ranging from concern about political ideology to typography and the staff's penchant for Scotch. Provides a nostalgic view of *Fortune*'s first decade.

Macdonald, Dwight. "*Fortune* Magazine." *The Nation* 144 (May 8, 1937): 528-532. After his widely publicized resignation in 1936 as a senior writer for *Fortune*, Macdonald wrote a three-part series in *The Nation* about Time Inc. In this article he concludes that despite its apparent objectivity, *Fortune* was dominated by capitalist ideology.

Okren, Daniel, ed. *"Fortune": The Art of Covering Business.* New York: Gibbs Smith, 1999. Presents reproductions of every *Fortune* cover from the first issue in February, 1930, to December, 1950, when the magazine changed its approach to cover art. Includes a brief introductory essay.

Whitfield, Stephen J. *A Critical American: The Politics of Dwight Macdonald.* Hamden, Conn.: Archon Books, 1984. Fascinating account of Macdonald's political changeability. In Archibald MacLeish's opinion, Macdonald was *Fortune*'s most valuable writer, but Luce began to doubt Macdonald's value as the writer tried to record his increasing radicalism in the pages of *Fortune*. Excellent description of the complicated interaction between Luce and his writers.

SEE ALSO: Nov. 7, 1914: Lippmann Helps to Establish *The New Republic*; Sept. 15, 1917: *Forbes* Magazine Is Founded; Feb., 1922: *Reader's Digest* Is Founded; Mar. 3, 1923: Luce Founds *Time* Magazine; Feb. 21, 1925: Ross Founds *The New Yorker*; Nov. 23, 1936: Luce Launches *Life* Magazine.